Handbook of
PHARMACEUTICAL
EXCIPIENTS

Handbook of
PHARMACEUTICAL EXCIPIENTS

Second Edition

Edited by
Ainley Wade and **Paul J Weller**

American Pharmaceutical Association
Washington

The Pharmaceutical Press
London

1994

A catalogue record for this book is available from the British Library.

Library of Congress Catalog Card Number: 94–79492.

International Standard Book Number (ISBN) in the UK: 0 85369 305 6
International Standard Book Number (ISBN) in the USA: 0 91730 66 8

Typeset in Great Britain by Alden Multimedia, Northampton.
Printed and bound in Great Britain by

Contents

Committees

Members of the UK Steering Committee
RF Weir (Chairman)
CG Cable
TM Jones
W Lund*
PC Record
JE Rees
RC Rowe
WG Thomas†
HEC Worthington
A Wade
PJ Weller

Members of the USA Steering Committee
A Palmieri (Chairman)
GS Banker
AA Belmonte
JC Boylan
WG Chambliss
PB Chemburkar
ZT Chowhan
AH Kibbe
GE Peck
CT Rhodes
BB Sheth

* Deceased, December 1992.
† Deceased, August 1993.

Contributors

UK Contributors

MC Allwood
NA Armstrong
ME Aulton
R Baird
S Behn
CG Cable
JH Collett
RS Cook
PJ Davies
PN Davies
SP Denyer
SZ Dziedzic
JE Fairbrother
FR Higton
N Hodges
JE Hogan
DA Hollingsbee
JM Horry
JE Jeffries

KA Khan
MJ Lawrence
MG Lee
SJ Lewis
RL Leyland
M Lynch
JQ Maclaine
MC Meyer
RC Moreton
A Pickard
G Rowley
JA Stead
DM Thurgood
RS Torr
KD Vaughan
PJ Weller
AJ Winfield
HEC Worthington
N Yussuf

USA Contributors

A Abdul-Rahman
R Abramowitz
KS Alexander
LV Allen
GE Amidon
KL Amsberry
A Athani
UV Banakar
AA Belmonte
LD Bighley
KD Brenner
EL Brunson
T-SH Chen
ZT Chowhan
TC Dahl
SA Daskalakis
B Farhadieh
J Fleitman
SO Freers
JS Fujiki
DL Gabriel
RD Gibson
FW Goodhart
MJ Groves
M Haase
EE Hamlow
W Han
D Harpaz
DJ Harper
RJ Harwood
S Hickok
JL Johnson
MJ Jozwiakowski
TN Julian
AS Kearney
SJ Kennedy
DL Kiser
NH Kobayashi
JC Lee
NG Lordi

PE Luner
AW Malick
L Mathur
MC McCaffrey-Manzo
JW McGinity
FH Merkle
N Mugharbel
RA Nash
PM Olinger
B Pagliocca
A Palmieri
HB Pandya
NH Parikh
NR Poola
DG Pope
JC Price
GW Radebaugh
GE Reier
AJ Repta
MM Rieger
S Scheindlin
J Schirmer
JJ Sciarra
RI Senderoff
E Shefter
AJ Shukla
JT Stewart
JG Strom
HM Unvala
RC Vasavada
NM Vemuri
DA Wadke
WD Walkling
TA Wheatley
DC White
JS White
W Wood
A Yu
CD Yu

Additions to the Second Edition

New Monographs

Acesulfame Potassium
Albumin
Alpha Tocopherol
Ascorbyl Palmitate
Aspartame
Benzethonium Chloride
Benzyl Benzoate
Bronopol
Canola Oil
Chlorodifluoroethane
Chlorodifluoromethane
Cresol
Croscarmellose Sodium
Crospovidone
Cyclodextrins
Dextrates
Dibutyl Sebacate
Difluoroethane
Dimethyl Ether
Ethyl Maltol
Ethyl Vanillin
Fructose
Glyceryl Monooleate
Glyceryl Palmitostearate
Imidurea
Lactic Acid
Hydrous Lanolin
Magnesium Oxide
Magnesium Trisilicate
Maltitol Solution
Maltodextrin
Maltol
Medium Chain Triglycerides
Meglumine
Menthol
Light Mineral Oil
Nitrogen
Nitrous Oxide
Oleic Acid
Phenol
Phenoxyethanol
Potassium Chloride
Propyl Gallate
Propylene Carbonate
Sodium Cyclamate
Dibasic Sodium Phosphate
Monobasic Sodium Phosphate
Sodium Propionate
Sodium Stearyl Fumarate
Soybean Oil
Sugar Spheres
Tartaric Acid
Tetrafluoroethane
Triacetin
Triethyl Citrate
Vanillin
Hydrogenated Vegetable Oil, Type I
Xanthan Gum

Related Substances

Acetyltributyl Citrate
Acetyltriethyl Citrate
Dehydrated Alcohol
Denatured Alcohol
Dilute Alcohol
Aleuritic Acid
d-Alpha Tocopherol
d-Alpha Tocopheryl Acetate
dl-Alpha Tocopheryl Acetate
d-Alpha Tocopheryl Acid Succinate
dl-Alpha Tocopheryl Acid Succinate
Amylopectin
α-Amylose
Bentonite Magma
Beta-carotene
Beta Tocopherol
Butylparaben Sodium
Calcium Alginate
Calcium Ascorbate
Calcium Cyclamate
Dibasic Calcium Phosphate Anhydrous
Calcium Propionate
Calcium Silicate
Calcium Sorbate
Calcium Sulfate Hemihydrate
Carboxymethylcellulose Sodium 12
Castor Oil
Cationic Emulsifying wax
Microcrystalline Cellulose and
    Carboxymethylcellulose Sodium
Cellulose Acetate
Ceresin
Chlorhexidine Acetate
Chlorhexidine Gluconate
Chlorhexidine Hydrochloride
Chlorobutanol Hemihydrate
Chlorophenoxyethanol
Chloroxylenol
Anhydrous Citric Acid
Corn Syrup Solids
m-Cresol
o-Cresol
p-Cresol
Cyclamic Acid
Delta Tocopherol
Dextrose Anhydrous
Diazolidinyl Urea
Dibutyl Phthalate
Dimethyl Phthalate
Dimethyl-β-cyclodextrin
Dipotassium Edetate
Disodium Edetate
Docusate Calcium
Docusate Potassium
Dodecyl Gallate
Dodecyltrimethylammonium Bromide
Edetate Calcium Disodium
Eglumine

Ethyl Gallate
Ethylparaben Potassium
Ethylparaben Sodium
Liquid Fructose
Powdered Fructose
High Fructose Syrup
Gamma Tocopherol
Glyceryl Behenate
Glyceryl Monostearate 40-50
Self-emulsifying Glyceryl Monostearate
Hexadecyltrimethylammonium Bromide
Dilute Hydrochloric Acid
2-Hydroxyethyl-β-Cyclodextrin
Low-substituted Hydroxypropyl Cellulose
2-Hydroxypropyl-β-Cyclodextrin
3-Hydroxypropyl-β-Cyclodextrin
Indigo Carmine
Iron Oxides
Lactitol
Lanolin Alcohols Ointment
Magnesium Carbonate Anhydrous
Magnesium Carbonate Hydroxide
Normal Magnesium Carbonate
Magnesium Lauryl Sulfate
Magnesium Silicate
Magnesium Trisilicate Anhydrous
D-Malic Acid
L-Malic Acid
Maltitol
Maltose
d-Menthol
l-Menthol
Methyl Methacrylate
Methyl Oleate
Methylparaben Potassium
Methylparaben Sodium
Montmorillonite
Octyl Gallate
Palmitic Acid
Synthetic Paraffin
White Petrolatum
Pharmaceutical Glaze
Liquefied Phenol
Phenoxypropanol
Polacrilin
Poly(methyl methacrylate)
Potassium Alginate
Potassium Bisulfite
Potassium Benzoate

Potassium Bicarbonate
Potassium Citrate Anhydrous
Potassium Metabisulfite
Dibasic Potassium Phosphate
Monobasic Potassium Phosphate
Potassium Propionate
Propan-1-ol
Propionic Acid
(*S*)-Propylene Carbonate
Propylparaben Potassium
Propylparaben Sodium
Rapeseed Oil
Saccharin Calcium
Saccharin Potassium
Saponite
Shellolic Acid
Sodium Bisulfite
Anhydrous Sodium Citrate
Sodium Edetate
Tribasic Sodium Phosphate
Anhydrous Sodium Propionate
Sodium Sorbate
Sodium Sulfite
Sorbitol Solution 70%
Purified Stearic Acid
Invert Sugar
Sunset Yellow FCF
D-(-)-Tartaric Acid
DL-($\pm$)-Tartaric Acid
Tartrazine
Theobroma Oil
Tocopherols Excipient
Tributyl Citrate
Trimethyl-β-Cyclodextrin
Trimethyltetradecylammonium Bromide
Trisodium Edetate
Hydrogenated Vegetable Oil, Type II
Bacteriostatic Water For Injection
Carbon Dioxide-Free Water
De-Aerated Water
Hard Water
Soft Water
Sterile Water For Inhalation
Water For Injection
Water For Injections In Bulk
Sterile Water For Injection
Sterile Water For Irrigation
Spermaceti Wax
Zinc Propionate

Preface

Excipients are the additives used to convert pharmacologically active compounds into pharmaceutical dosage forms suitable for administration to patients. A knowledge of the physical and chemical properties of each excipient is therefore essential for the selection of suitable excipients for the formulation of the many varieties of products used as medicines today. The growth of novel forms of drug delivery has resulted in an increase in the number of excipients now being used and as a result the number of excipient monographs has been increased considerably in this second edition of the *Handbook of Pharmaceutical Excipients*.

The *Handbook of Pharmaceutical Excipients*, originally published in 1986, was the first English-language publication to comprehensively and systematically describe the chemical and physical properties of pharmaceutical excipients. Published jointly, after some 10 years of work, by the American Pharmaceutical Association and the Pharmaceutical Society of Great Britain (now the Royal Pharmaceutical Society of Great Britain), the *Handbook* was based upon the Swiss *Katalog pharmazeutischer Hilfsstoffe* (*Catalog of Pharmaceutical Excipients*). The *Katalog* contained German-language monographs for nearly 100 Swiss pharmacopeial and non-pharmacopeial excipients and was published in 1974 by Ciba-Geigy, Hoffmann-La Roche and Sandoz Ltd.

The first edition of the *Handbook of Pharmaceutical Excipients* contained 145 monographs for pharmacopeial and non-pharmacopeial excipients and established itself worldwide as the primary single source of information on pharmaceutical excipients. A Japanese translation of the *Handbook* was also produced.

This second edition of the *Handbook*, has been greatly expanded and revised to include a new format for the monographs. The *Handbook* now contains 203 monographs for pharmacopeial and non-pharmacopeial excipients. This includes 58 new monographs in addition to the 145 monographs from the first edition of the *Handbook* which have themselves been completely revised and updated. Other material in the *Handbook* such as the Suppliers' Directory (Appendix I), Laboratory Methods (Appendix II), and the Index have similarly been revised and expanded.

This new edition of the *Handbook* has again been produced jointly by the American Pharmaceutical Association and the Royal Pharmaceutical Society of Great Britain and has been written by nearly 120 pharmaceutical scientists representing academic, hospital and industrial pharmacy in Europe and the USA. To help expedite the publishing plan, steering committees in the UK and USA were established to select excipients for inclusion in the *Handbook* and to advise on its content. The committees also critically reviewed all of the monographs and suggested changes where necessary. The overall editorial control of the project was the responsibility of staff from the Department of Pharmaceutical Sciences, Royal Pharmaceutical Society of Great Britain.

Interest in the physical effects and properties of the excipients used in pharmaceutical formulations has increased in recent years as pharmaceutical scientists have become increasingly aware of the fundamental effects that excipients can exert on the bioavailability, bioequivalence, and stability of formulations; excipients can no longer be regarded simply as 'inert' or 'inactive' substances. Relatively small variations in the physical properties of an excipient can produce significant differences in the behavior of formulated products and recent interest in pharmacopeial harmonization has concentrated on many of the most widely used excipients.

The *Handbook of Pharmaceutical Excipients* collects together in a systematic and uniform manner essential data on the physical properties of excipients such as: boiling point; bulk and tapped density; compression characteristics; hygroscopicity; flowability; melting point; particle size distribution; refractive index; specific surface area and solubility. Scanning electron microphotographs (SEMs) are also included for many of the excipients. The *Handbook* contains information assembled from a variety of international sources, but also includes laboratory data determined specifically for the *Handbook*, along with personal observations and comments made by the authors.

This new edition of the *Handbook* also contains additional information on the safe use of excipients and adverse reactions associated with them. Greater information concerning the handling precautions necessary with certain excipients is also presented.

All of the monographs in the *Handbook* are thoroughly cross referenced and indexed so that excipients may be identified by a chemical, nonproprietary, or trade name. Many of the monographs also contain 'mini-monographs' describing similar related substances, or are 'group monographs' describing a large group of excipients with similar uses and properties, such as Suppository Bases. The monographs additionally contain a revised selection of specific and general references.

The *Handbook of Pharmaceutical Excipients* is a comprehensive, uniform guide to the uses, properties, and safety of pharmaceutical excipients and is an essential reference source for those involved in the development, production, or control of pharmaceutical preparations. Since many pharmaceutical excipients are also used in other applications, the *Handbook* will also be of value to persons with an interest in the formulation or production of confectionery, cosmetics, and food products.

Arrangement

Each of the monographs in the *Handbook of Pharmaceutical Excipients* is divided into 22 sections as follows:

1. Nonproprietary Names
2. Synonyms
3. Chemical Name and CAS Registry Number
4. Empirical Formula and Molecular Weight
5. Structural Formula
6. Functional Category
7. Applications in Pharmaceutical Formulation or Technology
8. Description
9. Pharmacopeial Specifications
10. Typical Properties
11. Stability and Storage Conditions
12. Incompatibilities
13. Method of Manufacture
14. Safety

15. Handling Precautions
16. Regulatory Status
17. Pharmacopeias
18. Related Substances
19. Comments
20. Specific References
21. General References
22. Authors

Section 1, **Nonproprietary Names**, lists the excipient names used in the current British Pharmacopoeia, European Pharmacopoeia, and the United States Pharmacopeia and National Formulary. For non-pharmacopeial excipients the appropriate approved name, e.g. USAN, is indicated.

Section 2, **Synonyms**, lists other names for the excipient, including trade names used by suppliers, which appear in italic type, e.g. *Ac-Di-Sol*.

Section 3, **Chemical Name and CAS Registry Number**, indicates the unique Chemical Abstract Services number for an excipient along with the chemical name.

Sections 4 and 5 present, where appropriate, the **Empirical Formula and Molecular Weight** of the excipient along with a graphical representation of the **Structural Formula**. Many excipients are not pure chemical substances, in which case their composition is described either here or in Section 8.

The main applications of the excipient are described in Section 6, **Functional Category**, and Section 7, **Applications in Pharmaceutical Formulation or Technology**. Section 8, **Description**, includes details of the physical appearance of the excipient.

Section 9, **Pharmacopeial Specifications**, briefly presents the compendial standards for the excipient; '—' indicates that the test specified does not apply to a particular compendium, while '+' indicates that the test must be complied with (*see* the relevant compendia for further information). The physical properties of the excipient, not shown in section 9, are described in Section 10, **Typical Properties**. All data are for measurements made at 20°C unless otherwise indicated. Where the solubility of an excipient is described in words, the following terms describe the solubility ranges:

very soluble	1 part in less than 1
freely soluble	1 part in 1-10
soluble	1 part in 10-30
sparingly soluble	1 part in 30-100
slightly soluble	1 part in 100-1000
very slightly soluble	1 part in 1000-10 000
practically insoluble or insoluble	1 part in over 10 000

Experimental data determined specifically for the *Handbook* are also shown, the procedures used being described in **Appendix II: HPE Laboratory Methods**.

The stability and storage conditions of the excipient, in its bulk form (i.e. as received from a supplier), in solution, and in formulations is described in Section 11, **Stability and Storage Conditions**. Section 12, **Incompatibilities**, describes reported incompatibilities between the excipient and other substances.

The **Method of Manufacture** of the excipient is described in Section 13 and possible impurities that may be present are indicated.

Section 14, **Safety**, describes briefly the types of formulation in which the excipient has been used and presents relevant data concerning possible hazards and adverse reactions which have been reported. Relevant animal toxicity data are also shown.

Section 15, **Handling Precautions**, indicates possible hazards associated with handling the excipient and makes recommendations for suitable containment and protective methods. A familiarity with good laboratory practice and standard chemical handling procedures is assumed.

The **Regulatory Status** of the excipient is detailed in Section 16. The accepted uses in foods and licensed pharmaceutical applications are shown where applicable. Section 17, **Pharmacopeias**, lists pharmacopeias in which the excipient appears.

Section 18, **Related Substances**, lists excipients similar to the main excipient discussed within a monograph. Related substances which are also the subject of monographs are indicated using initial capital letters. Some data for the related substance may be included in a 'mini-monograph'.

Section 19, **Comments**, includes additional information and observations relevant to the excipient. Where appropriate, the different grades of excipient commercially available are also discussed.

The **Specific References** cited within a monograph are listed in Section 20, while **General References** are shown in Section 21. The **Author**(s) of the current monograph are shown in Section 22. The author(s) of the earlier monograph will be found in the first edition.

Appendix I: Suppliers' Directory is in two parts. The first part of the directory lists the excipients contained in the *Handbook* and indicates suppliers of a particular excipient. The suppliers are shown according to their geographical location, either in the UK, rest of Europe (Other European), USA or other countries (Others) and are alphabetically listed. The second part of the directory shows an alphabetical listing of the suppliers' name, address, telephone number, fax number and any trade names used for the excipients described in the *Handbook*. The suppliers are grouped in four sections according to their geographical location. Current trade names have been included where the manufacturer responded to requests for information.

Acknowledgements

This edition of the *Handbook of Pharmaceutical Excipients* has been produced by many pharmaceutical scientists throughout Europe and the USA who voluntarily acted as authors. The diligent and enthusiastic support of the members of the two steering committees, many of whom were also involved in the first edition of the *Handbook*, is gratefully acknowledged. Particularly thanked are the Chairmen of the UK and USA steering committees: Robert Weir and Anthony Palmieri. Thanks are due also to the many excipient suppliers who provided information on their products.

The Suppliers' Directory was compiled through the good offices of Bill Clark, Technical Director, Fisons plc, Pharmaceutical Division. The efforts of Philip Relton and Jonathan Marsh in the detailed compilation of the Directory are also acknowledged.

Many other individuals and organizations have helped in the preparation of the *Handbook* and their assistance is appreciated. Peter Drew, Arne Hölzer and Louis Trombetta provided some new SEMs for use in the *Handbook*, and Eric Donaldson provided helpful safety data used in the preparation of the Handling Precautions sections of some monographs. Metin Çelik is especially thanked for determining some new compaction data.

The staff of the American Pharmaceutical Association are thanked for the administration of the *Handbook* project in the USA: Julian Graubart; Naomi Kaminsky; Arthur Kibbe and Laura Lawson. Thanks are also extended to the staff of the Pharmaceutics Division and other colleagues from the Department of Pharmaceutical Sciences, The Pharmaceutical Press, and Library, Royal Pharmaceutical Society of Great Britain, who provided assistance with the preparation of the Handbook.

Ainley Wade and **Paul Weller**
London, June 1994

Notice to Readers

The *Handbook of Pharmaceutical Excipients* is a reference work containing a compilation of information on the uses and properties of pharmaceutical excipients and the reader is assumed to possess the necessary knowledge to interpret the information the *Handbook* contains. The *Handbook* has no official status and there is no intent, implied or otherwise, that any of the information presented should constitute standards for the substances. The inclusion of an excipient in the *Handbook*, or a description of its use in a particular application, is not intended as an endorsement of that excipient or application. Similarly, reports of incompatibilities or adverse reactions to an excipient, in a particular application, may not necessarily prevent its use in other applications. Formulators should perform suitable experimental studies to satisfy themselves and regulatory bodies that a formulation is efficacious and safe to use.

While considerable efforts were made to ensure the accuracy of the information presented in the *Handbook* neither the publishers nor the compilers can accept liability for any errors or omissions. In particular, the inclusion of a supplier within the Suppliers' Directory is not intended as an endorsement of that supplier or its products and similarly the unintentional omission of a supplier or product from the directory is not intended to reflect adversely on that supplier or its product.

Although diligent effort was made to use as recent compendial information as possible, compendia are frequently revised and the reader is urged to consult current compendia, or supplements, for up-to-date information, particularly as efforts are currently in progress to harmonize standards for excipients.

The laboratory data presented for a particular excipient reflects only the results of testing a particular batch or sample and may not be representative of other batches or samples.

Relevant data and constructive criticism are welcome and may be used to assist in the preparation of any future editions of the *Handbook*. The reader is asked to send any comments either to the Editor, Handbook of Pharmaceutical Excipients, Royal Pharmaceutical Society of Great Britain, 1 Lambeth High Street, London SE1 7JN, England or to the American Pharmaceutical Association, 2215 Constitution Avenue NW, Washington, DC 20037–2985, USA.

Selected Bibliography

A selection of publications which contain information on pharmaceutical excipients is listed below:

Banker GS, Rhodes CT, editors. Modern pharmaceutics, 2nd edition. New York: Marcel Dekker Inc, 1990.

British Pharmacopoeia 1993. London: HMSO, 1993; Addendum, 1994.

Budavari S, editor. The Merck index: an encyclopedia of chemicals, drugs, and biologicals, 11th edition. Rahway, NJ: Merck and Co Inc, 1989.

Council of Europe. European Pharmacopoeia, 2nd edition. Paris: Maisonneuve, 1980-1994.

Florence AT, Salole EG, editors. Formulation factors in adverse reactions. London: Butterworth and Co Ltd, 1990.

Food and Drug Administration. Inactive ingredients guide. Washington, DC: FDA, 1990.

Food Chemicals Codex, 3rd edition. Washington, DC: National Academy Press, 1981.

Gennaro AR, editor. Remington's pharmaceutical sciences, 18th edition. Easton, PA: Mack Publishing Company, 1990.

Health and Safety Executive. EH40/93: occupational exposure limits, 1993. London: HMSO, 1993.

Japan Pharmaceutial Excipients Council. Japansese pharmaceutical excipients 1993. Japan: Yakuji Nippon Ltd, 1994.

Lund W, editor. The Pharmaceutical Codex: principles and practice of pharmaceutics, 12th edition. London: The Pharmaceutical Press, 1994.

Reynolds JEF, editor. Martindale: the extra pharmacopoeia, 30th edition. London: The Pharmaceutical Press, 1993.

Smolinske SC. Handbook of food, drug, and cosmetic excipients. Boca Raton, FL: CRC Press Inc, 1992.

Swarbrick J, Boylan JC, editors. Encyclopedia of pharmaceutical technology, volumes 1-9. New York: Marcel Dekker Inc, 1988-1994.

Sweet DV, editor. Registry of toxic effects of chemical substances. Cincinnati: US Department of Health, 1987.

United States Pharmacopeia XXII and National Formulary XVII and Supplements. Rockville, MD: The United States Pharmacopeial Convention Inc, 1990; USP23 and NF18, 1994.

Weiner M, Bernstein IL. Adverse reactions to drug formulation agents: a handbook of excipients. New York: Marcel Dekker Inc, 1989.

Abbreviations

Some units, terms, and symbols are not included in this list as they are defined in the text. Common abbreviations have been omitted. The titles of journals are abbreviated according to the general style of the *Index Medicus*.

$\approx$–approximately.
Ad–Addendum.
ADI–acceptable daily intake.
approx–approximately.
atm–atmosphere.
Aust–Austrian.
BAN–British Approved Name.
Belg–Belgian.
b.p.–boiling point.
BP–British Pharmacopoeia 1993 and Addendum 1994.
BP Vet–British Pharmacopoeia (Veterinary) 1993.
Br–British.
Braz–Brazilian.
BS–British Standard (specification).
BSI–British Standards Institution.
cal–calorie(s).
CAS–Chemical Abstract Service.
Chin–Chinese.
cm–centimeter(s).
cm^2–square centimeter(s).
cm^3–cubic centimeter(s).
cmc–critical micelle concentration.
CNS–central nervous system.
cP–centipoise(s).
cSt–centistoke(s).
CTFA–The Cosmetic, Toiletry, and Fragrance Association.
Cz–former Czechoslavakian.
D&C–designation applied in USA to dyes permitted for use in drugs and cosmetics.
DoH–Department of Health (UK).
DSC–differential scanning calorimetry.
EC–European Community.
e.g.–*exempli gratia*, 'for example'.
Egypt–Egyptian.
et al–*et alii*, 'and others'.
Eur–European.
FAO–Food and Agriculture Organization of the United Nations.
FAO/WHO–Food and Agriculture Organization of the United Nations *and the* World Health Organization.
FDA–Food and Drug Administration of the USA.
FD&C–designation applied in USA to dyes permitted for use in foods, drugs, and cosmetics.
FFBE–Flat face bevelled edge.
Fr–French.
g–gram(s).
Ger–German.
GMP–Good Manufacturing Practice.
Gr–Greek.
GRAS–generally recognised as safe by the Food and Drugs Administration of the USA.
HIV–human immunodeficiency virus.

HLB–hydrophilic-lipophilic balance.
HSE–Health and Safety Executive (UK).
Hung–Hungarian.
i.e.–*id est*, 'that is'.
IM–intramuscular.
Ind–Indian.
INN–International Nonproprietary Name.
Int–International.
IP–intraperitoneal.
ISO–International Organization for Standardization.
It–Italian.
IV–intravenous.
J–joule(s).
Jpn–Japanese.
kcal–kilocalorie(s).
kg–kilogram(s).
kJ–kilojoule(s).
kPa–kilopascal(s).
L–liter(s).
LAL–*Limulus* amoebocyte lysate.
LC_{50}–a concentration in air lethal to 50% of the specified animals on inhalation.
LD_{50}–a dose lethal to 50% of the specified animals or microorganisms.
Ld_{Lo}–lowest lethal dose for the specified animals or microorganisms.
m–meter(s).
m^2–square meter(s).
m^3–cubic meter(s).
M–molar.
max–maximum.
MCA–Medicines Control Agency (UK).
Mex–Mexican.
mg–milligram(s).
MIC–minimum inhibitory concentration.
min–minute(s) *or* minimum.
mL–milliliter(s).
mm–millimeter(s).
mM–millimolar.
mm^2–square millimeter(s).
mm^3–cubic millimeter(s).
mmHg–millimeter(s) of mercury.
mmol–millimole(s).
mN–millinewton(s).
mol–mole(s).
m.p.–melting point.
mPa–millipascal(s).
MPa–megapascal(s).
μg–microgram(s).
μm–micrometer(s).
N–newton(s) *or* normal (concentration).
Neth–Netherlands.
nm–nanometer(s).
Nord–Nordic.
o/w–oil-in-water.
o/w/o–oil-in-water-in-oil.
Pa–pascal(s).
pH–the negative logarithm of the hydrogen ion concentration.
PhEur–European Pharmacopeia.

pK$_a$–the negative logarithm of the dissociation constant.
Port–Portuguese.
pph–parts per hundred.
ppm–parts per million.
psia–pounds per square inch absolute.
RDA–recommended dietary allowance (USA).
Rom–Romanian.
rpm–revolutions per minute.
Rus–former Soviet Union.
s–second(s).
SC–subcutaneous.
SEM–scanning electron microscopy *or* scanning electron microphotograph.
SI–Statutory Instrument *or* Système International d'Unites (International System of Units).
Suppl–supplement(s).
TPN–total parenteral nutrition.
Turk–Turkish.
TWA–time weighted average.

UK–United Kingdom.
US *or* USA–United States of America.
USAN–United States Adopted Name.
USP–The United States Pharmacopeia XXII, 1990, and Supplements 1 to 9.
USPNF-The United States National Formulary XVII, 1990 and Supplements 1 to 9. This designation is used in the *Handbook* where the monograph appears in the National Formulary section of the United States Pharmacopeia and National Formulary.
UV–ultraviolet.
v/v–volume in volume.
v/w–volume in weight.
WHO–World Health Organization.
w/o–water-in-oil.
w/o/w–water-in-oil-in-water.
w/v–weight in volume.
w/w–weight in weight.
Yug–former Yugoslavia.

Units of Measurement

The table below shows Imperial to SI unit conversions for the units of measurement most commonly used in the *Handbook*. SI units are used throughout the Handbook with, where appropriate, Imperial units reported in parenthesis.

Area

1 square inch (in^2) = 6.4516 x 10^{-4} square meter (m^2)
1 square foot (ft^2) = 9.29030 x 10^{-2} square meter (m^2)
1 square yard (yd^2) = 8.36127 x 10^{-1} square meter (m^2)

Density

1 pound per cubic foot (lb/ft^3) = 16.0185 kilograms per cubic meter (kg/m^3)

Energy

1 kilocalorie (kcal) = 4.1840 x 10^3 joules (J)

Force

1 dyne (dynes) = 1 x 10^{-5} newton (N)

Length

1 angstrom (Å) = 10^{-10} meter (m)
1 inch (in) = 2.54 x 10^{-2} meter (m)
1 foot (ft) = 3.048 x 10^{-1} meter (m)
1 yard (yd) = 9.144 x 10^{-1} meter (m)

Pressure

1 atmosphere (atm) = 0.101325 megapascal (MPa)
1 millimetre of mercury (mmHg) = 133.322 pascals (Pa)
1 pound per square inch (psi) = 6894.76 pascals (Pa)

Surface tension

1 dyne per centimeter (dyne/cm) = 1 millinewton per meter (mN/m)

Temperature

1 degree Fahrenheit (°F) = 5/9 degree Celsius (°C)

Viscosity (dynamic)

1 centipoise (cP) = 1 millipascal second (mPa s)
1 poise (P) = 0.1 pascal second (Pa s)

Viscosity (kinematic)

1 centistoke (cSt) = 1 square millimeter per second (mm^2/s)

Volume

1 cubic inch (in^3) = 1.63871 x 10^{-5} cubic meter (m^3)
1 cubic foot (ft^3) = 2.83168 x 10^{-2} cubic meter (m^3)
1 cubic yard (yd^3) = 7.64555 x 10^{-1} cubic meter (m^3)
1 pint (UK) = 5.68261 x 10^{-4} cubic meter (m^3)
1 pint (US) = 4.73176 x 10^{-4} cubic meter (m^3)
1 gallon (UK) = 4.54609 x 10^{-3} cubic meter (m^3)
1 gallon (US) = 3.78541 x 10^{-3} cubic meter (m^3)

Acacia

1. Nonproprietary Names

BP: Acacia
PhEur: Acaciae gummi
USPNF: Acacia

2. Synonyms

E414; gum acacia; gum arabic; talha gum.

3. Chemical Name and CAS Registry Number

Acacia [9000-01-5]

4. Empirical Formula   Molecular Weight

Acacia is a complex, loose aggregate of sugars and hemi-celluloses with a molecular weight of approximately 240 000-580 000. The aggregate consists essentially of an arabic acid nucleus to which are connected calcium, magnesium and potassium along with the sugars arabinose, galactose and rhamnose.

5. Structural Formula

See Section 4.

6. Functional Category

Emulsifying agent; stabilizing agent; suspending agent; tablet binder; viscosity-increasing agent.

7. Applications in Pharmaceutical Formulation or Technology

Acacia is mainly used in oral and topical pharmaceutical formulations as a suspending and emulsifying agent, often in combination with tragacanth. It is also used in the preparation of pastilles and lozenges, and as a tablet binder, although used incautiously it can produce tablets with a prolonged disintegration time.
Acacia is also used in cosmetics, confectionery and food products.
See also Section 19.

Use	Concentration (%)
Emulsifying agent	5-10
Pastille base	10-30
Suspending agent	5-10
Tablet binder	1-5

8. Description

Acacia occurs as white or yellowish-white colored thin flakes, spheroidal tears, granules or powder. It is odorless and has a bland taste.

9. Pharmacopeial Specifications

The BP 1993 includes monographs on acacia, powdered acacia and spray-dried acacia which differ only in their physical characteristics. The PhEur 1992 similarly has monographs on acacia and spray-dried acacia, while the USPNF XVII describes acacia in a single monograph which encompasses tears, flakes, granules and spray-dried powder.

Test	PhEur 1992	USPNF XVII
Identification	+	+
Botanic characteristics	+	+
Microbial limit	+	+
Water	⩽ 15%	⩽ 15%
	⩽ 10%[(a)]	—
Total ash	⩽ 4.0%	⩽ 4.0%
Acid-insoluble ash	—	⩽ 0.5%
Insoluble residue	⩽ 0.5%	⩽ 1.0%
Arsenic	—	⩽ 3 ppm
Lead	—	⩽ 0.001%
Heavy metals	—	⩽ 0.004%
Starch or dextrin	+	+
Tannin-bearing gums	+	+
Agar & tragacanth	+	—
Agar & sterculia gum	+	—
Sucrose & fructose	+	—

Note: a. Spray-dried acacia.

10. Typical Properties

Acidity/alkalinity:
pH = 4.5-5.0 (5% w/v aqueous solution)
Acid value: 2.5
Hygroscopicity: at relative humidities between 25-65%, the equilibrium moisture content of powdered acacia at 25°C is between 8-13% w/w, but at relative humidities above about 70% it absorbs substantial amounts of water.
Moisture content: see HPE Data.
Solubility: soluble 1 in 20 of glycerin, 1 in 20 of propylene glycol, 1 in 2.7 of water; practically insoluble in ethanol (95%).
Specific gravity: 1.35-1.49
Viscosity (dynamic): 100 mPa s (100 cP) for a 30% w/v aqueous solution at 20°C.
The viscosity of aqueous acacia solutions varies depending upon the source of the material, processing, storage conditions, pH and the presence of salts. Viscosity increases slowly up to about 25% w/v concentration and exhibits Newtonian behavior. Above this concentration, viscosity rapidly increases. Increasing temperature or prolonged heating of solutions results in a decrease of viscosity due to depolymerization or particle agglomeration. *See also* Section 12.

	HPE Laboratory Project Data		
	Method	Lab #	Results
Moisture content	MC-1	5	10.75%[(a)]
	MC-1	5	12.54%[(b)]
	MC-1	5	3.92%[(c)]

Supplier: a. Penick; b. EM Industries Inc; c. Fisher Scientific.

11. Stability and Storage Conditions

Aqueous solutions are subject to bacterial or enzymatic degradation but may be preserved by initially boiling the solution for a short time to inactivate any enzymes present; microwave irradiation can also be used.[(1)] Aqueous solutions may also be preserved by the addition of an antimicrobial preservative such as 0.1% w/v benzoic acid, 0.1% w/v sodium benzoate or a mixture of 0.17% w/v methylparaben and 0.03% propylparaben.
Powdered acacia should be stored in an airtight container in a cool, dry, place.

12. Incompatibilities

Acacia is incompatible with a number of substances including amidopyrine, cresol, ethanol (95%), ferric salts, morphine, phenol, physostigmine, tannins, thymol, and vanillin.

An oxidizing enzyme is present in acacia which may affect preparations containing easily oxidizable substances. The enzyme may however be inactivated by heating at 100°C for a short time, *see* Section 11.

Many salts reduce the viscosity of aqueous acacia solutions, while trivalent salts may initiate coagulation. Aqueous solutions carry a negative charge and will form coacervates with gelatin and other substances. In the preparation of emulsions, solutions of acacia are incompatible with soaps.

13. Method of Manufacture

Acacia is the dried gummy exudate obtained from the stems and branches of *Acacia senegal* (Linné) Willdenow or other related species of *Acacia* (Fam. Leguminosae) which grow mainly in the Sudan and Senegal regions of Africa.

The bark of the tree is incised and the exudate allowed to dry on the bark. The dried exudate is then collected, processed to remove bark, sand and other particulate matter, and graded. Various acacia grades differing in particle size and other physical properties are thus obtained. A spray-dried powder is also commercially available.

14. Safety

Acacia is used in cosmetics, foods, and oral and topical pharmaceutical formulations. Although generally regarded as an essentially nontoxic material, there have been a limited number of reports of hypersensitivity to acacia after inhalation or ingestion.[2,3] Severe anaphylactic reactions have occurred following the parenteral administration of acacia and it is now no longer used for this purpose.[2]

The WHO has not set an acceptable daily intake for acacia as a food additive since the levels necessary to achieve a desired effect were not considered to represent a hazard to health.[4]

LD_{50} (rabbit, oral): 8.0 g/kg[5]

15. Handling Precautions

Observe normal precautions appropriate to the circumstances and quantity of material handled. Acacia can be irritant to the eyes, skin, and upon inhalation. Gloves, eye protection and a dust respirator are recommended.

16. Regulatory Status

GRAS listed. Accepted for use in Europe as a food additive. Included in the FDA Inactive Ingredients Guide (oral preparations). Included in nonparenteral medicines licensed in the UK.

17. Pharmacopeias

Aust, Br, Cz, Egypt, Eur, Fr, Ger, Ind, It, Jpn, Neth, Nord, Port, Rom, Swiss, USPNF and Yug.
See also Section 9.

18. Related Substances

Tragacanth.

19. Comments

Concentrated aqueous solutions are used to prepare pastilles since on drying they form solid rubbery, or glass-like masses depending upon the concentration used.

20. Specific References

1. Richards RME, Al Shawa R. Investigation of the effect of microwave irradiation on acacia powder. J Pharm Pharmacol 1980; 32: 45P.
2. Maytum CK, Magath TB. Sensitivity to acacia. JAMA 1932; 99: 2251.
3. Smolinske SC. Handbook of food, drug, and cosmetic excipients. Boca Raton, FL: CRC Press Inc, 1992: 7-11.
4. FAO/WHO. Evaluation of certain food additives and contaminants: thirty-fifth report of the joint FAO/WHO expert committee on food additives. Tech Rep Ser Wld Hlth Org 1990; No. 789.
5. Sweet DV, editor. Registry of toxic effects of chemical substances. Cincinnati: US Department of Health, 1987.

21. General References

Anderson DMW, Dea ICM. Recent advances in the chemistry of acacia gums. J Soc Cosmet Chem 1971; 22: 61-76.
Anderson DM, Douglas DM, Morrison NA, Wang WP. Specifications for gum arabic (*Acacia Senegal*): analytical data for samples collected between 1904 and 1989. Food Add Contam 1990; 7: 303-321.
Aspinal GO. Gums and Mucilages. Adv Carbohydrate Chem Biochem 1969; 24: 333-379.
Whistler RL. Industrial gums. New York: Academic Press, 1959.

22. Authors

USA: E Shefter.

Acesulfame Potassium

1. Nonproprietary Names
BAN: Acesulfame potassium
INN: Acesulfame potassium

2. Synonyms
Acesulfame K; E950; 6-methyl-3,4-dihydro-1,2,3-oxathiazin-4(3*H*)-one 2,2-dioxide potassium salt; *Sunett.*

3. Chemical Name and CAS Registry Number
6-Methyl-1,2,3-oxathiazin-4(3*H*)-one-2,2-dioxide potassium salt [55589-62-3]

4. Empirical Formula   Molecular Weight
$C_4H_4KNO_4S$ 201.24

5. Structural Formula

$$CH_3$$

O=\quad\quad O

N^-—SO_2

K^+

6. Functional Category
Sweetening agent.

7. Applications in Pharmaceutical Formulation or Technology
Acesulfame potassium is used as an intense sweetening agent in cosmetics, foods, beverage products, table-top sweeteners, vitamin and pharmaceutical preparations including powder mixes, tablets and liquid products. The approximate sweetening power is 180-200 times that of sucrose. It enhances flavor systems and can be used to mask some unpleasant taste characteristics.

8. Description
Acesulfame potassium occurs as a colorless to white-colored, odorless, crystalline powder with an intensely sweet taste.

9. Pharmacopeial Specifications
See Section 19.

10. Typical Properties
Density (bulk): 1.1-1.3 g/cm³
Melting point: 250°C, decomposition can be observed at 225°C if slowly heated.

SEM: 1
Excipient: Acesulfame potassium
Magnification: 150x
Voltage: 5 kV

Solubility:

Solvent	Solubility at 20°C Unless otherwise stated
Ethanol	1 in 1000
Ethanol (50%)	1 in 100
Water	1 in 7.1 at 0°C
	1 in 3.7
	1 in 0.77 at 100°C

11. Stability and Storage Conditions
Acesulfame potassium possesses good stability. In the bulk form it shows no sign of decomposition, at ambient temperature, over many years. In aqueous solutions (pH 3-3.5 at 20°C) no reduction in sweetness was observed over a period of approximately 2 years. Stability at elevated temperatures is good, although some decomposition was noted following storage at 40°C for several months. Sterilization and pasteurization do not affect the taste of acesulfame potassium.[1]
The bulk material should be stored in a well-closed container in a cool, dry, place.

12. Incompatibilities
—

13. Method of Manufacture
Acesulfame potassium is synthesized from acetoacetic acid *tert*-butyl ester and fluorosulfonyl isocyanate. The resulting compound is transformed to fluorosulfonyl acetoacetic acid amide which is then cyclized, in the presence of potassium hydroxide, to form the oxathiazinone dioxide ring system. Because of the strong acidity of this compound the potassium salt is produced directly.

14. Safety

Pharmacokinetic studies have shown that acesulfame potassium is not metabolized and is rapidly excreted unchanged in the urine. Long-term feeding studies in rats and dogs showed no evidence to suggest acesulfame potassium is mutagenic or carcinogenic.[2]

The WHO has set an acceptable daily intake for acesulfame potassium of up to 15 mg/kg body-weight.[2]

LD_{50} (rat, IP): 2.2 g/kg[1]
LD_{50} (rat, oral): 6.9-8.0 g/kg

15. Handling Precautions

Observe normal precautions appropriate to the circumstances and quantity of material handled. Eye protection, gloves and a dust mask are recommended.

16. Regulatory Status

Acesulfame potassium is accepted for use in certain food products in Europe, the USA, and several countries in Central and South America, the Middle East, Africa, Asia and Australasia.

17. Pharmacopeias

—

18. Related Substances

Aspartame; Saccharin; Saccharin Sodium; Sodium Cyclamate.

19. Comments

The perceived intensity of sweeteners relative to sucrose depends upon their concentration, temperature of tasting, pH and on the flavor and texture of the product concerned.

Intense sweetening agents will not replace the bulk, textural or preservative characteristics of sugar, if the latter ingredient is removed from a formulation.

Synergistic effects for combinations of sweeteners have been reported, e.g. acesulfame potassium with aspartame or sodium cyclamate.

Note that free acesulfame acid is not suitable for use as a sweetener.

Although there are no pharmacopeial specifications for acesulfame potassium, the FAO, in 1983, set the following limits for acesulfame potassium purity:

Test	
Identification	+
Loss on Drying	$\leqslant 1\%$
Arsenic	$\leqslant 3$ ppm
Selenium	$\leqslant 30$ ppm
Fluoride	$\leqslant 30$ ppm
Heavy Metals (as lead)	$\leqslant 10$ ppm
Assay	99.0-101.0%

20. Specific References

1. Lipinski G-WvR, Huddart BE. Acesulfame K. Chem Ind 1983; (11): 427-432.
2. FAO/WHO. Evaluation of certain food additives and contaminants. Thirty-seventh report of the joint FAO/WHO expert committee on food additives. Tech Rep Ser Wld Hlth Org 1991; No. 806.

21. General References

Higginbotham JD. Recent developments in non-nutritive sweeteners. In: Grenby, Parker, Dindley, editors. Developments in sweeteners, volume 2. London: Applied Science, 1983: 130.
Lipinski G-WvR, Lück E. Acesulfame K: a new sweetener for oral cosmetics. Mfg Chem 1981; 52(5): 37.
Lipinski G-WvR, Mayer D. Acesulfame K. In: Hayes, Berndt, editors. Comments on toxicology, special issue: artificial sweeteners. New York: Gordon and Breach, 1989: 279.
Marie S. Sweeteners. In: Smith J, editor. Food additives user's handbook. Glasgow: Blackie, 1991: 47-74.

22. Authors

UK: FR Higton, DM Thurgood.

Albumin

1. Nonproprietary Names

BP: Albumin solution
PhEur: Albumini humani solutio
USP: Albumin human

2. Synonyms

Albuconn; albumin human solution; *Albuminar*; *Albumisol*; *Albuspan*; *Albutein*; *Buminate*; HSA; human serum albumin; normal human serum albumin; *Plasbumin*; plasma albumin; *Pro-Bumin*; *Proserum*.

3. Chemical Name and CAS Registry Number

Serum albumin [9048-49-1]

4. Empirical Formula Molecular Weight

The USP XXII describes albumin human as a sterile, non-pyrogenic preparation of serum albumin obtained from healthy human donors, *see* Section 13. It is available as a solution containing either 4, 5, 20 or 25 g of serum albumin in 100 mL of solution, with not less than 96% of the total protein content as albumin. The solutions contain no added antimicrobial preservative but may contain sodium acetyl-tryptophanate with or without sodium caprylate as a stabilizing agent.

The BP 1993 and PhEur 1990 similarly describe albumin solution as a sterile, aqueous solution of protein obtained from healthy human donors, *see* Section 13. It is available as a concentrated solution containing 15.0-25.0% w/v of total protein or as an isotonic solution containing 4.0-5.0% w/v of total protein. Not less than 95% of the total protein content is albumin. A suitable stabilizer, against the effects of heat, such as sodium caprylate at a suitable concentration, may be added but no antimicrobial preservative should be added.

The molecular weight of albumin is approximately 66 500.

See also Sections 5 and 8.

5. Structural Formula

Albumin is one of the smallest plasma proteins and consists of a polypeptide chain connecting four globular segments. It contains 584 amino acids, 7 disulfide bridges, and has an isoelectric point of 4.7.

The secondary structure of albumin contains about 48% α-helix, 15% β-pleated sheet, with the remainder as a random coil.

6. Functional Category

Stabilizing agent; therapeutic agent.

7. Applications in Pharmaceutical Formulation or Technology

Albumin is primarily used as an excipient in parenteral pharmaceutical formulations where it is used as a stabilizing agent for formulations containing proteins and enzymes, and to prepare microspheres for experimental drug delivery systems.[1-6]

As a stabilizing agent, albumin has been employed in protein formulations at concentrations as low as 0.003% although 1-5% concentration has also been used. Albumin has also been used as a cosolvent[7] for parenteral drugs, as a cryoprotectant during lyophilization, and to prevent adsorption of other proteins to surfaces.

Therapeutically, albumin solutions are used parenterally for plasma volume replacement and to treat severe acute albumin loss.

8. Description

In the solid state, albumin appears as brownish amorphous lumps, scales or powder. Aqueous albumin solutions are slightly viscous and range in color from almost colorless to amber, depending on the protein concentration.

9. Pharmacopeial Specifications

Test	PhEur 1990	USP XXII
Identification	+	—
pH (1% w/v solution)	6.7-7.3	+
Alkaline phosphatase	⩽ 0.1 unit/g of protein	—
Polymers and aggregates	+	—
Potassium	⩽ 50 μmol/g of protein	—
Sodium	⩽ 160 mmol/L	130-160 mEq/L
Heme	+	+
Aluminum	⩽ 200 μg/L	—
Sterility	+	+
Pyrogens	+	+
Assay of albumin	95-105%	—
For 4% w/v solution	—	93.75-106.25%
For > 4% w/v solutions	—	94.0-106.0%

10. Typical Properties

Acidity/alkalinity: pH = 6.7-7.3 for a 1% w/v solution, in 0.9% w/v sodium chloride solution, at 20°C.
Osmolarity: a 4-5% w/v aqueous solution is iso-osmotic with serum.
Solubility: freely soluble in dilute salt solutions, and water. Aqueous solutions containing 40% w/v albumin can be readily prepared at pH 7.4.

11. Stability and Storage Conditions

Albumin is a protein and is therefore susceptible to chemical degradation and denaturation by exposure to extremes of pH, high salt concentrations, heat, enzymes, organic solvents and other chemical agents.

Albumin solutions should be protected from light and stored at a temperature of 2-25°C. During preparation, albumin solutions are subjected to a heat treatment process (*see* Section 13); after this treatment, the albumin solution is stable for 5 years when stored at 2-8°C and for 3 years if stored at 25°C.

12. Incompatibilities

See Section 11.

13. Method of Manufacture

Albumin is obtained by the fractionation of blood, plasma, serum, or placentas from healthy human donors. The source material is tested for the absence of hepatitis B surface antigen and HIV antibodies.

Separation of the albumin is carried out under controlled conditions, particularly with respect to pH, ionic strength and temperature, so that the final product contains not less than

95% of the total protein as albumin, according to the BP 1993 and PhEur 1990, and not less than 96%, according to the USP XXII. A suitable stabilizer may then be added.

The albumin solution is sterilized by filtration and aseptically filled and sealed in sterile containers. The solution, in its final containers, is heated to 59.5-60.5°C and maintained at this temperature for 10 hours. The containers are then incubated for not less than 14 days at 30-32°C or at 20-25°C for 4 weeks and examined visually for signs of microbial contamination.

14. Safety

Albumin occurs naturally in the body, comprising about 60% of all the plasma proteins.

As an excipient, albumin is used primarily in parenteral formulations and is generally regarded as an essentially nontoxic and nonirritant material.

Therapeutically, an initial dose equivalent to 25 g of albumin is administered parenterally to adults, e.g. 500 mL of a 5% w/v solution. Adverse reactions to albumin infusion rarely occur but include nausea, vomiting, increased salivation, and febrile reactions. Allergic reactions, including anaphylactic shock can occur. Albumin infusions are contra-indicated in patients with severe anemia or cardiac failure. Albumin solutions with an aluminum content of less than 200 μg/L should be used in dialysis patients and premature infants.[8]

It has been suggested that albumin, as an excipient, is the cause of the pain experienced by patients following subcutaneous administration of erythropoietin injection.[9]

15. Handling Precautions

Observe handling precautions appropriate for a biologically derived blood product.

16. Regulatory Acceptance

Included in the FDA Inactive Ingredients Guide (IV injections). Included in parenteral products licensed in the UK.

17. Pharmacopeias

Br, Eur and US.

18. Related Substances

Albumins derived from animal sources are also commercially available, e.g. bovine serum albumin.

19. Comments

A 100 mL aqueous solution of albumin containing 25 g of serum albumin is osmotically equivalent to 500 mL of normal human plasma.

20. Specific References

1. Kramer PA. Albumin microspheres as vehicles for achieving specificity in drug delivery [letter]. J Pharm Sci 1974; 63: 1646-1647.
2. Lee TK, Sokoloski TD, Royer GP. Serum albumin beads: an injectable, biodegradable system for the sustained release of drugs. Science 1981; 213: 233-235.
3. Gallo JM, Hung CT, Perrier DG. Analysis of albumin microsphere preparation. Int J Pharmaceutics 1984; 22: 63-74.
4. Gupta PK, Hung CT, Perrier DG. Albumin microspheres II: effect of stabilization temperature on the release of adriamycin. Int J Pharmaceutics 1986; 33: 147-153.
5. Dhawan A, Vyas SP, Jain NK, Varma KC. In vitro evaluation of albumin microspheres containing actinomycin D. Drug Dev Ind Pharm 1991; 17: 2229-2237.
6. Öner L, Groves MJ. Properties of human albumin microparticles prepared by a chilled cross-linking technique. J Pharm Pharmacol 1993; 45: 866-870.
7. Olson WP, Faith MR. Human serum albumin as a cosolvent for parenteral drugs. J Parenter Sci Technol 1988; 42: 82-85.
8. Quagliaro DA, Geraci VA, Dwan RE, Kent RS, Olson WP. Aluminum in albumin for injection. J Parenter Sci Technol 1988; 42: 187-190.
9. Lui SF, Leung CB, Li PKT, Lai KN. Pain after subcutaneous injection of erythropoietin [letter]. Br Med J 1991; 303: 856.

21. General References

Putnam FW, editor. The plasma proteins, structure, function and genetic control. London: Academic Press, 1975.

22. Authors

USA: TN Julian.

Alcohol

1. Nonproprietary Names

BP: Ethanol (96%)
USP: Alcohol

2. Synonyms

Ethyl alcohol; ethyl hydroxide; grain alcohol; methyl carbinol.

3. Chemical Name and CAS Registry Number

Ethanol [64-17-5]

4. Empirical Formula   Molecular Weight

C_2H_6O 46.07

5. Structural Formula

C_2H_5OH

6. Functional Category

Antimicrobial preservative; disinfectant; skin penetrant; solvent.

7. Applications in Pharmaceutical Formulation or Technology

Ethanol and aqueous ethanol solutions of various concentrations (*see* Sections 8 and 18) are widely used in pharmaceutical formulations and cosmetics. Although ethanol is primarily used as a solvent it is also employed in solutions as an antimicrobial preservative.[1,2] Topical ethanol solutions are also used as penetration enhancers[3] and as disinfectants.

Use	Concentration (% v/v)
Antimicrobial preservative	$\geqslant 10$
Disinfectant	60-90
Extracting solvent in galenical manufacture	Up to 85
Solvent in film coating	Variable
Solvent in injectable solutions	Variable
Solvent in oral liquids	Variable
Solvent in topical products	60-90

8. Description

In the BP 1993, the term 'ethanol' used without other qualification refers to ethanol $\geqslant 99.5\%$ v/v. The term 'alcohol', without other qualification, refers to ethanol 96.0-96.6% v/v. Where other strengths are intended, the term 'alcohol' or 'ethanol' is used, followed by the statement of the strength.

In the USP XXII, the term 'dehydrated alcohol' refers to ethanol $\geqslant 99.5\%$ v/v. The term 'alcohol', without other qualification refers to ethanol 94.9-96.0% v/v.

In the *Handbook of Pharmaceutical Excipients*, the term 'alcohol' is used for either ethanol 95% v/v or ethanol 96% v/v.

Alcohol is a clear, colorless, mobile and volatile liquid with a slight, characteristic odor and burning taste.

See also Section 18.

9. Pharmacopeial Specifications

Test	BP 1993	USP XXII
Identification	+	+
Specific gravity	0.8038-0.8063	0.812-0.816
Acidity	+	+
Clarity of solution	+	—
Nonvolatile residue	$\leqslant 5$ mg/100 mL	$\leqslant 1$ mg/40 mL
Water-insoluble substances	—	+
Aldehydes	$\leqslant 10$ ppm	+
Amyl alcohol, etc	—	+
Benzene	$\leqslant 2$ ppm	—
Fusel oil constituents	—	+
Acetone and propan-2-ol	—	+
Methanol	—	+
Reducing substances	+	—
Volatile impurities	+	—

10. Typical Properties

Antimicrobial activity: ethanol is bactericidal in aqueous mixtures at concentrations between 60-95% v/v; the optimum concentration is generally considered to be 70% v/v. Antimicrobial activity is enhanced in the presence of edetic acid or edetate salts.[1] Ethanol is inactivated in the presence of nonionic surfactants and is ineffective against bacterial spores.

Boiling point: 78.15°C

Flammability: readily flammable, burning with a blue, smokeless flame.

Flash point: 14°C (closed cup)

Solubility: miscible with chloroform, ether, glycerin and water (with rise of temperature and contraction of volume).

Specific gravity: 0.8119-0.8139 at 20°C

Note: the above typical properties are for alcohol (ethanol 95% or 96% v/v). *See* Section 18 for typical properties of dehydrated alcohol.

11. Stability and Storage Conditions

Aqueous ethanol solutions may be sterilized by autoclaving or by filtration and should be stored in airtight containers, in a cool place.

12. Incompatibilities

In acidic conditions, ethanol solutions may react vigorously with oxidizing materials. Mixtures with alkali may darken in color due to a reaction with residual amounts of aldehyde. Organic salts or acacia may be precipitated from aqueous solutions or dispersions. Ethanol solutions are also incompatible with aluminum containers and may interact with some drugs.

13. Method of Manufacture

Ethanol is manufactured by the controlled enzymatic fermentation of starch, sugar or other carbohydrates. A fermented liquid is produced containing about 15% ethanol; ethanol 95% v/v is then obtained by fractional distillation. Ethanol may also be prepared by a number of synthetic methods.

14. Safety

Ethanol and aqueous ethanol solutions are widely used in a variety of pharmaceutical formulations and cosmetics. Ethanol is also consumed in alcoholic beverages.

Ethanol is rapidly absorbed from the gastrointestinal tract and vapor may be absorbed through the lungs. Ethanol is metabolized mainly in the liver to acetaldehyde, which is further oxidized to acetate.

Ethanol is a central nervous system depressant and ingestion of low to moderate quantities can lead to symptoms of intoxication including muscle incoordination, visual impairment, slurred speech, etc. Ingestion of higher concentrations may cause depression of medullary action, lethargy, amnesia, hypothermia, hypoglycemia, stupor, coma, respiratory depression and cardiovascular collapse. The lethal human blood-alcohol concentration is generally estimated to be 400-500 mg/100 mL.

Although symptoms of ethanol intoxication are usually encountered following deliberate consumption of ethanol containing beverages, many pharmaceutical products contain ethanol as a solvent which, if ingested in sufficiently large quantities, may cause adverse symptoms of intoxication.

Parenteral products containing up to 50% of alcohol (ethanol 95% or 96% v/v) have been formulated. However, such concentrations can produce pain on intramuscular injection and lower concentrations such as 5-10% v/v are preferred. Subcutaneous injection of alcohol (ethanol 95% v/v) similarly causes considerable pain followed by anesthesia. If injections are made close to nerves, neuritis and nerve degeneration may occur. This effect is used therapeutically to cause anesthesia in cases of severe pain although the practice of using alcohol in nerve blocks is controversial. Doses of 1 mL of absolute alcohol have been used for this purpose.[4]

Preparations containing greater than 50% v/v alcohol may cause skin irritation when applied topically.

LD_{50} (guinea pig, IP): 3.41 g/kg[5]
LD_{50} (guinea pig, IV): 2.3 g/kg
LD_{50} (guinea pig, oral): 5.56 g/kg
LD_{50} (hamster, IP): 5.07 g/kg
LD_{50} (mouse, IP): 0.93 g/kg
LD_{50} (mouse, IV): 1.97 g/kg
LD_{50} (mouse, oral): 7.5 g/kg
LD_{50} (mouse, SC): 8.29 g/kg
LD_{50} (rabbit, IP): 0.96 g/kg
LD_{50} (rabbit, IV): 2.37 g/kg
LD_{50} (rabbit, oral): 6.3 g/kg
LD_{50} (rat, IP): 3.75 g/kg
LD_{50} (rat, IV): 1.44 g/kg
LD_{50} (rat, oral): 7.06 g/kg

15. Handling Precautions

Observe normal precautions appropriate to the circumstances and quantity of material handled. Ethanol and aqueous ethanol solutions should be handled in a well-ventilated environment. In the UK, the long-term 8-hour TWA exposure limit for ethanol is 1900 mg/m^3 (1000 ppm).[6] Ethanol may be irritant to the eyes and mucous membranes and eye protection and gloves are therefore recommended. Ethanol is flammable and should be heated with care. Fixed storage tanks should be electrically grounded to avoid ignition from electrostatic discharges, when ethanol is transferred.

16. Regulatory Status

Included in the FDA Inactive Ingredients Guide (dental preparations, inhalations, IM and IV injections, nasal and ophthalmic preparations, oral capsules, solutions, suspensions, syrups and tablets, rectal, topical and transdermal preparations). Included in nonparenteral and parenteral medicines licensed in the UK.

17. Pharmacopeias

Aust, Br, Chin, Cz, Egypt, Fr, Ger, Hung, Ind, It, Jpn, Mex, Neth, Nord, Rom, Rus, Swiss, Turk, US and Yug. Also in BP Vet.

18. Related Substances

Dehydrated alcohol; denatured alcohol; dilute alcohol; Isopropyl Alcohol.

Dehydrated alcohol

Synonyms: absolute alcohol; ethanol.
Autoignition temperature: 365°C
Boiling point: 78.5°C
Explosive limits: 3.5-19.0% v/v in air
Flash point: 12°C (closed cup)
Hygroscopicity: absorbs water rapidly from the air.
Melting point: −112°C
Refractive index: n_D^{20} = 1.361
Specific gravity: 0.7904-0.7935 at 20°C
Surface tension: 22.75 mN/m at 20°C (ethanol/vapor)
Vapor density (relative): 1.59 (air = 1)
Vapor pressure: 5.8 Pa at 20°C
Viscosity (dynamic): 1.22 mPa s (1.22 cP) at 20°C
Comments: dehydrated alcohol is ethanol ≥ 99.5% v/v. *See* Section 8.

Denatured alcohol

Synonyms: industrial methylated spirit; surgical spirit.
Comments: denatured alcohol is alcohol, for external use only, that has been rendered unfit for human consumption by the addition of a denaturing agent such as methanol or methyl isobutyl ketone.

Dilute alcohol

Synonyms: dilute ethanol.
Specific gravity:

Strength of alcohol (% v/v)	Specific gravity at 20°C
90	0.8289-0.8319
80	0.8599-0.8621
70	0.8860-0.8883
60	0.9103-0.9114
50	0.9314-0.9326
45	0.9407-0.9417
25	0.9694-0.9703
20	0.9748-0.9759

Comments: the term 'dilute alcohol' refers to a mixture of ethanol and water of stated concentration. The BP 1993 lists eight strengths of dilute alcohol (dilute ethanol) containing 90, 80, 70, 60, 50, 45, 25 and 20% v/v respectively of ethanol.

19. Comments

Possession and use of non-denatured alcohols are usually subject to close control by excise authorities.

20. Specific References

1. Chiori CO, Ghobashy AA. A potentiating effect of EDTA on the bactericidal activity of lower concentrations of ethanol. Int J Pharmaceutics 1983; 17: 121-128.

2. Karabit MS, Juneskans OT, Lundgren P. The determination of antimicrobial characteristics of some pharmaceutical compounds in aqueous solutions. Int J Pharmaceutics 1989; 54: 51-56.
3. Liu P, Higuchi WI, Song W, Kurihara-Bergstrom T, Good WR. Quantitative evaluation of ethanol effects on diffusion and metabolism of β-estradiol in hairless mouse skin. Pharm Res 1991; 8: 865-872.
4. Lloyd JW. Use of anaesthesia: the anaesthetist and the pain clinic. Br Med J 1980; 281: 432-434.
5. Sweet DV, editor. Registry of toxic effects of chemical substances. Cincinnati: US Department of Health, 1987.
6. Health and Safety Executive. Occupational exposure limits 1993: EH40/93. London: HMSO, 1993.

21. General References

Lund W, editor. The Pharmaceutical Codex: principles and practice of pharmaceutics, 12th edition. London: The Pharmaceutical Press, 1994: 694-695.
Spiegel AJ, Noseworthy MN. Use of nonaqueous solvents in parenteral products. J Pharm Sci 1963; 52: 917-927.
Wade A, editor. Pharmaceutical handbook, 19th edition. London: The Pharmaceutical Press, 1980: 227-230.

22. Authors

UK: SJ Lewis.

Alginic Acid

1. Nonproprietary Names

BP: Alginic acid
PhEur: Acidum alginicum
USPNF: Alginic acid

2. Synonyms

E400; L-gulo-D-mannoglycuronan; *Kelacid*; polymannuronic acid; *Protacid*; *Satialgine*.

3. Chemical Name and CAS Registry Number

Alginic acid [9005-32-7]

4. Empirical Formula Molecular Weight

Alginic acid is a linear glycuronan polymer consisting of a mixture of β-(1→4)-D-mannosyluronic acid and α-(1→4)-L-gulosyluronic acid residues, of general formula $(C_6H_8O)_n$. The molecular weight is typically 20 000-200 000.

5. Structural Formula

See Section 4.

6. Functional Category

Stabilizing agent; tablet and capsule disintegrant; tablet binder; viscosity-increasing agent.

7. Applications in Pharmaceutical Formulation or Technology

Alginic acid is used in a variety of oral and topical pharmaceutical formulations. In tablet and capsule formulations, alginic acid is used as both a binder and disintegrating agent[1,2] at concentrations between 1-5%. Alginic acid is also widely used as a thickening and suspending agent in a variety of pastes, creams and gels, and as a stabilizing agent for oil-in-water emulsions. Therapeutically, alginic acid has been used in combination with an H_2-receptor antagonist in the management of gastroesophageal reflux.[3] Alginic acid is also used in cosmetics and extensively in food products, as an emulsifier and stabilizer.

8. Description

Alginic acid is a tasteless, practically odorless, white to yellowish-white colored, fibrous powder.

9. Pharmacopeial Specifications

Test	PhEur 1992	USPNF XVII
Identification	+	+
Microbial limits	⩽ 100/g	⩽ 200/g
pH (3% dispersion)	—	1.5-3.5
Loss on drying	⩽ 15.0%	⩽ 15.0%
Ash	—	⩽ 4.0%
Sulfated ash	⩽ 8.0%	—
Arsenic	—	⩽ 3 ppm
Chloride	⩽ 1.0%	—
Lead	—	⩽ 0.001%
Heavy metals	⩽ 20 ppm	⩽ 0.004%
Acid value (dried basis)	—	⩾ 230
Assay (of COOH groups)	19.0-25.0%	—

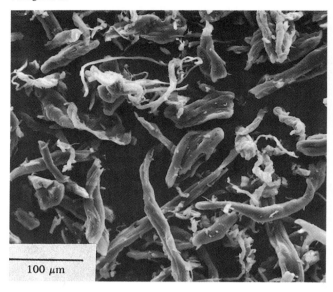

SEM: 1
Excipient: Alginic acid
Magnification: 200x
Voltage: 25 kV

100 μm

SEM: 2
Excipient: Alginic acid
Magnification: 600x
Voltage: 25 kV

10 μm

10. Typical Properties

Acidity/alkalinity:
pH = 1.5-3.5 for a 3% w/v aqueous dispersion.
Moisture content: see HPE Data.
Solubility: soluble in alkali hydroxides, producing viscous solutions; very slightly soluble or practically insoluble in ethanol (95%) and other organic solvents. Alginic acid swells in water but does not dissolve; it is capable of absorbing 200-300 times its own weight in water.
Viscosity (dynamic): various grades of alginic acid are commercially available which vary in their molecular weight and hence viscosity. Viscosity increases considerably with

increasing concentration; typically a 0.5% w/w aqueous dispersion will have a viscosity of approximately 20 mPa s, whilst a 2.0% w/w aqueous dispersion will have a viscosity of approximately 2000 mPa s. The viscosity of dispersions decreases with increasing temperature. As a general rule, a 1°C increase in temperature results in a 2.5% reduction in viscosity. At low concentrations, the viscosity of an alginic acid dispersion may be increased by the addition of a calcium salt, such as calcium citrate. This causes cross-linking of the alginic acid polymer to occur, resulting in an apparent increase in molecular weight. *See also* Sections 11 and 19.

HPE Laboratory Project Data			
	Method	Lab #	Results
Moisture content	MC-8	18	7.013%

Supplier: Edward Mendell Co Inc.

11. Stability and Storage Conditions

Alginic acid hydrolyzes slowly at warm temperatures producing a material with a lower molecular weight and lower dispersion viscosity.

Alginic acid dispersions are susceptible to microbial spoilage on storage which may result in some depolymerization and hence a decrease in viscosity. Dispersions should therefore be preserved with an antimicrobial preservative such as: benzoic acid; potassium sorbate; sodium benzoate; sorbic acid or parabens. Concentrations of 0.1-0.2% are usually used.

Alginic acid dispersions may be sterilized by autoclaving or filtration through a 0.22 μm filter. Autoclaving may result in a decrease in viscosity which can vary depending upon the nature of any other substances present.[4]

Alginic acid should be stored in a well-closed container in a cool, dry, place.

12. Incompatibilities

Incompatible with strong oxidizing agents. The alkaline earth metals and group III metals, with the exception of magnesium, all form insoluble alginate salts.

13. Method of Manufacture

Alginic acid is a hydrophilic colloid carbohydrate which occurs naturally in the cell walls and intercellular spaces of various species of brown seaweed (Phaeophyceae). The seaweed occurs widely throughout the world and is harvested, crushed, and treated with dilute alkali to extract the alginic acid.

14. Safety

Alginic acid is widely used in food products and topical and oral pharmaceutical formulations. It is generally regarded as a nontoxic and nonirritant material although excessive oral consumption may be harmful.

Inhalation of alginate dust may be irritant and has been associated with industrially related asthma in workers involved in alginate production. However, it appears that the cases of asthma were linked to exposure to seaweed dust rather than pure alginate dust.[5]

The WHO has set an estimated acceptable daily intake of alginic acid and alginate salts used as food additives at up to 25 mg/kg body-weight, calculated as alginic acid.[6]

LD_{50} (rat, IP): 1.6 g/kg[7]

15. Handling Precautions

Observe normal precautions appropriate to the circumstances and quantity of material handled. Alginic acid may be irritant to the eyes or respiratory system if inhaled as dust, *see* Section 14. Eye protection, gloves and a dust respirator are recommended. Alginic acid should be handled in a well-ventilated environment.

16. Regulatory Status

GRAS listed. Accepted in Europe for use as a food additive. Included in the FDA Inactive Ingredients Guide (ophthalmic preparations, oral capsules and tablets). Included in nonparenteral medicines licensed in the UK.

17. Pharmacopeias

Br, Eur, Fr, Ger, It, Mex, Neth, Nord, Swiss and USPNF.

18. Related Substances

Propylene Glycol Alginate; Sodium Alginate.

19. Comments

Alginic acid dispersions are best prepared by pouring the alginic acid slowly and steadily into vigorously stirred water. Dispersions should be stirred for approximately 30 minutes. Premixing the alginic acid with another powder, such as sugar, or a water miscible liquid such as ethanol (95%) or glycerin, aids dispersion.

When using alginic acid in tablet formulations the alginic acid is best incorporated or blended using a dry granulation process.

20. Specific References

1. Shotton E, Leonard GS. Effect of intragranular and extragranular disintegrating agents on particle size of disintegrated tablets. J Pharm Sci 1976; 65: 1170-1174.
2. Esezobo S. Disintegrants: effects of interacting variables on the tensile strengths and disintegration times of sulphaguanidine tablets. Int J Pharmaceutics 1989; 56: 207-211.
3. Stanciu C, Bennett JR. Alginate/antacid in the reduction of gastro-oesophageal reflux. Lancet 1974; i: 109-111.
4. Vandenbossche GMR, Remon J-P. Influence of the sterilization process on alginate dispersions. J Pharm Pharmacol 1993; 45: 484-486.
5. Henderson AK, et al. Pulmonary hypersensitivity in the alginate industry. Scott Med J 1984; 29(2): 90-95.
6. FAO/WHO. Toxicological evaluation of certain food additives with a review of general principles and of specifications. Seventeenth report of the joint FAO/WHO expert committee on food additives. Tech Rep Ser Wld Hlth Org 1974; No. 539.
7. Sweet DV, editor. Registry of toxic effects of chemical substances. Cincinnati: US Department of Health, 1987.

21. General References

Marshall PV, Pope DG, Carstensen JT. Methods for the assessment of the stability of tablet disintegrants. J Pharm Sci 1991; 80: 899-903.

22. Authors

USA: M Haase, JW McGinity.

Alpha Tocopherol

1. Nonproprietary Names

BP: Alpha tocopherol
PhEur: α-Tocopherolum
USP: Vitamin E
See also Sections 3, 9 and 18.

2. Synonyms

(±)-3,4-Dihydro-2,5,7,8-tetramethyl-2-(4,8,12-trimethyltride-cyl)-2*H*-1-benzopyran-6-ol; E307; synthetic alpha tocopherol; *all-rac*-α-tocopherol; *dl*-α-tocopherol; 5,7,8-trimethyltocol.

3. Chemical Name and CAS Registry Number

(±)-(2*RS*,4'*RS*,8'*RS*)-2,5,7,8-Tetramethyl-2-(4',8',12'-trime-thyltridecyl)-6-chromanol
[10191-41-0]
Note that alpha tocopherol has three chiral centres giving rise to eight isomeric forms. The naturally occurring form is known as *d*-alpha tocopherol or (2*R*,4'*R*,8'*R*)-alpha-tocopherol. The synthetic form, *dl*-alpha tocopherol or simply alpha tocopherol, occurs as a racemic mixture containing equimolar quantities of all the isomers.
Similar considerations apply to beta, delta and gamma tocopherol and tocopherol esters.
See Section 18 for further information.

4. Empirical Formula   Molecular Weight

$C_{29}H_{50}O_2$ 430.69

5. Structural Formula

Alpha tocopherol: $R_1 = R_2 = R_3 = CH_3$.
Beta tocopherol: $R_1 = R_3 = CH_3$; $R_2 = H$.
Delta tocopherol: $R_1 = CH_3$; $R_2 = R_3 = H$.
Gamma tocopherol: $R_1 = R_2 = CH_3$; $R_3 = H$.
* Indicates chiral centres.

6. Functional Category

Antioxidant; therapeutic agent.

7. Applications in Pharmaceutical Formulation or Technology

Alpha tocopherol is primarily recognised as a source of vitamin E and the commercially available materials and specifications reflect this purpose. Whilst alpha tocopherol also exhibits antioxidant properties, the beta, delta and gamma tocopherols are considered to be more effective as antioxidants.
Of widespread regulatory acceptability, tocopherols are of value in oil or fat-based pharmaceutical products and are normally used in the concentration range of 0.001-0.05%.

There is frequently an optimum concentration; thus the autoxidation of linoleic acid and methyl linolenate is reduced at low concentrations of alpha tocopherol but accelerated by higher concentrations. Antioxidant effectiveness can be increased by the addition of oil soluble synergists such as lecithin and ascorbyl palmitate.[1]

8. Description

Alpha tocopherol is a practically odorless, clear, colorless, yellow, yellowish-brown or greenish-yellow colored viscous oil. *See also* Section 18.

9. Pharmacopeial Specifications

Test	PhEur 1990	USP XXII
Identification	+	+
Acidity	—	+
Acid value	≤ 2	—
Heavy metals	≤ 20 ppm	—
Sulfated ash	≤ 0.1%	—
Assay	96.0-102.0%	96.0-102.0%

Note that the USP XXII describes vitamin E as comprising *d*- or *dl*-alpha tocopherol; *d*- or *dl*-alpha tocopheryl acetate; or *d*- or *dl*-alpha tocopheryl acid succinate. However, the PhEur 1990 and the BP 1993 describe alpha tocopherol and alpha tocopheryl acetate in separate monographs.
The diversity of the tocopherols described in the various pharmacopeial monographs makes a comparison of specifications difficult.

10. Typical Properties

Solubility: practically insoluble in water; freely soluble in acetone, ethanol, ether and vegetable oils.

11. Stability and Storage Conditions

Tocopherols are slowly oxidized by atmospheric oxygen and rapidly by ferric and silver salts. Oxidation products include tocopheroxide, tocopherylquinone and tocopherylhydroquinone, as well as dimers and trimers. Tocopherol esters are more stable to oxidation than the free tocopherols but are in consequence less effective antioxidants. *See also* Section 18.
Tocopherols should be stored under an inert gas, in an airtight container in a cool, dry, place and protected from light.

12. Incompatibilities

Tocopherols are incompatible with peroxides and metal ions especially iron, copper and silver. Tocopherols may be absorbed into plastic.[2]

13. Method of Manufacture

Naturally occurring tocopherols are obtained by the extraction or molecular distillation of steam distillates of vegetable oils, e.g. alpha tocopherol occurs in concentrations of 0.1-0.3% in corn, rapeseed, soybean, sunflower and wheat germ oils.[3] Beta tocopherol and gamma tocopherol are usually found in natural sources along with alpha tocopherol. Racemic synthetic tocopherols may be prepared by the condensation of the appropriate methylated hydroquinone with racemic isophytol.[4]

14. Safety

Tocopherols (vitamin E) occur in many food substances that are consumed as part of the normal diet. The daily nutritional requirement has not been clearly defined but is estimated to be 3-20 mg. Absorption from the gastrointestinal tract is dependent upon normal pancreatic function and the presence of bile. Tocopherols are widely distributed throughout the body with some ingested tocopherol metabolized in the liver; excretion of metabolites is via the urine or bile. Individuals with vitamin E deficiency are usually treated by oral administration of tocopherols although intramuscular and intravenous administration may sometimes be used.

Tocopherols are well tolerated although large oral doses may cause diarrhea or other gastrointestinal disturbances. Topical application of tocopherols may cause contact dermatitis.

The use of tocopherols as antioxidants in pharmaceuticals and food products is unlikely to pose any hazard to human health since the daily intake from such uses is small compared to the intake of naturally occurring tocopherols in the diet.

The WHO has set an acceptable daily intake of tocopherol used as an antioxidant at 0.15-2 mg/kg body-weight.[5]

15. Handling Precautions

Observe normal precautions appropriate to the circumstances and quantity of material handled. Gloves and eye protection are recommended.

16. Regulatory Status

GRAS listed. Accepted in Europe as a food additive. Included in the FDA Inactive Ingredients Guide (oral capsules, tablets, and topical preparations). Included in nonparenteral medicines licensed in the UK.

17. Pharmacopeias

Aust, Br, Braz, Chin, Cz, Egypt, Eur, Fr, Ger, Gr, Hung, Ind, It, Jpn, Neth, Nord, Rom, Rus, Swiss, US and Yug. Also in BP Vet.

Note that the nomenclature for tocopherols and tocopherol derivatives is confusing and many pharmacopeias do not specify clearly the isomer or form of the tocopherol.

18. Related Substances

d-Alpha tocopherol; *d*-alpha tocopheryl acetate; *dl*-alpha tocopheryl acetate; *d*-alpha tocopheryl acid succinate; *dl*-alpha tocopheryl acid succinate; beta tocopherol; delta tocopherol; gamma tocopherol; tocopherols excipient.

d-Alpha tocopherol: $C_{29}H_{50}O_2$
Molecular weight: 430.69
CAS number: [59-02-9]
Synonyms: natural alpha tocopherol; (+)-(2R,4'R,8'R)-2,5,7,8-tetramethyl-2-(4',8',12'-trimethyltridecyl)-6-chromanol; *d*-α-tocopherol; vitamin E.
Appearance: a practically odorless, clear, yellow or greenish-yellow colored viscous oil.
Solubility: practically insoluble in water; soluble in ethanol (95%). Miscible with acetone, chloroform, ether and vegetable oils.
Comments: this is the naturally occurring form of alpha tocopherol.

d-Alpha tocopheryl acetate: $C_{31}H_{52}O_3$
Molecular weight: 472.73
CAS number: [58-95-7]
Synonyms: (+)-(2R,4'R,8'R)-2,5,7,8-tetramethyl-2-(4',8',12'-trimethyltridecyl)-6-chromanyl acetate; *d*-α-tocopheryl acetate; vitamin E.
Appearance: a practically odorless, clear, yellow or greenish-yellow colored viscous oil which may solidify in the cold.

Melting point: 28°C
Solubility: practically insoluble in water; soluble in ethanol (95%). Miscible with acetone, chloroform, ether and vegetable oils.
Specific rotation $[\alpha]_D^{25}$:
+0.25° (10% w/v solution in chloroform)
Comments: unstable to alkalis.

dl-Alpha tocopheryl acetate: $C_{31}H_{52}O_3$
Molecular weight: 472.73
CAS number: [7695-91-2]
Synonyms: (±)-3,4-dihydro-2,5,7,8-tetramethyl-2-(4,8,12-trimethyltridecyl)-2H-1-benzopyran-6-ol acetate; (±)-(2RS,4'RS,8'RS)-2,5,7,8-tetramethyl-2-(4',8',12'-trimethyltridecyl)-6-chromanyl acetate; (±)-α-tocopherol acetate; α-tocopheroli acetas; *all-rac*-α-tocopheryl acetate; *dl*-α-tocopheryl acetate; vitamin E.
Appearance: a practically odorless, clear, yellow or greenish-yellow viscous oil.
Density: 0.953 g/cm³
Melting point: −27.5°C
Refractive index: n_D^{20} = 1.4950-1.4972
Solubility: practically insoluble in water; freely soluble in acetone, chloroform, ethanol, ether and vegetable oils; soluble in ethanol (95%).
Comments: unstable to alkali. However, unlike alpha tocopherol, the acetate is much less susceptible to the effects of air, light or ultraviolet light. Alpha tocopherol acetate concentrate, a powdered form of alpha tocopherol acetate, is described in some pharmacopeias, e.g. BP 1993. The concentrate may be prepared by either dispersing alpha tocopherol acetate in a suitable carrier such as acacia or gelatin, or by adsorbing alpha tocopherol acetate on silicic acid.

d-Alpha tocopheryl acid succinate: $C_{33}H_{54}O_5$
Molecular weight: 530.8
CAS number: [4345-03-3]
Synonyms: (+)-α-tocopherol hydrogen succinate; *d*-α-tocopheryl acid succinate; vitamin E.
Appearance: a practically odorless white powder.
Melting point: 76-77°C
Solubility: practically insoluble in water; slightly soluble in alkaline solutions; soluble in acetone, ethanol (95%), ether and vegetable oils; very soluble in chloroform.
Comments: unstable to alkalis.

dl-Alpha tocopheryl acid succinate: $C_{33}H_{54}O_5$
Molecular weight: 530.8
CAS number: [17407-37-3]
Synonyms: (±)-α-tocopherol hydrogen succinate; *dl*-α-tocopherol succinate; *dl*-α-tocopheryl acid succinate; vitamin E.
Appearance: a practically odorless white crystalline powder.
Solubility: practically insoluble in water; slightly soluble in alkaline solutions; soluble in acetone, ethanol (95%), ether and vegetable oils; very soluble in chloroform.
Comments: unstable to alkalis.

Beta tocopherol: $C_{28}H_{48}O_2$
Molecular weight: 416.66
CAS number: [148-03-8]
Synonyms: cumotocopherol; (±)-3,4-dihydro-2,5,8-trimethyl-2-(4,8,12-trimethyltridecyl)-2H-1-benzopyran-6-ol; 5,8-dimethyltocol; neotocopherol; *dl*-β-tocopherol; vitamin E; *p*-xylotocopherol.
Appearance: a pale yellow colored viscous oil.
Solubility: practically insoluble in water; freely soluble in acetone, chloroform, ethanol (95%), ether and vegetable oils.
Specific rotation $[\alpha]_D^{20}$: +6.37°

Comments: less active biologically than alpha tocopherol. Obtained along with alpha tocopherol and gamma tocopherol from natural sources. Beta tocopherol is very stable to heat and alkalis and is slowly oxidized by atmospheric oxygen.

Delta tocopherol: $C_{27}H_{46}O_2$
Molecular weight: 402.64
CAS number: [119-13-1]
Synonyms: ($\pm$)-3,4-dihydro-2,8-dimethyl-2-(4,8,12-trimethyltridecyl)-2*H*-1-benzopyran-6-ol; E309; 8-methyltocol; *dl-δ*-tocopherol; vitamin E.
Appearance: a pale yellow colored viscous oil.
Solubility: practically insoluble in water; freely soluble in acetone, chloroform, ethanol (95%), ether and vegetable oils.
Comments: occurs naturally as 30% of the tocopherol content of soybean oil. Delta tocopherol is said to be the most potent antioxidant of the tocopherols.

Gamma tocopherol: $C_{28}H_{48}O_2$
Molecular weight: 416.66
CAS number: [7616-22-0]
Synonyms: ($\pm$)-3,4-dihydro-2,7,8-trimethyl-2-(4,8,12-trimethyltridecyl)-2*H*-1-benzopyran-6-ol; 7,8-dimethyltocol; E308; *dl-γ*-tocopherol; vitamin E; *o*-xylotocopherol.
Appearance: a pale yellow colored viscous oil.
Melting point: $-30°C$
Solubility: practically insoluble in water; freely soluble in acetone, chloroform, ethanol (95%), ether and vegetable oils.
Specific rotation $[\alpha]_D^{20}$: $-2.4°$ (in ethanol(95%))
Comments: occurs in natural sources along with alpha and beta tocopherol. Gamma tocopherol is biologically less active than alpha tocopherol. Very stable to heat and alkalis; slowly oxidized by atmospheric oxygen and gradually darkens on exposure to light.

Tocopherols excipient
Synonyms: Embanox tocopherol.
Appearance: a pale yellow colored viscous oil.
Pharmacopeias: USPNF.

Comments: tocopherols excipient is described in the USPNF XVII as a vegetable oil solution containing not less than 50.0% of total tocopherols, of which not less than 80.0% consists of varying amounts of alpha, beta, delta and gamma tocopherols.

19. Comments

Note that most commercially available tocopherols are used as sources of vitamin E rather than as antioxidants in pharmaceutical formulations.

Various mixtures of tocopherols, and mixtures of tocopherols with other excipients are commercially available and individual manufacturers should be consulted for specific information on their products.

20. Specific References

1. Johnson DM, Gu LC. Autoxidation and antioxidants. In: Swarbrick J, Boylan JC, editors. Encyclopedia of pharmaceutical technology, volume 1. New York: Marcel Dekker, 1988: 415-450.
2. Allwood MC. Compatibility and stability of TPN mixtures in big bags. J Clin Hosp Pharm 1984; 9: 181-198.
3. Buck DF. Antioxidants. In: Smith J, editor. Food additive user's handbook. Blackie: Glasgow, 1991: 1-46.
4. Rudy BC, Senkowski BZ. *dl*-Alpha-tocopheryl acetate. In: Florey K, editor. Analytical profiles of drug substances, volume 3. New York: Academic Press, 1974: 111-126.
5. FAO/WHO. Evaluation of certain food additives and contaminants. Thirtieth report of the joint FAO/WHO expert committee on food additives. Tech Rep Ser Wld Hlth Org 1987; No. 751.

21. General References

US National Research Council Food and Nutrition Board. Recommended dietary allowances, 10th edition. Washington DC: National Academy Press, 1989: 99-105.

22. Authors

UK: JA Stead.

Ascorbic Acid

1. Nonproprietary Names
BP: Ascorbic acid
PhEur: Acidum ascorbicum
USP: Ascorbic acid

2. Synonyms
Cevitamic acid; *C-97*; 2,3-didehydro-L-*threo*-hexono-1,4-lactone; E300; 3-oxo-L-gulofuranolactone, enol form; vitamin C.

3. Chemical Name and CAS Registry Number
L-(+)-Ascorbic acid [50-81-7]

4. Empirical Formula   Molecular Weight
$C_6H_8O_6$ 176.13

5. Structural Formula

6. Functional Category
Antioxidant; therapeutic agent.

7. Applications in Pharmaceutical Formulation or Technology
Ascorbic acid is used as an antioxidant in aqueous pharmaceutical formulations at a concentration of 0.01-0.1% w/v. It is also widely used in foods as an antioxidant.

8. Description
Ascorbic acid occurs as a white to light yellow colored, nonhygroscopic, odorless, crystalline powder or colorless crystals with a sharp, acidic taste. It gradually darkens in color upon exposure to light.

9. Pharmacopeial Specifications

Test	PhEur 1984	USP XXII
Identification	+	+
Specific rotation (10% w/v solution)	+20.5° to +21.5°	+20.5° to +21.5°
Residue on ignition	—	≤ 0.1%
Sulfated ash	≤ 0.1%	—
Copper	≤ 5 ppm	—
Heavy metals	≤ 10 ppm	≤ 0.002%
Iron	≤ 2 ppm	—
Oxalic acid	+	—
Appearance of solution	+	—
Assay	99.0-100.5%	99.0-100.5%

SEM: 1
Excipient: Ascorbic acid USP (fine powder)
Manufacturer: Pfizer Ltd
Lot No.: 9A-3/G92040-CO 146
Magnification: 120x
Voltage: 20 kV

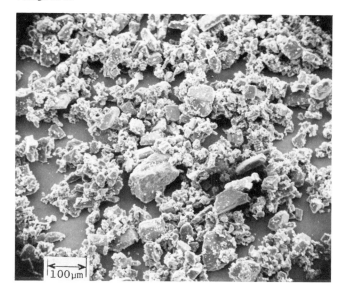

SEM: 2
Excipient: Ascorbic acid USP (fine powder)
Manufacturer: Pfizer Ltd
Lot No.: 9A-3/G92040-CO 146
Magnification: 600x
Voltage: 20 kV

SEM: 3
Excipient: Ascorbic acid USP (granular)
Manufacturer: Pfizer Ltd
Lot No.: 9A-1/G01260-CO 140
Magnification: 120x
Voltage: 20 kV

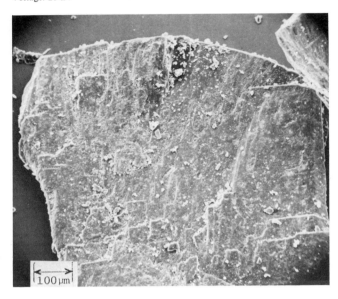

SEM: 5
Excipient: Ascorbic acid USP (fine granular)
Manufacturer: Pfizer Ltd
Lot No.: 9A-2/G01280-CO 148
Magnification: 120x
Voltage: 20 kV

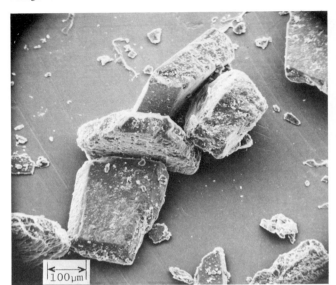

SEM: 4
Excipient: Ascorbic acid USP (granular)
Manufacturer: Pfizer Ltd
Lot No.: 9A-1/G01260-CO 140
Magnification: 600x
Voltage: 20 kV

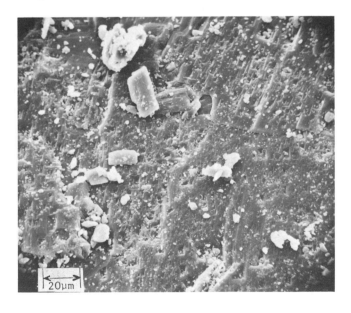

SEM: 6
Excipient: Ascorbic acid USP (fine granular)
Manufacturer: Pfizer Ltd
Lot No.: 9A-2/G01280-CO 148
Magnification: 600x
Voltage: 20 kV

10. Typical Properties

Acidity/alkalinity:
pH = 2.1-2.6 (5% w/v aqueous solution)
Density (bulk):
0.7-0.9 g/cm³ for crystalline material;
0.5-0.7 g/cm³ for powder.
Density (particle): 1.65 g/cm³
Density (tapped):
1.0-1.2 g/cm³ for crystalline material;
0.9-1.1 g/cm³ for powder.
Dissociation constant:
pK_{a1} = 4.17;
pK_{a2} = 11.57
Melting point: 190°C (with decomposition)
Moisture content: 0.1% w/w
Particle size distribution: various grades of ascorbic acid with different particle size distributions are commercially available. See Fig. 1.
Solubility:

Solvent	Solubility at 20°C
Chloroform	practically insoluble
Ethanol	1 in 50
Ethanol (95%)	1 in 25
Ether	practically insoluble
Fixed oils	practically insoluble
Glycerin	1 in 100
Propylene glycol	1 in 20
Water	1 in 3.5

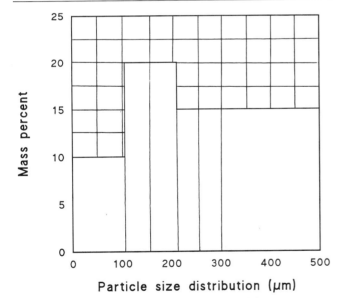

Fig. 1: Particle size distribution of ascorbic acid.

11. Stability and Storage Conditions

In powder form, ascorbic acid is relatively stable in air. In the absence of oxygen and other oxidizing agents it is also heat stable. Ascorbic acid is unstable in solution, especially alkaline solution, readily undergoing oxidation on exposure to the air.[1,2] The oxidation process is accelerated by light and heat and is catalyzed by traces of copper and iron. Ascorbic acid solutions exhibit maximum stability at about pH 5.4. Solutions may be sterilized by filtration.

The bulk material should be stored in a well-closed nonmetallic container, protected from light, in a cool, dry, place.

12. Incompatibilities

Incompatible with alkalis, heavy metal ions, especially copper and iron, oxidizing materials, methenamine, phenylephrine hydrochloride, pyrilamine maleate, salicylamide, sodium nitrite, sodium salicylate and theobromine salicylate.[3]

13. Method of Manufacture

Ascorbic acid is prepared synthetically or extracted from various vegetable sources in which it occurs naturally, such as rose hips, blackcurrants, the juice of citrus fruits and the ripe fruit of *Capsicum annuum* L. A common synthetic procedure involves the hydrogenation of D-glucose to D-sorbitol, followed by oxidation using *Acetobacter suboxydans* to form L-sorbose. A carboxyl group is then added at C_1 by air oxidation of the diacetone derivative of L-sorbose and the resulting diacetone-2-keto-L-gulonic acid converted to L-ascorbic acid by heating with hydrochloric acid.

14. Safety

Ascorbic acid is an essential part of the human diet with 40 mg the recommended daily dose in the UK[4] and 60 mg in the USA.[5] However, these figures are controversial with some advocating doses of 150 mg or 250 mg daily. Megadoses of 10 g daily have also been suggested to prevent illness.[6,7]
The body can absorb about 500 mg of ascorbic acid daily with any excess immediately excreted by the kidneys. Large doses may cause diarrhea or other gastrointestinal disturbances. Damage to the teeth has also been reported.[8] However, at the levels employed as an antioxidant in foods and pharmaceuticals no adverse effects have been reported. The WHO has set an acceptable daily intake of ascorbic acid, potassium ascorbate and sodium ascorbate, as antioxidants in food, at up to 15 mg/kg body-weight in addition to that naturally present in food.[9]
LD_{50} (mouse, IP): 0.64 g/kg[10]
LD_{50} (mouse, IV): 0.52 g/kg
LD_{50} (mouse, oral): 3.37 g/kg
LD_{50} (rat, oral): 11.9 g/kg

15. Handling Precautions

May be harmful if ingested in large quantities and may be irritating to the eyes. Observe normal precautions appropriate to the circumstances and quantity of material handled. Eye protection and rubber or plastic gloves are recommended.

16. Regulatory Status

GRAS listed. Accepted as a food additive in Europe. Included in the FDA Inactive Ingredients Guide (inhalations, injections, oral capsules, suspensions and tablets). Included in medicines licensed in the UK.

17. Pharmacopeias

Aust, Br, Braz, Chin, Cz, Egypt, Eur, Fr, Ger, Gr, Hung, Ind, Int, It, Jpn, Mex, Neth, Nord, Port, Rom, Rus, Swiss, Turk, US and Yug. Also in BP Vet.

18. Related Substances

Ascorbyl Palmitate; Sodium Ascorbate.

19. Comments

—

20. Specific References

1. Hajratwala BR. Stability of ascorbic acid. STP Pharma 1985; 1: 281-286.
2. Touitou E, Gilhar D, Alhaique F, Memoli A, Riccieri FM, Santucci E. Ascorbic acid in aqueous solution: bathochromic shift in dilution and degradation. Int J Pharmaceutics 1992; 78: 85-87.
3. Botha SA, Lötter AP, du Preez JL. DSC screening for drug-drug interactions in polypharmaceuticals intended for the alleviation of the symptoms of colds and flu. Drug Dev Ind Pharm 1987; 13: 345-354.
4. Department of Health. Dietary reference values for food energy and nutrients for the United Kingdom: report of the panel on dietary reference values of the committee on medical aspects of food policy. Report on health and social subjects 41. London: HMSO, 1991.
5. Subcommittee on the tenth edition of the RDAs, Food and Nutrition Board, Commission on Life Sciences, National Research Council. Recommended dietary allowances, 10th edition. Washington, DC: National Academy Press, 1989.
6. Ovesen L. Vitamin therapy in the absence of obvious deficiency: what is the evidence? Drugs 1984; 27: 148-170.
7. Bates CJ. Is there a maximum safe dose of vitamin C (ascorbic acid)? Br Med J 1992; 305: 32.
8. Giunta JL. Dental erosion resulting from chewable vitamin C tablets. J Am Dent Assoc 1983; 107: 253-256.
9. FAO/WHO. Toxicological evaluation of certain food additives with a review of general principles and of specifications. Seventeenth report of the joint FAO/WHO expert committee on food additives. Tech Rep Ser Wld Hlth Org 1974; No. 539.
10. Sweet DV, editor. Registry of toxic effects of chemical substances. Cincinnati: US Department of Health, 1987.

21. General References

Abramovici B, Molard F, Seguin B, Gromenil JC. Comparative study of the tabletability of different grades of vitamin C [in French]. STP Pharma 1987; 3: 16-22.
Allwood MC. Factors influencing the stability of ascorbic acid in total parenteral nutrition infusions. J Clin Hosp Pharm 1984; 9: 75-85.
Bhagavan HN, Wolkoff BI. Correlation between the disintegration time and the bioavailability of vitamin C tablets. Pharm Res 1993; 10: 239-242.
Davies MB, Austin J, Partridge DA. Vitamin C— its chemistry and biochemistry. London: Royal Society of Chemistry, 1991.
Martin J, editor. Handbook of pharmacy health education. London: The Pharmaceutical Press, 1991: 11-47.
Saleh SI, Stamm A. Contribution to the preparation of a directly compressible L-ascorbic acid granular form: comparison of granules prepared by three granulation methods and evaluation of their corresponding tablets. STP Pharma 1988; 4: 182-187.
Seta Y, Higuchi F, Otsuka T, Kawahara Y, Nishimura K, Okada R, Koike H. Preparation and pharmacological evaluation of Captopril sustained-release dosage forms using oily semisolid matrix. Int J Pharmaceutics 1988; 41: 255-262.

22. Authors

USA: A Abdul-Rahman.

Ascorbyl Palmitate

1. Nonproprietary Names

BP: Ascorbyl palmitate
PhEur: Ascorbylis palmitas
USPNF: Ascorbyl palmitate

2. Synonyms

L-Ascorbic acid 6-palmitate; E304; 3-oxo-L-gulofuranolactone 6-palmitate; vitamin C palmitate.

3. Chemical Name and CAS Registry Number

L-Ascorbic acid 6-hexadecanoate [137-66-6]

4. Empirical Formula   Molecular Weight

$C_{22}H_{38}O_7$ 414.54

5. Structural Formula

6. Functional Category

Antioxidant.

7. Applications in Pharmaceutical Formulation or Technology

Ascorbyl palmitate is primarily used either alone or in combination with alpha tocopherol as a stabilizer for oils in oral pharmaceutical formulations and food products. It may also be used in oral and topical preparations as an antioxidant for drugs unstable to oxygen. The combination of ascorbyl palmitate with alpha tocopherol shows marked synergism, which increases the effect of the components and allows the amount used to be reduced.
The solubility of ascorbyl palmitate in alcohol permits it to be used in nonaqueous and aqueous systems and emulsions.

8. Description

Ascorbyl palmitate is a practically odorless, white to yellowish powder.

9. Pharmacopeial Specifications

Test	PhEur 1993	USPNF XVII
Identification	+	+
Appearance of solution	+	—
Melting range	—	107-117°C
Specific rotation (10% w/v in methanol)	+21° to +24°	+21° to +24°
Loss on drying	$\leqslant 1.0\%$	$\leqslant 2.0\%$
Residue on ignition	—	$\leqslant 0.1\%$
Sulfated ash	$\leqslant 0.1\%$	—
Heavy metals	$\leqslant 10$ ppm	$\leqslant 0.001\%$
Assay (dried basis)	98.0-100.5%	95.0-100.5%

10. Typical Properties

Solubility:

Solvent	Solubility at 20°C[1] Unless otherwise stated
Acetone	1 in 15
Chloroform	1 in 3300
	1 in 11 at 60°C
Ethanol	1 in 8
	1 in 1.7 at 70°C
Ethanol (95%)	1 in 9.3
Ethanol (50%)	1 in 2500
Ether	1 in 132
Methanol	1 in 5.5
	1 in 1.7 at 60°C
Olive oil	1 in 3300
Peanut oil	1 in 3300
Propan-2-ol	1 in 20
	1 in 5 at 70°C
Sunflower oil	1 in 3300
Water	practically insoluble
	1 in 500 at 70°C
	1 in 100 at 100°C

11. Stability and Storage Conditions

Ascorbyl palmitate is stable in the dry state, but is gradually oxidized and becomes discolored when exposed to light and high humidity. In an unopened container, stored in a cool place, it has a shelf life of at least twelve months. During processing, temperatures greater than 65°C should be avoided. The bulk material should be stored in an airtight container, in a cool, dry place.

12. Incompatibilities

Incompatibilities are known with oxidizing agents, e.g. in solution oxidation is catalyzed by trace metal ions such as Cu^{2+} and Fe^{3+}.

13. Method of Manufacture

Ascorbyl palmitate is prepared synthetically by the reaction of ascorbic acid with sulfuric acid followed by reesterification with palmitic acid.

14. Safety

Ascorbyl palmitate is used in oral pharmaceutical formulations and food products and is generally regarded as an essentially nontoxic and nonirritant material.[2] The WHO has set an estimated acceptable daily intake for ascorbyl palmitate at up to 1.25 mg/kg body-weight.[3]

LD_{50} (mouse, oral): 25 g/kg[4]

LD_{50} (rat, oral): 10 g/kg

15. Handling Precautions

Observe normal precautions appropriate to the circumstances and quantity of material handled. Ascorbyl palmitate dust may cause irritation to the eyes and respiratory tract. Eye protection is recommended.

16. Regulatory Status

GRAS listed. Accepted for use as a food additive in Europe. Included in the FDA Inactive Ingredients Guide (oral, rectal, topical preparations). Included in nonparenteral medicines licensed in the UK.

17. Pharmacopeias

Br, Eur, Fr, Ger and USPNF.

18. Related Substances

Ascorbic Acid.

19. Comments

In order to maximize the stability and efficacy of ascorbyl palmitate the following precautions are recommended:

- stainless steel, enamel or glass should be used;
- deaeration (vacuum) procedures and inert gas treatment are recommended where feasible;
- protect from light and radiant energy.

20. Specific References

1. Kläui H. Tocopherol, carotene and ascorbyl palmitate. Int Flavours Food Add 1976; 7(4): 165-172
2. Simmon VF, Eckford SL. NTIS US Government Report. No.: PB89-178693.
3. FAO/WHO. Toxicological evaluation of certain food additives with a review of general principles and of specifications. Seventeenth report of the joint FAO/WHO expert committee on food additives. Tech Rep Ser Wld Hlth Org 1974; No. 539.
4. Sweet DV, editor. Registry of toxic effects of chemical substances. Cincinnati: US Department of Health, 1987.

21. General References

Johnson DM, Gu LC. Autoxidation and antioxidants. In: Swarbrick J, Boylan JC, editors. Encyclopedia of pharmaceutical technology, volume 1. New York: Marcel Dekker, 1988: 415-449.

Pongracz G. Antioxidant mixtures for use in food. Int J Vitam Nutr Res 1973; 43: 517-525.

Weller PJ, Newman CM, Middleton KR, Wicker SM. Stability of a novel dithranol ointment formulation, containing ascorbyl palmitate as an anti-oxidant. J Clin Pharm Ther 1990; 15: 419-423.

22. Authors

UK: HEC Worthington.

Aspartame

1. Nonproprietary Names

USPNF: Aspartame

2. Synonyms

3-Amino-*N*-(α-carboxyphenethyl)succinamic acid *N*-methyl ester; 3-amino-*N*-(α-methoxycarbonylphenethyl)succinamic acid; APM; aspartyl phenylamine methyl ester; *Canderel*; E951; *Equal*; methyl *N*-α-L-aspartyl-L-phenylalaninate; *NutraSweet*; *Sanecta*; SC-18862; *Tri-Sweet*.

3. Chemical Name and CAS Registry Number

N-α-L-Aspartyl-L-phenylalanine 1-methyl ester [22839-47-0]

4. Empirical Formula   Molecular Weight

$C_{14}H_{18}N_2O_5$ 294.31

5. Structural Formula

6. Functional Category

Sweetening agent.

SEM: 1
Excipient: Aspartame
Magnification: 70x
Voltage: 3 kV

7. Applications in Pharmaceutical Formulation or Technology

Aspartame is used as an intense sweetening agent in beverage products, food products, table-top sweeteners and in pharmaceutical preparations including tablets,[1,2] powder mixes and vitamin preparations. It enhances flavor systems and can be used to mask some unpleasant taste characteristics; the approximate sweetening power is 180-200 times that of sucrose.

Unlike some other intense sweeteners, aspartame is metabolized in the body and consequently has some nutritive value: 1 g provides approximately 17 kJ (4 kcal). However, in practice, the small quantity of aspartame consumed provides a minimal nutritive effect.

8. Description

Aspartame occurs as an off white, almost odorless crystalline powder with an intensely sweet taste.

9. Pharmacopeial Specifications

Test	USPNF XVII
Identification	+
Transmittance	+
Specific rotation	+ 14.5° to + 16.5°
Loss on drying	⩽ 4.5%
Residue on ignition	⩽ 0.2%
Arsenic	⩽ 3 ppm
Heavy metals	⩽ 0.001%
Other related substances	+
5-Benzyl-3,6-dioxo-2-piperazine-acetic acid	+
Assay (dried basis)	98.0-102.0%

10. Typical Properties

Acidity/alkalinity:
pH = 4.0-6.5 (0.8% w/v aqueous solution).
Density (bulk):
0.4-0.5 g/cm^3 for granular grade;
0.3-0.4 g/cm^3 for powder grade.
Melting point: 246-247°C
Solubility: slightly soluble in ethanol (95%); sparingly soluble in water. At 20°C the solubility is 1% w/v at the isoelectric point (pH 5.2). Solubility increases at higher temperature and at more acidic pH, e.g. at pH 2 and 20°C solubility is 10% w/v.
Specific rotation $[\alpha]_D^{22}$: −2.3° in 1N HCl

11. Stability and Storage Conditions

Aspartame is stable in dry conditions. In the presence of moisture, hydrolysis occurs to form the degradation products L-aspartyl-L-phenylalanine and 3-benzyl-6-carboxymethyl-2,5-diketopiperazine. A third degradation product is also known, β-L-aspartyl-L-phenylalanine methyl ester. For stability profile at 25°C in aqueous buffers *see* Fig. 1.

Stability in aqueous solutions has been enhanced by the addition of cyclodextrins,[3,4] and by the addition of polyethylene glycol 400 at pH 2.[5] However, at pH 3.5-4.5 stability is not enhanced by the replacement of water with organic solvents.[6]

Aspartame degradation also occurs during prolonged heat treatment; losses of aspartame may be minimized by using processes that employ high temperatures for a short time followed by rapid cooling.

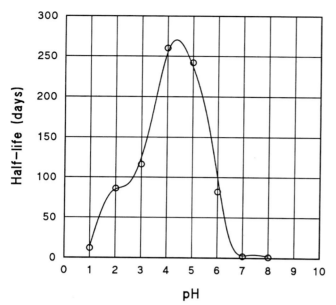

Fig. 1: Stability profile of aspartame in aqueous buffers at 25°C.[7]

The bulk material should be stored in a well-closed container, in a cool, dry, place.

12. Incompatibilities

Differential scanning calorimetry experiments with some directly compressible tablet excipients suggests that aspartame is incompatible with dibasic calcium phosphate and also with the lubricant magnesium stearate.[8]

13. Method of Manufacture

Aspartame is produced by coupling together L-phenylalanine (or L-phenylalanine methyl ester) and L-aspartic acid, either chemically or enzymatically. The former procedure yields both the sweet α-aspartame and nonsweet β-aspartame from which the α-aspartame has to be separated and purified. The enzymatic process yields only α-aspartame.

14. Safety

Aspartame is widely used in oral pharmaceutical formulations, beverages and food products as an intense sweetener and is generally regarded as a nontoxic material. However, the use of aspartame has been of some concern due to the formation of the potentially toxic metabolites methanol, aspartic acid and phenylalanine. Of these materials, only phenylalanine is produced in sufficient quantities, at normal aspartame intake levels to cause concern. In the normal healthy individual any phenylalanine produced is harmless, however it is recommended that aspartame be avoided or its intake restricted by those patients with phenylketonuria.[9]
The WHO has set an acceptable daily intake for aspartame at up to 40 mg/kg body-weight.[10] Additionally, the acceptable daily intake of diketopiperazine (an impurity found in aspartame) has been set, by the WHO, at up to 7.5 mg/kg body-weight.[11]
A number of adverse effects have been reported following the consumption of aspartame,[9,11] particularly in individuals who drink large quantities (up to 8 L per day in one case) of aspartame sweetened beverages. Reported adverse effects include: headaches;[12] grand mal seizure;[13] memory loss;[14] gastrointestinal symptoms and dermatological symptoms. Although aspartame has been reported to cause hyperactivity and behavioral problems in children, a double-blind controlled trial of 48 preschool age children fed diets containing a daily intake of 38 $\pm$ 13 mg/kg body-weight of aspartame for 3 weeks showed no adverse effects attributable to aspartame, or dietary sucrose, on children's behavior or cognitive function.[15]

15. Handling Precautions

Observe normal precautions appropriate to the circumstances and quantity of material handled. Measures should be taken to minimize the potential for dust explosion. Eye protection is recommended.

16. Regulatory Status

GRAS listed. Accepted for use as a food additive in Europe. Included in the FDA Inactive Ingredients Guide (oral powder for reconstitution). Included in nonparenteral medicines licensed in the UK.

17. Pharmacopeias

Fr, It and USPNF.

18. Related Substances

Acesulfame Potassium; Saccharin; Saccharin Sodium; Sodium Cyclamate.

19. Comments

The perceived intensity of sweeteners relative to sucrose depends upon their concentration, temperature of tasting, pH and on the flavor and texture of the product concerned.
Intense sweetening agents will not replace the bulk, textural or preservative characteristics of sugar if the latter ingredient is removed from a formulation.
Synergistic effects for combinations of sweeteners have been reported, e.g. aspartame with acesulfame potassium.

20. Specific References

1. Joachim J, et al. The compression of effervescent aspartame tablets: the influence of particle size on the strain applied on the punches during compression [in French]. J Pharm Belg 1987; 42: 17-28.
2. Joachim J, et al. The compression of effervescent aspartame tablets: the influence of particle size and temperature on the effervescence time and carbon dioxide liberation kinetics [in French]. J Pharm Belg 1987; 42: 303-314.
3. Brewster ME, Loftsson T, Baldvinsdóttir J, Bodor N. Stabilization of aspartame by cyclodextrins. Int J Pharmaceutics 1991; 75: R5-R8.
4. Prankerd RJ, Stone HW, Sloan KB, Perrin JH. Degradation of aspartame in acidic aqueous media and its stabilization by complexation with cyclodextrins or modified cyclodextrins. Int J Pharmaceutics 1992; 88: 189-199.
5. Yalkowsky SH, Davis E, Clark T. Stabilization of aspartame by polyethylene glycol 400. J Pharm Sci 1993; 82: 978.
6. Sanyude S, Locock RA, Pagliaro LA. Stability of aspartame in water: organic solvent mixtures with different dielectric constants. J Pharm Sci 1991; 80: 674-676.
7. The NutraSweet Company. Technical literature: *NutraSweet* technical bulletin, 1991.
8. El-Shattawy HE, Peck GE, Kildsig DO. Aspartame-direct compression excipients: preformulation stability screening using

differential scanning calorimetry. Drug Dev Ind Pharm 1981; 7: 605-619.

9. Golightly LK, Smolinske SS, Bennett ML, Sutherland EW, Rumack BH. Pharmaceutical excipients: adverse effects associated with inactive ingredients in drug products (part II). Med Toxicol 1988; 3: 209-240.

10. FAO/WHO. Evaluation of certain food additives and contaminants. Twenty-fifth report of the joint FAO/WHO expert committee on food additives. Tech Rep Ser Wld Hlth Org 1981; No. 669.

11. Butchkio HH, Kotsonis FN. Aspartame: review of recent research. Commen Toxicol 1989; 3(4): 253-278.

12. Schiffman SS, Buckley E, Sampson HA, Massey EW, Baraniuk JN, Follett JV, Warwick ZS. Aspartame and susceptibility to headache. N Engl J Med 1987; 317: 1181-1185.

13. Wurtman RJ. Aspartame: possible effect on seizure susceptibility [letter]. Lancet 1985; ii: 1060.

14. Sweetener blamed for mental illnesses. New Scientist 1988; February 18: 33.

15. Wolraich ML, et al. Effects of diets high in sucrose or aspartame on the behavior and cognitive performance of children. N Engl J Med 1994; 330: 301-307.

21. General References

Marie S. Sweeteners. In: Smith J, editor. Food additives user's handbook. Glasgow: Blackie, 1991: 47-74.

Roy GM. Taste masking in oral pharmaceuticals. Pharmaceut Technol Eur 1994; 6(6): 24, 26-28, 30-32, 34, 35.

Stegink LD, Filer LJ, editors. Aspartame, physiology and biochemistry. New York: Marcel Dekker Inc, 1984.

22. Authors

UK: FR Higton, DM Thurgood.

Bentonite

1. Nonproprietary Names

BP: Bentonite
PhEur: Bentonitum
USPNF: Bentonite

2. Synonyms

BentoPharm; E558; mineral soap; soap clay; taylorite; *Veegum HS*; wilkinite.

3. Chemical Name and CAS Registry Number

Bentonite [1302-78-9]

4. Empirical Formula   Molecular Weight

$Al_2O_3.4SiO_2.H_2O$ 359.16

Bentonite is a native colloidal hydrated aluminum silicate consisting mainly of montmorillonite, $Al_2O_3.4SiO_2.H_2O$; it may also contain calcium, magnesium, and iron. The average chemical analysis is conventionally expressed as oxides and is shown below, in comparison with magnesium aluminum silicate (*Veegum*).

	Bentonite	Magnesium aluminum silicate (*Veegum*)
Silicon dioxide	59.92%	61.1%
Aluminum oxide	19.78%	9.3%
Magnesium oxide	1.53%	13.7%
Ferric oxide	2.96%	0.9%
Calcium oxide	0.64%	2.7%
Sodium oxide	2.06%	2.9%
Potassium oxide	0.57%	0.3%

5. Structural Formula

See Section 4.

6. Functional Category

Adsorbent; stabilizing agent; suspending agent; viscosity-increasing agent

7. Applications in Pharmaceutical Formulation or Technology

Bentonite is a naturally occurring hydrated aluminum silicate used primarily in the formulation of suspensions, gels and sols, for topical pharmaceutical application. It is also used to suspend powders in aqueous preparations and to prepare cream bases containing oil-in-water emulsifying agents.

Bentonite may also be used in oral pharmaceutical preparations, cosmetics and food products. In oral preparations, bentonite, and other similar silicate clays, can be used to adsorb cationic drugs and so retard their release.[1-3] Adsorbents are also used to mask the taste of certain drugs. Bentonite has been investigated as a diagnostic agent for magnetic resonance imaging (MRI).[4]

Use	Concentration (%)
Adsorbent (clarifying agent)	1.0-2.0
Emulsion stabilizer	1.0
Suspending agent	0.5-5.0

8. Description

Bentonite is a crystalline, clay-like mineral, and is available as an odorless, pale buff or cream to grayish-colored fine powder, which is free from grit. It consists of particles about 50-150 μm in size along with numerous particles about 1-2 μm. Microscopic examination of samples stained with alcoholic methylene blue solution reveals strongly stained blue particles. Bentonite may have a slight earthy taste.

SEM: 1

Excipient: Bentonite
Manufacturer: American Colloid Co
Lot No.: NMD 11780
Magnification: 600x
Voltage: 10 kV

SEM: 2

Excipient: Bentonite
Manufacturer: American Colloid Co
Lot No.: NMD 11780
Magnification: 2400x
Voltage: 20 kV

9. Pharmacopeial Specifications

Test	PhEur 1990	USPNF XVII
Identification	+	+
Microbial limit	+	+
pH (2% w/v suspension)	+	9.5-10.5
Loss on drying	$\leqslant$ 15%	5.0-8.0%
Arsenic	—	$\leqslant$ 5 ppm
Lead	—	$\leqslant$ 0.004%
Heavy metals	$\leqslant$ 50 ppm	—
Gel formation	—	+
Sedimentation volume	+	—
Swelling power	+	+
Fineness of powder	+	+

10. Typical Properties

Acidity/alkalinity:
pH = 9.5-10.5 for a 2% w/v aqueous suspension.
Flowability: no flow, *see* HPE Data.
Hygroscopicity: bentonite is hygroscopic.[5] *See* HPE Data.
Moisture content: 5-12%, *see also* HPE Data.
Solubility: practically insoluble in ethanol, fixed oils, glycerin, propan-2-ol and water. Bentonite swells to about 12 times its original volume in water, to form viscous homogeneous suspensions, sols, or gels depending upon the concentration. Bentonite does not swell in organic solvents. Sols and gels may be conveniently prepared by sprinkling the bentonite on the surface of hot water and allowing to stand for 24 hours, stirring occasionally when the bentonite has become thoroughly wetted. Water should not be added to bentonite alone, but may be satisfactorily dispersed in water if the bentonite is first triturated with glycerin or mixed with a powder such as zinc oxide. A 7% w/v aqueous suspension of bentonite is just pourable. *See also* Section 12.
Viscosity (dynamic): 75-225 mPa s (75-225 cP) for a 5.5% w/v aqueous suspension at 25°C. Viscosity increases with increasing concentration.

| | HPE Laboratory Project Data | | |
	Method	Lab #	Results
Average flow rate	FLO-1	14	No flow[a]
Moisture content	MC-14	18	6.28%[a]
	MC-14	18	5.70%[b]
	EMC-1	18	*See* Fig. 1.[b]

Supplier:
a. American Colloid Co;
b. Whittaker, Clark & Daniels (Lot No.: NG3977).

11. Stability and Storage Conditions

Bentonite is hygroscopic, and sorption of atmospheric water should be avoided.
Aqueous bentonite suspensions may be sterilized by autoclaving. The solid material may be sterilized by maintaining it at 170°C for 1 hour after drying at 100°C.
Bentonite should be stored in an airtight container in a cool, dry, place.

12. Incompatibilities

Aqueous bentonite suspensions retain their viscosity above pH 6, but are precipitated by acids. Acid-washed bentonite does not have suspending properties. The addition of alkaline materials, such as magnesium oxide, increases gel formation.

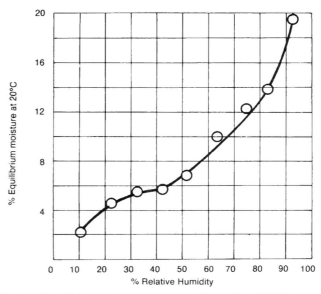

Fig. 1: Equilibrium moisture content of bentonite USPNF.

Addition of significant amounts of alcohol to aqueous preparations will precipitate bentonite, primarily by dehydration of the lattice structure, *see also* Section 19.
Bentonite particles are negatively charged and flocculation occurs when electrolytes or positively charged suspensions are added. Bentonite is thus said to be incompatible with strong electrolytes, although this effect is sometimes used beneficially to clarify turbid liquids.
The antimicrobial efficacy of cationic preservatives may be reduced in aqueous bentonite suspensions, but nonionic and anionic preservatives are unaffected.[6]
Bentonite is incompatible with acriflavine hydrochloride.

13. Method of Manufacture

Bentonite is a native, colloidal, hydrated aluminum silicate, found in regions of Canada and the US. The mined ore is processed to remove grit and non-swelling materials so that it is suitable for pharmaceutical applications.

14. Safety

Bentonite is mainly used in topical pharmaceutical formulations but has also been used in oral pharmaceutical preparations, food products and cosmetics.
Following oral administration, bentonite is not absorbed from the gastrointestinal tract; it has been used in the form of a gel as a bulk laxative. Bentonite is generally regarded as a nontoxic and nonirritant material.
LD_{50} (rat, IV): 0.035 g/kg[7]

15. Handling Precautions

Observe normal precautions appropriate to the circumstances and quantity of material handled. Eye protection, gloves and a dust mask are recommended. Bentonite should be handled in a well ventilated environment and dust generation minimized.

16. Regulatory Status

Accepted in Europe as a food additive in certain applications. Included in the FDA Inactive Ingredients Guide (oral capsules, tablets, topical emulsions and suspensions). Included in nonparenteral medicines licensed in the UK.

17. Pharmacopeias

Aust, Br, Cz, Egypt, Eur, Fr, Ger, Gr, Ind, It, Jpn, Mex, Neth, Port, Swiss and USPNF.

Some pharmacopeias, such as the USPNF XVII, also contain a separate monograph for purified bentonite. This is bentonite which has been processed to remove grit and non-swellable ore components.

18. Related Substances

Bentonite magma; Kaolin; Magnesium Aluminum Silicate; Magnesium Trisilicate; Talc.

Bentonite magma:
Comments: a 5% w/v suspension of bentonite in purified water appears in some pharmacopeias, such as the USPNF XVII.

19. Comments

Bentonite may be used with concentrations of up to 30% ethanol or propan-2-ol; 50% glycerin; 30% propylene glycol; or high molecular weight polyethylene glycols.

20. Specific References

1. Stul MS, Vliers DP, Uytterhoven JB. *In vitro* adsorption-desorption of phenethylamines and phenylimidazoles by a bentonite and a resin. J Pharm Sci 1984; 73: 1372-1375.
2. Shrivastava R, Jain SR, Frank SG. Dissolution dialysis studies of metronidazole-montmorillonite adsorbates. J Pharm Sci 1985; 74: 214-216.
3. Forni F, Iannuccelli V, Coppi G, Bernabei MT. Effect of montmorillonite on drug release from polymeric matrices. Arch Pharm 1989; 322: 789-793.
4. Listinsky JJ, Bryant RG. Gastrointestinal contrast agents: a diamagnetic approach. Magn Reson Med 1988; 8(3): 285-292.
5. Callahan JC, Cleary GW, Elefant M, Kaplan G, Kensler T, Nash RA. Equilibrium moisture content of pharmaceutical excipients. Drug Dev Ind Pharm 1982; 8: 355-369.
6. Harris WA. The inactivation of cationic antiseptics by bentonite suspensions. Aust J Pharm 1961; 42: 583-588.
7. Sweet DV, editor. Registry of toxic effects of chemical substances. Cincinnati: US Department of Health, 1987.

21. General References

Altagracia M, Ford I, Garzon ML, Kravzov J. A comparative mineralogical and physico-chemical study of some crude Mexican and pharmaceutical grade montmorillonites. Drug Dev Ind Pharm 1987; 13: 2249-2262.
Sadik F, Fincher JH, Hartman CW. X-Ray diffraction analysis for identification of kaolin NF and bentonite USP. J Pharm Sci 1971; 60: 916-918.

22. Authors

USA: AA Belmonte.

Benzalkonium Chloride

1. Nonproprietary Names

BP: Benzalkonium chloride
PhEur: Benzalkonii chloridum
USPNF: Benzalkonium chloride

2. Synonyms

Alkylbenzyldimethylammonium chloride; alkyl dimethyl benzyl ammonium chloride; BKC; *Catigene DC 100*; *Exameen 3580*; *Hyamine 3500*; *Pentonium*; *Roccal*; *Zephiran*.

3. Chemical Name and CAS Registry Number

Alkyldimethyl(phenylmethyl)ammonium chloride
[8001-54-5]

4. Empirical Formula Molecular Weight

The USPNF XVII describes benzalkonium chloride as a mixture of alkylbenzyldimethylammonium chlorides of the general formula $[C_6H_5CH_2N(CH_3)_2R]Cl$, where R represents a mixture of alkyls, including all or some of the group beginning with n-C_8H_{17} and extending through higher homologs, with n-$C_{12}H_{25}$, n-$C_{14}H_{29}$, and n-$C_{16}H_{33}$ comprising the major portion. The average molecular weight of benzalkonium chloride is 360.

5. Structural Formula

R = mixture of alkyls: n-C_8H_{17} to n-$C_{18}H_{37}$; mainly n-$C_{12}H_{25}$ (dodecyl), n-$C_{14}H_{29}$ (tetradecyl) and n-$C_{16}H_{33}$ (hexadecyl).

6. Functional Category

Antimicrobial preservative; antiseptic; disinfectant; solubilizing agent; wetting agent.

7. Applications in Pharmaceutical Formulation or Technology

Benzalkonium chloride is a quaternary ammonium compound used in pharmaceutical formulations as an antimicrobial preservative in applications similar to other cationic surfactants, such as cetrimide.
In ophthalmic preparations, benzalkonium chloride is one of the most widely used preservatives, at a concentration of 0.01-0.02% w/v. Often it is used in combination with other preservatives or excipients, particularly 0.1% w/v disodium edetate, to enhance its antimicrobial activity against strains of *Pseudomonas*.

In nasal and otic formulations a concentration of 0.002-0.02% is used, sometimes in combination with 0.002-0.005% w/v thimerosal. Benzalkonium chloride 0.01% w/v is also employed as a preservative in small volume parenteral products.
Benzalkonium chloride is additionally used as a preservative in cosmetics.

8. Description

Benzalkonium chloride occurs as a white or yellowish white amorphous powder, a thick gel, or gelatinous flakes. It is hygroscopic, soapy to the touch and has a mild aromatic odor and very bitter taste.

9. Pharmacopeial Specifications

Test	PhEur 1985	USPNF XVII
Identification	+	+
Acidity or alkalinity	+	—
Appearance of solution	+	—
Water	⩽ 10.0%	⩽ 15.0%
Residue on ignition	—	⩽ 2.0%
Sulfated ash	⩽ 0.1%	—
Water-insoluble matter	—	+
Foreign amines	+	+
Ratio of alkyl components	—	+
Assay (dried basis)		
of n-$C_{12}H_{25}$	—	⩾ 40.0%
of n-$C_{14}H_{29}$	—	⩾ 20.0%
of n-$C_{12}H_{25}$ & n-$C_{14}H_{29}$	—	⩾ 70.0%
for total alkyl content	95.0-104.0%	97.0-103.0%

10. Typical Properties

Acidity/alkalinity:
pH = 5-8 for a 10% w/v aqueous solution.
Antimicrobial activity: benzalkonium chloride solutions are active against a wide range of bacteria, yeasts and fungi. Activity is more marked against Gram-positive than Gram-negative bacteria and minimal against bacterial endospores and acid fast bacteria. The antimicrobial activity of benzalkonium chloride is significantly dependent upon the alkyl composition of the homolog mixture.[1] Benzalkonium chloride is ineffective against some *Pseudomonas aeruginosa* strains, *Mycobacterium tuberculosis*, *Trichophyton interdigitale* and *T. rubrum*. However, combined with disodium edetate (0.01-0.1% w/v), benzyl alcohol, phenylethanol or phenylpropanol, the activity against *Pseudomonas aeruginosa* is increased.[2] Antimicrobial activity may also be enhanced by the addition of phenylmercuric acetate, phenylmercuric borate, chlorhexidine, cetrimide or *m*-cresol.[3,4] In the presence of citrate and phosphate buffers (but not borate), activity against *Pseudomonas* can be reduced. *See also* Sections 11 and 12. Benzalkonium chloride is relatively inactive against spores and molds, but is active against some viruses, including HIV.[5] Inhibitory activity increases with pH although antimicrobial activity occurs between pH 4-10. Typical minimum inhibitory concentrations (MICs) are shown in Table I.

Table I: Minimum inhibitory concentrations (MICs) of benzalkonium chloride.

Microorganism	MIC (μg/mL)
Aerobacter aerogenes	64
Clostridium histolyticum	5
Clostridium oedematiens	5
Clostridium tetani	5
Clostridium welchii	5
Escherichia coli	16
Pneumococcus II	5
Proteus vulgaris	64
Pseudomonas aeruginosa	30
Salmonella enteritidis	30
Salmonella paratyphi	16
Salmonella typhosa	4
Shigella dysenteriae	2
Staphylococcus aureus	1.25
Streptococcus pyrogenes	1.25
Vibrio cholerae	2

Density: $\approx$ 0.98 g/cm^3 at 20°C
Melting point: $\approx$ 40°C
Partition coefficients: the octanol: water partition coefficient varies with the alkyl chain length of the homolog; 9.98 for C_{12}, 32.9 for C_{14} and 82.5 for C_{16}.
Solubility: practically insoluble in ether; very soluble in acetone, ethanol (95%), methanol, propanol and water. Aqueous solutions of benzalkonium chloride foam when shaken, have a low surface tension and possess detergent and emulsifying properties.

11. Stability and Storage Conditions

Benzalkonium chloride is hygroscopic and may be affected by light, air and metals.
Solutions are stable over a wide pH and temperature range and may be sterilized by autoclaving without loss of effectiveness. Solutions may be stored for prolonged periods at room temperature. Dilute solutions stored in polyvinyl chloride or polyurethane foam containers may lose antimicrobial activity. The bulk material should be stored in an airtight container, protected from light and contact with metals, in a cool, dry, place.

12. Incompatibilities

Incompatible with aluminum, anionic surfactants, citrates, cotton, fluorescein, hydrogen peroxide, hydroxypropyl methylcellulose,[6] iodides, kaolin, lanolin, nitrates, nonionic surfactants in high concentration, permanganates, protein, salicylates, silver salts, soaps, sulfonamides, tartrates, zinc oxide, zinc sulfate, some rubber mixes and some plastic mixes.

13. Method of Manufacture

Benzalkonium chloride is formed by the reaction of a solution of *N*-alkyl-*N*-methyl-benzamine with methyl chloride in an organic solvent suitable for precipitating the quaternary compound as it is formed.

14. Safety

Benzalkonium chloride is usually nonirritating, nonsensitizing and well tolerated in the dilutions normally employed on the skin and mucous membranes. However, benzalkonium chloride has been associated with adverse effects when used in some pharmaceutical formulations.[7]
Ototoxicity can occur when benzalkonium chloride is applied to the ear[8] and prolonged contact with the skin can occasionally cause irritation and hypersensitivity. Benzalkonium chloride is also known to cause bronchoconstriction in some asthmatics when used in nebulizer solutions.[9-13]
Toxicity experiments with rabbits have shown benzalkonium chloride, in concentrations higher than that normally used as a preservative, to be harmful to the eye. However, the human eye appears to be less affected than the rabbit eye and many ophthalmic products have been formulated with benzalkonium chloride 0.01% w/v as the preservative. Benzalkonium chloride is not suitable for use as a preservative in solutions used for storing and washing hydrophilic soft contact lenses, as the benzalkonium chloride can bind to the lenses and may later produce ocular toxicity when the lenses are worn.[14] Solutions stronger than 0.03% w/v concentration entering the eye require prompt medical attention.
Local irritation of the throat, esophagus, stomach and intestine can occur following contact with strong solutions (> 0.1% w/v). The fatal oral dose of benzalkonium chloride in humans is estimated to be 1-3 g. Adverse effects following oral ingestion include vomiting, collapse and coma. Toxic doses lead to paralysis of the respiratory muscles, dyspnea and cyanosis.

LD_{50} (guinea pig, oral): 200 mg/kg[15]
LD_{50} (mouse, IP): 10 mg/kg
LD_{50} (mouse, IV): 10 mg/kg
LD_{50} (mouse, oral): 175 mg/kg
LD_{50} (mouse, SC): 64 mg/kg
LD_{50} (rat, IP): 14.5 mg/kg
LD_{50} (rat, IV): 13.9 mg/kg
LD_{50} (rat, oral): 240 mg/kg
LD_{50} (rat, SC): 400 mg/kg
LD_{50} (rat, skin): 1.56 g/kg

15. Handling Precautions

Observe normal precautions appropriate to the circumstances and quantity of material handled. Benzalkonium chloride is irritant to the skin and eyes and repeated exposure to the skin may cause hypersensitivity. Concentrated benzalkonium chloride solutions accidentally spilled on the skin may produce corrosive skin lesions with deep necrosis and scarring, and should be washed immediately with water, followed by soap solutions applied freely. Gloves, eye protection and suitable protective clothing should be worn.

16. Regulatory Status

Included in the FDA Inactive Ingredients Guide (inhalations, IM injections, nasal, ophthalmic, otic and topical preparations). Included in nonparenteral medicines licensed in the UK.

17. Pharmacopeias

Aust, Br, Braz, Egypt, Eur, Fr, Gr, Hung, It, Jpn, Mex, Neth, Port, Swiss, Turk, Yug and USPNF. Also in BP Vet.

18. Related Substances

Benzethonium Chloride; Cetrimide.

19. Comments

—

20. Specific References

1. Euerby MR. High performance liquid chromatography of benzalkonium chlorides — variation in commercial preparations. J Clin Hosp Pharm 1985; 10: 73-77.
2. Richards RME, McBride RJ. Enhancement of benzalkonium chloride and chlorhexidine acetate activity against *Pseudomonas aeruginosa* by aromatic alcohols. J Pharm Sci 1973; 62: 2035-2037.
3. Hugbo PG. Additivity and synergism *in vitro* as displayed by mixtures of some commonly employed antibacterial preservatives. Can J Pharm Sci 1976; 11: 17-20.
4. McCarthy TJ, Myburgh JA, Butler N. Further studies on the influence of formulation on preservative activity. Cosmet Toilet 1977; 92(3): 33-36.
5. Chermann JC, Barre-Sinoussi F, Henin Y, Marechal V. HIV inactivation by a spermicide containing benzalkonium. AIDS Forsch 1987; 2: 85-86.
6. Richards RME. Effect of hypromellose on the antibacterial activity of benzalkonium chloride. J Pharm Pharmacol 1976; 28: 264.
7. Smolinske SC. Handbook of food, drug, and cosmetic excipients. Boca Raton, FL: CRC Press Inc, 1992: 31-39.
8. Honigman JL. Disinfectant ototoxicity [letter]. Pharm J 1975; 215: 523.
9. Beasley CRW, Rafferty P, Holgate ST. Bronchoconstrictor properties of preservatives in ipratropium bromide (Atrovent) nebuliser solution. Br Med J 1987; 294: 1197-1198.
10. Miszkiel KA, Beasley R, Rafferty P, Holgate ST. The contribution of histamine release to bronchoconstriction provoked by inhaled benzalkonium chloride in asthma. Br J Clin Pharmacol 1988; 25: 157-163.
11. Miszkiel KA, Beasley R, Holgate ST. The influence of ipratropium bromide and sodium cromoglycate on benzalkonium chloride-induced bronchoconstriction in asthma. Br J Clin Pharmacol 1988; 26: 295-301.
12. Worthington I. Bronchoconstriction due to benzalkonium chloride in nebulizer solutions. Can J Hosp Pharm 1989; 42: 165-166.
13. Boucher M, Roy MT, Henderson J. Possible association of benzalkonium chloride in nebulizer solutions with respiratory arrest. Ann Pharmacother 1992; 26: 772-774.
14. Gasset AR. Benzalkonium chloride toxicity to the human cornea. Am J Ophthalmol 1977; 84: 169-171.
15. Sweet DV, editor. Registry of toxic effects of chemical substances. Cincinnati: US Department of Health, 1987.

21. General References

Cowen RA, Steiger B. Why a preservative system must be tailored to a specific product. Cosmet Toilet 1977; 92(3): 15-20.
El-Falaha BMA, Rogers DT, Furr JR, Russell AD. Surface changes in *Pseudomonas aeruginosa* exposed to chlorhexidine diacetate and benzalkonium chloride. Int J Pharmaceutics 1985; 23: 239-243.
El-Falaha BMA, Russell AD, Furr JR, Rogers DT. Activity of benzalkonium chloride and chlorhexidine diacetate against wild-type and envelope mutants of *Escherichia coli* and *Pseudomonas aeruginosa*. Int J Pharmaceutics 1985; 23: 239-243.
Karabit MS, Juneskans OT, Lundgren P. Studies on the evaluation of preservative efficacy III: the determination of antimicrobial characteristics of benzalkonium chloride. Int J Pharmaceutics 1988; 46: 141-147.
Lien EJ, Perrin JH. Effect of chain length on critical micelle formation and protein binding of quaternary ammonium compounds. J Med Chem 1976; 19: 849-850.
Martin AR. Anti-infective agents. In: Doerge RF, editor. Wilson and Gisvold's textbook of organic, medicinal and pharmaceutical chemistry. Philadelphia: J.B. Lippincott Company, 1982: 141-142.
Pensé AM, Vauthier C, Puisieux F, Benoit JP. Microencapsulation of benzalkonium chloride. Int J Pharmaceutics 1992; 81: 111-117.
Prince HN, Nonemaker WS, Norgard RC, Prince DL. Drug resistance studies with topical antiseptics. J Pharm Sci 1978; 67: 1629-1631.
Wallhäusser KH. Benzalkonium chloride. In: Kabara JJ, editor. Cosmetic and drug preservation principles and practice. New York: Marcel Dekker Inc, 1984: 731-734.

22. Authors

USA: NM Vemuri.

Benzethonium Chloride

1. Nonproprietary Names

USP: Benzethonium chloride

2. Synonyms

Benzyldimethyl[2-[2-(*p*-1,1,3,3-tetramethylbutylphenoxy)ethoxy]ethyl]ammonium chloride; BZT; diisobutylphenoxyethoxyethyl dimethyl benzyl ammonium chloride; *Hyamine 1622.*

3. Chemical Name and CAS Registry Number

N,N-Dimethyl-*N*-[2-[2-[4-(1,1,3,3-tetramethylbutyl)phenoxy]ethoxy]ethyl]benzene-methanaminium chloride [121-54-0]

4. Empirical Formula   Molecular Weight

$C_{27}H_{42}ClNO_2$ 448.10

5. Structural Formula

6. Functional Category

Antimicrobial preservative; antiseptic; disinfectant.

7. Applications in Pharmaceutical Formulation or Technology

Benzethonium chloride is a quaternary ammonium compound used in pharmaceutical formulations as an antimicrobial preservative. Typically, it is used for this purpose in injections, ophthalmic and otic preparations at concentrations between 0.01-0.02% w/v. Benzethonium chloride may also be used as a wetting and solubilizing agent, and as a topical disinfectant.

In cosmetics such as deodorants, benzethonium chloride may be used as an antimicrobial preservative in concentrations up to 0.5% w/v.

The physical properties and applications of benzethonium chloride are similar to other cationic surfactants such as cetrimide.

8. Description

Benzethonium chloride occurs as a white crystalline material with a mild odor and very bitter taste.

9. Pharmacopeial Specifications

Test	USP XXII
Identification	+
Melting range	158-163°C
Loss on drying	≤ 5.0%
Residue on ignition	≤ 0.1%
Ammonium compounds	+
Assay (dried basis)	97.0-103.0%

10. Typical Properties

Acidity/alkalinity:
pH = 4.8-5.5 for a 1% w/v aqueous solution.
Antimicrobial activity: optimum antimicrobial activity occurs between pH 4-10. Preservative efficacy is enhanced by ethanol and reduced by soaps and other anionic surfactants. Typical minimum inhibitory concentrations (MICs) are shown below:[1]

Microorganism	MIC (μg/mL)
Aspergillus niger	128
Candida albicans	64
Escherichia coli	32
Penicillium notatum	64
Proteus vulgaris	64
Pseudomonas aeruginosa	250
Pseudomonas cepacia	250
Pseudomonas fluorescens	250
Staphylococcus aureus	0.5
Streptococcus pyogenes	0.5

Solubility: soluble 1 in less than 1 of acetone, chloroform, ethanol (95%) and water; soluble 1 in 6000 of ether. Dissolves in water to produce a foamy, soapy solution.

11. Stability and Storage Conditions

Benzethonium chloride is stable. Aqueous solutions may be sterilized by autoclaving.
The bulk material should be stored in an airtight container protected from light, in a cool, dry, place.

12. Incompatibilities

Benzethonium chloride is incompatible with soaps and other anionic surfactants and may be precipitated from solutions greater than 2% w/v concentration by the addition of mineral acids and some salt solutions.

13. Method of Manufacture

p-Diisobutylphenol is condensed in the presence of a basic catalyst with β,β'-dichlorodiethyl ether to yield 2-[2-[4-(1,1,3,3-tetramethylbutyl)phenoxy]ethoxy]ethyl chloride. Alkaline dimethylamination then produces the corresponding tertiary amine which, after purification by distillation, is dissolved in a suitable organic solvent and treated with benzyl chloride to precipitate benzethonium chloride.[2]

14. Safety

Benzethonium chloride is readily absorbed and is generally regarded as a toxic substance when administered orally. Ingestion may cause vomiting, collapse, convulsions and coma. The probable lethal human oral dose is estimated to be 50-500 mg/kg body-weight.

The topical use of solutions containing greater than 5% w/v benzethonium chloride can cause irritation although benzethonium chloride is not regarded as a sensitizer. The use of 0.5% w/v benzethonium chloride in cosmetics is associated with few adverse effects. A maximum concentration of 0.02% w/v benzethonium chloride is recommended for use in cosmetics used in the eye area and this is also the maximum concentration generally used in pharmaceutical formulations such as injections and ophthalmic preparations.[3]
See also Benzalkonium Chloride.

LD_{50} (mouse, IP): 8 mg/kg[4]
LD_{50} (mouse, IV): 30 mg/kg
LD_{50} (mouse, oral): 340 mg/kg
LD_{50} (rat, IP): 17 mg/kg
LD_{50} (rat, IV): 19 mg/kg
LD_{50} (rat, oral): 370 mg/kg
LD_{50} (rat, SC): 120 mg/kg

15. Handling Precautions

Observe normal precautions appropriate to the circumstances and quantity of material handled. Eye protection and gloves are recommended.

16. Regulatory Status

Included in the FDA Inactive Ingredients Guide (IM and IV injections, ophthalmic and otic preparations).

17. Pharmacopeias

Egypt, Jpn, Nord and US.

18. Related Substances

Benzalkonium Chloride; Cetrimide.

19. Comments

Benzethonium chloride has been used therapeutically in the past as a disinfectant and topical anti-infective agent. However, its use in these applications has largely been superseded by other more effective antimicrobials and it is now largely used solely as a preservative in a limited number of pharmaceutical and cosmetic formulations.

20. Specific References

1. Wallhäusser KH. Benzethonium chloride. In: Kabara JJ, editor. Cosmetic and drug preservation principles and practice. New York: Marcel Dekker Inc, 1984: 734-735.
2. Remington's pharmaceutical sciences, 15th edition. Easton, PA: Mack Publishing Co, 1975: 1089.
3. The Expert Panel of the American College of Toxicology. Final report on the safety assessment of benzethonium chloride and methylbenzethonium chloride. J Am Coll Toxicol 1985; 4: 65-106.
4. Sweet DV, editor. Registry of toxic effects of chemical substances. Cincinnati: US Department of Health, 1987.

21. General References

—

22. Authors

UK: PJ Weller.

Benzoic Acid

1. Nonproprietary Names

BP: Benzoic acid
PhEur: Acidum benzoicum
USP: Benzoic acid

2. Synonyms

Benzenecarboxylic acid; benzeneformic acid; carboxybenzene; dracylic acid; E210; phenylcarboxylic acid; phenylformic acid.

3. Chemical Name and CAS Registry Number

Benzoic acid [65-85-0]

4. Empirical Formula   Molecular Weight

$C_7H_6O_2$ 122.12

5. Structural Formula

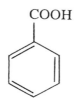

6. Functional Category

Antimicrobial preservative; therapeutic agent.

7. Applications in Pharmaceutical Formulation or Technology

Benzoic acid is widely used in cosmetics, foods and pharmaceuticals as an antimicrobial preservative. Greatest activity is seen at pH values between 2.5-4.5, *see* Section 10.

SEM: 1

Excipient: Benzoic acid
Manufacturer: Merck Ltd
Magnification: 60x

Benzoic acid also has a long history of use as an antifungal agent in topical therapeutic preparations such as Whitfield's ointment (benzoic acid 6% and salicylic acid 3%).

Use	Concentration (%)
IM and IV injections	0.17
Oral solutions	0.01-0.1
Oral suspensions	0.1
Oral syrups	0.15
Topical preparations	0.1-0.2
Vaginal preparations	0.1-0.2

8. Description

Benzoic acid occurs as feathery, light, white or colorless crystals or powder. It is essentially tasteless and odorless or with a slight characteristic odor suggestive of benzoin.

9. Pharmacopeial Specifications

Test	PhEur 1981	USP XXII
Identification	+	+
Congealing range	—	121-123°C
Water	—	⩽ 0.7%
Residue on ignition	—	⩽ 0.05%
Sulfated ash	⩽ 0.1%	—
Readily carbonizable substances	+	+
Readily oxidizable substances	+	+
Heavy metals	⩽ 10 ppm	⩽ 0.001%
Arsenic	—	⩽ 3 ppm
Halogenated compounds and halides	+	—
Appearance of solution	+	—
Assay	99.0-100.5%	99.5-100.5%

SEM: 2

Excipient: Benzoic acid
Manufacturer: Merck Ltd
Magnification: 600x

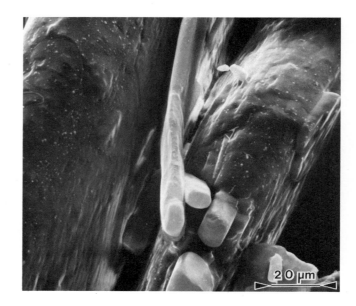

10. Typical Properties

Acidity/alkalinity:
pH = 2.8 (saturated aqueous solution at 25°C)
Antimicrobial activity: only the undissociated acid shows antimicrobial properties, therefore the activity depends on the pH of the medium. Optimum activity occurs at pH values below 4.5; at values above pH 5, benzoic acid is almost inactive.[1] It has been reported that antimicrobial activity is enhanced by the addition of protamine, a basic protein.[2]
Bacteria: moderate bacteriostatic activity against most species of Gram-positive bacteria. Typical MIC is 100 μg/mL. Less activity, in general, against Gram-negative bacteria. MIC for Gram-negative bacteria may be up to 1600 μg/mL.
Molds: moderate activity. Typical MICs are: 400-1000 μg/mL at pH 3; 1000-2000 μg/mL at pH 5.
Yeasts: moderate activity. Typical MIC is 1200 μg/mL. The addition of propylene glycol may enhance the fungistatic activity of benzoic acid.
Spores: inactive against spores.
Autoignition temperature: 570°C
Boiling point: 249.2°C
Density:
1.316 g/cm^3 for solid at 24°C;
1.075 g/cm^3 for liquid at 130°C.
Dissociation constant: the dissociation of benzoic acid in mixed solvents is dictated by specific solute-solvent interactions as well as by relative solvent basicity. Increasing the organic solvent fraction favors the free acid form.[3]
pK_a = 4.19 at 25°C;
pK_a = 5.54 in methanol 60%.
Flash point: 121-131°C
Melting point:
122°C (begins to sublime at 100°C).
Partition coefficients:
Benzene: water = 0.0044;[4]
Cyclohexane: water = 0.30;[5]
Octanol: water = 1.87.[6]
Refractive index:
n_D^{15} = 1.5397 for solid;
n_D^{132} = 1.504 for liquid.
Solubility: apparent aqueous solubility of benzoic acid may be enhanced by the addition of citric acid or sodium acetate to the solution. *See also* HPE Data.

Solvent	Solubility at 25°C Unless otherwise stated
Acetone	1 in 2.3
Benzene	1 in 9.4
Carbon disulfide	1 in 30
Carbon tetrachloride	1 in 15.2
Chloroform	1 in 4.5
Cyclohexane	1 in 14.6 [5]
Ethanol	1 in 2.7 at 15°C
	1 in 2.2
Ethanol (76%)	1 in 3.72 [7]
Ethanol (54%)	1 in 6.27 [7]
Ethanol (25%)	1 in 68 [7]
Ether	1 in 3
Fixed oils	freely soluble
Methanol	1 in 1.8
Toluene	1 in 11
Water	1 in 300

HPE Laboratory Project Data			
	Method	Lab #	Results
Density	DE-1	31	1.339 g/cm^3 [a]
Density	DE-1	31	1.315 g/cm^3 [b]
Moisture content	MC-3	25	0.168% [a]
Moisture content	MC-3	25	0.424% [b]
Solubility in mg/mL			
Ethanol (95%) at 25°C	SOL-5	11	327.9 ± 24.3
	SOL-6	23	309 [a]
	SOL-6	23	334 [b]
Ethanol (95%) at 37°C	SOL-5	11	418.6 ± 26.3
	SOL-6	23	380 [a]
	SOL-6	23	379 [b]
Hexane at 25°C	SOL-5	11	9.6 ± 0.2
	SOL-6	23	< 1 [a]
	SOL-6	23	< 1 [b]
Hexane at 37°C	SOL-5	11	15.8 ± 0.12
	SOL-6	23	< 1 [a]
	SOL-6	23	< 1 [b]
Propylene glycol at 25°C	SOL-5	11	189.4 ± 15.1
	SOL-6	23	225-325 [a]
	SOL-6	23	225-325 [b]
Propylene glycol at 37°C	SOL-5	11	319.8 ± 5.4
	SOL-6	23	225-325 [a]
	SOL-6	23	225-325 [b]
Water at 25°C	SOL-5	11	3.04 ± 0.11
	SOL-6	23	< 1 [a]
	SOL-6	23	< 1 [b]
Water at 37°C	SOL-5	11	4.67 ± 0.07
	SOL-6	23	< 1 [a]
	SOL-6	23	< 1 [b]

Supplier: a. Witco Corporation; b. Mallinckrodt Speciality Chemicals Co.

11. Stability and Storage Conditions

Aqueous solutions of benzoic acid may be sterilized by autoclaving or by filtration.
A 0.1% w/v aqueous solution of benzoic acid has been reported as being stable for at least 8 weeks when stored in polyvinyl chloride bottles, at room temperature.[8]
When added to a suspension benzoic acid dissociates with the benzoate anion adsorbing onto the suspended drug particles. This adsorption alters the charge at the surface of the particles which may in turn affect the physical stability of the suspension.[9]
The bulk material should be stored in a well-closed container in a cool, dry, place.

12. Incompatibilities

Undergoes typical reactions of an organic acid, e.g. with alkalis or heavy metals. Preservative activity may be reduced by interaction with kaolin.[10]

13. Method of Manufacture

Although benzoic acid occurs naturally, it is produced commercially by several synthetic methods. One process involves the continuous liquid-phase oxidation of toluene in the presence of a cobalt catalyst at 150-200°C and 0.5-5 MPa (5-50 atm) pressure to give a yield of approximately 90% benzoic acid.
Benzoic acid can also be produced commercially from benzotrichloride or phthalic anhydride. Benzotrichloride, produced by chlorination of toluene, is reacted with one

mole of benzoic acid to yield two moles of benzoyl chloride. The benzoyl chloride is then converted to two moles of benzoic acid by hydrolysis. Yield is 75-80%.

In another commercial process, phthalic anhydride is converted to benzoic acid, in about an 85% yield, by hydrolysis in the presence of heat and chromium and disodium phthalates.

Crude benzoic acid is purified by sublimation or recrystallization.

14. Safety

Ingested benzoic acid is conjugated with glycine in the liver to yield hippuric acid, which is then excreted in the urine. Benzoic acid is a gastric irritant and a mild irritant to the skin, eyes and mucous membranes. Allergic reactions to benzoic acid have been reported although a controlled study indicated that the incidence of urticaria in patients given benzoic acid is no greater than a lactose placebo.[11]

The WHO acceptable daily intake of benzoic acid and other benzoates, calculated as benzoic acid, has been set at up to 5 mg/kg of body-weight.[12,13] The minimum lethal human oral dose of benzoic acid is 500 mg/kg body-weight.[14]

LD_{50} (cat, oral): 2 g/kg[14]
LD_{50} (dog, oral): 2 g/kg
LD_{50} (mouse, IP): 1.46 g/kg
LD_{50} (mouse, oral): 1.94 g/kg
LD_{50} (rat, oral): 2.53 g/kg

See also Sodium Benzoate.

15. Handling Precautions

Observe normal precautions appropriate to the circumstances and quantity of material handled. Benzoic acid may be harmful by inhalation, ingestion or skin absorption and may be irritant to the eyes, skin and mucous membranes. Benzoic acid should be handled in a well-ventilated environment; eye protection, gloves and a dust mask or respirator are recommended. Benzoic acid is flammable.

16. Regulatory Status

GRAS listed. Accepted as a food additive in Europe. Included in the FDA Inactive Ingredients Guide (buccal solutions, IM and IV injections, oral solutions, syrups and tablets, rectal, topical and vaginal preparations). Included in nonparenteral medicines licensed in the UK.

17. Pharmacopeias

Aust, Belg, Br, Braz, Chin, Cz, Egypt, Eur, Fr, Ger, Gr, Hung, Ind, Int, It, Jpn, Mex, Neth, Nord, Port, Rom, Rus, Swiss, Turk, US and Yug.

18. Related Substances

Sodium Benzoate.

19. Comments

Benzoic acid is known to dimerize in many nonpolar solvents. This property, coupled with pH-dependent dissociation in aqueous media, comprises a classic textbook example of the effects of dissociation and molecular association on apparent partitioning behavior. The principles involved might be practically applied in determination of the total concentration of benzoate necessary to provide a bacteriostatic level of benzoic acid in the aqueous phase of an oil-in-water emulsion.

20. Specific References

1. Hurwitz SJ, McCarthy TJ. The effect of pH and concentration on the rates of kill of benzoic acid solutions against E. coli. J Clin Pharm Ther 1987; 12: 107-115.
2. Boussard P, Devleeschouwer MJ, Dony J. In vitro modification of antimicrobial efficacy by protamine. Int J Pharmaceutics 1991; 72: 51-55.
3. Ghosh SK, Hazra DK. Solvent effects on the dissociation of benzoic acid in aqueous mixtures of 2-methoxyethanol and 1,2-dimethoxyethane at 25°C. J Chem Soc Perkin Trans 1989; 2: 1021-1024.
4. Pawlowski W, Wieckowska E. Hydration of benzoic acid in benzene solution II: calculation of hydration constant. Z Phys Chem 1990; 168: 205-215.
5. Dearden JC, Roberts MJ. Cyclohexane-water partition coefficients of some pharmaceuticals. J Pharm Pharmacol 1989; 41: 102P.
6. Yalkowsky SH, Valvani SC, Roseman TJ. Solubility and partitioning VI: octanol solubility and octanol-water partition coefficients. J Pharm Sci 1983; 72: 866-870.
7. Pal A, Lahiri SC. Solubility and the thermodynamics of transfer of benzoic acid in mixed solvents. Indian J Chem 1989; 28A: 276-279.
8. The Pharmaceutical Society of Great Britain, Department of Pharmaceutical Sciences. Plastic medicine bottles of rigid PVC. Pharm J 1973; 210: 100.
9. Gallardo V, Salcedo J, Parera A, Delgado A. Effect of the preservatives antipyrin, benzoic acid and sodium metabisulfite on properties of the nitrofurantoin/solution interface. Int J Pharmaceutics 1991; 71: 223-227.
10. Clarke CD, Armstrong NA. Influence of pH on the adsorption of benzoic acid by kaolin. Pharm J 1972; 209: 44-45.
11. Lahti A, Hannuksela M. Is benzoic acid really harmful in cases of atopy and urticaria? Lancet 1981; ii: 1055.
12. FAO/WHO. Toxicological evaluation of certain food additives with a review of general principles and of specifications. Seventeenth report of the joint FAO/WHO expert committee on food additives. Tech Rep Ser Wld Hlth Org 1974; No. 539.
13. FAO/WHO. Evaluation of certain food additives and contaminants. Twenty-seventh report of the joint FAO/WHO expert committee on food additives. Tech Rep Ser Wld Hlth Org 1983; No. 696.
14. Sweet DV, editor. Registry of toxic effects of chemical substances. Cincinnati: US Department of Health, 1987.

21. General References

Garrett ER, Woods OR. The optimum use of acid preservatives in oil-water systems: benzoic acid in peanut oil-water. J Am Pharm Assoc (Sci) 1953; 42: 736-739.

22. Authors

USA: KL Amsberry.

Benzyl Alcohol

1. Nonproprietary Names

BP: Benzyl alcohol
PhEur: Alcohol benzylicus
USPNF: Benzyl alcohol

2. Synonyms

α-Hydroxytoluene; phenylcarbinol; phenylmethanol; α-toluenol.

3. Chemical Name and CAS Registry Number

Benzenemethanol [100-51-6]

4. Empirical Formula   Molecular Weight

C_7H_8O 108.14

5. Structural Formula

6. Functional Category

Antimicrobial preservative; disinfectant; solvent.

7. Applications in Pharmaceutical Formulation or Technology

Benzyl alcohol is an antimicrobial preservative used in cosmetics, foods and a wide range of pharmaceutical formulations,[1-3] including oral and parenteral preparations, at concentrations up to 2.0% v/v. In cosmetics, concentrations up to 3.0% v/v may be used as a preservative. Concentrations of 5% v/v or more are employed as a solubilizer, whilst a 10% v/v solution is used as a disinfectant.

Benzyl alcohol 10% v/v solutions also have some local anesthetic properties which are exploited in some parenterals, cough products, ophthalmic solutions, ointments, and dermatological aerosol sprays.

Although widely used as an antimicrobial preservative, benzyl alcohol, when administered to neonates, has been associated with some fatal adverse reactions. It is now recommended that parenteral products preserved with benzyl alcohol, or other antimicrobial preservatives, should not be used in newborn infants if at all possible, *see* Section 14.

8. Description

A clear, colorless, oily liquid with a faint aromatic odor and a sharp, burning taste.

9. Pharmacopeial Specifications

Test	PhEur 1990	USPNF XVII
Identification	+	+
Acidity	+	—
Clarity of solution	+	—
Specific gravity	1.043-1.049	1.042-1.047
Distilling range	—	202.5-206.5°C

Continued

Test	PhEur 1990	USPNF XVII
Refractive index	1.538-1.541	1.539-1.541
Residue on ignition	—	$\leqslant$ 0.005%
Nonvolatile matter	$\leqslant$ 0.05%	—
Chlorinated compounds	$\leqslant$ 300 ppm	+
Aldehyde	$\leqslant$ 0.2%	$\leqslant$ 0.2%
Peroxide value	$\leqslant$ 5	—
Assay	97.0-100.5%	—

10. Typical Properties

Acidity/alkalinity: aqueous solutions are neutral to litmus.

Antimicrobial activity: benzyl alcohol is bacteriostatic and is used as an antimicrobial preservative against Gram-positive bacteria, molds, fungi and yeasts although it possesses only modest bactericidal properties. Optimum activity occurs at less than pH 5; little activity is shown above pH 8. Antimicrobial activity is reduced in the presence of nonionic surfactants, such as polysorbate 80. However, the reduction in activity is less than is the case with either hydroxybenzoate esters or quaternary ammonium compounds. The activity of benzyl alcohol may also be reduced by incompatibilities with some packaging materials, particularly polyethylene, *see* Section 12. Reported minimum inhibitory concentrations (MICs) are shown in Table I.[4]

Bacteria: benzyl alcohol is moderately active against most Gram-positive organisms (typical MICs are 3-5 mg/mL), although some Gram-positive bacteria are very sensitive (MICs 0.025-0.05 mg/mL). In general, benzyl alcohol is less active against Gram-negative organisms.

Fungi: benzyl alcohol is effective against molds and yeasts, typical MICs are 3-5 mg/mL.

Spores: benzyl alcohol is inactive against spores, but activity may be enhanced by heating. Benzyl alcohol 1% v/v, at pH 5-6, has been claimed to be as effective as phenylmercuric nitrate 0.002% w/v against *Bacillus stearothermophilus* at 100°C for 30 minutes.

Table I: Minimum inhibitory concentrations (MICs) of benzyl alcohol.[4]

Microorganism	MIC (μg/mL)
Aspergillus niger	5000
Candida albicans	2500
Escherichia coli	2000
Pseudomonas aeruginosa	2000
Staphylococcus aureus	25

Autoignition temperature: 436.5°C
Boiling point: 204.7°C
Flammability: flammable. Limits in air 1.7-15.0% v/v.
Flash point:
100.6°C (closed cup);
104.5°C (open cup).
Freezing point: -15°C
Melting point: -15.2°C
Partition coefficients:
Liquid paraffin: water = 0.2;
Peanut oil: water = 1.3.
Refractive index: $n_D^{20} = 1.5404$

Solubility:

Solvent	Solubility at 20°C Unless otherwise stated
Chloroform	miscible in all proportions
Ethanol	miscible in all proportions
Ethanol (50%)	1 in 2.5
Ether	miscible in all proportions
Fixed and volatile oils	miscible in all proportions
Water	1 in 25 at 25°C
	1 in 14 at 90°C

Specific gravity: 1.0454 at 20°C
Surface tension: 38.8 mN/m (38.8 dynes/cm)
Vapor density (relative): 3.72 (air = 1)
Vapor pressure:
13.3 Pa (0.1 mmHg) at 30°C;
1.769 kPa (13.3 mmHg) at 100°C.
Viscosity (dynamic): 6 mPa s (6 cP) at 20°C

11. Stability and Storage Conditions

Benzyl alcohol oxidizes slowly in air to benzaldehyde and benzoic acid; it does not react with water. Aqueous solutions may be sterilized by filtration or autoclaving; some solutions may generate benzaldehyde during autoclaving.

Benzyl alcohol may be stored in metal or glass containers although plastic containers should not be used. Exceptions to this include polypropylene containers or vessels coated with inert fluorinated polymers such as Teflon, *see* Section 12.

Benzyl alcohol should be stored in an airtight container, protected from light, in a cool, dry, place.

12. Incompatibilities

Benzyl alcohol is incompatible with oxidizing agents and strong acids. It can also accelerate the autoxidation of fats.

Although antimicrobial activity is reduced in the presence of nonionic surfactants, such as polysorbate 80, the reduction is less than is the case with hydroxybenzoate esters or quaternary ammonium compounds.

Benzyl alcohol is compatible with methylcellulose and is only slowly sorbed by closures composed of natural rubber, Neoprene and butyl rubber closures, the resistance of which can be enhanced by coating with fluorinated polymers.[5] However, a 2% v/v aqueous solution in a polyethylene container, stored at 20°C, may lose up to 15% of its benzyl alcohol content in 13 weeks.[6] Losses to polyvinyl chloride and polypropylene containers under similar conditions are usually negligible.

13. Method of Manufacture

Benzyl alcohol is prepared commercially by the distillation of benzyl chloride with potassium or sodium carbonate. It may also be prepared by the Cannizzaro reaction of benzaldehyde and potassium hydroxide.

14. Safety

Benzyl alcohol is used in a wide variety of pharmaceutical formulations. It is metabolized to benzaldehyde and benzoic acid, with benzoic acid being further metabolized in the liver by conjugation with glycine to form hippuric acid which is excreted in the urine.

Ingestion or inhalation of benzyl alcohol may cause headache, vertigo, nausea, vomiting and diarrhea. Overexposure may result in CNS depression and respiratory failure. However, the concentrations of benzyl alcohol normally employed as a preservative are not associated with such adverse effects.

Reports of adverse reactions to benzyl alcohol[7-9] used as an excipient include: neurotoxicity in patients administered benzyl alcohol in intrathecal preparations;[10] hypersensitivity,[11,12] although relatively rare, and a fatal toxic syndrome in premature infants.[13-15]

The fatal toxic syndrome in low-birth-weight neonates, which includes symptoms of metabolic acidosis and respiratory depression, was attributed to the use of benzyl alcohol as a preservative in solutions used to flush umbilical catheters. As a result of this the FDA has recommended that benzyl alcohol should not be used in such flushing solutions and advised against the use of medicines containing preservatives in the newborn.[16,17]

The WHO has set the estimated acceptable daily intake of the benzyl/benzoic moiety at up to 5 mg/kg body-weight daily.[18]

LD_{50} (mouse, IV): 0.32 g/kg[19]
LD_{50} (mouse, oral): 1.58 g/kg
LD_{50} (rabbit, oral): 1.04 g/kg
LD_{50} (rabbit, skin): 2.0 g/kg
LD_{50} (rat, IP): 0.4 g/kg
LD_{50} (rat, IV): 0.06 g/kg
LD_{50} (rat, oral): 1.23 g/kg

15. Handling Precautions

Observe normal precautions appropriate to the circumstances and quantity of material handled. Benzyl alcohol (liquid and vapor) is irritant to the skin, eyes and mucous membranes. Eye protection, gloves and protective clothing are recommended. Benzyl alcohol should be handled in a well-ventilated environment; a self-contained breathing apparatus is recommended in areas of poor ventilation. Benzyl alcohol is flammable.

16. Regulatory Status

Included in the FDA Inactive Ingredients Guide (injections, oral capsules, solutions and tablets, topical and vaginal preparations). Included in parenteral and nonparenteral medicines licensed in the UK.

17. Pharmacopeias

Aust, Br, Egypt, Eur, Fr, Gr, Hung, Ind, It, Jpn, Mex, Neth, Nord, Port, Swiss and USPNF.

18. Related Substances

—

19. Comments

—

20. Specific References

1. Croshaw B. Preservatives for cosmetics and toiletries. J Soc Cosmet Chem 1977; 28: 3-16.
2. Karabit MS, Juneskans OT, Lundgren P. Studies on the evaluation of preservative efficacy II: the determination of antimicrobial characteristics of benzyl alcohol. J Clin Hosp Pharm 1986; 11: 281-289.
3. Shah AK, Simons KJ, Briggs CJ. Physical, chemical, and bioavailability studies of parenteral diazepam formulations containing propylene glycol and polyethylene glycol 400. Drug Dev Ind Pharm 1991; 17: 1635-1654.

4. Wallhäusser KH. Benzyl alcohol. In: Kabara JJ, editor. Cosmetic and drug preservation principles and practice. New York: Marcel Dekker, 1984: 627-628.

5. Royce A, Sykes G. Losses of bacteriostats from injections in rubber-closed containers. J Pharm Pharmacol 1957; 9: 814-823.

6. Roberts MS, Polack AE, Martin G, Blackburn HD. The storage of selected substances in aqueous solution in polyethylene containers: the effect of some physicochemical factors on the disappearance kinetics of the substances. Int J Pharmaceutics 1979; 2: 295-306.

7. Evens RP. Toxicity of intravenous benzyl alcohol [letter]. Drug Intell Clin Pharm 1975; 9: 154-155.

8. Reynolds RD. Nebulizer bronchitis induced by bacteriostatic saline [letter]. JAMA 1990; 264: 35.

9. Smolinske SC. Handbook of food, drug, and cosmetic excipients. Boca Raton, FL: CRC Press Inc, 1992: 47-54.

10. Hahn AF, Feasby TE, Gilbert JJ. Paraparesis following intrathecal chemotherapy. Neurology 1983; 33: 1032-1038.

11. Grant JA, Bilodeau PA, Guernsey BG, Gardner FH. Unsuspected benzyl alcohol hypersensitivity [letter]. N Engl J Med 1982; 306: 108.

12. Wilson JP, Solimando DA, Edwards MS. Parenteral benzyl alcohol-induced hypersensitivity reaction. Drug Intell Clin Pharm 1986; 20: 689-691.

13. Brown WJ, et al. Fatal benzyl alcohol poisoning in a neonatal intensive care unit [letter]. Lancet 1982; i: 1250.

14. Gershanik J, et al. The gasping syndrome and benzyl alcohol poisoning. N Engl J Med 1982; 307: 1384-1388.

15. McCloskey SE, Gershanik JJ, Lertora JJL, White L, George WJ. Toxicity of benzyl alcohol in adult and neonatal mice. J Pharm Sci 1986; 75: 702-705.

16. Benzyl alcohol may be toxic to newborns. FDA Drug Bull 1982; 12: 10-11.

17. Belson JJ. Benzyl alcohol questionnaire. Am J Hosp Pharm 1982; 39: 1850,1852.

18. FAO/WHO. Evaluation of certain food additives: twenty-third report of the joint FAO/WHO expert committee on food additives. Tech Rep Ser Wld Hlth Org 1980; No. 648.

19. Sweet DV, editor. Registry of toxic effects of chemical substances. Cincinnati: US Department of Health, 1987.

21. General References

Akers MJ. Considerations in selecting antimicrobial preservative agents for parenteral product development. Pharmaceut Technol 1984; 8(5): 36-40,43,44,46.

Bloomfield SF. Control of microbial contamination part 2: current problems in preservation. Br J Pharm Pract 1986; 8: 72,74-76,78,80.

Carter DV, Charlton PT, Fenton AH, Housley JR, Lessel B. The preparation and the antibacterial and antifungal properties of some substituted benzyl alcohols. J Pharm Pharmacol 1958; 10(Suppl): 149T-159T.

Harrison SM, Barry BW, Dugard PH. Benzyl alcohol vapour diffusion through human skin: dependence on thermodynamic activity in the vehicle. J Pharm Pharmacol 1982; 34(Suppl): 36P.

Russell AD, Jenkins J, Harrison IH. The inclusion of antimicrobial agents in pharmaceutical products. Adv Appl Microbiol 1967; 9: 1-38.

22. Authors

UK: PJ Weller.
USA: EL Brunson.

Benzyl Benzoate

1. Nonproprietary Names

BP: Benzyl benzoate
USP: Benzyl benzoate

2. Synonyms

Benzoic acid benzyl ester; benzylbenzenecarboxylate; benzyl phenylformate.

3. Chemical Name and CAS Registry Number

Benzoic acid phenylmethyl ester [120-51-4]

4. Empirical Formula   Molecular Weight

$C_{14}H_{12}O_2$ 212.24

5. Structural Formula

6. Functional Category

Plasticizer; solubilizing agent; solvent; therapeutic agent.

7. Applications in Pharmaceutical Formulation or Technology

Benzyl benzoate is used as a solubilizing agent and nonaqueous solvent in intramuscular injections at concentrations between 0.01-46.0% v/v.[1] It is also used as a solvent and plasticizer for cellulose and nitrocellulose. However, the most widespread pharmaceutical use of benzyl benzoate is as a topical therapeutic agent in the treatment of scabies. Benzyl benzoate is also used therapeutically as a parasiticide in veterinary medicine.[2]
Other applications of benzyl benzoate include its use as a solvent and fixative for flavors and perfumes in cosmetics and food products.

8. Description

Benzyl benzoate is a clear, colorless, oily liquid with a slightly aromatic odor. It produces a sharp, burning sensation on the tongue. At temperatures below 17°C it exists as clear, colorless crystals.

9. Pharmacopeial Specifications

Test	BP 1993	USP XXII
Identification	+	+
Specific gravity	1.118-1.122	1.116-1.120
Congealing temperature	$\geqslant$ 17.0°C	$\geqslant$ 18.0°C
Refractive index	1.568-1.570	1.568-1.570
Aldehyde	—	+
Acidity	+	+
Sulfated ash	$\leqslant$ 0.1%	—
Assay	99.0-100.5%	99.0-100.5%

10. Typical Properties

Autoignition temperature: 481°C
Boiling point: 323°C
Flash point: 148°C
Freezing point: 17°C
Melting point: 21°C
Refractive index: $n_D^{21} = 1.5681$
Solubility: practically insoluble in glycerin and water; miscible with chloroform, ethanol (95%), ether and oils.
Specific gravity: 1.12
Vapor density (relative): 7.3 (air = 1)

11. Stability and Storage Conditions

Benzyl benzoate is stable when stored in tight, well-filled, light-resistant containers. Exposure to excessive heat should be avoided.

12. Incompatibilities

Benzyl benzoate is incompatible with alkalis and oxidizing agents.

13. Method of Manufacture

Benzyl benzoate is a constituent of Peru balsam and occurs naturally in certain plant species. Commercially, it is produced synthetically by the dry esterification of sodium benzoate and benzoyl chloride in the presence of triethylamine or by the reaction of sodium benzylate on benzaldehyde.

14. Safety

Benzyl benzoate is metabolized by rapid hydrolysis to benzoic acid and benzyl alcohol. Benzyl alcohol is then further metabolized to hippuric acid which is excreted in the urine.
Benzyl benzoate is widely used as a 25% v/v topical application in the treatment of scabies and as an excipient in intramuscular injections and oral products. Adverse reactions to benzyl benzoate include skin irritation and hypersensitivity reactions. Oral ingestion may cause harmful stimulation of the CNS and convulsions.

LD_{50} (cat, oral): 2.24 g/kg[3-5]
LD_{50} (guinea pig, oral): 1.0 g/kg
LD_{50} (mouse, oral): 1.4 g/kg
LD_{50} (rabbit, oral): 1.68 g/kg
LD_{50} (rabbit, skin): 4.0 g/kg
LD_{50} (rat, oral): 0.5 g/kg
LD_{50} (rat, skin): 4.0 g/kg

15. Handling Precautions

Benzyl benzoate may be harmful if ingested and is irritating to the skin, eyes and mucous membranes. Observe normal precautions appropriate to the circumstances and quantity of material handled. Eye protection, gloves and a respirator are recommended. It is recommended that benzyl benzoate be handled in a fume cupboard. Benzyl benzoate is combustible.

16. Regulatory Status

Included in the FDA Inactive Ingredients Guide (IM injections and oral capsules). Included, as an active ingredient, in nonparenteral medicines licensed in the UK.

17. Pharmacopeias

Aust, Br, Braz, Cz, Egypt, Fr, Hung, Ind, Int, It, Jpn, Mex, Neth, Nord, Swiss, Turk, US and Yug. Also in the BP Vet.

18. Related Substances

—

19. Comments

—

20. Specific References

1. Spiegel AJ, Noseworthy MM. Use of nonaqueous solvents in parenteral products. J Pharm Sci 1963; 52: 917-927.
2. Debuf Y, editor. The veterinary formulary: handbook of medicines used in veterinary practice, 2nd edition. London: The Pharmaceutical Press, 1994: 152-153.
3. Graham BE, Kuizenga MH. Toxicity studies on benzyl benzoate and related benzyl compounds. J Pharmacol Exp Ther 1945; 84: 358-362.
4. Draize JH, et al. Toxicological investigations of compounds proposed for use as insect repellents. J Pharmacol Exp Ther 1948; 93: 26-39.
5. Sweet DV, editor. Registry of toxic effects of chemical substances. Cincinnati: US Department of Health, 1987.

21. General References

Gupta VD, Ho HW. Quantitative determination of benzyl benzoate in benzyl benzoate lotion NF. Am J Hosp Pharm 1976; 33: 665-666.
Hassan MMA, Mossa JS. Benzyl benzoate. In: Florey K, editor. Analytical profiles of drug substances, volume 10. New York: Academic Press, 1981: 55-74.

22. Authors

USA: SA Daskalakis.

Bronopol

1. Nonproprietary Names

BP: Bronopol

2. Synonyms

2-Bromo-2-nitro-1,3-propanediol; *β*-bromo-*β*-nitrotrimethyle-neglycol; *Bronopol-Boots*; *Bronosol*; BNPD; *Myacide*; *Tristat BNP*.

3. Chemical Name and CAS Registry Number

2-Bromo-2-nitropropane-1,3-diol [52-51-7]

4. Empirical Formula   Molecular Weight

$C_3H_6BrNO_4$ 200.00

5. Structural Formula

$$\underset{\underset{NO_2}{|}}{\overset{\overset{Br}{|}}{HOCH_2-C-CH_2OH}}$$

6. Functional Category

Antimicrobial preservative; antiseptic.

7. Applications in Pharmaceutical Formulation or Technology

Bronopol 0.01-0.1% is used as an antimicrobial preservative either alone or in combination with other preservatives in topical pharmaceutical formulations, cosmetics and toiletries.

8. Description

Bronopol is a white or almost white crystalline powder; odorless or with a faint characteristic odor.

9. Pharmacopeial Specifications

Test	BP 1993
Identification	+
Acidity or alkalinity (1% w/v solution)	+
Related substances	+
Sulfated ash	≤ 0.1%
Water	≤ 0.5%
Assay (anhydrous basis)	99.0-101.0

10. Typical Properties

Acidity/alkalinity:
pH = 5.0-6.0 (1% w/v aqueous solution)
Antimicrobial activity: bronopol is active against both Gram-positive and Gram-negative bacteria including *Pseudomonas aeruginosa*, with typical minimum inhibitory concentrations (MICs) between 10-50 μg/mL,[1-8] *see also* Table I. At room temperature a 0.08% w/v aqueous solution may reduce the viability of culture collection strains of *Escherichia coli* and

SEM: 1
Excipient: Bronopol
Manufacturer: Boots MicroCheck
Lot No.: 28-11-90-2346-B-479
Magnification: 20x
Voltage: 3 kV

Pseudomonas aeruginosa by 100 fold or more in 15 minutes. Antimicrobial activity is not markedly influenced by pH in the range 5.0-8.0, nor by common anionic and nonionic surfactants, lecithin or proteins.[2,5,6] Bronopol is less active against yeasts and molds with MICs of 50-400 μg/mL and has little or no useful activity against bacterial spores. *See also* Section 12.

Table I: Minimum inhibitory concentrations (MICs) of bronopol.[2]

Microorganism	Concentration (μg/mL)
Bacillus subtilis	12.5
Candida albicans	25-50
Escherichia coli	12.5-50
Klebsiella aerogenes	25
Penicillium roqueforti	400
Pityrosporum ovale	125
Proteus mirabilis	25-50
Proteus vulgaris	12.5-50
Pseudomonas aeruginosa	12.5-50
Pseudomonas cepacia	25
Salmonella gallinarum	25
Staphylococcus aureus	12.5-50
Staphylococcus epidermidis	50
Streptococcus faecalis	50
Trichophyton mentagrophytes	200

Melting point: 128-132°C
Partition coefficients:
Mineral oil: water = 0.043 at 22-24°C;
Peanut oil: water = 0.11 at 22-24°C.

Solubility:

Solvent	Solubility at 20°C
Ethanol (95%)	1 in 2
Cottonseed oil	slightly soluble
Glycerin	1 in 100
Isopropyl myristate	1 in 200
Mineral oil	slightly soluble
Propan-2-ol	1 in 4
Propylene glycol	1 in 2
Water	1 in 4

11. Stability and Storage Conditions

Bronopol is stable, and its antimicrobial activity practically unaffected, when stored as a solid at room temperature and ambient relative humidity for up to 2 years.[3]
The pH of a 1.0% w/v aqueous solution is 5.0-6.0 and falls slowly during storage; solutions are more stable in acid conditions. Half-lives at 20°C predicted from accelerated stability studies on 0.2% w/v aqueous solutions at pH 4.0, 6.0 and 8.0 are approximately 5 years, 1.5 years and 2 months respectively.[3] These data derive from HPLC assay, but microbiological assay results indicate longer half-lives and thus suggest that degradation products may contribute to antimicrobial activity; formaldehyde and nitrites are amongst the decomposition products. On exposure to light, especially under alkaline conditions, solutions become yellow or brown-colored but the degree of discoloration does not directly correlate with loss of antimicrobial activity.
The bulk material should be stored in a well-closed, non-aluminum container protected from light, in a cool, dry, place.

12. Incompatibilities

Sulfhydryl compounds cause significant reductions in the activity of bronopol and cysteine hydrochloride may be used as the deactivating agent in preservative efficacy tests; lecithin/polysorbate combinations are unsuitable for this purpose.[5] Bronopol is incompatible with sodium thiosulfate, sodium metabisulfite and with amine oxide or protein hydrolysate surfactants. Due to an incompatibility with aluminum, the use of aluminum in the packaging of products which contain bronopol should be avoided.

13. Method of Manufacture

Bronopol is synthesized by the reaction of nitromethane with paraformaldehyde in an alkaline environment followed by bromination. After crystallization bronopol powder may be milled to produce a powder of the required fineness.

14. Safety

Bronopol is used widely in topical pharmaceutical formulations and cosmetics as an antimicrobial preservative.
Although bronopol has been reported to cause both irritant and hypersensitivity adverse reactions following topical use[9-12] it is generally regarded as a nonirritant and nonsensitizing material at concentrations up to 0.1%. At a concentration of 0.02%, bronopol is frequently used as a preservative in 'hypoallergenic' formulations.
Animal toxicity studies have shown no evidence of photo-toxicity, mutagenicity *in vitro* or *in vivo*, nor any evidence of tumor occurrence when bronopol is applied to rodents topically or administered orally;[1] this is despite the demonstrated potential of bronopol to liberate nitrite on decomposition, which, in the presence of certain amines may generate nitrosamines. Formation of nitrosamines in formulations containing amines may be reduced by limiting the concentration of bronopol to 0.01% and including an antioxidant such as 0.2% alpha tocopherol or 0.05% butylated hydroxytoluene.[13]

LD_{50} (dog, oral): 25 mg/kg[14]
LD_{50} (mouse, IP): 15.5 mg/kg
LD_{50} (mouse, IV): 48 mg/kg
LD_{50} (mouse, oral): 250 mg/kg
LD_{50} (mouse, SC): 116 mg/kg
LD_{50} (mouse, skin): 4.75 g/kg
LD_{50} (rat, IP): 26 mg/kg
LD_{50} (rat, IV): 37.4 mg/kg
LD_{50} (rat, oral): 180 mg/kg
LD_{50} (rat, SC): 170 mg/kg
LD_{50} (rat, skin): 3.5 g/kg

15. Handling Precautions

Observe normal precautions appropriate to the circumstances and quantity of material handled. Bronopol may be harmful upon inhalation and the solid or concentrated solutions can be irritant to the skin and eyes. Eye protection, gloves and dust respirator are recommended. Bronopol burns to produce toxic fumes.

16. Regulatory Status

Included in topical pharmaceutical formulations licensed in the UK.

17. Pharmacopeias

Br.

18. Related Substances

—

19. Comments

Bronopol owes its usefulness as a preservative largely to its activity against *Pseudomonas aeruginosa*, and its affinity for polar solvents which prevents the loss of preservative into the oil phase of emulsions seen with some other preservatives. Other advantages include a relatively low incidence of microbial resistance and good compatibility with most surfactants, other excipients and preservatives, with which it can therefore be used in combination.
The major disadvantages of bronopol are relatively poor activity against yeasts and molds, instability at alkaline pH, and the production of formaldehyde and nitrite on decomposition, although there is no evidence of serious toxicity problems associated with bronopol which are attributable to these compounds.

20. Specific References

1. Croshaw B, Groves MJ, Lessel B. Some properties of bronopol, a new antimicrobial agent active against *Pseudomonas aeruginosa*. J Pharm Pharmacol 1964; 16(Suppl): 127T-130T.
2. Preservative properties of bronopol. Cosmet Toilet 1977; 92(3): 87-88.
3. Bryce DM, Croshaw B, Hall JE, Holland VR, Lessel B. The activity and safety of the antimicrobial agent bronopol (2-bromo-2-nitropropane-1,3-diol). J Soc Cosmet Chem 1978; 29: 3-24.
4. Moore KE, Stretton RJ. A method for studying the activity of preservatives and its application to bronopol. J Appl Bacteriol 1978; 45: 137-141.

5. Myburgh JA, McCarthy TJ. Effect of certain formulation factors on the activity of bronopol. Cosmet Toilet 1978; 93(2): 47-48.

6. Moore KE, Stretton RJ. The effect of pH, temperature and certain media constituents on the stability and activity of the preservative bronopol. J Appl Bacteriol 1981; 51: 483-494.

7. Sondossi M. The effect of fifteen biocides on formaldehyde resistant strains of Pseudomonas aeruginosa. J Ind Microbiol 1986; 1: 87-96.

8. Kumanova R, et al. Evaluating bronopol. Mfg Chem 1989; 60(9): 36-38.

9. Maibach HI. Dermal sensitization potential of 2-bromo-2-nitropropane-1,3-diol (bronopol). Contact Dermatitis 1977; 3: 99.

10. Elder RL. Final report on the safety assessment for 2-bromo-2-nitropropane-1,3,-diol. J Environ Pathol Toxicol 1980; 4: 47-61.

11. Storrs FJ, Bell DE. Allergic contact dermatitis to 2-bromo-2-nitropropane-1,3-diol in a hydrophilic ointment. J Am Acad Dermatol 1983; 8: 157-170.

12. Grattan CEH, Harman RRM. Bronopol contact dermatitis in a milk recorder. Br J Dermatol 1985; 113(Suppl 29): 43.

13. Dunnett PC, Telling GM. Study of the fate of bronopol and the effects of antioxidants on *N*-nitrosamine formation in shampoos and skin creams. Int J Cosmet Sci 1984; 6: 241-247.

14. Sweet DV, editor. Registry of toxic effects of chemical substances. Cincinnati: US Department of Health, 1987.

21. General References

Boots MicroCheck. Technical literature: *Bronopol-Boots*, 1992.

Croshaw B. Preservatives for cosmetics and toiletries. J Soc Cosmet Chem 1977; 28: 3-16.

Rossmore HW, Sondossi M. Applications and mode of action of formaldehyde condensate biocides. Adv Appl Microbiol 1988; 33: 223-273.

Toler JC. Preservative stability and preservative systems. Int J Cosmet Sci 1985; 7: 157-164.

Wallhäusser KH. Bronopol. In: Kabara JJ, editor. Cosmetic and drug preservation principles and practice. New York: Marcel Dekker, 1984: 635-638.

22. Authors

UK: MC Allwood, SP Denyer, N Hodges.

Butane

1. Nonproprietary Names
USPNF: Butane

2. Synonyms
A-17; *Aeropres 17*; *n*-butane.

3. Chemical Name and CAS Registry Number
Butane [106-97-8]

4. Empirical Formula   Molecular Weight
C_4H_{10} 58.12

5. Structural Formula

$$H_3C{-}CH_2{-}CH_2{-}CH_3$$

6. Functional Category
Aerosol propellant.

7. Applications in Pharmaceutical Formulation or Technology
Butane is used as an aerosol propellant, in combination with other hydrocarbon or chlorofluorocarbon propellants, primarily in topical pharmaceutical aerosols. *See also* Section 19. Depending upon the application, the concentration of hydrocarbon propellant used ranges from 5-95% w/w.
Only highly purified hydrocarbon grades can be used for pharmaceutical formulations since they may contain traces of unsaturated compounds which not only contribute a slight odor to a product but may also react with other ingredients. Butane is also used in food products and as a fuel.
See also Isobutane.

8. Description
Butane is a liquefied gas and exists as a liquid at room temperature when contained under its own vapor pressure, or as a gas when exposed to room temperature and atmospheric pressure. It is essentially a clear, colorless, odorless liquid, but may have a slight ethereal odor.

9. Pharmacopoeial Specifications

Test	USPNF XVII
Identification	+
Water	$\leqslant$ 0.001%
High-boiling residues	$\leqslant$ 5 ppm
Acidity of residue	+
Sulfur compounds	+
Assay	$\geqslant$ 97.0%

10. Typical Properties
Autoignition temperature: 405°C
Boiling point: −0.5°C
Critical pressure: 3.80 MPa (37.47 atm)
Critical temperature: 152°C
Density: 0.58 g/cm³ for liquid at 20°C

Explosive limits:
1.9% v/v lower limit;
8.5% v/v upper limit.
Flash point: −62°C
Freezing point: −138.3°C
Kauri-butanol value: 19.5
Solubility:

Solvent	Solubility at 17°C and 102.7 kPa (770 mmHg)
Chloroform	1 in 0.03
Ethanol (95%)	1 in 0.56
Ether	1 in 0.04
Water	1 in 6.67

Vapor density (absolute): 2.595 g/m³
Vapor density (relative): 2.05 (air = 1)
Vapor pressure: 113.8 kPa (16.5 psig) at 21°C

11. Stability and Storage Conditions
Butane and the other hydrocarbons used as aerosol propellants are stable compounds and are chemically nonreactive when used as propellants. They are however highly flammable and explosive when mixed with certain concentrations of air, *see* Section 10. Butane should be stored in a well ventilated area, in a tightly sealed cylinder. Exposure to excessive heat should be avoided.

12. Incompatibilities
Other than their lack of miscibility with water, butane and the other hydrocarbon propellants do not have any practical incompatibilities with the ingredients commonly used in pharmaceutical aerosol formulations. Hydrocarbon propellants are generally miscible with nonpolar materials and some semipolar compounds.

13. Method of Manufacture
Butane is obtained by the fractional distillation, under pressure, of crude petroleum and natural gas. It may be purified by passing through a molecular sieve to remove any unsaturated compounds that are present.

14. Safety
Butane and other hydrocarbon propellants have been associated with an increasing number of serious or fatal adverse reactions primarily due to deliberate inhalation.[1-5] However, they are not generally regarded as being toxic materials although they do have an anesthetic effect, hence inhalation in large quantities is hazardous.

LC_{50} (mouse, inhalation): 0.68 g/m³/2 hour[6]
LC_{50} (rat, inhalation): 0.658 g/m³/4 hour

15. Handling Precautions
Butane and the other hydrocarbon propellants are liquefied gases and should be handled with appropriate caution. Direct contact of liquefied gas with the skin is hazardous and may result in serious cold burn injuries. Protective clothing, rubber gloves and eye protection are recommended.
Hydrocarbon gases should be used in a well-ventilated environment. In the UK, the occupational exposure limits for butane are 1430 mg/m³ (600 ppm) long-term (8-hour TWA) and 1780 mg/m³ (750 ppm) short-term (10-minutes).[7]

It should be noted that butane vapors do not support life; therefore, when cleaning large tanks, adequate provisions for oxygen must be provided for personnel cleaning the tanks. Butane is highly flammable and explosive and must only be handled in an explosion-proof room which is equipped with adequate safety warning devices and explosion-proof equipment.

To fight fires the flow of gas should be stopped and dry powder extinguishers used at the flashing point.

16. Regulatory Status

GRAS listed. Included in the FDA Inactive Ingredients Guide (aerosol formulations for topical application). Included in nonparenteral medicines licensed in the UK.

17. Pharmacopeias

USPNF.

18. Related Substances

Dimethyl Ether; Isobutane; Propane.

19. Comments

Although hydrocarbon aerosol propellants are relatively cheap, nontoxic and environmentally friendly (since they are not damaging to the ozone layer and are not greenhouse gases) their use is limited by their flammability. Mixtures of hydrocarbons with varying amounts of dichlorodifluoromethane may however be classified as nonflammable.[8]

Whilst primarily used in topical aerosol formulations it is possible that butane may also become used in metered-dose inhalers as a replacement for chlorofluorocarbons.

Various blends of hydrocarbon propellants, that have a range of physical properties suitable for different applications are commercially available, e.g. *CAP30* (Calor Gas Ltd) is a mixture of 11% propane, 29% isobutane and 60% butane.

20. Specific References

1. Gunn J, Wilson J, Mackintosh AF. Butane sniffing causing ventricular fibrillation [letter]. Lancet 1989; i: 617.
2. Roberts MJD, McIvor RA, Adgey AAJ. Asystole following butane gas inhalation. Br J Hosp Med 1990; 44: 294.
3. Siegel E, Wason S. Sudden death caused by inhalation of butane and propane. N Eng J Med 1990; 323: 1638.
4. Rising deaths from volatile substance abuse. Pharm J 1992; 248: 539.
5. Russell J. Fuel of the forgotten deaths. New Scientist 1993; Feb 6: 21-23.
6. Sax NI, editor. Dangerous properties of industrial materials, 6th edition. New York: Van Nostrand Reinhold Company, 1984.
7. Health and Safety Executive. EH40/93: occupational exposure limits 1993. London: HMSO, 1993.
8. Dalby RN. Prediction and assessment of flammability hazards associated with metered-dose inhalers containing flammable propellants. Pharm Res 1992; 9: 636-642.

21. General References

Dalby RN. Possible replacements for CFC-propelled metered-dose inhalers. Med Device Tech 1991; May: 21-25.
Greaves J. Compressed gas aerosol systems. Mfg Chem 1984; 55(11): 47,49,52.
Johnson MA. The aerosol handbook, 2nd edition. Mendham: Wayne Dorland Company, 1982: 199-252, 335-361.
Randall DS. Solving the problems of hydrocarbon propellants. Mfg Chem Aerosol News 1979; 50(4): 43,44,47.
Sanders PA. Handbook of aerosol technology, 2nd edition. New York: Van Nostrand Reinhold Company, 1979: 36-44.
Sciarra JJ, Stoller L. The science and technology of aerosol packaging. New York: John Wiley and Sons, 1974: 131-137.

22. Authors

UK: PJ Davies.
USA: JJ Sciarra.

Butylated Hydroxyanisole

1. Nonproprietary Names

BP: Butylated hydroxyanisole
USPNF: Butylated hydroxyanisole

2. Synonyms

Antrancine 12; BHA; *tert*-butyl-4-methoxyphenol; 1,1-di-methylethyl-4-methoxyphenol; E320; *Embanox BHA*; *Nipanox BHA*; *Nipantiox 1-F*; *PM 1787*; *PM 1788*; *PM 12366*; *Sustane 1-F*; *Tenox BHA*.

3. Chemical Name and CAS Registry Number

2-*tert*-Butyl-4-methoxyphenol [25013-16-5]

4. Empirical Formula   Molecular Weight

$C_{11}H_{16}O_2$ 180.25

The BP 1993 describes butylated hydroxyanisole as 2-*tert*-butyl-4-methoxyphenol containing a variable amount of 3-*tert*-butyl-4-methoxyphenol.

5. Structural Formula

6. Functional Category

Antioxidant.

7. Applications in Pharmaceutical Formulation or Technology

Butylated hydroxyanisole is an antioxidant with some antimicrobial properties.[1] It is used in cosmetics, foods and pharmaceuticals particularly to delay or prevent oxidative rancidity of fats and oils and to prevent loss of activity of oil-soluble vitamins.

Butylated hydroxyanisole is frequently used in combination with other antioxidants, particularly butylated hydroxytoluene and alkyl gallates, and with sequestrants or synergists such as citric acid.

Antioxidant use	Concentration (%)
β-Carotene	0.01
Essential oils and flavoring agents	0.02-0.5
IM injections	0.03
IV injections	0.0002-0.0005
Oils and fats	0.02
Topical formulations	0.005-0.02
Vitamin A	10 mg per million units

8. Description

Butylated hydroxyanisole occurs as a white or almost white crystalline powder or a yellowish-white waxy solid with a faint, characteristic aromatic odor.

9. Pharmacopeial Specifications

Test	BP 1993 (Ad 1994)	USPNF XVII (Suppl 6)
Identification	+	+
Residue on ignition	—	⩽ 0.01%
Sulfated ash	⩽ 0.05%	—
Related substances	+	—
Arsenic	—	⩽ 3 ppm
Heavy metals	—	⩽ 0.001%
Organic volatile matter	—	+
Assay	—	⩾ 98.5%

10. Typical Properties

Antimicrobial activity: activity is similar to that of the *p*-hydroxybenzoate esters (parabens). The greatest activity is against molds and Gram-positive bacteria, with less activity against Gram-negative bacteria.
Boiling point: 264°C
Melting point: 47°C (for pure 2-*tert*-butyl-4-methoxyphenol), *see also* Section 19.
Solubility: practically insoluble in water; freely soluble in ⩾ 50% aqueous ethanol, propylene glycol, chloroform, ether, hexane, cottonseed oil, peanut oil, soybean oil and in solutions of alkali hydroxides. *See also* HPE Data.
Specific gravity: 1.05 at 20°C
Viscosity (kinematic): 3.3 mm^2/s (3.3 cSt) at 99°C

| | HPE Laboratory Project Data | | |
	Method	Lab #	Results
Density	DE-1	31	1.117 g/cm^3
Solubility			
Ethanol (95%) at 25°C	SOL-7	32	793.0 mg/mL
Ethanol (95%) at 37°C	SOL-7	32	834.0 mg/mL
Hexane at 25°C	SOL-7	32	48.0 mg/mL
Hexane at 37°C	SOL-7	32	10.0 mg/mL
Propylene glycol at 25°C	SOL-7	32	467.0 mg/mL
Propylene glycol at 37°C	SOL-7	32	456.0 mg/mL
Water at 25°C	SOL-7	32	0.32 mg/mL
Water at 37°C	SOL-7	32	0.78 mg/mL

Supplier: Eastman Fine Chemicals.

11. Stability and Storage Conditions

Exposure to light causes discoloration and loss of activity. Butylated hydroxyanisole should be stored in a well-closed container, protected from light, in a cool, dry, place.

12. Incompatibilities

Butylated hydroxyanisole is phenolic and undergoes reactions characteristic of phenols. It is incompatible with oxidizing agents and ferric salts. Trace quantities of metals, and exposure to light, cause discoloration and loss of activity.

13. Method of Manufacture

Prepared by the reaction of *p*-methoxyphenol with isobutene.

14. Safety

Butylated hydroxyanisole is absorbed from the gastrointestinal tract and is metabolized and excreted in the urine with less than 1% unchanged within 24 hours of ingestion.[2] Although there have been some isolated reports of adverse skin reactions to butylated hydroxyanisole[3,4] it is generally regarded as nonirritant and nonsensitizing at the levels employed as an antioxidant.

Concern over the use of butylated hydroxyanisole has occurred following long-term animal feeding studies. Although previous studies in rats and mice fed butylated hydroxyanisole at several hundred times the US permitted level in the human diet showed no adverse effects, a study in which rats, hamsters and mice were fed butylated hydroxyanisole at 1-2% of the diet produced benign and malignant tumors of the forestomach, but in no other sites. However, humans do not have any region of the stomach comparable to the rodent forestomach and studies in animals that also do not have a comparable organ (dogs, monkeys and guinea pigs) showed no adverse effects. Thus, the weight of evidence does not support any relevance to the human diet where butylated hydroxyanisole is ingested at much lower levels.[5] The WHO acceptable daily intake of butylated hydroxyanisole has been set at 500 μg/kg body-weight.[5]

LD_{50} (mouse, oral): 2.0 g/kg[6]
LD_{50} (rat, IP): 0.88 g/kg
LD_{50} (rat, oral): 2.2 g/kg

15. Handling Precautions

Observe normal precautions appropriate to the circumstances and quantity of material handled. Butylated hydroxyanisole may be irritant to the eyes, skin, and on inhalation. It should be handled in a well-ventilated environment; gloves and eye protection are recommended.

16. Regulatory Status

GRAS listed. Accepted as a food additive in Europe. Included in the FDA Inactive Ingredients Guide (inhalations, IM and IV injections, oral capsules and tablets, rectal, topical and vaginal preparations). Included in nonparenteral medicines licensed in the UK.

17. Pharmacopeias

Br, Fr, Ind, It, Mex and USPNF.

18. Related Substances

Butylated Hydroxytoluene.

19. Comments

The commercially available material can have a wide melting point range (47-57°C) due to the presence of varying amounts of 3-*tert*-butyl-4-methoxyphenol.

Tenox brands contain 0.1% w/w citric acid as a stabilizer.

20. Specific References

1. Lamikanra A, Ogunbayo TA. A study of the antibacterial activity of butyl hydroxy anisole (BHA). Cosmet Toilet 1985; 100(10): 69-74.
2. El-Rashidy R, Niazi S. A new metabolite of butylated hydroxyanisole in man. Biopharm Drug Dispos 1983; 4: 389-396.
3. Roed-Peterson J, Hjorth N. Contact dermatitis from antioxidants: hidden sensitizers in topical medications and foods. Br J Dermatol 1976; 94: 233-241.
4. Juhlin L. Recurrent urticaria: clinical investigation of 330 patients. Br J Dermatol 1981; 104: 369-381.
5. FAO/WHO. Evaluation of certain food additives and contaminants. Thirty-third report of the joint FAO/WHO expert committee on food additives. Tech Rep Ser Wld Hlth Org 1989; No. 776.
6. Sweet DV, editor. Registry of toxic effects of chemical substances. Cincinnati: US Department of Health, 1987.

21. General References

Babich H, Borenfreund E. Cytotoxic effects of food additives and pharmaceuticals on cells in culture as determined with the neutral red assay. J Pharm Sci 1990; 79: 592-594.
Verhagen H. Toxicology of the food additives BHA and BHT. Pharm Weekbl Sci 1990; 12: 164-166.

22. Authors

USA: MJ Groves.

Butylated Hydroxytoluene

1. Nonproprietary Names

BP: Butylated hydroxytoluene
PhEur: Butylhydroxytoluenum
USPNF: Butylated hydroxytoluene

2. Synonyms

Advastab-401; *Agidol*; *Annulex BHT*; *Antioxidant 30*; *Antrancine 8*; BHT; 2,6-bis(1,1-dimethylethyl)-4-methylphenol; butylhydroxytoluene; *Dalpac*; dibutylated hydroxytoluene; 2,6-di-*tert*-butyl-*p*-cresol; 3,5-di-*tert*-butyl-4-hydroxytoluene; E321; *Embanox BHT*; *Impruvol*; *Ionol CP*; *Nipanox BHT*; *OHS28890*; *Sustane*; *Tenox BHT*; *Topanol*; *Vianol*.

3. Chemical Name and CAS Registry Number

2,6-Di-*tert*-butyl-4-methylphenol [128-37-0]

4. Empirical Formula   Molecular Weight

$C_{15}H_{24}O$ 220.35

5. Structural Formula

6. Functional Category

Antioxidant.

7. Applications in Pharmaceutical Formulation or Technology

Butylated hydroxytoluene is used as an antioxidant in cosmetics, foods and pharmaceuticals. It is mainly used to delay or prevent oxidative rancidity of fats and oils and to prevent loss of activity of oil-soluble vitamins. Butylated hydroxytoluene is also used at 0.5-1% concentration in natural or synthetic rubber to provide enhanced color stability.
Butylated hydroxytoluene has some antiviral activity[1] and has been used therapeutically to treat herpes simplex labialis.[2]

Antioxidant use	Concentration (%)
β-Carotene	0.01
Edible vegetable oils	0.01
Essential oils and flavoring agents	0.02-0.5
Fats and oils	0.02
Fish oils	0.01-0.1
Inhalations	0.01
IM injections	0.03
IV injections	0.0009-0.002
Topical formulations	0.0075-0.1
Vitamin A	10 mg per million units

8. Description

Butylated hydroxytoluene occurs as a white or pale yellow crystalline solid or powder with a faint characteristic odor.

9. Pharmacopeial Specifications

Test	PhEur 1988	USPNF XVII
Identification	+	+
Appearance of solution	+	—
Congealing temperature	—	$\geqslant$ 69.2°C
Freezing-point	69-70°C	—
Residue on ignition	—	$\leqslant$ 0.002%
Sulfated ash	$\leqslant$ 0.1%	—
Arsenic	—	$\leqslant$ 3 ppm
Heavy metals	—	$\leqslant$ 0.001%
Related substances	+	—
Assay	—	$\geqslant$ 99.0%

10. Typical Properties

Boiling point: 265°C
Density (bulk): 0.48-0.60 g/cm^3
Flash point: 127°C (open cup)
Latent heat of fusion: 23.4 J/g (16.5 cal/g)
Melting point: 70°C
Partition coefficients: Octanol: water = 4.17-5.80
Refractive index: n_D^{75} = 1.4859
Solubility: practically insoluble in water, glycerin, propylene glycol, solutions of alkali hydroxides and dilute aqueous mineral acids. Freely soluble in acetone, benzene, ethanol (95%), ether, methanol, toluene, fixed oils and liquid paraffin. More soluble in food oils and fats than butylated hydroxyanisole. *See also* HPE Data.
Specific gravity:
1.006 at 20°C;
0.890 at 80°C;
0.883 at 90°C;
0.800 at 100°C.
Specific heat:
1.63 J/g/°C (0.39 cal/g/°C) for solid;
2.05 J/g/°C (0.49 cal/g/°C) for liquid.
Vapor density (relative): 7.6 (air = 1)
Vapor pressure:
1.33 Pa (0.01 mmHg) at 20°C;
266.6 Pa (2 mmHg) at 100°C.
Viscosity (kinematic): 3.47 mm^2/s (3.47 cSt) at 80°C

	HPE Laboratory Project Data		
	Method	Lab #	Results
Density	DE-1	31	1.031 g/cm^3
Solubility			
Ethanol (95%) at 25°C	SOL-7	32	108 mg/mL
Ethanol (95%) at 37°C	SOL-7	32	147 mg/mL
Hexane at 25°C	SOL-7	32	409 mg/mL
Hexane at 37°C	SOL-7	32	514 mg/mL
Propylene glycol at 25°C	SOL-7	32	Insoluble
Propylene glycol at 37°C	SOL-7	32	Insoluble
Water at 25°C	SOL-7	32	Insoluble
Water at 37°C	SOL-7	32	Insoluble

Supplier: Koppers Company Inc.

11. Stability and Storage Conditions

Exposure to light, moisture and heat cause discoloration and a loss of activity. Butylated hydroxytoluene should be stored in a well-closed container, protected from light, in a cool, dry, place.

12. Incompatibilities

Butylated hydroxytoluene is phenolic and undergoes reactions characteristic of phenols. It is incompatible with strong oxidizing agents such as peroxides and permanganates. Iron salts cause discoloration with loss of activity. Heating with catalytic amounts of acids causes rapid decomposition with the release of the flammable gas isobutylene.

13. Method of Manufacture

Prepared by the reaction of *p*-cresol with isobutylene.

14. Safety

Butylated hydroxytoluene is readily absorbed from the gastrointestinal tract and is metabolized and excreted in the urine mainly as glucuronide conjugates of oxidation products. Although there have been some isolated reports of adverse skin reactions, butylated hydroxytoluene is generally regarded as nonirritant and nonsensitizing at the levels employed as an antioxidant.[3,4]

The WHO has set a temporary estimated acceptable daily intake for butylated hydroxytoluene at up to 125 μg/kg body-weight.[5]

Ingestion of 4 g of butylated hydroxytoluene, although causing severe nausea and vomiting, has been reported to be nonfatal.[6]

LD_{50} (guinea pig, oral): 6.4-12.8 g/kg[7]
LD_{50} (mouse, IP): 0.14 g/kg
LD_{50} (mouse, IV): 0.18 g/kg
LD_{50} (mouse, oral): 0.8-1.6 g/kg
LD_{50} (rat, oral): 0.89 g/kg

15. Handling Precautions

Observe normal precautions appropriate to the circumstances and quantity of material handled. Butylated hydroxyanisole may be irritant to the eyes, skin, and on inhalation. It should be handled in a well-ventilated environment; gloves and eye protection are recommended.

16. Regulatory Status

GRAS listed. Accepted as a food additive in Europe. Included in the FDA Inactive Ingredients Guide (inhalations, IM and IV injections, oral capsules and tablets, rectal, topical and vaginal preparations). Included in nonparenteral medicines licensed in the UK.

17. Pharmacopeias

Br, Eur, Fr, Ger, Ind, Mex, Neth, Nord, Swiss and USPNF.

18. Related Substances

Butylated Hydroxyanisole.

19. Comments

—

20. Specific References

1. Snipes W, et al. Butylated hydroxytoluene inactivates lipid-containing viruses. Science 1975; 188: 64-66.
2. Freeman DJ, Wenerstrom G, Spruance SL. Treatment of recurrent herpes simplex labialis with topical butylated hydroxytoluene. Clin Pharmacol Ther 1985; 38: 56-59.
3. Roed-Peterson J, Hjorth N. Contact dermatitis from antioxidants: hidden sensitizers in topical medications and foods. Br J Dermatol 1976; 94: 233-241.
4. Juhlin L. Recurrent urticaria: clinical investigation of 330 patients. Br J Dermatol 1981; 104: 369-381.
5. FAO/WHO. Evaluation of certain food additives and contaminants. Thirty-seventh report of the joint FAO/WHO expert committee on food additives. Tech Rep Ser Wld Hlth Org 1991; No. 806.
6. Shlian DM, Goldstone J. Toxicity of butylated hydroxytoluene. N Eng J Med 1986; 314: 648-649.
7. Sweet DV, editor. Registry of toxic effects of chemical substances. Cincinnati: US Department of Health, 1987.

21. General References

Verhagen H. Toxicology of the food additives BHA and BHT. Pharm Weekbl (Sci) 1990; 12: 164-166.

22. Authors

USA: MJ Groves.

Butylparaben

1. Nonproprietary Names
BP: Butyl hydroxybenzoate
USPNF: Butylparaben

2. Synonyms
Butoben; *Butyl chemosept*; *n*-butyl-*p*-hydroxybenzoate; butyl parahydroxybenzoate; *Butyl parasept*; 4-hydroxybenzoic acid butyl ester; *Nipabutyl*; *Solbrol B*; *Tegosept B*.

3. Chemical Name and CAS Registry Number
Butyl-4-hydroxybenzoate [94-26-8]

4. Empirical Formula   Molecular Weight
$C_{11}H_{14}O_3$ 194.23

5. Structural Formula

HO—⟨benzene⟩—COOCH$_2$(CH$_2$)$_2$CH$_3$

6. Functional Category
Antimicrobial preservative.

7. Applications in Pharmaceutical Formulation or Technology
Butylparaben is widely used as an antimicrobial preservative in cosmetics and pharmaceutical formulations. It may be used either alone, in combination with other paraben esters, or with other antimicrobial agents. In cosmetics it is the fourth most frequently used preservative.[1]

The parabens are effective over a wide pH range and have a broad spectrum of antimicrobial activity although they are most effective against yeasts and molds, *see* Section 10.

Due to the poor solubility of the parabens, paraben salts, particularly the sodium salt, are frequently used in formulations. However, this may cause the pH of poorly buffered formulations to become more alkaline.

See Methylparaben for further information.

Use	Concentration (%)
Oral suspensions	0.006-0.05
Topical preparations	0.02-0.4

8. Description
Butylparaben occurs as colorless crystals or a white, crystalline, odorless or almost odorless, tasteless powder.

9. Pharmacopeial Specifications

Test	BP 1993	USPNF XVII
Identification	+	+
Melting range	≈ 69°C	68-72°C
Acidity	+	+
Loss on drying	—	⩽ 0.5%
Residue on ignition	—	⩽ 0.05%
Related substances	+	—
Sulfated ash	⩽ 0.1%	—
Assay (dried basis)	99.0-101.0%	99.0-100.5%

SEM: 1
Excipient: Butylparaben
Magnification: 240x

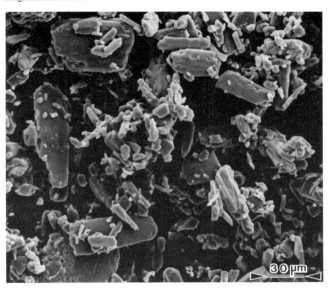

SEM: 2
Excipient: Butylparaben
Magnification: 2400x

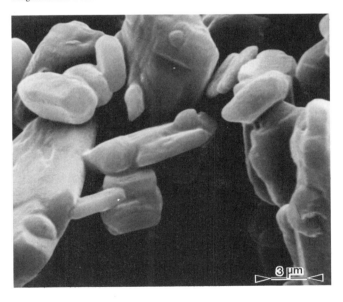

10. Typical Properties
Antimicrobial activity: butylparaben exhibits antimicrobial activity between pH 4-8. Preservative efficacy decreases with increasing pH due to the formation of the phenolate anion. Parabens are more active against yeasts and molds than against bacteria. They are also more active against Gram-positive than against Gram-negative bacteria.

The activity of the parabens increases with increasing chain length of the alkyl moiety; solubility however decreases. Butylparaben is thus more active than methylparaben. Activity may be improved by using combinations of parabens since additive effects occur. Activity has also been reported to be improved by the addition of other excipients, *see* Methylparaben for further information.

Reported minimum inhibitory concentrations (MICs) for butylparaben are shown in Table I:[2]

Table I: Minimum inhibitory concentrations (MICs) for butylparaben in aqueous solution.[2]

Microorganism	MIC (μg/mL)
Aerobacter aerogenes ATCC 8308	400
Aspergillus niger ATCC 9642	125
Aspergillus niger ATCC 10254	200
Bacillus cereus var. mycoides ATCC 6462	63
Bacillus subtilis ATCC 6633	250
Candida albicans ATCC 10231	125
Enterobacter cloacae ATCC 23355	250
Escherichia coli ATCC 8739	5000
Escherichia coli ATCC 9637	5000
Klebsiella pneumoniae ATCC 8308	250
Penicillium chrysogenum ATCC 9480	70
Penicillium digitatum ATCC 10030	32
Proteus vulgaris ATCC 13315	125
Pseudomonas aeruginosa ATCC 9027	> 1000
Pseudomonas aeruginosa ATCC 15442	> 1000
Pseudomonas stutzeri	500
Rhizopus nigricans ATCC 6227A	63
Saccharomyces cerevisiae ATCC 9763	35
Salmonella typhosa ATCC 6539	500
Serratia marcescens ATCC 8100	500
Staphylococcus aureus ATCC 6538P	125
Staphylococcus epidermidis ATCC 12228	250
Trichophyton mentagrophytes	35

Melting point: 68-72°C

Partition coefficients: values for different vegetable oils vary considerably and are affected by the purity of the oil, *see* Table II.

Table II: Partition coefficients for butylparaben between oils and water.[3]

Solvent	Partition coefficient Oil: water
Mineral oil	3.0
Peanut oil	280
Soybean oil	280

Solubility: *see* Table III and HPE Data.

Table III: Solubility of butylparaben in various solvents.[2]

Solvent	Solubility at 25°C Unless otherwise stated
Acetone	freely soluble
Ethanol	1 in 0.5
Ethanol (95%)	1 in 1
Ether	freely soluble
Glycerin	1 in 330
Methanol	1 in 0.5
Mineral oil	1 in 1000
Peanut oil	1 in 20
Propylene glycol	1 in 1
Water	1 in 6700
	1 in 670 at 80°C

HPE Laboratory Project Data			
	Method	Lab #	Results
Solubility			
Water at 25°C	SOL-8	30	0.2 mg/mL

11. Stability and Storage Conditions

Aqueous butylparaben solutions at pH 3-6 can be sterilized by autoclaving, without decomposition.[4] At pH 3-6 aqueous solutions are stable (less than 10% decomposition) for up to about four years at room temperature whilst solutions at pH 8 or above are subject to rapid hydrolysis (10% or more after about 60 days at room temperature).[5]

Butylparaben should be stored in a well-closed container, in a cool, dry, place.

12. Incompatibilities

The antimicrobial activity of butylparaben is considerably reduced in the presence of nonionic surfactants as a result of micellization.[6] Absorption of butylparaben by plastics has not been reported but appears probable given the behavior of other parabens. Some pigments, e.g. ultramarine blue, and yellow iron oxide, absorb butylparaben and thus reduce its preservative properties.[7]

Butylparaben is discolored in the presence of iron and is subject to hydrolysis by weak alkalis and strong acids.
See also Methylparaben.

13. Method of Manufacture

Butylparaben is prepared by esterification of *p*-hydroxybenzoic acid with *n*-butanol.

14. Safety

Butylparaben, and other parabens, are widely used as antimicrobial preservatives in cosmetics and oral and topical pharmaceutical formulations.

Systemically no adverse reactions to parabens have been reported although they have been associated with hypersensitivity reactions. *See* Methylparaben for further information.

LD_{50} (mouse, IP): 0.23 g/kg[8]

15. Handling Precautions

Observe normal precautions appropriate to the circumstances and quantity of material handled. Butylparaben may be irritant to the skin, eyes and mucous membranes and should be handled in a well-ventilated environment. Eye protection, gloves and a dust mask or respirator are recommended.

16. Regulatory Status

Included in the FDA Inactive Ingredients Guide (oral capsules, solutions, suspensions and tablets, rectal and topical preparations). Included in nonparenteral medicines licensed in the UK.

17. Pharmacopeias

Br, Jpn, Mex and USPNF.

18. Related Substances

Butylparaben sodium; Ethylparaben; Methylparaben; Propylparaben.

Butylparaben sodium: $C_{11}H_{13}NaO_3$
Molecular weight: 216.23
CAS number: [36457-20-2]
Synonyms: butyl 4-hydroxybenzoate sodium salt; sodium butyl hydroxybenzoate.
Pharmacopeias: Br.
Appearance: white, odorless or almost odorless, hygroscopic powder.
Acidity/alkalinity: pH = 9.5-10.5 (0.1% w/v aqueous solution)
Solubility: 1 in 10 of ethanol (95%); 1 in 1 of water.
Comments: butylparaben sodium may be used instead of butylparaben because of its greater aqueous solubility. However, it may cause the pH of a formulation to become more alkaline.

19. Comments

See Methylparaben for further information and references.

20. Specific References

1. Decker RL, Wenninger JA. Frequency of preservative use in cosmetic formulas as disclosed to FDA − 1987. Cosmet Toilet 1987; 102(12): 21-24.
2. Haag TE, Loncrini DF. Esters of para-hydroxybenzoic acid. In: Kabara JJ, editor. Cosmetic and drug preservation. New York: Marcel Dekker, 1984: 63-77.
3. Wan LSC, Kurup TRR, Chan LW. Partition of preservatives in oil/water systems. Pharm Acta Helv 1986; 61: 308-313.

4. Aalto TR, Firman MC, Rigler NE. *p*-Hydroxybenzoic acid esters as preservatives I: uses, antibacterial and antifungal studies, properties and determination. J Am Pharm Assoc (Sci) 1953; 42: 449-457.
5. Kamada A, Yata N, Kubo K, Arakawa M. Stability of *p*-hydroxybenzoic acid esters in acidic medium. Chem Pharm Bull 1973; 21: 2073-2076.
6. Aoki M, Kameta A, Yoshioka I, Matsuzaki T. Application of surface active agents to pharmaceutical preparations I: effect of Tween 20 upon the antifungal activities of p-hydroxybenzoic acid esters in solubilized preparations [in Japanese]. J Pharm Soc Jpn 1956; 76: 939-943.
7. Sakamoto T, Yanagi M, Fukushima S, Mitsui T. Effects of some cosmetic pigments on the bactericidal activities of preservatives. J Soc Cosmet Chem 1987; 38: 83-98.
8. Sweet DV, editor. Registry of toxic effects of chemical substances. Cincinnati: US Department of Health, 1987.

See also Methylparaben.

21. General References

Golightly LK, Smolinske SS, Bennett ML, Sutherland EW, Rumack BH. Pharmaceutical excipients associated with inactive ingredients in drug products (part I). Med Toxicol 1988; 3: 128-165.

See also Methylparaben.

22. Authors

USA: MM Rieger.

Calcium Carbonate

1. Nonproprietary Names

BP: Calcium carbonate
PhEur: Calcii carbonas
USP: Precipitated calcium carbonate

2. Synonyms

Cal-Carb; calcium carbonate (1:1); E170; *Millicarb*; precipitated carbonate of lime; *Pharma-Carb*; precipitated chalk; *Sturcal*.

3. Chemical Name and CAS Registry Number

Carbonic acid, calcium salt (1:1) [471-34-1]

4. Empirical Formula   Molecular Weight

$CaCO_3$ 100.09

5. Structural Formula

$CaCO_3$

6. Functional Category

Tablet and capsule diluent; therapeutic agent.

7. Applications in Pharmaceutical Formulation or Technology

Calcium carbonate, employed as a pharmaceutical excipient, is mainly used in solid dosage forms as a diluent.[1,2] It is also used as a base for medicated dental preparations, as a buffering and dissolution aid in dispersible tablets and as a bulking agent in sugar coating processes.
Calcium carbonate is also used as a food additive and therapeutically as an antacid and calcium supplement.[3]

8. Description

Calcium carbonate occurs as an odorless and tasteless white powder or crystals.

9. Pharmacopeial Specifications

Test	PhEur 1990	USP XXII
Identification	+	+
Loss on drying	≤ 2.0%	≤ 2.0%
Acid-insoluble substances	—	≤ 0.2%
Substances insoluble in acetic acid	≤ 0.2%	—
Fluoride	—	≤ 0.005%
Arsenic	≤ 4 ppm	≤ 3 ppm
Barium	+	+
Chloride	≤ 330 ppm	—
Lead	—	≤ 0.001%
Iron	≤ 200 ppm	≤ 0.05%
Heavy metals	≤ 20 ppm	≤ 0.003%
Magnesium & alkali salts	≤ 1.5%	≤ 1.0%
Sulfate	≤ 0.25%	—
Assay (dried basis)	98.5-100.5%	98.0-100.5%

SEM: 1
Excipient: Calcium carbonate
Manufacturer: Whittaker, Clark & Daniels
Lot No.: 15A-3
Magnification: 600x
Voltage: 20 kV

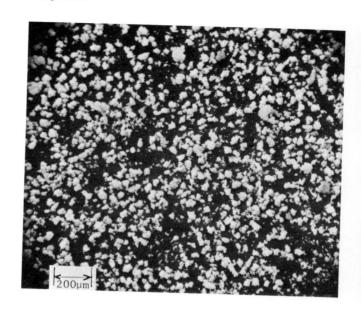

SEM: 2
Excipient: Calcium carbonate
Manufacturer: Whittaker, Clark & Daniels
Lot No.: 15A-3
Magnification: 2400x
Voltage: 20 kV

SEM: 3

Excipient: Calcium carbonate
Manufacturer: Whittaker, Clark & Daniels
Lot No.: 15A-4
Magnification: 600x
Voltage: 20 kV

SEM: 5

Excipient: Calcium carbonate
Manufacturer: Whittaker, Clark & Daniels
Lot No.: 15A-2
Magnification: 600x
Voltage: 20 kV

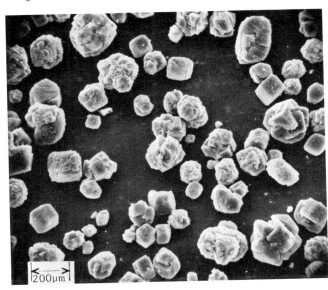

SEM: 4

Excipient: Calcium carbonate
Manufacturer: Whittaker, Clark & Daniels
Lot No.: 15A-4
Magnification: 2400x
Voltage: 20 kV

SEM: 6

Excipient: Calcium carbonate
Manufacturer: Whittaker, Clark & Daniels
Lot No.: 15A-2
Magnification: 2400x
Voltage: 20 kV

10. Typical Properties

Acidity/alkalinity:
pH = 9.0 (10% w/v aqueous dispersion)
Compressibility: *see* HPE Data.
Density (bulk): 0.8 g/cm³
Density (tapped): 1.2 g/cm³
Flowability: cohesive.
Hardness (Mohs): 3.0 for *Millicarb*.
Hygroscopicity: non-hygroscopic. See HPE Data.
Melting point: decomposes at 825-893°C.
Particle size distribution: *see* HPE Data and Fig. 4.
Average particle size = 3.5 μm for *Millicarb*.
Refractive index: 1.59
Solubility: practically insoluble in ethanol (95%) and water. Solubility in water is increased by the presence of ammonium salts or carbon dioxide. The presence of alkali hydroxides reduces the solubility.
Calcium carbonate dissolves with effervescence in dilute acetic acid, dilute hydrochloric acid and dilute nitric acid.
Specific gravity: 2.7 g/cm³
Specific surface area: 1.81 m²/g

HPE Laboratory Project Data			
	Method	Lab #	Results
Bulk/tap density	BTD-8	36	B: 0.391 g/cm³ (a)
			T: 0.485 g/cm³
Compressibility	COM-4,5,6	20	See Fig. 1. (b)
Moisture content	SI-1	13	See Fig. 2.
Particle size	PSD-5B	21	99.8% < 44 μm (a)
	PSD-2	5	See Fig. 3.

Supplier:
a. Charles B Chrystal Co Inc;
b. Whittaker, Clark & Daniels (Lot No.: 64).

11. Stability and Storage Conditions

Calcium carbonate is stable and should be stored in a well-closed container, in a cool, dry, place.

12. Incompatibilities

Incompatible with acids and ammonium salts. *See also* Sections 10 and 19.

13. Method of Manufacture

Calcium carbonate is prepared by double decomposition of calcium chloride and sodium bicarbonate in aqueous solution. Density and fineness are governed by the concentration of solutions. Calcium carbonate is also obtained from the naturally occurring minerals aragonite, calcite and vaterite.

14. Safety

Calcium carbonate is mainly used in oral pharmaceutical formulations and is generally regarded as a nontoxic material. However, calcium carbonate administered orally may cause constipation. Consumption of large quantities (4-60 g daily) may also result in hypercalcemia or renal impairment.[4] Therapeutically, oral daily doses of up to 1 g are employed as an antacid.
LD_{50} (rat, oral): 6.45 g/kg[5]

15. Handling Precautions

Observe normal precautions appropriate to the circumstances and quantity of material handled. Calcium carbonate may be

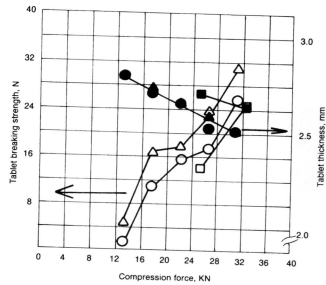

Fig. 1: Compression characteristics of calcium carbonate.
○● Unlubricated Carver laboratory press (COM-5).
△▲ Lubricated Carver laboratory press (COM-6).
□■ Lubricated, instrumented Stokes, model F, single punch press (COM-4).

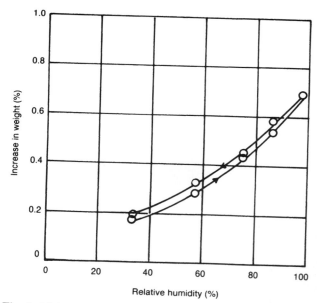

Fig. 2: Moisture sorption-desorption isotherm of calcium carbonate.

irritant to the eyes and on inhalation. Eye protection, gloves and a dust mask are recommended. Calcium carbonate should be handled in a well-ventilated environment. In the UK, the long-term (8-hour TWA) occupational exposure limit for calcium carbonate is 10 mg/m³ for total inhalable dust and 5 mg/m³ for respirable dust.[6]

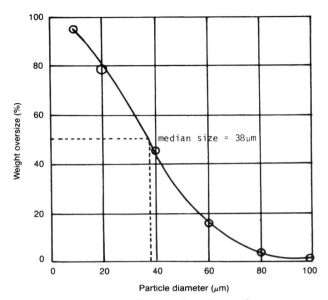

Fig. 3: Particle size distribution of calcium carbonate.

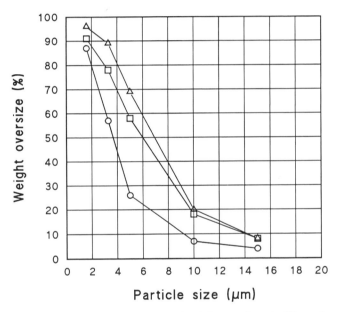

Fig. 4: Particle size distribution of calcium carbonate (*Sturcal*, Rhône-Poulenc Inc).
○ *Sturcal F.*
□ *Sturcal H.*
△ *Sturcal L.*

16. Regulatory Status

GRAS listed. Accepted for use as a food additive in Europe. Included in the FDA Inactive Ingredients Guide (oral capsules and tablets, and otic solutions). Included in nonparenteral medicines licensed in the UK.

17. Pharmacopeias

Aust, Belg, Br, Braz, Cz, Egypt, Eur, Fr, Ger, Gr, Hung, Ind, Int, It, Jpn, Mex, Neth, Nord, Port, Rom, Swiss, Turk, US and Yug.

18. Related Substances

Directly compressible tablet diluents containing calcium carbonate and other excipients are commercially available, e.g. *Cal-Carb* (Ingredients Technology Inc) is a blend containing 95% calcium carbonate and 5% maltodextrin; *Calcium 90* (Ingredients Technology Inc) is a blend containing 90% calcium carbonate and 5% starch.

19. Comments

When used in tablets containing aspirin and related substances, traces of iron may cause discoloration. This may be overcome by the inclusion of a suitable chelating agent.

20. Specific References

1. Haines-Nutt RF. The compression properties of magnesium and calcium carbonates. J Pharm Pharmacol 1976; 28: 468-470.
2. Gorecki DKJ, Richardson CJ, Pavlakidis P, Wallace SM. Dissolution rates in calcium carbonate tablets: a consideration in product selection. Can Pharm J 1989; 122: 484-487, 508.
3. Roberts DE, Rogers CM, Richards CE, Lee MG. Calcium carbonate mixture [letter]. Pharm J 1986; 236: 577.
4. Orwoll ES. The milk-alkali syndrome: current concepts. Ann Intern Med 1982; 97: 242-248.
5. Sweet DV, editor. Registry of toxic effects of chemical substances. Cincinnati: US Department of Health, 1987.
6. Health and Safety Executive. Occupational exposure limits 1993: EH40/93. London: HMSO, 1993.

21. General References

Czeisler JL, Perlman KP. Diluents. In: Swarbrick J, Boylan JC, editors. Encyclopedia of pharmaceutical technology, volume 4. New York: Marcel Dekker, 1988: 37-84.

22. Authors

UK: NA Armstrong.
USA: A Athani.

Dibasic Calcium Phosphate Dihydrate

1. Nonproprietary Names

BP: Calcium hydrogen phosphate
PhEur: Calcii hydrogenophosphas
USP: Dibasic calcium phosphate

2. Synonyms

Cafos; calcium hydrogen orthophosphate dihydrate; calcium monohydrogen phosphate dihydrate; *Calstar*; dicalcium orthophosphate; *Di-Cafos*; *DI-TAB*; E341; *Emcompress*; phosphoric acid calcium salt (1:1) dihydrate; secondary calcium phosphate.

3. Chemical Name and CAS Registry Number

Dibasic calcium phosphate dihydrate [7789-77-7]

4. Empirical Formula   Molecular Weight

$CaHPO_4.2H_2O$ 172.09

5. Structural Formula

$CaHPO_4.2H_2O$

6. Functional Category

Tablet and capsule diluent.

7. Applications in Pharmaceutical Formulation or Technology

Dibasic calcium phosphate is one of the most widely used tableting excipients in the US, particularly in the health food sector. However, it has historically been less frequently used in Europe. Although predominantly used in vitamin and mineral preparations dibasic calcium phosphate is increasingly being used in ethical pharmaceuticals due to its relatively low cost and desirable flow and compression characteristics.

The dihydrate is available in milled and unmilled forms, and is used primarily for direct compression or wet granulation processes. The dihydrate and anhydrous forms are nonhygroscopic at 25°C and relative humidities up to about 90%. In applications where the temperature exceeds about 45°C, and at high relative humidities, the anhydrous form (*see* Section 18) should be used since the dihydrate starts to lose water of crystallization.

Dibasic calcium phosphate has good compression characteristics, compaction taking place primarily by brittle fracture for both the dihydrate and anhydrous forms. Due to its abrasive nature it is essential that lubrication is provided during tableting processes, for example with 1% magnesium stearate.

Dibasic calcium phosphate is practically insoluble in water although it will dissolve in acids such as gastric acid. Tablets produced with dibasic calcium phosphate do not disintegrate readily and a disintegrant such as starch, povidone, sodium starch glycolate or croscarmellose sodium is necessary.[1-3]

Dibasic calcium phosphate is also used in nutritional supplements as a calcium source and in dental preparations for its abrasive qualities.

See also Section 19.

8. Description

Dibasic calcium phosphate dihydrate is a white, odorless, tasteless powder or crystalline solid.

SEM: 1

Excipient: Calcium phosphate dibasic dihydrate (*Emcompress*)
Manufacturer: Edward Mendell Co Inc
Lot No.: 16A-3 (B-392X)
Magnification: 120x
Voltage: 20 kV

SEM: 2

Excipient: Calcium phosphate dibasic dihydrate (*Emcompress*)
Manufacturer: Edward Mendell Co Inc
Lot No.: 16A-3 (B-392X)
Magnification: 600x
Voltage: 20 kV

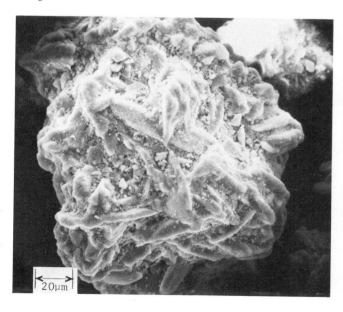

SEM: 3

Excipient: Calcium phosphate dibasic dihydrate
Manufacturer: Stauffer Chemical Co
Lot No.: 16A-1 (89)
Magnification: 120x
Voltage: 20 kV

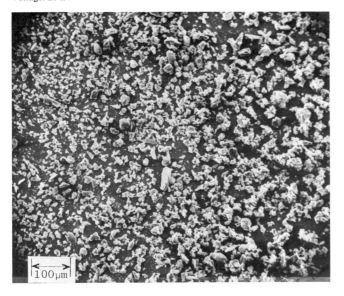

SEM: 4

Excipient: Calcium phosphate dibasic dihydrate
Manufacturer: Stauffer Chemical Co
Lot No.: 16A-1 (89)
Magnification: 600x
Voltage: 20 kV

9. Pharmacopeial Specifications

Test	PhEur 1981	USP XXII
Identification	+	+
Loss on ignition		
(for dihydrate)	—	24.5-26.5%
(for anhydrous)	—	6.6-8.5%
Acid-insoluble substances	—	$\leqslant$ 0.2%
Carbonate	+	+
Chloride	$\leqslant$ 330 ppm	$\leqslant$ 0.25%
Fluoride	$\leqslant$ 100 ppm	$\leqslant$ 0.005%
Sulfate	$\leqslant$ 0.5%	$\leqslant$ 0.5%
Arsenic	$\leqslant$ 10 ppm	$\leqslant$ 3 ppm
Barium	+	+
Heavy metals	$\leqslant$ 40 ppm	$\leqslant$ 0.003%
Iron	$\leqslant$ 400 ppm	—
Monocalcium & tricalcium phosphates	+	—
Assay		
(as CaHPO$_4$.2H$_2$O)	98.0-105.0%	—
(as Ca on ignited basis)	—	30.0-31.7%

10. Typical Properties

Acidity/alkalinity:
pH = 7.4 (20% slurry of *DI-TAB*)
Angle of repose: 28.3° for *Emcompress*.[4]
Compressibility: *see* HPE Data.
Density: 2.35 g/cm^3
Density (bulk):
0.87 g/cm^3 for *DI-TAB*;
0.86 g/cm^3 for *Emcompress*.[4]
Density (tapped):
0.93 g/cm^3 for *DI-TAB*;
0.93 g/cm^3 for *Emcompress*.[4]
Flowability:
27.3 g/s for *DI-TAB*;
11.4 g/s for *Emcompress*.[4]
Melting point: decomposes below 100°C with loss of water.
Moisture content: dibasic calcium phosphate dihydrate and the anhydrous material are both nonhygroscopic and absorb minimal amounts of water at up to approximately 90% relative humidity, *see* HPE Data. At temperatures greater than about 45°C the dihydrate starts to lose its water of crystallization. The anhydrous material, which cannot be rehydrated to form the dihydrate, is formed at temperatures in excess of 200°C.
Particle size distribution:
average particle diameter = 180 μm for *DI-TAB*;
average particle diameter = 9 μm for powder.
Powdered dibasic calcium phosphate consists of particles less than about 44 μm in size. The granular materials used for direct compression tableting are of generally uniform size with *DI-TAB* consisting of over 95% of granules between 44-420 μm in size and for *Emcompress* over 95% of granules are less than 420 μm in size. See also HPE Data.
Solubility: practically insoluble in ethanol (95%) and water; soluble in dilute acids.
Specific surface area: 1-2 m^2/g for *DI-TAB*

HPE Laboratory Project Data (Dihydrate)			
	Method	Lab #	Results
Average flow rate	FLO-3	24	No flow [a]
Average flow rate	FLO-3	24	6.03 g/s [b]
Bulk/tap density	BTD-8	36	B: 0.815 g/cm^3 [b]
			T: 0.904 g/cm^3 [b]
Bulk/tap density	BTD-8	36	B: 0.565 g/cm^3 [c]
			T: 0.772 g/cm^3 [c]
Compressibility	COM-All	20	No compression [a]
Compressibility	COM-4-6	29	*See* Fig. 1. [b]
Density	DE-1	31	2.597 g/cm^3 [a]
Density	DE-1	31	2.305 g/cm^3 [b]
Moisture content	MC-25	15	20.36% [c]
Moisture content	SI-1	13	*See* Fig. 2. [a]
Moisture content	SI-1	13	*See* Fig. 2. [b]
Particle friability	PF-1	36	0.019 [b]
Particle size	PSD-7	24	4.2 μm [a]
Particle size	PSD-5B	21	100% ≤ 44 μm [a]
Particle size	PSD-5A	21	*See* Fig. 3. [b]

Supplier:
    a. Stauffer Chemical Co (Lot No.: 89)
    b. Edward Mendell Co Inc (*Emcompress*, Lot No.: B-392X);
    c. Monsanto Co (Lot No.: 05587).

11. Stability and Storage Conditions

Both the dihydrate and anhydrous forms of dibasic calcium phosphate are nonhygroscopic, relatively stable materials. Tablets produced with these excipients show good storage characteristics although the anhydrous form is preferred in conditions of extreme heat due to loss of water from the dihydrate.[5-9]

The bulk material should be stored in a well-closed container in a cool, dry place.

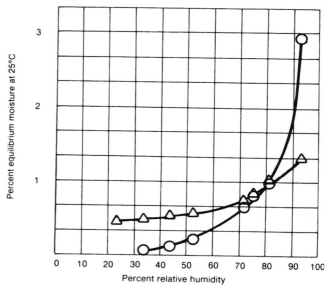

Fig. 2: Moisture sorption isotherm of dibasic calcium phosphate dihydrate.
○ Dibasic calcium phosphate dihydrate (Stauffer Chemical Co)
△ Dibasic calcium phosphate dihydrate (*Emcompress*, Edward Mendell Co Inc)

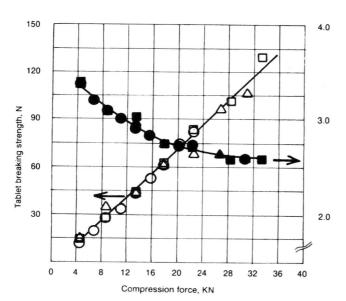

Fig. 1: Compression characteristics of lubricated and unlubricated dibasic calcium phosphate dihydrate (*Emcompress*).
○ ● Unlubricated Carver laboratory press (COM-5)
△ ▲ Lubricated Carver laboratory press (COM-6)
□ ■ Lubricated, instrumented Stokes model-F single punch press (COM-4)

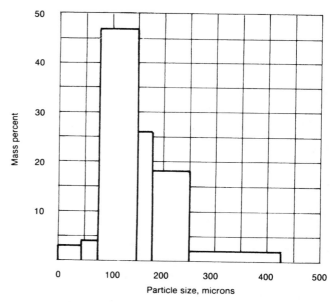

Fig. 3: Particle size distribution of dibasic calcium phosphate dihydrate (*Emcompress*).

12. Incompatibilities

Dibasic calcium phosphate is incompatible with tetracycline antibiotics and indomethacin.[10] Due to its alkaline nature dibasic calcium phosphate should also not be used with active ingredients that are sensitive to a pH of 7.3 or above.

13. Method of Manufacture

Calcium phosphates are usually manufactured by reacting very pure phosphoric acid with calcium hydroxide, $Ca(OH)_2$, obtained from limestone. In the correct molar ratios and under suitable conditions the desired calcium phosphate is precipitated. Dibasic calcium phosphate dihydrate can only be manufactured by precipitation at a suitable temperature. Production by means of hydration of the anhydrous material is not possible.[3]

14. Safety

Dibasic calcium phosphate is widely used in oral pharmaceutical formulations and food products and is generally regarded as a nontoxic and nonirritant material. However, oral ingestion of large quantities may cause abdominal discomfort.
LD_{50} (rat, oral): 4.6-10 g/kg[11]

15. Handling Precautions

Observe normal precautions appropriate to the circumstances and quantity of material handled. Eye protection and gloves are recommended. Handle in a well-ventilated environment since dust inhalation may be irritant. For processes generating large amounts of dust a respirator is recommended.

16. Regulatory Status

GRAS listed. Accepted as a food additive in Europe. Included in the FDA Inactive Ingredients Guide (oral capsules and tablets). Included in nonparenteral medicines licensed in the UK.

17. Pharmacopeias

Aust, Belg, Br, Eur, Fr, Ger, Gr, Hung, Ind, It, Jpn, Mex, Neth, Nord, Port, Rus, Swiss, US and Yug.
Note that the USP XXII permits dibasic calcium phosphate to be either the dihydrate or anhydrous material.

18. Related Substances

Dibasic calcium phosphate anhydrous; Tricalcium Phosphate.

Dibasic calcium phosphate anhydrous: $CaHPO_4$

Molecular weight: 136.06
CAS number: [7757-93-9]
Synonyms: *A-TAB*; calcium hydrogen orthophosphate anhydrous; calcium monohydrogen phosphate anhydrous; *Di-Cafos A*; dicalcium orthophosphate anhydrous; *Emcompress Anhydrous*; phosphoric acid calcium salt (1:1).
Acidity/alkalinity:
pH = 7.3 (20% slurry)
pH = 5.1 (20% slurry of *A-TAB*)
Compressibility: *see* HPE Data.
Density: 2.89 g/cm^3
Density (bulk): 0.78 g/cm^3 for *A-TAB*
Density (tapped):
0.82 g/cm^3 for *A-TAB*;
0.70 g/cm^3 for *Emcompress Anhydrous*.
Flowability: 18.9 g/s for *A-TAB*
Moisture content: *see* Section 10 and HPE Data.
Particle size distribution: *A-TAB* consists of granules of which over 95% are between 44-420 μm in size. *Emcompress Anhydrous* consists of granules of which over 95% are less than 420 μm in size.

Sample	Average particle diameter (μm)
A-TAB	180
Emcompress Anhydrous	136
Powder	15

Specific surface area: 20-30 m^2/g for *A-TAB*

	Method	Lab #	Results
	HPE Laboratory Project Data (Anhydrous)		
Compressibility	COM-2	21	*See* Fig. 4. [d]
Density	DE-1	31	2.873 g/cm^3 [d]
Moisture content	EMC-1	2	*See* Fig. 5. [e]
Moisture content	MC-28	18	0.142% [e]
Moisture content	MC-12	18	0.149% [e]
Moisture content	MC-23	21	0.187% [d]
Moisture content	MC-20	14	0.100% [e]
Particle size	PSD-7	24	9.4 μm [d]

Supplier:
d. Van Waters & Rogers Inc (Lot No.: DK9);
e. Monsanto Co (Lot No.: RNB 476S).

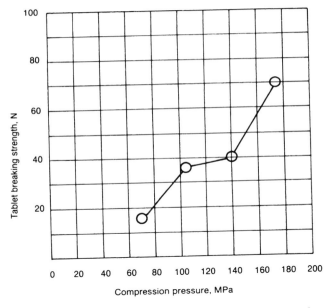

Fig. 4: Compression characteristics of dibasic calcium phosphate anhydrous.
Tablet weight: 750 mg

19. Comments

Dibasic calcium phosphate dihydrate forms available for direct compression include: *Calstar* (FMC Corp); *DI-TAB* (Rhône-Poulenc) and *Emcompress* (Edward Mendell Co Inc). Anhydrous forms include: *A-TAB* (Rhône-Poulenc) and *Emcompress Anhydrous* (Edward Mendell Co Inc).
Accelerated stability studies of formulations containing dibasic calcium phosphate dihydrate should not be performed at temperatures greater than 50-60°C since erroneous results will be obtained due to loss of water of crystallization from the dihydrate.

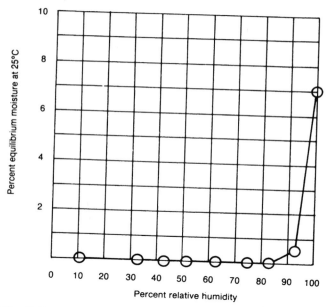

Fig. 5: Equilibrium moisture content of dibasic calcium phosphate anhydrous.

Each gram of dibasic calcium phosphate dihydrate represents approximately 5.8 mmol of calcium and phosphate. Also, 4.29 g of dibasic calcium phosphate dihydrate is approximately equivalent to 1 g of calcium.

20. Specific References

1. Rubinstein MH, Bodey DM. Disaggregation of compressed tablets. J Pharm Sci 1976; 65: 1749-1753.
2. Koparkar AD, Augsburger LL, Shangraw RF. Intrinsic dissolution rates of tablet filler-binders and their influence on the dissolution of drugs from tablet formulations. Pharm Res 1990; 7: 80-86.
3. Fischer E. Calcium phosphate as a pharmaceutical excipient. Mfg Chem 1992; 64(6): 25-27.
4. Çelik M, Okutgen E. A feasibility study for the development of a prospective compaction functionality test and the establishment of a compaction data bank. Drug Dev Ind Pharm 1993; 19: 2309-2334.
5. Horhota ST, Burgio J, Lonski L, Rhodes CT. Effect of storage at specified temperature and humidity on properties of three directly compressible tablet formulations. J Pharm Sci 1976; 65: 1746-1749.
6. Chowhan ZT. The effect of low- and high-humidity ageing on the hardness, disintegration time and dissolution rate of dibasic calcium phosphate-based tablets. J Pharm Pharmacol 1979; 32: 10-14.
7. Rudnic EM, Lausier JM, Rhodes CT. Comparative aging studies of tablets made with dibasic calcium phosphate dihydrate and spray dried lactose. Drug Dev Ind Pharm 1979; 5: 589-604.
8. Ahlneck C, Alderborn G. Moisture adsorption and tableting II. The effect on tensile strength and air permeability of the relative humidity during storage of tablets of 3 crystalline materials. Int J Pharmaceutics 1989; 56: 143-150.
9. de Haan P, Kroon C, Sam AP. Decomposition and stabilization of the tablet excipient calcium hydrogenphosphate dihydrate. Drug Dev Ind Pharm 1990; 16: 2031-2055.
10. Eerikäinen S, Yliruusi J, Laakso R. The behaviour of the sodium salt of indomethacin in the cores of film-coated granules containing various fillers. Int J Pharmaceutics 1991; 71: 201-211.
11. Rhône-Poulenc Basic Chemicals Co. Technical literature: calcium phosphate pharmaceutical ingredients, 1992.

21. General References

Bryan JW, McCallister JD. Matrix forming capabilities of three calcium diluents. Drug Dev Ind Pharm 1992; 18: 2029-2047.

Carstensen JT, Ertell C. Physical and chemical properties of calcium phosphates for solid state pharmaceutical formulations. Drug Dev Ind Pharm 1990; 16: 1121-1133.

Landín M, Martínez-Pacheco R, Gómez-Amoza JL, Souto C, Concheiro A, Rowe RC. The effect of country of origin on the properties of dicalcium phosphate dihydrate powder. Int J Pharmaceutics 1994; 103: 9-18.

Schmidt PC, Herzog R. Calcium phosphates in pharmaceutical tableting 1: physico-pharmaceutical properties. Pharm Wld Sci 1993; 15(3): 105-115.

Schmidt PC, Herzog R. Calcium phosphates in pharmaceutical tableting 2: comparison of tableting properties. Pharm Wld Sci 1993; 15(3): 116-122.

Shiromani PK, Bavitz JF. Studies on a dibasic calcium phosphate-mannitol matrix tablet formulation - a complementary combination. Drug Dev Ind Pharm 1988; 14: 1375-1387.

22. Authors

USA: NH Parikh.

Tribasic Calcium Phosphate

1. Nonproprietary Names

BP: Calcium phosphate
USPNF: Tribasic calcium phosphate

2. Synonyms

Calcium orthophosphate; E341; hydroxyapatite; phosphoric acid calcium salt (2:3); precipitated calcium phosphate; tertiary calcium phosphate; *Tri-Cafos*; tricalcium diorthophosphate; *TRI-CAL WG*; *TRI-TAB*.

3. Chemical Name and CAS Registry Number

Tribasic calcium phosphate is not a clearly defined chemical entity but is a mixture of calcium phosphates. Several chemical names, CAS registry numbers and molecular formulas have therefore been used to describe this material. Those most frequently cited are shown below.
Calcium hydroxide phosphate [12167-74-7]
Tricalcium orthophosphate [7758-87-4]
See also, Sections 4 and 8.

4. Empirical Formula   Molecular Weight

$Ca_3(PO_4)_2$ 310.20
$Ca_5(OH)(PO_4)_3$ 502.32

5. Structural Formula

See Sections 3 and 4.

6. Functional Category

Anticaking agent; glidant; tablet and capsule diluent.

7. Applications in Pharmaceutical Formulation or Technology

Tribasic calcium phosphate is widely used as a tablet and capsule diluent in either direct compression or wet granulation processes. As with dibasic calcium phosphate, a lubricant, such as magnesium stearate, and a disintegrant should be incorporated in capsule or tablet formulations which include tribasic calcium phosphate. Tribasic calcium phosphate is most widely used in vitamin and mineral preparations as a diluent and calcium source[1] but may also be used in some specialised applications as a disintegrant.[2]
Tribasic calcium phosphate is also widely used in food applications as an anticaking agent.
See also, Dibasic Calcium Phosphate Dihydrate.

8. Description

The BP 1993 states that tribasic calcium phosphate consists mainly of tricalcium diorthophosphate, $Ca_3(PO_4)_2$, together with calcium phosphates of more acidic or basic character. The USPNF XVII specifies that tribasic calcium phosphate consists of variable mixtures of calcium phosphates having the approximate composition $10CaO.3P_2O_5.H_2O$. This corresponds to a molecular formula of $Ca_5(OH)(PO_4)_3$ or $Ca_{10}(OH)_2(PO_4)_6$.

Tribasic calcium phosphate is a white, amorphous, odorless and tasteless powder.

9. Pharmacopeial Specifications

Test	BP 1993	USPNF XVII
Identification	+	+
Loss on ignition	—	$\leqslant 8.0\%$
Water-soluble substances	—	$\leqslant 0.5\%$
Acid-insoluble substances	$\leqslant 0.3\%$	$\leqslant 0.2\%$
Carbonate	+	+
Chloride	$\leqslant 0.35\%$	$\leqslant 0.14\%$
Fluoride	$\leqslant 50$ ppm	$\leqslant 0.0075\%$
Nitrate	—	+
Sulfate	$\leqslant 0.6\%$	$\leqslant 0.8\%$
Arsenic	$\leqslant 4$ ppm	$\leqslant 3$ ppm
Barium	—	+
Iron	$\leqslant 400$ ppm	—
Dibasic salt and calcium oxide	—	+
Heavy metals	$\leqslant 30$ ppm	$\leqslant 0.003\%$
Water	$\leqslant 2.5\%$	—
Assay as Ca	—	34.0-40.0%
Assay as $Ca_3(PO_4)_2$	$\geqslant 90.0\%$	—

10. Typical Properties

Acidity/alkalinity:
pH = 6.8 (20% slurry of *TRI-TAB*)
Compressibility: *see* Fig. 1.
Density: 3.14 g/cm^3
Density (bulk): 0.80 g/cm^3 for *TRI-TAB*.[3]
Density (tapped): 0.95 g/cm^3 for *TRI-TAB*.[3]
Flowability: 24.6 g/s for *TRI-TAB*.[3]
Melting point: 1670°C
Particle size distribution:
average particle diameter = 350 μm for *TRI-TAB*;
average particle diameter = 180 μm for *TRI-CAL WG*.
For *TRI-CAL WG* 99% of particles < 420 μm, 46% < 149 μm and 15% < 44 μm in size. For *TRI-TAB* 15% of particles < 149 μm and 5% < 44 μm in size.
Solubility: soluble in dilute mineral acids; very slightly soluble in water; practically insoluble in acetic acid and alcohols.
Specific surface area: 70-80 m^2/g[3]
Water content: slightly hygroscopic. A well-defined crystalline hydrate is not formed although surface moisture may be picked up or contained within small pores in the crystal structure. At relative humidities between about 15-65%, the equilibrium moisture content at 25°C is about 2.0%. At relative humidities above about 75%, tribasic calcium phosphate may absorb small amounts of moisture.

11. Stability and Storage Conditions

Tribasic calcium phosphate is a stable material and is not liable to cake.
The bulk material should be stored in a well-closed container in a cool, dry, place.

12. Incompatibilities

Calcium salts are incompatible with tetracycline antibiotics. Tribasic calcium phosphate is also incompatible with tocopheryl acetate (but not tocopheryl succinate). It influences the absorption of vitamin D and may form sparingly soluble phosphates with hormones.

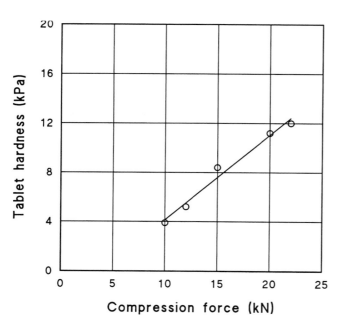

Fig. 1: Compression characteristics of tribasic calcium phosphate (*TRI-TAB*, Rhône-Poulenc Basic Chemicals Co).[3]
Tablet weight: 750 mg

13. Method of Manufacture

Tribasic calcium phosphate occurs naturally as the minerals oxydapatite, voelicherite and whitlockite. Commercially, it is prepared by treating phosphate-containing rock with sulfuric acid. Tribasic calcium phosphate is then precipitated by the addition of calcium hydroxide. Tribasic calcium phosphate may also be obtained from calcined animal bones in a similar process.[4]

14. Safety

Tribasic calcium phosphate is widely used in oral pharmaceutical formulations and food products and is generally regarded as nontoxic and nonirritant at the levels employed as a pharmaceutical excipient.

Ingestion or inhalation of excessive quantities may result in the deposition of tribasic calcium phosphate crystals in tissues. These crystals may lead to inflammation and cause tissue lesions in the areas of deposition.

Oral ingestion of large quantities of tribasic calcium phosphate may cause abdominal discomfort such as nausea and vomiting. No teratogenic effects were found in chicken embryos exposed to a dose of 2.5 mg of tribasic calcium phosphate.[5]

LD_{50} (rat, oral): > 1 g/kg[3]

15. Handling Precautions

Observe normal precautions appropriate to the circumstances and quantity of material handled. Eye protection and gloves are recommended. Handle in a well-ventilated environment since dust inhalation may be irritant. For processes generating large amounts of dust a respirator is recommended.

16. Regulatory Status

GRAS listed. Accepted for use as a food additive in Europe. Included in the FDA Inactive Ingredients Guide (oral capsules and tablets). Included in nonparenteral medicines licensed in the UK.

17. Pharmacopeias

Br, Fr, Hung, Ind, Mex, Rom, Swiss and USPNF.

18. Related Substances

Dibasic Calcium Phosphate Dihydrate.

19. Comments

Tribasic calcium phosphate provides a higher calcium load than dibasic calcium phosphate. Each gram of tribasic calcium phosphate represents approximately 9.7 mmol of calcium and 6.4 mmol of phosphate; a gram of calcium is contained in 2.58 g of tribasic calcium phosphate.

Directly compressible forms of tribasic calcium phosphate include *TRI-CAL WG* and *TRI-TAB* (both Rhône-Poulenc Basic Chemicals Co).

20. Specific References

1. Magid L. Stable multivitamin tablets containing tricalcium phosphate. US Patent 3564097. 1971.
2. Delonca H, Puech A, Segura G, Youakim J. Effect of excipients and storage conditions on drug stability I - acetylsalicylic acid-based tablets [in French]. J Pharm Belg 1969; 24: 243-252.
3. Rhône-Poulenc Basic Chemicals Co. Technical literature: calcium phosphate pharmaceutical ingredients, 1992.
4. Magami A. Basic pentacalcium triphosphate production. Japanese Patent 56022614. 1981.
5. Verrett MJ, Scott WF, Reynaldo EF, Alterman EK, Thomas CA. Toxicity and teratogenicity of food additive chemicals in the developing chicken embryo. Toxicol Appl Pharmacol 1980; 56: 265-273.

21. General References

Agnihotri VP. Solubilization of insoluble phosphates by some soil fungi isolated from nursery seed beds. Can J Microbiol 1970; 16: 877-880.

Bryan JW, McCallister JD. Matrix forming capabilities of three calcium diluents. Drug Dev Ind Pharm 1992; 18: 2029-2047.

Chowhan ZT, Amaro AA. The effect of low- and high-humidity aging on the hardness, disintegration time and dissolution rate of tribasic calcium phosphate-based tablets. Drug Dev Ind Pharm 1979; 5: 545-562.

Fischer E. Calcium phosphate as a pharmaceutical excipient. Mfg Chem 1992; 64(6): 25-27.

Kutty TRN. Thermal decomposition of hydroxylapatite. Indian J Chem 1973; 11: 695-697.

Molokhia AM, Moustafa MA, Gouda MW. Effect of storage conditions on the hardness, disintegration and drug release from some tablet bases. Drug Dev Ind Pharm 1982; 8: 283-292.

Schmidt PC, Herzog R. Calcium phosphates in pharmaceutical tableting 1: physico-pharmaceutical properties. Pharm Wld Sci 1993; 15(3): 105-115.

Schmidt PC, Herzog R. Calcium phosphates in pharmaceutical tableting 2: comparison of tableting properties. Pharm Wld Sci 1993; 15(3): 116-122.

22. Authors

USA: SA Daskalakis, NR Poola.

Calcium Stearate

1. Nonproprietary Names
USPNF: Calcium stearate

2. Synonyms
Calcium distearate; *HyQual*; stearic acid, calcium salt.

3. Chemical Name and CAS Registry Number
Octadecanoic acid calcium salt [1592-23-0]

4. Empirical Formula   Molecular Weight
$C_{36}H_{70}CaO_4$ 607.03
                                  (for pure material)

The USPNF XVII describes calcium stearate as a compound of calcium with a mixture of solid organic acids obtained from fats and consists chiefly of variable proportions of calcium stearate and calcium palmitate ($C_{32}H_{62}CaO_4$). It contains the equivalent of 9.0-10.5% of calcium oxide.

5. Structural Formula
$[CH_3(CH_2)_{16}COO]_2Ca$

6. Functional Category
Tablet and capsule lubricant.

7. Applications in Pharmaceutical Formulation or Technology
Calcium stearate is primarily used in pharmaceutical formulations as a lubricant in tablet and capsule manufacture at concentrations up to 1.0% w/w. Although it has good antiadherent and lubricant properties, calcium stearate has poor glidant properties.

Calcium stearate is also employed as an emulsifier, stabilizing agent and suspending agent. It is also used in cosmetics and food products.

8. Description
Calcium stearate occurs as a fine, white to yellowish white-colored, bulky powder having a slight, characteristic odor. It is unctuous and free from grittiness.

9. Pharmacopeial Specifications

Test	USPNF XVII (Suppl 5)
Identification	+
Loss on drying	$\leqslant 4.0\%$
Arsenic	$\leqslant 3$ ppm
Heavy metals	$\leqslant 0.001\%$
Assay (as CaO)	9.0-10.5%

10. Typical Properties
Acid value: 191-203
Ash: 9.9-10.3%
Chloride: < 200 ppm
Density: 1.04 g/cm^3

SEM: 1
Excipient: Calcium stearate (Standard)
Manufacturer: Durham Chemicals
Lot No.: 0364
Voltage: 20 kV

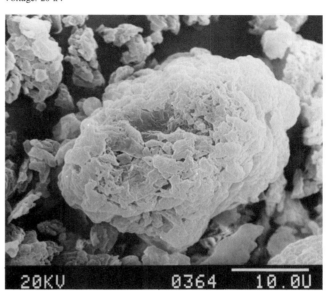

SEM: 2
Excipient: Calcium stearate (Precipitated)
Manufacturer: Witco Corporation
Lot No.: 0438
Voltage: 12 kV

SEM: 3

Excipient: Calcium stearate (EA)
Manufacturer: Witco Corporation
Voltage: 12 kV

SEM: 5

Excipient: Calcium stearate
Manufacturer: Mallinckrodt Speciality Chemicals Co
Lot No.: JMP
Magnification: 600x
Voltage: 5 kV

SEM: 4

Excipient: Calcium stearate (Fused)
Manufacturer: Witco Corporation
Voltage: 15 kV

SEM: 6

Excipient: Calcium stearate
Manufacturer: Mallinckrodt Speciality Chemicals Co
Lot No.: JMP
Magnification: 2400x
Voltage: 5 kV

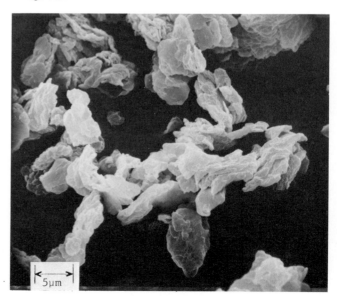

Density (bulk & tapped):

	Bulk Density g/cm³	Tapped Density g/cm³
Durham Chemicals		
(Standard)	—	0.26
(A)	—	0.45
(AM)	—	0.33
Witco Corporation		
(EA)	0.21	0.27
(Fused)	0.38	0.48
(Precipitated)	0.16	0.20

Flowability: 21.2-22.6% (Carr compressibility index)
Free fatty acid: 0.3-0.5%
Melting point: 149-160°C
Moisture content: see HPE Data.
Particle size distribution: 1.7-60 μm.
100% through a 73.7 μm (#200 mesh); 99.5% through a 44.5 μm (#325 mesh).
Shear strength: 14.71 MPa
Softening point: 160°C
Solubility: practically insoluble in ethanol (95%), ether and water.
Specific surface area: 5.76-7.44 m²/g
Sulfate: < 0.25%

HPE Laboratory Project Data			
	Method	Lab #	Results
Moisture content	MC-23	21	2.96% [a]
Moisture content	MC-12	18	2.97% [b]

Supplier: a. Witco Corporation; b. Mallinckrodt Speciality Chemicals Co.

11. Stability and Storage Conditions

Calcium stearate is stable and should be stored in a well-closed container in a cool, dry, place.

12. Incompatibilities

—

13. Method of Manufacture

Calcium stearate is prepared by the reaction of calcium chloride with a mixture of the sodium salts of stearic and palmitic acids. The calcium stearate formed is collected and washed with water to remove any sodium chloride.

14. Safety

Calcium stearate is used in oral pharmaceutical formulations and is generally regarded as a nontoxic and nonirritant material.

15. Handling Precautions

Observe normal precautions appropriate to the circumstances and quantity of material handled. Calcium stearate should be used in a well-ventilated environment; eye protection, gloves and a respirator are recommended.

16. Regulatory Status

GRAS listed. Included in the FDA Inactive Ingredients Guide (oral capsules and tablets). Included in nonparenteral medicines licensed in the UK.

17. Pharmacopeias

Jpn and USPNF.

18. Related Substances

Magnesium Stearate; Stearic Acid; Zinc Stearate.

19. Comments

See Magnesium Stearate for further information and references.

20. Specific References

—

21. General References

Büsch G, Neuwald F. Metallic soaps as water-in-oil emulsifiers [in German]. J Soc Cosmet Chem 1973; 24: 763-769.

22. Authors

USA: LV Allen.

Calcium Sulfate

1. Nonproprietary Names

USPNF: Calcium sulfate

2. Synonyms

Calcium sulfate anhydrous: anhydrite; anhydrous gypsum; anhydrous sulfate of lime; *Destab*; E516; karstenite; muriacite; *Snow White*; sulfuric acid, calcium salt.
Calcium sulfate dihydrate: alabaster; *Cal-Tab*; *Compactrol*; *Destab*; E516; gypsum; light spar; mineral white; native calcium sulfate; precipitated calcium sulfate; satinite; satin spar; selenite; terra alba; *USG Terra Alba*.

3. Chemical Name and CAS Registry Number

Calcium sulfate [7778-18-9]
Calcium sulfate dihydrate [10101-41-4]

4. Empirical Formula   Molecular Weight

$CaSO_4$ 136.14
$CaSO_4.2H_2O$ 172.17

5. Structural Formula

$CaSO_4$

6. Functional Category

Capsule and tablet diluent; desiccant.

7. Applications in Pharmaceutical Formulation or Technology

Calcium sulfate dihydrate is widely used in capsules and tablets as a diluent due to its good compression characteristics and disintegrant properties.[1,2]
Calcium sulfate hemihydrate is used in the preparation of plaster of Paris bandage which is used for the immobilization of limbs and fractures; it should not be used in tablets, *see* Section 18.
The anhydrous material is widely used as a desiccant.

8. Description

The USPNF XVII describes calcium sulfate as either the dihydrate or the anhydrous material.
Calcium sulfate is a white to yellowish-white, odorless and tasteless powder.

9. Pharmacopeial Specifications

Test	USPNF XVII
Identification	+
Loss on drying	
(anhydrous)	⩽ 1.5%
(dihydrate)	19.0-23.0%
Iron	⩽ 0.01%
Heavy metals	⩽ 0.001%
Assay (dried basis)	98.0-101.0%

10. Typical Properties

Acidity/alkalinity:
pH = 7.3 (10% slurry) for dihydrate;
pH = 10.4 (10% slurry) for anhydrous material.
Angle of repose: 37.6° for *Compactrol*.[2]
Compressibility: *see* HPE Data.
Density (bulk):
0.94 g/cm^3 for *Compactrol*;[2]
0.67 g/cm^3 for dihydrate;
0.70 g/cm^3 for anhydrous material.
Density (tapped):
1.10 g/cm^3 for *Compactrol*;[2]
1.12 g/cm^3 for dihydrate;
1.28 g/cm^3 for anhydrous material.
Flowability: 48.4% (Carr compressibility index); 5.2 g/s for *Compactrol*.[2]
Melting point: 1450°C for anhydrous material.
Particle size distribution: 93% less than 45 μm in size for the dihydrate (*USG Terra Alba*); 97% less than 45 μm in size for the anhydrous material (*Snow White*). Average particle size is 17 μm for the dihydrate and 8 μm for the anhydrous material. *See also* HPE Data.
Solubility:

Solvent	Solubility (for dihydrate) at 20°C Unless otherwise stated
Ethanol (95%)	practically insoluble
Water	1 in 375
	1 in 485 at 100°C

Specific gravity:
2.32 for dihydrate;
2.96 for anhydrous material.
Specific surface area:
3.15 m^2/g (Strohlein apparatus).

HPE Laboratory Project Data			
	Method	Lab #	Results
Compressibility	COM-2	21	*See* Fig. 1. [a]
Moisture content	MC-27	18	2.085% [b]
	MC-24	21	19.80% [c]
	MC-23	21	18.86% [c]
Particle size	PSD-8	33	*See* Fig. 2.
	PSD-9	3	*See* Fig. 3.

Supplier:
a. Fisher (Lot No.: 711313);
b. JT Baker (Lot No.: 7314100);
c. Canadian Lab Supply.

11. Stability and Storage Conditions

Calcium sulfate is a chemically stable material. Due to its hygroscopic nature, anhydrous calcium sulfate powder may absorb moisture and may cake. Calcium sulfate should be stored in a cool, dry place, in a well-closed, moisture-resistant container.

12. Incompatibilities

In the presence of moisture, calcium salts may be incompatible with amines, amino acids, peptides and proteins, which may form complexes. Calcium sulfate may react violently, at high temperatures, with phosphorus and aluminum powder; it can

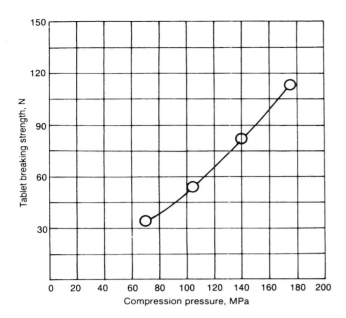

Fig. 1: Compression characteristics of calcium sulfate dihydrate. Tablet weight = 700 mg

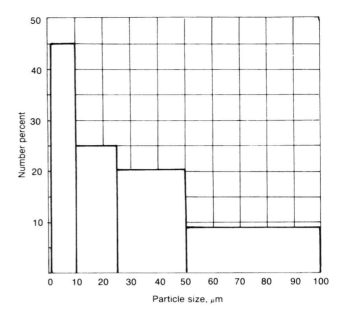

Fig. 3: Particle size distribution of calcium sulfate anhydrous.

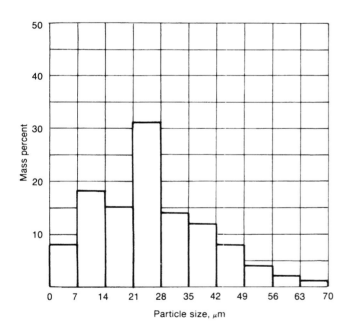

Fig. 2: Particle size distribution of calcium sulfate dihydrate.

react violently with diazomethane. The presence of calcium salts in certain formulations may cause bioavailability problems since calcium complexes with active ingredients may be formed, e.g tetracycline.[3]

13. Method of Manufacture

Anhydrous calcium sulfate occurs naturally as the mineral anhydrite. The naturally occurring rock gypsum may be crushed and ground for use as the dihydrate or calcined at about 150°C to produce the hemihydrate. A purer variety of calcium sulfate may also be obtained chemically by reacting calcium carbonate with sulfuric acid or by precipitation from calcium chloride and a soluble sulfate.

14. Safety

Calcium sulfate is widely used as an excipient in oral capsule and tablet formulations. At the levels employed as an excipient it is generally regarded as a nontoxic material. However, oral ingestion of a sufficient quantity may result in mechanical obstruction of patients' upper intestinal tract after absorption of moisture.

Due to the limited intestinal absorption of calcium from its salts, hypercalcemia cannot be induced even when massive oral doses are ingested. Calcium salts are also soluble in bronchial fluid and pure salts do not precipitate pneumoconiosis.

15. Handling Precautions

Observe normal precautions appropriate to the circumstances and quantity of material handled. Calcium sulfate may be irritant to the eyes or on inhalation. Gloves and eye protection are recommended along with a dust mask or respirator to prevent excessive inhalation of the powder, which may saturate the bronchial fluid and lead to precipitation of calcium sulfate, causing blockage of air passages. In the UK, the long-term (8 hour TWA) occupational exposure limit for calcium sulfate is 10 mg/m^3 for total dust and 5 mg/m^3 for respirable dust.[4]

16. Regulatory Status

GRAS listed. Accepted for use as a food additive in Europe. Included in the FDA Inactive Ingredients Guide (oral capsules and tablets). Included in nonparenteral medicines licensed in the UK.

17. Pharmacopeias

Fr and Jpn specify the dihydrate.
Mex and USPNF specify the dihydrate or the anhydrous material.

18. Related Substances

Calcium sulfate hemihydrate; Dibasic Calcium Phosphate Dihydrate; Tribasic Calcium Phosphate.

Calcium sulfate hemihydrate: $CaSO_4 \cdot H_2O$

Molecular weight: 145.14
CAS number: [26499-65-0]
Synonyms: annalin; dried calcium sulfate; dried gypsum; E516; exsiccated calcium sulfate; plaster of Paris.
Appearance: a white or almost white, odorless, crystalline powder.
Pharmacopeias: Aust, Br, Cz, Ger, Hung, Ind, Jpn, Swiss and Yug.
Solubility: practically insoluble in ethanol (95%); slightly soluble in water, more soluble in dilute mineral acids.
Comments: the BP 1993 defines dried calcium sulfate as predominantly the hemihydrate, produced by drying powdered gypsum ($CaSO_4.2H_2O$) at about 150°C, in a controlled manner, such that minimum quantities of the anhydrous material is produced. Dried calcium sulfate may also contain suitable setting accelerators or decelerators.

19. Comments

Calcium sulfate tends to absorb moisture and therefore should be used with caution in the formulation of products containing drugs which easily decompose in the presence of moisture.

20. Specific References

1. Bergman LA, Bandelin FJ. Effects of concentration, aging, and temperature on tablet disintegrants in a soluble direct-compression system. J Pharm Sci 1965; 54: 445-447.
2. Çelik M, Okutgen E. A feasibility study for the development of a prospective compaction functionality test and the establishment of a compaction data bank. Drug Dev Ind Pharm 1993; 19: 2309-2334.
3. Weiner M, Bernstein IL. Adverse reactions to drug formulation agents: a handbook of excipients. New York: Marcel Dekker Inc, 1989: 93-94.
4. Health and Safety Executive. EH40/93 occupational exposure limits 1993. London: HMSO, 1993.

21. General References

Bryan JW, McCallister JD. Matrix forming capabilities of three calcium diluents. Drug Dev Ind Pharm 1992; 18: 2029-2047.
Schwartz CJ, Suydam WL. Pilot plant vacuum drying of tablet excipients. J Pharm Sci 1965; 54: 1050-1054.

22. Authors

USA: HB Pandya.

Canola Oil

1. Nonproprietary Names
None adopted.

2. Synonyms
Calchem C-102; canbra oil; LEAR; *Lipex 108*; *Lipex 204*; low erucic acid colza oil; low erucic acid rapeseed oil.

3. Chemical Name and CAS Registry Number
Canola oil

4. Empirical Formula Molecular Weight
A typical analysis of canola oil indicates the composition of the acids, present as glycerides, to be: erucic acid 0.2-1.8%; linoleic acid 19.0-24.0%; linolenic acid 8.2-13.0%; oleic acid 56.0-62.0%; palmitic acid 3.0-4.5%; palmitoleic acid 0.2-0.3% and stearic acid 1.3-1.7%. Canola oil thus contains in total approximately 6% saturated acids, 52% monounsaturated acids and 32% polyunsaturated acids. *See also* Section 13.

5. Structural Formula
See Section 4.

6. Functional Category
Oleaginous vehicle.

7. Applications in Pharmaceutical Formulation or Technology
Canola oil is a refined rapeseed oil obtained from particular species of rapeseed that have been genetically selected for their low erucic acid content. In pharmaceutical formulations, canola oil is used mainly in topical preparations such as soft soaps and liniments. It is also used in cosmetics and as an edible oil in food products such as salad dressings, *see* Section 14.

8. Description
A clear, light yellow colored oily liquid with a bland taste.

9. Pharmacopeial Specifications
—

10. Typical Properties
Acid value: $\leqslant 0.5$
Density: 0.913-0.917 g/cm^3
Erucic acid: $\leqslant 2.0\%$
Flash point: 290-330°C
Free fatty acid: $\leqslant 0.05\%$ as oleic acid
Freezing point: -10 to -2°C
Iodine number: 94-126
Refractive index: $n_D^{40} = 1.465$-1.469
Saponification value: 186-198
Solubility: soluble in chloroform and ether; practically insoluble in ethanol (95%). Miscible with fixed oils.
Viscosity (dynamic): 77.3-78.3 mPa s at 20°C

11. Stability and Storage Conditions
Canola oil is stable and should be stored in an airtight, light-resistant container in a cool, dry, place.

12. Incompatibilities
—

13. Method of Manufacture
Canola oil is rapeseed oil low in erucic acid ($C_{22}H_{42}O_2$) and is obtained by mechanical expression or *n*-hexane extraction from the seeds of *Brassica napus* (*Brassica campestris*) var. *oleifera* and certain other species of *Brassica* (Cruciferae). The crude oil thus obtained is refined, bleached and deodorized to substantially remove free fatty acids, phospholipids, color, odor and flavor components and miscellaneous non-oil materials.

14. Safety
Rapeseed oil has been used for a number of years, predominantly in food applications, as a cheap alternative to olive oil. However, animal feeding studies in rats have suggested that erucic acid present in rapeseed oil is toxic to the heart and may be harmful to humans.[1] Canola oil, derived from genetically selected rapeseed plants that are low in erucic acid content, was thus developed to overcome this problem.[2] Feeding studies in rats have suggested that canola oil is nontoxic to the heart although it has also been claimed that the toxicological data is unclear.[2] Canola oil is generally regarded as an essentially nontoxic and nonirritant material and has been accepted by the FDA for use in cosmetics, foods and pharmaceuticals.

15. Handling Precautions
Observe normal precautions appropriate to the circumstances and quantity of material handled. Spillages of this material are very slippery and should be covered with an inert absorbent material prior to disposal. Canola oil poses a slight fire hazard.

16. Regulatory Status

Accepted for use by the FDA in cosmetics and foods. Included in the FDA Inactive Ingredients Guide (oral capsules).

17. Pharmacopeias
—

18. Related Substances
Corn Oil; Cottonseed Oil; Peanut Oil; rapeseed oil; Sesame Oil; Soybean Oil.

Rapeseed oil
CAS number: [8002-13-9]
Synonyms: *Calchem H-102*; colza oil; rape oil.
Appearance: a clear, yellow to dark yellow colored oily liquid.
Pharmacopeias: Jpn.
Iodine number: 94-120
Peroxide value: < 5
Saponification value: 168-181
Comments: rapeseed oil contains 40-55% erucic acid. It is an edible oil and has been primarily used as an alternative, in foods, to the more expensive olive oil. The safety of rapeseed oil as part of the diet has however been questioned, *see* Section 14.

19. Comments

—

20. Specific References

1. Rapeseed oil revisited. Lancet 1974; ii: 1359-1360.
2. Rapeseed oil and the heart. Lancet 1973; ii: 193.

21. General References

Hiltunen R, Huhtikangas A, Hovinen S. Breeding of a zero erucic spring turnip-rape cultivar, *Brassica campestris* L., adapted to Finnish climatic conditions. Acta Pharm Fenn 1979; 88: 31-34.

22. Authors

USA: KS Alexander.

Carbomer

1. Nonproprietary Names

BP: Carbomer
USPNF: Carbomer
Note that the USPNF XVII contains several carbomer monographs, *see* Sections 4 and 17.

2. Synonyms

Acritamer; acrylic acid polymer; *Carbopol*; carboxyvinyl polymer.

3. Chemical Name and CAS Registry Number

Carboxypolymethylene [54182-57-9]
[91315-32-1] for carbomer 910
[9007-16-3] for carbomer 934
[9003-01-4] for carbomer 934P
[76050-42-5] for carbomer 940

4. Empirical Formula Molecular Weight

Carbomers are synthetic high molecular weight polymers of acrylic acid cross-linked with either allylsucrose or allyl ethers of pentaerythritol. They contain between 56.0-68.0% of carboxylic acid (COOH) groups, calculated on the dry basis. The BP 1993 (Ad 1994) has a single monograph describing carbomer whilst the USPNF XVII has several monographs describing individual carbomer grades which vary in their aqueous viscosities.

Carbomer	Approximate molecular weight
Carbomer 934	3×10^6
Carbomer 940	4×10^6
Carbomer 941	1×10^6

5. Structural Formula

See Section 4.

6. Functional Category

Emulsifying agent; suspending agent; tablet binder; viscosity-increasing agent.

7. Applications in Pharmaceutical Formulation or Technology

Carbomers are used mainly in liquid or semisolid pharmaceutical formulations as suspending or viscosity-increasing agents. Formulations include creams, gels and ointments, and may be used in ophthalmic,[1,2] rectal[3] and topical preparations.[4] Carbomer grades with a low residual benzene content, such as carbomer 934P or 974P, may additionally be used in oral preparations, in suspensions, tablets, or sustained release tablet formulations.[5-7] In tablet formulations, carbomers are used as a binder in either direct compression or wet granulation processes. In wet granulation processes, water is used as the granulating fluid.
Carbomers are also employed as emulsifying agents in the preparation of oil-in-water emulsions for external use. For this purpose, the carbomer is neutralized partly with sodium hydroxide and partly with a long-chain amine such as stearylamine.
Carbomers are also used in cosmetics.

Use	Concentration (%)
Emulsifying agent	0.1-0.5
Gelling agent	0.5-2.0
Suspending agent	0.5-1.0
Tablet binder	5-10

8. Description

Carbomers are white-colored, 'fluffy', acidic, hygroscopic powders with a slight characteristic odor.

9. Pharmacopeial Specifications

Test	BP 1993 (Ad 1994)	USPNF XVII (Suppl 3,7,9)
Identification	+	+
Aqueous viscosity (mPa s)		
Carbomer 910 (1.0% w/v)	—	3000-7000
Carbomer 934 (0.5% w/v)	—	30 500-39 400
Carbomer 934P (0.5% w/v)	—	29 400-39 400
Carbomer 940 (0.5% w/v)	—	40 000-60 000
Carbomer 941 (0.5% w/v)	—	4000-11 000
Carbomer 1342 (1.0% w/v)	—	9500-26 500
Loss on drying	$\leqslant 2.0\%$	$\leqslant 2.0\%$
Sulfated ash	$\leqslant 4\%$	—
Heavy metals	$\leqslant 20$ ppm	$\leqslant 0.002\%$
Benzene		
Carbomer	$\leqslant 100$ ppm	—
Carbomer 910	—	$\leqslant 0.5\%$
Carbomer 934	—	$\leqslant 0.5\%$
Carbomer 934P	—	$\leqslant 0.01\%$
Carbomer 940	—	$\leqslant 0.5\%$
Carbomer 941	—	$\leqslant 0.5\%$
Carbomer 1342	—	$\leqslant 0.2\%$
Assay (of COOH)	56.0-68.0%	56.0-68.0%

Note that the USPNF XVII has several monographs for different carbomer grades whilst the BP 1993 has a single monograph. Unless otherwise indicated the test limits shown above apply to all grades of carbomer.

10. Typical Properties

Acidity/alkalinity:
pH = 2.7-3.5 for a 0.5% w/v aqueous dispersion;
pH = 2.5-3.0 for a 1% w/v aqueous dispersion.
Density (bulk): 1.76 g/cm^3
Density (tapped): 1.4 g/cm^3
Melting point: decomposition occurs at 260°C.
Moisture content: normal moisture content is up to 2% w/w. However, carbomers are hygroscopic and a typical equilibrium moisture content at 25°C and 50% relative humidity is 10% w/w. The moisture content of a carbomer does not affect its thickening efficiency, but an increase in the moisture content makes the carbomer more difficult to handle, i.e. it is less readily dispersed.
Particle size distribution: average particle size is 2-7 μm.
Solubility: soluble in water, and after neutralization, in ethanol (95%) and glycerin.
Specific gravity: 1.41

SEM: 1
Excipient: Carbomer 934P (*Carbopol 934P*)
Manufacturer: BFGoodrich Company
Magnification: 2000x
Voltage: 25 kV

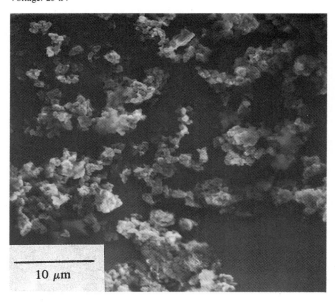

10 μm

SEM: 2
Excipient: Carbomer 934P (*Carbopol 934P*)
Manufacturer: BFGoodrich Company
Magnification: 5400x
Voltage: 25 kV

1 μm

Viscosity (dynamic): carbomers disperse in water to form acidic colloidal solutions of low viscosity which when neutralized produce highly viscous gels. Carbomer powder should first be dispersed into vigorously stirred water, taking care to avoid the formation of indispersible lumps, then neutralized by the addition of a base. Agents that may be used to neutralize carbomer include: amino acids; borax; potassium hydroxide; sodium bicarbonate; sodium hydroxide; polar organic amines, such as triethanolamine, and lauryl and stearyl amines, which are used as gelling agents in nonpolar systems. One gram of carbomer is neutralized by approximately 0.4 g of sodium hydroxide. During preparation of the gel the solution should be agitated slowly with a broad, paddle-like stirrer to avoid introducing air bubbles. Neutralized aqueous carbomer gels are more viscous at pH 6-11. The viscosity is considerably reduced if the pH is less than pH 3 or greater than pH 12; viscosity is also reduced in the presence of strong electrolytes. Gels rapidly lose viscosity on exposure to light, but this can be minimized by the addition of a suitable antioxidant. *See also* Section 11.

HPE Laboratory Project Data			
	Method	Lab #	Results
Bulk/tap density			(% Consolidated)
Carbomer 934	BTD-6	8	Volume: 13.0%
			Weight: 11.0%
Carbomer 941	BTD-6	8	Volume: 8.5%
			Weight: 8.0%

Supplier: BFGoodrich Company.

11. Stability and Storage Conditions

Carbomers are stable, though hygroscopic materials, and may be heated at temperatures below 104°C for up to two hours without affecting their thickening efficiency. However, exposure to excessive temperatures can result in discoloration and reduced stability. Complete decomposition occurs on heating for 30 minutes at 260°C.

Dry powder forms of carbomer do not support the growth of molds and fungi. However, microorganisms grow well in unpreserved aqueous carbomer dispersions and therefore an antimicrobial preservative such as 0.1% w/v chlorocresol, 0.1% w/v methylparaben or 0.1% w/v thimerosal should be added. The addition of certain antimicrobial preservatives, such as benzalkonium chloride, benzoic acid and sodium benzoate, or high concentrations of preservative, can cause a decrease in the viscosity of a dispersion. Aqueous gels may be sterilized by autoclaving.

At room temperature, carbomer dispersions maintain their viscosity during storage for prolonged periods of time. Similarly, dispersion viscosity is maintained, or only slightly reduced, at elevated storage temperatures if an antioxidant is included or if the dispersion is stored protected from light. Exposure to light causes oxidation, which is reflected in a decrease in dispersion viscosity. However, stability to light may be improved by the addition of 0.05-0.1% w/v of a water-soluble UV absorber such as benzophenone-2 or benzophenone-4 in combination with 0.05-0.1% edetic acid. The UV stability of carbomer gels may also be improved by using triethanolamine as the neutralizing base, *see* Section 10.

Carbomer powder should be stored in an airtight, corrosion-resistant container in a cool, dry, place.

12. Incompatibilities

Carbomers are discolored by resorcinol and are incompatible with phenol, cationic polymers, strong acids and high concentrations of electrolytes. Trace levels of iron and other transition metals can catalytically degrade carbomer dispersions. Intense heat may be generated if a carbomer is in contact with a strongly basic material such as ammonia, potassium hydroxide, sodium hydroxide, or strongly basic amines.

13. Method of Manufacture

Carbomers are synthetic, high molecular weight, cross-linked polymers of acrylic acid copolymerized with approximately 0.75-2% w/w of allylsucrose. The solvent used for the polymerization is normally benzene. However, some of the newer commercially available grades of carbomer are manufactured using either ethyl acetate or a cyclohexane/ethyl acetate mixture as the solvent.

14. Safety

Carbomers are extensively used in nonparenteral medicines, particularly topical liquid and semisolid preparations. Carbomers may also be used in oral formulations although only certain grades are commonly used, *see* Section 19.

Acute oral toxicity studies in animals indicate that carbomer 934P has a low oral toxicity with doses up to 8 g/kg being administered to dogs without fatalities occurring.

Carbomers are generally regarded as essentially nontoxic and nonirritant materials; there is no evidence in humans of hypersensitivity or allergic reaction to carbomers used topically. In humans, oral doses of 1-3 g of carbomer have been used as a bulk laxative.

LD_{50} (guinea pig, oral): 2.5 g/kg for carbomer 934.[8]

LD_{50} (mouse, IP): 0.04 g/kg for carbomer 934P.

LD_{50} (mouse, IV): 0.07 g/kg for carbomer 934P.

LD_{50} (mouse, oral): 4.6 g/kg for carbomer 934.

LD_{50} (rat, oral): 2.5 g/kg for carbomer 934P.

LD_{50} (rat, oral): 4.1 g/kg for carbomer 934.

LD_{50} (rat, oral): 10.25 g/kg for carbomer 910.

15. Handling Precautions

Observe normal precautions appropriate to the circumstances and quantity of material handled. Excessive dust generation should be minimized to avoid the risk of explosion; lowest explosive concentration is 100 g/m^3. Carbomer dust is irritant to the eyes, mucous membranes and respiratory tract. In contact with the eye, carbomer dust is difficult to remove with water due to the gelatinous film that forms and saline should therefore be used for irrigation purposes. Gloves, eye protection and a dust-respirator are recommended.

16. Regulatory Status

Included in the FDA Inactive Ingredients Guide (oral suspensions and tablets, ophthalmic, rectal and topical preparations). Included in nonparenteral medicines licensed in the UK.

17. Pharmacopeias

Br, It, Mex and USPNF.

Note that the USPNF XVII has separate monographs for carbomer 910, carbomer 934, carbomer 934P, carbomer 940, carbomer 941 and carbomer 1342.

18. Related Substances

—

19. Comments

A number of different carbomer grades are commercially available which vary in their molecular weight, degree of cross-linking and polymer structure. These differences account for the specific rheological characteristics of each grade.

Carbomer grades which have the polymer backbone modified with long chain alkyl methacrylates are also commercially available, as are the sodium salts of various carbomers. The sodium salts have similar rheological characteristics but the pH of a 0.5% w/v dispersion would typically be 7.0-8.2.

Carbomers designated with the letter 'P', e.g. carbomer 934P, are the only pharmaceutical grades of polymer accepted for oral or mucosal contact products.

Carbomers are particularly useful in the production of clear gels.

20. Specific References

1. Deshpande SG, Shirolkar S. Sustained release ophthalmic formulations of pilocarpine. J Pharm Pharmacol 1989; 41: 197-200.
2. Ünlü N, Ludwig A, van Ooteghem M, Hincal AA. Formulation of carbopol 940 ophthalmic vehicles, and in vitro evaluation of the influence of simulated lacrimal fluid on their physico-chemical properties. Pharmazie 1991; 46: 784-788.
3. Morimoto K, Morisaka K. In vitro release and rectal absorption of barbital and aminopyrine from aqueous polyacrylic acid gel. Drug Dev Ind Pharm 1987; 13: 1293-1305.
4. Chu JS, Yu DM, Amidon GL, Weiner ND, Goldberg AH. Viscoelastic properties of polyacrylic acid gels in mixed solvents. Pharm Res 1992; 9: 1659-1663.
5. Choulis NH, Papadopoulos H, Choulis M. Long acting methadone. Pharmazie 1976; 31: 466-470.
6. Graf E, Tsaktanis I, Fawzy AA. Studies on the direct compression of pharmaceuticals part 20: timed release tablets of diphenhydramine and dexachlorpheniramine. Pharm Ind 1986; 48: 661-665.
7. Perez Marcos B, et al. Mechanical and drug-release properties of atenolol-carbomer hydrophilic matrix tablets. J Controlled Release 1991; 17: 267-276.
8. Sweet DV, editor. Registry of toxic effects of chemical substances. Cincinnati: US Department of Health, 1987.

21. General References

Alexander P. Organic rheological additives. Mfg Chem 1986; 57(10): 81, 83, 84.
BFGoodrich Company. Technical literature: *Carbopol* resins handbook, 1991.
Pérez-Marcos B, et al. Interlot variability of carbomer 934. Int J Pharmaceutics 1993; 100: 207-212.
Secard DL. Carbopol pharmaceuticals. Drug Cosmet Ind 1962; 90(1): 28-30, 113, 115, 116.

22. Authors

USA: M Haase, JW McGinity.

Carbon Dioxide

1. Nonproprietary Names
BP: Carbon dioxide
PhEur: Carbonei dioxidum
USP: Carbon dioxide

2. Synonyms
Carbonic acid gas; carbonic anhydride; E290.

3. Chemical Name and CAS Registry Number
Carbon dioxide [124-38-9]

4. Empirical Formula   Molecular Weight
CO_2 44.01

5. Structural Formula
CO_2

6. Functional Category
Aerosol propellant; air displacement.

7. Applications in Pharmaceutical Formulation or Technology
Carbon dioxide and other compressed gases such as nitrogen and nitrous oxide are used as propellants for topical pharmaceutical aerosols. They are also used in other aerosol products that work satisfactorily with the coarse aerosol spray that is produced with compressed gases, e.g. cosmetics, furniture polish and window cleaner.[1-3]
The advantages of compressed gases as aerosol propellants are that they are inexpensive, of low toxicity and practically odorless and tasteless. Also, in contrast to liquefied gases, their pressures change relatively little with temperature. However, the disadvantages of compressed gases are that there is no reservoir of propellant in the aerosol and pressure consequently decreases as the product is used. This results in a change in spray characteristics. Additionally, if a product which contains a compressed gas as a propellant is actuated in an inverted position the vapor phase, instead of the liquid phase, is discharged. Since most of the propellant is contained in the vapor phase some of the propellant will be lost and hence the spray characteristics are also very wet. Sprays produced using compressed gases are generally very wet.
Carbon dioxide is also used to displace air from pharmaceutical products by sparging and hence inhibit oxidation. As a food additive it is used to carbonate beverages and to preserve foods such as bread from spoilage by mold formation, the gas being injected into the space between the product and its packaging.[4,5]
Solid carbon dioxide is also widely used to refrigerate products temporarily, whilst liquid carbon dioxide, which can be handled at temperatures up to 31°C under high pressure, is used as a solvent for flavors and fragrances primarily in the perfumery and food manufacturing industries.

8. Description
Carbon dioxide occurs naturally as approximately 0.03% v/v of the atmosphere. It is a colorless, odorless, noncombustible gas with a faint acid taste. Solid carbon dioxide, also known as dry ice, is usually encountered as white colored pellets or blocks.

9. Pharmacopeial Specifications

Test	PhEur 1985	USP XXII
Identification	+	+
Carbon monoxide	⩽ 10 ppm	⩽ 0.001%
Hydrogen sulfide	—	⩽ 1 ppm
Nitric oxide	—	⩽ 2.5 ppm
Nitrogen dioxide	—	⩽ 2.5 ppm
Ammonia	—	⩽ 0.0025%
Sulfur dioxide	—	⩽ 5 ppm
Water	—	⩽ 150 mg/m^3
Acidity	+	—
Phosphoric hydrides, hydrogen sulfide and organic reducing substances	+	—
Assay	⩾ 99.0%	⩾ 99.0%

10. Typical Properties
Boiling point: -56.6°C
Critical pressure: 7.39 MPa (72.9 atm)
Critical temperature: 31.3°C
Density:
0.714 g/cm^3 for liquid at 25°C;
0.742 g/cm^3 for vapor at 25°C.
Flammability: nonflammable
Melting point: sublimes at -78.5°C
Solubility: 1 in about 1 of water by volume at normal temperature and pressure.
Vapor density (absolute): 1.964 g/m^3
Vapor density (relative): 1.53 (air = 1)
Vapor pressure: 6.436 MPa at 25°C
Viscosity (kinematic): 0.14 mm^2/s (0.14 cSt) at -17.8°C

11. Stability and Storage Conditions
Extremely stable and chemically nonreactive. Store in a tightly sealed cylinder. Avoid exposure to excessive heat.

12. Incompatibilities
Carbon dioxide is generally compatible with most materials although it may react violently with various metal oxides or reducing metals such as aluminum, magnesium, titanium and zirconium. Mixtures with sodium and potassium will explode if shocked.

13. Method of Manufacture
Carbon dioxide is obtained industrially in large quantities as a by-product in the manufacture of lime, by incineration of coke or other carbonaceous material, and by the fermentation of glucose by yeast. In the laboratory it may be prepared by dropping acid on a carbonate.

14. Safety
In formulations, carbon dioxide is generally regarded as an essentially nontoxic material.
See also Section 15.

15. Handling Precautions

Handle in accordance with standard procedures for handling metal cylinders containing liquefied or compressed gases. Carbon dioxide is an asphyxiant and inhalation in large quantities is hazardous. It should therefore be handled in a well-ventilated environment equipped with suitable safety devices for monitoring vapor concentration.

In the UK, the occupational exposure limits for carbon dioxide are 9000 mg/m^3 (5000 ppm) long-term (8-hour TWA) and 27 000 mg/m^3 (15 000 ppm) short-term (10-minutes).[6] In the US, the permissible exposure limits are 9000 mg/m^3 (5000 ppm) long-term and the recommended exposure limits are 18 000 mg/m^3 (10 000 ppm) short-term and 54 000 mg/m^3 (30 000 ppm) maximum, short-term.[7]

Solid carbon dioxide can produce severe burns in contact with the skin and appropriate precautions, depending on the circumstances and quantity of material handled should be taken. A face shield and protective clothing, including thick gloves, are recommended.

16. Regulatory Status

GRAS listed. Accepted for use in Europe as a food additive. Included in the FDA Inactive Ingredients Guide (injections).

17. Pharmacopeias

Aust, Br, Braz, Chin, Cz, Egypt, Eur, Fr, Ger, Gr, Hung, It, Jpn, Mex, Neth, Port, Swiss, Turk, US and Yug. Also in BP Vet.

18. Related Substances

Nitrogen; Nitrous Oxide.

19. Comments

—

20. Specific References

1. Haase LW. Application of carbon dioxide in cosmetic aerosols. Cosmet Perfum 1975; 90(8): 31-32.
2. Sanders PA. Aerosol packaging of pharmaceuticals. In: Banker GS, Rhodes CT, editors. Modern pharmaceutics. New York: Marcel Dekker Inc, 1979: 591-626.
3. CO_2/acetone propellant kinder to ozone layer. Mfg Chem 1992; 63(1): 14.
4. King JS, Mabbitt LA. The use of carbon dioxide for the preservation of milk. In: Board RG, Allwood MC, Banks JG, editors. Preservatives in the food, pharmaceutical and environmental industries. Oxford: Blackwell Scientific Publications, 1987: 35-43.
5. Carbon dioxide breaks the mould. Chem Br 1992; 28: 506.
6. Health and Safety Executive. EH40/93: occupational exposure limits 1993. London: HMSO, 1993.
7. National Institute for Occupational Safety and Health. Recommendations for occupational safety and health. MMWR 1988; 37(Suppl S-7): 1-29.

21. General References

Johnson MA. The aerosol handbook, 2nd edition. New Jersey: WE Dorland Co, 1982: 361-372.

Mintzer H. Aerosols. In: Martin FW, editor. Dispensing of medication, 7th edition. Easton: Mack Publishing Co, 1971.

Sanders PA. Handbook of aerosol technology, 2nd edition. New York: Van Nostrand Reinhold Company, 1979: 44-54.

Sciarra JJ. Pharmaceutical and cosmetic aerosols. J Pharm Sci 1974; 63: 1815-1837.

Sciarra JJ. Pharmaceutical aerosols. In: Lachman L, Lieberman HA, Kanig JL, editors. The theory and practice of industrial pharmacy, 3rd edition. Philadelphia: Lea and Febiger, 1986: 589-591.

Sciarra JJ, Stoller L. The science and technology of aerosol packaging. New York: John Wiley and Sons, 1974: 137-145.

22. Authors

UK: PJ Davies.
USA: JJ Sciarra.

Carboxymethylcellulose Calcium

1. Nonproprietary Names

USPNF: Carboxymethylcellulose calcium

2. Synonyms

Calcium carboxymethylcellulose; calcium CMC; carmellose calcium; *ECG 505*; *Nymcel ZSC*.

3. Chemical Name and CAS Registry Number

Cellulose, carboxymethyl ether, calcium salt
[9050-04-8]

4. Empirical Formula   Molecular Weight

The USPNF XVII describes carboxymethylcellulose calcium as the calcium salt of a polycarboxymethyl ether of cellulose.

5. Structural Formula

Structure shown with a degree of substitution (DS) of 1.0.

6. Functional Category

Stabilizing agent; suspending agent; tablet and capsule disintegrant; viscosity-increasing agent.

7. Applications in Pharmaceutical Formulation or Technology

The main use of carboxymethylcellulose calcium is in tablet formulations where it is used as a binder, diluent and disintegrant.[1-3] Although carboxymethylcellulose calcium is insoluble in water it is an effective tablet disintegrant since it swells to several times its original bulk on contact with water. Concentrations up to 15% w/w may be used in tablet formulations; above this concentration tablet hardness is reduced.

Carboxymethylcellulose calcium is also used in other applications similarly to carboxymethylcellulose sodium for example, as a suspending or viscosity increasing agent in oral and topical pharmaceutical formulations.

Use	Concentration (%)
Tablet binder	5-15
Tablet disintegrant	1-15

8. Description

Carboxymethylcellulose calcium occurs as a white to yellowish-white colored, hygroscopic, fine powder.

9. Pharmacopeial Specifications

Test	USPNF XVII
Identification	+
Alkalinity	+
Loss on drying	$\leq 10.0\%$
Residue on ignition	10.0-20.0%
Chloride	$\leq 0.36\%$
Silicate	$\leq 1.5\%$
Sulfate	$\leq 0.96\%$
Arsenic	$\leq 0.001\%$
Heavy metals	$\leq 0.002\%$
Starch	+

10. Typical Properties

Acidity/alkalinity:
pH = 4.5-6.0 for a 1% w/v aqueous dispersion.
Particle size distribution:
95% through a 73.7 μm sieve (#200 mesh).
Solubility: practically insoluble in acetone, chloroform, ethanol (95%) and ether. Insoluble in water, but swells to twice its volume to form a suspension. Insoluble in 0.1N hydrochloric acid, but slightly soluble in 0.1N sodium hydroxide.

11. Stability and Storage Conditions

Carboxymethylcellulose calcium is a stable, though hygroscopic material. It should be stored in a well-closed container in a cool, dry, place.
See also Carboxymethylcellulose Sodium.

12. Incompatibilities

See Carboxymethylcellulose Sodium.

13. Method of Manufacture

Cellulose, obtained from wood pulp or cotton fibres is carboxymethylated, followed by conversion into the calcium salt. It is then graded on the basis of its degree of carboxymethylation and pulverized.

14. Safety

Carboxymethylcellulose calcium is used in oral and topical pharmaceutical formulations, similarly to carboxymethylcellulose sodium, and is generally regarded as a nontoxic and nonirritant material. However, like other cellulose derivatives, oral consumption of large amounts of carboxymethylcellulose calcium may have a laxative effect.
See also Carboxymethylcellulose Sodium.

15. Handling Precautions

Observe normal precautions appropriate to the circumstances and quantity of material handled. Carboxymethylcellulose calcium may be irritant to the eyes; eye protection is recommended.

16. Regulatory Status

Accepted for use as a food additive in Japan at concentrations up to 2% w/w. Included in the FDA Inactive Ingredients Guide (oral tablets). Included in nonparenteral medicines licensed in the UK.

17. Pharmacopeias
Jpn and USPNF.

18. Related Substances
Carboxymethylcellulose Sodium; Croscarmellose Sodium.

19. Comments
—

20. Specific References
1. Khan KA, Rooke DJ. Effect of disintegrant type upon the relationship between compressional pressure and dissolution efficiency. J Pharm Pharmacol 1976; 28: 633-636.
2. Kitamori N, Makino T. Improvement in pressure-dependent dissolution of trepibutone tablets by using intragranular disintegrants. Drug Dev Ind Pharm 1982; 8: 125-139.
3. Roe TS, Chang KY. The study of Key-Jo clay as a tablet disintegrator. Drug Dev Ind Pharm 1986; 12: 1567-1585.

21. General References
Doelker E. Cellulose derivatives. Adv Polymer Sci 1993; 107: 199-265.

22. Authors
UK: PJ Weller.

Carboxymethylcellulose Sodium

1. Nonproprietary Names

BP: Carmellose sodium
PhEur: Carboxymethylcellulosum natricum
USP: Carboxymethylcellulose sodium

2. Synonyms

Akucell; *Blanose*; *Cekol*; cellulose gum; CMC sodium; *Courlose*; E466; *Nymcel*; SCMC; sodium carboxymethylcellulose; sodium cellulose glycolate; sodium CMC; *Tylose CB*.

3. Chemical Name and CAS Registry Number

Cellulose, carboxymethyl ether, sodium salt [9004-32-4]

4. Empirical Formula   Molecular Weight

The USP XXII describes carboxymethylcellulose sodium as the sodium salt of a polycarboxymethyl ether of cellulose. Typical molecular weight is 90 000-700 000.

5. Structural Formula

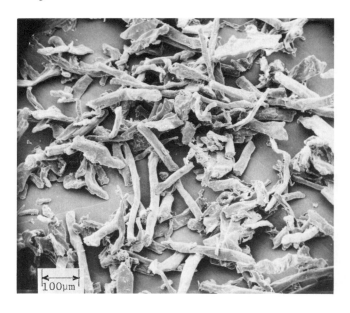

Structure shown with a degree of substitution (DS) of 1.0.

6. Functional Category

Coating agent; tablet and capsule disintegrant; tablet binder; stabilizing agent; suspending agent; viscosity-increasing agent.

7. Applications in Pharmaceutical Formulation or Technology

Carboxymethylcellulose sodium is widely used in oral and topical pharmaceutical formulations primarily for its viscosity-increasing properties. Viscous aqueous solutions are used to suspend powders intended for either topical application or oral and parenteral administration.[1] Carboxymethylcellulose sodium may also be used as a tablet binder and disintegrant,[2-4] and to stabilize emulsions.[5]
Higher concentrations, usually 4-6%, of the medium viscosity grade is used to produce gels which can be used as the base for applications and pastes; glycerin is often included in such gels to prevent drying out. Carboxymethylcellulose sodium is additionally one of the main ingredients of self adhesive ostomy, wound care and dermatological patches where it is used to absorb wound exudate or transepidermal water and sweat.
Carboxymethylcellulose sodium is also used in cosmetics, toiletries[6] and food products.

Use	Concentration (%)
Emulsifying agent	0.25-1.0
Gel-forming agent	4.0-6.0
Injections	0.05-0.75
Oral solutions	0.1-1.0
Tablet binder	1.0-6.0

8. Description

Carboxymethylcellulose sodium occurs as a white to almost white colored, odorless, granular powder. *See also* Section 19.

9. Pharmacopeial Specifications

Test	PhEur 1986	USP XXII (Suppl 8)
Identification	+	+
pH (1% w/v solution)	6.0-8.0	6.5-8.5
Appearance of solution	+	—
Viscosity	+	+
Loss on drying	$\leqslant 10.0\%$	$\leqslant 10.0\%$
Heavy metals	$\leqslant 20$ ppm	$\leqslant 0.004\%$
Chloride	$\leqslant 0.25\%$	—
Sodium glycolate	$\leqslant 0.4\%$	—
Sulfated ash	20.0-33.3%	—
Assay (of sodium)	6.5-10.8%	6.5-9.5%

SEM: 1

Excipient: Carboxymethylcellulose sodium
Manufacturer: Buckeye Cellulose Corp
Lot No.: 9247 AP
Magnification: 120x
Voltage: 10 kV

SEM: 2

Excipient: Carboxymethylcellulose sodium
Manufacturer: Buckeye Cellulose Corp
Lot No.: 9247 AP
Magnification: 600x
Voltage: 10 kV

SEM: 4

Excipient: Carboxymethylcellulose sodium
Manufacturer: Hercules Ltd
Lot No.: 21 A-1 (44390)
Magnification: 600x
Voltage: 20 kV

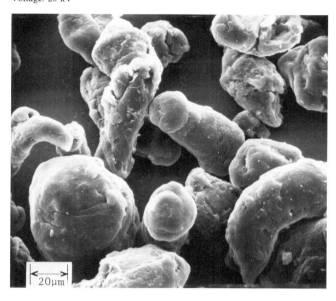

SEM: 3

Excipient: Carboxymethylcellulose sodium
Manufacturer: Hercules Ltd
Lot No.: 21 A-1 (44390)
Magnification: 120x
Voltage: 20 kV

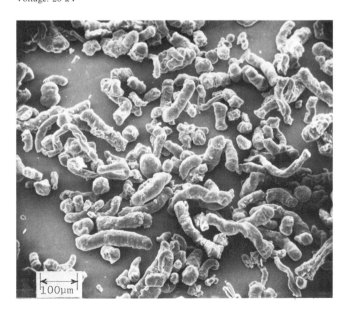

10. Typical Properties

Density (bulk): 0.75 g/cm^3
Dissociation constant: pK_a = 4.30
Melting point: browns at approximately 227°C, chars at approximately 252°C.
Moisture content: typically, contains less than 10% of water. However, carboxymethylcellulose sodium is hygroscopic and absorbs significant amounts of water at temperatures up to 37°C at relative humidities of about 80%. *See also* HPE Data and Section 11.
Solubility: practically insoluble in acetone, ethanol, ether and toluene. Easily dispersed in water at all temperatures, forming clear, colloidal solutions. The aqueous solubility varies with the degree of substitution (DS). *See* Section 19.
Viscosity: various grades of carboxymethylcellulose sodium are commercially available which have differing aqueous viscosities; aqueous 1% w/v solutions with viscosities of 5-4000 mPa s (5-4000 cP) may be obtained. An increase in concentration results in an increase in aqueous solution viscosity.[6] Viscosities of various grades of carboxymethyl-cellulose sodium are shown in Table I. *See also* Section 11.

Table I: Viscosity of aqueous carboxymethylcellulose sodium solutions at 25°C.

Grade	Concentration (% w/v)	Viscosity (mPa s)
Low viscosity	4	50-200
Medium viscosity	2	400-800
High viscosity	1	1500-3000

HPE Laboratory Project Data			
	Method	Lab #	Results
Moisture content	MC-10	10	8.5%
Moisture content	MC-7	5	6.5%
Moisture content	EMC-1	10	*See* Fig. 1.

Supplier: Hercules Ltd (Lot #76493).

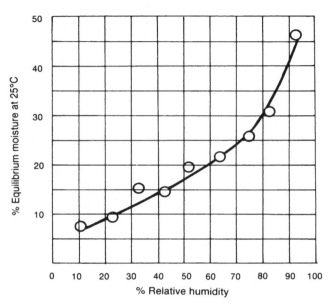

Fig. 1: Equilibrium moisture content of carboxymethylcellulose sodium.

11. Stability and Storage Conditions

Carboxymethylcellulose sodium is a stable, though hygroscopic material. Under high humidity conditions carboxymethylcellulose sodium can absorb a large quantity (> 50%) of water. In tablets, this has been associated with a decrease in tablet hardness and an increase in disintegration time.[7]

Aqueous solutions are stable between pH 2-10; below pH 2 precipitation can occur while above pH 10 solution viscosity rapidly decreases. Generally, solutions exhibit maximum viscosity and stability at pH 7-9.

Carboxymethylcellulose sodium may be sterilized in the dry state by maintaining it at a temperature of 160°C for 1 hour. However, this process results in a significant decrease in viscosity and some deterioration in the properties of solutions prepared from the sterilized material.

Aqueous solutions may similarly be sterilized by heating although this also results in some reduction in viscosity. After autoclaving, viscosity is reduced by about 25% although this reduction is less marked than for solutions prepared from material sterilized in the dry state. The extent of the reduction is dependent on the molecular weight and degree of substitution; higher molecular weight grades generally undergo a greater percentage reduction in viscosity. Sterilization of solutions by gamma irradiation also results in a reduction in viscosity.

Aqueous solutions stored for prolonged periods should contain an antimicrobial preservative.[8]

The bulk material should be stored in a well-closed container in a cool, dry, place.

12. Incompatibilities

Carboxymethylcellulose sodium is incompatible with strongly acidic solutions and with the soluble salts of iron and some other metals, such as aluminum, mercury and zinc; it is also incompatible with xanthan gum. Precipitation can occur at pH < 2 and when mixed with ethanol (95%).

Carboxymethylcellulose sodium also forms complex coacervates with gelatin and pectin. It additionally forms a complex with collagen and is capable of precipitating certain positively charged proteins.

13. Method of Manufacture

Alkali cellulose is prepared by steeping cellulose obtained from wood pulp or cotton fibres in sodium hydroxide solution. The alkali cellulose is then reacted with sodium monochloroacetate to produce carboxymethylcellulose sodium. Sodium chloride and sodium glycolate are obtained as by-products of this etherification.

14. Safety

Carboxymethylcellulose sodium is used in oral, topical and some parenteral formulations. It is also widely used in cosmetics, toiletries and food products and is generally regarded as a nontoxic and nonirritant material. However, oral consumption of large amounts of carboxymethylcellulose sodium can have a laxative effect; therapeutically 4-10 g, in daily divided doses, of the medium and high viscosity grades of carboxymethylcellulose sodium have been used as bulk laxatives.

The WHO has not specified an acceptable daily intake for carboxymethylcellulose sodium as a food additive since the levels necessary to achieve a desired effect were not considered to be a hazard to health.[9]

In animal studies, subcutaneous administration of carboxymethylcellulose sodium has been found to cause inflammation and in some cases of repeated injection fibrosarcomas have been found at the injection site.[10]

Hypersensitivity and anaphylactic reactions have occurred in cattle and horses which have been attributed to carboxymethylcellulose sodium in parenteral formulations such as vaccines and penicillins.[11,12]

LD$_{50}$ (guinea pig, oral): 16 g/kg[13]
LD$_{50}$ (mouse, oral): > 27 g/kg
LD$_{50}$ (rabbit, oral): > 27 g/kg
LD$_{50}$ (rat, oral): 27 g/kg

15. Handling Precautions

Observe normal precautions appropriate to the circumstances and quantity of material handled. Carboxymethylcellulose sodium may be irritant to the eyes. Eye protection is recommended.

16. Regulatory Status

GRAS listed. Accepted as a food additive in Europe. Included in the FDA Inactive Ingredients Guide (dental preparations, inhalations, intra-articular, intrabursal, intradermal, intralesional, IM, intrasynovial and SC injections, oral capsules, drops, solutions, suspensions, syrups and tablets, topical and vaginal preparations). Included in nonparenteral medicines licensed in the UK.

17. Pharmacopeias

Aust, Br, Braz, Cz, Egypt, Eur, Fr, Gr, Hung, Ind, It, Jpn, Mex, Neth, Nord, Rom, Swiss, US and Yug.

18. Related Substances

Carboxymethylcellulose Calcium; Carboxymethylcellulose sodium 12; Croscarmellose Sodium.

Carboxymethylcellulose sodium 12

Pharmacopeias: USPNF.

Comments: carboxymethylcellulose sodium 12 is the sodium salt of a polycarboxymethyl ether of cellulose. Its degree of substitution is between 1.15-1.45, corresponding to a sodium content, calculated on the dry basis, of 10.5-12.0%.

19. Comments

A number of grades of carboxymethylcellulose sodium are commercially available, the most frequently used grade having a degree of substitution (DS) of 0.7. The DS is defined as the average number of hydroxyl groups substituted per anhydroglucose unit and it is this which determines the aqueous solubility of the polymer.

Grades are typically classified as being either low, medium or high viscosity. The degree of substitution and the maximum viscosity of an aqueous solution of stated concentration should be indicated on any carboxymethylcellulose sodium labelling. Carboxymethylcellulose sodium has been reported to give false positive results in the LAL test for eudotoxins.[14]

20. Specific References

1. Hussain MA, Aungst BJ, Maurin MB, Wu LS. Injectable suspensions for prolonged release nalbuphine. Drug Dev Ind Pharm 1991; 17: 67-76.
2. Khan KA, Rhodes CT. Evaluation of different viscosity grades of sodium carboxymethylcellulose as tablet disintegrants. Pharm Acta Helv 1975; 50: 99-102.
3. Shah NH, Lazarus JH, Sheth PR, Jarowski CI. Carboxymethylcellulose: effect of degree of polymerization and substitution on tablet disintegration and dissolution. J Pharm Sci 1981; 70: 611-613.
4. Singh J. Effect of sodium carboxymethylcelluloses on the disintegration, dissolution and bioavailability of lorazepam tablets. Drug Dev Ind Pharm 1992; 18: 375-383.
5. Oza KP, Frank SG. Microcrystalline cellulose stabilized emulsions. J Disper Sci Technol 1986; 7(5): 543-561.
6. Mombellet H, Bale P. Sodium carboxymethylcellulose toothpaste. Mfg Chem 1988; 59(11): 47, 49, 52.
7. Khan KA, Rhodes CT. Water-sorption properties of tablet disintegrants. J Pharm Sci 1975; 64: 447-451.
8. Banker G, Peck G, Williams E, Taylor D, Pirakitikulr P. Microbiological considerations of polymer solutions used in aqueous film coating. Drug Dev Ind Pharm 1982; 8: 41-51.
9. FAO/WHO. Evaluation of certain food additives and contaminants. Thirty-fifth report of the joint FAO/WHO expert committee on food additives. Tech Rep Ser Wld Hlth Org 1990; No. 789.
10. Teller MN, Brown GB. Carcinogenicity of carboxymethylcellulose in rats. Proc Am Assoc Cancer Res 1977; 18: 225.
11. Schneider CH, de Weck AL, Stuble E. Carboxymethylcellulose additives in penicillins and the elicidation of anaphylactic reactions. Experentia 1971; 27: 167-168.
12. Aitken MM. Induction of hypersensitivity to carboxymethylcellulose in cattle. Res Vet Sci 1975; 19: 110-113.
13. Sweet DV, editor. Registry of toxic effects of chemical substances. Cincinnati: US Department of Health, 1987.
14. Tanaka S, Aketagawa J, Takahashi S, Shibata Y, Tsumuraya Y, Hashimoto Y. Activation of a limulus coagulation factor G by $(1 \rightarrow 3)$-β-D-glucans. Carbohydrate Res 1991; 218: 167-174.

21. General References

Doelker E. Cellulose derivatives. Adv Polymer Sci 1993; 107: 199-265.

22. Authors

UK: JE Fairbrother, DA Hollingsbee, PJ Weller.

Hydrogenated Castor Oil

1. Nonproprietary Names

USPNF: Hydrogenated castor oil

2. Synonyms

Castorwax; *Castorwax MP 70*; *Castorwax MP 80*; *Opalwax*; *Simulsol*.

3. Chemical Name and CAS Registry Number

Glyceryl-tri-(12-hydroxystearate) [8001-78-3]

4. Empirical Formula   Molecular Weight

The USPNF XVII describes hydrogenated castor oil as the refined, bleached, hydrogenated, and deodorized castor oil, consisting mainly of the triglyceride of hydroxystearic acid.

$C_{57}O_9H_{110}$ 939.50

5. Structural Formula

6. Functional Category

Extended release agent; stiffening agent; tablet and capsule lubricant.

7. Applications in Pharmaceutical Formulation or Technology

Hydrogenated castor oil is a hard, high melting point wax used in oral and topical pharmaceutical formulations.

In topical formulations, hydrogenated castor oil is used to provide stiffness to creams and emulsions.[1]

In oral formulations, hydrogenated castor oil is used to prepare sustained release tablet and capsule preparations;[2,3] the hydrogenated castor oil may be used as a coat or to form a solid matrix. Hydrogenated castor oil is additionally used to lubricate the die walls of tablet presses;[4,5] it is similarly used as a lubricant in food processing.

Hydrogenated castor oil is also used in cosmetics.

Use	Concentration (%)
Coating agent (delayed release)	5-20
Delayed release drug matrix	5-10
Tablet die lubricant	0.1-2

8. Description

Hydrogenated castor oil occurs as a white colored powder or flakes.

9. Pharmacopeial Specifications

Test	USPNF XVII
Melting range	85-88°C
Heavy metals	$\leqslant 0.001\%$
Free fatty acids	+
Hydroxyl value	154-162
Iodine value	$\leqslant 5$
Saponification value	176-182

10. Typical Properties

Acid value: $\leqslant 5$
Density (tapped): see HPE Data.
Flash point: 316°C (open cup)
Moisture content: $\leqslant 0.1\%$
Particle size distribution: see HPE Data.
Specific gravity: 1.023
Solubility: insoluble in water; soluble in acetone and chloroform.

HPE Laboratory Project Data			
	Method	Lab #	Results
Bulk/tap density			
Castorwax	BTD-6	8	Volume: 12.5% Weight: 9.0%
Castorwax MP 70	BTD-6	8	Volume: 12.5% Weight: 8.0%
Castorwax MP 80	BTD-6	8	Volume: 12.0% Weight: 9.0%
Density			
Castorwax	DE-1	7	1.03 ± 0.01 g/cm³
Castorwax MP 70	DE-1	7	1.07 ± 0.02 g/cm³
Castorwax MP 80	DE-1	7	0.985 ± 0.006 g/cm³
Particle size	PSD-4	17	97.7% $\geqslant 1000$ μm (for flakes)

Supplier: NL Industries Inc.

11. Stability and Storage Conditions

Hydrogenated castor oil is stable at temperatures up to 150°C. Clear, stable, chloroform solutions containing up to 15% w/v of hydrogenated castor oil may be produced. Hydrogenated castor oil may also be dissolved at temperatures greater than 90°C in polar solvents and mixtures of aromatic and polar solvents but the hydrogenated castor oil precipitates out on cooling below 90°C.

Store in a well-closed container in a cool, dry, place.

12. Incompatibilities

Hydrogenated castor oil is compatible with most natural vegetable and animal waxes. No incompatibilities are reported in the literature.

13. Method of Manufacture

Hydrogenated castor oil is prepared by the hydrogenation of castor oil using a catalyst.

14. Safety

Hydrogenated castor oil is used in oral and topical pharmaceutical formulations where it is generally regarded as an essentially nontoxic and nonirritant material.

Acute oral toxicity studies in animals have shown that hydrogenated castor oil is a relatively nontoxic material. Irritation tests with rabbits show that hydrogenated castor oil causes mild, transient irritation to the eye.

LD_{50} (rat, oral): > 5 g/kg

15. Handling Precautions

Observe normal precautions appropriate to the circumstances and quantity of material handled.

16. Regulatory Status

Accepted in the US as an indirect food additive. Included in the FDA Inactive Ingredients Guide (oral capsules, tablets and topical emulsions).

Included in nonparenteral medicines licensed in the UK.

17. Pharmacopeias

It, Mex and USPNF.

18. Related Substances

Castor oil; Hydrogenated Vegetable Oil, Type I.

Castor oil

CAS number: [8001-79-4]

Synonyms: ricinus oil; tangantangan.

Appearance: a pale yellow viscous oil with a slight characteristic odor. The crude oil has a slightly acrid taste with a nauseating after-taste.

Pharmacopeias: Aust, Belg, Br, Chin, Cz, Egypt, Eur, Fr, Ger, Gr, Hung, It, Jpn, Mex, Neth, Nord, Port, Rom, Rus, Swiss, Turk, US and Yug. Also in BP Vet.

Acid value: ⩽ 4

Autoignition temperature: 449°C

Boiling point: 313°C

Flash point: 230°C

Freezing point: -10 to -18°C

Hydroxyl value: 160-168

Iodine number: 83-88

Refractive index: $n_D^{25} = 1.473$-1.477

Saponification value: 176-182

Specific gravity: 0.957-0.961

Surface tension:
39.0 mN/m (39.0 dynes/cm) at 20°C;
35.2 mN/m (35.2 dynes/cm) at 80°C.

Solubility: miscible with chloroform, ethanol, ether, methanol; very soluble in ethanol (95%) and petroleum ether; insoluble in mineral oil unless mixed with another vegetable oil. On heating at 300°C for several hours, castor oil polymerizes and becomes soluble in mineral oil.

Stability: castor oil is stable and does not turn rancid unless subjected to excessive heat; it may be sterilized by dry heat.

Castor oil should be stored in a well-filled airtight container at a temperature not exceeding 15°C.

Safety: castor oil is a laxative and oral administration, particularly of large quantities, may cause nausea, vomiting and severe purgation. The seeds from which castor oil is obtained contain a toxic protein, ricin, which has caused severe adverse reactions, including fatalities. Allergic reactions attributed to handling the seeds of *Ricinus communis* have also been reported. However, refined castor oil contains no ricin and is free of such adverse effects.

Comments: castor oil is a fixed oil obtained from the seeds of *Ricinus communis* Linné (Fam. Euphorbiaceae). Approximate fatty acid composition is: 85-90% ricinoleic acid; 3-7% linoleic acid; 2-5% oleic acid; 1-3% stearic acid; 0.5-2% palmitic acid; up to 1% linolenic acid and up to 0.1% gadoleic acid.[6] Castor oil intended for parenteral administration should not contain antioxidants. Castor oil has been used as a solvent in some injections but is most widely used in topical formulations, including ophthalmic preparations, where it is used for its emollient effect.

19. Comments

Various different grades of hydrogenated castor oil are commercially available the composition of which may vary considerably. *Sterotex K* (Karlshamns Lipid Specialities), for example, is a mixture of hydrogenated castor oil and hydrogenated cottonseed oil. *See* Hydrogenated Vegetable Oil, Type I for further information.

20. Specific References

1. Kline CH. Thixcin R-thixotrope. Drug Cosmet Ind 1964; 95(6): 895-897, 960, 963, 973, 976.
2. Pommier AM, Brossard C, Ser J, Duchêne D. Optimization of a prolonged release tablet formulation of dyphylline by retention in a lipid matrix [in French]. STP Pharma 1988; 4: 384-391.
3. Boles MG, Deasy PB, Donnellan MF. Design and evaluation of a sustained-release aminophylline tablet. Drug Dev Ind Pharm 1993; 19: 349-370.
4. Danish FQ, Parrott EL. Effect of concentration and size of lubricant on flow rate of granules. J Pharm Sci 1971; 60: 752-754.
5. Hölzer AW, Sjögren J. Evaluation of some lubricants by the comparison of friction coefficients and tablet properties. Acta Pharm Suec 1981; 18: 139-148.
6. British Standards Institute. Specifications for crude vegetable fats, BS 7207. London: BSI, 1990.

21. General References

—

22. Authors

USA: A Yu.

Microcrystalline Cellulose

1. Nonproprietary Names

BP: Microcrystalline cellulose
PhEur: Cellulosum microcristallinum
USPNF: Microcrystalline cellulose

2. Synonyms

Avicel; cellulose gel; crystalline cellulose; E460; *Emcocel*; *Fibrocel*; *Tabulose*; *Vivacel*.

3. Chemical Name and CAS Registry Number

Cellulose [9004-34-6]

4. Empirical Formula   Molecular Weight

$(C_6H_{10}O_5)_n$ $\approx 36\,000$
Where $n \approx 220$.

5. Structural Formula

6. Functional Category

Adsorbent; suspending agent; tablet and capsule diluent; tablet disintegrant.

7. Applications in Pharmaceutical Formulation or Technology

Microcrystalline cellulose is widely used in pharmaceuticals primarily as a diluent in oral tablet and capsule formulations where it is used in both wet granulation and direct compression processes.[1-7] In addition to its use as a diluent, microcrystalline cellulose also has some lubricant[8] and disintegrant properties that make it useful in tableting. Microcrystalline cellulose is also used in cosmetics and food products.

Use	Concentration (%)
Adsorbent	20-90
Anti-adherent	5-20
Capsule diluent	20-90
Tablet disintegrant	5-15
Tablet diluent	20-90

8. Description

Microcrystalline cellulose is a purified, partially depolymerized cellulose that occurs as a white-colored, odorless, tasteless, crystalline powder composed of porous particles. It is commercially available in different particle size grades which have different properties and applications.

SEM: 1
Excipient: Microcrystalline cellulose (*Avicel PH 101*)
Manufacturer: FMC Corporation
Lot No.: 08345J
Magnification: 360x

50 µm

9. Pharmacopeial Specifications

Test	PhEur 1984	USPNF XVII (Suppl 9)
Identification	+	+
pH	5.0-7.5	5.0-7.0 [a]
		5.5-7.0 [b]
Solubility	+	—
Loss on drying	≤ 6.0%	—
Residue on ignition	—	≤ 5.0%
Sulfated ash	≤ 0.1%	≤ 0.05%
Ether-soluble substances	≤ 0.05%	—
Water-soluble substances	≤ 0.2%	≤ 0.24% [a]
		≤ 0.16% [b]
Heavy metals	≤ 10 ppm	≤ 0.001%
Starch	+	+
Organic impurities	+	+
Assay (dried basis)	—	97.0-102.0%

Note:

a. Grades with less than 5% retained on a 37 µm screen.
b. Grades with more than 5% retained on a 37 µm screen.

10. Typical Properties

Angle of repose: 34.4° for *Emcocel 90M*.[9]
Density (bulk):
0.32 g/cm³ for *Avicel PH 101*;[10]
0.29 g/cm³ for *Emcocel 90M*.[9]
Density (tapped):
0.45 g/cm³ for *Avicel PH 101*;[10]
0.35 g/cm³ for *Emcocel 90M*.[9]
Flowability: 1.41 g/s for *Emcocel 90M*.[9]
Melting point: chars at 260-270°C.
Moisture content: typically, less than 5% w/w. However, different grades may contain varying amounts of water. Microcrystalline cellulose is hygroscopic.[11] *See* HPE Data and Table I.

Table I: Properties of some commercially available grades of microcrystalline cellulose.

Grade	Nominal mean particle size (μm)	Particle size analysis		Moisture content (%)
		Mesh size	Amount retained (%)	
Avicel PH 101 [a]	50	60	$\leqslant 1.0$	$\leqslant 5.0$
		200	$\leqslant 30.0$	
Avicel PH 102 [a]	100	60	$\leqslant 8.0$	$\leqslant 5.0$
		200	$\geqslant 45.0$	
Avicel PH 103 [a]	50	60	$\leqslant 1.0$	$\leqslant 3.0$
		200	$\leqslant 30.0$	
Avicel PH 105 [a]	20	400	$\leqslant 1.0$	$\leqslant 5.0$
Avicel PH 112 [a]	100	60	$\leqslant 8.0$	$\leqslant 1.5$
		200	$\geqslant 45.0$	
Avicel PH 200 [a]	180	60	$\geqslant 10.0$	$\leqslant 5.0$
		100	$\geqslant 50.0$	
Emcocel 50M [b]	51	60	$\leqslant 0.25$	$\leqslant 5.0$
		200	$\leqslant 30.0$	
Emcocel 90M [b]	91	60	$\leqslant 8.0$	$\leqslant 5.0$
		200	$\geqslant 45.0$	
Vivacel 101 [c]	50	50	$\geqslant 35.0$	$\leqslant 5.0$
		150	$\leqslant 10.0$	
Vivacel 102 [c]	100	50	$\geqslant 50.0$	$\leqslant 5.0$
		150	$\leqslant 30.0$	
Vivacel 12 [c]	180	50	$\geqslant 70.0$	$\leqslant 5.0$
		500	$\leqslant 1.0$	
Vivacel 20 [c]	20	50	$\leqslant 2.0$	$\leqslant 5.0$
		150	$\leqslant 0.1$	

Suppliers: a. FMC Corporation; b. Edward Mendell Co Inc; c. J. Rettenmaier & Söhne GmbH.

HPE Laboratory Project Data			
Method	Grade*	Lab #	Results
Bulk/tap density			
BTD-8	PH 101	36	B: 0.320 g/cm^3
			T: 0.386 g/cm^3
BTD-8	PH 102	36	B: 0.307 g/cm^3
			T: 0.370 g/cm^3
BTD-8	PH 103	36	B: 0.301 g/cm^3
			T: 0.370 g/cm^3
BTD-8	PH 105	36	B: 0.260 g/cm^3
			T: 0.333 g/cm^3
Density			
DE-1	PH 101	31	1.618 g/cm^3
DE-1	PH 102	31	1.554 g/cm^3
DE-1	PH 103	31	1.571 g/cm^3
DE-1	PH 105	31	1.573 g/cm^3
Moisture content			
MC-3	PH 101	31	3.745%
MC-3	PH 105	31	4.655%
MC-3	PH 103	31	3.065%
MC-3	PH 102	31	3.315%
EMC-1	PH 101	5	See Fig. 1.
SI-1	PH 102	13	See Fig. 2.
SI-1	PH 103	13	See Fig. 2.
SI-1	PH 105	13	See Fig. 2.
Solubility in water at 25°C			
SOL-8	PH 101	30	1 mg/mL
SOL-8	PH 102	30	0.2 mg/mL

* Supplier: FMC Corporation (*Avicel*).

Particle size distribution: typical mean particle size is 20–200 μm. Different grades may have a different nominal mean particle size, *see* Table I.

Solubility: slightly soluble in 5% w/v sodium hydroxide solution; practically insoluble in water, dilute acids and most organic solvents.

Specific surface area: 1.18 m^2/g for *Avicel PH 101*.[10]

11. Stability and Storage Conditions

Microcrystalline cellulose is a stable, though hygroscopic material. The bulk material should be stored in a well-closed container in a cool, dry, place.

12. Incompatibilities

Incompatible with strong oxidizing agents.

13. Method of Manufacture

Microcrystalline cellulose is manufactured by the controlled hydrolysis, with dilute mineral acid solutions, of α-cellulose, obtained as a pulp from fibrous plant materials. Following hydrolysis, the hydrocellulose is purified by filtration and the aqueous slurry is spray-dried to form dry, porous particles of a broad size distribution.

14. Safety

Microcrystalline cellulose is widely used in oral pharmaceutical formulations and food products and is generally regarded as a nontoxic and nonirritant material.

Microcrystalline cellulose is not absorbed systemically following oral administration and thus has little toxic potential.

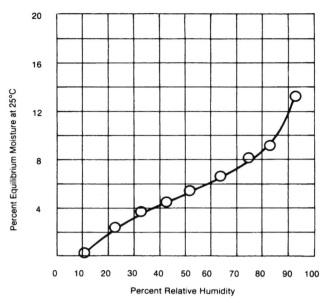

Fig. 1: Equilibrium moisture content of microcrystalline cellulose (*Avicel PH 101*, Lot #1929).

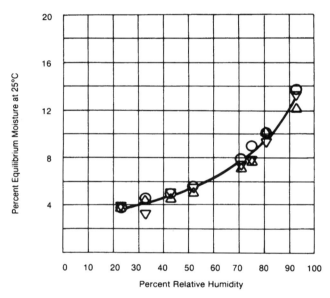

Fig. 2: Equilibrium moisture content of microcrystalline cellulose.
○ *Avicel PH 102*, Lot #2911-2904.
△ *Avicel PH 105*, Lot #5926.
▽ *Avicel PH 103*, Lot #3445.

Consumption of large quantities of cellulose may however have a laxative effect although this is unlikely to be a problem when cellulose is used as an excipient in pharmaceutical formulations.
Deliberate abuse of formulations containing cellulose, either by inhalation or injection, has resulted in the formation of cellulose granulomas.[12]

15. Handling Precautions

Observe normal precautions appropriate to the circumstances and quantity of material handled. Microcrystalline cellulose may be irritant to the eyes. Gloves, eye protection and a dust mask are recommended. In the UK, the occupational exposure limits for cellulose have been set at 10 mg/m^3 long-term (8-hour TWA) for total inhalable dust and 5 mg/m^3 for respirable dust; short-term the limit for total inhalable dust has been set at 20 mg/m^3.[13]

16. Regulatory Status

GRAS listed. Accepted in Europe for use as a food additive. Included in the FDA Inactive Ingredients Guide (inhalations, oral capsules, powders, suspensions, syrups and tablets, topical and vaginal preparations). Included in nonparenteral medicines licensed in the UK.

17. Pharmacopeias

Br, Eur, Fr, Gr, Hung, Ind, It, Jpn, Mex, Neth, Port, Swiss and USPNF.

18. Related Substances

Microcrystalline cellulose and carboxymethylcellulose sodium; Powdered Cellulose.

Microcrystalline cellulose and carboxymethylcellulose sodium
Synonyms: *Avicel RC-581*; *Avicel RC-591*; *Avicel CL-611*; colloidal cellulose; dispersible cellulose.
Appearance: white colored, odorless and tasteless hygroscopic powder.
Pharmacopeias: Br, Jpn and USPNF.
Acidity/alkalinity:
pH = 6-8 for a 1.2% w/v aqueous dispersion.
Moisture content: not more than 6.0% w/w.
Particle size distribution: ≤ 0.1% retained on a #60 mesh and ≤ 50% retained on a #325 mesh for *Avicel CL-611*; ≤ 0.1% retained on a #60 mesh and ≤ 35% retained on a #200 mesh for *Avicel RC-581*; ≤ 0.1% retained on a #60 mesh and ≤ 45% retained on a #325 mesh for *Avicel RC-591*.
Solubility: practically insoluble in dilute acids and organic solvents. Partially soluble in dilute alkali and water (carboxymethylcellulose sodium fraction).
Viscosity (dynamic): 5-20 mPa s (5-20 cP) for a 1.2% w/v aqueous dispersion of *Avicel CL-611*; 72-168 mPa s (72-168 cP) for *Avicel RC-581* and 39-91 mPa s (39-91 cP) for *Avicel RC-591* at the same concentration.
Comments: mixtures of microcrystalline cellulose and carboxymethylcellulose sodium that are dispersible in water and produce thixotropic gels are suitable as suspending vehicles in pharmaceutical formulations. The amount of carboxymethylcellulose present can vary between 8.3-18.8% w/w depending upon the grade of material.

19. Comments

Several different grades of microcrystalline cellulose are commercially available which differ in their method of manufacture,[14,15] particle size, moisture, flow, and other physical properties.[16-23] The larger particle size grades generally provide better flow properties in pharmaceutical machinery. Low moisture grades are used with moisture-sensitive materials.

20. Specific References

1. Enézian GM. Direct compression of tablets using microcrystalline cellulose [in French]. Pharm Acta Helv 1972; 47: 321-363.
2. Lerk CF, Bolhuis GK. Comparative evaluation of excipients for direct compression I. Pharm Weekbl 1973; 108: 469-481.
3. Lerk CF, Bolhuis GK, de Boer AH. Comparative evaluation of excipients for direct compression II. Pharm Weekbl 1974; 109: 945-955.
4. Lamberson RF, Raynor GE. Tableting properties of microcrystalline cellulose. Mfg Chem Aerosol News 1976; 47(6): 55-61.
5. Lerk CF, Bolhuis GK, de Boer AH. Effect of microcrystalline cellulose on liquid penetration in and disintegration of directly compressed tablets. J Pharm Sci 1979; 68: 205-211.
6. Chilamkurti RN, Rhodes CT, Schwartz JB. Some studies on compression properties of tablet matrices using a computerized instrumented press. Drug Dev Ind Pharm 1982; 8: 63-86.
7. Wallace JW, Capozzi JT, Shangraw RF. Performance of pharmaceutical filler/binders as related to methods of powder characterization. Pharmaceut Technol 1983; 7(9): 94-104.
8. Omray A, Omray P. Evaluation of microcrystalline cellulose as a glidant. Indian J Pharm Sci 1986; 48: 20-22.
9. Çelik M, Okutgen E. A feasibility study for the development of a prospective compaction functionality test and the establishment of a compaction data bank. Drug Dev Ind Pharm 1993; 19: 2309-2334.
10. Parker MD, York P, Rowe RC. Binder-substrate interactions in wet granulation 3: the effect of excipient source variation. Int J Pharmaceutics 1992; 80: 179-190.
11. Callahan JC, Cleary GW, Elefant M, Kaplan G, Kensler T, Nash RA. Equilibrium moisture content of pharmaceutical excipients. Drug Dev Ind Pharm 1982; 8: 355-369.
12. Cooper CB, Bai TR, Heyderman E, Corrin B. Cellulose granulomas in the lungs of a cocaine sniffer. Br Med J 1983; 286: 2021-2022.
13. Health and Safety Executive. EH40/93: occupational exposure limits 1993. London: HMSO, 1993.
14. Jain JK, Dixit VK, Varma KC. Preparation of microcrystalline cellulose from cereal straw and its evaluation as a tablet excipient. Indian J Pharm Sci 1983; 45: 83-85.
15. Singla AK, Sakhuja A, Malik A. Evaluation of microcrystalline cellulose prepared from absorbent cotton as a direct compression carrier. Drug Dev Ind Pharm 1988; 14: 1131-1136.
16. Doelker E, Mordier D, Iten H, Humbert-Droz P. Comparative tableting properties of sixteen microcrystalline celluloses. Drug Dev Ind Pharm 1987; 13: 1847-1875.
17. Bassam F, York P, Rowe RC, Roberts RJ. Effect of particle size and source on variability of Young's modulus of microcrystalline cellulose powders. J Pharm Pharmacol 1988; 40: 68P.
18. Dittgen M, Fricke S, Gerecke H. Microcrystalline cellulose in direct tabletting. Mfg Chem 1993; 64(7): 17, 19, 21.
19. Landín M, Martínez-Pacheco R, Gómez-Amoza JL, Souto C, Concheiro A, Rowe RC. Effect of country of origin on the properties of microcrystalline cellulose. Int J Pharmaceutics 1993; 91: 123-131.
20. Landín M, Martínez-Pacheco R, Gómez-Amoza JL, Souto C, Concheiro A, Rowe RC. Effect of batch variation and source of pulp on the properties of microcrystalline cellulose. Int J Pharmaceutics 1993; 91: 133-141.
21. Landín M, Martínez-Pacheco R, Gómez-Amoza JL, Souto C, Concheiro A, Rowe RC. Influence of microcrystalline cellulose source and batch variation on the tabletting behavior and stability of prednisone formulations. Int J Pharmaceutics 1993; 91: 143-149.
22. Podczeck F, Révész P. Evaluation of the properties of microcrystalline and microfine cellulose powders. Int J Pharmaceutics 1993; 91: 183-193.
23. Rowe RC, McKillop AG, Bray D. The effect of batch and source variation on the crystallinity of microcrystalline cellulose. Int J Pharmaceutics 1994; 101: 169-172.

21. General References

Doelker E. Comparative compaction properties of various microcrystalline cellulose types and generic products. Drug Dev Ind Pharm 1993; 19: 2399-2471.
FMC Corporation. Technical literature: *Avicel PH* microcrystalline cellulose, 1986.
Smolinske SC. Handbook of food, drug, and cosmetic excipients. Boca Raton, FL: CRC Press Inc, 1992: 71-74.
Staniforth JN, Baichwal AR, Hart JP, Heng PWS. Effect of addition of water on the rheological and mechanical properties of microcrystalline celluloses. Int J Pharmaceutics 1988; 41: 231-236.

22. Authors

USA: L Mathur.

Powdered Cellulose

1. Nonproprietary Names

BP: Powdered cellulose
PhEur: Cellulosi pulvis
USPNF: Powdered cellulose

2. Synonyms

Cepo; E460; *Elcema*; *Sanacel*; *Solka-Floc*.

3. Chemical Name and CAS Registry Number

Cellulose [9004-34-6]

4. Empirical Formula   Molecular Weight

$(C_6H_{10}O_5)_n$ $\approx 243\,000$
Where $n \approx 500$.
Since cellulose is derived from a natural polymer, it has variable chain length and thus variable molecular weight. *See also* Sections 8 and 13.

5. Structural Formula

6. Functional Category

Adsorbent; glidant; suspending agent; tablet and capsule diluent; tablet disintegrant.

7. Applications in Pharmaceutical Formulation or Technology

Powdered cellulose is used as a tablet diluent and a hard gelatin capsule filler. In both these contexts it acts as a bulking agent to increase the physical size of the dosage form for formulations containing a small amount of active substance. Powdered cellulose has acceptable compression properties although its flow properties are poor.

In soft gelatin capsules, powdered cellulose may be used to reduce the sedimentation of oily suspension fills.

Powdered cellulose is additionally used as the powder base material of powder dosage forms and as a suspending agent in aqueous suspensions for peroral delivery. It may also be used to reduce sedimentation during the manufacture of suppositories.

Powdered cellulose is also used in cosmetics and food products.

Use	Concentration (%)
Capsule filler	0-100
Tablet binder	5-20
Tablet disintegrant	5-15
Tablet glidant	1-2

8. Description

Powdered cellulose occurs as a white or almost white, odorless and tasteless powder of various particle sizes, ranging from a free-flowing fine or granular dense powder, to a coarse, fluffy, non-flowing material.

9. Pharmacopeial Specifications

Test	PhEur 1984	USPNF XVII (Suppl 9)
Identification	+	+
pH (10% w/w suspension)	5.0-7.5	5.0-7.5
Loss on drying	$\leqslant 6.0\%$	$\leqslant 7.0\%$
Residue on ignition	—	$\leqslant 0.3\%$
Sulfated ash	$\leqslant 0.3\%$	—
Solubility	+	—
Ether-soluble substances	+	—
Water-soluble substances	$\leqslant 1.0\%$	$\leqslant 1.5\%$
Heavy metals	$\leqslant 10$ ppm	$\leqslant 0.001\%$
Organic impurities	+	+
Starch	+	+
Assay (dried basis)	—	97.0-102.0%

10. Typical Properties

Density: 1.5 g/cm³
Density (tapped): *see* Table I and HPE Data.
Moisture content: powdered cellulose is slightly hygroscopic,[1] *see also* HPE Data.
Particle size distribution: powdered cellulose is commercially available in several different particle sizes, *see* Table I.
Solubility: practically insoluble in water, dilute acids and most organic solvents although it disperses in most liquids. Slightly soluble in 5% w/v sodium hydroxide solution. Powdered cellulose does not swell in water, but does in dilute bleach.

HPE Laboratory Project Data			
	Method	Lab #	Results
Bulk/tap density	BTD-8	36	B: 0.287 g/cm³ [a]
			T: 0.403 g/cm³
	BTD-8	36	B: 0.208 g/cm³ [a]
			T: 0.301 g/cm³
	BTD-8	36	B: 0.139 g/cm³ [a]
			T: 0.210 g/cm³
	BTD-8	36	B: 0.176 g/cm³ [a]
			T: 0.250 g/cm³
	BTD-8	36	B: 0.302 g/cm³ [a]
			T: 0.415 g/cm³
	BTD-8	36	B: 0.391 g/cm³ [a]
			T: 0.488 g/cm³
	BTD-5	6	B: 0.372 g/cm³ [b]
			T: 0.481 g/cm³
	BTD-5	6	B: 0.197 g/cm³ [b]
			T: 0.332 g/cm³
	BTD-5	6	B: 0.211 g/cm³ [b]
			T: 0.363 g/cm³
Compressibility	COM-3	20	*See* Fig. 1. [a]
Density	DE-1	31	1.509 [a]
Moisture content	EMC-1	18	*See* Fig. 2. [a]
	SI-1	13	*See* Figs. 3 and 4. [a]
Solubility			
Water at 24°C	SOL-8	30	0.6 mg/mL [a]

Supplier: a. Brown Chemical Co Inc (*Solka-Floc*);
             b. Degussa Ltd (*Elcema*).

Note: *Solka-Floc* now supplied by Edward Mendell Co Inc.

Table I: Typical properties of some commercially available grades of powdered cellulose.

Grade	Approximate particle size (μm)	Density (bulk) (g/cm^3)	Density (tapped) (g/cm^3)
Elcema P 050	40-70	0.23	—
Elcema P 100	50-100	0.22	—
Elcema F 150	100-200	0.18	—
Elcema G 250	200-300	0.35	—
Elcema G 400	130-260	0.36	—
Solka-Floc BW-40	60	—	0.35
Solka-Floc BW-100	40	—	0.46
Solka-Floc BW-200	35	—	0.46
Solka-Floc BW-2030	35	—	0.45
Solka-Floc Fine Granular	granules	—	0.68

Note: *Elcema* supplied by Degussa Ltd; *Solka-Floc* supplied by Edward Mendell Co Inc.

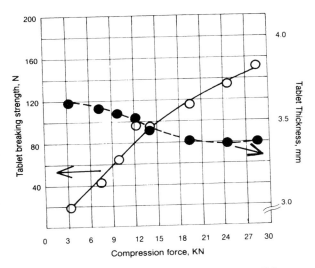

Fig. 1: Compression characteristics of powdered cellulose (*Solka-Floc Fine Granular*, Lot #9-10-8).
Mean tablet weight: 502 mg.
Minimum compressional force for compaction: 4.9 kN.
Compressional force resulting in capping: > 29.4 kN.

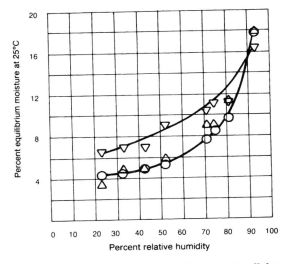

Fig. 3: Equilibrium moisture content of powdered cellulose at 25°C.
○ Powdered cellulose (*Solka-Floc BW-40*, Lot #8-10-30A).
△ Powdered cellulose (*Solka-Floc BW-20*, Lot #22A-19).
▽ Powdered cellulose (*Solka-Floc Fine Granular*, Lot #9-10-8).

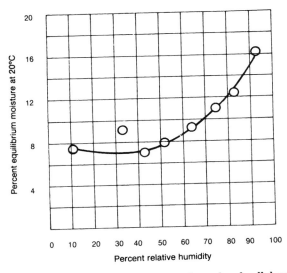

Fig. 2: Equilibrium moisture content of powdered cellulose at 20°C (*Solka-Floc*, Lot #30150).

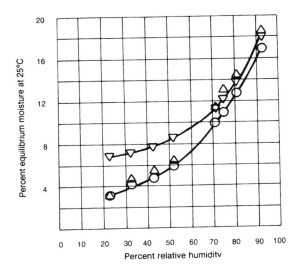

Fig. 4: Equilibrium moisture content of powdered cellulose at 25°C.
○ Powdered cellulose (*Solka-Floc BW-100*, Lot #9-7-18B).
△ Powdered cellulose (*Solka-Floc BW-200*, Lot #22A-20).
▽ Powdered cellulose (*Solka-Floc BW-2030*, Lot #240).

11. Stability and Storage Conditions

Powdered cellulose is a stable, slightly hygroscopic material. The bulk material should be stored in a well-closed container in a cool, dry, place.

12. Incompatibilities

Incompatible with strong oxidizing agents.

13. Method of Manufacture

Powdered cellulose is manufactured by the purification and mechanical size reduction of α-cellulose obtained as a pulp from fibrous plant materials.

14. Safety

Powdered cellulose is widely used in oral pharmaceutical formulations and food products and is generally regarded as a nontoxic and nonirritant material.

Powdered cellulose is not absorbed systemically following oral administration and thus has little toxic potential. Consumption of large quantities of cellulose may however have a laxative effect although this is unlikely to be a problem when cellulose is used as an excipient in pharmaceutical formulations.

Deliberate abuse of formulations containing cellulose, either by inhalation or injection, has resulted in the formation of cellulose granulomas.[2]

15. Handling Precautions

Observe normal precautions appropriate to the circumstances and quantity of material handled. Powdered cellulose may be irritant to the eyes. Gloves, eye protection and a dust mask are recommended. In the UK, the occupational exposure limits for cellulose have been set at 10 mg/m^3 long-term (8-hour TWA) for total inhalable dust and 5 mg/m^3 for respirable dust; short-term the limit for total inhalable dust has been set at 20 mg/m^3.[3]

16. Regulatory Status

GRAS listed. Accepted in Europe for use as a food additive. Included in nonparenteral medicines licensed in the UK.

17. Pharmacopeias

Br, Eur, Fr, Ger, Gr, It, Neth, Port, Swiss and USPNF.

18. Related Substances

Microcrystalline Cellulose.

19. Comments

—

20. Specific References

1. Callahan JC, Cleary GW, Elefant M, Kaplan G, Kensler T, Nash RA. Equilibrium moisture content of pharmaceutical excipients. Drug Dev Ind Pharm 1982; 8: 355-369.
2. Cooper CB, Bai TR, Heyderman E, Corrin B. Cellulose granulomas in the lungs of a cocaine sniffer. Br Med J 1983; 286: 2021-2022.
3. Health and Safety Executive. EH40/93: occupational exposure limits 1993. London: HMSO, 1993.

See also Microcrystalline Cellulose.

21. General References

Smolinske SC. Handbook of food, drug, and cosmetic excipients. Boca Raton, FL: CRC Press Inc, 1992: 71-74.

22. Authors

UK: ME Aulton.

Cellulose Acetate Phthalate

1. Nonproprietary Names

BP: Cellacephate
PhEur: Cellulosi acetas phthalas
USPNF: Cellulose acetate phthalate

2. Synonyms

Acetyl phthalyl cellulose; *Aquateric*; CAP; cellacefate; cellulose acetate hydrogen 1,2-benzenedicarboxylate; cellulose acetate hydrogen phthalate; cellulose acetate monophthalate; cellulose acetophthalate; cellulose acetylphthalate.

3. Chemical Name and CAS Registry Number

Cellulose, acetate, 1,2-benzenedicarboxylate
[9004-38-0]

4. Empirical Formula Molecular Weight

Cellulose acetate phthalate is a cellulose in which about half the hydroxyl groups are acetylated and about a quarter are esterified, with one of the two acid groups being phthalic acid. The other acid group is free. *See* Section 5.

5. Structural Formula

6. Functional Category

Coating agent.

7. Applications in Pharmaceutical Formulation or Technology

Cellulose acetate phthalate is used as an enteric film coating material, or as a matrix binder, for tablets and capsules.[1-8] Such coatings resist prolonged contact with the strongly acidic gastric fluid, but soften and swell in the mildly acidic or neutral intestinal environment.
Cellulose acetate phthalate is commonly applied to solid dosage forms either by coating from organic or aqueous solvent systems, or by direct compression. Concentrations used are 0.5-9.0% of the core weight. The addition of plasticizers improves the water resistance of this coating material, and such plasticized films are more effective than when cellulose acetate phthalate is used alone. Cellulose acetate phthalate is compatible with the following plasticizers: acetylated monoglyceride; butyl phthalylbutyl glycolate; dibutyl tartrate; diethyl phthalate; dimethyl phthalate; ethyl phthalylethyl glycolate; glycerin; propylene glycol; triacetin; triacetin citrate and tripropionin. It may also be used in combination with other coating agents to control drug release, e.g. ethylcellulose.

8. Description

Cellulose acetate phthalate is a hygroscopic, white, free-flowing powder or colorless flakes. It is tasteless and odorless, or may have a slight odor of acetic acid.

9. Pharmacopeial Specifications

Test	PhEur 1984	USPNF XVII (Suppl 2)
Identification	+	+
Appearance of solution	+	—
Appearance of a film	+	—
Solubility of a film	+	—
Viscosity at 25°C	—	45-90 cP
Water	≤ 5.0%	≤ 5.0%
Residue on ignition	—	≤ 0.1%
Sulfated ash	≤ 0.1%	—
Free acid	≤ 3.0%	≤ 6.0%
Heavy metals	≤ 10 ppm	—
Phthalyl content	30.0-40.0%	30.0-36.0%
Acetyl content	17.0-26.0%	21.5-26.0%

10. Typical Properties

Hygroscopicity: cellulose acetate phthalate is hygroscopic and precautions are necessary to avoid excessive absorption of moisture. *See* HPE Data.[9]
Melting point: 192°C. Glass transition temperature is 160-170°C.[10]
Solubility: practically insoluble in alcohols, chlorinated hydrocarbons, hydrocarbons, and water; soluble in cyclic ethers, esters, ether alcohols, ketones and certain solvent mixtures. Also soluble in certain buffered aqueous solutions at greater than pH 6. The list below shows some of the solvents and solvent mixtures in which cellulose acetate phthalate has a solubility of 1 in 10 parts or more.
Acetone
Acetone: Ethanol (1:1)
Acetone: Methanol (1:1/1:3)
Acetone: Methylene chloride (1:1/1:3)
Acetone: Water (97:3)
Benzene: Methanol (1:1)
Diacetone alcohol
Dioxane
Ethoxyethyl acetate
Ethyl acetate: Ethanol (1:1)
Ethyl acetate: Propan-2-ol (1:1/1:3)
Ethylene glycol monoacetate
Ethyl lactate
Methoxyethyl acetate
β-Methoxyethylene alcohol
Methyl acetate
Methylene chloride: Ethanol (3:1)
Methyl ethyl ketone
Viscosity (dynamic): 50-90 mPa s (50-90 cP) for a 15% w/w solution in acetone with a moisture content of 0.4%. This is a good coating solution with a honey-like consistency, but the viscosity is influenced by the purity of the solvent.

HPE Laboratory Project Data

	Method	Lab #	Results
Moisture content	MC-5	5	2.20% [a]
	EMC-1	5	*See* Fig. 1. [a]
	SDI-2	26	*See* Fig. 2. [b]
Solubility			
Water at 25°C	SOL-8	30	0.8 mg/mL [a]

Supplier:
a. Eastman Fine Chemicals (Lot No.: C-2104);
b. Eastman Fine Chemicals (Lot No.: S-2090).

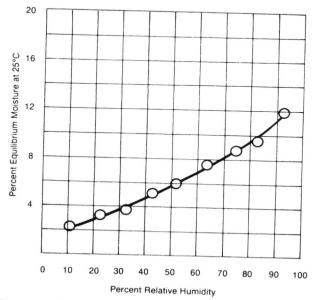

Fig. 1: Equilibrium moisture content of cellulose acetate phthalate.

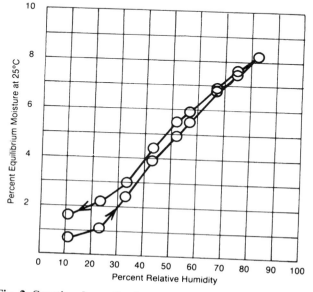

Fig. 2: Sorption-desorption isotherm of cellulose acetate phthalate.

11. Stability and Storage Conditions

Cellulose acetate phthalate hydrolyzes slowly under prolonged adverse conditions, such as high temperature and humidity, with a resultant increase in free acid content, viscosity and odor of acetic acid. If its moisture content is above about 6% w/w fairly rapid hydrolysis occurs. However, cellulose acetate phthalate is stable if stored in a well-closed container in a cool, dry, place.

12. Incompatibilities

Cellulose acetate phthalate is incompatible with ferrous sulfate, ferric chloride, silver nitrate, sodium citrate, aluminum sulfate, calcium chloride, mercuric chloride, barium nitrate, basic lead acetate, and strong oxidizing agents such as strong alkalis and acids.
It should be noted that one carboxylic acid group of the phthalic acid moiety remains unesterified and free for interactions. Accordingly, imcompatability with acid sensitive drugs may occur.[11]

13. Method of Manufacture

Cellulose acetate phthalate is produced by reacting the partial acetate ester of cellulose with phthalic anhydride in the presence of a tertiary organic base, such as pyridine.

14. Safety

Cellulose acetate phthalate is widely used in oral pharmaceutical products and is generally regarded as a nontoxic material, free of adverse effects.
Results of long-term feeding studies with cellulose acetate phthalate, in rats and dogs, have indicated a low oral toxicity. Rats survived daily feedings of up to 30% in the diet for up to one year without showing a depression in growth. Dogs fed 16 g daily in the diet for one year also remained normal.

15. Handling Precautions

Observe normal precautions appropriate to the circumstances and quantity of material handled. Cellulose acetate phthalate may be irritant to the eyes, mucous membranes and upper respiratory tract. Eye protection and gloves are recommended. Cellulose acetate phthalate should be handled in a well-ventilated environment; a respirator is recommended when handling large quantities.

16. Regulatory Status

Included in the FDA Inactive Ingredients Guide (oral capsules and tablets). Included in nonparenteral medicines licensed in the UK.

17. Pharmacopeias

Aust, Br, Braz, Cz, Eur, Fr, Ger, Gr, Hung, Ind, It, Jpn, Mex, Neth, Nord, Port, Swiss and USPNF.

18. Related Substances

Cellulose acetate; Hydroxypropyl Methylcellulose Phthalate.

Cellulose acetate:
Comments: a reconstituted colloidal dispersion of cellulose acetate in latex is available for use as a coating material instead of solvent based solutions. This consists of a white water-insoluble powder, composed of solid, or semisolid, polymer spheres. The spheres range in size from 0.05-3 μm, with an average particle size of 0.2 μm. A typical coating system made from this latex powder is a 10-30% solid-content aqueous

dispersion with a viscosity in the 50-100 mPa s (50-100 cP) range.

19. Comments

Any plasticizers which are used with cellulose acetate phthalate to improve performance should be carefully chosen on the basis of experimental evidence since the same plasticizer, used in a different tablet coating, may not yield a satisfactory product.

In using mixed solvents, it is important to dissolve the cellulose acetate phthalate in the solvent with the greater dissolving power, and then to add the second solvent. Cellulose acetate phthalate should always be added to the solvent, not the reverse.

Cellulose acetate phthalate films are permeable to certain ionic substances, such as potassium iodide and ammonium chloride. In such cases, an appropriate sealer subcoat should be used.

20. Specific References

1. Spitael J, Kinget R, Naessens K. Dissolution rate of cellulose acetate phthalate and Brönsted catalysis law. Pharm Ind 1980; 42: 846-849.
2. Takenaka H, Kawashima Y, Lin SY. Preparation of enteric-coated microcapsules for tableting by spray-drying technique and *in vitro* simulation of drug release from the tablet in GI tract. J Pharm Sci 1980; 69: 1388-1392.
3. Stricker H, Kulke H. Rate of disintegration and passage of enteric-coated tablets in gastrointestinal tract [in German]. Pharm Ind 1981; 43: 1018-1021.
4. Takenaka H, Kawashima Y, Lin SY. Polymorphism of spray-dried microencapsulated sulfamethoxazole with cellulose acetate phthalate and colloidal silica, montmorillonite, or talc. J Pharm Sci 1981; 70: 1256-1260.
5. Maharaj I, Nairn JG, Campbell JB. Simple rapid method for the preparation of enteric-coated microspheres. J Pharm Sci 1984; 73: 39-42.
6. Beyger JW, Nairn JG. Some factors affecting the microencapsulation of pharmaceuticals with cellulose acetate phthalate. J Pharm Sci 1986; 75: 573-578.
7. Lin S-Y, Kawashima Y. Drug release from tablets containing cellulose acetate phthalate as an additive or enteric-coating material. Pharm Res 1987; 4: 70-74.
8. Thoma K, Heckenmüller H. Effect of film formers and plasticizers on stability of resistance and disintegration behaviour. Part 4: pharmaceutical-technological and analytical studies of gastric juice resistant commercial preparations [in German]. Pharmazie 1987; 42: 837-841.
9. Callahan JC, Cleary GW, Elefant M, Kaplan G, Kensler T, Nash RA. Equilibrium moisture content of pharmaceutical excipients. Drug Dev Ind Pharm 1982; 8: 355-369.
10. Sakellariou P, Rowe RC, White EFT. The thermomechanical properties and glass transition temperatures of some cellulose derivatives used in film coating. Int J Pharmaceutics 1985; 27: 267-277.
11. Rawlins EA, editor. Bentley's textbook of pharmaceutics. London: Baillière, Tindall and Cox, 1977: 291.

21. General References

Doelker E. Cellulose derivatives. Adv Polymer Sci 1993; 107: 199-265.

O'Connor RE, Berryman WH. Evaluation of enteric film permeability: tablet swelling method and capillary rise method. Drug Dev Ind Pharm 1992; 18: 2123-2133.

Wyatt DM. Cellulose esters as direct compression matrices. Mfg Chem 1991; 62: 20, 21, 23.

22. Authors

USA: JC Lee.

Cetostearyl Alcohol

1. Nonproprietary Names

BP: Cetostearyl alcohol
PhEur: Alcohol cetylicus et stearylicus
USPNF: Cetostearyl alcohol

2. Synonyms

Cetearyl alcohol; *Crodacol CS.*

3. Chemical Name and CAS Registry Number

Cetostearyl alcohol [67762-27-0 and 8005-44-5]

4. Empirical Formula   Molecular Weight

Cetostearyl alcohol is a mixture of solid aliphatic alcohols consisting mainly of stearyl ($C_{18}H_{38}O$) and cetyl ($C_{16}H_{34}O$) alcohols with small quantities of other alcohols, chiefly myristyl alcohol. The proportion of stearyl to cetyl alcohol varies considerably but usually consists of about 50-70% stearyl alcohol and 20-35% cetyl alcohol. *See also* Section 9.

5. Structural Formula

See Section 4.

6. Functional Category

Emollient; emulsifying agent; viscosity-increasing agent.

7. Applications in Pharmaceutical Formulation or Technology

Cetostearyl alcohol is used in cosmetics and oral and topical pharmaceuticals. In topical pharmaceutical formulations cetostearyl alcohol is used as a stiffening agent and emulsifier in both water-in-oil and oil-in-water emulsions. It acts as an emulsion stabilizer when mixed with more hydrophilic primary emulsifiers, such as anionic emulsifying agents, to produce oil-in-water emulsions which are stable over a wide pH range. Cetostearyl alcohol is also used in the preparation of nonaqueous creams and sticks.

8. Description

Cetostearyl alcohol occurs as white or cream-colored unctuous masses, or almost white-colored flakes or granules. It has a faint characteristic odor and a bland taste. On heating, cetostearyl alcohol melts to a clear, colorless or pale yellow-colored liquid free of suspended matter.

9. Pharmacopeial Specifications

Test	PhEur 1991	USPNF XVII
Identification	+	+
Appearance of solution	+	—
Melting range	49-56°C	48-55°C
Acid value	⩽ 1.0	⩽ 2.0
Iodine value	⩽ 2.0	⩽ 4.0
Hydroxyl value	208-228	208-228
Saponification value	⩽ 2.0	—
Assay		
(of $C_{18}H_{38}O$)	⩾ 40.0%	⩾ 40.0%
(of $C_{16}H_{34}O$ and $C_{18}H_{38}O$)	⩾ 90.0%	⩾ 90.0%

10. Typical Properties

Boiling point: > 300°C
Density: ≈ 0.82 g/cm^3 at 60°C
Flash point: > 150°C (closed-cup)
Solubility: soluble in ethanol (95%), ether and petroleum spirit (boiling range 40-60°C); practically insoluble in water.
Water content: no more than trace amounts of water are present.

11. Stability and Storage Conditions

Cetostearyl alcohol is stable under normal storage conditions. It is not liable to fatty ester hydrolysis and does not become rancid.
Cetostearyl alcohol should be stored in a well-closed container in a cool, dry, place.

12. Incompatibilities

Incompatible with strong oxidizing agents.

13. Method of Manufacture

Cetostearyl alcohol is prepared by the reduction of the appropriate fatty acids.

14. Safety

Cetostearyl alcohol is mainly used in topical pharmaceutical formulations although it has also been used in oral preparations.
Cetostearyl alcohol is generally regarded as a nontoxic material and is not readily absorbed from the gastrointestinal tract. Although essentially nonirritant, hypersensitivity reactions to cetyl and stearyl alcohol, the main components of cetostearyl alcohol, have been reported, *see* Cetyl Alcohol and Stearyl Alcohol.

15. Handling Precautions

Observe normal precautions appropriate to the circumstances and quantity of material handled. Eye protection and gloves are recommended. Cetostearyl alcohol is flammable and on combustion may produce fumes containing carbon monoxide.

16. Regulatory Status

Included in the FDA Inactive Ingredients Guide (oral tablets and topical emulsions, lotions and ointments). Included in nonparenteral medicines licensed in the UK.

17. Pharmacopeias

Aust, Br, Cz, Eur, Ger, Hung, Ind, Rom, USPNF and Yug. Also in BP Vet.

18. Related Substances

Cetyl Alcohol; Stearyl Alcohol.

19. Comments

The composition of cetostearyl alcohol may vary considerably from different sources. This may result in different emulsification behavior, particularly with respect to emulsion consistency or stability.

20. Specific References

21. General References

Eccleston GM. Properties of fatty alcohol mixed emulsifiers and emulsifying waxes. In: Florence AT, editor. Materials used in pharmaceutical formulation: critical reports on applied chemistry, volume 6. Oxford: Blackwell Scientific Publications, 1984: 124-156.

Eccleston GM, Beattie L. Microstructural changes during the storage of systems containing cetostearyl alcohol/polyoxyethylene alkyl ether surfactants. In: Rubinstein MH, editor. Pharmaceutical technology: drug stability. Chichester: Ellis Horwood Ltd, 1989: 76-87.

Louden JD, Patel HK, Rowe RC. A preliminary examination of the structure of gels and emulsions containing cetostearyl alcohol and cetrimide using Laser Raman Spectroscopy. Int J Pharmaceutics 1985; 25: 179-190.

Louden JD, Rowe RC. A quantitative examination of the structure of emulsions prepared using cetostearyl alcohol and cetrimide using Fourier transform infrared microscopy. Int J Pharmaceutics 1990; 63: 219-225.

Patel HK, Rowe RC, McMahon J, Stewart RF. A comparison of the structure and properties of ternary gels containing cetrimide and cetostearyl alcohol obtained from both natural and synthetic sources. Acta Pharm Technol 1985; 31: 243-247.

Patel HK, Rowe RC, McMahon J, Stewart RF. A systematic microscopical examination of gels and emulsions containing cetrimide and cetostearyl alcohol. Int J Pharmaceutics 1985; 25: 13-25.

Patel HK, Rowe RC, McMahon J, Stewart RF. An investigation of the structural changes occurring in a cetostearyl alcohol/cetrimide/water gel after prolonged low temperature (4°C) storage. J Pharm Pharmacol 1985; 37: 899-902.

Rowe RC, Patel HK. The effect of temperature on the conductivity of gels and emulsions prepared from cetrimide and cetostearyl alcohol. J Pharm Pharmacol 1985; 37: 564-567.

Rowe RC, McMahon J. Cryogenic scanning electron microscopy - a novel method for the structural characterisation of semi-solid creams. Int Pharm J 1987; 1: 91-93.

22. Authors

USA: FH Merkle.

Cetrimide

1. Nonproprietary Names
BP: Cetrimide
PhEur: Cetrimidum

2. Synonyms
Bromat; Cetab; Cetavlon; Cetraol; Lissolamine V; Micol; Morpan CHSA; Morphans; Quammonium; Sucticide.

3. Chemical Name and CAS Registry Number
Cetrimide [8044-71-1]
Note that the above name, CAS registry number and synonyms refer to the PhEur 1989 (BP 1993) material which although it consists predominantly of trimethyltetradecylammonium bromide may also contain other bromides, *see* Section 4.
There is some confusion in the literature with the synonyms, CAS registry number and molecular weight applied to cetrimide. It is most common to find the molecular weight and CAS registry number of trimethyltetradecylammonium bromide used since it is the principal component of cetrimide. It should be noted however, that in the original BP 1953 material the principal component of cetrimide was hexadecyltrimethylammonium bromide.
The CAS registry number for hexadecyltrimethylammonium hydroxide [505-86-2] has also been widely applied to cetrimide. *See* Section 18 for further information.

4. Empirical Formula   Molecular Weight
Cetrimide consists mainly of trimethyltetradecylammonium bromide ($C_{17}H_{38}BrN$) and may contain smaller amounts of dodecyltrimethylammonium bromide ($C_{15}H_{34}BrN$) and hexadecyltrimethylammonium bromide ($C_{19}H_{42}BrN$).
$C_{17}H_{38}BrN$ 336.40
See also Section 18.

5. Structural Formula

$$H_3C\text{---}(CH_2)_n\text{---}N^+\text{---}CH_3Br^-$$
with CH_3 groups above and below the N^+.

Where,
n = 11 for dodecyltrimethylammonium bromide,
n = 13 for trimethyltetradecylammonium bromide,
n = 15 for hexadecyltrimethylammonium bromide.

6. Functional Category
Antimicrobial preservative; antiseptic; cationic surfactant; disinfectant.

7. Applications in Pharmaceutical Formulation or Technology
Cetrimide is a quaternary ammonium compound that is used in cosmetics and pharmaceutical formulations as an antimicrobial preservative, *see* Section 10. It may also be used as a cationic surfactant.[1] In eye-drops, it is used as a preservative at a concentration of 0.005% w/v.

Therapeutically cetrimide is used in relatively high concentrations, generally 0.1-1.0% w/v aqueous solutions, as a topical antiseptic for skin, burns and wounds. Solutions containing 1-3% w/v cetrimide are used as shampoos to remove the scales in seborrhea.
Cetrimide is also used as a cleanser and disinfectant for hard contact lenses although it should not be used on soft lenses; as an ingredient of cetrimide emulsifying wax and in o/w creams, e.g. cetrimide cream.

8. Description
Cetrimide is a white to creamy white, free-flowing powder, with a faint but characteristic odor and a bitter, soapy taste.

9. Pharmacopeial Specifications

Test	PhEur 1989
Identification	+
Acidity or alkalinity	+
Appearance of solution	+
Amines and amine salts	+
Loss on drying	⩽ 2.0%
Sulfated ash	⩽ 0.5%
Assay (as $C_{17}H_{38}BrN$, dried basis)	96.0-101.0%

10. Typical Properties
Acidity/alkalinity:
pH = 5-7.5 (1% w/v aqueous solution)
Antimicrobial activity: cetrimide has good bactericidal activity against Gram-positive species but is less active against Gram-negative species. *Pseudomonas* species, particularly *Pseudomonas aeruginosa*, may exhibit resistance. Cetrimide is most effective at neutral or slightly alkaline pH values with activity appreciably reduced in acidic media and in the presence of organic matter. However, activity is enhanced in the presence of alcohols. Cetrimide has variable antifungal activity, is effective against some viruses, and inactive against bacterial spores. Typical minimum inhibitory concentrations (MICs) are shown below:

Microorganism	MIC (μg/mL)
Escherichia coli	30
Pseudomonas aeruginosa	300
Staphylococcus aureus	10

Critical micelle concentration: ≈ 0.01%
Hygroscopicity: at 40-50% relative humidity and 20°C, cetrimide absorbs sufficient moisture to cause caking and retard flow properties.
Melting point: 232-247°C
Partition coefficients:
Liquid paraffin: water = < 1;
Vegetable oil: water = < 1.
Solubility: freely soluble in chloroform, ethanol (95%) and water; practically insoluble in ether.

11. Stability and Storage Conditions
Cetrimide is chemically stable in the dry state and in aqueous solution at ambient temperatures. Aqueous solutions may be sterilized by autoclaving. Water containing metal ions and organic matter may reduce the antimicrobial activity of cetrimide.

The bulk material should be stored in a well-closed container in a cool, dry, place.

12. Incompatibilities

Incompatible with soaps, anionic surfactants, high concentrations of nonionic surfactants, bentonite, iodine, phenylmercuric nitrate, alkali hydroxides and acid dyes. Aqueous solutions react with metals.

13. Method of Manufacture

Cetrimide is prepared by the condensation of suitable alkyl bromides and trimethylamine.

14. Safety

Most adverse effects reported relate to the therapeutic use of cetrimide. If ingested orally, cetrimide and other quaternary ammonium compounds can cause nausea, vomiting, muscle paralysis, CNS depression and hypotension; concentrated solutions may cause esophageal damage and necrosis. The fatal oral human dose is estimated to be 1-3 g.[2]

At the concentrations used topically, solutions do not generally cause irritation although concentrated solutions have occasionally been reported to cause burns. Cases of hypersensitivity have been reported following repeated application.[3]

Adverse effects which have been reported following irrigation of wounds with cetrimide solution include chemical peritonitis,[4] methemoglobinemia with cyanosis[5] and metabolic disorders.[6]

15. Handling Precautions

Observe normal precautions appropriate to the circumstances and quantity of material handled. Cetrimide powder, and concentrated cetrimide solutions are irritant; avoid inhalation, ingestion, skin and eye contact. Eye protection, gloves and a respirator are recommended.[7]

16. Regulatory Status

Included in nonparenteral medicines licensed in the UK.

17. Pharmacopeias

Aust, Br, Braz, Egypt, Eur, Fr, Ger, Gr, Ind, It, Neth, Port, Swiss, Turk, and Yug. Also in BP Vet.

18. Related Substances

Dodecyltrimethylammonium bromide; hexadecyltrimethylammonium bromide; trimethyltetradecylammonium bromide.

Dodecyltrimethylammonium bromide: $C_{15}H_{34}BrN$
Molecular weight: 308.35
CAS number: [1119-94-4]
Synonyms: DTAB; *N*-lauryl-*N*,*N*,*N*-trimethylammonium bromide; *N*,*N*,*N*- trimethyldodecylammonium bromide.

Hexadecyltrimethylammonium bromide: $C_{19}H_{42}BrN$
Molecular weight: 364.48
CAS number: [57-09-0]
Synonyms: cetrimide BP 1953; cetrimonium bromide; cetyltrimethylammonium bromide; CTAB; *N*,*N*,*N*-trimethylhexadecylammonium bromide.
Appearance: a white to creamy-white, voluminous, free-flowing powder, with a characteristic faint odor and bitter, soapy taste.
Melting point: 237-243°C

Safety: LD_{50} (guinea pig, SC): 100 mg/kg[8]
LD_{50} (mouse, IP): 106 mg/kg
LD_{50} (mouse, IV): 32 mg/kg
LD_{50} (rabbit, IP): 125 mg/kg
LD_{50} (rabbit, SC): 125 mg/kg
LD_{50} (rat, IV): 44 mg/kg
LD_{50} (rat, oral): 410 mg/kg
Solubility: freely soluble in ethanol (95%); soluble 1 in 10 parts of water.
Comments: the original cetrimide BP 1953 consisted largely of hexadecyltrimethylammonium bromide, with smaller amounts of analogous alkyltrimethylammonium bromides. It contained a considerable proportion of inorganic salts, chiefly sodium bromide, and was less soluble than the present product.

Trimethyltetradecylammonium bromide: $C_{17}H_{38}BrN$
Molecular weight: 336.40
CAS number: [1119-97-7]
Synonyms: cetrimide BP 1993; myristyltrimethylammonium bromide; tetradecyltrimethylammonium bromide; *N*,*N*,*N*-trimethyl-1-tetradecanaminium bromide.

19. Comments

As a precaution against contamination with *Pseudomonas* species resistant to cetrimide, stock solutions may be further protected by adding at least 7% v/v ethanol or 4% v/v propan-2-ol.

20. Specific References

1. Ford JL, et al. Hydroxypropylmethylcellulose matrix tablets containing propranolol hydrochloride and sodium dodecyl sulphate. Int J Pharmaceutics 1991; 71: 213-221.
2. Arena JM. Poisonings and other health hazards associated with the use of detergents. JAMA 1964; 190: 56-58.
3. Weiner M, Bernstein IL. Adverse reactions to drug formulation agents: a handbook of excipients. New York: Marcel Dekker, 1989.
4. Gilchrist DS. Chemical peritonitis after cetrimide washout in hydatid-cyst surgery [letter]. Lancet 1979; ii: 1374.
5. Baraka A, Yamut F, Wakid N. Cetrimide-induced methaemoglobinaemia after surgical excision of hydatid cyst [letter]. Lancet 1980; ii: 88-89.
6. Momblano P, Pradere B, Jarrige N, Concina D, Bloom E. Metabolic acidosis induced by cetrimonium bromide [letter]. Lancet 1984; ii: 1045.
7. Jacobs JY. Work hazards from drug handling. Pharm J 1984; 233: 195-196.
8. Sweet DV, editor. Registry of toxic effects of chemical substances. Cincinnati: US Department of Health, 1987.

21. General References

August PJ. Cutaneous necrosis due to cetrimide application. Br Med J 1975; 1: 70.
Eccleston GM. Phase transitions in ternary systems and oil-in-water emulsions containing cetrimide and fatty alcohols. Int J Pharmaceutics 1985; 27: 311-323.
Evans BK, Harding KG, Marks J, Ribeiro CD. The disinfection of silicone-foam dressings. J Clin Hosp Pharm 1985; 10: 289-295.
Louden JD, Rowe RC. A quantitative examination of the structure of emulsions prepared using cetostearyl alcohol and cetrimide using Fourier transform infrared microscopy. Int J Pharmaceutics 1990; 63: 219-225.
Rowe RC, Patel HK. The effect of temperature on the conductivity of gels and emulsions prepared from cetrimide and cetostearyl alcohol. J Pharm Pharmacol 1985; 37: 564-567.

Smith ARW, Lambert PA, Hammond SM, Jessup C. The differing effects of cetyltrimethylammonium bromide and cetrimide BP upon growing cultures of *Escherichia coli* NCIB 8277. J Appl Bacteriol 1975; 38: 143-149.

22. Authors

UK: MC Allwood, R Baird.

Cetyl Alcohol

1. Nonproprietary Names

BP: Cetyl alcohol
PhEur: Alcohol cetylicus
USPNF: Cetyl alcohol

2. Synonyms

Crodacol C70; *Crodacol C90*; *Crodacol C95*; ethal; ethol; 1-hexadecanol; *n*-hexadecyl alcohol; palmityl alcohol.

3. Chemical Name and CAS Registry Number

Hexadecan-1-ol [36653-82-4]

4. Empirical Formula   Molecular Weight

$C_{16}H_{34}O$ 242.44
                             (for pure material)

Cetyl alcohol, used in pharmaceutical formulations, is a mixture of solid aliphatic alcohols consisting chiefly of hexadecan-1-ol, $C_{16}H_{34}O$. The USPNF XVII specifies a maximum of 10% of other alcohols.
Commercially, many grades of cetyl alcohol are available which usually contain 60-70% cetyl alcohol and 20-30% stearyl alcohol, the remainder being related alcohols.

5. Structural Formula

$CH_3(CH_2)_{14}CH_2OH$

6. Functional Category

Coating agent; emulsifying agent; stiffening agent.

7. Applications in Pharmaceutical Formulation or Technology

Cetyl alcohol is widely used in pharmaceuticals and cosmetics.
In pharmaceutical formulations it is used in the preparation of suppositories, delayed-release solid dosage forms, emulsions, lotions, creams and ointments.
In suppositories, cetyl alcohol is used to raise the melting point of the suppository base whilst in delayed-release solid dosage forms, cetyl alcohol may be used to form a permeable barrier coating.
In lotions, creams and ointments, cetyl alcohol is used because of its emollient, water absorptive and emulsifying properties. It enhances stability, improves texture and increases consistency. The emollient properties are due to cetyl alcohol being absorbed and retained by the epidermis, where it lubricates and softens the skin while imparting a characteristic 'velvety' texture.
Cetyl alcohol is also used for its water absorption properties in water-in-oil emulsions. A mixture of 19 parts petrolatum and 1 part cetyl alcohol will, for example, absorb 40-50% of its weight of water.
Cetyl alcohol is a weak emulsifier of the water-in-oil type and this allows the quantity of other emulsifying agents used in a water-in-oil formulation to be reduced. Cetyl alcohol also increases the consistency of water-in-oil emulsions.
In oil-in-water emulsions cetyl alcohol improves stability by combining with the water-soluble emulsifying agent. The combined, mixed emulsifier produces a close packed, mono-molecular barrier at the oil-globule water interface which forms a mechanical barrier against droplet coalescence.
In semisolid emulsions, excess cetyl alcohol combines with the aqueous emulsifier solution to form a viscoelastic continuous phase. This imparts semisolid properties to the emulsions and also prevents droplet coalescence. Thus, cetyl alcohol is often referred to as a 'consistency improver' or a 'bodying agent', although it may be necessary for the cetyl alcohol to be coupled with a hydrophilic emulsifier to impart this property. It should be noted that pure or pharmacopeial grades of cetyl alcohol may not form stable semisolid emulsions and may not show the same physical properties as grades of cetyl alcohol which contain significant amounts of other similar alcohols.
See Section 4.

Use	Concentration (%)
Emollient	2-5
Emulsifying agent	2-5
Stiffening agent	2-10
Water absorption	5

8. Description

Cetyl alcohol occurs as waxy, white flakes, granules, cubes or castings. It has a faint characteristic odor and bland taste.

9. Pharmacopeial Specifications

Test	PhEur 1987	USPNF XVII (Suppl 4)
Identification	+	+
Melting range	46-52°C	—
Acid value	⩽ 1.0	⩽ 2.0
Iodine value	⩽ 2.0	⩽ 5.0
Hydroxyl value	218-238	218-238
Saponification value	⩽ 2.0	—
Clarity and color of solution	+	—
Assay	—	⩾ 90.0%

SEM: 1

Excipient: Cetyl alcohol, C-50
Manufacturer: RW Greeff & Co Inc
Magnification: 60x
Voltage: 10 kV

SEM: 2

Excipient: Cetyl alcohol, C-50
Manufacturer: RW Greeff & Co Inc
Magnification: 600x
Voltage: 10 kV

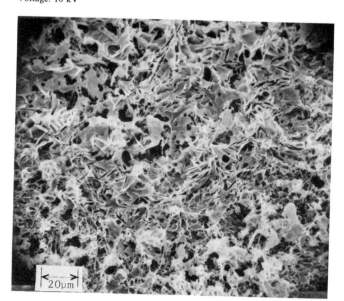

SEM: 4

Excipient: Cetyl alcohol USPNF
Manufacturer: Amend Drug & Chemical Co
Lot No.: B11030F09
Magnification: 600x
Voltage: 10 kV

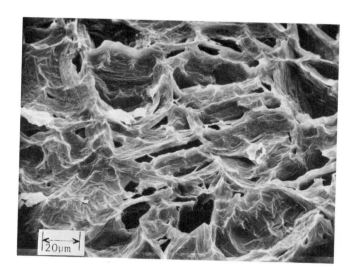

SEM: 3

Excipient: Cetyl alcohol USPNF
Manufacturer: Amend Drug & Chemical Co
Lot No.: B11030F09
Magnification: 60x
Voltage: 10 kV

SEM: 5

Excipient: Cetyl alcohol USPNF
Manufacturer: Aceto Corp
Magnification: 60x
Voltage: 10 kV

SEM: 6

Excipient: Cetyl alcohol USPNF
Manufacturer: Aceto Corp
Magnification: 600x
Voltage: 10 kV

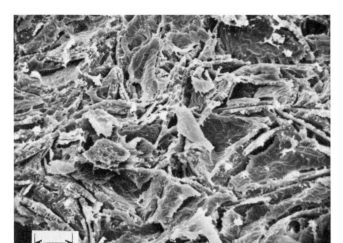

SEM: 8

Excipient: Cetyl alcohol USPNF
Manufacturer: Fallek Chemical Corp
Magnification: 600x
Voltage: 10 kV

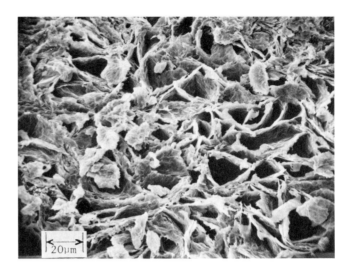

SEM: 7

Excipient: Cetyl alcohol USPNF
Manufacturer: Fallek Chemical Corp
Magnification: 60x
Voltage: 10 kV

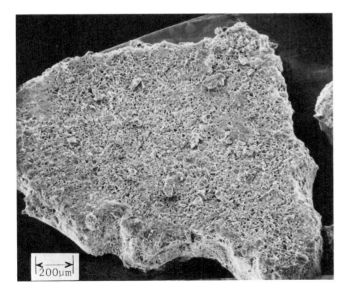

SEM: 9

Excipient: Cetyl alcohol
Manufacturer: Robinson-Wagner Co
Lot No.: 9153
Magnification: 60x
Voltage: 10 kV

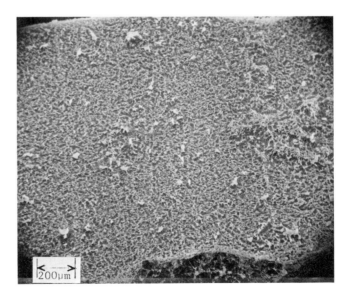

SEM: 10

Excipient: Cetyl alcohol
Manufacturer: Robinson-Wagner Co
Lot No.: 9153
Magnification: 600x
Voltage: 10 kV

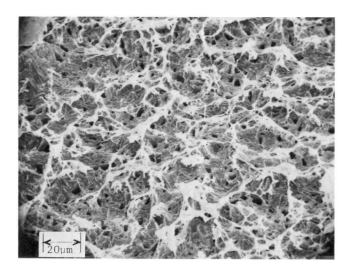

SEM: 12

Excipient: Cetyl alcohol (*Crodacol C95*)
Manufacturer: Croda Inc
Lot No.: 48020
Magnification: 600x
Voltage: 10 k

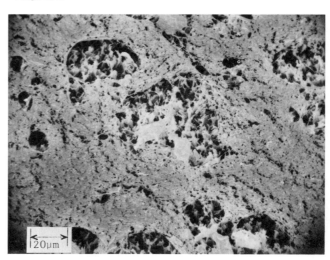

SEM: 11

Excipient: Cetyl alcohol (*Crodacol C95*)
Manufacturer: Croda Inc
Lot No.: 48020
Magnification: 60x
Voltage: 10 kV

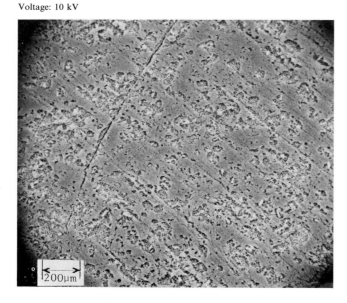

10. Typical Properties

Boiling point:
316-344°C;
344°C for pure material.
Density: 0.811-0.830 g/cm^3
Melting point:
45-52°C;
49°C for pure material.
Solubility: freely soluble in ethanol (95%) and ether, solubility increasing with increasing temperature; practically insoluble in water. Miscible when melted with fats, liquid and solid paraffins, and isopropyl myristate. *See also* HPE Data.
Refractive index:
n_D^{79} = 1.4283 for pure material.

HPE Laboratory Project Data			
	Method	**Lab #**	**Results**
Density	DE-1	7	0.907 ± 0.005 g/cm^3
Solubility			
Ethanol (95%)	SOL-7	32	208 mg/mL
Hexane	SOL-7	32	76 mg/mL
Propylene glycol	SOL-7	32	< 0.2 mg/mL
Water	SOL-7	32	< 10 mg/mL

Supplier: American Cyanamid.

11. Stability and Storage Conditions

Cetyl alcohol is stable in the presence of acids, alkalis, light and air; it does not become rancid.

Cetyl alcohol should be stored in a well-closed container in a cool, dry, place.

12. Incompatibilities

Incompatible with strong oxidizing agents.

13. Method of Manufacture

Cetyl alcohol may be manufactured by a number of methods such as esterification and hydrogenolysis of fatty acids or by catalytic hydrogenation of the triglycerides obtained from coconut oil or tallow. Cetyl alcohol may be purified by crystallization and distillation.

14. Safety

Cetyl alcohol is mainly used in topical pharmaceutical formulations although it has also been used in oral, rectal and other preparations, *see* Sections 7 and 16.

Cetyl alcohol has been associated with allergic delayed-type hypersensitivity reactions in patients with stasis dermatitis.[1] Cross sensitization with cetostearyl alcohol, lanolin and stearyl alcohol have also been reported.[2,3] It has been suggested that hypersensitivity may be caused by impurities in commercial grades of cetyl alcohol since in tests highly refined cetyl alcohol (99.5%) has not been associated with hypersensitivity reactions.[4]

LD_{50} (mouse, IP): 1.6 g/kg[5]
LD_{50} (mouse, oral): 3.2 g/kg
LD_{50} (rat, IP): 1.6 g/kg
LD_{50} (rat, oral): 6.4 g/kg

15. Handling Precautions

Observe normal precautions appropriate to the circumstances and quantity of material handled. Eye protection and gloves are recommended.

16. Regulatory Status

Included in the FDA Inactive Ingredients Guide (ophthalmic preparations, oral capsules and tablets, otic and rectal preparations, topical aerosols, creams, emulsions, ointments and solutions, and vaginal preparations). Included in non-parenteral medicines licensed in the UK.

17. Pharmacopeias

Aust, Br, Cz, Eur, Fr, Ger, It, Jpn, Mex, Neth, Nord, Swiss, USPNF and Yug.

18. Related Substances

Cetostearyl Alcohol; Stearyl Alcohol

19. Comments

—

20. Specific References

1. Smolinske SC. Handbook of food, drug and cosmetic excipients. Boca Raton, FL: CRC Press Inc, 1992: 75-77.
2. van Ketel WG, Wemer J. Allergy to lanolin and 'lanolin-free' creams. Contact Dermatitis 1983; 9(5): 420.
3. Degreef H, Dooms-Goossens A. Patch testing with silver sulfadiazine cream. Contact Dermatitis 1985; 12: 33-37.
4. Hannuksela M, Salo H. The repeated open application test (ROAT). Contact Dermatitis 1986; 14(4): 221-227.
5. Sweet DV, editor. Registry of toxic effects of chemical substances. Cincinnati: US Department of Health, 1987.

21. General References

Eccleston GM. Properties of fatty alcohol mixed emulsifiers and emulsifying waxes. In: Florence AT, editor. Materials used in pharmaceutical formulation: critical reports on applied chemistry, volume 6. Oxford: Blackwell Scientific Publications, 1984: 124-156.
Mapstone GE. Crystallization of cetyl alcohol from cosmetic emulsions. Cosmet Perfum 1974; 89(11): 31-33.

22. Authors

USA: HM Unvala.

Cetyl Esters Wax

1. Nonproprietary Names
USPNF: Cetyl esters wax

2. Synonyms
Crodamol SS; *Protachem MST*; *Ritachol SS*; spermaceti wax replacement; *Spermwax*; synthetic spermaceti.

3. Chemical Name and CAS Registry Number
Cetyl esters wax [977067-67-6]

4. Empirical Formula   Molecular Weight
$C_nH_{2n}O_2$ $\approx$ 470-490

Where n = 26-38.

The USPNF XVII describes cetyl esters wax as a mixture consisting primarily of esters of saturated fatty alcohols (C_{14}-C_{18}) and saturated fatty acids (C_{14}-C_{18}).

5. Structural Formula
See Section 4.

6. Functional Category
Emollient; stiffening agent.

7. Applications in Pharmaceutical Formulation or Technology
Cetyl esters wax is a stiffening agent and emollient used in creams and ointments as a replacement for naturally occurring spermaceti.

The physical properties of cetyl esters wax vary greatly from manufacturer to manufacturer due to differences between the mixtures of fatty acids and fatty alcohol esters that are used. Differences between products appear most obviously in the melting point which can range from 43-47°C (USPNF XVII range) to 51-55°C, depending on the mixture. Materials with a high melting point tend to contain predominantly cetyl and stearyl palmitates.

Use	Concentration (%)
Cold cream	12.5
Rose water ointment	12.5
Spermaceti ointment	20
Topical creams and ointments	1-15

8. Description
Cetyl esters wax occurs as white to off-white, somewhat translucent flakes (typically in the range of 5 μm to several millimeters in the largest dimension), having a crystalline structure and a pearly luster when caked. It has a faint, aromatic odor and a bland, mild taste.

9. Pharmacopeial Specifications

Test	USPNF XVII
Melting range	43-47°C
Acid value	$\leqslant$ 5
Iodine value	$\leqslant$ 1
Saponification value	109-120
Paraffin and free acids	+

10. Typical Properties
Solubility: high melting materials tend to be less soluble, *see also* HPE Data.

Solvent	Solubility at 20°C
Chloroform	soluble
Ethanol (95%)	practically insoluble
Fixed and volatile oils	soluble
Water	practically insoluble

Specific gravity: 0.820-0.840 at 50°C

HPE Laboratory Project Data	
	Results
Solubility*	
Acetone	2-3 mg/mL
Chloroform	400-500 mg/mL
Dichloromethane	300-400 mg/mL
Ethanol	0.6-1.2 mg/mL
Ethanol (95%)	< 0.1 mg/mL
Ethanol (95%) at 78°C	> 400 mg/mL
Ethyl acetate	12-15 mg/mL
Hexane	125-150 mg/mL
Mineral oil	14-22 mg/mL
Water	< 0.01 mg/mL

* Measured on a range of representative products from various manufacturers.

11. Stability and Storage Conditions
Store in a well-closed container in a cool, dry, place. Avoid exposure to excessive heat (over 40°C).

12. Incompatibilities
Incompatible with strong acids or bases.

13. Method of Manufacture
Cetyl esters wax is prepared by the direct esterification of the appropriate mixtures of fatty alcohols and fatty acids.

14. Safety
Cetyl esters wax is an innocuous material generally regarded as essentially nontoxic and nonirritant.

LD_{50} (rat, oral): > 16 g/kg

15. Handling Precautions
Observe normal precautions appropriate to the circumstances and quantity of material handled.

16. Regulatory Status

Included in the FDA Inactive Ingredients Guide (topical preparations). Included in nonparenteral medicines licensed in the UK.

17. Pharmacopeias

USPNF.

18. Related Substances

Spermaceti wax.

Spermaceti wax

CAS number: [8002-23-1]

Appearance: spermaceti is a waxy substance obtained from the head of the sperm whale. It consists of a mixture of the cetyl esters of fatty acids (C_{12}-C_{18}) with cetyl laurate, cetyl myristate, cetyl palmitate and cetyl stearate comprising at least 85% of the total esters. It occurs as white, translucent, slightly unctuous masses with a faint odor and mild, bland taste.

Iodine value: 3.0-4.4

Melting point: 44-52°C

Refractive index: $n_D^{80} = 1.4330$

Saponification value: 120-136

Solubility: soluble in chloroform, boiling ethanol (95%), ether and fixed or volatile oils; practically insoluble in ethanol (95%) and water.

Specific gravity: 0.938-0.944

19. Comments

In the interests of whale conservation, natural spermaceti wax has largely been superseded in pharmaceutical and cosmetics formulation by the synthetic material, cetyl esters wax.

20. Specific References

—

21. General References

Egan RR, Portwood O. Higher alcohols in skin lotions. Cosmet Perfum 1974; 89(3): 39-42.

Holloway PJ. The chromatographic analysis of spermaceti. J Pharm Pharmacol 1968; 20: 775-779.

Spencer GF, Kleiman R. Detection of spermaceti in a hand cream. J Am Oil Chem Soc 1978; 55: 837-838.

22. Authors

UK: PJ Weller.

Chlorhexidine

1. Nonproprietary Names

BAN: Chlorhexidine
INN: Chlorhexidine
Note that chlorhexidine is usually encountered as the acetate, gluconate or hydrochloride salt, and a number of pharmacopeias contain monographs for such materials.
See Sections 9, 17 and 18.

2. Synonyms

1,6-Bis[N'-(p-chlorophenyl)-N^5-biguanido] hexane; N,N''-bis(4-chlorophenyl)-3,12-diimino-2,4,11,13-tetraazatetradecanediimidamide; 1,6-di(4'-chlorophenyldiguanido) hexane.

3. Chemical Names and CAS Registry Number

1,1'-Hexamethylenebis[5-(4-chlorophenyl)biguanide]
[55-56-1]

4. Empirical Formula   Molecular Weight

$C_{22}H_{30}Cl_2N_{10}$ 505.48

5. Structural Formula

6. Functional Category

Antimicrobial preservative; antiseptic.

7. Applications in Pharmaceutical Formulation or Technology

Chlorhexidine salts are widely used in pharmaceutical formulations in Europe for their antimicrobial properties. Although mainly used as disinfectants, chlorhexidine salts are also used as antimicrobial preservatives.
As excipients, chlorhexidine salts are mainly used for the preservation of eye-drops at a concentration of 0.01% w/v; generally the acetate or gluconate salt is used for this purpose. Solutions containing between 0.002-0.006% w/v chlorhexidine gluconate have also been used for the disinfection of hydrophilic contact lenses.
For skin disinfection, chlorhexidine has been formulated as a 0.5% w/v solution in 70% v/v ethanol and in conjunction with detergents, as a 4% w/v surgical scrub. Chlorhexidine salts may also be used in topical antiseptic creams, mouthwashes, dental gels, and in urology for catheter sterilization and bladder irrigation.
Chlorhexidine salts have additionally been used as constituents of medicated dressings, dusting powders, sprays and creams.

8. Description

Chlorhexidine occurs as an odorless, bitter tasting, white crystalline powder. *See* Section 18 for information on chlorhexidine salts.

SEM: 1
Excipient: Chlorhexidine
Manufacturer: SST Corp
Magnification: 600x

SEM: 2
Excipient: Chlorhexidine
Manufacturer: SST Corp
Magnification: 2400X

9. Pharmacopeial Specifications

Test	PhEur 1990
Identification	+
Acidity or alkalinity	
Chlorhexidine acetate	—
Chlorhexidine gluconate solution	5.5-7.0
Chlorhexidine hydrochloride	—
Relative density	
Chlorhexidine acetate	—
Chlorhexidine gluconate solution	1.06-1.07
Chlorhexidine hydrochloride	—
4-Chloroaniline	$\leqslant$ 500 ppm
Related substances	+
Loss on drying	
Chlorhexidine acetate	$\leqslant$ 3.5%
Chlorhexidine gluconate solution	—
Chlorhexidine hydrochloride	$\leqslant$ 1.0%
Sulfated ash	
Chlorhexidine acetate	$\leqslant$ 0.15%
Chlorhexidine gluconate solution	—
Chlorhexidine hydrochloride	$\leqslant$ 0.1%
Assay	
Chlorhexidine acetate	98.0-101.0%
Chlorhexidine gluconate solution	19.0-21.0%
Chlorhexidine hydrochloride	98.0-101.0%

See also Sections 17 and 18.

10. Typical Properties

Antimicrobial activity: chlorhexidine and its salts exhibit antimicrobial activity against Gram-positive and Gram-negative microorganisms.[1] At the low concentrations normally used for preservation and antisepsis chlorhexidine salts are rapidly bactericidal. However, species of *Proteus* and *Pseudomonas* are less susceptible to chlorhexidine, which is also inactive against acid-fast bacilli, bacterial spores and some fungi. Chlorhexidine salts are effective against some lipophilic viruses such as: adenovirus; herpes virus and influenza virus. Optimum antimicrobial activity occurs at pH 5-7. Above pH 8, the chlorhexidine base may precipitate from aqueous solutions.

Bacteria (Gram-positive): chlorhexidine salts are active against most species; the minimum inhibitory concentration (MIC) is normally in the range of 1-10 μg/mL, although much higher concentrations are necessary for *Streptococcus faecalis*. Typical MIC values are shown below:

Microorganism	MIC (μg/mL)
Bacillus spp.	1.0-3
Clostridium spp.	1.8-70
Corynebacterium spp.	5.0-10
Staphylococcus spp.	0.5-6
Streptococcus faecalis	2000-5000
Streptococcus spp.	0.1-7

Bacteria (Gram-negative): chlorhexidine salts are less active against Gram-negative species than against Gram-positive species. Typical MICs are 1-15 μg/mL, but pseudomonads, particularly *Pseudomonas aeruginosa*, may be more resistant. *Serratia marcescens* may also be resistant. Combinations of chlorhexidine acetate with the following substances have shown enhanced or more than additive activity towards *Pseudomonas aeruginosa*: benzalkonium chloride; benzyl alcohol; bronopol; edetic acid; phenylethanol and phenylpropanol.[2,3] Typical MIC values are shown below:

Microorganism	MIC (μg/mL)
Escherichia coli	2.5-7.5
Klebsiella spp.	1.5-12.5
Proteus spp.	3-100
Pseudomonas spp.	3-60
Serratia marcescens	3-75
Salmonella spp.	1.6-15

Fungi: chlorhexidine salts are slowly active against molds and yeasts although they are generally less potent in their inhibitory activity against fungi than against bacteria. Typical MIC values are shown below:

Microorganism	MIC (μg/mL)
Aspergillus spp.	75-500
Candida albicans	7-15
Microsporum spp.	12-18
Penicillium spp.	150-200
Saccharomyces spp.	50-125
Trichophyton spp.	2.5-14

Spores: chlorhexidine salts are inactive against spores at normal room temperature.[4] At 98-100°C there is some activity against mesophilic spores.

Critical micelle concentration: $\approx$ 0.6% w/v (depends on other ions in solution).[5]

Melting point: 132-134°C

See also Section 18 for additional information.

11. Stability and Storage Conditions

Chlorhexidine and its salts, in the powdered form, are stable at normal storage temperatures. However, chlorhexidine hydrochloride is hygroscopic, absorbing significant amounts of moisture at temperatures up to 37°C and relative humidities up to 80%.

Heating to 150°C will cause decomposition of chlorhexidine and its salts, yielding trace amounts of 4-chloroaniline. However, chlorhexidine hydrochloride is more thermostable than the acetate and can be heated at 115°C for one hour without appreciable formation of 4-chloroaniline.

In aqueous solution, chlorhexidine salts may undergo hydrolysis to form 4-chloroaniline. Following autoclaving of a 0.02% w/v chlorhexidine gluconate solution at pH 9, for 30 minutes at 120°C, it was found that 1.56% w/w of the original chlorhexidine content had been converted into 4-chloroaniline; for solutions at pH 6.3 and 4.7 the 4-chloroaniline content was 0.27% w/w and 0.13% w/w of the original gluconate content respectively.[6] In buffered 0.05% w/v chlorhexidine acetate solutions, maximum stability occurs at pH 5.6.

When chlorhexidine solutions were autoclaved at various time and temperature combinations, the rate of hydrolysis increased markedly above 100°C and as pH increased or decreased from pH 5.6. At a given pH, chlorhexidine gluconate produced more 4-chloroaniline than did the acetate.

It was predicted that in an autoclaved solution containing 0.01% w/v chlorhexidine, the amount of 4-chloroaniline formed would be about 0.00003%. At these low concentrations there would be little likelihood of any toxic hazard as a result of the increase in 4-chloroaniline content in the autoclaved solution.

Chlorhexidine solutions and aqueous based products may be packaged in glass and high-density polyethylene or polypropylene bottles provided that they are protected from light. If not protected from light, chlorhexidine solutions containing 4-chloroaniline discolor due to polymerization of the 4-chloroaniline.[7-9]

Cork-based closures or liners should not be used in packaging in contact with chlorhexidine solutions.

As a precaution against contamination with *Pseudomonas* species resistant to chlorhexidine, stock solutions may be protected by the inclusion of 7% w/v ethanol or 4% w/v propan-2-ol.

Chlorhexidine salts, and their solutions, should be stored in well-closed containers, protected from light, in a cool, dry, place.

12. Incompatibilities

Chlorhexidine salts are cationic in solution and are therefore incompatible with soaps and other anionic species. Chlorhexidine salts are compatible with most cationic and nonionic surfactants, but in high concentrations of surfactant, chlorhexidine activity can be substantially reduced due to micellar binding.

Chlorhexidine salts of low aqueous solubility are formed and may precipitate from chlorhexidine solutions greater than 0.05% w/v concentration, when in the presence of inorganic acids, certain organic acids and salts, e.g. benzoates, bicarbonates, borates, carbonates, chlorides, citrates, iodides, nitrates, phosphates and sulfates.[10] At chlorhexidine concentrations below 0.01% w/v, precipitation is less likely to occur. In hard water, insoluble salts may form due to interaction with calcium and magnesium cations. Solubility may be enhanced by the inclusion of surfactants, such as cetrimide.

Other substances incompatible with chlorhexidine salts include viscous materials, such as: acacia; sodium alginate; sodium carboxymethylcellulose; starch and tragacanth.[11,12] Also incompatible are brilliant green, chloramphenicol, copper sulfate, fluorescein sodium, formaldehyde, silver nitrate and zinc sulfate.

Interaction has been reported between chlorhexidine gluconate and the hydrogel poly(2-hydroxyethyl methacrylate), which is a component of some hydrophilic contact lenses.[13,14]

13. Method of Manufacture

Chlorhexidine may be prepared by condensation of either polymethylene bisdicyandiamide with 4-chloroaniline hydrochloride or by condensation of 4-chlorophenyl dicyandiamine with hexamethylenediamine dihydrochloride. Chlorhexidine may also be synthesized from a series of biguanides.[15]

14. Safety

Chlorhexidine and its salts are widely used, primarily as topical disinfectants. As excipients, chlorhexidine salts are mainly used as antimicrobial preservatives in ophthalmic formulations.

Animal studies suggest that the acute oral toxicity of chlorhexidine is low, with little or no absorption from the gastrointestinal tract. However, although humans have consumed up to 2 g of chlorhexidine daily, for one week, without untoward symptoms, chlorhexidine is not generally used as an excipient in oral formulations. Recent reports have suggested that there may be some systemic effects, in humans, following oral consumption of chlorhexidine.[16-18] Similarly, the topical application of chlorhexidine or its salts, produced

evidence of very slight percutaneous absorption of chlorhexidine although the concentrations absorbed were insufficient to produce systemic adverse effects.[19]

Hypersensitivity to chlorhexidine used topically has been reported[20-22] although such instances are rare given the extensive use of chlorhexidine and it salts.

In ophthalmic preparations, irritation to the conjunctiva occurs with chlorhexidine solutions stronger than 0.1% w/v concentration. Accidental eye contact with 4% w/v chlorhexidine gluconate solution may result in corneal damage.[23]

The aqueous concentration of chlorhexidine normally recommended for contact with mucous surfaces is 0.05% w/v. At this concentration, there is no irritant effect on soft tissues, nor is healing delayed. The gluconate salt (1% w/v) is frequently used in creams, lotions and disinfectant solutions.

Direct instillation of chlorhexidine into the middle ear can result in ototoxicity[24] and when used in dental preparations, staining of teeth and oral lesions may occur.[25,26]

Chlorhexidine is extremely dangerous to use on the brain or meninges.

LD$_{50}$ (mouse, IV): 0.02 g/kg[27]
LD$_{50}$ (mouse, oral): 9.85 g/kg
LD$_{50}$ (mouse, SC): 0.63 g/kg
LD$_{50}$ (rat, IV): 0.02 g/kg
LD$_{50}$ (rat, oral): 9.2 g/kg

15. Handling Precautions

Observe normal precautions appropriate to the circumstances and quantity of material handled. The dust of chlorhexidine and its salts may be irritant to the skin, eyes and respiratory tract. Gloves, eye protection and a respirator are recommended.

16. Regulatory Status

Chlorhexidine salts are included in nonparenteral and parenteral medicines licensed in the UK.

17. Pharmacopeias

Specifications for chlorhexidine acetate, chlorhexidine gluconate solution and chlorhexidine hydrochloride are contained in certain pharmacopeias. *See* Sections 9 and 18.

18. Related Substances

Chlorhexidine acetate; chlorhexidine gluconate; chlorhexidine hydrochloride.

Chlorhexidine acetate: $C_{22}H_{30}Cl_2N_{10}.2C_2H_4O_2$
Molecular weight: 625.64
CAS number: [56-95-1]
Synonyms: chlorhexidini acetas; chlorhexidine diacetate; 1,1'-hexamethylenebis[5-(4-chlorophenyl)biguanide] diacetate; *Hibitane diacetate.*
Appearance: a white or almost white-colored, microcrystalline powder.
Pharmacopeias: Br, Chin, Eur, Ger, Int, Neth and Swiss. Also in BP Vet.
Melting point: 154°C
Moisture content: chlorhexidine acetate is hygroscopic, absorbing significant amounts of moisture at relative humidities up to about 80% and temperatures up to 37°C.
Partition coefficients:
Mineral oil: water = 0.075;
Peanut oil: water = 0.04.
Solubility: soluble 1 in 15 of ethanol (95%), 1 in 55 of water; slightly soluble in glycerin and propylene glycol.

Safety:
LD_{50} (mouse, IP): 0.04 g/kg[27]
LD_{50} (mouse, IV): 0.03 g/kg
LD_{50} (mouse, oral): 2 g/kg
LD_{50} (mouse, SC): 0.33 g/kg
Comments: aqueous solutions may be sterilized by autoclaving; the solutions should not be alkaline or contain other ingredients which affect the stability of chlorhexidine. *See* Sections 11 and 12.

Chlorhexidine gluconate: $C_{22}H_{30}Cl_2N_{10}.2C_6H_{12}O_7$
Molecular weight: 897.88
CAS number: [18472-51-0]
Synonyms: chlorhexidine digluconate; chlorhexidini gluconati; 1,1′-hexamethylenebis[5-(4-chlorophenyl)biguanide] digluco-nate; *Hibiclens*; *Hibiscrub*; *Hibitane*; *Unisept*.
Appearance: chlorhexidine gluconate is usually used as an almost colorless or pale yellow colored aqueous solution.
Pharmacopeias: Br, Eur, Ger, Jpn, Neth and Swiss. Also BP Vet. Note that these pharmacopeias include monographs on chlorhexidine gluconate solution, which contains 19-21% w/v of chlorhexidine gluconate.
Acidity/alkalinity: pH = 5.5-7.0 for a 5% w/v aqueous dilution.
Solubility: miscible with water; soluble in acetone and ethanol (95%).
Safety:
LD_{50} (mouse, IV): 0.01 g/kg[27]
LD_{50} (mouse, oral): 1.26 g/kg
LD_{50} (mouse, SC): 1.14 g/kg
LD_{50} (rat, IV): 0.02 g/kg
LD_{50} (rat, oral): 2 g/kg
LD_{50} (rat, SC): 3.32 g/kg
Comments: the commercially available 5% w/v chlorhexidine gluconate solution contains a nonionic surfactant to prevent precipitation and is not suitable for use in body cavities or for the disinfection of surgical instruments containing cemented glass components. Aqueous dilutions of commercially avail-able chlorhexidine gluconate solutions may be sterilized by autoclaving. *See* Sections 11 and 12.

Chlorhexidine hydrochloride: $C_{22}H_{30}Cl_2N_{10}.2HCl$
Molecular weight: 578.44
CAS number: [3697-42-5]
Synonyms: chlorhexidine dihydrochloride; chlorhexidini hy-drochloridum; 1,1′-hexamethylenebis[5-(4-chlorophe-nyl)biguanide] dihydrochloride.
Appearance: a white or almost white-colored crystalline powder.
Pharmacopeias: Br, Egypt, Eur, Ger, Int, Neth and Swiss. Also in BP Vet.
Melting point: 261°C, with decomposition.
Solubility: sparingly soluble in water; very slightly soluble in ethanol (95%); soluble 1 in 50 of propylene glycol.
Safety: LD_{50} (mouse, SC): > 5 g/kg[27]
Comments: chlorhexidine hydrochloride may be sterilized by dry heat. *See* Sections 11 and 12.

19. Comments

—

20. Specific References

1. Prince HN, Nonemaker WS, Norgard RC, Prince DL. Drug resistance studies with topical antiseptics. J Pharm Sci 1978; 67: 1629-1631.
2. Richards RME, McBride RJ. Enhancement of benzalkonium chloride and chlorhexidine activity against *Pseudomonas aeruginosa* by aromatic alcohols. J Pharm Sci 1973; 62: 2035-2037.
3. Russell AD, Furr JR. Comparitive sensitivity of smooth, rough and deep rough strains of *Escherichia coli* to chlorhexidine, quaternary ammonium compounds and dibromopropamidine isethionate. Int J Pharmaceutics 1987; 36: 191-197.
4. Shaker LA, Russell AD, Furr JR. Aspects of the action of chlorhexidine on bacterial spores. Int J Pharmaceutics 1986; 34: 51-56.
5. Heard DD, Ashworth RW. The colloidal properties of chlorhexidine and its interaction with some macromolecules. J Pharm Pharmacol 1968; 20: 505-512.
6. Jaminet F, Delattre L, Delporte JP, Moes A. Influence of sterilization temperature and pH on the stability of chlorhexidine solutions [in French]. Pharm Acta Helv 1970; 45: 60-63.
7. Goodall RR, Goldman J, Woods J. Stability of chlorhexidine in solutions. Pharm J 1968; 200: 33-34.
8. Dolby J, Gunnarsson B, Kronberg L, Wikner H. Stability of chlorhexidine when autoclaving. Pharm Acta Helv 1972; 47: 615-620.
9. Myers JA. Hospital infections caused by contaminated fluids [letter]. Lancet 1972; ii: 282.
10. Oelschläger H, Canenbley R. Clear indication of chlorhexidine dihydrochloride precipitate in isotonic eye-drops: report based on experience on the use of chlorhexidine as a preservative. Pharm Ztg 1983; 128: 1166-1168.
11. Yousef RT, El-Nakeeb MA, Salama S. Effect of some pharmaceutical materials on the bactericidal activities of preservatives. Can J Pharm Sci 1973; 8: 54-56.
12. McCarthy TJ, Myburgh JA. The effect of tragacanth gel on preservative activity. Pharm Weekbl 1974; 109: 265-268.
13. Plaut BS, Davies DJG, Meakin BJ, Richardson NE. The mechanism of interaction between chlorhexidine digluconate and poly(2-hydroxyethyl methacrylate). J Pharm Pharmacol 1981; 33: 82-88.
14. Stevens LE, Durrwachter JR, Helton DO. Analysis of chlorhex-idine sorption in soft contact lenses by catalytic oxidation of [^{14}C] chlorhexidine and by liquid chromatography. J Pharm Sci 1986; 75: 83-86.
15. Rose FL, Swain G. Bisguanides having antibacterial activity. J Chem Soc 1956; 4422-4425.
16. Massano G, et al. Striking aminotransferase rise after chlorhex-idine self-poisoning [letter]. Lancet 1982; i: 289.
17. Emerson D, Pierce C. A case of a single ingestion of 4% Hibiclens. Vet Hum Toxicol 1988; 30: 583.
18. Quinn MW, Bini RM. Bradycardia associated with chlorhexidine spray [letter]. Arch Dis Child 1989; 64: 892-893.
19. Alder VG, Burman D, Simpson RA, Fysh J, Gillespie WA. Comparison of hexachlorophane and chlorhexidine powders in prevention of neonatal infection. Arch Dis Child 1980; 55: 277-280.
20. Wahlberg JE, Wennersten G. Hypersensitivity and photosensi-tivity to chlorhexidine. Dermatologica 1971; 143: 376-379.
21. Okano M, et al. Anaphylactic symptoms due to chlorhexidine gluconate. Arch Dermatol 1989; 125: 50-52.
22. Evans RJ. Acute anaphylaxis due to topical chlorhexidine acetate. Br Med J 1992; 304: 686.
23. Tabor E, Bostwick DC, Evans CC. Corneal damage due to eye contact with chlorhexidine gluconate [letter]. JAMA 1989; 261: 557-558.
24. Honigman JL. Disinfectant ototoxicity [letter]. Pharm J 1975; 215: 523.
25. Addy M, Moran J, Griffiths AA, Wills-Wood NJ. Extrinsic tooth discoloration by metals and chlorhexidine I: surface protein

denaturation or dietary precipitation? Br Dent J 1985; 159: 281-285.

26. Addy M, Moran J. Extrinsic tooth discoloration by metals and chlorhexidine II: clinical staining produced by chlorhexidine, iron and tea. Br Dent J 1985; 159: 331-334.

27. Sweet DV, editor. Registry of toxic effects of chemical substances. Cincinnati: US Department of Health, 1987.

21. General References

Davies GE, Francis J, Martin AR, Rose FL, Swain G. 1,6-Di-4′-chlorophenyldiguanidohexane (Hibitane): laboratory investigation of a new antibacterial agent of high potency. Br J Pharmacol Chemother 1954; 9: 192-196.

McCarthy TJ. The influence of insoluble powders on preservatives in solution. J Mond Pharm 1969; 12: 321-328.

Senior N. Some observations on the formulation and properties of chlorhexidine. J Soc Cosmet Chem 1973; 24: 259-278.

22. Authors

UK: MC Allwood, R Baird.

Chlorobutanol

1. Nonproprietary Names

BP: Chlorbutol
PhEur: Chlorobutanolum anhydricum
USPNF: Chlorobutanol

2. Synonyms

Acetone chloroform; chlorbutanol; trichloro-*tert*-butanol; β,β,β-trichloro-*tert*-butyl alcohol.

3. Chemical Name and CAS Registry Number

1,1,1-Trichloro-2-methyl-2-propanol [57-15-8]

4. Empirical Formula   Molecular Weight

$C_4H_7Cl_3O$ 177.46

5. Structural Formula

$$\begin{array}{c} CH_3 \\ | \\ H_3C-C-CCl_3 \\ | \\ OH \end{array}$$

6. Functional Category

Antimicrobial preservative; plasticizer.

7. Applications in Pharmaceutical Formulation or Technology

Chlorobutanol is primarily used in ophthalmic or parenteral dosage forms as an antimicrobial preservative at concentrations up to 0.5%, *see* Section 10. It is commonly used as an antibacterial agent for epinephrine solutions, posterior pituitary extract solutions and ophthalmic preparations intended for the treatment of miosis. It is especially useful as an antibacterial agent in nonaqueous formulations. Chlorobutanol is also used as a preservative in cosmetics (*see* Section 16), as a plasticizer for cellulose esters and ethers, and has been used therapeutically as a mild sedative and local analgesic.

8. Description

Volatile, colorless or white crystals with a musty, camphoraceous odor.

9. Pharmacopeial Specifications

Test	PhEur 1985	USPNF XVII
Identification	+	+
Appearance of solution	+	—
Reaction to litmus	—	Neutral
Acidity	+	—
Water (anhydrous form)	$\leqslant 1.0\%$	$\leqslant 1.0\%$
Water (hemihydrate)	—	$\leqslant 6.0\%$
Chloride	$\leqslant 300$ ppm	$\leqslant 0.07\%$
Sulfated ash	$\leqslant 0.1\%$	—
Assay (anhydrous basis)	98.0-101.0%	98.0-100.5%

10. Typical Properties

Antimicrobial activity: chlorobutanol has both antibacterial and antifungal properties. It is effective against Gram-positive and Gram-negative bacteria and some fungi, e.g. *Candida albicans*, *Pseudomonas aeruginosa* and *Staphylococcus albus*. Antimicrobial activity is bacteriostatic, rather than bactericidal, and is considerably reduced above pH 5.5. In addition, activity may also be reduced by increasing heat, and incompatibilities between chlorobutanol and other excipients or packaging materials, *see* Sections 11 and 12. However, activity may be increased by combination with other antimicrobial preservatives, *see* Section 19. Typical minimum inhibitory concentrations (MICs) are: Gram-positive bacteria 650 μg/mL; Gram-negative bacteria 1000 μg/mL; yeasts 2500 μg/mL; fungi 5000 μg/mL.
Boiling point: 167°C
Melting point: 95-97°C
Moisture content: see HPE Data.
Refractive index: $n_D^{25} = 1.4339$
Solubility:

Solvent	Solubility at 20°C
Chloroform	freely soluble
Ethanol (95%)	1 in 0.6
Ether	freely soluble
Glycerin	1 in 10
Volatile oils	freely soluble
Water	1 in 125

	HPE Laboratory Project Data		
	Method	Lab #	Results
Moisture content	MC-3	25	0.808%[a]

Supplier: a. Stauffer Chemical Co.

11. Stability and Storage Conditions

Chlorobutanol is volatile and readily sublimes. In aqueous solution degradation is catalyzed by hydroxide ions. Stability is good at pH 3 but becomes progressively worse with increasing pH.[1] The half-life at pH 7.5 for a chlorobutanol solution stored at 25°C was determined to be approximately 3 months.[2] In a 0.5% aqueous chlorobutanol solution, at room temperature, chlorobutanol is almost saturated and may crystallize out of solution if the temperature is reduced.
Losses of chlorobutanol also occur due to its volatility, with appreciable amounts being lost during autoclaving; at pH 5 about 30% of chlorobutanol is lost.[3] Porous containers result in losses from solutions and polyethylene containers result in rapid loss. Losses of chlorobutanol during autoclaving in polyethylene containers may be reduced by pre-autoclaving the containers in a solution of chlorobutanol; the containers should then be immediately used.[4] There is also appreciable loss of chlorobutanol through stoppers in parenteral vials.
The bulk material should be stored in a well-closed container at a temperature between 8-15°C.

12. Incompatibilities

Due to problems associated with sorption, chlorobutanol is incompatible with plastic vials,[4-8] rubber stoppers, bentonite,[9] magnesium trisilicate,[9] polyethylene and polyhydroxyethylmethacrylate, which has been used in soft contact lenses.[10] To a lesser extent, carboxymethylcellulose and polysorbate 80 reduce antimicrobial activity by sorption or complex formation.

13. Method of Manufacture

Chlorobutanol is prepared by condensing acetone and chloroform in the presence of solid potassium hydroxide.

14. Safety

Chlorobutanol is widely used as a preservative in a number of pharmaceutical formulations, particularly ophthalmic preparations. Although animal studies have suggested that chlorobutanol may be harmful to the eye, in practice the widespread use of chlorobutanol as a preservative in ophthalmic preparations has been associated with few reports of adverse reactions. Adverse reactions to chlorobutanol that have been reported include: cardiovascular effects following intravenous administration of heparin sodium injection preserved with chlorobutanol;[11] neurological effects following administration of a large dose of morphine infusion preserved with chlorobutanol;[12] and hypersensitivity reactions, although these are regarded as rare.[13-15]
The lethal human dose of chlorobutanol is estimated to be 50-500 mg/kg.[16]
LD_{Lo} (dog, oral): 0.24 g/kg[17]
LD_{Lo} (rabbit, oral): 0.21 g/kg

15. Handling Precautions

Observe normal precautions appropriate to the circumstances and quantity of material handled. Chlorobutanol may be irritant to the skin, eyes and mucous membranes. Eye protection and gloves are recommended along with a respirator in poorly ventilated environments. There is a slight fire hazard when exposed to heat or flame.

16. Regulatory Status

Included in the FDA Inactive Ingredients Guide (IM, IV and SC injections, inhalations, nasal, otic, ophthalmic and topical preparations). Included in nonparenteral and parenteral medicines licensed in the UK.
In the UK, the maximum concentration of chlorobutanol permitted for use in cosmetics, other than foams, is 0.5%. It is not suitable for use in aerosols.

17. Pharmacopeias

Aust, Braz, Br, Chin, Cz, Egypt, Eur, Fr, Ger, Gr, Hung, Ind, It, Mex, Neth, Nord, Swiss, Turk, USPNF and Yug.

18. Related Substances

Chlorobutanol hemihydrate; Phenoxyethanol; Phenylethyl Alcohol.

Chlorobutanol hemihydrate: $C_4H_7Cl_3O.\frac{1}{2}H_2O$
Molecular weight: 186.46
CAS number: [6001-64-5]
Synonyms: 1,1,1-trichloro-2-methylpropan-2-ol hemihydrate.
Appearance: as for the anhydrous material, *see* Section 8.
Pharmacopeias: Aust, Braz, Br, Eur, Fr, Ger, Gr, It, Jpn, Mex, Neth, Swiss and USPNF.
Melting point: 76-78°C
Moisture content: *see* HPE Data.
Solubility: as for the anhydrous material, *see* Section 10.

HPE Laboratory Project Data			
	Method	Lab #	Results
Moisture content	MC-3	25	4.82%[a]
Moisture content	MC-3	25	4.84%[b]

Supplier: a. E. Merck; b. Stauffer Chemical Co.

19. Comments

It has been reported that a combination of chlorobutanol and phenylethanol, both at 0.5% concentration, has shown greater antibacterial activity than either compound alone. An advantage of the use of this combination is that chlorobutanol dissolves in the alcohol; the ensuing liquid can then be dissolved in an aqueous pharmaceutical preparation without the application of heat.

20. Specific References

1. Patwa NV, Huyck CL. Stability of chlorobutanol. J Am Pharm Assoc 1966; NS6: 372-373.
2. Nair AD, Lach JL. The kinetics of degradation of chlorobutanol. J Am Pharm Assoc (Sci) 1959; 48: 390-395.
3. Hecht G, et al. Design and evaluation of ophthalmic pharmaceutical products. In: Banker GS, Rhodes CT, editors. Modern Pharmaceutics, 2nd edition. New York: Marcel Dekker, 1990: 539-603.
4. Blackburn HD, Polack AE, Roberts MS. The affect of container pre-treatment on the interaction between chlorbutol and polyethylene during autoclaving. Aust J Hosp Pharm 1983; 13: 153-156.
5. Lachman L, et al. Stability of antibacterial preservatives in parenteral solutions I: factors influencing the loss of antimicrobial agents from solutions in rubber-stoppered containers. J Pharm Sci 1962; 51: 224-232.
6. Friesen WT, Plein EM. The antibacterial stability of chlorobutanol stored in polyethylene bottles. Am J Hosp Pharm 1971; 28: 507-512.
7. Blackburn HD, Polack AE, Roberts MS. Preservation of ophthalmic solutions: some observations on the use of chlorbutol in plastic containers [letter]. J Pharm Pharmacol 1978; 30: 666.
8. Holdsworth DG, Roberts MS, Polack AE. Fate of chlorbutol during storage in polyethylene dropper containers and simulated patient use. J Clin Hosp Pharm 1984; 9: 29-39.
9. Yousef RT, El-Nakeeb MA, Salama S. Effect of some pharmaceutical materials on the bactericidal activities of preservatives. Can J Pharm Sci 1973; 8: 54-56.
10. Richardson NE, Davies DJG, Meakin BJ, Norton DA. The interaction of preservatives with polyhydroxy-ethylmethacrylate (polyHEMA). J Pharm Pharmacol 1978; 30: 469-475.
11. Bowler GMR, Galloway DW, Meiklejohn BH, Macintyre CCA. Sharp fall in blood pressure after injection of heparin containing chlorbutol [letter]. Lancet 1986; i: 848-849.
12. DeChristoforo R, et al. High-dose morphine infusion complicated by chlorobutanol-induced somnolence. Ann Intern Med 1983; 98: 335-336.
13. Dux S, Pitlik S, Perry G, Rosenfeld JB. Hypersensitivity reaction to chlorobutanol-preserved heparin [letter]. Lancet 1981; i: 149.
14. Itabashi A, Katayama S, Yamaji T. Hypersensitivity to chlorobutanol in DDAVP solution [letter]. Lancet 1982; i: 108.
15. Hofmann H, Goerz G, Plewig G. Anaphylactic shock from chlorobutanol-preserved oxytocin. Contact Dermatitis 1986; 15: 241.
16. Gosselin RE, Hodge HC, Smith RP, Gleason MN. Clinical toxicology of commercial products, 4th edition. Baltimore: Williams and Wilkins, 1976: II-119.

17. Sweet DV, editor. Registry of toxic effects of chemical substances. Cincinnati: US Department of Health, 1987.

21. General References

Summers QA, Nesbit MR, Levin R, Holgate ST. A non-bronchoconstrictor, bacteriostatic preservative for nebuliser solutions. Br J Clin Pharmacol 1991; 31: 204-206.

22. Authors

USA: RA Nash.

Chlorocresol

1. Nonproprietary Names

BP: Chlorocresol
PhEur: Chlorocresolum
USPNF: Chlorocresol

2. Synonyms

p-Chloro-*m*-cresol; 2-chloro-5-hydroxytoluene; 6-chloro-3-hydroxytoluene; 4-chloro-*m*-cresol; 3-methyl-4-chlorophenol; *Nipacide PC*; parachlorometacresol; PCMC.

3. Chemical Name and CAS Registry Number

4-Chloro-3-methylphenol [59-50-7]

4. Empirical Formula   Molecular Weight

C_7H_7ClO 142.58

5. Structural Formula

6. Functional Category

Antimicrobial preservative; disinfectant.

7. Applications in Pharmaceutical Formulation or Technology

Chlorocresol is used as an antimicrobial preservative in cosmetics and pharmaceutical formulations. It is generally used in concentrations up to 0.2% in a variety of preparations except those intended for oral administration. Chlorocresol is effective against bacteria, spores, molds and yeasts; it is most active in acidic media. Preservative efficacy may be reduced in the presence of some other excipients, particularly nonionic surfactants, *see* Sections 10 and 12.

In higher concentrations, chlorocresol is an effective disinfectant.

Use	Concentration (%)
Eye-drops	0.05
Injections	0.1
Shampoos and other cosmetics	0.1-0.2
Topical creams and emulsions	0.075-0.12

8. Description

Colorless or almost colorless, dimorphous crystals or crystalline powder with a characteristic phenolic odor.

9. Pharmacopeial Specifications

Test	PhEur 1985	USPNF XVII
Identification	+	+
Completeness of solution	+	+
Melting range	64-67°C	63-66°C
Nonvolatile matter	⩽ 0.1%	⩽ 0.1%
Acidity or alkalinity	+	—
Related substances	⩽ 1.0%	—
Assay	98.0-101.0%	99.0-101.0%

10. Typical Properties

Antimicrobial activity: chlorocresol has bactericidal activity against both Gram-positive and Gram-negative organisms (including *Pseudomonas aeruginosa*), spores, molds and yeasts. It is most active in acidic solutions with antimicrobial effectiveness decreasing with increasing pH; it is inactive above pH 9. Antimicrobial activity may also be reduced by loss of chlorocresol from a formulation due to incompatibilities with packaging materials or other excipients, such as nonionic surfactants, *see* Section 12. Synergistic antimicrobial effects between chlorocresol and other antimicrobial preservatives, such as 2-phenylethanol, have been reported.[1,2] Reported minimum inhibitory concentrations (MICs) for chlorocresol are shown in Table I.[3]

Bacteria: concentrations of approximately 0.08%, with a contact time of 10 minutes, are bactericidal. A typical MIC is 0.02%.

Fungi: chlorocresol is active against molds and yeasts. Fungicidal concentrations (after 24 hours of contact) range between 0.01-0.04%.

Spores: at temperatures of 80°C or above and in concentrations greater than 0.012%, chlorocresol is active against spores. It is much less active at room temperature. Heating at 98-100°C for 30 minutes in the presence of 0.2% chlorocresol has previously been used as a compendial method for the sterilization of solutions of substances which would not withstand autoclaving.

Table I: Minimum inhibitory concentrations (MICs) for chlorocresol.[3]

Microorganism	MIC (μg/mL)
Aspergillus niger	2500
Candida albicans	2500
Escherichia coli	1250
Klebsiella pneumoniae	625
Pseudomonas aeruginosa	1250
Pseudomonas fluorescens	1250
Staphylococcus aureus	625

Boiling point: 235°C
Dissociation constant: $pK_a = 9.2$
Flash point: 110°C (open cup)
Melting point: dimorphous crystals with a melting point of 55.5°C and 65°C.
Partition coefficients: at 25°C
Liquid paraffin: water = 1.53;
Peanut oil: water = 117.

Solubility:

Solvent	Solubility at 25°C Unless otherwise stated
Acetone	soluble
Alkali hydroxide solutions	soluble
Chloroform	soluble
Ethanol	1 in 0.4
Ether	soluble
Fixed oils	soluble
Glycerin	soluble
Terpenes	soluble
Water	1 in 260*
	1 in 50 at 100°C*

*Aqueous solubility is decreased in the presence of electrolytes, particularly sodium chloride, potassium chloride and potassium sulfonate.[4]

Vapor pressure: 0.67 kPa at 100°C

11. Stability and Storage Conditions

Chlorocresol is stable at room temperature but is volatile in steam. Aqueous solutions may be sterilized by autoclaving. On exposure to air and light aqueous solutions may become yellow colored. Solutions in oil or glycerin may be sterilized by heating at 160°C for 1 hour. The bulk material should be stored in a well-closed container, protected from light, in a cool, dry, place.

12. Incompatibilities

Chlorocresol can decompose on contact with strong alkalis evolving heat and fumes which ignite explosively. It is also incompatible with solutions of calcium chloride, codeine phosphate, diamorphine hydrochloride, papaveretum and quinine hydrochloride.[5] Discoloration also occurs with iron salts. Chlorocresol additionally exhibits strong sorption or binding tendencies to organic materials such as rubber, certain plastics and nonionic surfactants.[6-9]

Chlorocresol may be lost from solutions to rubber closures, and in contact with polyethylene may initially be rapidly removed by sorption and then by permeation, the uptake being temperature dependent. Presoaking of components may reduce losses due to sorption, but not those by permeation.[10,11] Chlorocresol may also be taken up by polymethylmethacrylate and by cellulose acetate. Losses to polypropylene or rigid polyvinyl chloride are usually small.[12]

At a concentration of 0.1%, chlorocresol may be completely inactivated in the presence of nonionic surfactants, such as polysorbate 80.[7] Bactericidal activity is also reduced, due to binding, by cetomacrogol or methylcellulose.[7,9] In emulsified or solubilized systems, chlorocresol readily partitions into the oil phase, particularly into vegetable oils.[8]

13. Method of Manufacture

Chlorocresol is prepared by the chlorination of *m*-cresol.

14. Safety

Chlorocresol is used primarily as a preservative in topical pharmaceutical formulations but has also been used in nebulized solutions[13] and ophthalmic and parenteral preparations. It should not however be used in formulations for intrathecal, intracisternal or peridural injection.

Chlorocresol is metabolized by conjugation with glucuronic acid and sulfate and is excreted in the urine, mainly as the conjugate, with little chlorocresol being excreted unchanged. Although less toxic than phenol, chlorocresol may be irritant to the skin, eyes and mucous membranes and has been reported to cause some adverse reactions when used as an excipient.[14]

Sensitization reactions may follow the prolonged application of strong solutions to the skin although patch tests have shown that chlorocresol is not a primary irritant at concentrations up to 0.2%. Cross sensitization with the related preservative chloroxylenol has also been reported.[15,16]

When used systemically, notably in a heparin injection preserved with chlorocresol 0.15%, delayed irritant and hypersensitivity reactions attributed to chlorocresol have been reported.[17,18] *See also* Section 19.

LD$_{50}$ (rat, oral): 1.83 g/kg[19]
LD$_{50}$ (rat, SC): 0.4 g/kg

15. Handling Precautions

Observe normal precautions appropriate to the circumstances and quantity of material handled. Chlorocresol can be irritant to the skin, eyes and mucous membranes. Eye protection, gloves and protective clothing are recommended. Chlorocresol presents a slight fire hazard when exposed to heat or flame. It burns to produce highly toxic fumes containing phosgene and hydrogen chloride.

16. Regulatory Status

Included in the FDA Inactive Ingredients Guide (topical creams and emulsions). Included in nonparenteral and parenteral medicines licensed in the UK.

17. Pharmacopeias

Aust, Br, Eur, Fr, Gr, Ind, It, Neth, Nord, Port, Swiss, Turk, USPNF and Yug.

18. Related Substances

Cresol; chloroxylenol.

Chloroxylenol: C_8H_9ClO
Molecular weight: 156.61
CAS number: [88-04-0]
Synonyms: 4-chloro-3,5-dimethylphenol; 4-chloro-3,5-xylenol; *p*-chloro-*m*-xylenol; PCMX.
Appearance: white or cream colored crystals or crystalline powder with a characteristic phenolic odor. Volatile in steam.
Pharmacopeias: Br and US. Also in BP Vet.
Boiling point: 246°C
Melting point: 115.5°C
Solubility: soluble 1 in 1 of ethanol (95%), ether, terpenes and fixed oils; very slightly soluble in water. Dissolves in solutions of alkali hydroxides.
Incompatibilities: incompatible with nonionic surfactants and methylcellulose.
Comments: used as an antimicrobial preservative similarly to chlorocresol. Chloroxylenol is used in pharmaceutical creams in concentrations up to 1.0%. It is reported to be effective in concentrations of 0.05-0.1% and is considered to have a low order of toxicity.

19. Comments

Chlorocresol has a characteristic odor which is difficult to mask in formulations, even at concentrations of 0.05-0.1%.

Although used in Europe, chlorocresol is not used in the US in parenteral formulations.

20. Specific References

1. Denyer SP, Hugo WB, Harding VD. The biochemical basis of synergy between the antibacterial agents, chlorocresol and 2-phenylethanol. Int J Pharmaceutics 1986; 29: 29-36.
2. Abdelaziz AA, El-Nakeeb MA. Sporicidal activity of local anaesthetics and their binary combinations with preservatives. J Clin Pharm Ther 1988; 13: 249-256.
3. Wallhäusser KH. *p*-Chloro-*m*-cresol. In: Kabara JJ, editor. Cosmetic and drug preservation principles and practice. New York: Marcel Dekker Inc, 1984: 683-684.
4. Gadalla MAF, Saleh AM, Motawi MM. Effect of electrolytes on the solubility and solubilization of chlorocresol. Pharmazie 1974; 29: 105-107.
5. McEwan JS, Macmorran GH. The compatibility of some bactericides. Pharm J 1947; 158: 260-262.
6. Yousef RT, El-Nakeeb MA, Salama S. Effect of some pharmaceutical materials on the bactericidal activities of preservatives. Can J Pharm Sci 1973; 8: 54-56.
7. McCarthy TJ. Dissolution of chlorocresol from various pharmaceutical formulations. Pharm Weekbl 1975; 110: 101-106.
8. Kazmi SJA, Mitchell AG. Preservation of solubilized and emulsified systems I: correlation of mathematically predicted preservative availability with antimicrobial activity. J Pharm Sci 1978; 67: 1260-1266.
9. Kazmi SJA, Mitchell AG. Preservation of solubilized and emulsified systems II: theoretical development of capacity and its role in antimicrobial activity of chlorocresol in cetomacrogol-stabilized systems. J Pharm Sci 1978; 67: 1266-1271.
10. McCarthy TJ. Interaction between aqueous preservative solutions and their plastic containers III. Pharm Weekbl 1972; 107: 1-7.
11. Roberts MS, Polack AE, Martin G, Blackburn HD. The storage of selected substances in aqueous solution in polyethylene containers: the effect of some physicochemical factors on the disappearance kinetics of the substances. Int J Pharmaceutics 1979; 2: 295-306.
12. McCarthy TJ. Interaction between aqueous preservative solutions and their plastic containers. Pharm Weekbl 1970; 105: 557-563.
13. Summers QA, Nesbit MR, Levin R, Holgate ST. A non-bronchoconstrictor, bacteriostatic preservative for nebuliser solutions. Br J Clin Pharmacol 1991; 31: 204-206.
14. Smolinske SC. Handbook of food, drug and cosmetic excipients. Boca Raton, FL: CRC Press Inc, 1992: 87-90.
15. Burry JN, Kirk J, Reid JG, Turner T. Chlorocresol sensitivity. Contact Dermatitis 1975; 1: 41-42.
16. Andersen KE, Hamann K. How sensitizing is chlorocresol? Allergy tests in guinea pigs versus the clinical experience. Contact Dermatitis 1984; 11: 11-20.
17. Hancock BW, Naysmith A. Hypersensitivity to chlorocresol-preserved heparin. Br Med J 1975; 3: 746-747.
18. Ainley EJ, Mackie IG, Macarthur D. Adverse reaction to chlorocresol-preserved heparin [letter]. Lancet 1977; i: 705.
19. Sweet DV, editor. Registry of toxic effects of chemical substances. Cincinnati: US Department of Health, 1987.

21. General References

Denyer SP, Wallhäusser KH. Antimicrobial preservatives and their properties. In: Denyer SP, Baird R, editors. Guide to microbiological control in pharmaceuticals. Chichester: Ellis Horwood, 1990: 251-273.

22. Authors

UK: PJ Weller.

Chlorodifluoroethane

1. Nonproprietary Names
None adopted.

2. Synonyms
CFC 142b; 1,1-difluoro-1-chloroethane; *Dymel 142b*; *Isceon 142b*; propellant 142b; refrigerant 142b.

3. Chemical Name and CAS Registry Number
1-Chloro-1,1-difluoroethane [75-68-3]

4. Empirical Formula   Molecular Weight
$C_2H_3ClF_2$ 100.50

5. Structural Formula

$$Cl-\underset{\underset{F}{|}}{\overset{\overset{F}{|}}{C}}-\underset{\underset{H}{|}}{\overset{\overset{H}{|}}{C}}-H$$

6. Functional Category
Aerosol propellant.

7. Applications in Pharmaceutical Formulation or Technology

Chlorodifluoroethane is used as an aerosol propellant in topical pharmaceutical formulations. It is generally used in conjunction with difluoroethane to form a propellant blend with a specific gravity of one. Chlorodifluoroethane may also be used in combination with chlorodifluoromethane and hydrocarbon propellants. Chlorodifluoroethane may be used as a vehicle for dispersions and emulsions.

Under the terms of the Montreal Protocol, aimed at reducing damage to the ozone layer, the use of chlorofluorocarbons will be prohibited from January 1996.[1-5] However, this prohibition does not apply to essential uses such as existing pharmaceutical formulations for which no alternative chlorofluorocarbon-free product is available. New pharmaceutical formulations containing chlorofluorocarbons may also be exempted provided they demonstrate that there is no technically feasible alternative to their use, that the product is of a substantial health benefit, and that its usage would not involve release of significant quantities of chlorofluorocarbon into the atmosphere. Regulatory bodies in individual countries should be consulted for advice on chlorodifluoroethane use in formulations. Although chlorodifluoroethane has some potential for ozone depletion (approximately 5% that of trichloromonofluoromethane) it is not currently prohibited under the terms of the Montreal Protocol.

8. Description
Chlorodifluoroethane is a liquefied gas and exists as a liquid at room temperature when contained under its own vapor pressure, or as a gas when exposed to room temperature and atmospheric pressure. The liquid is practically odorless and colorless. Chlorodifluoroethane is noncorrosive and nonirritating.

9. Pharmacopeial Specifications
—

10. Typical Properties
Autoignition temperature: 632°C
Boiling point: -9.8°C
Critical temperature: 137.1°C
Density:
1.11 g/cm^3 for liquid at 25°C;
1.03 g/cm^3 for liquid at 54.5°C.
Flammability: flammable. Limits of flammability 6.2-17.9% v/v in air.
Melting point: -131°C
Solubility: soluble 1 in 715 parts of water at 20°C.
Vapor density (absolute): 4.487 g/m^3 at standard temperature and pressure.
Vapor density (relative): 3.48 (air = 1)
Vapor pressure:
339 kPa (49.2 psia) at 25°C;
772 kPa (112.0 psia) at 54.5°C.
Viscosity (dynamic): 0.33 mPa s (0.33 cP) for liquid at 21°C.

11. Stability and Storage Conditions
Chlorodifluoroethane is a nonreactive and stable material. The liquefied gas is stable when used as a propellant and should be stored in a metal cylinder in a cool, dry, place.

12. Incompatibilities
Compatible with the usual ingredients used in the formulation of pharmaceutical aerosols. Chlorodifluoroethane can react vigorously with oxidizing materials.

13. Method of Manufacture
Chlorodifluoroethane is prepared by the chlorination of difluoroethane in the presence of a suitable catalyst; hydrochloric acid is also formed. The chlorodifluoroethane is purified to remove all traces of water and hydrochloric acid, as well as traces of the starting and intermediate materials.

14. Safety
Chlorodifluoroethane may be used as an aerosol propellant in topical pharmaceutical formulations. It is generally regarded as an essentially nontoxic and nonirritant material.

Deliberate inhalation of excessive quantities of chlorofluorocarbon propellant may result in death, and the following 'warning' statements must appear on the label of all aerosols:

WARNING: Avoid inhalation. Keep away from eyes or other mucous membranes. (Aerosols designed specifically for oral and nasal inhalation need not contain this statement).

WARNING: Do not inhale directly; deliberate inhalation of contents can cause death.

OR

WARNING: Use only as directed; intentional misuse by deliberately concentrating and inhaling the contents can be harmful or fatal.

Additionally, the label should contain the following information:

WARNING: Contents under pressure. Do not puncture or incinerate container. Do not expose to heat or store at room temperature above 120°F (49°C). Keep out of the reach of children.

In the US, the Environmental Protection Agency (EPA) additionally requires the following information on all aerosols containing chlorofluorocarbons as the propellant:
WARNING: Contains a chlorofluorocarbon that may harm the public health and environment by reducing ozone in the upper atmosphere. (Metered-dose inhalers and nasal aerosols are exempt from this regulation).
When chlorofluorocarbon propellants are used in topical aerosols they may cause a chilling effect on the skin although this effect has been somewhat overcome by the use of vapor tap valves. The propellants quickly vaporize from the skin, and are nonirritating when used as directed.

15. Handling Precautions

Chlorodifluoroethane is usually encountered as a liquefied gas and appropriate precautions for handling such materials should be taken. Eye protection, gloves and protective clothing are recommended. Chlorodifluoroethane should be handled in a well-ventilated environment. Chlorofluorocarbon vapors are heavier than air and do not support life and therefore, when cleaning large tanks which have contained chlorofluorocarbons, adequate provisions for oxygen in the tanks must be made in order to protect workers cleaning the tanks.
Chlorodifluoroethane is flammable, *see* Section 10. When heated to decomposition chlorodifluoroethane emits toxic fumes.

16. Regulatory Status

Accepted in the US, by the FDA, for use as a topical aerosol propellant.

17. Pharmacopeias

—

18. Related Substances

Chlorodifluoromethane; Dichlorodifluoromethane; Dichlorotetrafluoroethane; Difluoroethane; Tetrafluoroethane; Trichloromonofluoromethane.

19. Comments

Chlorodifluoroethane is useful as an aerosol propellant in that it shows greater miscibility with water than some other chlorofluorocarbons and when combined with difluoroethane will produce a mixture with a specific gravity of one.
For a discussion of the numerical nomenclature applied to fluorocarbon aerosol propellants *see* Dichlorodifluoromethane.

20. Specific References

1. Fischer FX, Hess H, Sucker H, Byron PR. CFC propellant substitution: international perspectives. Pharmaceut Technol 1989; 13(9): 44, 48, 50, 52.
2. Kempner N. Metered dose inhaler CFCs under pressure. Pharm J 1990; 245: 428-429.
3. Dalby RN. Possible replacements for CFC-propelled metered-dose inhalers. Med Device Tech 1991; 2(4): 21-25.
4. CFC-free aerosols: the final hurdle. Mfg Chem 1992; 63(7): 22-23.
5. Mackenzie D. Large hole in the ozone agreement. New Scientist 1992; Nov 28: 5.

21. General References

Johnson MA. The aerosol handbook, 2nd edition. Caldwell: WE Dorland, 1982: 305-335.
Sanders PA. Handbook of aerosol technology, 2nd edition. New York: Van Nostrand Reinhold, 1979: 19-35.
Sciarra JJ. Pharmaceutical and cosmetic aerosols. J Pharm Sci 1974; 63: 1815-1836.
Sciarra JJ, Stoller L. The science and technology of aerosol packaging. New York: John Wiley and Sons, 1974: 97-130.
Sciarra JJ. Pharmaceutical aerosols. In: Lachman L, Lieberman HA, Kanig JL, editors. The theory and practice of industrial pharmacy, 3rd edition. Philadelphia: Lea and Febiger, 1986: 589-618.
Sciarra JJ, Cutie AJ. In: Banker GS, Rhodes CT, editors. Modern pharmaceutics, 2nd edition. New York: Marcel Dekker Inc, 1990: 605-634.

22. Authors

UK: PJ Davies.
USA: JJ Sciarra.

Chlorodifluoromethane

1. Nonproprietary Names

None adopted.

2. Synonyms

Arcton 22; difluorochloromethane; *Dymel 22*; *Frigen 22*; HCFC 22; *Isceon 22*; propellant 22; refrigerant 22.

3. Chemical Name and CAS Registry Number

Chlorodifluoromethane [75-45-6]

4. Empirical Formula   Molecular Weight

$CHClF_2$ 86.47

5. Structural Formula

$CHClF_2$

6. Functional Category

Aerosol propellant.

7. Applications in Pharmaceutical Formulation or Technology

Chlorodifluoromethane is used as an aerosol propellant in topical pharmaceutical formulations. Its relatively high vapor pressure precludes its use as the sole propellant in a preparation. Therefore, it is generally used in combination with chlorodifluoroethane, difluoroethane or hydrocarbons. By adjusting the ratio of chlorodifluoromethane to the propellants listed above, it is possible to produce nonflammable propellant blends.

An azeotropic mixture of chlorodifluoromethane and chloropentafluoroethane, called propellant 502, is also used as a propellant and refrigerant.

Under the terms of the Montreal Protocol, aimed at reducing damage to the ozone layer, the use of chlorofluorocarbons will be prohibited from January 1996.[1-5] However, this prohibition does not apply to essential uses such as existing pharmaceutical formulations for which no alternative chlorofluorocarbon-free product is available. New pharmaceutical formulations, containing chlorofluorocarbons may also be exempted provided they demonstrate that there is no technically feasible alternative to their use, that the product is of a substantial health benefit, and that its usage would not involve release of significant quantities of chlorofluorocarbon into the atmosphere. Regulatory bodies in individual countries should be consulted for advice on chlorodifluoromethane use in formulations. Chlorodifluoromethane is not currently covered by the Montreal Protocol.

8. Description

Chlorodifluoromethane is a liquefied gas and exists as a liquid at room temperature when contained under its own vapor pressure, or as a gas when exposed to room temperature and atmospheric pressure. The liquid is practically odorless and colorless. Chlorodifluoromethane is noncorrosive, nonirritating and nonflammable.

9. Pharmacopeial Specifications

10. Typical Properties

Boiling point: -40.8°C
Critical pressure: 4.9 MPa (48.7 atm)
Critical temperature: 96°C
Density: 1.19 g/cm³ for liquid at 25°C.
Flammability: nonflammable.
Heat of vaporization: 234 kJ/kg
Melting point: -146°C
Refractive index: n_D^{25} = 1.256
Solubility: freely soluble in acetone, chloroform, and ether; soluble 1 in 330 parts of water at 25°C.
Surface tension: 15 mN/m (15 dynes/cm) at -41°C.
Vapor density (absolute): 3.860 g/m³ at standard temperature and pressure.
Vapor density (relative): 2.98 (air = 1)
Vapor pressure:
1041 kPa (151 psia) at 25°C;
2137 kPa (310 psia) at 54.5°C.

11. Stability and Storage Conditions

Chlorodifluoromethane is a nonreactive and stable material. The liquefied gas is stable when used as a propellant and should be stored in a metal cylinder in a cool, dry, place.

12. Incompatibilities

Compatible with the usual ingredients used in the formulation of pharmaceutical aerosols. Incompatible with aluminum. On contact with acids highly toxic fumes are evolved.

13. Method of Manufacture

Chlorodifluoromethane is prepared by the reaction of chloroform with anhydrous hydrofluoric acid in the presence of an antimony chloride catalyst; dichlorofluoromethane and hydrochloric acid are also formed. The chlorofluorocarbons are separated by fractional distillation and the chlorodifluoromethane then further purified to remove all traces of water and hydrochloric acid, as well as traces of the starting and intermediate materials. Chlorodifluoromethane is commercially available greater than 99.9% pure.

14. Safety

Chlorodifluoromethane may be used as an aerosol propellant in topical pharmaceutical formulations. It is generally regarded as an essentially nontoxic and nonirritant material. Deliberate inhalation of excessive quantities of chlorofluorocarbon propellant may result in death, and the following 'warning' statements must appear on the label of all aerosols:

WARNING: Avoid inhalation. Keep away from eyes or other mucous membranes. (Aerosols designed specifically for oral and nasal inhalation need not contain this statement).

WARNING: Do not inhale directly; deliberate inhalation of contents can cause death.

OR

WARNING: Use only as directed; intentional misuse by deliberately concentrating and inhaling the contents can be harmful or fatal.

Additionally, the label should contain the following information:

WARNING: Contents under pressure. Do not puncture or incinerate container. Do not expose to heat or store at room temperature above 120°F (49°C). Keep out of the reach of children.

In the US, the Environmental Protection Agency (EPA) additionally requires the following information on all aerosols containing chlorofluorocarbons as the propellant:

WARNING: Contains a chlorofluorocarbon that may harm the public health and environment by reducing ozone in the upper atmosphere. (Metered-dose inhalers and nasal aerosols are exempt from this regulation).

When chlorofluorocarbon propellants are used in topical aerosols they may cause a chilling effect on the skin although this effect has been somewhat overcome by the use of vapor tap valves. The propellants quickly vaporize from the skin, and are nonirritating when used as directed.

LC_{50} (mouse, inhalation): 28 pph/30 min[6]
LC_{50} (rat, inhalation): 35 pph/15 min

15. Handling Precautions

Chlorodifluoromethane is usually encountered as a liquefied gas and appropriate precautions for handling such materials should be taken. Eye protection, gloves and protective clothing are recommended. Chlorodifluoromethane should be handled in a well-ventilated environment. Chlorofluorocarbon vapors are heavier than air and do not support life and therefore, when cleaning large tanks which have contained chlorofluorocarbons, adequate provisions for oxygen in the tanks must be made in order to protect workers cleaning the tanks.

In the UK, the long-term (8-hour TWA) occupational exposure limit for chlorodifluoromethane is 3500 mg/m^3 (1000 ppm).[7]

Although nonflammable, highly toxic fumes may be produced on heating chlorodifluoromethane.

16. Regulatory Status

Accepted in the US, by the FDA, for use as a topical aerosol propellant.

17. Pharmacopeias

—

18. Related Substances

Chlorodifluoroethane; Dichlorodifluoromethane; Dichlorotetrafluoroethane; Difluoroethane; Tetrafluoroethane; Trichloromonofluoromethane.

19. Comments

Chlorodifluoromethane is useful as an aerosol propellant in that it shows greater miscibility with water than other chlorofluorocarbons and when combined with chlorodifluoroethane will produce a mixture with a specific gravity of one. Since chlorodifluoromethane is not currently covered by the Montreal Protocol its use is projected to increase significantly. Based on 1992 figures, chlorodifluoromethane represents 30% of all fluorocarbon production in the US.

For a discussion of the numerical nomenclature applied to fluorocarbon aerosol propellants *see* Dichlorodifluoromethane.

20. Specific References

1. Fischer FX, Hess H, Sucker H, Byron PR. CFC propellant substitution: international perspectives. Pharmaceut Technol 1989; 13(9): 44, 48, 50, 52.
2. Kempner N. Metered dose inhaler CFCs under pressure. Pharm J 1990; 245: 428-429.
3. Dalby RN. Possible replacements for CFC-propelled metered-dose inhalers. Med Device Tech 1991; 2(4): 21-25.
4. CFC-free aerosols: the final hurdle. Mfg Chem 1992; 63(7): 22-23.
5. Mackenzie D. Large hole in the ozone agreement. New Scientist 1992; Nov 28: 5.
6. Sweet DV, editor. Registry of toxic effects of chemical substances. Cincinnati: US Department of Health, 1987.
7. Health and Safety Executive. EH40/93: occupational exposure limits 1993. London: HMSO, 1993.

21. General References

Johnson MA. The aerosol handbook, 2nd edition. Caldwell: WE Dorland, 1982: 305-335.
Sanders PA. Handbook of aerosol technology, 2nd edition. New York: Van Nostrand Reinhold, 1979: 19-35.
Sciarra JJ. Pharmaceutical and cosmetic aerosols. J Pharm Sci 1974; 63: 1815-1836.
Sciarra JJ, Stoller L. The science and technology of aerosol packaging. New York: John Wiley and Sons, 1974: 97-130.
Sciarra JJ. Pharmaceutical aerosols. In: Lachman L, Lieberman HA, Kanig JL, editors. The theory and practice of industrial pharmacy, 3rd edition. Philadelphia: Lea and Febiger, 1986: 589-618.
Sciarra JJ, Cutie AJ. In: Banker GS, Rhodes CT, editors. Modern pharmaceutics, 2nd edition. New York: Marcel Dekker Inc, 1990: 605-634.

22. Authors

UK: PJ Davies.
USA: JJ Sciarra.

Cholesterol

1. Nonproprietary Names
USPNF: Cholesterol

2. Synonyms
Cholesterin.

3. Chemical Name and CAS Registry Number
Cholest-5-en-3β-ol [57-88-5]

4. Empirical Formula
$C_{27}H_{46}O$

Molecular Weight
386.67

5. Structural Formula

6. Functional Category
Emollient; emulsifying agent.

7. Applications in Pharmaceutical Formulation or Technology
Cholesterol is used in cosmetics and topical pharmaceutical formulations at concentrations between 0.3-5.0% w/w as an emulsifying agent. It imparts water-absorbing power to an ointment and has emollient activity. Cholesterol additionally has a physiological role.

8. Description
White or faintly yellow, almost odorless, pearly leaflets, needles, powder or granules. On prolonged exposure to light and air cholesterol acquires a yellow to tan color.

9. Pharmacopeial Specifications

Test	USPNF XVII
Identification	+
Melting range	147-150°C
Specific rotation	-34° to -38°
Acidity	+
Loss on drying	$\leqslant 0.3\%$
Residue on ignition	$\leqslant 0.1\%$

10. Typical Properties
Boiling point: 360°C
Density: 1.052 g/cm^3 for anhydrous form.
Dielectric constant D^{20}: 5.41
Melting point: 147-150°C

SEM: 1
Excipient: Cholesterol
Manufacturer: Pfaltz & Bauer Inc.
Magnification: 240x

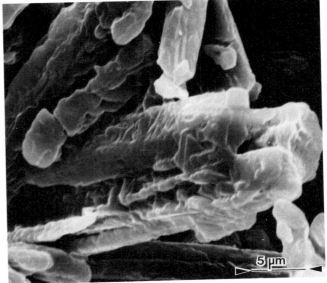

SEM: 2
Excipient: Cholesterol
Manufacturer: Pfaltz & Bauer Inc.
Magnification: 2400x

Solubility:

Solvent	Solubility at 20°C[1-3] Unless otherwise stated
Acetone	soluble
Benzene	1 in 7
Chloroform	1 in 4.5
Ethanol	1 in 147 at 0°C
	1 in 78 at 20°C
	1 in 29 at 40°C
	1 in 19 at 50°C
	1 in 13 at 60°C
Ethanol (95%)	1 in 78 (slowly)
	1 in 3.6 at 80°C
Ether	1 in 2.8
Hexane	1 in 52
Isopropyl myristate	1 in 19
Methanol	1 in 294 at 0°C
	1 in 153 at 20°C
	1 in 53 at 40°C
	1 in 34 at 50°C
	1 in 23 at 60°C
Vegetable oils	soluble
Water	practically insoluble

Specific rotation $[\alpha]_D^{20}$:
-39.5° (2% w/v solution in chloroform);
-31.5° (2% w/v solution in ether).

11. Stability and Storage Conditions

Cholesterol is stable and should be stored in a well-closed container, protected from light.

12. Incompatibilities

Precipitated by digitonin.

13. Method of Manufacture

The commercial material is normally obtained from the spinal cord of cattle by extraction with petroleum ethers but may also be obtained from wool fat. Purification is normally accomplished by repeated bromination. Cholesterol may also be produced by entirely synthetic means.

14. Safety

Cholesterol is generally regarded as an essentially nontoxic and nonirritant material at the levels employed as an excipient.[3]

15. Handling Precautions

May be harmful following inhalation or ingestion of large quantities, or over prolonged periods of time, due to the possible involvement of cholesterol in atherosclerosis and gallstones. May be irritant to the eyes. Observe normal precautions appropriate to the circumstances and quantity of material handled. Rubber or plastic gloves, eye protection and a respirator are recommended.

16. Regulatory Status

Included in the FDA Inactive Ingredients Guide (ophthalmic, topical and vaginal preparations).
Included in nonparenteral medicines licensed in the UK.

17. Pharmacopeias

Aust, Braz, Cz, Jpn, Rom and USPNF.

18. Related Substances

Lanolin Alcohols.

19. Comments

Cholesterol monohydrate becomes anhydrous at 70-80°C.

20. Specific References

1. Harwood RJ, Cohen EM. Solubility of cholesterol in isopropyl myristate. J Soc Cosmet Chem 1977; 28: 79-82.
2. Flynn GL, Shah Y, Prakongpan S, Kwan KH, Higuchi WI, Hofmann AF. Cholesterol solubility in organic solvents. J Pharm Sci 1979; 68: 1090-1097.
3. Cosmetic, Toiletry and Fragrance Association. Final report on the safety assessment of cholesterol. J Am Coll Toxicol 1986; 5(5): 491-516.

21. General References

Bogardus JB. Unusual cholesterol solubility in water/glyceryl-1-monooctanoate solutions. J Pharm Sci 1982; 71: 370-372.
Cadwallader DE, Madan DK. Effect of macromolecules on aqueous solubility of cholesterol and hormone drugs. J Pharm Sci 1981; 70: 442-446.
Feld KM, Higuchi WI, Su C-C. Influence of benzalkonium chloride on the dissolution behavior of several solid-phase preparations of cholesterol in bile acid solutions. J Pharm Sci 1982; 71: 182-188.
Singh VS, Gaur RC. Dispersion of cholesterol in aqueous surfactant solutions: interpretation of viscosity data. J Disper Sci Technol 1983; 4: 347-359.
Udupa N, Chandraprakash KS, Umadevi P, Pillai GK. Formulation and evaluation of methotrexate niosomes. Drug Dev Ind Pharm 1993; 19: 1331-1342.

22. Authors

USA: AJ Repta.

Citric Acid Monohydrate

1. Nonproprietary Names

BP: Citric acid monohydrate
PhEur: Acidum citricum monohydricum
USP: Citric acid

2. Synonyms

2-Hydroxypropane-1,2,3-tricarboxylic acid monohydrate.

3. Chemical Name and CAS Registry Number

2-Hydroxy-1,2,3-propanetricarboxylic acid monohydrate
[5949-29-1]

4. Empirical Formula   Molecular Weight

$C_6H_8O_7.H_2O$ 210.14

5. Structural Formula

$$\left[\begin{array}{c} CH_2-COOH \\ HO-C-COOH \\ CH_2-COOH \end{array} \right] \bullet H_2O$$

6. Functional Category

Acidifying agent; buffering agent; chelating agent; flavor enhancer.

7. Applications in Pharmaceutical Formulation or Technology

Citric acid, as either the monohydrate or anhydrous material, is widely used in pharmaceutical formulations and food products primarily to adjust the pH of solutions. Citric acid monohydrate is used in the preparation of effervescent granules whilst anhydrous citric acid is widely used in the preparation of effervescent tablets.[1]

In food products citric acid is used as a flavor enhancer, for its tart, acid taste. Citric acid monohydrate is also used as a sequestering agent and antioxidant synergist.

Therapeutically, preparations containing citric acid have been used to dissolve renal calculi.

Use	Concentration (%)
Flavor improver in liquid formulations	0.3-2.0
Sequestering agent	0.3-2.0

8. Description

Citric acid monohydrate occurs as colorless or translucent crystals, or as a white crystalline, efflorescent powder. It is odorless and has a strong acidic taste. Crystal structure is orthorhombic.

SEM: 1

Excipient: Citric acid monohydrate
Manufacturer: Pfizer Ltd
Magnification: 60x

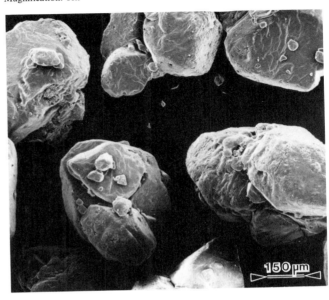

SEM: 2

Excipient: Citric acid monohydrate
Manufacturer: Pfizer Ltd
Magnification: 600x

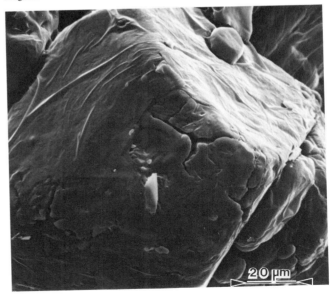

SEM: 3
Excipient: Anhydrous citric acid
Manufacturer: Pfizer Ltd
Magnification: 120x

SEM: 4
Excipient: Anhydrous citric acid
Manufacturer: Pfizer Ltd
Magnification: 600x

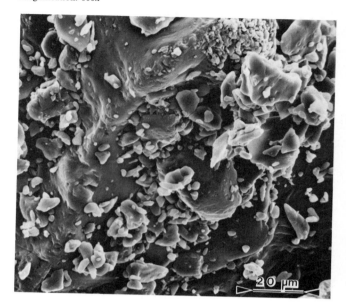

9. Pharmacopeial Specifications

Test	PhEur 1992	USP XXII
Identification	+	+
Clarity and color of solution	+	—
Water		
(hydrous form)	7.5-9.0%	⩽ 8.8%
(anhydrous form)	⩽ 1.0%	⩽ 0.5%
Residue on ignition	—	⩽ 0.05%
Sulfated ash	⩽ 0.1%	—
Barium	+	—
Calcium	⩽ 200 ppm	—
Oxalate	⩽ 350 ppm	—
Sulfate	⩽ 150 ppm	+
Arsenic	—	⩽ 3 ppm
Heavy metals	⩽ 10 ppm	⩽ 0.001%
Iron	⩽ 50 ppm	—
Chloride	⩽ 50 ppm	—
Readily carbonizable substances	+	+
Assay (anhydrous basis)	99.5-101.0%	99.5-100.5%

10. Typical Properties

Acidity/alkalinity:
pH = 2.2 (1% w/v aqueous solution)
Density: 1.542 g/cm^3
Heat of combustion:
-1972 kJ/mol (-471.4 kcal/mol)
Heat of solution:
-16.3 kJ/mol (-3.9 kcal/mol) at 25°C
Hygroscopicity: at relative humidities less than about 65% citric acid monohydrate effloresces at 25°C, the anhydrous acid being formed at relative humidities less than about 40%. At relative humidities between about 65-75%, citric acid monohydrate absorbs insignificant amounts of moisture but under more humid conditions substantial amounts of water are absorbed.
Melting point: ≈ 100°C (softens at 75°C)
Particle size distribution: various grades of citric acid monohydrate with different particle sizes are commercially available, e.g. for a granular grade (Roche Products Ltd) minimum of 99% through a 4 mm mesh (US #5 sieve) and maximum of 10% through a 590 μm mesh (US #30 sieve); for a powder grade (Roche Products Ltd) minimum of 95% through a 250 μm mesh (US #60 sieve) and minimum of 65% through a 73.7 μm mesh (US #200 sieve).
Solubility: soluble 1 in 1.5 parts of ethanol (95%) and 1 in less than 1 part of water; sparingly soluble in ether.
Viscosity (dynamic): 6.5 mPa s (6.5 cP) for a 50% w/v aqueous solution at 25°C
See also Section 18.

11. Stability and Storage Conditions

Citric acid monohydrate loses water of crystallization in dry air or when heated to about 40°C. It is slightly deliquescent in moist air. Dilute aqueous solutions of citric acid may ferment on standing.
The bulk monohydrate or anhydrous material should be stored in airtight containers in a cool, dry, place.

12. Incompatibilities

Citric acid is incompatible with potassium tartrate, alkali and alkaline earth carbonates and bicarbonates, acetates and sulfides. On storage, sucrose may crystallize from syrups in the presence of citric acid.

13. Method of Manufacture

Citric acid occurs naturally in a number of plant species and may be extracted from lemon juice, which contains 5-8% citric acid, or pineapple waste. Anhydrous citric acid may also be produced industrially by mycological fermentation of crude sugar solutions such as molasses, using strains of *Aspergillus niger*. Citric acid is purified by recrystallization; the anhydrous form is obtained from a hot concentrated aqueous solution and the monohydrate from a cold concentrated aqueous solution.

14. Safety

Citric acid is found naturally in the body, mainly in the bones, and is commonly consumed as part of a normal diet. Orally ingested citric acid is absorbed and is generally regarded as a nontoxic material when used as an excipient. Excessive or frequent consumption of citric acid has however been associated with erosion of the teeth.[2]

Citric acid and citrates also enhance intestinal aluminum absorption in renal patients which may lead to increased, harmful serum aluminum levels. It has therefore been suggested that patients with renal failure taking aluminum compounds to control phosphate absorption should not be prescribed citric acid or citrate containing products.[3]

See Section 18 for anhydrous citric acid animal toxicity data.

15. Handling Precautions

Observe normal precautions appropriate to the circumstances and quantity of material handled. Eye protection and gloves are recommended. Citric acid should be handled in a well-ventilated environment or a dust mask should be worn.

16. Regulatory Status

GRAS listed. The anhydrous form is accepted for use as a food additive in Europe. Included in the FDA Inactive Ingredients Guide (inhalations, IM, IV and other injections, ophthalmic preparations, oral capsules, solutions, suspensions and tablets, topical and vaginal preparations). Included in nonparenteral and parenteral medicines licensed in the UK.

17. Pharmacopeias

Aust, Br, Chin, Cz, Egypt, Eur, Fr, Ger, Gr, Hung, Ind, It, Jpn, Mex, Neth, Nord, Port, Rom, Swiss, Turk, US and Yug.

18. Related Substances

Anhydrous citric acid; Sodium Citrate Dihydrate.

Anhydrous citric acid: $C_6H_8O_7$
Molecular weight: 192.12
CAS number: [77-92-9]
Synonyms: acidum citricum anhydricum; citric acid; E330; 2-hydroxy-1,2,3-propanetricarboxylic acid; 2-hydroxypropane-1,2,3-tricarboxylic acid; β-hydroxytricarballylic acid.
Appearance: odorless or almost odorless, colorless crystals or a white crystalline powder. Crystal structure is monoclinic holohedra.

Pharmacopeias: Br, Eur, Fr, Ger, Gr, Ind, It, Jpn, Mex, Neth, Nord, Swiss, US and Yug.
Dissociation constant:
pk_{a1}: 3.128 at 25°C;
pk_{a2}: 4.761 at 25°C;
pk_{a3}: 6.396 at 25°C.
Density: 1.665 g/cm^3
Heat of combustion:
-1985 kJ/mol (-474.5 kcal/mol)
Hygroscopicity: at relative humidities between about 25-50% anhydrous citric acid absorbs insignificant amounts of water at 25°C. However, at relative humidities between 50-75% it absorbs significant amounts with the monohydrate being formed at relative humidities approaching 75%. At relative humidities greater than 75% substantial amounts of water are absorbed.
Melting point: 153°C
Solubility: soluble 1 in 1 parts of ethanol (95%) and 1 in 1 of water; sparingly soluble in ether.
Safety:
LD_{50} (mouse, IP): 0.96 g/kg[4]
LD_{50} (mouse, IV): 0.04 g/kg
LD_{50} (mouse, oral): 5.04 g/kg
LD_{50} (mouse, SC): 2.7 g/kg
LD_{50} (rabbit, IV): 0.33 g/kg
LD_{50} (rat, IP): 0.88 g/kg
LD_{50} (rat, oral): 6.73 g/kg
LD_{50} (rat, SC): 5.5 g/kg

19. Comments

—

20. Specific References

1. Anderson NR, Banker GS, Peck GE. Quantitative evaluation of pharmaceutical effervescent systems II: stability monitoring by reactivity and porosity measurements. J Pharm Sci 1982; 71: 7-13.
2. Citric acid: tooth enamel destruction. ClinAlert 1971; No. 151.
3. Main J, Ward MK. Potentiation of aluminium absorption by effervescent analgesic tablets in a haemodialysis patient. Br Med J 1992; 304: 1686.
4. Sweet DV, editor. Registry of toxic effects of chemical substances. Cincinnati: US Department of Health, 1987.

21. General References

Cho MJ, Scieszka JF, Burton PS. Citric acid as an adjuvant for transepithelial transport. Int J Pharmaceutics 1989; 52: 79-81.

Timko RJ, Lordi NG. Thermal characterization of citric acid solid dispersions with benzoic acid and phenobarbital. J Pharm Sci 1979; 68: 601-605.

22. Authors

USA: GE Amidon.

Coloring Agents

1. Nonproprietary Names
See Section 18, and Tables I, II, III and IV.

2. Synonyms
See Section 18 for specific, selected, coloring agents.

3. Chemical Name and CAS Registry Number
See Tables I, II, III and IV.

Table I: European Community list of coloring materials authorized for coloring medicinal products up to June 1992.

EC number	Common name	CAS number
E100	Curcumin	[458-37-7]
E101	Lactoflavin (riboflavin)	[83-88-5]
E102	Tartrazine	[1934-21-0]
E104	Quinoline yellow	[8004-92-0]
E110	Sunset yellow FCF	[2783-94-0]
E120	Cochineal carminic acid	[1260-17-9]
E122	Carmoisine	[3567-69-9]
E123	Amaranth	[915-67-3]
E124	Ponceau 4R	[2611-82-7]
E127	Erythrosine	[16423-68-0]
E131	Patent blue V	[3536-49-0]
E132	Indigo carmine	[860-22-0]
E140	Chlorophylls	[479-61-8] for a
		[519-62-0] for b
E141	Copper complexes of chlorophylls and chlorophyllins	—
E142	Acid brilliant green BS (lissamine green)	[3087-16-9]
E150	Caramel	[8028-89-5]
E151	Brilliant black BN, black PN	[2519-30-4]
E153	Carbo medicinalis vegetabilis (charcoal)	—
E160	Carotenoids:	
	Alpha-, beta-, gamma-carotene	[7235-40-7]
	Bixin, norbixin (roucou annatto)	[8015-67-6]
	Capsanthin	[465-42-9]
	Capsorubin	[470-38-2]
	Lycopene	[502-65-8]
	Beta-apo-8′ carotenal (C30)	[1107-26-2]
	Ethyl ester of beta-apo-8′ carotenoic acid (C30)	—
E161	Xanthophylls:	
	Flavoxanthin	[512-29-8]
	Lutein	[127-40-2]
	Kryptoxanthin	[472-70-8]
	Rubixanthin	[3763-55-1]
	Violaxanthin	[126-29-4]
	Rhodoxanthin	[116-30-3]
	Canthaxanthin	[514-78-3]
E162	Beetroot red, betanin	—
E163	Anthocyanins:	
E163a	Cyanidin	[528-58-5]
E163b	Delphidin	[528-53-0]
E163c	Malvidin	[643-84-5]

Continued

EC number	Common name	CAS number
E163d	Pelargonidin	[134-04-3]
E163e	Peonidin	[134-01-0]
E163f	Petunidin	[1429-30-7]
E170*	Calcium carbonate	[471-34-1]
E171	Titanium dioxide	[13463-67-7]
E172	Iron oxides and hydroxides	[977053-38-5]
E173*	Aluminum	[7429-90-5]
E174*	Silver	[7440-22-4]
E175*	Gold	[7440-57-5]

* For surface coloring only.

Note: List of colors taken from Annex I, Sections I and II of the Council Directive of 23 October 1962 concerning the approximation of legislation of Member States for coloring materials which can be utilized in foodstuffs destined for human consumption. (Official Journal EC 1962; 115: 2645-2662.)
Amended by:
Directive EC/65/469. Official Journal EC 1965; 178: 2793.
Directive EC/67/653. Official Journal EC 1967; 263: 4.
Directive EC/68/419. Official Journal EC 1968; L 309: 24.
Directive EC/70/358. Official Journal EC 1970; L 157: 36.
Act of Accession. Official Journal EC 1972; L 73: 14.
Directive EC/76/399. Official Journal EC 1976; L 108: 19.
Directive EC/78/144. Official Journal EC 1978; L 44.

4. Empirical Formula Molecular Weight
See Section 18 for specific, selected, coloring agents.

5. Structural Formula
See Section 18 for specific, selected, coloring agents.

6. Functional Category
Colorants; opacifiers.

7. Applications in Pharmaceutical Formulation or Technology
The primary purpose of coloring agents is to visually alter the appearance of a medicinal product by imparting a definite color or shade. This has the advantage to the manufacturer of making otherwise similar products more distinctive. Easier differentiation of a product is also of considerable benefit to the patient on multiple medication.[1]
The use of color in medicinal products, in conjunction with other factors, such as shape and packing, additionally serves to reinforce brand image and identity. This commercial distinctiveness also aids in preventing the counterfeiting of products. Colors used in some preparations can also serve to introduce a uniformity of appearance to a product, e.g. a tablet, where an ingredient in the formulation has itself a variable appearance from batch to batch.[2]
The classes of product most frequently colored are:
1. Coated tablets
2. Uncoated tablets
3. Hard and soft gelatin capsules
4. Liquid oral preparations.
The use of color is occasionally associated with topical preparations (especially over the counter remedies) and sustained release granules in transparent hard gelatin capsules. Some of the insoluble colors or pigments have the additional benefit when used in tablet coatings or gelatin shells of

Table II: List of permanently listed color additives subject to US certification in 1991.

Color	Common name	CAS number	21 CFR references to drug use
FD&C blue #1	Brilliant blue FCF	[2650-18-2]	74.1101
FD&C blue #2	Indigotine	[860-22-0]	74.1102
D&C blue #4	Alphazurine FG	[6371-85-3]	74.1104
D&C blue #9	Indanthrene blue	[130-20-1]	74.1109
FD&C green #3	Fast green FCF	[2353-45-9]	74.1203
D&C green #5	Alizarin cyanine Green F	[4403-90-1]	74.1205
D&C green #6	Quinizarine green SS	[128-80-3]	74.1206
D&C green #8	Pyranine concentrated	[6358-69-6]	74.1208
D&C orange #4	Orange II	[633-96-5]	74.1254
D&C orange #5	Dibromofluorescein	[596-03-2]	74.1255
D&C orange #10	Diiodofluorescein	[38577-97-8]	74.1260
D&C orange #11	Erythrosine yellowish Na	[38577-97-8]	74.1261
FD&C red #3	Erythrosine	[16423-68-0]	74.1303
FD&C red #4	Ponceau SX	[4548-53-2]	74.1304
D&C red #6	Lithol rubin B	[5858-81-1]	74.1306
D&C red #7	Lithol rubin B Ca	[5281-04-9]	74.1307
D&C red #17	Toney red	[85-86-9]	74.1317
D&C red #21	Tetrabromofluorescein	[15086-94-9]	74.1321
D&C red #22	Eosine	[17372-87-1]	74.1322
D&C red #27	Tetrachlorotetrabromo-fluorescein	[13473-26-2]	74.1327
D&C red #28	Phloxine B	[18472-87-2]	74.1328
D&C red #30	Helindone pink CN	[2379-74-0]	74.1330
D&C red #31	Brilliant lake red R	[6371-76-2]	74.1331
D&C red #33	Acid fuchsine	[3567-66-6]	74.1333
D&C red #34	Lake bordeaux B	[6417-83-0]	74.1334
D&C red #36	Flaming red	[2814-77-9]	74.1336
D&C red #39	Alba red	[6371-55-7]	74.1339
FD&C red #40	Allura red AC	[25956-17-6]	74.1340
FD&C red #40 lake	Allura red AC	[68583-95-9]	74.1340
D&C violet #2	Alizurol purple SS	[81-48-1]	74.1602
Ext. D&C violet #2	Alizarin violet	[4430-18-6]	—
FD&C yellow #5	Tartrazine	[1934-21-0]	74.1705
FD&C yellow #6	Sunset yellow FCF	[2783-94-0]	74.1706
D&C yellow #7	Fluorescein	[2321-07-5]	74.1707
Ext. D&C yellow #7	Napthol yellow S	[846-70-8]	74.1707
D&C yellow #8	Uranine	[518-47-8]	74.1708
D&C yellow #10	Quinoline yellow WS	[8004-92-0]	74.1710
D&C yellow #11	Quinoline yellow SS	[8003-22-3]	74.1711

providing useful opacity which can aid in the stability of light sensitive active materials in the tablet or capsule formulation. Pigments such as the iron oxides, titanium dioxide and some of the aluminum lakes are especially useful for this purpose.[3]

Of the many classifications possible for pharmaceutical coloring agents, one of the most useful is to simply divide the colors into those which are soluble in water (dyes) and those which are insoluble in water (pigments).

Colors for clear liquid preparations are limited to the dyes,[4] e.g. see Section 18.

For surface coloration, which includes coated tablets, the choice of color is usually restricted to insoluble pigments. The reasons for this include their lack of color migration, greater opacity and enhanced color stability over water soluble colors.[5]

Lakes are largely water insoluble forms of the common synthetic water soluble dyes. They are prepared by adsorbing a sodium or potassium salt of a dye onto a very fine substrate of hydrated alumina, followed by treatment with a further soluble aluminum salt. The lake is then purified and dried.[6]

Lakes are frequently used in coloring tablet coatings since, for this purpose, they have the general advantages of pigments over water soluble colors. See Table V.

8. Description

The physical appearance of coloring agents varies widely. See Section 18 for specific, selected, coloring agents.

9. Pharmacopeial Specifications

A number of materials used as pharmaceutical coloring agents are included in various pharmacopeias, see Section 17. In general, the pharmacopeial specifications are based on the purity requirements for pharmaceutical coloring agents shown

Table III: List of provisionally listed color additives subject to US certification in 1991.

Color	Common name	CAS number	21 CFR references to drug use
FD&C lakes	General	*See* individual color	82.51
D&C lakes	General	*See* individual color	82.1051
Ext. D&C lakes	General	*See* individual color	82.2051
FD&C blue #1 lake	Brilliant blue FCF	[53026-57-6]	82.101
FD&C blue #2 lake	Indigotine	[16521-38-3]	82.102
D&C blue #4 lake	Alphazurine FG	[6371-85-3]	82.1104
FD&C green #3 lake	Fast green FCF	[2353-45-9]	82.203
D&C green #5 lake	Alizarin cyanine Green F	[4403-90-1]	82.1205
D&C green #6 lake	Quinizarine Green SS	[128-80-3]	82.1206
D&C orange #4 lake	Orange II	[633-56-5]	82.1254
D&C orange #5 lake	Dibromofluorescein	[596-03-2]	82.1255
D&C orange #10 lake	Diiodofluorescein	[38577-97-8]	82.1260
D&C orange #11 lake	Erythosine yellowish Na	[38577-97-8]	82.1261
FD&C red #4 lake	Ponceau SX	[4548-53-2]	82.304
D&C red #6 lake	Lithol rubin B	[17852-98-1]	82.1306
D&C red #7 lake	Lithol rubin B Ca	[5281-04-9]	82.1307
D&C red #17 lake	Toney red	[85-86-9]	82.1317
D&C red #21 lake	Tetrabromofluorescein	[15086-94-9]	82.1321
D&C red #22 lake	Eosine	[17372-87-1]	82.1322
D&C red #27 lake	Tetrachlorotetrabromo-fluorescein	[13473-26-2]	82.1327
D&C red #28 lake	Phloxine B	[18472-87-2]	82.1328
D&C red #30 lake	Helindone pink CN	[2379-74-0]	82.1330
D&C red #31 lake	Brilliant lake red R	[6371-76-2]	82.1331
D&C red #33 lake	Acid fuchsine	[3567-66-6]	82.1333
D&C red #34 lake	Lake bordeaux B	[6417-83-0]	82.1334
D&C red #36 lake	Flaming red	[2814-77-9]	82.1336
D&C violet #2 lake	Alizurol purple SS	[81-48-1]	82.1602
FD&C yellow #5 lake	Tartrazine	[12225-21-7]	82.705
FD&C yellow #6 lake	Sunset yellow FCF	[15790-07-5]	82.706
D&C yellow #7 lake	Fluorescein	[2321-07-5]	82.1707
Ext. D&C yellow #7 lake	Napthol yellow S	[846-70-8]	82.2707
D&C yellow #8 lake	Uranine	[518-47-8]	82.1708
D&C yellow #10 lake	Quinoline yellow WS	[68814-04-0]	82.1710

in Table VI. Specifications for specific, selected, coloring agents are also shown in Section 18.

10. Typical Properties

Typical properties of specific, selected, coloring agents are shown in Section 18. Properties of lakes and general purity requirements for coloring agents are shown in Tables V and VI respectively.

11. Stability and Storage Conditions

Pharmaceutical coloring agents form a chemically diverse group of materials which have widely varying stability properties. Specific information for selected colors is shown in Table VII and in Woznicki and Schoneker.[4] *See also* Section 18.

Whilst some colors, notably the inorganic pigments, show excellent stability, other coloring agents, such as some organic colors, have poor stability properties but are used in formulations because of their low toxicity.[7]

Some natural and synthetic organic colors are particularly unstable in light. However, with appropriate manufacturing procedures, combined with effective product packaging these colors may be successfully used in formulations, thus making a wide choice of colors practically available.

Lakes, inorganic dyes, and synthetic dyes should be stored in well-closed, light-resistant containers at a temperature below 30°C.

For most natural and nature identical colors the storage conditions are more stringent and a manufacturers recommendations for a particular color should be followed.

To extend shelf life, some natural colors are supplied as gelatin or similarly encapsulated powders and/or sealed in containers under nitrogen.

12. Incompatibilities

See Section 18 for incompatibilities of specific selected coloring agents and also Woznicki and Schoneker,[4] and Walford.[8,9]

Table IV: List of color additives exempt from certification permitted for use in the US in 1991.

Color	CAS number	21 CFR references to drug use
Alumina	[1332-73-6]	73.1010
Aluminum powder	[7429-90-5]	73.1645
Annato extract	[8015-67-6]	73.1030
Beta-carotene	[7235-40-7]	73.1095
Bismuth oxychloride	[7787-59-9]	73.1162
Bronze powder	[7440-66-6]	73.1646
Calcium carbonate	[471-34-1]	73.1070
Canthaxanthin	[514-78-3]	73.1075
Caramel	[8028-89-5]	73.1085
Carmine	[1390-65-4]	73.1100
Chromium-cobalt-aluminum oxide	[68187-11-1]	73.1015
Chromium hydroxide green	[12182-82-0]	73.1326
Chromium oxide green	[1308-38-9]	73.1327
Cochineal extract	[1260-17-9]	73.1100
Copper powder	[7440-50-6]	73.1647
Dihydroxy acetone	[62147-49-3]	73.1150
Ferric ammonium citrate	[1185-57-5]	73.1025
Ferric ammonium ferrocyanide	[25869-00-5]	73.1298
Ferric ferrocyanide	[14038-43-8]	73.1299
Guanine	[68-94-0]	73.1329
	[73-40-5]	
Iron oxides synthetic	[977053-38-5]	73.1200
Logwood extract	[8005-33-2]	73.1410
Mica	[12001-26-2]	73.1496
Potassium sodium copper chlorophyllin	—	73.1125
Pyrogallol	[87-66-1]	73.1375
Pyrophyllite	[8047-76-5]	73.1400
Talc	[14807-96-6]	73.1550
Titanium dioxide	[13463-67-7]	73.1575
Zinc oxide	[1314-13-2]	73.1991

Table V: Characteristic properties of selected aluminum lakes.

	Indigo carmine	Sunset yellow FCF	Tartrazine
Appearance	Reddish blue powder	Reddish yellow powder	Greenish yellow powder
Pure dye content (%)	12-34	15-40	15-39
Solubility (% dye dissolved)			
pH 1.3	84.2	93.8	97.2
pH 3.0	13.2	5.7	18.8
Chemical resistance			
Alkali	F	F	F
Acid	F	G	G

Note: G = Good   F = Fair

13. Method of Manufacture

See Section 18, and Walford[8,9] for information on specific, selected, coloring agents.

14. Safety

Coloring agents are used in a variety of oral and topical pharmaceutical formulations, in addition to their use in cosmetics and food products.

Concerns over the safety of particular coloring agents in pharmaceutical formulations generally arise from adverse effects noticed as a result of the more widespread use of colors in food products. Although continuous review, over many years, by such bodies as the FDA, has resulted in a list of permitted colors which are generally regarded as free of serious adverse toxicological effects, a number of coloring agents in current use have been associated with adverse effects, although in a relatively small number of people.[10,11] Restrictions or bans on the use of some coloring agents have been imposed in some countries, whilst the same color may be permitted for use in a different country.

Erythrosine (FD&C red #3), for example, has been delisted (*see* Section 16) in the US since 1990, following studies in rats which suggested that it was carcinogenic. This was as a result of the Delaney Clause, which restricts the use of any color shown to induce cancer in humans or animals in any amount.

Table VI: General purity requirements for colors.

	EC*	FAO/WHO	USA FD&C	D&C
Water insoluble matter	—	≤ 0.2%	—	—
Ether extracts	—	≤ 0.2%	—	—
Lead	≤ 20 ppm	≤ 10 ppm	≤ 10 ppm[a]	≤ 20 ppm[a]
Arsenic	≤ 5 ppm	≤ 3 ppm	≤ 1.4 ppm[a]	≤ 2 ppm[a]
Subsidiary colors	≤ 4%	≤ 4%	—	—
Volatile matter (135°C)	—	≤ 15%	—	—
Chlorides and sulfates (as Na salts)	—	≤ 15%	—	—
Intermediates	≤ 0.5% (except free aromatic amines)	≤ 0.5%	—	—
Heavy metals[b]	—	—	≤ trace	≤ 30 ppm

^a For provisionally listed colors only.   ^b Except lead and arsenic, by precipitation as sulfides.
* Additional general EC requirements:

Inorganic Impurities: the colorants should contain not more than 100 mg/kg of the following substances, taken separately: antimony; copper; chromium; barium sulphate; zinc; and not more than 200 mg/kg of these products taken together. They should not contain: cadmium; mercury; selenium; tellurium; thallium; uranium or chromates; or soluble combinations of barium in detectable quantities.

Organic Impurities: the colorants should not contain amino-4-diphenyl (or xenylamine), benzidine, 2-naphthylamine or their derivatives; or polycyclic aromatic hydrocarbons. Synthetic organic coloring matters should in addition contain not more than 0.01% of free aromatic amines, while sulfonated organic coloring agents should contain not more than 0.2% of substances extractable by diethyl ether.

Table VII: Stability properties of selected dyes.

	Indigo carmine	Sunset yellow FCF	Tartrazine
Heat stability			
At 105°C	A	VG	O
At 205°C	P	VG	VG
Light stability	VP to P	G to VG	G to VG
pH stability	P	G	(≤ 10) G
Oxidizing agents	VP	—	—
Reducing agents	VP	P	—
Color stability of tablets*	> 3 days	1-3 days	> 3 days

* Measured on solid dosage forms (colored tablets), exposed to Xenotest of 200 000 lux irradiation (daylight is approximately 10 000 lux).
A = Acceptable P = Poor G = Good
VG = Very good VP = Very poor O = Outstanding

However, erythrosine was not regarded as being an immediate hazard to health and products containing it were permitted to be used until supplies were exhausted.[12]
Tartrazine (FD&C yellow #5) has also been the subject of controversy over its safety, and restrictions are imposed on its use in some countries, *see* Section 18.
In general, concerns over the safety of coloring agents in pharmaceuticals and foods are associated with reports of hypersensitivity[13-15] and hyperkinetic activity, especially among children.[16]

15. Handling Precautions

Pharmaceutical coloring agents form a diverse group of materials and manufacturers' data sheets should be consulted for safety and handling data for specific colors.
In general, inorganic pigments and lakes are of a low hazard and standard chemical handling precautions should be observed depending upon the circumstances and quantity of material handled. Care should be especially taken to prevent excessive dust generation and inhalation.
The organic dyes, natural colors and nature identical colors present a greater hazard and appropriate precautions should accordingly be taken.

16. Regulatory Status

In both the EC and US, pharmaceutical coloring agents are subject to regulations and legislation not generally encountered with other pharmaceutical excipients. Amongst other items this legislation specifies which colorants may be used in medicinal products, and also provides for purity specifications.
European Community legislation: Table I shows a list of colors permitted for use in medicinal products within the EC. It is derived from an unnumbered 1962 Directive[17] listing food colors and their specifications. Since 1962, this Directive has been extensively amended.

The important EC Directive, EC/78/25, limits the choice of pharmaceutical colours to those listed in Annex I of the 1962 Directive. However, small national differences do exist, and some states forbid certain colors, *see* Table VIII.

Within the EC, the use of pharmaceutical colors is regulated by food color legislation. Acceptable daily intakes for colors permitted for use in foods have been set by various expert committees of the FAO/WHO and are the subject of periodic review. The Scientific Committee on Food of the EC is also actively involved in a continuing safety review of all food additives, including colors.

A new EC Directive, to replace the 1962 Directive and its amendments is currently under consideration.

United States legislation: the 1960 Color Additive Amendment to the Food Drug and Cosmetic Act defines the responsibility of the Food and Drug Administration in the area of pharmaceutical colorants. Tables II, III and IV provide a list of permitted colors.[18] The list is superficially long but many of the coloring agents have a restricted use.

For the so called certified colors, the FDA operates a scheme whereby each batch of color produced is certified as analytically correct by the FDA prior to issuing a certification number and document which will permit sale of the batch in question. Colors requiring certification are described as FD&C (Food Drug and Cosmetic); D&C (Drug and Cosmetic) or External D&C. The remaining colors are described as uncertified colors and are mainly of natural origin.

The US also operates a system of division of certified colors into permanently and provisionally listed colors. Provisionally listed colors require the regular intervention of the FDA Commissioner to provide continued listing of these colors. Should the need arise, the legislative process for removal of these colors from use is comparatively easy.

Licensing authority approval: in addition to national approvals and lists, a pharmaceutical licensing authority can impose additional restrictions at the time of application review. Within the EC this generally takes the form of restricting colors, such as tartrazine and amaranth, in medicinal products for chronic administration, and especially in medicines for allergic conditions.

Table VIII: Additional restrictions imposed by EC member states on the use of colors specified in EC Directive EC/78/25.

Country	Restricted colors
Belgium	Amaranth
Denmark	Tartrazine
Greece	Lissamine green, tartrazine
Italy	Patent blue V, tartrazine
Luxembourg	Vegetable carbon black

17. Pharmacopeias

Pharmaceutical coloring agents are not widely represented in the pharmacopeias. Those which are included are shown in Table IX.

Table IX: Pharmaceutical coloring agents listed in pharmacopeias.

Coloring agent	Pharmacopeia
Black PN	Fr.
Caramel	USPNF.
Carmine	Arg, Belg, Fr, Port and Swiss.
Carmoisine	Fr.
Cochineal	Br, Egypt and Port.
Erythrosine	Fr.

Continued

Coloring agent	Pharmacopeia
Iron oxides	
(Black)	Fr.
(Red)	Fr and USPNF.
(Yellow)	Fr and USPNF.
Ponceau 4R	Fr.
Quinoline yellow	Fr.
Sunset yellow	Fr.
Titanium dioxide*	Aust, Br, Braz, Eur, Fr, Ind, It, Jpn, Neth, Swiss, US and Yug.

* Titanium dioxide frequently appears in pharmacopeias by virtue of its medicinal use as an ingredient in topical preparations. For use as a pharmaceutical coloring agent, additional purity criteria may need to be met. *See also* Section 19 and Titanium Dioxide.

18. Related Substances

Beta-carotene; indigo carmine; iron oxides; sunset yellow FCF; tartrazine; Titanium Dioxide.

Beta-carotene: $C_{40}H_{56}$
Molecular weight: 536.85
CAS number: [7235-40-7]
Synonyms: betacarotene; β-carotene; β,β-carotene; E160a.
Structure:

Appearance: occurs in the pure state as red crystals when recrystallized from light petroleum. A 1% w/v solution in chloroform is clear.
Color Index No.:
CI 75130 (natural);
CI 40800 (synthetic).
Melting point: 183°C
Purity (EC): general requirements only, *see* Table VI.
Purity (US):
Arsenic: $\leqslant$ 3 ppm
Assay: 96-101%
Lead: $\leqslant$ 10 ppm
Residue on ignition: $\leqslant$ 0.2%
Loss on drying: $\leqslant$ 0.2%
1% solution in chloroform: clear
Solubility: soluble 1 in 30 parts of chloroform; practically insoluble in ethanol, glycerin and water.
Incompatibilities: generally incompatible with oxidizing agents; decolorization will take place.
Stability: beta-carotene is very susceptible to oxidation and antioxidants such as ascorbic acid, sodium ascorbate or tocopherols should be added. Store protected from light at a low temperature (-20°C) in containers sealed under nitrogen.
Method of Manufacture: all industrial processes for preparing carotenoids are based on β-ionone. This material can be obtained by total synthesis from acetone and acetylene via dehydrolinalool. The commercially available material is usually 'extended' on a matrix such as acacia or maltodextrin. These extended forms of beta-carotene are dispersible in aqueous systems. Beta-carotene is also available as micronized crystals suspended in an edible oil such as peanut oil.

Comments: beta-carotene is capable of producing colors varying from pale yellow to dark orange. It can be used as a color for sugar coated tablets prepared by the ladle process. However, beta-carotene is very unstable to light and air, and products containing this material should be securely packaged to minimize degradation. Beta-carotene is particularly unstable when used in spray-coating processes, probably due to atmospheric oxygen attacking the finely dispersed spray droplets.

Because of its poor water solubility beta-carotene cannot be used to color clear aqueous systems, and co-solvents such as ethanol must be used.

Suppositories have been successfully colored with beta-carotene in approximately 0.1% concentration.

Indigo carmine: $C_{16}H_8N_2Na_2O_8S_2$
Molecular weight: 466.37
CAS number: [860-22-0]
Synonyms: 2-(1,3-dihydro-3-oxo-5-sulfo-2H-indol-2-ylidene)-2,3-dihydro-3-oxo-1H-indole-5-sulfonic acid disodium salt; disodium 5,5'-indigotin disulfonate; E132; FD&C blue #2; indigotine; sodium indigotin disulfonate; soluble indigo blue.
Structure:

Appearance: dark blue powder. Aqueous solutions are blue or bluish-purple colored.
Absorption maximum: 604 nm
Color Index No.: CI 73015
Purity (EC): general requirements (Table VI) and tests shown below.
Accessory colorings: $\leqslant$ 1.0%
Isatin-5-sulfonic acid: $\leqslant$ 1.0%
Water insoluble matter: $\leqslant$ 0.2%
Purity (US):
Arsenic: $\leqslant$ 3 ppm
2-(1,3-Dihydro-3-oxo-2H-indol-2-ylidene)-2,3-dihydro-3-oxo-1H-indole-5-sulfonic acid sodium salt: $\leqslant$ 2%
2-(1,3-Dihydro-3-oxo-7-sulfo-2H-indol-2-ylidene)-2,3-dihydro-3-oxo-1H-indole-5-sulfonic acid disodium salt: $\leqslant$ 18%
Isatin-5-sulfonic acid: $\leqslant$ 0.4%
Lead: $\leqslant$ 10 ppm
Mercury: $\leqslant$ 1 ppm
5-Sulfoanthranilic acid: $\leqslant$ 0.2%
Total color: $\geqslant$ 85%
Volatile matter, chlorides and sulfates (calculated as the sodium salts): $\leqslant$ 15.0% at 135°C
Water insoluble matter: $\leqslant$ 0.4%

Solubility:

Solvent	Solubility at 25°C Unless otherwise stated
Acetone	practically insoluble
Ethanol (75%)	1 in 1430
Glycerin	1 in 100
Propylene glycol	1 in 1000
Propylene glycol (50%)	1 in 167
Water	1 in 125 at 2°C
	1 in 63 at 25°C
	1 in 45 at 60°C

Incompatibilities: poorly compatible with citric acid and saccharose solution. Incompatible with ascorbic acid, gelatin, glucose, lactose, oxidizing agents, and saturated sodium bicarbonate solution.
Stability: sensitive to light.
Method of Manufacture: indigo is sulfonated with concentrated or fuming sulfuric acid.
Safety:
LD_{50} (mouse, oral): 2.5 g/kg[19]
LD_{50} (rat, oral): 2 g/kg
Comments: indigo carmine is an indigoid dye used to color oral and topical pharmaceutical preparations. It is used with yellow colors to produce green colors. Indigo carmine is also used to color nylon surgical sutures and is used diagnostically as a 0.8% w/v injection.

Iron oxides:
$Fe_2O_3.H_2O$ (yellow, 97-98% monohydrate);
Fe_2O_3 (red);
$FeO.Fe_2O_3$ (black or brown).
CAS number: [977053-38-5]
Synonyms: E172.
Appearance: yellow, red, black or brown powder. The color depends on the particle size, shape and the amount of combined water.
Color Index No.:
CI 77491 (red, brown);
CI 77492 (yellow);
CI 77499 (black).
Purity (EC): general requirements (Table VI) and tests shown below.
Mercury: $\leqslant$ 1 ppm
Selenium: $\leqslant$ 2 ppm
Purity (US):
Arsenic: $\leqslant$ 3 ppm
Lead: $\leqslant$ 10 ppm
Mercury: $\leqslant$ 3 ppm
Solubility: practically insoluble in water; partially soluble in strong mineral acids.
Incompatibilities: it has been reported that iron oxides make hard gelatin capsules brittle at higher temperatures when the residual moisture is 11-12%. This factor affects the use of iron oxides for coloring hard gelatin capsules and would limit the amount to be incorporated into the gelatin material.
Method of Manufacture: Fe^{2+} salt solutions are precipitated and oxidized to black (or brown) iron oxide.
Comments: iron oxides are gaining importance as mineral colorants as a result of the limitations affecting some synthetic organic dyestuffs. Nevertheless, the use of iron oxide colorants is limited in the US to a maximum ingestion of 5 mg of elemental iron per day. There are also some technical restrictions on the use of iron oxides, e.g. dullness and limitation of shade, and abrasiveness.

Sunset yellow FCF: $C_{16}H_{10}N_2Na_2O_7S_2$
Molecular weight: 452.37
CAS number: [2783-94-0]
Synonyms: E110; FD&C yellow #6; 6-hydroxy-5-[(4-sulfophe-nyl)azo]-2-napthalenesulfonic acid disodium salt; 1-*p*-sulfo-phenylazo-2-naphthol-6-sulfonic acid disodium salt; yellow orange S.
Structure:

Appearance: reddish yellow powder. Aqueous solutions are bright orange colored.
Absorption maximum: 482 nm
Color Index No.: CI 15985
Purity (EC): general requirements (Table VI) and tests shown below.
Water insoluble matter: $\leqslant$ 0.2%
Purity (US):
Chlorides and sulfates of sodium: $\leqslant$ 5.0%
Ether extracts: $\leqslant$ 0.2%
Mixed oxides: $\leqslant$ 1.0%
Subsidiary dyes: $\leqslant$ 5.0%
Total color: $\geqslant$ 85.0%
Volatile matter: $\leqslant$ 10.0% at 135°C
Water insoluble matter: $\leqslant$ 0.5%
Solubility:

Solvent	Solubility at 25°C Unless otherwise stated
Acetone	1 in 38.5
Ethanol (75%)	1 in 333
Glycerin	1 in 5
Propylene glycol	1 in 45.5
Propylene glycol (50%)	1 in 5
Water	1 in 5.3 at 2°C
	1 in 5.3 at 25°C
	1 in 5 at 60°C

Incompatibilities: poorly compatible with citric acid, saccharose solutions and saturated sodium bicarbonate solutions. Incompatible with ascorbic acid, gelatin and glucose.
Method of Manufacture: diazotized sulfanilic acid is coupled with Schaeffer's salt (sodium salt of β-naphthol-6-sulfonic acid).
Safety:
LD_{50} (mouse, IP): 4.6 g/kg[19]
LD_{50} (mouse, oral): > 6 g/kg
LD_{50} (rat, IP): 3.8 g/kg
LD_{50} (rat, oral): > 10 g/kg
Comments: sunset yellow FCF is a monoazo dye.

Tartrazine: $C_{16}H_9N_4Na_3O_9S_2$
Molecular weight: 534.39
CAS number: [1934-21-0]

Synonyms: 4,5-dihydro-5-oxo-(4-sulfophenyl) 4-[(4-sulfophe-nyl)azo]-1*H*-pyrazole-3-carboxylic acid trisodium salt; E102; FD&C yellow #5; hydrazine yellow.
Structure:

Appearance: yellow or orange-yellow powder. Aqueous solutions are yellow colored; the color is retained upon addition of hydrochloric acid solution, but with sodium hydroxide solution a reddish color is formed.
Absorption maximum: 425 nm
Color Index No.: CI 19140
Purity (EC): general requirements (Table VI) and tests shown below.
Accessory colorings: $\leqslant$ 1.0%
Water insoluble matter: $\leqslant$ 0.2%
Purity (US):
Arsenic: $\leqslant$ 3 ppm
Lead: $\leqslant$ 10 ppm
Other uncombined intermediates: $\leqslant$ 0.2%
Phenylhydrazine-*p*-sulfonic acid: $\leqslant$ 0.1%
Subsidiary dyes: $\leqslant$ 1.0%
Total color: $\geqslant$ 87.0%
Volatile matter, chlorides and sulfates (calculated as the sodium salts): $\leqslant$ 13.0% at 135°C
Water insoluble matter: $\leqslant$ 0.2%
Solubility:

Solvent	Solubility at 25°C Unless otherwise stated
Acetone	practically insoluble
Ethanol (75%)	1 in 91
Glycerin	1 in 5.6
Propylene glycol	1 in 14.3
Propylene glycol (50%)	1 in 5
Water	1 in 26 at 2°C
	1 in 5 at 25°C
	1 in 5 at 60°C

Incompatibilities: poorly compatible with citric acid solution. Incompatible with ascorbic acid, lactose, 10% glucose solution and saturated aqueous sodium bicarbonate solution. Gelatin accelerates the fading of the color.
Method of Manufacture: phenylhydrazine *p*-sulfonic acid is condensed with sodium ethyl oxalacetate; the product obtained from this reaction is then coupled with diazotized sulfanilic acid.
Safety:
LD_{50} (mouse, oral): 12.75 g/kg[19]
Comments: tartrazine is a monoazo, or pyrazolone dye. It is used to improve the appearance of a product and to impart a distinctive coloring for identification purposes.
US regulations require that prescription drugs for human use containing tartrazine bear the warning statement: 'This product contains FD&C yellow #5 (tartrazine) which may cause allergic-type reactions (including bronchial asthma) in certain susceptible persons.' Although the overall incidence of FD&C yellow #5 (tartrazine) sensitivity in the general

population is low, it is frequently seen in patients who are also hypersensitive to aspirin.

19. Comments

Titanium dioxide is used extensively to impart a white color to film coated tablets, sugar coated tablets, and gelatin capsules. It is also used in lakes as an opacifier, to 'extend' the color. *See* Titanium Dioxide monograph for further information.

In the EC, colors used in pharmaceutical formulations and colors used in cosmetics are controlled by separate regulations. Cosmetic colors are also classified according to their use, e.g. those which may be used in external products which are washed off after use.

20. Specific References

1. Hess H, Schrank J. Coloration of pharmaceuticals: possibilities and technical problems. Acta Pharm Technol 1979; 25(Suppl 8): 77-87.
2. Aulton ME, Abdul-Razzak MH, Hogan JE. The mechanical properties of hydroxypropylmethylcellulose films derived from aqueous systems part 1: the influence of solid inclusions. Drug Dev Ind Pharm 1984; 10: 541-561.
3. Rowe RC. The opacity of tablet film coatings. J Pharm Pharmacol 1984; 36: 569-572.
4. Woznicki EJ, Schoneker DR. Coloring agents for use in pharmaceuticals. In: Swarbrick J, Boylan JC, editors. Encyclopedia of pharmaceutical technology, volume 3. New York: Marcel Dekker, 1990: 65-100.
5. Porter SC. Tablet coating. Drug Cosmet Ind 1981; 128(5): 46, 48, 50, 53, 86-93.
6. Marmion DM. Handbook of US colorants for foods, drugs and cosmetics, 3rd edition. New York: Wiley-Interscience, 1991.
7. Delonca H, Laget J-P, Saunal H, Ahmed K. Stability of principal tablet coating colors II: effect of adjuvants on color stability [in French] Pharm Acta Helv 1983; 58: 332-337.
8. Walford J, editor. Developments in food colours, volume 1. New York: Elsevier, 1980.
9. Walford J, editor. Developments in food colours, volume 2. New York: Elsevier, 1980.
10. Weiner M, Bernstein IL. Adverse reactions to drug formulation agents: a handbook of excipients. New York: Marcel Dekker, 1989: 159-165.
11. Smolinske SC. Handbook of food, drug, and cosmetic excipients. Boca Raton, FL: CRC Press Inc, 1992.
12. Blumenthal D. Red No. 3 and other colorful controversies. FDA Consumer 1990; 21: 18.
13. Bell T. Colourants and drug reactions [letter]. Lancet 1991; 338: 55-56.
14. Lévesque H, Moore N, Courtois H. Reporting adverse drug reactions by proprietary name [letter]. Lancet 1991; 338: 393.
15. Dietemann-Molard A, Braun JJ, Sohier B, Pauli G. Extrinsic allergic alveolitis secondary to carmine [letter]. Lancet 1991; 338: 460.
16. Pollock I, Young E, Stoneham M, Slater N, Wilkinson JD, Warner JO. Survey of colourings and preservatives in drugs. Br Med J 1989; 299: 649-651.
17. Official Journal EC. 1962; 115: 2645-2662.
18. Code of Federal Regulations 1991; Title 21 Parts 74, 81, 82.
19. Sweet DV, editor. Registry of toxic effects of chemical substances. Cincinnati: US Department of Health, 1987.

21. General References

Jones BE. Colours for pharmaceutical products. Pharmaceut Technol Int 1993; 5(4): 14-16, 18-20.

22. Authors

UK: JE Hogan.

Corn Oil

1. Nonproprietary Names
USPNF: Corn oil

2. Synonyms
Calchem IVO-108; *Lipex 104*; maize oil.

3. Chemical Name and CAS Registry Number
Corn oil [8001-30-7]

4. Empirical Formula   Molecular Weight
Corn oil is composed of fatty acid esters with glycerol, known commonly as triglycerides. Typical corn oil produced in the US contains five major fatty acids: linoleic 58.9%; oleic 25.8%; palmitic 11.0%; stearic 1.7% and linolenic 1.1%. Corn grown outside the US corn belt, including other countries, yields corn oil with lower linoleic, higher oleic and higher saturated fatty acid levels. Corn oil also contains small quantities of plant sterols.

5. Structural Formula
See Section 4.

6. Functional Category
Oleaginous vehicle; solvent.

7. Applications in Pharmaceutical Formulation or Technology
Corn oil is used primarily in pharmaceutical formulations as a solvent for intramuscular injections or as a vehicle for topical preparations. Emulsions containing up to 67% corn oil are also used as oral nutritional supplements, *see also* Section 19. Corn oil has a long history of use as an edible oil.

8. Description
Clear, light yellow colored, oily liquid with a faint characteristic odor and slightly nutty, sweet taste resembling cooked sweet corn.

9. Pharmacopeial Specifications

Test	USPNF XVII
Specific gravity	0.914-0.921
Heavy metals	$\leqslant 0.001\%$
Cottonseed oil	+
Fatty acid composition	+
Free fatty acids	+
Iodine value	102-130
Saponification value	187-193
Unsaponifiable matter	$\leqslant 1.5\%$

10. Typical Properties
Acid value: 2-6
Autoignition temperature: 393°C
Density: see HPE Data.
Flash point: 321°C
Hydroxyl value: 8-12

Melting point: -18 to -10°C
Refractive index:
n_D^{25} = 1.470-1.474;
n_D^{40} = 1.464-1.468.
Solubility: slightly soluble in ethanol (95%); miscible with benzene, chloroform, ether and hexane.
Viscosity (dynamic): *see* HPE Data.

HPE Laboratory Project Data			
	Method	Lab #	Results
Density	DE-5	30	0.918 g/cm^3 [a]
	DE-5	30	0.915 g/cm^3 [b]
Viscosity	VIS-2	30	38.83 mPa s [a]
	VIS-2	30	37.36 mPa s [b]

Supplier: a. Welch, Holme & Clark Co; b. Capital.

11. Stability and Storage Conditions
Corn oil is stable when protected with nitrogen in tightly sealed bottles. On prolonged exposure to air it thickens and becomes rancid. Corn oil may be sterilized by dry heat, maintaining it at 150°C for one hour.[1]
Corn oil should be stored in an airtight, light-resistant container in a cool, dry, place.

12. Incompatibilities
—

13. Method of Manufacture
Refined corn oil is obtained from the germ or embryo of *Zea mays* Linné (Fam. Gramineae) which contains nearly 50% of the fixed oil, compared with 3.0-6.5% in the whole kernel. The oil is obtained from the embryo by expression and/or solvent extraction. The crude oil is then refined to remove free fatty acids, phospholipids and impurities. It is bleached with solid adsorbents to lighten its color, dewaxed by chilling (which removes any solid waxy components) and deodorized at high temperature, under vacuum, to produce a bland, odorless, edible product.

14. Safety
Based upon its extensive history of food usage corn oil is generally regarded as a nontoxic and nonirritant material.

15. Handling Precautions
Observe normal precautions appropriate to the circumstances and quantity of material handled. Spillages of this material are very slippery and should be covered with an inert absorbent material prior to disposal.

16. Regulatory Status
Included in the FDA Inactive Ingredients Guide (IM injections, oral capsules, suspensions, tablets and topical emulsions).

17. Pharmacopeias
Cz, Egypt, Fr, Jpn, Mex and USPNF.

18. Related Substances
Canola Oil; Cottonseed Oil; Peanut Oil; Sesame Oil; Soybean Oil.

19. Comments

Corn oil contains a high content of unsaturated acids and has been used to replace fats and oils containing a high content of saturated acids in the diets of patients with hypercholesterolemia.

20. Specific References

1. Pasquale D, Jaconia D, Eisman P, Lachman L. A study of sterilizing conditions for injectable oils. Bull Parenter Drug Assoc 1964; 18(3): 1-11.

21. General References

Mann JI, Carter R, Eaton P. Re-heating corn oil does not saturate its double bonds [letter]. Lancet 1977; ii: 401.

Strecker LR, Maza A, Winnie GF. Corn oil - composition, processing and utilization. In: Erickson DR, editor. World conference proceedings. Edible fats and oils processing: basic principles and modern practices. American Oil Chemist's Society, 1990: 309-323.

Watson SA, Ramstead PE, editors. Corn chemistry and technology. St. Paul: American Association of Cereal Chemists Inc, 1987: 53-78.

22. Authors

USA: KD Brenner.

Cottonseed Oil

1. Nonproprietary Names

USPNF: Cottonseed oil

2. Synonyms

Calchem IVO-109; cotton oil; *Lipex 109*; refined cottonseed oil.

3. Chemical Name and CAS Registry Number

Cottonseed oil [8001-29-4]

4. Empirical Formula   Molecular Weight

A typical analysis of refined cottonseed oil indicates the composition of the acids, present as glycerides, to be: linoleic acid 39.3%; oleic acid 33.1%; palmitic acid 19.1%; stearic acid 1.9%; arachidic acid 0.6% and myristic acid 0.3%. Also present are small quantities of phospholipid, phytosterols and pigments. The toxic polyphenolic pigment gossypol is present in raw cottonseed and in the oil cake remaining after expression of oil; it is not found in refined oil.

5. Structural Formula

See Section 4.

6. Functional Category

Oleaginous vehicle; solvent.

7. Applications in Pharmaceutical Formulation or Technology

Cottonseed oil is used in pharmaceutical formulations primarily as a solvent for intramuscular injections. Although it has been used in intravenous emulsions as a fat source in parenteral nutrition regimens its use for this purpose has been superseded by soybean oil emulsions, *see* Section 14.

8. Description

Pale yellow or bright golden yellow colored, clear oily liquid. It is odorless, or nearly so, with a bland, nutty taste. At temperatures below 10°C, particles of solid fat may separate from the oil and at about -5 to 0°C the oil becomes solid or nearly so. If it solidifies, the oil should be remelted and thoroughly mixed before use.

9. Pharmacopeial Specifications

Test	USPNF XVII
Identification	+
Specific gravity	0.915-0.921
Heavy metals	$\leq 0.001\%$
Trichloroethylene	+
Solidification range of fatty acids	31-35°C
Free fatty acids	+
Iodine value	109-120
Saponification value	190-198

10. Typical Properties

Autoignition temperature: 344°C

Density: *see* HPE Data.
Flash point: 321°C
Freezing point: -5 to 0°C
Heat of combustion: 37.1 kJ/g
Refractive index: n_D^{40} = 1.4645-1.4655
Solubility: slightly soluble in ethanol (95%); miscible with carbon disulfide, chloroform and hexane.
Surface tension:
35.4 mN/m (35.4 dynes/cm) at 20°C;
31.3 mN/m (31.3 dynes/cm) at 80°C.
Viscosity (dynamic): up to 70.4 mPa s (70.4 cP) at 20°C. *See also* HPE Data.

HPE Laboratory Project Data			
	Method	Lab #	Results
Density	DE-5	30	0.916 g/cm³
Viscosity	VIS-2	30	39.19 mPa s

Supplier: Welch, Home & Clark Co.

11. Stability and Storage Conditions

Cottonseed oil is stable if stored in a well-filled, airtight, light-resistant container in a cool, dry, place.

12. Incompatibilities

—

13. Method of Manufacture

Cottonseed oil is the refined fixed oil obtained from the seed of cultivated plants of various varieties of *Gossypium hirsutum* Linné or of other species of *Gossypium* (Fam. Malvaceae). The seeds contain about 15% oil. The testae of the seeds are first separated and the kernels then exposed to powerful expression in a hydraulic press. The crude oil thus obtained has a bright red or blackish-red color and requires purification before it is suitable for food or pharmaceutical purposes.

14. Safety

Cottonseed oil emulsions have in the past been used in long-term intravenous nutrition regimens.[1,2] However, a complex series of adverse reactions, called the 'overloading syndrome'[3] seen with chronic administration of cottonseed oil emulsions has led to the cessation in the use of this material for parenteral nutrition purposes. For such applications it has been replaced by soybean oil.[2,4-6]

15. Handling Precautions

Observe normal precautions appropriate to the circumstances and quantity of material handled. Spillages of this material are very slippery and should be covered with an inert absorbent material prior to disposal.

16. Regulatory Status

Included in the FDA Inactive Ingredients Guide (IM injections).

17. Pharmacopeias

Egypt, Mex and USPNF.

18. Related Substances

Canola Oil; Corn Oil; Hydrogenated Vegetable Oil, Type I; Peanut Oil; Sesame Oil; Soybean Oil.

19. Comments

—

20. Specific References

1. Cole WH. Fat emulsion for intravenous use. JAMA 1958; 166: 1042-1043.
2. McNiff BL. Clinical use of 10% soybean oil emulsion. Am J Hosp Pharm 1977; 34: 1080-1086.
3. Goulon M, Barois A, Grosbuis S, Schortgen G. Fat embolism after repeated perfusion of lipid emulsion. Nouv Presse Med 1974; 3: 13-18.
4. Davis SS. Pharmaceutical aspects of intravenous fat emulsions. J Hosp Pharm 1974; 32: 149-160.
5. Davis SS. Pharmaceutical aspects of intravenous fat emulsions. J Hosp Pharm 1974; 32: 165-171.
6. Singh M, Ravin LJ. Parenteral emulsions as drug carrier systems. J Parenter Sci Technol 1986; 40: 34-41.

21. General References

—

22. Authors

USA: MC McCaffrey-Manzo.

Cresol

1. Nonproprietary Names

BP: Cresol
USPNF: Cresol

2. Synonyms

Cresylic acid; hydroxytoluene.

3. Chemical Name and CAS Registry Number

Methylphenol [1319-77-3]

4. Empirical Formula   Molecular Weight

C_7H_8O 108.14

5. Structural Formula

m-Cresol structure shown.

6. Functional Category

Antimicrobial preservative; disinfectant.

7. Applications in Pharmaceutical Formulation or Technology

Cresol is used at 0.15-0.3% concentration as an antimicrobial preservative for intramuscular, intradermal and subcutaneous injectable pharmaceutical formulations. It is also used as a preservative in some topical formulations and as a disinfectant. Cresol is not suitable as a preservative for preparations that are to be freeze-dried.[1]

8. Description

Cresol consists of a mixture of cresol isomers and other phenols obtained from coal tar or petroleum; *m*-cresol predominates. It is a colorless, yellowish to pale brownish-yellow, or pink colored liquid, with a characteristic odor similar to phenol but more tar-like. An aqueous solution has a pungent taste.

9. Pharmacopeial Specifications

Test	BP 1993	USPNF XVII
Identification	+	+
Specific gravity	1.029-1.044	1.030-1.038
Distilling range	+	+
Acidity	+	—
Hydrocarbons	⩽ 0.15%	+
Volatile bases	⩽ 0.15%	—
Hydrocarbons and volatile bases combined	⩽ 0.25%	—
Phenol	—	⩽ 5.0%
Sulfur compounds	+	—
Non-volatile matter	⩽ 0.1%	—

10. Typical Properties

Acidity/alkalinity: a saturated aqueous solution is neutral or slightly acidic to litmus.
Antimicrobial activity: cresol is similar to phenol but has slightly more antimicrobial activity. It is moderately active against Gram-positive bacteria, less active against Gram-negative bacteria, yeasts and molds. Cresol is active below pH 9; optimum activity is obtained in acidic conditions. Synergistic effects between cresol and other preservatives have been reported.[2,3] When used as a disinfectant most common pathogens are killed within 10 minutes by 0.3-0.6% solutions. Cresol has no significant activity against bacterial spores.
Solubility:

Solvent	Solubility at 20°C
Chloroform	freely soluble
Ethanol (95%)	freely soluble
Ether	freely soluble
Fixed and volatile oils	freely soluble
Glycerin	miscible
Water	1 in 50

11. Stability and Storage Conditions

Cresol and aqueous cresol solutions darken in color with age and on exposure to air and light.
Cresol should be stored in a well-closed container, protected from light, in a cool, dry, place.

12. Incompatibilities

Cresol has been reported to be incompatible with chlorpromazine.[4] Antimicrobial activity is reduced in the presence of nonionic surfactants.

13. Method of Manufacture

Cresol may be obtained from coal tar or prepared synthetically by either sulfonation or oxidation of toluene.

14. Safety

Reports of adverse reactions to cresol are generally associated with the use of either the bulk material or cresol based disinfectants, which may contain up to 50% cresol, rather than for its use as a preservative.
Cresol is similar to phenol although it is less caustic and toxic. However, cresol is sufficiently caustic to be unsuitable for skin and wound disinfection. In studies in rabbits cresol was found to be metabolized and excreted primarily as the glucuronide.[5]
A patient has survived ingestion of 12 g of cresol though with severe adverse effects.[6]
LD_{50} (mouse, oral): 0.76 g/kg[7]
LD_{50} (rat, oral): 1.45 g/kg
LD_{50} (rat, skin): 2 g/kg
See also Sections 18 and 19.

15. Handling Precautions

Observe normal precautions appropriate to the circumstances and quantity of material handled. Cresol may be irritant to the skin, eyes and mucous membranes. Eye protection, gloves and a respirator are recommended. In the UK, the occupational exposure limit for cresol is 22 mg/m^3 (5 ppm) long-term (8-hour TWA).[8] In the US, the permissible and recommended exposure limits are 22 mg/m^3 long-term and 10 mg/m^3 long-term respectively.[9]

16. Regulatory Status

Included in the FDA Inactive Ingredients Guide (IM, intradermal and SC injections). Included in parenteral medicines licensed in the UK.

17. Pharmacopeias

Aust, Br, Chin, Hung, Ind, It, Jpn, Mex, Nord, Rom, Turk, USPNF and Yug.

18. Related Substances

Chlorocresol; *m*-cresol; *o*-cresol; *p*-cresol; Phenol.

m-**Cresol**: C$_7$H$_8$O
Molecular weight: 108.14
CAS number: [108-39-4]
Synonyms: *m*-cresylic acid; 3-hydroxytoluene; meta-cresol; 3-methylphenol.
Appearance: colorless or yellowish liquid with a characteristic phenolic odor.
Boiling point: 202°C
Density: 1.034 g/cm^3 at 20°C
Flash point: 86°C (closed cup)
Melting point: 11-12°C
Refractive index: n$_D^{20}$ = 1.5398
Solubility: soluble in organic solvents; very slightly soluble in water.
Safety:
LD$_{50}$ (cat, SC): 0.15 g/kg[10]
LD$_{50}$ (mouse, SC): 0.45 g/kg
LD$_{50}$ (rabbit, IV): 0.28 g/kg
LD$_{50}$ (rabbit, oral): 1.1 g/kg
LD$_{50}$ (rabbit, SC): 0.5 g/kg
LD$_{50}$ (rat, oral): 2.02 g/kg

o-**Cresol**: C$_7$H$_8$O
Molecular weight: 108.14
CAS number: [95-48-7]
Synonyms: *o*-cresylic acid; 2-hydroxytoluene; 2-methylphenol; ortho-cresol.
Appearance: colorless deliquescent solid with a characteristic odor; it becomes yellow on storage.
Boiling point: 191-192°C
Density: 1.047 g/cm^3 at 20°C
Flash point: 81-83°C (closed cup)
Melting point: 30°C
Refractive index: n$_D^{20}$ = 1.553
Safety:
LD$_{50}$ (cat, SC): 0.6 g/kg[10]
LD$_{50}$ (mouse, SC): 0.35 g/kg
LD$_{50}$ (rabbit, IV): 0.2 g/kg
LD$_{50}$ (rabbit, oral): 0.8 g/kg
LD$_{50}$ (rabbit, SC): 0.45 g/kg
LD$_{50}$ (rat, oral): 1.35 g/kg

p-**Cresol**: C$_7$H$_8$O
Molecular weight: 108.14
CAS number: [106-44-5]
Synonyms: *p*-cresylic acid; 4-hydroxytoluene; 4-methylphenol; para-cresol.

Appearance: crystalline solid.
Boiling point: 201.8°C
Density: 1.0341 g/cm^3 at 20°C
Flash point: 86°C (closed cup)
Melting point: 35.5°C
Refractive index: n$_D^{20}$ = 1.5395
Solubility: soluble in ethanol (95%) and ether; very slightly soluble in water.
Safety:
LD$_{50}$ (cat, SC): 0.08 g/kg[10]
LD$_{50}$ (mouse, SC): 0.15 g/kg
LD$_{50}$ (rabbit, IV): 0.16 g/kg
LD$_{50}$ (rabbit, oral): 1.1 g/kg
LD$_{50}$ (rabbit, SC): 0.3 g/kg
LD$_{50}$ (rat, oral): 1.8 g/kg

19. Comments

m-Cresol is generally considered the least toxic of the three cresol isomers.[10]

20. Specific References

1. FAO/WHO. WHO expert committee on biological standardization: thirty-seventh report. Tech Rep Ser Wld Hlth Org 1987; No. 760.
2. Denyer SP, Baird RM, editors. Guide to microbiological control in pharmaceuticals. Chichester: Ellis Horwood Ltd, 1990: 261.
3. Hugbo PG. Additive and synergistic actions of equipotent admixtures of some antimicrobial agents. Pharm Acta Helv 1976; 51: 284-288.
4. McSherry TJ. Incompatibility between chlorpromazine and metacresol [letter]. Am J Hosp Pharm 1987; 44: 1574.
5. Cresol. In: The Pharmaceutical Codex, 11th edition. London: The Pharmaceutical Press, 1979: 232.
6. Côté MA, Lyonnais J, Leblond PF. Acute Heinz-body anemia due to severe cresol poisoning: successful treatment with erythrocytapheresis. Can Med Assoc J 1984; 130: 1319-1322.
7. Sweet DV, editor. Registry of toxic effects of chemical substances. Cincinnati: US Department of Health, 1987.
8. Health and Safety Executive. EH40/93: occupational exposure limits 1993. London: HMSO, 1993.
9. NIOSH. Recommendations for occupational safety and health standard. MMWR 1988; 37(Suppl S-7): 1-29.
10. Deichmann WB, Keplinger ML. Phenols and phenolic compounds. In: Clayton GD, Clayton FE, editors. Patty's industrial hygiene and toxicology, 3rd edition. New York: John Wiley and Sons, 1981: 2597-2600.

21. General References

Chapman DG. *o*-Cresol. In: Board RG, Allwood MC, Banks JG, editors. Preservatives in the food, pharmaceutical and environmental industries. Oxford: Blackwell Scientific Publications, 1987: 184.
Russell AD, Jones BD, Milburn P. Reversal of the inhibition of bacterial spore germination and outgrowth by antibacterial agents. Int J Pharmaceutics 1985; 25: 105-112.

22. Authors

UK: MC Allwood, PJ Weller.

Croscarmellose Sodium

1. Nonproprietary Names

USPNF: Croscarmellose sodium

2. Synonyms

Ac-Di-Sol; cross-linked carboxymethylcellulose sodium; modified cellulose gum; *Nymcel ZSX*; *Primellose*; *Solutab*.

3. Chemical Name and CAS Registry Number

Cellulose, carboxymethyl ether, sodium salt, cross-linked [74811-65-7]

4. Empirical Formula   Molecular Weight

Croscarmellose sodium is a cross-linked polymer of carboxymethylcellulose sodium.
See Carboxymethylcellulose Sodium.

5. Structural Formula

See Carboxymethylcellulose Sodium.

6. Functional Category

Tablet and capsule disintegrant.

7. Applications in Pharmaceutical Formulation or Technology

Croscarmellose sodium is used in oral pharmaceutical formulations as a disintegrant for capsules,[1,2] tablets[3-12] and granules.

In tablet formulations, croscarmellose sodium may be used in both direct compression and wet granulation processes. When used in wet granulations the croscarmellose sodium is best added in both the wet and dry stages of the process (intra- and extragranularly) so that the wicking and swelling ability of the disintegrant is best utilized.[11,12] Concentrations of up to 5% w/w of croscarmellose sodium may be used as a tablet disintegrant although normally 2% w/w is used in tablets prepared by direct compression and 3% w/w in tablets prepared by a wet granulation process.

Use	Concentration (%)
Disintegrant in capsules	10-25
Disintegrant in tablets	0.5-5.0

8. Description

Croscarmellose sodium occurs as an odorless, white-colored powder.

9. Pharmacopeial Specifications

Test	USPNF XVII (Suppl 6)
Identification	+
pH (1% w/v dispersion)	5.0-7.0
Loss on drying	⩽ 10.0%
Heavy metals	⩽ 0.001%
Sodium chloride and sodium glycolate	⩽ 0.5%
Degree of substitution	0.60-0.85
Content of water-soluble material	1.0-10.0%
Settling volume	+

SEM 1

Excipient: Croscarmellose sodium (*Ac-Di-Sol*)
Manufacturer: FMC Europe NV
Magnification: 100x
Voltage: 5 kV

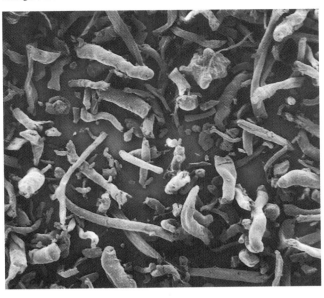

10. Typical Properties

Density (bulk): 0.48 g/cm^3 for *Ac-Di-Sol*[7]
Density (tapped): 0.67 g/cm^3 for *Ac-Di-Sol*[7]
Particle size distribution: not more than 2% retained on a #200 (73.7 μm) mesh and not more than 10% retained on a #325 (44.5 μm) mesh, for *Ac-Di-Sol*.
Solubility: insoluble in water, although croscarmellose sodium rapidly swells to 4-8 times its original volume on contact with water.

11. Stability and Storage Conditions

Croscarmellose sodium is a stable though hygroscopic material.

A model tablet formulation prepared by direct compression, with croscarmellose sodium as a disintegrant, showed no significant difference in drug dissolution after storage at 30°C for 14 months.[9]

Croscarmellose sodium should be stored in a well-closed container in a cool, dry, place.

12. Incompatibilities

The efficacy of disintegrants, such as croscarmellose sodium, may be slightly reduced in tablet formulations prepared by either wet granulation or direct compression processes which contain hygroscopic excipients such as sorbitol.[10]

13. Method of Manufacture

Alkali cellulose is prepared by steeping cellulose, obtained from wood pulp or cotton fibres, in sodium hydroxide solution. The alkali cellulose is then reacted with sodium monochloroacetate to obtain carboxymethylcellulose sodium. After the substitution reaction is completed and all of the sodium hydroxide has been used, the excess sodium monochloroacetate slowly hydrolyzes to glycolic acid. The glycolic acid changes a few of the sodium carboxymethyl groups to the free acid and catalyzes the formation of cross-links to produce croscarmellose sodium. The croscarmellose sodium is then extracted with aqueous alcohol and any remaining sodium chloride or sodium glycolate removed. After purification, croscarmellose sodium of greater than 99.5% purity is obtained.[4] The croscarmellose sodium may be milled to break the polymer fibres into shorter lengths and hence improve its flow properties.

14. Safety

Croscarmellose sodium is mainly used as a disintegrant in oral pharmaceutical formulations and is generally regarded as an essentially nontoxic and nonirritant material. However, oral consumption of large amounts of croscarmellose sodium may have a laxative effect although the quantities used in solid dosage formulations are unlikely to cause such problems.

The WHO has not specified an acceptable daily intake for the related substance carboxymethylcellulose sodium, used as a food additive, since the levels necessary to achieve a desired effect were not considered sufficient to be a hazard to health.[13]

See also Carboxymethylcellulose Sodium

15. Handling Precautions

Observe normal precautions appropriate to the circumstances and quantity of material handled. Croscarmellose sodium may be irritant to the eyes; eye protection is recommended.

16. Regulatory Status

Included in the FDA Inactive Ingredients Guide (oral capsules and tablets). Included in nonparenteral medicines licensed in the UK.

17. Pharmacopeias

USPNF.

18. Related Substances

Carboxymethylcellulose Calcium; Carboxymethylcellulose Sodium.

19. Comments

Typically, the degree of substitution (DS) for croscarmellose sodium is 0.7.

20. Specific References

1. Botzolakis JE, Augsburger LL. Disintegrating agents in hard gelatin capsules part I: mechanism of action. Drug Dev Ind Pharm 1988; 14: 29-41.
2. Dahl TC, Sue IT, Yum A. The influence of disintegrant level and capsule size on dissolution of hard gelatin capsules stored in high humidity conditions. Drug Dev Ind Pharm 1991; 17: 1001-1016.
3. Gissinger D, Stamm. A comparitive evaluation of the properties of some tablet disintegrants. Drug Dev Ind Pharm 1980; 6: 511-536.
4. Shangraw R, Mitrevej A, Shah M. A new era of tablet disintegrants. Pharmaceut Technol 1980; 4(10): 49-57.
5. Rudnic EM, Rhodes CT, Bavitz JF, Schwartz JB. Some effects of relatively low levels of eight tablet disintegrants on a direct compression system. Drug Dev Ind Pharm 1981; 7: 347-358.
6. Gorman EA, Rhodes CT, Rudnic EM. An evaluation of croscarmellose as a tablet disintegrant in direct compression systems. Drug Dev Ind Pharm 1982; 8: 397-410.
7. Rudnic EM, Rhodes CT, Welch S, Bernado P. Evaluations of the mechanism of disintegrant action. Drug Dev Ind Pharm 1982; 8: 87-109.
8. Gordon MS, Chowhan ZT. Effect of tablet solubility and hygroscopicity on disintegrant efficiency in direct compression tablets in terms of dissolution. J Pharm Sci 1987; 76: 907-909.
9. Gordon MS, Chowhan ZT. The effect of aging on disintegrant efficiency in direct compression tablets with varied solubility and hygroscopicity, in terms of dissolution. Drug Dev Ind Pharm 1990; 16: 437-447.
10. Johnson JR, Wang L-H, Gordon MS, Chowhan ZT. Effect of formulation solubility and hygroscopicity on disintegrant efficiency in tablets prepared by wet granulation, in terms of dissolution. J Pharm Sci 1991; 80: 469-471.
11. Gordon MS, Rudraraju VS, Dani K, Chowhan ZT. Effect of the mode of super disintegrant incorporation on dissolution in wet granulated tablets. J Pharm Sci 1993; 82: 220-226.
12. Khattab I, Menon A, Sakr A. Effect of mode of incorporation of disintegrants on the characteristics of fluid-bed wet-granulated tablets. J Pharm Pharmacol 1993; 45: 687-691.
13. FAO/WHO. Evaluation of certain food additives and contaminants: thirty-fifth report of the joint FAO/WHO expert committee on food additives. Tech Rep Ser Wld Hlth Org 1990; No. 789.

21. General References

FMC Corporation. Technical literature: *Ac-Di-Sol* croscarmellose sodium, 1988.

22. Authors

UK: PJ Weller.

Crospovidone

1. Nonproprietary Names

USPNF: Crospovidone

2. Synonyms

Cross-linked povidone; *Kollidon CL*; *Polyplasdone XL*; *Polyplasdone XL-10*; polyvinylpolypyrrolidone; PVPP; 1-vinyl-2-pyrrolidinone homopolymer.

3. Chemical Name and CAS Registry Number

1-Ethenyl-2-pyrrolidinone homopolymer [9003-39-8]

4. Empirical Formula　　Molecular Weight

$(C_6H_9NO)_n$　　　　$> 1\,000\,000$

Crospovidone is a water insoluble synthetic cross-linked homopolymer of *N*-vinyl-2-pyrrolidinone. An exact determination of the molecular weight has not been established because of the insolubility of the material.

5. Structural Formula

See Povidone.

6. Functional Category

Tablet disintegrant.

7. Applications in Pharmaceutical Formulation or Technology

Crospovidone is a water insoluble tablet disintegrant used at 2-5% concentration in tablets prepared by direct compression or wet and dry granulation methods.[1-4] It rapidly exhibits high capillary activity and pronounced hydration capacity with little tendency to gel formation.

8. Description

Crospovidone is a white to creamy-white, finely divided, free-flowing, practically tasteless, odorless or nearly odorless, hygroscopic powder.

9. Pharmacopeial Specifications

Test	USPNF XVII (Suppl 9)
Identification	+
pH (1% solution)	5.0-8.0
Water	⩽ 5.0%
Residue on ignition	⩽ 0.4%
Water-soluble substances	⩽ 1.5%
Heavy metals	⩽ 0.001%
Vinylpyrrolidinone	⩽ 0.1%
Nitrogen content (anhydrous basis)	11.0-12.8%

10. Typical Properties

Acidity/alkalinity:
pH = 5.0-8.0 (1% w/v aqueous slurry)
Density: 1.22 g/cm^3
Density (bulk):
0.363 g/cm^3 for *Kollidon CL*;
0.213 g/cm^3 for *Polyplasdone XL*;

SEM: 1
Excipient: Crospovidone (*Kollidon CL*)
Manufacturer: BASF Corporation
Lot No.: 80-3077
Magnification: 150x
Voltage: 20 kV

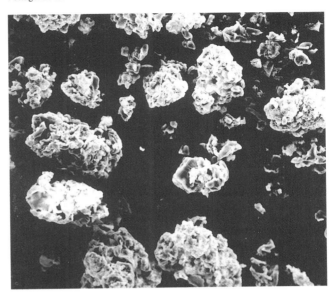

0.323 g/cm^3 for *Polyplasdone XL-10*.
Density (tapped):
0.534 g/cm^3 for *Kollidon CL*;
0.273 g/cm^3 for *Polyplasdone XL*;
0.461 g/cm^3 for *Polyplasdone XL-10*.
Moisture content: maximum moisture sorption is approximately 60%.
Particle size distribution: less than 400 μm for *Polyplasdone XL*; less than 74 μm for *Polyplasdone XL-10*. Approximately 50% greater than 50 μm and maximum of 1% greater than 250 μm in size for *Kollidon CL*.
Sodium content:
39 ppm *Kollidon CL*;
209 ppm *Polyplasdone XL*.
Solubility: practically insoluble in water and most common organic solvents.
Specific surface area: 1.03 m^2/g (BET method)

11. Stability and Storage Conditions

Crospovidone is stable. However, since it is hygroscopic it should be stored in an airtight container in a cool, dry, place.

12. Incompatibilities

Crospovidone is compatible with most organic and inorganic pharmaceutical ingredients. When exposed to a high water level crospovidone may form molecular adducts with some materials, *see* Povidone.

13. Method of Manufacture

Acetylene and formaldehyde are reacted in the presence of a highly active catalyst to form butynediol which is hydrogenated to butanediol and then cyclodehydrogenated to form butyrolactone. Pyrrolidone is produced by reacting butyrolactone with ammonia. This is followed by a vinylation reaction in which pyrrolidone and acetylene are reacted under pressure. The monomer vinylpyrrolidone is then polymerized, in solution, using a catalyst. Crospovidone is prepared by a 'popcorn polymerization' process.[5]

14. Safety

Crospovidone is used in oral pharmaceutical formulations and is generally regarded as a nontoxic and nonirritant material. Short-term animal toxicity studies have shown no adverse effects associated with crospovidone.[6] However, due to the lack of available data an acceptable daily intake in humans has not been specified by the WHO.[6]

LD_{50} (mouse, IP): 12 g/kg[7]

15. Handling Precautions

Observe normal precautions appropriate to the circumstances and quantity of material handled. Eye protection, gloves and a dust mask are recommended.

16. Regulatory Status

Included in the FDA Inactive Ingredients Guide (oral capsules and tablets, topical, transdermal and vaginal preparations).

17. Pharmacopeias

It, Mex and USPNF.

18. Related Substances

Povidone.

19. Comments

—

20. Specific References

1. Kornblum SS, Stoopak SB. A new tablet disintegrating agent: cross-linked polyvinylpyrrolidone. J Pharm Sci 1973; 62: 43-49.
2. Rudnic EM, Lausier JM, Chilamkurti RN, Rhodes CT. Studies of the utility of cross linked polyvinylpolypyrrolidine as a tablet disintegrant. Drug Dev Ind Pharm 1980; 6: 291-309.
3. Gordon MS, Chowhan ZT. Effect of tablet solubility and hygroscopicity on disintegrant efficiency in direct compression tablets in terms of dissolution. J Pharm Sci 1987; 76: 907-909.
4. Gordon MS, Rudraraju VS, Dani K, Chowhan ZT. Effect of the mode of super disintegrant incorporation on dissolution in wet granulated tablets. J Pharm Sci 1993; 82: 220-226.
5. BASF Corporation. Technical literature: *Kollidon* grades, polyvinylpyrrolidone for the pharmaceuticals industry, 1990.
6. FAO/WHO. Evaluation of certain food additives and contaminants. Twenty-seventh report of the joint FAO/WHO expert committee on food additives. Tech Rep Ser Wld Hlth Org 1983; No. 696.
7. Sweet DV, editor. Registry of toxic effects of chemical substances. Cincinnati: US Department of Health, 1987.

21. General References

ISP. Technical literature: *Polyplasdone XL* and *Polyplasdone XL-10*, 1992.
Wan LSC, Prasad KPP. Uptake of water by excipients in tablets. Int J Pharmaceutics 1989; 50: 147-153.

22. Authors

USA: JG Strom.

Cyclodextrins

1. Nonproprietary Names

USPNF: Beta cyclodextrin
Note: β-cyclodextrin is the only cyclodextrin to be currently described in a pharmacopeia. Alfadex is the rINN for α-cyclodextrin and betadex is the pINN for β-cyclodextrin.

2. Synonyms

Cyclodextrin: *Cavitron*; cyclic oligosaccharide; cycloamylose; cycloglucan; *Encapsin*; *Rhodocap*; Schardinger dextrin.
α-Cyclodextrin: alfadex; alpha-cycloamylose; alpha-cyclodextrin; alpha-dextrin; cyclohexaamylose; cyclomaltohexose.
β-Cyclodextrin: beta-cycloamylose; betadex; beta-dextrin; cycloheptaamylose; cycloheptaglucan; cyclomaltoheptose; *Kleptose*.
γ-Cyclodextrin: cyclooctaamylose; gamma cyclodextrin; *Gamma W8*.

3. Chemical Name and CAS Registry Number

α-Cyclodextrin: [10016-20-3]
β-Cyclodextrin: [7585-39-9]
γ-Cyclodextrin: [17465-86-0]

4. Empirical Formula   Molecular Weight

α-Cyclodextrin: $C_{36}H_{60}O_{30}$ 972
β-Cyclodextrin: $C_{42}H_{70}O_{35}$ 1135
γ-Cyclodextrin: $C_{48}H_{80}O_{40}$ 1297

5. Structural Formula

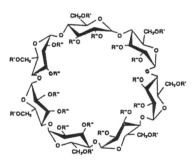

R', R'' = -H for 'natural' α-, β- and γ-cyclodextrins
R', R'' = $-CH_3$ for methyl cyclodextrins
R', R'' = $-CHOHCH_3$ for hydroxyethyl cyclodextrins
R', R'' = $-CH_2CHOHCH_3$ for 2-hydroxypropyl cyclodextrins
Note: structure of β-cyclodextrin (7 glucose units) shown.

6. Functional Category

Stabilizing agent; solubilizing agent.

7. Applications in Pharmaceutical Formulation or Technology

Cyclodextrins are crystalline, nonhygroscopic, cyclic oligosaccharides derived from starch. Among the most commonly used forms are α-, β-, and γ-cyclodextrin which have respectively 6, 7, and 8 glucose units, *see* Section 5. Substituted cyclodextrin derivatives are also available, *see* Section 18.

In shape, cyclodextrins are 'bucket-like' or 'cone-like', toroid molecules. They thus have a rigid structure with a central cavity whose size varies according to the cyclodextrin type, *see* Section 8. Due to the arrangement of hydroxyl groups within the molecule the internal surface of the cavity is hydrophobic whilst the outside of the torus is hydrophilic. This arrangement permits the cyclodextrin to accommodate a guest molecule within the cavity so forming an inclusion complex.

Cyclodextrins may thus be used to form inclusion complexes with a variety of drug molecules resulting primarily in improvements to dissolution and bioavailability due to enhanced solubility, and improved chemical and physical stability, *see* Section 19.

Cyclodextrin inclusion complexes have also been used to mask the unpleasant taste of active materials, and to convert a liquid substance into a solid material.

β-Cyclodextrin is the most commonly used cyclodextrin although it is the least soluble, *see* Section 10. It is the least expensive cyclodextrin, is commercially available from a number of sources and is able to form inclusion complexes with a number of molecules of pharmaceutical interest. However, β-cyclodextrin should not be used in parenteral formulations since it is nephrotoxic, *see* Section 14. β-Cyclodextrin is considered to be nontoxic when administered orally and has thus become primarily used in tablet and capsule formulations. β-Cyclodextrin derivatives tend to be nontoxic when used either orally or parenterally and the derivatives 2-hydroxypropyl-β-cyclodextrin and 3-hydroxypropyl-β-cyclodextrin are becoming of increasing importance in pharmaceutical formulations.[1-5]

α-Cyclodextrin is mainly used in parenteral formulations, although since it has the smallest cavity of the cyclodextrins it can only form inclusion complexes with relatively few, small sized molecules. In contrast, γ-cyclodextrin has the largest cavity and can be used to form inclusion complexes with large molecules. Although γ-cyclodextrin may also be used in parenteral formulations its relatively high cost has limited its use to date in pharmaceutical formulations.

In oral tablet formulations β-cyclodextrin may be used in both wet granulation and direct compression processes. Whilst the physical properties of β-cyclodextrin vary from manufacturer to manufacturer, β-cyclodextrin tends to possess poor flow properties and requires a lubricant, such as 0.1% w/w magnesium stearate, when it is directly compressed.[6, 7]

In parenteral formulations, cyclodextrins have been used to produce stable and soluble preparations of drugs that would otherwise have been formulated using a non-aqueous solvent. Cyclodextrins have also been used in the formulation of solutions,[8, 9] suppositories[10, 11] and cosmetics.[12]

8. Description

Cyclodextrins are cyclic oligosaccharides containing at least 6 D-(+)-glucopyranose units attached by α (1→4) glucoside bonds. The three natural cyclodextrins, α, β, and γ, differ in their ring size and solubility. They contain 6, 7 or 8 glucose units respectively.[12]

Cyclodextrins occur as white, practically odorless, fine crystalline powders, having a slightly sweet taste. Some cyclodextrin derivatives occur as amorphous powders.

Table I: Physical characteristics of cyclodextrins.

Characteristic	Cyclodextrin		
	α	β	γ
Cavity diameter (Å)	4.7-5.3	6.0-6.5	7.5-8.3
Height of torus (Å)	7.9	7.9	7.9
Diameter of periphery (Å)	14.6	15.4	17.5
Approximate volume of cavity (Å³)	174	262	472
Approximate cavity volume			
per mol cyclodextrin (mL)	104	157	256
per g cyclodextrin (mL)	0.1	0.14	0.20

Note: 1 nm = 10 Å.

9. Pharmacopeial Specifications

Test	USPNF XVII (Suppl 7)
Identification	+
Color and clarity of solution	+
Specific rotation	+160° to +164°
Microbial limits	+
Water	$\leqslant$ 14.0%
Residue on ignition	$\leqslant$ 0.1%
Heavy metals	$\leqslant$ 5 ppm
Reducing substances	$\leqslant$ 1.0%
Assay (anhydrous basis)	98.0-101.0%

10. Typical Properties

Compressibility: 21-44% for β-cyclodextrin.
Density (bulk): 0.42-0.70 g/cm³ for β-cyclodextrin.
Density (tapped): 0.63-0.85 g/cm³ for β-cyclodextrin.
Melting point:
250-260°C for α-cyclodextrin;
255-265°C for β-cyclodextrin;
240-245°C for γ-cyclodextrin.
Moisture content:
10.2% w/w for α-cyclodextrin;
13-15% w/w for β-cyclodextrin;
8-18% w/w for γ-cyclodextrin.
Particle size distribution:
7-45 µm for β-cyclodextrin.
Solubility:
α-cyclodextrin: soluble 1 in 7 parts of water at 20°C, 1 in 3 at 50°C.
β-cyclodextrin: soluble 1 in 200 parts of propylene glycol, 1 in 50 of water at 20°C, 1 in 20 at 50°C; practically insoluble in acetone and ethanol (95%).
γ-cyclodextrin: soluble 1 in 4.4 parts of water at 20°C, 1 in 2 at 45°C.
Specific rotation $[\alpha]_D^{25}$:
+150.5° for α-cyclodextrin;
+162.0° for β-cyclodextrin;
+177.4° for γ-cyclodextrin.
Surface tension:
71 mN/m (71 dynes/cm) for α-cyclodextrin at 25°C;
71 mN/m (71 dynes/cm) for β-cyclodextrin at 25°C;
71 mN/m (71 dynes/cm) for γ-cyclodextrin at 25°C.

11. Stability and Storage Conditions

β-Cyclodextrin, and other cyclodextrins, are stable in the solid state if protected from high humidity.
Cyclodextrins should be stored in a tightly sealed container, in a cool, dry, place.

12. Incompatibilities

The activity of some antimicrobial preservatives in aqueous solution can be reduced in the presence of hydroxypropyl-β-cyclodextrin.[13-15]

13. Method of Manufacture

Cyclodextrins are manufactured by the enzymatic degradation of starch using specialized bacteria. For example, β-cyclodextrin is produced by the action of the enzyme cyclodextrin glucosyltransferase upon starch or a starch hydrolysate. An organic solvent is used to direct the reaction to produce β-cyclodextrin and to prevent the growth of microorganisms during the enzymatic reaction. The insoluble β-cyclodextrin organic solvent complex is separated from the non-cyclic starch, and the organic solvent removed *in vacuo* so that less than 1 ppm of solvent remains in the β-cyclodextrin. The β-cyclodextrin is then carbon treated and crystallized from water, dried, and collected.
Hydroxyethyl-β-cyclodextrin is made by reacting β-cyclodextrin with ethylene oxide, whilst hydroxypropyl-β-cyclodextrin is made by reacting β-cyclodextrin with propylene oxide.

14. Safety

Cyclodextrins are starch derivatives and are mainly used in oral and parenteral pharmaceutical formulations. They are also used in cosmetics and food products and are generally regarded as essentially nontoxic and nonirritant materials. However, when parenterally administered, β-cyclodextrin is not metabolized but accumulates in the kidneys as insoluble cholesterol complexes, resulting in severe nephrotoxicity.[16] Other cyclodextrin derivatives, e.g. 2-hydroxypropyl-β-cyclodextrin, have been the subject of extensive toxicological studies and are not associated with nephrotoxicity and are reported to be safe for use in parenteral formulations.[3]
Cyclodextrin administered orally is metabolized by microflora in the colon forming the metabolites maltodextrin, maltose and glucose, which are themselves further metabolized before being finally excreted as carbon dioxide and water. Although a study published in 1957 suggested that orally administered cyclodextrins were highly toxic[17] more recent animal toxicity studies in rats and dogs have shown this not to be the case and cyclodextrins are now approved for use in food products and orally administered pharmaceuticals in a number of countries. Cyclodextrins are not irritant to the skin and eyes, or upon inhalation. There is also no evidence to suggest that cyclodextrins are mutagenic or teratogenic.
α-Cyclodextrin:
LD_{50} (rat, IP): 1.0 g/kg[18]
LD_{50} (rat, IV): 0.79 g/kg
β-Cyclodextrin:
LD_{50} (mouse, IP): 0.33 g/kg[18]
LD_{50} (mouse, SC): 0.41 g/kg
LD_{50} (rat, IP): 0.36 g/kg
LD_{50} (rat, IV): 1.0 g/kg
LD_{50} (rat, oral): 18.8 g/kg
LD_{50} (rat, SC): 3.7 g/kg

15. Handling Precautions

Observe normal precautions appropriate to the circumstances and quantity of material handled. Cyclodextrins are fine organic powders and should be handled in a well-ventilated environment. Efforts should be made to limit the generation of dust which can be explosive.

16. Regulatory Status

Included in oral and rectal pharmaceutical formulations licensed in Europe, Japan and the US.

17. Pharmacopeias

USPNF.

18. Related Substances

Dimethyl-β-cyclodextrin; 2-hydroxyethyl-β-cyclodextrin; 2-hydroxypropyl-β-cyclodextrin; 3-hydroxypropyl-β-cyclodextrin; trimethyl-β-cyclodextrin.

Dimethyl-β-cyclodextrin

Molecular weight: 1331
Synonyms: DM-β-CD.
Appearance: white crystalline powder.
Cavity diameter: 6 Å
Melting point: 295-300°C
Moisture content: $\leqslant$ 1% w/w
Solubility: soluble 1 in 135 parts of ethanol, and 1 in 1.75 of water at 25°C. Solubility decreases with increasing temperature.
Surface tension: 62 mN/m (62 dynes/cm) at 25°C
Method of manufacture: dimethyl-β-cyclodextrin is prepared from β-cyclodextrin by the selective methylation of all C2 secondary hydroxyl groups and all C6 primary hydroxyl groups (C3 secondary hydroxyl groups remain unsubstituted).
Comments: used in applications similar to β-cyclodextrin.[2, 3]

2-Hydroxyethyl-β-cyclodextrin

CAS number: [98513-20-3]
Synonyms: 2-HE-β-CD.
Appearance: white crystalline powder.
Solubility: greater than 1 in 2 parts of water at 25°C.
Surface tension: 68-71 mN/m (68-71 dynes/cm) at 25°C.
Comments: used in applications similar to β-cyclodextrin. The degree of substitution of hydroxyethyl groups can vary.[2,3,19]

2-Hydroxypropyl-β-cyclodextrin

CAS number: [128446-35-5]
Synonyms: 2-HP-β-CD.
Appearance: white crystalline powder.
Solubility: greater than 1 in 2 parts of water at 25°C.
Surface tension: 52-69 mN/m (52-69 dynes/cm) at 25°C.
Comments: used in applications similar to β-cyclodextrin, however, since it is not nephrotoxic it has been suggested for use in parenteral formulations. The degree of substitution of hydroxypropyl groups can vary.[1-5]

3-Hydroxypropyl-β-cyclodextrin

Synonyms: 3-HP-β-CD.
Appearance: white crystalline powder.
Solubility: greater than 1 in 2 parts of water at 25°C.
Surface tension: 70-71 mN/m (70-71 dynes/cm) at 25°C.
Comments: used in applications similar to β-cyclodextrin, however, since it is not nephrotoxic it has been suggested for use in parenteral formulations. The degree of substitution of hydroxypropyl groups can vary.[2, 3]

Trimethyl-β-cyclodextrin

Molecular weight: 1429
Synonyms: TM-β-CD.
Appearance: white crystalline powder.
Cavity diameter: 4-7 Å
Melting point: 157°C
Moisture content: $\leqslant$ 1% w/w
Solubility: soluble 1 in 3.2 parts of water at 25°C. Solubility decreases with increasing temperature.
Surface tension: 56 mN/m (56 dynes/cm) at 25°C
Method of manufacture: trimethyl-β-cyclodextrin is prepared from β-cyclodextrin by the complete methylation of all C2 and C3 secondary hydroxyl groups along with all C6 primary hydroxyl groups.
Comments: used in applications similar to β-cyclodextrin.[2, 3]

19. Comments

In addition to their use in pharmaceutical formulation, cyclodextrins have also been investigated for use in various industrial applications. Analytically, cyclodextrin polymers are used in chromatographic separations, particularly of chiral materials.

Cyclodextrins have been formulated with a number of drug substances, *see* Table II.

Table II: Selected list of drugs with improved pharmaceutical characteristics after inclusion complex formation with cyclodextrin.

Improvement	Drug
Enhancement of bioavailability	Aspirin, barbiturates, clofibrate, diazepam, diltiazem, famotidine, ibuprofen, piretamide, spironolactone.
Enhancement of solubility	Barbiturates, biphenylacetic acid, chloramphenicol, diazepam, digoxin, estradiol, furosemide, hydrochlorthiazide, hydrocortisone, ibuprofen, indomethacin, pancratistatin, phenytoin, prostaglandins, progesterone, sulfonamides, testosterone, tolbutamide.
Enhancement of stability	Against dehydration - mitomycin, prostaglandins. Against hydrolysis - aspirin, atropine, digoxin, procaine. Against oxidation - aldehydes, epinephrine, phenothiazines. Against photodecomposition - phenothiazines, ubiquinones.
Formation of solid inclusion complexes	Clofibrate, essential oils, nitroglycerin, oil-soluble vitamins.
Improvement in taste and odor	Chloral hydrate, chloramphenicol, prostaglandins, spironolactone.
Inhibition of sublimation	Camphor, chlorobutanol, iodine, menthol.
Inhibition of hemolysis	Flufenamic acid, menadione, phenothiazines, protriptyline.

20. Specific References

1. Brewster ME, Simpkins JW, Hora MS, Stern WC, Bodor N. The potential use of cyclodextrins in parenteral formulations. J Parenter Sci Technol 1989; 43: 231-240.
2. Duchêne D, Wouessidjewe D. Physicochemical characteristics and pharmaceutical uses of cyclodextrin derivatives, part I. Pharmaceut Technol 1990; 14(6): 26, 28, 34.
3. Duchêne D, Wouessidjewe D. Physicochemical characteristics and pharmaceutical uses of cyclodextrin derivatives, part II. Pharmaceut Technol 1990; 14(8): 14, 22, 24, 26.
4. Brewster ME, Hora MS, Simpkins JW, Bodor N. Use of 2-hydroxypropyl-β-cyclodextrin as a solubilizing and stabilizing excipient for protein drugs. Pharm Res 1991; 8: 792-795.
5. Choudhury S, Nelson KF. Improvement of oral bioavailability of carbamazepine by inclusion in 2-hydroxypropyl-β-cyclodextrin. Int J Pharmaceutics 1992; 85: 175-180.

6. El Shaboury MH. Physical properties and dissolution profiles of tablets directly compressed with β-cyclodextrin. Int J Pharmaceutics 1990; 63: 95-100.

7. Shangraw RF, Pande GS, Gala P. Characterization of the tableting properties of β-cyclodextrin and the effects of processing variables on inclusion complex formation, compactibility and dissolution. Drug Dev Ind Pharm 1992; 18: 1831-1851.

8. Prankerd RJ, Stone HW, Sloan KB, Perrin JH. Degradation of aspartame in acidic aqueous media and its stabilization by complexation with cyclodextrins or modified cyclodextrins. Int J Pharmaceutics 1992; 88: 189-199.

9. Palmieri GF, Wehrlé P, Stamm A. Inclusion of vitamin D2 in β-cyclodextrin. Evaluation of different complexation methods. Drug Dev Ind Pharm 1993; 19: 875-885.

10. Szente L, Apostol I, Szejtli J. Suppositories containing β-cyclodextrin complexes, part 1: stability studies. Pharmazie 1984; 39: 697-699.

11. Szente L, Apostol I, Gerloczy A, Szejtli J. Suppositories containing β-cyclodextrin complexes, part 2: dissolution and absorption studies. Pharmazie 1985; 40: 406-407.

12. Amann M, Dressnandt G. Solving problems with cyclodextrins in cosmetics. Cosmet Toilet 1993; 108(11): 90, 92-95.

13. Loftsson T, Stefánsdóttir Ó, Fridriksdóttir H, Gudmundsson Ö. Interactions between preservatives and 2-hydroxypropyl-β-cyclodextrin. Drug Dev Ind Pharm 1992; 18: 1477-1484.

14. Lehner SJ, M ller BW, Seydel JK. Interactions between *p*-hydroxybenzoic acid esters and hydroxypropyl-β-cyclodextrin and their antimicrobial effect against *Candida albicans*. Int J Pharmaceutics 1993; 93: 201-208.

15. Lehner SJ, Müller BW, Seydel JK. Effect of hydroxypropyl-β-cyclodextrin on the antimicrobial action of preservatives. J Pharm Pharmacol 1994; 46: 186-191.

16. Frank DW, Gray JE, Weaver RN. Cyclodextrin nephrosis in the rat. Am J Pathol 1976; 83: 367-382.

17. French D. The Schardinger dextrins. Adv Carbohydrate Chem 1957; 12: 189-260.

18. Sweet DV, editor. Registry of toxic effects of chemical substances. Cincinnati: US Department of Health, 1987.

19. Menard FA, Dedhiya MG, Rhodes CT. Potential pharmaceutical applications of a new beta cyclodextrin derivative. Drug Dev Ind Pharm 1988; 14: 1529-1547.

21. General References

Bekers O, Uijtendaal EV, Beijnen JH, Bult A, Underberg WJM. Cyclodextrins in the pharmaceutical field. Drug Dev Ind Pharm 1991; 17: 1503-1549.

Bender ML, Komiyama M. Cyclodextrin chemistry. New York: Springer-Verlag, 1978.

Darrouzet H. Preparing cyclodextrin inclusion compounds. Mfg Chem 1993; 64(11): 33-34.

Fenyvest É, Antal B, Zsadon B, Szejtli J. Cyclodextrin polymer, a new tablet disintegrating agent. Pharmazie 1984; 39: 473-475.

Leroy-Lechat F, Wouessidjewe D, Andreux J-P, Puisieux F, Duchêne D. Evaluation of the cytotoxicity of cyclodextrins and hydroxypropylated derivatives. Int J Pharmaceutics 1994; 101: 97-103.

Pande GS, Shangraw RF. Characterization of β-cyclodextrin for direct compression tableting. Int J Pharmaceutics 1994; 101: 71-80.

Pitha J, Szente L, Szejtli J. Molecular encapsulation by cyclodextrin and congeners. In: Bruck SD, editor. Controlled drug delivery, volume I. Boca Raton, FL: CRC Press, 1983.

Shao Z, Krishinamoorthy R, Mitra AK. Cyclodextrins as nasal absorption promoters of insulin: mechanistic evaluations. Pharm Res 1992; 9: 1157-1163.

Stoddard F, Zarycki R. Cyclodextrins. Boca Raton, FL: CRC Press, 1991.

Strattan CE. 2-Hydroxypropyl-β-cyclodextrin, part II: safety and manufacturing issues. Pharmaceut Technol 1992; 16(2): 52, 54, 56, 58.

Szejtli J. Cyclodextrins in drug formulations: part I. Pharmaceut Technol Int 1991; 3(2): 15-18, 20-22.

Szejtli J. Cyclodextrins in drug formulations: part II. Pharmaceut Technol Int 1991; 3(3): 16, 18, 20, 22, 24.

Yamamoto M, Yoshida A, Hirayama F, Uekama K. Some physicochemical properties of branched β-cyclodextrins and their inclusion characteristics. Int J Pharmaceutics 1989; 49: 163-171.

22. Authors

USA: RA Nash.

Dextrates

1. Nonproprietary Names
USPNF: Dextrates

2. Synonyms
Emdex.

3. Chemical Name and CAS Registry Number
Dextrates [39404-33-6]

4. Empirical Formula   Molecular Weight
The USPNF XVII describes dextrates as a purified mixture of saccharides resulting from the controlled enzymatic hydrolysis of starch. It may be either hydrated or anhydrous.

5. Structural Formula
See Section 4.

6. Functional Category
Tablet and capsule diluent.

7. Applications in Pharmaceutical Formulation or Technology
Dextrates is a directly compressible tablet diluent used in both chewable and nonchewable tablets.[1-3] It is a free flowing material and glidants are thus not necessary. However, lubrication with 0.5-1.0% w/w magnesium stearate is recommended. Dextrates may also be used as a binding agent by adding water, no further binder being required.

Tablets made from dextrates show an increase in crushing strength in the first few hours after manufacture but no further increase occurs on storage.

8. Description
Dextrates comprises white, spray-crystallized free-flowing porous spheres. It is odorless with a sweet taste about half that of sucrose.

9. Pharmacopeial Specifications

Test	USPNF XVII (Suppl 6)
pH (20% w/v aqueous solution)	3.8-5.8
Loss on drying	
(anhydrous form)	≤ 2.0%
(hydrated form)	7.8-9.2%
Residue on ignition	≤ 0.1%
Heavy metals	≤ 5 ppm
Organic volatile impurities	+
Dextrose equivalent (dried basis)	93.0-99.0%

10. Typical Properties
Angle of repose: 26.4°[4]
Compressibility: see Fig. 1.[4]
Density: 1.50 g/cm³
Density (bulk): 0.64 g/cm³
Density (tapped): 0.77 g/cm³

Flowability: 9.3 g/s[4]
Heat of combustion: 16.7-18.8 J/g (4.0-4.5 cal/g)
Heat of solution: -0.1 kJ/g (-25 cal/g)
Melting point: 141°C
Moisture content: 7.8-9.2% w/w for hydrated form.
See also Fig. 2.
Particle size distribution: ≤ 3% greater than 840 μm in size; ≤ 25% smaller than 150 μm. Average particle size is 211 μm.
Solubility: soluble 1 in 1 of water; practically insoluble in ethanol, propan-2-ol, and common organic solvents.
Specific surface area: 0.70 m²/g

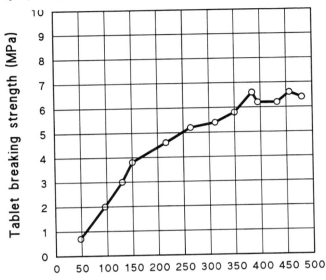

Fig. 1: Compression characteristics of dextrates (*Emdex*, Lot No.: L-53X).[4]
Tablet diameter: 10.3 mm
Punch velocity: 100 mm/s
Lubricant: 0.5% w/w magnesium stearate

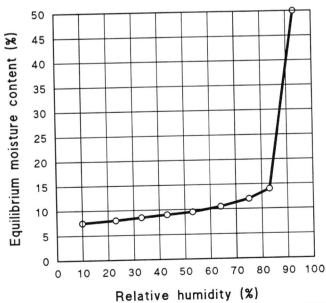

Fig. 2: Equilibrium moisture content of dextrates at 25°C (*Emdex*, Lot No.: M-10).[5]

11. Stability and Storage Conditions

Dextrates may be heated at 50°C without any appreciable darkening in color. Dextrates should be stored in a well-closed container, in a cool, dry place.

12. Incompatibilities

At high temperatures and humidities dextrates may react with substances containing a primary amine group. Also incompatible with strong oxidizing agents.

13. Method of Manufacture

Dextrates is produced by the controlled enzymatic hydrolysis of starch. The product is spray-crystallized and may be dried to produce an anhydrous form.

14. Safety

Dextrates is used in oral pharmaceutical formulations and is generally regarded as a nontoxic and nonirritant material.

15. Handling Precautions

Observe normal precautions appropriate to the circumstances and quantity of material handled. Eye protection, gloves and a dust mask are recommended.

16. Regulatory Status

Included in the FDA Inactive Ingredients Guide (oral tablets). Included in nonparenteral medicines licensed in the UK.

17. Pharmacopeias

USPNF.

18. Related Substances

Dextrose.

19. Comments

Only the hydrated form of dextrates is currently commercially available.

20. Specific References

1. Henderson NL, Bruno AJ. Lactose USP (beadlets) and dextrose (PAF 2011): two new agents for direct compression. J Pharm Sci 1970; 59: 1336-1340.
2. McGinity JW, Ku C-T, Bodmeier R, Harris MR. Dissolution and uniformity properties of ordered mixes of micronized griseofulvin and a directly compressible excipient. Drug Dev Ind Pharm 1985; 11: 891-900.
3. Shukla AJ, Price JC. Effect of moisture content on compression properties of two dextrose-based directly compressible diluents. Pharm Res 1991; 8: 336-340.
4. Çelik M, Okutgen E. A feasibility study for the development of a prospective compaction functionality test and the establishment of a compaction data bank. Drug Dev Ind Pharm 1993; 19: 2309-2334.
5. Callahan JC, Cleary GW, Elefant M, Kaplan G, Kensler T, Nash RA. Equilibrium moisture content of pharmaceutical excipients. Drug Dev Ind Pharm 1982; 8: 355-369.

21. General References

Blaug SM, Huang W-T. Browning of dextrates in solid-solid mixtures containing dextroamphetamine sulfate. J Pharm Sci 1974; 63: 1415-1418.
Czeisler JL, Perlman KP. Diluents. In: Swarbrick J, Boylan JC, editors. Encyclopedia of pharmaceutical technology, volume 4. New York: Marcel Dekker, 1988: 37-84.
Shangraw RF, Wallace JW, Bowers FM. Morphology and functionality in tablet excipients for direct compression: part I. Pharmaceut Technol 1981; 5(9): 69-78.

22. Authors

UK: NA Armstrong.

Dextrin

1. Nonproprietary Names

BP: Dextrin
USPNF: Dextrin

2. Synonyms

Avedex; British gum; *Caloreen*; canary dextrin; *Crystal Gum*; dextrinum album; starch gum; yellow dextrin; white dextrin.

3. Chemical Name and CAS Registry Number

Dextrin [9004-53-9]

4. Empirical Formula   Molecular Weight

$(C_6H_{10}O_5)_n.xH_2O$ $(162.14)_n$

The molecular weight is typically 4500-85 000 and depends on the number of $(C_6H_{10}O_5)$ units in the polymer chain.

5. Structural Formula

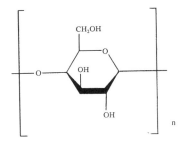

6. Functional Category

Suspending agent; tablet binder; tablet and capsule diluent.

7. Applications in Pharmaceutical Formulation or Technology

Dextrin is a dextrose polymer used as an adhesive and stiffening agent for surgical dressings. It is also used as a tablet and capsule diluent; a binder for tablet granulation; a sugar coating ingredient, which serves as a plasticizer and adhesive; and a thickening agent for suspensions.

Additionally, dextrin is sometimes used as a source of carbohydrate by people with special dietary requirements, since it has a low electrolyte content and is free of lactose and sucrose.[1]

Dextrin is also used in cosmetics.

8. Description

Dextrin is starch, or partially hydrolyzed starch. It is a white, pale yellow or brown-colored powder with a slight characteristic odor.

SEM: 1

Excipient: Dextrin
Manufacturer: Matheson Colleman & Bell
Magnification: 600x

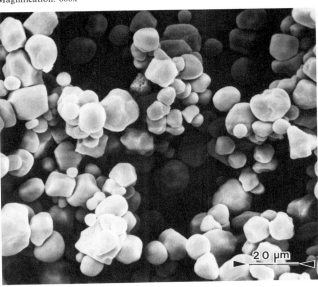

SEM: 2

Excipient: Dextrin
Manufacturer: Matheson Colleman & Bell
Magnification: 2400x

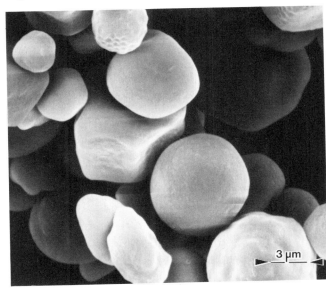

9. Pharmacopeial Specifications

Test	BP 1993	USPNF XVII (Suppl 6)
Identification	+	+
Loss on drying	$\leqslant$ 11.0%	$\leqslant$ 13.0%
Acidity	+	+
Residue on ignition	—	$\leqslant$ 0.5%
Ash	$\leqslant$ 0.5%	—
Chloride	$\leqslant$ 0.2%	$\leqslant$ 0.2%
Arsenic	—	$\leqslant$ 3 ppm
Heavy metals	$\leqslant$ 40 ppm	$\leqslant$ 0.004%
Protein	$\leqslant$ 0.5%	$\leqslant$ 1.0%
Organic volatile impurities	—	+
Reducing sugars/substances (calculated as $C_6H_{12}O_6$)	$\leqslant$ 10.0%	$\leqslant$ 10.0%

10. Typical Properties

Density (bulk): 0.80 g/cm^3
Density (tapped): 0.91 g/cm^3
Melting point: 178°C (with decomposition)
Moisture content: 5% w/w
Particle size distribution: see Fig. 1.
Solubility: practically insoluble in chloroform, ethanol (95%), ether and propan-2-ol; slowly soluble in water, very soluble in boiling water forming a mucilaginous solution.
Specific surface area: 0.14 m^2/g

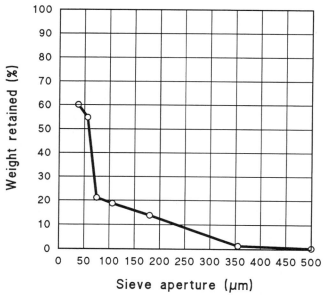

Fig. 1: Particle size distribution of dextrin.

11. Stability and Storage Conditions

In aqueous solutions, dextrin molecules tend to aggregate as density, temperature, pH, or other characteristics change. An increase in viscosity is caused by gelation or retrogradation as dextrin solutions age and is particularly noticeable in the less soluble corn starch dextrins. Dextrin solutions are thixotropic, becoming less viscous when sheared but changing to a soft paste or gel when allowed to stand. However, acids that are present in dextrin as residues from manufacturing can cause further hydrolysis which results in a gradual thinning of solutions. Residual acid, often found in less soluble dextrins as pyrodextrin, will also cause a reduction in viscosity during dry storage. To eliminate these problems, dextrin manufacturers neutralize dextrins of low solubility with ammonia or sodium carbonate in the cooling vessel.

The bulk material should be stored in a well-closed container in a cool, dry, place.

12. Incompatibilities

Incompatible with strong oxidizing agents.

13. Method of Manufacture

Dextrin is prepared by the incomplete hydrolysis of starch by heating in the dry state with or without the aid of suitable acids and buffers; during heating moisture may be added. The BP 1993 specifies that dextrin is derived from maize or potato starch.

14. Safety

Dextrin is generally regarded as a nontoxic and nonirritant material at the levels employed as an excipient. Larger quantities are used as a dietary supplement without adverse effects, although ingestion of very large quantities may be harmful.
LD_{50} (mouse, IV): 0.35 g/kg[2]

15. Handling Precautions

Observe normal precautions appropriate to the circumstances and quantity of material handled. Dextrin may be irritant to the eyes. Eye protection, gloves and a dust mask are recommended.

16. Regulatory Status

GRAS listed. Included in the FDA Inactive Ingredients Guide (oral tablets and topical preparations). Included in nonparenteral medicines licensed in the UK.

17. Pharmacopeias

Aust, Br, Chin, Cz, Fr, Ger, Jpn, Mex, USPNF and Yug.

18. Related Substances

See Section 19.

19. Comments

Dextrin is available from suppliers in a number of modified forms and mixtures such as dextri-maltose, a mixture of maltose and dextrin obtained by the enzymatic action of barley malt on corn flour. It is a light amorphous powder, readily soluble in milk or water.
Crystal Gum, is a grade of dextrin containing carbohydrate not less than 98% of dry weight, whilst *Caloreen*,[1] is a water soluble mixture of dextrins which consists predominantly of polysaccharides containing an average of 5 dextrose molecules, with a mean molecular weight of 840 which does not change after heating. A 22% w/v solution of *Caloreen* is iso-osmotic with serum.

20. Specific References

1. Berlyne GM, Booth EM, Brewis RAL, Mallick NP, Simons PJ. A soluble glucose polymer for use in renal failure and calorie-deprivation states. Lancet 1969; i: 689-692.

2. Sweet DV, editor. Registry of toxic effects of chemical substances. Cincinnati: US Department of Health, 1987.

21. General References

French D. Chemical and physical properties of starch. J Animal Sci 1973; 37: 1048-1061.

Satterthwaite RW, Iwinski DJ. Starch dextrins. In: Whistler RL, Bemiller JN, editors. Industrial gums. New York: Academic Press, 1973: 577-599.

22. Authors

UK: JQ Maclaine, RS Torr.

Dextrose

1. Nonproprietary Names

BP: Glucose
PhEur: Dextrosum (glucosum) monohydricum
USP: Dextrose

2. Synonyms

Blood sugar; *Caridex*; corn sugar; D-(+)-glucopyranose monohydrate; grape sugar; starch sugar; *Tabfine D-100*.

3. Chemical Name and CAS Registry Number

D-(+)-Glucose monohydrate [5996-10-1]
See also Section 18.

4. Empirical Formula

$C_6H_{12}O_6.H_2O$
See also Section 18.

Molecular Weight

198.17 (for monohydrate)

5. Structural Formula

Anhydrous material shown.

6. Functional Category

Tablet and capsule diluent; therapeutic agent; tonicity agent; sweetening agent.

7. Applications in Pharmaceutical Formulation or Technology

Dextrose is widely used in solutions to adjust tonicity and as a sweetening agent. Dextrose is also used as a direct compression tablet diluent and binder, primarily in chewable tablets. Although comparable as a tablet diluent to lactose, tablets produced with dextrose monohydrate require more lubrication, are less friable and have a tendency to harden.[1-3] The mildly reducing properties of dextrose may be used when tableting to improve the stability of active materials which are sensitive to oxidation.
Dextrose is also used therapeutically and is the preferred source of carbohydrate in parenteral nutrition regimens.

8. Description

Dextrose occurs as odorless, sweet-tasting, colorless crystals or as a white crystalline or granular powder.

9. Pharmacopeial Specifications

Test	PhEur 1983	USP XXII
Identification	+	+
Color of solution	+	+
Specific rotation	+ 52.5° to + 53.3°	+ 52.5° to + 53.5°
Acidity	+	+
Water (for monohydrate)	7.5-9.5%	7.5-9.5%

Continued

Test	PhEur 1983	USP XXII
Residue on ignition	⩽ 0.1%	⩽ 0.1%
Chloride	⩽ 125 ppm	⩽ 0.018%
Sulfate	⩽ 200 ppm	⩽ 0.025%
Arsenic	⩽ 1 ppm	⩽ 1 ppm
Barium	⩽ 1 ppm	—
Calcium	⩽ 200 ppm	—
Heavy metals	—	⩽ 5 ppm
Lead	⩽ 0.5 ppm	—
Dextrin	+	+
Soluble starch, and sulfites	+	+

SEM: 1.

Excipient: Dextrose anhydrous (granular)
Manufacturer: Mallinckrodt Speciality Chemicals Co
Lot No.: KLKZ
Magnification: 180x

10. Typical Properties

Data for dextrose monohydrate shown, *see* Section 18 and HPE Data for dextrose anhydrous data.
Acidity/alkalinity:
pH = 3.5-5.5 (20% w/v aqueous solution)
Compressibility: see HPE Data.
Density: 1.54 g/cm³
Flowability: see HPE Data.
Heat of solution: 105.4 J/g (25.2 cal/g)
Hygroscopicity: anhydrous dextrose absorbs significant amounts of moisture at 25°C and a relative humidity of about 85% to form the monohydrate. The monohydrate similarly only absorbs moisture at around 85% relative humidity and 25°C. *See* HPE Data.
Melting point: 83°C
Osmolarity: a 5.51% w/v aqueous solution is iso-osmotic with serum. However, it is not isotonic since dextrose can pass through the membrane of red cells and cause hemolysis.

Solubility:

Solvent	Solubility at 20°C
Chloroform	practically insoluble
Ethanol (95%)	1 in 60
Ether	practically insoluble
Glycerin	soluble
Water	1 in 1

	HPE Laboratory Project Data		
	Method	Lab #	Results
Dextrose anhydrous			
Average flow rate	FLO-1	14	No flow [a]
Density	DE-1	31	1.556 g/cm³ [a]
Moisture content	MC-30	14	0.31% [a]
	MC-30	14	0.22% [b]
	SDI-1	14	*See* Fig. 1.[b]
Dextrose monohydrate			
Average flow rate	FLO-1	14	35 g/s [a]
Compressibility	COM-3	20	*See* Fig. 2.[c]
Moisture content	EMC-1	10	*See* Fig. 3.[a]
	MC-10	10	8.30% [a]
	MC-10	28	8.73% [c]

Supplier:
a. Corn Products (*Cerelose*, Lot No.: CP44);
b. Mallinckrodt Speciality Chemicals Co (Lot No.: 4905);
c. AE Staley Mfg Co (*Staleydex*, Lot No.: 0F04Y).

11. Stability and Storage Conditions

Dextrose has good stability under dry storage conditions. Aqueous solutions may be sterilized by autoclaving. However, excessive heating can cause a reduction in pH and caramelization of solutions.[4-7]
The bulk material should be stored in a well-closed container in a cool, dry, place.

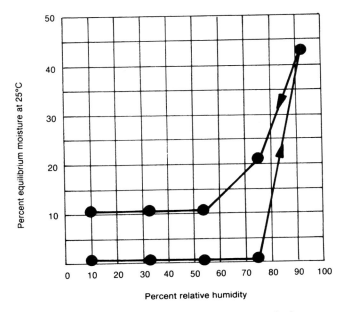

Fig. 1: Sorption-desorption isotherm of dextrose anhydrous.

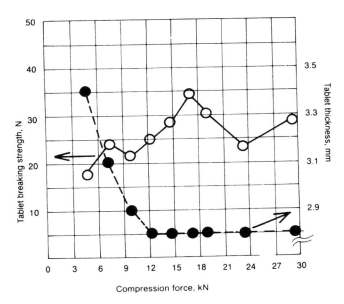

Fig. 2: Compression characteristics of dextrose monohydrate (*Staleydex*).
Mean tablet weight: 502 mg
Minimum compressional force for compaction: 4.9 kN
Compressional force resulting in capping: 7.35 kN
Lubricant: 0.5% w/w magnesium stearate

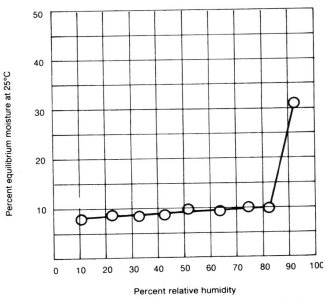

Fig. 3: Equilibrium moisture content of dextrose monohydrate (*Cerelose*).

12. Incompatibilities

Dextrose solutions are incompatible with a number of drugs such as: cyanocobalamin; kanamycin sulfate; novobiocin sodium and warfarin sodium.[8] Erythromycin gluceptate is unstable in dextrose solutions at a pH less than 5.05.[9] Decomposition of B-complex vitamins may occur if they are warmed with dextrose.

In the aldehyde form, dextrose can react with amines, amides, amino acids, peptides, and proteins. Brown coloration and decomposition occurs with strong alkali.

Dextrose may cause browning of tablets containing amines.

13. Method of Manufacture

Dextrose, a monosaccharide sugar, occurs widely in plants and is manufactured on a large scale by the acid and enzymatic hydrolysis of starch, usually corn starch. Below 50°C α-D-dextrose monohydrate is the stable crystalline form produced, above 50°C the anhydrous form is obtained and at still higher temperatures β-D-dextrose is formed which has a melting point of 148-155°C.

14. Safety

Dextrose is rapidly absorbed from the gastrointestinal tract. It is metabolized to carbon dioxide and water with the release of energy.

Concentrated dextrose solutions given by mouth may cause nausea and vomiting. Dextrose solutions greater than 5% w/v concentration are hyperosmotic and are liable to cause local vein irritation following intravenous administration. Thrombophlebitis has been observed following the intravenous infusion of iso-osmotic dextrose solution with low pH, probably due to the presence of degradation products formed by overheating during sterilization. The incidence of phlebitis may be reduced by adding sufficient sodium bicarbonate to raise the pH of the infusion above pH 7.

LD_{50} (mouse, IP): 18 g/kg[10]
LD_{50} (mouse, IV): 9 g/kg
LD_{50} (rat, oral): 25.8 g/kg

15. Handling Precautions

Observe normal precautions appropriate to the circumstances and quantity of material handled. Eye protection and gloves are recommended. Dust generation should be minimized to reduce the risk of explosion.

16. Regulatory Status

Included in the FDA Inactive Ingredients Guide (capsules, inhalations, IM, IV and SC injections, tablets, oral solutions and syrups). Included in nonparenteral and parenteral medicines licensed in the UK.

17. Pharmacopeias

Aust, Belg, Br, Braz, Chin, Eur, Fr, Ger, Gr, Ind, Int, It, Mex, Neth, Nord, Port, Rus, Swiss, Turk, US and Yug. Also in BP Vet.

Some pharmacopeias include separate monographs for dextrose anhydrous and/or dextrose monohydrate whilst others permit the anhydrous and/or monohydrate under a single monograph. The USPNF XVII also includes a monograph for dextrose excipient; this material is dextrose monohydrate not intended for parenteral use, and with a specific optical rotation of +52.5° to +53.5°.

18. Related Substances

Dextrates; Dextrin; dextrose anhydrous; Fructose; Liquid Glucose; Sucrose.

Dextrose anhydrous: $C_6H_{12}O_6$
Molecular weight: 180.16
CAS number: [50-99-7]
Synonyms: anhydrous D-(+)-glucopyranose; anhydrous glucose; anhydrous dextrose; dextrosum anhydricum.

Appearance: white, odorless, crystalline powder with a sweet taste.
Pharmacopeias: Aust, Br, Braz, Cz, Egypt, Eur, Fr, Ger, Gr, Hung, Ind, Int, It, Jpn, Neth, Mex, Port, Rom, Swiss, US and Yug. Also in BP Vet.
Acidity/alkalinity:
pH = 5.9 (10% w/v aqueous solution)
Density (bulk): 1.3-1.4 g/cm^3
Density (tapped): 1.1-1.2 g/cm^3
Melting point: 146°C
Osmolarity: a 5.05% w/v aqueous solution is iso-osmotic with serum. *See also* Section 10.
Refractive index:
n_D^{20} = 1.3479 (10% w/v aqueous solution)
Solubility:

Solvent	Solubility at 20°C Unless otherwise stated
Ethanol (95%)	sparingly soluble
Ether	sparingly soluble
Methanol	1 in 120
Water	1 in 1.1 at 25°C
	1 in 0.8 at 30°C
	1 in 0.41 at 50°C
	1 in 0.28 at 70°C
	1 in 0.18 at 90°C

Specific gravity:

Concentration of aqueous dextrose solution (% w/v)	Specific gravity at 17.5°C
5	1.019
10	1.038
20	1.076
30	1.113
40	1.149

19. Comments

The way in which the strengths of dextrose solutions are expressed varies from country to country. The USP XXII requires strengths to be expressed in terms of dextrose monohydrate whilst the BP 1993 requires strengths to be expressed in terms of anhydrous dextrose. Approximately 1.1 g of dextrose monohydrate is equivalent to 1 g of anhydrous dextrose.

20. Specific References

1. DuVall RN, Koshy KT, Dashiell RE. Comparative evaluation of dextrose and spray-dried lactose in direct compression systems. J Pharm Sci 1965; 54: 1196-1200.
2. Henderson NL, Bruno AJ. Lactose USP (beadlets) and dextrose (PAF 2011): two new agents for direct compression. J Pharm Sci 1970; 59: 1336-1340.
3. Armstrong NA, Patel A, Jones TM. The compressional properties of dextrose monohydrate and anhydrous dextrose of varying water contents. In: Rubinstein MH, editor. Pharmaceutical technology: tableting technology, volume 1. Chichester: Ellis Horwood, 1987: 127-138.
4. Wing WT. An examination of the decomposition of dextrose solution during sterilisation. J Pharm Pharmacol 1960; 12: 191T-196T.

5. Murty BSR, Kapoor JN, Smith FX. Levels of 5-hydroxymethyl-furfural in dextrose injection. Am J Hosp Pharm 1977; 34: 205-206.

6. Sturgeon RJ, Athanikar NK, Harbison HA, Henry RS, Jurgens RW, Welco AD. Degradation of dextrose during heating under simulated sterilization. J Parenter Drug Assoc 1980; 34: 175-182.

7. Durham DG, Hung CT, Taylor RB. Identification of some acids produced during autoclaving of D-glucose solutions using HPLC. Int J Pharmaceutics 1982; 12: 31-40.

8. Patel JA, Phillips GL. A guide to physical compatibility of intravenous drug admixtures. Am J Hosp Pharm 1966; 23: 409-411.

9. Edward M. pH - an important factor in the compatibility of additives in intravenous therapy. Am J Hosp Pharm 1967; 24: 440-449.

10. Sweet DV, editor. Registry of toxic effects of chemical substances. Cincinnati: US Department of Health, 1987.

21. General References

—

22. Authors

UK: JQ Maclaine, RS Torr.

Dibutyl Sebacate

1. Nonproprietary Names

USPNF: Dibutyl sebacate

2. Synonyms

Butyl sebacate; decanedioic acid, dibutyl ester; dibutyl decanedioate; dibutyl 1,8-octanedicarboxylate; *Kodaflex DBS*; sebacic acid, dibutyl ester.

3. Chemical Name and CAS Registry Number

Di-*n*-butyl sebacate [109-43-3]

4. Empirical Formula   Molecular Weight

$C_{18}H_{34}O_4$ 314.47

(for pure material)

The USPNF XVII (Suppl 3) describes dibutyl sebacate as consisting of the esters of *n*-butanol and saturated dibasic acids, principally sebacic acid.

5. Structural Formula

$$CH_3—(CH_2)_3—O—\overset{\displaystyle O}{\overset{\|}{C}}—(CH_2)_8—\overset{\displaystyle O}{\overset{\|}{C}}—O—(CH_2)_3—CH_3$$

6. Functional Category

Plasticizer.

7. Applications in Pharmaceutical Formulation or Technology

Dibutyl sebacate is used in oral pharmaceutical formulations as a plasticizer for film coatings on tablets, beads and granules, at concentrations of 10-30% by weight of polymer.[1,2]

Dibutyl sebacate is also used as a synthetic flavor and flavor adjuvant in food products, e.g. up to 5 ppm is used in ice cream and nonalcoholic beverages.

8. Description

Dibutyl sebacate is a clear, colorless, oily liquid with a bland to slight butyl odor.

9. Pharmacopeial Specifications

Test	USPNF XVII (Suppl 3)
Specific gravity	0.935-0.939
Refractive index	1.429-1.441
Acid value	$\leqslant 0.1\%$
Saponification value	352-357
Assay (of $C_{18}H_{34}O_4$)	$\geqslant 92.0\%$

10. Typical Properties

Acid value: 0.02
Boiling point: 344-349°C
Flash point: 193°C
Melting point: -10°C
Refractive index: $n_D^{25} = 1.4401$

Solubility: soluble in ethanol, propan-2-ol and mineral oil; practically insoluble in water.
Specific gravity: 0.937 at 20°C
Vapor density (relative): 10.8 (air = 1)
Vapor pressure: 0.4 kPa (3 mmHg) at 180°C

11. Stability and Storage Conditions

Dibutyl sebacate is stable. It is not reactive with water and hazardous polymerization does not occur. Dibutyl sebacate should be stored in a well-closed container, in a cool, dry, place.

12. Incompatibilities

Incompatible with strong oxidizing agents.

13. Method of Manufacture

Dibutyl sebacate is produced by the esterification of *n*-butanol and sebacic acid, in the presence of a suitable catalyst, and by the distillation of sebacic acid with *n*-butanol, in the presence of concentrated hydrochloric acid in benzene solution.

14. Safety

Dibutyl sebacate is used in cosmetics, foods and oral pharmaceutical formulations and is generally regarded as a nontoxic and nonirritant material. Following oral administration dibutyl sebacate is metabolized in the same way as fats.

In humans, direct eye contact and prolonged or repeated contact with the skin may cause very mild irritation.

Acute animal toxicity tests and long-term animal feeding studies have shown no serious adverse effects to be associated with orally administered dibutyl sebacate.

LD_{50} (rat, oral): 16 g/kg[3]

15. Handling Precautions

Observe normal precautions appropriate to the circumstances and quantity of material handled. Eye protection and nitrile gloves are recommended. Handle in a well-ventilated environment; a respirator is recommended when handling the heated product.

16. Regulatory Status

Included in the FDA Inactive Ingredients Guide (oral capsules and tablets).

17. Pharmacopeias

USPNF.

18. Related Substances

—

19. Comments

Since dibutyl sebacate is an emollient ester, the personnel care grade is recommended for use in cosmetics, hair products, lotions and creams.

20. Specific References

1. Goodhart FW, Harris MR, Murthy KS, Nesbitt RU. An evaluation of aqueous film-forming dispersions for controlled release. Pharmaceut Technol 1984; 8(4): 64, 66, 68, 70, 71.
2. Iyer U, Hong W-H, Das N, Ghebre-Sellassie I. Comparative evaluation of three organic solvent and dispersion-based ethylcellulose coating formulations. Pharmaceut Technol 1990; 14(9): 68, 70, 72, 74, 76, 78, 80, 82, 84, 86.

3. Sweet DV, editor. Registry of toxic effects of chemical substances. Cincinnati: US Department of Health, 1987.

21. General References

Appel LE, Zentner GM. Release from osmotic tablets coated with modified Aquacoat lattices. Proc Int Symp Control Rel Bioact Mater 1990; 17: 335-336.

Rowe RC. Materials used in the film coating of oral dosage forms. In: Florence AT, editor. Materials used in pharmaceutical formulation: critical reports on applied chemistry, volume 6. Oxford: Blackwell Scientific Publications, 1984: 1-36.

22. Authors

USA: TA Wheatley.

Dichlorodifluoro-methane

1. Nonproprietary Names
USPNF: Dichlorodifluoromethane

2. Synonyms
Arcton 12; difluorodichloromethane; *Dymel 12*; *Freon 12*; *Frigen 12*; *Genetron 12*; *Halon 12*; *Isceon 12*; *Isotron 12*; propellant 12; refrigerant 12.

3. Chemical Name and CAS Registry Number
Dichlorodifluoromethane [75-71-8]

4. Empirical Formula   Molecular Weight
CCl_2F_2 120.92

5. Structural Formula
CCl_2F_2

6. Functional Category
Aerosol propellant.

7. Applications in Pharmaceutical Formulation or Technology
Dichlorodifluoromethane is used as an aerosol propellant in metered-dose inhalant (MDI) oral and nasal aerosol formulations either as the sole propellant or in combination with dichlorotetrafluoroethane, trichloromonofluoromethane or mixtures of these other chlorofluorocarbons. Dichlorodifluoromethane may also be used as a propellant in various other pharmaceutical aerosols such as contraceptive foams and cytology sprays.

Dichlorodifluoromethane has also been used in foods and as a refrigerant.

Under the terms of the Montreal Protocol, aimed at reducing damage to the ozone layer, the use of chlorofluorocarbons, including dichlorodifluoromethane, will be prohibited from January 1996.[1-5] However, this prohibition does not apply to essential uses such as existing pharmaceutical formulations for which no alternative chlorofluorocarbon-free product is available. New pharmaceutical formulations, containing chlorofluorocarbons may also be exempted provided they demonstrate that there is no technically feasible alternative to their use, that the product is of a substantial health benefit, and that its usage would not involve release of significant quantities of chlorofluorocarbon into the atmosphere. Regulatory bodies in individual countries should be consulted for advice on chlorofluorocarbon use in formulations.

8. Description
Dichlorodifluoromethane is a liquefied gas and exists as a liquid at room temperature when contained under its own vapor pressure, or as a gas when exposed to room temperature and atmospheric pressure. The liquid is practically odorless and colorless. The gas in high concentrations has a faint ether-like odor. Dichlorodifluoromethane is noncorrosive, nonirritating and nonflammable.

9. Pharmacopeial Specifications

Test	USPNF XVII
Identification	+
Boiling temperature	-30°C
Water	$\leqslant 0.001\%$
High boiling residues	$\leqslant 0.01\%$
Inorganic chlorides	+

10. Typical Properties
Boiling point: -29.8°C
Critical pressure: 4.01 MPa (39.6 atm)
Critical temperature: 111.5°C
Density:
1.325 g/cm^3 for liquid at 21°C;
1.191 g/cm^3 for liquid at 54.5°C.
Flammability: nonflammable
Freezing point: -158°C
Kauri-butanol value: 18
Solubility:

Solvent	Solubility at 20°C Unless otherwise stated
Ethanol (95%)	soluble
Ether	soluble
Water	1 in 3570 at 25°C

Surface tension: 9 mN/m (9 dynes/cm) at 25°C
Vapor density (absolute): 5.398 g/m^3
Vapor density (relative): 4.19 (air = 1)
Vapor pressure:
585.4 kPa (84.9 psia) at 21°C;
1351.4 kPa (196.0 psia) at 54.5°C.
Viscosity (dynamic):
0.262 mPa s (0.262 cP) for liquid at 21°C;
0.227 mPa s (0.227 cP) for liquid at 54.5°C.

11. Stability and Storage Conditions
Dichlorodifluoromethane is nonreactive and stable at temperatures up to 550°C. The liquefied gas is stable when used as a propellant and should be stored in a metal cylinder in a cool, dry, place.

12. Incompatibilities
Compatible with the usual ingredients used in the formulation of pharmaceutical aerosols although it has poor miscibility with water, *see* Section 19.

13. Method of Manufacture
Dichlorodifluoromethane is prepared by the reaction of hydrogen fluoride with carbon tetrachloride in the presence of a suitable catalyst, such as polyvalent antimony. The dichlorodifluoromethane formed is further purified to remove all traces of water and hydrochloric acid as well as traces of the starting and intermediate materials. Trichloromonofluoromethane is also obtained by this process.

14. Safety
Dichlorodifluoromethane and other chlorofluorocarbons have been used for a number of years as propellants in topical, oral and nasal aerosol formulations and are generally regarded as nontoxic and nonirritant materials.[6-8]

The propellants used for oral and nasal aerosol products generally vaporize quickly and most of the vapors escape and are not inhaled. However, a small amount of the propellant may be inhaled with the active ingredient and be carried to the respiratory system. These amounts of propellant do not present a toxicological problem and are quickly cleared from the lungs. Deliberate inhalation of excessive quantities of fluorocarbon propellant may result in death, and the following 'warning' statements must appear on the label of all aerosols: WARNING: Avoid inhalation. Keep away from eyes or other mucous membranes. (Aerosols designed specifically for oral and nasal inhalation need not contain this statement).

WARNING: Do not inhale directly; deliberate inhalation of contents can cause death.

OR

WARNING: Use only as directed; intentional misuse by deliberately concentrating and inhaling the contents can be harmful or fatal.

Additionally, the label should contain the following information:

WARNING: Contents under pressure. Do not puncture or incinerate container. Do not expose to heat or store at room temperature above 120°F (49°C). Keep out of the reach of children.

In the US, the Environmental Protection Agency (EPA) additionally requires the following information on all aerosols containing chlorofluorocarbons as the propellant:

WARNING: Contains a chlorofluorocarbon that may harm the public health and environment by reducing ozone in the upper atmosphere. (Metered-dose inhalers and nasal aerosols are exempt from this regulation).

When chlorofluorocarbon propellants are used in topical aerosols they may cause a chilling effect on the skin although this effect has been somewhat overcome by the use of vapor tap valves. The propellants quickly vaporize from the skin, and are nonirritating when used as directed.

The WHO has set an estimated acceptable daily intake of dichlorodifluoromethane at up to 1.5 mg/kg body-weight.[9]

LC_{50} (guinea pig, inhalation): 80 pph/30 min[10]
LC_{50} (mouse, inhalation): 76 pph/30 min
LC_{50} (rabbit, inhalation): 80 pph/30 min
LC_{50} (rat, inhalation): 80 pph/30 min

15. Handling Precautions

Dichlorodifluoromethane is usually encountered as a liquefied gas and appropriate precautions for handling such materials should be taken. Eye protection, gloves and protective clothing are recommended. Dichlorodifluoromethane should be handled in a well-ventilated environment. Chlorofluorocarbon vapors are heavier than air and do not support life and therefore, when cleaning large tanks which have contained chlorofluorocarbons, adequate provisions for oxygen in the tanks must be made in order to protect workers cleaning the tanks.

Although nonflammable, when heated to decomposition dichlorodifluoromethane emits toxic fumes containing phosgene and fluorides.

In the UK, the long-term (8-hour TWA) occupational exposure limit for dichlorodifluoromethane is 4950 mg/m³ (1000 ppm) and the short-term (10-minutes) exposure limit is 6200 mg/m³ (1250 ppm).[11]

16. Regulatory Status

Included in the FDA Inactive Ingredients Guide (aerosol formulations for inhalation, nasal, oral, rectal, topical and vaginal applications). Included in nonparenteral medicines licensed in the UK.

17. Pharmacopeias

Mex and USPNF.
See also Section 19.

18. Related Substances

Chlorodifluoroethane; Chlorodifluoromethane; Dichlorotetrafluoroethane; Difluoroethane; Tetrafluoroethane; Trichloromonofluoromethane.

19. Comments

Dichlorodifluoromethane is frequently used in preference to other chlorofluorocarbon propellants in metered-dose aerosols since its vapor pressure is sufficient to dispense a product in the proper particle size distribution without the use of any other propellant.

The disadvantages of using dichlorodifluoromethane in aerosols include its poor miscibility with water. However, it is generally miscible with nonpolar materials and some semipolar materials. To overcome the lack of miscibility with water cosolvents are frequently employed in aerosol formulations, the most commonly used being ethanol, glycols and oils. Dichlorodifluoromethane has been omitted from the BP 1993, although it was present in the BP 1988.

Fluorocarbon aerosal propellants may be identified by a standardized numbering nomenclature, e.g. dichlorodifluoromethane is known as propellant 12, while dichlorotetrafluoroethane is known as propellant 114.

Usually, three digits are used to describe the propellant except when the first digit would be a zero, in which case only two digits are used. The first digit is a number one less than the number of carbon atoms in the molecule. Thus, if the molecule is a methane derivative the first digit would be a zero (1-1) and is ignored so that only two digits are used in the propellant description, e.g. propellant 12. For an ethane derivative, the first digit would be a one (2-1), e.g. propellant 114.

The second digit is a number one more than the number of hydrogen atoms in the molecule, while the third digit represents the number of fluorine atoms in the molecule. The difference between the sum of the fluorine and hydrogen atoms and the number of atoms required to saturate the carbon chain is the number of chlorine atoms in the molecule. Isomers of a compound have the same identifying number and an additional letter, a, b, c and so on. Cyclic derivatives are indicated by the letter C before the identifying number. With unsaturated propellants, the number one is used as the fourth digit from the right to indicate an unsaturated double bond. *see* Lund for further information.[12]

Thus for dichlorodifluoromethane (propellant 12):

First digit = 0, number of C atoms = 1
Second digit = 1, number of H atoms = 0
Third digit = 2, number of F atoms = 2.
The number of Cl atoms = 4 − (2 + 0) = 2

20. Specific References

1. Fischer FX, Hess H, Sucker H, Byron PR. CFC propellant substitution: international perspectives. Pharmaceut Technol 1989; 13(9): 44, 48, 50, 52.
2. Kempner N. Metered dose inhaler CFCs under pressure. Pharm J 1990; 245: 428-429.
3. Dalby RN. Possible replacements for CFC-propelled metered-dose inhalers. Med Device Tech 1991; 2(4): 21-25.
4. CFC-free aerosols: the final hurdle. Mfg Chem 1992; 63(7): 22-23.

5.   Mackenzie D. Large hole in the ozone agreement. New Scientist 1992; Nov 28: 5.

6.   Weiner M, Bernstein IL. Adverse reactions to drug formulation agents: a handbook of excipients. New York: Marcel Dekker, 1989: 184-190.

7.   Florence AT, Salole EG, editors. Formulation factors in adverse reactions. Sevenoaks: Wright, 1990: 116-118.

8.   Smolinske SC. Handbook of food, drug, and cosmetic excipients. Boca Raton, FL: CRC Press Inc, 1992: 91-97.

9.   FAO/WHO. Nineteenth report of the joint FAO/WHO expert committee on food additives. Tech Rep Ser Wld Hlth Org 1975; No. 576.

10. Sweet DV, editor. Registry of toxic effects of chemical substances. Cincinnati: US Department of Health, 1987.

11. Health and Safety Executive. EH40/93: occupational exposure limits 1993. London: HMSO, 1993.

12. Lund W, editor. The Pharmaceutical Codex: principles and practice of pharmaceutics, 12th edition. London: The Pharmaceutical Press, 1994: 121.

21. General References

Byron PR, editor. Respiratory drug delivery. Boca Raton, FL: CRC Press Inc, 1990.

Johnson MA. The aerosol handbook, 2nd edition. Caldwell: WE Dorland, 1982: 305-335.

Niazi S, Chiou WL. Fluorocarbon aerosol propellants XI: pharmacokinetics of dichlorodifluoromethane in dogs following single dose and multiple dosing. J Pharm Sci 1977; 66: 49-53.

Sanders PA. Handbook of aerosol technology, 2nd edition. New York: Van Nostrand Reinhold, 1979: 19-35.

Sciarra JJ. Pharmaceutical and cosmetic aerosols. J Pharm Sci 1974; 63: 1815-1836.

Sciarra JJ, Stoller L. The science and technology of aerosol packaging. New York: John Wiley and Sons, 1974: 97-130.

Sciarra JJ. Pharmaceutical aerosols. In: Lachman L, Lieberman HA, Kanig JL, editors. The theory and practice of industrial pharmacy, 3rd edition. Philadelphia: Lea and Febiger, 1986: 589-618.

Sciarra JJ, Cutie AJ. In: Banker GS, Rhodes CT, editors. Modern pharmaceutics, 2nd edition. New York: Marcel Dekker, 1990: 605-634.

22. Authors

UK: PJ Davies.
USA: JJ Sciarra.

Dichlorotetrafluoro-ethane

1. Nonproprietary Names

USPNF: Dichlorotetrafluoroethane

2. Synonyms

Arcton 114; cryofluorane; *Dymel 114*; *Freon 114*; *Frigen 114*; *Gentron 114*; *Isceon 114*; propellant 114; refrigerant 114.

3. Chemical Name and CAS Registry Number

1,2-Dichloro-1,1,2,2-tetrafluoroethane
[76-14-2]

4. Empirical Formula   Molecular Weight

$C_2Cl_2F_4$ 170.92

5. Structural Formula

$$\begin{array}{c} \quad Cl \quad Cl \\ \quad | \quad \ | \\ F-C-C-F \\ \quad | \quad \ | \\ \quad F \quad F \end{array}$$

6. Functional Category

Aerosol propellant.

7. Applications in Pharmaceutical Formulation or Technology

Dichlorotetrafluoroethane is used in combination with dichlorodifluoromethane, and in several cases with dichlorodifluoromethane and trichloromonofluoromethane, as the propellant in metered-dose oral and nasal aerosols.
Under the terms of the Montreal Protocol the use of chlorofluorocarbons will be prohibited from January 1996. However, this prohibition does not apply to essential uses in pharmaceutical formulations. For further information *see* Dichlorodifluoromethane.

8. Description

Dichlorotetrafluoroethane is a colorless, nonflammable liquefied gas with a faint, ethereal odor.

9. Pharmacopeial Specifications

Test	USPNF XVII
Identification	+
Boiling temperature	4°C
Water	≤ 0.001%
High boiling residues	≤ 0.01%
Chlorides	+

10. Typical Properties

Boiling point: 4.1°C
Critical pressure: 3268 kPa (474 psia)
Critical temperature: 145.7°C
Density:
1.468 g/cm^3 for liquid at 21°C;
1.360 g/cm^3 for liquid at 54.5°C.
Freezing point: -94°C
Solubility:

Solvent	Solubility at 20°C Unless otherwise stated
Ethanol (95%)	soluble
Ether	soluble
Water	1 in 7690 at 25°C

Surface tension: 13 mN/m (13 dynes/cm) at 25°C
Vapor density (absolute): 7.630 g/m^3
Vapor density (relative): 5.92 (air = 1)
Vapor pressure:
190.3 kPa (27.6 psia) at 21°C;
506.8 kPa (73.5 psia) at 54.5°C
Viscosity (dynamic):
0.386 mPa s (0.386 cP) for liquid at 21°C;
0.296 mPa s (0.296 cP) for liquid at 54.5°C.

11. Stability and Storage Conditions

Dichlorotetrafluoroethane is a nonreactive and stable material. The liquefied gas is stable when used as a propellant and should be stored in a metal cylinder in a cool, dry, place.

12. Incompatibilities

Dichlorotetrafluoroethane is compatible with most ingredients used in pharmaceutical aerosol propellants although it has poor miscibility with water, similar to dichlorodifluoromethane. *See* Dichlorodifluoromethane.

13. Method of Manufacture

Dichlorotetrafluoroethane is prepared by the reaction of hydrogen fluoride with chlorine and perchloroethylene in the presence of a catalyst, polyvalent antimony.

14. Safety

Dichlorotetrafluoroethane and other chlorofluorocarbons have been used for a number of years as propellants in topical, oral and nasal aerosol formulations and are generally regarded as nontoxic and nonirritant materials. For further information *see* Dichlorodifluoromethane.
LC_{50} (rabbit, inhalation): 75 pph/30 min[1]
LC_{50} (rat, inhalation): 72 pph/30 min

15. Handling Precautions

Dichlorotetrafluoroethane is usually encountered as a liquefied gas and appropriate precautions for handling such materials should be taken. Eye protection, gloves and protective clothing are recommended. Dichlorotetrafluoroethane should be handled in a well-ventilated environment.
Although nonflammable, when heated to decomposition toxic fumes may be released.
In the UK, the long-term (8-hour TWA) occupational exposure limit for dichlorotetrafluoroethane is 7000 mg/m^3 (1000 ppm) and the short-term (10-minutes) exposure limit is 8750 mg/m^3 (1250 ppm).[2]
See also Dichlorodifluoromethane.

16. Regulatory Status

Included in the FDA Inactive Ingredients Guide (aerosol formulations for inhalation, nasal, oral, rectal, topical and vaginal applications). Included in nonparenteral medicines licensed in the UK.

17. Pharmacopeias

Mex and USPNF.
See also Section 19.

18. Related Substances

Chlorodifluoroethane; Chlorodifluoromethane; Dichlorodifluoromethane; Difluoroethane; Tetrafluoroethane; Trichloromonofluoromethane.

19. Comments

Dichlorotetrafluoroethane is useful in formulating oral and nasal aerosol products. However, since it is highly fluorinated its solubility in water and other solvents is limited.
Dichlorotetrafluoroethane has been omitted from the BP 1993, although it was present in the BP 1988.

For a discussion of the numerical nomenclature applied to flurocarbon aerosol propellants *see* Dichlorodifluoromethane.

20. Specific References

1. Sweet DV, editor. Registry of toxic effects of chemical substances. Cincinnati: US Department of Health, 1987.
2. Health and Safety Executive. EH40/93: occupational exposure limits 1993. London: HMSO, 1993.
See also Dichlorodifluoromethane.

21. General References

Niazi S, Chiou WL. Fluorocarbon aerosol propellants X: pharmacokinetics of dichlorotetrafluoroethane in dogs. J Pharm Sci 1976; 65: 60-64.
See also Dichlorodifluoromethane.

22. Authors

UK: PJ Davies.
USA: JJ Sciarra.

Diethanolamine

1. Nonproprietary Names
USPNF: Diethanolamine

2. Synonyms
Bis(hydroxyethyl)amine; DEA; diethylolamine; 2,2'-dihydroxydiethylamine; diolamine; 2,2'-iminodiethanol.

3. Chemical Name and CAS Registry Number
2,2'-Iminobisethanol [111-42-2]

4. Empirical Formula   Molecular Weight
$C_4H_{11}NO_2$ 105.14

5. Structural Formula
$NH(CH_2CH_2OH)_2$

6. Functional Category
Alkalizing agent; emulsifying agent.

7. Applications in Pharmaceutical Formulation or Technology
Diethanolamine is primarily used in pharmaceutical formulations as a buffering agent, such as in the preparation of emulsions with fatty acids.
Diethanolamine has also been used to form the soluble salts of active compounds, such as iodinated organic acids which are used as contrast media. As a stabilizing agent diethanolamine prevents the discoloration of aqueous formulations containing hexamethylene-tetramine-1,3-dichloropropene salts.
Diethanolamine is also used in cosmetics.

8. Description
The USPNF XVII describes diethanolamine as a mixture of ethanolamines consisting largely of diethanolamine. At about room temperature it is a white, deliquescent solid. Above room temperature diethanolamine is a clear, viscous liquid with a mildly ammoniacal odor.

9. Pharmacopeial Specifications

Test	USPNF XVII
Identification	+
Refractive index at 30°C	1.473-1.476
Water	$\leqslant$ 0.15%
Triethanolamine	$\leqslant$ 1.0%
Assay (anhydrous basis)	98.5-101.0%

10. Typical Properties
Acidity/alkalinity:
pH = 11.0 for a 0.1N aqueous solution
Autoignition temperature: 662°C
Boiling point: 268.8°C
Density:
1.0881 g/cm³ at 30°C;
1.0693 g/cm³ at 60°C.
Dissociation constant: pK_a = 8.88

Flash point (open cup): 138°C
Hygroscopicity: very hygroscopic.
Melting point: 28°C
Refractive index: n_D^{30} = 1.4753
Solubility:

Solvent	Solubility at 20°C
Acetone	miscible
Benzene	1 in 24
Chloroform	miscible
Ether	1 in 125
Glycerin	miscible
Methanol	miscible
Water	1 in 1

Surface tension:
49.0 mN/m (49.0 dynes/cm) at 20°C
Vapor density (relative): 3.65 (air = 1)
Vapor pressure: < 1 Pa at 20°C
Viscosity (dynamic):
351.9 mPa s (351.9 cP) at 30°C;
53.85 mPa s (53.85 cP) at 60°C.

11. Stability and Storage Conditions
Diethanolamine, like monoethanolamine, is hygroscopic, light and oxygen sensitive and should be stored in an airtight container, protected from light, in a cool, dry, place.
See Monoethanolamine for further information.

12. Incompatibilities
Diethanolamine is a secondary amine which contains a hydroxy group. It is therefore capable of undergoing reactions typical of secondary amines and alcohols. The amine group usually exhibits the greater activity whenever it is possible for a reaction to take place at either the amine or the hydroxy group.
Diethanolamine will react with acids, acid anhydrides, acid chlorides and esters to form amide derivatives, and with propylene carbonate or other cyclic carbonates to give the corresponding carbonates. As a secondary amine, diethanolamine reacts with aldehydes and ketones to yield aldimines and ketimines. Diethanolamine also reacts with copper to form complex salts. Discoloration and precipitation will take place in the presence of heavy metal salts.

13. Method of Manufacture
Diethanolamine is prepared commercially by the ammonolysis of ethylene oxide. The reaction yields a mixture of monoethanolamine, diethanolamine and triethanolamine which is separated to obtain the pure products.

14. Safety
Diethanolamine is used in topical and parenteral pharmaceutical formulations, up to 0.3% w/v being used in intravenous infusions. Experimental studies in dogs have shown that intravenous administration of larger doses of diethanolamine produce sedation, coma and death.
Animal toxicity studies suggest that diethanolamine is less toxic than monoethanolamine although in rats the oral acute and subacute toxicity is greater.
Diethanolamine is irritant to the skin, eyes and mucous membranes when used undiluted or in high concentration.

However, in rabbits, aqueous solutions containing 10% w/v diethanolamine produce minor irritation.

The lethal human oral dose of diethanolamine is estimated to be 5-15 g/kg body-weight.

LD_{50} (guinea pig, oral): 2.0 g/kg[1]
LD_{50} (mouse, IP): 2.3 g/kg
LD_{50} (mouse, oral): 3.3 g/kg
LD_{50} (rabbit, oral): 2.2 g/kg
LD_{50} (rabbit, skin): 12.2 g/kg
LD_{50} (rat, IM): 1.5 g/kg
LD_{50} (rat, IP): 0.12 g/kg
LD_{50} (rat, IV): 0.78 g/kg
LD_{50} (rat, oral): 0.71 g/kg
LD_{50} (rat, SC): 2.2 g/kg

15. Handling Precautions

Diethanolamine is irritant to the skin, eyes and mucous membranes. Protective clothing, gloves, eye protection and a respirator are recommended. Ideally, diethanolamine should be handled in a fume cupboard. In the UK, the long-term (8-hour TWA) exposure limit for diethanolamine is 15 mg/m^3 (3 ppm).[2] Diethanolamine poses a slight fire hazard when exposed to heat or flame.

16. Regulatory Status

Included in the FDA Inactive Ingredients Guide (IV infusions). Included in medicines licensed in the UK.

17. Pharmacopeias

Yug and USPNF.

18. Related Substances

Monoethanolamine; Triethanolamine.

19. Comments

—

20. Specific References

1. Sweet DV, editor. Registry of toxic effects of chemical substances. Cincinnati: US Department of Health, 1987.
2. Health and Safety Executive. EH40/93: occupational exposure limits 1993. London: HMSO, 1993.

21. General References

—

22. Authors

USA: J Fleitman, JS Fujiki.

Diethyl Phthalate

1. Nonproprietary Names

BP: Diethyl phthalate
USPNF: Diethyl phthalate

2. Synonyms

Ethyl benzene-1,2-dicarboxylate; ethyl phthalate; *Kodaflex DEP*; *Palatinol A*; phthalic acid ethyl ester.

3. Chemical Name and CAS Registry Number

1,2-Benzenedicarboxylic acid, diethyl ester [84-66-2]

4. Empirical Formula   Molecular Weight

$C_{12}H_{14}O_4$ 222.24

5. Structural Formula

6. Functional Category

Solvent; plasticizer.

7. Applications in Pharmaceutical Formulation or Technology

Diethyl phthalate is used as a plasticizer for film coatings on tablets, beads and granules at concentrations of 10-30% by weight of polymer.
Diethyl phthalate is also used as an alcohol denaturant and as a solvent for cellulose acetate in the manufacture of varnishes and dopes. In perfumery, diethyl phthalate is used as a perfume fixative at a concentration of 0.1-0.5% the weight of the perfume used.

8. Description

Diethyl phthalate is a clear, colorless, oily liquid. It is practically odorless, or with a very slight aromatic odor and a bitter, disagreeable taste.

9. Pharmacopeial Specifications

Test	BP 1993	USPNF XVII
Identification	+	+
Specific gravity*	1.115-1.119	1.118-1.122
Refractive index	1.500-1.505	1.500-1.505
Acidity	+	+
Related substances	+	—
Water	⩽ 0.2%	⩽ 0.2%
Residue on ignition	—	⩽ 0.02%
Sulfated ash	⩽ 0.02%	—
Assay (anhydrous basis)	99.0-100.5%	98.0-102.0%

* Note: the BP 1993 states the test is performed at 20°C, while the USPNF XVII states the test is performed at 25°C.

10. Typical Properties

Boiling point: 295°C
Flash point: 160°C (open cup)
Melting point: -40°C
Refractive index: $n_D^{14} = 1.5049$
Solubility: miscible with ethanol, ether, and many other organic solvents; practically insoluble in water.
Specific gravity: 1.120 at 25°C
Vapor density (relative): 7.66 (air = 1)
Vapor pressure: 1.87 kPa (14 mmHg) at 163°C

11. Stability and Storage Conditions

Diethyl phthalate is stable when stored in a well-closed container, in a cool, dry, place.

12. Incompatibilities

Incompatible with strong oxidizing materials.

13. Method of Manufacture

Diethyl phthalate is produced by the reaction of ethanol with phthalic acid.

14. Safety

Diethyl phthalate is used in oral pharmaceutical formulations and is generally regarded as a nontoxic and nonirritant material at the levels employed as an excipient. However, if consumed in large quantities it can act as a narcotic and cause paralysis of the central nervous system.
LD_{50} (guinea pig, oral): 8.6 g/kg[1]
LD_{50} (mouse, IP): 2.8 g/kg
LD_{50} (mouse, oral): 6.2 g/kg
LD_{50} (rat, IP): 5.1 g/kg
LD_{50} (rat, oral): 8.6 g/kg

15. Handling Precautions

Observe normal precautions appropriate to the circumstances and quantity of material handled. Diethyl phthalate is irritant to the skin, eyes and mucous membranes. Protective clothing, eye protection and nitrile gloves are recommended. Diethyl phthalate should be handled in a fume-cupboard, or a well-ventilated environment; a respirator is recommended. In the UK, the long-term (8-hour TWA) exposure limit for diethyl phthalate is 5 mg/m^3. The short-term (10-minute) exposure limit is 10 mg/m^3.[2]

16. Regulatory Status

Included in the FDA Inactive Ingredients Guide (oral capsules and tablets). Included in nonparenteral medicines licensed in the UK.

17. Pharmacopeias

Br and USPNF.

18. Related Substances

Dibutyl phthalate; dimethyl phthalate.

Dibutyl phthalate: $C_{16}H_{22}O_4$
Molecular weight: 278.35
CAS number: [84-74-2]
Synonyms: 1,2-benzenedicarboxylic acid dibutyl ester; *n*-butyl phthalate; DBP; dibutyl benzene-1,2-dicarboxylate; di-*n*-butyl phthalate; *Kodaflex DBP*; phthalic acid dibutyl ester.
Appearance: a clear, colorless or faintly colored oily liquid.
Pharmacopeias: Br, Eur and Ind.

Boiling point: 340°C
Density: $\approx$ 1.05 g/cm^3
Flash point: 171°C (open cup)
Freezing point: -35°C
Refractive index: n_D^{20} = 1.491-1.493
Solubility: very soluble in acetone, benzene, ethanol (95%), and ether; soluble 1 in 2500 of water.
Viscosity (dynamic): 15 mPa s (15 cP) at 25°C.
Comments: dibutyl phthalate is used as a plasticizer in film coatings; has limited compatibility with cellulose acetate. It is also used as an insect repellant, primarily for the impregnation of clothing.

Dimethyl phthalate: C$_{10}$H$_{10}$O$_4$
Molecular weight: 194.20
CAS number: [131-11-3]
Synonyms: DMP; *Kodaflex DMP*; methyl benzene-1,2-dicar-boxylate; methyl phthalate.
Appearance: colorless or faintly colored, odorless liquid.
Pharmacopeias: Br and Nord.
Boiling point: $\approx$ 280°C (with decomposition)
Refractive index: n_D^{20} = 1.515-1.517
Solubility: miscible with ethanol (95%), ether, and most organic solvents; soluble 1 in 250 parts of water.
Specific gravity: 1.186-1.192
Comments: dimethyl phthalate is used as a plasticizer for film coatings.[3] Dimethyl phthalate is also used as an insect repellant; typically, a 40% cream or lotion, applied to the skin is effective for 3-5 hours. Dimethyl phthalate is irritant to the eyes and mucous membranes although it is less irritant than diethyl phthalate.

19. Comments

—

20. Specific References

1. Sweet DV, editor. Registry of toxic effects of chemical substances. Cincinnati: US Department of Health, 1987.
2. Health and Safety Executive. Occupational exposure limits 1993: EH40/93. London: HMSO, 1993.
3. Shah PS, Zatz JL. Plasticization of cellulose esters used in the coating of sustained release solid dosage forms. Drug Dev Ind Pharm 1992; 18: 1759-1772.

21. General References

Banker GS. Film coating theory and practice. J Pharm Sci 1966; 55: 81-89.
Berg JA, Mayor GH. Diethyl phthalate not dangerous [letter]. Am J Hosp Pharm 1991; 48: 1448-1449.
Cafmeyer NR, Wolfson BB. Possible leaching of diethyl phthalate into levothyroxine sodium tablets. Am J Hosp Pharm 1991; 48: 735-739.
Chambliss WG. The forgotten dosage form: enteric-coated tablets. Pharmaceut Technol 1983; 7(9): 124, 126, 128, 130, 132, 138.
Kamrin MA, Mayor GH. Diethyl phthalate: a perspective. J Clin Pharmacol 1991; 31: 484-489.
Porter SC, Ridgway K. The permeability of enteric coatings and the dissolution rates of coated tablets. J Pharm Pharmacol 1982; 34: 5-8.
Rowe RC. Materials used in the film coating of oral dosage forms. In: Florence AT, editor. Materials used in pharmaceutical formulation: critical reports on applied chemistry, volume 6. Oxford: Blackwell Scientific Publications, 1984: 1-36.

22. Authors

USA: TN Julian, TA Wheatley.

Difluoroethane

1. Nonproprietary Names

None adopted.

2. Synonyms

Dymel 152a; ethylene fluoride; halocarbon 152a; HFC 152a; propellant 152a; refrigerant 152a.

3. Chemical Name and CAS Registry Number

1,1-Difluoroethane [75-37-6]

4. Empirical Formula

$C_2H_4F_2$

Molecular Weight

66.05

5. Structural Formula

$$\begin{array}{ccccc} & H & & H & \\ & | & & | & \\ F & - & C & - & C & - H \\ & | & & | & \\ & F & & H & \end{array}$$

6. Functional Category

Aerosol propellant.

7. Applications in Pharmaceutical Formulation or Technology

Difluoroethane is used as an aerosol propellant in topical pharmaceutical formulations. It is generally used in conjunction with chlorodifluoroethane to form a propellant blend with a specific gravity of one. Difluoroethane may also be used in combination with chlorodifluoromethane and hydrocarbon propellants. Difluoroethane may be used as a vehicle for dispersions and emulsions.

Under the terms of the Montreal Protocol, aimed at reducing damage to the ozone layer, the use of fluorocarbons will be prohibited from January 1996.[1-5] However, this prohibition does not apply to essential uses such as existing pharmaceutical formulations for which no alternative fluorocarbon-free product is available. New pharmaceutical formulations, containing fluorocarbons may also be exempted provided they demonstrate that there is no technically feasible alternative to their use, that the product is of a substantial health benefit, and that its usage would not involve release of significant quantities of fluorocarbon into the atmosphere. Regulatory bodies in individual countries should be consulted for advice on difluoroethane use in formulations. Although difluoroethane has some potential for ozone depletion it is not currently prohibited under the terms of the Montreal Protocol.

8. Description

Difluoroethane is a liquefied gas and exists as a liquid at room temperature when contained under its own vapor pressure, or as a gas when exposed to room temperature and atmospheric pressure. The liquid is practically odorless and colorless. Difluoroethane is noncorrosive and nonirritating.

9. Pharmacopeial Specifications

—

10. Typical Properties

Boiling point: -24.7°C
Critical temperature: 113.5°C
Density:
0.90 g/cm³ for liquid at 25°C;
0.81 g/cm³ for liquid at 54.5°C.
Flammability: flammable. Limits of flammability 3.7-18.0% v/v in air.
Melting point: -117°C
Solubility: soluble 1 in 357 parts of water at 25°C.
Surface tension: 11.25 mN/m (11.25 dynes/cm) for liquid at 20°C.
Vapor density (absolute): 2.949 g/m³ at standard temperature and pressure.
Vapor density (relative): 2.29 (air = 1)
Vapor pressure:
600 kPa (87 psia) at 25°C;
1317 kPa (191 psia) at 54.5°C.
Viscosity (dynamic): 0.243 mPa s (0.243 cP) for liquid at 20°C.

11. Stability and Storage Conditions

Difluoroethane is a nonreactive and stable material. The liquefied gas is stable when used as a propellant and should be stored in a metal cylinder in a cool, dry, place.

12. Incompatibilities

Compatible with the usual ingredients used in the formulation of pharmaceutical aerosols.

13. Method of Manufacture

Difluoroethane is prepared from ethyne by the addition of hydrogen fluoride in the presence of a suitable catalyst. The difluoroethane formed is purified to remove all traces of water, as well as traces of the starting materials.

14. Safety

Difluoroethane may be used as an aerosol propellant in topical pharmaceutical formulations. It is generally regarded as an essentially nontoxic and nonirritant material.

Deliberate inhalation of excessive quantities of fluorocarbon propellant may result in death, and the following 'warning' statements must appear on the label of all aerosols:

WARNING: Avoid inhalation. Keep away from eyes or other mucous membranes. (Aerosols designed specifically for oral and nasal inhalation need not contain this statement).

WARNING: Do not inhale directly; deliberate inhalation of contents can cause death.

OR

WARNING: Use only as directed; intentional misuse by deliberately concentrating and inhaling the contents can be harmful or fatal.

Additionally, the label should contain the following information:

WARNING: Contents under pressure. Do not puncture or incinerate container. Do not expose to heat or store at room temperature above 120°F (49°C). Keep out of the reach of children.

When fluorocarbon propellants are used in topical aerosols they may cause a chilling effect on the skin although this effect has been somewhat overcome by the use of vapor tap valves.

The propellants quickly vaporize from the skin, and are nonirritating when used as directed.

15. Handling Precautions

Difluoroethane is usually encountered as a liquefied gas and appropriate precautions for handling such materials should be taken. Eye protection, gloves and protective clothing are recommended. Difluoroethane should be handled in a well-ventilated environment. Fluorocarbon vapors are heavier than air and do not support life and therefore, when cleaning large tanks which have contained fluorocarbons, adequate provisions for oxygen in the tanks must be made in order to protect workers cleaning the tanks.

Difluoroethane is flammable, *see* Section 10. When heated to decomposition toxic fumes of hydrogen fluoride may be formed.

16. Regulatory Status

Accepted in the US, by the FDA, for use as a topical aerosol propellant.

17. Pharmacopeias

—

18. Related Substances

Chlorodifluoroethane; Chlorodifluoromethane; Dichlorodifluoromethane; Dichlorotetrafluoroethane; Tetrafluoroethane; Trichloromonofluoromethane.

19. Comments

Difluoroethane is useful as an aerosol propellant in that it shows greater miscibility with water than some other fluorocarbons and when combined with chlorodifluoroethane will produce a mixture with a specific gravity of one.

For a discussion of the numerical nomenclature applied to fluorocarbon aerosol propellants *see* Dichlorodifluoromethane.

20. Specific References

1. Fischer FX, Hess H, Sucker H, Byron PR. CFC propellant substitution: international perspectives. Pharmaceut Technol 1989; 13(9): 44, 48, 50, 52.
2. Kempner N. Metered dose inhaler CFCs under pressure. Pharm J 1990; 245: 428-429.
3. Dalby RN. Possible replacements for CFC-propelled metered-dose inhalers. Med Device Tech 1991; 2(4): 21-25.
4. CFC-free aerosols: the final hurdle. Mfg Chem 1992; 63(7): 22-23.
5. Mackenzie D. Large hole in the ozone agreement. New Scientist 1992; Nov 28: 5.

21. General References

Johnson MA. The aerosol handbook, 2nd edition. Caldwell: WE Dorland, 1982: 305-335.
Sanders PA. Handbook of aerosol technology, 2nd edition. New York: Van Nostrand Reinhold, 1979: 19-35.
Sciarra JJ. Pharmaceutical and cosmetic aerosols. J Pharm Sci 1974; 63: 1815-1836.
Sciarra JJ, Stoller L. The science and technology of aerosol packaging. New York: John Wiley and Sons, 1974: 97-130.
Sciarra JJ. Pharmaceutical aerosols. In: Lachman L, Lieberman HA, Kanig JL, editors. The theory and practice of industrial pharmacy, 3rd edition. Philadelphia: Lea and Febiger, 1986: 589-618.
Sciarra JJ, Cutie AJ. In: Banker GS, Rhodes CT, editors. Modern pharmaceutics, 2nd edition. New York: Marcel Dekker Inc, 1990: 605-634.

22. Authors

UK: PJ Davies.
USA: JJ Sciarra.

Dimethyl Ether

1. Nonproprietary Names
None adopted.

2. Synonyms
Dimethyl oxide; DME; *Dymel A*; methoxymethane; methyl ether; oxybismethane; wood ether.

3. Chemical Name and CAS Registry Number
Dimethyl ether [115-10-6]

4. Empirical Formula   Molecular Weight
C_2H_6O 46.07

5. Structural Formula

$$H_3C-O-CH_3$$

6. Functional Category
Aerosol propellant.

7. Applications in Pharmaceutical Formulation or Technology
Dimethyl ether may be used as an aerosol propellant for topical aerosol formulations in combination with hydrocarbons and other propellants.[1-4] Generally, it cannot be used alone as a propellant due to its high vapor pressure. Since dimethyl ether is a good solvent and has the unique property, compared to other propellants, of high water solubility it has been used with aqueous aerosols. A coarse, wet, spray is formed when dimethyl ether is used as a propellant.
Dimethyl ether is also used as a propellant in cosmetics, such as hairsprays, and other aerosol products such as airfresheners and fly-sprays. Dimethyl ether is additionally used as a refrigerant.

8. Description
Dimethyl ether is a liquefied gas and exists as a liquid at room temperature when contained under its own vapor pressure, or as a gas when exposed to room temperature and pressure. It is a clear, colorless, virtually odorless liquid. In high concentrations, the gas has a faint ether-like odor.

9. Pharmacopeial Specifications
—

10. Typical Properties
Autoignition temperature: 350°C
Boiling point: -23.6°C
Critical temperature: 126.9°C
Density: 0.66 g/cm^3 for liquid at 25°C
Flammability: pure material is flammable, limit of flammability is 3.4-18.2% v/v in air. Aqueous mixtures are nonflammable.
Freezing point: -138.5°C
Flash point: -41°C
Heat of combustion: -28.9 kJ/g (-6900 cal/g)

Kauri-butanol value: 60
Solubility: soluble in acetone, chloroform, ethanol, ether and 1 in 3 parts of water. Dimethyl ether is generally miscible with water, nonpolar materials and some semipolar materials. For pharmaceutical aerosols, ethanol is the most useful cosolvent. Glycols, oils and other similar materials exhibit varying degrees of miscibility with dimethyl ether.
Surface tension: 16 mN/m (16 dynes/cm) at -10°C
Vapor density (absolute):
2.058 g/m^3 at standard temperature and pressure.
Vapor density (relative): 1.60 (air = 1)
Vapor pressure:
592 kPa at 25°C;
1301 kPa at 54°C.

11. Stability and Storage Conditions
The liquefied gas is stable when used as a propellant. However, explosive peroxides may be formed slowly upon long exposure to the air. Liquid dimethyl ether should not be concentrated either by distillation or evaporation. Dimethyl ether should be stored in tightly closed metal cylinders in a cool, dry, place.

12. Incompatibilities
Dimethyl ether is an aggressive solvent and may affect the gasket materials used in aerosol packaging. Oxidizing agents, acetic acid, organic acids and anhydrides should not be used with dimethyl ether.
See also Section 10.

13. Method of Manufacture
Dimethyl ether is prepared by the reaction of bituminous or lignite coals with steam in the presence of a finely divided nickel catalyst. This reaction produces formaldehyde which is then reduced to methanol and dimethyl ether. Dimethyl ether may also be prepared by the dehydration of methanol.

14. Safety
Dimethyl ether may be used as a propellant and solvent in topical pharmaceutical aerosols and is generally regarded as an essentially nontoxic and nonirritant material when used in such applications. However, inhalation of high concentrations of dimethyl ether vapor is harmful. Additionally, skin contact with dimethyl ether liquid may cause freezing of the skin and severe frostbite. When used in formulations applied topically, dimethyl ether may thus have a chilling effect on the skin although if used as directed the propellant quickly vaporizes and is nonirritating.
LC$_{50}$ (mouse, inhalation): 386 ppm/30 min[5]
LC$_{50}$ (rat, inhalation): 308 g/m^3

15. Handling Precautions
Dimethyl ether is usually encountered as a liquefied gas and appropriate precautions for handling such materials should be taken. Eye protection, gloves and protective clothing are recommended. Dimethyl ether should be handled in a well ventilated environment. Dimethyl ether vapor is heavier than air and does not support life and therefore, when cleaning large tanks which have contained this material, adequate provisions for oxygen in the tanks must be made in order to protect workers cleaning the tanks.
Dimethyl ether is flammable, *see* Section 10.

16. Regulatory Status
Accepted for use by the FDA in topical aerosol products.

17. Pharmacopeias

—

18. Related Substances

Butane; Isobutane; Propane.

19. Comments

Since the solubility of dimethyl ether in water is about 35%, it can be used to good effect in aqueous aerosol products.

20. Specific References

1. Bohnenn LJM. DME: an alternative propellant? Mfg Chem Aerosol News 1977; 48(9): 40.
2. Bohnenn LJM. DME: further data on this alternative propellant. Mfg Chem Aerosol News 1978; 49(8): 39, 63.
3. Bohnenn LJM. 'Alternative' aerosol propellant. Drug Cosmet Ind 1979; 125(Nov): 58,60,62,66,68,70,72,74.
4. Boulden ME. Use of dimethyl ether for reduction of VOC content. Spray Technol Market 1992; 2(May): 30,32,34,36.
5. Sweet DV, editor. Registry of toxic effects of chemical substances. Cincinnati: US Department of Health, 1987.

21. General References

Johnson MA. The aerosol handbook, 2nd edition. Caldwell: WE Dorland, 1982: 305-335.
Sanders PA. Handbook of aerosol technology, 2nd edition. New York: Van Nostrand Reinhold, 1979: 19-35.
Sciarra JJ, Stoller L. The science and technology of aerosol packaging. New York: John Wiley and Sons, 1974: 97-130.
Sciarra JJ. Pharmaceutical aerosols. In: Lachman L, Lieberman HA, Kanig JL, editors. The theory and practice of industrial pharmacy, 3rd edition. Philadelphia: Lea and Febiger, 1986: 589-618.
Sciarra JJ, Cutie AJ. In: Banker GS, Rhodes CT, editors. Modern pharmaceutics, 2nd edition. New York: Marcel Dekker, 1990: 605-634.

22. Authors

UK: PJ Davies.
USA: JJ Sciarra.

Docusate Sodium

1. Nonproprietary Names

BP: Docusate sodium
USP: Docusate sodium

2. Synonyms

Bis(2-ethylhexyl) sodium sulfosuccinate; *Cropol 35*; *Cropol 60*; *Cropol 70*; dioctyl sodium sulfosuccinate; dioctyl sodium sulphosuccinate; DSS; sodium dioctyl sulfosuccinate; sulfo-butanedioic acid 1,4-bis(2-ethylhexyl) ester, sodium salt.

3. Chemical Name and CAS Registry Number

Sodium 1,4-bis(2-ethylhexyl) sulfosuccinate
[577-11-7]

4. Empirical Formula   Molecular Weight

$C_{20}H_{37}NaO_7S$ 444.56

5. Structural Formula

6. Functional Category

Anionic surfactant; therapeutic agent; wetting agent.

7. Applications in Pharmaceutical Formulation or Technology

Docusate sodium and docusate salts are widely used as anionic surfactants in pharmaceutical formulations. Docusate sodium is mainly used in capsule and direct compression tablet formulations to assist in wetting and dissolution. Docusate salts are also widely used in oral formulations as laxatives and fecal softeners.

Use	Concentration (%)
IM injections	0.015
Surfactant (wetting/dispersing/emulsifying agent)	0.01-1.0
Tablet coating agent	20[*]
Tablet disintegrant	≈ 0.5

[*] Formulation of a tablet coating solution: 20% docusate sodium; 2-15% sodium benzoate; 0.5% propylene glycol; solution made in ethanol (70%).

8. Description

Docusate sodium is a white or almost white, wax-like, bitter tasting, plastic solid with a characteristic octanol-like odor. It is hygroscopic and usually available in the form of pellets, flakes or rolls of tissue-thin material. A 50-75% solution in various solvents is also available.

9. Pharmacopeial Specifications

Test	BP 1993 (Ad 1994)	USP XXII
Identification	+	+
Clarity of solution	—	+
Alkalinity	+	—
Water	—	≤ 2.0%
Loss on drying	≤ 3.0%	—
Residue on ignition	—	15.5-16.5%
Arsenic	—	≤ 3 ppm
Heavy metals	≤ 10 ppm	≤ 0.001%
Bis(2-ethylhexyl) maleate	—	≤ 0.4%
Chloride	+	—
Related nonionic substances	+	—
Sodium sulfate	≤ 2.0%	—
Assay	98.5-100.5%	99.0-100.5%

10. Typical Properties

Acidity/alkalinity:
pH = 5.8-6.9 (1% w/v aqueous solution).
Acid value: ≤ 2.5
Critical micelle concentration:
0.11% w/v aqueous solution at 25°C.
Density: 1.1 g/cm^3
Hydroxyl value: 6-8
Interfacial tension: in water versus mineral oil at 25°C, *see* table below.

Concentration (% w/v)	Interfacial tension (mN/m)
0.01	20.7
0.1	5.9
1.0	1.84

Iodine number: ≤ 0.25
Melting point: 153-157°C
Saponification value: 240-253
Solubility: see table below and also HPE Data.

Solvent	Solubility at 20°C Unless otherwise stated
Acetone	soluble
Chloroform	1 in 1
Ethanol (95%)	1 in 3
Ether	1 in 1
Glycerin	freely soluble
Vegetable oils	soluble
Water	1 in 70 at 25°C[*]
	1 in 56 at 30°C
	1 in 44 at 40°C
	1 in 33 at 50°C
	1 in 25 at 60°C
	1 in 18 at 70°C

[*] In water, higher concentrations form a thick gel.
Surface tension:

Concentration in water at 25°C (% w/v)	Surface tension (mN/m)
0.001	62.8
0.1	28.7
1.0	26.0

HPE Laboratory Project Data			
	Method	Lab #	Results
Density	DE-1	7	1.16 ± 0.03 g/cm^3
Moisture content	MC-29	23	1.51%
Solubility			
Ethanol (95%) at 25°C	SOL-6	23	> 1.0 g/mL
Ethanol (95%) at 37°C	SOL-6	23	> 1.0 g/mL
Hexane at 25°C	SOL-6	23	> 2.5 g/mL
Hexane at 37°C	SOL-6	23	> 2.5 g/mL
Propylene glycol at 25°C	SOL-6	23	0.80-1.25 g/mL
Propylene glycol at 37°C	SOL-6	23	0.80-1.25 g/mL
Water at 25°C	SOL-6	23	0.028 g/mL
Water at 37°C	SOL-6	23	0.107-0.111 g/mL

Supplier: American Cyanamid Co.

11. Stability and Storage Conditions

Docusate sodium is stable in the solid state when stored at room temperature. Dilute aqueous solutions of docusate sodium between pH 1 and pH 10 are stable at room temperature. However, at very low pH (pH < 1) and very high pH (pH > 10) docusate sodium solutions are subject to hydrolysis.

The solid material is hygroscopic and should be stored in an airtight container in a cool, dry, place.

12. Incompatibilities

Electrolytes, e.g. 3% sodium chloride, added to aqueous solutions of docusate sodium can cause turbidity.[1,2] However, docusate sodium possesses greater tolerance to calcium, magnesium and other polyvalent ions as compared to other surfactants. Docusate sodium is incompatible with acids at pH < 1 and alkalis at pH > 10.

13. Method of Manufacture

Maleic anhydride is treated with 2-ethylhexanol to produce dioctyl maleate, which is then reacted with sodium bisulfite.

14. Safety

Docusate salts are widely used in oral formulations as therapeutic agents for their fecal softening and laxative properties. As a laxative in adults, up to 500 mg of docusate sodium is administered daily in divided doses; in children over 6 months old up to 75 mg, in divided doses, is used. The quantity of docusate sodium used as an excipient in oral formulations should therefore be controlled to avoid unintended laxative effects. Adverse effects associated with docusate sodium include: diarrhea; nausea; vomiting; abdominal cramps and skin rashes.

Docusate salts are absorbed from the gastrointestinal tract and excreted in bile; they may cause alteration of the gastrointestinal epithelium.[3,4] The gastrointestinal or hepatic absorption of other drugs may also be affected by docusate salts, enhancing activity and possibly toxicity. Docusate sodium should not be administered with mineral oil as it may increase the absorption of the oil.

LD$_{50}$ (mouse, IV): 0.06 g/kg[5]
LD$_{50}$ (mouse, oral): 2.64 g/kg
LD$_{50}$ (rat, IP): 0.59 g/kg
LD$_{50}$ (rat, oral): 1.9 g/kg

15. Handling Precautions

Observe normal precautions appropriate to the circumstances and quantity of material handled. Docusate sodium may be irritant to the eyes, skin and on inhalation. Eye protection, gloves and a dust mask or respirator are recommended. When heated to decomposition docusate sodium emits toxic fumes.

16. Regulatory Status

GRAS listed. Included in the FDA Inactive Ingredients Guide (IM injections, oral capsules, suspensions and tablets, also topical formulations). Included in nonparenteral medicines licensed in the UK.

17. Pharmacopeias

Br and US.

18. Related Substances

Docusate calcium; docusate potassium.

Docusate calcium: $C_{40}H_{74}CaO_{14}S_2$
Molecular weight: 883.23
CAS number: [128-49-4]
Synonyms: 1,4-bis(2-ethylhexyl) sulfosuccinate, calcium salt; dioctyl calcium sulfosuccinate.
Appearance: white amorphous solid with a characteristic octanol-like odor.
Pharmacopeias: US.
Solubility: soluble 1 in 1 of ethanol (95%) and 1 in 3300 of water; very soluble in corn oil and polyethylene glycol 400.

Docusate potassium: $C_{20}H_{37}KO_7S$
Molecular weight: 460.67
CAS number: [7491-09-0]
Synonyms: dioctyl potassium sulfosuccinate; potassium 1,4-bis(2-ethylhexyl) sulfosuccinate.
Appearance: white amorphous solid with a characteristic octanol-like odor.
Pharmacopeias: US.
Solubility: soluble in ethanol (95%) and glycerin; sparingly soluble in water.

19. Comments

A convenient way of making a 1% w/v aqueous solution of docusate sodium is to add 1 g of solid to about 50 mL of water and to apply gentle heat. The docusate sodium dissolves in a short time and the resulting solution can be made up to 100 mL with water. Alternatively, 1 g may be soaked overnight in 50 mL of water and the additional water may then be added with gentle heating and stirring.

Docusate sodium may alter the dissolution characteristics of certain dosage forms and the bioavailability of some drugs.

20. Specific References

1. Ahuja S, Cohen J. Dioctyl sodium sulfosuccinate. In: Florey K, editor. Analytical profiles of drug substances, volume 2. New York: Academic Press, 1973: 199-219.
2. Ahuja S, Cohen J. Dioctyl sodium sulfosuccinate. In: Florey K, editor. Analytical profiles of drug substances, volume 12. New York: Academic Press, 1983: 713-720.
3. Chapman RW, Sillery J, Fontana DD, Matthys C. Effect of oral dioctyl sodium sulfosuccinate on intake-output studies of human small and large intestine. Gastroenterology 1985; 89: 489-493.
4. Moriarty KJ, Kelly MJ, Beetham R, Clark ML. Studies on the mechanism of action of dioctyl sodium sulphosuccinate in the human jejunum. Gut 1985; 26: 1008-1013.

5. Sweet DV, editor. Registry of toxic effects of chemical substances. Cincinnati: US Department of Health, 1987.

21. General References

Chambliss WG, Cleary RW, Fischer R, Jones AB, Skierkowski P, Nicholes W, Kibbe AH. Effect of docusate sodium on drug release from a controlled release dosage form. J Pharm Sci 1981; 70: 1248-1251.

Hogue DR, Zimmardi JA, Shah KA. High-performance liquid chromatographic analysis of docusate sodium in soft gelatin capsules. J Pharm Sci 1992; 81: 359-361.

Shah DN, Feldkamp JR, White JL, Hem SL. Effect of the pH-zero point of charge relationship on the interaction of ionic compounds and polyols with aluminum hydroxide gel. J Pharm Sci 1982; 71: 266-268.

22. Authors

USA: AW Malick.

Edetic Acid

1. Nonproprietary Names
USPNF: Edetic acid

2. Synonyms
Edathamil; EDTA; ethylenediaminetetraacetic acid; (ethylenedinitrilo)tetraacetic acid; *Questric acid 5286*; *Sequestrene AA*; *Versene Acid.*

3. Chemical Name and CAS Registry Numbers
N,N'-1,2-Ethanediylbis[*N*-(carboxymethyl)glycine] [60-00-4]

4. Empirical Formula   Molecular Weight
$C_{10}H_{16}N_2O_8$ 292.24

5. Structural Formula
$(HOOCCH_2)_2NCH_2CH_2N(CH_2COOH)_2$

6. Functional Category
Chelating agent; therapeutic agent.

7. Applications in Pharmaceutical Formulation or Technology
Edetic acid and edetate salts are used in pharmaceutical formulations, cosmetics and foods as chelating agents; that is, they form stable water-soluble complexes (chelates) with alkaline earth and heavy metal ions. The chelated form has few of the properties of the free ion, and for this reason chelating agents are often described as 'removing' ions from solution; this process is also called sequestering. The stability of the metal-edetate complex depends on the metal ion involved and also on the pH. The calcium chelate is relatively weak and will preferentially chelate heavy metals, such as iron, copper and lead, with the release of calcium ions. For this reason, edetate calcium disodium is used therapeutically in cases of lead poisoning, *see also* Section 19.

Edetic acid and edetates are primarily used as antioxidant synergists by sequestering trace amounts of metal ions, particularly copper, iron and manganese, which might otherwise catalyze autoxidation reactions. Edetic acid and edetates may be used alone or in combination with true antioxidants, the usual concentration employed being in the range 0.005-0.1% w/v. Edetates have been used to stabilize: ascorbic acid; corticosteroids; epinephrine; folic acid; formaldehyde; gums and resins; hyaluronidase; hydrogen peroxide; oxytetracycline; penicillin; salicylic acid and unsaturated fatty acids. Essential oils may be washed with a 2% w/v solution of edetate to remove trace metal impurities.

Edetic acid and edetates possess some antimicrobial activity but are most frequently used in combination with other antimicrobial preservatives due to their synergistic effects. Many solutions used for the cleaning, storage and wetting of contact lenses thus contain disodium edetate. Typically, edetic acid and edetates are used in concentrations of 0.01-0.1% w/v as antimicrobial preservative synergists, *see* Section 10.

Edetic acid and disodium edetate may also be used as water softeners since they will chelate the calcium and magnesium ions present in hard water; edetate calcium disodium is not effective. Many cosmetic and toiletry products, e.g. soaps, contain edetic acid as a water softener.

Disodium edetate is also used as an anticoagulant since it will chelate calcium and prevent the coagulation of blood *in vitro*. Concentrations of 0.1% w/v are used in small volumes for hematological testing and 0.3% w/v in transfusions.

8. Description
Edetic acid occurs as a white crystalline powder.

9. Pharmacopeial Specifications

Test	USPNF XVII
Identification	+
Residue on ignition	$\leqslant$ 0.2%
Heavy metals	$\leqslant$ 0.003%
Nitrilotriacetic acid	$\leqslant$ 0.3%
Iron	$\leqslant$ 0.005%
Assay	98.0-100.5%

10. Typical Properties
Acidity/alkalinity:
pH = 2.2 for a 0.2% w/v aqueous solution.
Antimicrobial activity: edetic acid has some antimicrobial activity against Gram-negative microorganisms, *Pseudomonas aeruginosa*, some yeasts and fungi, although this activity is insufficient for edetic acid to be used effectively as an antimicrobial preservative on its own.[1,2] However, when used with other antimicrobial preservatives edetic acid demonstrates a marked synergistic effect in its antimicrobial activity. Edetic acid and edetates are therefore frequently used in combination with such preservatives as: benzalkonium chloride; bronopol; cetrimide; imidurea; parabens and phenols, especially chloroxylenol. Typically, edetic acid is used at a concentration of 0.1-0.15% w/v. In the presence of some divalent metal ions, such as Ca^{2+} or Mg^{2+}, the synergistic effect may be reduced or lost altogether. The addition of disodium edetate to phenylmercuric nitrate[3] and thimerosal [3, 4] has also been reported to reduce the antimicrobial efficacy of the preservative. Edetic acid and iodine form a colorless addition compound which is bactericidal.
Dissociation constant:
pK_{a1} = 2.00;
pK_{a2} = 2.67;
pK_{a3} = 6.16;
pK_{a4} = 10.26.
Melting point: melts above 220°C, with decomposition.
Solubility: soluble in solutions of alkali hydroxides; soluble 1 in 500 of water.

11. Stability and Storage Conditions
Although edetic acid is fairly stable in the solid state, edetate salts are more stable than the free acid, which decarboxylates if heated above 150°C. Disodium edetate dihydrate loses water of crystallization when heated to 120°C. Edetate calcium disodium is slightly hygroscopic and should be protected from moisture.

Aqueous solutions of edetic acid or edetate salts may be sterilized by autoclaving, and should be stored in an alkali-free container.

Edetic acid and edetates should be stored in well-closed containers in a cool, dry, place.

12. Incompatibilities

Edetic acid and edetates are incompatible with strong oxidizing agents, strong bases and polyvalent metal ions such as copper, nickel and copper alloy.

Edetic acid and disodium edetate behave as weak acids, displacing carbon dioxide from carbonates and reacting with metals to form hydrogen.

Other incompatibilities include the inactivation of certain types of insulin due to the chelation of zinc, and the chelation of trace metals in TPN solutions following the addition of TPN additives stabilized with disodium edetate. Calcium disodium edetate has also been reported to be incompatible with amphotericin and with hydralazine hydrochloride in infusion fluids.

13. Method of Manufacture

Edetic acid may be prepared by the condensation of ethylenediamine with sodium monochloroacetate in the presence of sodium carbonate. An aqueous solution of the reactants is heated to about 90°C for ten hours, then cooled, and hydrochloric acid added to precipitate the edetic acid.

Edetic acid may also be prepared by the reaction of ethylenediamine with hydrogen cyanide and formaldehyde with subsequent hydrolysis of the tetranitrile, or under alkaline conditions with continuous extraction of ammonia.

See Section 18 for information on the preparation of edetate salts.

14. Safety

Edetic acid and edetates are widely used in topical, oral and parenteral pharmaceutical formulations. They are also extensively used in cosmetics and food products.

Edetic acid is generally regarded as an essentially nontoxic and nonirritant material although it has been associated with dose-related bronchoconstriction when used as a preservative in nebulizer solutions. It has therefore been recommended that nebulizer solutions for bronchodilation should not contain edetic acid.[5]

Edetates, particularly disodium edetate and edetate calcium disodium, are used in a greater number and variety of pharmaceutical formulations than the free acid. Both disodium edetate and edetate calcium disodium are poorly absorbed from the gastrointestinal tract and are associated with few adverse effects when used as excipients in pharmaceutical formulations.

Disodium edetate, trisodium edetate and edetic acid readily chelate calcium and can, in large doses, cause calcium depletion (hypocalcemia) if used over an extended period or if administered too rapidly by intravenous infusion. If used in preparations for the mouth, they can also leach calcium from the teeth. In contrast, edetate calcium disodium does not chelate calcium.

Edetate calcium disodium is nephrotoxic and should be used with caution in patients with renal impairment. Disodium edetate should similarly be used with caution in patients with renal impairment, tuberculosis and impaired cardiac function. The WHO has set an estimated acceptable daily intake for disodium edetate in foodstuffs at up to 2.5 mg/kg body-weight.[6]

See also Section 19.

LD$_{50}$ (mouse, IP): 0.25 g/kg[7]
LD$_{50}$ (mouse, oral): 0.03 g/kg
LD$_{50}$ (rat, IP): 0.397 g/kg

15. Handling Precautions

Observe normal precautions appropriate to the circumstances and quantity of material handled. Edetic acid and edetates are mildly irritant to the skin, eyes and mucous membranes. Ingestion, inhalation and contact with the skin and eyes should therefore be avoided. Eye protection, gloves and a dust mask are recommended.

16. Regulatory Status

Included in the FDA Inactive Ingredients Guide (otic, rectal and topical preparations). Included in nonparenteral medicines licensed in the UK.

See also Section 18.

17. Pharmacopeias

Rom and USPNF.

18. Related Substances

Dipotassium edetate; disodium edetate; edetate calcium disodium; sodium edetate; trisodium edetate.

Dipotassium edetate: $C_{10}H_{14}K_2N_2O_8$
Molecular weight: 368.46
CAS number: [2001-94-7]
Synonyms: dipotassium edathamil; dipotassium ethylenediaminetetraacetate; edathamil dipotassium; edetate dipotassium; edetic acid dipotassium salt; EDTA dipotassium; *N,N'*-1,2-ethanediylbis[*N*-(carboxymethyl)glycine] dipotassium salt; ethylenebis(iminodiacetic acid) dipotassium salt; ethylenediaminetetraacetic acid dipotassium salt; (ethylenedinitrilo)tetraacetic acid dipotassium salt; tetracemate dipotassium.
Appearance: white crystalline powder.

Disodium edetate: $C_{10}H_{14}N_2Na_2O_8$
Molecular weight: 336.21
CAS number:
[139-33-3] for the anhydrous material;
[6381-92-6] for the dihydrate.
Synonyms: disodium edathamil; disodium ethylenediaminetetraacetate; edathamil disodium; edetate disodium; edetic acid disodium salt; EDTA disodium; *N,N'*-1,2-ethanediylbis[*N*-(carboxymethyl)glycine] disodium salt; ethylenebis(iminodiacetic acid) disodium salt; ethylenediaminetetraacetic acid disodium salt; (ethylenedinitrilo)tetraacetic acid disodium salt; *Questal Di*; *Sequestrene NA2*; tetracemate disodium; *Versene disodium*.
Appearance: odorless white crystalline powder with a slightly acid taste.
Pharmacopeias: Belg, Br, Eur, Fr, Gr, Hung, Ind, It, Jpn, Mex, Neth, Nord, Port, Swiss, Turk, US and Yug.
Acidity/alkalinity: pH = 4.3-4.7 for a 1% w/v solution in carbon dioxide free water.
Freezing point depression:
0.14°C (1% w/v aqueous solution)
Melting point:
decomposition at 252°C for the dihydrate.
Refractive index:
1.335 for a 1% w/v aqueous solution.
Solubility: practically insoluble in chloroform and ether; slightly soluble in ethanol (95%); soluble 1 in 11 of water.
Specific gravity:
1.004 for a 1% w/v aqueous solution.
Viscosity (kinematic): 1.03 mm^2/s (1 cSt) for a 1% w/v aqueous solution.

Method of manufacture: disodium edetate may be prepared by the reaction of edetic acid and sodium hydroxide.

Safety: *see also* Section 14.

LD_{50} (mouse, IP): 0.26 g/kg[7]
LD_{50} (mouse, IV): 0.056 g/kg
LD_{50} (mouse, oral): 2.05 g/kg
LD_{50} (rabbit, IV): 0.047 g/kg
LD_{50} (rabbit, oral): 2.3 g/kg
LD_{50} (rat, oral): 2 g/kg
LD_{50} (rat, SC): 3.735 g/kg

Regulatory status: GRAS listed. Included in the FDA Inactive Ingredients Guide (inhalations, injections, ophthalmic preparations, oral capsules, solutions, suspensions, syrups and tablets, rectal, topical and vaginal preparations). Included in nonparenteral and parenteral medicines licensed in the UK.

Comments: in pharmaceutical formulations disodium edetate is used as a chelating agent typically at concentrations between 0.005-0.1% w/v.

Edetate calcium disodium: $C_{10}H_{12}CaN_2Na_2O_8$
Molecular weight: 374.28
CAS number:
[62-33-9] for the anhydrous material;
[23411-34-9] for the dihydrate.

Synonyms: 385; calcium disodium edetate; calcium disodium ethylenediaminetetraacetate; calcium disodium (ethylenedinitrilo)tetraacetate; edathamil calcium disodium; edetic acid calcium disodium salt; [[N,N'-1,2-ethanediylbis[N-(carboxymethyl)glycinat o]](4-)-N,N',O,O',O^N,-O^N]calciate(2-)disodium; EDTA calcium; ethylenediaminetetraacetic acid calcium disodium chelate; [(ethylenedinitrilo)tetraacetato] calciate(2-) disodium; sodium calciumedetate; *Versene CA*.

Appearance: white or creamy-white colored, slightly hygroscopic, crystalline powder or granules; odorless, or with a slight odor; tasteless, or with a faint saline taste.

Pharmacopeias: Belg, Br, Cz, Egypt, Eur, Fr, Gr, It, Mex, Neth, Nord, Port, Swiss, Turk, US and Yug. Also in BP Vet. Some pharmacopeias specify that edetate calcium disodium is the dihydrate, others that it is the anhydrous material. The USP XXII specifies that edetate calcium disodium is a mixture of the dihydrate and trihydrate but that the dihydrate predominates.

Acidity/alkalinity:
pH = 4-5 for a 1% w/v aqueous solution.

Density (bulk): 0.69 g/cm^3

Solubility: practically insoluble in chloroform, ether and other organic solvents; very slightly soluble in ethanol (95%); soluble 1 in 2 of water.

Method of manufacture: edetate calcium disodium may be prepared by the addition of calcium carbonate to a solution of disodium edetate.

Safety: *see also* Section 14.

LD_{50} (dog, oral): 12 g/kg[7]
LD_{50} (mouse, IP): 4.5 g/kg
LD_{50} (mouse, oral): 10 g/kg
LD_{50} (rabbit, IP): 6 g/kg
LD_{50} (rabbit, oral): 7 g/kg
LD_{50} (rat, IP): 3.85 g/kg
LD_{50} (rat, IV): 3.0 g/kg
LD_{50} (rat, oral): 10 g/kg

Regulatory status: GRAS listed. Accepted for use as a food additive in the UK. Included in the FDA Inactive Ingredients Guide (injections, oral capsules, solutions, suspensions, syrups and tablets).

Comments: used in pharmaceutical formulations as a chelating agent in concentrations between 0.01-0.1% w/v. Usually

edetate calcium disodium is used in pharmaceutical formulations in preference to disodium edetate or sodium edetate to prevent calcium depletion occurring in the body. In food products, edetate calcium disodium may also be used in flavors and as a color retention agent. Edetate calcium disodium occurs as the dihydrate, trihydrate and anhydrous material.

Sodium edetate: $C_{10}H_{12}N_2Na_4O_8$
Molecular weight: 380.20
CAS number: [64-02-8]

Synonyms: edetate sodium; edetic acid tetrasodium salt; EDTA tetrasodium; N,N'-1,2-ethanediylbis[N-(carboxymethyl)glycine] tetrasodium salt; ethylenebis(iminodiacetic acid) tetrasodium salt; ethylenediaminetetraacetic acid tetrasodium salt; (ethylenedinitrilo)tetraacetic acid tetrasodium salt; *Sequestrene NA4*; tetracemate tetrasodium; tetracemin; tetrasodium edetate; tetrasodium ethylenebis(iminodiacetate); tetrasodium ethylenediaminetetraacetate; *Versene*.

Appearance: white crystalline powder.

Acidity/alkalinity:
pH = 11.3 for a 1% w/v aqueous solution.

Melting point: > 300°C

Solubility: soluble 1 in 1 of water.

Safety: *see also* Section 14.

LD_{50} (mouse, IP): 0.33 g/kg[7]

Regulatory status: included in the FDA Inactive Ingredients Guide (inhalations, injections, ophthalmic preparations, oral capsules and tablets, and topical preparations).

Comments: sodium edetate reacts with most divalent and trivalent metallic ions to form soluble metal chelates and is used in pharmaceutical formulations in concentrations between 0.01-0.1% w/v.

Trisodium edetate: $C_{10}H_{13}N_2Na_3O_8$
Molecular weight: 358.20
CAS number: [150-38-9]

Synonyms: edetate trisodium; edetic acid trisodium salt; EDTA trisodium; N,N'-1,2-ethanediylbis[N-(carboxymethyl)glycine] trisodium salt; ethylenediaminetetraacetic acid trisodium salt; (ethylenedinitrilo)tetraacetic acid trisodium salt; *Sequestrene NA3*; trisodium ethylenediaminetetraacetate; *Versene-9*.

Appearance: white crystalline powder.

Acidity/alkalinity:
pH = 9.3 for a 1% w/v aqueous solution.

Melting point: > 300°C

Method of manufacture: trisodium edetate may be prepared by adding a solution of sodium hydroxide to disodium edetate.

Safety: *see also* Section 14.

LD_{50} (mouse, IP): 0.3 g/kg[7]
LD_{50} (mouse, oral): 2.15 g/kg
LD_{50} (rat, oral): 2.15 g/kg

Regulatory status: included in the FDA Inactive Ingredients Guide (topical preparations).

Comments: more soluble in water than either the disodium salt or the free acid. Trisodium edetate also occurs as the monohydrate and is used in pharmaceutical formulations as a chelating agent.

Other salts of edetic acid which are commercially available include diammonium, dimagnesium, dipotassium, ferric sodium and magnesium disodium edetates.

19. Comments

Therapeutically, a dose of 50 mg/kg body-weight of disodium edetate, as a slow infusion over a 24 hour period, with a maximum daily dose of 3 g, has been used as a treatment for hypercalcemia. For the treatment of lead poisoning, a dose of

60-80 mg/kg of edetate calcium disodium, as a slow infusion in two daily doses, for 5 days, has been used.

20. Specific References

1. Richards RME, Cavill RH. Electron microscope study of effect of benzalkonium chloride and edetate disodium on cell envelope of *Pseudomonas aeruginosa.* J Pharm Sci 1976; 65: 76-80.
2. Whalley G. Preservative properties of EDTA. Mfg Chem 1991; 62(9): 22-23.
3. Richards RME, Reary JME. Changes in antibacterial activity of thiomersal and PMN on autoclaving with certain adjuvants. J Pharm Pharmacol 1972; 24(Suppl): 84P-89P.
4. Morton DJ. EDTA reduces antimicrobial efficacy of thiomerosal. Int J Pharmaceutics 1985; 23: 357-358.
5. Beasley CRW, Rafferty P, Holgate ST. Bronchoconstrictor properties of preservatives in ipratropium bromide (Atrovent) nebuliser solution. Br Med J 1987; 294: 1197-1198.
6. FAO/WHO. Toxicological evaluation of certain food additives with a review of general principles and of specifications. Seventeenth report of the joint FAO/WHO expert committee on food additives. Tech Rep Ser Wld Hlth Org 1974; No. 539.
7. Sweet DV, editor. Registry of toxic effects of chemical substances. Cincinnati: US Department of Health, 1987.

21. General References

Chalmers L. The uses of EDTA and other chelates in industry. Mfg Chem 1978; 49(3): 79-80, 83.
Hart JR. Chelating agents in cosmetic and toiletry products. Cosmet Toilet 1978; 93(12): 28-30.
Hart JR. EDTA-type chelating agents in personal care products. Cosmet Toilet 1983; 98(4): 54-58.
Lachman L. Antioxidants and chelating agents as stabilizers in liquid dosage forms. Drug Cosmet Ind 1968; 102(2): 43-45, 146-149.

22. Authors

UK: RS Cook; N Yussuf.

Ethyl Maltol

1. Nonproprietary Names
None adopted.

2. Synonyms
E637; 2-ethyl pyromeconic acid; 3-hydroxy-2-ethyl-4-pyrone; *Veltol Plus*.

3. Chemical Name and CAS Registry Number
2-Ethyl-3-hydroxy-4*H*-pyran-4-one
[4940-11-8]

4. Empirical Formula   Molecular Weight
$C_7H_8O_3$ 140.14

5. Structural Formula

6. Functional Category
Flavor enhancer; flavoring agent.

7. Applications in Pharmaceutical Formulation or Technology
Ethyl maltol is used in pharmaceutical formulations and food products as a flavoring agent or flavor enhancer in applications similar to maltol. It has a flavor and odor 4-6 times as intense as maltol. Ethyl maltol is used in oral syrups at concentrations of about 0.004% w/v and also at low levels in perfumery.

8. Description
White crystalline solid with characteristic, very sweet, caramel-like odor and taste. In dilute solution it possesses a sweet, fruit-like flavor and odor.

9. Pharmacopeial Specifications
See Section 19.

10. Typical Properties
Melting point: 89-93°C
Solubility:

Solvent	Solubility at 25°C Unless stated otherwise
Chloroform	1 in 5 at 20°C
Ethanol (95%)	1 in 10
Glycerin	1 in 500
Propan-2-ol	1 in 11
Propylene glycol	1 in 17
Water	1 in 56

11. Stability and Storage Conditions
Solutions may be stored in glass or plastic containers. The bulk material should be stored in a well-closed container, protected from light, in a cool, dry, place.

12. Incompatibilities
—

13. Method of Manufacture
Unlike maltol, ethyl maltol does not occur naturally. It may be prepared by treating α-ethylfurfuryl alcohol with a halogen to produce 4-halo-6-hydroxy-2-ethyl-2*H*-pyran-3(6*H*)-one which is converted to ethyl maltol by hydrolysis.

14. Safety
In animal feeding studies, ethyl maltol has been shown to be well tolerated with no adverse toxic, reproductive or embryogenic effects. It has been reported that whilst the acute toxicity of ethyl maltol, in animal studies, is slightly greater than maltol, with repeated dosing the opposite is true.[1] Although an acceptable daily intake for ethyl maltol has not been set the WHO has set an acceptable daily intake for maltol at up to 1 mg/kg body-weight.[2]
LD_{50} (rat, oral): 1.15 g/kg[3]
LD_{50} (mouse, oral): 0.78 g/kg
LD_{50} (mouse, SC): 0.91 g/kg

15. Handling Precautions
Observe normal precautions appropriate to the circumstances and quantity of material handled. Ethyl maltol should be used in a well ventilated environment. Dust may be irritant and eye protection and gloves are recommended.

16. Regulatory Status
GRAS listed. Accepted for use as a food additive in Europe. Included in the FDA Inactive Ingredients Guide (oral syrup).

17. Pharmacopeias
—

18. Related Substances
Maltol.

19. Comments
See Maltol for further information.
Although not included in any pharmacopeias a specification for ethyl maltol is contained in the Food Chemicals Codex (FCC), *see* below.[4]

Test	FCC 1981
Identification	+
Arsenic	⩽ 3 ppm
Heavy metals (as lead)	⩽ 0.002%
Lead	⩽ 10 ppm
Residue on ignition	⩽ 0.2%
Water	⩽ 0.5%
Assay	⩾ 99.0%

20. Specific References

1. Gralla EJ, Stebbins RB, Coleman GL, Delahunt CS. Toxicity studies with ethyl maltol. Toxicol Appl Pharmacol 1969; 15: 604-613.
2. FAO/WHO. Evaluation of certain food additives. Twenty-fifth report of the joint FAO/WHO expert committee on food additives. Tech Rep Ser Wld Hlth Org 1981; No. 669.
3. Sweet DV, editor. Registry of toxic effects of chemical substances. Cincinnati: US Department of Health, 1987.
4. Food Chemicals Codex, 3rd edition. Washington, DC: National Academy Press, 1981: 114-115.

21. General References

—

22. Authors

UK: PJ Weller.

Ethyl Oleate

1. Nonproprietary Names

BP: Ethyl oleate
USPNF: Ethyl oleate

2. Synonyms

Ethyl 9-octadecenoate; *Kessco EO*; oleic acid, ethyl ester.

3. Chemical Name and CAS Registry Number

(Z)-9-Octadecenoic acid, ethyl ester [111-62-6]

4. Empirical Formula   Molecular Weight

$C_{20}H_{38}O_2$ 310.52

5. Structural Formula

$CH_3(CH_2)_7CH=CH(CH_2)_7COOC_2H_5$

6. Functional Category

Oleaginous vehicle; solvent.

7. Applications in Pharmaceutical Formulation or Technology

Ethyl oleate is primarily used as a vehicle in certain parenteral preparations intended for intramuscular administration. It has also been used as a solvent for drugs formulated as biodegradable capsules for subdermal implantation.[1]
Ethyl oleate is a suitable solvent for steroids and other lipophilic drugs. Its properties are similar to those of almond oil and peanut oil. However, it has the advantage that it is less viscous than fixed oils and is more rapidly absorbed by body tissues.[2]

8. Description

Ethyl oleate occurs as a pale yellow to almost colorless, mobile, oily liquid with a taste resembling that of olive oil. It has a slight, but not rancid odor.

9. Pharmacopeial Specifications

Test	BP 1993	USPNF XVII
Specific gravity	0.869-0.874	0.866-0.874
Viscosity	—	$\geq$ 5.15 cP
Refractive index	—	1.443-1.450
Acid value	$\leq$ 0.5	$\leq$ 0.5
Iodine value	75-84	75-85
Saponification value	—	177-188
Peroxides	+	—
Assay	100.0-105.0%	—

10. Typical Properties

Boiling point: 205-208°C (some decomposition)
Flash point: 175.3°C
Freezing point: $\approx$ -32°C
Moisture content: at 20°C and 52% relative humidity, the equilibrium moisture content of ethyl oleate is 0.08%. *See also* Fig. 1.

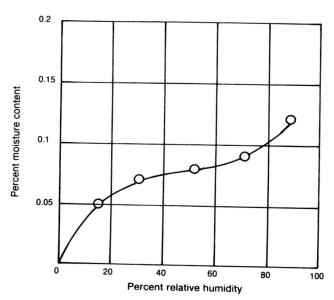

Fig. 1: Moisture sorption isotherm of ethyl oleate.
Values determined by Karl Fischer titration of samples at equilibrium after storage for five days in desiccators over saturated solutions of appropriate salts.

Solubility: miscible with chloroform, ethanol (95%), ether and fixed oils; practically insoluble in water.
Surface tension:
32.3 mN/m (32.3 dynes/cm) at 25°C[2]
Viscosity (dynamic): 3.9 mPa s (3.9 cP) at 25°C[2]
Viscosity (kinematic): 4.6 mm²/s (4.6 cSt) at 25°C[2]

11. Stability and Storage Conditions

Ethyl oleate should be stored in a cool, dry, place in a small, well-filled, well-closed container, protected from light. When a partially filled container is used, the air should be replaced by nitrogen or another inert gas. Ethyl oleate oxidizes on exposure to air, resulting in an increase in the peroxide value. It remains clear at 5°C, but darkens in color on standing. Antioxidants are frequently used to extend the shelf life of ethyl oleate. Protection from oxidation for over two years has been achieved by storage in amber glass bottles with the addition of combinations of propyl gallate, butylated hydroxyanisole, butylated hydroxytoluene and citric or ascorbic acid.[3,4] A concentration of 0.03% w/v of a mixture of propyl gallate (37.5%), butylated hydroxytoluene (37.5%) and butylated hydroxyanisole (25%) was found to be the best antioxidant for ethyl oleate.[4]
Ethyl oleate may be sterilized by heating at 150°C for 1 hour.

12. Incompatibilities

Ethyl oleate dissolves certain types of rubber and causes others to swell.[5,6] It may also react with oxidizing agents.

13. Method of Manufacture

Ethyl oleate is prepared by the reaction of ethanol with oleoyl chloride in the presence of a suitable hydrogen chloride acceptor.

14. Safety

Generally considered to be of low toxicity, but ingestion should be avoided. Ethyl oleate has been found to cause minimal tissue irritation.[7] No reports of intramuscular irritation during use have been recorded.

15. Handling Precautions

Observe normal precautions appropriate to the circumstances and quantity of material handled. Eye protection and nitrile gloves are recommended. Ethyl oleate is flammable.

16. Regulatory Status

Included in the FDA Inactive Ingredients Guide (transdermal preparation). Included in parenteral medicines licensed in the UK.

17. Pharmacopeias

Br, Egypt, Fr, Hung, Ind, It, Mex and USPNF.

18. Related Substances

Methyl oleate; Oleic Acid.

Methyl oleate: $C_{19}H_{36}O_2$
Molecular weight: 296.49
CAS number: [112-69-9]
Synonyms: methyl 9-octadecenoate; (Z)-9-octadecenoic acid, methyl ester.
Boiling point: 168-170°C
Density: 0.879 g/cm^3
Iodine number: 85.6
Refractive index: $n_D^{26} = 1.4510$
Solubility: miscible with ethanol and ether.
Comments: prepared by refluxing oleic acid with *p*-toluene sulfonic acid in methanol.

19. Comments

—

20. Specific References

1. Ory SJ, Hammond CB, Yancy SG, Hendren RW, Pitt CG. Effect of a biodegradable contraceptive capsule (Capronor) containing levonorgestrel on gonadotropin, estrogen and progesterone levels. Am J Obstet Gynecol 1983; 145: 600-605.
2. Howard JR, Hadgraft J. The clearance of oily vehicles following intramuscular and subcutaneous injections in rabbits. Int J Pharmaceutics 1983; 16: 31-39.
3. Alemany P, Del Pozo A. Autoxidation of ethyl oleate: protection with antioxidants [in Spanish]. Galenica Acta 1963; 16: 335-338.
4. Nikolaeva NM, Gluzman MK. Conditions for stabilizing ethyl oleate during storage [in Russian]. Farmatsiya 1977; 26: 25-28.
5. Dexter MB, Shott MJ. The evaluation of the force to expel oily injection vehicles from syringes. J Pharm Pharmacol 1979; 31: 497-500.
6. Halsall KG. Calciferol injection and plastic syringes [letter]. Pharm J 1985; 235: 99.
7. Hem SL, Bright DR, Banker GS, Pogue JP. Tissue irritation evaluation of potential parenteral vehicles. Drug Dev Comm 1974-75; 1(5): 471-477.

21. General References

Spiegel AJ, Noseworthy MM. Use of nonaqueous solvents in parenteral products. J Pharm Sci 1963; 52: 917-927.

22. Authors

UK: PJ Weller.

Ethyl Vanillin

1. Nonproprietary Names
USPNF: Ethyl vanillin

2. Synonyms
Ethylprotocatechuic aldehyde; 4-hydroxy-3-ethoxybenzaldehyde; *Rhodiarôme*.

3. Chemical Name and CAS Registry Number
3-Ethoxy-4-hydroxybenzaldehyde [121-32-4]

4. Empirical Formula   Molecular Weight
$C_9H_{10}O_3$ 166.18

5. Structural Formula

6. Functional Category
Flavoring agent.

7. Applications in Pharmaceutical Formulation or Technology
Ethyl vanillin is used as an alternative to vanillin, i.e. as a flavoring agent in foods, beverages, confectionery and pharmaceuticals. It is also used in perfumery.

Ethyl vanillin possesses a flavor and odor approximately three times as intense as vanillin, hence the quantity of material necessary to produce an equivalent vanilla flavor may be reduced, causing less discoloration to a formulation and potential savings in material costs. However, exceeding certain concentration limits may impart an unpleasant, slightly bitter taste to a product due to the intensity of the ethyl vanillin flavor.

Use	Concentration (%)
Foods and confectionery	0.002-0.025
Oral syrups	0.01

8. Description
White or slightly yellowish crystals with a characteristic intense vanilla odor and flavor.

9. Pharmacopeial Specifications

Test	USPNF XVII
Identification	+
Melting range	76-78°C
Loss on drying	$\leqslant$ 1.0%
Residue on ignition	$\leqslant$ 0.1%
Assay (dried basis)	98.0-101.0%

10. Typical Properties
Boiling point: 285°C
Density (bulk): 1.05 g/cm^3
Flash point: 127°C
Melting point: 76-78°C
Solubility:

Solvent	Solubility at 20°C Unless otherwise stated
Alkaline hydroxide solutions	freely soluble
Chloroform	freely soluble
Ethanol (95%)	1 in 2
Ether	freely soluble
Glycerin	soluble
Propylene glycol	soluble
Water	1 in 250
	1 in 100 at 50°C

11. Stability and Storage Conditions
Store in a well-closed container, protected from light, in a cool, dry, place. *See* Vanillin for further information.

12. Incompatibilities
Unstable in contact with iron or steel forming a red colored, flavorless compound. *See* Vanillin for other potential incompatibilities.

13. Method of Manufacture
Unlike vanillin, ethyl vanillin does not occur naturally. It may be prepared synthetically by the same methods as vanillin, using guethol instead of guaiacol as a starting material, *see* Vanillin.

14. Safety
Ethyl vanillin is generally regarded as an essentially nontoxic and nonirritant material. However, cross-sensitization with other structurally similar molecules may occur, *see* Vanillin. The WHO has set a temporary estimated acceptable daily intake, for ethyl vanillin, of up to 5 mg/kg body-weight.[1]
LD_{50} (mouse, IP): 0.75 g/kg[2]
LD_{50} (rabbit, oral): 3 g/kg
LD_{50} (rabbit, SC): 2.5 g/kg
LD_{50} (rat, oral): 1.59 g/kg
LD_{50} (rat, SC): 3.5-4.0 g/kg

15. Handling Precautions
Observe normal precautions appropriate to the circumstances and quantity of material handled. Eye protection is recommended. Heavy airborne concentrations of dust may present an explosion hazard.

16. Regulatory Status
GRAS listed. Included in the FDA Inactive Ingredients Guide (capsules, oral suspensions and syrups). Included in nonparenteral medicines licensed in the UK.

17. Pharmacopeias
Fr, Mex and USPNF.

18. Related Substances
Vanillin.

19. Comments

Ethyl vanillin can be distinguished analytically from vanillin by the yellow color developed in the presence of concentrated sulfuric acid.

20. Specific References

1. FAO/WHO. Evaluation of certain food additives and contaminants. Thirty-fifth report of the joint FAO/WHO expert committee on food additives. Tech Rep Ser Wld Hlth Org 1990; No. 789.

2. Sweet DV, editor. Registry of toxic effects of chemical substances. Cincinnati: US Department of Health, 1987.

21. General References

—

22. Authors

UK: PJ Weller.

Ethylcellulose

1. Nonproprietary Names

BP: Ethylcellulose
PhEur: Ethylcellulosum
USPNF: Ethylcellulose

2. Synonyms

Aquacoat; E462; *Ethocel*; *Surelease.*

3. Chemical Names and CAS Registry Number

Cellulose ethyl ether [9004-57-3]

4. Empirical Formula   Molecular Weight

Ethylcellulose is an ethyl ether of cellulose, a long-chain polymer consisting of anhydroglucose units joined together by acetal linkages. Each anhydroglucose unit has three replaceable hydroxyl groups which are substituted to the extent of 2.25-2.60 ethoxyl groups (OC_2H_5) per unit, equivalent to an ethoxyl content of 44-51%.

5. Structural Formula

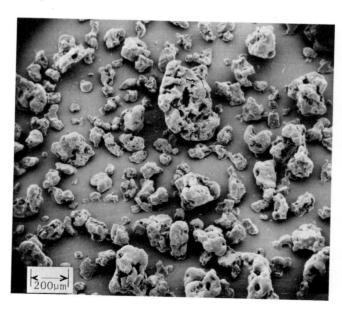

Structure shown with complete ethoxyl substitution. *See also* Section 4.

6. Functional Category

Coating agent; tablet binder; viscosity-increasing agent.

7. Applications in Pharmaceutical Formulation or Technology

Ethylcellulose is widely used in oral and topical pharmaceutical formulations.

The main use of ethylcellulose in oral formulations is as a hydrophobic coating agent for tablets and granules.[1-5] Ethylcellulose coatings are used to modify the release of a drug,[5] to mask an unpleasant taste, or to improve the stability of a formulation, e.g. ethylcellulose dissolved in propan-2-ol is used to coat ascorbic acid granules to prevent oxidation. Modified release tablet formulations may also be produced using ethylcellulose as a matrix former.[6]

Ethylcellulose, dissolved in an organic solvent, or solvent mixture, can be used on its own to produce water-insoluble films. Higher viscosity ethylcellulose grades tend to produce stronger, tougher films. Ethylcellulose films may be modified, to alter their solubility, by the addition of hydroxypropyl-methylcellulose[7] or a plasticizer, *see* Section 19. An aqueous polymer dispersion (or latex) of ethylcellulose such as *Aquacoat* (FMC Corporation) may also be used to produce

ethylcellulose films without the need for organic solvents. With coats of hydrated ethylcellulose, drug release is via diffusion. This can be a slow process unless a large surface area is utilized and aqueous ethylcellulose dispersions tend therefore to be used to coat granules.[8,9]

Ethylcellulose is also widely used in drug microencapsulation,[10-14] high viscosity grades usually being used. Release of a drug from an ethylcellulose microcapsule is a function of the microcapsule wall thickness.[12]

In tablet formulations, ethylcellulose may additionally be employed as a binder, the ethylcellulose being blended dry or wet-granulated with a solvent such as ethanol (95%). Ethylcellulose produces hard tablets, with low friability; they may however demonstrate poor dissolution.

In topical formulations, ethylcellulose is used as a thickening agent in creams, lotions or gels, provided an appropriate solvent is used.

Ethylcellulose is additionally used in cosmetics and food products.

Use	Concentration (%)
Microencapsulation	10.0-20.0
Sustained release tablet coating	3.0-10.0
Tablet coating	1.0-3.0
Tablet granulation	1.0-3.0

8. Description

Ethylcellulose is a tasteless, free-flowing, white to light tan colored powder.

SEM: 1
Excipient: Ethylcellulose
Manufacturer: Hercules Ltd
Lot No.: 57911
Magnification: 60x
Voltage: 10 kV

SEM: 2

Excipient: Ethylcellulose
Manufacturer: Hercules Ltd
Lot No.: 57911
Magnification: 600x
Voltage: 10 kV

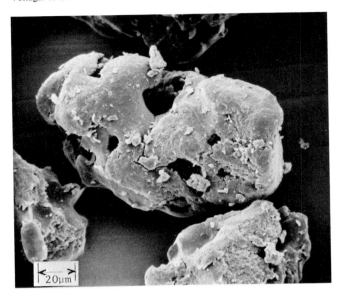

SEM: 4

Excipient: Ethylcellulose (*Ethocel*)
Manufacturer: Dow Chemical Company
Lot No.: 103051
Magnification: 600x
Voltage: 10 kV

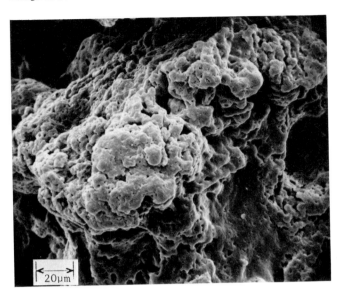

SEM: 3

Excipient: Ethylcellulose (*Ethocel*)
Manufacturer: Dow Chemical Company
Lot No.: 103051
Magnification: 60x
Voltage: 10 kV

9. Pharmacopeial Specifications

Test	PhEur 1993	USPNF XVII
Identification	+	+
pH (2% w/w suspension)	5.0-7.5	—
Viscosity	+	+
Loss on drying	⩽ 3.0%	⩽ 3.0%
Residue on ignition	—	⩽ 0.4%
Sulfated ash	⩽ 0.5%	—
Arsenic	—	⩽ 3 ppm
Lead	—	⩽ 10 ppm
Heavy metals	⩽ 20 ppm	⩽ 40 ppm
Acetaldehyde	⩽ 100 ppm	—
Chlorides	⩽ 0.05%	—
Assay (of ethoxyl groups)	—	44.0-51.0%

10. Typical Properties

Density (bulk): 0.4 g/cm^3
Glass transition temperature: 130-133°C[3]
Hygroscopicity: ethylcellulose absorbs very little water at high relative humidities or during immersion; any absorbed water evaporates readily.[15] *See also* HPE Data.
Solubility: practically insoluble in glycerin, propylene glycol and water. Ethylcellulose that contains less than 46.5% of ethoxyl groups is freely soluble in chloroform, methyl acetate, tetrahydrofuran, and in mixtures of aromatic hydrocarbons with ethanol (95%). Ethylcellulose that contains not less than 46.5% of ethoxyl groups is freely soluble in chloroform, ethanol (95%), ethyl acetate, methanol and toluene.
Specific gravity: 1.12-1.15
Viscosity: various grades of ethylcellulose are commercially available which differ in their ethoxyl content and degree of polymerization. They may be used to produce 5% w/v

solutions, in organic solvents, with viscosities of 6-110 mPa s (6-110 cP), *see also* Section 19. Specific ethylcellulose grades, or blends of different grades, may be used to obtain solutions of a desired viscosity. Solutions of higher viscosity tend to be composed of longer polymer chains and produce stronger, tougher films. The viscosity of solutions increases with an increase in concentration of ethylcellulose, e.g. the viscosity at 25°C of a 5% w/v solution of *Ethocel* in an 80/20 toluene/ethanol solvent blend is 4 mPa s (4 cP), whilst a 25% w/v solution in the same solvent mixture has a viscosity of 850 mPa s (850 cP). Solutions with a lower viscosity may be obtained by incorporating a higher percentage (up to 35%) of a low molecular weight aliphatic alcohol, such as methanol or ethanol, in a solvent mixture. The viscosity of such solutions depends almost entirely on the alcohol content and is independent of the other aromatic solvent.

HPE Laboratory Project Data			
	Method	Lab #	Results
Average flow rate	FLO-3	24	1.66 g/s [b]
Moisture content	MC-29	23	1.853% [a]
	MC-20	15	0.700% [a]
	MC-29	23	1.020% [b]
	EMC-1	15	*See* Fig. 1. [a]
Particle friability	PF-1	36	0.068% [b]
Particle size	PSD-6	23	*See* Fig. 2. [a]
	PSD-6	23	*See* Fig. 3. [b]
Solubility	SOL-6	23	
Ethanol (95%) at 25°C			53 mg/mL [a]
Ethanol (95%) at 25°C			15 mg/mL [b]
Ethanol (95%) at 37°C			66 mg/mL [a]
Ethanol (95%) at 37°C			25 mg/mL [b]
Hexane at 25°C			< 2 mg/mL [a]
Hexane at 25°C			< 2 mg/mL [b]
Hexane at 37°C			< 6 mg/mL [a]
Hexane at 37°C			< 6 mg/mL [b]
Propylene glycol at 25°C			25 mg/mL [a]
Propylene glycol at 25°C			25 mg/mL [b]
Propylene glycol at 37°C			25 mg/mL [a]
Propylene glycol at 37°C			25 mg/mL [b]
Water at 25°C			< 1 mg/mL [a]
Water at 25°C			10 mg/mL [b]
Water at 37°C			< 1 mg/mL [a]
Water at 37°C			10 mg/mL [b]

Supplier: a. Hercules Ltd (Lot No.: 58587); b. Dow Chemical Company.

11. Stability and Storage Conditions

Ethylcellulose is a stable, slightly hygroscopic material. It is chemically resistant to alkalis, both dilute and concentrated, and to salt solutions, although it is more sensitive to acidic materials than cellulose esters.

Ethylcellulose is subject to oxidative degradation in the presence of sunlight or UV light at elevated temperatures. This may be prevented by the use of an antioxidant and a compound with light absorption properties between 230-340 nm.

The bulk material should be stored in a dry place, in a well-closed container at a temperature between 7-32°C.

12. Incompatibilities

Incompatible with paraffin wax and microcrystalline wax.

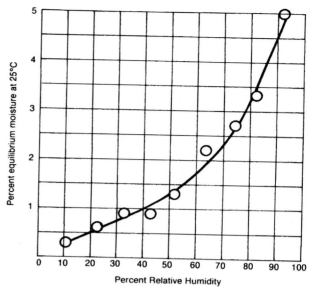

Fig. 1: Equilibrium moisture content of ethylcellulose.[15]

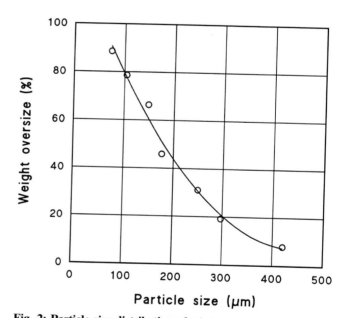

Fig. 2: Particle size distribution of ethylcellulose.

13. Method of Manufacture

Ethylcellulose is prepared from wood pulp by treatment with alkali followed by ethylation of the alkali cellulose with chloroethane.

14. Safety

Ethylcellulose is widely used in oral and topical pharmaceutical formulations. It is also used in food products.

Ethylcellulose is not metabolized following oral consumption and is therefore a noncaloric substance. It is generally regarded as a nontoxic, nonallergenic and nonirritant material. Since ethylcellulose is not metabolized it is not recommended for use in parenteral products; parenteral use may be harmful to the kidneys.

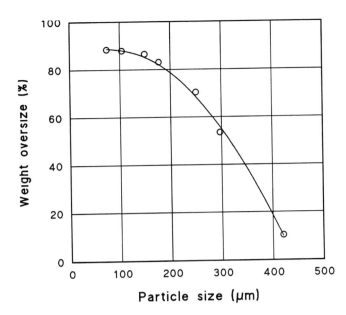

Fig. 3: Particle size distribution of ethylcellulose (*Ethocel*).

Table I: Comparison of different grades of ethylcellulose.

Grade	Viscosity (mPa s)*	Mean particle diameter (μm)
Aqualon N7	5.3	160 [a]
Aqualon N10	5.5	225 [a]
Aqualon N100	80.0	194 [a]
Ethocel Std 4	5.4	204 [b]
Ethocel Std 7	6.4	210 [b]
Ethocel Std 10	10.6	212 [b]
Ethocel Std 20	19.3	243 [b]
Ethocel Std 45	47.6	305 [b]
Ethocel Std 100	95.9	280 [b]
Ethocel Med 50	55.0	262 [b]
Ethocel Med 70	66.9	280 [b]
Ethocel Med 100	98.6	286 [b]

* Viscosities are for a 5% w/v solution at 25°C. Solvent is the supplier's recommended blend of toluene/ethanol.
Supplier: a. Aqualon Company; b. Dow Chemical Company.

The WHO has not specified an acceptable daily intake of ethylcellulose since the level of use in foods was not considered to be a hazard to health.[16]

15. Handling Precautions

Observe normal precautions appropriate to the circumstances and quantity of material handled. Dust may be irritant to the eyes and eye protection should therefore be worn. Excessive dust generation should be avoided to minimize the risk of explosions. Ethylcellulose is combustible.

16. Regulatory Status

GRAS listed. Accepted for use as a food additive in Europe. Included in the FDA Inactive Ingredients Guide (oral capsules, suspensions and tablets, topical emulsions and vaginal preparations). Included in nonparenteral medicines licensed in the UK.

17. Pharmacopeias

Br, Eur, Mex and USPNF.

18. Related Substances

Methylcellulose.

19. Comments

Ethylcellulose is compatible with the following plasticizers: dibutyl phthalate; diethyl phthalate; dimethyl phthalate; benzyl benzoate; butyl and glycol esters of fatty acids; refined mineral oils; oleic acid; stearic acid; cetyl alcohol; stearyl alcohol; castor oil; corn oil; camphor and numerous other materials.
Various grades of ethylcellulose are commercially available which differ in their ethoxyl content and physical properties, *see* Table I.

20. Specific References

1. Donbrow M, Friedman M. Timed release from polymeric films containing drugs and kinetics of drug release. J Pharm Sci 1975; 64: 76-80.
2. Kent DJ, Rowe RC. Solubility studies on ethyl cellulose used in film coating. J Pharm Pharmacol 1978; 30: 808-810.
3. Sakellariou P, Rowe RC, White EFT. The thermomechanical properties and glass transition temperatures of some cellulose derivatives used in film coating. Int J Pharmaceutics 1985; 27: 267-277.
4. Sarisuta N, Sirithunyalug J. Release rate of indomethacin from coated granules. Drug Dev Ind Pharm 1988; 14: 683-687.
5. Porter SC. Controlled-release film coatings based on ethylcellulose. Drug Dev Ind Pharm 1989; 15: 1495-1521.
6. Upadrashta SM, Katikaneni PR, Hileman GA, Keshary PR. Direct compression controlled release tablets using ethylcellulose matrices. Drug Dev Ind Pharm 1993; 19: 449-460.
7. Rowe RC. The prediction of compatibility/incompatibility in blends of ethyl cellulose with hydroxypropyl methylcellulose or hydroxypropyl cellulose using 2-dimensional solubility parameter maps. J Pharm Pharmacol 1986; 38: 214-215.
8. Appel LE, Zentner GM. Release from osmotic tablets coated with modified Aquacoat lattices. Proceed Intern Symp Control Rel Bioact Mater 1990; 17: 335-336.
9. Parikh NH, Porter SC, Rohera BD. Aqueous dispersion of ethylcellulose I: evaluation of coating process variables. Pharm Res 1993; 10: 525-534.
10. Jalsenjak I, Nicolaidou CF, Nixon JR. The *in vitro* dissolution of phenobarbitone sodium from ethyl cellulose microcapsules. J Pharm Pharmacol 1976; 28: 912-914.
11. Oya Alpar H, Walters V. The prolongation of the in vitro dissolution of a soluble drug (phenethicillin potassium) by microencapsulation with ethylcellulose. J Pharm Pharmacol 1981; 33: 419-422.
12. Benita S, Donbrow M. Effect of polyisobutylene on ethylcellulose-walled microcapsules: wall structure and thickness of salicylamide and theophylline microcapsules. J Pharm Sci 1982; 71: 205-210.
13. Robinson DH. Ethyl cellulose-solvent phase relationships relevant to coacervation microencapsulation processes. Drug Dev Ind Pharm 1989; 15: 2597-2620.
14. Tirkkonen S, Paronen P. Enhancement of drug release from ethylcellulose microcapsules using solid sodium chloride in the wall. Int J Pharmaceutics 1992; 88: 39-51.

15. Callahan JC, Cleary GW, Elefant M, Kaplan G, Kensler T, Nash RA. Equilibrium moisture content of pharmaceutical excipients. Drug Dev Ind Pharm 1982; 8: 355-369.

16. FAO/WHO. Evaluation of certain food additives and contaminants: thirty-fifth report of the joint FAO/WHO expert committee on food additives. Tech Rep Ser Wld Hlth Org 1990; No. 789.

21. General References

Aqualon Company. Technical literature: ethylcellulose, 1989.

Dow Chemical Company. Technical literature: Ethocel, ethylcellulose in pharmaceutical applications, 1991.

Doelker E. Cellulose derivatives. Adv Polymer Sci 1993; 107: 199-265.

Iyer U, Hong W-H, Das N, Ghebre-Sellassie I. Comparative evaluation of three organic solvent and dispersion-based ethylcellulose coating formulations. Pharmaceut Technol 1990; 14(9): 68, 70, 72, 74, 76, 78, 80, 82, 84, 86.

Rowe RC. Molecular weight studies on ethyl cellulose used in film coating. Acta Pharm Suec 1982; 19: 157-160.

Rowe RC. Materials used in the film coating of oral dosage forms. In: Florence AT, editor. Critical reports on applied chemistry, volume 6: materials used in pharmaceutical formulation. Oxford: Blackwell Scientific Publications, 1984: 1-36.

22. Authors

USA: TC Dahl.

Ethylparaben

1. Nonproprietary Names
BP: Ethyl hydroxybenzoate
USPNF: Ethylparaben

2. Synonyms
E214; ethyl *p*-hydroxybenzoate; ethyl parahydroxybenzoate; *Ethyl parasept*; 4-hydroxybenzoic acid ethyl ester; *Nipagin A*; *Solbrol A*; *Tegosept E*.

3. Chemical Name and CAS Registry Number
Ethyl 4-hydroxybenzoate [120-47-8]

4. Empirical Formula   Molecular Weight
$C_9H_{10}O_3$ 166.18

5. Structural Formula

6. Functional Category
Antimicrobial preservative.

7. Applications in Pharmaceutical Formulation or Technology
Ethylparaben is widely used as an antimicrobial preservative in cosmetics, food products and pharmaceutical formulations. It may be used either alone, in combination with other paraben esters, or with other antimicrobial agents. In cosmetics it is the sixth most frequently used preservative.[1]
The parabens are effective over a wide pH range and have a broad spectrum of antimicrobial activity although they are most effective against yeasts and molds, *see* Section 10.
Due to the poor solubility of the parabens, paraben salts, particularly the sodium salt, are frequently used in formulations. However, this may cause the pH of poorly buffered formulations to become more alkaline.
See Methylparaben for further information.

8. Description
Ethylparaben occurs as a white-colored, odorless or almost odorless, crystalline powder.

9. Pharmacopeial Specifications

Test	BP 1993	USPNF XVII (Suppl 9)
Identification	+	+
Melting range	≈ 117°C	115-118°C
Acidity	+	+
Loss on drying	—	≤ 0.5%
Residue on ignition	—	≤ 0.05%
Sulfated ash	≤ 0.1%	—

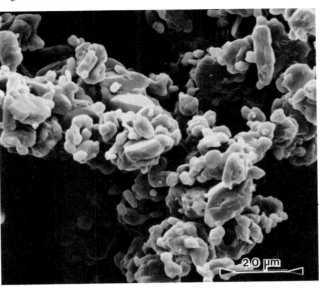

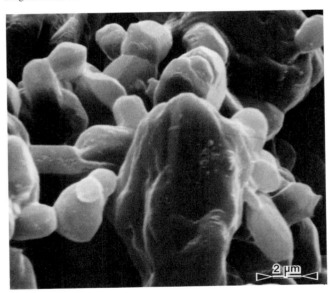

Continued

Test	BP 1993	USPNF XVII (Suppl 9)
Related substances	+	—
Organic volatile impurities	—	+
Assay (dried basis)	99.0-101.0%	99.0-100.5%

10. Typical Properties

Antimicrobial activity: ethylparaben exhibits antimicrobial activity between pH 4-8. Preservative efficacy decreases with increasing pH due to the formation of the phenolate anion. Parabens are more active against yeasts and molds than against bacteria. They are also more active against Gram-positive than against Gram-negative bacteria.

The activity of the parabens increases with increasing chain length of the alkyl moiety; solubility however decreases. Activity may be improved by using combinations of parabens since additive effects occur. Ethylparaben is thus commonly used with methyl and propylparaben in oral and topical formulations. (Such mixtures are commercially available, e.g. *Nipasept* (Nipa Laboratories Inc)). Activity has also been reported to be improved by the addition of other excipients, *see* Methylparaben for further information.

Reported minimum inhibitory concentrations (MICs) for ethylparaben are shown in Table I:[2]

Table I: Minimum inhibitory concentrations (MICs) for ethylparaben in aqueous solution.[2]

Microorganism	MIC (μg/mL)
Aerobacter aerogenes ATCC 8308	1200
Aspergillus niger ATCC 9642	500
Aspergillus niger ATCC 10254	400
Bacillus cereus var. mycoides ATCC 6462	1000
Bacillus subtilis ATCC 6633	1000
Candida albicans ATCC 10231	500
Enterobacter cloacae ATCC 23355	1000
Escherichia coli ATCC 8739	1000
Escherichia coli ATCC 9637	1000
Klebsiella pneumoniae ATCC 8308	500
Penicillium chrysogenum ATCC 9480	250
Penicillium digitatum ATCC 10030	250
Proteus vulgaris ATCC 13315	500
Pseudomonas aeruginosa ATCC 9027	> 2000
Pseudomonas aeruginosa ATCC 15442	> 2000
Pseudomonas stutzeri	1000
Rhizopus nigricans ATCC 6227A	250
Saccharomyces cerevisiae ATCC 9763	500
Salmonella typhosa ATCC 6539	1000
Serratia marcescens ATCC 8100	1000
Staphylococcus aureus ATCC 6538P	1000
Staphylococcus epidermidis ATCC 12228	1000
Trichophyton mentagrophytes	125

Boiling point: 297-298°C with decomposition
Melting point: 115-118°C
Partition coefficients: values for different vegetable oils vary considerably and are affected by the purity of the oil, *see* Table II.

Table II: Partition coefficients for ethylparaben in vegetable oil and water.[3]

Solvent	Partition coefficient Oil: water
Corn oil	14.0
Mineral oil	0.13
Peanut oil	16.1
Soybean oil	18.8

Solubility: *see* Table III and HPE Data.

Table III: Solubility of ethylparaben in various solvents.[2]

Solvent	Solubility at 25°C Unless otherwise stated
Acetone	freely soluble
Ethanol	1 in 1.4
Ethanol (95%)	1 in 2
Ether	1 in 3.5
Glycerin	1 in 200
Methanol	1 in 0.9
Mineral oil	1 in 4000
Peanut oil	1 in 100
Propylene glycol	1 in 4
Water	1 in 1250 at 15°C
	1 in 910
	1 in 120 at 80°C

HPE Laboratory Project Data			
	Method	Lab #	Results
Solubility			
Water at 25°C	SOL-8	30	0.85 mg/mL

11. Stability and Storage Conditions

Aqueous ethylparaben solutions at pH 3-6 can be sterilized by autoclaving, without decomposition.[4] At pH 3-6 aqueous solutions are stable (less than 10% decomposition) for up to about four years at room temperature whilst solutions at pH 8 or above are subject to rapid hydrolysis (10% or more after about 60 days at room temperature).[5]

Ethylparaben should be stored in a well-closed container in a cool, dry, place.

12. Incompatibilities

The antimicrobial properties of ethylparaben are considerably reduced in the presence of nonionic surfactants as a result of micellization.[6] Absorption of ethylparaben by plastics has not been reported but appears probable given the behavior of other parabens. Ethylparaben is coabsorbed on silica in the presence of ethoxylated phenols.[7] Yellow iron oxide, ultramarine blue and aluminum silicate extensively absorb ethylparaben in simple aqueous systems, thus reducing preservative efficacy.[8,9]

Ethylparaben is discolored in the presence of iron and is subject to hydrolysis by weak alkalis and strong acids.
See also Methylparaben.

13. Method of Manufacture

Ethylparaben is prepared by the esterification of *p*-hydroxybenzoic acid with ethanol.

14. Safety

Ethylparaben, and other parabens, are widely used as antimicrobial preservatives in cosmetics, food products, and oral and topical pharmaceutical formulations.

Systemically no adverse effects to parabens have been reported although they have been associated with hypersensitivity reactions. The WHO has set an estimated total acceptable daily intake for methyl, ethyl and propylparabens at up to 10 mg/kg body-weight.[10]

LD$_{50}$ (mouse, IP): 0.52 g/kg[11]
LD$_{50}$ (mouse, oral): 3.0 g/kg

15. Handling Precautions

Observe normal precautions appropriate to the circumstances and quantity of material handled. Ethylparaben may be irritant to the skin, eyes and mucous membranes and should be handled in a well-ventilated environment. Eye protection, gloves and a dust mask or respirator are recommended.

16. Regulatory Status

Accepted as a food additive in Europe. Included in the FDA Inactive Ingredients Guide (oral and topical preparations). Included in nonparenteral medicines licensed in the UK.

17. Pharmacopeias

Br, Chin, Fr, Jpn and USPNF.

18. Related Substances

Butylparaben; ethylparaben potassium; ethylparaben sodium; Methylparaben; Propylparaben.

Ethylparaben potassium: $C_9H_9KO_3$
Molecular weight: 204.28
CAS number: [36547-19-9]
Synonyms: ethyl 4-hydroxybenzoate potassium salt; potassium ethyl hydroxybenzoate.

Ethylparaben sodium: $C_9H_9NaO_3$
Molecular weight: 188.17
CAS number: [35285-68-8]
Synonyms: E215; ethyl 4-hydroxybenzoate sodium salt; sodium ethyl hydroxybenzoate.

19. Comments

See Methylparaben for further information and references.

20. Specific References

1. Decker RL, Wenninger JA. Frequency of preservative use in cosmetic formulas as disclosed to FDA - 1987. Cosmet Toilet 1987; 102(12): 21-24.

2. Haag TE, Loncrini DF. Esters of para-hydroxybenzoic acid. In: Kabara JJ, editor. Cosmetic and drug preservation. New York: Marcel Dekker, 1984: 63-77.
3. Wan LSC, Kurup TRR, Chan LW. Partition of preservatives in oil/water systems. Pharm Acta Helv 1986; 61: 308-313.
4. Aalto TR, Firman MC, Rigler NE. *p*-Hydroxybenzoic acid esters as preservatives I: uses, antibacterial and antifungal studies, properties and determination. J Am Pharm Assoc (Sci) 1953; 42: 449-457.
5. Kamada A, Yata N, Kubo K, Arakawa M. Stability of *p*-hydroxybenzoic acid esters in acidic medium. Chem Pharm Bull 1973; 21: 2073-2076.
6. Aoki M, Kameta A, Yoshioka I, Matsuzaki T. Application of surface active agents to pharmaceutical preparations I: effect of Tween 20 upon the antifungal activities of p-hydroxybenzoic acid esters in solubilized preparations [in Japanese]. J Pharm Soc Jpn 1956; 76: 939-943.
7. Daniels R, Rupprecht H. Effect of coadsorption on sorption and release of surfactant paraben mixtures from silica dispersions. Acta Pharm Technol 1985; 31: 236-242.
8. Sakamoto T, Yanagi M, Fukushima S, Mitsui T. Effects of some cosmetic pigments on the bactericidal activities of preservatives. J Soc Cosmet Chem 1987; 38: 83-98.
9. Allwood MC. The adsorption of esters of p-hydroxybenzoic acid by magnesium trisilicate. Int J Pharmaceutics 1982; 11: 101-107.
10. FAO/WHO. Toxicological evaluation of certain food additives with a review of general principles and of specifications. Seventeenth report of the FAO/WHO expert committee on food additives. Tech Rep Ser Wld Hlth Org 1974; No. 539.
11. Sweet DV, editor. Registry of toxic effects of chemical substances. Cincinnati: US Department of Health, 1987.

21. General References

Golightly LK, Smolinske SS, Bennett ML, Sutherland EW, Rumack BH. Pharmaceutical excipients: adverse effects associated with inactive ingredients in drug products (part I). Med Toxicol 1988; 3: 128-165.

22. Authors

USA: MM Rieger.

Fructose

1. Nonproprietary Names
BP: Fructose
PhEur: Laevulosum (Fructosum)
USP: Fructose

2. Synonyms
D-(-)-Fructopyranose; β-D-fructose; fruit sugar; *Krystar*; laevulose; levulose.

3. Chemical Name and CAS Registry Number
D-Fructose [57-48-7]

4. Empirical Formula   Molecular Weight
$C_6H_{12}O_6$ 180.16

5. Structural Formula

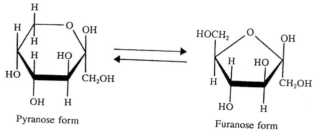

Pyranose form   Furanose form

See Section 19.

6. Functional Category
Flavor enhancer; sweetening agent; tablet diluent.

7. Applications in Pharmaceutical Formulation or Technology

Fructose is used in tablets, syrups and solutions as a flavoring and sweetening agent.
The sweetness response profile of fructose is perceived in the mouth more rapidly than that for sucrose and dextrose which may account for the ability of fructose to enhance syrup or tablet fruit flavors and mask certain unpleasant vitamin or mineral 'off-flavors'.
The increased solubility of fructose in comparison to sucrose is advantageous in syrup or solution formulations that must be refrigerated since ingredient settling or crystallization is retarded. Similarly, the greater solubility and hygroscopicity of fructose over sucrose and dextrose helps to avoid 'cap-locking' (sugar crystallization around the bottle cap) in elixir preparations. Fructose also has greater solubility in alcohol and is therefore used to sweeten alcoholic formulations.
Fructose is sweeter than the sugar alcohols mannitol and sorbitol which are commonly used as tableting excipients. Although fructose is effective at masking unpleasant flavors in tablet formulations, tablets of satisfactory hardness and friability can only be produced by direct compression if tablet presses are operated at relatively slow speeds. However, by combining crystalline fructose with tablet grade sorbitol in a 3:1 ratio satisfactory direct compression characteristics can be

achieved. Pre-granulation of fructose with 3.5% povidone also produces a satisfactory tablet excipient.[1] The added sweetness of fructose may also be used to advantage by coating the surface of chewable tablets, lozenges or medicinal gums with powdered fructose.

8. Description
Fructose occurs as odorless, colorless crystals or a white crystalline powder with a very sweet taste.

9. Pharmacopeial Specifications

Test	PhEur 1983	USP XXII
Identification	+	+
Color of solution	+	+
Acidity	+	+
Specific optical rotation	-91.0° to -93.5°	—
Foreign sugars	+	—
Loss on drying	≤ 0.5%	≤ 0.5%
Residue on ignition	—	≤ 0.5%
Sulfated ash	≤ 0.1%	—
Chloride	—	≤ 0.018%
Sulfate	—	≤ 0.025%
Arsenic	—	≤ 1 ppm
Barium	+	—
Calcium and magnesium (as calcium)	—	≤ 0.005%
Lead	≤ 0.5 ppm	—
Heavy metals	—	≤ 5 ppm
Hydroxymethylfurfural	+	+
Assay (dried basis)	—	98.0-102.0%

10. Typical Properties
Acidity/alkalinity:
pH = 5.35 (9% w/v aqueous solution)
Density: 1.58 g/cm³
Heat of combustion: 15.3 kJ/g (3.66 kcal/g)
Heat of solution: 50.2 kJ/g (12 kcal/g)
Hygroscopicity: at 25°C and relative humidities above approximately 60%, fructose absorbs significant amounts of moisture, *see* Fig. 1.
Melting point: ≈ 103°C (with decomposition)
Osmolarity: a 5.05% w/v aqueous solution is iso-osmotic with serum.
Particle size distribution: the average particle size of powdered fructose is 25-40 μm (*Krystar*, AE Staley Mfg Co). Other grades are available, e.g. *Krystar 300* and *Krystar 450* with average particle sizes of 300 μm and 450 μm respectively.
Refractive index:
n_D^{20} = 1.3477 (10% w/v aqueous solution)
Solubility:

Solvent	Solubility at 20°C
Ethanol (95%)	1 in 15
Methanol	1 in 14
Water	1 in 0.3

Specific rotation $[\alpha]_D^{20}$:
-132° to -92° (2% w/v aqueous solution).
Note that fructose shows rapid and anomalous mutarotation involving pyranose-furanose interconversion. The final value may be obtained in the presence of hydroxide ions. *See also* Section 19.

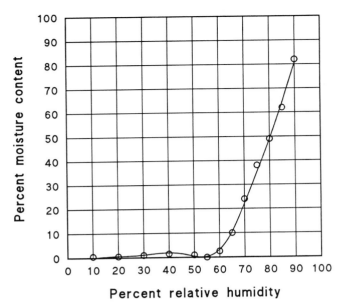

Fig. 1: Equilibrium moisture content of fructose at 25°C.

11. Stability and Storage Conditions

Fructose is hygroscopic and absorbs significant amounts of moisture at relative humidities greater than 60%. Under dry storage conditions it has good stability. Aqueous solutions are most stable at pH 3-4 and temperatures of 4-70°C; they may be sterilized by autoclaving. The bulk material should be stored in a well-closed container in a cool, dry, place.

12. Incompatibilities

Incompatible with strong acids or alkalis, forming a brown coloration. In the aldehyde form, fructose can react with amines, amino acids, peptides and proteins. Fructose may cause browning of tablets containing amines.

13. Method of Manufacture

Fructose, a monosaccharide sugar, occurs naturally in honey and a large number of fruits. It may be prepared from inulin, dextrose or sucrose by a number of methods. Commercially, fructose is mainly manufactured by crystallization from high fructose syrup derived from hydrolyzed and isomerized cereal starch or cane and beet sugar.

14. Safety

Although absorbed more slowly than dextrose from the gastrointestinal tract fructose is metabolized more rapidly. Metabolism of fructose occurs mainly in the liver where it is converted partially to dextrose and the metabolites lactic acid and pyruvic acid. Insulin is required for complete metabolism. Excessive oral fructose consumption (> 75 g daily) in the absence of dietary dextrose in any form (e.g. sucrose, starch, dextrin, etc) may cause malabsorption in susceptible individuals which may result in flatulence, abdominal pain and diarrhea. Except in patients with hereditary fructose intolerance,[2,3] there is no evidence to indicate that oral fructose intake at current levels is a risk factor in any particular disease, other than dental caries.[4]

Fructose is no longer used for parenteral applications since fatalities have occurred as a result of lactic acidosis and hyperuricemia.
See also Section 19.

15. Handling Precautions

Observe normal precautions appropriate to the circumstances and quantity of material handled. Fructose may be irritant to the eyes. Eye protection and gloves are recommended.

16. Regulatory Status

Included in the FDA Inactive Ingredients Guide (oral solutions and suspensions).

17. Pharmacopeias

Aust, Belg, Br, Cz, Egypt, Eur, Fr, Ger, Gr, Hung, It, Jpn, Neth, Port, Swiss, US and Yug.

18. Related Substances

Dextrose; high fructose syrup; liquid fructose; powdered fructose; Sucrose.

High fructose syrup:
Description: a syrup most commonly containing 42% or 55% fructose, with the remainder consisting of dextrose and small amounts of oligosaccharides. It is a colorless, odorless, very viscous syrup with a sweet taste.

Liquid fructose:
Description: a syrup containing $\geq$ 99.5% fructose made by solubilizing crystalline fructose in water. It is a colorless, odorless, very viscous syrup with a sweet taste.

Powdered fructose:
Description: finely ground crystalline fructose containing $\leq$ 2% silicon dioxide as a glidant.

19. Comments

Fructose can occur in both the furanose and pyranose forms. Fructose present in natural products occurs in the furanose form, while that produced by crystallization occurs in the pyranose form. An aqueous solution at 20°C contains about 20% of the furanose form.
Although fructose has been proposed for use in the diabetic diet it is not regarded as a suitable source of carbohydrate although it does have value as a sweetening agent.[5] The British Diabetic Association has recommended that intake of fructose be limited to 25 g daily.[6]
Fructose is the sweetest of all sugars; *see below.*

Sugar	Relative sweetness at 25°C (10% solids)
Fructose	117
Sucrose	100
High fructose syrup-55	99
High fructose syrup-42	92
Dextrose	65

20. Specific References

1. Osberger TF. Tableting characteristics of pure crystalline fructose. Pharmaceut Technol 1979; 3(6): 81-86.
2. Cox TM. An independent diagnosis: a treatable metabolic disorder diagnosed by molecular analysis of human genes. Br Med J 1990; 300: 1512-1514.

3. Collins J. Time for fructose solutions to go. Lancet 1993; 341: 600.

4. Glinsman WH, Irausquin H, Park YK. Evaluation of health aspects of sugars contained in carbohydrate sweeteners: report of sugars task force. Washington DC: Health and Human Services Center for Food Safety and Applied Nutrition, Food and Drug Administration, 1986.

5. Has fructose a place in the diabetic diet? Drug Ther Bull 1980; 18: 67-68.

6. Clarke BP. Is it harmful to a juvenile diabetic to substitute sorbitol and fructose for ordinary sugar? Br Med J 1987; 294: 422.

21. General References

Ahmed SU, Madan PL. Evaluation of the in vitro release profile of digoxin from drug-carbohydrate coprecipitates. Drug Dev Ind Pharm 1991; 17: 831-842.

22. Authors

USA: DC White, JS White.

Fumaric Acid

1. Nonproprietary Names

USPNF: Fumaric acid

2. Synonyms

Allomaleic acid; allomalenic acid; boletic acid; *trans*-butene-dioic acid; E297; 1,2-ethenedicarboxylic acid; lichenic acid.

3. Chemical Name and CAS Registry Number

(*E*)-2-Butenedioic acid [110-17-8]

4. Empirical Formula   Molecular Weight

$C_4H_4O_4$ 116.07

5. Structural Formula

6. Functional Category

Acidulant; antioxidant; flavoring agent; therapeutic agent.

7. Applications in Pharmaceutical Formulation or Technology

Fumaric acid is used primarily in liquid pharmaceutical preparations as an acidulant and flavoring agent. Other uses include: as the acid part of effervescent tablet formulations and as a chelating agent, in combination with other antioxidants. Fumaric acid is also used as a food additive at concentrations up to 3600 ppm, and as a therapeutic agent in the treatment of psoriasis.[1]

8. Description

Fumaric acid occurs as white, odorless or nearly odorless, granules or as a crystalline powder.

9. Pharmacopeial Specifications

Test	USPNF XVII (Suppl 6)
Identification	+
Water	⩽ 0.5%
Residue on ignition	⩽ 0.1%
Heavy metals	⩽ 0.001%
Maleic acid	⩽ 0.1%
Organic volatile impurities	+
Assay (dried basis)	99.5-100.5%

10. Typical Properties

Acidity/alkalinity:
pH = 2.45 (saturated aqueous solution at 20°C)

Density: 1.635 g/cm³ at 20°C
Density (bulk): 0.77 g/cm³
Density (tapped): 0.93 g/cm³
Dissociation constant:
$pK_{a1} = 3.03$ at 25°C;
$pK_{a2} = 4.54$ at 25°C.
Melting point: 287°C (closed capillary); sublimes at 200°C.
Solubility:

Solvent	Solubility at 20°C Unless otherwise stated
Benzene	very slightly soluble
Carbon tetrachloride	very slightly soluble
Chloroform	very slightly soluble
Ethanol	1 in 28
Ether	slightly soluble
Olive oil	very slightly soluble
Propylene glycol	1 in 33
Water	1 in 222
	1 in 159 at 25°C
	1 in 94 at 40°C
	1 in 42 at 60°C
	1 in 10 at 100°C

11. Stability and Storage Conditions

Fumaric acid is stable although it is subject to degradation by both aerobic and anaerobic microorganisms.
The bulk material should be stored in a well-closed container in a cool, dry, place.

12. Incompatibilities

Fumaric acid undergoes reactions typical of an organic acid.

13. Method of Manufacture

Commercially, fumaric acid may be prepared from dextrose by the action of fungi such as *Rhizopus nigricans*; as a by-product in the manufacture of maleic and phthalic anhydrides; and by the isomerization of maleic acid using heat or a catalyst.

14. Safety

Fumaric acid is used in oral pharmaceutical formulations and food products and is generally regarded as a nontoxic and nonirritant material. However, acute renal failure and other adverse reactions have occurred following the therapeutic use of fumaric acid, and fumaric acid derivatives, in the treatment of psoriasis.[1]
Since fumaric acid is a normal constituent of tissues, and is metabolised by the body, the WHO has stated that the establishment of an estimated acceptable daily intake of fumaric acid or its salts was unnecessary.[2]
LD_{50} (mouse, IP): 0.1 g/kg[3]
LD_{50} (rat, oral): 10.7 g/kg

15. Handling Precautions

Observe normal precautions appropriate to the circumstances and quantity of material handled. Fumaric acid may be irritating to the skin, eyes and respiratory system and should be handled in a well ventilated environment. Gloves and eye protection are recommended.

16. Regulatory Status

GRAS listed. Accepted as a food additive in Europe. Included in the FDA Inactive Ingredients Guide (capsules, tablets and oral liquids).

17. Pharmacopeias

USPNF.

18. Related Substances

Citric Acid Monohydrate; Malic Acid; Tartaric Acid.

19. Comments

—

20. Specific References

1. Reynolds JEF, editor. Martindale: the extra pharmacopoeia, 30th edition. London: The Pharmaceutical Press, 1993: 759.
2. FAO/WHO. Evaluation of certain food additives and contaminants. Thirty-fifth report of the joint FAO/WHO expert committee on food additives. Tech Rep Ser Wld Hlth Org 1990; No. 789.
3. Sweet DV, editor. Registry of toxic effects of chemical substances. Cincinnati: US Department of Health, 1987.

21. General References

Malic and Fumaric Acids. Mfg Chem Aerosol News 1964; 35(12): 56-59.
Robinson WD, Mount RA. In: Kirk-Othmer encyclopedia of chemical technology, volume 14; 3rd edition. New York: Wiley-Interscience, 1981: 770-793.

22. Authors

UK: M Lynch.

Gelatin

1. Nonproprietary Names

BP: Gelatin
PhEur: Gelatina
USPNF: Gelatin

2. Synonyms

Crodyne BY19; gelatine; *Pharmagel A*; *Pharmagel B*; *Vee Gee*.

3. Chemical Name and CAS Registry Number

Gelatin [9000-70-8]

4. Empirical Formula   Molecular Weight

Gelatin is a generic term for a mixture of purified protein fractions obtained either by partial acid hydrolysis (type A gelatin) or by partial alkaline hydrolysis (type B gelatin) of animal collagen. Gelatin may be a mixture of both types.
The protein fractions consist almost entirely of amino acids joined together by amide linkages to form linear polymers, varying in molecular weight from 15 000-250 000.

5. Structural Formula

See Section 4.

6. Functional Category

Coating agent; film-former; gelling agent; suspending agent; tablet binder; viscosity-increasing agent.

7. Applications in Pharmaceutical Formulation or Technology

Gelatin is widely used in a variety of pharmaceutical formulations (*see* Section 16) although it is most frequently used to form either hard or soft gelatin capsules.[1,2]
Gelatin capsules are unit dosage forms, which are filled with an active drug and generally designed for oral administration. Whilst gelatin is poorly soluble in cold water, a gelatin capsule will swell in gastric fluid to rapidly release its contents.
Hard capsules are manufactured in two pieces by dipping stainless steel pins into a gelatin solution which is distributed evenly around the pin. The gelatin is then set with a blast of chilled air and dried to remove any moisture. The capsule halves are then removed, trimmed and filled before they are joined and closed with a tamper-evident seal. The USPNF XVII permits gelatin, used to produce hard capsules, to contain various coloring agents, antimicrobial preservatives and sodium lauryl sulfate. Manufacturers may also add a hardening agent, such as sucrose, to hard gelatin capsules. Capsules varying in size from 0.13-1.37 mL volume are commercially available.
Soft gelatin capsules are formed from an aqueous gelatin solution which contains a plasticizer such as glycerin or sorbitol. Two soft gelatin strips are formed which run between suitable dies. As the dies meet, capsules are formed by injecting the filling material, followed by the capsule halves being sealed together.
Gelatin is also used for the microencapsulation of drugs, where the active drug is sealed inside a microsized capsule that may then be handled as a powder. Gelatin forms simple coacervates at temperatures above 40°C with dehydrating agents such as ethanol or 7% sodium sulfate solution. A gelatin solution is first adjusted to its isoelectric point and then a dehydrating agent added slowly over a period of one hour. Complex coacervation between gelatin and acacia requires dilute solutions of equal concentration. The temperature should be controlled at 40°C and the pH adjusted to between 3.8-4.6, depending on the system being encapsulated. The concentration of the two colloid solutions should not be greater than 2%.
Low molecular weight gelatin has been investigated for its ability to enhance the dissolution of orally ingested drugs.[3] Other uses of gelatin include the preparation of pastes, pastilles, pessaries and suppositories. In addition, it is used as a vehicle for parenteral formulations, as a tablet binder and coating agent, and as a viscosity-increasing agent for solutions and semi-solids.
Therapeutically, gelatin has been used as a plasma substitute and in the preparation of wound dressings.[4]
Gelatin is also widely used in food products and photographic emulsions.

8. Description

Gelatin occurs as a light-amber to faintly yellow-colored, vitreous, brittle solid. It is practically odorless and tasteless and is available as translucent sheets and granules, or as a powder.

9. Pharmacopeial Specifications

Test	PhEur 1986	USPNF XVII (Suppl 8)
Identification	+	+
Microbial limits	+	+
Residue on ignition	≤ 2.0%	≤ 2.0%
Loss on drying	≤ 15.0%	—
Odor & water-insoluble substances	—	+
Acidity or alkalinity	+	—
Clarity and color of solution	+	—
Sulfur dioxide	≤ 200 ppm	≤ 0.15%
Arsenic	≤ 1 ppm	≤ 0.8 ppm
Heavy metals	≤ 50 ppm	≤ 0.005%
Peroxides	≤ 100 ppm	—
Phenolic preservatives	+	—
Jelly strength	+	—

10. Typical Properties

Acidity/alkalinity:
for a 1% w/v aqueous solution at 25°C.
pH = 3.8-6.0 (type A);
pH = 5.0-7.4 (type B).
Density:
1.325 g/cm³ for type A;
1.283 g/cm³ for type B.
Iso-electric point:
7-9 for type A;
4.7-5.3 for type B.
Moisture content: see HPE Data.[5]
Solubility: practically insoluble in acetone, chloroform, ethanol (95%), ether, and methanol.
Soluble in glycerin, acids and alkalis, although strong acids or alkalis cause precipitation. In water, gelatin swells and softens, gradually absorbing between 5-10 times its own weight of water. Gelatin is soluble in hot water, forming a jelly, or gel,

on cooling to 35-40°C. At temperatures > 40°C, the system exists as a sol. This gel-sol system is heat reversible, the melting temperature being slightly higher than the setting point; the melting point can be varied by the addition of glycerin.
Viscosity (dynamic): 4.3-4.7 mPa s (4.3-4.7 cP) for a 6.67% w/v aqueous solution at 60°C; 18.5-20.5 mPa s (18.5-20.5 cP) for a 12.5% w/v aqueous solution at 60°C.

	HPE Laboratory Project Data		
	Method	Lab #	Results
Moisture content	MC-11	14	10.6% [a]
	MC-26	18	10.6% [b]
	MC-10	28	8.82% [b]
	MC-10	28	11.02% [b]
	MC-10	28	11.75% [a]
	EMC-1	18	*See* Fig. 1. [b]
	SDI-1	14	*See* Fig. 2. [a]

Supplier:
a. Leiner (Lot No.: 627);
b. Kind & Knox (*Pharmagel A*).

11. Stability and Storage Conditions

Dry gelatin is stable in air.
Aqueous gelatin solutions are also stable for long periods if stored under cool, sterile conditions. At temperatures above about 50°C aqueous gelatin solutions may undergo slow depolymerization and a reduction in gel strength on resetting may occur. Depolymerization becomes more rapid at temperatures above 65°C, and gel strength may be reduced by half when a solution is heated at 80°C for 1 hour. The rate and extent of depolymerization depends on the molecular weight of the gelatin, with a lower molecular weight material decomposing more rapidly.[6]
Gelatin may be sterilized by dry heat.
The bulk material should be stored in an airtight container in a cool, dry, place.

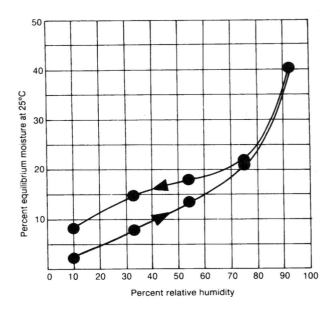

Fig. 2: **Sorption-desorption isotherm of gelatin.**

12. Incompatibilities

Gelatin is an amphoteric material and will thus react with both acids and bases. It is also a protein and thus exhibits chemical properties characteristic of such materials, e.g. gelatin may be hydrolyzed by most proteolytic systems to yield its amino acid components.
Gelatin will also react with aldehydes and aldehydic sugars, anionic and cationic polymers, electrolytes, metal ions, plasticizers, preservatives and surfactants. It is precipitated by alcohols, chloroform, ether, mercury salts and tannic acid. Gels can be liquefied by bacteria unless preserved.
Some of these interactions are exploited to favorably alter the physical properties of gelatin, e.g. gelatin is mixed with a plasticizer, such as glycerin, to produce soft gelatin capsules and suppositories, *see* Section 7.

13. Method of Manufacture

Gelatin is extracted from animal tissues rich in collagen such as skin, sinews and bone. Although it is possible to extract gelatin from these materials using boiling water it is more practical to first pretreat the animal tissues with either acid or alkali. Gelatin obtained from the acid process is called type A, whilst that obtained from the alkali process is called type B.
In the US, most type A gelatin is obtained from pig skins. This material is washed in cold water for a few hours to remove extraneous matter and is then digested in dilute mineral acid (either HCl, H_2SO_4, H_2SO_3 or H_3PO_4) at pH 1-3 and 15-20°C until maximum swelling has occurred. This process takes approximately 24 hours. The swollen stock is then washed with water to remove excess acid and the pH adjusted to pH 3.5-4.0 for the conversion to gelatin by hot water extraction.
The hydrolytic extraction is carried out in a batch-type operation, with successive portions of hot water, at progressively higher temperatures until the maximum yield of gelatin is obtained. The gelatin solution is then chilled to form jelled sheets which are dried in temperature-controlled ovens. The dried gelatin is then ground to the desired particle size.
In the alkali process, demineralized bones (ossein) or cattle skins are usually used. The animal tissue is held in a calcium

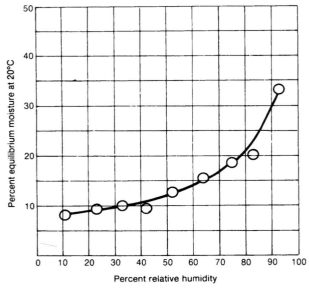

Fig. 1: **Equilibrium moisture content of gelatin (*Pharmagel A*).**

hydroxide (lime) slurry for a period of one to three months at 15-20°C. At the end of the liming, the stock is washed with cold water to remove as much of the lime as possible. The stock solution is then neutralized with acid (HCl, H_2SO_4, H_3PO_4) and the gelatin extracted with water in an identical manner to the acid process.

14. Safety

Gelatin is widely used in a variety of pharmaceutical formulations including oral and parenteral products.

In general, when used in oral formulations gelatin may be regarded as a nontoxic and nonirritant material. However, there have been rare reports of gelatin capsules adhering to the esophageal lining which may cause local irritation.[7] Hypersensitivity reactions, including serious anaphylactoid reactions, have been reported following the use of gelatin in parenteral products.[8]

15. Handling Precautions

Observe normal precautions appropriate to the circumstances and quantity of material handled. Eye protection and gloves are recommended. Gelatin should be handled in a well-ventilated environment.

16. Regulatory Status

Included in the FDA Inactive Ingredients Guide (dental preparations, inhalations, injections, oral capsules, solutions, syrups and tablets, topical and vaginal preparations). Included in medicines licensed in the UK.

17. Pharmacopeias

Aust, Br, Braz, Chin, Cz, Egypt, Eur, Fr, Ger, Gr, Hung, Ind, It, Jpn, Mex, Neth, Nord, Port, Rom, Rus, Swiss, Turk, USPNF and Yug.

18. Related Substances

—

19. Comments

Various grades of gelatin are commercially available with different particle sizes, molecular weights, etc. Grading is usually by jelly strength, expressed as 'Bloom strength', which is the weight in grams which, when applied under controlled conditions to a plunger 12.7 mm in diameter, will produce a depression exactly 4 mm deep in a matured jelly containing 6.66% w/w of gelatin in water.

20. Specific References

1. Armstrong NA, James KC, Pugh WKL. Drug migration in soft gelatin capsules. J Pharm Pharmacol 1982; 34(Suppl.): 5P.
2. Ridgway K, editor. Hard capsules: development and technology. London: The Pharmaceutical Press, 1987.
3. Kimura S, Imai T, Otagiri M. Evaluation of low-molecular gelatin as a pharmaceutical additive for rapidly absorbed oral dosage formulations. Chem Pharm Bull 1991; 39: 1328-1329.
4. Thomas S. Wound management and dressings. London: The Pharmaceutical Press, 1990.
5. Callahan JC, Cleary GW, Elefant M, Kaplan G, Kensler T, Nash RA. Equilibrium moisture content of pharmaceutical excipients. Drug Dev Ind Pharm 1982; 8: 355-369.
6. Ling WC. Thermal degradation of gelatin as applied to processing of gel mass. J Pharm Sci 1978; 67: 218-223.
7. Weiner M, Bernstein IL. Adverse reactions to drug formulation agents: a handbook of excipients. New York: Marcel Dekker Inc, 1989: 121-123.
8. Blanloeil Y, Gunst JP, Spreux A, Cozian A, Dixneuf B. Severe anaphylactoid reactions after infusion of modified gelatin solution [in French]. Therapie 1983; 38: 539-546.

21. General References

Fassihi AR, Parker MS. Influence of gamma radiation on the gel rigidity index and binding capability of gelatin. J Pharm Sci 1988; 77: 876.
Hawley AR, Rowley G, Lough WJ, Chatham S. Physical and chemical characterization of thermosoftened bases for molten filled hard gelatin capsule formulations. Drug Dev Ind Pharm 1992; 18: 1719-1739.
Jones RT. The role of gelatin in pharmaceuticals. Mfg Chem Aerosol News 1977; 48(7): 23-24.
Nadkarni SR, Yalkowsky SH. Controlled delivery of pilocarpine 1: *in vitro* characterization of gelfoam matrices. Pharm Res 1993; 10: 109-112.
Ofner CM, Schott H. Swelling studies of gelatin II: effect of additives. J Pharm Sci 1987; 76: 715-723.
Ray-Johnson ML, Jackson IM. Temperature-related incompatibility between gelatin and calcium carbonate in sugar-coated tablets. J Pharm Pharmacol 1976; 28: 309-310.
Voigt R, Werchan D. Radioinduced changes of the properties of gelatin [in German]. Pharmazie 1986; 41: 120-123.
Ward AG, Courts A, editors. The science and technology of gelatin. London: Academic Press, 1977.

22. Authors

USA: JC Price.

Liquid Glucose

1. Nonproprietary Names
USPNF: Liquid glucose

2. Synonyms
Corn syrup; glucose syrup; starch syrup.

3. Chemical Name and CAS Registry Number
Liquid glucose

4. Empirical Formula   Molecular Weight
See Section 8.

5. Structural Formula
See Section 8.

6. Functional Category
Coating agent; sweetening agent; tablet binder.

7. Applications in Pharmaceutical Formulation or Technology
Liquid glucose is used as a base in oral solutions and syrups and also as a granulating and coating agent in tablet manufacture. In sugar solutions for tablet coating, liquid glucose is used to retard the crystallization of the sucrose. Liquid glucose is also used in confectionery products.

Use	Concentration (%)
Granulating agent	5-10
Oral syrup vehicle	20-60
Tablet coating	10-20

8. Description
Liquid glucose is an aqueous solution of several compounds, principally dextrose, dextrin and maltose. It is a colorless, odorless and viscous sweet-tasting liquid.
Liquid glucose is classified according to its dextrose equivalent (DE) into four types:
Type I: 20-38 DE
Type II: 38-58 DE
Type III: 58-73 DE
Type IV: > 73 DE

9. Pharmacopeial Specifications

Test	USPNF XVII
Identification	+
Acidity	+
Water	$\leqslant 21.0\%$
Residue on ignition	$\leqslant 0.5\%$
Sulfite	+
Arsenic	$\leqslant 1$ ppm
Heavy metals	$\leqslant 0.001\%$
Starch	+
Organic volatile impurities	+

10. Typical Properties
Density: 1.43 g/cm^3 at 20°C
Solubility: miscible with water; partially miscible with ethanol (90%).
Viscosity (dynamic):
13.0-14.5 mPa s (13.0-14.5 cP) at 21°C

11. Stability and Storage Conditions
Liquid glucose should be stored in a well-closed container in a cool, dry, place.

12. Incompatibilities
Incompatible with strong oxidizing agents.

13. Method of Manufacture
Liquid glucose is prepared by the incomplete acidic or enzymatic hydrolysis of starch.

14. Safety
Liquid glucose is used in oral pharmaceutical formulations and confectionery products and is generally regarded as a nontoxic and nonirritant material. It may be consumed by diabetics.
See also Dextrose.

15. Handling Precautions
Observe normal precautions appropriate to the circumstances and quantity of material handled.

16. Regulatory Status
Included in the FDA Inactive Ingredients Guide (oral solutions, syrups and tablets). Included in nonparenteral medicines licensed in the UK.

17. Pharmacopeias
USPNF.

18. Related Substances
Dextrin; Dextrose; maltose.

Maltose: $C_{12}H_{22}O_{11}$
Molecular weight: 342.31
CAS number:
[69-79-4] for anhydrous maltose;
[6363-53-7] for maltose monohydrate.
Synonyms: 4-(α-D-glucopyranosido)-D-glucopyranose; 4-*O*-α-D-glucopyranosyl-β-D-glucopyranose; malt sugar.
Melting point: 102-103°C for monohydrate
Solubility: soluble in water; slightly soluble in ethanol (95%); practically insoluble in ether.
Specific rotation $[\alpha]_D^{20}$: 111.7° to 130.4° for 4% w/v aqueous solution. Shows mutarotation.
Comments: maltose is a disaccharide composed of two dextrose molecules. It is obtained from starch or glycogen by hydrolysis with amylase. The hydration of maltose depends on the solvent from which it is crystallized. Maltose is approximately one third as sweet as sucrose.

19. Comments
—

20. Specific References

21. General References

Dziedzic SZ, Kearsley MW, editors. Glucose syrups: science and technology. New York: Elsevier Applied Science, 1984.

Hoynak RX, Bolcenback GN. This is liquid sugar, 2nd edition. Yonkers: Refined Syrup and Sugars Inc, 1966: 205, 226.

Inglett GE, editor. Symposium on sweeteners. New York: AVI, 1974.

22. Authors

UK: JQ Maclaine, RS Torr.

Glycerin

1. Nonproprietary Names

BP: Glycerol
PhEur: Glycerolum
USP: Glycerin

2. Synonyms

Croderol; E422; glycerine; *Glycon G-100*; *Kemstrene*; *Pricerine*; 1,2,3-propanetriol; trihydroxypropane glycerol.

3. Chemical Name and CAS Registry Number

Propane-1,2,3-triol [56-81-5]

4. Empirical Formula   Molecular Weight

$C_3H_8O_3$ 92.09

5. Structural Formula

$$CH_2\text{---}OH$$
$$|$$
$$CH\text{---}OH$$
$$|$$
$$CH_2\text{---}OH$$

6. Functional Category

Antimicrobial preservative; emollient; humectant; plasticizer; solvent; sweetening agent; tonicity agent.

7. Applications in Pharmaceutical Formulation or Technology

Glycerin is used in a wide variety of pharmaceutical formulations including oral, otic, ophthalmic, topical and parenteral preparations. It is also used in cosmetics and as a food additive.

In topical pharmaceutical formulations and cosmetics, glycerin is used primarily for its humectant and emollient properties. In parenteral formulations glycerin is mainly used as a solvent,[1] whilst in oral solutions glycerin is used as a sweetening agent, antimicrobial preservative and viscosity-increasing agent. Glycerin is also used as a plasticizer of gelatin in the production of soft gelatin capsules and gelatin suppositories. Glycerin is additionally employed as a therapeutic agent in a variety of clinical applications.

Use	Concentration (%)
Antimicrobial preservative	> 20
Emollient	up to 30
Humectant	up to 30
Ophthalmic formulations	0.5-3.0
Plasticizer in tablet film coating	variable
Solvent for parenteral formulations	up to 50
Sweetening agent in alcoholic elixirs	up to 20

8. Description

Glycerin is a clear, colorless, odorless, viscous, hygroscopic liquid; it has a sweet taste, approximately 0.6 times as sweet as sucrose.

9. Pharmacopeial Specifications

Test	PhEur 1991	USP XXII (Suppl 7)
Identification	+	+
Specific gravity	—	$\geqslant$ 1.249
Color	—	+
Appearance of solution	+	—
Acidity or alkalinity	+	—
Refractive index	1.470-1.475	—
Residue on ignition	—	$\leqslant$ 0.01%
Sulfated ash	$\leqslant$ 0.01%	—
Chloride	$\leqslant$ 10 ppm	$\leqslant$ 0.001%
Sulfate	—	$\leqslant$ 0.002%
Arsenic	—	$\leqslant$ 1.5 ppm
Heavy metals	$\leqslant$ 5 ppm	$\leqslant$ 5 ppm
Chlorinated compounds (as Cl)	+	$\leqslant$ 0.003%
Organic volatile impurities	—	+
Aldehydes	+	—
Fatty acids and esters	+	+
Sugars	+	—
Water	$\leqslant$ 2.0%	—
Assay	98.0-101.0%	95.0-101.0%

10. Typical Properties

Boiling point: 290°C (with decomposition)
Density:
1.2656 g/cm^3 at 15°C;
1.2636 g/cm^3 at 20°C;
1.2620 g/cm^3 at 25°C.
Flash point: 176°C (open cup)
Freezing point:

Concentration of aqueous glycerin solution (% w/w)	Freezing point (°C)
10	-1.6
20	-4.8
30	-9.5
40	-15.4
50	-23
60	-34.7
66.7	-46.5
80	-20.3
90	-1.6

Hygroscopicity: hygroscopic.
Melting point: 17.8°C
Osmolarity: a 2.6% v/v aqueous solution is iso-osmotic with serum.
Refractive index:
$n_D^{15} = 1.4758$;
$n_D^{20} = 1.4746$;
$n_D^{25} = 1.4730$.

Solubility:

Solvent	Solubility at 20°C
Acetone	slightly soluble
Benzene	practically insoluble
Chloroform	practically insoluble
Ethanol (95%)	miscible
Ether	1 in 500
Ethyl acetate	1 in 11
Methanol	miscible
Oils	practically insoluble
Water	miscible

Specific gravity:

Concentration of aqueous glycerin solution (% w/w)	Specific gravity at 20°C
10	1.024
20	1.049
30	1.075
40	1.101
50	1.128
60	1.156

Surface tension:
63.4 mN/m (63.4 dynes/cm) at 20°C.
Vapor density (relative): 3.17 (air = 1)
Viscosity (dynamic): *see also* HPE Data.

Concentration of aqueous glycerin solution (% w/w)	Viscosity at 20°C (mPa s)
5	1.143
10	1.311
25	2.095
50	6.05
60	10.96
70	22.94
83	111

HPE Laboratory Project Data	Method	Lab #	Results
Viscosity	VIS-1	27	515 ± 19 mPa s [a]
Viscosity	VIS-1	27	1034 ± 19 mPa s [b]

Supplier: a. Star; b. Superol.

11. Stability and Storage Conditions

Glycerin is hygroscopic. Pure glycerin is not prone to oxidation by the atmosphere under ordinary storage conditions, but decomposes on heating, with the evolution of toxic acrolein. Mixtures of glycerin with water, ethanol and propylene glycol are chemically stable.
Glycerin may crystallize if stored at low temperatures; the crystals do not melt until raised to 20°C.
Glycerin should be stored in an airtight container, in a cool, dry, place.

12. Incompatibilities

Glycerin may explode if mixed with strong oxidizing agents, such as chromium trioxide, potassium chlorate or potassium permanganate. In dilute solution, the reaction proceeds at a slower rate, with several oxidation products being formed. Black discoloration of glycerin occurs, in the presence of light, on contact with zinc oxide or basic bismuth nitrate.
An iron contaminant in glycerin is responsible for the darkening in color of mixtures containing phenols, salicylates and tannin.
Glycerin forms a boric acid complex, glyceroboric acid, which is a stronger acid than boric acid.

13. Method of Manufacture

Glycerin is mainly obtained from oils and fats as a by-product in the manufacture of soaps and fatty acids. It may also be obtained from natural sources by fermentation of, for example, sugar beet molasses in the presence of large quantities of sodium sulfite. Synthetically, glycerin may be prepared by the chlorination and saponification of propylene.

14. Safety

Glycerin occurs naturally in animal and vegetable fats and oils that are consumed as part of a normal diet. Glycerin is readily absorbed from the intestine and is either metabolized to carbon dioxide and glycogen or is used in the synthesis of body fats.
Glycerin is used in a wide variety of pharmaceutical formulations including oral, ophthalmic, parenteral and topical preparations. Adverse effects are mainly due to the dehydrating properties of glycerin.
Oral doses are demulcent and mildly laxative in action. Large doses may produce headache, thirst, nausea and hyperglycemia. The therapeutic parenteral administration of very large glycerin doses, 70-80 g over 30-60 minutes in adults to reduce cranial pressure, may induce hemolysis, hemoglobinuria and renal failure.[2] Slower administration has no deleterious effects.[3]
Glycerin may also be used orally in doses of 1.0-1.5 g/kg body-weight to reduce intraocular pressure.
When used as an excipient or food additive, glycerin is not usually associated with any adverse effects and is generally regarded as a nontoxic and nonirritant material.
LD_{50} (guinea pig, oral): 7.75 g/kg[4]
LD_{50} (mouse, IP): 8.98 g/kg
LD_{50} (mouse, IV): 6.2 g/kg
LD_{50} (mouse, oral): 4.1 g/kg
LD_{50} (mouse, SC): 0.09 g/kg
LD_{50} (rat, IP): 8.3 g/kg
LD_{50} (rat, IV): 5.6 g/kg
LD_{50} (rat, oral): 12.6 g/kg
LD_{50} (rat, SC): 0.1 g/kg

15. Handling Precautions

Observe normal precautions appropriate to the circumstances and quantity of material handled. Eye protection and gloves are recommended. In the UK, the recommended long-term (8-hour TWA) exposure limit for glycerin mist is 10 mg/m³.[5]
Glycerin is combustible and may react explosively with strong oxidizing agents, *see* Section 12.

16. Regulatory Status

GRAS listed. Accepted as a food additive in Europe. Included in the FDA Inactive Ingredients Guide (inhalations, injections, nasal, ophthalmic, oral capsules, solutions, suspensions and tablets, otic, rectal, topical, transdermal and vaginal preparations). Included in nonparenteral and parenteral medicines licensed in the UK.

17. Pharmacopeias

Aust, Br, Braz, Chin, Cz, Egypt, Eur, Fr, Ger, Gr, Hung, Ind, It, Jpn, Mex, Neth, Nord, Port, Rom, Swiss, Turk and US. Also in BP Vet.
Glycerin (85%) is also included in the following pharmacopeias: Br; Eur; Fr; Gr; It; Neth; Port; Swiss and Yug. Also in BP Vet.

18. Related Substances

—

19. Comments

—

20. Specific References

1. Spiegel AJ, Noseworthy MM. Use of nonaqueous solvents in parenteral products. J Pharm Sci 1963; 52: 917-927.
2. Hägnevik K, Gordon E, Lins LE, Wilhelmsson S, Forster D. Glycerol-induced haemolysis with haemoglobinuria and acute renal failure. Lancet 1974; i: 75-77.
3. Welch KMA, Meyer JS, Okamoto S, Mathew NT, Rivera VM, Bond J. Glycerol-induced haemolysis [letter]. Lancet 1974; i: 416-417.
4. Sweet DV, editor. Registry of toxic effects of chemical substances. Cincinnati: US Department of Health, 1987.
5. Health and Safety Executive. EH40/93: occupational exposure limits 1993. London: HMSO, 1993.

21. General References

Grissom CB, Chagovetz AM, Wang Z. Use of viscosigens to stabilize vitamin B_{12} solutions against photolysis. J Pharm Sci 1993; 82: 641-643.

Jungermann E, Sonntag NOV, editors. Glycerine: a key cosmetic ingredient. New York: Marcel Dekker Inc, 1991.

Smolinske SC. Handbook of food, drug, and cosmetic excipients. Boca Raton, FL: CRC Press Inc, 1992: 199-204.

Staples R, Misher A, Wardell J. Gastrointestinal irritant effect of glycerin as compared with sorbitol and propylene glycol in rats and dogs. J Pharm Sci 1967; 56: 398-400.

22. Authors

USA: JC Price.

Glyceryl Monooleate

1. Nonproprietary Names
None adopted.

2. Synonyms
Aldo MO; *Arlacel 186*; *Atlas G-695*; *Cithrol GMO N/E*; glycerol-1-oleate; glyceryl mono-oleate; *Hodag GMO*; mono-olein; α-mono-olein glycerol; monolein; *Myverol 18-99*; *Priolube 1408*; *Tegin*.

3. Chemical Name and CAS Registry Number
9-Octadecenoic acid (Z)-monoester with 1,2,3-propanetriol [25496-72-4]

4. Empirical Formula   Molecular Weight
$C_{21}H_{40}O_4$ 356.55
(for pure material)
Glyceryl monooleate is a mixture of the glycerides of oleic acid and other fatty acids, consisting mainly of the monooleate.

5. Structural Formula

$$CH_2-OOCC_{17}H_{33}$$
$$|$$
$$CHOH$$
$$|$$
$$CH_2OH$$

6. Functional Category
Nonionic surfactant.

7. Applications in Pharmaceutical Formulation or Technology
Glyceryl monooleate is a polar lipid which swells in water to give several phases with different rheological properties.[1,2] It is available in both non-emulsifying and self-emulsifying grades, the self-emulsifying grade containing about 5% of an anionic surfactant.
The non-emulsifying grade is used in topical formulations as an emollient and as an emulsifying agent for water-in-oil emulsions. It is also a stabilizer for oil-in-water emulsions. The self-emulsifying grade is used as a primary emulsifier for oil-in-water systems.
Glyceryl monooleate also gels in excess water, forming a highly ordered cubic phase which can be used to sustain the release of various water soluble drugs.[1,2]

8. Description
Glyceryl monooleate occurs as a yellow to yellow-brown oily liquid or paste with a characteristic odor.

9. Pharmacopeial Specifications
—

10. Typical Properties
Acid value: < 2.0
Boiling point: 238-240°C
Density: 0.942 g/cm³

Flash point: 216°C
Free glycerin: ⩽ 5.0%
HLB value:
3.3 for non-emulsifying grade;
4.1 for self-emulsifying grade.
Iodine number: 90-100
Melting point: 35°C, *see also* Section 13.
Monoglyceride content:
38-42% for non-emulsifying grade;
30-35% for self-emulsifying grade.
Refractive index: 1.4626
Saponification value:
160-170 for non-emulsifying grade;
150-160 for self-emulsifying grade.
Soap content:
0.5% for non-emulsifying grade;
5.0-5.5% for self-emulsifying grade.
Solubility: soluble in chloroform, ethanol (95%), ether, mineral oil and vegetable oils. Practically insoluble in water; the self-emulsifying grade is dispersible in water.
Water content:
⩽ 1.0% for non-emulsifying grade;
< 2.0% for self-emulsifying grade.
See also Section 13.

11. Stability and Storage Conditions
Glyceryl monooleate should be stored in an airtight container protected from light, in a cool, dry, place.

12. Incompatibilities
Incompatible with strong oxidizing agents. The self-emulsifying grade is incompatible with cationic surfactants.

13. Method of Manufacture
Glyceryl monooleate is prepared by the esterification of glycerin with fatty acids, chiefly oleic acid. As the fatty acids used are not pure substances, but rather a mixture of fatty acids, the product obtained from the esterification process contains a mixture of esters, including stearic and palmitic. Di- and tri-esters may also be present. The composition and therefore the physical properties of glyceryl monooleate may thus vary considerably from manufacturer to manufacturer, e.g. the melting point may vary from 10-35°C.

14. Safety
Glyceryl monooleate is generally regarded as a nonirritant and nontoxic excipient.

15. Handling Precautions
Observe normal precautions appropriate to the circumstances and quantity of material handled.

16. Regulatory Status
GRAS listed. Included in the FDA Inactive Ingredients Guide (oral capsules and tablets). Included in nonparenteral medicines licensed in the UK.

17. Pharmacopeias
Nord.

18. Related Substances
Glyceryl Monostearate; Medium Chain Triglycerides.

19. Comments

—

20. Specific References

1. Engström S, Lindahl L, Wallin R, Engblom J. A study of polar lipid drug carrier systems undergoing a thermoreversible lamellar-to-cubic phase transition. Int J Pharmaceutics 1992; 86: 137-145.
2. Wyatt DM, Dorschel D. A cubic-phase delivery system composed of glyceryl monooleate and water for sustained release of water-soluble drugs. Pharmaceut Technol 1992; 16(10): 116, 118, 120, 122, 130.

21. General References

Eccleston GM. Emulsions. In: Swarbrick J, Boylan JC, editors. Encyclopaedia of pharmaceutical technology, volume 5. New York: Marcel Dekker, 1992: 137-188.

22. Authors

UK: NA Armstrong.

Glyceryl Monostearate

1. Nonproprietary Names

USPNF: Glyceryl monostearate

2. Synonyms

Aldo MS; *Arlacel 129*; *Atmos 150*; *Cithrol GMS N/E*; *Estol 1473*; glycerol monostearate; glycerol stearate; glyceryl stearate; GMS; *Hodag GMS*; *Imwitor*; monostearin; *Myvaplex 600P*; *Protachem GMS-450*; *Rita-GMS*; *Simulsol 165*.

3. Chemical Name and CAS Registry Number

Octadecanoic acid, monoester with 1,2,3-propane-triol [31566-31-1]

4. Empirical Formula   Molecular Weight

$C_{21}H_{42}O_4$

358.57
(for pure material)

See Section 8.

5. Structural Formula

$$CH_2—OOCC_{17}H_{35}$$
$$CHOH$$
$$CH_2OH$$

6. Functional Category

Emollient; emulsifying agent; solubilizing agent; stabilizing agent; tablet and capsule lubricant.

7. Applications in Pharmaceutical Formulation or Technology

Glyceryl monostearate is used as a nonionic emulsifier, stabilizer, emollient and plasticizer in a variety of food, pharmaceutical and cosmetic applications. It acts as an effective stabilizer, i.e. as a mutual solvent for polar and nonpolar compounds which may form water-in-oil or oil-in-water emulsions.[1] These properties also make it useful as a dispersing agent of pigments in oils or of solids in fats, or as a solvent for phospholipids, such as lecithin.

Glyceryl monostearate is also used as a lubricant and to sustain the release of active ingredients in tablet formulations.

8. Description

The USPNF XVII describes glyceryl monostearate as consisting of not less than 90% of monoglycerides, chiefly glyceryl monostearate ($C_{21}H_{42}O_4$) and glyceryl monopalmitate ($C_{19}H_{38}O_4$). It should be noted that glyceryl monostearate from European sources usually refers to glyceryl monostearate 40-50, *see* Section 18.

Glyceryl monostearate is a white to cream-colored, wax-like solid in the form of beads, flakes or powder. It is waxy to the touch and has a slight fatty odor and taste.

9. Pharmacopeial Specifications

Test	USPNF XVII
Melting range	$\geqslant 55°C$
Residue on ignition	$\leqslant 0.5\%$
Arsenic	$\leqslant 3$ ppm
Heavy metals	$\leqslant 0.001\%$
Acid value	$\leqslant 6.0$
Iodine value	$\leqslant 3.0$
Saponification value	155-165
Hydroxyl value	300-330
Free glycerin	$\leqslant 1.2\%$
Assay (for monoglycerides)	$\geqslant 90.0\%$

10. Typical Properties

A wide variety of glyceryl monostearate grades are commercially available, including self-emulsifying grades which contain small amounts of soap or other surfactants. Most grades are tailored for specific applications or made to user specifications and thus have varied physical properties.

Flash point: $\approx 240°C$
HLB value: 3.8
Melting point: 55-60°C
Solubility: soluble in hot ethanol (95%), ether, chloroform, hot acetone, mineral oil and fixed oils. Practically insoluble in water, but readily dispersible in hot water with the aid of an anionic or cationic agent.
Specific gravity: 0.92

11. Stability and Storage Conditions

Glyceryl monostearate increases in acid value upon aging, if stored at warm temperatures, due to the saponification of the ester with trace amounts of water. Effective antioxidants that may be added are butylated hydroxytoluene and propyl gallate.

Glyceryl monostearate should be stored in a light-resistant, tightly sealed container at a cool temperature.

12. Incompatibilities

The self-emulsifying grades of glyceryl monostearate are incompatible with acidic substances.

13. Method of Manufacture

Glyceryl monostearate is prepared by esterification of glycerin with fatty acids, chiefly stearic acid, and by interesterification of hydrogenated edible oils such as tallow, lard or palm oil with glycerin.

As the fatty acids used are not pure substances, but a mixture of fatty acids, the product obtained from the esterification processes contains a mixture of esters, including palmitic and oleic. The composition and therefore the physical properties of glyceryl monostearate may thus vary considerably from manufacturer to manufacturer.

14. Safety

Glyceryl monostearate is used in cosmetics, foods and oral and topical pharmaceutical formulations and is generally regarded as a nontoxic and nonirritant excipient.

LD_{50} (mouse, IP): 0.2 g/kg[2]

15. Handling Precautions

Observe normal precautions appropriate to the circumstances and quantity of material handled.

16. Regulatory Status

GRAS listed. Included in the FDA Inactive Ingredients Guide (oral capsules and tablets, ophthalmic, otic, rectal, topical, transdermal and vaginal preparations). Included in nonparenteral medicines licensed in the UK.

17. Pharmacopeias

Hung and USPNF.

A number of other pharmacopeias contain monographs for glyceryl monostearate 40-50. *See* Section 18.

18. Related Substances

Glyceryl Monooleate; glyceryl monostearate 40-50; Glyceryl Palmitostearate; self-emulsifying glyceryl monostearate.

Glyceryl monostearate 40-50

Synonyms: *Drewmulse SE 200K*; *Kessco GMS*; glyceroli monostearas 40-50; mono- and di-glycerides USPNF.

CAS number: [31566-31-1]

Pharmacopeias: Aust, Br, Eur, Fr, Ger, Ind, It, Swiss and USPNF.

Acid value: $\leqslant 3$

Iodine number: $\leqslant 3$

Melting point: 55-60°C

Saponification value: 158-177

Comments: the PhEur 1986 describes glyceryl monostearate 40-50 as a mixture of mono-, di- and triglycerides of stearic and palmitic acids. It contains not less than 40% and not more than 50% of monoglycerides calculated as 2,3-dihydroxypropyl stearate ($C_{21}H_{42}O_4$). The monograph 'Mono- and Diglycerides' in the USPNF XVII encompasses the PhEur 1986 material.

Self-emulsifying glyceryl monostearate

Synonyms: *Arlacel 165*; *Arlatone 983*; *Cithrol GMS S/E*; glyceryl stearate SE; GMS SE; *Hodag GMS-D*.

Pharmacopeias: Br.

Acid value: $\leqslant 6$

Acidity/alkalinity:

pH = 8.0-10.0 (5% w/v dispersion in hot water)

HLB value: 11-12

Iodine number: $\leqslant 3$

Melting point: 55-60°C

Comments: self-emulsifying glyceryl monostearate is a grade of glyceryl monostearate which has had added to it an emulsifying agent which may be a soluble soap, a salt of a sulfated alcohol, a nonionic surfactant or a quaternary compound. It is used primarily as an emulsifying agent for oils, fats, solvents and waxes. It should not be used in formulations for internal use. Aqueous preparations should contain an antimicrobial preservative.

19. Comments

Glyceryl monostearate and monoesters of other fatty acids are not efficient emulsifiers as such. They are best regarded as useful emollients which are readily emulsified by the usual emulsifying agents and when other fatty materials are incorporated into a formulation. The monoesters in general endow creams with smoothness, a fine texture, and improve stability. In topical applications, glyceryl monostearate does not have as great a drying effect as straight stearate creams, and is not drying when used in protective applications.

20. Specific References

1. O'Laughlin R, et al. Effects of variations in physicochemical properties of glyceryl monostearate on the stability of an oil-in-water cream. J Soc Cosmet Chem 1989; 40: 215-229.
2. Sweet DV, editor. Registry of toxic effects of chemical substances. Cincinnati: US Department of Health, 1987.

21. General References

Eccleston GM. Emulsions. In: Swarbrick J, Boylan JC, editors. Encyclopaedia of pharmaceutical technology, volume 5. New York: Marcel Dekker, 1992: 137-188.

Rieger MM. Glyceryl stearate: chemistry and use. Cosmet Toilet 1990; 105(Nov): 51-54, 56-57.

Schumacher GE. Glyceryl monostearate in some pharmaceuticals. Am J Hosp Pharm 1967; 24: 290-291.

Wiśniewski W, Golucki Z. Stability of glyceryl monostearate [in Polish]. Acta Pol Pharm 1965; 22: 293-298.

22. Authors

USA: B Pagliocca.

Glyceryl Palmitostearate

1. Nonproprietary Names
None adopted.

2. Synonyms
Glycerin palmitostearate; glycerol palmitostearate; *Precirol ATO 5*.

3. Chemical Name and CAS Registry Number
Glyceryl palmitostearate [8067-32-1]

4. Empirical Formula   Molecular Weight
Glyceryl palmitostearate is a mixture of mono-, di- and triglycerides of C_{16} and C_{18} fatty acids.

5. Structural Formula
See Section 4.

6. Functional Category
Tablet and capsule diluent; tablet and capsule lubricant.

7. Applications in Pharmaceutical Formulation or Technology
Glyceryl palmitostearate is used in oral solid dosage pharmaceutical formulations as a lubricant[1-3] and lipophilic matrix for sustained release tablet and capsule formulations.[4-10] When used as a tablet lubricant disintegration times increase with increasing mixing times.[2] Sustained release tablet formulations that contain glyceryl palmitostearate as the base may be prepared either by granulation or by a hot melt technique. Granulation methods produce tablets that have a faster release profile; release rate also decreases with increased glyceryl palmitostearate content.[8] Glyceryl palmitostearate may also be used to form microspheres which may be used in capsules or compressed to form tablets.[10]

Use	Concentration (%)
Matrix for sustained release	10-50
Tablet lubricant	0.5-5

8. Description
Glyceryl palmitostearate occurs as a fine white powder with a faint odor.

9. Pharmacopeial Specifications
—

10. Typical Properties
Acid value: < 6.0
Boiling point: 200°C
Color: < 3 (Gardner scale)
Free glycerin content: < 1.0%
Heavy metals: < 10 ppm
Hydroxyl value: 60-115
Iodine number: < 3
Melting point: 52-55°C
1-Monoglycerides content: 8.0-17.0%
Peroxide value: < 3.0
Saponification value: 175-195
Solubility: freely soluble in chloroform and dichloromethane; practically insoluble in ethanol (95%), mineral oil and water.
Sulfated ash: < 0.1%
Unsaponifiable matter: < 1.0%
Water content: < 1.0%

11. Stability and Storage Conditions
Glyceryl palmitostearate should not be stored at temperatures above 35°C. For storage periods greater than one month, glyceryl palmitostearate should be stored at a temperature of 5-15°C, in an airtight container, protected from light and moisture.

12. Incompatibilities
Glyceryl palmitostearate is incompatible with ketoprofen[11] and naproxen.[12]

13. Method of Manufacture
Glyceryl palmitostearate is manufactured, without a catalyst, by the direct esterification of palmitic and stearic acids with glycerin.

14. Safety
Glyceryl palmitostearate is used in oral pharmaceutical formulations and is generally regarded as an essentially nontoxic and nonirritant material.
LD_{50} (rat, oral): > 6 g/kg[13]

15. Handling Precautions
Observe normal precautions appropriate to the circumstances and quantity of material handled.

16. Regulatory Status
Included in the FDA Inactive Ingredients Guide (oral preparations). Included in nonparenteral medicines licensed in Europe.

17. Pharmacopeias
—

18. Related Substances
Glyceryl behenate; Glyceryl Monostearate.

Glyceryl behenate: $C_{69}H_{134}O_6$
Molecular weight: 1060.03
CAS number: [18641-57-1]
Synonyms: *Compritol 888*; docosanoic acid, 1,2,3-propanetriyl ester; glyceryl tribehenate.
Appearance: fine white powder with a faint odor.
Pharmacopeias: USPNF.
Acid value: < 4.0
Color: < 5 (Gardner scale)
Free glycerin: < 1.0%
Heavy metals: < 10 ppm
Iodine number: < 3
Melting point: ≈ 70°C
1-Monoglycerides: 12.0-18.0%
Saponification value: 145-165

Solubility: soluble, when heated, in chloroform and dichloromethane; practically insoluble in ethanol (95%), hexane, mineral oil and water.

Sulfated ash: < 0.1%

Safety: LD_{50} (mouse, oral): 5 g/kg[14]

Comments: glyceryl behenate is a mixture of glycerides of fatty acids, mainly behenic acid, and is used as a tablet and capsule lubricant.[15,16]

19. Comments

—

20. Specific References

1. Hölzer AW, Sjögren J. Evaluation of some lubricants by the comparison of friction coefficients and tablet properties. Acta Pharm Suec 1981; 18: 139-148.

2. Sekulović D, Samardžić Z. The effect of the mixing time of lubricants on the properties of acetylsalicylic acid tablets prepared by the method of direct compression. Pharmazie 1986; 41: 667-668.

3. Sekulović D. Effect of Precirol ATO 5 on the properties of tablets. Pharmazie 1987; 42: 61-62.

4. Terrier JL, Cruaud-Mangenot O, Duchène D, Puisieux F. Effects of pressure on the *in vitro* release of sodium salicylate from a sustained action tablet [in French]. Pharm Acta Helv 1976; 51: 144-152.

5. Hausmann K, Soliva M, Speiser PP. Studies on oral iron formulations [in German]. Pharm Ind 1979; 41: 274-278.

6. Parab PV, Oh CK, Ritschel WA. Sustained release from Precirol (glycerol palmito-stearate) matrix. Effect of mannitol and hydroxypropyl methylcellulose on the release of theophylline. Drug Dev Ind Pharm 1986; 12: 1309-1327.

7. Bodmeier R, Paeratakul O, Chen H, Zhang W. Formation of sustained release wax matrices within hard gelatin capsules in a fluidized bed. Drug Dev Ind Pharm 1990; 16: 1505-1519.

8. Saraiya D, Bolton S. The use of Precirol to prepare sustained release tablets of theophylline and quinidine gluconate. Drug Dev Ind Pharm 1990; 16: 1963-1969.

9. Malamataris S, Panagopoulou A, Hatzipantou P. Controlled release from glycerol palmito-stearate matrices prepared by dry-heat granulation and compression at elevated temperature. Drug Dev Ind Pharm 1991; 17: 1765-1777.

10. Shaikh NH, De Yanes SE, Shukla AJ, Block LH, Collins CC, Price JC. Effect of different binders on release characteristics of theophylline from compressed microspheres. Drug Dev Ind Pharm 1991; 17: 793-804.

11. Botha SA, Lötter AP. Compatibility study between ketoprofen and tablet excipients using differential scanning calorimetry. Drug Dev Ind Pharm 1989; 15: 415-426.

12. Botha SA, Lötter AP. Compatibility study between naproxen and tablet excipients using differential scanning calorimetry. Drug Dev Ind Pharm 1990; 16: 673-683.

13. Gattefossé SA. Technical literature: Precirol ATO 5, 1993.

14. Sweet DV, editor. Registry of toxic effects of chemical substances. Cincinnati: US Department of Health, 1987.

15. Abramovici B, Groménil J-C, Molard F, Blanc F. Comparative study of the lubricant properties of a new excipient, glyceryl tribehenate (Compritol 888), compared with magnesium stearate [in French]. STP Pharma 1986; 2: 403-409.

16. Shah NH, Stiel D, Weiss M, Infeld MH, Malick AW. Evaluation of two new tablet lubricants sodium stearyl fumarate and glyceryl behenate. Measurement of physical parameters (compaction, ejection and residual forces) in the tableting process and the effect on the dissolution rate. Drug Dev Ind Pharm 1986; 12: 1329-1346.

21. General References

Edimo A, Leterme P, Denis J, Traisnel M, Gayot AT. Capacity of lipophilic auxiliary substances to give spheres by extrusion-spheronization. Drug Dev Ind Pharm 1993; 19: 827-842.

Stampf G, Karoliny V. Contribution to the galenical use of a fatty acid ester (Precirol) [in Hungarian]. Acta Pharm Hung 1974; 44: 283-288.

22. Authors

UK: NA Armstrong.

Glycofurol

1. Nonproprietary Names

None adopted.

2. Synonyms

Glycofurol 75; tetraglycol; α-(tetrahydrofuranyl)-ω-hydroxy-poly(oxyethylene); tetrahydrofurfuryl alcohol polyethylene glycol ether.
Note: tetraglycol is also used as a synonym for tetrahydrofurfuryl alcohol.

3. Chemical Name and CAS Registry Number

α-[(Tetrahydro-2-furanyl)methyl]-ω-hydroxy-poly(oxy-1,2-ethanediyl)
[31692-85-0]

4. Empirical Formula   Molecular Weight

$C_9H_{18}O_4$ (average)   190.24 (average)

5. Structural Formula

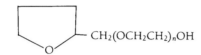

Glycofurol 75: $n = 1$-2

6. Functional Category

Solvent.

7. Applications in Pharmaceutical Formulation or Technology

Glycofurol is used as a solvent in parenteral products for intravenous or intramuscular injection in concentrations up to 50% v/v.

8. Description

Glycofurol is a clear, colorless, almost odorless liquid, with a bitter taste; it produces a warm sensation on the tongue.

9. Pharmacopeial Specifications

—

10. Typical Properties

Boiling point: 80-100°C for *Glycofurol 75*.
Density: 1.070-1.090 g/cm^3 at 20°C
Hydroxyl value: 300-400
Refractive index: $n_D^{40} = 1.4545$
Solubility:

Solvent	Solubility at 20°C
Arachis oil	immiscible
Castor oil	miscible*
Ethanol (95%)	miscible in all proportions
Glycerin	miscible in all proportions

Continued

Solvent	Solubility at 20°C
Isopropyl ether	immiscible
Petroleum ether	immiscible
Polyethylene glycol 400	miscible in all proportions
Propan-2-ol	miscible in all proportions
Propylene glycol	miscible in all proportions
Water	miscible in all proportions*

* Cloudiness may occur.

Viscosity:
8-18 mPa s (8-18 cP) at 20°C for *Glycofurol 75*.
Water content: 0.2-5% at ambient temperature and 30% relative humidity.

11. Stability and Storage Conditions

Stable if stored under nitrogen in a well-closed container protected from light, in a cool, dry, place.

12. Incompatibilities

Incompatible with oxidizing agents.

13. Method of Manufacture

Glycofurol is prepared by the reaction of tetrahydrofurfuryl alcohol with ethylene oxide (followed by a special purification process in the case of *Glycofurol 75*).

14. Safety

Glycofurol is used as a solvent in parenteral pharmaceutical formulations and is generally regarded as a nontoxic and nonirritant material. However, it is irritant if injected undiluted.
The quantity of glycofurol administered parenterally should not exceed 0.07 mL/kg body-weight daily.
LD$_{50}$ (mouse, IV): 3.5 mL/kg

15. Handling Precautions

Observe normal precautions appropriate to the circumstances and quantity of material handled.

16. Regulatory Status

Included in parenteral medicines licensed in Europe.

17. Pharmacopeias

—

18. Related Substances

—

19. Comments

Grades other than *Glycofurol 75* may contain significant amounts of tetrahydrofurfuryl alcohol and other impurities. *Glycofurol 75* meets an analytical specification which includes a requirement that the fraction in which $n = 1$ or 2 amounts to a minimum of 95%, *see* Section 5.

20. Specific References

—

21. General References

Anschel J. Solvents and solubilisers in injections. Pharm Ind 1965; 27: 781-787.

Fiedler HP. Lexikon der Hilfsstoffe für Pharmazie, Kosmetik und angrenzende Gebiete, 3rd Edition. Aulendorf: Editio Cantor, 1989.

Jørgensen L, Artursson P, Bechgaard E. Toxicological and absorption enhancing effects of glycofurol 75 and sodium glycocholate in monolayers of human intestinal epithelial (Caco-2) cells. Int J Pharmaceutics 1993; 95: 209-217.

Spiegel AJ, Noseworthy MM. Use of non-aqueous solvents in parenteral products. J Pharm Sci 1963; 52: 917-927.

Spiegelberg H, Schläpfer R, Zbinden G, Studer A. A new injectable solvent (glycofurol) [in German]. Arzneimittelforschung 1956; 6: 75-77.

Yalkowsky SH, Roseman TJ. Solubilisation of drugs by co-solvents. In: Yalkowsky SH, editor. Techniques of solubilisation of drugs. New York: Marcel Dekker, 1981: 91-134.

22. Authors

UK: HEC Worthington.

Guar Gum

1. Nonproprietary Names

USPNF: Guar gum

2. Synonyms

E412; guar flour; jaguar gum.

3. Chemical Name and CAS Registry Number

Galactomannan polysaccharide [9000-30-0]

4. Empirical Formula   Molecular Weight

$(C_6H_{12}O_6)_n$ $\approx$ 220 000

See Section 5.

5. Structural Formula

Guar gum consists of linear chains of $(1\rightarrow4)$-β-D-mannopyr-anosyl units with α-D-galactopyranosyl units attached by $(1\rightarrow6)$ linkages. The ratio of D-galactose to D-mannose is 1:2. *See also* Section 8.

6. Functional Category

Suspending agent; tablet binder; tablet disintegrant; viscosity-increasing agent.

7. Applications in Pharmaceutical Formulation or Technology

Guar gum is used in cosmetics, food products and pharmaceutical formulations.

In pharmaceuticals, guar gum is used in solid dosage forms as a binder and disintegrant[1-3] and in liquid oral and topical products as a suspending, thickening and stabilizing agent. Therapeutically, guar gum has been used as part of the diet of patients with diabetes mellitus.[4,5] Guar gum has also been used as an appetite suppressant although its use for this purpose, in tablet form, is now banned in the UK,[6,7] *see* Section 14.

Use	Concentration (%)
Emulsion stabilizer	1
Tablet binder	up to 10
Thickener for lotions & creams	up to 2.5

8. Description

The USPNF XVII describes guar gum as a gum obtained from the ground endosperms of *Cyamopsis tetragonolobus* (Linné) Taub. (Fam. Leguminosae). It consists chiefly of a high molecular weight hydrocolloidal polysaccharide, composed of galactan and mannan units combined through glycoside linkages, which may be described chemically as a galactomannan.

Guar gum occurs as an odorless or nearly odorless, white to yellowish-white powder with a bland taste.

9. Pharmacopeial Specifications

Test	USPNF XVII
Identification	+
Loss on drying	$\leqslant$ 15%
Ash	$\leqslant$ 1.5%
Acid-insoluble matter	$\leqslant$ 7%
Arsenic	$\leqslant$ 3 ppm
Lead	$\leqslant$ 0.001%
Heavy metals	$\leqslant$ 0.002%
Protein	$\leqslant$ 10%
Starch	+
Galactomannans	$\geqslant$ 66.0%

10. Typical Properties

Acidity/alkalinity:
pH = 5.0-7.0 (1% w/v aqueous dispersion)

Solubility: practically insoluble in organic solvents. In cold or hot water guar gum disperses and swells almost immediately to form a highly viscous, thixotropic sol. The optimum rate of hydration occurs between pH 7.5-9.0. Finely-milled powders swell more rapidly and are more difficult to disperse. Two to four hours in water at room temperature are required to develop maximum viscosity.

Viscosity (dynamic): 2-3.5 Pa s (2000-3500 cP) for a 1% w/v dispersion. Viscosity is dependent upon temperature, time, concentration, pH, rate of agitation and particle size of the guar gum powder. Synergistic rheological effects may occur with other suspending agents such as xanthan gum, *see* Xanthan Gum.

11. Stability and Storage Conditions

Aqueous guar gum dispersions have a buffering action and are stable between pH 4-10.5. However, prolonged heating reduces the viscosity of dispersions.

Bacteriological stability of guar gum dispersions may be improved by the addition of a mixture of 0.15% methylparaben and 0.02% propylparaben as a preservative. In food applications benzoic acid, citric acid, sodium benzoate or sorbic acid may be used.

Guar gum powder should be stored in a well-closed container in a cool, dry, place.

12. Incompatibilities

Guar gum is compatible with most other plant hydrocolloids such as tragacanth. It is incompatible with acetone, alcohol, tannins, strong acids and alkalis. Borate ions, if present in the dispersing water, will prevent the hydration of guar gum. However, the addition of borate ions to hydrated guar gum produces cohesive structural gels and further hydration is then prevented. The gel formed can be liquefied by reducing the pH to below pH 7 or by heating.

Guar gum may reduce the absorption of penicillin V from some formulations by a quarter.[8]

13. Method of Manufacture

Guar gum is obtained from the ground endosperm of the guar plant, *Cyamopsis tetragonolobus* (Linné) Taub. (Fam. Leguminosae), which is grown in India, Pakistan and the semi-arid southwestern region of the USA.

The seed hull can be removed by grinding, after soaking in sulfuric acid or water, or by charring. The embryo (germ) is removed by differential grinding, since each component possesses a different hardness. The separated endosperm, containing 80% galactomannan is then ground to different particle sizes depending upon final application.

14. Safety

Guar gum is widely used in foods and oral and topical pharmaceutical formulations. Excessive consumption may cause gastrointestinal disturbance such as flatulence, diarrhea or nausea. Therapeutically, daily oral doses of up to 25 g of guar gum have been administered to patients with diabetes mellitus.[4]

Although generally regarded as a nontoxic and nonirritant material the safety of guar gum when used as an appetite suppressant has been questioned. When consumed the gum swells in the stomach to promote a feeling of fullness. However, it is claimed that premature swelling of guar gum tablets may occur and cause obstruction or damage to the oesophagus. Consequently, appetite suppressants containing guar gum in tablet form have been banned in the UK.[7] Appetite suppressants containing microgranules of guar gum are however claimed to be safe.[6] The use of guar gum for pharmaceutical purposes is unaffected by the ban.

In food applications an acceptable daily intake of guar gum has not been specified by the WHO.[9]

LD_{50} (hamster, oral): 6 g/kg[10]
LD_{50} (mouse, oral): 8.1 g/kg
LD_{50} (rabbit, oral): 7 g/kg
LD_{50} (rat, oral): 7.06 g/kg

15. Handling Precautions

Observe normal precautions appropriate to the circumstances and quantity of material handled. Guar gum may be irritating to the eyes. Eye protection, gloves and a dust mask or respirator are recommended.

16. Regulatory Status

GRAS listed. Accepted for use as a food additive in Europe. Included in the FDA Inactive Ingredients Guide (oral suspensions, syrups and tablets). Included in nonparenteral medicines licensed in the UK.

17. Pharmacopeias

Fr, Ind and USPNF.

18. Related Substances

—

19. Comments

—

20. Specific References

1. Feinstein W, Bartilucci AJ. Comparative study of selected disintegrating agents. J Pharm Sci 1966; 55: 332-334.
2. Sakr AM, Elsabbagh HM. Evaluation of guar gum as a tablet additive: a preliminary report. Pharm Ind 1977; 39(4): 399-403.
3. Duru C, et al. A comparative study of the disintegrating efficiency of polysaccharides in a directly-tabletable formulation. Pharmaceut Technol Int 1992; 4(5): 15,16,20,22,23.
4. Jenkins DJA, et al. Treatment of diabetes with guar gum. Lancet 1977; ii: 779-780.
5. Uusitupa MIJ. Fibre in the management of diabetes [letter]. Br Med J 1990; 301: 122.
6. Levin R. Guar gum [letter]. Pharm J 1989; 242: 153.
7. Guar slimming tablets ban. Pharm J 1989; 242: 611.
8. Does guar reduce penicillin V absorption? Pharm J 1987; 239: 123.
9. WHO. Toxicological evaluation of some food additives including anticaking agents, antimicrobials, antioxidants, emulsifiers and thickening agents. WHO Food Add Ser 1974; No. 5: 321-323.
10. Sweet DV, editor. Registry of toxic effects of chemical substances. Cincinnati: US Department of Health, 1987.

21. General References

Ben-Kerrour L, Dûchene D, Puisieux F, Carstensen JT. Temperature- and concentration-dependence in pseudoplastic rheological equations for gum guar solutions. Int J Pharmaceutics 1980; 5: 59-65.
Goldstein AM, Alter EN, Seaman JK. Guar gum. In: Whistler RL, editor. Industrial gums, 2nd edition. New York: Academic Press, 1973: 303-321.
Vemuri S. Flow and consistency index dependence of pseudoplastic guar gum solutions. Drug Dev Ind Pharm 1988; 14: 905-914.

22. Authors

USA: T-SH Chen.

Hydrochloric Acid

1. Nonproprietary Names

BP: Hydrochloric acid
PhEur: Acidum hydrochloricum concentratum
USPNF: Hydrochloric acid

2. Synonyms

Concentrated hydrochloric acid; E507.

3. Chemical Name and CAS Registry Number

Hydrochloric acid [7647-01-0]

4. Empirical Formula   Molecular Weight

HCl   36.46

5. Structural Formula

HCl

6. Functional Category

Acidifying agent.

7. Applications in Pharmaceutical Formulation or Technology

Hydrochloric acid is widely used as an acidifying agent, in a variety of pharmaceutical and food preparations. It may also be used to prepare dilute hydrochloric acid which in addition to its use as an excipient has some therapeutic use, intravenously in the management of metabolic alkalosis, and orally for the treatment of achlorhydria. *See* Section 18.

8. Description

Hydrochloric acid occurs as a clear, colorless, fuming aqueous solution of hydrogen chloride, with a pungent odor.
The BP 1993 and PhEur 1980 specify that hydrochloric acid contains 35.0-39.0% w/w of HCl, while the USPNF XVII specifies that it contains 36.5-38.0% w/w of HCl. *See also* Section 9.

9. Pharmacopeial Specifications

Test	PhEur 1980	USPNF XVII
Identification	+	+
Appearance of solution	+	—
Residue on ignition	—	⩽ 0.008%
Residue on evaporation	⩽ 0.01%	—
Bromide or iodide	—	+
Free bromine	—	+
Free chlorine	⩽ 4 ppm	+
Sulfate	⩽ 20 ppm	+
Sulfite	—	+
Arsenic	⩽ 2 ppm	⩽ 1 ppm
Heavy metals	⩽ 2 ppm	⩽ 5 ppm
Assay (of HCl)	35.0-39.0%	36.5-38.0%

10. Typical Properties

Acidity/alkalinity:
pH = 0.1 (10% v/v aqueous solution)

Boiling point: 110°C (constant boiling mixture of 20.24% w/w HCl)
Density: ≈ 1.18 at 20°C g/cm^3
Freezing point: ≈ -24°C
Refractive index: n_D^{20} = 1.342 (10% v/v aqueous solution)
Solubility: miscible with water.

11. Stability and Storage Conditions

Hydrochloric acid should be stored in a well-closed, glass or other inert container at a temperature below 30°C. Storage in close proximity to concentrated alkalis, metals and cyanides should be avoided.

12. Incompatibilities

Hydrochloric acid reacts violently with alkalis, with the evolution of a large amount of heat. Hydrochloric acid also reacts with many metals, liberating hydrogen.

13. Method of Manufacture

Hydrochloric acid is an aqueous solution of hydrogen chloride gas produced by a number of methods including: from the reaction of sodium chloride and sulfuric acid; from the constituent elements; as a by-product from the electrolysis of sodium hydroxide, or as a by-product during the chlorination of hydrocarbons.

14. Safety

When used diluted, at low concentration, hydrochloric acid is not usually associated with any adverse effects. However, the concentrated solution is corrosive and can cause severe damage on contact with the eyes and skin, or if ingested.

15. Handling Precautions

Caution should be exercised when handling hydrochloric acid and suitable protection against inhalation and spillage should be taken. Eye protection, gloves, face-mask, apron and respirator are recommended, depending on the circumstances and quantity of hydrochloric acid handled. Spillages should be diluted with copious amounts of water and run to waste. Splashes on the skin and eyes should be treated by immediate and prolonged washing with copious amounts of water and medical attention should be sought. Fumes can cause irritation to the eyes, nose and respiratory system; prolonged exposure to fumes may damage the lungs. In the UK, the recommended short-term exposure limit for hydrogen chloride vapor is 7 mg/m^3 (5 ppm).[1]

16. Regulatory Status

GRAS listed. Accepted as a food additive in Europe. Included in the FDA Inactive Ingredients Guide (IM, IV and SC injections, inhalations, ophthalmic preparations, oral solutions, otic and topical preparations). Included in parenteral and nonparenteral medicines licensed in the UK.

17. Pharmacopeias

Aust, Belg, Br, Chin, Egypt, Eur, Fr, Ger, Gr, Ind, It, Jpn, Mex, Neth, Nord, Port, Rom, Swiss, Turk and USPNF. Also in BP Vet.
Note: Cz, Rus, Swiss and Yug also contain monographs for hydrochloric acid 25%.
See also Section 18.

18. Related Substances

Dilute hydrochloric acid.

Dilute hydrochloric acid

Synonyms: acidum hydrochloricum dilutum; diluted hydro-chloric acid.

Pharmacopeias: Aust, Belg, Br, Chin, Cz, Egypt, Eur, Fr, Ger, Gr, Hung, Ind, It, Jpn, Neth, Port, Rom, Rus, Swiss, Turk, USPNF and Yug.

Comments: the BP 1993 and PhEur 1980 specify that dilute hydrochloric acid contains 9.5-10.5% w/w of HCl and is prepared by mixing 274 g of hydrochloric acid with 726 g of water. The USPNF XVII specifies 9.5-10.5% w/v of HCl, prepared by mixing 226 mL of hydrochloric acid with sufficient water to make 1000 mL.

19. Comments

In pharmaceutical formulations, dilute hydrochloric acid is usually used as an acidifying agent in preference to hydrochloric acid.

20. Specific References

1. Health and Safety Executive. EH40/93: occupational exposure limits 1993. London: HMSO, 1993.

21. General References

—

22. Authors

UK: JE Jeffries.

Hydroxyethyl Cellulose

1. Nonproprietary Names

BP: Hydroxyethylcellulose
PhEur: Hydroxyethylcellulosum
USPNF: Hydroxyethyl cellulose

2. Synonyms

Alcoramnosan; *Cellosize*; cellulose, hydroxyethyl ether; HEC; *Idroramnosan*; *Liporamnosan*; *Natrosol*.

3. Chemical Name and CAS Registry Number

Cellulose, 2-hydroxyethyl ether [9004-62-0]

4. Empirical Formula   Molecular Weight

The USPNF XVII describes hydroxyethyl cellulose as a partially substituted poly(hydroxyethyl) ether of cellulose. It is available in several grades, varying in viscosity and degree of substitution, and some grades are modified to improve their dispersion in water. The grades are distinguished by appending a number indicative of the apparent viscosity, in mPa s, of a 2% w/v solution measured at 20°C. Hydroxyethyl cellulose may also contain a suitable anticaking agent.
See Section 5.

5. Structural Formula

Where R is H or $[-CH_2CH_2O-]_mH$

6. Functional Category

Coating agent; suspending agent; tablet binder; thickening agent; viscosity-increasing agent.

7. Applications in Pharmaceutical Formulation or Technology

Hydroxyethyl cellulose is a nonionic, water soluble polymer widely used in pharmaceutical formulations. It is primarily used as a thickening agent in ophthalmic[1] and topical formulations[2] although it is also used as a binder[3] and film-coating agent for tablets.[4]
The concentration of hydroxyethyl cellulose used in a formulation is dependent upon the solvent and the molecular weight of the grade.
Hydroxyethyl cellulose is also widely used in cosmetics.

8. Description

Hydroxyethyl cellulose occurs as a light tan or cream to white-colored, odorless and tasteless, hygroscopic powder.
See Sections 4 and 5.

SEM: 1
Excipient: Hydroxyethyl cellulose (*Natrosol*)
Manufacturer: Aqualon
Magnification: 120x

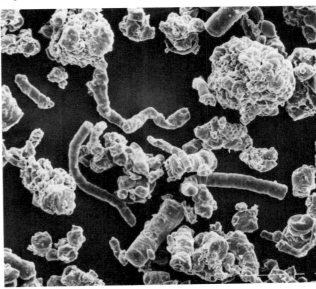

SEM: 2
Excipient: Hydroxyethyl cellulose (*Natrosol*)
Manufacturer: Aqualon
Magnification: 600x

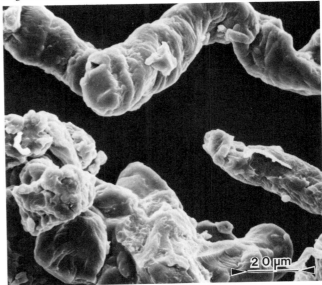

9. Pharmacopeial Specifications

Test	PhEur 1984	USPNF XVII (Suppl 6)
Identification	+	+
Appearance of solution	+	—
Viscosity	+	+
pH (1 in 100)	5.5-8.5	6-8.5
Loss on drying	⩽ 10.0%	⩽ 10.0%
Lead	—	⩽ 0.001%
Residue on ignition	—	⩽ 5.0%
Sulfated ash	⩽ 4.0%	—
Arsenic	—	⩽ 3ppm
Chlorides	⩽ 1.0%	—
Heavy metals	⩽ 20 ppm	⩽ 0.004%
Organic volatile impurities	—	+
Nitrates	+	—

10. Typical Properties

Acidity/alkalinity: pH = 5.5-8.5 for a 1% w/v aqueous solution.

Ash:
2.5% w/w for *Cellosize*;
3.5% w/w for *Natrosol*.

Autoignition temperature: 420°C

Density (bulk):
0.35-0.61 g/cm^3 for *Cellosize*;
0.60 g/cm^3 for *Natrosol*.

Melting point: softens at 135-140°C, decomposes at about 205°C.

Moisture content: commercially available grades of hydroxyethyl cellulose contain less than 5% w/w of water. However, hydroxyethyl cellulose is hygroscopic, the amount of water absorbed depending upon the initial moisture content and the relative humidity of the surrounding air. Typical equilibrium moisture values for *Natrosol 250* at 25°C are: 6% w/w at 50% relative humidity and 29% w/w at 84% relative humidity.

Particle size distribution: for *Cellosize*, 100% through a US #80 mesh (177 μm); for *Natrosol* (regular grind), 10% retained on a US #40 mesh (420 μm); for *Natrosol* (X-grind) 0.5% retained on a US #60 mesh (250 μm).

Refractive index:
n_D^{20} = 1.336 for a 2% w/v aqueous solution.

Solubility: hydroxyethyl cellulose is soluble in either hot or cold water, forming clear, smooth, uniform solutions. Practically insoluble in acetone, ethanol, ether, toluene and most other organic solvents. In some polar organic solvents, such as the glycols, hydroxyethyl cellulose either swells or is partially soluble.

Specific gravity: 1.38-1.40 for *Cellosize*; 1.0033 for a 2% w/v aqueous hydroxyethyl cellulose solution.

Surface tension: see Table I.

Table I: Surface tension (mN/m) of different *Cellosize* (Amerchol Corp) grades at 25°C.

Concentration of aqueous solution (% w/v)	WP-02	*Cellosize* grade 09	300	QP4400	52000	100M
0.01	65.8	65.7	66.4	66.3	65.9	66.1
0.1	65.3	65.4	65.8	65.3	65.4	65.4
1.0	64.4	65.1	65.5	65.8	66.1	66.3

Table I: *Continued*

Concentration of aqueous solution (% w/v)	WP-02	*Cellosize* grade 09	300	QP4400	52000	100M
2.0	64.2	65.0	66.3	67.3	—	—
5.0	64.1	64.7	—	—	—	—
10.0	64.4	65.9	—	—	—	—

Viscosity (dynamic): hydroxyethyl cellulose is available in a wide range of viscosity types, e.g. *Cellosize* is manufactured in eleven regular viscosity grades. Hydroxyethyl cellulose grades differ principally in their aqueous solution viscosities which range from 2-20 000 mPa s for a 2% w/v aqueous solution. Two types of *Cellosize* are produced, a WP-type, which is a normal-dissolving material, and a QP-type, which is a rapid-dispersing material. The lowest viscosity grade (02) is available only in the WP-type. Five viscosity grades (09, 3, 40, 300 and 4400) are produced in both WP- and QP-types. Five high-viscosity grades (10000, 15000, 30000, 52000, and 100M) are produced only in the QP-type. Table II shows the standard *Cellosize* grades and types available and their respective viscosity ranges in aqueous solution.

Natrosol 250 has a degree of substitution of 2.5 and is produced in ten viscosity types. The suffix 'R' denotes that *Natrosol* has been surface treated with glyoxal to aid in solution preparation, see Table III.

Aqueous solutions made using a rapidly dispersing material may be prepared by dispersing the hydroxyethyl cellulose in mildly agitated water at 20-25°C. When the hydroxyethyl cellulose has been thoroughly wetted the temperature of the solution may be increased to 60-70°C to increase the rate of dispersion. Making the solution slightly alkaline also increases the dispersion process. Typically, complete dispersion may be achieved in approximately an hour by controlling the temperature, pH and rate of stirring.

Normally dispersing grades of hydroxyethyl cellulose require more careful handling to avoid agglomeration during dispersion; the water should be vigorously stirred. Alternatively, a slurry of hydroxyethyl cellulose may be prepared in a nonaqueous solvent, such as ethanol, prior to dispersion in water.

See also Section 11 for information on solution stability.

Table II: Approximate viscosities of various grades of aqueous *Cellosize* (Amerchol Corp) solutions at 25°C.

Type	Grade	Concentration (% w/v)	Viscosity (mPa s)[*] Low	High
WP	02	5	7-14	14-20
WP &	09	5	60-100	100-140
QP	3	5	220-285	285-350
	40	2	70-110	110-150
	300	2	250-325	325-400
	4400	2	4200-4700	4700-5200
QP	10000	2	5700	6500
	15000	2	15 000-18 000	18 000-21 000
	30000	1	950-1230	1230-1500
	52000	1	1500-1800	1800-2100
	100M	1	2500	3000

[*] *Cellosize* viscosity grades are available in narrower ranges, as noted by the Low and High designation.

Table III: Approximate viscosities of various grades of aqueous *Natrosol 250* (Aqualon) solutions at 25°C.

| Type | Viscosity (mPa s) for varying concentrations (% w/v). | | |
	1%	2%	5%
HHR	3400-5000	—	—
H4R	2600-3300	—	—
HR	1500-2500	—	—
MHR	800-1500	—	—
MR	—	4500-6500	—
KR	—	1500-2500	—
GR	—	150-400	—
ER	—	25-105	—
JR	—	—	150-400
LR	—	—	75-150

| HPE Laboratory Project Data | | | |
	Method	Lab#	Results
Particle Friability			
Natrosol 250L	PF-1	36	0.050%
Natrosol 250HHR	PF-1	36	0.008%
Viscosity			
Natrosol 250L (5%)	VIS-4	6	150-225 mPa s
Natrosol 250MR (1%)	VIS-4	6	190-375 mPa s
Natrosol 250MR (2%)	VIS-4	6	4250-7250 mPa s
Natrosol 250HHR (1%)	VIS-4	6	3275-5875 mPa s

Supplier: Aqualon.

11. Stability and Storage Conditions

Hydroxyethyl cellulose powder is a stable, though hygroscopic, material.

Aqueous solutions of hydroxyethyl cellulose are relatively stable between pH 2-12 with the viscosity of solutions being largely unaffected. However, solutions are less stable below pH 5 due to hydrolysis. At high pH, oxidation may occur.

Increasing temperature reduces the viscosity of aqueous hydroxyethyl cellulose solutions. However, on cooling, the original viscosity is restored. Solutions may be subjected to freeze-thawing, high temperature storage or boiling without precipitation or gelation occurring.

Hydroxyethyl cellulose is subject to enzymatic degradation, with consequent loss in viscosity of its solutions.[5] Enzymes which catalyze this degradation are produced by many bacteria and fungi present in the environment. For prolonged storage, an antimicrobial preservative should therefore be added to aqueous solutions. Aqueous solutions of hydroxyethyl cellulose may also be sterilized by autoclaving.

Hydroxyethyl cellulose powder should be stored in a well-closed container, in a cool, dry, place.

12. Incompatibilities

Hydroxyethyl cellulose is insoluble in most organic solvents. Hydroxyethyl cellulose is incompatible with zein and partially compatible with the following water-soluble compounds: casein; gelatin; methylcellulose; polyvinyl alcohol and starch.

Hydroxyethyl cellulose can be used with a wide variety of water-soluble antimicrobial preservatives. However, sodium pentachlorophenate produces an immediate viscosity increase when added to hydroxyethyl cellulose solutions.

Hydroxyethyl cellulose has good tolerance for dissolved electrolytes although it may be salted out of solution when mixed with certain salt solutions, e.g. the following salt solutions will precipitate a 10% w/v solution of *Cellosize WP-09* and a 2% w/v solution of *Cellosize WP-4400*: sodium carbonate 50%; and saturated solutions of aluminum sulfate; ammonium sulfate; chromic sulfate; disodium phosphate; magnesium sulfate; potassium ferrocyanide; sodium sulfate; sodium sulfite; sodium thiosulfate and zinc sulfate.

Natrosol is soluble in most 10% salt solutions, except sodium carbonate and sodium sulfate, and many 50% salt solutions except: aluminum sulfate; ammonium sulfate; diammonium phosphate; disodium phosphate; ferric chloride; magnesium sulfate; potassium ferrocyanide; sodium metaborate; sodium nitrate; sodium sulfite; trisodium phosphate and zinc sulfate. *Natrosol 150* is generally more tolerant of dissolved salts than *Natrosol 250*.

Hydroxyethyl cellulose is also incompatible with certain fluorescent dyes or optical brighteners, and certain quaternary disinfectants which will increase the viscosity of aqueous solutions.

13. Method of Manufacture

A purified form of cellulose is reacted with sodium hydroxide to produce a swollen alkali cellulose which is chemically more reactive than untreated cellulose. The alkali cellulose is then reacted with ethylene oxide, to produce a series of hydroxyethyl cellulose ethers.

The manner in which ethylene oxide is added to cellulose can be described by two terms: the degree of substitution (DS) and the molar substitution (MS). The degree of substitution designates the average number of hydroxyl positions on the anhydroglucose unit that have been reacted with ethylene oxide. Since each anhydroglucose unit of the cellulose molecule has three hydroxyl groups, the maximum value for DS is 3. Molar substitution is defined as the average number of ethylene oxide molecules that have reacted with each anhydroglucose unit. Once a hydroxyethyl group is attached to each unit, it can further react with additional groups in an end-to-end formation. This reaction can continue and, theoretically, there is no limit for molar substitution.

14. Safety

Hydroxyethyl cellulose is primarily used in ophthalmic and topical pharmaceutical formulations. It is generally regarded as an essentially nontoxic and nonirritant material.[6,7]

Acute and subacute oral toxicity studies, in rats, have shown no toxic effects attributable to hydroxyethyl cellulose consumption, the hydroxyethyl cellulose being neither absorbed nor hydrolyzed in the rat gastrointestinal tract. However, although used in oral pharmaceutical formulations hydroxyethyl cellulose has not been approved for direct use in food products, *see* Section 16.

Glyoxal-treated hydroxyethyl cellulose is not recommended for use in oral pharmaceutical formulations or topical preparations which may be used on mucous membranes. Hydroxyethyl cellulose is also not recommended for use in parenteral products.

15. Handling Precautions

Observe normal precautions appropriate to the circumstances and quantity of material handled. Hydroxyethyl cellulose dust may be irritant to the eyes and therefore eye protection is recommended. Excessive dust generation should be avoided to minimize the risks of explosions. Hydroxyethyl cellulose is combustible.

16. Regulatory Status

Included in the FDA Inactive Ingredients Guide (ophthalmic preparations, oral syrups and tablets, otic and topical preparations). Included in nonparenteral medicines licensed in the UK.

Hydroxyethyl cellulose is not currently approved for use in food products in Europe or the US although it is permitted for use in indirect applications such as packaging. This restriction is due to the high levels of ethylene glycol residues which are formed during the manufacturing process.

17. Pharmacopeias

Br, Eur, Fr, Ger, Gr, Hung, It, Neth, Port, Swiss and USPNF.

18. Related Substances

Ethylcellulose; Hydroxypropyl Cellulose; Hydroxypropyl Methylcellulose; Methylcellulose.

19. Comments

The limited scope for the use of hydroxyethyl cellulose in foodstuffs is in stark contrast to its widespread application as an excipient in oral pharmaceutical formulations.

20. Specific References

1. Grove J, Durr M, Quint M-P, Plazonnet B. The effect of vehicle viscosity on the ocular bioavailability of L-653328. Int J Pharmaceutics 1990; 66: 23-28.
2. Gauger LJ. Hydroxyethylcellulose gel as a dinoprostone vehicle. Am J Hosp Pharm 1984; 41: 1761-1762.
3. Delonca H, Joachim J, Mattha A. Influence of temperature on disintegration and dissolution time of tablets with a cellulose component as binder [in French]. J Pharm Belg 1978; 33: 171-178.
4. Kovács B, Merényi G. Evaluation of tack behavior of coating solutions. Drug Dev Ind Pharm 1990; 16: 2302-2323.
5. Wirick MG. Study of the substitution pattern of hydroxyethyl cellulose and its relationship to enzymic degradation. J Polymer Sci 1968; 6(Part A-1): 1705-1718.
6. Final report on the safety assessment of hydroxyethylcellulose, hydroxypropylcellulose, methylcellulose, hydroxypropyl methylcellulose and cellulose gum. J Am Coll Toxicol 1986; 5(3): 1-60.
7. Durand-Cavagna G, Delort P, Duprat P, Bailly Y, Plazonnet B, Gordon LR. Corneal toxicity studies in rabbits and dogs with hydroxyethyl cellulose and benzalkonium chloride. Fundam Appl Toxicol 1989; 13: 500-508.

21. General References

Amerchol Corp. Technical literature: *Cellosize*, hydroxyethyl cellulose, 1993.

Aqualon. Technical literature: *Natrosol*, hydroxyethyl cellulose, 1993.

Chauveau C, Maillols H, Delonca H. Natrosol 250 part 1: characterization and modeling of rheological behavior [in French]. Pharm Acta Helv 1986; 61: 292-297.

Doelker E. Cellulose derivatives. Adv Polymer Sci 1993; 107: 199-265.

Haugen P, Tung MA, Runikis JO. Steady shear flow properties, rheological reproducibility and stability of aqueous hydroxyethylcellulose dispersions. Can J Pharm Sci 1978; 13: 4-7.

Klug ED. Some properties of water-soluble hydroxyalkyl celluloses and their derivatives. J Polymer Sci 1971; 36(Part C): 491-508.

Rufe RG. Cellulose polymers in cosmetics and toiletries. Cosmet Perfum 1975; 90(3): 93-94, 99-100.

22. Authors

USA: RJ Harwood, JL Johnson.

Hydroxypropyl Cellulose

1. Nonproprietary Names

BP: Hydroxypropylcellulose
PhEur: Hydroxypropylcellulosum
USPNF: Hydroxypropyl cellulose

2. Synonyms

Cellulose, hydroxypropyl ether; E463; hyprolose; *Klucel*; *Methocel*; *Nisso HPC*; oxypropylated cellulose.

3. Chemical Name and CAS Registry Number

Cellulose, 2-hydroxypropyl ether [9004-64-2]

4. Empirical Formula　　Molecular Weight

The USPNF XVII describes hydroxypropyl cellulose as a partially substituted poly(hydroxypropyl) ether of cellulose. It may contain not more than 0.6% of silica or some other suitable anticaking agent. Hydroxypropyl cellulose is commercially available in a number of different grades which have different solution viscosities. Molecular weight ranges from 50 000-1 250 000, *see also* Section 10.

5. Structural Formula

Where R is H or $[-CH_2-CH(CH_3)-O]_mH$

6. Functional Category

Coating agent; emulsifying agent; stabilizing agent; suspending agent; tablet binder; thickening agent; viscosity-increasing agent.

7. Applications in Pharmaceutical Formulation or Technology

Hydroxypropyl cellulose is widely used in oral and topical pharmaceutical formulations.

In oral products, hydroxypropyl cellulose is primarily used in tableting as a binder, film-coating and extended release matrix former. Concentrations of between 2-6% w/w of hydroxypropyl cellulose may be used as a binder in either wet granulation or dry, direct compression tableting processes.[1-5] Concentrations of between 15-35% w/w of hydroxypropyl cellulose may be used to produce tablets with an extended drug release.[6] The release rate of a drug increases with decreasing viscosity of hydroxypropyl cellulose. The addition of an anionic surfactant similarly increases the hydroxypropyl cellulose viscosity and hence decreases the release rate of a drug. Typically, a 5% w/w solution of hydroxypropyl cellulose may be used to film-coat tablets. Either aqueous solutions, containing hydroxypropyl cellulose along with some methylcellulose, or ethanolic solutions may be used.[7-9] Stearic acid or palmitic acid may be added to ethanolic hydroxypropyl cellulose solutions as plasticizers. A low-substituted hydroxypropyl cellulose is used as a tablet disintegrant, *see* Section 18.

Hydroxypropyl cellulose is also used in microencapsulation processes and as a thickening agent. In topical formulations, hydroxypropyl cellulose is used in transdermal patches and ophthalmic preparations.[10-12]

Hydroxypropyl cellulose is also used in cosmetics and in food products as an emulsifier and stabilizer.

Use	Concentration (%)
Extended release matrix former	15-35
Tablet binder	2-6
Tablet film coating	5

8. Description

Hydroxypropyl cellulose is a white to slightly yellow-colored, odorless and tasteless powder. *See also* Sections 4 and 5.

SEM: 1
Excipient: Hydroxypropyl cellulose (*Klucel*)
Manufacturer: Aqualon
Magnification: 60x

SEM: 2

Excipient: Hydroxypropyl cellulose (*Klucel*)
Manufacturer: Åqualon
Magnification: 600x

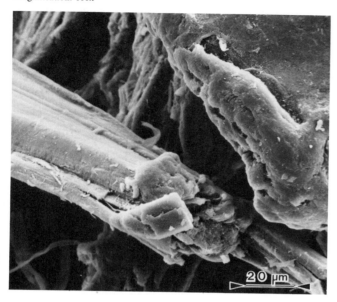

20 μm

9. Pharmacopeial Specifications

Test	PhEur 1992	USPNF XVII (Suppl 6)
Identification	+	+
Apparent viscosity	+	+
Appearance of solution	+	—
pH (1 in 100)	5.0-8.5	5.0-8.0
Loss on drying	≤ 7.0%	≤ 5.0%
Residue on ignition	—	≤ 0.2%
Sulfated ash	≤ 1.6%	—
Arsenic	—	≤ 3 ppm
Chlorides	≤ 0.5%	—
Lead	—	≤ 0.001%
Heavy metals	≤ 20 ppm	≤ 0.004%
Silica	≤ 0.6%	≤ 0.6%
Organic volatile impurities	—	+
Assay of hydroxypropoxy groups	—	≤ 80.5%

10. Typical Properties

Acidity/alkalinity:
pH = 5.0-8.5 for a 1% w/v aqueous solution.
Density (bulk): ≈ 0.5 g/cm^3
Interfacial tension: 12.5 mN/m for a 0.1% w/v aqueous solution versus mineral oil.
Melting point: softens at 130°C; chars at 260-275°C.
Moisture content: hydroxypropyl cellulose absorbs moisture from the atmosphere, the amount of water absorbed depending upon the initial moisture content, and the temperature and relative humidity of the surrounding air.

Typical equilibrium moisture content values at 25°C are: 4% w/w at 50% relative humidity and 12% w/w at 84% relative humidity. *See also* HPE Data.
Molecular weight:
for *Klucel EF* ≈ 80 000
for *Klucel LF* ≈ 95 000
for *Klucel JF* ≈ 140 000
for *Klucel GF* ≈ 370 000
for *Klucel MF* ≈ 850 000
for *Klucel HF* ≈ 1 150 000.
Particle size distribution: for *Klucel* (regular grind), 95% through a US #30 mesh (590 μm) and 99% through a US #20 mesh (840 μm); for *Klucel* (X-grind), 100% through a US #60 mesh (250 μm) and 80% through a US #100 mesh (149 μm).
Refractive index:
n_D^{20} = 1.3353 for a 2% w/v aqueous solution.
Solubility: soluble 1 in 10 parts dichloromethane, 1 in 2.5 parts ethanol, 1 in 2 parts methanol, 1 in 5 parts propan-2-ol, 1 in 5 parts propylene glycol and 1 in 2 parts water; practically insoluble in aliphatic hydrocarbons, aromatic hydrocarbons, carbon tetrachloride, petroleum distillates, glycerin and oils.
Hydroxypropyl cellulose is freely soluble in water below 38°C forming a smooth, clear, colloidal solution. In hot water, it is insoluble and is precipitated as a highly swollen floc at a temperature between 40-45°C.
Hydroxypropyl cellulose is soluble in many cold or hot polar organic solvents such as: dimethyl formamide; dimethyl sulfoxide; dioxane; ethanol; methanol; propan-2-ol (95%) and propylene glycol. There is no tendency for precipitation in hot organic solvents. However, the grade of hydroxypropyl cellulose can have a marked effect upon solution quality in some organic liquids which are borderline solvents, such as: acetone; butyl acetate; cyclohexanol; dichloromethane; lactic acid; methylacetate; methylethyl ketone; propan-2-ol (99%) and *tert*-butanol. The higher viscosity grades of hydroxypropyl cellulose tend to produce slightly inferior solutions. However, the solution quality in borderline solvents can often be greatly improved by the use of small quantities (5-15%) of a cosolvent. For example, dichloromethane is a borderline solvent for *Klucel HF* and solutions have a granular texture, but by adding 10% methanol a smooth solution may be produced.
Hydroxypropyl cellulose is compatible with a number of high molecular weight, high boiling waxes and oils, and can be used to modify certain properties of these materials. Examples of materials that are good solvents for hydroxypropyl cellulose at an elevated temperature are: acetylated monoglycerides; glycerides; pine oil; polyethylene glycol and polypropylene glycol.
Specific gravity: 1.2224 for particles; 1.0064 for a 2% w/v aqueous solution at 20°C.
Surface tension: *see* Table I.

Table I: Surface tension (mN/m) of aqueous solutions of *Nisso HPC* (Nippon Soda Co Ltd) at 20°C.

Grade	Surface tension at 20°C (mN/m) Concentration			
	0.01%	0.1%	1.0%	10.0%
Nisso HPC-L	51.0	49.1	46.3	45.8
Nisso HPC-M	54.8	49.7	46.3	—

Viscosity (dynamic): a wide range of viscosity types are commercially available, *see* Table II and HPE Data. Solutions should be prepared by gradually adding the hydroxypropyl cellulose to a vigorously stirred solvent. Increasing concentration produces solutions of increased viscosity. *See also* Section 11 for information on solution stability.

Table II: Viscosity of aqueous solutions of *Klucel* (Aqualon) at 25°C.

Grade	Viscosity (mPa s) of various aqueous solutions Concentration			
	1%	**2%**	**5%**	**10%**
Klucel HF	1500-3000	—	—	—
Klucel MF	—	4000-6500	—	—
Klucel GF	—	150-400	—	—
Klucel JF	—	—	150-400	—
Klucel LF	—	—	75-150	—
Klucel EF	—	—	—	200-600

	HPE Laboratory Project Data		
	Method	**Lab #**	**Results**
Moisture content			
Type LH-21[*]	MC-7	14	3.81% [a]
Klucel HF	MC-7	14	4.27% [b]
Klucel MF	MC-7	14	1.52% [b]
Klucel GF	MC-7	14	1.67% [b]
Klucel JF	MC-7	14	1.44% [b]
Klucel LF	MC-7	14	2.21% [b]
Klucel EF	MC-7	14	0.59% [b]
Klucel	EMC-1	15	*See* Fig. 1. [b]
Type LH-11[*]	SDI-1	14	*See* Fig. 2. [a]
Klucel HF	SDI-1	14	*See* Fig. 2. [b]
Klucel MF	SDI-1	14	*See* Fig. 2. [b]
Klucel EF	SDI-1	14	*See* Fig. 3. [b]
Klucel GF	SDI-1	14	*See* Fig. 3. [b]
Klucel JF	SDI-1	14	*See* Fig. 3. [b]
Klucel LF	SDI-1	14	*See* Fig. 3. [b]
Particle friability	PF-1	36	0.125% [c]
Solubility [c]			
Ethanol (95%) at 25°C	SOL-7	32	0.14 mg/mL
Ethanol (95%) at 37°C	SOL-7	32	0.24 mg/mL
Hexane at 25°C	SOL-7	32	1.0 mg/mL
Hexane at 37°C	SOL-7	32	1.0 mg/mL
Propylene glycol at 25°C	SOL-7	32	1.0 mg/mL
Propylene glycol at 37°C	SOL-7	32	1.0 mg/mL
Water at 25°C	SOL-7	32	500 mg/mL
Water at 37°C	SOL-7	32	500 mg/mL
Viscosity [b]			
Klucel EF (10% w/v)	VIS-1	6	410-740 mPa s
Klucel GF (2% w/v)	VIS-1	6	360-615 mPa s
Klucel GF (3% w/v)	VIS-1	6	1350-1625 mPa s
Klucel HF (1% w/v)	VIS-1	6	1800-3250 mPa s
Klucel HF (2% w/v)	VIS-1	6	2325-3300 mPa s

Supplier: a. Biddle Sawyer Corporation; b. Aqualon; c. Shin-Etsu Chemical Co Ltd.

[*] Note that *Type LH-11* and *LH-21* are low-substituted grades of hydroxypropyl cellulose, *see also* Section 18.

11. Stability and Storage Conditions

Hydroxypropyl cellulose powder is a stable material although it is hygroscopic after drying.

Aqueous solutions of hydroxypropyl cellulose are stable between pH 6.0-8.0 with the viscosity of solutions being relatively unaffected. However, at low pH aqueous solutions may undergo acid hydrolysis, which causes chain scission and hence a decrease in solution viscosity. The rate of hydrolysis

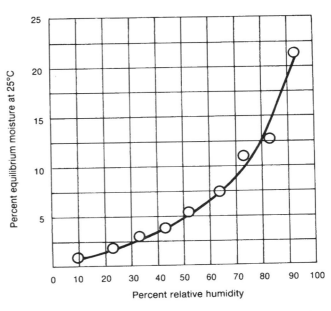

Fig. 1: Equilibrium moisture content of hydroxypropyl cellulose (*Klucel*).

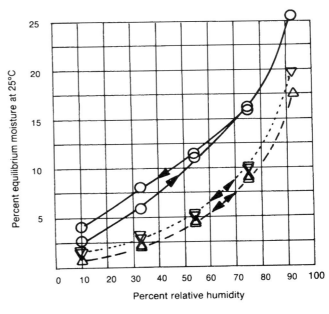

Fig. 2: Equilibrium moisture content of various grades of hydroxypropyl cellulose.
○ *Type LH-11* (Biddle Sawyer Corporation, Lot #8069).
△ *Klucel HF* (Aqualon, Lot #1061).
▽ *Klucel MF* (Aqualon, Lot #1294).
Note that *Type LH-11* is a low-substituted grade of hydroxypropyl cellulose.

increases with increasing temperature and hydrogen ion concentration. At high pH, alkali-catalyzed oxidation may degrade the polymer and result in a decrease in viscosity of solutions. This degradation can occur due to the presence of dissolved oxygen or oxidizing agents in a solution.

Increasing temperature causes the viscosity of aqueous solutions to gradually decrease until the viscosity drops

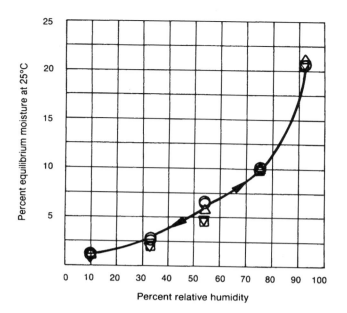

Fig. 3: Equilibrium moisture content of various grades of hydroxypropyl cellulose.
○ *Klucel GF* (Aqualon, Lot #4996).
△ *Klucel JF* (Aqualon, Lot #4753).
▽ *Klucel LF* (Aqualon, Lot #4965).
□ *Klucel EF* (Aqualon, Lot #1223).

suddenly at about 45°C due to the limited solubility of hydroxypropyl cellulose. However, this process is reversible and on cooling the original viscosity is restored.

The high level of substitution of hydroxypropyl cellulose improves the resistance of the polymer to degradation by molds and bacteria.[9] However, aqueous solutions are susceptible to degradation under severe conditions and a viscosity decrease may thus occur. Certain enzymes, produced by microbial action, will degrade hydroxypropyl cellulose in solution.[13] For prolonged storage, an antimicrobial preservative should therefore be added to aqueous solutions. Solutions of hydroxypropyl cellulose in organic solvents do not generally require preservatives.

Ultraviolet light will also degrade hydroxypropyl cellulose and aqueous solutions may therefore slightly decrease in viscosity if exposed to light for several months.

Aqueous hydroxypropyl cellulose solutions thus have optimum stability when the pH is maintained between pH 6.0-8.0 and the solution is protected from light, heat and the action of microorganisms.

Hydroxypropyl cellulose powder should be stored in a well-closed container in a cool, dry, place.

12. Incompatibilities

Hydroxypropyl cellulose in solution demonstrates some incompatibility with substituted phenol derivatives, such as methylparaben and propylparaben. The presence of anionic polymers may increase the viscosity of hydroxypropyl cellulose solutions.

The compatibility of hydroxypropyl cellulose with inorganic salts varies depending upon the salt and its concentration, *see* Table III; hydroxypropyl cellulose may not tolerate high concentrations of other dissolved materials. The balance of the

hydrophilic-lipophilic properties of the polymer, which are required for dual solubility, reduces its ability to hydrate with water and it therefore tends to be salted out in the presence of high concentrations of other dissolved materials.

The precipitation temperature of hydroxypropyl cellulose is lower in the presence of relatively high concentrations of other dissolved materials that compete for the water in the system, *see* Table IV.

Table III: Compatibility of hydroxypropyl cellulose (*Nisso HPC*) with inorganic salts in aqueous solutions.

Salt	Concentration of salt (% w/w)						
	2	3	5	7	10	30	50
Aluminum sulfate	S	S	I	I	I	I	I
Ammonium nitrate	S	S	S	S	S	I	I
Ammonium sulfate	S	S	I	I	I	I	I
Calcium chloride	S	S	S	S	S	T	I
Dichromic acid	S	S	S	S	S	S	S
Disodium hydrogenphosphate	S	S	I	I	I	I	I
Ferric chloride	S	S	S	S	S	I	I
Potassium ferrocyanide	S	S	S	I	I	I	I
Silver nitrate	S	S	S	S	S	S	T
Sodium acetate	S	S	S	S	I	I	I
Sodium carbonate	S	S	I	I	I	I	I
Sodium chloride	S	S	S	S	I	I	I
Sodium nitrate	S	S	S	S	S	I	I
Sodium sulfate	S	S	I	I	I	I	I
Sodium sulfite	S	S	I	I	I	I	I
Sodium thiosulfate	T	T	T	I	I	I	I

S: completely soluble   T: turbid white   I: insoluble

Table IV: Variation in precipitation temperature of hydroxypropyl cellulose (*Klucel H*) in the presence of other materials.

Ingredients and concentrations	Precipitation temperature (°C)
1% *Klucel H*	41
1% *Klucel H* + 1.0% NaCl	38
1% *Klucel H* + 5.0% NaCl	30
0.5% *Klucel H* + 10% Sucrose	41
0.5% *Klucel H* + 30% Sucrose	32
0.5% *Klucel H* + 40% Sucrose	20
0.5% *Klucel H* + 50% Sucrose	7

13. Method of Manufacture

A purified form of cellulose is reacted with sodium hydroxide to produce a swollen alkali cellulose which is chemically more reactive than untreated cellulose. The alkali cellulose is then reacted with propylene oxide at elevated temperature and pressure. The propylene oxide can be substituted on the cellulose through an ether linkage at the three reactive hydroxyls present on each anhydroglucose monomer unit of the cellulose chain. Etherification takes place in such a way that hydroxypropyl substituent groups contain almost entirely secondary hydroxyls. The secondary hydroxyl present in the side chain is available for further reaction with the propylene oxide, and 'chaining-out' may take place. This results in the formation of side chains containing more than one mole of combined propylene oxide.

14. Safety

Hydroxypropyl cellulose is widely used as an excipient in oral and topical pharmaceutical formulations. It is also extensively used in cosmetics and food products.

Hydroxypropyl cellulose is generally regarded as an essentially nontoxic and nonirritant material.[14] However, the use of hydroxypropyl cellulose as a solid ocular insert has been associated with rare reports of discomfort or irritation, including hypersensitivity and edema of the eyelids. Adverse reactions to hydroxypropyl cellulose are rare but have included a report, in a single patient, of allergic contact dermatitis due to hydroxypropyl cellulose in a transdermal estradiol patch.[15] The WHO has not specified an acceptable daily intake for hydroxypropyl cellulose since the levels consumed were not considered to represent a hazard to health.[16] Excessive consumption of hydroxypropyl cellulose may however have a laxative effect.

LD_{50} (mouse, IP): > 25 g/kg[17]
LD_{50} (mouse, IV): > 0.5 g/kg
LD_{50} (mouse, oral): > 5 g/kg
LD_{50} (rat, IP): > 25 g/kg
LD_{50} (rat, IV): 0.25 g/kg
LD_{50} (rat, oral): 10.2 g/kg

15. Handling Precautions

Observe normal precautions appropriate to the circumstances and quantity of material handled. Hydroxypropyl cellulose dust may be irritant to the eyes; eye protection is recommended. Excessive dust generation should be avoided to minimize the risks of explosions.

16. Regulatory Status

GRAS listed. Accepted as a food additive in Europe. Included in the FDA Inactive Ingredients Guide (oral capsules and tablets, topical and transdermal preparations). Included in nonparenteral medicines licensed in the UK.

17. Pharmacopeias

Br, Eur, Fr, Ger, Hung, It, Jpn, Neth, Port, Swiss and USPNF.

18. Related Substances

Hydroxyethyl Cellulose; Hydroxypropyl Methylcellulose; low-substituted hydroxypropyl cellulose.

Low-substituted hydroxypropyl cellulose:
CAS number: [78214-41-2]
Synonyms: cellulose, 2-hydroxypropyl ether (low-substituted); L-HPC.
Pharmacopeias: Jpn and USPNF.
Angle of repose:
49° for *L-HPC Type LH-11*;
45° for *L-HPC Type LH-21*.
Density (bulk):
0.34 g/cm³ for *L-HPC Type LH-11*;
0.40 g/cm³ for *L-HPC Type LH-21*.
Density (tapped):
0.57 g/cm³ for *L-HPC Type LH-11*;
0.65 g/cm³ for *L-HPC Type LH-21*.
Moisture content: ⩽ 5.0% w/w
Particle size distribution: average particle size for *L-HPC Type LH-11* is 50.6 μm; for *L-HPC Type LH-21* it is 41.7 μm.[18]
Solubility: insoluble in water but swells.
Specific gravity: 1.46

Specific surface area:[18]
L-HPC Type LH-11 = 2.70 m²/g;
L-HPC Type LH-21 = 3.20 m²/g;
L-HPC Type LH-31 = 5.24 m²/g;
L-HPC Type LH-41 = 31.60 m²/g.
Safety: LD_{50} (rat, oral): > 15 g/kg[17]
Comments: a low-substituted hydroxypropyl cellulose containing 5-16% of hydroxypropoxy groups. Used as a sustained release tablet matrix former and as a tablet disintegrant.[18,19]

19. Comments

Hydroxypropyl cellulose is a thermoplastic polymer that can be processed by virtually all fabrication methods used for plastics.

20. Specific References

1. Machida Y, Nagai T. Directly compressed tablets containing hydroxypropyl cellulose in addition to starch or lactose. Chem Pharm Bull 1974; 22: 2346-2351.
2. Delonca H, Joachim J, Mattha AG. Binding activity of hydroxypropyl cellulose (200,000 and 1,000,000 mol. wt.) and its effect on the physical characteristics of granules and tablets. Farmaco (Prat) 1977; 32: 157-171.
3. Delonca H, Joachim J, Mattha A. Effect of temperature on disintegration and dissolution time of tablets with a cellulose component as a binder [in French]. J Pharm Belg 1978; 33: 171-178.
4. Stafford JW, Pickard JF, Zink R. Temperature dependence of the disintegration times of compressed tablets containing hydroxypropyl cellulose as binder. J Pharm Pharmacol 1978; 30: 1-5.
5. Kitamori N, Makino T. Improvement in pressure-dependent dissolution of trepibutone tablets by using intragranular disintegrants. Drug Dev Ind Pharm 1982; 8: 125-139.
6. Johnson JL, Holinej J, Williams MD. Influence of ionic strength on matrix integrity and drug release from hydroxypropyl cellulose compacts. Int J Pharmaceutics 1993; 90: 151-159.
7. Lindberg NO. Water vapour transmission through free films of hydroxypropyl cellulose. Acta Pharm Suec 1971; 8: 541-548.
8. Banker G, Peck G, Williams E, Taylor D, Pirakitikulr P. Evaluation of hydroxypropylcellulose and hydroxypropylmethylcellulose as aqueous based film coatings. Drug Dev Ind Pharm 1981; 7: 693-716.
9. Banker G, Peck G, Williams E, Taylor D, Pirakitikulr P. Microbiological considerations of polymer solutions used in aqueous film coating. Drug Dev Ind Pharm 1982; 8: 41-51.
10. Cohen EM, Grim WM, Harwood RJ, Mehta GN. Solid state ophthalmic medication. US Patent 4179497, 1979.
11. Harwood RJ, Schwartz JB. Drug release from compression molded films: preliminary studies with pilocarpine. Drug Dev Ind Pharm 1982; 8: 663-682.
12. Dumortier G, Zuber M, Chast F, Sandouk P, Chaumeil JC. Systemic absorption of morphine after ocular administration: evaluation of morphine salt insert in vitro and in vivo. Int J Pharmaceutics 1990; 59: 1-7.
13. Wirick MG. Study of the enzymic degradation of CMC and other cellulose ethers. J Polymer Sci 1968; 6(Part A-1): 1965-1974.
14. Final report on the safety assessment of hydroxyethylcellulose, hydroxypropylcellulose, methylcellulose, hydroxypropyl methylcellulose and cellulose gum. J Am Coll Toxicol 1986; 5(3): 1-60.
15. Schwartz BK, Clendenning WE. Allergic contact dermatitis from hydroxypropyl cellulose in a transdermal estradiol patch. Contact Dermatitis 1988; 18: 106-107.
16. FAO/WHO. Evaluation of certain food additives and contaminants: thirty-fifth report of the joint FAO/WHO expert

committee on food additives. Tech Rep Ser Wld Hlth Org 1990; No. 789.

17. Sweet DV, editor. Registry of toxic effects of chemical substances. Cincinnati: US Department of Health, 1987.

18. Kawashima Y, Takeuchi H, Hino T, Niwa T, Lin T-L, Sekigawa F, Kawahara K. Low-substituted hydroxypropylcellulose as a sustained-drug release matrix base or disintegrant depending on its particle size and loading in formulation. Pharm Res 1993; 10: 351-355.

19. Kleinebudde P. Application of low substituted hydroxypropyl-cellulose (L-HPC) in the production of pellets using extrusion/spheronization. Int J Pharmaceutics 1993; 96: 119-128.

21. General References

Aqualon. Technical literature: *Klucel*, hydroxypropyl cellulose, a nonionic water-soluble polymer, physical and chemical properties, 1987.

Doelker E. Cellulose derivatives. Adv Polymer Sci 1993; 107: 199-265.

Ganz AJ. Thermoplastic food production. US Patent 3769029, 1973.

Klug ED. Some properties of water-soluble hydroxyalkyl celluloses and their derivatives. J Polymer Sci 1971; 36(Part C): 491-508.

Nippon Soda Co Ltd. Technical literature: *Nisso HPC*, 1993.

Opota O, Maillols H, Acquier R, Delonca H, Fortune R. Rheological behavior of aqueous solutions of hydroxypropylcellulose: influence of concentration and molecular mass [in French]. Pharm Acta Helv 1988; 63: 26-32.

Shin-Etsu Chemical Co Ltd. Technical literature: *L-HPC*, low-substituted hydroxypropyl cellulose, 1991.

22. Authors

USA: RJ Harwood, JL Johnson.

Hydroxypropyl Methylcellulose

1. Nonproprietary Names

BP: Hypromellose
PhEur: Methylhydroxypropylcellulosum
USP: Hydroxypropyl methylcellulose

2. Synonyms

Cellulose, hydroxypropyl methyl ether; *Culminal MHPC*; E464; HPMC; *Methocel*; methylcellulose propylene glycol ether; methyl hydroxypropylcellulose; *Metolose*; *Pharmacoat*.

3. Chemical Name and CAS Registry Number

Cellulose, 2-Hydroxypropyl methyl ether
[9004-65-3]

4. Empirical Formula Molecular Weight

The PhEur 1992 describes hydroxypropyl methylcellulose as a partly *O*-methylated and *O*-(2-hydroxypropylated) cellulose. It is available in several grades which vary in viscosity and extent of substitution. Grades may be distinguished by appending a number indicative of the apparent viscosity, in mPa s, of a 2% w/w aqueous solution at 20°C. Hydroxypropyl methylcellulose defined in the USP XXII specifies the substitution type by appending a four digit number to the nonproprietary name, e.g. hydroxypropyl methylcellulose 1828. The first two digits refer to the approximate percentage content of the methoxy group (OCH_3). The second two digits refer to the approximate percentage content of the hydroxypropoxy group ($OCH_2CHOHCH_3$), calculated on a dried basis. Molecular weight is approximately 10 000-1 500 000.

5. Structural Formula

Where R is H, CH_3 or [$CH_3CH(OH)CH_2$].

6. Functional Category

Coating agent; film-former; stabilizing agent; suspending agent; tablet binder; viscosity-increasing agent.

7. Applications in Pharmaceutical Formulation or Technology

Hydroxypropyl methylcellulose is widely used in oral and topical pharmaceutical formulations.

In oral products, hydroxypropyl methylcellulose is primarily used as a tablet binder,[1] in film-coating[2-7] and as an extended release tablet matrix.[8-12] Concentrations of between 2-5% w/w may be used as a binder in either wet or dry granulation processes. High viscosity grades may be used to retard the release of water-soluble drugs from a matrix.

Depending upon the viscosity grade, concentrations between 2-10% w/w are used as film-forming solutions to film-coat tablets. Lower viscosity grades are used in aqueous film-coating solutions while higher viscosity grades are used with organic solvents.

Hydroxypropyl methylcellulose is also used as a suspending and thickening agent in topical formulations, particularly ophthalmic preparations. Compared with methylcellulose, hydroxypropyl methylcellulose produces solutions of greater clarity, with fewer undispersed fibres present, and is therefore preferred in formulations for ophthalmic use. Concentrations of between 0.45-1.0% w/w may be added as a thickening agent to vehicles for eye-drops and artificial tear solutions.

Hydroxypropyl methylcellulose is also used as an emulsifier, suspending agent and stabilizing agent in topical gels and ointments. As a protective colloid, it can prevent droplets and particles from coalescing or agglomerating, thus inhibiting the formation of sediments.

In addition, hydroxypropyl methylcellulose is used as an adhesive in plastic bandages and as a wetting agent for hard contact lenses. It is also widely used in cosmetics and food products.

8. Description

Hydroxypropyl methylcellulose is an odorless and tasteless, white or creamy-white colored fibrous or granular powder.

9. Pharmacopeial Specifications

Test	PhEur 1992	USP XXII (Suppl 2)
Identification	+	+
Appearance of solution	+	—
pH (1% w/w solution)	5.5-8.0	—
Apparent viscosity	+	+
Loss on drying	≤ 10.0%	≤ 5.0%
Residue on ignition		
for viscosity grade > 50 mPa s	—	≤ 1.5%
for viscosity grade ≤ 50 mPa s	—	≤ 3.0%
for type 1828 of all viscosities	—	≤ 5.0%
Sulfated ash	≤ 1.0%	—
Arsenic	—	≤ 3 ppm
Chlorides	≤ 0.5%	—
Heavy metals	≤ 20 ppm	≤ 0.001%
Methoxy content		
Type 1828	—	16.5-20.0%
Type 2208	—	19.0-24.0%
Type 2906	—	27.0-30.0%
Type 2910	—	28.0-30.0%
Hydroxypropoxy content		
Type 1828	—	23.0-32.0%
Type 2208	—	4.0-12.0%
Type 2906	—	4.0-7.5%
Type 2910	—	7.0-12.0%

10. Typical Properties

Acidity/alkalinity:
pH = 5.5-8.0 for a 1% w/w aqueous solution.

SEM: 1

Excipient: Hydroxypropyl methylcellulose
Manufacturer: Shin-Etsu Chemical Co Ltd
Lot No.: 83214
Magnification: 60x
Voltage: 10kV

SEM: 2

Excipient: Hydroxypropyl methylcellulose
Manufacturer: Shin-Etsu Chemical Co Ltd
Lot No.: 83214
Magnification: 600x
Voltage: 10kV

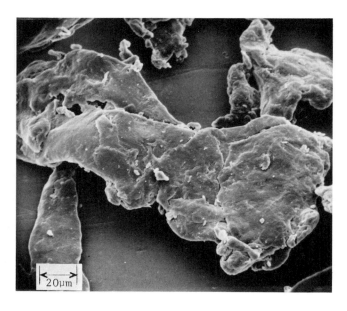

Ash: 1.5-3.0%, depending upon the grade.
Autoignition temperature: 360°C
Density (tapped): 0.50-0.70 g/cm^3 for *Pharmacoat*.
Melting point: browns at 190-200°C; chars at 225-230°C. Glass transition temperature is 170-180°C.
Moisture content: hydroxypropyl methylcellulose absorbs moisture from the atmosphere, the amount of water absorbed depending upon the initial moisture content and the temperature and relative humidity of the surrounding air. *See also* HPE Data.
Solubility: soluble in cold water, forming a viscous colloidal solution; practically insoluble in chloroform, ethanol (95%) and ether, but soluble in mixtures of ethanol and dichloromethane, and mixtures of methanol and dichloromethane. Certain grades of hydroxypropyl methylcellulose are soluble in aqueous acetone solutions, mixtures of dichloromethane and propan-2-ol, and other organic solvents. *See also* Section 11.
Specific gravity: 1.26
Viscosity (dynamic): a wide range of viscosity types are commercially available. Aqueous solutions are most commonly prepared although hydroxypropyl methylcellulose may also be dissolved in aqueous alcohols such as ethanol and propan-2-ol provided the alcohol content is less than 50% w/w. Dichloromethane and ethanol mixtures may also be used to prepare viscous hydroxypropyl methylcellulose solutions. Solutions prepared using organic solvents tend to be more viscous; increasing concentration also produces more viscous solutions, *see* Table I.
To prepare an aqueous solution, it is recommended that hydroxypropyl methylcellulose is dispersed and thoroughly hydrated in about 20-30% of the required amount of water. The water should be vigorously stirred and heated to 80-90°C then the remaining hydroxypropyl methylcellulose added. Cold water should then be added to produce the required volume.
When a water-miscible organic solvent such as ethanol, glycol, or mixtures of ethanol and dichloromethane is used, the hydroxypropyl methylcellulose should first be dispersed into the organic solvent, at a ratio of 5-8 parts of solvent to 1 part of hydroxypropyl methylcellulose. Cold water is then added to produce the required volume.

Table I: Dynamic viscosity (mPa s) of *Pharmacoat 603* (Shin-Etsu Chemical Co Ltd) solutions in various solvents at 20°C.

Solvent	Viscosity (mPa s) at 20°C Concentration (% w/w)			
	2	**6**	**10**	**14**
Dichloromethane: ethanol (50:50)	4	28	150	580
Ethanol: water (50:50)	8	32	120	350
Water	3	15	45	100

	HPE Laboratory Project Data		
	Method	**Lab #**	**Results**
Moisture content	MC-20	15	2.10% [a]
Moisture content	MC-20	15	3.10% [b]
Moisture content	EMC-1	15	*See* Fig. 1. [a]

Supplier: a. Dow Chemical Company; b. Aqualon.

11. Stability and Storage Conditions

Hydroxypropyl methylcellulose powder is a stable material although it is hygroscopic after drying.

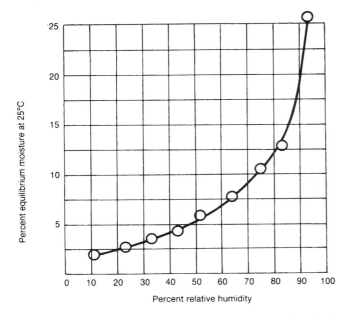

Fig. 1: Equilibrium moisture content of hydroxypropyl methylcellulose, *Methocel E15* **(Dow Chemical Company, Lot No.: QP0502-801-E).**

Solutions are stable between pH 3-11. Increasing temperature reduces the viscosity of solutions. Hydroxypropyl methylcellulose undergoes a reversible sol to gel transformation upon heating and cooling respectively. The gel point is 50-90°C, depending upon the grade of material.
Aqueous solutions are comparatively enzyme-resistant, providing good viscosity stability during long-term storage.[13] However, aqueous solutions are liable to microbial spoilage and should be preserved with an antimicrobial preservative. When used as a viscosity-increasing agent in ophthalmic solutions, benzalkonium chloride is commonly used for this purpose. Aqueous solutions may also be sterilized by autoclaving; the coagulated polymer must be redispersed on cooling by shaking.
Hydroxypropyl methylcellulose powder should be stored in a well-closed container, in a cool, dry, place.

12. Incompatibilities

Hydroxypropyl methylcellulose is incompatible with some oxidizing agents. Since it is nonionic, hydroxypropyl methylcellulose will not complex with metallic salts and ionic organics to form insoluble precipitates.

13. Method of Manufacture

A purified form of cellulose, obtained from cotton waste or wood pulp, is reacted with sodium hydroxide solution to produce a swollen alkali cellulose which is chemically more reactive than untreated cellulose. The alkali cellulose is then treated with chloromethane and propylene oxide to produce methylhydroxypropyl ethers of cellulose. The fibrous reaction product is then purified and ground to a fine, uniform powder or granules.

14. Safety

Hydroxypropyl methylcellulose is widely used as an excipient in oral and topical pharmaceutical formulations. It is also used extensively in cosmetics and food products.

Hydroxypropyl methylcellulose is generally regarded as a nontoxic and nonirritant material although excessive oral consumption may have a laxative effect.[14] The WHO has not specified an acceptable daily intake for hydroxypropyl methylcellulose since the levels consumed were not considered to represent a hazard to health.[15]
LD_{50} (mouse, IP): 5 g/kg[16]
LD_{50} (rat, IP): 5.2 g/kg

15. Handling Precautions

Observe normal precautions appropriate to the circumstances and quantity of material handled. Hydroxypropyl methylcellulose dust may be irritant to the eyes and eye protection is recommended. Excessive dust generation should be avoided to minimize the risks of explosions. Hydroxypropyl methylcellulose is combustible.

16. Regulatory Status

GRAS listed. Accepted as a food additive in Europe. Included in the FDA Inactive Ingredients Guide (ophthalmic preparations, oral capsules, suspensions, syrups and tablets, topical and vaginal preparations). Included in nonparenteral medicines licensed in the UK.

17. Pharmacopeias

Br, Eur, Fr, Gr, It, Jpn, Neth, Port, Swiss and US.

18. Related Substances

Hydroxyethyl Cellulose; Hydroxypropyl Cellulose; Hydroxypropyl Methylcellulose Phthalate.

19. Comments

Powdered or granular, surface-treated grades of hydroxypropyl methylcellulose are also available which are dispersible in cold water. The dissolution rate of these materials can be controlled by a shift in pH and they are thus useful for slow-release or enteric coated formulations.

20. Specific References

1. Chowhan ZT. Role of binders in moisture-induced hardness increase in compressed tablets and its effect on *in vitro* disintegration and dissolution. J Pharm Sci 1980; 69: 1-4.
2. Rowe RC. The adhesion of film coatings to tablet surfaces - the effect of some direct compression excipients and lubricants. J Pharm Pharmacol 1977; 29: 723-726.
3. Rowe RC. The molecular weight and molecular weight distribution of hydroxypropyl methylcellulose used in the film coating of tablets. J Pharm Pharmacol 1980; 32: 116-119.
4. Banker G, Peck G, Jan S, Pirakitikulr P. Evaluation of hydroxypropyl cellulose and hydroxypropyl methyl cellulose as aqueous based film coatings. Drug Dev Ind Pharm 1981; 7: 693-716.
5. Okhamafe AO, York P. Moisture permeation mechanism of some aqueous-based film coats. J Pharm Pharmacol 1982; 34(Suppl): 53P.
6. Alderman DA, Schulz GJ. Method of making a granular, cold water dispersible coating composition for tablets. US Patent 4816298, 1989.
7. Patell MK. Taste masking pharmaceutical agents. US Patent 4916161, 1990.
8. Hardy JG, Kennerley JW, Taylor MJ, Wilson CG, Davis SS. Release rates from sustained-release buccal tablets in man. J Pharm Pharmacol 1982; 34(Suppl): 91P.

9. Hogan JE. Hydroxypropylmethylcellulose sustained release technology. Drug Dev Ind Pharm 1989; 15: 975-999.

10. Shah AC, Britten NJ, Olanoff LS, Badalamenti JN. Gel-matrix systems exhibiting bimodal controlled release for oral delivery. J Controlled Release 1989; 9: 169-175.

11. Wilson HC, Cuff GW. Sustained release of isomazole from matrix tablets administered to dogs. J Pharm Sci 1989; 78: 582-584.

12. Dahl TC, Calderwood T, Bormeth A, Trimble K, Piepmeier E. Influence of physicochemical properties of hydroxypropyl methylcellulose on naproxen release from sustained release matrix tablets. J Controlled Release 1990; 14: 1-10.

13. Banker G, Peck G, Williams E, Taylor D, Pirakitikulr P. Microbiological considerations of polymer solutions used in aqueous film coating. Drug Dev Ind Pharm 1982; 8: 41-51.

14. Final report on the safety assessment of hydroxyethylcellulose, hydroxypropylcellulose, methylcellulose, hydroxypropyl methylcellulose and cellulose gum. J Am Coll Toxicol 1986; 5(3): 1-60.

15. FAO/WHO. Evaluation of certain food additives and contaminants: thirty-fifth report of the joint FAO/WHO expert committee on food additives. Tech Rep Ser Wld Hlth Org 1990; No. 789.

16. Sweet DV, editor. Registry of toxic effects of chemical substances. Cincinnati: US Department of Health, 1987.

21. General References

Dow Chemical Company. Technical literature: *Methocel*, 1993.

Doelker E. Cellulose derivatives. Adv Polymer Sci 1993; 107: 199-265.

Malamataris S, Karidas T, Goidas P. Effect of particle size and sorbed moisture on the compression behavior of some hydroxypropyl methylcellulose (HPMC) polymers. Int J Pharmaceutics 1994; 103: 205-215.

Papadimitriou E, Buckton G, Efentakis M. Probing the mechanisms of swelling of hydroxypropylmethylcellulose matrices. Int J Pharmaceutics 1993; 98: 57-62.

Parab PV, Nayak MP, Ritschel WA. Influence of hydroxypropyl methylcellulose and of manufacturing technique on *in vitro* performance of selected antacids. Drug Dev Ind Pharm 1985; 11: 169-185.

Radebaugh GW, Murtha JL, Julian TN, Bondi JN. Methods for evaluating the puncture and shear properties of pharmaceutical polymeric films. Int J Pharmaceutics 1988; 45: 39-46.

Rowe RC. Materials used in the film coating of oral dosage forms. In: Florence AT, editor. Critical reports on applied chemistry, volume 6: materials used in pharmaceutical formulation. Oxford: Blackwell Scientific Publications, 1984: 1-36.

Sebert P, Andrianoff N, Rollet M. Effect of gamma irradiation on hydroxypropylmethylcellulose powders: consequences on physical, rheological and pharmacotechnical properties. Int J Pharmaceutics 1993; 99: 37-42.

Shin-Etsu Chemical Co Ltd. Technical literature: *Metolose*, 1977.

Shin-Etsu Chemical Co Ltd. Technical literature: *Pharmacoat* hydroxypropyl methylcellulose, 1990.

Wan LSC, Heng PWS, Wong LF. The effect of hydroxypropylmethylcellulose on water penetration into a matrix system. Int J Pharmaceutics 1991; 73: 111-116.

22. Authors

USA: RJ Harwood, JL Johnson.

Hydroxypropyl Methylcellulose Phthalate

1. Nonproprietary Names

BP: Hypromellose phthalate
PhEur: Methylhydroxypropylcellulosi phthalas
USPNF: Hydroxypropyl methylcellulose phthalate

2. Synonyms

Cellulose phthalate hydroxypropyl methyl ether; HPMCP; 2-hydroxypropyl methylcellulose phthalate; methylhydroxypropylcellulose phthalate.

3. Chemical Name and CAS Registry Number

Cellulose, hydrogen 1,2-benzenedicarboxylate, 2-hydroxypropyl methyl ether.
[9050-31-1]

4. Empirical Formula   Molecular Weight

Hydroxypropyl methylcellulose phthalate is a cellulose in which some of the hydroxyl groups are replaced with methyl ethers, 2-hydroxypropyl ethers or phthalyl esters. The USPNF XVII describes two types, type 200731 and type 220824, which have varying degrees of substitution, *see* Sections 9 and 19. Several different types of hydroxypropyl methylcellulose phthalate are commercially available with molecular weights in the range 20 000-200 000. Typical average values are 80 000-130 000.[1]
See also Sections 5 and 19.

5. Structural Formula

6. Functional Category

Coating agent.

7. Applications in Pharmaceutical Formulation or Technology

Hydroxypropyl methylcellulose phthalate is widely used in oral pharmaceutical formulations as an enteric coating material for tablets or granules.[2-7] Hydroxypropyl methylcellulose phthalate is insoluble in gastric fluid but will swell and dissolve rapidly in the upper intestine. Generally, concentrations of 5-10% of hydroxypropyl methylcellulose phthalate are employed with the material being dissolved in either a dichloromethane: ethanol (50:50) or an ethanol: water (80:20) solvent mixture. Hydroxypropyl methylcellulose phthalate can normally be applied to tablets and granules without the addition of a plasticizer or other film formers, using established coating techniques.[1] However, the addition of a small amount of plasticizer or water can avoid film cracking problems; many commonly used plasticizers such as diacetin, triacetin, diethyl and dibutyl phthalate, castor oil, acetyl monoglyceride and polyethylene glycols are compatible with hydroxypropyl methylcellulose phthalate. Tablets coated with hydroxypropyl methylcellulose phthalate disintegrate more rapidly than tablets coated with cellulose acetate phthalate.

Hydroxypropyl methylcellulose phthalate can be applied to tablet surfaces using a dispersion of the micronized hydroxypropyl methylcellulose phthalate powder in an aqueous dispersion of a suitable plasticizer such as triacetin, triethyl citrate or diethyl tartrate along with a wetting agent.[9]

Hydroxypropyl methylcellulose phthalate may be used alone or in combination with other soluble or insoluble binders in the preparation of granules with sustained drug release properties; the release rate is pH dependent. Since hydroxypropyl methylcellulose phthalate is tasteless and insoluble in saliva, it can also be used as a coating to mask the unpleasant taste of some tablet formulations.

8. Description

Hydroxypropyl methylcellulose phthalate occurs as white to slightly off-white colored, free-flowing flakes or as a granular powder. It is odorless or with a slightly acidic odor, and a barely detectable taste.

9. Pharmacopeial Specifications

Test	PhEur 1984	USPNF XVII (Suppl 2)
Identification	+	+
Clarity and color of solution	+	+
Appearance of a film	+	—
Solubility of a film	+	—
Viscosity	—	+
Loss on drying	⩽ 5.0%	⩽ 5.0%
Residue on ignition	—	⩽ 0.20%
Sulfated ash	⩽ 0.1%	—
Chloride	—	⩽ 0.07%
Arsenic	—	⩽ 2 ppm
Heavy metals	⩽ 10 ppm	⩽ 0.001%
Free phthalic acid	⩽ 2.0%	⩽ 1.0%
Phthalyl content		
Type not specified	20.0-35.0%	—
Type 200731	—	27.0-35.0%
Type 220824	—	21.0-27.0%
Methoxy content		
Type 200731	—	18.0-22.0%
Type 220824	—	20.0-24.0%
Hydroxypropoxy content		
Type 200731	—	5.0-9.0%
Type 220824	—	6.0-10.0%

SEM: 1

Excipient: Hydroxypropyl methylcellulose phthalate (HP-55)
Manufacturer: Shin-Etsu Chemical Co Ltd
Magnification: 60x

SEM: 2

Excipient: Hydroxypropyl methylcellulose phthalate (HP-55)
Manufacturer: Shin-Etsu Chemical Co Ltd
Magnification: 600x

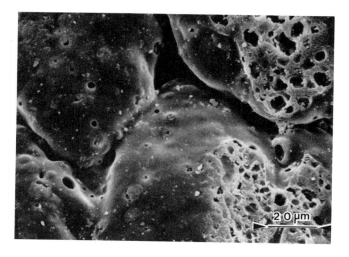

10. Typical Properties

Angle of repose:
37° for HP-50;
39° for HP-55;
38° for HP-55S.[10]

Density:
1.82 g/cm^3 for HP-50;
1.65 g/cm^3 for HP-55.
Density (bulk):
0.278 g/cm^3 for HP-50;
0.275 g/cm^3 for HP-55;
0.239 g/cm^3 for HP-55S.[10]
Density (tapped):
0.343 g/cm^3 for HP-50;
0.306 g/cm^3 for HP-55;
0.288 g/cm^3 for HP-55S.[10]
Hygroscopicity: hydroxypropyl methylcellulose phthalate is hygroscopic, *see* Fig. 1.
Melting point: 150°C. Glass transition temperature is 137°C for HP-50 and 133°C for HP-55.[11]
Particle size distribution: see Fig. 2.
Solubility: practically insoluble in ethanol and water; very slightly soluble in acetone, and toluene; soluble in aqueous alkalis, a mixture of equal volumes of acetone and methanol, and in a mixture of equal volumes of dichloromethane and methanol. The solubilities of the HP-50 and HP-55 grades, in various solvents and solvent mixtures, are shown in the table below.[10]

Solvent	Solubility	
	HP-50	HP-55
Acetone	S/I	S
Acetone: dichloromethane	S/I	S
Acetone: ethanol	S/S	S
Acetone: methanol	S	S
Acetone: propan-2-ol	S/S	S
Acetone: water (95:5)	S	S
Benzene: methanol	S	S
Dichloromethane	S/I	S/I
Dichloromethane: ethanol	S	S
Dichloromethane: methanol	S	S
Dichloromethane: propan-2-ol	S/S	S
Dioxane	S	S
Ethanol	S/I	S/I
Ethyl acetate	X	S/I
Ethyl acetate: ethanol	S/S	S
Ethyl acetate: methanol	S	S
Ethyl acetate: propan-2-ol	S/I	S
Methanol	S/I	S/I
Methyl ethyl ketone	S/I	S
Propan-2-ol	X	S/I

Note: solubilities are for the pure solvent, or a (1:1) solvent mixture, unless otherwise indicated.

S   = soluble, clear solution.
S/S = slightly soluble, cloudy solution.
S/I = swells but insoluble.
X   = insoluble.

Viscosity (dynamic): see Fig. 3 and 4.

11. Stability and Storage Conditions

Hydroxypropyl methylcellulose phthalate is chemically and physically stable at ambient temperature and humidity for 3-4 years, and for 2-3 months at 40°C and 75% relative humidity.[10] It is stable on exposure to UV light for up to 3 months at 25°C and 70% relative humidity.[10] In general, hydroxypropyl methylcellulose phthalate is more stable than cellulose acetate phthalate. At ambient storage conditions

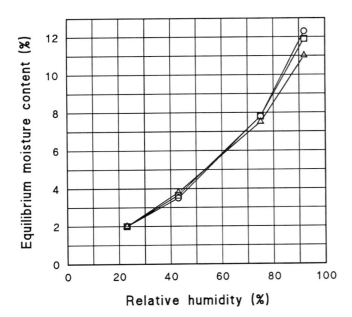

Fig. 1: Equilibrium moisture content of hydroxypropyl methyl-cellulose phthalate (Shin-Etsu Chemical Co Ltd) at 25°C.[10]

○ = HP-50
□ = HP-55
△ = HP-55S

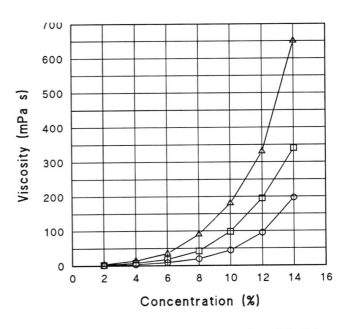

Fig. 3: Dynamic viscosity of hydroxypropyl methylcellulose phthalate (HP-50) in various solvent mixtures at 20°C.[10]

○ = Acetone: ethanol (1:1)
□ = Dichloromethane: ethanol (1:1)
△ = Ethanol: water (7:3)

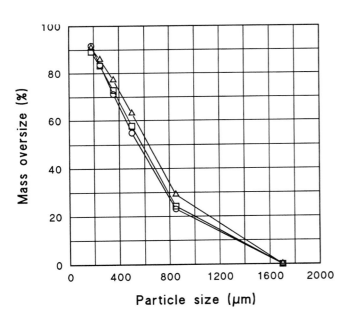

Fig. 2: Particle size distribution of hydroxypropyl methylcellu-lose phthalate (Shin-Etsu Chemical Co Ltd).[10]

○ = HP-50
□ = HP-55
△ = HP-55S

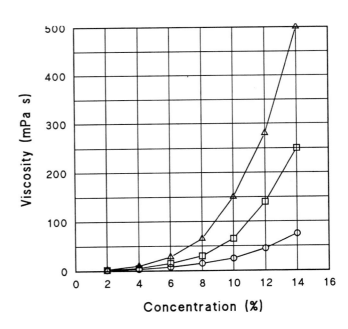

Fig. 4: Dynamic viscosity of hydroxypropyl methylcellulose phthalate (HP-55) in various solvent mixtures at 20°C.[10]

○ = Acetone: ethanol (1:1)
□ = Dichloromethane: ethanol (1:1)
△ = Ethanol: water (8:2)

hydroxypropyl methylcellulose phthalate is not susceptible to microbial attack. Hydroxypropyl methylcellulose should be stored in a well-closed container in a cool, dry, place.

12. Incompatibilities

Incompatible with strong oxidizing agents.

Splitting of film coatings has been reported rarely, most notably with coated tablets which contain microcrystalline cellulose and calcium carboxymethylcellulose. Film splitting has also occurred when a mixture of acetone: propan-2-ol or dichloromethane: propan-2-ol has been used as the coating solvent, or when coatings have been applied in conditions of low temperature and humidity. However, film splitting may be avoided by careful selection of the coating solvent used, by using a higher molecular weight grade of polymer,[1] or by the addition of a plasticizer, such as acetyl monoglyceride or triacetin.

The addition of more than about 10% titanium dioxide to a coating solution of hydroxypropyl methylcellulose phthalate, that is used to produce a colored film coating, may result in coatings with decreased elasticity and gastric fluid resistance.[10]

13. Method of Manufacture

Hydroxypropyl methylcellulose phthalate is prepared by the esterification of hydroxypropyl methylcellulose with phthalic anhydride. The degree of methoxy and phthalyl substitution determines the properties of the polymer and in particular the pH at which it dissolves in aqueous media.

14. Safety

Hydroxypropyl methylcellulose phthalate is widely used, primarily as an enteric coating agent, in oral pharmaceutical formulations. Chronic and acute animal feeding studies, on several different species, have shown no evidence of teratogenicity or toxicity associated with hydroxypropyl methylcellulose phthalate.[12-16] Hydroxypropyl methylcellulose phthalate is generally regarded as a nonirritant and nontoxic material.

LD_{50} (rat, oral): > 15 g/kg[12]

15. Handling Precautions

Observe normal precautions appropriate to the circumstances and quantity of material handled. Eye protection and gloves are recommended. Although no threshold limit value has been set for hydroxypropyl methylcellulose phthalate it should be handled in a well-ventilated environment and the generation of dust minimized.

16. Regulatory Status

Included in the FDA Inactive Ingredients Guide (oral capsules and tablets). Included in nonparenteral medicines licensed in the UK.

17. Pharmacopeias

Br, Eur, Fr, Gr, It, Jpn, Neth, Port, Swiss and USPNF.

18. Related Substances

Cellulose Acetate Phthalate; Hydroxypropyl Methylcellulose.

19. Comments

Various grades of hydroxypropyl methylcellulose phthalate are available with differing degrees of substitution and physical properties, e.g. grades HP-50, HP-55 and HP-55S (Shin-Etsu Chemical Co Ltd). *See* table below.

| Property | Grade of *HPMCP* | | |
	HP-50	HP-55	HP-55S
Substitution type	220824	200731	200731
Hydroxypropoxy content	6-10%	5-9%	5-9%
Methoxy content	20-24%	18-22%	18-22%
Phthalyl content	21-27%	27-35%	27-35%
Molecular weight	84 000	78 000	132 000

The number following 'HP' in each grade designation refers to the pH value (x10) at which the polymer dissolves in aqueous buffer solutions. The designation 'S' in HP-55S indicates a higher molecular weight grade, which produces films with a greater resistance to cracking.

In the US, the substitution type is indicated by a 6 digit number; the first 2 digits represent the approximate percentage content of methoxy groups, the next 2 digits the approximate percentage content of hydroxypropoxy groups and the final 2 digits the approximate percentage content of phthalyl groups. To dissolve hydroxypropyl methylcellulose phthalate in acetone: alcohol or dichloromethane: alcohol solvent systems, the hydroxypropyl methylcellulose phthalate should first be well dispersed in alcohol before adding the acetone or dichloromethane. When using acetone: dichloromethane, hydroxypropyl methylcellulose phthalate should be first dispersed in the dichloromethane and then the acetone added.

20. Specific References

1. Rowe RC. Molecular weight studies on hydroxypropyl methylcellulose phthalate (HP55). Acta Pharm Technol 1982; 28(2): 127-130.
2. Ehrhardt L, Patt L, Schindler E. Optimization of film coating systems [in German]. Pharm Ind 1973; 35: 719-722.
3. Delporte JP, Jaminet F. Influence of formulation of enteric coated tablets on the bioavailability of the drug [in French]. J Pharm Belg 1976; 31: 263-276.
4. Patt L, Hartmann V. Solvent residues in film forming agents [in German]. Pharm Ind 1976; 38: 902-906.
5. Stafford JW. Enteric film coating using completely aqueous dissolved hydroxypropyl methyl cellulose phthalate spray solutions. Drug Dev Ind Pharm 1982; 8: 513-530.
6. Thoma K, Heckenmüller H, Oschmann R. Resistance and disintegration behaviour of gastric juice resistant drugs [in German]. Pharmazie 1987; 42: 832-836.
7. Thoma K, Heckenmüller H. Impact of film formers and plasticizers on stability of resistance and disintegration behaviour [in German]. Pharmazie 1987; 42: 837-841.
8. Takada K, Oh-Hashi M, Furuya Y, Yoshikawa H, Muranishi S. Enteric solid dispersion of ciclosporin A (CiA) having potential to deliver CiA into lymphatics. Chem Pharm Bull 1989; 37: 471-474.
9. Muhammad NA, Boisvert W, Harris MR, Weiss J. Evaluation of hydroxypropyl methylcellulose phthalate 50 as film forming polymer from aqueous dispersion systems. Drug Dev Ind Pharm 1992; 18: 1787-1797.
10. Shin-Etsu Chemical Co Ltd. Technical literature: hydroxypropyl methylcellulose phthalate, 1993.
11. Sakellariou P, Rowe RC, White EFT. The thermomechanical properties and glass transition temperature of some cellulose derivatives used in film coating. Int J Pharmaceutics 1985; 27: 267-277.

12. Kitagawa H, Kawana H, Satoh T, Fukuda Y. Acute and subacute toxicities of hydroxypropyl methylcellulose phthalate. Pharmacometrics 1970; 4(6): 1017-1025.

13. Kitagawa H, Satoh T, Yokoshima T, Nanbo T. Absorption, distribution and excretion of hydroxypropyl methylcellulose phthalate in the rat. Pharmacometrics 1971; 5(1): 1-4.

14. Ito R, Toida S. Studies on the teratogenicity of a new enteric coating material, hydroxypropyl methylcellulose phthalate (HPMCP) in rats and mice. J Med Soc Toho-Univ 1972; 19(5): 453-461.

15. Kitagawa H, Yano H, Fukuda Y. Chronic toxicity of hydroxypropylmethylcellulose phthalate in rats. Pharmacometrics 1973; 7(5): 689-701.

16. Kitagawa H, Yokoshima T, Nanbo T, Hasegawa M. Absorption, distribution, excretion and metabolism of ^{14}C-hydroxypropyl methylcellulose phthalate. Pharmacometrics 1974; 8(8): 1123-1132.

21. General References

Deasy PB, O'Connell MJM. Correlation of surface characteristics with ease of production and *in vitro* release of sodium salicylate from various enteric coated microcapsules prepared by pan coating. J Micorencapsulation 1984; 1(3): 217-227.

Doelker E. Cellulose derivatives. Adv Polymer Sci 1993; 107: 199-265.

Rowe RC. Materials used in the film coating of oral dosage forms. In: Florence AT, editor. Critical reports on applied chemistry, volume 6: materials used in pharmaceutical formulation. Oxford: Blackwell Scientific Publications, 1984: 1-36.

22. Authors

USA: JC Lee.

Imidurea

1. Nonproprietary Names

USPNF: Imidurea

2. Synonyms

Biopure 100; *Germall 115*; imidazolidinyl urea; methane-bis[*N*,*N'*(5-ureido-2,4-diketotetrahydroimidazole)*N*,*N*-di-methylol]; 1,1'-methylenebis{3-[3-(hydroxymethyl)-2,5-dioxo-4-imidazolidinyl]urea}; *Tri-Stat IU*.

3. Chemical Name and CAS Registry Number

N,*N'*–Methylenebis{*N'*-[3-(hydroxymethyl)-2,5-dioxo-4-imida-zolidinyl] urea} [39236-46-9]

4. Empirical Formula   Molecular Weight

$C_{11}H_{16}N_8O_8$ 388.30

$C_{11}H_{16}N_8O_8 \cdot H_2O$ 406.33 (for monohydrate)

5. Structural Formula

Monohydrate shown.

6. Functional Category

Antimicrobial preservative.

7. Applications in Pharmaceutical Formulation or Technology

Imidurea is a broad spectrum antimicrobial preservative used in cosmetics and topical pharmaceutical formulations; typical concentrations used are 0.03-0.5% w/w. It is effective between pH 3.0-9.0 and is reported to have synergistic effects when used with parabens, *see* Section 10.

8. Description

Imidurea is a white, free flowing powder, with a faint characteristic odor.

9. Pharmacopeial Specifications

Test	USPNF XVII (Suppl 6)
Identification	+
Color and clarity of solution	+
pH (1% w/v solution)	6.0-7.5
Loss on drying	≤ 3.0%

Continued

Test	USPNF XVII (Suppl 6)
Residue on ignition	≤ 3.0%
Heavy metals	≤ 0.001%
Organic volatile impurities	+
Nitrogen content (dried basis)	26.0-28.0%

10. Typical Properties

Acidity/alkalinity: pH = 6.0-7.5 (1% w/v aqueous solution).
Antimicrobial activity: predominantly an antibacterial preservative, imidurea also has some selective antifungal properties. Used at concentrations between 0.03-0.5% w/w it is effective between pH 3.0-9.0 although preservative efficacy is best seen in slightly acidic solutions. Synergistic effects have been reported and preservative activity is considerably enhanced, particularly against fungi, when used in combination with parabens.[1,2] A cosmetic formulation containing 0.5% imidurea, 0.2% methylparaben and 0.1% propylparaben was effectively preserved against various *pseudomonas* species.[3] Reported minimum inhibitory concentrations (MICs) are shown below:[4]

Microorganism	MIC (μg/mL)
Aspergillus niger	8000
Candida albicans	8000
Escherichia coli	2000
Klebsiella pneumoniae	2000
Penicillium notatum	8000
Pseudomonas aeruginosa	2000
Pseudomonas cepacia	2000
Pseudomonas fluorescens	2000
Staphylococcus aureus	1000

Solubility: very soluble in water, but insoluble in almost all organic solvents.[4]

Solvent	Solubility at 25°C
Ethanol	very slightly soluble
Ethanol (90%)	very slightly soluble
Ethanol (70%)	1 in 330
Ethanol (60%)	1 in 25
Ethanol (50%)	1 in 2.5
Ethanol (30%)	1 in 0.8
Ethylene glycol*	1 in 0.7
Glycerin*	1 in 1
Methanol	very slightly soluble
Mineral oil	practically insoluble
Propan-2-ol	practically insoluble
Propylene glycol*	1 in 0.8
Sesame oil	very slightly soluble
Water	1 in 0.5

* Slow to dissolve and requires heating and stirring.

11. Stability and Storage Conditions

Imidurea is hygroscopic and should be stored in a well-closed container in a cool, dry, place.

12. Incompatibilities

Imidurea is compatible with other preservatives including sorbic acid and quaternary ammonium compounds.[5] It is also compatible with other pharmaceutical and cosmetic excipients including proteins, nonionic surfactants and lecithin.[6]

13. Method of Manufacture

Imidurea is commercially prepared by a complex synthetic route.

14. Safety

Imidurea is widely used in cosmetics and topical pharmaceutical formulations and is generally regarded as a nontoxic and nonirritant material.[5] However, there have been some reports of contact dermatitis associated with imidurea, although these are relatively few considering its widespread use in cosmetics.[7-10]

Although imidurea releases formaldehyde it does not appear to be associated with cross sensitization with formaldehyde or other formaldehyde releasing compounds.

LD$_{50}$ (mouse, oral): 7.2 g/kg[11,12]
LD$_{50}$ (rabbit, skin): > 8 g/kg
LD$_{50}$ (rat, oral): 11.3 g/kg

15. Handling Precautions

Observe normal precautions appropriate to the circumstances and quantity of material handled. Imidurea may be irritant to the eyes. Eye protection and gloves are recommended.

16. Regulatory Status

Included in the FDA Inactive Ingredients Guide (topical preparations). Accepted for use in cosmetics in Europe and the US.

17. Pharmacopeias

USPNF.

18. Related Substances

Diazolidinyl urea.

Diazolidinyl urea: $C_8H_{14}N_4O_7$
Molecular weight: 278.23
CAS number: [78491-02-8]
Synonyms: Germall II; *N*-(hydroxymethyl)-*N*-(1,3-dihydroxymethyl-2,5-dioxo-4-imidazolidinyl)-*N'*-(hydroxymethyl)urea.
Appearance: white, free flowing powder, with a faint characteristic odor.
Antimicrobial activity: similar to imidurea.[13,14] Diazolidinyl urea is the most active of the imidazolidinyl family of preservatives. Used in concentrations of 0.1-0.5% w/w, at pH 3.0-9.0, it has predominantly antibacterial properties. Typical MICs are: *Aspergillus niger* 4000 μg/mL; *Candida albicans* 8000 μg/mL; *Escherichia coli* 1000 μg/mL; *Pseudomonas aeruginosa* 1000 μg/mL; *Staphylococcus aureus* 250 μg/mL.
Solubility: soluble in water.

19. Comments

Imidurea is the best known of a family of heterocyclic urea derivatives that are effective antimicrobial preservatives. Diazolidinyl urea has most antimicrobial activity.

20. Specific References

1. Jacobs G, Henry SM, Cotty VF. The influence of pH, emulsifier, and accelerated ageing upon preservative requirements of o/w emulsions. J Soc Cosmet Chem 1975; 26: 105-117.
2. Rosen WE, Berke PA, Matzin T, Peterson AF. Preservation of cosmetic lotions with imidazolidinyl urea plus parabens. J Soc Cosmet Chem 1977; 28: 83-87.
3. Berke PA, Rosen WE. Imidazolidinyl urea activity against pseudomonas. J Soc Cosmet Chem 1978; 29: 757-766.
4. Wallhäusser KH. Imidazolidinyl urea. In: Kabara JJ, editor. Cosmetic and drug preservation principles and practice. New York: Marcel Dekker, 1984: 655-657.
5. Rosen WE, Berke PA. Germall 115 - a safe and effective modern preservative. Cosmet Toilet 1977; 92(3): 88-89.
6. Rosen WE, Berke PA. Germall 115 and nonionic emulsifiers. Cosmet Toilet 1979; 94(12): 47-48.
7. Fisher AA. Cosmetic dermatitis: part II. Reactions to some commonly used preservatives. Cutis 1980; 26: 136-137, 141-142, 147-148.
8. Dooms-Goossens A, De Boulle K, Dooms M, Degreef H. Imidazolidinyl urea dermatitis. Contact Dermatitis 1986; 14(5): 322-324.
9. O'Brien TJ. Imidazolidinyl urea (Germall 115) causing cosmetic dermatitis. Aust J Dermatol 1987; 28(1): 36-37.
10. Ziegler V, Ziegler B, Kipping D. Dose-response sensitization experiments with imidazolidinyl urea. Contact Dermatitis 1988; 19(3): 236-237.
11. Elder RL. Final report of the safety assessment for imidazolidinyl urea. J Environ Pathol Toxicol 1980; 4(4): 133-146.
12. Sweet DV, editor. Registry of toxic effects of chemical substances. Cincinnati: US Department of Health, 1987.
13. Berke PA, Rosen WE. Germall II - a new broad-spectrum cosmetic preservative. Cosmet Toilet 1982; 97(6): 49-53.
14. Wallhäusser KH. Germall II. In: Kabara JJ, editor. Cosmetic and drug preservation principles and practice. New York: Marcel Dekker, 1984: 657-659.

21. General References

Berke PA, Rosen WE. Germall, a new family of antimicrobial preservatives for cosmetics. Am Perfum Cosmet 1970; 85(3): 55-59.
Croshaw B. Preservatives for cosmetics and toiletries. J Soc Cosmet Chem 1977; 28: 3-16.
Decker RL, Wenninger JA. Frequency of preservative use in cosmetic formulas as disclosed to FDA-1987. Cosmet Toilet 1987; 102(12): 21-24.
Rosen WE, Berke PA. Germall 115: a safe and effective preservative. In: Kabara JJ, editor. Cosmetic and drug preservation principles and practice. New York: Marcel Dekker, 1984: 191-205.

22. Authors

UK: MC Allwood.

Isobutane

1. Nonproprietary Names
USPNF: Isobutane

2. Synonyms
A-31; Aeropres 31.

3. Chemical Name and CAS Registry Number
2-Methylpropane [75-28-5]

4. Empirical Formula   Molecular Weight
C_4H_{10} 58.12

5. Structural Formula

$$H_3C-\underset{\underset{CH_3}{|}}{\overset{\overset{H}{|}}{C}}-CH_3$$

6. Functional Category
Aerosol propellant.

7. Applications in Pharmaceutical Formulation or Technology
Isobutane is used as an aerosol propellant, in combination with other hydrocarbon or chlorofluorocarbon propellants, primarily in topical pharmaceutical aerosols (particularly aqueous products).

Depending upon the application, the concentration of hydrocarbon propellant used ranges from 5-95% w/w. Foam aerosols generally use about 4-5% of a hydrocarbon propellant consisting of isobutane (84.1%) and propane (15.9%). Spray type aerosols utilize propellant concentrations of 50% and higher.

Isobutane is also used in cosmetics and food products as an aerosol propellant.

See also Butane.

8. Description
Isobutane is a liquefied gas and exists as a liquid at room temperature when contained under its own vapor pressure, or as a gas when exposed to room temperature and atmospheric pressure. It is essentially a clear, colorless, odorless liquid but may have a slight ethereal odor.

9. Pharmacopeial Specifications

Test	USPNF XVII
Identification	+
Water	≤ 0.001%
High-boiling residues	≤ 5 ppm
Acidity of residue	+
Sulfur compounds	+
Assay	≥ 95.0%

10. Typical Properties
Autoignition temperature: 420°C
Boiling point: -11.7°C
Critical pressure: 3.65 MPa (36 atm)
Critical temperature: 135°C
Density: 0.56 g/cm^3 for liquid at 20°C
Explosive limits:
1.8% v/v lower limit;
8.4% v/v upper limit.
Flash point: -83°C
Freezing point: -159.7°C
Kauri-butanol value: 17.5
Vapor density (absolute): 2.595 g/m^3
Vapor density (relative): 2.01 (air = 1)
Vapor pressure:
209.6 kPa (30.4 psig) at 21°C;
661.9 kPa (96.0 psig) at 54.5°C.

11. Stability and Storage Conditions
See Butane.

12. Incompatibilities
See Butane.

13. Method of Manufacture
See Butane.

14. Safety
See Butane.

15. Handling Precautions
See Butane.

16. Regulatory Status
GRAS listed. Included in the FDA Inactive Ingredients Guide (aerosol formulations for topical application). Included in nonparenteral medicines licensed in the UK.

17. Pharmacopeias
USPNF.

18. Related Substances
Butane; Dimethyl Ether; Propane.

19. Comments
See Butane.

20. Specific References
See Butane.

21. General References
See Butane.

22. Authors
UK: PJ Davies.
USA: JJ Sciarra.

Isopropyl Alcohol

1. Nonproprietary Names

BP: Isopropyl alcohol
USP: Isopropyl alcohol

2. Synonyms

Dimethyl carbinol; IPA; isopropanol; petrohol; 2-propanol; *sec*-propyl alcohol.

3. Chemical Name and CAS Registry Number

Propan-2-ol [67-63-0]

4. Empirical Formula   Molecular Weight

C_3H_8O 60.1

5. Structural Formula

$(CH_3)_2CHOH$

6. Functional Category

Disinfectant; solvent.

7. Applications in Pharmaceutical Formulation or Technology

Isopropyl alcohol (propan-2-ol) is used in cosmetics and pharmaceutical formulations primarily as a solvent in topical formulations. It is not recommended for oral use due to its toxicity, *see* Section 14.
Although used in lotions, the marked degreasing properties of isopropyl alcohol may limit its usefulness in preparations used repeatedly. Isopropyl alcohol is also used as a solvent both for tablet film-coating and tablet granulation where the isopropyl alcohol is subsequently removed by evaporation.
Isopropyl alcohol has some antimicrobial activity (*see* Section 10) and a 70% v/v aqueous solution is used as a topical disinfectant.

8. Description

Isopropyl alcohol is a clear, colorless, mobile, volatile, flammable liquid with a characteristic, spirituous odor resembling that of a mixture of ethanol and acetone; it has a slightly bitter taste.

9. Pharmacopeial Specifications

Test	BP 1993	USP XXII
Identification	+	+
Specific gravity	0.784-0.786	0.783-0.787
Refractive index	1.377-1.378	1.376-1.378
Acidity or alkalinity	+	+
Water	⩽ 0.5%	—
Nonvolatile residue	⩽ 0.0016%	⩽ 0.005%
Distillation range	81-83°	—
Water-insoluble matter	+	—
Benzene	+	—
Aldehydes and ketones	+	—
Assay	—	⩾ 99.0%

10. Typical Properties

Antimicrobial activity: isopropyl alcohol is bactericidal; at concentrations greater than 70% v/v it is a more effective antibacterial preservative than alcohol. The bactericidal effect of aqueous solutions increases steadily as the concentration approaches 100% v/v. Isopropyl alcohol is ineffective against bacterial spores.
Autoignition temperature: 425°C
Boiling point: 82.4°C
Dielectric constant: $D^{20} = 18.62$
Explosive limits: 2.5-12.0% v/v in air.
Flammability: flammable.
Flash point: 11.7°C (closed cup); 13°C (open cup). The water azeotrope has a flash point of 16°C.
Freezing point: -89.5°C
Melting point: -88.5°C
Moisture content: 0.1-13% w/w for commercial grades (13% w/w corresponds to the water azeotrope).
Refractive index: $n_D^{20} = 1.3776$; $n_D^{25} = 1.3749$.
Solubility: miscible with benzene, chloroform, ethanol, ether, glycerin and water. Soluble in acetone; insoluble in salt solutions. Forms an azeotrope with water, containing 87.4% w/w isopropyl alcohol (boiling point = 80.37°C).
Specific gravity: 0.786
Vapor density (relative): 2.07 (air = 1)
Vapor pressure:
133.3 Pa (1 mmHg) at -26.1°C;
4.32 kPa (32.4 mmHg) at 20°C;
5.33 kPa (40 mmHg) at 23.8°C;
13.33 kPa (100 mmHg) at 39.5°C.
Viscosity (dynamic): 2.43 mPa s (2.43 cP) at 20°C

11. Stability and Storage Conditions

Isopropyl alcohol should be stored in an airtight container in a cool, dry, place.

12. Incompatibilities

Incompatible with oxidizing agents such as hydrogen peroxide and nitric acid which cause decomposition. Isopropyl alcohol may be salted out from aqueous mixtures by the addition of sodium chloride, sodium sulfate and other salts, or by the addition of sodium hydroxide.

13. Method of Manufacture

Isopropyl alcohol may be prepared from propylene; by the catalytic reduction of acetone, or by fermentation of certain carbohydrates.

14. Safety

Isopropyl alcohol is widely used in cosmetics and topical pharmaceutical formulations. It is readily absorbed from the gastrointestinal tract and may be slowly absorbed through intact skin. Isopropyl alcohol is metabolized more slowly than ethanol, primarily to acetone. Metabolites and unchanged isopropyl alcohol are mainly excreted in the urine.
Isopropyl alcohol is about twice as toxic as ethanol and should therefore not be administered orally; isopropyl alcohol also has an unpleasant taste. Symptoms of isopropyl alcohol toxicity are similar to those for ethanol except that isopropyl alcohol has no initial euphoric action and gastritis and vomiting are more prominent, *see* Alcohol. The lethal oral dose is estimated to be about 250 mL although toxic symptoms may be produced by 20 mL.

Adverse effects following parenteral administration of up to 20 mL of isopropyl alcohol diluted with water have included only a sensation of heat and a slight lowering of blood pressure. However, isopropyl alcohol is not commonly used in parenteral products.

Isopropyl alcohol is most frequently used in topical pharmaceutical formulations where it may act as a local irritant.[1] When applied to the eye it can cause corneal burns and eye damage.

LD_{50} (dog, oral): 4.80 g/kg[2]
LD_{50} (guinea pig, IP): 2.56 g/kg
LD_{50} (hamster, IP): 3.44 g/kg
LD_{50} (mouse, oral): 3.6 g/kg
LD_{50} (mouse, IP): 4.48 g/kg
LD_{50} (mouse, IV): 1.51 g/kg
LD_{50} (rabbit, IP): 0.67 g/kg
LD_{50} (rabbit, IV): 1.18 g/kg
LD_{50} (rabbit, skin): 12.8 g/kg
LD_{50} (rat, IP): 2.74 g/kg
LD_{50} (rat, IV): 1.09 g/kg
LD_{50} (rat, oral): 5.05 g/kg

15. Handling Precautions

Observe normal precautions appropriate to the circumstances and quantity of material handled. Isopropyl alcohol may be irritant to the skin, eyes and mucous membranes upon inhalation. Eye protection and gloves are recommended. Isopropyl alcohol should be handled in a well-ventilated environment. In the UK, the long-term (8-hour TWA) exposure limit for isopropyl alcohol is 980 mg/m³ (400 ppm); the short-term (10-minute) exposure limit is 1225 mg/m³ (500 ppm).[3] Isopropyl alcohol is flammable and produces toxic fumes on combustion.

16. Regulatory Status

Included in the FDA Inactive Ingredients Guide (oral capsules, tablets and topical preparations). Included in nonparenteral medicines licensed in the UK.

17. Pharmacopeias

Aust, Belg, Br, Egypt, Hung, Jpn, Mex, Swiss and US.

18. Related Substances

Alcohol; propan-1-ol.

Propan-1-ol: C_3H_8O
Molecular weight: 60.1
CAS number: [71-23-8]
Synonyms: propanol; *n*-propanol; propyl alcohol; propylic alcohol.
Autoignition temperature: 540°C
Boiling point: 97.2°C
Dielectric constant: $D^{25} = 22.20$
Explosive limits: 2.15-13.15% v/v in air.
Flash point: 15°C (closed cup)
Melting point: -127°C
Refractive index: $n_D^{20} = 1.3862$
Solubility: miscible with ethanol, ether and water.
Specific gravity: 0.8053 at 20°C
Viscosity (dynamic): 2.3 mPa s (2.3 cP) at 20°C
Comments: propan-1-ol is more toxic than isopropyl alcohol. In the UK, the long-term (8-hour TWA) exposure limit for propan-1-ol is 500 mg/m³ (200 ppm); the short-term (10-minute) exposure limit is 625 mg/m³ (250 ppm).[3]

19. Comments

—

20. Specific References

1. Diem P. Allergy to insulin [letter]. Br Med J 1980; 281: 1068-1069.
2. Sweet DV, editor. Registry of toxic effects of chemical substances. Cincinnati: US Department of Health, 1987.
3. Health and Safety Executive. EH40/93: occupational exposure limits 1993. London: HMSO, 1993.

21. General References

—

22. Authors

UK: SJ Lewis.
USA: J Schirmer.

Isopropyl Myristate

1. Nonproprietary Names

BP: Isopropyl myristate
PhEur: Isopropylis myristas
USPNF: Isopropyl myristate

2. Synonyms

Bisomel; *Crodamol IPM*; *Deltyl Extra*; *Emcol-IM*; *Emerest 2314*; *Estergel*; *Estol 1514*; *Isomyst*; isopropyl ester of myristic acid; *Ja-Fa IPM*; *Kessco IPM 95*; *Kesscomir*; myristic acid isopropyl ester; *Plymouth IPM*; *Promyr*; *Protachem IPM*; *Sinnoester MIP*; *Starfol IPM*; *Stepan D-50*; *Tegester*; tetradecanoic acid, 1-methylethyl ester; *Unimate IPM*; *Wickenol 101*.

3. Chemical Name and CAS Registry Number

1-Methylethyl tetradecanoate [110-27-0]

4. Empirical Formula   Molecular Weight

$C_{17}H_{34}O_2$ 270.51

5. Structural Formula

$CH_3(CH_2)_{12}COOCH(CH_3)_2$

6. Functional Category

Emollient; oleaginous vehicle; skin penetrant; solvent.

7. Applications in Pharmaceutical Formulation or Technology

Isopropyl myristate is a non-oleaginous emollient that is absorbed readily by the skin. It is used as a component of semi-solid bases and as a solvent for many substances applied topically. Applications in topical pharmaceutical and cosmetic formulations include: bath oils; make-up; hair and nail care products; creams; lotions; lip products; shaving products; suntan preparations; skin lubricants; deodorants; otic suspensions and vaginal creams.

Use	Concentration (%)
Detergent	0.003-0.03
Otic suspension	0.024
Perfumes	0.5-2.0
Soap	0.03-0.3
Topical aerosols	2-98
Topical creams and lotions	1-10

8. Description

Isopropyl myristate is a clear, colorless, practically odorless, mobile liquid with a bland taste. It consists of esters of propan-2-ol and saturated high molecular weight fatty acids, principally myristic acid.

9. Pharmacopeial Specifications

Test	PhEur 1991	USPNF XVII
Identification	+	+
Specific gravity	—	0.846-0.854
Relative density	0.850-0.855	—
Refractive index	1.434-1.437	1.432-1.436
Residue on ignition	—	$\leqslant 0.1\%$
Sulfated ash	$\leqslant 0.1\%$	—
Acid value	$\leqslant 1.0$	$\leqslant 1.0$
Saponification value	202-212	202-212
Iodine value	$\leqslant 1.0$	$\leqslant 1.0$
Appearance of solution	+	—
Viscosity	5-6 mPa s	—
Water	$\leqslant 0.1\%$	—
Assay (of $C_{17}H_{34}O_2$)	$\geqslant 90.0\%$	$\geqslant 90.0\%$

10. Typical Properties

Boiling point: 140.2°C at 266 Pa (2 mmHg)
Flash point: 153.5°C (closed cup)
Freezing point: ≈ 3°C
Solubility: miscible with acetone, chloroform, ethanol, ethyl acetate, fats, fatty alcohols, fixed oils, liquid hydrocarbons, toluene and waxes. Practically insoluble in glycerin, propylene glycol and water.
Viscosity (dynamic): 5-7 mPa s (5-7 cP) at 25°C

11. Stability and Storage Conditions

Isopropyl myristate is resistant to oxidation and hydrolysis and does not become rancid. It should be stored in a well-closed container in a cool, dry, place and protected from light.

12. Incompatibilities

When isopropyl myristate comes into contact with rubber, there is a drop in viscosity with concomitant swelling and partial dissolution of the rubber; contact with plastics, e.g. nylon and polyethylene, results in swelling. Isopropyl myristate is incompatible with hard paraffin, producing a granular mixture. Also incompatible with strong oxidizing agents.

13. Method of Manufacture

Isopropyl myristate may be prepared either by the esterification of myristic acid with propan-2-ol or by the reaction of myristoyl chloride and propan-2-ol with the aid of a suitable dehydrochlorinating agent. A high purity material is also commercially available which is produced by enzymatic esterification at low temperature.

14. Safety

Isopropyl myristate is widely used in cosmetics and topical pharmaceutical formulations and is generally regarded as a nontoxic and nonirritant material.[1-4]
LD_{50} (mouse, oral): 49.7 g/kg[5]
LD_{50} (mouse, SC): 50.2 g/kg
LD_{50} (rabbit, skin): 5 g/kg

15. Handling Precautions

Observe normal precautions appropriate to the circumstances and quantity of material handled.

16. Regulatory Status

Included in the FDA Inactive Ingredients Guide (otic, topical and vaginal preparations). Used in nonparenteral medicines licensed in the UK.

17. Pharmacopeias

Aust, Br, Eur and USPNF.

18. Related Substances

Isopropyl Palmitate.

19. Comments

—

20. Specific References

1. Fitzgerald JE, Kurtz SM, Schardein JL, Kaump DH. Cutaneous and parenteral studies with vehicles containing isopropyl myristate and peanut oil. Toxicol Appl Pharmacol 1968; 13: 448-453.
2. Stenbäck F, Shubik P. Lack of toxicity and carcinogenicity of some commonly used cutaneous agents. Toxicol Appl Pharmacol 1974; 30: 7-13.
3. Opdyke DL. Monographs on fragrance raw materials. Food Cosmet Toxicol 1976; 14(4): 307-338.
4. Guillot JP, Martini MC, Giauffret JY. Safety evaluation of cosmetic raw materials. J Soc Cosmet Chem 1977; 28: 377-393.
5. Sweet DV, editor. Registry of toxic effects of chemical substances. Cincinnati: US Department of Health, 1987.

21. General References

Armstrong NA, Griffiths H-A, James KC. Migration of ephedrine and salicylic acid from lipid mixtures containing isopropyl myristate. Int J Pharmaceutics 1988; 41: 205-211.
Platcow EL, Voss E. A study of the adaptability of isopropyl myristate for use as a vehicle for parenteral injections. J Am Pharm Assoc (Sci) 1954; 43: 690-692.

22. Authors

USA: DG Pope.

Isopropyl Palmitate

1. Nonproprietary Names

BP: Isopropyl palmitate
PhEur: Isopropylis palmitas
USPNF: Isopropyl palmitate

2. Synonyms

Crodamol IPP; *Deltyl*; *Deltyl Prime*; *Emcol-IP*; *Emerest 2316*; *Estol 1517*; hexadecanoic acid isopropyl ester; hexadecanoic acid 1-methylethyl ester; *Isopal*; *Isopalm*; isopropyl hexadecanoate; *Ja-Fa IPP*; *Kessco IPP*; palmitic acid isopropyl ester; *Plymouth IPP*; *Propal*; *Protachem IPP*; *Starfol IPP*; *Stepan D-70*; *Tegester Isopalm*; *Unimate IPP*; *USAF KE-5*; *Wickenol 111*.

3. Chemical Name and CAS Registry Number

1-Methylethyl hexadecanoate [142-91-6]

4. Empirical Formula   Molecular Weight

$C_{19}H_{38}O_2$ 298.51

5. Structural Formula

$CH_3(CH_2)_{14}COOCH(CH_3)_2$

6. Functional Category

Emollient; oleaginous vehicle; solvent.

7. Applications in Pharmaceutical Formulation or Technology

Isopropyl palmitate is a non-oleaginous emollient with good spreading characteristics used in topical pharmaceutical formulations and cosmetics such as: bath oils; creams; lotions; make-up; hair care products; deodorants; lip products; suntan preparations and pressed powders. Isopropyl palmitate has also been used in a controlled release percutaneous film.

Use	Concentration (%)
Detergent	0.005-0.02
Perfume	0.2-0.8
Soap	0.05-0.2
Topical aerosol spray	3.36
Topical creams and lotions	0.05-5.5

8. Description

Isopropyl palmitate is a clear, colorless to pale yellow-colored, practically odorless viscous liquid which solidifies at less than 16°C.

9. Pharmacopeial Specifications

Test	PhEur 1993	USPNF XVII
Identification	+	+
Specific gravity	—	0.850-0.855
Relative density	0.850-0.855	—
Refractive index	1.436-1.440	1.435-1.438
Residue on ignition	—	$\leqslant 0.1\%$
Sulfated ash	$\leqslant 0.1\%$	—
Acid value	$\leqslant 1.0$	$\leqslant 1.0$
Iodine value	$\leqslant 1.0$	$\leqslant 1.0$
Saponification value	183-193	183-193
Appearance of solution	+	—
Viscosity	5-10 mPa s	—
Water	$\leqslant 0.1\%$	—
Assay (of $C_{19}H_{38}O_2$)	$\geqslant 90.0\%$	$\geqslant 90.0\%$

10. Typical Properties

Boiling point: 160°C at 266 Pa (2 mmHg)
Freezing point: ≈ 13-15°C
Solubility: soluble in acetone, chloroform, ethanol, ethyl acetate, mineral oil, propan-2-ol, silicone oils, vegetable oils, and aliphatic and aromatic hydrocarbons. Practically insoluble in glycerin, glycols and water.
Viscosity (dynamic): 5-10 mPa s (5-10 cP) at 25°C

11. Stability and Storage Conditions

Isopropyl palmitate is resistant to oxidation and hydrolysis and does not become rancid. It should be stored in a well-closed container, above 16°C, and protected from light.

12. Incompatibilities

See Isopropyl Myristate.

13. Method of Manufacture

Isopropyl palmitate is prepared by the reaction of palmitic acid with propan-2-ol in the presence of an acid catalyst. A high purity material is also commercially available which is produced by enzymatic esterification at low temperatures.

14. Safety

Isopropyl palmitate is widely used in cosmetics and topical pharmaceutical formulations and is generally regarded as a nontoxic and nonirritant material.[1-3]
LD_{50} (mouse, IP): 0.1 g/kg[4]
LD_{50} (rabbit, skin): > 5 g/kg
LD_{50} (rat, oral): > 5 g/kg

15. Handling Precautions

Observe normal precautions appropriate to the circumstances and quantity of material handled.

16. Regulatory Status

Included in the FDA Inactive Ingredients Guide (topical and transdermal preparations). Used in nonparenteral medicines licensed in the UK.

17. Pharmacopeias

Br, Eur and USPNF.

18. Related Substances

Isopropyl Myristate.

19. Comments

—

20. Specific References

1. Frosch PJ, Kligman AM. The chamber-scarification test for irritancy. Contact Dermatitis 1976; 2: 314-324.
2. Guillot JP, Martini MC, Giauffret JY. Safety evaluation of cosmetic raw materials. J Soc Cosmet Chem 1977; 28: 377-393.
3. Opdyke DL, Letizia C. Monographs on fragrance raw materials. Food Cosmet Toxicol 1982; 20(Suppl): 633-852.
4. Sweet DV, editor. Registry of toxic effects of chemical substances. Cincinnati: US Department of Health, 1987.

21. General References

—

22. Authors

USA: DG Pope.

Kaolin

1. Nonproprietary Names

BP: Light kaolin
USP: Kaolin
Note that the PhEur 1986 contains a monograph on heavy kaolin (kaolinum ponderosum). The BP 1993 in addition to the monograph for light kaolin also contains monographs for light kaolin (natural) and heavy kaolin.
See also Sections 4 and 9.

2. Synonyms

Argilla; bolus alba; china clay; E559; kaolinite; porcelain clay; *Vanclay*; white bole.

3. Chemical Name and CAS Registry Number

Hydrated aluminum silicate [1332-58-7]

4. Empirical Formula   Molecular Weight

$Al_2H_4O_9Si_2$ 258.16

The USP XXII describes kaolin as a native hydrated aluminum silicate, powdered and freed from gritty particles by elutriation. The BP 1993 similarly describes light kaolin but additionally states that it contains a suitable dispersing agent. Light kaolin (natural) BP contains no dispersing agent. Heavy kaolin is described in the BP 1993 and PhEur 1986 as a purified, natural, hydrated aluminum silicate of variable composition.

5. Structural Formula

$Al_2O_3.2SiO_2.2H_2O$

6. Functional Category

Adsorbent; suspending agent; tablet and capsule diluent.

7. Applications in Pharmaceutical Formulation or Technology

Kaolin is a naturally occurring mineral used in oral and topical pharmaceutical formulations.
In oral medicines, kaolin has been used as a diluent in tablet and capsule formulations; it has also been used as a suspending vehicle. In topical preparations, sterilized kaolin has been used in poultices and as a dusting powder.

8. Description

Kaolin occurs as a white to greyish-white colored, unctuous powder free from gritty particles. It has a characteristic earthy or clay-like taste and when moistened with water, becomes darker in color and develops a clay-like odor.

SEM: 1
Excipient: Kaolin USP
Manufacturer: Georgia Kaolin Co.
Lot No.: 1672
Magnification: 60x
Voltage: 10 kV

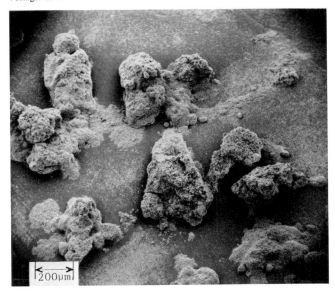

SEM: 2
Excipient: Kaolin USP
Manufacturer: Georgia Kaolin Co.
Lot No.: 1672
Magnification: 600x
Voltage: 10 kV

9. Pharmacopeial Specifications

Test	BP 1993 Light kaolin*	PhEur 1986 Heavy kaolin	USP XXII Kaolin
Identification	+	+	+
Acidity or alkalinity	—	+	—
Microbial limit	—	+	+
Coarse particles	+	—	—
Loss on drying	⩽ 1.5%	—	—
Fine particles	+	—	—
Loss on ignition	⩽ 15.0%	—	⩽ 15.0%
Acid-soluble substances	—	⩽ 1.0%	⩽ 2.0%
Organic impurities	—	+	—
Adsorption power	—	+	—
Swelling power	—	+	—
Arsenic	⩽ 2 ppm	—	—
Calcium	—	⩽ 250 ppm	—
Carbonate	—	—	+
Chloride	⩽ 330 ppm	⩽ 250 ppm	—
Heavy metals	⩽ 20 ppm	⩽ 25 ppm	—
Iron	—	—	+
Lead	—	—	⩽ 0.001%
Sulfate	—	⩽ 0.1%	—

* Tests for Light kaolin (natural) BP are the same.

10. Typical Properties

Acidity/alkalinity:
pH = 4.0-7.5 for a 20% w/v aqueous slurry.
Hardness (Mohs): 2.0, very low.
Hygroscopicity: at relative humidities between about 15-65%, the equilibrium moisture content at 25°C is about 1% w/w, but at relative humidities above about 75%, kaolin absorbs small amounts of moisture.
Particle size distribution: median size = 0.6-0.8 μm.
Refractive index: 1.56
Solubility: practically insoluble in water, organic solvents, cold dilute acids and solutions of alkali hydroxides.
Specific gravity: 2.6
Viscosity (dynamic): 300 mPa s (300 cP) for a 70% w/v aqueous suspension.
Whiteness: 85-90% of the brightness of MgO.

11. Stability and Storage Conditions

Kaolin is a stable material. Since it is a naturally occurring material, kaolin is commonly contaminated with microorganisms such as *Bacillus anthracis*, *Clostridium tetani* and *Clostridium welchii*. However, kaolin may be sterilized by heating at a temperature greater than 160°C for not less than one hour.
Kaolin should be stored in a well-closed container in a cool, dry, place.

12. Incompatibilities

The adsorbent properties of kaolin may influence the absorption of other orally administered drugs. Drugs reportedly affected by kaolin include: amoxicillin;[1] ampicillin;[1] cimetidine;[2] digoxin;[3] lincomycin; phenytoin[4] and tetracycline. Warfarin absorption by rat intestine *in vitro* was reported not to be affected by kaolin.[5] With clindamycin, the rate (but not the amount) of absorption was affected by kaolin.[6]

13. Method of Manufacture

Kaolin is a hydrated aluminum silicate obtained by mining naturally occurring mineral deposits. Large deposits are found in Georgia, USA and in Cornwall, England.
Mined kaolin is powdered and freed of coarse, gritty particles either by elutriation or screening. Impurities such as ferric oxide, calcium carbonate and magnesium carbonate are removed with an electromagnet and by treatment with hydrochloric acid and/or sulfuric acid.

14. Safety

Kaolin has been used in oral and topical pharmaceutical formulations and is generally regarded as an essentially nontoxic and nonirritant material.
Therapeutically, oral doses of up to about 24 g of kaolin have been administered in the treatment of diarrhea.

15. Handling Precautions

Observe normal precautions appropriate to the circumstances and quantity of material handled. The chronic inhalation of kaolin dust can cause diseases of the lung (silicosis or kaolinosis).[7] Eye protection and a dust mask are recommended.

16. Regulatory Status

Accepted in Europe as a food additive in certain applications. Included in the FDA Inactive Ingredients Guide (oral capsules, powders, syrups and tablets). Included in nonparenteral medicines licensed in the UK.

17. Pharmacopeias

Aust, Br, Chin, Egypt, Eur, Fr, Ger, Gr, Hung, Ind, It, Jpn, Mex, Neth, Nord, Port, Rus, Swiss, US and Yug. Also in BP Vet.
Note that some pharmacopeias do not distinguish between the light and the heavy material.

18. Related Substances

Bentonite; Talc.

19. Comments

Kaolin is considered in most countries to be an archaic diluent. The name kaolinite was historically used to describe the processed mineral whilst the name kaolin was used for the unprocessed clay. However, the two names have effectively become synonymous and kaolin is now generally the only name used.

20. Specific References

1. Khalil SAH, Mortada LM, El-Khawas M. Decreased bioavailability of ampicillin and amoxicillin in presence of kaolin. Int J Pharmaceutics 1984; 19: 233-238.
2. Ganjian F, Cutie AJ, Jochsberger T. *In vitro* adsorption studies of cimetidine. J Pharm Sci 1980; 69: 352-353.
3. Albert KS, et al. Influence of kaolin-pectin suspension on digoxin bioavailability. J Pharm Sci 1978; 67: 1582-1586.
4. McElnay JC, D'Arcy PF, Throne O. Effect of antacid constituents, kaolin and calcium citrate on phenytoin absorption. Int J Pharmaceutics 1980; 7: 83-88.
5. McElnay JC, Harron DW, D'Arcy PF, Collier PS. The interaction of warfarin with antacid constituents in the gut. Experientia 1979; 35: 1359-1360.

6. Albert KS, DeSante KA, Welch RD, DiSanto AR. Pharmacokinetic evaluation of a drug interaction between kaolin-pectin and clindamycin. J Pharm Sci 1978; 67: 1579-1582.

7. Lesser M, Zia M, Kilburn KH. Silicosis in kaolin workers and firebrick makers. South Med J 1978; 71: 1242-1246.

21. General References

Allwood MC. The adsorption of esters of *p*-hydroxybenzoic acid by magnesium trisilicate. Int J Pharmaceutics 1982; 11: 101-107.

22. Authors

USA: A Palmieri.

Lactic Acid

1. Nonproprietary Names

BP: Lactic acid
PhEur: Acidum lacticum
USP: Lactic acid

2. Synonyms

E270; *Eco-Lac*; 2-hydroxypropanoic acid; α-hydroxypropionic acid; 2-hydroxypropionic acid; *L18*; DL-lactic acid; milk acid; *Patlac LA*; *Purac 88 PH*; racemic lactic acid.

3. Chemical Name and CAS Registry Number

2-Hydroxypropionic acid [50-21-5]
(R)-(-)-2-Hydroxypropionic acid [10326-41-7]
(S)-(+)-2-Hydroxypropionic acid [79-33-4]
(RS)-(±)-2-Hydroxypropionic acid [598-82-3]
See also Section 8.

4. Empirical Formula   Molecular Weight

$C_3H_6O_3$ 90.08

5. Structural Formula

$$CH_3—CH—COOH$$
$$|$$
$$OH$$

6. Functional Category

Acidifying agent; acidulant.

7. Applications in Pharmaceutical Formulation or Technology

Lactic acid is used in beverages, foods, cosmetics and pharmaceuticals as an acidifying agent and acidulant.
In topical formulations, particularly cosmetics, it is used for its softening and conditioning effect on the skin. It is also used as a food preservative; in injections, in the form of lactate, as a source of bicarbonate for the treatment of metabolic acidosis; as a spermicidal agent; in pessaries for the treatment of leucorrhea; in infant feeds and in topical formulations for the treatment of warts.

Use	Concentration (%)
Injections	0.012-1.16
Topical preparations	0.015-6.6

8. Description

Lactic acid consists of a mixture of 2-hydroxypropionic acid, its condensation products, such as lactoyl-lactic acid and other polylactic acids, and water. It is usually in the form of the racemate, (RS)-lactic acid, but in some cases the (S)-(+)-isomer is predominant.
Lactic acid is a practically odorless, colorless or slightly yellow-colored, viscous, hygroscopic, nonvolatile liquid.

9. Pharmacopeial Specifications

Test	PhEur 1986	USP XXII
Identification	+	+
Color	+	—
Specific rotation	—	-0.05° to +0.05°
Calcium	≤ 200 ppm	—
Heavy metals	≤ 10 ppm	≤ 0.001%
Sulfate	≤ 200 ppm	+
Chloride	—	+
Citric, oxalic and phosphoric acids	+	+
Ether-insoluble substances	+	—
Sugars	—	+
Methanol and methyl esters	≤ 500 ppm	—
Reducing substances	+	—
Readily carbonizable substances	—	+
Volatile fatty acids	+	—
Residue on ignition	—	≤ 0.05%
Sulfated ash	≤ 0.1%	—
Assay	88.0-92.0	85.0-90.0%

10. Typical Properties

Boiling point: 122°C at 2 kPa (15 mmHg)
Dissociation constant: $pK_a = 4.14$ at 22.5°C
Flash point: > 110°C
Heat of combustion: 15.13 kJ/kg (3615 cal/kg)
Melting point: 17°C
Osmolarity: a 2.3% w/v aqueous solution is iso-osmotic with serum.
Refractive index: $n_D^{20} = 1.4251$
Solubility: miscible with ethanol (95%), ether and water; practically insoluble in chloroform.
Specific heat: 2.11 J/g (0.505 cal/g) at 20°C
Specific gravity: 1.21
Specific rotation $[\alpha]_D^{21}$:
-2.6° (8% w/v aqueous solution) for (R)-form;
+2.6° (2.5% w/v aqueous solution) for (S)-form.
Viscosity (dynamic): 28.5 mPa s (28.5 cP) for 85% aqueous solution at 25°C.

11. Stability and Storage Conditions

Lactic acid is hygroscopic and will form condensation products, such as polylactic acids on contact with water; the equilibrium between the polylactic acids and lactic acid is dependent on concentration and temperature. At elevated temperatures lactic acid will form lactide which is readily hydrolyzed back to lactic acid.
Lactic acid should be stored in a well-closed container in a cool, dry, place.

12. Incompatibilities

Incompatible with oxidising agents, iodides and albumin. Reacts violently with hydrofluoric acid and nitric acid.

13. Method of Manufacture

Lactic acid is prepared by the fermentation of carbohydrates, such as glucose, sucrose and lactose, with *Bacillus acidi lacti* or related microorganisms. On a commercial scale whey, corn starch, potatoes or molasses are used as a source of carbohydrate. Lactic acid may also be prepared synthetically by the reaction between acetaldehyde and carbon monoxide at

130-200°C and high pressure, or by the hydrolysis of hexoses with sodium hydroxide.

Lactic acid prepared by the fermentation of sugars is levorotatory; that prepared synthetically is racemic. However, lactic acid prepared by fermentation becomes dextrorotatory on dilution with water due to the hydrolysis of (R)-lactic acid lactate to (S)-lactic acid.

14. Safety

Lactic acid occurs in appreciable quantities in the body as an end product of the anaerobic metabolism of carbohydrates and whilst harmful in the concentrated form (*see* Section 15) can be considered nontoxic at the levels used as an excipient. A 1% solution, for example, is harmless when applied to the skin. There is no evidence that lactic acid is carcinogenic, teratogenic or mutagenic.

See also Section 19.

LD_{50} (guinea pig, oral): 1.81 g/kg[1]
LD_{50} (mouse, oral): 4.88 g/kg
LD_{50} (mouse, SC): 4.5 g/kg
LD_{50} (rat, oral): 3.73 g/kg

15. Handling Precautions

Lactic acid is caustic in concentrated form and can cause burns on contact with the skin and eyes. It is harmful if swallowed, inhaled or absorbed through the skin. Observe precautions appropriate to the circumstances and quantity of material handled. Eye protection, rubber gloves and respirator are recommended. It is advisable to handle in a chemical fume hood and to avoid repeated or prolonged exposure. Spillages should be diluted with copious quantities of water. In case of excessive inhalation, remove to a well-ventilated environment and seek medical attention. Lactic acid presents no fire or explosion hazard but emits acrid smoke and fumes when heated to decomposition.

16. Regulatory Status

GRAS listed. Accepted for use as a food additive in Europe. Included in the FDA Inactive Ingredients Guide (IM, IV and SC injections, oral syrups and tablets, topical and vaginal preparations). Included in medicines licensed in the UK.

17. Pharmacopeias

Aust, Br, Braz, Chin, Cz, Egypt, Eur, Fr, Ger, Gr, Hung, Ind, It, Jpn, Mex, Neth, Nord, Port, Rom, Swiss, Turk, US and Yug.

18. Related Substances

-

19. Comments

There is evidence that neonates have difficulty in metabolising (R)-lactic acid and this isomer and the racemate should therefore not be used in foods for infants aged less than 3 months old.[2]

20. Specific References

1. Sweet DV, editor. Registry of toxic effects of chemical substances. Cincinnati: US Department of Health, 1987.
2. FAO/WHO. Toxicological evaluation of certain food additives with a review of general principles and specifications. Seventeenth report of the FAO/WHO expert committee on food additives. Tech Rep Ser Wld Hlth Org 1974; No. 539.

21. General References

Al-Shammary FJ, Mian NAZ, Mian MS. Lactic acid. In: Brittain HG, editor. Analytical profiles of drug substances and excipients, volume 22. San Diego: Academic Press Inc, 1993: 263-316.

22. Authors

UK: MG Lee.

Lactose

1. Nonproprietary Names

BP: Lactose monohydrate
PhEur: Lactosum
USPNF: Lactose monohydrate
Note that the USPNF XVII (Suppl 9) also contains a monograph for anhydrous lactose, see Sections 9 and 19.

2. Synonyms

Fast-Flo; 4-(β-D-galactosido)-D-glucose; *Lactochem*; *Microtose*; milk sugar; *Pharmatose*; saccharum lactis; *Tablettose*; *Zeparox*.

3. Chemical Name and CAS Registry Number

O-β-D-Galactopyranosyl-(1→4)-α-D-glucopyranose anhydrous [63-42-3]
O-β-D-Galactopyranosyl-(1→4)-α-D-glucopyranose monohydrate [64044-51-5]

4. Empirical Formula   Molecular Weight

$C_{12}H_{22}O_{11}$ 342.30 (anhydrous)
$C_{12}H_{22}O_{11}.H_2O$ 360.31 (monohydrate)

5. Structural Formula

α - lactose   β - lactose

6. Functional Category

Tablet and capsule diluent.

7. Applications in Pharmaceutical Formulation or Technology

Lactose is widely used as a filler or diluent in tablets, capsules, and to a more limited extent in lyophilized products and infant feed formulas.[1-15]

Spray-dried lactose was first developed over 30 years ago for use in solid dosage pharmaceutical formulations. Today, many other lactose grades are commercially available, including anhydrous α-lactose, α-lactose monohydrate, and to a minor extent, anhydrous β-lactose.

Generally, the grade of lactose chosen is dependent on the type of dosage form being developed. Direct compression grades are often used to carry small quantities of drug and this permits tablets to be made without granulating.

Direct compression grades of lactose are more fluid and more compressible than crystalline or powdered lactose and are generally composed of spray-dried lactoses which contain specially prepared pure α-lactose monohydrate along with a small amount of amorphous lactose. The amorphous lactose improves the compression force/hardness profile of the lactose. Other specially produced direct compression grades of lactose do not contain amorphous material but may contain glassy or vitreous areas which impart improved compressibility. Direct compression grades of lactose may also be combined with microcrystalline cellulose or starch, and usually require a tablet lubricant such as 0.5% w/w magnesium stearate. The use of direct compression grades of lactose results in tablets of higher breaking strength than standard lactose. Concentrations of lactose generally used in these formulations are from 65-85%.

Various lactose grades are commercially available which have different physical properties such as particle size distribution and flow characteristics. This permits the selection of the most suitable material for a particular application, e.g. the particle size range selected for capsules is often dependent upon the type of encapsulating machine used. Usually, fine grades of lactose are used in the preparation of tablets by the wet granulation method or when milling during processing is carried out, since the fine size permits better mixing with other formulation ingredients and utilizes the binder more efficiently.

Other applications of lactose include as a carrier/diluent for inhalation products and in lyophilized products, where lactose is added to freeze-dried solutions to increase plug size and aid caking. Lactose is also used in combination with sucrose (approximately 1:3) to prepare sugar-coating solutions.

8. Description

White to off-white crystalline particles or powder. Lactose is odorless and slightly sweet-tasting; α-lactose is approximately 15% as sweet as sucrose, while β-lactose is sweeter than the α-form.

Several different forms of lactose are commercially available: anhydrous α-lactose, α-lactose monohydrate, and to a lesser extent, anhydrous β-lactose which typically contains 70% anhydrous β-lactose and 30% anhydrous α-lactose, although grades containing a greater quantity of anhydrous β-lactose are also available, e.g. *Pharmatose DCL 21* (DMV International). α-Lactose may also contain a small quantity of the β-form.

SEM: 1

Excipient: Lactose monohydrate (*Lactose D30*)
Manufacturer: Meggle GmbH

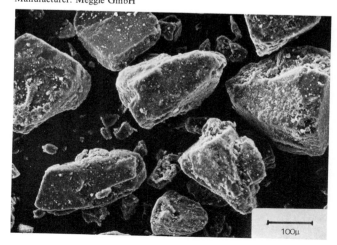

100µ

SEM: 2

Excipient: Lactose monohydrate (*Lactose G200*)
Manufacturer: Meggle GmbH

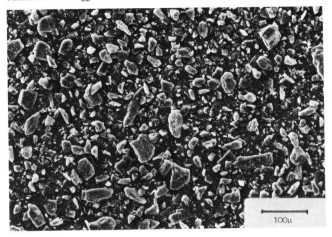

SEM: 3

Excipient: Lactose monohydrate (*Tablettose*)
Manufacturer: Meggle GmbH

SEM: 4

Excipient: Lactose monohydrate (*Lactose monohydrate 60S*)
Manufacturer: Quest International Inc (Sheffield Products)
Lot No.: 58A-13 (9 NJ 16)
Magnification: 120x
Voltage: 20 kV

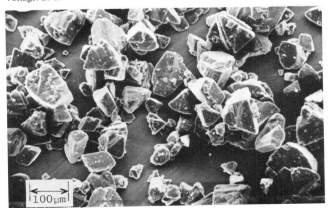

SEM: 5

Excipient: Lactose monohydrate (*Lactose monohydrate 80S*)
Manufacturer: Quest International Inc (Sheffield Products)
Lot No.: 58A-12 (9 NK 18)
Magnification: 120x
Voltage: 20 kV

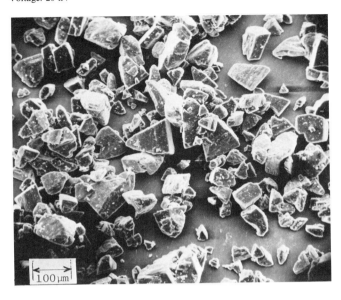

SEM: 6

Excipient: Lactose monohydrate (*Lactose monohydrate 80M*)
Manufacturer: Quest International Inc (Sheffield Products)
Lot No.: 58A-11 (9 NL 18)
Magnification: 120x
Voltage: 20 kV

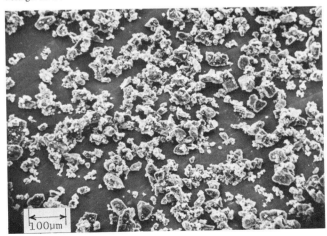

SEM: 7

Excipient: Lactose monohydrate (*Lactose monohydrate capsulating*)
Manufacturer: Quest International Inc (Sheffield Products)
Lot No.: 58A-10 (9 NL 20)
Magnification: 120x
Voltage: 20 kV

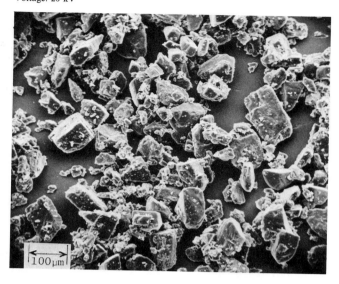

SEM: 8

Excipient: Lactose monohydrate (*Lactose monohydrate impalpable*)
Manufacturer: Quest International Inc (Sheffield Products)
Lot No.: 58A-14 (9 NH 22)
Magnification: 120x
Voltage: 20 kV

9. Pharmacopeial Specifications

Test	PhEur 1994	USPNF XVII (Suppl 9)
Identification	+	+
Appearance of solution	+	+
Specific rotation (anhydrous basis)	+ 54.4° to + 55.9°	+ 54.8° to + 55.5°
Microbial limits	100/g	100/g
Acidity or alkalinity	+	+
Loss on drying		
Anhydrous form	—	⩽ 0.1%
Monohydrate	—	⩽ 0.5%
Water		
Anhydrous form	—	⩽ 1.0%
Monohydrate	4.5-5.5%	4.5-5.5%
Residue on ignition	—	⩽ 0.1%
Sulfated ash	⩽ 0.1%	—
Heavy metals	⩽ 5 ppm	⩽ 5 ppm
Organic volatile impurities	—	+
Protein and light-absorbing impurities	+	+

10. Typical Properties

Angle of repose: *see* Table I.
Compressibility: *see* HPE Data.
Density:
1.540 for α-lactose monohydrate;
1.589 for anhydrous β-lactose.
Density (bulk): *see* Table I and HPE Data.
Density (tapped): *see* Table I and HPE Data.
Flowability: *see* HPE Data.
Hygroscopicity: lactose monohydrate is stable in air and is unaffected by humidity at room temperature. However, the amorphous form, depending upon how it is dried, may be affected by humidity and can be converted to the monohydrate. *See also* HPE Data.
Melting point:
201-202°C for α-lactose monohydrate;
223°C for anhydrous α-lactose;
252.2°C for anhydrous β-lactose.
Moisture content: anhydrous lactose normally contains up to 1% w/w water. Lactose monohydrate contains approximately 5% w/w water of crystallization and normally ranges between 4.5-5.5% w/w water content. *See also* Table I and HPE Data.
Osmolarity: a 9.75% w/v aqueous solution is iso-osmotic with serum.
Particle size distribution: *see* Table II.
Solubility:

Solvent	Solubility at 25°C Unless otherwise stated
Chloroform	practically insoluble
Ethanol	practically insoluble
Ether	practically insoluble
Water	1 in 4.63
	1 in 3.14 at 40°C
	1 in 2.04 at 50°C
	1 in 1.68 at 60°C
	1 in 1.07 at 80°C

Specific rotation $[\alpha]_D^{20}$: + 54.8° to + 55.5° for anhydrous lactose, as a 10% w/v aqueous solution.

Table I: Typical physical properties of selected commercially available lactoses.

Supplier/Grade	Angle of repose (°)	Density (g/cm³) Bulk	Density (g/cm³) Tapped	Specific surface area (m²/g)	Water content (%)
Borculo Whey Products					
(Lactochem)					
Microfine	—	—	—	—	⩽ 5.5
Zeparox[a]	—	0.6-0.7	—	—	⩽ 5.5
DMV International					
Pharmatose 50M	36	0.80	0.95	—	5.2
Pharmatose 80M	38	0.76	0.91	—	5.2
Pharmatose 90M	39	0.76	0.91	—	5.2
Pharmatose 100M	39	0.75	0.90	—	5.2
Pharmatose 110M	40	0.73	0.89	—	5.2
Pharmatose 125M	44	0.68	0.87	—	5.2
Pharmatose 150M	—	0.58	0.89	0.45	5.2
Pharmatose 200M	—	0.55	0.85	0.50	5.2
Pharmatose 325M	40	0.67	0.84	—	5.2
Pharmatose 350M	—	0.50	0.82	0.60	5.2
Pharmatose 450M	—	0.47	0.77	1.0	5.2
Pharmatose DCL 11[b]	31	0.61	0.73	—	4.8
Pharmatose DCL 21[c]	39	0.67	0.85	0.35	0.5
Foremost Ingredients Group					
Impalpable #312	—	0.53	0.81	—	4.8-5.2
Impalpable #313	—	0.48	0.78	—	4.8-5.2
Spray Process #315	—	0.67	0.78	—	4.8-5.2
Fast-Flo #316	—	0.58	0.70	—	4.8-5.2
Meggle GmbH					
Lactose D10	35	0.50	0.59	—	5.1
Lactose D20	33	0.59	0.68	—	5.1
Lactose D30	34	0.72	0.85	—	5.1
Lactose GK	—	0.72	0.87	—	5.1
Lactose G200	—	0.46	0.51	—	5.1
Microtose	—	0.34	0.41	—	5.1
Tablettose	32	0.53	0.65	—	5.1
Quest International Inc					
(Sheffield Products)					
Monohydrate 60S	—	—	—	—	⩽ 5.5
Monohydrate 80S	—	—	—	—	⩽ 5.5
Monohydrate 80M	—	—	—	—	⩽ 5.5
Monohydrate Capsulating	—	—	—	—	⩽ 5.5
Monohydrate Impalpable	—	—	—	—	⩽ 5.5
Anhydrous Direct Tableting	—	—	—	—	⩽ 1.0
Anhydrous 60M	—	—	—	—	⩽ 1.0
Anhydrous 80M	—	—	—	—	⩽ 1.0
Anhydrous Impalpable	—	—	—	—	⩽ 1.0

Note:
a. Direct compression grade of lactose.
b. Spray-dried lactose monohydrate.
c. Anhydrous lactose containing 82% β-lactose.
Unless otherwise stated all of the above grades are α-lactose monohydrate.

Table II: Particle size distribution of selected commercially available lactoses.

Supplier/Grade	Typical particle size distribution (%) less than stated size.												
	10μm	32μm	45μm	63μm	75μm	100μm	150μm	200μm	250μm	315μm	400μm	600μm	800μm
Borculo Whey Products (Lactochem)													
Microfine	99.9	—	—	—	—	—	—	—	—	—	—	—	—
Zeparox[a]	—	—	—	—	10-20	40-65	70-95	95-100	—	—	—	—	—
DMV International													
Pharmatose 50M	—	—	—	—	—	—	—	10	—	—	92	—	—
Pharmatose 80M	—	—	—	6	—	10	65	—	84	99	—	—	—
Pharmatose 90M	—	—	—	9	—	21	65	—	—	100	—	—	—
Pharmatose 100M	—	—	—	—	—	—	68	—	99.7	—	—	—	—
Pharmatose 110M	—	—	—	15	—	40	85	—	—	100	—	—	—
Pharmatose 125M	—	—	25	55	—	97	—	—	—	100	—	—	—
Pharmatose 150M	—	—	45	—	—	75	90	—	—	100	—	—	—
Pharmatose 200M	—	—	60	—	83	92	98	—	100	—	—	—	—
Pharmatose 325M	—	8	—	78	—	100	—	—	—	—	—	—	—
Pharmatose 350M	—	—	75	—	—	98	—	—	100	—	—	—	—
Pharmatose 450M	—	—	95	99	—	—	100	—	—	—	—	—	—
Pharmatose DCL 11[b]	—	—	10	—	—	—	—	—	100	—	—	—	—
Pharmatose DCL 21[c]	—	—	15	—	—	45	50	—	85	—	—	—	—
Foremost Ingredients Group													
Impalpable #312	—	—	—	—	94	99	—	—	—	—	—	—	—
Impalpable #313	—	—	90	—	99	—	—	—	—	—	—	—	—
Spray Process #315	—	—	—	—	15-50	40-70	—	—	—	—	—	—	—
Fast-Flo #316	—	—	—	—	15-45	35-75	—	—	98	—	—	100	—
Meggle GmbH													
Lactose D10	—	—	—	—	—	—	—	—	—	—	—	—	—
Lactose D20	—	—	—	—	—	2	—	4	—	—	12-35	—	100
Lactose D30	—	—	—	—	—	25-50	—	10-35	—	—	—	100	—
Lactose GK	—	—	—	—	—	45-55	—	—	100	—	—	—	—
Lactose G200	—	—	—	—	—	100	—	—	—	—	100	—	—
Microtose	—	98	—	100	—	—	—	—	—	—	—	—	—
Tablettose	—	—	—	12	—	—	—	—	—	—	93	100	—
Quest International Inc (Sheffield Products)													
Monohydrate 60S	—	—	—	—	15-35	70-85	80-90	—	97-100	—	—	—	—
Monohydrate 80S	—	—	—	—	20-35	—	80-95	—	99.3-100	—	—	—	—
Monohydrate 80M	—	—	—	—	65-90	95-98	95-99.5	—	99.5-100	—	—	—	—
Monohydrate Capsulating	—	—	—	—	58-70	—	94-100	—	—	—	—	—	—
Monohydrate Impalpable	—	—	—	—	90	97-99	98.5-100	—	—	—	—	—	—
Anhydrous Direct Tableting	—	—	—	—	15-30	75-90	85-93	—	—	—	—	—	—
Anhydrous 60M	—	—	—	—	20-40	75-90	85-93	—	—	—	—	—	—
Anhydrous 80M	—	—	—	—	70	—	85-93	—	95-98	—	—	—	—
Anhydrous Impalpable	—	—	—	—	90	—	—	—	—	—	—	—	—

Note:
a. Direct compression grade of lactose.
b. Spray-dried lactose monohydrate.
c. Anhydrous lactose containing 82% β-lactose.
Unless otherwise stated all of the above grades are α-lactose monohydrate.

Specific rotation $[\alpha]_D^{25}$: $+52°$ to $+52.6°$ for lactose monohydrate, as a 10% w/v aqueous solution. Lactose exhibits mutarotation and an equilibrium mixture containing 62% β-lactose and 38% α-lactose is obtained instantly on the addition of a trace of ammonia.

	HPE Laboratory Project Data		
	Method	**Lab #**	**Results**
Average flow rate			
Fast-Flo #316	FLO-1	14	3.9 g/s [a]
Impalpable #312	FLO-1	14	No flow [a]
Impalpable #313	FLO-1	14	No flow [a]
Spray process #315	FLO-1	14	4.1 g/s [a]
Bulk/tap density			
Fast-Flo #316	BTD-8	36	B: 0.69 g/cm³ [a]
			T: 0.74 g/cm³
Impalpable #313	BTD-8	36	B: 0.44 g/cm³ [a]
			T: 0.64 g/cm³
Spray process #315	BTD-8	36	B: 0.73 g/cm³ [a]
			T: 0.78 g/cm³
Monohydrate 60S	BTD-5	6	B: 0.73 g/cm³ [b]
			T: 0.90 g/cm³
Monohydrate 80S	BTD-5	6	B: 0.71 g/cm³ [b]
			T: 0.90 g/cm³
Compressibility			
Fast-Flo #316	COM-4,5,6	29	*See* Fig. 1. [a]
Impalpable #312	COM-4,5,6	29	*See* Fig. 2. [a]
Impalpable #313	COM-4,5,6	29	*See* Fig. 3. [a]
Spray process #315	COM-3	20	*See* Fig. 4. [a]
Spray process #315	COM-4,5,6	29	*See* Fig. 5. [a]
Moisture content			
Anhydrous impalpable	SDI-1	14	*See* Fig. 6. [b]
Fast-Flo #316	EMC-1	2	*See* Fig. 7. [a]
Impalpable #313	MC-3	14	5.12% [a]
Impalpable #313	MC-16	14	5.04% [a]
Spray process #315	EMC-1	2	*See* Fig. 7. [a]
Spray process #315	SDI-1	14	*See* Fig. 6. [a]
Particle friability			
Spray process #315	PF-1	36	0.018 [a]

Supplier: a. Foremost Ingredients Group; b. Quest International Inc (Sheffield Products).

11. Stability and Storage Conditions

Under humid conditions (80% relative humidity and above), mold growth may occur. Lactose may develop a brown coloration on storage, the reaction being accelerated by warm, damp conditions, *see also* Section 12. The purity of different lactoses can vary and color evaluation may thus be important, particularly if white tablets are being formulated. The color stability of various lactoses also differ.

Saturated solutions of β-lactose may precipitate crystals of α-lactose on standing. Solutions also shown mutarotation, *see* Section 10.

Lactose should be stored in a well-closed container in a cool, dry, place.

12. Incompatibilities

A Maillard-type condensation reaction is likely to occur between lactose and compounds with a primary amine group to form brown-colored products.[16] This reaction occurs more readily with the amorphous material rather than with crystalline lactose. The spray-dried material, which contains about 10% amorphous lactose, is also prone to discoloration.

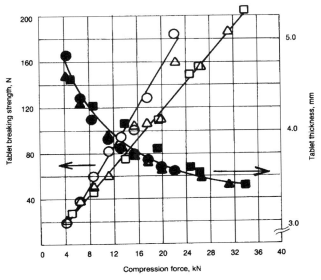

Fig. 1: Compression characteristics of spray-dried lactose (*Fast-Flo #316*, Lot #RK923).
○ ● Unlubricated, Carver Laboratory Press (COM-5)
△ ▲ Lubricated, Carver Laboratory Press (COM-6)
□ ■ Lubricated, Instrumented Stokes Model F-single punch press (COM-4)

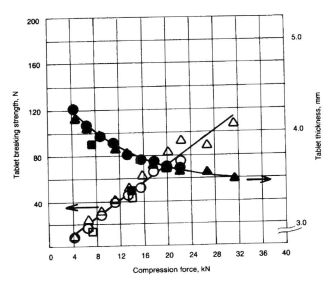

Fig. 2: Compression characteristics of lactose (*Impalpable #312*, Lot #SG923).
○ ● Unlubricated, Carver Laboratory Press (COM-5)
△ ▲ Lubricated, Carver Laboratory Press (COM-6)
□ ■ Lubricated, Instrumented Stokes Model F-single punch press (COM-4)

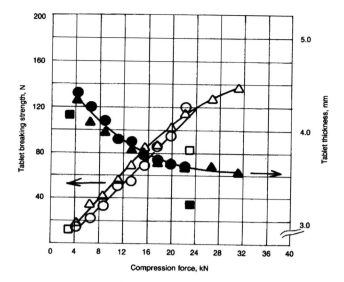

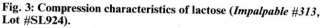

Fig. 3: Compression characteristics of lactose (*Impalpable #313, Lot #SL924*).
○ ● Unlubricated, Carver Laboratory Press (COM-5)
△ ▲ Lubricated, Carver Laboratory Press (COM-6)
□ ■ Lubricated, Instrumented Stokes Model F-single punch press (COM-4)

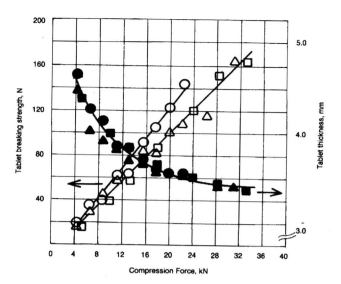

Fig. 5: Compression characteristics of lactose (*Spray Process #315, Lot #RH914*).
○ ● Unlubricated, Carver Laboratory Press (COM-5)
△ ▲ Lubricated, Carver Laboratory Press (COM-6)
□ ■ Lubricated, Instrumented Stokes Model F-single punch press (COM-4)

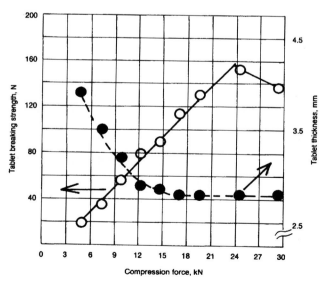

Fig. 4: Compression characteristics of lactose (*Spray Process #315, Lot #RL921*).
Mean tablet weight = 511 mg
Minimum compressional force for compaction = 4.9 kN
Compressional force resulting in capping = 29.4 kN

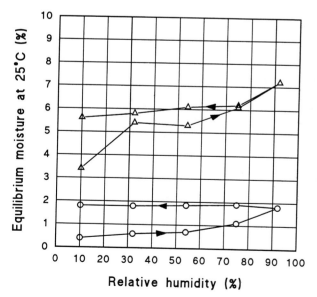

Fig. 6: Moisture sorption-desorption isotherms of different grades of lactose.
○ Anhydrous lactose, *Anhydrous Impalpable* (Lot #7N4868)
△ Lactose, *Spray Process #315* (Lot #RH914)

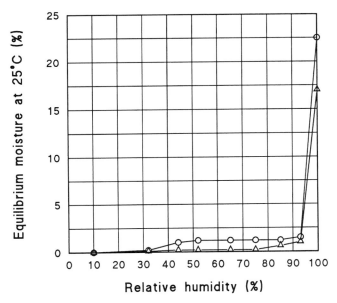

Fig. 7: Equilibrium moisture content of different grades of lactose.

○ Lactose, *Spray Process #315* (Lot #56165)
△ Lactose, *Fast-Flo #316* (Lot #RB806)

The 'browning reaction' is base-catalyzed and may therefore be accelerated if alkaline lubricants are used. Lactose may also develop a yellow-brown color, in the absence of amines, with browning again occurring most rapidly in the spray-dried material, possibly due to the formation of 5-hydroxymethyl-2-furfural.

Lactose is incompatible with amino acids, aminophylline[17] and amphetamines.[18]

13. Method of Manufacture

Lactose is a natural disaccharide consisting of galactose and glucose and is present in the milk of most mammals. Commercially, lactose is produced from the whey of cows' milk, whey being the residual liquid of the milk following cheese and casein production. Cows' milk contains 4.4-5.2% lactose and it is 38% of the total solid content of milk.

Lactose exists as two anomeric forms, α and β, which are normally handled as respectively the monohydrate and the anhydrous material. α-Lactose is prepared by crystallization from supersaturated solutions below 93.5°C, whereas β-lactose is prepared from solutions above this temperature. The commercially available β-lactose typically contains 70% of the β-form and 30% of the α-form and is prepared by roller drying. Other grades containing greater amounts of the β-form are also available.

α-Lactose is available primarily as the monohydrate but two anhydrous forms also exist. Anhydrous forms which are commercially available may exhibit hygroscopicity. An unstable hygroscopic form can also be prepared using special drying techniques, however this material is not used or available in normal practice.

An amorphous or glassy form of lactose is present in lactose when it is either spray-dried from a suspension or lyophilized. This noncrystalline portion is responsible for the improved compressibility of spray-dried lactose.

α-Lactose monohydrate has also been prepared by special commercial crystallization procedures which improve compressibility over the normally prepared material. These special grades may be readily identified by microscopic examination. Various crystalline shapes are prism, pyramidal, and tomahawk; these are dependent on the method of precipitation and crystallization.

14. Safety

Lactose is widely used in pharmaceutical formulations as a diluent in oral capsule and tablet formulations. It may also be used in intravenous injections.

Adverse reactions to lactose are largely attributed to lactose intolerance, which occurs in persons with a deficiency of the intestinal enzyme lactase.[19-21] This results in lactose being undigested and may lead to clinical symptoms including abdominal cramps, diarrhea, distension and flatulence.

In lactose-tolerant individuals, the enzyme lactase hydrolyzes lactose in the small intestine to glucose and galactose, which are then absorbed. Lactose is excreted unchanged when administered intravenously.

Lactase is normally high at birth but declines rapidly in early childhood. Malabsorption of lactose (hypolactasia) may thus occur at an early age, e.g. 4-8 years old, and varies among different ethnic groups.

The symptoms of lactose intolerance are caused by the osmotic effect of the unabsorbed lactose which increases water and sodium levels in the lumen. Unabsorbed lactose, upon reaching the colon, can be fermented by colonic flora, which produces gas, thus causing abdominal distention and discomfort.

A lactase tolerance test has been developed based upon the measurement of the blood glucose level, and the hydrogen level in the breath. However, this test is based on a 50 g dose of lactose, hence its usefulness has been questioned.

Approximately 10-20% of lactose-intolerant individuals, in two studies, showed clinical symptoms of intolerance after ingestion of 3-5 g of lactose.[19,20] In one of these studies,[19] 75% of the subjects had symptoms with 12 g of lactose (equivalent to 8 ounces of milk). In the other study,[20] 8 out of 13 individuals developed diarrhea after the administration of 20 g of lactose, and 9 out of 13 after the administration of 25 g. Lower doses of lactose produce fewer adverse effects, and lactose is better tolerated if taken with other foods. As a result, there is a significant population with lactose malabsorption who can still ingest normal amounts of lactose, such as that in milk, without the development of significant adverse effects. Although the quantities of lactose ingested as an excipient in oral pharmaceutical formulations are less than might be consumed in certain foods, drug-induced diarrhea due to lactose intolerance has been reported following administration of pharmaceutical preparations containing lactose.

LD_{50} (rat, IP): > 10 g/kg[22]
LD_{50} (rat, oral): > 10 g/kg
LD_{50} (rat, SC): > 5 g/kg

15. Handling Precautions

Observe normal precautions appropriate to the circumstances and quantity of material handled. Excessive dust generation, or dust inhalation, should be avoided.

16. Regulatory Status

Included in the FDA Inactive Ingredients Guide (IV injections, oral capsules and tablets). Included in nonparenteral and parenteral medicines licensed in the UK.

17. Pharmacopeias

Aust, Belg, Br, Braz, Chin, Cz, Egypt, Eur, Fr, Ger, Gr, Hung, Ind, It, Jpn, Mex, Neth, Nord, Port, Rom, Rus, Swiss, Turk, USPNF and Yug. Also in BP Vet.

18. Related Substances

A number of excipient mixtures intended for direct compression use are commercially available, e.g. *Cellactose* (Meggle GmbH) is a mixture of lactose and cellulose.[23,24]

19. Comments

A number of different grades of lactose are commercially available which vary in their physical properties and many studies have been reported in the literature comparing the behavior of these various materials in different formulations.[7-9,13]

Lactose, depending on its form, may exhibit complex thermoanalytical transitions because of its several crystalline, as well as amorphous forms. Differential scanning calorimetry (DSC) can effectively be used to characterize the composition.[25] For example, α-Lactose monohydrate becomes anhydrous at 120°C and has a melting point of 201-202°C; endothermic peaks occur at approximately 150°C and vary depending upon the particle size of the material.

The complex nature of the lactose grades used for direct compression tableting, which contain both crystalline and amorphous fractions, has been recognised, and recent compendia now have new monographs which distinguish between the various types of lactose, e.g. the BP 1993 (Ad 1994) has a single monograph for lactose monohydrate while the USPNF XVII (Suppl 9) has two monographs for anhydrous lactose and lactose monohydrate.[26,27] Lactose, being one of the most widely used excipients, has become the first excipient to bear a global, standardized monograph which harmonizes the analytical specifications of the major pharmacopeias.[27]

20. Specific References

1. Batuyios NH. Anhydrous lactose in direct tablet compression. J Pharm Sci 1966; 55: 727-730.
2. Alpar O, Hersey JA, Shotton E. The compression properties of lactose. J Pharm Pharmacol 1970; 22(Suppl): 1S-7S.
3. Fell JT, Newton JM. The characterization of the form of lactose in spray dried lactose. Pharm Acta Helv 1970; 45: 520-522.
4. Fell JT, Newton JM. The production and properties of spray dried lactose, part 1: the construction of an experimental spray drier and the production of spray dried lactose under various conditions of operation. Pharm Acta Helv 1971; 46: 226-247.
5. Fell JT, Newton JM. The production and properties of spray dried lactose, part 2: the physical properties of samples of spray dried lactose produced on an experimental drier. Pharm Acta Helv 1971; 46: 425-430.
6. Fell JT, Newton JM. The production and properties of spray dried lactose, part 3: the compaction properties of samples of spray dried lactose produced on an experimental drier. Pharm Acta Helv 1971; 46: 441-447.
7. Bolhuis GK, Lerk CF. Comparative evaluation of excipients for direct compression, I. Pharm Weekbl 1973; 108: 469-481.
8. Lerk CF, Bolhuis GK, de Boer AH. Comparative evaluation of excipients for direct compression, II. Pharm Weekbl 1974; 109: 945-955.
9. Vromans H, de Boer AH, Bolhuis GK, Lerk CF, Kussendrager KD. Studies on the tableting properties of lactose: the effect of initial particle size on binding properties and dehydration

characteristics of α-lactose monohydrate. In: Rubinstein MH, editor. Pharmaceutical technology: tableting technology, volume 1. Chichester, England: Ellis Horwood, 1987: 31-42.
10. Shukla AJ, Price JC. Effect of moisture content on compression properties of directly compressible high beta-content anhydrous lactose. Drug Dev Ind Pharm 1991; 17: 2067-2081.
11. Thwaites PM, Mashadi AB, Moore WD. An investigation of the effect of high speed mixing on the mechanical and physical properties of direct compression lactose. Drug Dev Ind Pharm 1991; 17: 503-517.
12. Riepma KA, Dekker BG, Lerk CF. The effect of moisture sorption on the strength and internal surface area of lactose tablets. Int J Pharmaceutics 1992; 87: 149-159.
13. Çelik M, Okutgen E. A feasibility study for the development of a prospective compaction functionality test and the establishment of a compaction data bank. Drug Dev Ind Pharm 1993; 19: 2309-2334.
14. Lerk CF. Consolidation and compaction of lactose. Drug Dev Ind Pharm 1993; 19: 2359-2398.
15. Otsuka M, Ohtani H, Otsuka K, Kaneniwa N. Effect of humidity on solid-state isomerization of various kinds of lactose during grinding. J Pharm Pharmacol 1993; 45: 2-5.
16. Castello RA, Mattocks AM. Discoloration of tablets containing amines and lactose. J Pharm Sci 1962; 51: 106-108.
17. Hartauer KJ, Guillory JK. A comparison of diffuse reflectance FT-IR spectroscopy and DSC in the characterization of a drug-excipient interaction. Drug Dev Ind Pharm 1991; 17: 617-630.
18. Blaug SM, Huang W. Interaction of dextroamphetamine sulphate with spray-dried lactose. J Pharm Sci 1972; 61: 1770-1775.
19. Bedine MS, Bayless TM. Intolerance of small amounts of lactose by individuals with low lactase levels. Gastroenterology 1973; 65: 735-743.
20. Gudmand-Hoyer E, Simony K. Individual sensitivity to lactose in lactose malabsorption. Am J Dig Dis 1977; 22(3): 177-181.
21. Pray WS. Lactose intolerance. US Pharm 1990; 15(11): 24,26,28,29.
22. Sweet DV, editor. Registry of toxic effects of chemical substances. Cincinnati: US Department of Health, 1987.
23. Meggle GmbH. Technical literature: *Cellactose*, 1992.
24. Reimerdes D, Aufmuth KP. Tabletting with co-processed lactose-cellulose excipient. Mfg Chem 1992; 63(12): 21, 23, 24.
25. Lerk CF, et al. Alterations of α-lactose during differential scanning calorimetry [letter]. J Pharm Sci 1984; 73: 856-857.
26. Chowhan ZT. Revision of the lactose monograph. Pharmacopeial Forum 1990; 16(6): 1281-1282.
27. Artiges A, Schorn PJ. International harmonisation. Pharmeuropa 1994; 6(1): 29-35.

21. General References

Blair TC, Buckton G, Bloomfield SF. On the mechanism of kill of microbial contaminants during tablet compression. Int J Pharmaceutics 1991; 72: 111-115.
DMV International. Technical literature: *Pharmatose*, 1993.
Foremost Ingredients Group. Technical literature: Foremost lactose, 1993.
Meggle GmbH. Technical literature: lactose EP, 1992.
Pearce S. Lactose: the natural excipient. Mfg Chem 1986; 57(10): 77-80.
Quest International Inc (Sheffield Products). Technical literature: tabletting characteristics of lactose, 1993.
Timsina MP, Martin GP, Marriott C, Ganderton D, Yianneskis M. Drug delivery to the respiratory tract using dry powder inhalers. Int J Pharmaceutics 1994; 101: 1-13.

Zuurman K, Riepma KA, Bolhuis GK, Vromans H, Lerk CF. The relationship between bulk density and compactibility of lactose granulations. Int J Pharmaceutics 1994; 102: 1-9.

22. Authors

USA: FW Goodhart.

Lanolin

1. Nonproprietary Names

BP: Wool fat
PhEur: Adeps lanae
USP: Lanolin

2. Synonyms

Corona; lanolin anhydrous; purified lanolin; refined wool fat.

3. Chemical Name and CAS Registry Number

Anhydrous Lanolin [8006-54-0]

4. Empirical Formula   Molecular Weight

The USP XXII (Suppl 9) describes lanolin as the purified wax-like substance obtained from the wool of the sheep, *Ovis aries* Linné (Fam. Bovidae), that has been cleaned, decolorized, and deodorized. It contains not more than 0.25% w/w of water and may contain 0.02% w/w of a suitable antioxidant; the PhEur 1982 specifies up to 200 ppm of butylated hydroxytoluene as an antioxidant.
See also Section 19.

5. Structural Formula

See Section 4.

6. Functional Category

Emulsifying agent; ointment base.

7. Applications in Pharmaceutical Formulation or Technology

Lanolin is widely used in topical pharmaceutical formulations and cosmetics.
Lanolin may be used as a hydrophobic vehicle and in the preparation of water-in-oil creams and ointments. When mixed with suitable vegetable oils or with soft paraffin it produces emollient creams which penetrate the skin and hence facilitate the absorption of drugs. Lanolin mixes with about twice its own weight of water, without separation, to produce stable emulsions which do not readily become rancid on storage.
See also Section 19.

8. Description

Lanolin is a pale yellow colored, unctuous, waxy substance with a faint, characteristic odour. Melted lanolin is a clear or almost clear, yellow liquid.

9. Pharmacopeial Specifications

Test	PhEur 1982	USP XXII (Suppl 9)
Identification	+	+
Melting range	38-44°C	38-44°C
Acidity	—	+
Alkalinity	—	+
Water	—	≤ 0.25%
Loss on drying	≤ 0.5%	—
Residue on ignition	—	≤ 0.1%

Continued

Test	PhEur 1982	USP XXII (Suppl 9)
Sulfated ash	≤ 0.15%	—
Water-soluble acids and alkalies	+	+
Water-soluble oxidisable substances	+	—
Chloride	≤ 150 ppm	≤ 0.035%
Ammonia	—	+
Acid value	≤ 1.0	—
Iodine value	—	18-36
Peroxide value	≤ 20	—
Saponification value	90-105	—
Water absorption capacity	+	—
Paraffins	+	—
Petrolatum	—	+
Foreign substances	—	+
Butylated hydroxytoluene	≤ 200 ppm	—

10. Typical Properties

Autoignition temperature: 445°C
Density: 0.932-0.945 g/cm^3 at 15°C
Flash point: 238°C
Refractive index: n_D^{40} = 1.478-1.482
Solubility: freely soluble in benzene, chloroform, ether and petroleum spirit; sparingly soluble in cold ethanol (95%), more soluble in boiling ethanol (95%); practically insoluble in water.

11. Stability and Storage Conditions

Lanolin may gradually undergo autoxidation during storage. To inhibit this process the inclusion of butylated hydroxytoluene is permitted as an antioxidant. Exposure to excessive or prolonged heating may cause anhydrous lanolin to darken in color and develop a strong rancid-like odor. However, lanolin may be sterilized by dry heat at 150°C. Sterile ophthalmic ointments containing lanolin may be sterilized by filtration or by exposure to gamma irradiation.[1]
Lanolin should be stored in a well-filled, well-closed container protected from light, in a cool, dry, place. Normal storage life is two years.

12. Incompatibilities

Lanolin may contain pro-oxidants, which may affect the stability of certain active drugs.

13. Method of Manufacture

Lanolin is a naturally occurring fat-like material obtained from the wool of sheep, *Ovis aries* Linné (Fam. Bovidae).
Crude lanolin is saponified with a weak alkali and the resultant saponified fat emulsion centrifuged to remove the aqueous phase. The aqueous phase contains a soap solution from which, on standing, a layer of partially purified lanolin separates. This material is then further refined by treating with calcium chloride, followed by fusion with unslaked lime to dehydrate the lanolin. The lanolin is then finally extracted with acetone and the solvent removed by distillation.

14. Safety

Lanolin is widely used in cosmetics and a variety of topical pharmaceutical formulations.
Although generally regarded as a nontoxic and nonirritant material lanolin, and lanolin derivatives, are associated with skin hypersensitivity reactions and the use of lanolin in subjects with known sensitivity should be avoided.[2,3]

However, skin hypersensitivity is relatively uncommon; the incidence of hypersensitivity to lanolin in the general population is estimated to be around 5 per million.[4] Sensitivity is thought to be associated with the content of free fatty alcohols present in lanolin products rather than the total alcohol content.[5] The safety of pesticide residues in lanolin products has also been of concern.[6,7] However, highly refined hypoallergenic grades of lanolin and grades with low pesticide residues are commercially available.

15. Handling Precautions

Observe normal precautions appropriate to the circumstances and quantity of material handled.

16. Regulatory Status

Included in the FDA Inactive Ingredients Guide (ophthalmic, otic, topical and vaginal preparations). Included in nonparenteral medicines licensed in the UK.

17. Pharmacopeias

Aust, Belg, Br, Braz, Chin, Cz, Egypt, Eur, Fr, Ger, Gr, Hung, Ind, It, Jpn, Mex, Neth, Nord, Port, Rom, Rus, Swiss, Turk, US and Yug. Also in BP Vet.

18. Related Substances

Cholesterol; Hydrous Lanolin; Lanolin Alcohols.
See also Section 19.

19. Comments

Lanolin (the anhydrous material) may be confused in some instances with hydrous lanolin since the USP formerly contained monographs for 'lanolin' and 'anhydrous lanolin' in which the name 'lanolin' referred to the material containing 25-30% w/w of purified water. However, in the USP XXII (Suppl 5) the former lanolin monograph (hydrous lanolin) was deleted and the monograph for anhydrous lanolin renamed 'lanolin'.

Since lanolin is a natural product obtained from various geographical sources, its physical characteristics such as color, consistency, iodine value, saponification value and hydroxyl value may vary from different sources. Consequently, formulations containing lanolin from different sources may also have different physical properties.

A wide range of lanolin grades are commercially available which have been refined to different extents in order to produce hypoallergenic grades or grades with low pesticide contents.

Many lanolin derivatives are also commercially available which have properties similar to the parent compound and include: acetylated lanolin; ethoxylated lanolin (water-soluble); hydrogenated lanolin; liquid lanolin and water soluble lanolin.

20. Specific References

1. Smith GG, Fonner DE, Griffin JC. New process for the manufacture of sterile ophthalmic ointments. Bull Parenter Drug Assoc 1975; 29: 18-25.
2. Lanolin allergy. Br Med J 1973; 2: 379-380.
3. Breit J, Bandmann H-J. Dermatitis from lanolin. Br J Dermatol 1973; 88: 414-416.
4. Clark EW. Estimation of the general incidence of specific lanolin allergy. J Soc Cosmet Chem 1975; 26: 323-335.
5. Clark EW, Cronin E, Wilkinson DS. Lanolin with reduced sensitizing potential: a preliminary note. Contact Dermatitis 1977; 3(2): 69-74.
6. Copeland CA, Raebel MA, Wagner SL. Pesticide residue in lanolin [letter]. JAMA 1989; 261: 242.
7. Cade PH. Pesticide residue in lanolin [letter]. JAMA 1989; 262: 613.

21. General References

Lanolin and anhydrous lanolin monographs: proposed addition of standards for pesticide residues and change in the title - comments received. Pharmacopeial Forum 1990; 16(2): 316-319.
Barnett G. Lanolin and derivatives. Cosmet Toilet 1986; 101(3): 23-44.
Osborne DW. Phase behavior characterization of ointments containing lanolin or a lanolin substitute. Drug Dev Ind Pharm 1993; 19: 1283-1302.
Smolinske SC. Handbook of food, drug, and cosmetic excipients. Boca Raton, FL: CRC Press Inc, 1992: 225-229.

22. Authors

UK: AJ Winfield.

Lanolin Alcohols

1. Nonproprietary Names

BP: Wool alcohols
PhEur: Alcoholes adipis lanae
USPNF: Lanolin alcohols

2. Synonyms

Argowax; *Hartolan*; *Ritawax*; wool wax alcohols.

3. Chemical Name and CAS Registry Number

Lanolin alcohols [8027-33-6]

4. Empirical Formula   Molecular Weight

Lanolin alcohols is a crude mixture of steroidal and triterpene alcohols, including not less than 30% cholesterol, and 10-13% isocholesterol. The USPNF XVII permits the inclusion of up to 0.1% w/w of a suitable antioxidant whilst the PhEur 1989 specifies that lanolin alcohols may contain up to 200 ppm of butylated hydroxytoluene as an antioxidant.

5. Structural Formula

See Section 4.

6. Functional Category

Emulsifying agent; ointment base.

7. Applications in Pharmaceutical Formulation or Technology

Lanolin alcohols is used in topical pharmaceutical formulations and cosmetics as a hydrophobic vehicle with emollient properties. It is also used in the preparation of water-in-oil creams and ointments. The proportion of water that can be incorporated into petrolatum is increased three-fold by the addition of 5% lanolin alcohols. Such emulsions do not crack upon the addition of citric, lactic or tartaric acid.

8. Description

Lanolin alcohols is a pale yellow to golden-brown colored solid which is plastic when warm, but brittle when cold. It has a faint characteristic odor. *See also* Section 4.

9. Pharmacopeial Specifications

Test	PhEur 1989	USPNF XVII
Identification	+	+
Melting range	$\geqslant$ 58°C	$\geqslant$ 56°C
Acidity and alkalinity	+	+
Clarity of solution	+	—
Loss on drying	$\leqslant$ 0.5%	$\leqslant$ 0.5%
Residue on ignition	—	$\leqslant$ 0.15%
Ash	$\leqslant$ 0.1%	—
Copper	—	$\leqslant$ 5 ppm
Acid value	$\leqslant$ 2.0	$\leqslant$ 2.0
Hydroxyl value	120-180	—
Peroxide value	$\leqslant$ 15	—
Saponification value	$\leqslant$ 12	$\leqslant$ 12
Water absorption capacity	+	—
Butylated hydroxytoluene	$\leqslant$ 200 ppm	—
Assay (of cholesterol)	$\geqslant$ 30.0%	$\geqslant$ 30.0%

10. Typical Properties

Solubility: freely soluble in chloroform, ether and light petroleum; soluble 1 in 25 parts of boiling ethanol; slightly soluble in ethanol (90%); practically insoluble in water.

11. Stability and Storage Conditions

Lanolin alcohols may gradually undergo autoxidation during storage. Store in a well-closed, well-filled container, protected from light, in a cool, dry, place. Normal storage life is approximately two years.

12. Incompatibilities

Incompatible with coal tar, ichthammol, phenol and resorcinol.

13. Method of Manufacture

Lanolin alcohols is prepared by the saponification of lanolin followed by the separation of the fraction containing cholesterol and other alcohols.

14. Safety

Lanolin alcohols is widely used in cosmetics and topical pharmaceutical formulations and is generally regarded as a nontoxic material. However, lanolin alcohols may be irritant to the skin and hypersensitivity can occur in some individuals. *See also* Lanolin.

15. Handling Precautions

Observe normal precautions appropriate to the circumstances and quantity of material handled.

16. Regulatory Status

Included in the FDA Inactive Ingredients guide (ophthalmic and topical preparations). Included in nonparenteral medicines licensed in the UK.

17. Pharmacopeias

Aust, Br, Cz, Egypt, Eur, Fr, Ger, Hung, Neth, Rom, Swiss, USPNF and Yug.

18. Related Substances

Cholesterol; Hydrous Lanolin; Lanolin; Petrolatum and Lanolin Alcohols.

19. Comments

Water-in-oil emulsions prepared with lanolin alcohols, unlike those made with lanolin, do not show surface darkening, nor do they develop an objectionable odor in hot weather.

20. Specific References

See Lanolin.

21. General References

Khan AR, Iyer BV, Cirelli RA, Vasavada RC. *In vitro* release of salicylic acid from lanolin alcohols-ethylcellulose films. J Pharm Sci 1984; 73: 302-305.
See also Lanolin.

22. Authors

UK: AJ Winfield.

Hydrous Lanolin

1. Nonproprietary Names

BP: Hydrous wool fat
PhEur: Adeps lanae cum aqua

2. Synonyms

Lanolin hydrous.

3. Chemical Name and CAS Registry Number

Hydrous lanolin [8020-84-6]

4. Empirical Formula   Molecular Weight

Hydrous lanolin is a mixture of lanolin and 25% w/w purified water, *see also* Section 17. The PhEur 1982 permits the inclusion of up to 150 ppm of butylated hydroxytoluene as an antioxidant.
See also Lanolin.

5. Structural Formula

See Section 4.

6. Functional Category

Emulsifying agent; ointment base.

7. Applications in Pharmaceutical Formulation or Technology

Hydrous lanolin is widely used in topical pharmaceutical formulations and cosmetics in applications similar to lanolin. Hydrous lanolin is commonly used in the preparation of water-in-oil creams and ointments. In comparison with lanolin, more water may be incorporated into hydrous lanolin. *See also* Section 19.

8. Description

Hydrous lanolin is a pale yellow colored, unctuous substance with a faint characteristic odor.

9. Pharmacopeial Specifications

Test	PhEur 1982
Identification	+
Melting point	38-44°C
Water absorption capacity	+
Water-soluble acids and alkalies	+
Water-soluble oxidisable substances	+
Chloride	⩽ 115 ppm
Paraffins	+
Acid value	⩽ 0.8
Peroxide value	⩽ 15
Saponification value	67-79
Butylated hydroxytoluene	⩽ 150 ppm
Non-volatile matter	+
Sulfated ash	⩽ 0.1%

10. Typical Properties

Solubility: practically insoluble in chloroform, ether and water. Only the fat component of hydrous lanolin is soluble in organic solvents.

11. Stability and Storage Conditions

Hydrous lanolin should be stored in a well-filled, well-closed container protected from light, in a cool, dry, place. Normal storage life is two years.
See also Lanolin.

12. Incompatibilities

See Lanolin.

13. Method of Manufacture

Lanolin is melted, and sufficient purified water gradually added with constant stirring.

14. Safety

Hydrous lanolin is used in cosmetics and a number of topical pharmaceutical formulations and is generally regarded as a nontoxic and nonirritant material although it has been associated with hypersensitivity reactions. *See* Lanolin for further information.

15. Handling Precautions

Observe normal precautions appropriate to the circumstances and quantity of material handled.

16. Regulatory Status

Included in the FDA Inactive Ingredients Guide (ophthalmic, topical, transdermal and vaginal preparations). Included in nonparenteral medicines licensed in the UK.

17. Pharmacopeias

Aust, Br, Braz, Cz, Eur, Ger, Ind, It, Jpn, Neth, Nord, Pol, Rom, Rus, Span and Swiss.
Note that in some pharmacopeias hydrous lanolin contains differing amounts of water and sometimes additional materials. For example, in the German Pharmacopeia, hydrous lanolin consists of 65% w/w anhydrous lanolin, 20% w/w water and 15% w/w mineral oil, whilst in the Swiss Pharmacopeia hydrous lanolin consists of 70% w/w lanolin, 20% w/w water and 10% w/w olive oil.

18. Related Substances

Cholesterol; Lanolin; Lanolin Alcohols.

19. Comments

Lanolin (the anhydrous material) may be confused in some instances with hydrous lanolin since the USP formerly contained monographs for 'lanolin' and 'anhydrous lanolin' in which the name 'lanolin' referred to the material containing 25-30% w/w of purified water. However, in the USP XXII (Suppl 5) the former lanolin monograph (hydrous lanolin) was deleted and the monograph for anhydrous lanolin renamed 'lanolin'.

20. Specific References

See Lanolin.

21. General References

See Lanolin.

22. Authors

UK: AJ Winfield.

Lecithin

1. Nonproprietary Names

USPNF: Lecithin
See also Section 4.

2. Synonyms

E322; egg lecithin; *Epikuron*; *Espholip*; *LSC*; mixed soybean phosphatides; ovolecithin; *Ovothin*; soybean lecithin; soybean phospholipids; vegetable lecithin.

3. Chemical Name and CAS Registry Number

Lecithin [8002-43-5]
The chemical nomenclature and CAS registry numbering of lecithin is complex. The commercially available lecithin, used in cosmetics, pharmaceuticals and food products, although a complex mixture of phospholipids and other materials, may be referred to in some literature sources as 1,2-diacyl-*sn*-glycero-3-phosphocholine (trivial chemical name, phosphatidylcholine). This material is the principal constituent of egg lecithin and has the same CAS registry number. The name lecithin and the CAS registry number above are thus used to refer to both lecithin and phosphatidylcholine in some literature sources.
See also Section 4.

4. Empirical Formula   Molecular Weight

The USPNF XVII describes lecithin as a complex mixture of acetone-insoluble phosphatides, which consist chiefly of phosphatidylcholine, phosphatidylethanolamine, phosphatidylserine and phosphatidylinositol, combined with various amounts of other substances such as triglycerides, fatty acids and carbohydrates as separated from a crude vegetable oil source.
The composition of lecithin and hence its physical properties varies enormously depending upon the source of the lecithin and the degree of purification. Egg lecithin, for example, contains 69% phosphatidylcholine and 24% phosphatidylethanolamine, whilst soybean lecithin contains 21% phosphatidylcholine, 22% phosphatidylethanolamine and 19% phosphatidylinositol, along with other components.[1]

5. Structural Formula

$$CH_2—O—\overset{\overset{O}{\|}}{C}—R_1$$

$$CH—O—\overset{\overset{O}{\|}}{C}—R_2$$

$$CH_2—O—\overset{\overset{O^-}{|}}{\underset{\underset{O}{\|}}{P}}—OCH_2CH_2N^+(CH_3)_3$$

α-phosphatidylcholine
Where, R_1 and R_2 are fatty acids which may be different or identical.

Lecithin is a complex mixture of materials, *see* Section 4. The structure above shows phosphatidylcholine, the principal component of egg lecithin, in its α-form. In the β-form the phosphorus containing group and the R_2 group exchange positions.

6. Functional Category

Emollient; emulsifying agent; solubilizing agent.

7. Applications in Pharmaceutical Formulation or Technology

Lecithins are used in a wide variety of pharmaceutical applications. They are also used in cosmetics[2] and food products.
Lecithins are mainly used in pharmaceutical products as dispersing, emulsifying and stabilizing agents and are included in intramuscular and intravenous injections, parenteral nutrition formulations and topical products, such as creams and ointments.
Lecithins are also used in suppository bases,[3] to reduce the brittleness of suppositories and have been investigated for their absorption enhancing properties in an intranasal insulin formulation.[4] Lecithins are also commonly used as a component of enteral and parenteral nutrition formulations. Liposomes in which lecithin is included as a component of the bilayer have been used to encapsulate drug substances and their potential as novel delivery systems has been investigated.[5]
Therapeutically, lecithin and derivatives have been used as a pulmonary surfactant in the treatment of neonatal respiratory distress syndrome.

Use	Concentration (%)
Aerosol inhalation	0.1
IM injection	0.3-2.3
Oral suspensions	0.25-10.0

8. Description

Lecithins vary greatly in their physical form, from viscous semiliquids to powders, depending upon the free fatty acid content. They may also vary in color from brown to light yellow, depending upon whether they are bleached or unbleached.
Lecithins have practically no odor. Those derived from vegetable sources have a bland or nut-like taste, similar to soybean oil.

9. Pharmacopeial Specifications

Test	USPNF XVII (Suppl 6)
Water	≤ 1.5%
Arsenic	≤ 3 ppm
Lead	≤ 0.001%
Heavy metals	≤ 0.004%
Acid value	≤ 36
Hexane-insoluble matter	≤ 0.3%
Acetone-insoluble matter	≥ 50.0%

10. Typical Properties

Density:
0.97 g/cm^3 for liquid lecithin;
0.5 g/cm^3 for powdered lecithin.
Iodine number:
95-100 for liquid lecithin;
82-88 for powdered lecithin.
Isoelectric point: $\approx$ 3.5
Saponification value: 196
Solubility: lecithins are soluble in aliphatic and aromatic hydrocarbons, halogenated hydrocarbons, mineral oil and fatty acids. They are practically insoluble in cold vegetable and animal oils, polar solvents and water. When mixed with water however, lecithins hydrate to form emulsions.

11. Stability and Storage Conditions

Lecithins decompose at extreme pH. They are also hygroscopic and subject to microbial degradation. When heated, lecithins oxidize, darken and decompose. Temperatures of 160-180°C will cause degradation within 24 hours.

Fluid, or waxy, lecithin grades should be stored at room temperature or above; temperatures below 10°C may cause separation.

All lecithin grades should be stored in well-closed containers protected from light.

12. Incompatibilities

Incompatible with esterases due to hydrolysis.

13. Method of Manufacture

Lecithins are essential components of cell membranes and may thus in principle be obtained from a wide variety of living matter. In practice however, lecithins are usually obtained from vegetable products such as soybean, peanut, cottonseed, sunflower, rapeseed, corn or groundnut oil. Soybean lecithin is the most commercially important vegetable lecithin. Lecithin obtained from eggs is also commercially important and was the first lecithin to be discovered.

Vegetable lecithins are obtained as a by-product in the vegetable oil refining process. Polar lipids are extracted with hexane and after removal of the solvent a crude vegetable oil obtained. Lecithin is then removed from the crude oil by water extraction. Following drying the lecithin may then be further purified.[1]

With egg lecithin, a different manufacturing process must be used since the lecithin in egg yolks is more tightly bound to proteins than in vegetable sources. Egg lecithin is thus obtained by solvent extraction from liquid egg yolks using acetone or from freeze dried egg yolks using ethanol.[1]

Synthetic lecithins may also be produced.

14. Safety

Lecithin is a component of cell membranes and is therefore consumed as a normal part of the diet. Although excessive consumption may be harmful, oral doses of up to 80 g daily have been used therapeutically in the treatment of tardive dyskinesia.[6] When used in topical formulations lecithin is generally regarded as a nonirritant and nonsensitizing material.[2]

15. Handling Precautions

Observe normal precautions appropriate to the circumstances and quantity of material handled. Lecithins may be irritant to the eyes; eye protection and gloves are recommended.

16. Regulatory Status

GRAS listed. Accepted as a food additive in Europe. Included in the FDA Inactive Ingredients Guide (inhalations, IM and IV injections, oral capsules, suspensions and tablets, rectal, topical and vaginal preparations). Included in nonparenteral and parenteral medicines licensed in the UK.

17. Pharmacopeias

Aust, Mex and USPNF.

18. Related Substances

-

19. Comments

Lecithins contain a variety of unspecified materials and care should therefore be exercised in the use of unpurified lecithin in injectable or topical dosage forms as interaction with the active substance or other excipients may occur. Unpurified lecithins may also have a greater potential for irritancy in formulations.

Supplier's literature should be consulted for information on the different grades of lecithin available and their applications in formulations.

20. Specific References

1. Schneider M. Achieving purer lecithin. Drug Cosmet Ind 1992; 150(2): 54, 56, 62, 64, 66, 101-103.
2. Lecithin: its composition, properties and use in cosmetic formulations. Cosmet Perfum 1974; 89(7): 31-35.
3. Novak E, et al. Evaluation of cefmetazole rectal suppository formulations. Drug Dev Ind Pharm 1991; 17: 373-389.
4. Intranasal insulin formulation reported to be promising. Pharm J 1991; 247: 17.
5. Grit M, Zuidam NJ, Underberg WJM, Crommelin DJA. Hydrolysis of partially saturated egg phosphatidylcholine in aqueous liposome dispersions and the effect of cholesterol incorporation on hydrolysis kinetics. J Pharm Pharmacol 1993; 45: 490-495.
6. Growdon JH, et al. Lecithin can suppress tardive dyskinesia [letter]. N Engl J Med 1978; 298: 1029-1030.

21. General References

Ansell GB, Hawthorne JN. Phospholipids. New York: Elsevier, 1964.
Arias C, Rueda C. Comparative study of lipid systems from various sources by rotational viscometry and potentiometry. Drug Dev Ind Pharm 1992; 18: 1773-1786.
Hanin I, Pepeu G, editors. Phospholipids: biochemical, pharmaceutical and analytical considerations. New York: Plenum, 1990.

22. Authors

USA: W Han.

Magnesium Aluminum Silicate

1. Nonproprietary Names

BP: Aluminium magnesium silicate
USPNF: Magnesium aluminum silicate

2. Synonyms

Aluminum magnesium silicate; *Carrisorb*; *Gelsorb*; magnesium aluminosilicate; magnesium aluminum silicate, colloidal; magnesium aluminum silicate, complex colloidal; *Veegum*.

3. Chemical Name and CAS Registry Number

Aluminum magnesium silicate [12511-31-8]
Magnesium aluminum silicate [1327-43-1]

4. Empirical Formula   Molecular Weight

A polymeric complex of magnesium, aluminum, silicon, oxygen and water. The average chemical analysis is conventionally expressed as oxides:

Silicon dioxide	61.1%
Magnesium oxide	13.7%
Aluminum oxide	9.3%
Titanium dioxide	0.1%
Ferric oxide	0.9%
Calcium oxide	2.7%
Sodium oxide	2.9%
Potassium oxide	0.3%
Carbon dioxide	1.8%
Water of combination	7.2%

5. Structural Formula

The complex is composed of a three-lattice layer of octahedral alumina and two tetrahedral silica sheets. The aluminum is substituted to varying degrees by magnesium (with sodium or potassium for balance of electrical charge). Additional elements present in small amounts include: iron; lithium; titanium; calcium and carbon.

6. Functional Category

Adsorbent; stabilizing agent; suspending agent; tablet and capsule disintegrant; tablet binder; viscosity-increasing agent.

7. Applications in Pharmaceutical Formulation or Technology

Magnesium aluminum silicate has been used for many years in the formulation of tablets, ointments and creams. It is used in oral and topical formulations as a suspending and stabilizing agent either alone or in combination with other suspending agents.[1,2] Viscosity of aqueous dispersions may be greatly increased by combination with other suspending agents, such as xanthan gum, due to synergistic effects, *see* Xanthan Gum. In tablets, magnesium aluminum silicate is used as a binder and disintegrant in conventional or slow-release formulations.[3,4]

Magnesium aluminum silicate may cause bioavailability problems with certain drugs, *see* Section 11.

Use	Concentration (%)
Adsorbent	10-50
Binding agent	2-10
Disintegrating agent	2-10
Emulsion stabilizer (oral)	1-5
Emulsion stabilizer (topical)	2-5
Suspending agent (oral)	0.5-2.5
Suspending agent (topical)	1-10
Stabilizing agent	0.5-2.5
Viscosity modifier	2-10

8. Description

The USPNF XVII describes magnesium aluminum silicate as a blend of colloidal montmorillonite and saponite that has been processed to remove grit and non-swellable ore components. Four types of magnesium aluminum silicate are defined: type IA; IB; IC and IIA. These types differ according to their viscosity and ratio of aluminum and magnesium content, *see* Table I. The BP 1993 describes aluminum magnesium silicate as native colloidal hydrated saponite.

Magnesium aluminum silicate occurs as off-white to creamy white, odorless, tasteless, soft, slippery small flakes or as a fine, micronized, powder. Flakes vary in shape and size from about 0.3 by 0.4 mm to 1.0 by 2.0 mm and from about 25-240 μm thick. Many flakes are perforated by scattered circular holes ranging from 20-120 μm in diameter. Under dark field polarized light, innumerable bright specks are observed scattered over the flakes. The powder varies from 45-297 μm in size.

Table I: Magnesium aluminum silicate types defined in the USPNF XVII.

Type	Viscosity (mPa s)	Al content/Mg content
IA	225-600	0.5-1.2
IB	150-450	0.5-1.2
IC	800-2200	0.5-1.2
IIA	100-300	1.4-2.8

9. Pharmacopeial Specifications

Test	BP 1993	USPNF XVII
Identification	+	+
Viscosity	250 mPa s	*see* Table I
(5% w/v suspension)		
Microbial limits	—	+
pH		
(5% w/v suspension)		9.0-10.0
(4% w/v suspension)	$\approx$ 9	—
Acid demand	—	+
Alkalinity	+	—
Loss on drying	$\leqslant$ 10.0%	$\leqslant$ 8.0%
Loss on ignition	$\leqslant$ 17.0%	—
Arsenic	—	$\leqslant$ 3 ppm
Lead	—	$\leqslant$ 0.0015%
Assay for Al and Mg content	—	+

10. Typical Properties

Acid demand: 6-8 mL of 0.1 N HCl is required to reduce the pH of 1 g to pH 4.
Moisture content: *see* HPE Data.

SEM: 1

Excipient: Magnesium aluminum silicate (*Veegum*)
Manufacturer: RT Vanderbilt Co Inc
Lot No.: 61A-1
Magnification: 600x
Voltage: 10 kV

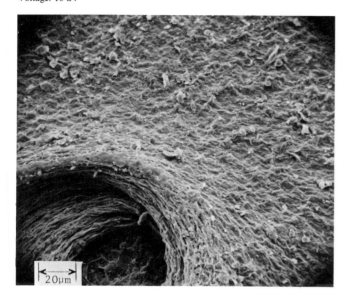

SEM: 3

Excipient: Magnesium aluminum silicate (*Veegum F*)
Manufacturer: RT Vanderbilt Co Inc
Lot No.: 61A-2
Magnification: 600x
Voltage: 10 kV

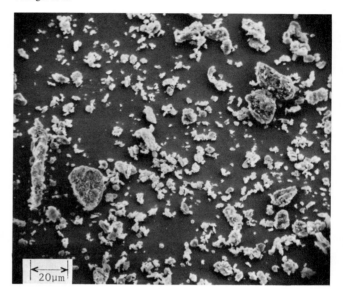

SEM: 2

Excipient: Magnesium aluminum silicate (*Veegum*)
Manufacturer: RT Vanderbilt Co Inc
Lot No.: 61A-1
Magnification: 2400x
Voltage: 10 kV

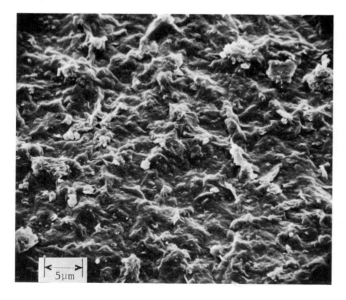

SEM: 4

Excipient: Magnesium aluminum silicate (*Veegum F*)
Manufacturer: RT Vanderbilt Co Inc
Lot No.: 61A-2
Magnification: 2400x
Voltage: 10 kV

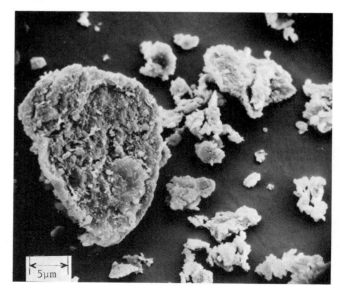

Particle size distribution: *see* HPE Data. *See also* Section 8.
Solubility: practically insoluble in alcohols, water and organic solvents.
Swelling capacity: swelling properties are reversible. Magnesium aluminum silicate swells to many times its original volume in water to form colloidal dispersions and may be dried and rehydrated any number of times.
Viscosity (dynamic): dispersions in water at the 1-2% level are thin colloidal suspensions. At 3% and above, dispersions are opaque. As the concentration is increased above 3%, the viscosity of aqueous dispersions increases rapidly; at 4-5%, dispersions are thick, white colloidal sols while at 10% firm gels are formed. Dispersions are thixotropic at concentrations greater than 3%. The viscosity of the suspension increases with heating, addition of electrolytes and at higher concentrations with aging. *See* Table II.

Table II: Viscosity of various grades of magnesium aluminum silicate (*Veegum*, RT Vanderbilt Co Inc).

Grade	Viscosity (mPa s)*	Al/Mg content	Acid demand
Veegum	225-600	0.5-1.2	6-8
Veegum F	150-450	0.5-1.2	6-8
Veegum HV	800-2200	0.5-1.2	6-8
Veegum K	100-300	1.4-2.8	< 3.5
Veegum S728	250-500	3.5-5.5	6.9
Veegum HS	40-200	3.5-5.5	< 2.5

* For a 5% w/v aqueous suspension.

HPE Laboratory Project Data

	Method	Lab #	Results
Moisture content	MC-22	2	6.00% [a]
	MC-13	18	6.85% [a]
	MC-13	18	9.98% [a]
	EMC-1	2	*See* Fig. 1. [a]
	SDI-2	26	*See* Fig. 2. [b]
	SDI-2	26	*See* Fig. 3. [c]
	SDI-2	26	*See* Fig. 4. [d]
Particle size	PSD-2	5	260 μm [a]
	PSD-2	5	636 μm [a]

Supplier:
a. RT Vanderbilt Co Inc (*Veegum HV*, Lot No.: NV1640);
b. Engelhard (*Pharmasorb*, Lot No.: 160-9-5);
c. ICD (Lot No.: MAK-378);
d. Engelhard (*Pharmasorb colloidal*, Lot No.: 349-9-3).

11. Stability and Storage Conditions

Magnesium aluminum silicate is stable indefinitely when stored under dry conditions. It is stable over a wide pH range, has base-exchange capacity, absorbs some organic substances and is compatible with organic solvents.
Magnesium aluminum silicate should be stored in a well-closed container, in a cool, dry, place.

12. Incompatibilities

Due to its inert nature, magnesium aluminum silicate has few incompatibilities but is generally unsuitable for acidic solutions below pH 3.5. Magnesium aluminum silicate, as with other clays, may absorb some drugs.[5,6] This can result in low bioavailability if the drug is tightly bound or slowly desorbed,

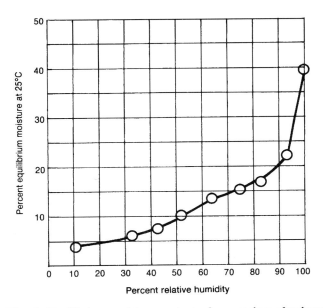

Fig. 1: Equilibrium moisture content of magnesium aluminum silicate (*Veegum HV*).

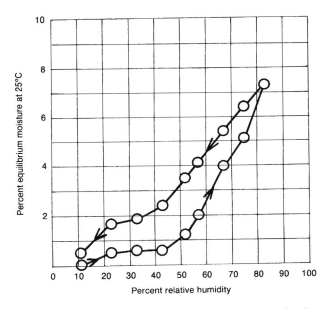

Fig. 2: Sorption-desorption isotherm of magnesium aluminum silicate (*Pharmasorb*).

e.g. amphetamine sulfate,[3] tolbutamide,[7] warfarin sodium[8] and diazepam.[9]

13. Method of Manufacture

Magnesium aluminum silicate is obtained from silicate ores of the montmorillonite group which show high magnesium content. The ore is blended with water to form a slurry to remove impurities and separate out the colloidal fraction. The refined colloidal dispersion is drum-dried to form a small flake which is then micro-atomized to form various powder grades.

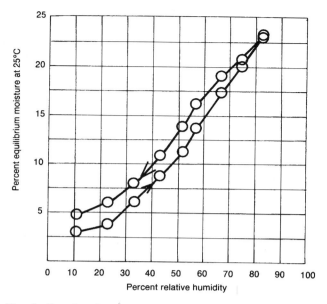

Fig. 3: Sorption-desorption isotherm of magnesium aluminum silicate.

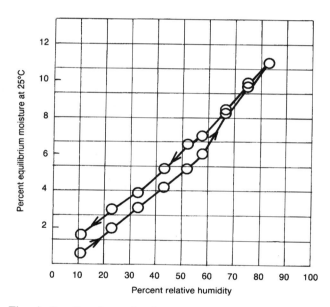

Fig. 4: Sorption-desorption isotherm of magnesium aluminum silicate (*Pharmasorb colloidal*).

14. Safety

Magnesium aluminum silicate is generally regarded as nontoxic and nonirritating at the levels employed as a pharmaceutical excipient. Sub-acute animal feeding studies in rats and dogs fed magnesium aluminum silicate at 10% of the diet, for 90 days, were negative, including autopsy and histopathological examinations.[10]

LD_{50} (rat, oral): > 16 g/kg[11]

15. Handling Precautions

Observe normal precautions appropriate to the circumstances and quantity of material handled. Eye protection and gloves

are recommended. Adequate ventilation should be provided and dust generation minimized.

16. Regulatory Status

Included in the FDA Inactive Ingredients Guide (oral capsules, solutions, suspensions and tablets; rectal and topical preparations). Included in nonparenteral medicines licensed in the UK.

17. Pharmacopeias

Br and USPNF.

18. Related Substances

Bentonite; Kaolin; Magnesium Trisilicate; montmorillonite; saponite; Talc.

Montmorillonite: $Al.\frac{1}{2}H_6O_{11}Si_4.\frac{1}{2}H_2O$
CAS number: [1318-93-0]
Comments: a naturally occurring silicate clay.

Saponite: $Mg_{18}(Al_4Si_{21}O_{66}).6H_2O$
CAS number: [1319-41-1]
Comments: a naturally occurring silicate clay.

19. Comments

—

20. Specific References

1. Polon JA. The mechanisms of thickening by inorganic agents. J Soc Cosmet Chem 1970; 21: 347-363.
2. Farley CA, Lund W. Suspending agents for extemporaneous dispensing: evaluation of alternatives to tragacanth. Pharm J 1976; 216: 562-566.
3. McGinity JW, Lach JL. Sustained-release applications of montmorillonite interaction with amphetamine sulfate. J Pharm Sci 1977; 66: 63-66.
4. McGinity JW, Harris MR. Optimization of slow-release tablet formulations containing montmorillonite I: properties of tablets. Drug Dev Ind Pharm 1980; 6: 399-410.
5. McGinity JW, Lach JL. *In vitro* adsorption of various pharmaceuticals to montmorillonite. J Pharm Sci 1976; 65: 896-902.
6. McGinity JW, Harris MR. Increasing dissolution rates of poorly-soluble drugs by adsorption to montmorillonite. Drug Dev Ind Pharm 1980; 6: 35-48.
7. Varley AB. The generic inequivalence of drugs. JAMA 1968; 206: 1745-1748.
8. Wagner JG, Welling PG, Lee KP, Walker JE. *In vivo* and *in vitro* availability of commercial warfarin tablets. J Pharm Sci 1971; 60: 666-677.
9. Munzel K. The desorption of medicinal substances from adsorbents in oral pharmaceutical suspensions. Acta Pharmacol Toxicol 1971; 29(Suppl 3): 81-87.
10. Sakai K, Moriguchi K. Effect of magnesium aluminosilicate administered to pregnant mice on pre- and postnatal development of offsprings. Oyo Yakri 1975; 9: 703.
11. Sweet DV, editor. Registry of toxic effects of chemical substances. Cincinnati: US Department of Health, 1987.

21. General References

RT Vanderbilt Co Inc. Technical literature: Veegum, the versatile ingredient for pharmaceutical formulations, 1992.
Wai K, DeKay HG, Banker GS. Applications of the montmorillonites in tablet making. J Pharm Sci 1966; 55: 1244-1248.

Yokoi H, Enomoto S, Takahashi H. Effect of magnesium alumino-silicate on fluidity of pharmaceutical powders [in Japanese]. J Pharm Soc Japan 1978; 98: 418-425.

22. Authors

USA: A Palmieri.

Magnesium Carbonate

1. Nonproprietary Names

BP: Heavy magnesium carbonate and
    Light magnesium carbonate
PhEur: Magnesii subcarbonas ponderosus and
      Magnesii subcarbonas levis
USP: Magnesium carbonate

2. Synonyms

See Sections 4 and 18.

3. Chemical Name and CAS Registry Number

Magnesium carbonate anhydrous [546-93-0]
See also Sections 4 and 18.

4. Empirical Formula   Molecular Weight

Magnesium carbonate is not a homogeneous material but may consist of the rarely encountered anhydrous material, $MgCO_3$, the normal hydrate and the basic hydrate. Basic magnesium carbonate, probably the commonest form, may vary in formula between light magnesium carbonate, $(MgCO_3)_3.Mg(OH)_2.3H_2O$ and magnesium carbonate hydroxide, $(MgCO_3)_4.Mg(OH)_2.5H_2O$. Normal magnesium carbonate is a hydrous magnesium carbonate with a varying amount of water, $MgCO_3.xH_2O$.
See also Sections 8, 13 and 18.

5. Structural Formula

—

6. Functional Category

Tablet and capsule diluent.

7. Applications in Pharmaceutical Formulation or Technology

As an excipient, magnesium carbonate is mainly used as a directly compressible tablet diluent in concentrations up to 45% w/w.[1-3] It is also used to adsorb liquids, such as flavors, in tableting processes.
Magnesium carbonate is additionally used as a food additive and therapeutically as an antacid.

Use	Concentration (%)
Adsorbent of liquid, in tableting	0.5-1.0
Tablet excipient (direct compression)	≤ 45

8. Description

Magnesium carbonate occurs as light, white-colored friable masses or as a bulky, white-colored powder. It has a slightly earthy taste and is odorless, but since it has a highly absorptive ability magnesium carbonate can absorb odors.
The USP XXII describes magnesium carbonate as either a basic magnesium carbonate or a normal hydrated magnesium carbonate. However, the PhEur 1983 describes magnesium carbonate in two separate monographs, heavy magnesium carbonate and light magnesium carbonate, as being a hydrated basic magnesium carbonate. The molecular for-

mula for heavy magnesium carbonate and light magnesium carbonate varies, but heavy magnesium carbonate may be regarded as the tetrahydrate $[(MgCO_3)_3.Mg(OH)_2.4H_2O]$, while light magnesium carbonate may be regarded as the trihydrate $[(MgCO_3)_3.Mg(OH)_2.3H_2O]$. The molecular weights of the heavy and light forms of magnesium carbonate are 383.32 and 365.30 respectively.

SEM: 1
Excipient: Magnesium carbonate USP
Manufacturer: Mallinckrodt Speciality Chemicals Co
Lot No.: KJGJ
Magnification: 60x
Voltage: 20 kV

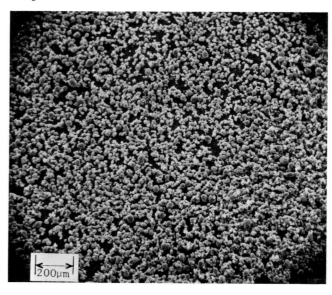

SEM: 2
Excipient: Magnesium carbonate USP
Manufacturer: Mallinckrodt Speciality Chemicals Co
Lot No.: KJGJ
Magnification: 600x
Voltage: 20 kV

9. Pharmacopeial Specifications

Test	PhEur 1983	USP XXII
Identification	+	+
Microbial limits	—	+
Color of solution	+	—
Soluble salts	⩽ 1.0%	⩽ 1.0%
Acid-insoluble substances	⩽ 0.05%	⩽ 0.05%
Arsenic	⩽ 2 ppm	⩽ 4 ppm
Calcium	⩽ 0.75%	⩽ 0.45%
Heavy metals	⩽ 20 ppm	⩽ 0.003%
Iron	⩽ 400 ppm	⩽ 0.02%
Chloride	⩽ 0.07%	—
Sulfate		
Heavy magnesium carbonate	⩽ 0.6%	—
Light magnesium carbonate	⩽ 0.3%	—
Assay (as MgO)	40.0-45.0%	40.0-43.5%

Note that except where indicated all of the PhEur 1983 test limits apply to both the heavy and light forms of magnesium carbonate.

10. Typical Properties

Angle of repose: 42-50° for granular heavy magnesium carbonate; 56-60° for spray-dried heavy magnesium carbonate.[3]

Compressibility: *see* HPE Data.

Density (bulk):
≈ 0.5 g/cm³ for heavy magnesium carbonate;
≈ 0.12 g/cm³ for light magnesium carbonate.

Density (tapped):
≈ 0.21 g/cm³ for light magnesium carbonate.

Moisture content: at relative humidities of between 15-65% the equilibrium moisture content of heavy magnesium carbonate at 25°C is about 1% w/w; at relative humidities above 75% the equilibrium moisture content at 25°C is about 5% w/w.[3]

Particle size distribution: 99.95% through a 44.5 μm (#350 mesh) sieve for light magnesium carbonate.

Solubility: practically insoluble in water but soluble in water containing carbon dioxide. Insoluble in ethanol (95%) and other solvents. Magnesium carbonate dissolves and effervesces on contact with dilute acids.

Specific surface area: 7.8-18.2 m²/g for granular heavy magnesium carbonate; 4.4-15.5 m²/g for spray-dried heavy magnesium carbonate.[3]

	HPE Laboratory Project Data		
	Method	Lab #	Results
Compressibility	COM-4-6	29	*See* Fig. 1 [a]
Compressibility	COM-1	21	*See* Fig. 2 [b]
Compressibility	COM-7	12	*See* Fig. 3 [a]

Supplier:
a. Mallinckrodt Speciality Chemicals Co (Lot No.: KJGJ);
b. Merck Ltd (Lot No.: 351386).

11. Stability and Storage Conditions

Magnesium carbonate is stable in dry air and on exposure to light. The bulk material should be stored in a well-closed container in a cool, dry, place.

12. Incompatibilities

Acids will dissolve magnesium carbonate, with the liberation of carbon dioxide. Slight alkalinity is imparted to water.

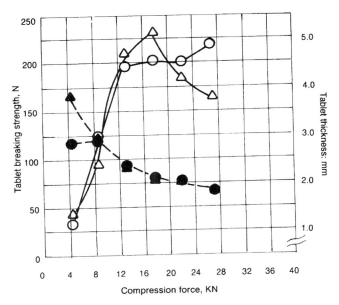

Fig. 1: Compression characteristics of heavy magnesium carbonate USP.
○●: Unlubricated, Carver laboratory press (COM-5)
△▲: Lubricated, Carver laboratory press (COM-6)

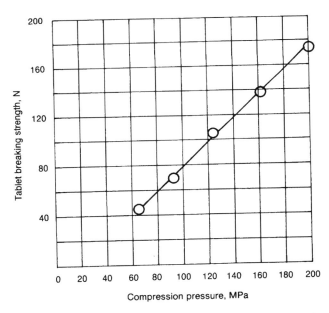

Fig. 2: Compression characteristics of heavy magnesium carbonate BP.
Weight range of tablets: 625-650 mg

13. Method of Manufacture

Depending upon the manufacturing process used, the composition of the magnesium carbonate obtained may vary from normal hydrated magnesium carbonate to basic hydrated magnesium carbonate.

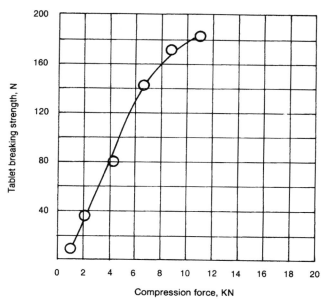

Fig. 3: Compression characteristics of magnesium carbonate USP.
Tablet weight: 300 mg

Light magnesium carbonate may be manufactured by saturating an aqueous suspension of dolomite ($MgCO_3.CaCO_3$) with carbon dioxide under pressure. On increasing the temperature calcium carbonate precipitates almost entirely. The filtered solution is then heated to boiling. The magnesium bicarbonate in the solution loses carbon dioxide and water, and light magnesium carbonate precipitates.

Heavy magnesium carbonate may be manufactured by mixing a hot concentrated solution of magnesium chloride or magnesium sulfate with a solution of sodium carbonate. The heavy magnesium carbonate may be either precipitated to produce a granular material or spray-dried. Varying the temperature of the reaction solutions produces heavy magnesium carbonate with differing physical properties, e.g. material with a higher specific surface area is produced at a lower reaction temperature.[3] If dilute magnesium chloride or magnesium sulfate solutions are used for the reaction a less dense material is produced.

14. Safety

Magnesium carbonate is used as an excipient in oral solid dosage pharmaceutical formulations and is generally regarded as an essentially nontoxic and nonirritant material. However, the use of magnesium salts, such as magnesium carbonate, is contraindicated in patients with renal impairment.

On contact with gastric acid, magnesium carbonate reacts in the stomach to form soluble magnesium chloride and carbon dioxide. Magnesium carbonate should therefore not be used as an antacid by those individuals whose stomachs cannot tolerate the evolution of carbon dioxide. Some magnesium is absorbed but is usually excreted in the urine. As with other magnesium salts, magnesium carbonate has a laxative effect and may cause diarrhea.

Therapeutically, the usual dose of magnesium carbonate as an antacid is 250-500 mg and as a laxative, 2-5 g.

15. Handling Precautions

Observe normal precautions appropriate to the circumstances and quantity of material handled. Magnesium carbonate may be irritant to the eyes; eye protection is recommended.

16. Regulatory Status

GRAS listed. Accepted as a food additive in Europe. Included in the FDA Inactive Ingredients Guide (oral capsules and tablets). Included in nonparenteral medicines licensed in the UK.

17. Pharmacopeias

Aust, Belg, Br, Braz, Chin, Cz, Egypt, Eur, Fr, Ger, Gr, Hung, Ind, It, Jpn, Mex, Neth, Nord, Port, Rom, Rus, Swiss, Turk, US and Yug. Also in BP Vet.

Some pharmacopeias have a single monograph which permits both the light and heavy forms of magnesium carbonate. Other pharmacopeias have two separate monographs.

18. Related Substances

Magnesium carbonate anhydrous; magnesium carbonate hydroxide; normal magnesium carbonate.

Magnesium carbonate anhydrous: $MgCO_3$
Molecular weight: 84.31
CAS number: [546-93-0]
Synonyms: carbonic acid, magnesium salt anhydrous (1:1); E504; magnesite.
Appearance: odorless, white-colored bulky powder or light friable masses.
Melting point: decomposes at 350°C.

Magnesium carbonate hydroxide: $(MgCO_3)_4.Mg(OH)_2.5H_2O$
Molecular weight: 485.65
CAS number: [39409-82-0]
Synonyms: carbonic acid, magnesium salt (1:1), mixture with magnesium hydroxide and magnesium hydrate; E504.
Appearance: odorless, white-colored bulky powder or light friable masses.
Melting point: on heating at 700°C is converted into magnesium oxide.
Specific gravity: 1.45

Normal magnesium carbonate: $MgCO_3.xH_2O$
CAS number: [23389-33-5]
Synonyms: carbonic acid, magnesium salt (1:1), hydrate; E504; magnesium carbonate, normal hydrate.
Appearance: odorless, white-colored bulky powder or light friable masses.

19. Comments

—

20. Specific References

1. Haines-Nutt RF. The compression properties of magnesium and calcium carbonates. J Pharm Pharmacol 1976; 28: 468-470.
2. Armstrong NA, Cham T-M. Changes in the particle size and size distribution during compaction of two pharmaceutical powders with dissimilar consolidation mechanisms. Drug Dev Ind Pharm 1986; 12: 2043-2059.
3. Cham T-M. The effect of the specific surface area of heavy magnesium carbonate on its tableting properties. Drug Dev Ind Pharm 1987; 13: 1989-2015.

21. General References

—

22. Authors

USA: NR Poola.

Magnesium Oxide

1. Nonproprietary Names

BP: Heavy magnesium oxide and
  Light magnesium oxide
PhEur: Magnesii oxidum ponderosum and
  Magnesii oxidum leve
USP: Magnesium oxide
See Section 8.

2. Synonyms

Calcined magnesia; *Destab*; E530; magnesia; magnesia usta; *Magnyox*; periclase.

3. Chemical Name and CAS Registry Number

Magnesium oxide [1309-48-4]

4. Empirical Formula   Molecular Weight
MgO   40.30

5. Structural Formula

MgO

6. Functional Category

Tablet and capsule diluent.

7. Applications in Pharmaceutical Formulation or Technology

Magnesium oxide is used as an alkaline diluent in solid dosage forms. It is also used as a food additive and as an antacid, either alone or in conjunction with aluminum hydroxide. Magnesium oxide is additionally used as an osmotic laxative.

8. Description

Two forms of magnesium oxide exist, a bulky form termed light magnesium oxide and a dense form termed heavy magnesium oxide. The USP XXII defines both forms in a single monograph whilst other pharmacopeias have separate monographs for each form. For the heavy variety, 15 g occupies a volume of about 30 mL and for the light variety, 20 g occupies a volume of about 150 mL.
Both forms of magnesium oxide occur as fine, white, odorless powders. They possess a cubic crystal structure.

9. Pharmcopeial Specifications

Test	PhEur 1983	USP XXII
Identification	+	+
Loss on ignition	≤ 8.0%	≤ 10.0%
Color of solution	+	—
Free alkali and soluble salts	—	≤ 2.0%
Soluble substances	≤ 2.0%	—
Acid-insoluble substances	≤ 0.1%	—
Arsenic	≤ 4 ppm	≤ 3 ppm
Calcium	≤ 1.5%	≤ 1.1%
Heavy metals	≤ 30 ppm	≤ 0.004%
Iron	≤ 0.07%	≤ 0.05%
Chloride	≤ 0.1%	—
Sulfate	≤ 1.0%	—
Assay	98.0-100.5%	96.0-100.5%

10. Typical Properties

Acidity/alkalinity:
pH = 10.3 (saturated aqueous solution).
Boiling point: 3600°C
Melting point: 2800°C
Particle size distribution: 99.98% less than 45 μm in size (light magnesium oxide).
Refractive index: 1.732
Solubility: soluble in dilute acids and ammonium salt solutions; very slightly soluble in pure water, solubility is increased by carbon dioxide; practically insoluble in ethanol (95%).
Specific gravity: 3.58 at 25°C

11. Stability and Storage Conditions

Magnesium oxide is stable at normal temperatures and pressures. However, it forms magnesium hydroxide in the presence of water. Magnesium oxide is hygroscopic and rapidly absorbs water and carbon dioxide on exposure to the air, the light form more readily than the heavy form.
The bulk material should be stored in an airtight container in a cool, dry, place.

12. Incompatibilities

Magnesium oxide is a basic oxide and as such can react with acidic compounds in the solid state to form salts such as Mg(ibuprofen)$_2$[1] or degrade alkaline-labile drugs. Adsorption of various drugs such as antihistamines,[2] antibiotics (especially tetracyclines),[3] salicylates,[4] and anthranilic acid derivatives onto magnesium oxide has been reported. Magnesium oxide can complex with polymers, e.g. *Eudragit RS*, to retard drug release.[5]

13. Method of Manufacture

Magnesium oxide occurs naturally as the mineral periclase. It may be manufactured by calcining either the mineral magnesite or magnesium hydroxide which is obtained, by liming, from seawater or brine. Purification methods include crushing and size separation, heavy-media separation and froth flotation. Magnesium oxide may also be produced by the thermal decomposition of magnesium chloride, magnesium sulfate, magnesium sulfite, nesquehonite and the basic carbonate $5MgO.4CO_2.5H_2O$. Purification is carried out by filtration or sedimentation.

14. Safety

Magnesium oxide is widely used in oral formulations as an excipient and as a therapeutic agent. Therapeutically, 250-500 mg is administered orally as an antacid and 2-5 g as an osmotic laxative. Magnesium oxide is generally regarded as a nontoxic material when employed as an excipient although adverse effects, due to its laxative action, may occur if high doses are ingested orally.

15. Handling Precautions

Observe normal precautions appropriate to the circumstances and quantity of material handled. Magnesium oxide may be harmful if inhaled or ingested in quantity and is irritating to the eyes and respiratory system. Gloves, eye protection and a dust mask or respirator are recommended. In the UK, the long-term (8-hour TWA) occupational exposure limits for magnesium oxide, calculated as magnesium, are 10 mg/m^3 for total dust and 5 mg/m^3 for respirable dust.[6] The short-term (10-minutes) limit for respirable dust is 10 mg/m^3.[6]

16. Regulatory Status

GRAS listed. Accepted for use as a food additive in Europe. Included in the FDA Inactive Ingredients Guide (oral capsules and tablets). Included in nonparenteral medicines licensed in the UK.

17. Pharmacopeias

Aust, Belg, Br, Chin, Cz, Egypt, Eur, Fr, Ger, Gr, Hung, Ind, Int, It, Jpn, Mex, Neth, Nord, Port, Rom, Rus, Swiss, Turk, US and Yug.

Some pharmacopeias include a single monograph which permits both the light and heavy forms of magnesium oxide whilst some have two separate monographs for the two forms.

18. Related Substances

—

19. Comments

—

20. Specific References

1. Tugrul TK, Needham TE, Seul CJ, Finnegan PM. Solid-state interaction of magnesium oxide and ibuprofen to form a salt. Pharm Res 1989; 6(9): 804-808.
2. Nada AH, Etman MA, Ebian AR. In vitro adsorption of mepyramine maleate onto some adsorbents and antacids. Int J Pharmaceutics 1989; 53: 175-179.
3. Khalil SA, Daabis NA, Naggar VF, Motawi MM. The in vitro adsorption of some antibiotics on antacids. Pharmazie 1976; 31: 105-109.
4. Naggar VF, Khalil SA, Daabis NA. The in-vitro adsorption of some antirheumatics on antacids. Pharmazie 1976; 31: 461-465.
5. Sanghavi NM, Bijlani CP, Kamath PR, Sarwade VB. Matrix tablets of salbutamol sulphate. Drug Dev Ind Pharm 1990; 16: 1955-1961.
6. Health and Safety Executive. EH40/93 occupational exposure limits 1993. London: HMSO, 1993.

21. General References

—

22. Authors

USA: DL Gabriel.

Magnesium Stearate

1. Nonproprietary Names

BP: Magnesium stearate
PhEur: Magnesii stearas
USPNF: Magnesium stearate

2. Synonyms

E572; *HyQual*; magnesium octadecanoate; stearic acid magnesium salt.

3. Chemical Name and CAS Registry Number

Octadecanoic acid magnesium salt [557-04-0]

4. Empirical Formula   Molecular Weight

$C_{36}H_{70}MgO_4$ 591.27
                             (for pure material)

The USPNF XVII describes magnesium stearate as a compound of magnesium with a mixture of solid organic acids obtained from fats and consists chiefly of variable proportions of magnesium stearate and magnesium palmitate ($C_{32}H_{62}MgO_4$). The BP 1993 and PhEur 1983 describe magnesium stearate as consisting mainly of magnesium stearate with variable proportions of magnesium palmitate and magnesium oleate ($C_{36}H_{66}MgO_4$).

5. Structural Formula

$[CH_3(CH_2)_{16}COO]_2Mg$

6. Functional Category

Tablet and capsule lubricant.

7. Applications in Pharmaceutical Formulation or Technology

Magnesium stearate is widely used in cosmetics, foods and pharmaceutical formulations. It is primarily used as a lubricant in capsule and tablet manufacture at concentrations between 0.25-5.0%.

8. Description

Magnesium stearate is a fine, white, precipitated or milled, impalpable powder of low bulk density, having a faint, characteristic odor and taste. The powder is greasy to the touch and readily adheres to the skin.

9. Pharmacopeial Specifications

Test	PhEur 1983	USPNF XVII (Suppl 9)
Identification	+	+
Microbial limits	—	+
Acidity or alkalinity	+	—
Color of solution	+	—
Acid value of the fatty acids	195-210	—
Clarity and color of solution of the fatty acids	+	—
Loss on drying	≤ 6.0%	≤ 4.0%
Heavy metals	≤ 20 ppm	—

Continued

Test	PhEur 1983	USPNF XVII (Suppl 9)
Lead	—	≤ 0.001%
Organic volatile impurities	—	+
Chloride	≤ 250 ppm	—
Sulfate	≤ 0.5%	—
Assay (dried basis, as Mg)	3.8-5.0%	—
Assay (as MgO)	—	6.8-8.3%

SEM: 1
Excipient: Magnesium stearate
Magnification: 600x

SEM: 2
Excipient: Magnesium stearate
Magnification: 2400x

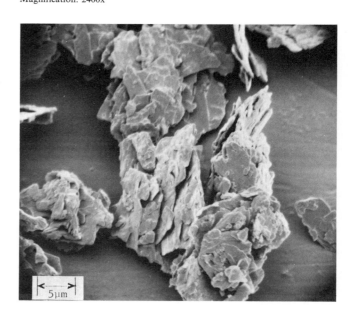

10. Typical Properties

Compressibility: *see* HPE Data.
Density: 1.03-1.08 g/cm³, *see also* HPE Data.
Density (tapped): 0.30 g/cm³, *see also* HPE Data.
Flash point: 250°C
Flowability: poorly flowing, cohesive powder.
Melting point: 88.5°C
Moisture content: *see* HPE Data.
Polymorphism: a trihydrate, acicular form and a dihydrate, lamellar form have been isolated, with the latter possessing the better lubricating properties.
Solubility: practically insoluble in ethanol, ethanol (95%), ether and water; slightly soluble in warm benzene and warm ethanol (95%). *See also* HPE Data.
Specific surface area: 2.45-16.0 m²/g.

HPE Laboratory Data

	Method	Lab #	Results
Compressibility			
at 63.5-235 MPa	COM-1	21	No compacts [a]
at 500 MPa	COM-7	12	Lamination [b]
Density	DE-1	7	1.06-1.1 g/cm³ [b]
Density (bulk & tapped)	BTD-2	1	B: 0.143 g/cm³ [b]
			T: 0.224 g/cm³ [b]
Density (bulk & tapped)	BTD-7	14	B: 0.160 g/cm³ [b]
			T: 0.180 g/cm³ [b]
Moisture content	EMC-1	5	*See* Fig. 1. [c]
Moisture content	MC-12	1	3.85% [b]
Moisture content	MC-12	5	3.00% [c]
Solubility			
Ethanol (95%) at 25°C	SOL-1	1	0.160 mg/mL [b]
n-Hexane at 25°C	SOL-1	1	0.018 mg/mL [b]
Water at 25°C	SOL-1	1	0.040 mg/mL [b]

Supplier:
a. Witco Corporation;
b. Mallinckrodt Speciality Chemicals Co;
c. Penick (Lot No.: 338-NB5-003).

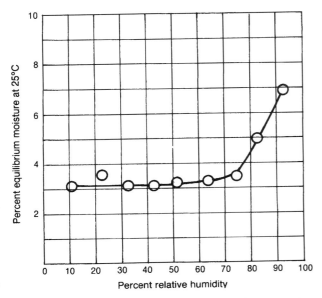

Fig. 1: Equilibrium moisture content of magnesium stearate.

11. Stability and Storage Conditions

Magnesium stearate is stable and should be stored in a well-closed container in a cool, dry place.

12. Incompatibilities

Incompatible with strong acids, alkalis and iron salts. Avoid mixing with strong oxidizing materials.

13. Method of Manufacture

Magnesium stearate is prepared either by the interaction of aqueous solutions of magnesium chloride with sodium stearate, or by the interaction of magnesium oxide, hydroxide or carbonate with stearic acid at elevated temperatures.

14. Safety

Magnesium stearate is widely used as a pharmaceutical excipient and is generally regarded as being nontoxic following oral administration. However, oral consumption of large quantities may result in some laxative effect or mucosal irritation. Inhalation of magnesium stearate powder is harmful and has resulted in fatalities, *see also* Section 15.

15. Handling Precautions

Observe normal precautions appropriate to the circumstances and quantity of material handled. Eye protection and gloves are recommended. Magnesium stearate should be handled in a well-ventilated environment; a respirator is recommended.

16. Regulatory Status

GRAS listed. Accepted as a food additive in Europe. Included in the FDA Inactive Ingredients Guide (oral capsules and tablets). Included in nonparenteral medicines licensed in the UK.

17. Pharmacopeias

Aust, Belg, Br, Braz, Chin, Cz, Eur, Fr, Ger, Hung, Ind, It, Jpn, Mex, Neth, Nord, Port, Rom, Swiss, Yug and USPNF.

18. Related Substances

Calcium Stearate; Stearic Acid; Zinc Stearate.

19. Comments

Magnesium stearate is hydrophobic and may retard the dissolution of a drug from a solid dosage form; the lowest possible concentration is therefore used in such formulations.[1-6] Since there may be variation between batches of magnesium stearate, it has not been possible to conclusively correlate the dissolution rate retardation with the observed lubricity.[7] The physical properties of different batches of magnesium stearate, such as specific surface area, have however been correlated with lubricant efficacy.[8-11]

There is evidence to suggest that the hydrophobic nature of magnesium stearate can vary from batch to batch due to the presence of water-soluble, surface-active impurities such as sodium stearate. Batches containing very low concentrations of these impurities have been shown to retard the dissolution of a drug to a greater extent than when using batches which contain higher levels of impurities.

An increase in the coefficient of variation of mixing and a decrease in the dissolution rate has been observed following blending of magnesium stearate with a tablet granulation. Tablet dissolution rate and crushing strength decreased as the time of blending increased; magnesium stearate may also increase tablet friability. Blending times with magnesium stearate should thus be carefully controlled.[12-26]

20. Specific References

1. Levy G, Gumtow RH. Effect of certain formulation factors on dissolution rate of the active ingredient III: tablet lubricants. J Pharm Sci 1963; 52: 1139-1144.
2. Ganderton D. The effect of distribution of magnesium stearate on the penetration of a tablet by water. J Pharm Pharmacol 1969; 21: 9S-18S.
3. Caldwell HC. Dissolution of lithium and magnesium from lithium carbonate capsules containing magnesium stearate. J Pharm Sci 1974; 63: 770-773.
4. Chowhan ZT, Amaro AA, Chow YP. Tablet-to-tablet dissolution variability and its relationship to the homogeneity of a water soluble drug. Drug Dev Ind Pharm 1982; 8: 145-168.
5. Lerk CF, Bolhuis GK, Smallenbroek AJ, Zuurman K. Interaction of tablet disintegrants and magnesium stearate during mixing II: effect on dissolution rate. Pharm Acta Helv 1982; 57: 282-286.
6. Hussain MSH, York P, Timmins P. Effect of commercial and high purity magnesium stearates on in-vitro dissolution of paracetamol DC tablets. Int J Pharmaceutics 1992; 78: 203-207.
7. Billany MR, Richards JH. Batch variation of magnesium stearate and its effect on the dissolution rate of salicylic acid from solid dosage forms. Drug Dev Ind Pharm 1982; 8: 497-511.
8. Frattini C, Simioni L. Should magnesium stearate be assessed in the formulation of solid dosage forms by weight or by surface area? Drug Dev Ind Pharm 1984; 10: 1117-1130.
9. Bos CE, Vromans H, Lerck CF. Lubricant sensitivity in relation to bulk density for granulations based on starch or cellulose. Int J Pharmaceutics 1991; 67: 39-49.
10. Phadke DS, Eichorst JL. Evaluation of particle size distribution and specific surface area of magnesium stearate. Drug Dev Ind Pharm 1991; 17: 901-906.
11. Steffens KJ, Koglin J. The magnesium stearate problem. Mfg Chem 1993; 64(12): 16, 17, 19.
12. Ragnarsson G, Hölzer AW, Sjögren J. The influence of mixing time and colloidal silica on the lubricating properties of magnesium stearate. Int J Pharmaceutics 1979; 3: 127-131.
13. Bolhuis GK, Lerk CF, Broersma P. Mixing action and evaluation of tablet lubricants in direct compression. Drug Dev Ind Pharm 1980; 6: 15-33.
14. Bossert J, Stamm A. Effect of mixing on the lubrication of crystalline lactose by magnesium stearate. Drug Dev Ind Pharm 1980; 6: 573-589.
15. Bolhuis GK, Smallenbroek AJ, Lerk CF. Interaction of tablet disintegrants and magnesium stearate during mixing I: effect on tablet disintegration. J Pharm Sci 1981; 70: 1328-1330.
16. Sheikh-Salem M, Fell JT. The influence of magnesium stearate on time dependent strength changes in tablets. Drug Dev Ind Pharm 1981; 7: 669-674.
17. Stewart PJ. Influence of magnesium stearate on the homogeneity of a prednisone granule ordered mix. Drug Dev Ind Pharm 1981; 7: 485-495.
18. Jarosz PJ, Parrott EL. Effect of tablet lubricants on axial and radial work of failure. Drug Dev Ind Pharm 1982; 8: 445-453.
19. Mitrevej KT, Augsburger LL. Adhesion of tablets in a rotary tablet press II: effects of blending time, running time, and lubricant concentration. Drug Dev Ind Pharm 1982; 8: 237-282.
20. Khan KA, Musikabhumma P, Rubinstein MH. The effect of mixing time of magnesium stearate on the tableting properties of dried microcrystalline cellulose. Pharm Acta Helv 1983; 58: 109-111.
21. Johansson ME. Investigations of the mixing time dependence of the lubricating properties of granular and powdered magnesium stearate. Acta Pharm Suec 1985; 22: 343-350.
22. Johansson ME. Influence of the granulation technique and starting material properties on the lubricating effect of granular magnesium stearate. J Pharm Pharmacol 1985; 37: 681-685.
23. Chowhan ZT, Chi LH. Drug-excipient interactions resulting from powder mixing III: solid state properties and their effect on drug dissolution. J Pharm Sci 1986; 75: 534-541.
24. Chowhan ZT, Chi LH. Drug-excipient interactions resulting from powder mixing IV: role of lubricants and their effect on in vitro dissolution. J Pharm Sci 1986; 75: 542-545.
25. Johansson ME, Nicklasson M. Influence of mixing time, particle size and colloidal silica on the surface coverage and lubrication of magnesium stearate. In: Rubinstein MH, editor. Pharmaceutical technology: tableting technology. Chichester: Ellis Horwood, 1987: 43-50.
26. Wang LH, Chowhan ZT. Drug-excipient interactions resulting from powder mixing V: role of sodium lauryl sulfate. Int J Pharmaceutics 1990; 60: 61-78.

21. General References

Bohidar NR, Restaino FA, Schwartz JB. Selecting key pharmaceutical formulation factors by regression analysis. Drug Dev Ind Pharm 1979; 5: 175-216.
Butcher AE, Jones TM. Some physical characteristics of magnesium stearate J Pharm Pharmacol 1972; 24: 1P-9P.
Dansereau R, Peck GE. The effect of the variability in the physical and chemical properties of magnesium stearate on the properties of compressed tablets. Drug Dev Ind Pharm 1987; 13: 975-999.
Ertel KD, Carstensen JT. Chemical, physical, and lubricant properties of magnesium stearate. J Pharm Sci 1988; 77: 625-629.
Ford JL, Rubinstein MH. An investigation into some pharmaceutical interactions by differential scanning calorimetry. Drug Dev Ind Pharm 1981; 7: 675-682.
Johansson ME. Granular magnesium stearate as a lubricant in tablet formulations. Int J Pharmaceutics 1984; 21: 307-315.
Jones TM. The effect of glidant addition on the flowability of bulk particulate solids. J Soc Cosmet Chem 1970; 21: 483-500.
Leinonen UI, Jalonen HU, Vihervaara PA, Laine ESU. Physical and lubrication properties of magnesium stearate. J Pharm Sci 1992; 81: 1194-1198.
Miller TA, York P, Jones TM. Manufacture and characterisation of magnesium stearate and palmitate powders of high purity. J Pharm Pharmacol 1982; 34: 8P.
Pilpel N. Metal stearates in pharmaceuticals and cosmetics. Mfg Chem Aerosol News 1971; 42(10): 37-40.

22. Authors

USA: LV Allen, PE Luner.

Magnesium Trisilicate

1. Nonproprietary Names

BP: Magnesium trisilicate
PhEur: Magnesii trisilicas
USP: Magnesium trisilicate

2. Synonyms

553(a); magnesium mesotrisilicate; silicic acid, magnesium salt (1:2), hydrate.

3. Chemical Name and CAS Registry Number

Magnesium trisilicate hydrate [39365-87-2]

4. Empirical Formula   Molecular Weight

$Mg_2Si_3O_8.xH_2O$ 260.86
(anhydrous)

5. Structural Formula

$2MgO.3SiO_2.xH_2O$

6. Functional Category

Anticaking agent; glidant; therapeutic agent.

7. Applications in Pharmaceutical Formulation or Technology

Magnesium trisilicate is used in oral pharmaceutical formulations and food products as a glidant. It is also extensively used therapeutically as an antacid.

8. Description

The USP XXII describes magnesium trisilicate as a compound of magnesium oxide and silicon dioxide with varying proportions of water.
Magnesium trisilicate occurs as an odorless and tasteless, fine, white-colored powder which is free from grittiness.

9. Pharmacopeial Specifications

Test	PhEur 1985	USP XXII
Identification	+	+
Water	17.0-34.0%	17.0-34.0%
Soluble salts	⩽ 1.5%	⩽ 1.5%
Chloride	⩽ 500 ppm	⩽ 0.055%
Sulfate	⩽ 0.5%	⩽ 0.5%
Free alkali	+	+
Arsenic	⩽ 4 ppm	⩽ 8 ppm
Heavy metals	⩽ 40 ppm	⩽ 0.003%
Acid-consuming capacity	+	+
Assay of MgO	⩾ 29.0%*	⩾ 20.0%
Assay of SiO_2	⩾ 65.0%*	⩾ 45.0%
Ratio of SiO_2 to MgO	—	2.10-2.37

* With reference to the ignited substance.

10. Typical Properties

Moisture content: magnesium trisilicate is slightly hygroscopic. At relative humidities of 15-65%, the equilibrium moisture content at 25°C is 17-23%; at relative humidities of 75-95%, the equilibrium moisture content is 24-30%.
Solubility: practically insoluble in ethanol (95%) and water.

11. Stability and Storage Conditions

Stable if stored in a well-closed container in a cool, dry, place.

12. Incompatibilities

Magnesium trisilicate may decrease the bioavailability of drugs such as mebeverine hydrochloride,[1] sucralfate and tetracycline, via chelation or binding, when they are taken together. The dissolution rate of folic acid tablets may be retarded by adsorption of the folic acid on to magnesium trisilicate.[2] Antimicrobial preservatives, such as the parabens, may be inactivated by the addition of magnesium trisilicate.[3]
Magnesium trisilicate is readily decomposed by mineral acids.

13. Method of Manufacture

Magnesium trisilicate may be prepared from sodium silicate and magnesium sulfate. The silicate also occurs in nature as the minerals meerschaum, parasepiolite and sepiolite.

14. Safety

Magnesium trisilicate is used in oral pharmaceutical formulations and is generally regarded as an essentially nontoxic and nonirritant material.
Orally administered magnesium trisilicate is neutralized in the stomach to form magnesium chloride and silicon dioxide; some magnesium is absorbed. Caution should be used when greater than 50 mEq of magnesium is given daily to persons with impaired renal function, due to the risk of hypermagnesemia.
Therapeutically, up to about 2 g of magnesium trisilicate may be taken daily as an antacid.
Reported adverse effects include the formation of bladder and renal calculi following the regular use, for many years, of magnesium trisilicate as an antacid.[4,5]

15. Handling Precautions

Observe normal precautions appropriate to the circumstances and quantity of material handled. Eye protection is recommended.

16. Regulatory Status

GRAS listed. Accepted for used as a food additive in the UK. Included in the FDA Inactive Ingredients Guide (oral tablets). Included in nonparenteral medicines licensed in the UK.

17. Pharmacopeias

Aust, Br, Braz, Chin, Cz, Egypt, Eur, Fr, Ger, Gr, Hung, Ind, It, Jpn, Mex, Neth, Nord, Port, Rus, Swiss, Turk, US and Yug.

18. Related Substances

Calcium silicate; magnesium silicate; magnesium trisilicate anhydrous; Talc.

Calcium silicate

Appearance: white to off-white colored, free-flowing powder that remains free-flowing after absorbing relatively large amounts of water or other liquids.
Pharmacopeias: USPNF.

Solubility: practically insoluble in water. Forms a gel with mineral acids.

Handling precautions: in the UK, the long-term (8-hour TWA) occupational exposure standards for calcium silicate are 10 mg/m^3 for total inhalable dust and 5 mg/m^3 for respirable dust.[6]

Comments: many different forms of calcium silicate are known such as $CaSiO_3$, Ca_2SiO_4 and Ca_3SiO_5. Usually these occur in the hydrated form and contain varying amounts of water of crystallization. Calcium silicate is used in pharmaceutical formulations as a glidant and anticaking agent. Also used in food products (GRAS listed).

Magnesium silicate

Appearance: an odorless and tasteless, fine, white-colored powder which is free from grittiness.

Pharmacopeias: USPNF.

Comments: several magnesium silicates are known such as magnesium metasilicate (MgO_3Si), magnesium orthosilicate (Mg_2O_4Si) and magnesium trisilicate. Magnesium silicate is used in pharmaceutical formulations as a glidant and anticaking agent. Also used in food products (GRAS listed).

Magnesium trisilicate anhydrous: $Mg_2Si_3O_8$

Molecular weight: 260.86

CAS number: [14987-04-3]

19. Comments

—

20. Specific References

1. Al-Gohary OMN. An in vitro study of the interaction between mebeverine hydrochloride and magnesium trisilicate powder. Int J Pharmaceutics 1991; 67: 89-95.
2. Iwuagwu MA, Jideonwo A. Preliminary investigations into the in-vitro interaction of folic acid with magnesium trisilicate and edible clay. Int J Pharmaceutics 1990; 65: 63-67.
3. Allwood MC. The adsorption of esters of *p*-hydroxybenzoic acid by magnesium trisilicate. Int J Pharmaceutics 1982; 11: 101-107.
4. Joekes AM, Rose GA, Sutor J. Multiple renal silica calculi. Br Med J 1973; 1: 146-147.
5. Levison DA, Crocker PR, Banim S, Wallace DMA. Silica stones in the urinary bladder. Lancet 1982; i: 704-705.
6. Health and Safety Executive. EH40/93: occupational exposure limits 1993. London: HMSO, 1993.

21. General References

—

22. Authors

USA: AS Kearney.

Malic Acid

1. Nonproprietary Names

USPNF: Malic acid

2. Synonyms

Apple acid; E296; 2-hydroxy-1,4-butanedioic acid; 1-hydroxy-1,2-ethanedicarboxylic acid; 2-hydroxysuccinic acid; DL-malic acid.

3. Chemical Name and CAS Registry Number

Hydroxybutanedioic acid [6915-15-7] also
(RS)-$(\pm)$-Hydroxybutanedioic acid [617-48-1]

4. Empirical Formula   Molecular Weight

$C_4H_6O_5$ 134.09

5. Structural Formula

$HOOC - CHOH - CH_2 - COOH$

6. Functional Category

Acidulant; antioxidant; flavoring agent; sialagogue; therapeutic agent.

7. Applications in Pharmaceutical Formulation or Technology

Malic acid is used in pharmaceutical formulations as a general purpose acidulant. It possesses a slight apple flavor and is used as a flavoring agent to mask bitter tastes and provide tartness. Malic acid is also used as an alternative to citric acid in effervescent powders, mouthwashes and tooth-cleaning tablets. In addition, malic acid has chelating and antioxidant properties and may be used as a synergist, with butylated hydroxytoluene, to retard oxidation in vegetable oils. In food products, it may be used in concentrations up to 420 ppm.
Therapeutically, malic acid has been used topically in combination with benzoic acid and salicylic acid to deslough burns, ulcers and wounds. It has also been used orally and parenterally, either intravenously or intramuscularly, in the treatment of liver disorders.

8. Description

White or nearly white, crystalline powder or granules having a slight odor and a strongly acidic taste. The synthetic material produced commercially in Europe and the USA is a racemic mixture; the naturally occurring material, found in apples and many other fruits and plants, is levorotatory.

9. Pharmacopeial Specifications

Test	USPNF XVII
Identification	+
Specific rotation (8.5% w/v aqueous solution)	-0.1° to +0.1°
Residue on ignition	⩽ 0.1%
Water insoluble substances	⩽ 0.1%
Heavy metals	⩽ 0.002%
Fumaric acid	⩽ 1.0%
Maleic acid	⩽ 0.05%
Assay	99.0-100.5%

10. Typical Properties

Data shown below is for the racemate. *See* Section 18 for other data for the D- and L-forms.
Acidity/alkalinity:
pH = 2.35 (1% w/v aqueous solution at 25°C)
Density (bulk): 0.81 g/cm^3
Density (tapped): 0.92 g/cm^3
Dissociation constant:
pK_{a1} = 3.40 at 25°C;
pK_{a2} = 5.05 at 25°C.
Melting point: 130-132°C
Solubility: freely soluble in ethanol (95%) and water. A saturated aqueous solution contains about 56% malic acid at 20°C.

Solvent	Solubility at 25°C
Ethanol (95%)	1 in 2.6*
Methanol	1 in 1.2
Propylene glycol	1 in 1.9
Water	1 in 1.5-2.0*

* Note that there is considerable variability in compendial values for solubility in ethanol and water.

Specific gravity:
1.601 at 20°C;
1.250 (saturated aqueous solution at 25°C).
Viscosity (dynamic): 6.5 mPa s (6.5 cP) for a 50% w/v aqueous solution at 25°C.

11. Stability and Storage Conditions

Malic acid is stable at temperatures up to 150°C. At temperatures above 150°C it begins to lose water very slowly to yield fumaric acid; complete decomposition occurs at about 180°C to give fumaric acid and maleic anhydride.
Malic acid is readily degraded by many aerobic and anaerobic microorganisms, and conditions of high humidity and elevated temperatures should be avoided to prevent caking.
The bulk material should be stored in a well-closed container, in a cool, dry, place.

12. Incompatibilities

Malic acid can react with oxidizing materials. Aqueous solutions are mildly corrosive to carbon steels.

13. Method of Manufacture

Malic acid is manufactured by hydrating maleic and fumaric acids in the presence of suitable catalysts. The malic acid formed is then separated from the equilibrium product mixture.

14. Safety

Malic acid is used in oral, topical and parenteral pharmaceutical formulations in addition to food products, and is generally regarded as a nontoxic and nonirritant material. However, concentrated solutions may be irritant.
LD_{50} (mouse, oral): 1.6 g/kg[1]
LD_{50} (rat, oral): 4.73 g/kg

15. Handling Precautions

Observe normal precautions appropriate to the circumstances and quantity of material handled. Malic acid, and concentrated malic acid solutions may be irritant to the skin, eyes and mucous membranes. Gloves and eye protection are recommended.

16. Regulatory Status

GRAS listed. Both the racemic mixture and the levorotatory isomer are accepted as food additives in Europe (the code number E296, applies to either the DL- or L-form). The DL- and L-forms are Included in the FDA Inactive Ingredients Guide (oral and rectal preparations). Included in nonparenteral and parenteral medicines licensed in the UK.

17. Pharmacopeias

Ger and USPNF.

18. Related Substances

Citric Acid Monohydrate; Fumaric Acid; D-malic acid; L-malic acid; Tartaric Acid.

D-Malic acid: $C_4H_6O_5$
Molecular weight: 134.09
CAS number: [636-61-3]
Synonyms: (*R*)-(+)-hydroxybutanedioic acid; D-(+)-malic acid.
Melting point: 99-101°C
Specific rotation $[\alpha]_D^{20}$: +5.2° (in acetone at 18°C).

L-Malic acid: $C_4H_6O_5$
Molecular weight: 134.09
CAS number: [97-67-6]
Synonyms: (*S*)-(-)-hydroxybutanedioic acid; L-(-)-malic acid.
Boiling point: ≈ 140°C (with decomposition)
Melting point: 99-100°C
Specific rotation $[\alpha]_D^{20}$: -5.7° (in acetone at 18°C)

19. Comments

—

20. Specific References

1. Sweet DV, editor. Registry of toxic effects of chemical substances. Cincinnati: US Department of Health, 1987.

21. General References

Malic and Fumaric Acids. Mfg Chem Aerosol News 1964; 35(12): 56-59.
Berger SE. In: Kirk-Othmer encyclopedia of chemical technology, volume 13; 3rd edition. New York: Wiley-Interscience, 1981: 103.

22. Authors

UK: M Lynch.

Maltitol Solution

1. Nonproprietary Names

USPNF: Maltitol solution

2. Synonyms

Hydrogenated glucose syrup; *Finmalt L*; *Lycasin 80/55*; maltitol syrup.

3. Chemical Name and CAS Registry Number

Maltitol solution [9053-46-7]

4. Empirical Formula   Molecular Weight

The USPNF XVII (Suppl 8) describes maltitol solution as an aqueous solution of a hydrogenated, partially hydrolyzed starch. It contains, on the anhydrous basis, not less than 50% w/w of D-maltitol ($C_{12}H_{24}O_{11}$) and not more than 16.0% w/w of D-sorbitol ($C_6H_{14}O_6$). See also Section 19.

5. Structural Formula

See Section 4.

6. Functional Category

Suspending agent; sweetening agent.

7. Applications in Pharmaceutical Formulation or Technology

Maltitol solution is used in oral pharmaceutical formulations as a bulk sweetening agent, either alone or in combination with other excipients, such as sorbitol. Maltitol solution is also used as a suspending agent in oral suspensions as an alternative to sucrose syrup since it is viscous, noncariogenic and has a low calorific value. It is also noncrystallizing and therefore prevents 'cap-locking' in syrups and elixirs.

Maltitol solution is additionally used in the preparation of pharmaceutical lozenges and is also used in confectionery and food products.

8. Description

Maltitol solution is a colorless and odorless, clear viscous liquid. It is sweet-tasting (approximately 75% the sweetness of sucrose).

9. Pharmacopeial Specifications

Test	USPNF XVII (Suppl 8)
Identification	+
Water	⩽ 30.0%
Residue on ignition	⩽ 0.1%
Chloride	⩽ 0.005%
Sulfate	⩽ 0.010%
Arsenic	⩽ 2.5 ppm
Heavy metals	⩽ 0.001%
Reducing sugars	+
Assay (dried basis) of maltitol	⩾ 50.0%
Assay (dried basis) of sorbitol	⩽ 16.0%

10. Typical Properties

Density: 1.36 g/cm^3 at 20°C
Heat of combustion: 10.0 kJ/g (2.4 kcal/g)
Osmolarity: the osmolarity of an aqueous maltitol solution is similar to that of a sucrose solution of the same concentration. A 10% v/v aqueous solution of *Lycasin 80/55* (Roquette Frères) is iso-osmotic with serum.
Refractive index: $n_D^{20} = 1.478$
Solubility: miscible with ethanol provided the ethanol concentration is less than 55%.
Viscosity (dynamic): maltitol solution is a viscous, syrupy, liquid. At 20°C, a solution of *Lycasin 80/55* (Roquette Frères) containing 75% of dry substances has a viscosity of approximately 2000 mPa s (2000 cP). With increasing temperature the viscosity of a maltitol solution is reduced, *see* Fig. 1. The viscosity of maltitol solutions also decreases with decreasing concentration of dry solids, at a constant temperature. Maltitol solution may also be mixed with sorbitol solution to obtain blends of a desired viscosity.

11. Stability and Storage Conditions

Maltitol solution is stable for at least two years at room temperature and pH 2-9. Following storage for three months at 50°C, maltitol solution at pH 2 underwent slight hydrolysis (1.2%) and became yellow colored. At pH 3, and the same storage conditions, no color change was apparent although very slight hydrolysis occurred (0.2%). At pH 4-9, no hydrolysis occurred although a very slight yellow color was formed under alkaline conditions.[1]

Formulations containing maltitol solution should be preserved with an antimicrobial preservative such as sodium benzoate or a mixture of parabens. Maltitol solution is noncrystallizing.

Maltitol solution should be stored in a well-closed container, in a cool, dry, place.

12. Incompatibilities

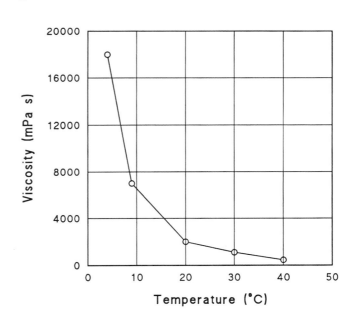

Fig. 1: Viscosity of maltitol solution (*Lycasin 80/55*), containing 75% of dry substances, at different temperatures.

13. Method of Manufacture

Maltitol solution is prepared by the hydrogenation of a high maltose syrup which is obtained from starch by enzymatic hydrolysis. The maltitol solution produced from this process consists of the hydrogenated homologues of the oligosaccharides contained in the original syrup.

14. Safety

Maltitol solution is used in oral pharmaceutical formulations, confectionery and food products and is considered to be less cariogenic than sucrose.[2-5] It is generally regarded as a nontoxic, nonallergenic and nonirritant material. However, excessive oral consumption (more than 50 g daily) may cause flatulence and diarrhea.

The WHO, in considering the safety of maltitol solution did not set a value for the acceptable daily intake for maltitol and hydrogenated glucose syrup since the levels used in food to achieve a desired effect were not considered a hazard to health.[6]

LD_{50} (rat, IP): 20 g/kg[7]

15. Handling Precautions

Observe normal precautions appropriate to the circumstances and quantity of material handled.

16. Regulatory Status

Accepted for use in confectionery, foods and nonparenteral pharmaceutical formulations in Europe and the US.

17. Pharmacopeias

USPNF.

18. Related Substances

Lactitol; maltitol; Sorbitol.

Lactitol: $C_{12}H_{24}O_{11}$
Molecular weight: 344.36
CAS number: [585-86-4]
Synonyms: 4-*O*-(β-D-galactopyranosyl)-D-glucitol; β-galactosido-sorbitol; lactositol.
Appearance: sweet-tasting, colorless, viscous, syrup. The dried material consists of lactitol monohydrate and lactitol dihydrate which are odorless, sweet-tasting, white crystalline solids.
Comments: lactitol is a disaccharide analogue of lactulose used as an intense and bulk sweetener in foods and pharmaceutical formulations. Lactitol monohydrate has laxative properties and is used therapeutically for this purpose; single daily doses of 10-20 g being used in adults.

Maltitol: $C_{12}H_{24}O_{11}$
Molecular weight: 344.36
CAS number: [585-88-6]
Synonyms: α-D-glucopyranosyl-1,4-D-glucitol; hydrogenated maltose; D-maltitol.
Appearance: a sweet-tasting, white crystalline powder.
Solubility: very soluble in water; slightly soluble in ethanol (95%).
Safety: LD_{50} (rabbit, oral): 65 mg/kg[7]

19. Comments

Hydrogenated glucose syrup is a generic term used to describe aqueous mixtures containing mainly D-maltitol, along with D-sorbitol and hydrogenated oligo- and polysaccharides. Such mixtures can vary widely in their composition and hence physical and chemical properties. Products containing up to 90% of maltitol are usually known as maltitol syrup or maltitol solution. Preparations containing a minimum of 98% of maltitol are designated maltitol.

20. Specific References

1. Roquette Frères. Technical literature: *Lycasin* the sweetener for sugarless pharmaceuticals; 1993.
2. Frostell G, Birkhed D. Acid production from Swedish Lycasin (candy quality) and French Lycasin (80/55) in human dental plaques. Caries Res 1978; 12: 256-263.
3. Grenby TH. Dental and nutritional effects of Lycasins replacing sucrose in the diet of laboratory rats. J Dent Res 1982; 61: 557.
4. Würsch P, Koellreutter. Maltitol and maltotriitol as inhibitors of acid production in human dental plaque. Caries Res 1982; 16: 90-95.
5. Havenaar R, Drost JS, de Stoppelaar JD, Huis in't Veld JHJ, Backer Dirks O. Potential cariogenicity of Lycasin 80/55 in comparison to starch, sucrose, xylitol, sorbitol and L-sorbose in rats. Caries Res 1984; 18: 375-384.
6. FAO/WHO. Evaluation of certain food additives and contaminants: thirty-third report of the joint FAO/WHO expert committee on food additives. Tech Rep Ser Wld Hlth Org 1989; No. 776.
7. Sweet DV, editor. Registry of toxic effects of chemical substances. Cincinnati: US Department of Health, 1987.

21. General References

Le Bot Y. Lycasin for confections. Manufacturing Confectioner 1983; Dec: 69-74.

22. Authors

UK: SZ Dziedzic.

Maltodextrin

1. Nonproprietary Names

USPNF: Maltodextrin

2. Synonyms

Glucidex; *Lo-Dex*; *Lycatab DSH*; *Maltagran*; *Maltrin*; *Paselli*.

3. Chemical Name and CAS Registry Number

Maltodextrin [9050-36-6]

4. Empirical Formula   Molecular Weight

$(C_6H_{10}O_5)_n.H_2O$ 900-9000

The USPNF XVII (Suppl 8) describes maltodextrin as a nonsweet, nutritive saccharide mixture of polymers that consist of D-glucose units, with a dextrose equivalent (DE) less than 20, *see also* Section 19. The D-glucose units are linked primarily by α-(1→4) bonds, but having branched segments linked by α-(1→6) bonds.

5. Structural Formula

See Section 4.

6. Functional Category

Coating agent; tablet and capsule diluent; tablet binder; viscosity-increasing agent.

7. Applications in Pharmaceutical Formulation or Technology

Maltodextrin is used in tablet formulations as a binder and diluent in both direct compression and wet granulation processes.[1-7] Maltodextrin appears to have no adverse effect on the rate of dissolution of tablet and capsule formulations; magnesium stearate 0.5-1.0% may be used as a lubricant. Maltodextrin may also be used as a tablet film former in aqueous film coating processes. Maltodextrin grades with a high DE value are particularly useful in chewable tablet formulations.

Maltodextrin may also be used in pharmaceutical formulations to increase the viscosity of solutions and to prevent the crystallization of syrups. Therapeutically, maltodextrin is often used as a carbohydrate source in oral nutritional supplements since solutions with a lower osmolarity than isocaloric dextrose solutions can be prepared.

Maltodextrin is also widely used in confectionery and food products.

Use	Concentration (%)
Aqueous film coating	2-10
Carrier	10-99
Crystallization inhibitor for lozenges and syrups	5-20
Osmolarity regulator for solutions	10-50
Spray-drying aid	20-80
Tablet binder (direct compression)	2-40
Tablet binder (wet granulation)	3-10

8. Description

Maltodextrin occurs as a nonsweet, odorless, white powder or granules. The sweetness of maltodextrin increases as the DE increases.

SEM: 1

Excipient: Maltodextrin (*Maltrin M100*)
Manufacturer: Grain Processing Corporation
Magnification: 100x

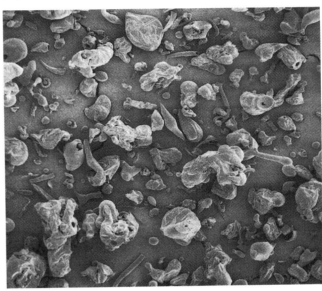

SEM: 2

Excipient: Maltodextrin (*Maltrin M500*)
Manufacturer: Grain Processing Corporation
Magnification: 100x

9. Pharmacopeial Specifications

Test	USPNF XVII (Suppl 8)
Microbial limits	+
pH (20% w/v solution)	4.0-7.0
Loss on drying	$\leqslant$ 6.0%
Residue on ignition	$\leqslant$ 0.5%
Heavy metals	$\leqslant$ 5 ppm
Protein	$\leqslant$ 0.1%
Sulfur dioxide	$\leqslant$ 0.004%
Dextrose equivalent	< 20

10. Typical Properties

Angle of repose:
35.2° for *Maltrin M500*;[5]
28.4° for *Maltrin M510*.[5]
Density:
1.410 g/cm^3 for *Maltrin M500*;[5]
1.425 g/cm^3 for *Maltrin M510*.[5]
Density (bulk):
0.43 g/cm^3 for *Lycatab DSH*;
0.51 g/cm^3 for *Maltrin M040*;
0.58 g/cm^3 for *Maltrin M150*;
0.26 g/cm^3 for *Maltrin M500*;[5]
0.48 g/cm^3 for *Maltrin M510*;[5]
0.37 g/cm^3 for *Maltrin M550*;
0.13 g/cm^3 for *Maltrin M700*.
Density (tapped):
0.32 g/cm^3 for *Maltrin M500*;[5]
0.54 g/cm^3 for *Maltrin M510*.[5]
Hygroscopicity: hygroscopicity increases as DE increases. Maltodextrin is slightly hygroscopic at relative humidities less than 50%. At relative humidities greater than 50% maltodextrin is very hygroscopic.
Particle size distribution: Maltrin is available in various grades with different particle size distributions. Maximum of 5% greater than 200 μm, and minimum of 90% greater than 50 μm in size for *Lycatab DSH*.
Solubility: freely soluble in water; slightly soluble in ethanol. Solubility increases as DE increases.
Specific surface area:
0.54 m^2/g for *Maltrin M500*;[5]
0.31 m^2/g for *Maltrin M510*.[5]
Viscosity (dynamic): less than 20 mPa s (20 cP) for a 20% w/v aqueous solution of *Lycatab DSH*. The viscosity of maltodextrin solutions decreases as the DE increases.

11. Stability and Storage Conditions

Maltodextrin is stable for at least one year when stored at a cool temperature (< 30°C) and less than 50% relative humidity. Maltodextrin solutions may require the addition of an antimicrobial preservative.
Maltodextrin should be stored in a well-closed container in a cool, dry, place.

12. Incompatibilities

Under certain pH and temperature conditions maltodextrin may undergo Maillard reactions with amino acids to cause yellowing or browning.

13. Method of Manufacture

Maltodextrin is prepared by heating and treating starch with acid and/or enzymes in the presence of water. This process partially hydrolyzes the starch to produce a solution of glucose polymers of varying chain length. This solution is then filtered and dried, or concentrated, to obtain maltodextrin.

14. Safety

Maltodextrin is a readily digestible carbohydrate with a nutritional value of approximately 17 kJ/g (4 kcal/g). As an excipient, maltodextrin is generally regarded as a nonirritant and nontoxic material.

15. Handling Precautions

Observe normal precautions appropriate to the circumstances and quantity of material handled. Eye protection and gloves are recommended. Maltodextrin should be handled in a well-ventilated environment and excessive dust generation avoided.

16. Regulatory Status

GRAS listed. Included in nonparenteral medicines licensed in the UK.

17. Pharmacopeias

USPNF.

18. Related Substances

Corn syrup solids; Dextrates; Dextrin; Starch.

Corn syrup solids

Comments: corn syrup solids are saccharide polymers with a DE equal to or greater than 20 and are prepared, in a similar manner to maltodextrin, by the partial hydrolysis of starch.

19. Comments

Various different grades of maltodextrin are commercially available for food and pharmaceutical applications from a number of suppliers, e.g. *Lycatab DSH* (Roquette Frères) and *Maltrin* (Grain Processing Corporation). The grades have different physical properties such as solubility and viscosity, depending upon their DE value. The dextrose equivalent (DE) value is a measure of the extent of starch polymer hydrolysis and is defined as the reducing power of a substance expressed in grams of D-glucose per 100 g of the dry substance.

20. Specific References

1. Li LC, Peck GE. The effect of moisture content on the compression properties of maltodextrins. J Pharm Pharmacol 1990; 42: 272-275.
2. Li LC, Peck GE. The effect of agglomeration methods on the micrometric properties of a maltodextrin product Maltrin 150. Drug Dev Ind Pharm 1990; 16: 1491-1503.
3. Papadimitriou E, Efentakis M, Choulis NH. Evaluation of maltodextrins as excipients for direct compression tablets and their influence on the rate of dissolution. Int J Pharmaceutics 1992; 86: 131-136.
4. Visavarungroj N; Remon JP. Evaluation of maltodextrin as binding agent. Drug Dev Ind Pharm 1992; 18: 1691-1700.
5. Mollan MJ, Çelik M. Characterization of directly compressible maltodextrins manufactured by three different processes. Drug Dev Ind Pharm 1993; 19: 2335-2358.
6. Muñoz-Ruiz A, Monedero Perales MC, Velasco Antequera MV, Jiménez-Castellanos MR. Physical and rheological properties of raw materials. STP Pharma (Sci) 1993; 3: 307-312.
7. Symecko CW; Romero AJ; Rhodes CT. Comparative evaluation of two pharmaceutical binders in the wet granulation of hydrochlorothiazide: Lycatb DSH versus Kollidon 30. Drug Dev Ind Pharm 1993; 19: 1131-1141.

21. General References

Grain Processing Corporation. Technical literature: *Maltrin* carbohydrates for pharmaceutical formulations, 1993.

Roquette Frères. Technical literature: *Lycatab DSH* excipient for wet granulation, 1992.

22. Authors

USA: DL Kiser, SO Freers.

Maltol

1. Nonproprietary Names

None adopted.

2. Synonyms

3-Hydroxy-2-methyl-(1,4-pyran); 3-hydroxy-2-methyl-4-pyrone; E636; larixinic acid; 2-methyl-3-hydroxy-4-pyrone; 2-methyl pyromeconic acid; *Veltol*.

3. Chemical Name and CAS Registry Number

3-Hydroxy-2-methyl-4*H*-pyran-4-one
[118-71-8]

4. Empirical Formula   Molecular Weight

$C_6H_6O_3$ 126.11

5. Structural Formula

6. Functional Category

Flavor enhancer; flavoring agent.

7. Applications in Pharmaceutical Formulation or Technology

Maltol is used in pharmaceutical formulations and food products as a flavoring agent or flavor enhancer. In foods, it is used at concentrations up to 30 ppm, particularly with fruit flavorings, although it is also used to impart a freshly baked odor and flavor to bread and cakes. When used at concentrations between 5-75 ppm maltol potentiates the sweetness of a food product permitting a reduction in sugar content of up to 15% whilst maintaining the same level of sweetness. Maltol is also used at low levels in perfumery.

8. Description

White crystalline solid with a characteristic, caramel-like odor and taste. In dilute solution it possesses a sweet, strawberry or pineapple-like flavor and odor.

9. Pharmacopeial Specifications

See Section 19.

10. Typical Properties

Acidity/alkalinity:
pH = 5.3 (0.5% w/v aqueous solution)
Melting point: 162-164°C (begins to sublime at 93°C)

Solubility:

Solvent	Solubility at 25°C
Ethanol (95%)	1 in 30
Glycerin	1 in 87
Propan-2-ol	1 in 53
Propylene glycol	1 in 28
Water	1 in 83

11. Stability and Storage Conditions

Maltol solutions may be stored in glass or plastic containers. The bulk material should be stored in a well-closed container, protected from light, in a cool, dry, place.

12. Incompatibilities

—

13. Method of Manufacture

Maltol is mainly isolated from naturally occurring sources such as: beechwood and other wood tars; pine needles; chicory; and the bark of young larch trees. It may also be synthesized by the alkaline hydrolysis of streptomycin salts or by a number of other synthetic methods.

14. Safety

Maltol is generally regarded as an essentially nontoxic and nonirritant material. In animal feeding studies, it has been shown to be well tolerated with no adverse toxic, reproductive or embryogenic effects observed in rats and dogs fed daily intakes of up to 200 mg/kg of maltol, for two years.[1] The WHO has set an acceptable daily intake for maltol at up to 1 mg/kg body-weight.[2]
LD_{50} (chicken, oral): 3.72 g/kg[3]
LD_{50} (guinea pig, oral): 1.41 g/kg
LD_{50} (mouse, oral): 0.55 g/kg
LD_{50} (mouse, SC): 0.82 g/kg
LD_{50} (rabbit, oral): 1.62 g/kg
LD_{50} (rat, oral): 1.41 g/kg

15. Handling Precautions

Observe normal precautions appropriate to the circumstances and quantity of material handled. Maltol should be used in a well-ventilated environment. Eye protection is recommended.

16. Regulatory Status

GRAS listed. Accepted for use as a food additive in Europe. Included in the FDA Inactive Ingredients Guide (oral solutions and syrups).

17. Pharmacopeias

—

18. Related Substances

Ethyl Maltol.

19. Comments

Maltol is a good chelating agent and various metal complexes, e.g. aluminum maltol and ferric maltol have been investigated as potentially useful therapeutic or experimental agents.[4-6]

Although not included in any pharmacopeias a specification for maltol is contained in the Food Chemicals Codex (FCC), *see* below.[7]

Test	FCC 1981
Identification	+
Arsenic	$\leqslant$ 3 ppm
Heavy metals (as lead)	$\leqslant$ 0.002%
Lead	$\leqslant$ 10 ppm
Melting range	160-164°C
Residue on ignition	$\leqslant$ 0.2%
Water	$\leqslant$ 0.5%
Assay	$\geqslant$ 99.0%

20. Specific References

1. Gralla EJ, Stebbins RB, Coleman GL, Delahunt CS. Toxicity studies with ethyl maltol. Toxicol Appl Pharmacol 1969; 15: 604-613.
2. FAO/WHO. Evaluation of certain food additives. Twenty-fifth report of the joint FAO/WHO expert committee on food additives. Tech Rep Ser Wld Hlth Org 1981; No. 669.
3. Sweet DV, editor. Registry of toxic effects of chemical substances. Cincinnati: US Department of Health, 1987.
4. Finnegan MM, Rettig SJ, Orvig C. A neutral water-soluble aluminium complex of neurological interest. J Am Chem Soc 1986; 108: 5033-5035.
5. Singh RK, Barrand MA. Lipid peroxidation effects of a novel iron compound, ferric maltol. A comparison with ferrous sulfate. J Pharm Pharmacol 1990; 42: 276-279.
6. Kelsey SM, Hider RC, Bloor JR, Blake DR, Gutteridge CN, Newland AC. Absorption of low and therapeutic doses of ferric maltol, a novel ferric iron compound, in iron deficient subjects using a single dose iron absorption test. J Clin Pharm Ther 1991; 16: 117-122.
7. Food Chemicals Codex, 3rd edition. Washington, DC: National Academy Press, 1981: 184-185.

21. General References

—

22. Authors

UK: PJ Weller.

Mannitol

1. Nonproprietary Names

BP: Mannitol
PhEur: Mannitolum
USP: Mannitol

2. Synonyms

Cordycepic acid; E421; 1,2,3,4,5,6-hexanehexol; manita; manna sugar; mannite; *Pearlitol*.

3. Chemical Name and CAS Registry Number

D-Mannitol [69-65-8]

4. Empirical Formula   Molecular Weight

$C_6H_{14}O_6$ 182.17

5. Structural Formula

$$
\begin{array}{c}
CH_2OH \\
HO-C-H \\
HO-C-H \\
H-C-OH \\
H-C-OH \\
CH_2OH
\end{array}
$$

6. Functional Category

Sweetening agent; tablet and capsule diluent; tonicity agent; vehicle (bulking agent) for lyophilized preparations.

7. Applications in Pharmaceutical Formulation or Technology

Mannitol is widely used in pharmaceutical formulations and food products. In pharmaceutical preparations it is primarily used as a diluent (10-90% w/w) in tablet formulations, where it is of particular value since it is not hygroscopic and may thus be used with moisture sensitive active ingredients.

Mannitol may be used in direct compression tablet applications,[1-5] for which the granular form was especially developed, or wet granulations,[6] which may be readily dried. A lubricant, such as magnesium stearate 1-2% w/w should be used in direct compression processes, *see also* Section 19. Specific tablet applications include antacid formulations, glyceryl trinitrate tablets and vitamin preparations.

Mannitol is commonly used as an excipient in the manufacture of chewable tablet formulations because of its negative heat of solution, sweetness and 'mouth feel'.[7,8]

In lyophilized preparations, mannitol (20-90% w/w) has been included as a carrier to produce a stiff, homogeneous cake that improves the appearance of the lyophilized plug in a vial.[9-12]

Mannitol has also been used to prevent thickening in aqueous antacid suspensions of aluminum hydroxide (< 7% w/v). In addition, mannitol has been suggested as a plasticizer in soft gelatin capsules, as a component of sustained release tablet formulations[13] and is used in food applications as a bulking agent.

Therapeutically, supersaturated aqueous solutions of mannitol (20-25% w/v) are widely used as osmotic diuretics.

8. Description

Mannitol is D-mannitol. It is a hexahydric alcohol related to mannose and is isomeric with sorbitol.

Mannitol occurs as a white, odorless, crystalline powder, or free-flowing granules. It has a sweet taste, approximately as sweet as glucose and half as sweet as sucrose, and imparts a cooling sensation in the mouth. Microscopically, it appears as orthorhombic needles when crystallized from alcohol.

SEM: 1

Excipient: Mannitol
Manufacturer: Triangle Import & Export Co
Magnification: 120x

SEM: 2

Excipient: Mannitol
Manufacturer: Triangle Import & Export Co
Magnification: 600x

9. Pharmacopeial Specifications

Test	PhEur 1987	USP XXII (Suppl 8)
Identification	+	+
Melting range	165-168°C	165-169°C
Specific rotation*	+23° to +24°	+137° to 145°
Acidity	+	+
Loss on drying	≤ 0.5%	≤ 0.3%
Chloride	≤ 70 ppm	≤ 0.007%
Sulfate	≤ 120 ppm	≤ 0.01%
Arsenic	≤ 2 ppm	≤ 1 ppm
Reducing sugars	+	+
Sulfated ash	≤ 0.1%	—
Assay	98.0-102.0%	96.0-101.5%

* Note that the preparation and concentration of the mannitol solution used to measure the specific optical rotation is different in the PhEur 1987 and USP XXII.

10. Typical Properties

Compressibility: see HPE Data and Fig. 1.
Density (bulk):
0.66 g/cm³ for *Pearlitol FG*;
0.72 g/cm³ for *Pearlitol MG*;
0.67 g/cm³ for *Pearlitol GG2*.[14]
See also HPE Data.
Density (particle): 1.48 g/cm³
Density (tapped):
0.76 g/cm³ for *Pearlitol FG*;
0.82 g/cm³ for *Pearlitol MG*;
0.78 g/cm³ for *Pearlitol GG2*.[14]
See also HPE Data.
Dissociation constant: pK_a = 13.5 at 18°C
Flash point: > 150°C
Flowability: powder is cohesive, granules are free flowing.
Heat of combustion: 16.57 kJ/g (3960 cal/g)
Heat of solution: -120.9 J/g (-28.9 cal/g) at 25°C
Melting point: 166-168°C
Moisture content: see HPE Data and Fig. 2.
Osmolarity: a 5.07% w/v aqueous solution is iso-osmotic with serum.
Particle size distribution: maximum of 0.1% greater than 500 μm and minimum of 90% greater than 200 μm in size for *Pearlitol FG*; maximum of 20% greater than 500 μm and minimum of 85% greater than 100 μm in size for *Pearlitol MG*; maximum of 0.5% greater than 841 μm and minimum of 90% greater than 150 μm in size for *Pearlitol GG2*.[14] Average particle diameter is 250 μm for *Pearlitol FG*, 360 μm for *Pearlitol MG* and 520 μm for *Pearlitol GG2*.[14] See also HPE Data.
Refractive index: n_D^{20} = 1.333
Solubility:

Solvent	Solubility at 20°C
Alkalis	soluble
Ethanol (95%)	1 in 83
Ether	practically insoluble
Glycerin	1 in 18
Propan-2-ol	1 in 100
Water	1 in 5.5

Specific surface area: 0.60 m²/g

HPE Laboratory Project Data

	Method	Lab #	Results
Average flow rate	FLO-3	24	No flow [a]
Bulk/tap density	BTD-5	6	B: 0.381 g/cm³ [b]
			T: 0.599 g/cm³
	BTD-5	6	B: 0.429 g/cm³ [c]
			T: 0.679 g/cm³
	BTD-5	6	B: 0.420 g/cm³ [a]
			T: 0.633 g/cm³
Compressibility	COM-3	20	See Fig. 3. [c]
Moisture content	MC-29	23	0.277% [a]
Particle size	PSD-7	24	12.5 μm [a]
			See also Fig. 4.
Solubility [a]			
Ethanol (95%) at 25°C	SOL-6	23	0.0133 g/mL
Ethanol (95%) at 37°C	SOL-6	23	0.0139 g/mL
Hexane at 25°C	SOL-6	23	< 0.001 g/mL
Hexane at 37°C	SOL-6	23	< 0.001 g/mL
Propylene glycol at 25°C	SOL-6	23	0.100-0.200 g/mL
Propylene glycol at 37°C	SOL-6	23	0.100-0.200 g/mL
Water at 25°C	SOL-6	23	0.1798 g/mL
Water at 37°C	SOL-6	23	0.2234 g/mL

Supplier:
a. Pfizer Inc;
b. George Lihe;
c. Atlas Chemical Industries (UK) Ltd (Lot No.: 2022BO).

11. Stability and Storage Conditions

Mannitol is stable in the dry state and in aqueous solutions. Solutions may be sterilized by filtration or by autoclaving and if necessary may be autoclaved repeatedly with no adverse physical or chemical effects.[15] In solution, mannitol is not attacked by cold, dilute acids or alkalis, nor by atmospheric oxygen in the absence of catalysts. Mannitol does not undergo Maillard reactions.
The bulk material should be stored in a well-closed container in a cool, dry, place.

12. Incompatibilities

None reported in the dry state. Mannitol solutions, 20% w/v or stronger, may be salted out by potassium or sodium chloride.[16] Precipitation has been reported to occur when a 25% w/v mannitol solution was allowed to contact plastic.[17] Sodium cephapirin at 2 mg/mL and 30 mg/mL is incompatible with 20% w/v aqueous mannitol solution. Mannitol is incompatible with xylitol infusion and may form complexes with some metals (Fe, Al, Cu).

13. Method of Manufacture

Mannitol may be extracted from the dried sap of manna and other natural sources by means of hot alcohol or other selective solvents. It is commercially produced by the catalytic or electrolytic reduction of monosaccharides such as mannose and glucose.

14. Safety

Mannitol is a naturally occurring sugar alcohol found in animals and plants; it is present in small quantities in almost all vegetables. Only small amounts are absorbed from the gastrointestinal tract following oral consumption. When consumed orally in large quantities laxative effects may occur.[18] If used in foods as a bodying agent and daily

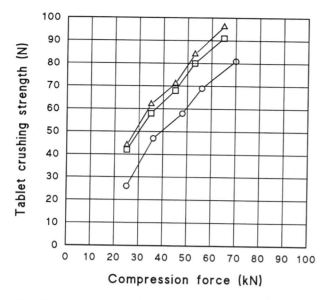

Fig. 1: Compression characteristics of granular mannitol (*Pearlitol*, Roquette Frères).[14]
○ *Pearlitol FG*
□ *Pearlitol MG*
△ *Pearlitol GG2*
Tablet diameter: 20 mm
Lubricant: magnesium stearate 0.7% w/w for *Pearlitol MG* and *Pearlitol GG2*, magnesium stearate 1% w/w for *Pearlitol FG*.

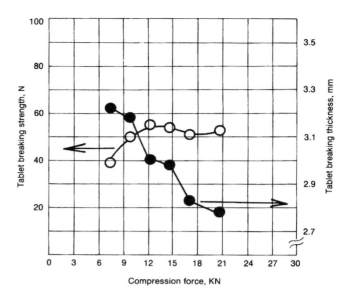

Fig. 3: Compression characteristics of granular mannitol.
Mean tablet weight: 500 mg
Minimum compressional force for compaction: 7.35 kN
Compressional force resulting in capping: 24.5 kN

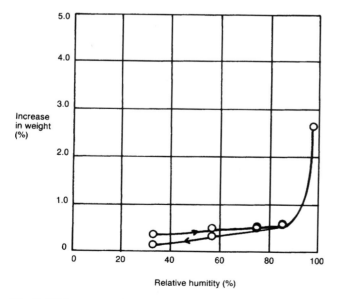

Fig. 2: Moisture sorption-desorption isotherm of mannitol.
Sample dried at 60°C for 24 hours over silica gel.

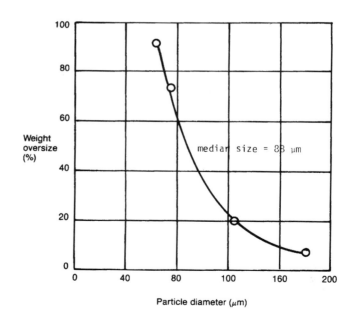

Fig. 4: Particle size distribution of mannitol powder.
Median size is 88 μm.

ingestion of over 20 g is foreseeable, the product label should bear the statement 'excessive consumption may have a laxative effect'. After intravenous injection, mannitol is not metabolized to any appreciable extent and is minimally reabsorbed by the renal tubule, about 80% of a dose being excreted in the urine in three hours.[19]

A number of adverse reactions to mannitol have been reported primarily following the therapeutic use of 20% w/v aqueous intravenous infusions.[20] The quantity of mannitol used as an excipient is considerably less than that used therapeutically and is consequently associated with a lower incidence of adverse reactions. However, allergic, hypersensitive type reactions may occur when mannitol is used as an excipient.

An acceptable daily intake of mannitol has not been specified by the WHO since the amount consumed as a sweetening agent was not considered to represent a hazard to health.[21]

LD_{50} (mouse, IP): 14 g/kg [22]
LD_{50} (mouse, IV): 7.47 g/kg
LD_{50} (mouse, oral): 22 g/kg
LD_{50} (rat, IV): 9.69 g/kg
LD_{50} (rat, oral): 13.5 g/kg

15. Handling Precautions

Observe normal precautions appropriate to the circumstances and quantity of material handled. Mannitol may be irritant to the eyes; eye protection is recommended.

16. Regulatory Status

GRAS listed. Accepted for use as a food additive in Europe. Included in the FDA Inactive Ingredients Guide (IP, IM, IV and SC injections, infusions, buccal, oral and sublingual tablets and capsules). Included in nonparenteral and parenteral medicines licensed in the UK.

17. Pharmacopeias

Aust, Br, Braz, Chin, Cz, Egypt, Eur, Fr, Gr, Hung, Ind, Int, It, Jpn, Mex, Neth, Nord, Rom, Swiss, Turk, US and Yug.

18. Related Substances

Sorbitol.

19. Comments

Mannitol is an isomer of sorbitol, the difference between the two polyols occurring in the planar orientation of the OH group on the second carbon atom. Each isomer is characterized by its own individual set of properties, the most important difference being the response to moisture. Sorbitol is hygroscopic while mannitol resists moisture sorption, even at high relative humidities.

Granular mannitol flows well and imparts improved flow properties to other materials. However, it usually cannot be used with concentrations of other materials exceeding 25% by weight. Recommended levels of lubricant are 1% w/w calcium stearate or 1-2% w/w magnesium stearate. Suitable binders for preparing granulations of powdered mannitol are gelatin, methylcellulose 400, starch paste, povidone and sorbitol. Usually, 3-6 times as much magnesium stearate or 1.5-3 times as much calcium stearate is needed for lubrication of mannitol granulations than is needed for other excipients.

20. Specific References

1. Kanig JL. Properties of fused mannitol in compressed tablets. J Pharm Sci 1964; 53: 188-192.
2. Ward DR, Lathrop LB, Lynch MJ. Dissolution and compatibility considerations for the use of mannitol in solid dosage forms. J Pharm Sci 1969; 58: 1464-1467.
3. Ghanem AH, Sakr FM, Abdel-Ghany G. Mechanical and physical properties of sulphamethoxazole-mannitol solid dispersion in tablet form. Acta Pharm Fenn 1986; 95: 167-172.
4. Debord B, Lefebvre C, Guyot-Hermann AM, Hubert J, Bouché R, Guyot JC. Study of different crystalline forms of mannitol: comparative behaviour under compression. Drug Dev Ind Pharm 1987; 13: 1533-1546.
5. Molokhia AM, Al-Shora HI, Hammad AA. Aging of tablets prepared by direct compression of bases with different moisture content. Drug Dev Ind Pharm 1987; 13: 1933-1946.
6. Mendes RW, Goll S, An CQ. Wet granulation: a comparison of Manni-Tab and mannitol. Drug Cosmet Ind 1978; 122(3): 36, 38, 40, 44, 87-88.
7. Daoust RG, Lynch MJ. Mannitol in chewable tablets. Drug Cosmet Ind 1963; 93(1): 26-28, 88, 92, 128-129.
8. Herman J, Remon JP. Aluminium-magnesium hydroxide tablets: effect of processing and composition of granulating solution on the granule properties and in vitro antacid performance. Drug Dev Ind Pharm 1988; 14: 1221-1234.
9. Couriel B. Advances in lyophilization technology. Bull Parenter Drug Assoc 1977; 31: 227-236.
10. Williams NA, Lee Y, Polli GP, Jennings TA. The effects of cooling rate on solid phase transitions and associated vial breakage occurring in frozen mannitol solutions. J Parenter Sci Technol 1986; 40: 135-141.
11. Stella VJ, Umprayn K, Waugh WN. Development of parenteral formulations of experimental cytotoxic agents I: rhizoxin (NSC-332598). Int J Pharmaceutics 1988; 43: 191-199.
12. Williams NA, Dean T. Vial breakage by frozen mannitol solutions: correlation with thermal characteristics and effect of stereoisomerism, additives, and vial configuration. J Parenter Sci Technol 1991; 45: 94-100.
13. Parab PV, Oh CK, Ritschel WA. Sustained release from Precirol (glycerol palmito-stearate) matrix. Effect of mannitol and hydroxypropyl methylcellulose on the release of theophylline. Drug Dev Ind Pharm 1986; 12: 1309-1327.
14. Roquette Frères. Technical literature: *Pearlitol* granulated mannitol for direct compression, 1992.
15. Murty BSR, Kapoor JN. Properties of mannitol injection (25%) after repeated autoclavings. Am J Hosp Pharm 1975; 32: 826-827.
16. Jacobs J. Factors influencing drug stability in intravenous infusions. J Hosp Pharm 1969; 27: 341-347.
17. Epperson E. Mannitol crystallization in plastic containers [letter]. Am J Hosp Pharm 1978; 35: 1337.
18. Flatulence, diarrhoea, and polyol sweeteners. Lancet 1983; ii: 1321.
19. Porter GA, et al. Mannitol hemodilution-perfusion: the kinetics of mannitol distribution and excretion during cardiopulmonary bypass. J Surg Res 1967; 7: 447-456.
20. McNeill IY. Hypersensitivity reaction to mannitol. Drug Intell Clin Pharm 1985; 19: 552-553.
21. FAO/WHO. Evaluation of certain food additives and contaminants: thirtieth report of the joint FAO/WHO expert committee on food additives. Tech Rep Ser Wld Hlth Org 1987; No. 751.
22. Sweet DV, editor. Registry of toxic effects of chemical substances. Cincinnati: US Department of Health, 1987.

21. General References

Czeisler JL, Perlman KP. Diluents. In: Swarbrick J, Boylan JC, editors. Encyclopedia of pharmaceutical technology, volume 4. New York: Marcel Dekker, 1988: 37-84.

Mendes RW, Anaebolam AO. Chewable tablets. In: Swarbrick J, Boylan JC, editors. Encyclopedia of pharmaceutical technology, volume 2. New York: Marcel Dekker, 1988: 397-418.

Pigman W, Horton D. The carbohydrates, chemistry and biochemistry, volume IA. New York: Academic Press, 1972: 479-518.

22. Authors

UK: NA Armstrong.

USA: GE Reier, DA Wadke.

Medium Chain Triglycerides

1. Nonproprietary Names

BP: Fractionated coconut oil
PhEur: Triglycerida saturata media

2. Synonyms

Caprylic/capric triglyceride; *Crodamol GTC/C*; glyceryl tricaprylate/caprate; *Miglyol 810*; *Miglyol 812*; MCT oil; *Neobee M5*; *Nesatol*; oleum neutrale; oleum vegetable tenue; thin vegetable oil.

3. Chemical Name and CAS Registry Number

Medium chain triglycerides

4. Empirical Formula   Molecular Weight

The PhEur 1993 describes medium chain triglycerides as the fixed oil extracted from the hard, dried fraction of the endosperm of *Cocos nucifera* L. by hydrolysis, fractionation of the fatty acids obtained and re-esterification. It consists of a mixture of exclusively short or medium chain triglycerides of fatty acids, of which not less than 95% are the saturated fatty acids octanoic (caprylic) acid and decanoic (capric) acid.

5. Structural Formula

$$
\begin{array}{l}
H \\
| \\
H-C-O-R_1 \\
| \\
H-C-O-R_2 \\
| \\
H-C-O-R_3 \\
| \\
H
\end{array}
$$

Where, $R_1 = -\overset{\displaystyle O}{\overset{\|}{C}}-(CH_2)_n CH_3$

$R_2 = -\overset{\displaystyle O}{\overset{\|}{C}}-(CH_2)_n CH_3$

$R_3 = -\overset{\displaystyle O}{\overset{\|}{C}}-(CH_2)_n CH_3$

$n = 6\text{-}8$

See also Section 4.

6. Functional Category

Emulsifying agent; solvent; suspending agent; therapeutic agent.

7. Applications in Pharmaceutical Formulation or Technology

Medium chain triglycerides have been used in a variety of pharmaceutical formulations including oral, parenteral and topical preparations.

In oral formulations, medium chain triglycerides are used as the base for the preparation of oral emulsions, solutions or suspensions of drugs unstable or insoluble in aqueous media, e.g. calciferol. Medium chain triglycerides have also been investigated as intestinal absorption enhancers[1] and have additionally been used as a filler in capsules and sugar-coated tablets, and as a lubricant or antiadhesion agent in tablets.

In parenteral formulations, medium chain triglycerides have similarly been used in the production of emulsions, solutions or suspensions intended for intravenous administration.[2,3] Medium chain triglycerides have been particularly investigated for their use in total parenteral nutrition (TPN) regimens in combination with long chain triglycerides.[3]

In cosmetics and topical pharmaceutical preparations, medium chain triglycerides are used as a component of ointments, creams and liquid emulsions.[4] In rectal formulations, medium chain triglycerides have been used in the preparation of suppositories containing labile materials.

Therapeutically, medium chain triglycerides have been used as nutritional agents.[5] Diets containing medium chain triglycerides are used in conditions associated with the malabsorption of fat, such as cystic fibrosis, since medium chain triglycerides are more readily digested than long chain triglycerides. Medium chain triglycerides provide 35 kJ (8.3 kcal) of energy per gram.

Although similar to long chain triglycerides, medium chain triglycerides have a number of advantages in pharmaceutical formulations which include: better spreading properties on the skin; no impedance of skin respiration; good penetration properties; good emollient and cosmetic properties; no visible film on the skin surface; good compatibility; good solvent properties and good stability against oxidation.

8. Description

A colorless to slightly yellowish oily liquid which is practically odorless and tasteless. It solidifies at about 0°C and has a low viscosity even at temperatures near its solidification point. The oil is free from catalytic residues or the products of cracking.

9. Pharmacopeial Specifications

Test	PhEur 1993
Identification	+
Alkaline impurities	+
Relative density	0.93-0.96
Refractive index	1.440-1.452
Viscosity	25-33 mPa s
Acid value	$\leqslant 0.2$
Hydroxyl value	$\leqslant 10$
Iodine value	$\leqslant 1.0$
Peroxide value	$\leqslant 1.0$
Saponification value	310-360
Unsaponifiable matter	$\leqslant 0.5$
Composition of fatty acids	
caproic acid	$\leqslant 2$
caprylic acid	50-80
capric acid	20-50
lauric acid	$\leqslant 3$
myristic acid	$\leqslant 1$
Heavy metals*	$\leqslant 10$ ppm
Water	$\leqslant 0.2$
Total ash	$\leqslant 0.1$
Chromium	$\leqslant 0.05$ ppm
Copper	$\leqslant 0.1$ ppm
Lead	$\leqslant 0.1$ ppm
Nickel	$\leqslant 0.1$ ppm
Tin	$\leqslant 0.1$ ppm

* For medium chain triglycerides intended for use in medical nutrition, the test for heavy metals is replaced by the tests for chromium, copper, lead, nickel and tin.

10. Typical Properties

Acid Value:
$\leq$ 0.1 for *Crodamol GTC/C*;
$\leq$ 0.1 for *Miglyol 810*;
$\leq$ 0.1 for *Miglyol 812*;
$\leq$ 0.05 for *Neobee M5*.

Cloud Point:
$\leq$ 5°C for Crodamol GTC/C;
$\approx$ 10°C for Miglyol 810;
$\approx$ 10°C for Miglyol 812.

Color:
$\leq$ 60 (Hazen color index) for *Crodamol GTC/C*;
$\leq$ 90 (Hazen color index) for *Miglyol 810*;
$\leq$ 2.0 (Iodine color index) for *Miglyol 810*;
$\leq$ 60 (Hazen color index) for *Miglyol 812*;
$\leq$ 2.0 (Iodine color index) for *Miglyol 812*;
$\leq$ 100 (Hazen color index) for *Neobee M5*.

Density:
0.94-0.96 g/cm^3 for *Crodamol GTC/C* at 20°C;
0.94-0.95 g/cm^3 for *Miglyol 810* at 20°C;
0.94-0.95 g/cm^3 for *Miglyol 812* at 20°C;
0.94 g/cm^3 for *Neobee M5* at 20°C.

Freezing point: -5°C for *Neobee M5*
Hydroxyl value: $\leq$ 8 for *Neobee M5*

Iodine number:
$\leq$ 1.0 for *Crodamol GTC/C*;
$\leq$ 0.5 for *Miglyol 810*;
$\leq$ 0.5 for *Miglyol 812*;
$\leq$ 0.5 for *Neobee M5*.

Moisture content:
$\leq$ 0.15% w/w for *Crodamol GTC/C*;
$\leq$ 0.10% w/w for *Miglyol 810*;
$\leq$ 0.10% w/w for *Miglyol 812*;
$\leq$ 0.15% w/w for *Neobee M5*.

Peroxide value: $\leq$ 0.5 for *Neobee M5*

Refractive index:
1.4485-1.4500 for *Crodamol GTC/C* at 20°C;
1.4485-1.4505 for *Miglyol 810* at 20°C;
1.4490-1.4510 for *Miglyol 812* at 20°C;
1.4480-1.4510 for *Neobee M5* at 20°C.

Saponification value:
325-345 for *Crodamol GTC/C*;
340-360 for *Miglyol 810*;
325-345 for *Miglyol 812*;
335-360 for *Neobee M5*.

Solubility: soluble, in all proportions at 20°C, in acetone, benzene, 2-butanone, carbon tetrachloride, chloroform, dichloromethane, ethanol, ethanol (95%), ether, ethyl acetate, petroleum ether, special petroleum spirit (boiling range 80-110°C), propan-2-ol, toluene, xylene and miscible with long chain hydrocarbons and triglycerides; practically insoluble in water.

Surface tension:
32.2 mN/m for *Crodamol GTC/C* at 25°C;
31.0 mN/m for *Miglyol 810* at 20°C;
31.1 mN/m for *Miglyol 812* at 20°C;
32.3 mN/m for *Neobee M5* at 25°C.

Viscosity (dynamic):
27-30 mPa s (27-30 cP) for *Miglyol 810* at 20°C;
28-32 mPa s (28-32 cP) for *Miglyol 812* at 20°C;
23 mPa s (23 cP) for *Neobee M5* at 25°C.

11. Stability and Storage Conditions

Medium chain triglycerides are stable over the wide range of storage temperatures that can be experienced in tropical and temperate climates. Ideally however, they should be stored at temperatures not exceeding 25°C and not exposed to temperatures above 40°C for long periods of time.

When preparing emulsions or aqueous suspensions of medium chain triglycerides, care should be taken to avoid microbiological contamination of the preparation, since lipase-producing microorganisms, which become active in the presence of moisture, can cause hydrolysis of the triglycerides. Hydrolysis of the triglycerides is revealed by the characteristic unpleasant odor of free medium chain fatty acids.

Medium chain triglycerides may be sterilized by maintaining at 170°C for 1 hour.

At low temperatures, samples of medium chain triglycerides may become viscous or solidify. Samples should therefore be well melted and mixed before use, although overheating should be avoided.

Medium chain triglycerides should be stored protected from light in a well-filled and well-closed container. When stored dry, in sealed containers, medium chain triglycerides remain stable for many years.

12. Incompatibilities

Preparations containing medium chain triglycerides should not come into contact with polystyrene containers or packaging components since the plastic rapidly becomes brittle upon contact. High-density polyethylene should also not be used as a packaging material as the medium chain triglycerides readily penetrate the plastic, especially at high temperatures, forming an oily film on the outside. Closures based on phenol resins should be tested before use for compatibility with medium chain triglycerides. Polyvinyl chloride packaging should also be tested for compatibility since medium chain triglycerides can dissolve some plasticisers, such as phthalates, out of the plastic.

Materials recommended as safe for packaging medium chain triglycerides are: low-density polyethylene; polypropylene; glass and metal.

13. Method of Manufacture

Medium chain triglycerides are obtained from the fixed oil extracted from the hard, dried fraction of the endosperm of *cocos nucifera* L. Hydrolysis of the fixed oil followed by fractionation yields the required fatty acids which are then re-esterified to produce the medium chain triglycerides.

Although the PhEur 1993 specifies that medium chain triglycerides are obtained from coconut oil, medium chain triglycerides are also to be found in substantial amounts in the kernel oils of certain other types of palm-tree, e.g. palm kernel oil and babassu oil. Some animal products, such as milk-fat, also contain small amounts (up to 4%) of the medium chain fatty acid esters.

14. Safety

Medium chain triglycerides are used in a variety of pharmaceutical formulations including oral, parenteral and topical products and are generally regarded as essentially nontoxic and nonirritant materials.

In acute toxicology studies in animals and humans no irritant or other adverse reactions have been observed, e.g. when patch-tested on more than 100 individuals no irritation was produced on either healthy or eczematous skin. Medium chain triglycerides are not irritant to the eyes.

Similarly, chronic toxicology studies in animals have shown no harmful adverse effects associated with medium chain triglycerides following inhalation, intraperitoneal, oral and parenteral administration.

In humans, administration of 0.5 g/kg body-weight medium chain triglycerides to healthy individuals produced no change in blood or serum triglycerides compared to subjects receiving the same dose of the long chain triglyceride, triolein.

In patients consuming diets based on medium chain triglycerides adverse effects reported include abdominal pain and diarrhea.

LD_{50} (mouse, IV): 3.7 g/kg[6]
LD_{50} (mouse, oral): 29.6 g/kg
LD_{50} (rat, oral): 33.3 g/kg

15. Handling Precautions

Observe normal precautions appropriate to the circumstances and quantity of material handled.

16. Regulatory Status

GRAS listed. Included in the FDA Inactive Ingredients Guide (topical preparations). Included in nonparenteral medicines licensed in the UK.

17. Pharmacopeias

Br, Eur, Fr and Ger.

18. Related Substances

Suppository Bases.
See also the monographs on naturally occurring long chain triglyceride oils such as Soybean Oil.

19. Comments

–

20. Specific References

1. Swenson ES, Curatolo WJ. Intestinal permeability enhancement for proteins, peptides and other drugs: mechanisms and potential toxicity. Adv Drug Del Rev 1992; 8: 39-92.
2. Bach A, Guisard D, Metais P, Debry G. Metabolic effects following a short and medium chain triglycerides load in dogs I: infusion of an emulsion of short and medium chain triglycerides. Arch Sci Physiol 1972; 26: 121-129.
3. Hatton J, et al. Safety and efficacy of a lipid emulsion containing medium-chain triglycerides. Clin Pharm 1990; 9: 366-371.
4. Adams U, Neuwald F. Comparative studies of the release of salicylic acid from medium chain triglyceride gel and paraffin ointment bases: in vitro and in vivo. Pharm Ind 1982; 44: 625-629.
5. Ruppin DC, Middleton WRJ. Clinical use of medium chain triglycerides. Drugs 1980; 20: 216-224.
6. Sweet DV, editor. Registry of toxic effects of chemical substances. Cincinnati: US Department of Health, 1987.

21. General References

–

22. Authors

UK: MJ Lawrence.

Meglumine

1. Nonproprietary Names
BP: Meglumine
USP: Meglumine

2. Synonyms
N-Methylglucamine; *N*-methyl-D-glucamine.

3. Chemical Name and CAS Registry Number
1-Deoxy-1-(methylamino)-D-glucitol
[6284-40-8]

4. Empirical Formula   Molecular Weight
$C_7H_{17}NO_5$ 195.21

5. Structural Formula

$$CH_2NHCH_3$$
$$H-C-OH$$
$$HO-C-H$$
$$H-C-OH$$
$$H-C-OH$$
$$CH_2OH$$

6. Functional Category
Organic base.

7. Applications in Pharmaceutical Formulation or Technology
Meglumine is an organic base used in the preparation of soluble salts of iodinated organic acids for use as X-ray contrast media.

8. Description
Meglumine occurs as a white to slightly yellow-colored microcrystalline powder; it is odorless or with a slight odor.

9. Pharmacopeial Specifications

Test	BP 1993	USP XXII
Identification	+	+
Completeness and color of solution	—	+
Melting point	128-131°C	128-132°C
Specific optical rotation (10% w/v aqueous solution)	-16.0 to -17.0°	-15.7 to -17.3°
Reducing sugars	+	—
Loss on drying	$\leqslant$ 1.0%	$\leqslant$ 1.0%
Residue on ignition	—	$\leqslant$ 0.1%
Sulfated ash	$\leqslant$ 0.1%	—
Absence of reducing substances	—	+
Heavy metals	—	$\leqslant$ 0.002%
Pyrogens	+	—
Assay (dried basis)	99.0-100.5%	99.0-100.5%

10. Typical Properties
Acidity/alkalinity:
pH = 10.5 (1% w/v aqueous solution).
Dissociation constant: pK_a = 9.5 at 20°C
Melting point: 128-132°C
Osmolarity: a 5.02% w/v aqueous solution is iso-osmotic with serum.
Solubility:

Solvent	Solubility at 25°C Unless otherwise stated
Chloroform	practically insoluble
Ethanol (95%)	1 in 80
	1 in 4.8 at 70°C
Ether	practically insoluble
Water	1 in 1

Specific rotation $[\alpha]_D^{20}$:
-16.5° (10% w/v aqueous solution)

11. Stability and Storage Conditions
Meglumine does not polymerize or dehydrate unless heated above 150°C for prolonged periods.
The bulk material should be stored in a well-closed container in a cool, dry, place. Meglumine should not be stored in aluminum containers since it reacts to evolve hydrogen gas; it discolors if stored in containers made from copper or copper alloys. Stainless steel containers are recommended.

12. Incompatibilities
Incompatible with aluminum, copper, mineral acids and oxidizing materials.

13. Method of Manufacture
Meglumine is prepared by the imination of glucose and monomethylamine, in an alcoholic solution, followed by catalytic hydrogenation.

14. Safety
Meglumine is widely used in parenteral pharmaceutical formulations and is generally regarded as a nontoxic material at the levels usually employed as an excipient.
LD_{50} (mouse, IP): 1.68 g/kg

15. Handling Precautions
Observe normal precautions appropriate to the circumstances and quantity of material handled. Meglumine should be handled in a well-ventilated environment and eye protection, gloves and a respirator are recommended. Exposure to meglumine dust should be kept below 10 mg/m^3 for total inhalable dust (8-hour TWA) or 5 mg/m^3 for respirable dust (8 hour TWA). There is a risk of explosion when meglumine dust is mixed with air.

16. Regulatory Status

Included in the FDA Inactive Ingredients Guide (injections). Included in parenteral medicines licensed in the UK.

17. Pharmacopeias
Br, Braz, Chin, Cz, Jpn, Nord, US and Yug.

18. Related Substances

Eglumine.

Eglumine: $C_8H_{19}NO_5$
Molecular weight: 209.24
CAS number: [14216-22-9]
Synonyms: 1-deoxy-1-(ethylamino)-D-glucitol; *N*-ethylglucamine.
Melting point: ≈ 138°C
Comments: prepared as for meglumine except monoethylamine is used as the precursor, instead of monomethylamine.

19. Comments

—

20. Specific References

—

21. General References

Bremecker KD, Seidel K, Böhner A. Polyacrylate gels: use of new bases in drug formulation [in German]. Dtsch Apoth Ztg 1990; 130(8): 401-403.

Chromy V, Kulhanek V, Fischer J. D-(-)-*N*-Methylglucamine buffer for pH 8.5 to 10.5. Clin Chem 1978; 24(2): 379-381.

Chromy V, Zahradniček L, Vozniček J. Use of *N*-methyl-D-glucamine as buffer in the determination of serum alkaline phosphatase activity. Clin Chem 1981; 27(10): 1729-1732.

22. Authors

UK: RS Cook; N Yussuf.

Menthol

1. Nonproprietary Names
BP: Racementhol
PhEur: Mentholum racemicum
USP: Menthol

2. Synonyms
Hexahydrothymol; 2-isopropyl-5-methylcyclohexanol; 4-iso-propyl-1-methylcyclohexan-3-ol; 3-*p*-menthanol; *p*-menthan-3-ol; *dl*-menthol; peppermint camphor; racemic menthol.

3. Chemical Name and CAS Registry Number
(1*RS*,2*RS*,5*RS*)-(±)-5-Methyl-2-(1-methylethyl)cyclohexanol [15356-70-4]
Note that the following CAS numbers have also been used: [1490-04-6] and [89-78-1].

4. Empirical Formula   Molecular Weight
$C_{10}H_{20}O$ 156.27

5. Structural Formula

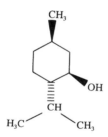

and enantiomer
Note structure shown is *l*-menthol.

6. Functional Category
Flavoring agent; therapeutic agent.

7. Applications in Pharmaceutical Formulation or Technology
Menthol is widely used in pharmaceuticals, confectionery and toiletry products as a flavoring agent or odor enhancer. In addition to its characteristic peppermint flavor, *l*-menthol, which occurs naturally, also exerts a cooling or refreshing sensation which is exploited in many topical preparations. Unlike mannitol, which exerts a similar effect due to a negative heat of solution, *l*-menthol interacts directly with the body's coldness receptors. *d*-Menthol has no cooling effect, while racemic menthol imparts an effect approximately half that of *l*-menthol.
When used to flavor tablets menthol is generally dissolved in ethanol (95%) and sprayed on tablet granules and not used as a solid excipient.
Menthol is also used in perfumery, tobacco products and as a therapeutic agent.

Use	Concentration (%)
Pharmaceutical products	
Inhalation	0.02-0.05
Oral suspension	0.003
Oral syrup	0.005-0.015
Tablets	0.2-0.4
Topical formulations	0.05-1.0
Cosmetic products	
Toothpaste	0.4
Mouthwash	0.1-2.0
Oral spray	0.3

8. Description
Racemic menthol is a mixture of equal parts of the (1*R*,2*S*,5*R*)- and (1*S*,2*R*,5*S*)- isomers of menthol. It is a free flowing or agglomerated crystalline powder or colorless, prismatic or acicular shiny crystals, with a strong characteristic odor and taste. The crystalline form may change with time due to sublimation within a closed vessel. The USP XXII specifies that menthol may be either naturally occurring *l*-menthol or synthetically prepared racemic or *l*-menthol. However, the BP 1993 and PhEur 1989 include two separate monographs for racemic and *l*-menthol.

9. Pharmacopeial Specifications

Test	PhEur 1989	USP XXII
Identification	+	+
Acidity or alkalinity	+	—
Congealing range	—	+
Melting point		
dl-menthol	≈ 34°C	—
l-menthol	≈ 43°C	41-44°C
Specific optical rotation		
dl-menthol	-0.2° to +0.2°	-2° to +2°
l-menthol	-48° to -51°	-45° to -51°
Readily oxidizable substances	—	+
Chromatographic purity	—	+
Related substances	+	—
Clarity and color of solution	+	—
Nonvolatile residue	—	≤ 0.05%
Residue on evaporation	≤ 0.05%	—

10. Typical Properties
Boiling point: 212°C
Flash point: 93°C
Melting point: 34-36°C
Refractive index: $n_D^{20} = 1.4615$
Solubility: very soluble in ethanol (95%), chloroform and ether; very slightly soluble in glycerin; practically insoluble in water.
Specific rotation $[\alpha]_D^{20}$:
-2 to +2° (10% w/v alcoholic solution)
See also Section 18.

11. Stability and Storage Conditions
Store in a well-closed container at a temperature not exceeding 25°C, since methanol sublimes readily.

12. Incompatibilities
Incompatible with β-naphthol, butylchloral hydrate, camphor, chloral hydrate, chromium trioxide, phenol, potassium permanganate, pyrogallol, resorcinol and thymol.

13. Method of Manufacture

Menthol occurs widely in nature as *l*-menthol and is the principal component of peppermint and cornmint oils obtained from the *Mentha piperita* and *Mentha arvensis* species. Commercially, *l*-menthol is mainly produced by extraction from these volatile oils. It may also be prepared by partial or total synthetic methods.

Racemic menthol is prepared synthetically via a number of routes, e.g. by hydrogenation of thymol.

14. Safety

Almost all toxicological data for menthol refer to its use as a therapeutic agent rather than as an excipient. Inhalation of large doses has resulted in serious adverse reactions such as ataxia[1] and CNS depression.[2] Although menthol is essentially nonirritant there have been some reports of hypersensitivity following topical application;[3] in a Polish study approximately 1% of individuals were determined as being sensitive to menthol.[4]

LD_{50} (mouse, IP): 14.2 g/kg[5]
LD_{50} (mouse, oral): 3.1 g/kg
LD_{50} (rat, IP): 0.67 g/kg
LD_{50} (rat, oral): 2.9 g/kg

15. Handling Precautions

May be harmful by inhalation or ingestion in large quantities; may be irritant to the skin, eyes and mucous membranes. Observe normal precautions appropriate to the circumstances and quantity of material handled. Eye protection and gloves are recommended.

16. Regulatory Status

Included in the FDA Inactive Ingredients Guide (buccal and dental preparations, inhalations, nasal preparations, oral solutions, suspensions, syrups and tablets, also topical preparations). Included in nonparenteral medicines licensed in the UK. Accepted for use in foods and confectionery as a flavoring agent of natural origin.

17. Pharmacopeias

Aust, Belg, Br, Braz, Chin, Cz, Egypt, Eur, Fr, Ger, Hung, Ind, It, Jpn, Mex, Neth, Nord, Rom, Rus, Swiss, Turk, US and Yug.

18. Related Substances

d-Menthol; *l*-menthol.

d-**Menthol**: $C_{10}H_{20}O$
Molecular weight: 156.27
CAS number: [15356-60-2]

Synonyms: (1*S*,2*R*,5*S*)-(+)-5-methyl-2-(1-methylethyl)cyclohexanol.
Appearance: colorless, prismatic or acicular, shiny crystals, without the characteristic odor, taste and cooling effect of *l*-menthol. The crystalline form may change with time due to sublimation within a closed vessel.
Flash point: 91°C
Melting point: 43-44°C
Specific rotation $[\alpha]_D^{23}$: +48° (10% w/v alcoholic solution)

l-**Menthol**: $C_{10}H_{20}O$
Molecular weight: 156.27
CAS number: [2216-51-5]
Synonyms: levomenthol; levomentholum; (1*R*,2*S*,5*R*)-(-)-5-methyl-2-(1-methylethyl)cyclohexanol.
Appearance: colorless, prismatic or acicular, shiny crystals, with a strong, characteristic odor, taste and cooling effect. The crystalline form may change with time due to sublimation within a closed vessel.
Pharmacopeias: Aust, Br, Eur, Fr, Ger, Jpn, Neth and Swiss.
Flash point: > 100°C
Melting point: 41-44°C
Refractive index: $n_D^{20} = 1.4600$
Specific rotation $[\alpha]_D^{20}$: -50° (10% w/v alcoholic solution)

19. Comments

It should be noted that considerable variation in the chemical composition of natural menthol oils can occur depending upon their country of origin.

20. Specific References

1. Luke E. Addiction to mentholated cigarettes [letter]. Lancet 1962; i: 110-111.
2. O'Mullane NM, Joyce P, Kamath SV, Tham MK, Knass D. Adverse CNS effects of menthol-containing olabas oil [letter]. Lancet 1982; i: 1121.
3. Papa CM, Shelley WB. Menthol hypersensitivity. JAMA 1964; 189: 546-548.
4. Rudzki E, Kleniewska D. The epidemiology of contact dermatitis in Poland. Br J Dermatol 1970; 83: 543-545.
5. Sweet DV, editor. Registry of toxic effects of chemical substances. Cincinnati: US Department of Health, 1987.

21. General References

Bauer K, Garbe D, Surburg H. Common fragrance and flavor materials. Weinheim: VCH Publishers, 1990: 43-46.
Eccles R. Menthol and related cooling compounds. J Pharm Pharmacol 1994; 46: 618–630

22. Authors

UK: PJ Weller.

Methylcellulose

1. Nonproprietary Names

BP: Methylcellulose
PhEur: Methylcellulosum
USP: Methylcellulose

2. Synonyms

Benecel; Celacol; Culminal MC; E461; Methocel; Metolose.

3. Chemical Name and CAS Registry Number

Cellulose methyl ether [9004-67-5]

4. Empirical Formula   Molecular Weight

Methylcellulose is a long-chain substituted cellulose in which approximately 27-32% of the hydroxyl groups are in the form of the methyl ether. It contains between 50-1500 anhydroglucose units. The degree of substitution of methylcellulose is defined as the average number of methoxyl (CH_3O) groups attached to each of the anhydroglucose units along the chain and is characteristic of material from a particular source. The degree of substitution also affects the physical properties of methylcellulose, such as its solubility.

5. Structural Formula

Structure shown with complete methoxyl substitution. *See* Section 4.

6. Functional Category

Coating agent; emulsifying agent; suspending agent; tablet and capsule disintegrant; tablet binder; viscosity-increasing agent.

7. Applications in Pharmaceutical Formulation or Technology

Methylcellulose is widely used in oral and topical pharmaceutical formulations.

In tablet formulations, low or medium viscosity grades of methylcellulose are used as binding agents, the methylcellulose being added either as a dry powder or in solution.[1-3] High viscosity grades of methylcellulose may also be incorporated in tablet formulations as a disintegrant.[4] Methylcellulose may also be added to a tablet formulation to produce sustained release preparations.[5] The methylcellulose is uniformly incorporated throughout a tablet in a hydrophilic matrix. Upon contact with water the outer tablet skin partially hydrates to form a gel layer. The rate of erosion of this coating or diffusion of an active ingredient through it thus controls the overall dissolution rate.

Tablet cores may also be spray-coated with either aqueous or organic solutions of highly substituted, low viscosity grades of methylcellulose, the coats being used to mask an unpleasant taste or to modify the release of a drug.[6] Methylcellulose coats are also used for sealing tablet cores prior to sugar coating.

Low viscosity grades of methylcellulose are used to emulsify olive, peanut and mineral oils.[7] They are also used as suspending or thickening agents for orally administered liquids, methylcellulose being commonly used in place of sugar-based syrups or other suspension bases.[8] The methylcellulose is used to delay the settling of suspensions and to increase the contact time of drugs, such as antacids, in the stomach.

High viscosity grades of methylcellulose are used to thicken topically applied products such as creams and gels.

In ophthalmic preparations, a 0.5-1.0% w/v solution of a highly substituted, high viscosity grade of methylcellulose has been used as a vehicle for eye-drops.[9] An antimicrobial preservative, such as benzalkonium chloride should also be included. However, hydroxypropyl methylcellulose based formulations are now preferred for ophthalmic preparations. Therapeutically, methylcellulose is used as a bulk laxative. Methylcellulose is also widely used in cosmetics and in food products as an emulsifier and stabilizer.

Use	Concentration (%)
Bulk laxative	5-30
Creams, gels and ointments	1-5
Emulsifying agent	1-5
Ophthalmic preparations	0.5-1.0
Suspensions	1-2
Sustained release tablet matrix	5-75
Tablet binder	2-6
Tablet coating	0.5-5
Tablet disintegrant	2-10

8. Description

Methylcellulose occurs as practically odorless and tasteless, white to yellowish-white colored granules or as a powder.

9. Pharmacopeial Specifications

Test	PhEur 1992	USP XXII (Suppl 9)
Identification	+	+
Appearance of solution	+	—
pH (1% w/v solution)	5.5-8.0	—
Apparent viscosity	+	+
Loss on drying	$\leqslant 10.0\%$	$\leqslant 5.0\%$
Residue on ignition	—	$\leqslant 1.5\%$
Sulfated ash	$\leqslant 1.0\%$	—
Arsenic	—	$\leqslant 3$ ppm
Chlorides	$\leqslant 0.5\%$	—
Heavy metals	$\leqslant 20$ ppm	$\leqslant 0.001\%$
Organic volatile impurities	—	+
Assay (of methoxyl groups)	—	27.5-31.5%

10. Typical Properties

Acidity/alkalinity:
pH = 5.5-8.0 for a 1% w/v aqueous suspension.
Angle of repose: 40-50°
Autoignition temperature: $\approx 360°C$

SEM: 1

Excipient: Methylcellulose
Manufacturer: Dow Chemical Company
Lot No.: MM-090271-A
Magnification: 60x
Voltage: 10 kV

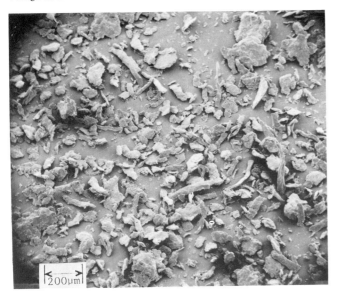

SEM: 2

Excipient: Methylcellulose
Manufacturer: Dow Chemical Company
Lot No.: MM-090271-A
Magnification: 600x
Voltage: 10 kV

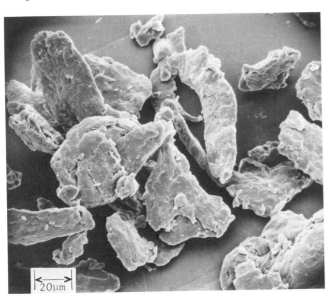

Degree of substitution: 1.1-2.0 for *Methocel*.

Hygroscopicity: methylcellulose is hygroscopic, *see* HPE Data.

Melting point: begins to char at 280-300°C.

Particle friability: *see* HPE Data.

Solubility: practically insoluble in acetone, chloroform, ethanol, ether, saturated salt solutions, toluene and hot water. Soluble in glacial acetic acid and in a mixture of equal volumes of ethanol and chloroform. In cold water, methylcellulose swells and disperses slowly to form a clear to opalescent, viscous, colloidal dispersion.

Specific gravity: 1.26-1.31 for powder; 1.0012 for 1% w/v solution; 1.0117 for 5% w/v solution; 1.0245 for 10% w/v solution.

Surface tension: 50-60 mN/m (50-60 dynes/cm) for a 2% w/v solution at 20°C.

Viscosity (dynamic): various grades of methylcellulose are commercially available which produce 2% w/v solutions with viscosities of 10-10 000 mPa s (10-10 000 cP). Individual grades of methylcellulose have a stated, narrowly defined viscosity range measured for a 2% w/v solution. For example, *Metolose SM-15* has a viscosity of 15 mPa s (15 cP), while *Metolose SM-4000* has a viscosity of 4000 mPa s (4000 cP). The viscosity of solutions may be increased by increasing the concentration of methylcellulose. Increased temperatures reduce the viscosity of solutions until gel formation occurs at 50-60°C. The process of thermogelation is reversible, with a viscous solution being reformed on cooling.

HPE Laboratory Project Data			
	Method	Lab #	Results
Moisture content	MC-14	28	3.87% [a]
	SI-1	13	*See* Fig. 1.[a]
Particle friability			
Metolose SM-15	PF-1	36	0.261% [b]
Metolose SM-400	PF-1	36	0.323% [b]
Metolose SM-4000	PF-1	36	0.204% [b]

Supplier: a. Dow Chemical Company (Lot No.: MM032364-A); b. Shin-Etsu Chemical Company Ltd.

11. Stability and Storage Conditions

Methylcellulose powder is stable although it is slightly hygroscopic.

Solutions of methylcellulose are stable to alkalis and dilute acids between pH 3-11, at room temperature. At less than pH 3, the viscosity of methylcellulose solutions are reduced.[10] On heating, solution viscosity is reduced until gel formation occurs at approximately 50°C, *see* Section 10.

Methylcellulose solutions are liable to microbial spoilage and should be preserved with an antimicrobial preservative. Solutions may also be sterilized by autoclaving although this process can decrease the viscosity of a solution.[11,12] The change in viscosity, after autoclaving, is related to solution pH; solutions at less than pH 4 had their viscosities reduced by greater than 20%.[11]

The bulk material should be stored in an airtight container in a cool, dry, place.

12. Incompatibilities

Methylcellulose is reported to be incompatible with: aminacrine hydrochloride; chlorocresol; mercuric chloride; phenol; resorcinol; tannic acid; silver nitrate; cetylpyridinium chloride; *p*-hydroxybenzoic acid; *p*-aminobenzoic acid; methylparaben; propylparaben and butylparaben. Salts of mineral acids and

Fig. 1: Moisture sorption isotherm of methylcellulose.

particularly of polybasic acids, phenols and tannins, coagulate solutions of methylcellulose. However, this can be prevented by the addition of ethanol (95%) or glycol diacetate. Complexation of methylcellulose occurs with highly surface-active compounds, such as tetracaine and dibutoline sulfate. High concentrations of electrolytes increase the viscosity of methylcellulose mucilages owing to the salting out of methylcellulose. With very high concentrations of electrolytes, the methylcellulose may be completely precipitated in the form of a discrete or continuous gel.

13. Method of Manufacture

Methylcellulose is prepared from wood pulp by treatment with alkali followed by methylation of the alkali cellulose with chloromethane.

14. Safety

Methylcellulose is widely used in a variety of oral and topical pharmaceutical formulations. It is also extensively used in cosmetics and food products and is generally regarded as a nontoxic, nonallergenic and nonirritant material.[13]
Following oral consumption, methylcellulose is not digested or absorbed and is therefore a noncaloric material. Ingestion of excessive amounts of methylcellulose may temporarily increase flatulence and gastrointestinal distension.
In the normal individual, oral consumption of large amounts of methylcellulose has a laxative action and medium or high viscosity grades are therefore used as bulk laxatives; divided, oral, daily doses of 1-6 g of methylcellulose in the form of granules or tablets, administered with plenty of fluid, are used. In certain individuals however, consumption of methylcellulose may aggravate obstructive gastrointestinal diseases. Oesophageal obstruction may also occur if methylcellulose is swallowed with an insufficient quantity of fluid. Consumption of large quantities of methylcellulose may additionally interfere with the normal absorbtion of some minerals. However, this and the other adverse effects discussed above relate mainly to the use of methylcellulose as a bulk laxative

and are not significant factors when methylcellulose is used as an excipient in oral preparations.
Methylcellulose is not commonly used in parenteral products although it has been used in intra-articular and intramuscular injections. Studies, in rats, have suggested that parenterally administered methylcellulose may cause glomerulonephritis and hypertension.
The WHO has not specified an acceptable daily intake of methylcellulose since the level of use in foods was not considered to be a hazard to health.[14]

15. Handling Precautions

Observe normal precautions appropriate to the circumstances and quantity of material handled. Dust may be irritant to the eyes and eye protection should therefore be worn. Excessive dust generation should be avoided to minimize the risk of explosions. Methylcellulose is combustible.

16. Regulatory Status

GRAS listed. Accepted as a food additive in Europe. Included in the FDA Inactive Ingredients Guide (buccal tablets, IM injections, ophthalmic preparations, oral capsules, suspensions and tablets, topical and vaginal preparations). Included in nonparenteral medicines licensed in the UK.

17. Pharmacopeias

Aust, Br, Braz, Cz, Eur, Fr, Hung, It, Jpn, Neth, Port, Rom, Swiss, US and Yug.

18. Related Substances

Ethylcellulose.

19. Comments

Methylcellulose is best dissolved in water by one of three methods, the most suitable being chosen for a particular application. The most commonly used method is to add methylcellulose initially to hot water. The appropriate quantity of methylcellulose, to produce a solution of required viscosity, is mixed with water at 70°C; about half the desired final volume of water is used. Cold, or ice water, is then added to the hot methylcellulose slurry in order to cool it to below 20°C. A clear, aqueous methylcellulose solution is obtained.
Alternatively, methylcellulose powder may be either dry blended with another powder prior to mixing with cold water or methylcellulose powder may be moistened with an organic solvent such as ethanol (95%) prior to the addition of water.

20. Specific References

1. Wan LSC, Prasad KPP. Uptake of water by excipients in tablets. Int J Pharmaceutics 1989; 50: 147-153.
2. Funck JAB, Schwartz JB, Reilly WJ, Ghali ES. Binder effectiveness for beads with high drug levels. Drug Dev Ind Pharm 1991; 17: 1143-1156.
3. Itiola OA, Pilpel N. Formulation effects on the mechanical properties of metronidazole tablets. J Pharm Pharmacol 1991; 43: 145-147.
4. Esezobo S. Disintegrants: effects of interacting variables on the tensile strengths and dissolution times of sulphaguanidine tablets. Int J Pharmaceutics 1989; 56: 207-211.
5. Sanghavi NM, Kamath PR, Amin DS. Sustained release tablets of theophylline. Drug Dev Ind Pharm 1990; 16: 1843-1848.
6. Wan LSC, Lai WF. Factors affecting drug release from drug-coated granules prepared by fluidized-bed coating. Int J Pharmaceutics 1991; 72: 163-174.

7. Wojdak H, Drobnicka B, Zientarska G, Gadomska-Nowak M. The influence of selected properties on the stability of pharmaceutical emulsions. Pharmazie 1991; 46: 120-125.

8. Dalal PS, Narurkar MM. In vitro and in vivo evaluation of sustained release suspensions of ibuprofen. Int J Pharmaceutics 1991; 73: 157-162.

9. El Gawad A, Ramadan EM, El Helw AM. Formulation and stability of saluzide eye drops. Pharm Ind 1987; 49: 751-754.

10. Huikari A, Karlsson A. Viscosity stability of methylcellulose solutions at different pH and temperature. Acta Pharm Fenn 1989; 98(4): 231-238.

11. Huikari A. Effect of heat sterilization on the viscosity of methylcellulose solutions. Acta Pharm Fenn 1986; 95(1): 9-17.

12. Huikari A, Hinkkanen R, Michelsson H, Uotila J, Kristoffersson E. Effect of heat sterilization on the molecular weight of methylcellulose determined using high pressure gel filtration chromatography and viscometry. Acta Pharm Fenn 1986; 95(3): 105-111.

13. Final report on the safety assessment of hydroxyethylcellulose, hydroxypropylcellulose, methylcellulose, hydroxypropyl methylcellulose and cellulose gum. J Am Coll Toxicol 1986; 5(3): 1-60.

14. FAO/WHO. Evaluation of certain food additives and contaminants: thirty-fifth report of the joint FAO/WHO expert committee on food additives. Tech Rep Ser Wld Hlth Org 1990; No. 789.

21. General References

Doelker E. Cellulose derivatives. Adv Polymer Sci 1993; 107: 199-265.

Huikari A, Kristoffersson E. Rheological properties of methylcellulose solutions: general flow properties and effects of added substances. Acta Pharm Fenn 1985; 94(4): 143-154.

Rowe RC. The molecular weight of methyl cellulose used in pharmaceutical formulation. Int J Pharmaceutics 1982; 11: 175-179.

22. Authors

USA: RI Senderoff.

Methylparaben

1. Nonproprietary Names

BP: Methyl hydroxybenzoate
PhEur: Methylis parahydroxybenzoas
USPNF: Methylparaben

2. Synonyms

E218; 4-hydroxybenzoic acid methyl ester; *Methyl Chemosept*; methyl *p*-hydroxybenzoate; methyl parahydroxybenzoate; *Methyl Parasept*; *Nipagin M*; *Solbrol M*; *Tegosept M*.

3. Chemical Name and CAS Registry Number

Methyl 4-hydroxybenzoate [99-76-3]

4. Empirical Formula   Molecular Weight

$C_8H_8O_3$ 152.15

5. Structural Formula

6. Functional Category

Antimicrobial preservative.

7. Applications in Pharmaceutical Formulation or Technology

Methylparaben is widely used as an antimicrobial preservative in cosmetics, food products and pharmaceutical formulations. It may be used either alone, in combination with other parabens, or with other antimicrobial agents. In cosmetics, methylparaben is the most frequently used antimicrobial preservative.[1]

The parabens are effective over a wide pH range and have a broad spectrum of antimicrobial activity although they are most effective against yeasts and molds. Antimicrobial activity increases as the chain length of the alkyl moiety is increased, aqueous solubility however decreases. A mixture of parabens is thus frequently used to provide effective preservation. Preservative efficacy is also improved by the addition of 2-5% propylene glycol, or by using parabens in combination with other antimicrobial agents such as imidurea, *see* Section 10.

Due to the poor solubility of the parabens, paraben salts, particularly the sodium salt, are frequently used in formulations. However, this may cause the pH of poorly buffered formulations to become more alkaline.

Methylparaben (0.18%) together with propylparaben (0.02%) has been used for the preservation of various parenteral pharmaceutical formulations, *see* Section 14.

Use	Concentration (%)
IM, IV, SC injections*	0.065-0.25
Ophthalmic preparations*	0.015-0.05
Oral solutions and suspensions	0.015-0.2
Topical preparations	0.02-0.3
Vaginal preparations	0.1-0.18

* *See* Section 14.

8. Description

Methylparaben occurs as colorless crystals or a white crystalline powder. It is odorless or almost odorless and has a slight burning taste.

SEM: 1
Excipient: Methylparaben
Supplier: Bate Chemical Co Ltd
Magnification: 600x

9. Pharmacopeial Specifications

Test	PhEur 1990	USPNF XVII
Identification	+	+
Melting range	125-128°C	125-128°C
Acidity	+	+
Loss on drying	—	⩽ 0.5%
Residue on ignition	—	⩽ 0.05%
Sulfated ash	⩽ 0.1%	—
Appearance of solution	+	—
Related substances	+	—
Assay (dried basis)	99.0-101.0%	99.0-100.5%

10. Typical Properties

Antimicrobial activity: methylparaben exhibits antimicrobial activity between pH 4-8. Preservative efficacy decreases with increasing pH due to the formation of the phenolate anion. Parabens are more active against yeasts and molds than against bacteria. They are also more active against Gram-positive bacteria than against Gram-negative bacteria.

Methylparaben is the least active of the parabens; antimicrobial activity increases with increasing chain length of the alkyl moiety. Activity may be improved by using combinations of parabens, since additive effects occur. Therefore, combinations of methyl, ethyl, propyl and butylparaben are often used together. Activity has also been reported to be enhanced by the addition of other excipients such as: propylene glycol (2-5%);[2] phenylethyl alcohol;[3] and edetic acid.[4] Activity may also be enhanced, due to synergistic effects, by using

combinations of parabens with other antimicrobial preservatives such as imidurea.[5]
The hydrolysis product, *p*-hydroxybenzoic acid, has practically no antimicrobial activity.
See also Section 12.
Reported minimum inhibitory concentrations (MICs) for methylparaben are shown in Table I.[4]

Table I: Minimum inhibitory concentrations (MICs) for methylparaben in aqueous solution.[4]

Microorganism	MIC (μg/mL)
Aerobacter aerogenes ATCC 8308	2000
Aspergillus oryzae	600
Aspergillus niger ATCC 9642	1000
Aspergillus niger ATCC 10254	1000
Bacillus cereus var. *mycoides* ATCC 6462	2000
Bacillus subtilis ATCC 6633	2000
Candida albicans ATCC 10231	2000
Enterobacter cloacae ATCC 23355	1000
Escherichia coli ATCC 8739	1000
Escherichia coli ATCC 9637	1000
Klebsiella pneumoniae ATCC 8308	1000
Penicillium chrysogenum ATCC 9480	500
Penicillium digitatum ATCC 10030	500
Proteus vulgaris ATCC 8427	2000
Proteus vulgaris ATCC 13315	1000
Pseudomonas aeruginosa ATCC 9027	4000
Pseudomonas aeruginosa ATCC 15442	4000
Pseudomonas stutzeri	2000
Rhizopus nigricans ATCC 6227A	500
Saccharomyces cerevisiae ATCC 9763	1000
Salmonella typhosa ATCC 6539	1000
Sarcina lutea	4000
Serratia marcescens ATCC 8100	1000
Staphylococcus aureus ATCC 6538P	2000
Staphylococcus epidermidis ATCC 12228	2000
Trichoderma lignorum ATCC 8678	250
Trichoderma mentagrophytes	250

Dissociation constant: pK_a = 8.4 at 22°C
Melting point: 125-128°C
Partition coefficients: values for different vegetable oils vary considerably and are affected by the purity of the oil, *see* Table II.

Table II: Partition coefficients for methylparaben in vegetable oil and water.[6,7]

Solvent	Partition coefficient Oil: water
Almond oil	7.5
Castor oil	6.0
Corn oil	4.1
Diethyl adipate	200
Isopropyl myristate	18.0
Lanolin	7.0
Mineral oil	0.1
Peanut oil	4.2
Soybean oil	6.1

Solubility: *see* Table III and HPE Data.

Table III: Solubility of methylparaben in various solvents.[4]

Solvent	Solubility at 25°C Unless otherwise stated
Ethanol	1 in 2
Ethanol (95%)	1 in 3
Ethanol (50%)	1 in 6
Ethanol (10%)	1 in 200
Ether	1 in 10
Glycerin	1 in 60
Methanol	1 in 2
Mineral oil	practically insoluble
Peanut oil	1 in 200
Propylene glycol	1 in 5
Water	1 in 400
	1 in 50 at 50°C
	1 in 30 at 80°C

HPE Laboratory Project Data			
	Method	Lab #	Results
Solubility Water at 25°C	SOL-8	30	2.4 mg/mL

11. Stability and Storage Conditions

Aqueous solutions of methylparaben, at pH 3-6, may be sterilized by autoclaving at 120°C for 20 minutes, without decomposition.[8] Aqueous solutions at pH 3-6 are stable (less than 10% decomposition) for up to about four years at room temperature, whilst aqueous solutions at pH 8 or above are subject to rapid hydrolysis (10% or more after about 60 days storage at room temperature).[9]
Predicted rate constants and half-lives at 25°C, for methylparaben dissolved in dilute hydrochloric acid solution at the initial pH shown below:[9]

Initial pH of solution	Rate constant $k \pm \sigma^*$ (hour^{-1})	Half-life $t_{\frac{1}{2}} \pm \sigma^*$ (day)
1	$(1.086 \pm 0.005) \times 10^{-4}$	266 ± 13
2	$(1.16 \pm 0.12) \times 10^{-5}$	2490 ± 260
3	$(6.1 \pm 1.5) \times 10^{-7}$	47000 ± 12000
4	$(3.27 \pm 0.64) \times 10^{-7}$	88000 ± 17000

* Indicates the standard error.

The predicted amount of methylparaben remaining after autoclaving is shown below for methylparaben dissolved in dilute hydrochloric acid solution at the initial pH shown:[9]

Initial pH of solution	Rate constant $k \pm \sigma^*$ (hour^{-1})	Predicted residual amount after sterilization (%)
1	$(4.96 \pm 0.16) \times 10^{-1}$	84.77 ± 0.46
2	$(4.49 \pm 0.37) \times 10^{-2}$	98.51 ± 0.12
3	$(2.79 \pm 0.57) \times 10^{-3}$	99.91 ± 0.02
4	$(1.49 \pm 0.22) \times 10^{-3}$	99.95 ± 0.01

* Indicates the standard error.

Methylparaben should be stored in a well-closed container in a cool, dry, place.

12. Incompatibilities

The antimicrobial activity of methylparaben and other parabens is considerably reduced in the presence of nonionic surfactants, such as polysorbate 80, as a result of micellization.[10,11]

However, propylene glycol (10%) has been shown to potentiate the antimicrobial activity of the parabens in the presence of nonionic surfactants and prevents the interaction between methylparaben and polysorbate 80.[12]

Incompatibilities with other substances such as bentonite,[13] magnesium trisilicate,[14] talc, tragacanth,[15] sodium alginate,[16] essential oils,[17] sorbitol[18] and atropine[19] have been reported.

Absorption of methylparaben by plastics has also been reported; the amount absorbed is dependent upon the type of plastic and the vehicle. It has been claimed that low and high density polyethylene bottles do not absorb methylparaben.[20]

Methylparaben is discolored in the presence of iron and is subject to hydrolysis by weak alkalis and strong acids.

13. Method of Manufacture

Methylparaben is prepared by the esterification of *p*-hydroxybenzoic acid with methanol.

14. Safety

Methylparaben, and other parabens, are widely used as antimicrobial preservatives in cosmetics and oral and topical pharmaceutical formulations. Although parabens have also been used as preservatives in injections and ophthalmic preparations they are now generally regarded as being unsuitable for these types of formulation due to the irritant potential of the parabens.

Hypersensitivity reactions to parabens, generally of the delayed type, and appearing as contact dermatitis have been reported. However, given the widespread use of parabens as preservatives such reactions are relatively uncommon and the classification of parabens in some sources as high-rate sensitizers may thus be somewhat overstated.[21]

Immediate hypersensitivity reactions following injection of preparations containing parabens have also been reported.[22-24] Delayed contact dermatitis occurs more frequently when parabens are used topically, but has also been reported to occur after oral administration.[25-27]

Unusually, preparations containing parabens may be used by patients who have reacted previously with contact dermatitis, provided they are applied to another unaffected site. This has been termed the paraben paradox.[28]

Concern has been expressed over the use of methylparaben in infant parenteral products since bilirubin binding may be affected, which is potentially hazardous in hyperbilirubinemic neonates.[29]

Systemically no adverse effects to parabens have been reported. The WHO has set an estimated total acceptable daily intake for methyl, ethyl and propylparabens at up to 10 mg/kg body-weight.[30]

LD$_{50}$ (dog, oral): 3.0 g/kg[31]
LD$_{50}$ (mouse, IP): 0.96 g/kg
LD$_{50}$ (mouse, SC): 1.20 g/kg

15. Handling Precautions

Observe normal precautions appropriate to the circumstances and quantity of material handled. Methylparaben may be irritant to the skin, eyes and mucous membranes and should be handled in a well-ventilated environment. Eye protection, gloves and a dust mask or respirator are recommended.

16. Regulatory Status

GRAS listed. Accepted for use as a food additive in Europe. Included in the FDA Inactive Ingredients Guide (IM, IV, and SC injections, ophthalmic preparations, oral capsules, tablets, solutions and suspensions, otic, rectal, topical and vaginal preparations). Included in medicines licensed in the UK.

17. Pharmacopeias

Aust, Br, Braz, Egypt, Eur, Fr, Ger, Gr, Hung, Ind, It, Jpn, Mex, Neth, Nord, Port, Rom, Swiss, USPNF and Yug.

18. Related Substances

Butylparaben; Ethylparaben; methylparaben potassium; methylparaben sodium; Propylparaben.

Methylparaben potassium: $C_8H_7KO_3$
Molecular weight: 190.25
CAS number: [26112-07-2]
Synonyms: methyl 4-hydroxybenzoate potassium salt; potassium methyl hydroxybenzoate.
Comments: methylparaben potassium may be used instead of methylparaben because of its greater aqueous solubility.

Methylparaben sodium: $C_8H_7NaO_3$
Molecular weight: 174.14
CAS number: [5026-62-0]
Synonyms: E219; methyl 4-hydroxybenzoate sodium salt; sodium methyl hydroxybenzoate; soluble methyl hydroxybenzoate.
Pharmacopeias: Br, Fr, It and USPNF.
Appearance: a white odorless, or almost odorless, hygroscopic crystalline powder.
Acidity/alkalinity: pH = 9.5-10.5 (0.1% aqueous solution).
Solubility: 1 in 50 of ethanol (95%); 1 in 2 of water; practically insoluble in fixed oils.
Comments: methylparaben sodium may be used instead of methylparaben because of its greater aqueous solubility. However, it may cause the pH of a formulation to become more alkaline.

19. Comments

—

20. Specific References

1. Decker RL, Wenninger JA. Frequency of preservative use in cosmetic formulas as disclosed to FDA - 1987. Cosmet Toilet 1987; 102(12): 21-24.
2. Prickett PS, Murray HL, Mercer NH. Potentiation of preservatives (parabens) in pharmaceutical formulations by low concentrations of propylene glycol. J Pharm Sci 1961; 50: 316-320.
3. Richards RME, McBride RJ. Phenylethanol enhancement of preservatives used in ophthalmic preparations. J Pharm Pharmacol 1971; 23: 141S-146S.
4. Haag TE, Loncrini DF. Esters of para-hydroxybenzoic acid. In: Kabara JJ, editor. Cosmetic and drug preservation. New York: Marcel Dekker, 1984: 63-77.
5. Rosen WE, Berke PA, Matzin T, Peterson AF. Preservation of cosmetic lotions with imidazolidinyl urea plus parabens. J Soc Cosmet Chem 1977; 28: 83-87.
6. Hibbott HW, Monks J. Preservation of emulsions - *p*-hydroxybenzoic ester partition coefficient. J Soc Cosmet Chem 1961; 12: 2-10.

7. Wan LSC, Kurup TRR, Chan LW. Partition of preservatives in oil/water systems. Pharm Acta Helv 1986; 61: 308-313.

8. Aalto TR, Firman MC, Rigler NE. *p*-Hydroxybenzoic acid esters as preservatives I: uses, antibacterial and antifungal studies, properties and determination. J Am Pharm Assoc (Sci) 1953; 42: 449-457.

9. Kamada A, Yata N, Kubo K, Arakawa M. Stability of *p*-hydroxybenzoic acid esters in acidic medium. Chem Pharm Bull 1973; 21: 2073-2076.

10. Aoki M, Kameta A, Yoshioka I, Matsuzaki T. Application of surface active agents to pharmaceutical preparations I: effect of Tween 20 upon the antifungal activities of *p*-hydroxybenzoic acid esters in solubilized preparations [in Japanese]. J Pharm Soc Jpn 1956; 76: 939-943.

11. Patel N, Kostenbauder HB. Interaction of preservatives with macromolecules I: binding of parahydroxybenzoic acid esters by polyoxyethylene 20 sorbitan monooleate (Tween 80). J Am Pharm Assoc (Sci) 1958; 47: 289-293.

12. Poprzan J, deNavarre MG. The interference of nonionic emulsifiers with preservatives VIII. J Soc Cosmet Chem 1959; 10: 81-87.

13. Yousef RT, El-Nakeeb MA, Salama S. Effect of some pharmaceutical materials on the bactericidal activities of preservatives. Can J Pharm Sci 1973; 8: 54-56.

14. Allwood MC. The adsorption of esters of *p*-hydroxybenzoic acid by magnesium trisilicate. Int J Pharmaceutics 1982; 11: 101-107.

15. Eisman PC, Cooper J, Jaconia D. Influence of gum tragacanth on the bactericidal activity of preservatives. J Am Pharm Assoc (Sci) 1957; 46: 144-147.

16. Myburgh JA, McCarthy TJ. The influence of suspending agents on preservative activity in aqueous solid/liquid dispersions. Pharm Weekbl (Sci) 1980; 2: 143-148.

17. Chemburkar PB, Joslin RS. Effect of flavoring oils on preservative concentrations in oral liquid dosage forms. J Pharm Sci 1975; 64: 414-417.

18. Runesson B, Gustavii K. Stability of parabens in the presence of polyols. Acta Pharm Suec 1986; 23: 151-162.

19. Deeks T. Oral atropine sulphate mixtures. Pharm J 1983; 230: 481.

20. Kakemi K, Sezaki H, Arakawa E, Kimura K, Ikeda K. Interactions of parabens and other pharmaceutical adjuvants with plastic containers. Chem Pharm Bull 1971; 19: 2523-2529.

21. Weiner M, Bernstein IL. Adverse reactions to drug formulation agents: a handbook of excipients. New York: Marcel Dekker, 1989: 298-300.

22. Aldrete JA, Johnson DA. Allergy to local anesthetics. JAMA 1969; 207: 356-357.

23. Latronica RJ, Goldberg AF, Wightman JR. Local anesthetic sensitivity: report of a case. Oral Surg 1969; 28: 439-441.

24. Nagel JE, Fuscaldo JT, Fireman P. Paraben allergy. JAMA 1977; 237: 1594-1595.

25. Michäelsson G, Juhlin L. Urticaria induced by preservatives and dye additives in food and drugs. Br J Dermatol 1973; 88: 525-532.

26. Warin RP, Smith RJ. Challenge test battery in chronic urticaria. Br J Dermatol 1976; 94: 401-406.

27. Kaminer Y, Apter A, Tyano S, Livni E, Wijsenbeek H. Delayed hypersensitivity reactions to orally administered methylparaben. Clin Pharm 1982; 1: 469-470.

28. Fisher AA. Cortaid cream dermatitis and the paraben paradox [letter]. J Am Acad Dermatol 1982; 6: 116-117.

29. Loria CJ, Escheverria P, Smith AL. Effect of antibiotic formulations in serum protein: bilirubin interaction of newborn infants. J Pediatr 1976; 89: 479-482.

30. FAO/WHO. Toxicological evaluation of certain food additives with a review of general principles and of specifications. Seventeenth report of the joint FAO/WHO expert committee on food additives. Tech Rep Ser Wld Hlth Org 1974; No. 539.

31. Sweet DV, editor. Registry of toxic effects of chemical substances. Cincinnati: US Department of Health, 1987.

21. General References

Forster S, Buckton G, Beezer AE. The importance of chain length on the wettability and solubility of organic homologs. Int J Pharmaceutics 1991; 72: 29-34.

Golightly LK, Smolinske SS, Bennett ML, Sutherland EW, Rumack BH. Pharmaceutical excipients: adverse effects associated with inactive ingredients in drug products (part I). Med Toxicol 1988; 3: 128-165.

Grant DJW, Mehdizadeh M, Chow AH-L, Fairbrother JE. Non-linear van't Hoff solubility-temperature plots and their pharmaceutical interpretation. Int J Pharmaceutics 1984; 18: 25-38.

Jian L, Li Wan Po A. Ciliotoxicity of methyl- and propyl-*p*-hydroxybenzoates: a dose-response and surface-response study. J Pharm Pharmacol 1993; 45: 925-927.

Jones PS, Thigpen D, Morrison JL, Richardson AP. *p*-Hydroxybenzoic acid esters as preservatives III: the physiological disposition of p-hydroxybenzoic acid and its esters. J Am Pharm Assoc (Sci) 1956; 45: 268-273.

Kostenbauder HB. Physical chemical aspects of preservative selection for pharmaceutical and cosmetic emulsions. Dev Ind Microbiol 1962; 1: 286-296.

Marouchoc SR. Cosmetic preservation. Cosmet Technol 1980; 2(10): 38-44.

Matthews C, Davidson J, Bauer E, Morrison JL, Richardson AP. *p*-Hydroxybenzoic acid esters as preservatives II: acute and chronic toxicity in dogs, rats and mice. J Am Pharm Assoc (Sci) 1956; 45: 260-267.

Sakamoto T, Yanagi M, Fukushima S, Mitsui T. Effects of some cosmetic pigments on the bactericidal activities of preservatives. J Soc Cosmet Chem 1987; 38: 83-98.

Sokol H. Recent developments in the preservation of pharmaceuticals. Drug Standards 1952; 20: 89-106.

22. Authors

USA: MM Rieger.

Mineral Oil

1. Nonproprietary Names

BP: Liquid paraffin
PhEur: Paraffinum liquidum
USP: Mineral oil

2. Synonyms

905 (mineral hydrocarbons); *Avatech*; *Citation*; heavy liquid petrolatum; heavy mineral oil; liquid petrolatum; paraffin oil; white mineral oil.

3. Chemical Name and CAS Registry Number

Mineral oil [8012-95-1]

4. Empirical Formula   Molecular Weight

Mineral oil is a mixture of refined liquid saturated hydrocarbons obtained from petroleum.

5. Structural Formula

See Section 4.

6. Functional Category

Emollient; solvent; tablet and capsule lubricant; therapeutic agent; oleaginous vehicle.

7. Applications in Pharmaceutical Formulation or Technology

Mineral oil is used primarily as an excipient in topical pharmaceutical formulations where its emollient properties are exploited as an ingredient in ointment bases. It is additionally used in oil-in-water emulsions,[1-5] as a solvent, and as a lubricant in capsule and tablet formulations, and to a limited extent, as a mold release agent for cocoa butter suppositories.

Therapeutically, mineral oil is used in ophthalmic formulations for its lubricant properties and has been used in the treatment of constipation, *see* Section 14. Mineral oil is also used in cosmetics and food products.[6]

Use	Concentration (%)
Ophthalmic ointments	3.0-60.0
Otic preparations	0.5-3.0
Topical emulsions	1.0-32.0
Topical lotions	1.0-20.0
Topical ointments	0.1-95.0

8. Description

Mineral oil is a transparent, colorless, viscous liquid, free from fluorescence in daylight. It is practically tasteless and odorless when cold, and has a faint odor when heated.

9. Pharmacopeial Specifications

Test	PhEur 1983	USP XXII
Specific gravity	0.827-0.890	0.845-0.905
Viscosity (kinematic) at 40°C	—	$\geqslant$ 34.5 cSt
Viscosity (dynamic) at 20°C	110-230 mPa s	—
Acidity or alkalinity	+	—
Neutrality	—	+
Readily carbonizable substances	+	+
Limit of polynuclear compounds	+	+
Solid paraffin	+	+

10. Typical Properties

Boiling point: > 360°C
Flash point: 210-224°C
Pour point: -12.2 to -9.4°C
Refractive index: n_D^{20} = 1.4756-1.4800
Surface tension: $\approx$ 35 mN/m (dynes/cm) at 25°C.
Solubility: practically insoluble in ethanol (95%), glycerin, and water; soluble in acetone, benzene, chloroform, carbon disulfide, ether, and petroleum ether. Miscible with volatile oils and fixed oils, with the exception of castor oil. The addition of a small amount of a suitable surfactant may promote miscibility/solubilization.
Viscosity (dynamic): 110-230 mPa s at 20°C. *See also* HPE Data.

	HPE Laboratory Project Data		
Sample	Method	Lab #	Results
Kaydol	VIS-1	27	163 $\pm$ 2.0 mPa s [a]
Primol 355	VIS-1	27	158 $\pm$ 2.0 mPa s [b]

Supplier: a. Witco Corporation; b. Exxon.

11. Stability and Storage Conditions

Mineral oil undergoes oxidation when exposed to heat and light. Oxidation begins with the formation of peroxides, exhibiting an 'induction period'. Under ordinary conditions, the induction period may take months or years. However, once a trace of peroxide is formed, further oxidation is autocatalytic and proceeds very rapidly. Oxidation results in the formation of aldehydes and organic acids, which impart taste and odor. Stabilizers may be added to retard oxidation; butylated hydroxyanisole, butylated hydroxytoluene and α-tocopherol being the most commonly used antioxidants.

Mineral oil may be sterilized by dry heat.

Mineral oil should be stored in an airtight container, protected from light, in a cool, dry, place.

12. Incompatibilities

Incompatible with strong oxidizing agents.

13. Method of Manufacture

Mineral oil is obtained by distillation of petroleum. The lighter hydrocarbons are first removed by distillation and the residue then redistilled between 330-390°C. The distillate is chilled and the solid fractions removed by filtration. The filtrate is then further purified and decolorized by high pressure hydrogenation or sulfuric acid treatment; the purified filtrate is then filtered through adsorbents. The liquid portion obtained is distilled and the portion boiling below 360°C discarded. A suitable stabilizer may be added to the mineral oil, *see* Section 11.

14. Safety

Mineral oil is used as an excipient in a wide variety of pharmaceutical formulations, *see* Section 16. It is also used extensively in cosmetics and in some food products.[6] Therapeutically, mineral oil has been used in the treatment of constipation since it acts as a lubricant and stool softener when taken orally. Daily doses of up to 45 mL have been administered orally while doses of up to 120 mL have been used as an enema. However, excessive dosage of mineral oil, either orally or rectally can result in anal seepage and irritation and its oral use as a laxative is not considered desirable.

Chronic oral consumption of mineral oil may impair the appetite and interfere with the absorption of fat-soluble vitamins and prolonged use should be avoided. Mineral oil is absorbed to some extent when emulsified and can lead to granulomatous reactions. Similar reactions also occur upon injection of the oil;[7] injection may also cause vasospasm.

The most serious adverse reaction to mineral oil is lipoid pneumonia caused by aspiration of the oil.[8,9] With the reduction in the use of mineral oil in nasal formulations the number of instances of lipoid pneumonia has been greatly reduced. However, lipoid pneumonia has also been associated with the use of mineral oil-containing cosmetics[10] and ophthalmic preparations[11] in addition to the chronic ingestion of mineral oil. It is therefore recommended that mineral oil-containing products not be used in very young children, the elderly or persons with debilitating illnesses.

Given its widespread use in many topical products, mineral oil has been associated with few instances of allergic reactions. The WHO has not specified an acceptable daily intake of mineral oil given the low concentration consumed in foods.[12]

LD_{50} (mouse, oral): 22 g/kg[13]

15. Handling Precautions

Observe normal precautions appropriate to the circumstances and quantity of material handled. Inhalation of mineral oil vapors may be harmful. In the UK, the recommended occupational exposure limit for mineral oil mist is 5 mg/m^3 long-term (8-hour TWA) and 10 mg/m^3 short-term.[14] Mineral oil is combustible.

16. Regulatory Status

GRAS listed. Accepted in the UK for use in certain food applications. Included in the FDA Inactive Ingredients Guide (dental preparations, IV injections, ophthalmic preparations, oral capsules and tablets, otic, topical, transdermal, and vaginal preparations). Included in nonparenteral medicines licensed in the UK.

17. Pharmacopeias

Aust, Belg, Br, Braz, Chin, Cz, Egypt, Eur, Fr, Ger, Gr, Hung, Ind, It, Jpn, Mex, Neth, Nord, Port, Rom, Rus, Swiss, Turk, US and Yug. Also in BP Vet.

18. Related Substances

Light Mineral Oil; Mineral Oil and Lanolin Alcohols; Paraffin; Petrolatum.

19. Comments

Mineral oil, in completely filled soft plastic tubes, showed bubbles of gas after gamma irradiation. The bubbles were larger at higher levels of radiation. The iodine value also increased after high and low levels of irradiation.

20. Specific References

1. Eccleston GM. Structure and rheology of cetomacrogol creams: the influence of alcohol chain length and homologue composition. J Pharm Pharmacol 1977; 29: 157-162.
2. Zatz JL. Effect of formulation additives on flocculation of dispersions stabilized by a non-ionic surfactant. Int J Pharmaceutics 1979; 4: 83-86.
3. Wepierre J, Adrangui M, Marty JP. Factors in the occlusivity of aqueous emulsions. J Soc Cosmet Chem 1982; 33: 157-167.
4. Fong-Spaven F, Hollenbeck RG. Thermal rheological analysis of triethanolamine-stearate stabilized mineral oil in water emulsions. Drug Dev Ind Pharm 1986; 12: 289-302.
5. Abd Elbary A, Nour SA, Ibrahim I. Physical stability and rheological properties of w/o/w emulsions as a function of electrolytes. Pharm Ind 1990; 52: 357-363.
6. Mineral hydrocarbons to be banned from foods. Pharm J 1989; 242: 187.
7. Bloem JJ, van der Waal I. Paraffinoma of the face: a diagnostic and therapeutic problem. Oral Surg 1974; 38: 675-680.
8. Volk BW, Nathanson L, Losner S, Slade WR, Jacobi M. Incidence of lipoid pneumonia in a survey of 389 chronically ill patients. Am J Med 1951; 10: 316-324.
9. Smolinske SC. Handbook of food, drug, and cosmetic excipients. Boca Raton, FL: CRC Press Inc, 1992: 231-234.
10. Becton DL, Lowe JE, Falleta JM. Lipoid pneumonia in an adolescent girl secondary to use of lip gloss. J Pediatr 1984; 105: 421-423.
11. Prakash UBS, Rosenow EC. Pulmonary complications from ophthalmic preparations. Mayo Clin Proc 1990; 65: 521.
12. FAO/WHO. Evaluation of certain food additives and contaminants: thirty-seventh report of the joint FAO/WHO expert committee on food additives. Tech Rep Ser Wld Hlth Org 1991; No. 806.
13. Sweet DV, editor. Registry of toxic effects of chemical substances. Cincinnati: US Department of Health, 1987.
14. Health and Safety Executive. EH40/93: occupational exposure limits 1993. London: HMSO, 1993.

21. General References

Davis SS, Khanderia MS. Rheological characterization of Plastibases and the effect of formulation variables on the consistency of these vehicles part 3: oscillatory testing. Int J Pharm Technol Prod Manuf 1981; 2(Apr): 13-18.
Rhodes RK. Highly refined petroleum products in skin lotions. Cosmet Perfum 1974; 89(3): 53-56.

22. Authors

USA: GE Reier, DA Wadke.

Light Mineral Oil

1. Nonproprietary Names

BP: Light liquid paraffin
PhEur: Paraffinum perliquidum
USPNF: Light mineral oil

2. Synonyms

905 (mineral hydrocarbons); *Citation*; light liquid petrolatum; light paraffin oil.

3. Chemical Name and CAS Registry Number

Light mineral oil

4. Empirical Formula   Molecular Weight

Light mineral oil is a mixture of refined liquid saturated hydrocarbons obtained from petroleum. It is less viscous and has a lower specific gravity than mineral oil.

5. Structural Formula

See Section 4.

6. Functional Category

Emollient; solvent; tablet and capsule lubricant; therapeutic agent; oleaginous vehicle.

7. Applications in Pharmaceutical Formulation or Technology

Light mineral oil is used in applications similar to mineral oil. It is used primarily as an excipient in topical pharmaceutical formulations where its emollient properties are exploited as an ingredient in ointment bases.[1,2] It is also used in ophthalmic formulations.[3] Light mineral oil is additionally used as a solvent and lubricant in capsules and tablets; as a solvent and penetration enhancer in transdermal preparations;[4] and as the oily medium used in the microencapsulation of many drugs.[5-13]

Light mineral oil is also used in cosmetics and certain food products.

Use	Concentration (%)
Ophthalmic ointments	≤ 15
Otic preparations	≤ 50
Topical emulsions	1-20
Topical lotions	7-16
Topical ointments	0.2-23

8. Description

Light mineral oil is a transparent, colorless liquid, free from fluorescence in daylight. It is practically tasteless and odorless when cold, and has a faint odor when heated.

9. Pharmacopeial Specifications

Test	PhEur 1983	USPNF XVII
Specific gravity	0.810-0.875	0.818-0.880
Viscosity (kinematic) at 40°C	—	≤ 33.5 cSt
Viscosity (dynamic) at 20°C	25-80 mPa s	—
Acidity or alkalinity	+	—
Neutrality	—	+
Readily carbonizable substances	+	+
Limit of polynuclear compounds	+	+
Solid paraffin	+	+

10. Typical Properties

Solubility: soluble in chloroform, ether, and hydrocarbons; sparingly soluble in ethanol (95%); practically insoluble in water.

11. Stability and Storage Conditions

Light mineral oil undergoes oxidation when exposed to heat and light. Oxidation begins with the formation of peroxides, exhibiting an 'induction period'. Under typical storage conditions, the induction period may take months or years. However, once a trace of peroxide is formed, further oxidation is autocatalytic and proceeds very rapidly. Oxidation results in the formation of aldehydes and organic acids, which impart taste and odor. The USPNF XVII permits the addition of suitable stabilizers to retard oxidation, butylated hydroxyanisole, butylated hydroxytoluene and α-tocopherol being the most commonly used antioxidants.

Light mineral oil may be sterilized by dry heat.

Light mineral oil should be stored in an airtight container, protected from light, in a cool, dry, place.

12. Incompatibilities

Incompatible with strong oxidizing agents.

13. Method of Manufacture

Light mineral oil is obtained by the distillation of petroleum. A suitable stabilizer may be added to the oil, *see* Section 11. *See also* Mineral Oil for further information.

14. Safety

Light mineral oil is used in applications similar to mineral oil. Oral ingestion of large doses of light mineral oil or chronic consumption may be harmful. Aspiration of light mineral oil may cause lipoid pneumonia.

See Mineral Oil for further information.

15. Handling Precautions

Observe normal precautions appropriate to the circumstances and quantity of material handled. Inhalation of mineral oil vapors may be harmful. In the UK, the recommended occupational exposure limit for mineral oil mist is 5 mg/m³ long-term (8-hour TWA) and 10 mg/m³ short-term.[14] Light mineral oil is combustible.

16. Regulatory Status

Mineral oil is GRAS listed and accepted in the UK for use in certain food applications.

Light mineral oil is included in the FDA Inactive Ingredients Guide (ophthalmic preparations, oral capsules and tablets, otic, rectal, topical and transdermal preparations). Included in nonparenteral medicines licensed in the UK.

17. Pharmacopeias

Belg, Br, Eur, Fr, Ger, Gr, Ind, It, Jpn, Neth, Port, Swiss and USPNF. Also in BP Vet.

18. Related Substances

Mineral Oil; Mineral Oil and Lanolin Alcohols; Paraffin; Petrolatum.

19. Comments

—

20. Specific References

1. Magdassi S, Frenkel M, Garti N. Correlation between nature of emulsifier and multiple emulsion stability. Drug Dev Ind Pharm 1985; 11: 791-798.
2. Tanaka S, Takashima Y, Murayama H, Tsuchiya S. Solubility and distribution of dexamethasone acetate in oil-in-water creams and its release from the creams. Chem Pharm Bull 1985; 33: 3929-3934.
3. Jay WM, Green K. Multiple-drop study of topically applied 1% delta 9-tetrahydrocannabinol in human eyes. Arch Ophthalmol 1983; 101: 591-593.
4. Pfister WR, Hsieh DST. Permeation enhancers compatible with transdermal drug delivery systems part II: system design considerations. Pharm Technol 1990; 14(10): 54, 56-58, 60.
5. Beyger JW, Nairn JG. Some factors affecting the microencapsulation of pharmaceuticals with cellulose acetate phthalate. J Pharm Sci 1986; 75: 573-578.
6. Pongpaibul Y, Whitworth CW. Preparation and in vitro dissolution characteristics of propranolol microcapsules. Int J Pharmaceutics 1986; 33: 243-248.
7. Sheu M-T, Sokoloski TD. Entrapment of bioactive compounds within native albumin beads III: evaluation of parameters affecting drug release. J Parenter Sci Technol 1986; 40: 259-265.
8. Huang HP, Ghebre Sellassie I. Preparation of microspheres of water-soluble pharmaceuticals. J Microencapsulation 1989; 6(2): 219-225.
9. Ghorab MM, Zia H, Luzzi LA. Preparation of controlled release anticancer agents I: 5-fluorouracil-ethyl cellulose microspheres. J Microencapsulation 1990; 7(4): 447-454.
10. Ruiz R, Sakr A, Sprockel OL. A study on the manufacture and in vitro dissolution of terbutaline sulfate microcapsules and their tablets. Drug Dev Ind Pharm 1990; 16: 1829-1842.
11. Sanghvi SP, Nairn JG. Phase diagram studies for microencapsulation of pharmaceuticals using cellulose acetate trimellitate. J Pharm Sci 1991; 80: 394-398.
12. Iwata M, McGinity JW. Preparation of multi-phase microspheres of poly(D,L-lactic acid) and poly(D,L-lactic co-glycolic acid) containing a w/o emulsion by a multiple emulsion solvent evaporation technique. J Microencapsulation 1992; 9(2): 201-214.
13. Sanghvi SP, Nairn JG. Effect of viscosity and interfacial tension on particle size of cellulose acetate trimellitate microspheres. J Microencapsulation 1992; 9(2): 215-227.
14. Health and Safety Executive. EH40/93: occupational exposure limits 1993. London: HMSO, 1993.

See also Mineral Oil.

21. General References

See Mineral Oil.

22. Authors

USA: R Abramowitz, GE Reier, DA Wadke.

Mineral Oil and Lanolin Alcohols

1. Nonproprietary Names

CTFA: Mineral oil and lanolin alcohol

2. Synonyms

Amerchol L-101; liquid paraffin and lanolin alcohols; *Protalan M-16*; *Protalan M-26*.

3. Chemical Name and CAS Registry Number

Mineral oil [8012-95-1] and
Lanolin alcohols [8027-33-6]

4. Empirical Formula   Molecular Weight

A mixture of mineral oil and lanolin alcohols.

5. Structural Formula

See Section 4.

6. Functional Category

Emollient; emulsifying agent; plasticizer.

7. Applications in Pharmaceutical Formulation or Technology

Mineral oil and lanolin alcohols is an oily liquid used in topical pharmaceutical formulations and cosmetics as an emulsifying agent with emollient properties. It is used as a primary emulsifier in the preparation of water-in-oil creams and lotions and as an auxiliary emulsifier and stabilizing agent in oil-in-water creams and lotions.

Use	Concentration (%)
Emollient	3.0-6.0
Emulsifier in w/o creams and lotions	5.0-15.0
Emulsifier in o/w creams and lotions	0.5-6.0

8. Description

A pale yellow-colored, oily liquid with a faint characteristic sterol odor.

9. Pharmacopeial Specifications

—

10. Typical Properties

Acid value: $\leqslant 1$
Arsenic: $\leqslant 2$ ppm
Ash: $\leqslant 0.2\%$
Heavy metals: $\leqslant 20$ ppm
HLB value: ≈ 8
Hydroxyl value: 10-15
Iodine number: $\leqslant 12$
Microbiological count: the total bacterial count, when packaged, is less than 10 per gram of sample.
Moisture content: $\leqslant 0.2\%$
Saponification value: $\leqslant 2$
Solubility: soluble 1 in 2 parts of chloroform, 1 in 4 parts of castor oil, and 1 in 4 parts of corn oil. Practically insoluble in ethanol (95%), and water. Precipitation occurs in hexane.
Specific gravity: 0.840-0.860 at 25°C

11. Stability and Storage Conditions

Mineral oil and lanolin alcohols is stable and should be stored in a well-closed container in a cool, dry, place.

12. Incompatibilities

Lanolin alcohols is incompatible with coal tar, ichthammol, phenol and resorcinol.

13. Method of Manufacture

Lanolin alcohols is dissolved in mineral oil.

14. Safety

Mineral oil and lanolin alcohols is generally regarded as an essentially nontoxic and nonirritant material. However, lanolin alcohols may be irritant to the skin and cause hypersensitivity in some individuals.

15. Handling Precautions

Observe normal precautions appropriate to the circumstances and quantity of material handled.

16. Regulatory Status

Accepted for use in topical pharmaceutical formulations and cosmetics.

17. Pharmacopeias

—

18. Related Substances

Lanolin Alcohols; Mineral Oil; Petrolatum and Lanolin Alcohols.

19. Comments

See individual monographs on Lanolin Alcohols, and Mineral Oil for further information.

20. Specific References

—

21. General References

Davis SS. Viscoelastic properties of pharmaceutical semisolids I: ointment bases. J Pharm Sci 1969; 58: 412-418.
Prosperio G, Gatti S, Genesi P. Lanolin and its derivatives for cosmetic creams and lotions. Cosmet Toilet 1980; 95(4): 81-85.

22. Authors

USA: S Scheindlin.

Monoethanolamine

1. Nonproprietary Names
BP: Ethanolamine
USPNF: Monoethanolamine

2. Synonyms
β-Aminoethyl alcohol; colamine; ethylolamine; β-hydroxyethylamine; 2-hydroxyethylamine.

3. Chemical Name and CAS Registry Number
2-Aminoethanol [141-43-5]

4. Empirical Formula Molecular Weight
C_2H_7NO 61.08

5. Structural Formula
$HOCH_2CH_2NH_2$

6. Functional Category
Alkalizing agent; emulsifying agent.

7. Applications in Pharmaceutical Formulation or Technology

Monoethanolamine is used primarily in pharmaceutical formulations for buffering purposes, and in the preparation of emulsions. Other uses include as a solvent for fats and oils and as a stabilizing agent in an injectable dextrose solution of phenytoin sodium.

Monoethanolamine is also used to produce a variety of salts with therapeutic uses. For example, a salt of monoethanolamine with vitamin C is used for intramuscular injection, whilst the salicylate and undecenoate monoethanolamine salts are utilized respectively in the treatment of rheumatism and as an antifungal agent. However, the most common therapeutic use of monoethanolamine is in the production of ethanolamine oleate injection, which is used as a sclerosing agent.[1]

Monoethanolamine has also been used to form an addition compound with theophylline which is more soluble than theophylline alone.

8. Description
Monoethanolamine is a clear, colorless or pale yellow-colored, moderately viscous liquid with a mild, ammoniacal odor.

9. Pharmacopeial Specifications

Test	BP 1993	USPNF XVII
Identification	+	—
Specific gravity	1.014-1.023	1.013-1.016
Distilling range	—	167-173°C
Residue on ignition	—	$\leqslant 0.1\%$
Refractive index	1.453-1.459	—
Related substances	$\leqslant 2.0\%$	—
Assay	98.0-100.5%	98.0-100.5%

10. Typical Properties
Acidity/alkalinity:
pH = 12.1 for a 0.1N aqueous solution.
Autoignition temperature: 410°C
Boiling point: 170.8°C
Critical temperature: 341°C
Density:
1.0117 g/cm³ at 25°C;
0.9998 g/cm³ at 40°C;
0.9844 g/cm³ at 60°C.
Dissociation constant: pK_a = 9.4 at 25°C
Flash point (open cup): 93°C
Hygroscopicity: very hygroscopic.
Melting point: 10.3°C
Refractive index: n_D^{20} = 1.4539
Solubility:

Solvent	Solubility at 25°C
Acetone	miscible
Benzene	1 in 72
Chloroform	miscible
Ethanol (95%)	miscible
Ether	1 in 48
Fixed oils	immiscible
Glycerin	miscible
Methanol	miscible
Water	miscible

Surface tension:
48.8 mN/m (48.8 dynes/cm) at 20°C
Vapor density (relative): 2.1 (air = 1)
Vapor pressure: 53.3 Pa (0.4 mmHg) at 20°C
Viscosity (dynamic):
18.95 mPa s (18.95 cP) at 25°C;
5.03 mPa s (5.03 cP) at 60°C.

11. Stability and Storage Conditions
Monoethanolamine is very hygroscopic and is unstable when exposed to light. Aqueous monoethanolamine solutions may be sterilized by autoclaving.

When stored in large quantities, milled steel vessels are satisfactory for a short period of time although, to prevent discoloration of the monoethanolamine, stainless steel is preferable for long-term storage. Color formation may be due to the absorption of atmospheric oxygen which can be prevented by sealing the monoethanolamine under an inert gas. This also prevents water uptake from the atmosphere.

Smaller quantities of monoethanolamine should be stored in an airtight container, protected from light, in a cool, dry, place.

12. Incompatibilities
Monoethanolamine contains both a hydroxy and primary amine group and will thus undergo reactions characteristic of both alcohols and amines. Where it is possible for a reaction to take place at either the amine or hydroxy group the amine group usually exhibits the greater activity.

As a primary amine, monoethanolamine will react with aldehydes and ketones to yield aldimines and ketimines. Monoethanolamine will also react with acids, acid anhydrides, acid chlorides and esters to form amide derivatives and with propylene carbonate or other cyclic carbonates to give the corresponding carbonates.

Additionally, monoethanolamine will react with aluminum, copper, and copper alloys to form complex salts. Discoloration and precipitation will also take place in the presence of heavy metal salts.

Violent reactions can occur between monoethanolamine and acrolein, acrylonite, epichlorohydrin, β-propiolactone and vinyl acetate.

13. Method of Manufacture

Monoethanolamine is prepared commercially by the ammonolysis of ethylene oxide. The reaction yields a mixture of monoethanolamine, diethanolamine and triethanolamine which is separated to obtain the pure products. Monoethanolamine is also produced from the reaction between nitromethane and formaldehyde.

14. Safety

Although monoethanolamine is an irritant, caustic material, when used in neutralized parenteral and topical pharmaceutical formulations it is not usually associated with adverse effects although hypersensitivity reactions have been reported. Monoethanolamine salts are generally regarded as being less toxic than monoethanolamine.

LD$_{50}$ (guinea pig, oral): 0.62 g/kg[2]
LD$_{50}$ (mouse, IP): 0.05 g/kg
LD$_{50}$ (mouse, oral): 0.7 g/kg
LD$_{50}$ (rabbit, oral): 1 g/kg
LD$_{50}$ (rat, IM): 1.75 g/kg
LD$_{50}$ (rat, IP): 0.07 g/kg
LD$_{50}$ (rat, IV): 0.23 g/kg
LD$_{50}$ (rat, oral): 1.72 g/kg
LD$_{50}$ (rat, SC): 1.5 g/kg

15. Handling Precautions

Monoethanolamine is irritant to mucous membranes, skin and the eyes. Inhalation of monoethanolamine vapor is also harmful, resulting in respiratory difficulties, headache, nausea and vomiting. Protective clothing, gloves, eye protection and an appropriate respirator are recommended. Ideally, monoethanolamine should be handled in a fume cupboard. In the UK, the recommended long-term (8-hour TWA) exposure limit for monoethanolamine is 8 mg/m^3 (3 ppm), and 15 mg/m^3 (6 ppm) short-term.[3] Monoethanolamine is flammable.

16. Regulatory Status

Included in medicines licensed in the UK and USA.

17. Pharmacopeias

Aust, Br and USPNF.

18. Related Substances

Diethanolamine; Triethanolamine.

19. Comments

–

20. Specific References

1. Crotty B, et al. The management of acutely bleeding varices by injection sclerotherapy. Med J Aust 1986; 145: 130-133.
2. Sweet DV, editor. Registry of toxic effects of chemical substances. Cincinnati: US Department of Health, 1987.
3. Health and Safety Executive. EH40/93: occupational exposure limits 1993. London: HMSO, 1993.

21. General References

Kubis A, Jadach W, Malecka K. Studies on the release of solubilized drugs from ointment bases. Pharmazie 1984; 39: 168-170.

22: Authors

USA: J Fleitman, JS Fujiki, JC Lee.

Nitrogen

1. Nonproprietary Names

USPNF: Nitrogen

2. Synonyms

Azote; E941; nitrogenium.

3. Chemical Name and CAS Registry Number

Nitrogen [7727-37-9]

4. Empirical Formula   Molecular Weight

N_2 28.01

5. Structural Formula

N_2

6. Functional Category

Air displacement; aerosol propellant.

7. Applications in Pharmaceutical Formulation or Technology

Nitrogen and other compressed gases such as carbon dioxide and nitrous oxide are used as propellants for topical pharmaceutical aerosols. They are also used in other aerosol products that work satisfactorily with the coarse aerosol spray that is produced with compressed gases, e.g. furniture polish and window cleaner. Nitrogen is insoluble in water and other solvents and therefore remains separated from the actual pharmaceutical formulation.

Advantages of compressed gases as aerosol propellants are that they are inexpensive, of low toxicity and practically odorless and tasteless. In contrast to liquefied gases, their pressures change relatively little with temperature. Disadvantages are that there is no reservoir of propellant in the aerosol; as a result the pressure decreases as the product is used and the spray characteristics change. Misuse of a product by the consumer, e.g. using a product inverted, results in the discharge of the vapor phase instead of the liquid phase. Since most of the propellant is contained in the vapor phase some of the propellant will be lost and hence the spray characteristics altered. Additionally, the sprays produced using compressed gases are very wet.

Nitrogen is also used to displace air from solutions subject to oxidation, by sparging, and to replace air in the headspace above products in their final packaging, e.g. in parenteral products packaged in glass ampoules. Nitrogen is also used for the same purpose in many food products.

8. Description

Nitrogen occurs naturally as approximately 78% v/v of the atmosphere. It is a nonreactive, noncombustible, colorless, tasteless and odorless gas. It is usually handled as a compressed gas, stored in metal cylinders.

9. Pharmacopeial Specifications

Test	USPNF XVII
Identification	+
Odor	+
Carbon monoxide	$\leqslant 0.001\%$

Continued

Test	USPNF XVII
Oxygen	$\leqslant 1.0\%$
Assay	$\geqslant 99.0\%$

See also Section 17.

10. Typical Properties

Boiling point: -195.8°C
Critical pressure: 3.39 MPa (33.49 atm)
Critical temperature: -147.2°C
Density: 0.967 g/cm^3 for vapor at 21°C
Flammability: nonflammable
Melting point: -210°C
Solubility: practically insoluble in water and most solvents; soluble in water under pressure.
Vapor density (absolute):
1.250 g/m^3 at standard temperature and pressure.
Vapor density (relative): 0.97 (air = 1)

11. Stability and Storage Conditions

Nitrogen is stable and chemically nonreactive. It should be stored in tightly sealed metal cylinders in a cool, dry, place.

12. Incompatibilities

Generally compatible with most materials encountered in pharmaceutical formulations and food products.

13. Method of Manufacture

Nitrogen is obtained commercially, in large quantities, by the fractional distillation of liquefied air.

14. Safety

Nitrogen is generally regarded as a nontoxic and nonirritant material. However, it is an asphyxiant and inhalation of large quantities is therefore hazardous. *See also* Section 19.

15. Handling Precautions

Handle in accordance with procedures for handling metal cylinders containing liquefied or compressed gases. Eye protection, gloves and protective clothing are recommended. Nitrogen is an asphyxiant and should be handled in a well-ventilated environment. The oxygen content of air in the working environment should be monitored and not permitted to fall below 18% v/v at normal atmospheric pressure.[1]

16. Regulatory Status

GRAS listed. Accepted for use as a food additive in Europe. Included in parenteral and nonparenteral medicines licensed in the UK and US.

17. Pharmacopeias

Aust, Cz, Fr, Hung, Jpn, Mex, Nord, Swiss, USPNF and Yug. The USPNF contains two nitrogen monographs, one for nitrogen of not less than 99% v/v purity and one for nitrogen of not less than 97% v/v purity.

18. Related Substances

Carbon Dioxide; Nitrous Oxide.

19. Comments

Different grades of nitrogen are commercially available which have, for example, specially low moisture levels.

Nitrogen is commonly used as a component of the gas mixtures breathed by divers. Under high pressure, such as when diving at great depths, nitrogen will dissolve in blood and lipid. If decompression is too rapid decompression sickness may occur where the nitrogen effervesces from body stores to form gas emboli.

20. Specific References

1. Health and Safety Executive. EH40/93: occupational exposure limits 1993. London: HMSO, 1993.

21. General References

Johnson MA. The aerosol handbook, 2nd edition. New Jersey: WE Dorland Co, 1982: 361-372.

Mintzer H. Aerosols. In: Martin FW, editor. Dispensing of medication, 7th edition. Easton: Mack Publishing Co, 1971.

Sanders PA. Handbook of aerosol technology, 2nd edition. New York: Van Nostrand Reinhold Company, 1979, 44-54.

Sciarra JJ. The science and technology of aerosol packaging. New York: John Wiley and Sons, 1974: 137-145.

Sciarra JJ. Pharmaceutical and cosmetic aerosols. J Pharm Sci 1974; 63: 1815-1837.

Sciarra JJ. Pharmaceutical aerosols. In: Lachman L, Lieberman HA, Kanig JL, editors. The theory and practice of industrial pharmacy, 3rd edition. Philadelphia: Lea and Febiger, 1986: 589-591.

Sciarra JJ, Cutie AJ. Pharmaceutical aerosols. In: Banker GS, Rhodes CT, editors. Modern pharmaceutics, 2nd edition. New York: Marcel Dekker Inc, 1990: 605-634.

22. Authors

UK: PJ Davies.
USA: JJ Sciarra.

Nitrous Oxide

1. Nonproprietary Names
BP: Nitrous oxide
PhEur: Nitrogenii oxidum
USP: Nitrous oxide

2. Synonyms
Dinitrogen monoxide; E942; laughing gas; nitrogen monoxide.

3. Chemical Name and CAS Registry Number
Dinitrogen oxide [10024-97-2]

4. Empirical Formula   Molecular Weight
N_2O 44.01

5. Structural Formula
N_2O

6. Functional Category
Aerosol propellant; therapeutic agent.

7. Applications in Pharmaceutical Formulation or Technology
Nitrous oxide and other compressed gases such as carbon dioxide and nitrogen are used as propellants for topical pharmaceutical aerosols. They are also used in other aerosol products that work satisfactorily with the coarse aerosol spray that is produced with compressed gases, e.g. furniture polish and window cleaner.

The advantages of compressed gases as aerosol propellants are that they are inexpensive, of low toxicity and practically odorless and tasteless. In contrast to liquefied gases, their pressures change relatively little with temperature. Disadvantages are that there is no reservoir of propellant in the aerosol; as a result the pressure decreases as the product is used and the spray characteristics change. Misuse of a product by the consumer, e.g. using a product inverted, results in the discharge of the vapor phase instead of the liquid phase. Since most of the propellant is contained in the vapor phase some of the propellant will be lost and the spray characteristics altered. Additionally, the sprays produced using compressed gases are very wet.

Therapeutically, nitrous oxide is best known as an anesthetic administered by inhalation. When used as an anesthetic it has strong analgesic properties but produces little muscle relaxation. Nitrous oxide is always administered in conjunction with oxygen since on its own it is hypoxic.

8. Description
Nitrous oxide is a nonflammable, colorless and odorless, sweet-tasting gas. It is usually handled as a compressed gas, stored in metal cylinders.

9. Pharmacopeial Specifications

Test	PhEur 1985	USP XXII
Identification	+	+
Acidity or alkalinity	+	—
Carbon dioxide	≤ 300 ppm	≤ 0.03%
Carbon monoxide	≤ 10 ppm	≤ 0.001%

Continued

Test	PhEur 1985	USP XXII
Nitric oxide	—	≤ 1 ppm
Nitrogen dioxide	—	≤ 1 ppm
Nitric oxide and nitrogen dioxide	≤ 2 ppm	—
Halogens	—	≤ 1 ppm
Halogens and hydrogen sulfide	≤ 10 ppm	—
Ammonia	—	≤ 0.0025%
Water	≤ 120 ppm	+
Assay	≥ 98.0%	≥ 99.0%

10. Typical Properties
Boiling point: -88.5°C
Critical pressure: 7.27 MPa (71.7 atm)
Critical temperature: 36.5°C
Density: 1.53 g/cm³
Flammability: nonflammable, but supports combustion.
Freezing point: -90.8°C
Solubility: freely soluble in chloroform, ethanol (95%), ether and oils; soluble 1 in 1.5 volumes of water at 20°C and 101.3 kPa pressure.
Vapor density (absolute): 1.964 g/m³ at standard temperature and pressure.
Vapor density (relative): 1.52 (air = 1)

11. Stability and Storage Conditions
Nitrous oxide is essentially nonreactive and stable except at high temperatures; at a temperature greater than 500°C nitrous oxide decomposes to nitrogen and oxygen. Explosive mixtures may be formed with other gases such as ammonia, hydrogen and other fuels. Nitrous oxide should be stored in a tightly sealed metal cylinder in a cool, dry, place.

12. Incompatibilities
Generally compatible with most materials encountered in pharmaceutical formulations although it may react as a mild oxidizing agent.

13. Method of Manufacture
Nitrous oxide is prepared by heating ammonium nitrate to about 170°C. This reaction also forms water.

14. Safety
Nitrous oxide is most commonly used therapeutically as an anesthetic and analgesic. Reports of adverse reactions to nitrous oxide therefore generally concern its therapeutic use, where relatively large quantities of the gas may be inhaled, rather than its use as an excipient.

The main complications associated with nitrous oxide inhalation occur as a result of hypoxia. Prolonged administration may also be harmful. Nitrous oxide is rapidly absorbed on inhalation.

Although animal studies have shown nitrous oxide to be fetotoxic in rats[1] no fetotoxicity has been shown in man following nitrous oxide anesthesia.[2] However, it has been reported that occupational exposure to high levels of nitrous oxide may adversely affect a woman's ability to become pregnant.[3]

15. Handling Precautions
Handle in accordance with procedures for handling metal cylinders containing liquefied or compressed gases. Eye

protection, gloves and protective clothing are recommended. Nitrous oxide is an anesthetic gas and should be handled in a well-ventilated environment. In the UK, the recommended long-term (8-hour TWA) occupational exposure limit for nitrous oxide is 180 mg/m^3 (100 ppm).[4]

16. Regulatory Status

GRAS listed. Accepted for use as a food additive in Europe. Included in nonparenteral medicines licensed in the UK and US.

17. Pharmacopeias

Aust, Br, Braz, Chin, Cz, Egypt, Eur, Fr, Ger, Gr, Hung, Ind, It, Jpn, Neth, Nord, Port, Rus, Swiss, Turk, US and Yug.

18. Related Substances

Carbon Dioxide; Nitrogen.

A mixture of 50% nitrous oxide and 50% oxygen (*Entonox*, BOC) is commonly used as an analgesic administered by inhalation.

19. Comments

-

20. Specific References

1. Lane GA, et al. Anesthetics as teratogens: nitrous oxide is fetotoxic, xenon is not. Science 1980; 210: 899-901.
2. Aldridge LM, Tunstall ME. Nitrous oxide and the fetus: a review and the results of a retrospective study of 175 cases of anesthesia for insertion of Shirodkar suture. Br J Anaesth 1986; 58: 1348-1356.
3. Rowland AS, et al. Reduced fertility among women employed as dental assistants exposed to high levels of nitrous oxide. N Eng J Med 1992; 327: 993-997.
4. Health and Safety Executive. EH40/93: occupational exposure limits 1993. London: HMSO, 1993.

21. General References

Johnson MA. The aerosol handbook, 2nd edition. New Jersey: WE Dorland Co, 1982: 361-372.

Mintzer H. Aerosols. In: Martin FW, editor. Dispensing of medication, 7th edition. Easton: Mack Publishing Co, 1971.

Sanders PA. Handbook of aerosol technology, 2nd edition. New York: Van Nostrand Reinhold Company, 1979, 44-54.

Sciarra JJ. The science and technology of aerosol packaging. New York: John Wiley and Sons, 1974: 137-145.

Sciarra JJ. Pharmaceutical and cosmetic aerosols. J Pharm Sci 1974; 63: 1815-1837.

Sciarra JJ. Pharmaceutical aerosols. In: Lachman L, Lieberman HA, Kanig JL, editors. The theory and practice of industrial pharmacy, 3rd edition. Philadelphia: Lea and Febiger, 1986: 589-591.

Sciarra JJ, Cutie AJ. Pharmaceutical aerosols. In: Banker GS, Rhodes CT, editors. Modern pharmaceutics, 2nd edition. New York: Marcel Dekker Inc, 1990: 605-634.

22. Authors

UK: PJ Davies.
USA: JJ Sciarra.

Oleic Acid

1. Nonproprietary Names
BP: Oleic acid
USPNF: Oleic acid

2. Synonyms
Crodolene; elaic acid; *Emersol*; *Glycon*; *Groco*; *Hy-Phi*; *Industrene*; *Metaupon*; *Neo-Fat*; cis-9-octadecenoic acid; 9,10-octadecenoic acid; oleinic acid; *Priolene*.

3. Chemical Name and CAS Registry Number
(Z)-9-Octadecenoic acid [112-80-1]

4. Empirical Formula   Molecular Weight
$C_{18}H_{34}O_2$ 282.47

5. Structural Formula
$CH_3(CH_2)_7CH=CH(CH_2)_7COOH$

6. Functional Category
Emulsifying agent; skin penetrant.

7. Applications in Pharmaceutical Formulation or Technology
Oleic acid is used as an emulsifying agent in foods and topical pharmaceutical formulations. It has also been used as penetration enhancer in transdermal formulations,[1-6] to improve the bioavailability of poorly water soluble drugs in tablet formulations,[7] and as part of a vehicle in soft gelatin capsules.
Oleic acid labelled with ^{131}I and ^3H is used in medical imaging.

8. Description
A yellowish to pale brown, oily liquid with a characteristic odor.

9. Pharmacopeial Specifications

Test	BP 1993	USPNF XVII
Specific gravity	0.889-0.895	0.889-0.895
Congealing temperature	4-10°C	$\leqslant 10°C$
Residue on ignition	—	$\leqslant 0.01\%$
Sulfated ash	$\leqslant 0.1\%$	—
Mineral acids	+	+
Neutral fat or mineral oil	+	+
Acid value	195-202	196-204
Iodine value	85-95	85-95

10. Typical Properties
Autoignition temperature: 363°C
Boiling point: 286°C at 13.3 kPa (100 mmHg) (decomposition at 80-100°C)
Density: 0.895 g/cm^3
Flash point: 189°C
Melting point: 4°C
Refractive index: $n_D^{26} = 1.4585$

Solubility: very soluble in benzene, chloroform, ethanol (95%), ether, hexane, and fixed and volatile oils; practically insoluble in water.
Vapor pressure: 133 Pa (1 mmHg) at 176.5°C
Viscosity (dynamic): 26 mPa s (26 cP) at 25°C

11. Stability and Storage Conditions
On exposure to air oleic acid darkens in color and its odor becomes more pronounced.
Oleic acid should be stored in a well-filled, well-closed container, protected from light, in a cool, dry, place.

12. Incompatibilities
Incompatible with aluminum, calcium, heavy metals, iodine solutions, perchloric acid and oxidizing agents. Oleic acid reacts with alkalis to form soaps.

13. Method of Manufacture
Oleic acid is obtained by the hydrolysis of various animal and vegetable fats or oils, such as olive oil, followed by separation of the liquid acids. It consists chiefly of (Z)-9-octadecenoic acid. Oleic acid which is to be used systemically should be prepared from edible sources.

14. Safety
Oleic acid is used in oral and topical pharmaceutical formulations.
In vitro tests have shown that oleic acid causes rupture of red blood cells (hemolysis) and intravenous injection or ingestion of a large quantity of oleic acid can therefore be harmful. Oleic acid is a moderate skin irritant; it should not be used in eye preparations.
An acceptable daily intake for the calcium, sodium and potassium salts of oleic acid was not specified by the WHO since the total daily intake of these materials in foods was such that they did not pose a hazard to health.[8]
LD_{50} (mouse, IV): 0.23 g/kg[9]
LD_{50} (rat, IV): 2.4 mg/kg
LD_{50} (rat, oral): 74 g/kg

15. Handling Precautions
Observe normal precautions appropriate to the circumstances and quantity of material handled. Gloves and eye protection are recommended.

16. Regulatory Status
GRAS listed. Included in the FDA Inactive Ingredients Guide (inhalations, tablets and topical preparations). Included in nonparenteral medicines licensed in the UK.

17. Pharmacopeias
Aust, Br, Braz, Egypt, Hung, Ind, Mex, Swiss and USPNF. Also in BP Vet.

18. Related Substances
Ethyl Oleate.

19. Comments
Several grades of oleic acid are commercially available ranging in color from pale yellow to reddish brown. Different grades become turbid at varying temperatures dependant upon the amount of saturated acid present. Usually, oleic acid contains

7-12% saturated acids, such as stearic and palmitic acid, together with other unsaturated acids, such as linoleic acid.

20. Specific References

1. Cooper ER, Merritt EW, Smith RL. Effect of fatty acids and alcohols on the penetration of acyclovir across human skin in vitro. J Pharm Sci 1985; 74: 688-689.
2. Francoeur ML, Golden GM, Potts RO. Oleic acid: its effects on stratum corneum in relation to (trans)dermal drug delivery. Pharm Res 1990; 7: 621-627.
3. Lewis D, Hadgraft J. Mixed monolayers of dipalmitoylphosphatidylcholine with azone or oleic acid at the air-water interface. Int J Pharmaceutics 1990; 65: 211-218.
4. Niazy EM. Influence of oleic acid and other permeation promoters on transdermal delivery of dihydroergotamine through rabbit skin. Int J Pharmaceutics 1991; 67: 97-100.
5. Ongpipattanakul B, Burnette RR, Potts RO, Francoeur ML. Evidence that oleic acid exists in a separate phase within stratum corneum lipids. Pharm Res 1991; 8: 350-354.
6. Walker M, Hadgraft J. Oleic acid: membrane fluidiser or fluid within the membrane? Int J Pharmaceutics 1991; 71: R1-R4.
7. Tokumura T, Tsushima Y, Tatsuishi K, Kayamo M, Machida Y, Nagai T. Enhancement of the oral bioavailability of cinnarizine in oleic acid in beagle dogs. J Pharm Sci 1987; 76: 286-288.
8. FAO/WHO. Evaluation of certain food additives and contaminants. Thirty-third report of the joint FAO/WHO expert committee on food additives. Tech Rep Ser Wld Hlth Org 1989; No. 776.
9. Sweet DV, editor. Registry of toxic effects of chemical substances. Cincinnati: US Department of Health, 1987.

21. General References

—

22. Authors

UK: PJ Weller.

Paraffin

1. Nonproprietary Names
BP: Hard paraffin
USPNF: Paraffin

2. Synonyms
905 (mineral hydrocarbons); hard wax; paraffinum durum; paraffinum solidum; paraffin wax.
See also Section 17.

3. Chemical Name and CAS Registry Number
Paraffin [8002-74-2]

4. Empirical Formula   Molecular Weight
Paraffin is a purified mixture of solid saturated hydrocarbons having the general formula C_nH_{2n+2}, and is obtained from petroleum or shale oil.

5. Structural Formula
See Section 4.

6. Functional Category
Ointment base; stiffening agent.

7. Applications in Pharmaceutical Formulation or Technology
Paraffin is mainly used in topical pharmaceutical formulations as a component of creams and ointments. In ointments, it may be used to increase the melting point of a formulation or to add stiffness. Paraffin is additionally used as a coating agent for capsules and tablets and is used in some food applications.

8. Description
Paraffin is an odorless and tasteless, translucent, colorless or white solid. It feels slightly greasy to the touch and may show a brittle fracture. Microscopically, it is a mixture of bundles of microcrystals. Paraffin burns with a luminous, sooty flame. When melted, paraffin is essentially free from fluorescence in daylight; a slight odor may be apparent.

9. Pharmacopeial Specifications

Test	BP 1993	USPNF XVII
Identification	+	+
Congealing range	50-57°C	47-65°C
Reaction	—	+
Readily carbonizable substances	—	+
Sulfated ash	⩽ 0.1%	—
Acidity or alkalinity	+	—

10. Typical Properties
Density: ≈ 0.84-0.89 g/cm³ at 20°C
Melting point: various grades with different specified melting ranges are commercially available.
Solubility: soluble in chloroform, ether, volatile oils and most warm fixed oils; slightly soluble in ethanol; practically insoluble in acetone, ethanol (95%) and water. Paraffin can be mixed with most waxes if melted and cooled.

11. Stability and Storage Conditions
Paraffin is stable, although repeated melting and congealing may alter its physical properties. Paraffin should be stored at a temperature not exceeding 40°C in well-closed container.

12. Incompatibilities
—

13. Method of Manufacture
Paraffin is manufactured by the distillation of crude petroleum or shale oil, followed by purification by acid treatment and filtration. Paraffins with different properties may be produced by controlling the distillation and subsequent congealing conditions.
Synthetic paraffin, synthesized from carbon monoxide and hydrogen is also available, *see* Section 18.

14. Safety
Paraffin is generally regarded as an essentially nontoxic and nonirritant material when used in topical ointments and as a coating agent for tablets and capsules. However, granulomatous reactions (paraffinomas) may occur following injection of paraffin into tissue for cosmetic purposes or to relieve pain.[1-3]
See also Mineral Oil for further information.

15. Handling Precautions
Observe normal precautions appropriate to the circumstances and quantity of material handled. In the UK, the recommended occupational exposure limits for paraffin wax fumes are 2 mg/m³ long-term (8-hour TWA) and 6 mg/m³ short-term.[4]

16. Regulatory Status
Accepted in the UK for use in certain food applications. Included in the FDA Inactive Ingredients Guide (oral capsules and tablets, topical emulsions, and ointments). Included in nonparenteral medicines licensed in the UK.

17. Pharmacopeias
Aust, Br, Chin, Egypt, Fr, Ger, Hung, Ind, It, Jpn, Mex, Neth, Nord and USPNF. Also in BP Vet.
Note that the title paraffinum solidum, in certain pharmacopeias (Span, Swiss and Yug) refers to ceresin.

18. Related Substances
Ceresin; Light Mineral Oil; Microcrystalline Wax; Mineral Oil; Petrolatum; synthetic paraffin.

Ceresin
Comments: see Microcrystalline Wax.

Synthetic paraffin
Molecular weight: 400-1400
Pharmacopeias: USPNF.
Appearance: a hard, odorless, white wax consisting of a mixture of mostly long-chain, unbranched, saturated hydrocarbons along with a small amount of branched hydrocarbons.
Comments: the USPNF (Suppl 5) states that synthetic paraffin is synthesized by the Fischer-Tropsch process from carbon monoxide and hydrogen, which are catalytically converted to a mixture of paraffin hydrocarbons. The lower molecular weight fractions are removed by distillation and the residue is

hydrogenated and further treated by percolation through activated charcoal. This mixture may be fractionated into its components by a solvent separation method. Synthetic paraffin may contain not more than 0.005% of a suitable antioxidant.

19. Comments

The more highly purified waxes are used in preference to paraffin in many applications because of their specifically controlled physical properties such as, hardness, malleability and melting range.

20. Specific References

1. Crosbie RB, Kaufman HD. Self-inflicted oleogranuloma of breast. Br Med J 1967; 3: 840-841.
2. Bloem JJ, van der Waal I. Paraffinoma of the face: a diagnostic and therapeutic problem. Oral Surg 1974; 38: 675-680.
3. Greaney MG, Jackson PR. Oleogranuloma of the rectum produced by Lasonil ointment. Br Med J 1977; 2: 997-998.
4. Health and Safety Executive. EH40/93: occupational exposure limits 1993. London: HMSO, 1993.

21. General References

—

22. Authors

USA: ZT Chowhan.

Peanut Oil

1. Nonproprietary Names

BP: Arachis oil
PhEur: Arachidis oleum
USPNF: Peanut oil

2. Synonyms

Calchem IVO-112; earthnut oil; groundnut oil; katchung oil; *Lipex 101*; nut oil.

3. Chemical Name and CAS Registry Number

Peanut oil [8002-03-7]

4. Empirical Formula   Molecular Weight

A typical analysis of refined peanut oil indicates the composition of the acids, present as glycerides, to be: arachidic acid 2.4%; behenic acid 3.1%; palmitic acid 8.3%; stearic acid 3.1%; lignoceric acid 1.1%; linoleic acid 26.0% and oleic acid 56.0%.[1]

5. Structural Formula

See Section 4.

6. Functional Category

Oleaginous vehicle; solvent.

7. Applications in Pharmaceutical Formulation or Technology

Peanut oil is used as an excipient in pharmaceutical formulations primarily as a solvent for sustained-release intramuscular injections. It is also used as a vehicle for topical preparations and as a solvent for vitamins and hormones.

Therapeutically, emulsions containing peanut oil have been used in nutrition regimens, in enemas as a fecal softener and in otic drops to soften ear wax. Peanut oil is also used as an edible oil.

8. Description

Peanut oil is a colorless or pale yellow colored liquid which has a faint nutty odor and a bland, nutty taste. At about 3°C it becomes cloudy, whilst at lower temperatures it partially solidifies.

9. Pharmacopeial Specifications

Test	PhEur 1984	USPNF XVII
Identification	+	+
Specific gravity	0.912-0.918	0.912-0.920
Refractive index	—	1.462-1.464
Heavy metals	—	⩽ 0.001%
Cottonseed oil	—	+
Sesame oil	+	—
Foreign fixed oils	+	—
Semi-drying oils	+	—
Rancidity	—	+
Solidification range of fatty acids	—	26-33°C

Continued

Test	PhEur 1984	USPNF XVII
Free fatty acids	—	+
Acid value	⩽ 0.5	—
Iodine value	—	84-100
Peroxide value	⩽ 5.0	—
Saponification value	—	185-195
Alkaline impurities	+	—
Unsaponifiable matter	⩽1.0%	⩽ 1.5%
Water	⩽ 0.3%	—

10. Typical Properties

Autoignition temperature: 443°C
Density: 0.910-0.915 g/cm^3 at 25°C. *See also* HPE Data.
Flash point: 283°C
Freezing point: -5°C
Hydroxyl value: 2.5-9.5
Interfacial tension: 19.9 mN/m at 25°C[2]
Refractive index: n_D^{25} = 1.466-1.470
Solubility: very slightly soluble in ethanol (95%); soluble in benzene, carbon tetrachloride and oils; miscible with carbon disulfide, chloroform, ether and hexane.
Surface tension: 37.5 mN/m at 25°C[2]
Viscosity (dynamic):
35.2 mPa s (35.2 cP) at 37°C.[2]
See also HPE Data.
Viscosity (kinematic):
39.0 mm^2/s (39.0 cSt) at 37°C[2]

	HPE Laboratory Project Data		
	Method	Lab #	Results
Density	DE-5	30	0.914 g/cm^3 [a]
	DE-5	30	0.915 g/cm^3 [b]
Viscosity	VIS-2	30	39.44 mPa s [a]
	VIS-2	30	42.96 mPa s [b]

Supplier: a. Capital; b. Welch.

11. Stability and Storage Conditions

Peanut oil is an essentially stable material.[3] However, on exposure to air, it can slowly thicken and may become rancid. Solidified peanut oil should be completely melted and mixed before use. Peanut oil may be sterilized by aseptic filtration or by dry heat, e.g. maintaining it at 150°C for one hour.[4]

Peanut oil should be stored in a well-filled, airtight, light-resistant container, at a temperature not exceeding 40°C. Material intended for use in parenteral dosage forms should be stored in a glass container.

12. Incompatibilities

Peanut oil may be saponified by alkali hydroxides.

13. Method of Manufacture

Refined peanut oil is obtained from the seeds of *Arachis hypogaea* Linné (Fam. Leguminosae). The seeds are separated from the peanut shells and are exposed to powerful expression in a hydraulic press. The crude oil thus obtained, which has a light yellow to light brown color, is then purified to make it suitable for food or pharmaceutical purposes.

14. Safety

Peanut oil is used mainly in intramuscular injections and topical pharmaceutical formulations. It is also consumed as an edible oil.

Peanut oil is mildly laxative at a dosage of 15-60 mL orally or 100-500 mL rectally, as an enema.

Adverse reactions to peanut oil include severe allergic skin rashes in infants fed milk formulas containing peanut oil[5,6] and anaphylactic shock following consumption of peanut butter.[7] It has therefore been suggested, in order to avoid sensitization in infancy, that peanut oil should be banned from infant feeds or medications.[5-7]

Peanut oil is harmful if administered intravenously and it should not be used in such formulations.[8]

15. Handling Precautions

Observe normal precautions appropriate to the circumstances and quantity of material handled. Spillages of peanut oil are slippery and should be covered with an inert absorbent material prior to disposal.

16. Regulatory Status

Included in the FDA Inactive Ingredients Guide (IM injections, intratracheal suspensions, oral capsules and vaginal emulsions). Included in parenteral and nonparenteral medicines licensed in the UK.

17. Pharmacopeias

Aust, Br, Cz, Egypt, Eur, Fr, Ger, Gr, Ind, It, Jpn, Mex, Neth, Nord, Port, Swiss and USPNF. Also in the BP Vet.

18. Related Substances

Canola Oil; Corn Oil; Cottonseed Oil; Sesame Oil; Soybean Oil.

19. Comments

–

20. Specific References

1. Allen A, Padley GH, Whalley GR. Fatty acid composition of some soapmaking fats and oils. Part 4: groundnut (peanut oil). Soap Perfum Cosm 1969; 42: 725-726.
2. Howard JR, Hadgraft J. The clearance of oily vehicles following intramuscular and subcutaneous injections in rabbits. Int J Pharmaceutics 1983; 16: 31-39.
3. Selles E, Ruiz A. Study of the stability of peanut oil [in Spanish]. Ars Pharm 1981; 22: 421-427.
4. Pasquale D, Jaconia D, Eisman P, Lachman L. A study of sterilizing conditions for injectable oils. Bull Parent Drug Assoc 1964; 18(3): 1-11.
5. Moneret-Vautrin DA, Hatahet R, Kanny G, Ait-Djafer Z. Allergenic peanut oil in milk formulas [letter]. Lancet 1991; 338: 1149.
6. Brown HM. Allergenic peanut oil in milk formulas [letter]. Lancet 1991; 338: 1523.
7. De Montis G, Gendrel D, Chemillier-Truong M, Dupont C. Sensitization to peanut and vitamin D oily preparations [letter]. Lancet 1993; 341: 1411.
8. Lynn KL. Acute rhabdomyolysis and acute renal failure after intravenous self-administration of peanut oil. Br Med J 1975; 4: 385-386.

21. General References

–

22. Authors

USA: KS Alexander.

Petrolatum

1. Nonproprietary Names

BP: Yellow soft paraffin
USP: Petrolatum

2. Synonyms

905 (mineral hydrocarbons); mineral jelly; petroleum jelly; *Snow white*; *Soft white*; vaselinum flavum; yellow petrolatum; yellow petroleum jelly.

3. Chemical Name and CAS Registry Number

Petrolatum [8009-03-8]

4. Empirical Formula   Molecular Weight

Petrolatum is a purified mixture of semisolid saturated hydrocarbons having the general formula C_nH_{2n+2}, and is obtained from petroleum. The hydrocarbons consist mainly of branched and unbranched chains although some cyclic alkanes and aromatic molecules with paraffin side chains may also be present.

5. Structural Formula

See Section 4.

6. Functional Category

Emollient; ointment base.

7. Applications in Pharmaceutical Formulation or Technology

Petrolatum is mainly used in topical pharmaceutical formulations as an emollient ointment base; it is poorly absorbed by the skin. Petrolatum is also used in creams and transdermal formulations and as an ingredient in lubricant formulations for medicated confectionery together with mineral oil.

Therapeutically, sterile gauze dressings containing petrolatum may be used for non-adherent wound dressings or as a packing material. Petrolatum is additionally widely used in cosmetics and in some food applications.

Use	Concentration (%)
Emollient topical creams	10-30
Topical emulsions	4-25
Topical ointments	up to 100

8. Description

Petrolatum is a pale yellow to yellow colored, translucent, soft unctuous mass. It is odorless, tasteless and not more than slightly fluorescent by daylight, even when melted.

9. Pharmacopeial Specifications

Test	BP 1993	USP XXII
Specific gravity at 60°C	—	0.815-0.880
Melting range	—	38-60°C
Drop point	42-60°C	—
Consistency	—	+

Test	BP 1993	USP XXII
Alkalinity	+	+
Acidity	+	+
Residue on ignition	—	$\leqslant 0.1\%$
Sulfated ash	$\leqslant 0.1\%$	—
Organic acids	—	+
Polycyclic aromatic hydrocarbons	+	—
Foreign organic matter	+	—
Fixed oils, fats and rosin	—	+
Color	—	+
Light absorption	+	—

10. Typical Properties

Refractive index: $n_D^{60} = 1.460\text{-}1.474$
Solubility: practically insoluble in acetone, ethanol, hot or cold ethanol (95%), glycerin and water; soluble in benzene, carbon disulfide, chloroform, ether, hexane and most fixed and volatile oils.
Viscosity (dynamic): the rheological properties of petrolatum are determined by the ratio of the unbranched chains to the branched chains and cyclic components of the mixture. Petrolatum contains relatively high amounts of branched and cyclic hydrocarbons, in contrast to paraffin, which accounts for its softer character and makes it an ideal ointment base.[1-4]

11. Stability and Storage Conditions

Petrolatum is an inherently stable material due to the unreactive nature of its hydrocarbon components; most stability problems occur due to the presence of small quantities of impurities. On exposure to light these impurities may be oxidized to discolor the petrolatum and produce an undesirable odor. The extent of the oxidation varies depending upon the source of the petrolatum and the degree of refinement. Oxidation may be inhibited by the inclusion of a suitable antioxidant such as butylated hydroxyanisole, butylated hydroxytoluene or alpha tocopherol.

Petrolatum should not be heated for extended periods above the temperature necessary to achieve complete fluidity (approximately 70°C). *See also* Section 19.

Petrolatum may be sterilized by dry heat. Although petrolatum may also be sterilized by gamma irradiation this process affects the physical properties of the petrolatum such as swelling, discoloration, odor and rheological behavior.[5,6]

Petrolatum should be stored in a well-closed container, protected from light, in a cool, dry, place.

12. Incompatibilities

Petrolatum is an inert material with few incompatibilities.

13. Method of Manufacture

Petrolatum is manufactured from the semisolid residue that remains after the steam or vacuum distillation of petroleum.[7] This residue is dewaxed and/or blended with stock from other sources, along with lighter fractions, to give a product with the desired consistency. Final purification is performed by a combination of high-pressure hydrogenation or sulfuric acid treatment followed by filtration through adsorbents. A suitable antioxidant may be added.

14. Safety

Petrolatum is mainly used in topical pharmaceutical formulations and is generally considered to be a nonirritant and nontoxic material.

Animal studies, in mice, have shown petrolatum to be nontoxic and noncarcinogenic following administration of a single subcutaneous 100 mg dose. Similarly, no adverse effects were observed in a two-year feeding study with rats fed a diet containing 5% of petrolatum blends.[8]

Although petrolatum is generally nonirritant in humans following topical application rare instances of allergic hypersensitivity reactions have been reported,[9-11] as have cases of acne, in susceptible individuals following repeated use on facial skin.[12] However, given the widespread use of petrolatum in topical products there are few reports of irritant reactions. The allergic components of petrolatum appear to be polycyclic aromatic hydrocarbons present as impurities. The quantities of these materials found in petrolatum vary depending upon the source and degree of refining. Hypersensitivity appears to occur less with white petrolatum and it is therefore the preferred material for use in cosmetics and pharmaceuticals.

Petrolatum has also been tentatively implicated in the formation of spherulosis of the upper respiratory tract following use of a petrolatum based ointment packing after surgery.[13] Other adverse reactions to petrolatum include granulomas (paraffinomas) following injection into soft tissue.[14] Also, when taken orally petrolatum acts as a mild laxative and may inhibit the absorption of lipids and lipid-soluble nutrients. For further information *see* Mineral Oil and Paraffin.

15. Handling Precautions

Observe normal precautions appropriate to the circumstances and quantity of material handled. For recommended occupational exposure limits *see* Mineral Oil and Paraffin.

16. Regulatory Status

GRAS listed. Accepted for use in certain food applications in the UK. Included in the FDA Inactive Ingredients Guide (ophthalmic preparations, oral capsules and tablets, otic, topical and transdermal preparations). Included in nonparenteral medicines licensed in the UK.

17. Pharmacopeias

Aust, Br, Chin, Cz, Egypt, Hung, Ind, Jpn, Neth, Nord, Swiss, US and Yug. Also in BP Vet.

Note that some pharmacopeias use the title vaselinum flavum to describe petrolatum. In the UK, USA, and many other countries, Vaseline is a trademark.

18. Related Substances

Mineral Oil; Paraffin; Petrolatum and Lanolin Alcohols; white petrolatum.

White petrolatum

Synonyms: vaselinum album; white petroleum jelly; white soft paraffin.

Appearance: white petrolatum is a white-colored, translucent, soft unctuous mass. It is odorless and tasteless and not more than slightly fluorescent by daylight, even when melted.

Method of Manufacture: white petrolatum is petrolatum that has been highly refined so that it is wholly or nearly decolorized.

Pharmacopeias: Aust, Br, Chin, Cz, Egypt, Fr, Ger, Hung, Ind, It, Jpn, Mex, Neth, Nord, Rom, Swiss, Turk, US and Yug. Also in BP Vet.

Comments: white petrolatum is associated with fewer instances of hypersensitivity reactions and is the preferred petrolatum for use in cosmetics and pharmaceuticals, *see* Section 14.

19. Comments

Various grades of petrolatum are commercially available which vary in their physical properties depending upon their source and refining process. Petrolatum obtained from different sources may therefore behave differently in a formulation.[15]

Care is required in heating petrolatum because of its large coefficient of thermal expansion. It has been shown by both rheological and spectrophotometric methods that petrolatum undergoes phase transition at temperatures between 30-40°C. Additives, such as microcrystalline wax, may be used to add body to petrolatum.

20. Specific References

1. Boylan JC. Rheological estimation of the spreading characteristics of pharmaceutical semisolids. J Pharm Sci 1967; 56: 1164-1169.
2. Longworth AR, French JD. Quality control of white soft paraffin. J Pharm Pharmacol 1969; 21(Suppl): 1S-5S.
3. Barry BW, Grace AJ. Grade variation in the rheology of white soft paraffin BP. J Pharm Pharmacol 1970; 22(Suppl): 147S-156S.
4. Barry BW, Grace AJ. Structural, rheological and textural properties of soft paraffins. J Texture Studies 1971; 2: 259-279.
5. Jacob BP, Leupin K. Sterilization of eye-nose ointments by gamma radiation [in German]. Pharm Acta Helv 1974; 49: 12-20.
6. Davis SS, Khanderia MS, Adams I, Colley IR, Cammack J, Sanford P. Effect of gamma radiation on rheological properties of pharmaceutical semisolids. J Texture Studies 1977; 8: 61-80.
7. Schindler H. Petrolatum for drugs and cosmetics. Drug Cosmet Ind 1961; 89(1): 36, 37, 76, 78-80, 82.
8. Oser BL, Oser M, Carson S, Sternberg SS. Toxicologic studies of petrolatum in mice and rats. Toxicol Appl Pharmacol 1965; 7: 382-401.
9. Dooms-Goossens A, Degreef H. Contact allergy to petrolatums I: sensitivity capacity of different brands of yellow and white petrolatums. Contact Dermatitis 1983; 9: 175-185.
10. Dooms-Goossens A, Degreef H. Contact allergy to petrolatums II: attempts to identify the nature of the allergens. Contact Dermatitis 1983; 9: 247-256.
11. Dooms-Goossens A, Dooms M. Contact allergy to petrolatums III: allergenicity prediction and pharmacopoeial requirements. Contact Dermatitis 1983; 9: 352-359.
12. Verhagen AR. Pomade acne in black skin [letter]. Arch Dermatol 1974; 110: 465.
13. Rosai J. The nature of myospherulosis of the upper respiratory tract. Am J Clin Pathol 1978; 69: 475-481.
14. Crosbie RB, Kaufman HD. Self-inflicted oleogranuloma of breast. Br Med J 1967; 3: 840-841.
15. Kneczke M, Landersjö L, Lundgren P, Führer C. *In vitro* release of salicylic acid from two different qualities of white petrolatum. Acta Pharm Suec 1986; 23: 193-204.

21. General References

Barker G. New trends in formulating with mineral oil and petrolatum. Cosmet Toilet 1977; 92(1): 43-46.
Davis SS. Viscoelastic properties of pharmaceutical semisolids I: ointment bases. J Pharm Sci 1969; 58: 412-418.

De Muynck C, Lalljie SPD, Sandra P, De Rudder D, Van Aerde P, Remon JP. Chemical and physicochemical characterization of petrolatums used in eye ointment formulations. J Pharm Pharmacol 1993; 45: 500-503.

De Rudder D, Remon JP, Van Aerde P. Structural stability of ophthalmic ointments containing soft paraffin. Drug Dev Ind Pharm 1987; 13: 1799-1806.

Smolinske SC. Handbook of food, drug, and cosmetic excipients. Boca Raton, FL: CRC Press Inc, 1992: 265-269.

Sucker H. Petrolatums - technological properties and quality assessment. Cosmet Perfum 1974; 89(2): 37-43.

22. Authors

UK: PJ Weller.

Petrolatum and Lanolin Alcohols

1. Nonproprietary Names
None adopted.

2. Synonyms
Amerchol CAB; *Forlan 200*; petrolatum and wool alcohols; white soft paraffin and lanolin alcohols; yellow soft paraffin and lanolin alcohols.

3. Chemical Name and CAS Registry Number
Petrolatum [8009-03-8] and
Lanolin alcohols [8027-33-6]

4. Empirical Formula   Molecular Weight
A mixture of petrolatum and lanolin alcohols.

5. Structural Formula
See Section 4.

6. Functional Category
Emollient; ointment base; plasticizer.

7. Applications in Pharmaceutical Formulation or Technology
Petrolatum and lanolin alcohols is a soft solid used in topical pharmaceutical formulations and cosmetics as an ointment base with emollient properties. It is also used in the preparation of creams and lotions. Petrolatum and lanolin alcohols can be used to absorb wound exudates.

Use	Concentration (%)
Absorption base component	10.0-50.0
Emollient and plasticizer in ointments	5.0-50.0

8. Description
A pale ivory-colored, soft solid with a faint, characteristic sterol odor.

9. Pharmacopeial Specifications
—

10. Typical Properties
Acid value: ⩽ 1
Arsenic: ⩽ 2 ppm
Ash: ⩽ 0.2%
Heavy metals: ⩽ 20 ppm
HLB value: ≈ 9
Hydroxyl value: 11-15
Melting range: 40-46°C
Microbiological count: the total bacterial count, when packaged, is less than 10 per gram of sample.
Moisture content: ⩽ 0.2%
Saponification value: ⩽ 2

Solubility: soluble 1 in 20 parts of chloroform, and 1 in 100 parts of mineral oil, precipitates at higher concentrations. Precipitation occurs in ethanol (95%), hexane, and water. May be dispersed in isopropyl palmitate. Forms a gel in castor oil and corn oil.

11. Stability and Storage Conditions
Petrolatum and lanolin alcohols is stable and should be stored in a well-closed container in a cool, dry, place.

12. Incompatibilities
Lanolin alcohols is incompatible with coal tar, ichthammol, phenol and resorcinol.

13. Method of Manufacture
Lanolin alcohols is blended together with petrolatum.

14. Safety
Petrolatum and lanolin alcohols is generally regarded as an essentially nontoxic and nonirritant material. However, lanolin alcohols may be irritant to the skin and cause hypersensitivity in some individuals.

15. Handling Precautions
Observe normal precautions appropriate to the circumstances and quantity of material handled.

16. Regulatory Status
Accepted for use in topical pharmaceutical formulations and cosmetics.

17. Pharmacopeias
—

18. Related Substances
Lanolin Alcohols; Mineral Oil and Lanolin Alcohols; lanolin alcohols ointment; Petrolatum.

Lanolin alcohols ointment
Synonyms: *Argobase EU*; wool alcohols ointment.
Appearance: white-colored ointment if prepared using white petrolatum, a yellow-colored ointment if yellow petrolatum is used in its preparation.
Pharmacopeias: Br.
Comments: The BP 1993 describes lanolin alcohols ointment (wool alcohols ointment BP) as a mixture consisting of:

Lanolin alcohols	60 g
Paraffin	240 g
Yellow petrolatum or white petrolatum	100 g
Mineral oil	600 g

However, the proportions of paraffin, petrolatum and mineral oil may be varied to produce an ointment of the desired physical properties.

19. Comments
See individual monographs on Lanolin Alcohols, and Petrolatum for further information.

20. Specific References
—

21. General References

Davis SS. Viscoelastic properties of pharmaceutical semisolids I: ointment bases. J Pharm Sci 1969; 58: 412-418.

22. Authors

USA: S Scheindlin.

Phenol

1. Nonproprietary Names

BP: Phenol
PhEur: Phenolum
USP: Phenol

2. Synonyms

Carbolic acid; hydroxybenzene; oxybenzene; phenic acid; phenyl hydrate; phenyl hydroxide; phenylic acid; phenylic alcohol.

3. Chemical Name and CAS Registry Number

Phenol [108-95-2]

4. Empirical Formula   Molecular Weight

C_6H_6O 94.11

5. Structural Formula

6. Functional Category

Antimicrobial preservative; disinfectant.

7. Applications in Pharmaceutical Formulation or Technology

Phenol is used mainly as an antimicrobial preservative in parenteral pharmaceutical products although it has also been used in topical pharmaceutical formulations and cosmetics. It should not be used to preserve preparations that are to be freeze-dried.[1] Phenol is also widely used as an antiseptic, disinfectant and therapeutic agent.

Use	Concentration (%)
Disinfectant	5.0
Injections (preservative)	0.5
Local anesthetic	0.5-1.0
Mouthwash	up to 1.4

8. Description

Phenol occurs as colorless to light pink, caustic, deliquescent needle-shaped crystals or crystalline masses with a characteristic odor. When heated gently phenol melts forming a highly refractive liquid. The USP XXII permits the addition of a suitable stabilizer; the name and amount of substance used for this purpose must be clearly stated on the label.

9. Pharmacopeial Specifications

Test	PhEur 1989	USP XXII
Identification	+	+
Clarity of solution	+	+

Continued

Test	PhEur 1989	USP XXII
Acidity	+	—
Congealing temperature	40-41°C	⩾ 39°C
Water	—	⩽ 0.5%
Nonvolatile residue	⩽ 0.05%	⩽ 0.05%
Assay	99.0-100.5%	99.0-100.5%

10. Typical Properties

Acidity/alkalinity:
pH = 6.0 (saturated aqueous solution)
Antimicrobial activity: phenol exhibits antimicrobial activity against a wide range of microorganisms such as Gram-negative and Gram-positive bacteria, mycobacteria and some fungi and viruses; it is only very slowly effective against spores. Aqueous solutions of 1% w/v concentration are bacteriostatic while stronger solutions are bactericidal. Phenol shows most activity in acidic solutions; increasing temperature also increases antimicrobial activity. Phenol is inactivated by the presence of organic matter.
Autoignition temperature: 715°C
Boiling point: 181.8°C
Density: 1.071 g/cm^3
Dissociation constant: pK_a = 10 at 25°C
Flash point: 79°C (closed cup)
Explosive limits: 2% lower limit; 9% upper limit.
Freezing point: 40.9°C
Melting point: 43°C
Osmolarity:
a 2.8% w/v solution is iso-osmotic with serum.
Refractive index: n_D^{41} = 1.5425
Solubility:

Solvent	Solubility at 20°C
Chloroform	very soluble
Ethanol (95%)	1 in 6
Ether	very soluble
Fixed oils	very soluble
Glycerin	very soluble
Mineral oil	1 in 70
Volatile oils	very soluble
Water	1 in 12

Vapor density (relative): 3.24 (air = 1)
Vapor pressure: 133 Pa (1 mmHg) at 40°C

11. Stability and Storage Conditions

When exposed to air and light phenol turns a red or brown color, the color being influenced by the presence of metallic impurities. Oxidizing agents also hasten the color change. Aqueous solutions of phenol are stable. Oily solutions for injection may be sterilized in hermetically sealed containers by dry heat. The bulk material should be stored in a well-closed container at a temperature not exceeding 15°C.

12. Incompatibilities

Phenol undergoes a number of chemical reactions characteristic of alcohols; however, it possesses a tautomeric enol structure that is weakly acidic. It will form salts with sodium hydroxide or potassium hydroxide, but not with their carbonates or bicarbonates. Phenol is a reducing agent and is capable of reacting with ferric salts in neutral to acidic solutions to form a greenish colored complex. Phenol decolorizes dilute iodine solutions, forming hydrogen iodide and iodophenol; stronger solutions of iodine react with phenol to form the insoluble 2,4,6-triiodophenol.

Phenol is incompatible with albumin and gelatin since they are precipitated. It forms a liquid or soft mass when triturated with some compounds, e.g. camphor, menthol, thymol, acetaminophen, phenacetin, chloral hydrate, phenazone, ethyl aminobenzoate, methenamine, phenyl salicylate, resorcinol, terpin hydrate, sodium phosphate or other eutectic formers. Phenol also softens cocoa butter in suppository mixtures.

13. Method of Manufacture

Historically, phenol was produced by the distillation of coal tar. Today, phenol is prepared by one of several synthetic methods, e.g. the fusion of sodium benzenesulfonate with sodium hydroxide followed by acidification; the hydrolysis of chlorobenzene by dilute sodium hydroxide at high temperature and pressure to give sodium phenate which on acidification liberates phenol (Dow process); or the catalytic vapor phase reaction of steam and chlorobenzene at 500°C (Raschig process).

14. Safety

Phenol is very corrosive and toxic, the main effects being on the CNS. The lethal human oral dose is estimated to be 1 g for an adult.

Phenol is absorbed from the gastrointestinal tract, skin and mucous membranes and is metabolized to phenylglucuronide and phenyl sulfate which are excreted in the urine.

Although there are a number of reports describing the toxic effects of phenol these largely concern instances of accidental poisoning[2] or adverse reactions during its use as a therapeutic agent.[3,4] Adverse reactions associated with phenol used as a preservative are less likely due to the smaller quantities that are used. It has been suggested however that the body burden of phenol should not exceed 50 mg in a 10-hour period.[5] This amount could be exceeded following administration of large volumes of phenol-preserved medicines.

LD$_{50}$ (mouse, IP): 0.36 g/kg[6]
LD$_{50}$ (mouse, IV): 0.11 g/kg
LD$_{50}$ (mouse, oral): 0.3 g/kg
LD$_{50}$ (mouse, SC): 0.34 g/kg
LD$_{50}$ (rabbit, skin): 0.85 g/kg
LD$_{50}$ (rat, skin): 0.67 g/kg
LD$_{50}$ (rat, IP): 0.25 g/kg
LD$_{50}$ (rat, oral): 0.41 g/kg

15. Handling Precautions

Phenol is toxic in contact with the skin and if swallowed or inhaled and is strongly corrosive, producing possibly irreversible damage to the cornea and severe skin burns. Skin burns are painless due the anesthetic effects of phenol.

Phenol should be handled with caution, particularly when hot, due to the release of corrosive and toxic fumes. The use of fume cupboards, enclosed plants, or other environmental containment is recommended. Protective polyvinyl chloride or rubber clothing is recommended together with gloves, eye protection and respirator. Spillages on the skin or eyes should be washed with copious amounts of water. Affected areas of the skin should be washed with water followed by application of a vegetable oil. Medical attention should be sought.

Phenol poses a slight fire hazard when cold and a moderate hazard when hot and exposed to heat or flame.

In the UK, the occupational exposure limits for phenol are 19 mg/m^3 (5 ppm) long-term (8-hour TWA) and 38 mg/m^3 (10 ppm) short-term (10-minutes).[7] In the US, the permissible exposure limit is 19 mg/m^3 long-term and the recommended exposure limits are 20 mg/m^3 long-term and 60 mg/m^3 maximum, short-term.

16. Regulatory Status

Included in the FDA Inactive Ingredients Guide (injections). Included in medicines licensed in the UK.

17. Pharmacopeias

Aust, Belg, Br, Braz, Chin, Cz, Egypt, Eur, Fr, Ger, Hung, Ind, It, Jpn, Mex, Neth, Nord, Swiss, Turk, US and Yug.

18. Related Substances

Liquefied phenol.

Liquefied phenol

Appearance: liquefied phenol is phenol maintained as a liquid by the presence of 10% of water. It is a colorless liquid, with a characteristic aromatic odor, which may develop a red coloration on exposure to air and light.

Pharmacopeias: Br, Mex and US.

Specific gravity: 1.065 at 25°C

Comments: liquefied phenol is often more convenient to use in a formulation than the crystalline form. However, liquefied phenol should not be used with fixed or mineral oils although the crystalline solid may be used.

19. Comments

Although phenol is soluble in approximately 12 parts of water at ambient temperatures, larger amounts of phenol in water produce a two phase system of phenol solution floating on a lower layer of wet phenol. At 20°C, 100 parts of phenol may be liquefied by the addition of 10 parts of water. At 84°C phenol is miscible with water in all proportions.

20. Specific References

1. WHO. WHO expert committee on biological standardization: thirty-seventh report. Tech Rep Ser Wld Hlth Org 1987; No. 760.
2. Foxall PJD, Bending MR, Gartland KPR, Nicholson JR. Acute renal failure following accidental cutaneous absorption of phenol: application of NMR urinalysis to monitor the disease process. Hum Toxicol 1989; 9: 491-496.
3. Warner MA, Harper JV. Cardiac dysrhythmias associated with chemical peeling with phenol. Anesthesiology 1985; 62: 366-367.
4. Ho S-L, Hollinrake K. Acute epiglottitis and Chloraseptic. Br Med J 1989; 298: 1584.
5. Brancato DJ. Recognizing potential toxicity of phenol. Vet Hum Toxicol 1982; 24: 29-30.
6. Sax NI. Dangerous properties of industrial materials, sixth edition. New York: Van Nostrand Reinhold Company, 1984.
7. Health and Safety Executive. EH40/93: occupational exposure limits 1993. London: HMSO, 1993.

21. General References

Karabit MS. Studies on the evaluation of preservative efficacy V. Effect of concentration of micro-organisms on the antimicrobial activity of phenol. Int J Pharmaceutics 1990; 60: 147-150.

22. Authors

USA: GW Radebaugh.

Phenoxyethanol

1. Nonproprietary Names

BP: Phenoxyethanol
PhEur: Phenoxyethanolum

2. Synonyms

Ethyleneglycol monophenyl ether; β-hydroxyethyl phenyl ether; 1-hydroxy-2-phenoxyethane; *Phenoxetol*; β-phenoxyethyl alcohol.

3. Chemical Name and CAS Registry Number

2-Phenoxyethanol [122-99-6]

4. Empirical Formula   Molecular Weight

$C_8H_{10}O_2$ 138.16

5. Structural Formula

6. Functional Category

Antimicrobial preservative; disinfectant.

7. Applications in Pharmaceutical Formulation or Technology

Phenoxyethanol is an antimicrobial preservative used in cosmetics and topical pharmaceutical formulations at a concentration of 0.5–1.0%; it may also be used as a preservative for vaccines.[1] Therapeutically, a 2.2% solution or 2.0% cream has been used as a disinfectant for superficial wounds and burns.[2-4]
Phenoxyethanol has a narrow spectrum of activity and is thus frequently used in combination with other preservatives, *see* Section 10.

8. Description

Phenoxyethanol is a colorless, slightly viscous liquid with a faint pleasant odor and burning taste.

9. Pharmacopeial Specifications

Test	PhEur 1992
Identification	+
Refractive index	1.537–1.539
Relative density	1.105–1.110
Phenol	⩽ 0.1%
Related substances	+
Assay	99.0–100.5%

10. Typical Properties

Acidity/alkalinity: pH = 6.0 for a 1% v/v aqueous solution.
Antimicrobial activity: phenoxyethanol is an antibacterial preservative effective over a wide pH range against strains of *Pseudomonas aeruginosa* and to a lesser extent against *Proteus vulgaris* and other Gram-negative organisms. It is most frequently used in combination with other preservatives, such as parabens, to obtain a wider spectrum of antimicrobial activity.[5-7] *See also* Section 12. Reported minimum inhibitory concentrations (MICs) are shown below:[8]

Microorganism	MIC (μg/mL)
Aspergillus niger ATCC 16404	3300
Candida albicans ATCC 10231	5400
Escherichia coli ATCC 8739	3600
Pseudomonas aeruginosa ATCC 9027	3200
Staphylococcus aureus ATCC 6538	8500

Autoignition temperature: 135°C
Boiling point: 245.2°C
Flash point: 121°C (open cup)
Melting point: 14°C
Partition coefficients:
Isopropyl palmitate: water = 2.9;
Mineral oil: water = 0.3;
Peanut oil: water = 2.6.
Refractive index: n_D^{20} = 1.537–1.539
Solubility:

Solvent	Solubility at 20°C
Acetone	miscible
Ethanol (95%)	miscible
Glycerin	miscible
Isopropyl palmitate	1 in 26
Mineral oil	1 in 143
Olive oil	1 in 50
Peanut oil	1 in 50
Water	1 in 43

Specific gravity: 1.11 at 20°C

11. Stability and Storage Conditions

Aqueous phenoxyethanol solutions are stable and may be sterilized by autoclaving. The bulk material is also stable and should be stored in a well-closed container in a cool, dry, place.

12. Incompatibilities

The antimicrobial activity of phenoxyethanol may be reduced by interaction with nonionic surfactants and possibly by absorption by polyvinyl chloride.[9]

13. Method of Manufacture

Phenoxyethanol is prepared by treating phenol with ethylene oxide in an alkaline medium.

14. Safety

Phenoxyethanol produces a local anesthetic effect on the lips, tongue and other mucous membranes. The pure material is a moderate irritant to the skin and eyes. In animal studies, a 10% v/v solution was not irritant to rabbit skin and a 2% v/v solution was not irritant to the rabbit eye.[10]
LD$_{50}$ (rabbit, skin): 5 g/kg[11]
LD$_{50}$ (rat, oral): 1.26 g/kg

15. Handling Precautions

Observe normal precautions appropriate to the circumstances and quantity of material handled. Phenoxyethanol may be irritant to the skin and eyes; eye protection and gloves are recommended.

16. Regulatory Status

Included in nonparenteral medicines licensed in the UK.

17. Pharmacopeias

Br and Eur.

18. Related Substances

Chlorophenoxyethanol; phenoxypropanol.

Chlorophenoxyethanol: $C_8H_9ClO_2$
Molecular weight: 172.60
CAS number: [29533-21-9]

Phenoxypropanol: $C_9H_{12}O_2$
Molecular weight: 152.18
CAS number: [4169-04-4]
Synonyms: 1-phenoxypropan-2-ol.

19. Comments

Aqueous solutions are best prepared by shaking phenoxyethanol with hot water until dissolved, followed by cooling and adjusting the volume to the required concentration.

20. Specific References

1. Pivnick H, Tracy JM, Tosoni AL, Glass DG. Preservatives for poliomyelitis (Salk) vaccine III: 2-phenoxyethanol. J Pharm Sci 1964; 53: 899-901.
2. Thomas B, Sykes L, Stickler DJ. Sensitivity of urine-grown cells of *Providencia stuartii* to antiseptics. J Clin Pathol 1978; 31: 929-932.
3. Lawrence JC, Cason JS, Kidson A. Evaluation of phenoxetol-chlorhexidine cream as a prophylactic antibacterial agent in burns. Lancet 1982; i: 1037-1040.
4. Bollag U. Phenoxetol-chlorhexidine cream as a prophylactic antibacterial agent in burns [letter]. Lancet 1982; ii: 106.
5. Abdelaziz AA, El-Nakeeb MA. Sporicidal activity of local anaesthetics and their binary combinations with preservatives. J Clin Pharm Ther 1988; 13: 249-256.
6. Denyer SP, Hugo WB, Harding VD. Synergy in preservative combinations. Int J Pharmaceutics 1985; 25: 245-253.
7. Onawunmi GO. In vitro studies on the antibacterial activity of phenoxyethanol in combination with lemon grass oil. Pharmazie 1988; 43: 42-44.
8. Hall AL. Cosmetically acceptable phenoxyethanol. In: Kabara JJ, editor. Cosmetic and drug preservation principles and practice. New York: Marcel Dekker, 1984: 79-108.
9. Lee MG. Phenoxyethanol absorption by polyvinyl chloride. J Clin Hosp Pharm 1984; 9: 353-355.
10. Nipa Laboratories Ltd. Technical literature: *phenoxetol*, 1992.
11. Sweet DV, editor. Registry of toxic effects of chemical substances. Cincinnati: US Department of Health, 1987.

21. General References

Baird RM. A proposed alternative to calamine cream BPC. Pharm J 1974; 213: 153-154.
Denyer SP, Baird RM, editors. Guide to microbiological control in pharmaceuticals. Chichester: Ellis Horwood Ltd, 1990.
Fitzgerald KA, Davies A, Russell AD. Effect of chlorhexidine and phenoxyethanol, alone and in combination, on leakage from Gram-negative bacteria. J Pharm Pharmacol 1990; 42(Suppl): 104P.
Gilbert P, Beveridge EG, Crone PB. The action of phenoxyethanol upon respiration and dehydrogenase enzyme systems in Escherichia coli. J Pharm Pharmacol 1976; 28(Suppl): 51P.
Hall AL. Phenoxyethanol: a cosmetically acceptable preservative. Cosmet Toilet 1981; 96(3): 83-85.

22. Authors

UK: MC Allwood, PJ Weller.

Phenylethyl Alcohol

1. Nonproprietary Names
USP: Phenylethyl alcohol

2. Synonyms
Benzeneethanol; benzyl carbinol; benzylmethanol; β-hydroxyethyl benzene; phenethanol; β-phenylethyl alcohol; 2-phenylethyl alcohol; phenylethanol; PEA.

3. Chemical Name and CAS Registry Number
2-Phenylethanol [60-12-8]

4. Empirical Formula   Molecular Weight
$C_8H_{10}O$ 122.17

5. Structural Formula

6. Functional Category
Antimicrobial preservative.

7. Applications in Pharmaceutical Formulation or Technology
Phenylethyl alcohol is used as an antimicrobial preservative in parenteral and ophthalmic formulations at 0.25-0.5% v/v concentration; it is generally used in combination with other preservatives.[1,2] Phenylethyl alcohol has also been used on its own as an antimicrobial preservative at concentrations up to 1% v/v in topical preparations. At this concentration, mycoplasmas are inactivated within 20 minutes although enveloped viruses are resistant.[3] Phenylethyl alcohol is also used in flavors and as a perfumery component, especially in rose perfumes.

8. Description
Phenylethyl alcohol is a clear, colorless liquid with an odor of rose oil. It has a burning taste which irritates and then anesthetizes mucous membranes.

9. Pharmacopeial Specifications

Test	USP XXII
Identification	+
Specific gravity	1.017-1.020
Refractive index	1.531-1.534
Residue on ignition	$\leqslant$ 0.005%
Chlorinated compounds	+
Aldehyde	+

10. Typical Properties
Antimicrobial activity: phenylethyl alcohol has moderate antimicrobial activity although it is relatively slow acting; it is not sufficiently active to be used alone.[4] Greatest activity occurs at less than pH 5; it is inactive above pH 8. Synergistic effects have been reported when combined with benzalkonium chloride, chlorhexidine gluconate or diacetate, polymyxin B sulfate and phenylmercuric nitrate.[5-9] With either benzalkonium chloride or chlorhexidine, synergistic effects were observed against *Pseudomonas aeruginosa* and apparently additive effects against Gram-positive organisms. With phenylmercuric nitrate, the effect was additive against *Pseudomonas aeruginosa*. Additive effects against *Pseudomonas cepacia* in combination with either benzalkonium chloride or chlorhexidine have also been reported.[10] *See also* Section 12.
Bacteria: fair activity against Gram-positive bacteria; for *Staphylococcus aureus*, the minimum inhibitory concentration (MIC) may be more than 5 mg/mL. Greater activity is shown against Gram-negative organisms.[11] Typical MIC values are: *Salmonella typhi* 1.25 mg/mL; *Pseudomonas aeruginosa* 2.5 mg/mL; *Escherichia coli* 5.0 mg/mL.
Fungi: poor activity against molds and fungi.
Spores: inactive, e.g. at 0.6% v/v concentration, reported to be ineffective against spores of *Bacillus stearothermophilus* at 100°C for 30 minutes.
Boiling point: 219-221°C
Melting point: -27°C
Partition coefficients:
Chloroform: water = 15.2;
Heptane: water = 0.58;
Octanol: water = 21.5.
Flash point: 102°C (open cup)
Solubility:

Solvent	Solubility at 20°C
Benzyl benzoate	very soluble
Chloroform	very soluble
Diethyl phthalate	very soluble
Ethanol (95%)	very soluble
Ether	very soluble
Fixed oils	very soluble
Glycerin	very soluble
Mineral oil	slightly soluble
Propylene glycol	very soluble
Water	1 in 60

11. Stability and Storage Conditions
Phenylethyl alcohol is stable in bulk, but is volatile and sensitive to light and oxidizing agents. It is reasonably stable in both acidic and alkaline solutions. Aqueous solutions may be sterilized by autoclaving. If stored in low density polyethylene containers, phenylethyl alcohol may be absorbed by the containers. Losses to polypropylene containers have been reported to be insignificant over 12 weeks at 30°C. Sorption to rubber closures is generally small.
The bulk material should be stored in a well-closed container, protected from light, in a cool, dry, place.

12. Incompatibilities
Incompatible with oxidizing agents and protein, e.g. serum. Phenylethyl alcohol is partially inactivated by polysorbates, although this is not as great as the reduction in antimicrobial activity that occurs with parabens and polysorbates.[12]

13. Method of Manufacture
Phenylethyl alcohol is prepared either by reduction of ethyl phenylacetate with sodium in absolute alcohol; hydrogenation

of phenylacetaldehyde in the presence of a nickel catalyst; or by addition of ethylene oxide or ethylene chlorohydrin to phenylmagnesium bromide, followed by hydrolysis. Phenylethyl alcohol also occurs naturally in a number of essential oils, especially rose oil.

14. Safety

Phenylethyl alcohol is used as an antimicrobial preservative in parenteral, topical and ophthalmic preparations and is generally regarded as a nontoxic and nonirritant material. However, at the concentration used to preserve eye-drops (about 0.5% v/v) or above, eye irritation may occur.[13]

LD$_{50}$ (mouse, IP): 0.2 g/kg[14]
LD$_{50}$ (mouse, oral): 0.8 g/kg
LD$_{50}$ (rabbit, skin): 0.79 g/kg
LD$_{50}$ (rat, oral): 1.79 g/kg

15. Handling Precautions

Observe normal precautions appropriate to the circumstances and quantity of material handled. Eye protection and gloves are recommended.

16. Regulatory Status

Included in the FDA Inactive Ingredients Guide (nasal, ophthalmic, otic, topical and vaginal preparations). Included in nonparenteral medicines licensed in the UK.

17. Pharmacopeias

Nord and US.

18. Related Substances

—

19. Comments

—

20. Specific References

1. Goldstein SW. Antibacterial agents in compounded ophthalmic solutions. J Am Pharm Assoc (Pract Pharm) 1953; 14: 498-524.
2. Heller WM, Foss NE, Shay DE and Ichniowski CT. Preservatives in solutions. J Am Pharm Assoc (Pract Pharm) 1955; 16: 29-36.
3. Staal SP, Rowe WP. Differential effect of phenylethyl alcohol on mycoplasmas and enveloped viruses. J Virol 1974; 14: 1620-1622.
4. Kohn SR, Gershenfeld L, Barr M. Effectiveness of antibacterial agents presently employed in ophthalmic preparations as preservatives against *Pseudomonas aeruginosa*. J Pharm Sci 1963; 52: 967-974.
5. Richards RME, McBride RJ. Cross-resistance in *Pseudomonas aeruginosa* resistant to phenylethanol. J Pharm Sci 1972; 61: 1075-1077.
6. Richards RME, McBride RJ. The preservation of ophthalmic solutions with antibacterial combinations. J Pharm Pharmacol 1972; 24: 145-148.
7. Richards RME, McBride RJ. Effect of 3-phenylpropan-1-ol, 2-phenylethanol, and benzyl alcohol on *Pseudomonas aeruginosa*. J Pharm Sci 1973; 62: 585-587.
8. Richards RME, McBride RJ. Enhancement of benzalkonium chloride and chlorhexidine acetate activity against *Pseudomonas aeruginosa* by aromatic alcohols. J Pharm Sci 1973; 62: 2035-2037.
9. Richards RME, McBride RJ. Antipseudomonal effect of polymyxin and phenylethanol. J Pharm Sci 1974; 63: 54-56.
10. Richards RME, Richards JM. *Pseudomonas cepacia* resistance to antibacterials. J Pharm Sci 1979; 68: 1436-1438.
11. Lilley BD, Brewer JH. The selective antibacterial action of phenylethyl alcohol. J Am Pharm Assoc (Sci) 1953; 42: 6-8.
12. Bahal CK, Kostenbauder HB. Interaction of preservatives with macromolecules V: binding of chlorobutanol, benzyl alcohol, and phenylethyl alcohol by nonionic agents. J Pharm Sci 1964; 53: 1027-1029.
13. Boer Y. Irritation by eyedrops containing 2-phenylethanol. Pharm Weekbl (Sci) 1981; 3: 826-827.
14. Sweet DV, editor. Registry of toxic effects of chemical substances. Cincinnati: US Department of Health, 1987.

21. General References

Silver S, Wendt L. Mechanism of action of phenylethyl alcohol: breakdown of the cellular permeability barrier. J Bacteriol 1967; 93: 560-566.

22. Authors

UK: MC Allwood, R Baird.

Phenylmercuric Acetate

SEM: 1
Excipient: Phenylmercuric acetate
Manufacturer: Eastman Fine Chemicals
Magnification: 600x

1. Nonproprietary Names
USPNF: Phenylmercuric acetate

2. Synonyms
(Acetato-*O*)phenylmercury; acetoxyphenylmercury; phenylmercury acetate; PMA.

3. Chemical Name and CAS Registry Number
(Acetato)phenylmercury [62-38-4]

4. Empirical Formula   Molecular Weight
$C_8H_8HgO_2$ 336.74

5. Structural Formula

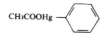

6. Functional Category
Antimicrobial preservative; antiseptic.

7. Applications in Pharmaceutical Formulation or Technology
Phenylmercuric acetate is used as an alternative antimicrobial preservative to phenylmercuric borate or phenylmercuric nitrate in cosmetics and pharmaceuticals. It may be used in preference to phenylmercuric nitrate due to its greater solubility.
Phenylmercuric acetate is also used as a spermicide.
See also Phenylmercuric Nitrate.

Use	Concentration (%)
Bactericide in parenterals and eye-drops	0.001-0.002
Spermicide in vaginal suppositories and jellies (active ingredient)	0.02

SEM: 2
Excipient: Phenylmercuric acetate
Manufacturer: Eastman Fine Chemicals
Magnification: 1800x

8. Description
Phenylmercuric acetate occurs as a white to creamy white, odorless or almost odorless, crystalline powder, or as small white prisms or leaflets.

9. Pharmacopeial Specifications

Test	USPNF XVII
Identification	+
Mercury salts and heavy metals	+
Polymercurated benzene compounds	$\leqslant 1.5\%$
Melting range	149-153°C
Residue on ignition	$\leqslant 0.2\%$
Assay	98.0-100.5%

10. Typical Properties
Acidity/alkalinity: pH $\approx$ 4 for a saturated aqueous solution at 20°C.

Antimicrobial activity: phenylmercuric acetate is a broad spectrum antimicrobial preservative with slow bactericidal and fungicidal activity similar to phenylmercuric nitrate, *see* Phenylmercuric Nitrate.
Dissociation constant: $pK_a = 3.3$
Melting point: 150°C
Partition coefficients: Mineral oil: water = 0.1

Solubility:

Solvent	Solubility at 20°C*
Acetone	1 in 19
Chloroform	1 in 6.8
Ethanol (95%)	1 in 225
Ether	1 in 200
Water	1 in 180

* Compendial values for solubility vary considerably and in most instances do not show close agreement with laboratory determined values, which also vary.

11. Stability and Storage Conditions

As for other phenylmercuric salts, *see* Phenylmercuric Nitrate. Phenylmercuric acetate should be stored in a well-closed container, protected from light, in a cool, dry, place.

12. Incompatibilities

As for other phenylmercuric salts, *see* Phenylmercuric Nitrate. Incompatible with: halides; anionic emulsifying agents and suspending agents; tragacanth; starch; talc; sodium metabisulfite; sodium thiosulfate; disodium edetate; silicates; aluminum and other metals; amino acids; ammonia and ammonium salts; sulfur compounds; rubber and some plastics.

13. Method of Manufacture

Phenylmercuric acetate is readily formed by heating benzene with mercuric acetate.

14. Safety

Phenylmercuric acetate is mainly used as an antimicrobial preservative in topical pharmaceutical formulations. A number of adverse reactions to mercury containing preservatives have been reported, *see* Phenylmercuric Nitrate.

LD_{50} (mouse, IP): 13 mg/kg[1]
LD_{50} (mouse, IV): 18 mg/kg
LD_{50} (mouse, oral): 50 mg/kg
LD_{50} (mouse, SC): 61 mg/kg
LD_{50} (rat, oral): 30 mg/kg

15. Handling Precautions

Observe normal precautions appropriate to the circumstances and quantity of material handled. Phenylmercuric acetate may be irritant to the skin, eyes and mucous membranes. Eye protection, gloves and a respirator are recommended. In the UK, the occupational exposure limit for mercury containing compounds, calculated as mercury, is 0.05 mg/m^3 long-term (8-hour TWA) and 0.15 mg/m^3 short-term.[2]

16. Regulatory Status

Included in the FDA Inactive Ingredients Guide (nasal and ophthalmic preparations). Included in nonparenteral medicines licensed in the UK. In France, a maximum concentration of 0.01% is permitted for use in pharmaceuticals. The use of phenylmercuric acetate in cosmetics is restricted in the UK, *see* Phenylmercuric Nitrate.

17. Pharmacopeias

Aust, Fr, Ind and USPNF.

18. Related Substances

Phenylmercuric Borate; Phenylmercuric Nitrate; Thimerosal.

19. Comments

—

20. Specific References

1. Sweet DV, editor. Registry of toxic effects of chemical substances. Cincinnati: US Department of Health, 1987.
2. Health and Safety Executive. EH40/93: occupational exposure limits 1993. London: HMSO, 1993.
See also Phenylmercuric Nitrate.

21. General References

See Phenylmercuric Nitrate.

22. Authors

UK: MC Allwood.

Phenylmercuric Borate

1. Nonproprietary Names

BP: Phenylmercuric borate
PhEur: Phenylhydrargyri boras

2. Synonyms

(Dihydrogen borato)phenylmercury;
phenylmercuriborate; phenylmercury borate; PMB.

3. Chemical Name and CAS Registry Number

[Orthoborato(3-)-*O*]-phenylmercurate(2-)dihydrogen[102-98-7]
The above chemical name, CAS registry number and
synonyms refer to phenylmercuric borate alone rather than
the compound. The name phenylmercuric borate and the
synonyms may however be applied to mean the PhEur
material which is a compound, or a mixture of compounds,
see Section 4. Unique CAS registry numbers for phenylmercuric borate and the compounds are:
$C_6H_7BHgO_3$ [102-98-7]
$C_{12}H_{13}BHg_2O_4$ [8017-88-7]
$C_{12}H_{11}BHg_2O_3$ [6273-99-0]

4. Empirical Formula   Molecular Weight

The BP 1993 and PhEur 1981 material is a compound
consisting of equimolecular proportions of phenylmercuric
orthoborate and phenylmercuric hydroxide ($C_{12}H_{13}BHg_2O_4$)
or of the dehydrated form (metaborate, $C_{12}H_{11}BHg_2O_3$) or a
mixture of the two compounds.
Phenylmercuric hydroxide and phenylmercuric orthoborate:
$C_{12}H_{13}BHg_2O_4$ 633.2
Phenylmercuric hydroxide and phenylmercuric metaborate:
$C_{12}H_{11}BHg_2O_3$ 615.2

5. Structural Formula

Phenylmercuric orthoborate and phenylmercuric hydroxide

Phenylmercuric metaborate and phenylmercuric hydroxide

6. Functional Category

Antimicrobial preservative; antiseptic.

7. Application in Pharmaceutical Formulation or Technology

Phenylmercuric borate is used as an alternative antimicrobial
preservative to phenylmercuric acetate or phenylmercuric
nitrate. It is more soluble than phenylmercuric nitrate and

has also been reported to be less irritant than either
phenylmercuric acetate or phenylmercuric nitrate.[1]
See also Phenylmercuric Nitrate.

Use	Concentration (%)
Antimicrobial agent in ophthalmics	0.002-0.004
Antimicrobial agent in parenterals	0.002

8. Description

Phenylmercuric borate occurs as colorless, shiny flakes or as a
white or slightly yellow, odorless, crystalline powder.

9. Pharmacopeial Specifications

Test	PhEur 1981
Identification	+
Appearance of solution	+
Ionized mercury (as heavy metals)	+
Loss on drying (at 45°C)	$\leqslant 3.5\%$
Assay (dried basis)	
of mercury	64.5-66.0%
of borates (as H_3BO_3)	9.8-10.3%

10. Typical Properties

Acidity/alkalinity: pH = 5.0-7.0 for 0.6% w/v aqueous
solution at 20°C.
Antimicrobial activity: phenylmercuric borate is a broad
spectrum antimicrobial preservative with slow bactericidal
and fungicidal activity similar to phenylmercuric nitrate, *see*
Phenylmercuric Nitrate.
Dissociation constant: $pK_a = 3.3$
Melting point: 112-113°C
Solubility:

Solvent	Solubility at 20°C* Unless otherwise stated
Ethanol (95%)	1 in 150
Glycerin	soluble
Propylene glycol	soluble
Water	1 in 125
	1 in 100 at 100°C

* Compendial values for solubility vary considerably.

11. Stability and Storage Conditions

As for other phenylmercuric salts, *see* Phenylmercuric Nitrate.
Solutions may be sterilized by autoclaving.
Phenylmercuric borate should be stored in a well-closed
container, protected from light, in a cool, dry, place.

12. Incompatibilities

As for other phenylmercuric salts, *see* Phenylmercuric Nitrate.
Incompatible with: halides; anionic emulsifying agents and
suspending agents; tragacanth; starch; talc; sodium metabisulfite; sodium thiosulfate; disodium edetate; silicates; aluminum and other metals; amino acids; ammonia and ammonium
salts; sulfur compounds; rubber and some plastics.

13. Method of Manufacture

Phenylmercuric borate may be prepared by heating mercuric
borate with benzene or by evaporating to dryness, under

vacuum, an alcoholic solution containing equimolar proportions of phenylmercuric hydroxide and boric acid.

14. Safety

Phenylmercuric borate is mainly used as an antimicrobial preservative in topical pharmaceutical formulations. A number of adverse reactions to mercury containing preservatives have been reported, *see* Phenylmercuric Nitrate.

Although phenylmercuric borate is an irritant it has been reported to be less so than either phenylmercuric acetate or phenylmercuric nitrate.[1] There is however some cross sensitization potential with other mercurial preservatives.

Systemic absorption has been reported following regular use of a hand disinfectant soap containing 0.04% phenylmercuric borate resulting in an increase in the estimated total daily body load of mercury from 30 μg to 100 μg per 24 hours.[2]

15. Handling Precautions

Observe normal precautions appropriate to the circumstances and quantity of material handled. Phenylmercuric borate may be irritant to the skin, eyes and mucous membranes. Eye protection, gloves and a respirator are recommended. In the UK, the occupational exposure limit for mercury containing compounds, calculated as mercury, is 0.05 mg/m^3 long-term (8-hour TWA) and 0.15 mg/m^3 short-term.[3]

16. Regulatory Status

Included in nonparenteral medicines licensed in Europe. In France, a maximum concentration of up to 0.01% is permitted for use in pharmaceutical formulations. In the UK, the use of phenylmercuric borate in cosmetics is restricted,[4] *see* Phenylmercuric Nitrate.

17. Pharmacopeias

Aust, Belg, Br, Cz, Eur, Fr, Gr, Hung, It, Neth, Port, Swiss, Turk and Yug.

18. Related Substances

Phenylmercuric Acetate; Phenylmercuric Nitrate; Thimerosal.

19. Comments

—

20. Specific References

1. Marzulli FN, Maibach HI. Antimicrobials: experimental contact sensitization in man. J Soc Cosmet Chem 1973; 24: 399-421.
2. Peters-Haefeli L, Michod JJ, Aelhg A, Varone JJ, Schelling JL, Peters G. Urinary excretion of mercury after the use of an antiseptic soap containing 0.04% of phenylmercuric borate [in French]. Schweiz Med Wochenschr 1976; 106(6): 171-178.
3. Health and Safety Executive. EH40/93: occupational exposure limits 1993. London: HMSO, 1993.
4. Statutory Instrument 2233. Consumer protection: the consumer products (safety) regulations 1989. London: HMSO, 1989.

See also Phenylmercuric Nitrate.

21. General References

See Phenylmercuric Nitrate.

22. Authors

UK: MC Allwood.

Phenylmercuric Nitrate

1. Nonproprietary Names

BP: Phenylmercuric nitrate
PhEur: Phenylhydrargyri nitras
USPNF: Phenylmercuric nitrate

2. Synonyms

Basic phenylmercury nitrate; merphenyl nitrate; nitratophenylmercury; phenylmercury nitrate; PMN.

Note that the synonyms above are usually used to refer to phenylmercuric nitrate alone. However, confusion with nomenclature and CAS registry number has lead to these synonyms also being applied to the BP, PhEur and USPNF material which is a mixture of phenylmercuric nitrate and phenylmercuric hydroxide.

3. Chemical Name and CAS Registry Number

There are two CAS registry numbers associated with phenylmercuric nitrate. One refers to the mixture of phenylmercuric nitrate and phenylmercuric hydroxide ($C_{12}H_{11}Hg_2NO_4$) whilst the other refers to phenylmercuric nitrate alone ($C_6H_5HgNO_3$). The BP 1993, PhEur 1992 and USPNF XVII use the name phenylmercuric nitrate to describe the mixture and use the CAS number [55-68-5].

$C_{12}H_{11}Hg_2NO_4$
Hydroxyphenylmercury mixture with (nitrato-*O*)phenylmercury [8003-05-2]
$C_6H_5HgNO_3$
(Nitrato-*O*)phenylmercury [55-68-5]

4. Empirical Formula   Molecular Weight

$C_{12}H_{11}Hg_2NO_4$ 634.45

5. Structural Formula

HgNO3HO—Hg

6. Functional Category

Antimicrobial preservative; antiseptic.

7. Applications in Pharmaceutical Formulation or Technology

Phenylmercuric salts are used as antimicrobial preservatives mainly in ophthalmic preparations, but are also used in cosmetics (*see* Section 16), parenteral and topical pharmaceutical formulations.

Phenylmercuric salts are active over a wide pH range against bacteria and fungi and are usually used in neutral to alkaline solutions although they have also been used effectively at slightly acid pH, *see* Section 10. In acidic formulations, phenylmercuric nitrate may be preferred to phenylmercuric acetate or phenylmercuric borate since it does not precipitate. Phenylmercuric nitrate is also an effective spermicide although its use in vaginal contraceptives is no longer recommended, *see* Section 14.

A number of adverse reactions to phenylmercuric salts have been reported and concern at the toxicity of mercury compounds may preclude the use of phenylmercuric salts under certain circumstances, *see* Section 14.

Use	Concentration (%)
Bactericide in parenterals	0.001
Bactericide in vaginal suppositories and jellies	0.02
Preservative in eye-drops	0.002

8. Description

Phenylmercuric nitrate BP, PhEur and USPNF is an equimolecular compound of phenylmercuric hydroxide and phenylmercuric nitrate; it occurs as a white, crystalline powder with a slight aromatic odor.

SEM: 1
Excipient: Phenylmercuric nitrate
Manufacturer: Eastman Fine Chemicals
Magnification: 180x

SEM: 2
Excipient: Phenylmercuric nitrate
Manufacturer: Eastman Fine Chemicals
Magnification: 1800x

9. Pharmacopeial Specifications

Test	PhEur 1992	USPNF XVII (Suppl 1)
Identification	+	+
Loss on drying	⩽ 1.0%	—
Residue on ignition	—	⩽ 0.1%
Mercury ions	—	+
Assay (dried basis)		
of mercury	62.5-64.0%	62.75-63.50%
of phenylmercuric ion	—	87.0-87.9%

10. Typical Properties

Acidity/alkalinity: a saturated aqueous solution is acidic to litmus.

Antimicrobial activity: phenylmercuric salts are broad spectrum, growth-inhibiting agents at the concentrations normally used for the preservation of pharmaceuticals and possess slow bactericidal and fungicidal activity. Antimicrobial activity tends to increase with increasing pH; however, in solutions of pH 6 and below activity against *Pseudomonas aeruginosa* has been demonstrated and phenylmercuric salts are included in several compendial eye-drop formulations of acid pH. Activity is also increased in the presence of phenylethyl alcohol and in the presence of sodium metabisulfite at acid pH, but decreased in the presence of sodium metabisulfite at alkaline pH.[1-3] As a preservative in topical creams, phenylmercuric salts are active at pH 5-8.[4]

Bacteria (Gram-positive): good inhibition, more moderate cidal activity. Minimum inhibitory concentration (MIC) against *Staphylococcus aureus* is 0.5 μg/mL.

Bacteria (Gram-negative): inhibitory activity for most Gram-negative bacteria is similar to that for Gram-positive bacteria (MIC is approximately 0.3-0.5 μg/mL). Phenylmercuric salts are less active against some *Pseudomonas* species, and particularly *Pseudomonas aeruginosa* (MIC is approximately 12 μg/mL).

Fungi: most fungi are inhibited by 0.3-1 μg/mL; phenylmercuric salts exhibit both inhibitory and fungicidal activity, e.g. phenylmercuric acetate against *Candida albicans*, MIC is 0.8 μg/mL; phenylmercuric acetate against *Aspergillus niger*, MIC is approximately 10 μg/mL.

Spores: phenylmercuric salts may be active in conjunction with heat. The BP 1980 included heating at 100°C for 30 minutes in the presence of 0.002% w/v phenylmercuric acetate or phenylmercuric nitrate as a sterilization method. However, in practice this may not be sufficient to kill spores and heating with a bactericide no longer appears as a sterilization method in the BP 1993.

Dissociation constant: $pK_a = 3.3$

Melting point: 187-190°C with decomposition.

Partition coefficients:
Mineral oil: water = 0.58;
Peanut oil: water = 0.4.

Solubility: more soluble in the presence of either nitric acid or alkali hydroxides.

Solvent	Solubility at 20°C* Unless otherwise stated
Ethanol (95%)	1 in 1000
Fixed oils	soluble
Glycerin	slightly soluble
Water	1 in 600-1500
	1 in 160 at 100°C

* Compendial values for solubility vary considerably.

11. Stability and Storage Conditions

All phenylmercuric compound solutions form a black residue of metallic mercury when exposed to light or after prolonged storage. Solutions may be sterilized by autoclaving although significant amounts of phenylmercuric salts may be lost, hence reducing preservative efficacy, due to incompatibilities with packaging components or other excipients, e.g. sodium metabisulfite.[5-7] *See* Section 12.

Phenylmercuric nitrate should be stored in a well-closed container, protected from light, in a cool, dry, place.

12. Incompatibilities

The antimicrobial activity of phenylmercuric salts may be reduced in the presence of anionic emulsifying agents and suspending agents, tragacanth, starch, talc, sodium metabisulfite,[8] sodium thiosulfate,[2] disodium edetate[2] and silicates (bentonite, aluminum magnesium silicate, magnesium trisilicate and kaolin).[9,10]

Phenylmercuric salts are incompatible with halides, particularly bromides and iodides, since they form less soluble halogen compounds. At concentrations of 0.002% w/v precipitation may not occur in the presence of chlorides. Phenylmercuric salts are also incompatible with aluminum and other metals, ammonia and ammonium salts, amino acids, and with some sulfur compounds, e.g. in rubber.

Phenylmercuric salts are absorbed by rubber stoppers and some types of plastic packaging components; uptake is usually greatest to natural rubbers and polyethylene and least to polypropylene.[11-16]

Incompatibilities with some types of filter membranes may also result in loss of phenylmercuric salts following sterilization by filtration.[17]

13. Method of Manufacture

Phenylmercuric nitrate is readily formed by heating benzene with mercuric acetate, then treating the resulting acetate with an alkali nitrate.[18]

14. Safety

Phenylmercuric nitrate and other phenylmercuric salts are widely used as antimicrobial preservatives in parenteral and topical pharmaceutical formulations. However, concern over the use of phenylmercuric salts in pharmaceuticals has increased as a result of greater awareness of the toxicity of mercury and other mercury compounds. This concern must however be balanced by the effectiveness of these materials as antimicrobial preservatives and the low concentrations in which they are employed.

Phenylmercuric salts are irritant to the skin at 0.1% w/w concentration in petrolatum.[19] In solution, they may give rise to erythema and blistering 6-12 hours later. In a modified repeated insult patch test, a 2% w/v solution was found to produce extreme sensitization of the skin.[20]

Eye-drops containing phenylmercuric nitrate as a preservative should not be used continuously for prolonged periods as mercurialentis, a brown pigmentation of the anterior capsule of the lens may occur. Incidence is 6% in patients using eye-drops for greater than 6 years; the condition is not however associated with visual impairment.[21,22] Cases of atypical band keratopathy have also been attributed to phenylmercuric nitrate preservative in eye-drops.[23]

Concern that the absorption of mercury from the vagina may be harmful has led to the recommendation that phenylmercuric nitrate should not be used in intravaginal formulations.[24]

LD$_{50}$ (mouse, IV): 27 mg/kg[25]
LD$_{50}$ (mouse, oral): 50 mg/kg
LD$_{50}$ (rat, SC): 63 mg/kg

15. Handling Precautions

Observe normal precautions appropriate to the circumstances and quantity of material handled. Phenylmercuric nitrate may be irritant to the skin, eyes and mucous membranes. Eye protection, gloves and a respirator are recommended. In the UK, the occupational exposure limit for mercury containing compounds, calculated as mercury, is 0.05 mg/m^3 long-term (8-hour TWA) and 0.15 mg/m^3 short-term.[26]

16. Regulatory Status

Included in the FDA Inactive Ingredients Guide (IM and ophthalmic preparations). Included in nonparenteral medicines licensed in the UK. In the UK, the use of phenylmercuric salts in cosmetics is limited to 0.003% (calculated as mercury, equivalent to approximately 0.0047% of phenylmercuric nitrate) as a preservative in shampoos and hair-creams, which contain nonionic emulsifiers that would render other preservatives ineffective. Total permitted concentration, as mercury, when mixed with other mercury compounds is 0.007% (equivalent up to approximately 0.011% of phenylmercuric nitrate).[27]

17. Pharmacopeias

Br, Braz, Egypt, Eur, Fr, Nord, Turk, USPNF and Yug. Also in BP Vet.

18. Related Substances

Phenylmercuric Acetate; Phenylmercuric Borate; Thimerosal.

19. Comments

Phenylmercuric salts should be used in preference to benzalkonium chloride as a preservative for salicylates and nitrates and in solutions of salts of physostigmine and epinephrine that contain 0.1% sodium sulfite.

20. Specific References

1. Buckles J, Brown MW, Porter GS. The inactivation of phenylmercuric nitrate by sodium metabisulphite. J Pharm Pharmacol 1971; 23(Suppl): 237S-238S.
2. Richards RME, Reary JME. Changes in antibacterial activity of thiomersal and PMN on autoclaving with certain adjuvants. J Pharm Pharmacol 1972; 24(Suppl): 84P-89P.
3. Richards RME, Fell AF, Butchart JME. Interaction between sodium metabisulphite and PMN. J Pharm Pharmacol 1972; 24: 999-1000.
4. Parker MS. The preservation of pharmaceuticals and cosmetic products. In: Russell AD, Hugo WB, Ayliffe GAJ, editors. Principles and practice of disinfection, preservation and sterilization. Oxford: Blackwell Scientific Publications, 1982: 287-305.
5. Hart A. Antibacterial activity of phenylmercuric nitrate in zinc sulphate and adrenaline eye drops BPC 1968. J Pharm Pharmacol 1973; 25: 507-508.
6. Miezitis EO, Polack AE, Roberts MS. Concentration changes during autoclaving of aqueous solutions in polyethylene containers: an examination of some methods for reduction of solute loss. Aust J Pharm Sci 1979; 8(3): 72-76.
7. Parkin JE, Marshall CA. The instability of phenylmercuric nitrate in APF ophthalmic products containing sodium metabisulphite. Aust J Hosp Pharm 1991; 20: 434-436.
8. Collins AJ, Lingham P, Burbridge TA, Bain R. Incompatibility of phenylmercuric acetate with sodium metabisulphite in eye drop formulations. J Pharm Pharmacol 1985; 37(Suppl): 123P.
9. Yousef RT, El-Nakeeb MA, Salama S. Effect of some pharmaceutical materials on the bactericidal activities of preservatives. Can J Pharm Sci 1973; 8: 54-56.
10. Horn NR, McCarthy TJ, Ramsted E. Interactions between powder suspensions and selected quaternary ammonium and organomercurial preservatives. Cosmet Toilet 1980; 95(2): 69-73.
11. Ingversen J, Andersen VS. Transfer of phenylmercuric compounds from dilute aqueous solutions to vials and rubber closures. Dansk Tidsskr Farm 1968; 42: 264-271.
12. Eriksson K. Loss of organomercurial preservatives from medicaments in different kinds of containers. Acta Pharm Suec 1967; 4: 261-264.
13. Christensen K, Dauv E. Absorption of preservatives by drip attachments in eye drop packages. J Mond Pharm 1969; 12(1): 5-11.
14. Aspinall JA, Duffy TD, Saunders MB, Taylor CG. The effect of low density polyethylene containers on some hospital-manufactured eye drop formulations I: sorption of phenylmercuric acetate. J Clin Hosp Pharm 1980; 5: 21-29.
15. McCarthy TJ. Interaction between aqueous preservative solutions and their plastic containers, III. Pharm Weekbl 1972; 107: 1-7.
16. Aspinall JA, Duffy TD, Taylor CG. The effect of low density polyethylene containers on some hospital-manufactured eye drop formulations II: inhibition of the sorption of phenylmercuric acetate. J Clin Hosp Pharm 1983; 8: 223-240.
17. Naido NT, Price CH, McCarthy TJ. Preservative loss from ophthalmic solutions during filtration sterilization. Aust J Pharm Sci 1972 1(1): 16-18.
18. Pyman FL, Stevenson HA. Phenylmercuric nitrate. Pharm J 1934; 133: 269.
19. Koby GA Fisher AA. Phenylmercuric acetate as primary irritant. Arch Dermatol 1972; 106: 129.
20. Kligman AM. The identification of contact allergens by human assay, III. The maximization test: a procedure for screening and rating contact sensitizers. J Invest Dermatol 1966; 47: 393-409.
21. Garron LK, Wood IS, Spencer WH, et al. A clinical and pathologic study of mercurialentis medicamentosus. Trans Am Ophthalmol Soc 1977; 74: 295.
22. Winder AF, Astbury NJ, Sheraidah GAK, Ruben M. Penetration of mercury from ophthalmic preservatives into the human eye. Lancet 1980; ii: 237-239.
23. Brazier DJ, Hitchings RA. Atypical band keratopathy following long-term pilocarpine treatment. Br J Ophthalmol 1989; 73: 294-296.
24. Lohr L. Mercury controversy heats up. Am Pharm 1978; 18(9): 23.
25. Sweet DV, editor. Registry of toxic effects of chemical substances. Cincinnati: US Department of Health, 1987.
26. Health and Safety Executive. EH40/93: occupational exposure limits 1993. London: HMSO, 1993.
27. Statutory Instrument 2233. Consumer protection: the consumer products (safety) regulations 1989. London: HMSO, 1989.

21. General References

Abdelaziz AA, El-Nakeeb MA. Sporicidal activity of local anaesthetics and their binary combinations with preservatives. J Clin Pharm Ther 1988; 13: 249-256.
Barkman R, Germanis M, Karpe G, Malmborg AS. Preservatives in eye drops. Acta Ophthalmol 1969; 47: 461-475.

Board RG, Allwood MC, Banks JG, editors. Preservatives in the food, pharmaceutical and environmental industries. Oxford: Blackwell Scientific Publications, 1987.

Grier N. Mercurials inorganic and organic. In: Block SS, editor. Disinfection, Sterilization and Preservation, 3rd edition. Philadelphia: Lea and Febiger, 1983: 346-374.

Mullins JD, Hecht G. Ophthalmic preparations. In: Gennaro AR, et al, editors. Remington's Pharmaceutical Sciences, 18th edition. Easton: Mack Publishing Company, 1990: 1581-1595.

Parkin JE, Button KL, Maroudas PA. The decomposition of phenylmercuric nitrate caused by disodium edetate in neomycin eye drops during the process of heat sterilization. J Clin Pharm Ther 1992; 17: 191-196.

Parkin JE, Duffy MB, Loo CN. The chemical degradation of phenylmercuric nitrate by disodium edetate during heat sterilization at pH values commonly encountered in ophthalmic products. J Clin Pharm Ther 1992; 17: 307-314.

Parkin JE. The decomposition of phenylmercuric nitrate in sulphacetamide drops during heat sterilization. J Pharm Pharmacol 1993; 45: 1024-1027.

22. Authors

UK: MC Allwood.

Polacrilin Potassium

1. Nonproprietary Names

USPNF: Polacrilin potassium

2. Synonyms

Amberlite IRP-88; methacrylic acid polymer with divinylbenzene, potassium salt.

3. Chemical Name and CAS Registry Number

2-Methyl-2-propenoic acid polymer with divinylbenzene, potassium salt
[39394-76-5]

4. Empirical Formula   Molecular Weight

The USPNF XVII describes polacrilin potassium as the potassium salt of a unifunctional low-cross-linked carboxylic cation-exchange resin. *See* Sections 5, 13 and 19.

5. Structural Formula

6. Functional Category

Tablet and capsule disintegrant.

7. Applications in Pharmaceutical Formulation or Technology

Polacrilin potassium (*Amberlite IRP-88*) is a cation-exchange resin used in oral pharmaceutical formulations as a tablet disintegrant.[1-3] Concentrations of between 2-10% w/w have been used for this purpose although 2% w/w of polacrilin potassium is usually sufficient. Other polacrilin ion-exchange resins have been used as excipients to stabilize drugs, to mask or modify the taste of drugs, and in the preparation of sustained-release dosage forms[4] and drug carriers.

Polacrilin resins are also used in the analysis and manufacture of pharmaceuticals and food products. Therapeutically, certain resins, e.g *Amberlite XAD-4*, have been used for hemoperfusion in cases of drug poisoning.

8. Description

Polacrilin potassium occurs as a cream-colored, odorless and tasteless, free flowing powder. Aqueous dispersions have a bitter taste.

9. Pharmacopeial Specifications

Test	USPNF XVII
Identification	+
Loss on drying	$\leqslant$ 10.0%
Powder fineness	$\leqslant$ 1.0% on a #100 mesh
	$\leqslant$ 30.0% on a #200 mesh
Arsenic	$\leqslant$ 3 ppm
Iron	$\leqslant$ 0.01%

Continued

Test	USPNF XVII
Sodium	$\leqslant$ 0.20%
Heavy metals	$\leqslant$ 0.002%
Assay of potassium (dried basis)	20.6%-25.1%

10. Typical Properties

Density (bulk):
0.48 g/cm^3 for *Amberlite IRP-88*.[3]
Density (tapped):
0.62 g/cm^3 for *Amberlite IRP-88*.[3]
Particle size distribution: see Fig. 1.[3]
Solubility: practically insoluble in water and most other liquids, although polacrilin resins swell rapidly when wetted.

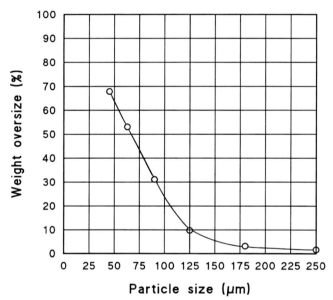

Fig. 1: Particle size distribution of polacrilin potassium (*Amberlite IRP-88*).

11. Stability and Storage Conditions

Polacrilin potassium and other polacrilin resins are stable to light, air and heat up to their maximum operation temperature, *see* Table I. Excessive heating can cause thermal decomposition of the resins and may yield one or more oxides of carbon, nitrogen, sulfur and/or amines.

Polacrilin resins should be stored in well-closed containers in a cool, dry, place.

12. Incompatibilities

Incompatible with strong oxidizing agents. Amines, particularly tertiary amines, and some other substances which interact with polacrilin resins.[5]

13. Method of Manufacture

Polacrilin resin (*Amberlite IRP-64*) is prepared by the copolymerization of methacrylic acid with divinylbenzene (DVB). Polacrilin potassium (*Amberlite IRP-88*) is then produced by neutralizing this resin with potassium hydroxide. Other resins are similarly produced by copolymerization between styrene and divinylbenzene (*Amberlite IRP-69*,

Table I: Summary of physico-chemical properties of pharmaceutical grade *Amberlite* resins.

Amberlite Grade	Copolymer	Type	Functional structure	Ionic form	Particle size (mesh)	Parent resin	Maximum moisture (%)	pH range	Maximum temperature (°C)	Application
Cation-exchange resins										
IRP-69	Styrene & DVB	Strongly acidic	$SO_3^-Na^+$	Na^+	100-500	*IR-120*	10	0-14	120	Carrier for cationic drugs which are bases or salts.
IRP-64	Methacrylic acid & DVB	Weakly acidic	COO^-H^+	H^+	100-500	*IRC-50*	10	5-14	120	Carrier for cationic drugs which are bases.
IRP-88	Methacrylic acid & DVB	Weakly acidic	COO^-K^+	K^+	100-500	*IRC-50*	10	5-14	120	Tablet disintegrant.
Anion-exchange resins										
IRP-58	Phenolic polyamine	Weakly basic	NH_2NH_2	Free base	100-500	*IR-4B*	10	0-7	60	Carrier for anionic drugs which are acids.
IRP-67	Styrene & DVB	Strongly basic	$N(CH_3)_3^+Cl^-$	Cl^-	100-500	*IRA-400*	10	0-12	60	Carrier for anionic drugs which are acids or salts.

Note that all of the above grades, with the exception of *Amberlite IRP-88*, are available in particle size grades < 325 mesh.

Amberlite IRP-67, Amberlite IR-120, and *Amberlite IRA-400).* Phenolic-based polyamine condensates (*Amberlite IRP-58*) may also be produced.

The homogeneity of the resin structure depends on the purity, nature, and properties of the copolymers used as well as the controls and conditions employed during the polymerization reaction. The nature and degree of cross-linking have significant influence on the physico-chemical properties of the resin matrix. The functional groups introduced on the matrix confer the property of ion-exchange. Depending upon the acidity or basicity of the functional groups, strongly acidic to strongly basic types of ion exchange resins may be produced.

14. Safety

Polacrilin potassium and other polacrilin resins are used in oral pharmaceutical formulations and are generally regarded as nontoxic and nonirritant materials. However, excessive ingestion of polacrilin resins may disturb the electrolyte balance of the body.

15. Handling Precautions

Observe normal precautions appropriate to the circumstances and quantity of material handled. Polacrilin potassium may be irritant to the eyes; eye protection and gloves are recommended.

16. Regulatory Status

Included in the FDA Inactive Ingredients Guide (oral capsules and tablets).

17. Pharmacopeias

USPNF.

18. Related Substances

Polacrilin.

Polacrilin

CAS number: [54182-62-6]
Synonyms: *Amberlite IRP-64*; methacrylic acid polymer with divinylbenzene; 2-methyl-2-propenoic acid polymer with divinylbenzene.
See also Section 19.

19. Comments

A number of other polacrilin (*Amberlite*) resins are commercially available which have a variety of industrial and pharmaceutical applications, *see* Table I.

20. Specific References

1. Van Abbé NJ, Rees JT. Amberlite resin XE-88 as a tablet disintegrant. J Am Pharm Assoc (Sci) 1958; 47: 487-489.
2. Khan KA, Rhodes CT. Effect of disintegrant concentration on disintegration and compression characteristics of two insoluble direct compression systems. Can J Pharm Sci 1973; 8: 77-80.
3. Rudnic EM, Rhodes CT, Welch S, Bernardo P. Evaluation of the mechanism of disintegrant action. Drug Dev Ind Pharm 1982; 8: 87-109.
4. Smith HA, Evanson RV, Sperandio GJ. The development of a liquid antihistaminic preparation with sustained release properties. J Am Pharm Assoc (Sci) 1960; 49: 94-97.
5. Borodkin S, Yunker MH. Interaction of amine drugs with a polycarboxylic acid ion-exchange resin. J Pharm Sci 1970; 59: 481-486.

21. General References

Dorfner K. Ion exchangers, properties and applications, 3rd edition. Michigan: Ann Arbour Science Publishers, 1972.
Nachod FC, Schubert J. Ion exchange technology. New York: Academic Press Inc, 1956.

22. Authors

USA: A Palmieri.

Poloxamer

1. Nonproprietary Names

USPNF: Poloxamer

2. Synonyms

Lutrol; *Monolan*; *Pluronic*; poloxalkol; polyethylene-propylene glycol copolymer; polyoxyethylene-polyoxypropylene copolymer; *Supronic*; *Synperonic*.

3. Chemical Name and CAS Registry Number

α-Hydro-ω-hydroxypoly(oxyethylene)poly(oxypropylene) poly(oxyethylene) block copolymer
[9003-11-6]

4. Empirical Formula   Molecular Weight

The poloxamer polyols are a series of closely related block copolymers of ethylene oxide and propylene oxide conforming to the general formula:

$$HO(C_2H_4O)_a(C_3H_6O)_b(C_2H_4O)_aH$$

The grades included in the USPNF XVII are shown below:

Poloxamer	Physical form	a	b	Average molecular weight
124	liquid	12	20	2090-2360
188	solid	80	27	7680-9510
237	solid	64	37	6840-8830
338	solid	141	44	12 700-17 400
407	solid	101	56	9840-14 600

5. Structural Formula

See Section 4.

6. Functional Category

Emulsifying agent; solubilizing agent; wetting agent.

7. Applications in Pharmaceutical Formulation or Technology

Poloxamers are nonionic polyoxyethylene-polyoxypropylene copolymers used primarily in pharmaceutical formulations as emulsifying or solubilizing agents.[1-6] The polyoxyethylene segment is hydrophilic whilst the polyoxypropylene segment is hydrophobic. All of the poloxamers are chemically similar in composition, differing only in the relative amounts of propylene and ethylene oxides added during manufacture. Their physical and surface active properties vary over a wide range and a number of different types are commercially available, *see* Sections 4, 9, 10 and 19.

Poloxamers are used as emulsifying agents in intravenous fat emulsions, and as solubilizing and stabilizing agents to maintain the clarity of elixirs and syrups. Poloxamers may also be used as wetting agents, in ointments, suppository bases, gels,[7-9] and as tablet binders and coatings.

Poloxamer 188 has also been used as an emulsifying agent for fluorocarbons used as artificial blood substitutes.[10,11]

Therapeutically, poloxamer 188 is administered orally as a wetting agent and stool lubricant in the treatment of constipation; it is usually used in combination with a laxative such as danthron. Poloxamers may also be used therapeutically as wetting agents in eye-drop formulations, in the treatment of kidney stones and as skin wound cleansers.

Use	Concentration (%)
Fat emulsifier	0.3
Flavor solubilizer	0.3
Fluorocarbon emulsifier	2.5
Gelling agent	15-50
Spreading agent	1
Stabilizing agent	1-5
Suppository base	4-6 or 90
Tablet coating	10
Tablet excipient	5-10
Wetting agent	0.01-5

8. Description

Poloxamers generally occur as white-colored, waxy, free flowing prilled granules or as cast solids. They are practically odorless and tasteless. At room temperature, poloxamer 124 occurs as a colorless liquid.

9. Pharmacopeial Specifications

Test	USPNF XVII (Suppl 8)
Average molecular weight	+
Weight percent oxyethylene	
For poloxamer 124	46.7 ± 1.9
For poloxamer 188	81.8 ± 1.9
For poloxamer 237	72.4 ± 1.9
For poloxamer 407	73.2 ± 1.7
pH (1 in 40 solution)	5.0-7.5
Unsaturation (mEq/g)	
For poloxamer 124	0.020 ± 0.008
For poloxamer 188	0.026 ± 0.008
For poloxamer 237	0.034 ± 0.008
For poloxamer 407	0.048 ± 0.017
Heavy metals	$\leqslant 0.002\%$
Free ethylene oxide, propylene oxide and 1,4-dioxane	$\leqslant 5$ ppm

10. Typical Properties

Acidity/alkalinity:
pH = 6.0-7.4 for a 2.5% w/v aqueous solution.
Cloud point: > 100°C for a 1% w/v aqueous solution, and a 10% w/v aqueous solution of poloxamer 188.
Density: 1.06 g/cm^3 at 25°C
Flash point: 260°C
Flowability: solid poloxamers are free flowing.
HLB value: 0.5-30; 29 for poloxamer 188.
Melting point:
16°C for poloxamer 124;
52°C for poloxamer 188;
49°C for poloxamer 237;
57°C for poloxamer 338;
56°C for poloxamer 407.
Moisture content: poloxamers generally contain less than 0.5% w/w water and are hygroscopic only at greater than 80% relative humidity. *See also* HPE Data.
Solubility: solubility varies according to the poloxamer type, *see* Table I.

Table I: Solubility at 25°C for various types of poloxamer in different solvents.

Type	Solvent				
	Ethanol (95%)	Propan-2-ol	Propylene glycol	Water	Xylene
Poloxamer 124	freely soluble	freely soluble	freely soluble	freely soluble	freely soluble
Poloxamer 188	freely soluble	—	—	freely soluble	—
Poloxamer 237	freely soluble	sparingly soluble	—	freely soluble	sparingly soluble
Poloxamer 338	freely soluble	—	sparingly soluble	freely soluble	—
Poloxamer 407	freely soluble	freely soluble	—	freely soluble	—

Surface tension: 19.8 mN/m (19.8 dynes/cm) for a 0.1% w/v aqueous poloxamer 188 solution at 25°C; 24.0 mN/m (24.0 dynes/cm) for a 0.01% w/v aqueous poloxamer 188 solution at 25°C; 26.0 mN/m (26.0 dynes/cm) for a 0.001% w/v aqueous poloxamer solution at 25°C.

Viscosity (dynamic):
1000 mPa s (1000 cP) as a melt at 77°C.

HPE Laboratory Project Data[*]			
	Method	Lab #	Results
Moisture content	MC-3	32	0.33%
Moisture content	EMC-1	15	*See* Fig. 1.
Solubility			
Ethanol (95%) at 25°C	SOL-7	32	398 mg/mL
Ethanol (95%) at 37°C	SOL-7	32	396 mg/mL
Hexane at 25°C	SOL-7	32	0.05 mg/mL
Hexane at 37°C	SOL-7	32	0.09 mg/mL
Propylene glycol at 25°C	SOL-7	32	1.0 mg/mL
Propylene glycol at 37°C	SOL-7	32	1.0 mg/mL
Water at 25°C	SOL-7	32	500 mg/mL
Water at 37°C	SOL-7	32	500 mg/mL

[*] For poloxamer 188.
Supplier: BASF Corp (*Pluronic F-68*, Lot No.: WPEA535B).

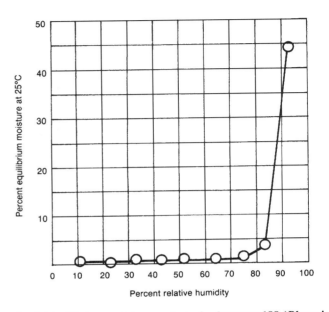

Fig. 1: Equilibrium moisture content of poloxamer 188 (*Pluronic F-68*).

11. Stability and Storage Conditions

Poloxamers are stable materials. Aqueous solutions are stable in the presence of acids, alkalis and metal ions. However, aqueous solutions do support mold growth.
The bulk material should be stored in a well-closed container in a cool, dry, place.

12. Incompatibilities

Depending on the relative concentrations, poloxamer 188 is incompatible with phenols and parabens.

13. Method of Manufacture

Poloxamer polymers are prepared by reacting propylene oxide with propylene glycol to form polyoxypropylene glycol. Ethylene oxide is then added to form the block copolymer.

14. Safety

Poloxamers are used in a variety of oral, parenteral and topical pharmaceutical formulations and are generally regarded as nontoxic and nonirritant materials. Poloxamers are not metabolized in the body.
Animal toxicity studies, with dogs and rabbits, have shown poloxamers to be nonirritant and nonsensitizing when applied, in 5% w/v and 10% w/v concentration, to the eyes, gums and skin.

In a 14-day study of intravenous administration to rabbits, at concentrations up to 0.5 g/kg/day, no overt adverse effects were noted. A similar study with dogs also showed no adverse effects at dosage levels up to 0.5 g/kg/day. In a longer term study, rats fed 3% w/w or 5% w/w of poloxamer in food, for up to two years, did not exhibit any significant symptoms of toxicity. However, rats receiving 7.5% w/w of poloxamer in their diet showed some decrease in growth rate.
No hemolysis of human blood cells was observed over 18 hours at 25°C, with 0.001-10% w/v poloxamer solutions.
Acute animal toxicity data for poloxamer 188:[12]
LD_{50} (mouse, IV): 1 g/kg
LD_{50} (mouse, oral): 15 g/kg
LD_{50} (mouse, SC): 5.5 g/kg
LD_{50} (rat, IV): 7.5 g/kg
LD_{50} (rat, oral): 9.4 g/kg

15. Handling Precautions

Observe normal precautions appropriate to the circumstances and quantity of material handled. Eye protection and gloves are recommended.

16. Regulatory Status

Included in the FDA Inactive Ingredients Guide (IV injections, inhalations, ophthalmic preparations, oral powders, solutions, suspensions and syrups, also topical preparations). Included in nonparenteral medicines licensed in the UK.

17. Pharmacopeias

USPNF.

18. Related Substances

—

19. Comments

Although the USPNF XVII contains specifications for 5 poloxamer grades many more different poloxamers are commercially available which vary in their molecular weight and the proportion of oxyethylene present in the polymer. A series of poloxamers with greatly varying physical properties are thus available.

The nonproprietary name 'poloxamer' is followed by a number, the first 2 digits of which, when multiplied by 100, correspond to the approximate average molecular weight of the polyoxypropylene portion of the copolymer and the third digit, when multiplied by 10, corresponds to the percentage by weight of the polyoxyethylene portion.

Similarly, with many of the trade names used for poloxamers, e.g. *Pluronic F-68* (BASF Corp), the first digit arbitrarily represents the molecular weight of the polyoxypropylene portion and the second digit represents the weight percent of the oxyethylene portion. The letters 'L', 'P', and 'F', stand for the physical form of the poloxamer, either liquid, paste or flakes, *see also* Table II.

Note that in the US the trade name *Pluronic* is used by BASF Corp for pharmaceutical and industrial grade poloxamers, whilst in the UK and Europe the trade name *Lutrol* is used for the pharmaceutical grade material.

Table II: Nonproprietary name and corresponding commercial grade.

Nonproprietary name	Commercial grade
Poloxamer 124	L-44
Poloxamer 188	F-68
Poloxamer 237	F-87
Poloxamer 338	F-108
Poloxamer 407	F-127

20. Specific References

1. Reddy RK, Khalil SA, Gouda MW. Effect of dioctyl sodium sulfosuccinate and poloxamer 188 on dissolution and intestinal absorption of sulfadiazine and sulfisoxazole in rats. J Pharm Sci 1976; 65: 115-118.
2. Collett JH, Tobin EA. Relationships between poloxamer structure and the solubilization of some *para*-substituted acetanilides. J Pharm Pharmacol 1979; 31: 174-177.
3. Collett JH, Rees JA, Buckley DL. The influence of some structurally related Pluronics on the hydrolysis of aspirin. J Pharm Pharmacol 1979; 31(Suppl): 80P.
4. Lin S-Y, Kawashima Y. The influence of three poly(oxyethylene) poly(oxypropylene) surface-active block copolymers on the solubility behavior of indomethacin. Pharm Acta Helv 1985; 60: 339-344.
5. El Shaboury MH. Effect of surfactant treated diluents on the dissolution and bioavailability of frusemide from capsules and tablets. Acta Pharm Fenn 1989; 98: 253-259.
6. Wang P-L, Johnston TP. Thermal-induced denaturation of two model proteins: effect of poloxamer 407 on solution stability. Int J Pharmaceutics 1993; 96: 41-49.
7. Hadgraft J, Howard JR. Drug release from pluronic gels. J Pharm Pharmacol 1982; 34(Suppl): 3P.
8. Miller SC, Donovan MD. Effect of poloxamer 407 gel on the miotic activity of pilocarpine nitrate in rabbits. Int J Pharmaceutics 1982; 12: 147-152.
9. Tomida H, Shinohara M, Kuwada N, Kiryu S. *In vitro* release characteristics of diclofenac and hydrocortisone from Pluronic F-127 gels. Acta Pharm Suec 1987; 24: 263-272.
10. Geyer RP. Bloodless rats through the use of artificial blood substitutes. Fedn Proc 1975; 34: 1499-1505.
11. Lowe KC, Washington C. Emulsified perfluorochemicals as respiratory gas carriers: recovery of perfluorodecalin emulsion droplets from rat tissues. J Pharm Pharmacol 1993; 45: 938-941.
12. Sweet DV, editor. Registry of toxic effects of chemical substances. Cincinnati: US Department of Health, 1987.

21. General References

Attwood D, Collett JH, O'Connor CA. Influence of gamma irradiation on the rheological properties of gels of the poloxamine, Synperonic T908. Int J Pharmaceutics 1991; 70: 147-152.

Bentley PK, Davis SS, Johnson OL, Lowe KC, Washington C. Purification of Pluronic F-68 for perfluorochemical emulsification. J Pharm Pharmacol 1989; 41: 661-663.

Chi SC, Jun HW. Release rates of ketoprofen from poloxamer gels in a membraneless diffusion cell. J Pharm Sci 1991; 80: 280-283.

Johnston TP, Miller SC. Toxicological evaluation of poloxamer vehicles for intramuscular use. J Parenter Sci Technol 1985; 39: 83-88.

Law TK, Florence AT, Whateley TL. Release from multiple w/o/w emulsions stabilized by interfacial complexation. J Pharm Pharmacol 1984; 36(Suppl): 50P.

Nurnberg E, Friess S. Poloxamers - what is that? Characteristics and possibilities of application [in German]. Dtsch Apoth Ztg 1989; 129: 2183-2187.

Schmolka IR. Applications of Pluronic polyols in the cosmetic industry. Am Perfum Cosmet 1967; 82(7): 25-30.

Tait CJ, Houston JB, Attwood D, Collett JH. Pharmacokinetics of cimetidine following delivery from implanted poloxamer gels in rats. J Pharm Pharmacol 1987; 39(Suppl): 57P.

22. Authors

UK: JH Collett, PJ Weller.

Polyethylene Glycol

1. Nonproprietary Names

BP: Macrogol 300
    Macrogol 400
    Macrogol 1000
    Macrogol 1540
    Macrogol 4000
PhEur: Macrogolum 300
      Macrogolum 400
      Macrogolum 1000
USPNF: Polyethylene glycol

2. Synonyms

Breox PEG; *Carbowax*; *Hodag PEG*; *Lutrol E*; PEG; polyoxyethylene glycol; *Renex*.

3. Chemical Name and CAS Registry Number

α-Hydro-ω-hydroxy-poly(oxy-1,2-ethanediyl)
[25322-68-3]

4. Empirical Formula   Molecular Weight

$HOCH_2(CH_2OCH_2)_mCH_2OH$
Where m represents the average number of oxyethylene groups.
Alternatively, the general formula $H(OCH_2CH_2)_nOH$ may be used to represent polyethylene glycol, where n is a number 1 more than the value of m in the previous formula.
See Table I for the average molecular weights of typical polyethylene glycols. Note that the number which follows PEG indicates the average molecular weight of the polymer.

Table I: Structural formula and molecular weight of typical polyethylene glycol polymers.

Grade	m	Average molecular weight
PEG 200	4.2	190-210
PEG 300	6.4	285-315
PEG 400	8.7	380-420
PEG 540 (blend)	—	500-600
PEG 600	13.2	570-613
PEG 900	15.3	855-900
PEG 1000	22.3	950-1050
PEG 1450	32.5	1300-1600
PEG 1540	28-36	1300-1600
PEG 2000	40-50	1800-2200
PEG 3000	60-75	2700-3300
PEG 3350	75.7	3000-3700
PEG 4000	69-84	3000-4800
PEG 4600	104.1	4400-4800
PEG 8000	181.4	7000-9000

5. Structural Formula

See Section 4.

6. Functional Category

Ointment base; plasticizer; solvent; suppository base; tablet and capsule lubricant.

7. Applications in Pharmaceutical Formulation or Technology

Polyethylene glycols are widely used in a variety of pharmaceutical formulations including parenteral, topical, ophthalmic, oral and rectal preparations.

Polyethylene glycols are stable, hydrophilic substances that are essentially nonirritant to the skin, *see* Section 14. Although they do not readily penetrate the skin, polyethylene glycols are water soluble and as such are easily removed from the skin by washing; they are therefore useful as ointment bases.[1] Solid grades are generally employed in topical ointments with the consistency of the base being adjusted by the addition of liquid grades of polyethylene glycol.

Mixtures of polyethylene glycols can be used as suppository bases[2] where they have the following advantages over fats: the melting point of the suppository can be made higher to withstand exposure to warmer climates; release of the drug is not dependent upon melting point; physical stability on storage is better; suppositories are readily miscible with rectal fluids. Disadvantages of using polyethylene glycols are: they are chemically more reactive than fats; greater care is needed in processing to avoid inelegant contraction holes in the suppositories; the rate of release of water-soluble medications decreases with the increasing molecular weight of the polyethylene glycol; polyethylene glycols tend to be more irritating to mucous membranes than fats.

Aqueous polyethylene glycol solutions can be used either as suspending agents or to adjust the viscosity and consistency of other suspending vehicles. When used in conjunction with other emulsifiers, polyethylene glycols can act as emulsion stabilizers.

Liquid polyethylene glycols are used as water-miscible solvents for the contents of soft gelatin capsules. However, they may cause hardening of the capsule shell by preferential absorption of moisture from gelatin in the shell.

In concentrations up to approximately 30% v/v, PEG 300 and PEG 400 have been used as the vehicle for parenteral dosage forms.

In solid dosage formulations, higher molecular weight polyethylene glycols can enhance the effectiveness of tablet binders and impart plasticity to granules.[3] However, they have only limited binding action when used alone, and can prolong disintegration if present in concentrations greater than 5% w/w. When used for thermoplastic granulations,[4-6] a mixture of the powdered constituents with 10-15% w/w PEG 6000 is heated to 70-75°C. The mass becomes paste-like and forms granules if stirred while cooling. This technique is useful for the preparation of dosage forms such as lozenges when prolonged disintegration is required.

Polyethylene glycols can also be used to enhance the aqueous solubility or dissolution characteristics of poorly soluble compounds by making solid dispersions with an appropriate polyethylene glycol.[7] Animal studies have also been performed using polyethylene glycols as solvents for steroids in osmotic pumps.

In film coatings, solid grades of polyethylene glycol can be used alone for the film coating of tablets or can be useful as hydrophilic polishing materials. Solid grades are also widely used as plasticizers in conjunction with film forming polymers.[8] The presence of polyethylene glycols, especially liquid grades, in film coats tends to increase their water permeability and may reduce protection against low pH in enteric coating films. Polyethylene glycols are useful as plasticizers in micro-encapsulated products to avoid rupture

Table II: Pharmacopeial specifications of polyethylene glycol.

Test	BP 1993 (Ad 1994) & PhEur 1993					USPNF XVII (Suppl 8)
	PEG 300	PEG 400	PEG 1000	PEG 1540	PEG 4000	
Appearance of solution	+	+	+	+	+	+
Freezing point	—	—	35-40°C	42-46°C	53-56°C	—
Viscosity	+	+	+	+	+	*See* Table III
Average molecular weight	+	+	+	+	+	*See* Table III
Acidity/alkalinity	+	+	+	—	—	—
pH (5% w/v solution)	—	—	—	4.0-7.0	4.5-7.5	4.5-7.5
Hydroxyl value	340-394	264-300	107-118	70-86	30-36	—
Reducing substances	+	+	+	—	—	—
Residue on ignition	—	—	—	—	—	≤ 0.1%
Sulfated ash	≤ 0.2%	≤ 0.2%	≤ 0.2%	≤ 0.1%	≤ 0.1%	—
Arsenic	—	—	—	—	—	≤ 3 ppm
Limit of ethylene glycol and diethylene glycol	≤ 0.4%	≤ 0.4%	—	—	—	≤ 0.25%
Ethylene oxide	≤ 1 ppm	≤ 1 ppm	≤ 1 ppm	—	—	≤ 0.02%
Heavy metals	≤ 20 ppm	≤ 20 ppm	≤ 20 ppm	—	—	≤ 5 ppm
Water	≤ 2.0%	≤ 2.0%	≤ 2.0%	—	—	—

of the coating film when the microcapsules are compressed into tablets.

Polyethylene glycol grades with molecular weights of 6000 and above can be used as lubricants, particularly for soluble tablets. The lubricant action is not as good as that of magnesium stearate, and stickiness may develop if the material becomes too warm during compression. An anti-adherent effect is also exerted, again subject to the avoidance of over-heating.

In addition, polyethylene glycols have been used in the preparation of urethane hydrogels which are used as controlled release agents.

8. Description

The USPNF XVII describes polyethylene glycol as being an addition polymer of ethylene oxide and water. Polyethylene glycol grades 200-600 are liquids whilst grades 1000 and above are solids at ambient temperatures.

Liquid grades (PEG 200-600) occur as clear, colorless or slightly yellow-colored, viscous liquids. They have a slight, but characteristic odor and a bitter, slightly burning taste. PEG 600 can occur as a solid at ambient temperatures.

Solid grades (PEG ≥ 1000) are white or off-white in color, and range in consistency from pastes to waxy flakes. They have a faint, sweet odor. Grades of PEG 6000 and above are available as free flowing milled powders.

9. Pharmacopeial Specifications

See Table II.

Table III: Specification for viscosity of polyethylene glycol of nominal molecular weight at 98.9°C ± 0.3°C from the USPNF XVII (Suppl 8).

Nominal average molecular weight	Viscosity range in mm²/s (cSt)
200	3.9-4.8
300	5.4-6.4
400	6.8-8.0
500	8.3-9.6
600	9.9-11.3
700	11.5-13.0
800	12.5-14.5

Table III: *Continued*

Nominal average molecular weight	Viscosity range in mm²/s (cSt)
900	15.0-17.0
1000	16.0-19.0
1100	18.0-22.0
1200	20.0-24.5
1300	22.0-27.5
1400	24-30
1450	25-32
1500	26-33
1600	28-36
1700	31-39
1800	33-42
1900	35-45
2000	38-49
2100	40-53
2200	43-56
2300	46-60
2400	49-65
2500	51-70
2600	54-74
2700	57-78
2800	60-83
2900	64-88
3000	67-93
3250	73-105
3350	76-110
3500	87-123
3750	99-140
4000	110-158
4250	123-177
4500	140-200
4750	155-228
5000	170-250
5500	206-315
6000	250-390
6500	295-480
7000	350-590
7500	405-735
8000	470-900

10. Typical Properties

Density:
1.11-1.14 g/cm^3 at 25°C for liquid PEGs;
1.15-1.21 g/cm^3 at 25°C for solid PEGs.
Flash point:
182°C for PEG 200;
213°C for PEG 300;
238°C for PEG 400;
250°C for PEG 600.
Freezing point:
< -65°C PEG 200 sets to a glass;
-15 to -8°C for PEG 300;
4-8°C for PEG 400;
15-25°C for PEG 600.
Melting point:
37-40°C for PEG 1000;
44-48°C for PEG 1500;
40-48°C for PEG 1540;
45-50°C for PEG 2000;
48-54°C for PEG 3000;
50-58°C for PEG 4000;
55-63°C for PEG 6000;
60-63°C for PEG 8000;
60-63°C for PEG 20000.
Moisture content: liquid polyethylene glycols are very hygroscopic, although hygroscopicity decreases with increasing molecular weight. Solid grades, e.g. PEG 4000 and above, are not hygroscopic. *See also* HPE Data.
Refractive index:
n_D^{25} = 1.459 for PEG 200;
n_D^{25} = 1.463 for PEG 300;
n_D^{25} = 1.465 for PEG 400;
n_D^{25} = 1.467 for PEG 600.
Solubility: all grades of polyethylene glycol are soluble in water and miscible in all proportions with other polyethylene glycols (after melting, if necessary). Aqueous solutions of higher molecular weight grades may form gels. Liquid polyethylene glycols are soluble in acetone, alcohols, benzene, glycerin and glycols. Solid polyethylene glycols are soluble in acetone, dichloromethane, ethanol and methanol; they are slightly soluble in aliphatic hydrocarbons and ether, but insoluble in fats, fixed oils and mineral oil. *See also* HPE Data.
Surface tension: approximately 44 mN/m (44 dynes/cm) for liquid polyethylene glycols; approximately 55 mN/m (55 dynes/cm) for 10% w/v aqueous solution of solid polyethylene glycol.
Viscosity (kinematic): *see also* HPE Data and Table III.

Grade	Viscosity in mm^2/s (cSt)	
	25°C	99°C
PEG 200	39.9	4.4
PEG 300	68.8	5.9
PEG 400	90.0	7.4
PEG 600	131	11.0
PEG 1000	solid	19.5
PEG 2000	solid	47
PEG 4000	solid	180
PEG 6000	solid	580
PEG 20000	solid	6900

HPE Laboratory Project Data			
	Method	Lab #	Results
Bulk/tap density			
PEG 4000 (flakes)	BTD-3	1	B: 0.485 g/cm^3 [c] T: 0.575 g/cm^3
PEG 4000 (powder)	BTD-1	1	B: 0.581 g/cm^3 [c] T: 0.704 g/cm^3
PEG 4000 (powder)	BTD-7	14	B: 0.610 g/cm^3 [c] T: 0.750 g/cm^3
PEG 6000 (flakes)	BTD-3	1	B: 0.476 g/cm^3 [c] T: 0.562 g/cm^3
PEG 6000 (powder)	BTD-1	1	B: 0.481 g/cm^3 [c] T: 0.581 g/cm^3
PEG 6000 (powder)	BTD-7	14	B: 0.510 g/cm^3 [c] T: 0.570 g/cm^3
Density			
PEG 4000 (prilled)	DE-1	31	1.043 g/cm^3 [a]
PEG 4000 (powder)	DE-1	31	1.205 g/cm^3 [c]
PEG 6000 (powder)	DE-1	31	1.122 g/cm^3 [c]
Moisture content			
PEG 1540	MC-3	28	0.585% [c]
PEG 4000 (flakes)	MC-19	1	0.290% [c]
PEG 4000 (powder)	MC-19	1	0.290% [c]
PEG 4000 (powder)	MC-20	2	0.300% [b]
PEG 4000	EMC-1	2	See Fig. 1. [b]
PEG 4000 (powder)	SDI-2	26	See Fig. 2. [c]
PEG E-4000	SDI-2	26	See Fig. 2. [a]
PEG 6000 (flakes)	MC-19	1	0.120% [c]
PEG 6000 (powder)	MC-19	1	0.150% [c]
PEG 6000 (powder)	SDI-2	26	See Fig. 3. [c]
PEG E-6000	SDI-2	26	See Fig. 3. [a]
Particle size			
PEG 4000 (flakes)	PSD-1	1	See Fig. 4. [c]
PEG 4000 (powder)	PSD-1	1	See Fig. 5. [c]
PEG 6000 (flakes)	PSD-1	1	See Fig. 6. [c]
PEG 6000 (powder)	PSD-1	1	See Fig. 7. [c]
Solubility in ethanol (95%) at 25°C			
PEG 4000 (flakes)	SOL-2	1	0.575 mg/mL [c]
PEG 4000 (powder)	SOL-2	1	0.575 mg/mL [c]
PEG 6000 (flakes)	SOL-2	1	0.500 mg/mL [c]
PEG 6000 (powder)	SOL-2	1	0.420 mg/mL [c]
Solubility in *n*-hexane at 25°C			
PEG 4000 (flakes)	SOL-1	1	0.006 mg/mL [c]
PEG 4000 (powder)	SOL-1	1	0.013 mg/mL [c]
PEG 6000 (flakes)	SOL-1	1	0.011 mg/mL [c]
PEG 6000 (powder)	SOL-1	1	0.055 mg/mL [c]
Solubility in water at 25°C			
PEG 4000 (flakes)	SOL-2	1	2100 mg/mL [c]
PEG 4000 (powder)	SOL-2	1	2100 mg/mL [c]
PEG 6000 (flakes)	SOL-2	1	1900 mg/mL [c]
PEG 6000 (powder)	SOL-2	1	1900 mg/mL [c]
Viscosity			
PEG 4000 (flakes)	VIS-1	27	1.26 ± 0.1 mPa s [a]
PEG 4000 (flakes)	VIS-1	27	1.26 ± 0.1 mPa s [b]
PEG 4000 (powder)	VIS-1	27	1.26 ± 0.1 mPa s [b]

Supplier: a. BASF; b. McKesson; c. Union Carbide Corporation.

11. Stability and Storage Conditions

Polyethylene glycols are chemically stable in air and in solution although grades with a molecular weight less than 2000 are hygroscopic. Polyethylene glycols do not support microbial growth, nor do they become rancid.
Polyethylene glycols and aqueous polyethylene glycol solutions can be sterilized by autoclaving, filtration or gamma

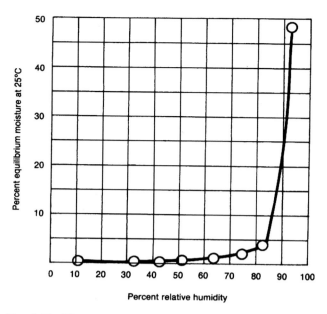

Fig. 1: Equilibrium moisture content of PEG 4000 (McKesson, Lot #B192-8209) at 25°C.

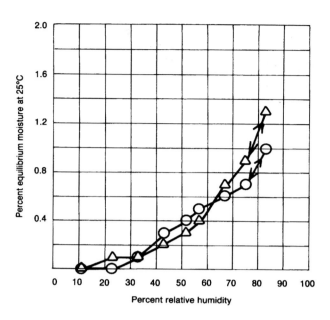

Fig. 3: Equilibrium moisture content of PEG 6000 at 25°C.
○ PEG 6000 powder (Union Carbide Corporation, Lot #B-507).
△ PEG E-6000 (BASF, Lot #WPNY-124B).

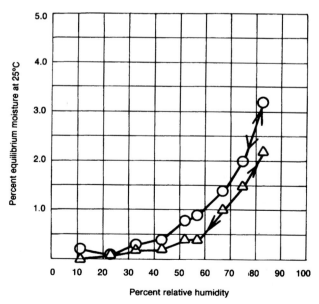

Fig. 2: Equilibrium moisture content of PEG 4000 at 25°C.
○ PEG 4000 powder (Union Carbide Corporation, Lot #B-251).
△ PEG E-4000 (BASF, Lot #WPYA-575B).

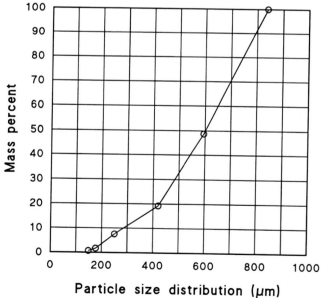

Fig. 4: Particle size distribution of PEG 4000 flakes.

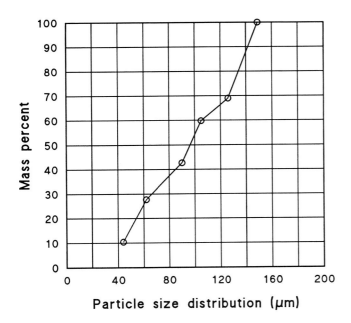

Fig. 5: Particle size distribution of PEG 4000 powder.

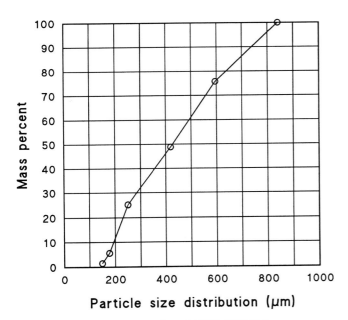

Fig. 6: Particle size distribution of PEG 6000 flakes.

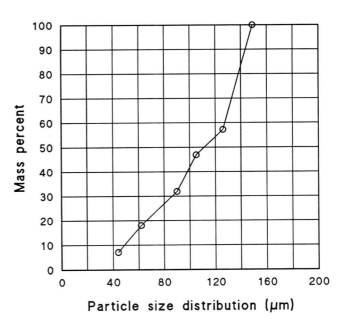

Fig. 7: Particle size distribution of PEG 6000 powder.

irradiation.[9] Sterilization of solid grades by dry heat at 150°C for one hour may induce oxidation, darkening and the formation of acidic degradation products. Ideally, sterilization should be carried out in an inert atmosphere. Oxidation of polyethylene glycols may also be inhibited by the inclusion of a suitable antioxidant.

If heated tanks are used to maintain solid polyethylene glycols in a molten state, care must be taken to avoid contamination with iron, which can lead to discoloration. The temperature must be kept to the minimum necessary to ensure fluidity; oxidation may occur if polyethylene glycols are exposed for long periods to temperatures exceeding 50°C. However, storage under nitrogen reduces the possibility of oxidation.

Polyethylene glycols should be stored in well-closed containers in a cool, dry, place. Stainless steel, aluminum, glass or lined steel containers are preferred for the storage of liquid grades.

12. Incompatibilities

The chemical reactivity of polyethylene glycols is mainly confined to the two terminal hydroxyl groups, which can be either esterified or etherified. However, all grades can exhibit some oxidizing activity due to the presence of peroxide impurities and secondary products formed by autoxidation.

Liquid and solid polyethylene glycol grades may be incompatible with some colors.

The antibacterial activity of certain antibiotics, particularly penicillin and bacitracin, is reduced in polyethylene glycol bases. The preservative efficacy of the parabens may also be impaired due to binding with polyethylene glycols.

Physical effects caused by polyethylene glycol bases include softening and liquefaction in mixtures with phenol, tannic acid and salicylic acid. Discoloration of sulfonamides and dithranol can also occur and sorbitol may be precipitated from mixtures. Plastics, such as polyethylene, phenolformaldehyde, polyvinyl chloride and cellulose-ester membranes (in filters) may be softened or dissolved by polyethylene glycols. Migration of polyethylene glycol can occur from tablet film coatings, leading to interaction with core components.

13. Method of Manufacture

Polyethylene glycols are condensation polymers formed by the reaction of ethylene oxide and water under pressure in the presence of a catalyst.

14. Safety

Polyethylene glycols are widely used in a variety of pharmaceutical formulations. Generally, they are regarded as nontoxic and nonirritant materials.[10-12] However, adverse reactions to polyethylene glycols have been reported and although of relatively low toxicity, any toxicity appears to be greatest with polyethylene glycols of low molecular weight.

Table IV: Animal toxicity data (LD$_{50}$) for various grades of polyethylene glycol.[17]

PEG grade	Guinea pig (oral)	Mouse (IP)	Mouse (IV)	Mouse (oral)	Rabbit (oral)	Rabbit (SC)	Rat (IP)	Rat (IV)	Rat (oral)	Rat (SC)
			LD$_{50}$ in g/kg							
PEG 200	—	7.5	—	38.3	19.9	—	—	—	28.9	—
PEG 300	19.6	—	—	—	17.3	—	17	—	27.5	—
PEG 400	15.7	10.0	8.6	28.9	26.8	—	9.7	7.3	30.2	—
PEG 810	—	—	—	—	—	—	—	13	—	16
PEG 1000	22.5	20	—	—	—	—	—	—	42	—
PEG 1540	—	—	—	—	—	—	15.4	—	51.2	—
PEG 4000	50.9	—	16	—	76	18	11.6	—	50	—
PEG 6000	50	—	—	—	—	—	6.8	—	50	—

Polyethylene glycols administered topically may cause stinging, especially when applied to mucous membranes. Hypersensitivity reactions to polyethylene glycols applied topically, including urticaria and delayed allergic reactions, have also been reported.[13] However, the most serious adverse effects associated with polyethylene glycols are hyperosmolarity, metabolic acidosis and renal failure following the topical use of polyethylene glycols in burn patients.[14] Topical preparations containing polyethylene glycols should therefore be used cautiously in patients with renal failure, extensive burns, or open wounds.

Oral administration of large quantities of polyethylene glycols can have a laxative effect. Therapeutically, up to 6 L of an aqueous mixture of electrolytes and high molecular weight polyethylene glycol is consumed by patients undergoing bowel cleansing.[15]

Liquid polyethylene glycols may be absorbed when taken orally, but the higher molecular weight polyethylene glycols are not significantly absorbed from the gastrointestinal tract. Absorbed polyethylene glycol is excreted largely unchanged in the urine although polyethylene glycols of low molecular weight may be partially metabolized.

The WHO has set an estimated acceptable daily intake of polyethylene glycols at up to 10 mg/kg body-weight.[16]

In parenteral products, the maximum recommended concentration of PEG 300 is approximately 30% v/v since hemolytic effects have been observed at concentrations greater than about 40% v/v.

For animal toxicity data *see* Table IV.

15. Handling Precautions

Observe normal precautions appropriate to the circumstances and quantity of material handled. Eye protection is recommended.

16. Regulatory Status

Included in the FDA Inactive Ingredients Guide (dental preparations, IM and IV injections, ophthalmic preparations, oral capsules, solutions, syrups and tablets, rectal, topical and vaginal preparations). Included in nonparenteral medicines licensed in the UK.

17. Pharmacopeias

Arg, Aust, Belg, Br, Braz, Cz, Eur, Fr, Ger, Hung, It, Jpn, Neth, Nord, Pol, Port, Rom, Swiss, USPNF and Yug.
Some pharmacopeias, such as the USPNF XVII, have a single monograph describing various different grades; other pharmacopeias have individual monographs. The BP 1993 (Ad 1994) for example has separate monographs for PEG 300, PEG 400, PEG 1000, PEG 1540 and PEG 4000.

18. Related Substances

Polyoxyethylene Alkyl Ethers; Polyoxyethylene Sorbitan Fatty Acid Esters; Suppository Bases.

19. Comments

—

20. Specific References

1. Hadia IA, Ugriné HE, Farouk AM, Shayoub M. Formulation of polyethylene glycol ointment bases suitable for tropical and subtropical climates I. Acta Pharm Hung 1989; 59: 137-142.
2. Kellaway IW, Marriott C. Correlations between physical and drug release characteristics of polyethylene glycol suppositories. J Pharm Sci 1975; 64: 1162-1166.
3. Wells JI, Bhatt DA, Khan KA. Improved wet massed tableting using plasticized binder. J Pharm Pharmacol 1982; 34(Suppl): 46P.
4. Chiou WL, Riegelman S. Pharmaceutical applications of solid dispersion systems. J Pharm Sci 1971; 60: 1281-1302.
5. Ford JL, Rubinstein MH. Formulation and ageing of tablets prepared from indomethacin-polyethylene glycol 6000 solid dispersions. Pharm Acta Helv 1980; 55: 1-7.
6. Vila-Jato JL, Blanco J, Alonso MJ. The effect of the molecular weight of polyethylene glycol on the bioavailabilty of paracetamol-polyethylene glycol solid dispersions. J Pharm Pharmacol 1986; 38: 126-128.
7. Miralles MJ, McGinity JW, Martin A. Combined water-soluble carriers for coprecipitates of tolbutamide. J Pharm Sci 1982; 71: 302-304.
8. Okhamafe AO, York P. Moisture permeation mechanism of some aqueous-based film coats. J Pharm Pharmacol 1982; 34(Suppl): 53P.
9. Bhalla HL, Menon MR, Gopal NGS. Radiation sterilization of polyethylene glycols. Int J Pharmaceutics 1983; 17: 351-355.
10. Smyth HF, Carpenter CP, Weil CS. The toxicology of the polyethylene glycols. J Am Pharm Assoc (Sci) 1950; 39: 349-354.
11. Tusing TW, Elsea JR, Sauveur AB. The chronic dermal toxicity of a series of polyethylene glycols. J Am Pharm Assoc (Sci) 1954; 43: 489-490.
12. Smyth HF, Carpenter CP, Weil CS. The chronic oral toxicology of the polyethylene glycols. J Am Pharm Assoc (Sci) 1955; 44: 27-30.
13. Fisher AA. Immediate and delayed allergic contact reactions to polyethylene glycol. Contact Dermatitis 1978; 4: 135-138.
14. Topical PEG in burn ointments. FDA Drug Bull 1982; 12: 25-26.

15. Reynolds JEF, editor. Martindale: the extra pharmacopoeia, 30th edition. London: The Pharmaceutical Press, 1993: 1384-1385.

16. FAO/WHO. Evaluation of certain food additives: twenty-third report of the joint FAO/WHO expert committee on food additives. Tech Rep Ser Wld Hlth Org 1980; No. 648.

17. Sweet DV, editor. Registry of toxic effects of chemical substances. Cincinnati: US Department of Health, 1987.

21. General References

Donovan MD, Flynn GL, Amidon GL. Absorption of polyethylene glycols 600 through 2000: molecular weight dependence of gastrointestinal and nasal absorption. Pharm Res 1990; 7: 863-867.

Union Carbide Corporation. Technical literature: *Carbowax* polyethylene glycols, 1986.

Van Dam J, Daenens P. Molecular weight identification of polyethylene glycols in pharmaceutical preparations by gel permeation chromatography. J Pharm Sci 1993; 82: 938-941.

Yamaoka T, Tabata Y, Ikada Y. Distribution and tissue uptake of poly(ethylene glycol) with different molecular weights after intravenous administration to mice. J Pharm Sci 1994; 83: 601-606.

22. Authors

USA: JC Price.

Polymethacrylates

1. Nonproprietary Names
USPNF: Ammonio methacrylate copolymer
USPNF: Methacrylic acid copolymer
Note that two separate monographs applicable to polymethacrylates are contained in the USPNF, *see* Section 9.

2. Synonyms
Eudragit; polymeric methacrylates.

3. Chemical Name and CAS Registry Number
See Table I.

4. Empirical Formula   Molecular Weight
The USPNF XVII describes methacrylic acid copolymer as a fully polymerized copolymer of methacrylic acid and an acrylic or methacrylic ester. Three types, type A (*Eudragit L*), type B (*Eudragit S*), and type C (*Eudragit L 30 D-55*), are defined which vary in their methacrylic acid content and solution viscosity. Two additional polymers, type A (*Eudragit RL*) and type B (*Eudragit RS*), also referred to as ammonio methacrylate copolymers, consisting of fully polymerized copolymers of acrylic acid and methacrylic acid esters with a low content of quaternary ammonium groups, are also described in the USPNF XVII. *See* Section 9.
Typically, the molecular weight of the polymer is $\geqslant 100\,000$.

5. Structural Formula

For *Eudragit E*:
$R_1, R_3 = CH_3$
$R_2 = CH_2CH_2N(CH_3)_2$
$R_4 = CH_3, C_4H_9$
For *Eudragit L* and *S*:
$R_1, R_3 = CH_3$
$R_2 = H$
$R_4 = CH_3$
For *Eudragit RL* and *RS*:
$R_1 = H, CH_3$
$R_2 = CH_3, C_2H_5$
$R_3 = CH_3$
$R_4 = CH_2CH_2N(CH_3)_3{}^+Cl^-$
For *Eudragit NE 30 D*:
$R_1, R_3 = H, CH_3$
$R_2, R_4 = CH_3, C_2H_5$
For *Eudragit L 30 D-55* and *L 100-55*:
$R_1, R_3 = H, CH_3$
$R_2 = H$
$R_4 = CH_3, C_2H_5$

6. Functional Category
Film-former; tablet binder; tablet diluent.

7. Applications in Pharmaceutical Formulation or Technology
Polymethacrylates are primarily used in oral capsule and tablet formulations as film coating agents.[1-10] Depending on the type of polymer used, films of different solubility characteristics can be produced, *see* Table III.
Eudragit E is used as a plain or insulating film former; it is soluble in gastric fluid below pH 5. In contrast, *Eudragit L* and *S* types are used as enteric coating agents since they are resistant to gastric fluid. Different types are available which are soluble at different pH values, e.g. *Eudragit L 100* is soluble at > pH 6, *Eudragit S 100* is soluble at > pH 7.
Eudragit RL, *RS* and *NE 30 D* are used to form water-insoluble film coats for sustained release products. *Eudragit RL* films are more permeable than those of *Eudragit RS*, and by mixing the two types together films of varying permeability can be obtained. *Eudragit L 100-55* is a redispersible powder and is an alternative to *Eudragit L 30 D-55* for aqueous enteric coating.
Polymethacrylates are also used as binders in both aqueous and organic wet-granulation processes. Larger quantities (5-20%) of dry polymer are used to control the release of an active substance from a tablet matrix. Solid polymers may be used in direct compression processes in quantities of 10-50%. Polymethacrylate polymers may additionally be used to form the matrix layers of transdermal delivery systems and have also been used to prepare novel gel formulations for rectal administration.[11]
See also Section 19.

8. Description
Polymethacrylates are synthetic cationic and anionic polymers of dimethylaminoethylmethacrylates, methacrylic acid and methacrylic acid esters in varying ratios. Several different types are commercially available and may be obtained as the dry powder, an aqueous dispersion, or as an organic solution. A (60:40) mixture of acetone and propan-2-ol is most commonly used as the organic solvent. *See* Tables I and II.
Eudragit E is cationic polymer based on dimethylaminoethyl methacrylate and other neutral methacrylic acid esters. It is soluble in gastric fluid as well as in weakly acidic buffer solutions (up to approximately pH 5). *Eudragit E* is available as a 12.5% ready-to-use solution in propan-2-ol/acetone (60:40). It is light yellow in color with the characteristic odor of the solvents. Solvent-free granules contain $\geqslant 98\%$ dried weight content of *Eudragit E*.
Eudragit L and *S*, also referred to as methacylic acid copolymers in the USPNF monograph, are anionic copolymerization products of methacrylic acid and methyl methacrylate. The ratio of free carboxyl groups to the ester is approximately 1:1 in *Eudragit L* and approximately 1:2 in *Eudragit S*. Both polymers are readily soluble in neutral to weakly alkaline conditions (pH 6-7) and form salts with alkalis, thus affording film coats which are resistant to gastric media but soluble in intestinal fluid. They are available as a 12.5% solution in propan-2-ol without plasticizer (*Eudragit L 12.5* and *S 12.5*); and as a 12.5% ready-to-use solution in propan-2-ol with 1.25% dibutyl phthalate as plasticizer (*Eudragit L 12.5 P* and *S 12.5 P*). Solutions are colorless, with the characteristic odor of the solvent. *Eudragit L-100* and

Table I: Chemical name and CAS registry number of polymethacrylates.

Chemical name	Trade name	CAS number
Poly(butyl methacrylate, (2-dimethyl aminoethyl) methacrylate, methyl methacrylate) 1:2:1	*Eudragit E 100* *Eudragit E 12.5*	[24938-16-7]
Poly(ethyl acrylate, methyl methacrylate) 2:1	*Eudragit NE 30 D* (formerly *Eudragit 30 D*)	[9010-88-2]
Poly(methacrylic acid, methyl methacrylate) 1:1	*Eudragit L 100* *Eudragit L 12.5* *Eudragit L 12.5 P*	[25806-15-1]
Poly(methacrylic acid, ethyl acrylate) 1:1	*Eudragit L 30 D-55* *Eudragit L 100-55*	[25212-88-8]
Poly(methacrylic acid, methyl methacrylate) 1:2	*Eudragit S 100* *Eudragit S 12.5* *Eudragit S 12.5 P*	[25086-15-1]
Poly(ethyl acrylate, methyl methacrylate, trimethylammonioethyl methacrylate chloride) 1:2:0.2	*Eudragit RL 100* *Eudragit RL PO* *Eudragit RL 30 D* *Eudragit RL 12.5*	[33434-24-1]
Poly(ethyl acrylate, methyl methacrylate, trimethylammonioethyl methacrylate chloride) 1:2:0.1	*Eudragit RS 100* *Eudragit RS PO* *Eudragit RS 30 D* *Eudragit RS 12.5*	[33434-24-1]

Eudragit S-100 are white free flowing powders with at least 95% of dry polymers.

Eudragit RL and *Eudragit RS*, also referred to as ammonio-methacrylate copolymers in the USPNF monograph, are copolymers synthesized from acrylic acid and methacrylic acid esters with *Eudragit RL* (type A) having 10% of functional quaternary ammonium groups and *Eudragit RS* (type B) having 5% of functional quaternary ammonium groups. The ammonium groups are present as salts and give rise to pH-independent permeability of the polymers. Both polymers are water-insoluble, and films prepared from *Eudragit RL* are freely permeable to water, whereas, films prepared from *Eudragit RS* are only slightly permeable to water. They are available as 12.5% ready-to-use solutions in propan-2-ol/acetone (60:40). Solutions are colorless or slightly yellow in color, and may be clear or slightly turbid; they have an odor characteristic of the solvents. Solvent-free granules (*Eudragit RL 100* and *Eudragit RS 100*) contain ≥ 97% of the dried weight content of the polymer.

Eudragit RL PO and *Eudragit RS PO* are fine, white powders with a slight amine-like odor. They are characteristically the same polymers as *Eudragit RL* and *RS*. They contain ≥ 97% of dry polymer.

Eudragit RL 30 D and *Eudragit RS 30 D* are aqueous dispersions of copolymers of acrylic acid and methacrylic acid esters with a low content of quaternary ammonium groups. The dispersions contain 30% polymer. The quaternary groups occur as salts and are responsible for the permeability of films made from these polymers. Films prepared from *Eudragit RL 30 D* are readily permeable to water and to dissolved active substances, whereas films prepared from *Eudragit RS 30 D* are less permeable to water. Film coatings prepared from both polymers give pH-independent release of active substance. Plasticizers are usually added to improve film properties.

Eudragit NE 30 D is an aqueous dispersion of a neutral copolymer consisting of polymethacrylic acid esters. The dispersions are milky-white liquids of low viscosity and have a weak aromatic odor. Films prepared from the lacquer swell in water, to which they become permeable. Thus, films produced are insoluble in water, but give pH-independent drug release.

Eudragit L 30 D-55 is an aqueous dispersion of an anionic copolymer based on methacrylic acid and acrylic acid ethyl ester. The polymer corresponds to USPNF methacrylic acid copolymer, type C. The ratio of free carboxyl groups to ester groups is 1:1. Films dissolve above pH 5.5 forming salts with alkalis, thus affording coatings which are insoluble in gastric media, but soluble in the small intestine.

Eudragit L 100-55 (prepared by spray-drying *Eudragit L 30 D-55*) is a white, free-flowing powder which is redispersible in water to form a latex which has properties similar to *Eudragit L 30 D-55*.

9. Pharmacopeial Specifications

Specifications for methacrylic acid copolymers (*Eudragit L, S* and *L 30 D-55*).

Test	USPNF XVII (Suppl 6)
Identification	+
Viscosity	
Type A	50-200 mPa s
Type B	50-200 mPa s
Type C	100-200 mPa s
Loss on drying	
Type A	≤ 5.0%
Type B	≤ 5.0%
Type C	≤ 3.0%
Residue on ignition	
Type A	≤ 0.1%
Type B	≤ 0.1%
Type C	≤ 0.4%
Arsenic	≤ 2 ppm
Heavy metals	≤ 0.002%
Monomers	≤ 0.3%
Assay of methacrylic acid units (dried basis)	
Type A	46.0-50.6%
Type B	27.6-30.7%
Type C	46.0-50.6%

Specifications for ammonio methacrylate copolymers (*Eudragit RL* and *RS*).

Test	USPNF XVII (Suppl 4)
Identification	+
Viscosity	
Types A and B	⩽ 15 mPa s
Loss on drying	
Types A and B	⩽ 3.0%
Residue on ignition	
Types A and B	⩽ 0.1%
Arsenic	⩽ 2 ppm
Heavy metals	⩽ 0.002%
Monomers	⩽ 0.3%
Assay of ammonio methacrylate units (dried basis)	
Type A	8.85-11.96%
Type B	4.48-6.77%

10. Typical Properties

Acid value: 315 for *Eudragit L 12.5, L 12.5 P, L 100, L 30 D-55,* and *L 100-55*; 180-200 for *Eudragit S 12.5, S 12.5 P,* and *S 100*.

Alkali value:
162-198 for *Eudragit E 12.5* and *E 100*;
23.9-32.3 for *Eudragit RL 12.5, RL 100,* and *RL PO*;
27.5-31.7 for *Eudragit RL 30 D*;
12.1-18.3 for *Eudragit RS 12.5, RS 100,* and *RS PO*;
16.5-22.3 for *Eudragit RS 30 D*.
Density:
0.81-0.82 g/cm^3 for *Eudragit E*;
0.83-0.85 g/cm^3 for *Eudragit L, S 12.5* and *12.5 P*;
0.83-0.85 g/cm^3 for *Eudragit L, S 100*;
1.06-1.07 g/cm^3 for *Eudragit L 30 D-55*;
0.82-0.84 g/cm^3 for *Eudragit L 100-55*;
0.815-0.835 g/cm^3 for *Eudragit RL* and *RS 12.5*;
0.815-0.835 g/cm^3 for *Eudragit RL* and *RS PO*;
1.045-1.055 g/cm^3 for *Eudragit RL* and *RS 30 D*.
Refractive index:
n_D^{20} = 1.38-1.385 for *Eudragit E*;
n_D^{20} = 1.39-1.395 for *Eudragit L* and *S*;
n_D^{20} = 1.387-1.392 for *Eudragit L 100-55*;
n_D^{20} = 1.38-1.385 for *Eudragit RL* and *RS*.
Solubility: *see* Table II.
Viscosity (dynamic):
3-12 mPa s for *Eudragit E*;
50-200 mPa s for *Eudragit L* and *S*;
⩽ 50 mPa s for *Eudragit L 30 D-55*;
100-200 mPa s for *Eudragit L 100-55*;
⩽ 15 mPa s for *Eudragit RL* and *RS*;
⩾ 200 mPa s for *Eudragit RL* and *RS D*.

Table II: Solubility of commercially available polymethacrylates (*Eudragit*, Röhm Pharma GmbH) in various solutions.

Type	Acetone and alcohols[a]	Dichloromethane	Solvent Ethyl acetate	1N HCl	1N NaOH	Petroleum ether	Water
Eudragit E 12.5	M	M	M	M	—	M	—
Eudragit E 100	S	S	S	—	—	I	I
Eudragit L 12.5 P	M	M	M	—	M	P	P
Eudragit L 12.5	M	M	M	—	M	P	P
Eudragit L 100-55	S	I	I	—	S	I	I
Eudragit L 100	S	I	I	—	S	I	I
Eudragit L 30 D-55[b]	M[c]	—	—	—	M[d]	—	M
Eudragit S 12.5 P	M	M	M	—	M	P	P
Eudragit S 12.5	M	M	M	—	M	P	P
Eudragit S 100	S	I	I	—	S	I	I
Eudragit RL 12.5	M	M	M	—	—	P	M
Eudragit RL 100	S	S	S	—	—	I	I
Eudragit RL PO	S	S	S	—	I	I	I
Eudragit RL 30 D	M[e]	M	M	—	I	I	M
Eudragit RS 12.5	M	M	M	—	—	P	M
Eudragit RS 100	S	S	S	—	—	I	I
Eudragit RS PO	S	S	S	—	I	I	I
Eudragit RS 30 D	M[e]	M	M	—	I	I	M

Where: S = soluble;
M = miscible;
I = insoluble or immiscible;
P = precipitates.
Note: a. Alcohols including ethanol, methanol and propan-2-ol.
b. Supplied as a milky-white colored aqueous dispersion.
c. A 1:5 mixture forms a clear, viscous, solution.
d. A 1:2 mixture forms a clear or slightly opalescent, viscous liquid.
e. A 1 part of both *Eudragit RL 30 D* and *Eudragit RS 30 D* dissolve completely in 5 parts acetone, ethanol or propan-2-ol to form a clear or slightly turbid solution. However, when mixed in a ratio of 1:5 with methanol, *Eudragit RL 30 D* dissolves completely, whereas *Eudragit RS 30 D* only partially.

11. Stability and Storage Conditions

Dry powder polymer forms are stable at temperatures less than 30°C. Above this temperature, powders tend to form clumps although this does not affect the quality of the substance and the clumps can be readily broken up. Dry powders are stable for at least two years if stored in a tightly closed container at less than 30°C.

Dispersions are sensitive to extreme temperatures and phase separation occurs below 0°C. Dispersions should therefore be stored at temperatures between 5-25°C and are stable for at least one year after shipping from the manufacturer's warehouse if stored in a tightly closed container at the above conditions.

12. Incompatibilities

Incompatibilities occur with certain polymethacrylate dispersions depending upon the ionic and physical properties of the polymer and solvent. For example, coagulation may be caused by soluble electrolytes, pH changes, some organic solvents and extremes of temperature, *see* Table II. Dispersions of *Eudragit*

L 30 D, *RL 30 D*, *L 100-55* and *RS 30 D* are also incompatible with magnesium stearate.

Interactions between polymethacrylates and some drugs can occur although solid polymethacrylates and organic solutions are generally more compatible than aqueous dispersions.

13. Method of Manufacture

Prepared by the polymerization of acrylic and methacrylic acids or their esters, e.g. butyl ester or dimethylaminoethyl ester.

14. Safety

Polymethacrylate copolymers are widely used as film coating materials in oral pharmaceutical formulations. They are also used to a lesser extent in topical formulations and are generally regarded as nontoxic and nonirritant materials.

A daily intake of 2 mg/kg body-weight of *Eudragit* (equivalent to approximately 150 mg for an average adult) may be regarded as essentially safe in humans.

See also Section 15.

Table III: Summary of properties and uses of commercially available polymethacrylates (*Eudragit*, Röhm Pharma GmbH).

Type	Supply form	Polymer dry weight content	Recommended solvents or diluents	Solubility	Applications
Eudragit E 12.5	Organic solution	12.5%	Acetone, alcohols	Soluble in gastric fluid to pH 5	Film coating
Eudragit E 100	Granules	98%	Acetone, alcohols	Soluble in gastric fluid to pH 5	Film coating
Eudragit L 12.5 P	Organic solution	12.5%	Acetone, alcohols	Soluble in intestinal fluid from pH 6	Enteric coatings
Eudragit L 12.5	Organic solution	12.5%	Acetone, alcohols	Soluble in intestinal fluid from pH 6	Enteric coatings
Eudragit L 100	Powder	95%	Acetone, alcohols	Soluble in intestinal fluid from pH 6	Enteric coatings
Eudragit L 100-55	Powder	95%	Acetone, alcohols	Soluble in intestinal fluid from pH 5.5	Enteric coatings
Eudragit L 30 D-55	Aqueous dispersion	30%	Water	Soluble in intestinal fluid from pH 5.5	Enteric coatings
Eudragit S 12.5 P	Organic solution	12.5%	Acetone, alcohols	Soluble in intestinal fluid from pH 7	Enteric coatings
Eudragit S 12.5	Organic solution	12.5%	Acetone, alcohols	Soluble in intestinal fluid from pH 7	Enteric coatings
Eudragit S 100	Powder fluid	95%	Acetone, alcohols	Soluble in intestinal from pH 7	Enteric coatings
Eudragit RL 12.5	Organic solution	12.5%	Acetone, alcohols	High permeability	Sustained release
Eudragit RL 100	Granules	97%	Acetone, alcohols	High permeability	Sustained release
Eudragit RL PO	Powder	97%	Acetone, alcohols	High permeability	Sustained release
Eudragit RL 30 D	Aqueous dispersion	30%	Water	High permeability	Sustained release
Eudragit RS 12.5	Organic solution	12.5%	Acetone, alcohols	Low permeability	Sustained release
Eudragit RS 100	Granules	97%	Acetone, alcohols	Low permeability	Sustained release
Eudragit RS PO	Powder	97%	Acetone, alcohols	Low permeability	Sustained release
Eudragit RS 30 D	Aqueous dispersion	30%	Water	Low permeability	Sustained release
Eudragit NE 30 D	Aqueous dispersion	30% or 40%	Water	Swellable, permeable	Sustained release, tablet matrix

Note: Recommended plasticizers for the above types of *Eudragit* polymers include dibutyl phthalate, polyethylene glycols and triethyl citrate. Approximately 20% plasticizer is required for *Eudragit RL 30 D* and *Eudragit RS 30 D*. A plasticizer is not necessary with *Eudragit E 12.5*, *Eudragit E 100* and *Eudragit NE 30 D*.

15. Handling Precautions

Observe normal precautions appropriate to the circumstances and quantity of material handled. Additional measures should be taken when handling organic solutions of polymethacrylates. Eye protection, gloves and a dust mask or respirator are recommended. Polymethacrylates should be handled in a well-ventilated environment and measures taken to prevent dust formation.

Acute and chronic adverse effects have been observed in workers handling the related substances methyl methacrylate and poly(methyl methacrylate) (PMMA).[12,13] In the UK, the occupational exposure limit for methyl methacrylate has been set at 410 mg/m^3 (100 ppm) long-term (8-hour TWA), and 510 mg/m^3 (125 ppm) short-term.[14]

See also Section 18.

16. Regulatory Status

Included in the FDA Inactive Ingredients Guide (oral capsules and tablets). Included in nonparenteral medicines licensed in the UK.

17. Pharmacopeias

Fr and USPNF.

18. Related Substances

Methyl methacrylate; poly(methyl methacrylate).

Methyl methacrylate: $C_5H_8O_2$
Molecular weight: 100.13
CAS number: [80-62-6]
Synonyms: methacrylic acid, methyl ester; methyl 2-methacrylate; methyl 2-methylpropenoate; MME.
Comments: methyl methacrylate forms the basis of acrylic bone cements used in orthopaedic surgery.

Poly(methyl methacrylate): $(C_5H_8O_2)_n$
Synonyms: methyl methacrylate polymer; PMMA.
Comments: poly(methyl methacrylate) has been used as a material for intra-ocular lenses, for denture bases and as a cement for dental prostheses.

19. Comments

A number of different polymethacrylates are commercially available which have different applications and properties, *see* Table III.

For spray-coating, polymer solutions and dispersions should be diluted with suitable solvents. Some products need the addition of a plasticizer such as: dibutyl sebacate; dibutyl phthalate; glyceryl triacetate and polyethylene glycol. Different types of plasticizer may be mixed to optimize the polymer properties for special requirements.

20. Specific References

1. Lehmann K, Dreher D. The use of aqueous synthetic-polymer dispersions for coating pharmaceutical dosage forms. Drugs Made Ger 1973; 16: 126, 131, 132, 134, 136.
2. Lehmann K. Acrylic coatings in controlled release tablet manufacture I. Mfg Chem Aerosol News 1973; 44(5): 36-38.
3. Lehmann K. Acrylic coatings in controlled release tablet manufacture II. Mfg Chem Aerosol News 1973; 44(6): 39-41.
4. Lehmann K. Polymer coating of tablets - a versatile technique. Mfg Chem Aerosol News 1974; 45(5): 48, 50.
5. Gurny R, Guitard P, Buri P, Sucker H. Realization and theoretical development of controlled-release drug forms using methacrylate films 3: preparation and characterization of controlled-release drug forms [in French]. Pharm Acta Helv 1977; 52: 182-187.
6. Lehmann K, Dreher D. Coating of tablets and small particles with acrylic resins by fluid bed technology. Int J Pharm Technol Prod Manuf 1981; 2(4): 31-43.
7. Dew MJ, Hughes PJ, Lee MG, Evans BK, Rhodes J. An oral preparation to release drugs in the human colon. Br J Clin Pharmacol 1982; 14: 405-408.
8. Lehmann K. Formulation of controlled release tablets with acrylic resins. Acta Pharm Fenn 1984; 93: 55-74.
9. Lehmann K. Acrylic latices from redispersible powders for peroral and transdermal drug formulations. Drug Dev Ind Pharm 1986; 12: 265-287.
10. Lehmann K, Dreher D. Mixtures of aqueous polymethacrylate dispersions for drug coating. Drugs Made Ger 1988; 31: 101-102.
11. Umejima H, Kim N-S, Ito T, Uchida T, Goto S. Preparation and evaluation of Eudragit gels VI: in vivo evaluation of Eudispert rectal hydrogel and Xerogel containing salicylamide. J Pharm Sci 1993; 82: 195-199.
12. Routledge R. Possible hazard of contact lens manufacture [letter]. Br Med J 1973; 1: 487-488.
13. Burchman S, Wheater RH. Hazard of methyl methacrylate to operating room personnel. JAMA 1976; 235: 2652.
14. Health and Safety Executive. EH40/93: occupational exposure limits, 1993. London: HMSO, 1993.

21. General References

McGinity JW. Aqueous polymeric coatings for pharmaceutical dosage forms. New York: Marcel Dekker Inc, 1989.
Röhm Pharma GmbH. Technical literature: *Eudragit*, 1990.

22. Authors

USA: AJ Shukla.

Polyoxyethylene Alkyl Ethers

1. Nonproprietary Names

The polyoxyethylene alkyl ethers are a series of polyoxyethylene glycol ethers of *n*-alcohols (lauryl, myristyl, cetyl and stearyl alcohol). Of the large number of different materials commercially available two types are listed in the USPNF XVII, one of which is equivalent to a type listed in the BP 1993.
BP: Cetomacrogol 1000
USPNF: Poloxyl 20 cetostearyl ether
USPNF: Poloxyl 10 oleyl ether
Polyoxyethylene alkyl ethers are extensively employed in cosmetics where the CTFA names laureth-N, myreth-N, ceteth-N and steareth-N are commonly used. In this nomenclature, N is the number of ethylene oxide groups, e.g. steareth-20.
See also Sections 2, 3, 4, 5 and 17.

2. Synonyms

Polyoxyethylene alkyl ethers are nonionic surfactants produced by the polyethoxylation of linear fatty alcohols. Products tend to be mixtures of polymers of slightly varying molecular weights and the numbers used to describe polymer lengths are average values.
Two systems of nomenclature are used to describe these materials. The number '10' in the name *Texofor A10* refers to the approximate polymer length in oxyethylene units (i.e. *y*, *see* Section 5). The number '1000' in the name 'cetomacrogol 1000' refers to the average molecular weight of the polymer chain.
Synonyms applicable to polyoxyethylene alkyl ethers are shown below:
Brij; *Cremophor A*; *Cyclogol 1000*; *Empilan KB*; *Empilan KM*; *Ethylan C*; macrogol ethers; *Marlowet*; *Plurafac*; *Procol*; *Texofor A*; *Volpo*.
Table I shows synonyms for specific materials.

Table I: Synonyms of selected polyoxyethylene alkyl ethers.

Name	Synonym
Poloxyl 20 cetostearyl ether	*Atlas G-3713*; cetomacrogol 1000; polyethylene glycol 1000 monocetyl ether.
Poloxyl 2 cetyl ether	*Brij 52*; ceteth-2.
Poloxyl 10 cetyl ether	*Brij 56*; ceteth-10.
Poloxyl 20 cetyl ether	*Brij 58*; ceteth-20.
Poloxyl 4 lauryl ether	*Brij 30*; laureth-4.
Poloxyl 23 lauryl ether	*Brij 35*; laureth-23.
Poloxyl 2 oleyl ether	*Brij 92*; *Brij 93*; oleth-2.
Poloxyl 10 oleyl ether	*Brij 96*; *Brij 97*; oleth-10; polyethylene glycol monooleyl ether.
Poloxyl 20 oleyl ether	*Brij 98*; *Brij 99*; oleth-20.
Poloxyl 2 stearyl ether	*Brij 72*; steareth-2.

Table I: *Continued.*

Name	Synonym
Poloxyl 10 stearyl ether	*Brij 76*; steareth-10.
Poloxyl 20 stearyl ether	*Brij 78*; steareth-20.
Poloxyl 100 stearyl ether	*Brij 700*; steareth-100.

3. Chemical Name and CAS Registry Number

Polyethylene glycol monocetyl ether [9004-95-9]
Polyethylene glycol monolauryl ether [9002-92-0]
Polyethylene glycol monooleyl ether [9004-98-2]
Polyethylene glycol monostearyl ether [9005-00-9]

4. Empirical Formula   Molecular Weight

See Sections 1, 2 and 5.

5. Structural Formula

$CH_3(CH_2)_x(OCH_2CH_2)_yOH$
Where $(x + 1)$ is the number of carbon atoms in the alkyl chain, typically:
12 lauryl (dodecyl)
14 myristyl (tetradecyl)
16 cetyl (hexadecyl)
18 stearyl (octadecyl)
and *y* is the number of ethylene oxide groups in the hydrophilic chain, typically 10-60.
The polyoxyethylene alkyl ethers tend to be mixtures of polymers of slightly varying molecular weights, and the numbers quoted are average values. In cetomacrogol 1000, for example, *x* is 15 or 17, and *y* is 20-24.

6. Functional Category

Emulsifying agent; solubilizing agent; wetting agent.

7. Applications in Pharmaceutical Formulation or Technology

Polyoxyethylene alkyl ethers are nonionic surfactants widely used in topical pharmaceutical formulations and cosmetics primarily as emulsifying agents for water-in-oil and oil-in-water emulsions.
Polyoxyethylene alkyl ethers are also used in other applications such as: solubilizing agents for essential oils, perfumery chemicals, vitamin oils and drugs of low water solubility; gelling and foaming agents, e.g. *Brij 72* gives a quick-breaking foam, while *Brij 97* (and others) gives clear gels at 15-20% concentration; anti-dusting agents for powders; wetting and dispersing agents for coarse-particle liquid dispersions; and detergents, especially in shampoos and similar cosmetic cleaning preparations.

8. Description

Polyoxyethylene alkyl ethers vary considerably in their physical appearance from liquids, to pastes, to solid waxy substances. They are colorless, white or cream-colored materials with a slight odor.

9. Pharmacopeial Specifications

Test	BP 1993 Cetomacrogol 1000	USPNF XVII Poloxyl 20 cetostearyl ether	USPNF XVII Poloxyl 10 oleyl ether
Identification	+	+	+
Water	$\leqslant$ 1.0%	$\leqslant$ 1.0%	$\leqslant$ 3.0%
pH (10% solution)	—	4.5-7.5	—
Alkalinity	+	—	—
Melting point	$\geqslant$ 38°C	—	—
Refractive index	1.448-1.452 at 60°C	—	—
Residue on ignition	—	$\leqslant$ 0.4%	$\leqslant$ 0.4%
Arsenic	—	$\leqslant$ 2 ppm	$\leqslant$ 2 ppm
Heavy metals	—	$\leqslant$ 0.002%	$\leqslant$ 0.002%
Acid value	$\leqslant$ 0.5	$\leqslant$ 0.5	$\leqslant$ 1.0
Hydroxyl value	40.0-52.5	42-60	75-95
Iodine value	—	—	23-40
Saponification value	$\leqslant$ 1.0	$\leqslant$ 2	$\leqslant$ 3
Free polyethylene glycols	—	$\leqslant$ 7.5%	$\leqslant$ 7.5%
Free ethylene oxide	—	$\leqslant$ 0.01%	$\leqslant$ 0.01%
Average polymer length	—	17.2-25.0	8.6-10.4

10. Typical Properties

See Tables II and III.

11. Stability and Storage Conditions

Polyoxyethylene alkyl ethers are chemically stable in strongly acidic or alkaline conditions. The presence of strong electrolytes may however adversely affect the physical stability of emulsions containing polyoxyethylene alkyl ethers.

On storage, polyoxyethylene alkyl ethers can undergo autoxidation, resulting in the formation of peroxides with an increase in acidity. Many commercially available grades are thus supplied with added antioxidants. Typically, a mixture of 0.01% butylated hydroxyanisole and 0.005% citric acid is used for this purpose.

Polyoxyethylene alkyl ethers should be stored in an airtight container, in a cool, dry, place.

12. Incompatibilities

Discoloration and/or precipitation occurs with iodides, mercury salts, phenolic substances, salicylates, sulfonamides, and tannins. Polyoxyethylene alkyl ethers are also incompatible with benzocaine and oxidizable drugs.[1]

The antimicrobial efficacy of some phenolic preservatives, such as the parabens, is reduced due to hydrogen bonding. Cloud points are similarly depressed by phenols due to hydrogen bonding between ether oxygen atoms and phenolic hydroxyl groups. Salts, other than nitrates, iodides and thiocyanates (which cause an increase), can also depress cloud points.[2]

13. Method of Manufacture

Polyoxyethylene alkyl ethers are prepared by the condensation of linear fatty alcohols with ethylene oxide. The reaction is controlled so that the required ether is formed with the polyethylene glycol of the desired molecular weight.

14. Safety

Polyoxyethylene alkyl ethers are used as nonionic surfactants in a variety of topical pharmaceutical formulations and cosmetics. The polyoxyethylene alkyl ethers form a series of materials with varying physical properties and manufacturers' literature should be consulted for information on the applications and safety of specific materials.

Although generally regarded as essentially nontoxic and nonirritant materials some polyoxyethylene alkyl ethers, particularly when used in high concentration ($>$ 20%), appear to have a greater irritant potential than others.

Animal toxicity studies suggest that polyoxyethylene alkyl ethers have a similar oral toxicity to other surfactants and can be regarded as being moderately toxic. In rats, the oral LD_{50} values range from about 2-4 g/kg body-weight.

15. Handling Precautions

Observe normal precautions appropriate to the circumstances and quantity of material handled. Eye protection and gloves are recommended.

16. Regulatory Status

Included in nonparenteral medicines licensed in the US. Included in nonparenteral medicines licensed in the UK.

17. Pharmacopeias

Name	Pharmacopeia*
Poloxyl 20 cetostearyl ether	Br and USPNF.
Poloxyl 10 oleyl ether	USPNF.

*Polyoxyethylene alkyl ethers are also included in the Japanese Pharmacopeia.

18. Related Substances

Nonionic Emulsifying Wax.

Many other polyoxyethylene ethers, such as diethers and polyethers, are commercially available and are also used as surfactants. In addition to their surfactant properties, the series of polyoxyethylene ethers with alkyllauryl side chains, e.g. nonoxynol 10, are also widely used as spermicides.

Table II: Typical properties of selected commercially available grades of polyoxyethylene alkyl ethers.

Name	Physical form	Acid value	HLB value	Hydroxyl value	Iodine number	Saponification value	Density g/cm³ at 20°C	Water content (%)	Melting point or pour point (°C)	Cloud point (°C) for 1% aqueous solution
Brij 30	Liquid	⩽ 2	9.7	145-165	—	—	≈ 0.95	⩽ 1.0	—	—
Brij 35	Solid	⩽ 5	16.9	40-60	—	—	≈ 1.05	⩽ 3.0	33	—
Brij 52	Solid	⩽ 1	5.3	160-180	—	—	—	⩽ 1.0	33	—
Brij 56	Solid	⩽ 1	12.9	75-90	—	—	—	⩽ 3.0	31	—
Brij 58	Solid	⩽ 1	15.7	45-60	—	—	—	⩽ 3.0	38	—
Brij 72	Solid	⩽ 1	4.9	150-170	—	—	—	⩽ 1.0	43	—
Brij 76	Solid	⩽ 1	12.4	75-90	—	—	—	⩽ 3.0	38	—
Brij 78	Solid	⩽ 1	15.3	45-60	—	—	—	⩽ 3.0	38	—
Brij 93		⩽ 1	4.9	160-180	—	—	—	⩽ 1.0	10	—
Brij 97		⩽ 1	12.4	80-95	—	—	—	⩽ 3.0	16	—
Brij 99		⩽ 1	15.3	50-65	—	—	—	⩽ 3.0	33	—
Cremophor A6		⩽ 1	10-12	115-135	⩽ 1	⩽ 3	0.896-0.906 at 60°C	⩽ 1.0	41-43	—
Cremophor A11		⩽ 1	12-14	70-80	⩽ 1	⩽ 1	0.964-0.968 at 60°C	⩽ 1.0	34-36	—
Cremophor A25		⩽ 1	15-17	35-45	⩽ 1	⩽ 3	1.020-1.028 at 60°C	⩽ 1.0	44-46	—
Ethosperse 1A4		⩽ 2	—	145-160	—	—	0.95	⩽ 0.5	—	—
Ethosperse 1A12		⩽ 2	—	72-82	—	—	1.10	⩽ 1.0	—	—
Ethosperse TDA6		⩽ 1	—	118-133	—	—	0.98	⩽ 1.0	—	—
Ethosperse S120		⩽ 0.5	—	385-430	—	—	1.16	⩽ 1.0	—	—
Ethosperse G26		⩽ 2	—	133-142	—	—	1.12 at 38°C	⩽ 0.5	—	—
Ethylan D252	Liquid	—	5.6	—	—	—	0.903	⩽ 0.5	5	Insoluble
Ethylan 253	Liquid	—	7.8	—	—	—	0.930	⩽ 0.5	3	Insoluble
Ethylan 254	Liquid	—	9.8	—	—	—	0.948	⩽ 3.0	5	Insoluble
Ethylan 256	Liquid	—	11.4	—	—	—	0.972	⩽ 0.5	15	43
Ethylan 257	Liquid	—	12.2	—	—	—	0.974 at 40°C	⩽ 0.5	21	49
Ethylan 2512	Solid	—	14.2	—	—	—	1.001	⩽ 0.5	29	92
Ethylan 2560	Solid	—	18.6	—	—	—	—	⩽ 0.5	45	>100
Plurafac RA20		—	—	69-78	—	—	0.9965	⩽ 0.1	4	—
Plurafac RA30		—	—	85-95	—	—	0.976	⩽ 0.1	-6	—
Plurafac RA40		—	—	65-75	—	—	0.978	⩽ 0.2	-27	—
Plurafac RA340		—	—	73	—	—	0.977	—	-23	—
Renex 30	Cloudy liquid	⩽ 1	14.5	75-85	—	—	1.0	⩽ 3.0	14	18.4
Renex 31		⩽ 1	15.4	60-74	—	—	1.0	⩽ 3.0	16	99
Renex 36		⩽ 1	11.4	118-133	—	—	1.0	⩽ 1.0	40	< 32
Texofor A1P	Solid		16.2		—	—	1.025 at 60°C	—	31	> 100
Texofor AP					—	—	0.875	—	26	Insoluble
Texofor A6	Solid				—	—	0.140	—	30	Insoluble
Texofor A10	Solid				—	—	0.970	—	35	75
Texofor A14	Solid				—	—	0.995	—	43	100
Texofor A30	Solid				—	—	1.035	—	47	> 100
Texofor A45	Solid				—	—	1.055	—	48	> 100
Texofor A60	Solid				—	—	1.065	—		> 100

Table III: Typical properties of selected commercially available grades of polyoxyethylene alkyl ethers (continued).

Name	Critical micelle concentration (%)	Surface tension of aqueous solution at 20°C (mN/m) (0.05%)	(0.1%)	(0.2%)	Dynamic viscosity at 25°C or pour point (mPa s)	Refractive index at 60°C	Solubility Ethanol	Fixed oils	Propylene glycol	Water
Brij 30	—	—	—	—	30	—	S	S	S	I
Brij 35	0.013	—	—	—	—	—	S	I	S	S
Brij 52	—	—	—	—	—	—	S	S	I	I
Brij 56	—	—	—	—	—	—	S	I	I	I
Brij 58	—	—	—	—	—	—	S	I	S	S
Brij 72	—	—	—	—	—	—	S	S	I	I
Brij 76	—	—	—	—	—	—	S	I	S	I
Brij 78	—	—	—	—	—	—	S	I	I	I
Brij 93	—	—	—	—	30	—	S	S	S	I
Brij 97	—	—	—	—	100	—	S	I	I	S
Brij 99	—	—	—	—	—	—	S	I	S	S
Cremophor A6	—	—	—	—	—	—	S	I	—	S
Cremophor A11	—	—	—	—	—	1.4420-1.4424	S	I	—	S
Cremophor A25	—	—	—	—	—	1.4464-1.4474	S	I	—	S
Ethosperse 1A4	—	—	—	—	30	1.4512-1.4520	S	S	—	S
Ethosperse 1A12	—	—	—	—	1000	—	S	S	—	S
Ethosperse TDA6	—	—	—	—	80	—	S	SH	—	S
Ethosperse S120	—	—	—	—	460	—	S	I	—	D
Ethosperse G26	—	—	—	—	150 at 38°C	—	S	I	—	S
Ethylan D252	—	—	—	—	—	—	S	I	—	S
Ethylan 253	—	—	—	—	—	—	—	—	—	I
Ethylan 254	—	—	—	—	—	—	—	—	—	I
Ethylan 256	—	—	—	—	—	—	—	—	—	I
Ethylan 257	—	—	—	—	—	—	—	—	—	S
Ethylan 2512	—	—	—	—	—	—	—	—	—	S
Ethylan 2560	—	—	—	—	—	—	—	—	—	S
Plurafac RA20	—	—	30.7	—	—	—	—	—	—	S
Plurafac RA30	—	—	28.6	—	—	—	—	—	—	—
Plurafac RA40	—	—	30.3	—	—	—	—	—	—	—
Plurafac RA340	—	—	30.5	—	—	—	—	—	—	—
Renex 30	—	—	—	—	60	—	S	I	—	S
Renex 31	—	—	—	—	130	—	S	I	—	S
Renex 36	—	—	—	—	80	—	S	I	—	S
Texofor A1P	0.006	42.9	—	42.3	—	—	S	—	—	D
Texofor AP	—	—	—	—	—	—	S	—	—	S
Texofor A6	—	—	—	—	—	—	S	—	—	I
Texofor A10	0.004	36.5	—	36.7	—	—	S	—	—	I
Texofor A14	—	36.9	—	36.6	—	—	S	—	—	S
Texofor A30	0.003	46.0	—	46.0	—	—	S	—	—	S
Texofor A45	0.004	47.5	—	47.0	—	—	S	—	—	S
Texofor A60	0.003	48.3	—	48.3	—	—	S	—	—	S

Key S = Soluble I = Insoluble
D = Dispersible SH = Soluble on heating.
Suppliers: ICI Surfactants (*Brij*).

19. Comments

—

20. Specific References

1. Azaz E, Donbrow M, Hamburger R. Incompatibility of non-ionic surfactants with oxidisable drugs. Pharm J 1973; 211: 15.
2. McDonald C, Richardson C. The effect of added salts on solubilization by a non-ionic surfactant. J Pharm Pharmacol 1981; 33: 38-39.

21. General References

Elworthy PH, Guthrie WG. Adsorption of non-ionic surfactants at the griseofulvin-solution interface. J Pharm Pharmacol 1970; 22(Suppl): 114S-120S.

Guveli D, Davis SS, Kayes JB. Viscometric studies on surface agent solutions and the examination of hydrophobic interactions. J Pharm Pharmacol 1974; 26(Suppl): 127P-128P.

Walters KA, Dugard PH, Florence AT. Non-ionic surfactants and gastric mucosal transport of paraquat. J Pharm Pharmacol 1981; 33: 207-213.

22. Authors

USA: CD Yu.

Polyoxyethylene Castor Oil Derivatives

1. Nonproprietary Names

Polyoxyethylene castor oil derivatives are a series of materials obtained by reacting varying amounts of ethylene oxide with either castor oil or hydrogenated castor oil. Several different types of material are commercially available the best known being the *Cremophors* (BASF Corporation). Of these, two castor oil derivatives are listed in the USPNF XVII.
USPNF: Polyoxyl 35 castor oil
USPNF: Polyoxyl 40 hydrogenated castor oil
See also Sections 2, 3, 4 and 17.

2. Synonyms

Synonyms applicable to polyoxyethylene castor oil derivatives are shown below. Table I shows synonyms for specific materials.
Arlatone; *Cremothon*; *Mapeg*; *Marlowet*; *Simulsol*.

3. Chemical Name and CAS Registry Number

Polyethoxylated castor oil [61791-12-6]

4. Empirical Formula   Molecular Weight

Polyoxyethylene castor oil derivatives are complex mixtures of various hydrophobic and hydrophilic components.
In polyoxyl 35 castor oil (*Cremophor EL*) the hydrophobic constituents comprise about 83% of the total mixture, the main component being glycerol polyethylene glycol ricinoleate. Other hydrophobic constituents include fatty acid esters of polyethylene glycol along with some unchanged castor oil. The hydrophilic part (17%) consists of polyethylene glycols and glycerol ethoxylates.
In polyoxyl 40 hydrogenated castor oil (*Cremophor RH 40*), approximately 75% of the components of the mixture are hydrophobic. These comprise mainly fatty acid esters of glycerol polyethylene glycol and fatty acid esters of polyethylene glycol. The hydrophilic portion consists of polyethylene glycols and glycerol ethoxylates.

5. Structural Formula

See Section 4.

6. Functional Category

Emulsifying agent; solubilizing agent; wetting agent.

7. Applications in Pharmaceutical Formulation or Technology

Polyoxyethylene castor oil derivatives are nonionic surfactants used in oral, topical and parenteral pharmaceutical formulations. They are also used in cosmetics and animal feeds.
Polyoxyl 35 castor oil (*Cremophor EL*) is mainly used as an emulsifing and solubilizing agent, and is particularly suitable for the production of aqueous liquid preparations containing volatile oils, fat-soluble vitamins and other hydrophobic substances.[1,2] In 1 mL of a 25% v/v aqueous polyoxyl 35 castor oil (*Cremophor EL*) solution it is possible to incorporate: approximately 10 mg of vitamin A palmitate; approximately 10 mg of vitamin D; approximately 120 mg of vitamin E acetate; or approximately 120 mg of vitamin K$_1$.
To solubilize fat-soluble vitamins, the active ingredient or ingredients should first be dissolved in polyoxyl 35 castor oil (*Cremophor EL*). Water should then be added very slowly with vigorous stirring. As the water is added, the viscosity increases, reaching a maximum at a water content of approximately 40% v/v. Solubilization can be facilitated by heating to approximately 60°C for a short time and in some cases by adding polyethylene glycol and/or propylene glycol. In oral formulations the taste of polyoxyl 35 castor oil (*Cremophor EL*) can be masked by a banana flavor.
Polyoxyl 35 castor oil (*Cremophor EL*) has also been used as a solvent in proprietary injections of diazepam, propanidid and alfaxalone with alfadolone acetate, *see* Section 14. Polyoxyl 35 castor oil (*Cremophor EL*) is also used in the production of glycerin suppositories.
In veterinary practice, polyoxyl 35 castor oil (*Cremophor EL*) can be used to emulsify cod liver oil, and oils and fats incorporated into animal feeding stuffs.
In cosmetics, polyoxyl 35 castor oil (*Cremophor EL*) is mainly used as a solubilizing agent for perfume bases and volatile oils in vehicles containing 30-50% v/v alcohol (ethanol or propan-2-ol). In hand lotions it can be used to replace castor oil.
Polyoxyl 40 hydrogenated castor oil (*Cremophor RH 40*) may be used in preference to polyoxyl 35 castor oil (*Cremophor EL*) in oral formulations since it is almost tasteless. In aqueous

Table I: Synonyms of selected polyoxyethylene castor oil derivatives.

Name	Synonym
Polyoxyl 5 castor oil	*Acconon CA-5*; PEG-5 castor oil; polyoxyethylene 5 castor oil.
Polyoxyl 9 castor oil	*Acconon CA-9*; castor oil POE-9; PEG-9 castor oil; polyoxyethylene 9 castor oil; *Protachem CA-9.*
Polyoxyl 15 castor oil	*Acconon CA-15*; castor oil POE-15; PEG-15 castor oil; polyoxyethylene 15 castor oil; *Protachem CA-15.*
Polyoxyl 35 castor oil	*Cremophor EL*; *Etocas 35*; glycerol polyethyleneglycol ricinoleate; polyethoxylated castor oil; polyoxyethylene 35 castor oil.
Polyoxyl 40 castor oil	Castor oil POE-40; *Croduret 40*; *Nonionic GR-40*; PEG-40 castor oil; polyoxyethylene 40 castor oil; *Protachem CA-40.*
Polyoxyl 40 hydrogenated castor oil	*Cremophor RH 40*; glycerol polyethyleneglycol oxystearate; hydrogenated castor oil POE-40; PEG-40 hydrogenated castor oil; polyethoxylated hydrogenated castor oil; polyoxyethylene 40 hydrogenated castor oil; *Nonionic GRH-40*; *Protachem CAH-40.*
Polyoxyl 60 hydrogenated castor oil	*Cremophor RH 60*; hydrogenated castor oil POE-60; PEG-60 hydrogenated castor oil; polyoxyethylene 60 hydrogenated castor oil; *Protachem CAH-60.*

alcoholic or completely aqueous solutions, polyoxyl 40 hydrogenated castor oil (*Cremophor RH 40*) can be used to solubilize vitamins, essential oils and certain drugs. Using 1 mL of a 25% v/v aqueous solution of polyoxyl 40 hydrogenated castor oil (*Cremophor RH 40*) it is possible to solubilize: approximately 88 mg of vitamin A palmitate; approximately 160 mg of vitamin A propionate. Other materials which can be solubilized are: alfadolone; alfaxalone; hexachlorophane; hexetidine; methotrimeprazine; miconazole; propanidid; and thiopentone.

In aerosol vehicles which include water, the addition of polyoxyl 40 hydrogenated castor oil (*Cremophor RH 40*) improves the solubility of the propellant in the aqueous phase. This enhancement applies both to dichlorodifluoromethane and to propane/butane mixtures.

Foam formation in aqueous ethanol solutions containing polyoxyl 40 hydrogenated castor oil (*Cremophor RH 40*) can be suppressed by the addition of small amounts of polypropylene glycol 2000.

Polyoxyl 40 hydrogenated castor oil (*Cremophor RH 40*) is also used as an emulsifier of fatty acids and alcohols.

8. Description

Polyoxyl 35 castor oil (*Cremophor EL*) occurs as a pale yellow, viscous liquid, which is clear at temperatures above 26°C. It has a slight but characteristic odor and can be completely liquefied by heating to 26°C.

Polyoxyl 40 hydrogenated castor oil (*Cremophor RH 40*) occurs as a white, semisolid paste which liquefies at 30°C. It has a very faint characteristic odor and a slight taste in aqueous solution.

Polyoxyl 60 hydrogenated castor oil (*Cremophor RH 60*) occurs as a white paste at room temperature. It has little taste or odor in aqueous solution.

9. Pharmacopeial Specifications

| Test | USPNF XVII | |
	Polyoxyl 35 castor oil	Polyoxyl 40 hydrogenated castor oil
Identification	+	+
Specific gravity	1.05-1.06	—
Congealing temperature	—	20-30°C
Viscosity at 25°C	650-850 mPa s	—
Water	$\leqslant$ 3.0%	$\leqslant$ 3.0%
Residue on ignition	$\leqslant$ 0.3%	$\leqslant$ 0.3%
Heavy metals	$\leqslant$ 0.001%	$\leqslant$ 0.001%
Acid value	$\leqslant$ 2.0	$\leqslant$ 2.0
Hydroxyl value	65-80	60-80
Iodine value	25-35	$\leqslant$ 2.0
Saponification value	60-75	45-69

10. Typical Properties

See Tables II, III and IV.

Table II: Typical physical properties of selected commercially available polyoxyethylene castor oil derivatives.

Name	Acid value	HLB value	Hydroxyl value	Iodine number	Saponification value	Water content	Melting point (°C)	Solidification point (°C)	Cloud point for a 1% aqueous solution (°C)
Polyoxyl 35 castor oil (*Cremophor EL*)	$\leqslant$ 2.0	12-14	65-78	28-32	65-70	$\leqslant$ 3%	19-20	—	72.5
Polyoxyl 40 hydrogenated castor oil (*Cremophor RH 40*)	$\leqslant$ 1.0	14-16	60-80	$\leqslant$ 1	50-60	$\leqslant$ 2%	$\approx$ 30	21-23	95.6
Polyoxyl 60 hydrogenated castor oil (*Cremophor RH 60*)	$\leqslant$ 1.0	15-17	50-70	$\leqslant$ 1	40-50	$\leqslant$ 2%	$\approx$ 40	—	—

Table III: Typical physical properties of selected commercially available polyoxyethylene castor oil derivatives (continued).

Name	Density g/cm³	pH	Refractive index at 20°C	Surface tension of 0.1% w/v aqueous solution (mN/m)	Viscosity at 25°C (mPa s)	Critical micelle concentration (%)
Polyoxyl 35 castor oil (*Cremophor EL*)	1.05-1.06	6-8	$\approx$ 1.471	40.9	650-800	$\approx$ 0.009
Polyoxyl 40 hydrogenated castor oil (*Cremophor RH 40*)	—	6-7	1.453-1.457	43.0	20-40[a]	$\approx$ 0.039
Polyoxyl 60 hydrogenated castor oil (*Cremophor RH 60*)	—	6-7	—	—	—	—

a. 30% w/v aqueous solution.

Table IV: Solubility of selected commercially available polyoxyethylene castor oil derivatives.

Name	Castor oil	Chloroform	Solubility Ethanol	Fatty acids	Fatty alcohols	Olive oil	Water
Polyoxyl 35 castor oil (*Cremophor EL*)	S	S	S	S	S	S	S
Polyoxyl 40 hydrogenated castor oil (*Cremophor RH 40*)	S	S	S	S	S	S	S
Polyoxyl 60 hydrogenated castor oil (*Cremophor RH 60*)	S	—	S[a]	S	S	S	S

Key S = Soluble

a. Need to add 0.5-1.0% water to maintain a clear solution.

11. Stability and Storage Conditions

Polyoxyl 35 castor oil (*Cremophor EL*) forms stable solutions in many organic solvents such as chloroform, ethanol and propan-2-ol; it also forms clear, stable, aqueous solutions. Polyoxyl 35 castor oil (*Cremophor EL*) is miscible with other polyoxyethylene castor oil derivatives and on heating with fatty acids, fatty alcohols and some animal and vegetable oils. Solutions of polyoxyl 40 hydrogenated castor oil (*Cremophor RH 40*) in aqueous alcohols are also stable.

On heating an aqueous solution the solubility of polyoxyl 35 castor oil (*Cremophor EL*) is reduced and the solution becomes turbid. Aqueous solutions of polyoxyl hydrogenated castor oil (*Cremophor RH* grades) heated for prolonged periods may separate into solid and liquid phases on cooling. However, the product can be restored to its original form by homogenization.

Aqueous solutions of polyoxyl 35 castor oil (*Cremophor EL*) are stable in the presence of low concentrations of electrolytes such as acids or salts, with the exception of mercuric chloride, *see* Section 12.

Aqueous solutions of polyoxyl 35 castor oil (*Cremophor EL*) can be sterilized by autoclaving for 20 minutes at 121°C. In this process a product may acquire a deeper color although this has no significance for product stability. Aqueous solutions of polyoxyl hydrogenated castor oil (*Cremophor RH*) can similarly be sterilized by autoclaving at 121°C, but this may cause a slight decrease in the pH value.

Although the method of manufacture used for polyoxyethylene castor oil derivatives ensures that they are near-sterile, microbial contamination can occur on storage.

Polyoxyethylene castor oil derivatives should be stored in a well-filled, airtight container, protected from light, in a cool, dry, place.

12. Incompatibilities

In strongly acidic or alkaline solutions the ester components of polyoxyethylene hydrogenated castor oil (*Cremophor RH*) are liable to saponify.

In aqueous solution, polyoxyl 35 castor oil (*Cremophor EL*) is stable towards most electrolytes in the concentrations normally employed. However, it is incompatible with mercuric chloride since precipitation occurs.

Some organic substances may cause precipitation at certain concentrations, especially compounds containing phenolic hydroxyl groups, e.g. phenol, resorcinol and tannins.

Polyoxyl 40 hydrogenated castor oil (*Cremophor RH 40*) and polyoxyl 60 hydrogenated castor oil (*Cremophor RH 60*) are largely unaffected by the salts that cause hardness in water.

13. Method of Manufacture

Polyoxyethylene castor oil derivatives are prepared by reacting varying amounts of ethylene oxide with either castor oil or hydrogenated castor oil under controlled conditions.

Polyoxyl 35 castor oil (*Cremophor EL*) is thus produced by reacting 1 mole of castor oil with 35-40 moles of ethylene oxide.

Polyoxyl 40 hydrogenated castor oil (*Cremophor RH 40*) is produced by reacting 1 mole of hydrogenated castor oil with 40-45 moles of ethylene oxide. Polyoxyl 60 hydrogenated castor oil (*Cremophor RH 60*) is similarly produced by reacting 1 mole of hydrogenated castor oil with 60 moles of ethylene oxide.

14. Safety

Polyoxyethylene castor oil derivatives are used in a variety of oral, topical and parenteral pharmaceutical formulations.

Acute and chronic toxicity tests in animals have shown polyoxyethylene castor oil derivatives to be essentially nontoxic and nonirritant materials, *see* Table V.[3,4] However, several serious anaphylactic reactions have been observed in humans and animals following parenteral, and more rarely, oral administration of formulations containing polyoxyethylene castor oil derivatives.[5-14] The precise mechanism of the reaction is not known.

Table V: LD_{50} values of selected polyoxyethylene castor oil derivatives.[3,4,15]

Name	Animal and route	LD_{50} g/kg body-weight
Polyoxyl 35 castor oil (*Cremophor EL*)	Cat (oral)	> 10
	Dog (IV)	0.64
	Mouse (IV)	2.5
	Rabbit (oral)	> 10
	Rat (oral)	> 6.4
Polyoxyl 40 hydrogenated castor oil (*Cremophor RH 40*)	Mouse (IP)	> 12.5
	Mouse (IV)	> 12.0
	Rat (oral)	> 16.0
Polyoxyl 60 hydrogenated castor oil (*Cremophor RH 60*)	Mouse (IP)	> 12.5
	Rat (oral)	> 16.0

15. Handling Precautions

Observe normal precautions appropriate to the circumstances and quantity of material handled. Eye protection and gloves are recommended.

16. Regulatory Status

Included in the FDA Inactive Ingredients Guide (IV injections). Inclued in parenteral medicines licensed in the UK.

17. Pharmacopeias

Name	Pharmacopeia
Polyoxyl 35 castor oil	USPNF.
Polyoxyl 40 hydrogenated castor oil	USPNF.

18. Related Substances

Poloxyethylene Alkyl Ethers; Polyoxyethylene Stearates.

Mixtures of different polyoxyethylene castor oil derivatives are commercially available. For example, *Cremophor RH 410* is a mixture of 90% polyoxyl 40 hydrogenated castor oil (*Cremophor RH 40*) with 10% water, and *Cremophor RH 455* is a mixture of 90% polyoxyl 40 hydrogenated castor oil (*Cremophor RH 40*), 5% propylene glycol and 5% water. At room temperature, *Cremophor RH 410* and *Cremophor 455* are viscous, slightly opalescent liquids.

19. Comments

Note that the trade name *Cremophor* (BASF Corporation) is also used for other polyoxyethylene derivatives, e.g. the *Cremophor A* series are polyoxyethylene alkyl ethers.

20. Specific References

1. Macek TJ. Preparation of parenteral dispersions. J Pharm Sci 1963; 52: 694-699.
2. Webb NE. Method for solubilization of selected drug substances. Bull Parenter Drug Assoc 1976; 30: 180-186.
3. BASF Corporation. Technical literature: *Cremophor EL*, 1988.
4. BASF Corporation. Technical literature: *Cremophor RH* grades, 1988.
5. Forrest ARW, Watrasiewicz K, Moore CJ. Long-term althesin infusion and hyperlipidaemia. Br Med J 1977; 2: 1357-1358.
6. Dye D, Watkins J. Suspected anaphylactic reaction to cremophor EL. Br Med J 1980; 280: 1353.
7. Knell AJ, Turner P, Chalmers EPD. Potential hazard of steroid anaesthesia for prolonged sedation [letter]. Lancet 1983; i: 526.
8. Lawler PGP, McHutchon A, Bamber PA. Potential hazards of prolonged steroid anaesthesia [letter]. Lancet 1983; i: 1270-1271.
9. Moneret-Vautrin DA, Laxenaire MC, Viry-Babel F. Anaphylaxis caused by anti-cremophor EL IgG STS antibodies in a case of reaction to althesin. Br J Anaesth 1983; 55: 469-471.
10. Howrie DL, et al. Anaphylactoid reactions associated with parenteral cyclosporine use: possible role of cremophor EL. Drug Intell Clin Pharm 1985; 19: 425-427.
11. van Hooff JP, Bessems P, Beuman GH, Leunissen KML. Absence of allergic reaction to cyclosporin capsules in patient allergic to standard oral and intravenous solution of cyclosporin [letter]. Lancet 1987; ii: 1456.
12. McCormick PA, Hughes JE, Burroughs AK, McIntyre N. Reformulation of injectable vitamin A: potential problems. Br Med J 1990; 301: 924.
13. Fjällskog M-L, Frii L, Bergh J. Is cremophor EL solvent for paclitaxel, cytotoxic? Lancet 1993; 342: 873.
14. Liebmann J, Cook JA, Mitchell JB. Cremophor EL, solvent for paclitaxel, and toxicity. Lancet 1993; 342: 1428.
15. Sweet DV, editor. Registry of toxic effects of chemical substances. Cincinnati: US Department of Health, 1987.

21. General References

—

22. Authors

USA: CD Yu.

Polyoxyethylene Sorbitan Fatty Acid Esters

1. Nonproprietary Names

BP: Polysorbates 20, 60 and 80
PhEur: Polysorbatum 20, 60 and 80
USPNF: Polysorbates 20, 40, 60 and 80

2. Synonyms

Synonyms of selected polysorbates are shown below, *see also* Section 3.

Polysorbate	Synonym
Polysorbate 20	*Armotan PML 20*; *Capmul POE-L*; *Crillet 1*; *E432*; *Glycosperse L-20*; *Hodag PSML-20*; *Liposorb L-20*; *Liposorb L-20K*; *Montanox 20*; sorbitan monododecanoate poly(oxy-1,2-ethanediyl) derivatives; polyoxyethylene 20 laurate; *Protasorb L-20*; *Tween 20*.
Polysorbate 21	*Crillet 11*; *Hodag PSML-4*; *Protasorb L-5*; *Tween 21*.
Polysorbate 40	*Crillet 2*; *E434*; *Glycosperse S-20*; *Hodag PSMP-20*; *Liposorb P-20*; *Montanox 40*; *Protasorb P-20*; sorbitan monohexadecanoate poly(oxy-1,2-ethanediyl) derivatives; *Tween 40*.
Polysorbate 60	*Armotan PMS 20*; *Capmul POE-S*; *Crillet 3*; *E435*; *Glycosperse S-20*; *Hodag PSMS-20*; *Liposorb S-20*; *Liposorb S-20K*; *Montanox 60*; *Polycon T 60 K*; polyoxyethylene 20 stearate; sorbitan monooctadecanoate poly(oxy-1,2-ethanediyl) derivatives; *Protasorb S-20*; *Tween 60*.
Polysorbate 61	*Crillet 31*; *Hodag PSMS-4*; *Protasorb S-4*; *Tween 61*.
Polysorbate 65	*Crillet 35*; *E436*; *Glycosperse TS-20*; *Hodag PSTS-20*; *Liposorb TS-20*; *Liposorb TS-20K*; *Montanox 65*; sorbitan trioctadecanoate poly(oxy-1,2-ethanediyl) derivatives; *Protasorb STS-20*; *Tween 65*.
Polysorbate 80	*Armotan PMO 20*; *Capmul POE-O*; *Crillet 4*; *Crillet 50*; *E433*; *Glycosperse O-20*; *Hodag PSMO-20*; *Liposorb O-20*; *Liposorb O-20K*; *Montanox 80*; polyoxyethylene 20 oleate; (Z)-sorbitan mono-9-octadecenoate poly(oxy-1,2-ethanediyl) derivatives; *Protasorb O-20*; *Tween 80*.
Polysorbate 81	*Crillet 41*; *Hodag PSMO-5*; sorbitan mono-9-octadecenoate poly(oxy-1,2-ethanediyl) derivatives; *Protasorb O-5*; *Tween 81*.
Polysorbate 85	*Crillet 45*; *Hodag PSTO-20*; *Liposorb TO-20*; *Montanox 85*; sorbitan tri-9-octadecenoate poly(oxy-1,2-ethanediyl) derivatives; *Protasorb TO-20*; *Tween 85*.
Polysorbate 120	*Crillet 6*.

3. Chemical Names and CAS Registry Numbers

See Table I.

Table I: Chemical name and CAS registry number of selected polysorbates.

Polysorbate	Chemical name	CAS number
Polysorbate 20	Polyoxyethylene 20 sorbitan monolaurate	[9005-64-5]
Polysorbate 21	Polyoxyethylene (4) sorbitan monolaurate	[9005-64-5]
Polysorbate 40	Polyoxyethylene 20 sorbitan monopalmitate	[9005-66-7]
Polysorbate 60	Polyoxyethylene 20 sorbitan monostearate	[9005-67-8]
Polysorbate 61	Polyoxyethylene (4) sorbitan monostearate	[9005-67-8]
Polysorbate 65	Polyoxyethylene 20 sorbitan tristearate	[9005-71-4]
Polysorbate 80	Polyoxyethylene 20 sorbitan monooleate	[9005-65-6]
Polysorbate 81	Polyoxyethylene (5) sorbitan monooleate	[9005-65-6]
Polysorbate 85	Polyoxyethylene 20 sorbitan trioleate	[9005-70-3]
Polysorbate 120	Polyoxyethylene 20 sorbitan monoisostearate	[66794-58-9]

4. Empirical Formula   Molecular Weight

Approximate molecular weights for selected polysorbates are shown below in Table II.

Table II: Empirical formula and molecular weight of selected polysorbates.

Polysorbate	Formula	Molecular weight
Polysorbate 20	$C_{58}H_{114}O_{26}$	1128
Polysorbate 21	$C_{26}H_{50}O_{10}$	523
Polysorbate 40	$C_{62}H_{122}O_{26}$	1284
Polysorbate 60	$C_{64}H_{126}O_{26}$	1312
Polysorbate 61	$C_{32}H_{62}O_{10}$	607
Polysorbate 65	$C_{100}H_{194}O_{28}$	1845
Polysorbate 80	$C_{64}H_{124}O_{26}$	1310
Polysorbate 81	$C_{34}H_{64}O_{11}$	649
Polysorbate 85	$C_{100}H_{188}O_{28}$	1839
Polysorbate 120	$C_{64}H_{126}O_{26}$	1312

5. Structural Formula

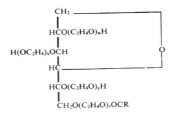

Polyoxyethylene sorbitan monoester

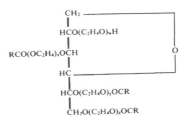

Polyoxyethylene sorbitan triester

$w+x+y+z = 20$ Polysorbate 20, 40, 60, 65, 80 and 85)
$w+x+y+z = 5$ (Polysorbate 81)
$w+x+y+z = 4$ (Polysorbate 21 and 61)

6. Functional Category

Emulsifying agent; nonionic surfactant; solubilizing agent; wetting agent.

7. Applications in Pharmaceutical Formulation or Technology

Polyoxyethylene sorbitan fatty acid esters (polysorbates) are a series of fatty acid esters of sorbitol and its anhydrides copolymerized with approximately 20 moles of ethylene oxide for each mole of sorbitol and its anhydrides.

Polysorbates are hydrophilic nonionic surfactants used widely as emulsifying agents in the preparation of stable oil-in-water pharmaceutical emulsions. They may also be used as solubilizing agents for a variety of substances including essential oils and oil soluble vitamins, and as wetting agents in the formulation of oral and parenteral suspensions.

Polysorbates are also widely used in cosmetics and food products.

Use	Concentration (%)
Emulsifying agent	
Used alone in oil-in-water emulsions	1-15
Used in combination with hydrophilic emulsifiers in oil-in-water emulsions	1-10
Used to increase the water holding properties of ointments	1-10
Solubilizing agent	
For poorly soluble active constituents in lipophilic bases	1-10
Wetting agent	
For insoluble active constituents in lipophilic bases	0.1-3

8. Description

Polysorbates have a characteristic odor and a warm, somewhat bitter taste. Their colors and physical forms at 25°C are shown below in Table III.

Table III: Color and physical form of selected polysorbates at 25°C

Polysorbate	Color and form at 25°C
Polysorbate 20	Yellow oily liquid
Polysorbate 21	Yellow oily liquid
Polysorbate 40	Yellow oily liquid
Polysorbate 60	Yellow oily liquid
Polysorbate 61	Tan solid
Polysorbate 65	Tan solid
Polysorbate 80	Yellow oily liquid
Polysorbate 81	Amber liquid
Polysorbate 85	Amber liquid
Polysorbate 120	Yellow liquid

9. Pharmacopeial Specifications

Test	PhEur 1985	USPNF XVII
Identification		
Polysorbate 20	+	+
Polysorbate 40*	—	+
Polysorbate 60	+	+
Polysorbate 80	+	+
Saponification value		
Polysorbate 20	40-50	40-50
Polysorbate 40*	—	41-52
Polysorbate 60	45-55	45-55
Polysorbate 80	45-55	45-55
Hydroxyl value		
Polysorbate 20	96-108	96-108
Polysorbate 40*	—	89-105
Polysorbate 60	81-96	81-96
Polysorbate 80	65-80	65-80
Water		
Polysorbate 20	≤ 3.0%	≤ 3.0%
Polysorbate 40*	—	≤ 3.0%
Polysorbate 60	≤ 3.0%	≤ 3.0%
Polysorbate 80	≤ 3.0%	≤ 3.0%
Residue on ignition		
Polysorbate 20	—	≤ 0.25%
Polysorbate 40*	—	≤ 0.25%
Polysorbate 60	—	≤ 0.25%
Polysorbate 80	—	≤ 0.25%
Sulfated ash		
Polysorbate 20	≤ 0.2%	—
Polysorbate 60	≤ 0.2%	—
Polysorbate 80	≤ 0.2%	—
Arsenic		
Polysorbate 20	—	≤ 1 ppm
Polysorbate 40*	—	≤ 1 ppm
Polysorbate 60	—	≤ 1 ppm
Polysorbate 80	—	≤ 1 ppm
Heavy metals		
Polysorbate 20	≤ 10 ppm	≤ 0.001%
Polysorbate 40*	—	≤ 0.001%
Polysorbate 60	≤ 10 ppm	≤ 0.001%
Polysorbate 80	≤ 10 ppm	≤ 0.001%
Acid value		
Polysorbate 20	≤ 2.0	≤ 2.2
Polysorbate 40*	—	≤ 2.2
Polysorbate 60	≤ 2.0	≤ 2.2
Polysorbate 80	≤ 2.0	≤ 2.2
Iodine value		
Polysorbate 20	≤ 5.0	—
Polysorbate 60	≤ 5.0	—
Polysorbate 80	18-24	—
Reducing substances		
Polysorbate 20	+	—
Polysorbate 60	+	—
Polysorbate 80	+	—
Specific gravity		
Polysorbate 20	1.10	—
Polysorbate 60	1.10	—
Polysorbate 80	1.08	1.06-1.09
Viscosity at 25°C		
Polysorbate 80	400 mPa s	300-500 mm²/s

* Note that the BP 1993 and PhEur 1985 contain monographs for polysorbate 20, 60 and 80; the USPNF XVII contains monographs for polysorbate 20, 40, 60 and 80.

10. Typical Properties

Acid value: see Table IV.
Acidity/alkalinity: pH = 6.0-8.0 for a 5% w/v aqueous solution.
Flash point: 149°C
HLB value: see Table V.
Hydroxyl value: see Table IV.
Moisture content: see Table IV.
Saponification value: see Table IV.
Solubility: see Table VI.
Specific gravity: see Table V.
Surface tension: for 0.1% w/v solutions, see table below.

Polysorbate	Surface tension at 20°C (mN/m)
Polysorbate 21	34.7
Polysorbate 40	41.5
Polysorbate 60	42.5
Polysorbate 61	41.5
Polysorbate 80	42.5
Polysorbate 85	41.0

Viscosity (dynamic): see Table V.

Table IV: Typical properties of selected polysorbates.

Polysorbate	Acid value	Hydroxyl value	Moisture content (%)	Saponifcation value
Polysorbate 20	2.0	96-108	3.0	40-50
Polysorbate 21	3.0	225-255	3.0	100-115
Polysorbate 40	2.0	90-105	3.0	41-52
Polysorbate 60	2.0	81-96	3.0	45-55
Polysorbate 61	2.0	170-200	3.0	95-115
Polysorbate 65	2.0	44-60	3.0	88-98
Polysorbate 80	2.0	65-80	3.0	45-55
Polysorbate 81	2.0	134-150	3.0	96-104
Polysorbate 85	2.0	39-52	3.0	80-95
Polysorbate 120	2.0	65-85	5.0	40-50

Table V: Typical properties of selected polysorbates (continued).

Polysorbate	HLB value	Specific gravity at 25°C	Viscosity (mPa s)
Polysorbate 20	16.7	1.1	400
Polysorbate 21	13.3	1.1	500
Polysorbate 40	15.6	1.08	500
Polysorbate 60	14.9	1.1	600
Polysorbate 61	9.6	1.06	solid
Polysorbate 65	10.5	1.05	solid
Polysorbate 80	15.0	1.08	425
Polysorbate 81	10.0	—	450
Polysorbate 85	11.0	1.00	300
Polysorbate 120	14.9	—	—

Table VI: Solubilities of selected polysorbates in various solvents.

Polysorbate	Ethanol	Solvent Mineral oil	Vegetable oil	Water
Polysorbate 20	S	I	I	S
Polysorbate 21	S	I	I	D
Polysorbate 40	S	I	I	S
Polysorbate 60	S	I	I	S
Polysorbate 61	SW	SW	SWT	D
Polysorbate 65	SW	SW	DW	D
Polysorbate 80	S	I	I	S
Polysorbate 81	S	S	ST	D
Polysorbate 85	S	I	ST	D
Polysorbate 120	S	I	I	S

D = dispersible; I = insoluble; S = soluble;
T = turbid; W = on warming .

11. Stability and Storage Conditions

Polysorbates are stable to electrolytes and weak acids and bases; gradual saponification occurs with strong acids and bases. The oleic acid esters are sensitive to oxidation.
Polysorbates should be stored in a well-closed container, protected from light, in a cool, dry, place.

12. Incompatibilities

Discoloration and/or precipitation occurs with various substances, especially phenols, tannins, tars and/or tar-like materials. The antimicrobial activity of paraben preservatives is reduced in the presence of polysorbates.[1] See Methylparaben.

13. Method of Manufacture

Polysorbates are prepared from sorbitol in a three step process. Water is initially removed from the sorbitol to form a sorbitan (a cyclic sorbitol anhydride). The sorbitan is then partially esterified with a fatty acid, such as oleic or stearic acid, to yield a hexitan ester. Finally, ethylene oxide is then chemically added in the presence of a catalyst to yield the polysorbate.

14. Safety

Polysorbates are widely used in cosmetics, food products and oral, parenteral and topical pharmaceutical formulations and are generally regarded as nontoxic and nonirritant materials. There have however been occasional reports of hypersensitivity to polysorbates following their topical use. Polysorbates have also been associated with serious adverse effects, including some deaths, in low-birthweight infants administered intravenously a vitamin E preparation containing a mixture of polysorbate 20 and 80.[2,3]
The WHO has set an estimated acceptable daily intake for polysorbates 20, 40, 60, 65 and 80, calculated as total polysorbate esters, at up to 25 mg/kg body-weight.[4]

15. Handling Precautions

Observe normal precautions appropriate to the circumstances and quantity of material handled. Eye protection and gloves are recommended.

16. Regulatory Status

Polysorbates 60, 65 and 80 are GRAS listed. Polysorbates 20, 40, 60, 65 and 80 are accepted as food additives in Europe. Polysorbates 20, 40, 60 and 80 are included in the FDA Inactive Ingredients Guide (IM, IV, oral, rectal, topical and vaginal preparations). Polysorbates are included in parenteral and nonparenteral medicines licensed in the UK.

17. Pharmacopeias

Polysorbate	Pharmacopeia
Polysorbate 20	Aust, Br, Eur, Fr, Ger, Gr, Hung, Ind, It, Neth, Port, Swiss and USPNF.
Polysorbate 40	USPNF.
Polysorbate 60	Aust, Br, Cz, Eur, Fr, Ger, Gr, Hung, It, Neth, Port, Swiss and USPNF.
Polysorbate 80	Aust, Br, Braz, Chin, Cz, Eur, Fr, Ger, Gr, Hung, Ind, It, Jpn, Neth, Nord, Port, Rom, Swiss and USPNF.

18. Related Substances

Sorbitan Esters (Sorbitan Fatty Acid Esters)

19. Comments

—

20. Specific References

1. Blanchard J. Effect of polyols on interaction of paraben preservatives with polysorbate 80. J Pharm Sci 1980; 69: 169-173.
2. Alade SL, Brown RE, Paquet A. Polysorbate 80 and E-Ferol toxicity. Pediatrics 1986; 77: 593-597.
3. Balistreri WF, Farrell MK, Bove KE. Lessons from the E-Ferol tragedy. Pediatrics 1986; 78: 503-506.
4. FAO/WHO. Toxicological evaluation of certain food additives with a review of general principles and of specifications: seventeenth report of the joint FAO/WHO expert committee on food additives. Tech Rep Ser Wld Hlth Org 1974; No. 539.

21. General References

Allen LV, Levinson RS, Robinson C, Lau A. Effect of surfactant on tetracycline absorption across everted rat intestine. J Pharm Sci 1981; 70: 269-271.

Chowhan ZT, Pritchard R. Effect of surfactants on percutaneous absorption of naproxen I: comparisons of rabbit, rat, and human excised skin. J Pharm Sci 1978; 67: 1272-1274.

Donbrow M, et al. Autoxidation of polysorbates. J Pharm Sci 1978; 67: 1676-1681.

Smolinske SC. Handbook of food, drug, and cosmetic excipients. Boca Raton, FL: CRC Press Inc, 1992: 295-301.

22. Authors

UK: RL Leyland.

Polyoxyethylene Stearates

1. Nonproprietary Names

The polyoxyethylene stearates are a series of polyethoxylated derivatives of stearic acid. Of the large number of different materials commercially available two types are listed in the USPNF XVII.
USPNF: Poloxyl 40 stearate
USPNF: Poloxyl 50 stearate
See also Sections 2, 3, 4, 5 and 17.

2. Synonyms

Polyoxyethylene stearates are nonionic surfactants produced by polyethoxylation of stearic acid. Two systems of nomenclature are used for these materials. The number '8' in the names 'poloxyl 8 stearate' or 'polyoxyethylene 8 stearate' refers to the approximate polymer length in oxyethylene units. The same material may also be designated 'polyoxyethylene glycol 400 stearate' or 'macrogol stearate 400' in which case, the number '400' refers to the average molecular weight of the polymer chain.
Synonyms applicable to polyoxyethylene stearates are shown below:
Ethoxylated fatty acid esters; macrogol stearates; *Marlosol*; PEG fatty acid esters; PEG stearates; polyethylene glycol stearates; poly(oxy-1,2-ethanediyl) α-hydro-ω-hydroxy-octadecanoate; polyoxyethylene glycol stearates.
Table I shows synonyms for specific materials.

Table I: Synonyms of selected polyoxyethylene stearates and distearates.

Name	Synonym
Poloxyl 2 stearate	*Hodag DGS*; PEG-2 stearate.
Poloxyl 4 stearate	*Acconon 200-MS*; *Hodag 20-S*; PEG-4 stearate; polyoxyethylene (4) monostearate; polyethylene glycol 200 monostearate; *Protamate 200-DPS*.
Poloxyl 6 stearate	*Cerasynt 616*; *Kessco PEG 300 Monostearate*; *Lipal 300S*; *Lipo PEG 3-S*; PEG-6 stearate; polyethylene glycol 300 monostearate; *Polystate C*; polyoxyethylene (6) monostearate; *Protamate 300-DPS*.
Poloxyl 8 stearate	*Acconon 400-MS*; *Cerasynt 660*; *Cithrol 4MS*; *Crodet S8*; *Emerest 2640*; *Grocor 400*; *Hodag 40-S*; *Kessco PEG-400 Monostearate*; macrogol stearate 400; *Myrj 45*; PEG-8 stearate; *Pegosperse 400 MS*; polyethylene glycol 400 monostearate; polyoxyethylene (8) monostearate; *Protamate 400-DPS*; *Ritapeg 400 MS*.
Poloxyl 12 stearate	*Hodag 60-S*; *Kessco PEG 600 Monostearate*; *Lipo-PEG 6-S*; PEG-12 stearate; *Pegosperse 600 MS*; polyethylene glycol 600 monostearate; polyoxyethylene (12) monostearate; *Protamate 600-DPS*.
Poloxyl 20 stearate	*Cerasynt 840*; *Hodag 100-S*; *Kessco PEG 1000 Monostearate*; *Lipo-PEG 10-S*;

Name	Synonym
	Myrj 49; *Pegosperse 1000 MS*; PEG-20 stearate; polyethylene glycol 1000 monostearate; polyoxyethylene (20) monostearate; *Protamate 1000-DPS*.
Poloxyl 30 stearate	*Myrj 51*; PEG-30 stearate; polyoxyethylene (30) stearate.
Poloxyl 40 stearate	*Crodet S40*; E431; *Emerest 2672*; *Hodag POE (40) MS*; *Lipal 395*; macrogol stearate 2000; *Myrj 52*; PEG-40 stearate; polyethylene glycol 2000 monostearate; polyoxyethylene (40) monostearate; *Protamate 2000-DPS*.
Poloxyl 50 stearate	*Atlas G-2153*; *Crodet S50*; *Lipal 505*; *Myrj 53*; PEG-50 stearate; polyoxyethylene (50) monostearate.
Poloxyl 100 stearate	*Myrj 59*; PEG-100 stearate; polyethylene glycol 4400 monostearate; polyoxyethylene (100) monostearate; *Protamate 4400-DPS*.
Poloxyl 150 stearate	*Hodag 600-S*; PEG-150 stearate.
Poloxyl 4 distearate	*Hodag 22-S*; PEG-4 distearate.
Poloxyl 8 distearate	*Hodag 42-S*; *Kessco PEG 400 DS*; PEG-8 distearate; polyethylene glycol 400 distearate; *Protamate 400-DS*.
Poloxyl 12 distearate	*Hodag 62-S*; *Kessco PEG 600 Distearate*; PEG-12 distearate; polyethylene (12) distearate; polyethylene glycol 600 distearate; *Protamate 600-DS*.
Poloxyl 32 distearate	*Hodag 154-S*; *Kessco PEG 1540 Distearate*; PEG-32 distearate; polyethylene glycol 1540 distearate; polyoxyethylene (32) distearate.
Poloxyl 150 distearate	*Hodag 602-S*; *Kessco PEG 6000 DS*; PEG-150 distearate; polyethylene glycol 6000 distearate; polyoxyethylene (150) distearate; *Protamate 6000-DS*.

3. Chemical Name and CAS Registry Number

Polyethylene glycol stearate [9004-99-3]
Polyethylene glycol distearate [9005-08-7]

4. Empirical Formula Molecular Weight

Table II: Empirical formula and molecular weight of selected polyoxyethylene stearates.

Name	Empirical formula	Molecular weight
Poloxyl 6 stearate	$C_{30}H_{60}O_8$	548.80
Poloxyl 8 stearate	$C_{34}H_{68}O_{10}$	636.91
Poloxyl 12 stearate	$C_{42}H_{84}O_{14}$	813.12
Poloxyl 20 stearate	$C_{58}H_{116}O_{22}$	1165.55
Poloxyl 40 stearate	$C_{98}H_{196}O_{42}$	2046.61
Poloxyl 50 stearate	$C_{118}H_{236}O_{52}$	2487.15
Poloxyl 100 stearate	$C_{218}H_{436}O_{102}$	4689.80

5. Structural Formula

$$R-\overset{\overset{\textstyle O}{\|}}{C}-(OCH_2CH_2)_n-OH$$

For the monostearate; where the average value of *n* is 6 for poloxyl 6 stearate, 8 for poloxyl 8 stearate, etc.

$$R—\overset{\overset{\displaystyle O}{\|}}{C}—(OCH_2CH_2)_n—O—\overset{\overset{\displaystyle O}{\|}}{C}—R$$

For the distearate; where the average value of n is 12 for poloxyl 12 distearate, 32 for poloxyl 32 distearate, etc.

In both structures, R represents the alkyl group of the parent fatty acid. With stearic acid, R is $CH_3(CH_2)_{16}$. However, it should be noted that stearic acid usually contains other fatty acids, primarily palmitic acid, and consequently a polyoxyethylene stearate may also contain varying amounts of other fatty acid derivatives such as palmitates.

6. Functional Category

Emulsifying agent; solubilizing agent; wetting agent.

7. Applications in Pharmaceutical Formulation or Technology

Polyoxyethylene stearates are generally used as emulsifiers in oil-in-water type creams and lotions. Their hydrophilicity or lipophilicity depends on the number of ethylene oxide units present: the larger the number, the greater the hydrophilic properties. Poloxyl 40 stearate has also been used as an emulsifying agent in intravenous infusions.[1]

Polyoxyethylene stearates are particularly useful as emulsifying agents when astringent salts or other strong electrolytes are present. They can also be blended with other surfactants to obtain any hydrophilic-lipophilic balance for lotions or ointment formulations.

Use	Concentration (%)
Auxiliary emulsifier for o/w intravenous fat emulsion	0.5-5
Emulsifier for o/w creams or lotions	0.5-10
Ophthalmic ointment	7
Suppository component	1-10
Tablet lubricant	1-2

8. Description

Name	Description
Poloxyl 6 stearate	Soft solid
Poloxyl 8 stearate	Waxy cream
Poloxyl 12 stearate	Pasty solid
Poloxyl 20 stearate	Waxy solid
Poloxyl 40 stearate	Waxy solid, with a faint, bland, fat-like odor, off-white to light tan in color.
Poloxyl 50 stearate	Solid, with a bland, fat-like odor or odorless.
Poloxyl 100 stearate	Solid
Poloxyl 12 distearate	Paste
Poloxyl 32 distearate	Solid
Poloxyl 150 distearate	Solid

9. Pharmacopeial Specifications

Test	USPNF XVII	
	Poloxyl 40 stearate	Poloxyl 50 stearate
Identification	+	+
Congealing range	37-47°C	—
Water	⩽ 3.0%	⩽ 3.0%

Continued

Test	USPNF XVII	
	Poloxyl 40 stearate	Poloxyl 50 stearate
Arsenic	⩽ 3 ppm	⩽ 3 ppm
Heavy metals	⩽ 0.001%	⩽ 0.001%
Acid value	⩽ 2	⩽ 2
Hydroxyl value	25-40	23-35
Saponification value	25-35	20-28
Free polyethylene glycols	17-27%	17-27%

10. Typical Properties

Flash point: > 149°C for poloxyl 8 stearate (*Myrj 45*).
Solubility:

Name	Solvent		
	Ethanol (95%)	Mineral oil	Water
Poloxyl 6 stearate	S	S	DH
Poloxyl 8 stearate	S	I	D
Poloxyl 12 stearate	S	I	S
Poloxyl 20 stearate	S	I	S
Poloxyl 40 stearate	S	I	S
Poloxyl 50 stearate	S	I	S
Poloxyl 100 stearate	S	I	S
Poloxyl 12 distearate	S	—	DH
Poloxyl 32 distearate	S	—	S
Poloxyl 150 distearate	I	—	S

Where,
D = dispersible   I = insoluble
S = soluble   DH = dispersible (with heat)

See also Table III.

11. Stability and Storage Conditions

Polyoxyethylene stearates are generally stable in the presence of electrolytes and weak acids or bases. Strong acids and bases can cause gradual hydrolysis and saponification.

The bulk material should be stored in a well-closed container, in a dry place, at room temperature.

12. Incompatibilities

Polyoxyethylene stearates are unstable in hot alkaline solutions due to hydrolysis, and will also saponify with strong acids or bases. Discoloration or precipitation can occur with salicylates, phenolic substances, iodine salts and salts of bismuth, silver and tannins.[2-4] Complex formation with preservatives may also occur.[5]

The antimicrobial activity of some materials such as bacitracin, chloramphenicol, phenoxymethylpenicillin, sodium penicillin and tetracycline may be reduced in the presence of polyoxyethylene stearate concentrations greater than 5% w/w.[6,7]

13. Method of Manufacture

Polyoxyethylene stearates are prepared by the direct reaction of fatty acids, particularly stearic acid, with ethylene oxide.

14. Safety

Although polyoxyethylene stearates are primarily used as emulsifying agents in topical pharmaceutical formulations

Table III: Typical properties of polyoxyethylene stearates.

Name	Acid value	Free ethylene oxide	HLB value	Hydroxyl value	Iodine number	Melting point (°C)	Saponification value	Water content (%)
Poloxyl 6 stearate	≤ 5.0	≤ 100 ppm	9.7	—	≤ 0.5	28-32	95-110	—
Poloxyl 8 stearate	≤ 2.0	≤ 100 ppm	11.1	87-105	≤ 1.0	28-33	82-95	≤ 3.0
Poloxyl 12 stearate	≤ 8.5	≤ 100 ppm	13.6	55-75	≤ 1.0	≈ 37	62-78	≤ 1.0
Poloxyl 20 stearate	≤ 1.0	≤ 100 ppm	14	50-62	≤ 1.0	≈ 28	46-56	≤ 1.0
Poloxyl 30 stearate	≤ 2.0	—	16	35-50	—	—	30-45	≤ 3.0
Poloxyl 40 stearate	≤ 1.0	—	16.9	27-40	—	≈ 38	25-35	≤ 3.0
Poloxyl 50 stearate	≤ 2.0	—	17.9	23-35	—	≈ 42	20-28	≤ 3.0
Poloxyl 100 stearate	≤ 1.0	≤ 100 ppm	18.8	15-30	—	≈ 46	9-20	≤ 3.0
Poloxyl 8 distearate	≤ 10.0	—	—	≤ 15	≤ 0.5	≈ 36	115-124	—
Poloxyl 12 distearate	≤ 10.0	≤ 100 ppm	10.6	≤ 20	≤ 1.0	≈ 39	93-102	≤ 1.0
Poloxyl 32 distearate	≤ 10.0	≤ 100 ppm	14.8	≤ 20	≤ 0.25	≈ 45	50-62	≤ 1.0
Poloxyl 150 distearate	7-9	≤ 100 ppm	18.4	≤ 15	≤ 0.1	53-57	14-20	≤ 1.0

certain materials, particularly poloxyl 40 stearate, have also been used in intravenous injections and oral preparations.[1,4] Polyoxyethylene stearates have been extensively tested for toxicity in animals[8-13] and are widely used in pharmaceutical formulations and cosmetics. They are generally regarded as essentially nontoxic and nonirritant materials.

Poloxyl 8 stearate:
LD_{50} (hamster, oral): 27 g/kg[14]
LD_{50} (rat, oral): 64 g/kg
Poloxyl 20 stearate:
LD_{50} (mouse, IP): 0.2 g/kg[14]
LD_{50} (mouse, IV): 0.87 g/kg

15. Handling Precautions

Observe normal precautions appropriate to the circumstances and quantity of material handled.

Polyoxyethylene stearates that contain greater than 100 ppm of free ethylene oxide may present an explosion hazard when stored in a closed container. This is due to the release of ethylene oxide into the container headspace where it can accumulate, and so exceed the explosion limit.

16. Regulatory Status

Certain polyoxyethylene stearates are accepted for use as food additives in Europe. Included in the FDA Inactive Ingredients Guide (dental solutions, IV injections, ophthalmic preparations, oral capsules and tablets, otic suspensions, topical creams, emulsions, lotions, ointments and solutions, and vaginal preparations). Included in nonparenteral medicines licensed in the UK.

17. Pharmacopeias

Name	Pharmacopeia
Poloxyl 8 stearate	Aust, Ger and Swiss.
Poloxyl 40 stearate	Braz, Hung, Jpn, Turk and USPNF.
Poloxyl 50 stearate	USPNF.

18. Related Substances

Polyethylene Glycol; Stearic Acid.

19. Comments

—

20. Specific References

1. Cohn I, Singleton S, Hartwig QL, Atik M. New intravenous fat emulsion. JAMA 1963; 183: 755-757.
2. Thoma K, Ullmann E, Fickel O. The antibacterial activity of phenols in the presence of polyoxyethylene stearates and polyethylene glycols [in German]. Arch Pharm 1970; 303: 289-296.
3. Thoma K, Ullmann E, Fickel O. Dimensions and cause of the reaction between phenols and polyoxyethylene stearates [in German]. Arch Pharm 1970; 303: 297-304.
4. Duchêne D, Djiane A, Puisieux F. Tablet study III: influence of nonionic surfactants with ester linkage on the quality of sulfanilamide grains and tablets [in French]. Ann Pharm Fr 1970; 28: 289-298.
5. Chakravarty D, Lach JL, Blaug SM. Study of complex formation between poloxyl 40 stearate and some pharmaceuticals. Drug Standards. 1957; 25: 137-140.
6. Ullmann E, Moser B. Effect of polyoxyethylene stearates on the antibacterial activity of antibiotics [in German]. Arch Pharm 1962; 295: 136-143.
7. Thoma K, Ullmann E, Zelfel G. Investigation of the stability of penicillin G sodium in the presence of nonionic surface active agents (polyethylene glycol derivatives) [in German]. Arch Pharm 1962; 295: 670-678.
8. Culver PJ, Wilcox CS, Jones CM, Rose RS. Intermediary metabolism of certain polyoxyethylene derivatives in man I: recovery of the polyoxyethylene moiety from urine and feces following ingestion of polyoxyethylene (20) sorbitan monooleate and of polyoxyethylene (40) mono-stearate. J Pharmacol Exp Ther 1951; 103: 377-381.
9. Oser BL, Oser M. Nutritional studies on rats on diets containing high levels of partial ester emulsifiers I: general plan and procedures; growth and food utilization. J Nutr 1956; 60: 367-390.
10. Oser BL, Oser M. Nutritional studies on rats on diets containing high levels of partial ester emulsifiers II: reproduction and lactation. J Nutr 1956; 60: 489-505.
11. Oser BL, Oser M. Nutritional studies on rats on diets containing high levels of partial ester emulsifiers III: clinical and metabolic observations. J Nutr 1957; 61: 149-166.
12. Oser BL, Oser M. Nutritional studies on rats on diets containing high levels of partial ester emulsifiers IV: mortality and post-mortem pathology; general conclusions. J Nutr 1957; 61: 235-252.
13. Fitzhugh OG, Bourke AR, Nelson AA, Frawley JP. Chronic oral toxicities of four stearic acid emulsifiers. Toxicol Appl Pharmacol 1959; 1: 315-331.

14. Sweet DV, editor. Registry of toxic effects of chemical substances. Cincinnati: US Department of Health, 1987.

21. General References

Satkowski WB, Huang SK, Liss RL. Polyoxyethylene esters of fatty acids. In: Schick MJ, editor. Nonionic surfactants. New York: Marcel Dekker, 1967: 142-174.

22. Authors

USA: CD Yu.

Polyvinyl Alcohol

1. Nonproprietary Names
USP: Polyvinyl alcohol

2. Synonyms
Airvol; *Elvanol*; *Polyviol*; *Poval*; PVA; vinyl alcohol polymer.

3. Chemical Name and CAS Registry Number
Ethenol, homopolymer [9002-89-5]

4. Empirical Formula   Molecular Weight
$(C_2H_4O)_n$ 30 000-20 0000

Polyvinyl alcohol is a polymer in which the average value of n lies between 500-5000. Various grades with different viscosities and molecular weights are commercially available; typical values are shown below.

Grade	Molecular weight
High viscosity	$\approx 200\,000$
Medium viscosity	$\approx 130\,000$
Low viscosity	$\approx 30\,000$

5. Structural Formula

6. Functional Category
Coating agent; nonionic surfactant; viscosity-increasing agent.

7. Applications in Pharmaceutical Formulation or Technology
Polyvinyl alcohol is used primarily in topical pharmaceutical formulations, particularly ophthalmic products.[1-3] It is a nonionic surfactant and is used as a stabilizing agent for emulsions. Polyvinyl alcohol is also used as a viscosity-increasing agent, especially in ophthalmic products, where it is generally preferable to have slightly viscous formulations. Polyvinyl alcohol also has desirable lubricant properties which are utilized in many ophthalmic products such as artificial tears and contact lens solutions.

Polyvinyl alcohol is additionally used in the preparation of various jellies which dry rapidly when applied to the skin. It is also used in the preparation of sustained release tablet formulations,[4] and in transdermal patches.[5]

Cross-linked polyvinyl alcohol microspheres, used for the controlled release of oral drugs, may be prepared by mixing 30% aqueous polyvinyl alcohol solution with an active drug and glutaraldehyde solution.[6] Cross-linked polyvinyl alcohol hydrogels[7] may also be formed by repeated freezing and thawing of polyvinyl alcohol solutions.[8]

Polyvinyl alcohol is also used in cosmetics.

Use	Concentration (%)
Emulsions	0.5
Ophthalmic formulations	0.25-3.0
Topical lotions	2.5

8. Description
Polyvinyl alcohol occurs as an odorless, white to cream-colored granular powder.

9. Pharmacopeial Specifications

Test	USP XXII (Suppl 6)
Viscosity	+
pH (4% aqueous solution)	5.0-8.0
Loss on drying	$\leqslant$ 5.0%
Residue on ignition	$\leqslant$ 2.0%
Water-insoluble substances	$\leqslant$ 0.1%
Organic volatile impurities	+
Degree of hydrolysis	85-89%

10. Typical Properties
Melting point:
228°C for fully hydrolyzed grades;
180-190°C for partially hydrolyzed grades.
Refractive index: $n_D^{25} = 1.49$-1.53
Solubility: soluble in hot or cold water; solubility in water increases as the molecular weight decreases. Effective dissolution of partially hydrolyzed grades requires the dispersion and continued mixing of the solid in cold or tepid water followed by sustained heating at 85-95°C until dissolved. Very slightly soluble in some polyhydroxy compounds, certain amines and amides. Practically insoluble in aliphatic, aromatic and chlorinated hydrocarbons, esters, ketones, and oils.
Specific gravity:
1.19-1.31 for solid at 25°C;
1.02 for 10% w/v aqueous solution at 25°C.
Specific heat: 1.67 J/g (0.4 cal/g)
Viscosity (dynamic):

Grade	Dynamic viscosity of 4% w/w aqueous solution at 20°C (mPa s)
High viscosity	40-65
Medium viscosity	21-33
Low viscosity	4-7

11. Stability and Storage Conditions
Polyvinyl alcohol undergoes slow degradation at 100°C and rapid degradation at 200°C; it is stable on exposure to light. Aqueous solutions are stable and should be stored in corrosion-resistant containers. For extended storage periods, an antimicrobial preservative should be added to polyvinyl alcohol solutions.

The bulk material should be stored in a well-closed container, in a cool, dry, place.

12. Incompatibilities
Polyvinyl alcohol will undergo reactions typical of a compound with secondary hydroxy groups, such as esterification.

Polyvinyl alcohol decomposes in strong acids and softens or dissolves in weak acids and alkalis. Incompatible at high concentration with most inorganic salts, especially sulfates and phosphates. Phosphates will cause 5% polyvinyl alcohol to precipitate from aqueous solution. Borax is a particularly effective gelling agent for polyvinyl alcohol solutions.

13. Method of Manufacture

Polyvinyl alcohol is a polymer prepared from polyvinyl acetate by replacement of the acetate groups with hydroxy groups. The alcoholysis proceeds most rapidly in a methanol and methyl acetate mixture in the presence of catalytic amounts of alkali or mineral acids. For partially hydrolyzed grades, the polyvinyl acetate is usually about 88% hydrolyzed.

14. Safety

Polyvinyl alcohol is generally regarded as a nontoxic material. At concentrations up to 10% it is nonirritant to the skin and eyes. Concentrations up to 7% may be used in cosmetics. Studies in rats have shown that 5% polyvinyl alcohol aqueous solution injected subcutaneously can cause anemia and infiltrate various organs and tissues.[9]

LD$_{50}$ (mouse, oral): 14.7 g/kg [10]
LD$_{50}$ (rat, oral): > 20 g/kg

15. Handling Precautions

Observe normal precautions appropriate to the circumstances and quantity of material handled. Eye protection and gloves are recommended. Polyvinyl alcohol dust may be irritant on inhalation. Handle in a well-ventilated environment.

16. Regulatory Status

Included in the FDA Inactive Ingredients Guide (ophthalmic preparations, oral tablets, topical, transdermal and vaginal preparations). Included in nonparenteral medicines licensed in the UK.

17. Pharmacopeias

Hung, Mex, US and Yug.

18. Related Substances

—

19. Comments

Various grades of polyvinyl alcohol are commercially available. Two main parameters determine their physical properties, the degree of polymerization and the degree of hydrolysis. The pharmaceutical grade is a partially hydrolyzed material although fully hydrolyzed polyvinyl alcohols are also available

for various industrial applications. Commercial grades may be named according to a coding system in which the first number following a trade name refers to the degree of hydrolysis and the second set of numbers indicates the approximate viscosity, in mPa s, of a 4% aqueous solution at 20°C.

20. Specific References

1. Krishna N, Brow F. Polyvinyl alcohol as an ophthalmic vehicle: effect on regeneration of corneal epithelium. Am J Ophthalmol 1964; 57: 99-106.
2. Patton TF, Robinson JR. Ocular evaluation of polyvinyl alcohol vehicle in rabbits. J Pharm Sci 1975; 64: 1312-1316.
3. New method of ocular drug delivery launched. Pharm J 1993; 250: 174.
4. Carstensen JT, Marty JP, Puisieux F, Fessi H. Bonding mechanisms and hysteresis areas in compression cycle plots. J Pharm Sci 1981; 70: 222-223.
5. Wan LSC, Lim LY. Drug release from heat-treated polyvinyl alcohol films. Drug Dev Ind Pharm 1992; 18: 1895-1906.
6. Thanoo BC, Sunny MC, Jayakrishnan A. Controlled release of oral drugs from cross-linked polyvinyl alcohol microspheres. J Pharm Pharmacol 1993; 45: 16-20.
7. Morimoto K, et al. Design of a polyvinyl alcohol hydrogel containing phospholipid as controlled-release vehicle for rectal administration of ($\pm$)-propranolol HCl. J Pharm Pharmacol 1990; 42: 720-722.
8. Urushizaki F, et al. Swelling and mechanical properties of poly(vinyl alcohol) hydrogels. Int J Pharmaceutics 1990; 58: 135-142.
9. Hall CE, Hall O. Polyvinyl alcohol: relationship of physicochemical properties to hypertension and other pathophysiologic sequelae. Lab Invest 1963; 12: 721-736.
10. Sweet DV, editor. Registry of toxic effects of chemical substances. Cincinnati: US Department of Health, 1987.

21. General References

Chudzikowski R. Polyvinyl alcohol. Mfg Chem Aerosol News 1970; 41(7): 31-37.
Finch CA, editor. Polyvinyl alcohol developments. Chichester: John Wiley & Sons Ltd, 1992.
Okhamafe AO, York P. Moisture permeation mechanism of some aqueous-based film coats. J Pharm Pharmacol 1982; 34(Suppl): 53P.

22. Authors

USA: S Hickok.

Potassium Chloride

1. Nonproprietary Names

BP: Potassium chloride
PhEur: Kalii chloridum
USP: Potassium chloride

2. Synonyms

Chloride of potash; E508.

3. Chemical Name and CAS Registry Number

Potassium chloride [7447-40-7]

4. Empirical Formula   Molecular Weight

KCl   74.55

5. Structural Formula

KCl

6. Functional Category

Tablet and capsule diluent; therapeutic agent; tonicity agent.

7. Applications in Pharmaceutical Formulation or Technology

Potassium chloride is widely used in a variety of parenteral and nonparenteral pharmaceutical formulations. Its primary use, in parenteral and ophthalmic preparations, is to produce isotonic solutions.
Potassium chloride is also used as a tablet and capsule diluent and therapeutically in the treatment of hypokalemia.
Many solid dosage forms of potassium chloride exist including: tablets prepared by direct compression[1-4] and granulation;[5,6] effervescent tablets; coated, sustained release tablets;[7-10] sustained release wax matrix tablets;[11] microcapsules;[12] pellets and osmotic pump formulations.[13,14]
Experimentally, potassium chloride is frequently used as a model drug in the development of new solid dosage forms, particularly for sustained or modified release products.

8. Description

Potassium chloride occurs as odorless, colorless crystals or a white crystalline powder, with an unpleasant, saline taste. The crystal lattice is a face centered cubic structure.

9. Pharmacopeial Specifications

Test	PhEur 1993	USP XXII (Suppl 6)
Identification	+	+
Acidity or alkalinity	+	+
Appearance of solution	+	—
Loss on drying	⩽ 1.0%	⩽ 1.0%
Iodide or bromide	+	+
Aluminum	⩽ 1 ppm	⩽ 1 ppm
Arsenic	—	⩽ 3 ppm
Barium	+	—
Calcium and magnesium	⩽ 200 ppm	+
Heavy metals	⩽ 10 ppm	⩽ 0.001%
Iron	⩽ 20 ppm	—

Continued

Test	PhEur 1993	USP XXII (Suppl 6)
Sodium	⩽ 0 .1%	+
Sulfates	⩽ 300 ppm	—
Organic volatile impurities	—	+
Assay (dried basis)	99.0-100.5%	99.0-100.5%

10. Typical Properties

Acidity/alkalinity:
pH ≈ 7 for a saturated aqueous solution at 15°C.
Boiling point: sublimes at 1500°C
Compressibility: see Fig. 1.[3,4]
Density: 1.99 g/cm^3; 1.17 g/cm^3 for a saturated aqueous solution at 15°C.
Melting point: 790°C
Osmolarity: a 1.19% w/v solution is iso-osmotic with serum.
Particle size distribution: typical distribution[5] is 10% less than 30 μm, 50% less than 94 μm and 90% less than 149 μm in size. Mean particle diameter is 108 μm. Finer powders may be obtained by milling.
Solubility:

Solvent	Solubility at 20°C Unless otherwise stated
Acetone	practically insoluble
Ethanol (95%)	1 in 250
Ether	practically insoluble
Glycerin	1 in 14
Water	1 in 2.8
	1 in 1.8 at 100°C

Specific surface area: 0.084 m^2/g (BET method)[5]

11. Stability and Storage Conditions

Potassium chloride tablets become increasingly hard on storage at low humidities. However, tablets stored at 76% relative humidity showed no increase or only a slight increase in hardness.[2] The addition of lubricants, such as 2% w/w magnesium stearate,[1] reduces tablet hardness and hardness on aging.[2] Aqueous potassium chloride solutions may be sterilized by autoclaving or by filtration.
Potassium chloride is stable and should be stored in a well-closed container in a cool, dry, place.

12. Incompatibilities

Potassium chloride reacts violently with bromine trifluoride and with a mixture of sulfuric acid and potassium permanganate. The presence of hydrochloric acid, sodium chloride and magnesium chloride decreases the solubility of potassium chloride in water. Aqueous solutions of potassium chloride form precipitates with lead and silver salts.
Intravenous aqueous potassium chloride solutions are incompatible with protein hydrolysate.

13. Method of Manufacture

Potassium chloride occurs naturally as the mineral sylvite or sylvine; it also occurs in other minerals such as sylvinite, carnallite and kainite. Commercially, potassium chloride is obtained by the solar evaporation of brine or by the mining of mineral deposits.

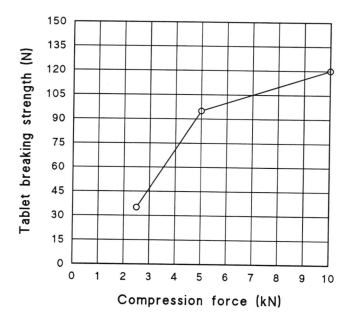

Fig. 1. Compression characteristics of potassium chloride.[3]
Tablet diameter = 10 mm

14. Safety

Potassium chloride is used in a large number of pharmaceutical formulations including oral, parenteral and topical preparations both as an excipient and as a therapeutic agent. Potassium ions play an important role in cellular metabolism and imbalances can result in serious clinical effects. Orally ingested potassium chloride is rapidly absorbed from the gastrointestinal tract and excreted by the kidneys. Following oral administration, potassium chloride is more irritant than sodium chloride and ingestion of large quantities of potassium chloride can cause gastrointestinal irritation, nausea, vomiting and diarrhea. High localized concentrations of potassium chloride in the gastrointestinal tract can cause ulceration hence the development of the many enteric coated and wax matrix sustained release preparations that are available.[15] Although it is claimed that some formulations cause less ulceration than others it is often preferred to administer potassium chloride as an aqueous solution. However, solutions have also been associated with problems due to their unpleasant taste.

Parenterally, rapid injection of strong potassium chloride solutions can cause cardiac arrest; in the adult, solutions should be infused at a rate not greater than 750 mg/hour.

Therapeutically, in adults, up to 10 g orally, in divided doses has been administered daily, while intravenously up to 6 g daily has been used.

LD_{50} (guinea pig, oral): 2.5 g/kg[16]
LD_{50} (mouse, IP): 1.18 g/kg
LD_{50} (mouse, IV): 0.12 g/kg
LD_{50} (mouse, oral): 1.5 g/kg
LD_{50} (rat, IP): 0.66 g/kg
LD_{50} (rat, IV): 0.14 g/kg
LD_{50} (rat, oral): 2.6 g/kg

15. Handling Precautions

Observe normal precautions appropriate to the circumstances and quantity of material handled.

16. Regulatory Status

GRAS listed. Accepted as a food additive in Europe. Included in the FDA Inactive Ingredients Guide (injections, ophthalmic preparations, oral capsules and tablets). Included in nonparenteral and parenteral medicines licensed in the UK.

17. Pharmacopeias

Aust, Belg, Br, Braz, Chin, Cz, Egypt, Eur, Fr, Ger, Gr, Hung, Ind, Int, It, Jpn, Mex, Neth, Nord, Port, Rom, Rus, Swiss, Turk, US and Yug.

18. Related Substances

Sodium Chloride.

For diets where the intake of sodium chloride is restricted, salt substitutes for use in cooking or as table salt are available and contain mainly potassium chloride, e.g. *LoSalt* (Klinge Chemicals Ltd) is a blend of 2/3 potassium chloride and 1/3 sodium chloride with magnesium carbonate added as a flow promoting agent.

19. Comments

Each gram of potassium chloride represents approximately 13.4 mmol of potassium. Potassium chloride 1.91 g is approximately equivalent to 1 g of potassium.

20. Specific References

1. Hirai Y, Okada J. Calculated stress and strain conditions of lubricated potassium chloride powders during die-compression. Chem Pharm Bull 1982; 30: 2202-2207.
2. Lordi N, Shiromani P. Mechanism of hardness of aged compacts. Drug Dev Ind Pharm 1984; 10: 729-752.
3. Pintye-Hodi K, Sohajda-Szücs E. Study on the compressibility of potassium chloride part 1: direct pressing without auxiliary products [in German]. Pharm Ind 1984; 46: 767-769.
4. Pintye-Hodi K, Sohajda-Szücs E. Study on the compressibility of potassium chloride part 2: direct compressing with microgranulous celluloses [in German]. Pharm Ind 1984; 46: 1080-1083.
5. Niskanen T, Yliruusi J, Niskanen M, Kontro O. Granulation of potassium chloride in instrumental fluidized bed granulator part 1: effect of flow rate. Acta Pharm Fenn 1990; 99: 13-22.
6. Niskanen T, Yliruusi J, Niskanen M, Kontro O. Granulation of potassium chloride in instrumental fluidized bed granulator part 2: evaluation of the effects of two independent process variables using 3^2-factorial design. Acta Pharm Fenn 1990; 99: 23-30.
7. Fee JV, Grant DJW, Newton JM. The effect of surface coatings on the dissolution rate of a non-disintegrating solid (potassium chloride). J Pharm Pharmacol 1973; 25(Suppl): 149P-150P.
8. Thomas WH. Measurement of dissolution rates of potassium chloride from various slow release potassium chloride tablets using a specific ion electrode. J Pharm Pharmacol 1973; 25: 27-34.
9. Cartwright AC, Shah C. An *in vitro* dissolution test for slow release potassium chloride tablets. J Pharm Pharmacol 1977; 29: 367-369.
10. Beckett AH, Samaan SS. Sustained release potassium chloride products *in vitro-in vivo* correlations. J Pharm Pharmacol 1978; 30(Suppl): 69P.
11. Flanders P, Dyer GA, Jordan D. The control of drug release from conventional melt granulation matrices. Drug Dev Ind Pharm 1987; 13: 1001-1022.
12. Harris MS. Preparation and release characteristics of potassium chloride microcapsules. J Pharm Sci 1981; 70: 391-394.
13. Ramadan MA, Tawashi R. The effect of hydrodynamic conditions and delivery orifice size on the rate of drug release

from the elementary osmotic pump system (EOP). Drug Dev Ind Pharm 1987; 13: 235-248.

14. Lindstedt B, Sjöberg M, Hjärtstam J. Osmotic pumping release from KCl tablets coated with porous and non-porous ethylcellulose. Int J Pharmaceutics 1991; 67: 21-27.

15. McMahon FG, Ryan JR, Akdamar K, Ertan A. Effect of potassium chloride supplements on upper gastrointestinal mucosa. Clin Pharmacol Ther 1984; 35: 852-855.

16. Sweet DV, editor. Registry of toxic effects of chemical substances. Cincinnati: US Department of Health, 1987.

21. General References

Staniforth JN, Rees JE. Segregation of vibrated powder mixes containing different concentrations of fine potassium chloride and tablet excipients. J Pharm Pharmacol 1983; 35: 549-554.

22. Authors

UK: PJ Weller.

Potassium Citrate

1. Nonproprietary Names

BP: Potassium citrate
PhEur: Kalii citras
USP: Potassium citrate

2. Synonyms

Citrate of potash; citric acid potassium salt; E332; 2-hydroxy-1,2,3-propanetricarboxylic acid tripotassium salt monohydrate; tripotassium citrate monohydrate.

3. Chemical Name and CAS Registry Number

Tripotassium 2-hydroxy-propane-1,2,3-tricarboxylate monohydrate.
[6100-05-6]

4. Empirical Formula   Molecular Weight

$C_6H_5K_3O_7.H_2O$ 324.41

5. Structural Formula

$$\left[\begin{array}{c} CH_2-COOK \\ | \\ HO-C-COOK \\ | \\ CH_2-COOK \end{array} \right] \cdot H_2O$$

6. Functional Category

Alkalizing agent; buffering agent; sequestering agent.

7. Applications in Pharmaceutical Formulation or Technology

Potassium citrate is used in beverages, foods and oral pharmaceutical formulations as a buffering and alkalizing agent. It is also used as a sequestering agent and as a therapeutic agent to alkalinize the urine and to relieve the painful irritation caused by cystitis.[1-3]

Use	Concentration (%)
Buffer for solutions	0.3-2.0
Sequestering agent	0.3-2.0

8. Description

Transparent prismatic crystals or a white, granular, powder. Potassium citrate is hygroscopic, odorless and has a cooling, saline taste.

9. Pharmacopeial Specifications

Test	PhEur 1985	USP XXII (Suppl 6)
Identification	+	+
Acidity or alkalinity	+	+
Loss on drying	—	3.0-6.0%
Water content	4.0-7.0%	—
Appearance of solution	+	—

Continued

Test	PhEur 1985	USP XXII (Suppl 6)
Tartrate	—	+
Heavy metals	⩽ 10 ppm	⩽ 0.001%
Sodium	⩽ 0.3%	—
Chlorides	⩽ 50 ppm	—
Oxalates	⩽ 300 ppm	—
Sulfates	⩽ 150 ppm	—
Organic volatile impurities	—	+
Readily carbonizable substances	+	—
Assay (dried basis)	99.0-101.0%	99.0-100.5%

10. Typical Properties

Acidity/alkalinity:
pH = 8.5 (saturated aqueous solution).
Density: 1.98 g/cm^3
Melting point: 230°C (loses water of crystallization at 180°C).
Solubility:

Solvent	Solubility at 20°C
Ethanol (95%)	practically insoluble
Glycerin	1 in 2.5
Water	1 in 0.65

11. Stability and Storage Conditions

Potassium citrate is a stable, though hygroscopic material, and should be stored in an airtight container in a cool, dry, place.

12. Incompatibilities

Aqueous potassium citrate solutions are slightly alkaline and will react with acidic substances. Potassium citrate may also precipitate alkaloidal salts from their aqueous or alcoholic solutions. Calcium and strontium salts will cause precipitation of the corresponding citrates.

13. Method of Manufacture

Potassium citrate is prepared by adding either potassium bicarbonate or potassium carbonate to a solution of citric acid until effervescence ceases. The resulting solution is then filtered and evaporated to dryness to obtain potassium citrate.

14. Safety

Potassium citrate is used in oral pharmaceutical formulations and is generally regarded as a nontoxic and nonirritant material. Most potassium citrate safety data relates to its use as a therapeutic agent where up to 10 g may be administered daily, in divided doses, as a treatment for cystitis. Although there are adverse effects associated with excessive ingestion of potassium salts the quantities of potassium citrate used as a pharmaceutical excipient are insignificant in comparison to those used therapeutically.

15. Handling Precautions

Observe normal precautions appropriate to the circumstances and quantity of material handled. Potassium citrate may be irritant to the skin and eyes and should be handled in a well-ventilated environment. Eye protection and gloves are recommended.

16. Regulatory Status

GRAS listed. Accepted as a food additive in Europe. Included in the FDA Inactive Ingredients Guide (oral solutions). Included in nonparenteral medicines licensed in the UK.

17. Pharmacopeias

Aust, Br, Chin, Egypt, Eur, Fr, Ger, Gr, Hung, Ind, Int, It, Neth, Nord, Port, Swiss and US.

18. Related Substances

Potassium citrate anhydrous.

Potassium citrate anhydrous: $C_6H_5K_3O_7$
Molecular weight: 306.40
CAS number: [866-84-2]

19. Comments

Each gram of potassium citrate monohydrate represents approximately 9.25 mmol of potassium and 3.08 mmol of citrate. Each gram of potassium citrate anhydrous represents approximately 9.79 mmol of potassium and 3.26 mmol of citrate.

20. Specific References

1. Elizabeth JE, Carter NJ. Potassium citrate mixture: soothing but not harmless? Br Med J 1987; 295: 993.
2. Gabriel R. Potassium sorbate mixture: soothing but not harmless? [letter] Br Med J 1987; 295: 1487.
3. Liak TL, Li Wan Po A, Irwin WJ. The effects of drug therapy on urinary pH - excipient effects and bioactivation of methenamine. Int J Pharmaceutics 1987; 36: 233-242.

21. General References

—

22. Authors

UK: RS Cook; N Yussuf.

Potassium Sorbate

1. Nonproprietary Names

BP: Potassium sorbate
PhEur: Kalii sorbas
USPNF: Potassium sorbate

2. Synonyms

E202; 2,4-hexadienoic acid (*E,E*)-potassium salt; 2,4-hexadienoic acid potassium salt; potassium (*E,E*)-sorbate; *Sorbistat K.*

3. Chemical Name and CAS Registry Number

Potassium (*E,E*)-hexa-2,4-dienoate
[24634-61-5]

4. Empirical Formula   Molecular Weight

$C_6H_7O_2K$ 150.22

5. Structural Formula

6. Functional Category

Antimicrobial preservative.

7. Applications in Pharmaceutical Formulation or Technology

Potassium sorbate is an antimicrobial preservative, with antibacterial and antifungal properties used in pharmaceuticals, foods, enteral preparations and cosmetics. Generally, it is used at concentrations of 0.1–0.2% in oral and topical formulations, especially those containing nonionic surfactants. Potassium sorbate is used in approximately twice as many pharmaceutical formulations as sorbic acid due to its greater solubility and stability in water. Like sorbic acid, potassium sorbate has minimal antibacterial properties in formulations above pH 6.

8. Description

Potassium sorbate occurs as a white crystalline powder with a faint, characteristic odor.

9. Pharmacopeial Specifications

Test	PhEur 1993	USPNF XVII (Suppl 6)
Identification	+	+
Appearance of solution	+	—
Acidity or alkalinity	+	+
Loss on drying	⩽ 1.0%	⩽ 1.0%
Heavy metals	⩽ 10 ppm	⩽ 0.001%
Organic volatile impurities	—	+
Aldehyde (as C_2H_4O)	⩽ 0.15%	—
Assay (anhydrous basis)	99.0–101.0%	98.0–101.0%

10. Typical Properties

Antimicrobial activity: potassium sorbate is predominantly used as an antifungal preservative although it also has antibacterial properties. Similar to sorbic acid, antimicrobial activity is dependent on the degree of dissociation; there is practically no antibacterial activity above pH 6. Preservative efficacy is increased with increasing temperature,[1] and increasing concentration of potassium sorbate.[1] The efficacy of potassium sorbate is also increased when used in combination with other antimicrobial preservatives or glycols since synergistic effects occur.[2] Reported minimum inhibitory concentrations (MICs) at the pH values indicated are shown below:[2]

Microorganism	MIC (μg/mL) at the stated pH		
	pH = 5.5	pH = 6.0	pH = 7.0
Escherichia coli	1400	1500	3800
Pseudomonas aeruginosa	1600–2300	1900–2500	5600–9000
Staphylococcus aureus	1200	1000	3800

Density: 1.363 g/cm^3
Melting point: 270°C with decomposition.
Solubility:

Solvent	Solubility at 20°C Unless otherwise stated
Acetone	1 in 1000
Benzene	practically insoluble
Chloroform	very slightly soluble
Corn oil	very slightly soluble
Ethanol	1 in 50
Ethanol (95%)	1 in 35
Ethanol (5%)	1 in 1.7
Ether	very slightly soluble
Propylene glycol	1 in 1.8
	1 in 2.1 at 50°C
	1 in 5 at 100°C
Water	1 in 1.72
	1 in 1.64 at 50°C
	1 in 1.56 at 100°C

11. Stability and Storage Conditions

Potassium sorbate is more stable in aqueous solution than sorbic acid; aqueous solutions may be sterilized by autoclaving.
The bulk material should be stored in a well-closed container, protected from light, at a temperature not exceeding 40°C.

12. Incompatibilities

Some loss of antimicrobial activity occurs in the presence of nonionic surfactants and some plastics. *See also* Sorbic Acid.

13. Method of Manufacture

Potassium sorbate is prepared from sorbic acid and potassium hydroxide.

14. Safety

Potassium sorbate is used as an antimicrobial preservative in oral and topical pharmaceutical formulations and is generally regarded as a nontoxic material. However, some adverse reactions to potassium sorbate have been reported including irritant skin reactions which may be of the allergic, hypersensitive type. There have been no reports of adverse systemic reactions following oral consumption of potassium sorbate.

The WHO has set an estimated total acceptable daily intake for sorbic acid, calcium sorbate, potassium sorbate and sodium sorbate expressed as sorbic acid at up to 25 mg/kg body-weight.[3,4]

LD_{50} (mouse, IP): 1.3 g/kg[5]
LD_{50} (rat, oral): 4.92 g/kg
See also Sorbic Acid.

15. Handling Precautions

Observe normal precautions appropriate to the circumstances and quantity of material handled. Potassium sorbate is irritant to the skin, eyes and mucous membranes; eye protection and gloves are recommended. In areas of limited ventilation a respirator is also recommended.

16. Regulatory Status

GRAS listed. Accepted for use as a food additive in Europe. Included in the FDA Inactive Ingredients Guide (oral capsules, solutions, suspensions, syrups, tablets, rectal and topical preparations). Included in nonparenteral medicines licensed in the UK.

17. Pharmacopeias

Br, Eur, Fr, It, Neth, Swiss and USPNF.

18. Related Substances

Sorbic Acid.

19. Comments

Much of the information contained in the sorbic acid monograph on safety, incompatibilities and references also applies to potassium, calcium and sodium sorbate. *See* Sorbic Acid for further information.

20. Specific References

1. Lusher P, Denyer SP, Hugo WB. A note on the effect of dilution and temperature on the bactericidal activity of potassium sorbate. J Appl Bacteriol 1984; 57: 179-181.
2. Woodford R, Adams E. Sorbic acid. Am Perfum Cosmet 1970; 85(3): 25-30.
3. FAO/WHO. Toxicological evaluation of certain food additives with a review of general principles and of specifications: seventeenth report of the joint FAO/WHO expert committee on food additives. Tech Rep Ser Wld Hlth Org 1974; No. 539.
4. FAO/WHO. Evaluation of certain food additives and contaminants: twenty-ninth report of the joint FAO/WHO expert committee on food additives. Tech Rep Ser Wld Hlth Org 1986; No. 733.
5. Sweet DV, editor. Registry of toxic effects of chemical substances. Cincinnati: US Department of Health, 1987.

21. General References

Fagerman KE, Paauw JD, McCamish MA, Dean RE. Effects of time, temperature, and preservative on bacterial growth in enteral nutrient solutions. Am J Hosp Pharm 1984; 41: 1122-1126.
Sofos JN, Busta FF. Sorbates. In: Branen AL, Davidson PM, editors. Antimicrobials in foods. New York: Marcel Dekker, 1983: 141-175.
Walker R. Toxicology of sorbic acid and sorbates. Food Add Contam 1990; 7(5): 671-676.

22. Authors

UK: PJ Weller.

Povidone

1. Nonproprietary Names
BP: Povidone
PhEur: Polyvidonum
USP: Povidone

2. Synonyms
E1201; *Kollidon*; *Plasdone*; poly[1-(2-oxo-1-pyrrolidi-nyl)ethylene]; polyvidone; polyvinylpyrrolidone; PVP; 1-vinyl-2-pyrrolidinone polymer.

3. Chemical Name and CAS Registry Number
1-Ethenyl-2-pyrrolidinone homopolymer
[9003-39-8]

4. Empirical Formula   Molecular Weight
$(C_6H_9NO)_n$ 2500-3 000 000
The USP XXII (Suppl 9) describes povidone as a synthetic polymer consisting essentially of linear 1-vinyl-2-pyrrolidinone groups, the degree of polymerization of which results in polymers of various molecular weights. It is characterized by its viscosity in aqueous solution, relative to that of water, expressed as a K-value, ranging from 10-120. The K-value is calculated using Fikentscher's equation[1] shown below:

$$\log z = c\left(\frac{75k^2}{1+1.5kc}\right) + k$$

where z is the relative viscosity of the solution of concentration c, k is the K-value x 10^{-3}, and c is the concentration in % w/v. Alternatively, the K-value may be determined from the following equation:

$$K-value = \frac{\sqrt{300c\log z + (c+1.5c\log z)^2} + 1.5}{0.15c + 0.03c^2}$$

where z is the relative viscosity of the solution of concentration c, k is the K-value x 10^{-3}, and c is the concentration in % w/v. Approximate molecular weights for different povidone grades are shown below:

K-value	Approximate molecular weight
12	2500
15	8000
17	10 000
25	30 000
30	50 000
60	400 000
90	1 000 000
120	3 000 000

See also Section 8.

5. Structural Formula

6. Functional Category
Suspending agent; tablet binder.

7. Applications in Pharmaceutical Formulation or Technology
Although povidone is used in a variety of pharmaceutical formulations it is primarily used in solid dosage forms. In tableting, povidone solutions are used as binders in wet granulation processes. Povidone is also added to powder blends in the dry form and granulated *in situ* by the addition of water, alcohol or hydroalcoholic solutions. Povidone solutions may also be used as coating agents.
Povidone is additionally used as a suspending, stabilizing or viscosity-increasing agent in a number of topical and oral suspensions and solutions. The solubility of a number of poorly soluble active drugs may be increased by mixing with povidone.
Special grades of pyrogen free povidone are available and have been used in parenteral formulations, *see* Section 14.

Use	Concentration (%)
Carrier for drugs	10-25
Dispersing agent	up to 5
Eye-drops	2-10
Suspending agent	up to 5
Tablet binder, tablet diluent, or coating agent	0.5-5

8. Description
Povidone is a fine, white to creamy-white colored, odorless or almost odorless, hygroscopic powder. Povidones with K-values equal to or lower than 30 are manufactured by spray-drying and exist as spheres. Povidone K-90 and higher K-value povidones are manufactured by drum drying and exist as plates.

9. Pharmacopeial Specifications

Test	PhEur 1990	USP XXII (Suppl 9)
Identification	+	+
pH	—	3.0-7.0
Appearance of solution	+	—
Water	⩽ 5.0%	⩽ 5.0%
Residue on ignition	—	⩽ 0.1%
Sulfated ash	⩽ 0.1%	—
Lead	—	⩽ 10 ppm
Heavy metals	⩽ 10 ppm	—
Aldehydes	⩽ 0.2%	⩽ 0.2%
Hydrazine	—	⩽ 1 ppm
Vinylpyrrolidinone	⩽ 0.2%	⩽ 0.2%
K-value		
⩽ 15	85.0-115.0%	85.0-115.0%
> 15	90.0-108.0%	90.0-108.0%
Nitrogen content	11.5-12.8%	11.5-12.8%

10. Typical Properties
Acidity/alkalinity:
pH = 3.0-7.0 (5% w/v aqueous solution)
Compressibility: *see* HPE Data.
Density: 1.17-1.18 g/cm^3

SEM: 1

Excipient: Povidone K-15 (*Plasdone* K-15)
Manufacturer: ISP
Lot No.: 82A-1
Magnification: 60x
Voltage: 5 kV

SEM: 3

Excipient: Povidone K-26/28 (*Plasdone* K-26/28)
Manufacturer: ISP
Lot No.: 82A-2
Magnification: 60x
Voltage: 5 kV

SEM: 2

Excipient: Povidone K-15 (*Plasdone* K-15)
Manufacturer: ISP
Lot No.: 82A-1
Magnification: 600x
Voltage: 5 kV

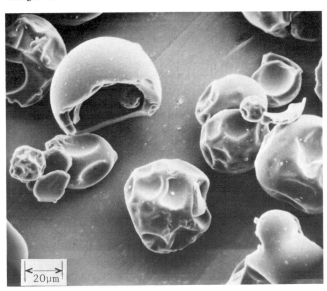

SEM: 4

Excipient: Povidone K-26/28 (*Plasdone* K-26/28)
Manufacturer: ISP
Lot No.: 82A-2
Magnification: 600x
Voltage: 10 kV

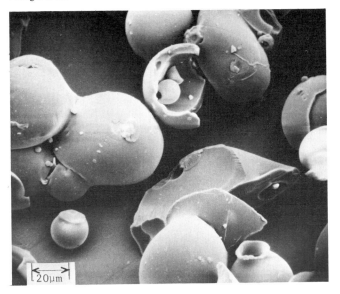

SEM: 5

Excipient: Povidone K-30 (*Plasdone* K-30)
Manufacturer: ISP
Lot No.: 82A-4
Magnification: 60x
Voltage: 10 kV

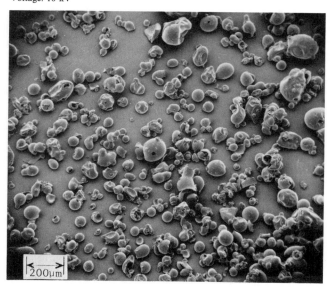

SEM: 7

Excipient: Povidone K-30 (*Kollidon* K-30)
Manufacturer: BASF Corporation
Magnification: 60x
Voltage: 2 kV

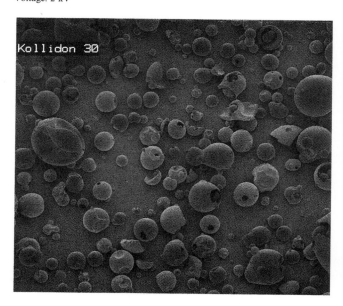

SEM: 6

Excipient: Povidone K-30 (*Plasdone* K-30)
Manufacturer: ISP
Lot No.: 82A-4
Magnification: 600x
Voltage: 10 kV

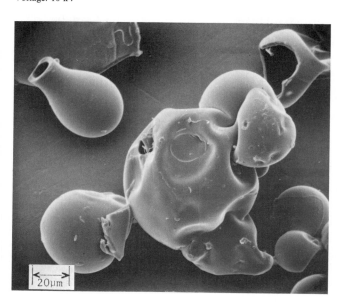

SEM: 8

Excipient: Povidone K-30 (*Kollidon* K-30)
Manufacturer: BASF Corporation
Magnification: 600x
Voltage: 5 kV

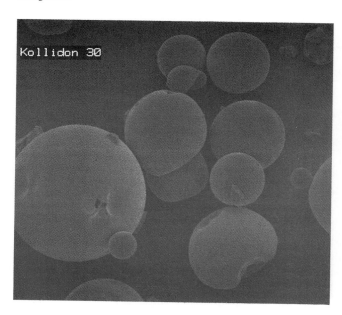

SEM: 9

Excipient: Povidone K-29/32 (*Plasdone* K-29/32)
Manufacturer: ISP
Lot No.: 82A-3
Magnification: 60x
Voltage: 5 kV

SEM: 11

Excipient: Povidone K-90F (*Kollidon* K-90F)
Manufacturer: BASF Corporation
Magnification: 60x
Voltage: 5 kV

SEM: 10

Excipient: Povidone K-29/32 (*Plasdone* K-29/32)
Manufacturer: ISP
Lot No.: 82A-3
Magnification: 600x
Voltage: 10 kV

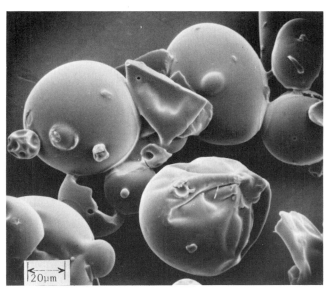

SEM: 12

Excipient: Povidone K-90F (*Kollidon* K-90F)
Manufacturer: BASF Corporation
Magnification: 600x
Voltage: 5 kV

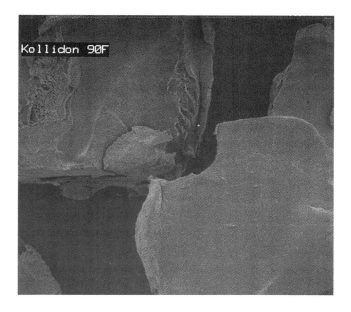

Density (bulk):
0.44 g/cm³ for *Kollidon 25*;
0.11-0.25 g/cm³ for *Kollidon 90*;
0.31 g/cm³ for *Plasdone K-30*.
See also HPE Data.
Density (tapped):
0.53 g/cm³ for *Kollidon 25*;
0.40 g/cm³ for *Plasdone K-30*.
See also HPE Data.
Flowability: see HPE Data.
Hygroscopicity: povidone is very hygroscopic, significant amounts of moisture being absorbed at low relative humidities. *See* HPE data.
Melting point: softens at 150°C
Particle size distribution: 90% > 50μm, 50% > 100 μm, 5% > 200 μm in size for *Kollidon 25/30*; 90% > 200 μm, 95% > 250 μm in size for *Kollidon 90*.[2]
Solubility: freely soluble in acids, chloroform, ethanol, ketones, methanol and water; practically insoluble in ether, hydrocarbons and mineral oil. In water the concentration of a solution is limited only by the viscosity of the resulting solution which is a function of the K-value. *See also* HPE Data.
Viscosity (dynamic): the viscosity of aqueous povidone solutions depends on both the concentration and molecular weight of the polymer employed, *see* Fig. 1. *See also* Tables I and II.[2]

Table I: Dynamic viscosity of 10% w/v aqueous povidone (*Kollidon*) solutions at 20°C.[2]

Grade	Dynamic viscosity (mPa s)
K-11/14	1.3-2.3
K-16/18	1.5-3.5
K-24/27	3.5-5.5
K-28/32	5.5-8.5
K-85/95	300-700

Table II: Dynamic viscosity of 5% w/v povidone (*Kollidon*) solutions in ethanol and propan-2-ol at 25°C.[2]

Grade	Dynamic viscosity (mPa s)	
	Ethanol	Propan-2-ol
K-12PF	1.4	2.7
K-17PF	1.9	3.1
K-25	2.7	4.7
K-30	3.4	5.8
K-90	53.0	90.0

HPE Laboratory Project Data			
	Method	Lab #	Results
Average flow rate			
Povidone K-15	FLO-1	14	20 g/s
Povidone K-29/32	FLO-1	14	16 g/s
Povidone K-30	FLO-1	14	Poor flow
Bulk/tap density			
Povidone K-15	BTD-1	1	B: 0.467 g/cm³
			T: 0.568 g/cm³
Povidone K-15	BTD-7	14	B: 0.490 g/cm³
			T: 0.570 g/cm³
Povidone K-29/32	BTD-1	1	B: 0.368 g/cm³
			T: 0.472 g/cm³
Povidone K-29/32	BTD-7	14	B: 0.400 g/cm³
			T: 0.479 g/cm³

Continued

HPE Laboratory Project Data			
	Method	Lab #	Results
Povidone K-30	BTD-1	1	B: 0.316 g.cm³
			T: 0.410 g/cm³
Povidone K-30	BTD-7	14	B: 0.350 g/cm³
			T: 0.420 g/cm³
Compressibility			
Povidone K-15	COM-4,5,6	29	See Fig. 2 [a]
Povidone K-29/32	COM-4,5,6	20	See Fig. 3 [b]
Povidone K-29/32	COM-7	12	See Fig. 4 [c]
Povidone K-30	COM-4,5,6	29	See Fig. 5 [d]
Moisture content			
Povidone K-15	MC-3	1	5.31%
Povidone K-29/32	MC-3	1	4.43%
Povidone K-26/28	MC-15	15	4.50%
Povidone K-30	MC-3	1	3.36%
Povidone USP	EMC-1	15	See Fig. 6
Povidone K-15	SDI-2	26	See Fig. 7 [a]
Povidone K-29/32	SDI-2	26	See Fig. 8 [c]
Povidone K-30	SDI-2	26	See Fig. 9 [d]
Solubility for povidone K-15			
Ethanol (95%)	SOL-2	1	1 g/mL
n-Hexane	SOL-1	1	0.012 mg/mL
Water	SOL-2	1	1 g/mL
Solubility for povidone K-29/32			
Ethanol (95%)	SOL-2	1	1 g/mL
n-Hexane	SOL-1	1	0.016 mg/mL
Water	SOL-2	1	1 g/mL
Solubility for povidone K-30			
Ethanol (95%)	SOL-2	1	1 g/mL
n-Hexane	SOL-1	1	0.010 mg/mL
Water	SOL-2	1	1 g/mL

Supplier:
a. ISP (*Plasdone K-15*, Lot No.: G-453);
b. ISP (*Plasdone K-29/32*, Lot No.: G-90920B-79);
c. ISP (*Plasdone K-29/32*, Lot No.: G-90920B-76);
d. ISP (*Plasdone K-30*, Lot No.: G-80905A-105).
All other samples ISP (*Plasdone*, unspecified lot number).

11. Stability and Storage Conditions

Povidone darkens to some extent on heating at 150°C, with a reduction in aqueous solubility. It is stable to a short cycle of heat exposure around 110-130°C; steam sterilization of an aqueous solution does not alter its properties. Aqueous solutions are susceptible to mold growth and consequently require the addition of suitable preservatives.
Povidone may be stored under ordinary conditions without undergoing decomposition or degradation. However, since the powder is hygroscopic, it should be stored in an airtight container in a cool, dry, place.

12. Incompatibilities

Povidone is compatible in solution with a wide range of inorganic salts, natural and synthetic resins and other chemicals. It forms molecular adducts in solution with sulfathiazole, sodium salicylate, salicylic acid, phenobarbital, tannin and other compounds, *see* Section 19. The efficacy of some preservatives, e.g. thimerosal, may be adversely affected by the formation of complexes with povidone.

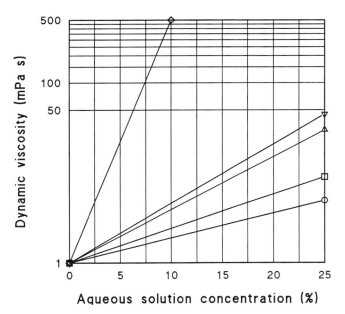

Fig. 1: Dynamic viscosity of various grades of povidone (*Kollidon*) in water at 25°C.[2]
○ Kollidon K-12PF
□ Kollidon K-17PF
△ Kollidon K-25
▽ Kollidon K-30
◇ Kollidon K-90

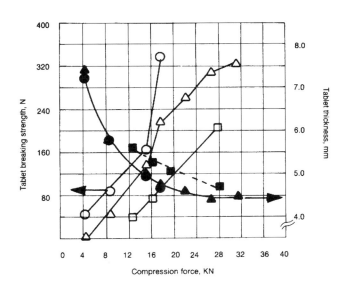

Fig. 3: Compression characteristics of povidone K-29/32 (*Plasdone K-29/32*).
○ ● Unlubricated, Carver laboratory press (COM-5)
△ ▲ Lubricated, Carver laboratory press (COM-6)
□ ■ Lubricated, instrumented Stokes model F-single punch press (COM-4)

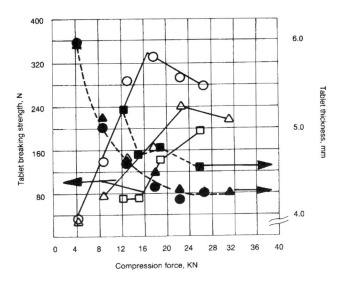

Fig. 2: Compression characteristics of povidone K-15 (*Plasdone K-15*).
○ ● Unlubricated, Carver laboratory press (COM-5)
△ ▲ Lubricated, Carver laboratory press (COM-6)
□ ■ Lubricated, instrumented Stokes model F-single punch press (COM-4)

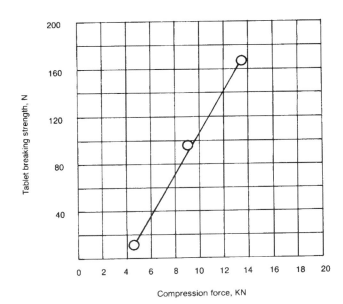

Fig. 4: Compression characteristics of povidone K-29/32 (*Plasdone K-29/32*).
Tablet weight: 500 mg

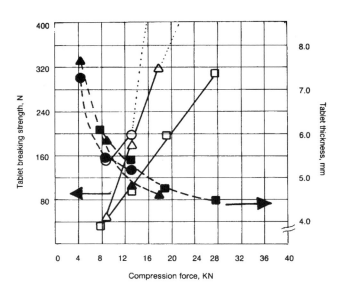

Fig. 5: Compression characteristics of povidone K-30 (*Plasdone K-30*).

○● Unlubricated, Carver laboratory press (COM-5)
△▲ Lubricated, Carver laboratory press (COM-6)
□■ Lubricated, instrumented Stokes model F-single punch press (COM-4)

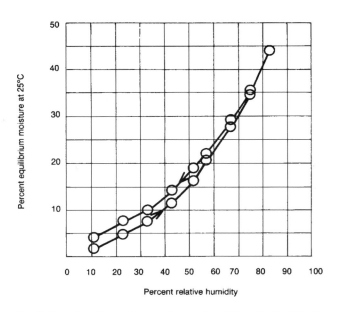

Fig. 7: Sorption-desorption isotherm of povidone K-15 (*Plasdone K-15*).

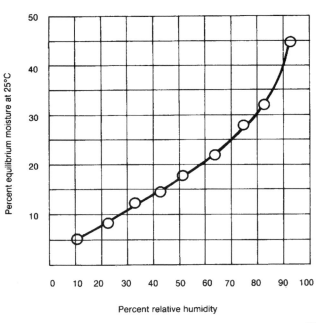

Fig. 6: Equilibrium moisture content of povidone (*Plasdone*).[3]

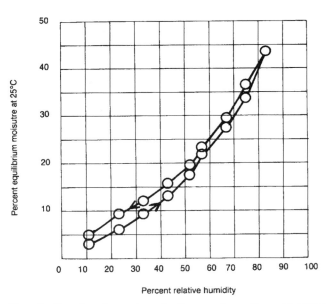

Fig. 8: Sorption-desorption isotherm of povidone K-29/32 (*Plasdone K-29/32*).

13. Method of Manufacture

Povidone is manufactured by the Reppe process. Acetylene and formaldehyde are reacted in the presence of a highly active copper acetylide catalyst to form butynediol which is hydrogenated to butanediol and then cyclodehydrogenated to form butyrolactone. Pyrrolidone is produced by reacting butyrolactone with ammonia. This is followed by a vinylation reaction in which pyrrolidone and acetylene are reacted under pressure. The monomer, vinylpyrrolidone, is then polymerized in the presence of a combination of catalysts to produce povidone.

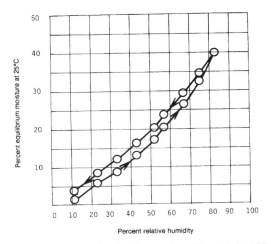

Fig. 9: Sorption-desorption isotherm of povidone K-30 (*Plasdone K-30*).

14. Safety

Povidone has been used in pharmaceutical formulations for many years, being first used in the 1940s as a plasma expander, although it has now been superseded for this purpose by dextran.[4]

Povidone is widely used as an excipient, particularly in oral tablets and solutions. When consumed orally, povidone may be regarded as essentially nontoxic since it is not absorbed from the gastrointestinal tract or mucous membranes.[4] Povidone additionally has no irritant effect on the skin and causes no sensitization.

Reports of adverse reactions to povidone primarily concern the formation of subcutaneous granulomas at the injection site of intramuscular injections formulated with povidone.[5] Evidence also exists that povidone may accumulate in the organs of the body following intramuscular injection.[6]

A temporary acceptable daily intake for povidone has been set by the WHO at up to 25 mg/kg body-weight.[7]

LD_{50} (mouse, IP): 12 g/kg[8]
LD_{50} (mouse, IV): > 11 g/kg
LD_{50} (rat, oral): 8.25 g/kg

15. Handling Precautions

Observe normal precautions appropriate to the circumstances and quantity of material handled. Eye protection, gloves and a dust mask are recommended.

16. Regulatory Status

Accepted in Europe as a food additive in certain applications. Included in the FDA Inactive Ingredients Guide (IM and IV injections, ophthalmic preparations, oral capsules, suspensions and tablets, topical and vaginal preparations). Included in nonparenteral medicines licensed in the UK.

17. Pharmacopeias

Br, Cz, Eur, Fr, Ger, Hung, Ind, It, Jpn, Mex, Neth, Rom, Swiss and US.

18. Related Substances

Crospovidone.

19. Comments

The molecular adduct formation properties of povidone may be used advantageously in solutions, slow release solid dosage forms and parenteral formulations. Perhaps the best known example of povidone complex formation is povidone-iodine which is used as a topical disinfectant.

For accurate standardization of solutions the water content of the solid povidone must be determined before use and taken into account for any calculations.

20. Specific References

1. Fikentscher H, Herrle K. Polyvinylpyrrolidone. Modern Plastics 1945; 23(3): 157-161,212,214,216,218.
2. BASF Corporation. Technical literature: *Kollidon* grades, polyvinylpyrrolidone for the pharmaceutical industry, 1990.
3. Callahan JC, Cleary GW, Elefant M, Kaplan G, Kensler T, Nash RA. Equilibrium moisture content of pharmaceutical excipients. Drug Dev Ind Pharm 1982; 8: 355-369.
4. Wessel W, Schoog M, Winkler E. Polyvinylpyrrolidone (PVP), its diagnostic, therapeutic and technical application and consequences thereof. Arzneimittelforschung 1971; 21: 1468-1482.
5. Hizawa K, Otsuka H, Inaba H, Izumi K, Nakanishi S. Subcutaneous pseudosarcomatous polyvinylpyrrolidone granuloma. Am J Surg Path 1984; 8: 393-398.
6. Christensen M, Johansen P, Hau C. Storage of polyvinylpyrrolidone (PVP) in tissues following long-term treatment with a PVP containing vasopressin preparation. Acta Med Scand 1978; 204: 295-298.
7. FAO/WHO. Evaluation of certain food additives and contaminants. Twenty-seventh report of the joint FAO/WHO expert committee on food additives. Tech Rep Ser Wld Hlth Org 1983; No. 696.
8. Sweet DV, editor. Registry of toxic effects of chemical substances. Cincinnati: US Department of Health, 1987.

21. General References

Adeyeye CM, Barabas E. Povidone. In: Brittain HG, editor. Analytical profiles of drug substances and excipients, volume 22. San Diego: Academic Press Inc, 1993: 555-685.
Horn D, Ditter W. Chromatographic study of interactions between polyvinylpyrrolidone and drugs. J Pharm Sci 1982; 71: 1021-1026.
Hsiao CH, Rhodes HJ, Blake MI. Fluorescent probe study of sulfonamide binding to povidone. J Pharm Sci 1977; 66: 1157-1159.
ISP. Technical literature: tableting with *Plasdone*, povidone USP, 1986.
Jager KF, Bauer KH. Polymer blends from PVP as a means to optimize properties of fluidized bed granulates and tablets. Acta Pharm Technol 1984; 30(1): 85-92.
Plaizier-Vercammen JA, DeNève RE. Interaction of povidone with aromatic compounds III: thermodynamics of the binding equilibria and interaction forces in buffer solutions at varying pH values and varying dielectric constant. J Pharm Sci 1982; 71: 552-556.
Robinson BV, Sullivan FM, Borzelleca JF, Schwartz SL. PVP: a critical review of the kinetics and toxicology of polyvinylpyrrolidone (povidone). Chelsea, MI: Lewis Publishers, 1990.
Shefter E, Cheng KC. Drug-polyvinylpyrrolidone (PVP) dispersions. A differential scanning calorimetric study. Int J Pharmaceutics 1980; 6: 179-182.
Smolinske SC. Handbook of food, drug, and cosmetic excipients. Boca Raton, FL: CRC Press Inc, 1992: 303-305.

22. Authors

USA: WD Walkling.

Propane

1. Nonproprietary Names

USPNF: Propane

2. Synonyms

A-70; *Aeropres 108*; dimethylmethane; propyl hydride.

3. Chemical Name and CAS Registry Number

Propane [74-98-6]

4. Empirical Formula   Molecular Weight

C_3H_8 44.10

5. Structural Formula

$$H_3C—CH_2—CH_3$$

6. Functional Category

Aerosol propellant.

7. Applications in Pharmaceutical Formulation or Technology

Propane is used as an aerosol propellant, in combination with other hydrocarbon or chlorofluorocarbon propellants, primarily in topical pharmaceutical aerosols (particularly aqueous products).

Depending upon the application, the concentration of hydrocarbon propellant used ranges from 5-95% w/w. Foam aerosols generally use about 4-5% of a hydrocarbon propellant consisting of isobutane (84.1%) and propane (15.9%). Spray type aerosols utilize propellant concentrations of 50% and higher.

Propane is also used in cosmetics and food products as an aerosol propellant and is additionally used as a refrigerant, a fuel, and in organic synthesis.

8. Description

Propane is a liquefied gas and exists as a liquid at room temperature when contained under its own vapor pressure, or as a gas when exposed to room temperature and atmospheric pressure. It is essentially a clear, colorless, odorless liquid but may have a slight ethereal odor.

9. Pharmacopeial Specifications

Test	USPNF XVII
Identification	+
Water	$\leqslant 0.001\%$
High-boiling residues	$\leqslant 5$ ppm
Acidity of residue	+
Sulfur compounds	+
Assay	$\geqslant 98.0\%$

10. Typical Properties

Autoignition temperature: 468°C
Boiling point: -42.1°C
Critical pressure: 4.26 MPa (42.01 atm)

Critical temperature: 96.8°C
Density: 0.50 g/cm³ for liquid at 20°C
Explosive limits:
2.2% v/v lower limit;
9.5% v/v upper limit.
Flash point: -104.5°C
Freezing point: -187.7°C
Heat of combustion: 2211 kJ/mol (528.4 kcal/mol)
Kauri-butanol value: 15.2
Solubility: soluble in ethanol; practically insoluble in water.
Vapor density (absolute): 1.969 g/m³
Vapor density (relative): 1.53 (air = 1)
Vapor pressure:
758.4 kPa (110.0 psig) at 21°C;
1765.1 kPa (256 psig) at 54.5°C.

11. Stability and Storage Conditions

See Butane.

12. Incompatibilities

See Butane.

13. Method of Manufacture

Propane is obtained by fractional distillation, under pressure, of crude petroleum and natural gas. It may also be prepared by a variety of synthetic methods.

14. Safety

Propane and other hydrocarbon propellants have been associated with an increasing number of serious or fatal adverse reactions primarily due to deliberate inhalation.[1-6] However, propane is not generally regarded as being a toxic material although inhalation in large quantities is hazardous since it is an asphyxiant.

15. Handling Precautions

Propane is usually encountered as a liquefied gas and should be handled accordingly with appropriate caution. Direct contact of liquefied gas with the skin is hazardous and may result in serious cold burn injuries.[2] Protective clothing, rubber gloves and eye protection are recommended.

Propane is an asphyxiant and should be handled in a well-ventilated environment; it is recommended that environmental oxygen levels are monitored and not permitted to fall below a concentration of 18% v/v.[7]

Propane is flammable and explosive and should be handled with appropriate caution. To fight fires the flow of gas should be stopped and dry powder extinguishers used at the flashing point.

16. Regulatory Status

GRAS listed. Included in the FDA Inactive Ingredients Guide (aerosol formulations for topical application). Included in nonparenteral medicines licensed in the UK.

17. Pharmacopeias

Mex and USPNF.

18. Related Substances

Butane; Dimethyl Ether; Isobutane.

19. Comments

Although hydrocarbon aerosol propellants are relatively cheap, nontoxic and 'environmentally friendly' (since they are not damaging to the ozone layer and are not greenhouse gases) their use is limited by their flammability. Mixtures of hydrocarbons with varying amounts of dichlorodifluoromethane may however be classified as nonflammable.[8]

Various blends of hydrocarbon propellants, that have a range of physical properties suitable for different applications are commercially available, e.g. *CAP30* (Calor Gas Ltd) is a mixture of 11% propane, 29% isobutane and 60% butane.

See also Butane.

20. Specific References

1. Gunn J, Wilson J, Mackintosh AF. Butane sniffing causing ventricular fibrillation [letter]. Lancet 1989; i: 617.
2. James NK, Moss ALH. Cold injury from liquid propane. Br Med J 1989; 299: 950-951.
3. Roberts MJD, McIvor RA, Adgey AAJ. Asystole following butane gas inhalation. Br J Hosp Med 1990; 44: 294.
4. Siegel E, Wason S. Sudden death caused by inhalation of butane and propane. N Eng J Med 1990; 323: 1638.
5. Rising deaths from volatile substance abuse. Pharm J 1992; 248 : 539.
6. Russell J. Fuel of the forgotten deaths. New Scientist 1993; Feb 6: 21-23.
7. Health and Safety Executive. EH40/93: occupational exposure limits 1993. London: HMSO, 1993.
8. Dalby RN. Prediction and assessment of flammability hazards associated with metered-dose inhalers containing flammable propellants. Pharm Res 1992; 9: 636-642.

21. General References

See Butane.

22. Authors

UK: PJ Davies.
USA: JJ Sciarra.

Propyl Gallate

1. Nonproprietary Names

BP: Propyl gallate
USPNF: Propyl gallate

2. Synonyms

E310; gallic acid propyl ester; *Progallin P*;
n-propyl gallate; propyl 3,4,5-trihydroxybenzoate; *Tenox PG*.

3. Chemical Name and CAS Registry Number

3,4,5-Trihydroxybenzoic acid propyl ester
[121-79-9]

4. Empirical Formula   Molecular Weight

$C_{10}H_{12}O_5$ 212.20

5. Structural Formula

6. Functional Category

Antioxidant.

7. Applications in Pharmaceutical Formulation or Technology

Propyl gallate has become widely used as an antioxidant in cosmetics, perfumes, foods and pharmaceuticals since its use in preventing autoxidation of oils was first described in 1943.[1,2] It is primarily used, in concentrations up to 0.1% w/v, to prevent the rancidity of oils and fats; it may also be used at concentrations of 0.002% w/v to prevent peroxide formation in ether and at 0.01% w/v to prevent the oxidation of paraldehyde. Synergistic effects with other antioxidants such as butylated hydroxyanisole and butylated hydroxytoluene have been reported. Propyl gallate is also said to possess some antimicrobial properties, *see* Section 10.

Other alkyl gallates are also used as antioxidants and have approximately equivalent antioxidant properties when used in equimolar concentration; solubilities however vary, *see* Section 18.

8. Description

Propyl gallate is a white, odorless or almost odorless crystalline powder, with a bitter astringent taste which is not normally noticeable at the concentrations employed as an antioxidant.

9. Pharmacopeial Specifications

Test	BP 1993	USPNF XVII
Identification	+	+
Melting range	148-151°C	146-150°C
Loss on drying	⩽ 1.0%	⩽ 0.5%
Residue on ignition	—	⩽ 0.1%
Sulfated ash	⩽ 0.1%	—
Chloride	⩽ 330 ppm	—
Sulfate	⩽ 0.12%	—
Heavy metals	—	⩽ 0.001%
Assay (dried basis)	—	98.0-102.0%

10. Typical Properties

Antimicrobial activity: propyl gallate has been reported to possess some antimicrobial activity against Gram-negative, Gram-positive and fungal species.[3] Its effectiveness as a preservative may be improved when used in combination with zinc salts, such as zinc sulfate, due to synergistic effects.[4] Reported minimum inhibitory concentrations (MICs) for aqueous solutions containing 4% v/v ethanol as cosolvent are shown below:[3]

Microorganism	MIC (μg/mL)
Candida albicans	1500
Escherichia coli	330
Staphylococcus aureus	600

Melting point: 150°C
Solubility:

Solvent	Solubility at 20°C Unless otherwise stated
Almond oil	1 in 44
Castor oil	1 in 4.5
Cottonseed oil	1 in 81 at 30°C
Ethanol (95%)	1 in 3
	1 in 0.98 at 25°C
Ether	1 in 3
	1 in 1.2 at 25°C
Lanolin	1 in 16.7 at 25°C
Lard	1 in 88 at 45°C
Mineral oil	1 in 200
Peanut oil	1 in 2000
Propylene glycol	1 in 2.5 at 25°C
Soybean oil	1 in 100 at 25°C
Water	1 in 1000
	1 in 286 at 25°C

11. Stability and Storage Conditions

Propyl gallate is unstable at high temperatures and is rapidly destroyed in oils that are used for frying purposes.

The bulk material should be stored in a well-closed, nonmetallic container, protected from light, in a cool, dry, place.

12. Incompatibilities

The alkyl gallates, are incompatible with metals, e.g. sodium, potassium and iron, forming intensely colored complexes. Complex formation may be prevented, under some circumstances, by the addition of a sequestering agent, typically citric acid. Propyl gallate may also react with oxidizing materials.

13. Method of Manufacture

Propyl gallate is prepared by the esterification of 3,4,5-trihydroxybenzoic acid (gallic acid) with *n*-propanol. Other alkyl gallates are similarly prepared using an appropriate alcohol of the desired alkyl chain length.

14. Safety

It has been reported, following animal studies, that propyl gallate has a strong contact sensitization potential.[5] However, despite this, there have been few reports of adverse reactions.[6] Those that have been described include: contact dermatitis; allergic contact dermatitis;[7] and methemoglobinemia in neonates.[8]

The WHO has set an estimated acceptable daily intake for propyl gallate at up to 2.5 mg/kg body-weight.[9]

LD_{50} (cat, oral): 0.4 g/kg[10]
LD_{50} (mouse, oral): 1.7 g/kg
LD_{50} (rat, oral): 3.8 g/kg
LD_{50} (rat, IP): 0.38 g/kg

15. Handling Precautions

Observe normal precautions appropriate to the circumstances and quantity of material handled. Eye protection and gloves are recommended. When heated to decomposition propyl gallate may emit toxic fumes and smoke.

16. Regulatory Status

GRAS listed. Accepted for use as a food additive in Europe. Included in the FDA Inactive Ingredients Guide (IM injections and topical preparations). Included in nonparenteral medicines licensed in the UK.

17. Pharmacopeias

Aust, Br, Cz, Egypt, Fr, Ind, Nord and USPNF.

18. Related Substances

Dodecyl gallate; ethyl gallate; octyl gallate.

Dodecyl gallate: $C_{19}H_{30}O_5$
Molecular weight: 338.44
CAS number: [1166-52-5]
Synonyms: dodecyl 3,4,5-trihydroxybenzoate; E312; lauryl gallate.
Pharmacopeias: Aust, Br and Fr.
Appearance: white, odorless or almost odorless crystalline powder.
Melting point: 96-97.5°C
Solubility:

Solvent	Solubility at 20°C
Acetone	1 in 2
Chloroform	1 in 60
Ethanol (95%)	1 in 3.5
Ether	1 in 4
Methanol	1 in 1.5
Peanut oil	1 in 30
Propylene glycol	1 in 60
Water	practically insoluble

Ethyl gallate: $C_9H_{10}O_5$
Molecular weight: 198.17
CAS number: [831-61-8]
Synonyms: ethyl 3,4,5-trihydroxybenzoate.
Pharmacopeias: Br.
Appearance: white, odorless or almost odorless, crystalline powder.
Melting point: 151-154°C
Solubility:

Solvent	Solubility at 20°C
Ethanol (95%)	1 in 3
Ether	1 in 3
Peanut oil	practically insoluble
Water	slightly soluble

Octyl gallate: $C_{15}H_{22}O_5$
Molecular weight: 282.34
CAS number: [1034-01-1]
Synonyms: E311; octyl 3,4,5-trihydroxybenzoate.
Pharmacopeias: Br and Fr.
Appearance: white, odorless or almost odorless crystalline powder.
Melting point: 100-102°C
Solubility:

Solvent	Solubility at 20°C
Acetone	1 in 1
Chloroform	1 in 30
Ethanol (95%)	1 in 2.5
Ether	1 in 3
Methanol	1 in 0.7
Peanut oil	1 in 33
Propylene glycol	1 in 7
Water	practically insoluble

19. Comments

Propyl gallate has been reported to impart an 'off' flavor to corn and cottonseed oils when used as an antioxidant.[11]

An acceptable daily intake for dodecyl gallate and octyl gallate was not set by the WHO due to insufficient data. The use of octyl gallate in beer and other widely consumed beverages was however not recommended by the WHO due to the possibility of adverse reactions in the buccal mucosa of individuals previously sensitized by cutaneous contact with this compound.[9]

20. Specific References

1. Boehm E, Williams R. The action of propyl gallate on the autoxidation of oils. Pharm J 1943; 151: 53.
2. Boehm E, Williams R. A study of the inhibiting actions of propyl gallate (normal propyl trihydroxy benzoate) and certain other trihydric phenols on the autoxidation of animal and vegetable oils. Chemist Drugg 1943; 140: 146-147.
3. Zeelie JJ, McCarthy TJ. The potential antimicrobial properties of antioxidants in pharmaceutical systems. S Afr Pharm J 1982; 49: 552-554.
4. McCarthy TJ, Zeelie JJ, Krause DJ. The antimicrobial action of zinc ion/antioxidant combinations. J Clin Pharm Ther 1992; 17: 51-54.

5. Kahn G, Phanuphak P, Claman HN. Propyl gallate contact sensitization and orally induced tolerance. Arch Dermatol 1979, 104: 506-509.
6. Golightly LK, Smolinske SS, Bennett ML, Sutherland EW, Rumack BH. Pharmaceutical excipients: adverse effects associated with 'inactive' ingredients in drug products (part II). Med Toxicol 1988; 3: 209-240.
7. Bojs G, Nicklasson B, Svensson A. Allergic contact dermatitis to propyl gallate. Contact Dermatitis 1987; 17: 294-298.
8. Nitzan M, Volovitz B, Topper E. Infantile methemoglobinemia caused by food additives. Clin Toxicol 1979; 15(3): 273-280.
9. FAO/WHO. Evaluation of certain food additives and contaminants: thirteenth report of the joint FAO/WHO expert committee on food additives. Tech Rep Ser Wld Hlth Org 1987; No. 751.
10. Sweet DV, editor. Registry of toxic effects of chemical substances. Cincinnati: US Department of Health, 1987.
11. McConnell JEW, Esselen WB. Effect of storage conditions and antioxidants on the keeping quality of packaged oils. J Am Oil Chem Soc 1947; 24: 6-14.

21. General References

Johnson DM, Gu LC. Autoxidation and antioxidants. In: Swarbrick J, Boylan JC, editors. Encyclopedia of pharmaceutical technology, volume 1. New York: Marcel Dekker Inc, 1988: 415-449.

22. Authors

UK: PJ Weller.

Propylene Carbonate

1. Nonproprietary Names
USPNF: Propylene carbonate

2. Synonyms
Carbonic acid, cyclic propylene ester; cyclic methylethylene carbonate; cyclic propylene carbonate; 4-methyl-2-oxo-1,3-dioxolane; 1,2-propanediol cyclic carbonate; 1,2-propylene carbonate.

3. Chemical Name and CAS Registry Number
($\pm$)-4-Methyl-1,3-dioxolan-2-one [108-32-7]

4. Empirical Formula
$C_4H_6O_3$

Molecular Weight
102.09

5. Structural Formula

6. Functional Category
Gelling agent; solvent.

7. Applications in Pharmaceutical Formulation or Technology
Propylene carbonate is used mainly as a solvent in oral and topical pharmaceutical formulations.

In topical applications, propylene carbonate has been used in combination with propylene glycol as a solvent for corticosteroids. The corticosteroid is dissolved in the solvent mixture to yield microdroplets which can then be dispersed in petrolatum.[1]

Propylene carbonate has also been used in hard gelatin capsules as a nonvolatile, stabilizing, liquid carrier. For formulations with a low dosage of active drug, a uniform drug content may be obtained by dissolving the drug in propylene carbonate then spraying this solution on to a solid carrier such as compressible sugar; the sugar may then be filled into hard gelatin capsules.[2]

Propylene carbonate may additionally be used as a solvent, at room and elevated temperatures, for many cellulose based polymers and plasticizers.

Propylene carbonate is also used in cosmetics.

8. Description
Propylene carbonate is a clear, colorless, mobile liquid, with a faint odor.

9. Pharmacopeial Specifications

Test	USPNF XVII (Suppl 6)
Identification	+
Specific gravity	1.203-1.210
pH (10% v/v aqueous solution)	6.0-7.5
Residue on ignition	$\leqslant 0.01\%$
Organic volatile impurities	+
Assay	99.0-100.5%

10. Typical Properties
Boiling point: 242°C
Flash point: 132°C
Freezing point: -49.2°C
Heat of combustion: 14.21 kJ/mol (3.40 kcal/mol)
Heat of vaporization:
55.2 kJ/mol (13.2 kcal/mol) at 150°C
Refractive index: $n_D^{20} = 1.420\text{-}1.422$
Solubility: practically insoluble in hexane; freely soluble in water. Miscible with acetone, benzene, chloroform, ethanol, ethanol (95%) and ether.
Specific heat: 2.57 J/g/°C (0.62 cal/g/°C) at 20°C
Vapor pressure: 4 Pa (0.03 mmHg) at 20°C.
Viscosity (dynamic): 2.5 mPa s (2.5 cP) at 25°C.

11. Stability and Storage Conditions
Propylene carbonate and its aqueous solutions are stable, but may degrade in the presence of acids or bases, or upon heating, *see also* Section 12.

Store in a well-closed container in a cool, dry, place.

12. Incompatibilities
Propylene carbonate hydrolyzes rapidly in the presence of strong acids and bases forming mainly propylene oxide and carbon dioxide. Propylene carbonate can also react with primary and secondary amines to yield carbamates.

13. Method of Manufacture
Propylene carbonate may be prepared by the reaction of sodium bicarbonate with propylene chlorohydrin.[3]

14. Safety
Propylene carbonate is used as a solvent in oral and topical pharmaceutical formulations and is generally regarded as an essentially nontoxic and nonirritant material.

In animal studies, propylene carbonate was found to cause tissue necrosis after parenteral administration.[4]

LD_{50} (mouse, oral): 20.7 g/kg[5]
LD_{50} (mouse, SC): 15.8 g/kg
LD_{50} (rabbit, skin): > 20 g/kg
LD_{50} (rat, oral): 29 g/kg
LD_{50} (rat, SC): 11.1 g/kg

15. Handling Precautions
Observe normal precautions appropriate to the circumstances and quantity of material handled. Propylene carbonate may be irritant to the eyes and mucous membranes. Eye protection and gloves are recommended.

16. Regulatory Status
Included in the FDA Inactive Ingredients Guide (topical ointments).

17. Pharmacopeias

USPNF.

18. Related Substances

(*S*)-Propylene carbonate.

(*S*)-Propylene carbonate: $C_4H_6O_3$
Molecular weight: 102.09
CAS number: [51260-39-0]
Specific rotation:
$[\alpha]_D^{25}$ = -1.7° (0.92 % v/v solution in ethanol)
Comments: the (*S*)-enantiomer of (±)-propylene carbonate.[6]

19. Comments

—

20. Specific References

1. Burdick KH, Haleblian JK, Poulsen BJ, Cobner SE. Corticosteroid ointments: comparison by two human bioassays. Curr Ther Res 1973; 15: 233-242.
2. Dahl TC, Burke G. Feasibility of manufacturing a solid dosage form using a liquid nonvolatile drug carrier: a physico-chemical characterization. Drug Dev Ind Pharm 1990; 16: 1881-1891.
3. Najer H, Chabrier P, Giudicelli R. Study of organic cyclic carbonates and their derivatives [in French]. Bull Soc Chim Fr 1954: 1142-1148.
4. Hem SL, Bright DR, Banker GS, Pogue JP. Tissue irritation evaluation of potential parenteral vehicles. Drug Dev Comm 1974-75; 1: 471-477.
5. Sweet DV, editor. Registry of toxic effects of chemical substances. Cincinnati: US Department of Health, 1987.
6. Usieli V, Pilersdorf A, Shor S, Katzhendler J, Sarel S. Chiroptical properties of cyclic esters and ketals derived from (*S*)-1,2-propylene glycol and (*S*,*S*)- and (*R*,*R*)-2,3-butylene glycol. J Org Chem 1974; 39: 2073-2079.

21. General References

Cheng H, Gadde RR. Determination of propylene carbonate in pharmaceutical formulations using liquid chromatography. J Pharm Sci 1985; 74: 695-696.

22. Authors

UK: PJ Weller.

Propylene Glycol

1. Nonproprietary Names

BP: Propylene glycol
PhEur: Propylenglycolum
USP: Propylene glycol

2. Synonyms

1,2-Dihydroxypropane; 2-hydroxypropanol; methyl ethylene glycol; methyl glycol; propane-1,2-diol.

3. Chemical Name and CAS Registry Number

1,2-Propanediol [57-55-6]
(R)-(-)-1,2-Propanediol [4254-14-2]
(S)-(+)-1,2-Propanediol [4254-15-3]
(RS)-($\pm$)-1,2-Propanediol [4254-16-4]

4. Empirical Formula   Molecular Weight

$C_3H_8O_2$ 76.09

5. Structural Formula

$CH_3CHOHCH_2OH$

6. Functional Category

Antimicrobial preservative; disinfectant; humectant; plasticizer; solvent; stabilizer for vitamins; water-miscible cosolvent.

7. Applications in Pharmaceutical Formulation or Technology

Propylene glycol has become widely used as a solvent, extractant and preservative in a variety of parenteral and nonparenteral pharmaceutical formulations. It is a better general solvent than glycerin and dissolves a wide variety of materials, such as corticosteroids, phenols, sulfa drugs, barbiturates, vitamins (A and D), most alkaloids and many local anesthetics.

As an antiseptic it is similar to ethanol, and against molds it is similar to glycerin and only slightly less effective than ethanol. Propylene glycol is also used in cosmetics and in the food industry as a carrier for emulsifiers and as a vehicle for flavors in preference to ethanol, since its lack of volatility provides a more uniform flavor.

Use	Dosage form	Concentration (%)
Humectant	Topicals	≈ 15
Preservative	Solutions, semisolids	15-30
Solvent or cosolvent	Aerosol solutions	10-30
	Oral solutions	10-25
	Parenterals	10-60
	Topicals	5-80

8. Description

Propylene glycol is a clear, colorless, viscous, practically odorless liquid with a sweet, slightly acrid taste resembling glycerin.

9. Pharmacopeial Specifications

Test	PhEur 1985	USP XXII (Suppl 8)
Identification	+	+
Appearance	+	+
Specific gravity	1.035-1.040	1.035-1.037
Acidity	+	+
Water	$\leqslant 0.2\%$	$\leqslant 0.2\%$
Residue on ignition	—	$\leqslant 0.007\%$
Sulfated ash	$\leqslant 0.01\%$	—
Chloride	—	$\leqslant 0.007\%$
Sulfate	—	$\leqslant 0.006\%$
Arsenic	—	$\leqslant 3$ ppm
Heavy metals	$\leqslant 5$ ppm	$\leqslant 5$ ppm
Organic volatile impurities	—	+
Refractive index	1.431-1.433	—
Oxidizing substances	+	—
Reducing substances	+	—
Assay	—	$\geqslant 99.5\%$

10. Typical Properties

Autoignition temperature: 371°C
Boiling point: 188°C
Density: 1.038 g/cm^3 at 20°C
Flammability: upper limit, 12.6% v/v in air; lower limit, 2.6% v/v in air.
Flash point: 99°C (open cup)
Heat of combustion: 1803.3 kJ/mol (431.0 kcal/mol)
Heat of vaporization: 705.4 J/g (168.6 cal/g) at b.p.
Melting point: -59°C
Osmolarity: a 2.0% v/v aqueous solution is iso-osmotic with serum.
Refractive index: $n_D^{20} = 1.4324$
Specific rotation $[\alpha]_D^{20}$:
-15.0° (neat) for (R)-form;
+15.8° (neat) for (S)-form.
Solubility: miscible with acetone, chloroform, ethanol (95%), glycerin and water; soluble 1 in 6 parts of ether; not miscible with light mineral oil or fixed oils, but will dissolve some essential oils.
Specific heat: 2.47 J/g (0.590 cal/g) at 20°C
Surface tension: 40.1 mN/m (40.1 dynes/cm) at 25°C
Vapor density (relative): 2.62 (air = 1)
Vapor pressure: 9.33 Pa (0.07 mmHg) at 20°C
Viscosity (dynamic): 58.1 mPa s (0.581 P) at 20°C

11. Stability and Storage Conditions

At cool temperatures, propylene glycol is stable in a well-closed container, but at high temperatures, in the open, it tends to oxidize, giving rise to products such as propionaldehyde, lactic acid, pyruvic acid and acetic acid. Propylene glycol is chemically stable when mixed with ethanol (95%), glycerin, or water; aqueous solutions may be sterilized by autoclaving.

Propylene glycol is hygroscopic and should be stored in an airtight container, protected from light, in a cool, dry, place.

12. Incompatibilities

Propylene glycol is incompatible with oxidizing reagents such as potassium permanganate.

13. Method of Manufacture

Propylene is converted to chlorohydrin by chlorine water and hydrolyzed to 1,2-propylene oxide. With further hydrolysis, 1,2-propylene oxide is converted to propylene glycol.

14. Safety

Propylene glycol is used in a wide variety of pharmaceutical formulations and is generally regarded as a nontoxic material. Probably as a consequence of its metabolism and excretion, propylene glycol is less toxic than other glycols.

In topical preparations, propylene glycol is regarded as minimally irritant although it is more irritant than glycerin. Some local irritation is produced upon application to mucous membranes or when used under occlusive conditions.[1] Parenteral administration may cause pain or irritation when used in high concentration.

Propylene glycol is estimated to be one third as intoxicating as ethanol, with administration of large volumes being associated with adverse effects most commonly on the central nervous system, especially in neonates and children.[2-4] Other adverse reactions reported, though generally isolated, include: ototoxicity;[5] cardiovascular effects; seizures; hyperosmolarity[6] and lactic acidosis, both of which occur most frequently in patients with renal impairment.

Based on metabolic and toxicological data, the WHO has set an acceptable daily intake of propylene glycol at up to 25 mg/kg body-weight.[7]

In animal studies, there has been no evidence that propylene glycol is teratogenic or mutagenic. Rats can tolerate a repeated oral daily dose of up to 30 mL/kg in the diet over 6 months, whilst the dog is unaffected by a repeated oral daily dose of 2 g/kg in the diet for 2 years.[8]

LD_{50} (dog, IV): 25.9 g/kg[8-10]
LD_{50} (dog, oral): 10-20 g/kg
LD_{50} (guinea pig, oral): 18.4-19.6 g/kg
LD_{50} (guinea pig, SC): 13-15.5 g/kg
LD_{50} (mouse, IP): 6.8-13.6 g/kg
LD_{50} (mouse, IV): 7.6-8.3 g/kg
LD_{50} (mouse, oral): 23.9 g/kg
LD_{50} (mouse, SC): 15.5-19.2 g/kg
LD_{50} (rabbit, IM): 6 g/kg
LD_{50} (rabbit, IV): 5-6.5 g/kg
LD_{50} (rabbit, oral): 15.7-19.2 g/kg
LD_{50} (rat, IM): 13-20.7 g/kg
LD_{50} (rat, IP): 13-16.8 g/kg
LD_{50} (rat, IV): 6.2-12.7 g/kg
LD_{50} (rat, oral): 21-33.7 g/kg
LD_{50} (rat, SC): 21.7-29 g/kg

15. Handling Precautions

Observe normal precautions appropriate to the circumstances and quantity of material handled. Propylene glycol should be handled in a well-ventilated environment; eye protection is recommended. In the UK, the long-term (8-hour TWA) occupational exposure limit for propylene glycol vapor and particulates is 470 mg/m^3 (150 ppm) and 10 mg/m^3 for particulates.[11]

16. Regulatory Status

GRAS listed. Accepted for use as a food additive in Europe (does not have a code number). Included in the FDA Inactive Ingredients Guide (dental preparations, IM and IV injections, inhalations, ophthalmic, oral, otic, percutaneous, rectal, topical and vaginal preparations). Included in nonparenteral and parenteral medicines licensed in the UK.

17. Pharmacopeias

Aust, Br, Braz, Cz, Egypt, Eur, Fr, Ger, Gr, Hung, Ind, It, Jpn, Mex, Neth, Nord, Port, Swiss, Turk, US and Yug. Also in BP Vet.

18. Related Substances

—

19. Comments

In addition to its uses as an excipient, propylene glycol is used in veterinary medicine as an oral glucogenic in ruminants.[12]

20. Specific References

1. Motoyoshi K, Nozawa S, Yoshimura M, Matsuda K. The safety of propylene glycol and other humectants. Cosmet Toilet 1984; 99(10): 83-91.
2. Arulanantham K, Genel M. Central nervous system toxicity associated with ingestion of propylene glycol. J Pediatr 1978; 93: 515-516.
3. MacDonald MG, Getson PR, Glasgow AM, Miller MK, Boeckx RL, Johnson EL. Propylene glycol: increased incidence of seizures in low birth weight infants. Pediatrics 1987; 79: 622-625.
4. Martin G, Finberg L. Propylene glycol: a potentially toxic vehicle in liquid dosage form. J Pediatr 1970; 77: 877-878.
5. Morizono T, Johnstone BM. Ototoxicity of chloramphenicol ear drops with propylene glycol as solvent. Med J Aust 1975; 2: 634-638.
6. Fligner CL, Jack R, Twiggs GA, Raisys VA. Hyperosmolality induced by propylene glycol: a complication of silver sulfadiazine therapy. JAMA 1985; 253: 1606-1609.
7. FAO/WHO. Toxicological evaluation of certain food additives with a review of general principles and of specifications. Seventeenth report of the FAO/WHO expert committee on food additives. Tech Rep Ser Wld Hlth Org 1974; No. 539.
8. Clayton GD, Clayton FE, editors. Patty's industrial hygiene and toxicology, 3rd edition. Chichester: John Wiley and Sons, 1987.
9. Rubino JT. Cosolvents and cosolvency. In: Swarbrick J, Boylan JC, editors. Encyclopedia of pharmaceutical technology; volume 3. New York: Marcel Dekker, 1990: 375-398.
10. Ruddick JA. Toxicology, metabolism and biochemistry of 1,2-propanediol. Toxicol Appl Pharmacol 1972; 21: 102-111.
11. Health and Safety Executive. EH40/93: occupational exposure limits 1993. London: HMSO, 1993.
12. Debuf Y, editor. The veterinary formulary, 2nd edition. London: The Pharmaceutical Press, 1994: 329-330.

21. General References

Wells JI, Bhatt DA, Khan KA. Improved wet massed tableting using plasticized binder. J Pharm Pharmacol 1982; 34(Suppl): 46P.
Yu CD, Kent JS. Effect of propylene glycol on subcutaneous absorption of a benzimidazole hydrochloride. J Pharm Sci 1982; 71: 476-478.

22. Authors

UK: HEC Worthington.

Propylene Glycol Alginate

1. Nonproprietary Names

USPNF: Propylene glycol alginate

2. Synonyms

Alginic acid, propylene glycol ester; E405; hydroxypropyl alginate; *Kelcoloid*; *Manucol ester*; *Pronova*; propane-1,2-diol alginate; *Protanal*.

3. Chemical Name and CAS Registry Number

Propylene glycol alginate [9005-37-2]

4. Empirical Formula   Molecular Weight

Propylene glycol alginate is a propylene glycol ester of alginic acid, a linear glycuronan polymer consisting of a mixture of β-$(1\rightarrow4)$-D-mannosyluronic acid and α-$(1\rightarrow4)$-L-gulosyluronic acid residues.

5. Structural Formula

See Section 4.

6. Functional Category

Emulsifying agent; stabilizing agent; suspending agent; viscosity-increasing agent.

7. Applications in Pharmaceutical Formulation or Technology

Propylene glycol alginate is used as a stabilizing, suspending, gelling and emulsifying agent in oral and topical pharmaceutical formulations. Typically, a concentration of 1-5% is used although this may vary depending upon the specific application and the grade of propylene glycol alginate used.
Propylene glycol alginate is also used in cosmetics and food products.

8. Description

Propylene glycol alginate occurs as a white to yellowish colored, practically odorless and tasteless, fibrous or granular powder.

9. Pharmacopeial Specifications

Test	USPNF XVII (Suppl 6)
Identification	+
Microbial limits	$\leqslant 200/g$
Loss on drying	$\leqslant 20.0\%$
Ash	$\leqslant 10.0\%$
Arsenic	$\leqslant 3$ ppm
Lead	$\leqslant 0.001\%$
Heavy metals	$\leqslant 0.004\%$
Free carboxyl groups	+
Esterified carboxyl groups	+
Assay (of alginates)	+

10. Typical Properties

Solubility: soluble in dilute organic acids and water, forming stable, viscous, colloidal solutions at pH 3. Depending upon the degree of esterification, propylene glycol alginate is also soluble in aqueous ethanol/water mixtures containing up to 60% w/w of ethanol.
Viscosity (dynamic): the viscosity of aqueous solutions vary depending upon the grade of material used. Typically, a 1% w/v aqueous solution has a viscosity of 20-400 mPa s (20-400 cP). Viscosity may vary depending upon concentration, pH, temperature or the presence of metal ions. *See also* Sodium Alginate.

11. Stability and Storage Conditions

Propylene glycol alginate is a stable material although it will gradually become less soluble if stored at elevated temperatures for extended periods of time.
Propylene glycol alginate solutions are most stable at pH 3-6. In alkaline solutions, propylene glycol alginate is rapidly saponified. Alginate solutions are susceptible to microbial spoilage and should be sterilized or preserved with an antimicrobial preservative. Sterilization processes may however adversely affect the viscosity of propylene glycol alginate solutions, *see* Sodium Alginate.
The bulk material should be stored in an airtight container in a cool, dry, place.

12. Incompatibilities

—

13. Method of Manufacture

Alginic acid, extracted from brown seaweed, is reacted with propylene oxide to form propylene glycol alginate. Various different grades may be obtained which vary in composition according to the degree of esterification and the percentage of free and neutralized carboxyl groups present in the molecule; complete esterification of alginic acid is impractical.

14. Safety

Propylene glycol alginate is used in oral and topical pharmaceutical formulations, cosmetics and food products. It is generally regarded as a nontoxic and nonirritant material although excessive oral consumption may be harmful. A study in five healthy male volunteers fed a daily intake of 175 mg/kg body-weight of propylene glycol alginate for 7 days, followed by a daily intake of 200 mg/kg body-weight of propylene glycol alginate for a further 16 days, showed no significant adverse effects.[1]
The WHO has set an estimated acceptable daily intake of alginate salts and alginic acid, used as food additives, at up to 25 mg/kg body-weight, calculated as alginic acid.[2]
Inhalation of alginate dust may be irritant and has been associated with industrially related asthma in workers involved in alginate production. However, it appears that the cases of asthma were linked to exposure to seaweed dust rather than pure alginate dust.[3]
LD$_{50}$ (hamster, oral): 7.0 g/kg[4]
LD$_{50}$ (mouse, oral): 7.8 g/kg
LD$_{50}$ (rabbit, oral): 7.6 g/kg
LD$_{50}$ (rat, oral): 7.2 g/kg

15. Handling Precautions

Observe normal precautions appropriate to the circumstances and quantity of material handled. Propylene glycol alginate may be irritant to the eyes or respiratory system if inhaled as dust, *see* Section 14. Eye protection, gloves and a dust respirator are recommended. Propylene glycol alginate should be handled in a well-ventilated environment.

16. Regulatory Status

GRAS listed. Accepted in Europe for use as a food additive. Included in the FDA Inactive Ingredients Guide (oral preparations). Included in nonparenteral medicines licensed in the UK.

17. Pharmacopeias

USPNF.

18. Related Substances

Alginic Acid; Sodium Alginate.

19. Comments

A number of different grades of propylene glycol alginate which have different solution viscosities are commercially available.

See Alginic Acid and Sodium Alginate for further information.

20. Specific References

1. Anderson DM, Brydon WG, Eastwood MA, Sedgwick DM. Dietary effects of propylene glycol alginate in humans. Food Add Contam 1991; 8(3): 225-236.
2. FAO/WHO. Toxicological evaluation of certain food additives with a review of general principles and of specifications. Seventeenth report of the joint FAO/WHO expert committee on food additives. Tech Rep Ser Wld Hlth Org 1974; No. 539.
3. Henderson AK, et al. Pulmonary hypersensitivity in the alginate industry. Scott Med J 1984; 29(2): 90-95.
4. Sweet DV, editor. Registry of toxic effects of chemical substances. Cincinnati: US Department of Health, 1987.

21. General References

McDowell RH. New reactions of propylene glycol alginate. J Soc Cosmet Chem 1970; 21: 441-457.

22. Authors

UK: PJ Weller.

Propylparaben

1. Nonproprietary Names

BP: Propyl hydroxybenzoate
PhEur: Propylis parahydroxybenzoas
USPNF: Propylparaben

2. Synonyms

Chemocide PK; E216; 4-hydroxybenzoic acid propyl ester; *Nipasol M*; *Propyl chemosept*; propyl *p*-hydroxybenzoate; propyl parahydroxybenzoate; *Propyl parasept*; *Solbrol P*; *Tegosept P*.

3. Chemical Name and CAS Registry Number

Propyl 4-hydroxybenzoate [94-13-3]

4. Empirical Formula   Molecular Weight

$C_{10}H_{12}O_3$ 180.20

5. Structural Formula

6. Functional Category

Antimicrobial preservative.

7. Applications in Pharmaceutical Formulation or Technology

Propylparaben is widely used as an antimicrobial preservative in cosmetics, food products and pharmaceutical formulations. It may be used alone, in combination with other paraben esters, or with other antimicrobial agents. In cosmetics it is the second most frequently used preservative.[1]

The parabens are effective over a wide pH range and have a broad spectrum of antimicrobial activity although they are most effective against yeasts and molds, *see* Section 10.

Due to the poor solubility of the parabens, paraben salts, particularly the sodium salt, are frequently used in formulations. However, this may cause the pH of poorly buffered formulations to become more alkaline.

Propylparaben (0.02%) together with methylparaben (0.18%) has been used for the preservation of various parenteral pharmaceutical formulations, *see* Section 14.

See Methylparaben for further information.

Use	Concentration (%)
IM, IV, SC injections[*]	0.005–0.2
Ophthalmic preparations	0.005–0.01
Oral solutions and suspensions	0.01–0.02
Topical preparations	0.01–0.6
Vaginal preparations	0.02–0.1

[*] *See* Section 14.

8. Description

Propylparaben occurs as a white, crystalline, odorless and tasteless powder.

SEM: 1

Excipient: Propylparaben
Supplier: Bate Chemical Co Ltd
Magnification: 60x

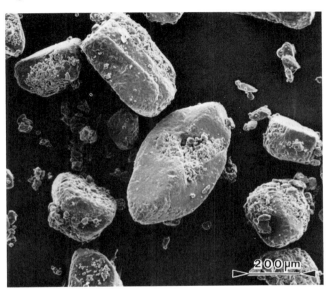

SEM: 2

Excipient: Propylparaben
Supplier: Bate Chemical Co Ltd
Magnification: 600x

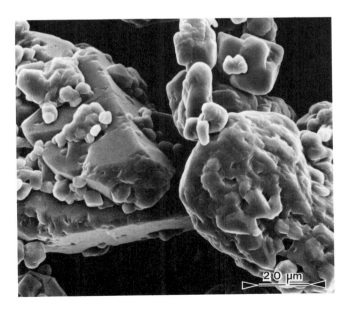

9. Pharmacopeial Specifications

Test	PhEur 1990	USPNF XVII (Suppl 6)
Identification	+	+
Melting range	96-99°C	95-98°C
Acidity	+	+
Loss on drying	—	≤ 0.5%
Residue on ignition	—	≤ 0.05%
Sulfated ash	≤ 0.1%	—
Appearance of solution	+	—
Related substances	+	—
Organic volatile impurities	—	+
Assay (dried basis)	99.0-101.0%	99.0-100.5%

10. Typical Properties

Antimicrobial activity: propylparaben exhibits antimicrobial activity between pH 4-8. Preservative efficacy decreases with increasing pH due to the formation of the phenolate anion. Parabens are more active against yeasts and molds than against bacteria. They are also more active against Gram-positive than against Gram-negative bacteria.

The activity of the parabens increases with increasing chain length of the alkyl moiety; solubility however decreases. Activity may be improved by using combinations of parabens since additive effects occur. Propylparaben has thus been used with methylparaben in parenteral preparations and is used with combinations of other parabens in topical and oral formulations. Activity has also been reported to be improved by the addition of other excipients, *see* Methylparaben for further information.

Reported minimum inhibitory concentrations (MICs) for propylparaben are shown in Table I:[2]

Table I: Minimum inhibitory concentrations (MICs) for propylparaben in aqueous solution.[2]

Microorganism	MIC (μg/mL)
Aerobacter aerogenes ATCC 8308	1000
Aspergillus niger ATCC 9642	500
Aspergillus niger ATCC 10254	200
Bacillus cereus var. mycoides ATCC 6462	125
Bacillus subtilis ATCC 6633	500
Candida albicans ATCC 10231	250
Enterobacter cloacae ATCC 23355	1000
Escherichia coli ATCC 8739	500
Escherichia coli ATCC 9637	100
Klebsiella pneumoniae ATCC 8308	500
Penicillium chrysogenum ATCC 9480	125
Penicillium digitatum ATCC 10030	63
Proteus vulgaris ATCC 13315	250
Pseudomonas aeruginosa ATCC 9027	> 1000
Pseudomonas aeruginosa ATCC 15442	> 1000
Pseudomonas stutzeri	500
Rhizopus nigricans ATCC 6227A	125
Saccharomyces cerevisiae ATCC 9763	125
Salmonella typhosa ATCC 6539	500
Serratia marcescens ATCC 8100	500
Staphylococcus aureus ATCC 6538P	500
Staphylococcus epidermidis ATCC 12228	500
Trichophyton mentagrophytes	65

Boiling point: 295°C
Dissociation constant: pKa = 8.4 at 22°C

Flash point: 140°C
Partition coefficients: values for different vegetable oils vary considerably and are affected by the purity of the oil, *see* Table II.

Table II: Partition coefficients for ethylparaben in vegetable oil and water.[3]

Solvent	Partition coefficient Oil: water
Corn oil	58.0
Mineral oil	0.5
Peanut oil	51.8
Soybean oil	65.9

Refractive index: n_D^{14} = 1.5049
Solubility: *see* Table III and HPE Data.

Table III: Solubility of ethylparaben in various solvents.[2]

Solvent	Solubility at 25°C Unless otherwise stated
Acetone	freely soluble
Ethanol	1 in 1.1
Ethanol (50%)	1 in 5.6
Ethanol (10%)	1 in 1000
Ether	freely soluble
Glycerin	1 in 250
Methanol	1 in 0.8
Mineral oil	1 in 3330
Peanut oil	1 in 70
Propylene glycol	1 in 3.9
Propylene glycol (50%)	1 in 110
Propylene glycol (10%)	1 in 1670
Water	1 in 4350 at 15°C
	1 in 2500
	1 in 225 at 80°C

HPE Laboratory Project Data			
	Method	Lab #	Results
Solubility			
Water at 25°C	SOL-8	30	0.4 mg/mL

11. Stability and Storage Conditions

Aqueous propylparaben solutions at pH 3-6 can be sterilized by autoclaving, without decomposition.[4] At pH 3-6 aqueous solutions are stable (less than 10% decomposition) for up to about four years at room temperature whilst solutions at pH 8 or above are subject to rapid hydrolysis (10% or more after about 60 days at room temperature).[5]

Predicted rate constants and half-lives at 25°C, for propylparaben dissolved in dilute hydrochloric acid solution at the initial pH shown:[5]

Initial pH of solution	Rate constant $k \pm \sigma^*$ (hour^{-1})	Half-life $t_{\frac{1}{2}} \pm \sigma^*$ (day)
1	$(1.255 \pm 0.042) \times 10^{-4}$	230 ± 7.6
2	$(1.083 \pm 0.081) \times 10^{-5}$	2670 ± 200
3	$(8.41 \pm 0.96) \times 10^{-7}$	$34\,300 \pm 3900$
4	$(2.23 \pm 0.37) \times 10^{-7}$	$130\,000 \pm 22\,000$

* Indicates the standard error.

The predicted amount of propylparaben remaining after autoclaving is shown below for propylparaben dissolved in dilute hydrochloric acid solution at the pH shown:[5]

Initial pH of solution	Rate constant $k \pm \sigma^*$ (hour^{-1})	Predicted residual amount after sterilization (%)
1	$(4.42 \pm 0.10) \times 10^{-1}$	86.30 ± 0.30
2	$(4.67 \pm 0.19) \times 10^{-2}$	98.46 ± 0.06
3	$(2.96 \pm 0.24) \times 10^{-3}$	99.90 ± 0.01
4	$(7.8 \pm 1.1) \times 10^{-4}$	99.97 ± 0.004

* Indicates the standard error.

Propylparaben should be stored in a well-closed container in a cool, dry, place.

12. Incompatibilities

The antimicrobial activity of propylparaben is considerably reduced in the presence of nonionic surfactants as a result of micellization.[6] Absorption of propylparaben by plastics has been reported, with the amount absorbed dependent upon the type of plastic and the vehicle.[7] Magnesium aluminum silicate, magnesium trisilicate, yellow iron oxide and ultramarine blue have also been reported to absorb propylparaben, thereby reducing preservative efficacy.[8,9]
Propylparaben is discolored in the presence of iron and is subject to hydrolysis by weak alkalis and strong acids.
See also Methylparaben.

13. Method of Manufacture

Propylparaben is prepared by the esterification of *p*-hydroxybenzoic acid with *n*-propanol.

14. Safety

Propylparaben, and other parabens, are widely used as antimicrobial preservatives in cosmetics, food products and oral and topical pharmaceutical formulations. Although propylparaben and methylparaben have been used as preservatives in injections and ophthalmic preparations they are now generally regarded as being unsuitable for these types of formulation due to the irritant potential of the parabens. Systemically, no adverse reactions to parabens have been reported although they have been associated with hypersensitivity reactions. The WHO has set an estimated acceptable total daily intake for methyl, ethyl and propylparabens at up to 10 mg/kg body-weight.[10]
LD$_{50}$ (dog, oral): 6.0 g/kg[11]
LD$_{50}$ (mouse, IP): 0.2 g/kg
LD$_{50}$ (mouse, SC): 1.65 g/kg

15. Handling Precautions

Observe normal precautions appropriate to the circumstances and quantity of material handled. Proylparaben may be irritant to the skin, eyes and mucous membranes and should be handled in a well-ventilated environment. Eye protection, gloves and a dust mask or respirator are recommended.

16. Regulatory Status

GRAS listed. Accepted as a food additive in Europe. Included in the FDA Inactive Ingredients Guide (IM, IV and SC injections, inhalations, ophthalmic preparations, oral capsules, solutions, suspensions and tablets, otic, rectal, topical and vaginal preparations). Included in parenteral and nonparenteral medicines licensed in the UK.

17. Pharmacopeias

Aust, Br, Braz, Cz, Egypt, Eur, Fr, Ger, Gr, Ind, It, Jpn, Mex, Neth, Nord, Port, Rom, Swiss, USPNF and Yug.

18. Related Substances

Butylparaben; Ethylparaben; Methylparaben; propylparaben potassium; propylparaben sodium.

Propylparaben potassium: $C_{10}H_{11}KO_3$
Molecular weight: 218.30
CAS number: [84930-16-5]
Synonyms: potassium propyl hydroxybenzoate; propyl 4-hydroxybenzoate potassium salt.

Propylparaben sodium: $C_{10}H_{11}NaO_3$
Molecular weight: 202.20
CAS number: [35285-69-9]
Synonyms: E217; propyl 4-hydroxybenzoate sodium salt; sodium propyl hydroxybenzoate; soluble propyl hydroxybenzoate.
Pharmacopeias: Br, Fr, It and USPNF.
Appearance: white odorless, or almost odorless, hygroscopic crystalline powder.
Acidity/alkalinity: pH = 9.5-10.5 (0.1% w/v aqueous solution)
Solubility: 1 in 50 of ethanol (95%); 1 in 2 ethanol (50%); 1 in 1 of water; practically insoluble in fixed oils.
Comments: propylparaben sodium may be used instead of propylparaben because of its greater aqueous solubility. However, it may cause the pH of a formulation to become more alkaline.

19. Comments

See Methylparaben for further information and references.

20. Specific References

1. Decker RL, Wenninger JA. Frequency of preservative use in cosmetic formulas as disclosed to FDA - 1987. Cosmet Toilet 1987; 102(12): 21-24.
2. Haag TE, Loncrini DF. Esters of para-hydroxybenzoic acid. In: Kabara JJ, editor. Cosmetic and drug preservation. New York: Marcel Dekker, 1984: 63-77.
3. Wan LSC, Kurup TRR, Chan LW. Partition of preservatives in oil/water systems. Pharm Acta Helv 1986; 61: 308-313.
4. Aalto TR, Firman MC, Rigler NE. *p*-Hydroxybenzoic acid esters as preservatives I: uses, antibacterial and antifungal studies, properties and determination. J Am Pharm Assoc (Sci) 1953, 42: 449-457.
5. Kamada A, Yata N, Kubo K, Arakawa M. Stability of *p*-hydroxybenzoic acid esters in acidic medium. Chem Pharm Bull 1973; 21: 2073-2076.
6. Aoki M, Kameta A, Yoshioka I, Matsuzaki T. Application of surface active agents to pharmaceutical preparations I: effect of Tween 20 upon the antifungal activities of *p*-hydroxybenzoic acid esters in solubilized preparations [in Japanese]. J Pharm Soc Jpn 1956; 76: 939-943.
7. Kakemi K, Sezaki H, Arakawa E, Kimura K, Ikeda K. Interactions of parabens and other pharmaceutical adjuvants with plastic containers. Chem Pharm Bull 1971; 19: 2523-2529.
8. Allwood MC. The adsorption of esters of *p*-hydroxybenzoic acid by magnesium trisilicate. Int J Pharmaceutics 1982; 11: 101-107.
9. Sakamoto T, Yanagi M, Fukushima S, Mitsui T. Effects of some cosmetic pigments on the bactericidal activities of preservatives. J Soc Cosmet Chem 1987; 38: 83-98.

10. FAO/WHO. Toxicological evaluation of certain food additives with a review of general principles and of specifications. Seventeenth report of the joint FAO/WHO expert committee on food additives. Tech Rep Ser Wld Hlth Org 1974; No. 539.

11. Sweet DV, editor. Registry of toxic effects of chemical substances. Cincinnati: US Department of Health, 1987.

21. General References

Golightly LK, Smolinske SS, Bennett ML, Sutherland EW, Rumack BH. Pharmaceutical excipients: adverse effects associated with inactive ingredients in drug products (part I). Med Toxicol 1988; 3: 128-165.

Jian L, Li Wan Po A. Ciliotoxicity of methyl- and propyl-*p*-hydroxybenzoates: a dose-response and surface-response study. J Pharm Pharmacol 1993; 45: 925-927.

22. Authors

USA: MM Rieger.

Saccharin

1. Nonproprietary Names

BP: Saccharin
USPNF: Saccharin

2. Synonyms

1,2-Benzisothiazolin-3-one 1,1-dioxide; benzoic sulfimide; benzosulfimide; 1,2-dihydro-2-ketobenzisosulfonazole; 2,3-dihydro-3-oxobenzisosulfonazole; E954; *Garantose*; *Glucid*; gluside; *Hermesetas*; *Sacarina*; *Saccarina*; saccharin insoluble; *Saccharinol*; *Saccharinose*; *Saccharol*; *Saxin*; *o*-sulfobenzimide; *o*-sulfobenzoic acid imide; *Sykose*; *Zaharina*.

3. Chemical Name and CAS Registry Number

1,2-Benzisothiazol-3(2*H*)-one 1,1-dioxide [81-07-2]

4. Empirical Formula   Molecular Weight

$C_7H_5NO_3S$ 183.18

5. Structural Formula

6. Functional Category

Sweetening agent.

7. Applications in Pharmaceutical Formulation or Technology

Saccharin is an intense sweetening agent used in beverages, food products, table-top sweeteners and oral hygiene products such as toothpastes and mouthwashes. In oral pharmaceutical formulations, it is used at a concentration of 0.02-0.5% w/w. Saccharin can be used to mask some unpleasant taste characteristics or to enhance flavor systems. Its sweetening power is approximately 500 times that of sucrose.

8. Description

Saccharin occurs as odorless white crystals or a white crystalline powder. It has an intensely sweet taste, with a metallic aftertaste which at normal levels of use can be detected by approximately 25% of the population.

9. Pharmacopeial Specifications

Test	BP 1993	USPNF XVII (Suppl 9)
Identification	+	+
Melting range	226-230°C	226-230°C
Loss on drying	⩽ 1.0%	⩽ 1.0%
Residue on ignition	—	⩽ 0.2%
Sulfated ash	⩽ 0.2%	—
Toluenesulfonamides	—	⩽ 0.0025%
Arsenic	⩽ 2 ppm	⩽ 3 ppm
Selenium	—	⩽ 0.003%
Heavy metals	⩽ 10 ppm	⩽ 0.001%

SEM: 1
Excipient: Saccharin
Magnification: 600x

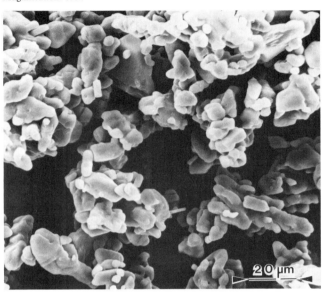

SEM: 2
Excipient: Saccharin
Magnification: 2400x

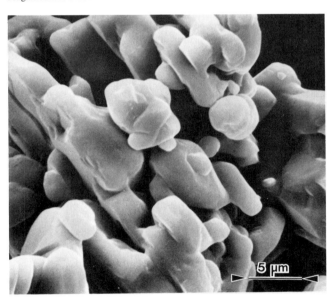

Continued

Test	BP 1993	USPNF XVII (Suppl 9)
Readily carbonizable substances	+	+
Benzoic and salicylic acids	—	+
Organic volatile impurities	—	+
Related substances	+	—
Assay (dried basis)	99.0-100.5%	98.0-101.0%

10. Typical Properties

Acidity/alkalinity: pH = 2.0 (0.35% w/v aqueous solution)
Density (bulk): 0.7–1.0 g/cm^3
Density (tapped): 0.9–1.2 g/cm^3
Dissociation constant: pK$_a$ = 1.6 at 25°C
Heat of combustion: 3644.3 kJ/mol (871 kcal/mol)
Moisture content: see HPE Data.
Solubility: readily dissolved by dilute ammonia solutions, alkali hydroxide solutions, or alkali carbonate solutions (with the evolution of carbon dioxide).

Solvent	Solubility at 20°C Unless otherwise stated
Acetone	1 in 12
Chloroform	slightly soluble
Ethanol (95%)	1 in 31
Ether	slightly soluble
Glycerin	1 in 50
Water	1 in 290
	1 in 25 at 100°C

HPE Laboratory Project Data			
	Method	Lab #	Results
Moisture content	MC-9	5	0.10%

11. Stability and Storage Conditions

Saccharin is stable under the normal range of conditions employed in formulations. In the bulk form it shows no detectable decomposition and it is only when exposed to a high temperature (125°C) at a low pH (pH 2) for over 1 hour that significant decomposition occurs. The decomposition product formed is (ammonium-*o*-sulfo)benzoic acid.[1]
Saccharin should be stored in a well-closed container in a cool, dry, place.

12. Incompatibilities

—

13. Method of Manufacture

Saccharin is prepared from toluene by the following series of reactions known as the Remsen-Fahlberg method. Toluene is first reacted with chlorosulfonic acid to form *o*-toluene sulfonyl chloride, which is reacted with ammonia to form the sulfonamide. The methyl group is then oxidized with dichromate, yielding *o*-sulfamoylbenzoic acid which, when heated, forms the cyclic imide, saccharin.
An alternative method involves a refined version of the Maumee process. Methyl anthranilate is initially diazotized to form 2-carbomethoxybenzenediazonium chloride, sulfonation followed by oxidation then yields 2-carbomethoxybenzenesulfonyl chloride. Amidation of this material, followed by acidification, forms insoluble acid saccharin.

14. Safety

There has been considerable controversy concerning the safety of saccharin which has led to extensive studies since the mid-1970s.
Two-generation studies in rats exposed to diets containing 5–7.5% total saccharin (equivalent to 175 g daily in humans) suggested that the incidence of bladder tumors was signifi-cantly greater in saccharin-treated males of the second generation than in controls.[2,3] Further experiments in rats suggested that a contaminant of commercial saccharin, *o*-toluene sulfonamide, might also account for carcinogenic effects. In view of these studies a ban on the use of saccharin was proposed in several countries. However, in 1977 a ban by the FDA led to a Congressional moratorium which permitted the continued use of saccharin in the US.
From the available data it now appears that the development of tumors is a sex, species, and organ specific phenomenon and extensive epidemiological studies have shown that saccharin intake is not related to bladder cancer in humans.[4,5]
The WHO has set a temporary acceptable daily intake for saccharin, including its calcium, potassium and sodium salts at up to 2.5 mg/kg body-weight.[6] In the UK, the Committee on Toxicity of Chemicals in Food, Consumer Products and the Environment (COT) has set an acceptable daily intake for saccharin and its calcium, potassium and sodium salts (expressed as saccharin sodium) at up to 5 mg/kg body-weight.[7]
Adverse reactions to saccharin, although relatively few in relation to its widespread use, include: urticaria with pruritus following ingestion of saccharin sweetened beverages[8] and photosensitization reactions.[9]

15. Handling Precautions

Observe normal precautions appropriate to the circumstances and quantity of material handled. Eye protection and a dust mask are recommended.

16. Regulatory Status

Accepted for use as a food additive in Europe and many other countries. Note that the EC number 'E954' is applied to both saccharin and saccharin salts. Included in the FDA Inactive Ingredients Guide (oral solutions, syrups, tablets and topical preparations). Included in nonparenteral medicines licensed in the UK.

17. Pharmacopeias

Br, Egypt, Fr, Ind, It, Mex, Rom, Swiss and USPNF.

18. Related Substances

Saccharin calcium; saccharin potassium; Saccharin Sodium.

Saccharin calcium: $C_{14}H_8CaN_2O_6S_2 \cdot 3\frac{1}{2}H_2O$
Molecular weight: 467.48
CAS number: [6381-91-5] for the hydrated form; [6485-34-3] for the anhydrous form.
Synonyms: Syncal CAS.
Appearance: white, odorless crystals or crystalline powder with an intensely sweet taste.
Pharmacopeias: US.
Solubility: 1 in 4.7 ethanol (95%); 1 in 2.6 of water.

Saccharin potassium: $C_7H_5NO_3SK$
Molecular weight: 222.29
CAS number: [10332-51-1]

19. Comments

The perceived intensity of sweeteners relative to sucrose depends upon their concentration, temperature of tasting, pH and on the flavor and texture of the product concerned.
Intense sweetening agents will not replace bulk, textural or preservative characteristics of sugar, if the latter ingredient is removed from a formulation.

Synergistic effects for combinations of sweeteners have been reported. Saccharin is often used in combination with cyclamtes and aspartame since saccharin content may be reduced to minimize any aftertaste.

20. Specific References

1. DeGarmo O, Ashworth GW, Eaker CM, Munch RH. Hydrolytic stability of saccharin. J Am Pharm Assoc (Sci) 1952; 41: 17-18.
2. Arnold DL, Moodie CA, Grice HC, et al. Long-term toxicity of ortho-toluenesulfonamide and sodium saccharin in the rat. Toxicol Appl Pharmacol 1980; 52: 113-152.
3. Arnold DL. Two-generation saccharin bioassays. Environ Health Perspect 1983; 50: 27-36.
4. Council on Scientific Affairs. Saccharin: review of safety issues. JAMA 1985; 254: 2622-2624.
5. Morgan RW, Wong O. A review of epidemiological studies on artificial sweeteners and bladder cancer. Food Chem Toxicol 1985; 23: 529-533.
6. FAO/WHO. Evaluation of certain food additives and contaminants. Twenty-eighth report of the FAO/WHO expert committee on food additives. Tech Rep Ser Wld Hlth Org 1984; No. 710.
7. Food Advisory Committee. FAC further advice on saccharin. FdAC/REP/9. London: MAFF, 1990.
8. Miller R, White LW, Schwartz HJ. A case of episodic urticaria due to saccharin ingestion. J Allergy Clin Immunol 1974; 53: 240-242.
9. Gordon HH. Photosensitivity to saccharin. J Am Acad Dermatol 1983; 8: 565.

21. General References

Lindley MG. Sweetener markets, marketing and product development. In: Marie, Piggot, editors. Handbook of sweeteners. Glasgow: Blackie, 1991: 186.
Zubair MU, Hassan MMA. Saccharin. In: Florey K, editor. Analytical profiles of drug substances, volume 13. Orlando: Academic Press, 1984: 487-519.

22. Authors

UK: FR Higton, DM Thurgood.

Saccharin Sodium

1. Nonproprietary Names

BP: Saccharin sodium
PhEur: Saccharinum natricum
USP: Saccharin sodium

2. Synonyms

1,2-Benzisothiazolin-3-one 1,1-dioxide, sodium salt; *Britsol*; *Crystallose*; *Dagutan*; E954; *Kristallose*; sodium *o*-benzosulfimide; soluble gluside; soluble saccharin; *Sucaryl*; *Sucromat*; *Syncal S*.

3. Chemical Name and CAS Registry Number

1,2-Benzisothiazol-3(2*H*)-one 1,1-dioxide, sodium salt
[6155-57-3] for the dihydrate.
[128-44-9] for the anhydrous material.
See also Section 8.

4. Empirical Formula   Molecular Weight

$C_7H_4NNaO_3S$	205.16
$C_7H_4NNaO_3S.2/3H_2O$ (84%)	217.24
$C_7H_4NNaO_3S.2H_2O$ (76%)	241.19

5. Structural Formula

·2H$_2$O   76% saccharin sodium (dihydrate)

·⅔H$_2$O   84% saccharin sodium

6. Functional Category

Sweetening agent.

7. Applications in Pharmaceutical Formulation or Technology

Saccharin sodium is an intense sweetening agent used in beverages, food products, table-top sweeteners and pharmaceutical formulations such as tablets, powders, medicated confectionery, gels, suspensions and liquids. It is also used in vitamin preparations.

Saccharin sodium is considerably more soluble in water than saccharin and is also more frequently used in pharmaceutical formulations. Sweetening power is approximately 300 times that of sucrose. Saccharin sodium enhances flavor systems and may be used to mask some unpleasant taste characteristics.

An injection of saccharin sodium has been used to measure the arm-to-tongue circulation time.

Use	Concentration (%)
Dental paste/gel	0.12-0.3
IM/IV injections	0.9
Oral solution	0.075-0.6
Oral syrup	0.04-0.25

8. Description

Saccharin sodium occurs as a white, odorless or faintly aromatic, efflorescent, crystalline powder. It has an intensely sweet taste, with a metallic aftertaste which at normal levels of use can be detected by approximately 25% of the population. Saccharin sodium can contain variable amounts of water.

SEM: 1
Excipient: Saccharin sodium
Magnification: 35x
Voltage: 5 kV

9. Pharmacopeial Specifications

Test	PhEur 1992	USP XXII (Suppl 3)
Identification	+	+
Water	≤ 15.0%	≤ 15.0%
Benzoate and salicylate	—	+
Arsenic	—	≤ 3 ppm
Selenium	—	≤ 0.003%
Acidity or alkalinity	—	+
Toluenesulfonamides	+	≤ 0.0025%
Heavy metals	≤ 20 ppm	≤ 0.001%
Readily carbonizable substances	+	+
Assay (anhydrous basis)	99.0-101.0%	98.0-101.0%

10. Typical Properties

Unless stated, data refers to either 76% or 84% saccharin sodium.

Acidity/alkalinity: pH = 6.6 (10% w/v aqueous solution)
Density (bulk):
0.8-1.1 g/cm^3 (76% saccharin sodium);
0.86 g/cm^3 (84% saccharin sodium).
Density (particle):
1.70 g/cm^3 (84% saccharin sodium)
Density (tapped):
0.9-1.2 g/cm^3 (76% saccharin sodium);
0.96 g/cm^3 (84% saccharin sodium).

Melting point: decomposes upon heating.
Moisture content: 9.00%. *See also* HPE Data. Saccharin sodium 76% contains 14.5% w/w water; saccharin sodium 84% contains 5.5% w/w water. During drying, water evolution occurs in two distinct phases. The 76% material dries under ambient conditions to approximately 5.5% moisture (84% saccharin sodium); remaining moisture is then removed only by heating.
Solubility:

Solvent	Solubility at 25°C Unless otherwise stated
Buffer solutions:	
pH 2.2 (phthalate)	1 in 1.15
	1 in 0.66 at 60°C
pH 4.0 (citrate-phosphate)	1 in 1.21
	1 in 0.69 at 60°C
pH 7.0 (citrate-phosphate)	1 in 1.21
	1 in 0.66 at 60°C
pH 9.0 (borate)	1 in 1.21
	1 in 0.69 at 60°C
Ethanol	1 in 102
Ethanol (95%)	1 in 50
Propylene glycol	1 in 3.5
Propan-2-ol	practically insoluble
Water	1 in 1.2

Specific surface area: 0.25 m^2/g

	HPE Laboratory Project Data		
	Method	Lab #	Results
Moisture Content	MC-3	5	9.00%

11. Stability and Storage Conditions

Saccharin sodium is stable under the normal range of conditions employed in formulations. It is only when exposed to a high temperature (125°C) at a low pH (pH 2) for over 1 hour that significant decomposition occurs. The 84% grade is the most stable form of saccharin sodium since the 76% form will dry further under ambient conditions.
Saccharin sodium should be stored in a well-closed container in a cool, dry, place.

12. Incompatibilities

—

13. Method of Manufacture

Saccharin is produced by the oxidation of *o*-toluene sulfonamide by potassium permanganate in a solution of sodium hydroxide. Acidification of the solution precipitates saccharin, which is then dissolved in water at 50°C and neutralized by the addition of sodium hydroxide. Rapid cooling of the solution initiates crystallization of saccharin sodium from the liquors.

14. Safety

There has been considerable controversy concerning the safety of saccharin and saccharin sodium in recent years, however it is now generally regarded as a safe intense sweetener. *See* Saccharin for further information.
The WHO has set a temporary acceptable daily intake of up to 2.5 mg/kg body-weight for saccharin, including its salts.[1] In the UK, the Committee on Toxicity of Chemicals in Food, Consumer Products and the Environment (COT) has set an acceptable daily intake for saccharin and its salts (expressed as saccharin sodium) at up to 5 mg/kg body-weight.[2]

15. Handling Precautions

Observe normal precautions appropriate to the circumstances and quantity of material handled. Eye protection and a dust mask are recommended.

16. Regulatory Status

Accepted for use as a food additive in Europe and many other countries. Note that the EC number 'E954' is applied to both saccharin and saccharin salts. Included in the FDA Inactive Ingredients Guide (buccal and dental preparations, IM and IV injections, oral and topical preparations). Included in nonparenteral medicines licensed in the UK.

17. Pharmacopeias

Aust, Br, Chin, Egypt, Eur, Fr, Ger, Hung, Ind, It, Jpn, Mex, Neth, Nord, Swiss, Turk, US and Yug.

18. Related Substances

Saccharin.

19. Comments

The perceived intensity of sweeteners relative to sucrose depends upon their concentration, temperature of tasting, pH and on the flavor and texture of the product concerned.
Intense sweetening agents will not replace bulk, textural or preservative characteristics of sugar if the latter ingredient is removed from a formulation.
Synergistic effects for combinations of sweeteners have been reported. Saccharin sodium is often used in combination with cyclamates and aspartame since saccharin sodium content may be reduced to minimize any aftertaste.

20. Specific References

1. FAO/WHO. Evaluation of certain food additives and contaminants. Twenty-eighth report of the FAO/WHO expert committee on food additives. Tech Rep Ser Wld Hlth Org 1984; No. 710.
2. Food Advisory Committee. FAC further advice on saccharin. FdAC/REP/9. London: MAFF, 1990.
See Saccharin for further references.

21. General References

Lindley MG. Sweetener markets, marketing and product developments. In: Marie, Piggot, editors. Handbook of sweeteners. Glasgow: Blackie, 1991: 186.

22. Authors

UK: FR Higton, DM Thurgood.

Sesame Oil

1. Nonproprietary Names

BP: Sesame oil
PhEur: Sesami oleum
USPNF: Sesame oil

2. Synonyms

Benne oil; gingelly oil; gingili oil; jinjili oil; teel oil.

3. Chemical Name and CAS Registry Number

Sesame oil [8008-74-0]

4. Empirical Formula   Molecular Weight

A typical analysis of refined sesame oil indicates the composition of the acids, present as glycerides, to be: arachidic acid 0.8%; linoleic acid 40.4%; oleic acid 45.4%; palmitic acid 9.1% and stearic acid 4.3%. Sesamin, a complex cyclic ether, and sesamolin, a glycoside, are also present in small amounts.
Note that other reported analyses may vary slightly from that above.[1]

5. Structural Formula

See Section 4.

6. Functional Category

Oleaginous vehicle; solvent.

7. Applications in Pharmaceutical Formulation or Technology

The major use of sesame oil in pharmaceutical formulations is as a solvent in the preparation of sustained-release intramuscular injections of certain steroids, such as estradiol valerate, hydroxyprogesterone caproate, testosterone enanthate and nandrolone decanoate,[2] or other oil soluble drug substances, for example the decanoates or enanthate esters of fluphenazine.
In addition, sesame oil may be used as a solvent in the preparation of subcutaneous injections,[3] oral capsules,[4,5] rectal capsules[6] and ophthalmic preparations;[7] it may also be used in the formulation of suspensions,[8] and emulsions.[8-10] Sesame oil is additionally used as an edible oil and in the preparation of oleomargarine.

8. Description

Refined sesame oil is a clear, pale yellow colored liquid with a slight, pleasant odor and a bland taste. It solidifies at about -4°C.

9. Pharmacopeial Specifications

Test	PhEur 1985	USPNF XVII
Identification	+	+
Specific gravity	0.915-0.923	0.916-0.921
Refractive index at 20°C	1.472-1.476	
Heavy metals	—	≤ 0.001%
Cottonseed oil	—	+

Continued

Test	PhEur 1985	USPNF XVII
Solidification range of fatty acids	—	20-25°C
Free fatty acids	—	+
Acid value	≤ 0.3	—
Iodine value	—	103-116
Peroxide value	≤ 5.0	—
Saponification value	—	188-195
Unsaponifiable matter	≤ 1.8%	≤ 1.5%
Alkaline impurities	+	—
Foreign fixed oils	+	—
Water	≤ 0.05%	—

10. Typical Properties

Density: 0.916-0.920 g/cm^3. *See also* HPE Data.
Flash point: 338°C (open cup)
Freezing point: -5°C
Refractive index: n_D^{40} = 1.4650-1.4665
Solubility: insoluble in water; practically insoluble in ethanol (95%); miscible with carbon disulfide, chloroform, ether and hexane.
Specific rotation $[\alpha]_D^{25}$: +1° to +9°
Viscosity (dynamic): *see* HPE Data.

HPE Laboratory Project Data			
	Method	Lab #	Results
Density	DE-5	30	0.914 g/cm^3
Viscosity	VIS-2	30	43.37 mPa s

11. Stability and Storage Conditions

Sesame oil is more stable than most other fixed oils and does not readily become rancid; this has been attributed to the antioxidant effect of some of its characteristic constituents. The BP 1993 also permits the addition of a suitable antioxidant to sesame oil used for certain applications.
Sesame oil may be sterilized by aseptic filtration or dry heat. It has been reported that suitable conditions for the sterilization of injections containing sesame oil are a temperature of 170°C for two hours; it was suggested that 150°C for one hour is inadequate.[11]
Sesame oil should be stored in a well-filled, airtight, light-resistant container, at a temperature not exceeding 40°C. Sesame oil intended for use in a parenteral dosage form should be stored in a glass container.

12. Incompatibilities

Sesame oil may be saponified by alkali hydroxides.

13. Method of Manufacture

Refined sesame oil is obtained from the seeds of one or more cultivated varieties of *Sesamum indicum* Linné (Fam. Pedaliaceae) by expression in a hydraulic press or solvent extraction. The crude oil thus obtained is refined to obtain an oil suitable for food or pharmaceutical use.

14. Safety

Sesame oil is mainly used in intramuscular and subcutaneous injections. It is also used in topical pharmaceutical formulations and consumed as an edible oil.

Although generally regarded as an essentially nontoxic and nonirritant material[12] there have been rare reports of hypersensitivity to sesame oil, with sesamin suspected as being the primary allergen.[13,14] Anaphylactic reactions to sesame seeds have also been reported. However, it is thought that the allergens in the seeds may be inactivated or destroyed by heating as heat extracted sesame seed oil or baked sesame seeds do not cause anaphylactic reactions in sesame seed allergic individuals.[15]

LD_{50} (rabbit, IV): 678 μg/kg[16]

15. Handling Precautions

Observe normal precautions appropriate to the circumstances and quantity of material handled. Spillages of sesame oil are slippery and should be covered with an inert absorbent material prior to disposal.

16. Regulatory Status

Included in the FDA Inactive Ingredients Guide (IM and SC injections, oral capsules, emulsions and tablets, also topical preparations). Included in parenteral and nonparenteral medicines licensed in the UK.

17. Pharmacopeias

Aust, Br, Chin, Egypt, Eur, Fr, Ger, Gr, It, Jpn, Mex, Neth, Port, Swiss and USPNF.

18. Related Substances

Canola Oil; Corn Oil; Cottonseed Oil; Peanut Oil; Soybean Oil.

19. Comments

—

20. Specific References

1. British Standards Institute. Specification for crude vegetable fats, BS 7207. London: BSI, 1990.
2. Williams JS, Stein JH, Ferris TH. Nandrolone decanoate therapy for patients receiving hemodialysis. Arch Intern Med 1974; 134: 289-292.
3. Hirano K, Ichihashi T, Yamada H. Studies on the absorption of practically water-insoluble drugs following injection V: subcutaneous absorption in rats from solutions in water immiscible oils. J Pharm Sci 1982; 71: 495-500.
4. Perez-Reyes M, et al. Pharmacology of orally administered $\triangle^9$-tetrahydrocannabinol. Clin Pharmacol Ther 1973; 14: 48-55.
5. Sallan SE, Zinberg NE, Frei E. Antiemetic effect of delta-9-tetrahydrocannabinol in patients receiving cancer chemotherapy. N Engl J Med 1975; 293: 795-797.
6. Tanabe K, Sawanoi M, Yamazaki M, Kamada A. Effect of different suppository bases on release of indomethacin [in Japanese]. Yakuzaigaku 1984; 44: 115-120.
7. Chien DS, Schoenwald RD. Ocular pharmacokinetics and pharmacodynamics of phenylephrine and phenylephrine oxazolidine in rabbit eyes. Pharm Res 1990; 7: 476-483.
8. Shinkuma D, et al. Bioavailability of phenytoin from oil suspension and emulsion in dogs. Int J Pharmaceutics 1981; 9: 17-28.
9. Rosenkrantz H, Thompson GR, Braude MC. Oral and parenteral formulations of marijuana constituents. J Pharm Sci 1972; 61: 1106-1112.
10. Unno K, Goto A, Kagaya S, Murota H, Echigo M. Preparation and tissue distribution of 5-fluorouracil emulsion [in Japanese]. J Nippon Hosp Pharm Assoc 1980; 6(1): 14-20.
11. Pasquale D, Jaconia D, Eisman P, Lachman L. A study of sterilizing conditions for injectable oils. Bull Parenter Drug Assoc 1964; 18(3): 1-11.
12. Hem SL, Bright DR, Banker GS, Pogue JP. Tissue irritation evaluation of potential parenteral vehicles. Drug Dev Comm 1974-75; 1: 471-477.
13. Neering H, Vitanyi BE, Malten KE, van Ketel WG, van Dijk E. Allergens in sesame oil contact dermatitis. Acta Dermatol Venerol 1975; 55: 31-34.
14. Weiner M, Bernstein IL. Adverse reactions to drug formulation agents: a handbook of excipients. New York: Marcel Dekker Inc, 1989: 212-213.
15. Kägi MK, Wüthrich B. Falafel-burger anaphylaxis due to sesame seed allergy [letter]. Lancet 1991; 338: 582.
16. Sweet DV, editor. Registry of toxic effects of chemical substances. Cincinnati: US Department of Health, 1987.

21. General References

—

22. Authors

UK: CG Cable, PJ Weller.

Shellac

1. Nonproprietary Names

USPNF: Shellac

2. Synonyms

Dewaxed orange shellac; E904; lac; lacca; *Mantrolac R-49*; orange shellac; refined bleached shellac; regular bleached shellac.

3. Chemical Name and CAS Registry Number

Shellac [9000-59-3]

4. Empirical Formula   Molecular Weight

Shellac is a naturally occurring material, consisting of a complex mixture of constituents, and may be obtained in various refined or modified forms, *see* Section 13.

Although its composition has not been fully elucidated, the main component of shellac (about 95%) is a resin which on mild basic hydrolysis gives a mixture of aliphatic and alicyclic hydroxy acids and polyesters, amongst which aleuritic, butolic, kerrolic and shellolic acids have been identified and named. The major component of the aliphatic fraction is aleuritic acid whilst the major component of the alicyclic fraction is shellolic acid. Shellac also contains about 5-6% wax along with gluten, other impurities, and a small amount of pigment. The exact composition of shellac may vary depending upon the country of origin and method of manufacture.[1,2]

5. Structural Formula

See Section 4.

6. Functional Category

Coating agent.

7. Applications in Pharmaceutical Formulation or Technology

Shellac is used in pharmaceutical formulations for the enteric coating of tablets and beads, the material usually being applied as a 35% w/v alcoholic solution, *see also* Section 19.

Shellac, applied as a 40% w/v alcoholic solution, has also been used to apply one or two sealing coats to tablet cores to protect them from moisture before being film or sugar-coated.

Shellac may also be used in food products and cosmetics.

8. Description

Shellac is a naturally occurring material which may be obtained in a variety of refined or modified forms, *see* Sections 4 and 13.

Generally, shellac occurs as hard, brittle, transparent, pale lemon-yellow to brownish-orange colored flakes of varying size and shape; it is also available as a powder. Shellac is tasteless and odorless, or may have a faint odor.

9. Pharmacopeial Specifications

Test	USPNF XVII
Identification	+
Arsenic	⩽ 1.5 ppm

Continued

Test	USPNF XVII
Heavy metals	⩽ 0.001%
Rosin	+
Acid value (on dried basis)	
Dewaxed orange shellac	71-79
Orange shellac	68-76
Refined bleached shellac	75-91
Regular bleached shellac	73-89
Loss on drying	
Dewaxed orange shellac	⩽ 2.0%
Orange shellac	⩽ 2.0%
Refined bleached shellac	⩽ 6.0%
Regular bleached shellac	⩽ 6.0%
Wax	
Dewaxed orange shellac	⩽ 0.2%
Orange shellac	⩽ 5.5%
Refined bleached shellac	⩽ 0.2%
Regular bleached shellac	⩽ 5.5%

10. Typical Properties

Alcohol-insoluble matter: ⩽ 1.0%
Ash: ⩽ 1.0%
Density: 1.035-1.140 g/cm^3
Hydroxyl value: 230-280
Iodine number: 10-18
Melting point: 115-120°C
Refractive index: n_D^{20} = 1.5210-1.5272
Saponification value: 185-210
Solubility:

Solvent	Solubility at 25°C
Alkalis	soluble
Aqueous ethanolamine solution	soluble
Benzene	1 in 10
Ethanol	1 in 2
Ethanol (95%)	1 in 1.2 (very slowly soluble)
Ether	1 in 8
Hexane	practically insoluble
Propylene glycol	1 in 10
Water	practically insoluble

11. Stability and Storage Conditions

After long storage, shellac becomes less readily soluble in alcohol, less fluid on heating, and darker in color. Shellac coated tablets may have increased disintegration times following prolonged storage due to changes in the physical characteristics of the coating, *see* Section 19.[3]

Shellac should be stored in a well-closed container at temperatures below 27°C. Wax containing grades should be mixed before use to ensure uniform distribution of the wax.

12. Incompatibilities

Shellac is chemically reactive with aqueous alkalis, organic bases, alcohols and agents which esterify hydroxyl groups. Therefore, shellac should be used with caution in the presence of such compounds.

13. Method of Manufacture

Shellac is a naturally occurring material obtained from lac, a resinous secretion of the insect *Laccifer lacca* Kerr (Coccidae). The insect lives on the sap of the stems of various trees;

secretions are found most abundantly on the smaller branches and twigs which are broken off and constitute sticklac. After scraping the twigs and soaking in water, the water-soluble components are removed by treatment with dilute alkali. The resulting water-insoluble material is called seed lac.

Historically, seed lac was processed into shellac by melting the seed lac in a muslin bag suspended over a fire. Shellac could then be squeezed out from the bag, by hand, and poured into molds to produce button shellac. Alternatively the molten shellac might be collected and allowed to cool as discs or wafer thin sheets.

Today, most shellac is produced on a commercial scale using machine processes involving extraction from seed lac using steam heat or solvent extraction with hot ethanol. Shellac produced by the heat and solvent extraction processes cannot usually be differentiated by chemical tests.

Various different grades of modified or refined shellac are available which may be broadly defined as either bleached or orange shellac. Orange shellac is essentially the crude shellac obtained from seed lac, as described above. It may retain most of its wax, or be dewaxed, and may contain lesser amounts of the natural color than was originally present. The quantities of wax, coloring material and other impurities present may vary and hence the physical properties of orange shellac may also vary depending upon its source or the processing methods used.

Bleached or white shellac is obtained by dissolving shellac in aqueous sodium carbonate, bleaching the solution with sodium hypochlorite and precipitating the bleached shellac with 2N sulfuric acid. Removal of wax, by filtration, results in a refined bleached shellac.

Most commercial shellac is produced in India and Thailand; smaller amounts come from Burma and Malaya.

14. Safety

Shellac is used in oral pharmaceutical formulations, food products and cosmetics. It is generally regarded as an essentially nonirritant and nontoxic material at the levels employed as an excipient. However, excessive consumption of shellac may be harmful.

15. Handling Precautions

Shellac may be harmful if ingested in large quantities. It is irritating to the eyes and if inhaled as dust. Observe normal precautions appropriate to the circumstances and quantity of material handled. Eye protection, gloves and a dust respirator are recommended. Shellac should be handled in a well-ventilated environment.

16. Regulatory Status

Accepted as a food additive in Europe. Included in the FDA Inactive Ingredients Guide (oral capsules and tablets). Included in nonparenteral medicines licensed in the UK.

17. Pharmacopeias

Fr, Ind, Jpn, Mex and USPNF.

18. Related Substances

Aleuritic acid; pharmaceutical glaze; shellolic acid.

Aleuritic acid: $C_{16}H_{32}O_5$
Molecular weight: 304.42
CAS number: [533-87-9]

Synonyms: DL-erythro-9,10,16-trihydroxyhexadecanoic acid; 9,10,16-trihydroxypalmitic acid; 8,9,15-trihydroxypentadecane-1-carboxylic acid.
Melting point: 100-101°C
Solubility: soluble in methanol.
Comments: component of shellac.

Pharmaceutical glaze
Pharmacopeias: USPNF.
Comments: pharmaceutical glaze is a specially denatured alcoholic solution of shellac containing between 20-57% of anhydrous shellac. It may be prepared using either ethanol or ethanol (95%) and may contain waxes and titanium dioxide as an opacifying agent.

Shellolic acid: $C_{15}H_{20}O_6$
Molecular weight: 296.33
CAS number: [4448-95-7]
Synonyms: 10β,13-dihydroxycedr-8-ene-12,15-dioic acid; 2,3,4,7,8,8α-hexahydro-4-hydroxy-8-(hydroxymethyl)-8-methyl-1*H*-3α,7-methanoazulene-3,6-dicarboxylic acid.
Melting point: 204-207°C
Comments: component of shellac.

19. Comments

Since shellac is insoluble in acidic conditions but soluble at higher pH it would appear to be a suitable enteric coating material. However, in practice, delayed disintegration and drug release may occur *in vivo* since shellac is insoluble in the slightly acidic environment of the upper intestine. Additives such as lauric acid may be added to plasticize and improve disintegration of shellac films.

Studies using the USP disintegration test for enteric-coated tablets have indicated that there is a marked increase in the disintegration time, over a six-month storage period, for shellac-coated tablets.[3] It is likely that this effect is due to the polymerization of shellac which occurs over storage periods of this duration.

20. Specific References

1. Yates P, Field GF. Lac-I: the structure of shellolic acid. Tetrahedron 1970; 26: 3135-3158.
2. Yates P, Burke PM, Field GF. Lac-II: the stereochemistry of shellolic and epishellolic acids. Tetrahedron 1970; 26: 3159-3170.
3. Luce GT. Disintegration of tablets enteric coated with CAP. Mfg Chem Aerosol News 1978; 49(7): 50, 52, 67.

21. General References

Chang R-K, Iturrioz G, Luo C-W. Preparation and evaluation of shellac pseudolatex as an aqueous enteric coating system for pellets. Int J Pharmaceutics 1990; 60: 171-173.
Cockeram HS, Levine SA. The physical and chemical properties of shellac. J Soc Cosmet Chem 1961; 12: 316-323.
Labhasetwar VD, Puranik PK, Dorle AK. Study of shellac-glycerol esters as anhydrous binding agents in tablet formulations. Indian J Pharm Sci 1988; 50: 343-345.
Martin J. Shellac. In: Kirk-Othmer, editor. Encyclopedia of chemical technology, 3rd edition, volume 20. New York: Wiley-Interscience, 1982: 737-747.

22. Authors

USA: RC Vasavada.

Colloidal Silicon Dioxide

1. Nonproprietary Names

BP: Colloidal anhydrous silica
PhEur: Silica colloidalis anhydrica
USPNF: Colloidal silicon dioxide

2. Synonyms

Aerosil; *Cab-O-Sil*; colloidal silica; fumed silica; light anhydrous silicic acid; silicic anhydride; silicon dioxide fumed; *Wacker HDK*.

3. Chemical Name and CAS Registry Number

Silica [7631-86-9]

4. Empirical Formula   Molecular Weight

SiO_2 60.08

5. Structural Formula

SiO_2

6. Functional Category

Adsorbent; anticaking agent; glidant; suspending agent; tablet disintegrant; viscosity-increasing agent.

7. Applications in Pharmaceutical Formulation or Technology

Colloidal silicon dioxide is widely used in pharmaceuticals, cosmetics and food products. Its small particle size and large specific surface area give it desirable flow characteristics which are exploited to improve the flow properties of dry powders in a number of processes, e.g. tableting.[1-3]

Colloidal silicon dioxide is also used to stabilize emulsions and as a thixotropic thickening and suspending agent in gels and semisolid preparations.[4] With other ingredients of similar refractive index transparent gels may be formed. The degree of viscosity increase depends on the polarity of the liquid (polar liquids generally require a greater concentration of colloidal silicon dioxide than nonpolar liquids). Viscosity is largely independent of temperature. However, changes to the pH of a system may affect the viscosity, *see* Section 11.

In aerosols, other than those for inhalation, colloidal silicon dioxide is used to promote particulate suspension, eliminate hard settling and minimize the clogging of spray nozzles. Colloidal silicon dioxide is also used as a tablet disintegrant and as an adsorbent dispersing agent for liquids in powders or suppositories.[5]

Use	Concentration (%)
Aerosols	0.5-2
Emulsion stabilizer	1-5
Glidant	0.1-0.5
Suspending and thickening agent	2-10

8. Description

Colloidal silicon dioxide is a submicroscopic fumed silica with a particle size of about 15 nm. It is a light, loose, bluish-white colored, odorless, tasteless, nongritty amorphous powder.

SEM: 1

Excipient: Colloidal silicon dioxide (*Aerosil A-200*)
Manufacturer: Degussa
Lot No.: 87A-1 (04169C)
Magnification: 600x
Voltage: 20 kV

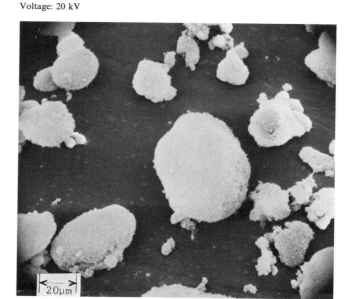

SEM: 2

Excipient: Colloidal silicon dioxide (*Aerosil A-200*)
Manufacturer: Degussa
Lot No.: 87A-1 (04169C)
Magnification: 2400x
Voltage: 20 kV

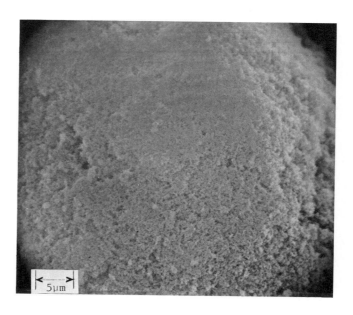

9. Pharmacopeial Specifications

Test	PhEur 1985	USPNF XVII
Identification	+	+
pH	3.5-5.5	3.5-4.4
Loss on drying	—	≤ 2.5%
Loss on ignition	≤ 5.0%	≤ 2.0%
Arsenic	—	≤ 8 ppm
Heavy metals	≤ 25 ppm	—
Chloride	≤ 250 ppm	—
Assay (on ignited sample)	99.0-100.5%	99.0-100.5%

10. Typical Properties

Acidity/alkalinity:
pH = 3.5-4.4 (4% w/v aqueous dispersion)
Density (bulk): see HPE Data.
Density (tapped): see HPE Data and Tables I-III.
Flowability: 35.52% (Carr compressibility index)
Moisture content: see HPE Data.[6]
Particle size distribution: 7-16 nm. *See also* HPE Data.
Refractive index: 1.46
Solubility: practically insoluble in organic solvents, water and acids, except hydrofluoric acid; soluble in hot solutions of alkali hydroxide. Forms a colloidal dispersion with water.
Specific gravity: 2.2
Specific surface area: 200-400 m^2/g (Stroehlein apparatus, single point); 50-380 m^2/g (BET method). *See also* Tables I-III.

Several grades of colloidal silicon dioxide are commercially available which are produced by modifying the manufacturing process. The modifications do not affect the silica content, specific gravity, refractive index, color or amorphous form. However, particle size, surface areas and densities are affected. The physical properties of three commercially available colloidal silicon dioxides, *Aerosil* (Degussa), *Cab-O-Sil* (Cabot Corporation) and *Wacker HDK* (Wacker-Chemie GmbH) are shown below in Tables I, II and III, respectively.

Table I: *Aerosil* physical properties.

Grade	Specific surface area[*] (m^2/g)	Density (tapped) (g/cm^3)
130	130 ± 25	0.05
130vs	130 ± 25	0.12
200	200 ± 25	0.05
200vs	200 ± 25	0.12
300	300 ± 30	0.05
380	380 ± 30	0.05

[*] BET method.

Table II: *Cab-O-Sil* physical properties.[7]

Grade	Specific surface area[*] (m^2/g)	Density (tapped) (g/cm^3)
LM-5	130 ± 25	0.04
LM-50	150 ± 25	0.04
M-5	200 ± 25	0.04
H-5	325 ± 25	0.04
EH-5	390 ± 40	0.04
M-7D	200 ± 25	0.10

[*] BET method.

Table III: *Wacker HDK* physical properties.[8]

Grade	Specific surface area[*] (m^2/g)	Density (tapped) (g/cm^3)
S13	125 ± 15	0.05
V15	150 ± 20	0.05
N20	200 ± 30	0.04
T30	300 ± 30	0.04
T40	400 ± 40	0.04
H15	120 ± 20	0.04
H20	170 ± 30	0.04
H30	250 ± 30	0.04
H2000	140 ± 30	0.22
H2000/4	120 ± 20	0.23
H3004	200 ± 30	0.08
H2015EP	100 ± 30	0.20
H2050EP	100 ± 30	0.20

[*] BET method.

	HPE Laboratory Project Data		
	Method	Lab #	Results
Bulk/tap density	BTD-4	1	B: 0.029 g/cm^3 [a]
			T: 0.040 g/cm^3
	BTD-7	14	B: 0.042 g/cm^3 [a]
			T: 0.069 g/cm^3
	BTD-6	8	Not measurable [b]
Moisture content	SDI-2	26	See Fig. 1 [a]
	EMC-1	2	See Fig. 2 [b]
Particle size	PSD-8	33	See Fig. 3 [a]

Supplier:
a. Degussa (*Aerosil A-200*, Lot No.: 0146 9C);
b. Cabot Corporation (*Cab-O-Sil M-5*, Lot No.: 1L 288).

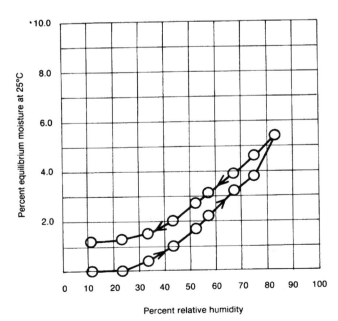

Fig. 1: Sorption-desorption isotherm of colloidal silicon dioxide (*Aerosil A-200*).

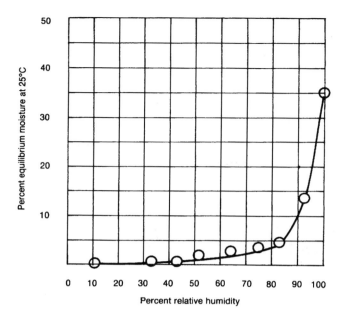

Fig. 2: Equilibrium moisture content of colloidal silicon dioxide (*Cab-O-Sil M-5*).

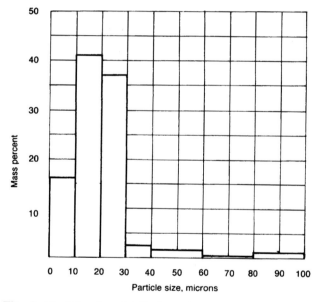

Fig. 3: Particle size distribution of colloidal silicon dioxide (*Aerosil A-200*).

11. Stability and Storage Conditions

Colloidal silicon dioxide is hygroscopic, but adsorbs large quantities of water without liquefying. When used in aqueous systems at a pH between 0-7.5 colloidal silicon dioxide is effective in increasing the viscosity of a system. However, at a pH greater than 7.5 the viscosity increasing properties of colloidal silicon dioxide are reduced and at a pH greater than 10.7 this ability is lost entirely since the silicon dioxide dissolves to form silicates.[7] Colloidal silicon dioxide powder should be stored in a well-closed container.

12. Incompatibilities

Incompatible with diethylstilbestrol preparations.[9]

13. Method of Manufacture

Colloidal silicon dioxide is prepared by the vapor hydrolysis of chlorosilanes, such as silicon tetrachloride, at 1800°C using a hydrogen-oxygen flame.

14. Safety

Colloidal silicon dioxide is widely used in oral and topical pharmaceutical products and is generally regarded as an essentially nontoxic and nonirritant excipient. However, intraperitoneal and subcutaneous injection may produce local tissue reactions and/or granulomas. Colloidal silicon dioxide should therefore not be administered parenterally.

LD_{50} (rat, IV): 15 mg/kg[10]
LD_{50} (rat, oral): 3.16 g/kg

15. Handling Precautions

Observe normal precautions appropriate to the circumstances and quantity of material handled. Eye protection and gloves are recommended. Precautions should be taken to avoid inhalation of colloidal silicon dioxide. In the absence of suitable containment facilities, a dust mask should be worn when handling small quantities of material. For larger quantities, a dust respirator is recommended.

Inhalation of colloidal silicon dioxide dust may cause irritation to the respiratory tract but it is not associated with fibrosis of the lungs (silicosis) which can occur upon exposure to crystalline silica. In the UK, the 8-hour TWA occupational exposure limits for colloidal silicon dioxide are 6 mg/m^3 for total inhalable dust and 3 mg/m^3 for respirable dust.[11]

16. Regulatory Status

GRAS listed. Included in the FDA Inactive Ingredients Guide (oral capsules, suspensions and tablets, transdermal and vaginal preparations). Included in nonparenteral medicines licensed in the UK.

17. Pharmacopeias

Aust, Br, Eur, Fr, Ger, Gr, Hung, It, Jpn, Mex, Neth, Port, Swiss and USPNF.

18. Related Substances

—

19. Comments

The incidence of microbial contamination of colloidal silicon dioxide is low.

20. Specific References

1. Lerk CF, Bolhuis GK, Smedema SS. Interaction of lubricants and colloidal silica during mixing with excipients I: its effect on tabletting. Pharm Acta Helv 1977; 52: 33-39.
2. Lerk CF, Bolhuis GK. Interaction of lubricants and colloidal silica during mixing with excipients II: its effect on wettability and dissolution velocity. Pharm Acta Helv 1977; 52: 39-44.
3. Gore AY, Banker GS. Surface chemistry of colloidal silica and a possible application to stabilize aspirin in solid matrixes. J Pharm Sci 1979; 68: 197-202.
4. Sherriff M, Enever RP. Rheological and drug release properties of oil gels containing colloidal silicon dioxide. J Pharm Sci 1979; 68: 842-845.

5. Ettlinger M, Ferch H, Mathias J. Adsorption at the surface of fumed silica [in German]. Arch Pharm 1987; 320: 1-15.

6. Callahan JC, Cleary GW, Elefant M, Kaplan G, Kensler T, Nash RA. Equilibrium moisture content of pharmaceutical excipients. Drug Dev Ind Pharm 1982; 8: 355-369.

7. Cabot Corporation. Technical literature: *Cab-O-Sil* fumed silica, properties and functions, 1990.

8. Wacker-Chemie GmbH. Technical literature: *Wacker HDK* the fumed silica, 1993.

9. Johansen H, Møller N. Solvent deposition of drugs on excipients II: interpretation of dissolution, adsorption and absorption characteristics of drugs. Arch Pharm Chemi (Sci) 1977; 5: 33-42.

10. Sweet DV, editor. Registry of toxic effects of chemical substances. Cincinnati: US Department of Health, 1987.

11. Health and Safety Executive. EH40/93: occupational exposure limits 1993. London: HMSO, 1993.

21. General References

Yang KY, Glemza R, Jarowski CI. Effects of amorphous silicon dioxides on drug dissolution. J Pharm Sci 1979; 68: 560-565.

22. Authors

USA: D Harpaz.

Sodium Alginate

1. Nonproprietary Names

BP: Sodium alginate
PhEur: Natrii alginas
USPNF: Sodium alginate

2. Synonyms

Algin; alginic acid, sodium salt; E401; *Kelcosol*; *Keltone*; *Manucol*; *Manugel*; *Pronova*; *Protanal*; *Satialgine-H8*; sodium polymannuronate.

3. Chemical Name and CAS Registry Number

Sodium alginate [9005-38-3]

4. Empirical Formula   Molecular Weight

Sodium alginate consists chiefly of the sodium salt of alginic acid, a linear glycuronan polymer consisting of a mixture of β-$(1\rightarrow4)$-D-mannosyluronic acid and α-$(1\rightarrow4)$-L-gulosyluronic acid residues.

5. Structural Formula

See Section 4.

6. Functional Category

Stabilizing agent; suspending agent; tablet and capsule disintegrant; tablet binder; viscosity-increasing agent.

7. Applications in Pharmaceutical Formulation or Technology

Sodium alginate is used in a variety of oral and topical pharmaceutical formulations. In tablet formulations, sodium alginate may be used as both a binder and disintegrant.[1] Sodium alginate has also been used in the preparation of sustained release oral formulations since it can delay the dissolution of a drug from tablets[2] and aqueous suspensions.[3]

In topical formulations, sodium alginate is widely used as a thickening and suspending agent in a variety of pastes, creams and gels, and as a stabilizing agent for oil-in-water emulsions. Recently, sodium alginate has been used for the aqueous microencapsulation of drugs,[4] in contrast with the more conventional microencapsulation techniques which use organic solvent systems.

Therapeutically, sodium alginate has been used in combination with an H_2-receptor antagonist in the management of gastroesophageal reflux,[5] and as a hemostatic agent in surgical dressings.[6]

Sodium alginate is also used in cosmetics and food products.

Use	Concentration (%)
Pastes and creams	5-10
Stabilizer in emulsions	1-3
Suspending agent	1-5
Tablet binder	1-3
Tablet disintegrant	2.5-10

8. Description

Sodium alginate occurs as an odorless and tasteless, white to pale yellowish-brown colored powder.

9. Pharmacopeial Specifications

Test	PhEur 1992	USPNF XVII
Identification	+	+
Appearance of solution	+	—
Microbial limits	$\leqslant 1000/g$	$\leqslant 200/g$
Loss on drying	$\leqslant 15.0\%$	$\leqslant 15.0\%$
Ash	—	18.0-24.0%
Sulfated ash	30.0-36.0%	—
Arsenic	—	$\leqslant 1.5$ ppm
Calcium	$\leqslant 1.5\%$	—
Chlorides	$\leqslant 1.0\%$	—
Lead	—	$\leqslant 0.001\%$
Heavy metals	$\leqslant 20$ ppm	$\leqslant 0.004\%$
Assay (dried basis)	—	90.8-106.0%

10. Typical Properties

Acidity/alkalinity:
pH $\approx$ 7.2 for a 1% w/v aqueous solution.
Solubility: practically insoluble in ethanol, ether and ethanol/water mixtures in which the ethanol content is greater than 30%. Also, practically insoluble in other organic solvents and acids, in which the pH of the resultant solution is less than pH 3. Slowly soluble in water, forming a viscous colloidal solution.
Viscosity (dynamic): various grades of sodium alginate are commercially available which yield aqueous solutions of varying viscosity. Typically, a 1% w/v aqueous solution, at 20°C, will have a viscosity of 20-400 mPa s (20-400 cP). Viscosity may vary depending upon concentration, pH, temperature or the presence of metal ions. Above pH 10, viscosity decreases, *see also* Alginic Acid and Section 11.

HPE Laboratory Project Data		
Method	Lab #	Results
Viscosity (2% w/v aqueous solution)		
VIS-3	28	2.16 Pa s [a]
VIS-3	28	2.05 Pa s [a]
VIS-3	28	2.00 Pa s [b]
VIS-3	28	3.04 Pa s [b]
Viscosity (3% w/v aqueous solution)		
VIS-3	28	9.85 Pa s [b]
VIS-3	28	8.35 Pa s [b]
VIS-3	28	8.64 Pa s [b]
VIS-3	28	7.20 Pa s [b]

Supplier: a. Edward Mendell Co Inc; b. Algum.

11. Stability and Storage Conditions

Sodium alginate is a hygroscopic material although it is stable if stored at low relative humidities and a cool temperature.

Aqueous solutions of sodium alginate are most stable between pH 4-10; below pH 3, alginic acid is precipitated. A 1% w/v aqueous solution of sodium alginate exposed to differing temperatures had a viscosity 60-80% its original value after storage for two years.[7] Solutions should not be stored in metal containers.

Sodium alginate solutions are susceptible on storage to microbial spoilage which may affect solution viscosity. Solutions are ideally sterilized using ethylene oxide, although filtration using a 0.45 μm filter also has only a slight adverse effect on solution viscosity.[8] Autoclaving of solutions can cause a decrease in viscosity which may vary depending upon the nature of any other substances present.[8,9] Gamma irradiation should not be used to sterilize sodium alginate solutions since this process severely reduces solution viscosity.[8,10]

Preparations for external use may be preserved by the addition of 0.1% chlorocresol, 0.1% chloroxylenol or parabens. If the medium is acidic, benzoic acid may also be used.

The bulk material should be stored in an airtight container in a cool, dry, place.

12. Incompatibilities

Sodium alginate is incompatible with acridine derivatives, crystal violet, phenylmercuric acetate and nitrate, calcium salts, heavy metals and ethanol in concentrations greater than 5%. High concentrations of electrolytes cause an increase in viscosity until salting-out of sodium alginate occurs; salting-out occurs if more than 4% of sodium chloride is present.

13. Method of Manufacture

Alginic acid is extracted from brown seaweed and neutralized with sodium bicarbonate to form sodium alginate.

14. Safety

Sodium alginate is widely used in cosmetics, food products and pharmaceutical formulations, such as tablets and topical products, including wound dressings. It is generally regarded as a nontoxic and nonirritant material although excessive oral consumption may be harmful. A study in five healthy male volunteers fed a daily intake of 175 mg/kg body-weight of sodium alginate for 7 days, followed by a daily intake of 200 mg/kg body-weight of sodium alginate for a further 16 days, showed no significant adverse effects.[11]

The WHO has set an estimated acceptable daily intake of alginate salts and alginic acid, used as food additives, at up to 25 mg/kg body-weight, calculated as alginic acid.[12]

Inhalation of alginate dust may be irritant and has been associated with industrially related asthma in workers involved in alginate production. However, it appears that the cases of asthma were linked to exposure to seaweed dust rather than pure alginate dust.[13]

LD_{50} (cat, IP): 0.25 g/kg[14]
LD_{50} (rabbit, IV): 0.1 g/kg
LD_{50} (rat, IV): 1 g/kg
LD_{50} (rat, oral): > 5 g/kg

15. Handling Precautions

Observe normal precautions appropriate to the circumstances and quantity of material handled. Sodium alginate may be irritant to the eyes or respiratory system if inhaled as dust, *see* Section 14. Eye protection, gloves and a dust respirator are recommended. Sodium alginate should be handled in a well-ventilated environment.

16. Regulatory Status

GRAS listed. Accepted in Europe for use as a food additive. Included in the FDA Inactive Ingredients Guide (oral suspensions and tablets). Included in nonparenteral medicines licensed in the UK.

17. Pharmacopeias

Aust, Br, Eur, Fr, Ger, It, Mex, Neth, Swiss and USPNF.

18. Related Substances

Alginic Acid; calcium alginate; potassium alginate; Propylene Glycol Alginate.

Calcium alginate
CAS number: [9005-35-0]
Synonyms: alginic acid, calcium salt; calcium polymannuronate; calginate; E404.
Comments: calcium alginate is used in applications similarly to sodium alginate, such as in sustained release formulations[15] and hemostatic wound dressings which can be washed off with sterile sodium chloride solution.[6]

Potassium alginate
CAS number: [9005-36-1]
Synonyms: alginic acid, potassium salt; E402; potassium polymannuronate.

19. Comments

A number of different grades of sodium alginate, which have different solution viscosities, are commercially available. Many different alginate salts and derivatives are also commercially available including: ammonium alginate; calcium alginate; magnesium alginate and potassium alginate.

See also Alginic Acid for further information.

20. Specific References

1. Sakr AM, Elsabbagh HM, Shalaby AH. Effect of the technique of incorporating sodium alginate on its binding and/or disintegrating effectiveness in sulfathiazole tablets. Pharm Ind 1978; 40(10): 1080-1086.
2. Klaudianos S. Alginate sustained-action tablets [in German]. Dtsch Apoth Ztg 1978; 118: 683-684.
3. Zatz JL, Woodford DW. Prolonged release of theophylline from aqueous suspensions. Drug Dev Ind Pharm 1987; 13: 2159-2178.
4. Bodmeier R, Wang J. Microencapsulation of drugs with aqueous colloidal polymer dispersions. J Pharm Sci 1993; 82: 191-194.
5. Stanciu C, Bennett JR. Alginate/antacid in the reduction of gastro-oesophageal reflux. Lancet 1974; i: 109-111.
6. Thomas S. Wound management and dressings. London: The Pharmaceutical Press, 1990: 43-49.
7. Pávics L. Comparison of rheological properties of mucilages [in Hungarian]. Acta Pharm Hung 1970; 40: 52-59.
8. Coates D, Richardson G. A note on the production of sterile solutions of sodium alginate. Can J Pharm Sci 1974; 9: 60-61.
9. Vandenbossche GMR, Remon J-P. Influence of the sterilization process on alginate dispersions. J Pharm Pharmacol 1993; 45: 484-486.
10. Hartman AW, Nesbitt RU, Smith FM, Nuessle NO. Viscosities of acacia and sodium alginate after sterilization by cobalt-60. J Pharm Sci 1975; 64: 802-805.
11. Anderson DM, Brydon WG, Eastwood MA, Sedgwick DM. Dietary effects of sodium alginate in humans. Food Add Contam 1991; 8(3): 237-248.
12. FAO/WHO. Toxicological evaluation of certain food additives with a review of general principles and of specifications. Seventeenth report of the joint FAO/WHO expert committee on food additives. Tech Rep Ser Wld Hlth Org 1974; No. 539.
13. Henderson AK, et al. Pulmonary hypersensitivity in the alginate industry. Scott Med J 1984; 29(2): 90-95.
14. Sweet DV, editor. Registry of toxic effects of chemical substances. Cincinnati: US Department of Health, 1987.
15. Badwan AA, et al. Sustained-release drug delivery system using calcium alginate beads. Drug Dev Ind Pharm 1985; 11: 239-256.

21. General References

—

22. Authors

UK: PJ Weller.

Sodium Ascorbate

1. Nonproprietary Names
USP: Sodium ascorbate

2. Synonyms
L-Ascorbic acid monosodium salt; E301; 3-oxo-L-gulofurano-lactone sodium enolate; *SA-99*; vitamin C sodium.

3. Chemical Name and CAS Registry Number
Monosodium L-(+)-ascorbate [134-03-2]

4. Empirical Formula   Molecular Weight
$C_6H_7NaO_6$ 198.11

5. Structural Formula

CH₂OH
|
HOCH
|
NaO   OH
O

6. Functional Category
Antioxidant; therapeutic agent.

7. Applications in Pharmaceutical Formulation or Technology
Sodium ascorbate is used as an antioxidant in pharmaceutical formulations and food products. It is also used therapeutically as a source of vitamin C in tablets and parenteral preparations.

8. Description
Sodium ascorbate occurs as a white or slightly yellow-colored, practically odorless, crystalline powder with a pleasant saline taste.

9. Pharmacopeial Specifications

Test	USP XXII
Identification	+
Specific rotation (10% w/v aqueous solution)	+103° to +108°
pH (10% solution)	7.0-8.0
Loss on drying	≤ 0.25%
Heavy metals	≤ 0.002%
Assay (dried basis)	99.0-101.0%

10. Typical Properties
Acidity/alkalinity:
pH = 7-8 (10% w/v aqueous solution).
Density (tapped):
0.6-1.1 g/cm³ for fine powder;
0.8-1.1 g/cm³ for fine granular grade.
Hygroscopicity: not hygroscopic. Sodium ascorbate adsorbs practically no water up to 80% relative humidity at 20°C and less than 1% w/w of water at 90% relative humidity.

SEM: 1
Excipient: Sodium ascorbate USP
Manufacturer: Pfizer Ltd
Lot No.: 9B-1 (C92220-C4025)
Magnification: 120x
Voltage: 20 kV

100μm

SEM: 2
Excipient: Sodium ascorbate USP
Manufacturer: Pfizer Ltd
Lot No.: 9B-1 (C92220-C4025)
Magnification: 600x
Voltage: 20 kV

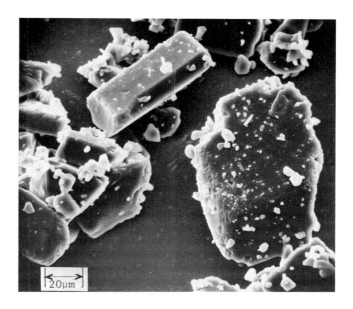

20μm

Melting point: 218°C (with decomposition)
Particle size distribution: various grades of sodium ascorbate with different particle size distributions are commercially available, e.g. approximately 98% passes through a 149 μm mesh for a fine powder grade (Takeda Europe GmbH), and approximately 95% passes through a 840 μm mesh for a standard grade (Takeda Europe GmbH).
Solubility:

Solvent	Solubility at 20°C Unless otherwise stated
Chloroform	practically insoluble
Ethanol (95%)	very slightly soluble
Ether	practically insoluble
Water	1 in 1.6
	1 in 1.3 at 75°C

Specific gravity:
1.782 for powder at 20°C;
1.005 for 1% w/v aqueous solution at 25°C;
1.026 for 5% w/v aqueous solution at 25°C.
Specific rotation $[\alpha]_D^{20}$:
+104.4°(10% w/v aqueous solution).

11. Stability and Storage Conditions

Sodium ascorbate is relatively stable in air although it gradually darkens on exposure to light. Aqueous solutions are unstable and subject to rapid oxidation in air at pH > 6.0. The bulk material should be stored in a well-closed nonmetallic container, protected from light, in a cool, dry, place.

12. Incompatibilities

Incompatible with oxidizing agents, heavy metal ions, especially copper and iron, methenamine, sodium nitrite, sodium salicylate and theobromine salicylate.

13. Method of Manufacture

An equivalent amount of sodium bicarbonate is added to a solution of ascorbic acid in water. Following the cessation of effervescence, the addition of propan-2-ol precipitates sodium ascorbate.

14. Safety

The parenteral administration of between 0.25-1.0 g of sodium ascorbate, given daily in divided doses, is recommended in the treatment of vitamin C deficiencies.
Various adverse reactions have been reported following the administration of 1 g or more of sodium ascorbate although ascorbic acid and sodium ascorbate are usually well tolerated, *see* Ascorbic Acid. There have been no reports of adverse effects associated with the much lower concentrations of sodium ascorbate and ascorbic acid that are employed as antioxidants.
The WHO has set an acceptable daily intake of ascorbic acid, potassium ascorbate and sodium ascorbate, as antioxidants in food, at up to 15 mg/kg body-weight in addition to that naturally present in food.[1]

15. Handling Precautions

Observe normal precautions appropriate to the circumstances and quantity of material handled. Sodium ascorbate may be irritant to the eyes. Eye protection and rubber or plastic gloves are recommended.

16. Regulatory Status

GRAS listed. Accepted for use as a food additive in Europe. Included in the FDA Inactive Ingredients Guide (IV preparations). Included in nonparenteral and parenteral medicines licensed in the UK.

17. Pharmacopeias

Fr, Ind and US.

18. Related Substances

Ascorbic Acid; Ascorbyl Palmitate; calcium ascorbate.

Calcium ascorbate: $C_{12}H_{14}O_{12}Ca$

Molecular weight: 390.31
CAS number: [5743-27-1]
Synonyms: calcium L-(+)-ascorbate; *CCal-97*; E302.

19. Comments

1 mg of sodium ascorbate is equivalent to 0.8890 mg of ascorbic acid (1 mg of ascorbic acid is equivalent to 1.1248 mg of sodium ascorbate).
1 g of sodium ascorbate contains approximately 5 mmol of sodium.

20. Specific References

1. FAO/WHO. Toxicological evaluation of certain food additives with a review of general principles and of specifications. Seventeenth report of the FAO/WHO expert committee on food additives. Tech Rep Ser Wld Hlth Org 1974; No. 539.

21. General References

Buck GW, Wolfe KR. Interaction of sodium ascorbate with stainless steel particulate filter needles [letter]. Am J Hosp Pharm 1991; 48: 1191.
Dahl GB, Jeppsson RI, Tengborn HJ. Vitamin stability in a TPN mixture stored in an EVA plastic bag. J Clin Hosp Pharm 1986; 11: 271-279.
DeRitter E, Magid L, Osadca M, Rubin SH. Effect of silica gel on stability and biological availability of ascorbic acid. J Pharm Sci 1970; 59: 229-232.
Dettman IC. Sterilization of ascorbates by heat and absolute ethanol. US Patent 4816223. 1989.
Iida S, Kita K, Ootsuki H. Stable ascorbic acid solutions. Japanese Patent 61130205. 1986.
Kitamori N, Hemmi K, Maeno M, Mima H. Direct compression of chewable vitamin C tablets. Pharmaceut Technol 1982; 6(10): 56-64.
Pfeifer HJ, Webb JW. Compatibility of penicillin and ascorbic acid injection. Am J Hosp Pharm 1976; 33: 448-450.
Sekine K, Araki D, Suzuki Y. Powdery pharmaceutical compositions containing ascorbic acids for intranasal administration. Japanese Patent 63115820. 1988.
Thielemann AM, Arata R, Morasso MI, Arancibia A. Biopharmaceutical study of a vitamin C controlled-release formulation. Farmaco (Prat) 1988; 43: 387-395.

22. Authors

USA: N Mugharbel.

Sodium Benzoate

1. Nonproprietary Names

BP: Sodium benzoate
PhEur: Natrii benzoas
USPNF: Sodium benzoate

2. Synonyms

Benzoate of soda; benzoic acid sodium salt; E211.

3. Chemical Name and CAS Registry Number

Sodium benzoate [532-32-1]

4. Empirical Formula   Molecular Weight

$C_7H_5NaO_2$ 144.11

5. Structural Formula

6. Functional Category

Antimicrobial preservative; tablet and capsule lubricant.

7. Applications in Pharmaceutical Formulation or Technology

Sodium benzoate is used primarily as an antimicrobial preservative in cosmetics, foods and pharmaceuticals. It is used in concentrations of 0.02-0.5% in oral medicines, 0.5% in parenteral products and 0.1-0.5% in cosmetics. The usefulness of sodium benzoate as a preservative is limited by its effectiveness over a narrow pH range, *see* Section 10.
Sodium benzoate is used in some circumstances, in preference to benzoic acid, due to its greater solubility. However, in some applications it may impart an unpleasant flavor to a product. Sodium benzoate has also been used as a tablet lubricant,[1] at 2-5% concentration and clinically, solutions of sodium benzoate, administered either orally or by intravenous injection, have been used to determine liver function.

8. Description

Sodium benzoate occurs as a white granular or crystalline, slightly hygroscopic powder. It is odorless, or with faint odor of benzoin and has an unpleasant sweet, and saline taste.

9. Pharmacopeial Specifications

Test	PhEur 1981	USPNF XVII
Identification	+	+
Water	⩽ 2.0%	⩽ 1.5%
Heavy metals	⩽ 10 ppm	⩽ 0.001%
Arsenic	—	⩽ 3 ppm
Chloride	⩽ 200 ppm	—
Total Chlorine	⩽ 300 ppm	—
Alkalinity	—	+

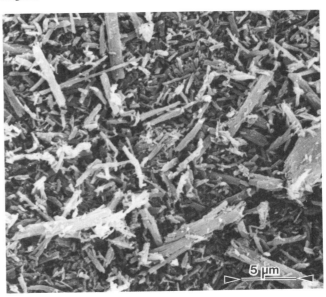

Continued

Test	PhEur 1981	USPNF XVII
Acidity or alkalinity	+	—
Appearance of solution	+	—
Assay (dried basis)	99.0-100.5%	99.0-100.5%

10. Typical Properties

Acidity/alkalinity:
pH = 8.0 (saturated aqueous solution at 25°C)
Antimicrobial activity: sodium benzoate has both bacteriostatic and antifungal properties attributed to undissociated benzoic acid, hence preservative efficacy is best seen in acidic solutions (pH 2-5). In alkaline conditions it is almost without effect.
Density: 1.15 g/cm^3 at 24°C
Freezing point depression: 0.24°C (1.0% w/v)
Osmolarity: a 2.25% w/v aqueous solution is iso-osmotic with serum.
Partition coefficients: Vegetable oil: water = 3-6
Solubility:

Solvent	Solubility at 25°C Unless otherwise stated
Ethanol (95%)	1 in 75
Ethanol (90%)	1 in 50
Water	1 in 1.8
	1 in 1.4 at 100°C

11. Stability and Storage Conditions

Aqueous solutions may be sterilized by autoclaving or filtration.
The bulk material should be stored in a well-closed container, in a cool, dry, place.

12. Incompatibilities

Incompatible with quaternary compounds, gelatin, ferric salts, calcium salts and salts of heavy metals, including silver, lead and mercury. Preservative activity may be reduced by interactions with kaolin[2] or nonionic surfactants.

13. Method of Manufacture

Prepared by the treatment of benzoic acid with either sodium carbonate or sodium bicarbonate.

14. Safety

Ingested sodium benzoate is conjugated with glycine in the liver to yield hippuric acid, which is excreted in the urine. Symptoms of systemic toxicity to benzoates resemble those of salicylates.[3] Whereas oral administration of the free acid form may cause severe gastric irritation, benzoate salts are well tolerated in large quantities, e.g. 6 g of sodium benzoate in 200 mL of water is administered orally as a liver function test. Adverse reactions to sodium benzoate, as an excipient, include anaphylaxis[4] and urticarial reactions[5,6] although a controlled study has shown that the incidence of urticaria in patients given benzoic acid is no greater than a lactose placebo.[7]
It has been recommended that caffeine and sodium benzoate injection should not be used in neonates,[8] however sodium benzoate has been used by others in the treatment of some neonatal metabolic disorders.[9]
The WHO acceptable daily intake of total benzoates, calculated as benzoic acid, has been estimated at up to 5 mg/kg of body-weight.[10,11]
LD$_{50}$ (rat, IV): 1.7 g/kg[12]
LD$_{50}$ (rat, oral): 4.1 g/kg
See also Benzoic Acid.

15. Handling Precautions

Observe normal precautions appropriate to the circumstances and quantity of material handled. Sodium benzoate may be irritant to the eyes and skin. Eye protection and rubber or plastic gloves are recommended.

16. Regulatory Status

GRAS listed. Accepted as a food additive in Europe. Included in the FDA Inactive Ingredients Guide (dental preparations, IM and IV injections, oral capsules, solutions and tablets, rectal and topical preparations). Included in nonparenteral medicines licensed in the UK.

17. Pharmacopeias

Aust, Belg, Br, Braz, Chin, Cz, Egypt, Eur, Fr, Gr, Hung, Ind, It, Jpn, Mex, Neth, Nord, Port, Rom, Rus, Swiss, Turk, USPNF and Yug.

18. Related Substances

Benzoic Acid; potassium benzoate.

Potassium benzoate: $C_7H_5KO_2$
Molecular weight: 160.21
CAS number: [582-25-2]
Synonyms: benzoic acid, potassium salt; E212.
Pharmacopeias: USPNF.
Solubility: 1 in 75 of ethanol (95%) and 1 in 50 ethanol (90%); 1 in 2 of water.
Comments: has been used as a tablet lubricant.

19. Comments

—

20. Specific References

1. Saleh SI, Wehrlé P, Stamm A. Improvement of lubrication capacity of sodium benzoate: effects of milling and spray drying. Int J Pharmaceutics 1988; 48: 149-157.
2. Clarke CD, Armstrong NA. Influence of pH on the adsorption of benzoic acid by kaolin. Pharm J 1972; 209: 44-45.
3. Michils A, Vandermoten G, Duchateau J, Yernault J-C. Anaphylaxis with sodium benzoate [letter]. Lancet 1991; 337: 1424-1425.
4. Rosenhall L. Evaluation of intolerance to analgesics, preservatives and food colorants with challenge tests. Eur J Respir Dis 1982; 63: 410-419.
5. Michaëlsson G, Juhlin L. Urticaria induced by preservatives and dye additives in food and drugs. Br J Dermatol 1973; 88: 525-532.
6. Warin RP, Smith RJ. Challenge test battery in chronic urticaria. Br J Dermatol 1976; 94: 401-406.
7. Lahti A, Hannuksela M. Is benzoic acid really harmful in cases of atopy and urticaria? Lancet 1981; ii: 1055.
8. Edwards RC, Voegeli CJ. Inadvisability of using caffeine and sodium benzoate in neonates. Am J Hosp Pharm 1984; 41: 658.
9. Brusilow SW, et al. Treatment of episodic hyperammonemia in children with inborn errors of urea synthesis. N Eng J Med 1984; 310: 1630-1634.
10. FAO/WHO. Toxicological evaluation of certain food additives with a review of general principles and of specifications. Seventeenth report of the joint FAO/WHO expert committee on food additives. Tech Rep Ser Wld Hlth Org 1974; No. 539.
11. FAO/WHO. Evaluation of certain food additives and contaminants. Twenty-seventh report of the joint FAO/WHO expert committee on food additives. Tech Rep Ser Wld Hlth Org 1983; No. 696.

12. Sweet DV, editor. Registry of toxic effects of chemical substances. Cincinnati: US Department of Health, 1987.

21. General References

Denyer S, Baird R. Guide to microbiological control in pharmaceuticals. New York: Ellis Horwood, 1990: 251-273.

Grayson M, editor. Encyclopedia of chemical technology, 3rd edition, volume 3. New York: John Wiley and Sons, 1978: 778-792.

Nishijo J, Yonetani I. Interaction of theobromine with sodium benzoate. J Pharm Sci 1982; 71: 354-356.

22. Authors

UK: MC Allwood.

Sodium Bicarbonate

1. Nonproprietary Names

BP: Sodium bicarbonate
PhEur: Natrii hydrogenocarbonas
USP: Sodium bicarbonate

2. Synonyms

Baking soda; E500; monosodium carbonate; sodium acid carbonate; sodium hydrogen carbonate.

3. Chemical Name and CAS Registry Number

Carbonic acid monosodium salt [144-55-8]

4. Empirical Formula   Molecular Weight

$NaHCO_3$ 84.01

5. Structural Formula

$NaHCO_3$

6. Functional Category

Alkalizing agent; therapeutic agent.

7. Applications in Pharmaceutical Formulation or Technology

Sodium bicarbonate is generally used in pharmaceutical formulations as a source of carbon dioxide in effervescent tablets and granules. It is also widely used to produce or maintain an alkaline pH in a preparation.

In effervescent tablets and granules, sodium bicarbonate is usually formulated with either citric or tartaric acid;[1] when the tablets or granules come into contact with water a chemical reaction occurs, carbon dioxide is evolved and the product disintegrates.[2,3] Tablets may also be prepared with sodium bicarbonate alone since the acid of gastric fluid is sufficient to cause effervescence and disintegration. Sodium bicarbonate is also used in tablet formulations to buffer drug molecules that are weak acids, thereby increasing the rate of tablet dissolution and reducing gastric irritation.[4-6]

Additionally, sodium bicarbonate is used in solutions as a buffering agent.[7] In some parenteral formulations, e.g. niacin, sodium bicarbonate is used to produce a sodium salt of the active ingredient which has enhanced solubility.

Therapeutically, sodium bicarbonate may be used as an antacid, and as a source of the bicarbonate anion in the treatment of metabolic acidosis. Sodium bicarbonate may also be used as a component of oral rehydration salts.

Sodium bicarbonate is used in food products as an alkali or as a leavening agent, e.g. baking soda.

Use	Concentration (%)
Buffer in tablets	10-40
Effervescent tablets	25-50
Isotonic injection/infusion	1.39

8. Description

Sodium bicarbonate occurs as an odorless, white crystalline powder with a saline, slightly alkaline taste. The crystal structure is monoclinic prisms. Grades with different particle sizes, from a fine powder to free flowing uniform granules, are commercially available.

SEM: 1

Excipient: Sodium bicarbonate
Manufacturer: Merck Ltd
Magnification: 120x

SEM: 2

Excipient: Sodium bicarbonate
Manufacturer: Merck Ltd
Magnification: 600x

9. Pharmacopeial Specifications

Test	PhEur 1983	USP XXII
Identification	+	+
Loss on drying	—	⩽ 0.25%
Insoluble substances	—	+
Clarity and color of solution	+	—
Carbonate	+	⩽ 0.23%
Normal carbonate	—	+
Chloride	⩽ 150 ppm	⩽ 0.015%
Sulfate	⩽ 150 ppm	⩽ 0.015%
Ammonia	—	+
Ammonium	⩽ 20 ppm	—
Aluminum	—	⩽ 2 ppm
Arsenic	⩽ 2 ppm	⩽ 2 ppm
Calcium	⩽ 100 ppm	⩽ 0.01%
Magnesium	—	⩽ 0.004%
Copper	—	⩽ 1 ppm
Iron	⩽ 20 ppm	⩽ 5 ppm
Heavy metals	⩽ 10 ppm	⩽ 5 ppm
Organics	—	⩽ 0.01%
Assay (dried basis)	99.0-101.0%	99.0-100.5%

10. Typical Properties

Acidity/alkalinity: pH = 8.3 for a freshly prepared 0.1M aqueous solution at 25°C.

Density: 2.159 g/cm^3

Freezing point depression: 0.381°C (1% w/v solution).

Hygroscopicity: below 80% relative humidity, the moisture content is less than 1% w/w. Above 85% relative humidity, sodium bicarbonate rapidly absorbs excessive amounts of water and may start to decompose with loss of carbon dioxide.

Melting point: 270°C (with decomposition).

Osmolarity: a 1.39% w/v aqueous solution is iso-osmotic with serum.

Refractive index:
n_D^{20} = 1.3344 (1% w/v aqueous solution).

Solubility:

Solvent	Solubility at 20°C Unless otherwise stated
Ethanol (95%)	practically insoluble
Ether	practically insoluble
Water	1 in 11
	1 in 4 at 100°C*

* Note that in hot water, sodium bicarbonate is converted into the carbonate.

11. Stability and Storage Conditions

When heated to about 50°C, sodium bicarbonate begins to dissociate into carbon dioxide, sodium carbonate and water; on heating to 250-300°C, for a short while, sodium bicarbonate is completely converted into anhydrous sodium carbonate. However, the process is both time and temperature dependent with conversion 90% complete within 75 minutes at 93°C. The reaction proceeds via surface controlled kinetics; when sodium bicarbonate crystals are heated for a short period of time, very fine needle shaped crystals of anhydrous sodium carbonate are formed on the sodium bicarbonate surface.[8]

At ambient temperatures, aqueous solutions slowly decompose with partial conversion into the carbonate; the decomposition is accelerated by agitation or heat.

Aqueous solutions of sodium bicarbonate may be sterilized by filtration or autoclaving. To minimise decomposition of sodium bicarbonate by decarboxylation on autoclaving, carbon dioxide is passed through the solution in its final container which is then hermetically sealed and autoclaved. The sealed container should not be opened for at least two hours after it has returned to ambient temperature to allow time for the complete reformation of the bicarbonate from the carbonate produced during the heating process.

Aqueous solutions of sodium bicarbonate stored in glass containers may develop deposits of small glass particles. Sediments of calcium carbonate with traces of magnesium or other metal carbonates have been found in injections sterilized by autoclaving; this is due to impurities in the bicarbonate or to extraction of calcium and magnesium ions from the glass container. Sedimentation may be retarded by the inclusion of 0.01-0.02% disodium edetate.[9-11]

Sodium bicarbonate is stable in dry air but slowly decomposes in moist air and should therefore be stored in a well-closed container in a cool, dry, place.

12. Incompatibilities

Sodium bicarbonate reacts with acids, acidic salts and many alkaloidal salts, with the evolution of carbon dioxide. Sodium bicarbonate can also intensify the darkening of salicylates.

In powder mixtures, atmospheric moisture or water of crystallization from another ingredient is sufficient for sodium bicarbonate to react with compounds such as boric acid or alum. In liquid mixtures containing bismuth subnitrate, sodium bicarbonate reacts with the acid formed by hydrolysis of the bismuth salt.

13. Method of Manufacture

Sodium bicarbonate is manufactured either by passing carbon dioxide into a cold saturated solution of sodium carbonate, or by the ammonia-soda (Solvay) process, where first ammonia and then carbon dioxide is passed into a sodium chloride solution to precipitate sodium bicarbonate while the more soluble ammonium chloride remains in solution.

14. Safety

Sodium bicarbonate is used in a number of pharmaceutical formulations including injections, ophthalmic, otic, topical and oral preparations.

Sodium bicarbonate is metabolized to the sodium cation, which is eliminated from the body by renal excretion, and the bicarbonate anion which becomes part of the body's bicarbonate store. Any carbon dioxide formed is eliminated via the lungs. Administration of excessive amounts of sodium bicarbonate may thus disturb the body's electrolyte balance leading to metabolic alkalosis or possibly sodium overload with potentially serious consequences. The amount of sodium present in antacids and effervescent formulations has been sufficient to exacerbate chronic heart failure, especially in elderly patients.[12]

Orally ingested sodium bicarbonate neutralizes gastric acid with the evolution of carbon dioxide and may cause stomach cramps and flatulence.

When used as an excipient, sodium bicarbonate is generally regarded as an essentially nontoxic and nonirritant material. LD$_{50}$ (rat, oral): 4.22 g/kg[13]

15. Handling Precautions

Observe normal precautions appropriate to the circumstances and quantity of material handled. Eye protection and gloves are recommended.

16. Regulatory Status

GRAS listed. Accepted for use as a food additive in Europe. Included in the FDA Inactive Ingredients Guide (injections, ophthalmic preparations, oral capsules, solutions and tablets). Included in parenteral and nonparenteral medicines licensed in the UK.

17. Pharmacopeias

Aust, Belg, Br, Braz, Chin, Cz, Egypt, Eur, Fr, Ger, Gr, Hung, Ind, Int, It, Jpn, Mex, Neth, Nord, Port, Rom, Rus, Swiss, Turk, US and Yug. Also in BP Vet.

18. Related Substances

Potassium bicarbonate.

Potassium bicarbonate: $KHCO_3$
Molecular weight: 100.11
CAS number: [298-14-6]
Synonyms: E501; kalii hydrogencarbonas; monopotassium carbonate; potassium hydrogen carbonate.
Appearance: colorless, odorless, transparent prisms or white granular powder.
Pharmacopeias: Belg, Braz, Ger, Gr, Mex, Nord, Swiss and US.
Acidity/alkalinity: pH = 8.2 for a 0.1M aqueous solution.
Solubility: soluble 1 in 2.8 of water at 20°C, 1 in 2 of water at 50°C; practically insoluble in ethanol (95%).
Comments: used in applications as an alternative to sodium bicarbonate and as a potassium supplement.

19. Comments

Each gram of sodium bicarbonate represents approximately 11.9 mmol of sodium and of bicarbonate. Each gram of sodium bicarbonate will neutralize 12 mEq of gastric acid in 60 minutes.
The yield of carbon dioxide from sodium bicarbonate is approximately 52% by weight.
It requires 3 molecules of sodium bicarbonate to neutralize 1 molecule of citric acid, and 2 molecules of sodium bicarbonate to neutralize 1 molecule of tartaric acid.

20. Specific References

1. Usui F, Carstensen JT. Interactions in the solid state I: interactions of sodium bicarbonate and tartaric acid under compressed conditions. J Pharm Sci 1985; 74: 1293-1297.
2. Anderson NR, Banker GS, Peck GE. Quantitative evaluation of pharmaceutical effervescent systems I: design of testing apparatus. J Pharm Sci 1982; 71: 3-6.
3. Anderson NR, Banker GS, Peck GE. Quantitative evaluation of pharmaceutical effervescent systems II: stability monitoring by reactivity and porosity measurements. J Pharm Sci 1982; 71: 7-13.
4. Javaid KA, Cadwallader DE. Dissolution of aspirin from tablets containing various buffering agents. J Pharm Sci 1972; 61: 1370-1373.
5. Rainsford KD. Gastric mucosal ulceration induced in pigs by tablets but not suspensions or solutions of aspirin. J Pharm Pharmacol 1978; 30: 129-131.
6. Mason WD, Winer N. Kinetics of aspirin, salicylic acid and salicyluric acid following oral administration of aspirin as a tablet and two buffered solutions. J Pharm Sci 1981; 70: 262-265.
7. Allwood MC. The influence of buffering on the stability of erythromycin injection in small-volume infusions. Int J Pharmaceutics 1992; 80: R7-R9.
8. Shefter E, Lo A, Ramalingam S. A kinetic study of the solid state transformation of sodium bicarbonate to sodium carbonate. Drug Dev Comm 1974; 1: 29-38.
9. Hadgraft JW, Hewer BD. Molar injection of sodium bicarbonate [letter]. Pharm J 1964; 192: 544.
10. Hadgraft JW. Unsatisfactory infusions of sodium bicarbonate [letter]. Lancet 1966; i: 603.
11. Smith G. Unsatisfactory infusions of sodium bicarbonate [letter]. Lancet 1966; i: 658.
12. Panchmatia K, Jolobe OM. Contra-indications of Solpadol [letter]. Pharm J 1993; 251: 73.
13. Sweet DV, editor. Registry of toxic effects of chemical substances. Cincinnati: US Department of Health, 1987.

21. General References

Hannula A-M, Marvola M, Aho E. Release of ibuprofen from hard gelatin capsule formulations: effect of sodium bicarbonate as a disintegrant. Acta Pharm Fenn 1989; 98: 131-134.
Sendall FEJ, Staniforth JN, Rees JE, Leatham MJ. Effervescent tablets. Pharm J 1983; 230: 289-294.
Travers DN, White RC. The mixing of micronized sodium bicarbonate with sucrose crystals. J Pharm Pharmacol 1971; 23: 260S-261S.

22. Authors

UK: CG Cable, PJ Weller.

Sodium Chloride

1. Nonproprietary Names

BP: Sodium chloride
PhEur: Natrii chloridum
USP: Sodium chloride

2. Synonyms

Common salt; natural halite; rock salt; salt; sea salt; table salt.

3. Chemical Name and CAS Registry Number

Sodium chloride [7647-14-5]

4. Empirical Formula   Molecular Weight

NaCl   58.44

5. Structural Formula

NaCl

6. Functional Category

Tablet and capsule diluent; tonicity agent.

7. Applications in Pharmaceutical Formulation or Technology

Sodium chloride is widely used in a variety of parenteral and nonparenteral pharmaceutical formulations. Its primary use, in parenteral and ophthalmic preparations, is to produce isotonic solutions.

In capsules and direct compression tablet formulations, sodium chloride is used as a lubricant and diluent.[1-4] Sodium chloride is additionally used to control drug release from microcapsules.[5] It may also be used to control micelle size,[6-8] and to adjust the viscosity of polymer dispersions by altering the ionic character of a formulation.[9,10]

Use	Concentration (%)
Capsule diluent	10-80
Controlled flocculation of suspensions	up to 1
Direct compression tablet diluent	10-80
To produce isotonic solutions in intravenous or ophthalmic preparations	up to 0.9
Water-soluble tablet lubricant	5

8. Description

Sodium chloride occurs as a white crystalline powder or colorless crystals; it has a saline taste. The crystal lattice is a face centered cubic structure.

SEM: 1

Excipient: Sodium chloride, powder
Manufacturer: Mallinckrodt Speciality Chemicals Co
Magnification: 600x

SEM: 2

Excipient: Sodium chloride, powder
Manufacturer: Mallinckrodt Speciality Chemicals Co
Magnification: 2400x

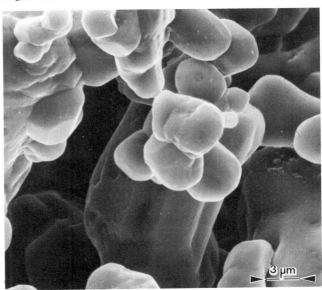

SEM: 3

Excipient: Sodium chloride, granular
Manufacturer: Van Waters & Rogers Inc
Magnification: 120x

SEM: 4

Excipient: Sodium chloride, granular
Manufacturer: Van Waters & Rogers Inc
Magnification: 600x

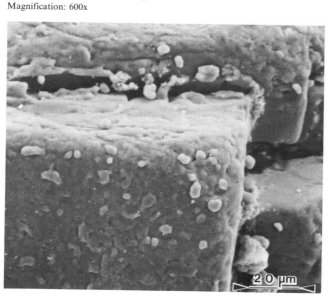

9. Pharmacopeial Specifications

Test	PhEur 1993	USP XXII (Suppl 7)
Identification	+	+
Acidity or alkalinity	+	+
Loss on drying	≤ 1.0%	≤ 0.5%
Arsenic	≤ 1 ppm	≤ 3 ppm
Barium	+	+
Iodide or bromide	+	+
Aluminum	—	≤ 0.2 ppm
Calcium and magnesium	100 ppm	≤ 0.005%
Iron	≤ 20 ppm	≤ 2 ppm
Sulfate	≤ 250 ppm	≤ 0.015%
Sodium ferrocyanide	+	+
Heavy metals	≤ 10 ppm	≤ 5 ppm
Phosphate	≤ 25 ppm	—
Organic volatile impurities	—	+
Assay (dried basis)	99.0-100.5%	99.0-101.0%

10. Typical Properties

Acidity/alkalinity:
pH = 6.7-7.3 (saturated aqueous solution)
Angle of repose: 38° for cubic crystals
Boiling point: 1439°C
Compressibility: with sodium chloride powder of less than 30 μm particle size, tablets are formed by plastic deformation. Above this size both plastic deformation and fracture occur.[1,3,4] *See also* Fig. 1.
Density:
2.17 g/cm^3;
1.20 g/cm^3 for saturated aqueous solution.
Density (bulk): 0.93 g/cm^3
Density (tapped): 1.09 g/cm^3
Freezing point depression:

Aqueous sodium chloride solution (% w/v)	Freezing point depression (°C)
11.69	6.90
17.53	10.82
23.38	15.14
30.39	21.12

Hardness (Mohs): 2-2.5
Hygroscopicity: hygroscopic above 75% RH.
Melting point: 801°C
Osmolarity: a 0.9% w/v aqueous solution is iso-osmotic with serum.
Refractive index:
n_D^{20} = 1.343 for a 1M aqueous solution.
Solubility:

Solvent	Solubility at 25°C Unless otherwise stated
Ethanol	slightly soluble
Ethanol (95%)	1 in 250
Glycerin	1 in 10
Water	1 in 2.8
	1 in 2.6 at 100°C

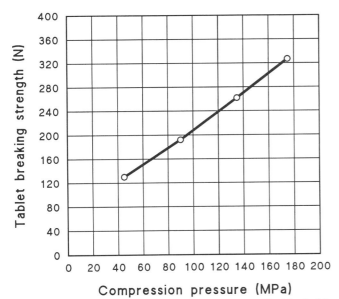

Fig. 1: Compression characteristics of sodium chloride (cubic crystals).[3]

Tablet diameter = 12 mm.

Vapor pressure:
133.3 Pa at 865°C for solid;
1759.6 Pa at 20°C for a saturated aqueous solution (equivalent to 75.3% RH).

11. Stability and Storage Conditions

Aqueous sodium chloride solutions are stable but may cause the separation of glass particles from certain types of glass containers. Aqueous solutions may be sterilized by autoclaving or filtration. The solid material is stable and should be stored in a well-closed container, in a cool, dry, place.

12. Incompatibilities

Aqueous sodium chloride solutions are corrosive to iron, they also react to form precipitates with silver, lead and mercury salts. Strong oxidizing agents liberate chlorine from acidified solutions of sodium chloride. The solubility of the antimicrobial preservative methylparaben is decreased in aqueous sodium chloride solutions.[11]

13. Method of Manufacture

Sodium chloride occurs naturally as the mineral halite. Commercially, it is obtained by the solar evaporation of sea water, by mining, or by the evaporation of brine from underground salt deposits.

14. Safety

Sodium chloride is the most important salt in the body for maintaining the osmotic tension of blood and tissues. About 5-12 g of sodium chloride is consumed daily, in the normal adult diet, and a corresponding amount excreted in the urine. As an excipient, sodium chloride may be regarded as an essentially nontoxic and nonirritant material. However, toxic effects following the oral ingestion of 0.5-1.0 g/kg body-weight in adults may occur. The oral ingestion of larger quantities of sodium chloride, e.g. 1000 g in 600 mL of water,[12] is harmful and can induce irritation of the gastrointestinal tract, vomiting, hypernatremia, respiratory distress, convulsions or death.

In rats, the minimum lethal intravenous dose is 2.5 g/kg body-weight.

LD_{50} (mouse, IP): 6.61 g/kg [13]
LD_{50} (mouse, IV): 0.65 g/kg
LD_{50} (mouse, oral): 4.0 g/kg
LD_{50} (mouse, SC): 3.0 g/kg
LD_{50} (rat, oral): 3.0 g/kg

15. Handling Precautions

Observe normal precautions appropriate to the circumstances and quantity of material handled. Sodium chloride evolves a vapor irritating to the eyes if heated to high temperatures.

16. Regulatory Status

GRAS listed. Included in the FDA Inactive Ingredients Guide (injections, inhalations, nasal, ophthalmic, oral, otic, rectal and topical preparations). Included in nonparenteral and parenteral medicines licensed in the UK.

17. Pharmacopeias

Aust, Belg, Br, Braz, Chin, Cz, Egypt, Eur, Fr, Ger, Gr, Hung, Ind, It, Jpn, Mex, Neth, Nord, Port, Rom, Rus, Swiss, Turk, US and Yug. Also in BP Vet.

18. Related Substances

Potassium Chloride.

19. Comments

Domestic salt may contain sodium iodide (as a prophylactic substance against goiter) and agents such as magnesium carbonate, calcium phosphate or starch, which reduce the hygroscopic characteristics of the salt and maintain the powder in a free-flowing state.

Food grade dendritic salt, which is porous, can be used as an absorbent for liquid medications and as a tablet diluent in specific formulations.

Each gram of sodium chloride represents approximately 17.1 mmol of sodium and 17.1 mmol of chloride. Sodium chloride 2.54 g is approximately equivalent to 1 g of sodium.

20. Specific References

1. Leigh S, Carless JE, Burt BW. Compression characteristics of some pharmaceutical materials. J Pharm Sci 1967; 56: 888-892.
2. Rees JE, Shotton E. Some observations on the ageing of sodium chloride compacts. J Pharm Pharmacol 1970; 22: 17S-23S.
3. Shotton E, Obiorah BA. The effect of particle shape and crystal habit on the properties of sodium chloride. J Pharm Pharmacol 1973; 25, 37P-43P.
4. Roberts RJ, Rowe RC, Kendall K. Brittle-ductile transitions in die compaction of sodium chloride. Chem Eng Sci 1989; 44: 1647-1651.
5. Tirkkonen S, Paronen P. Enhancement of drug release from ethylcellulose microcapsules using solid sodium chloride in the wall. Int J Pharmaceutics 1992; 88: 39-51.
6. Shah D, Ecanow B, Balagot R. Coacervate formation by inorganic salts with benzalkonium chloride. J Pharm Sci 1973; 62: 1741-1742.
7. Richard AJ. Ultracentrifugal study of effect of sodium chloride on micelle size of fusidate sodium. J Pharm Sci 1975; 64: 873-875.
8. McDonald C, Richardson C. The effect of added salts on solubilization by a non-ionic surfactant. J Pharm Pharmacol 1981; 33: 38-39.

9. Mattha AG. Rheological studies on Plantago albicans (Psyllium) seed gum dispersions II: effect of some pharmaceutical additives. Pharm Acta Helv 1977; 52: 214-217.

10. Okor RS. The effect of phenol on the electrolyte flocculation of certain polymeric dispersions to thixotropic gels. Pharm Res 1993; 10: 220-222.

11. McDonald C, Lindstrom RE. The effect of urea on the solubility of methyl *p*-hydroxybenzoate in aqueous sodium chloride solution. J Pharm Pharmacol 1974; 26: 39-45.

12. Calam J, Krasner N, Haqqani M. Extensive gastrointestinal damage following a saline emetic. Dig Dis Sci 1982; 27: 936-940.

13. Sweet DV, editor. Registry of toxic effects of chemical substances: Cincinnati: US Department of Health, 1987.

21. General References

—

22. Authors

UK: PJ Weller.

Sodium Citrate Dihydrate

1. Nonproprietary Names

BP: Sodium citrate
PhEur: Natrii citras
USP: Sodium citrate

2. Synonyms

Citric acid trisodium salt; E331; trisodium citrate.

3. Chemical Name and CAS Registry Number

Trisodium 2-hydroxypropane-1,2,3-
tricarboxylate dihydrate
[6132-04-3]

4. Empirical Formula   Molecular Weight

$C_6H_5Na_3O_7.2H_2O$ 294.10

5. Structural Formula

$$\left[\begin{array}{c} CH_2-COONa \\ | \\ HO-C-COONa \\ | \\ CH_2-COONa \end{array}\right] \bullet 2H_2O$$

6. Functional Category

Alkalizing agent; buffering agent; sequestering agent.

7. Applications in Pharmaceutical Formulation or Technology

Sodium citrate, as either the dihydrate or anhydrous material, is widely used in pharmaceutical formulations and food products primarily to adjust the pH of solutions. It is also used as a sequestering agent. The anhydrous material is used in effervescent tablet formulations.[1] Sodium citrate is additionally used as a blood anticoagulant either alone or in combination with other citrates such as disodium hydrogen citrate. Therapeutically, sodium citrate is used to relieve the painful irritation caused by cystitis, *see* Section 14.

Use	Concentration (%)
Buffering agent	0.3-2.0
Injections	0.02-4.0
Ophthalmic solutions	0.1-2.0
Sequestering agent	0.3-2.0

8. Description

Sodium citrate dihydrate consists of odorless, colorless, monoclinic crystals, or a white crystalline powder with a cooling, saline taste. It is slightly deliquescent in moist air and

in warm dry air it is efflorescent. Although most pharmacopeias specify that sodium citrate is the dihydrate the USP XXII states that sodium citrate may be either the dihydrate or anhydrous material.

SEM: 1
Excipient: Sodium citrate dihydrate (granular)
Manufacturer: Pfizer Ltd
Magnification: 60x

SEM: 2
Excipient: Sodium citrate dihydrate (granular)
Manufacturer: Pfizer Ltd
Magnification: 600x

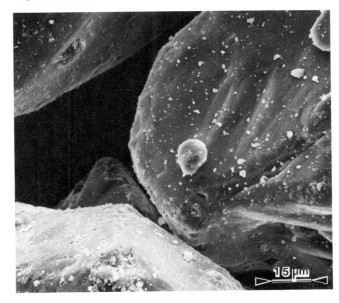

9. Pharmacopeial Specifications

Test	PhEur 1985	USP XXII
Identification	+	+
Alkalinity	+	+
Water		
(anhydrous)	—	$\leqslant$ 1.0%
(dihydrate)	11.0-13.0%	10.0-13.0%
Clarity & color of solution	+	—
Tartrate	—	+
Heavy metals	$\leqslant$ 10 ppm	$\leqslant$ 0.001%
Chloride	$\leqslant$ 50 ppm	—
Oxalate	$\leqslant$ 300 ppm	—
Sulfate	$\leqslant$ 150 ppm	—
Readily carbonizable substances	+	—
Assay (anhydrous basis)	99.0-101.0%	99.0-100.5%

10. Typical Properties

Acidity/alkalinity:
pH = 7.0-9.0 (5% w/v aqueous solution)
Density: 1.19 g/cm^3
Melting point: converts to the anhydrous form at 150°C.
Osmolarity: a 3.02% w/v aqueous solution is iso-osmotic with serum.
Particle size distribution: various grades of sodium citrate dihydrate with different particle sizes are commercially available, e.g. for a granular grade (Roche Products Ltd) minimum of 97% through a 1.2 mm mesh (US #16 sieve) and a maximum of 3% through a 104 μm mesh (US #140 sieve); for a powder grade (Roche Products Ltd) minimum of 95% through a 250 μm mesh (US #60 sieve) and a minimum of 65% through a 73.7 μm mesh (US #200 sieve).
Solubility: soluble 1 in 1.5 of water, 1 in 0.6 of boiling water; practically insoluble in ethanol (95%).

11. Stability and Storage Conditions

Sodium citrate dihydrate is stable. Aqueous solutions may be sterilized by autoclaving. On storage aqueous solutions may cause the separation of small, solid particles from glass containers.
The bulk material should be stored in an airtight container in a cool, dry, place.

12. Incompatibilities

Aqueous solutions are slightly alkaline and will react with acidic substances. Alkaloidal salts may be precipitated from their aqueous or hydro-alcohol solutions. Calcium and strontium salts will cause precipitation of the corresponding citrates.

13. Method of Manufacture

Sodium citrate is prepared by adding sodium carbonate to a solution of citric acid until effervescence ceases. The resulting solution is filtered and evaporated to dryness.

14. Safety

After ingestion sodium citrate is absorbed and metabolized to bicarbonate. Although generally regarded as a nontoxic and nonirritant excipient, excessive consumption may cause gastrointestinal discomfort or diarrhea. Therapeutically, in adults, up to 15 g daily of sodium citrate dihydrate may be administered orally, in divided doses, as an aqueous solution to relieve the painful irritation caused by cystitis.

Citrates and citric acid enhance intestinal aluminum absorption in renal patients which may lead to increased, harmful serum aluminum levels. It has therefore been suggested that patients with renal failure taking aluminum compounds to control phosphate absorption should not be prescribed citrate or citric acid containing products.[2]
See Section 18 for anhydrous sodium citrate animal toxicity data.

15. Handling Precautions

Observe normal precautions appropriate to the circumstances and quantity of material handled. Sodium citrate dihydrate dust may be irritant to the eyes and respiratory tract. Eye protection and gloves are recommended. Sodium citrate should be handled in a well-ventilated environment or a dust mask worn.

16. Regulatory Status

GRAS listed. Accepted for use as a food additive in Europe. Included in the FDA Inactive Ingredients Guide (inhalations, injections, ophthalmic products, oral solutions, suspensions, syrups and tablets, otic, rectal, topical, transdermal and vaginal preparations). Included in nonparenteral and parenteral medicines licensed in the UK.

17. Pharmacopeias

Aust, Br, Chin, Cz, Egypt, Eur, Fr, Ger, Gr, Hung, Ind, Int, It, Jpn, Mex, Neth, Nord, Port, Rom, Swiss, Turk, US and Yug. Also in BP Vet.
Note: Russian Pharmacopeia specifies that sodium citrate contains $5\frac{1}{2}H_2O$.

18. Related Substances

Anhydrous sodium citrate; Citric Acid Monohydrate.

Anhydrous sodium citrate: $C_6H_5Na_3O_7$
Molecular weight: 258.07
CAS number: [68-04-2]
Synonyms: anhydrous trisodium citrate; citric acid trisodium salt anhydrous; trisodium 2-hydroxy-1,2,3-propanetricarboxylic acid.
Appearance: colorless crystals or a white crystalline powder.
Pharmacopeias: Braz, Int, Mex and US.
Safety:
LD$_{50}$ (mouse, IP): 1.36 g/kg[3]
LD$_{50}$ (mouse, IV): 0.17 g/kg
LD$_{50}$ (rabbit, IV): 0.45 g/kg
LD$_{50}$ (rat, IP): 1.55 g/kg

19. Comments

Each gram of sodium citrate dihydrate represents approximately 10.2 mmol of sodium and 3.4 mmol of citrate. Each gram of anhydrous sodium citrate represents approximately 11.6 mmol of sodium and 3.9 mmol of citrate.

20. Specific References

1. Anderson NR, Banker GS, Peck GE. Quantitative evaluation of pharmaceutical effervescent systems II: stability monitoring of reactivity and porosity measurements. J Pharm Sci 1982; 71: 7-13.
2. Main J, Ward MK. Potentiation of aluminium absorption by effervescent analgesic tablets in a haemodialysis patient. Br Med J 1992; 304: 1686.
3. Sweet DV, editor. Registry of toxic effects of chemical substances. Cincinnati: US Department of Health, 1987.

21. General References

—

22. Authors

USA: GE Amidon.

Sodium Cyclamate

1. Nonproprietary Names
PhEur: Natrii cyclamas

2. Synonyms
Assugrin; cyclohexylsulfamic acid monosodium salt; E952; sodium cyclohexanesulfamate; *Sucaryl sodium*; *Sucrosa*.

3. Chemical Name and CAS Registry Number
Sodium *N*-cyclohexylsulfamate [139-05-9]

4. Empirical Formula   Molecular Weight
$C_6H_{12}NNaO_3S$ 201.22

5. Structural Formula

6. Functional Category
Sweetening agent.

7. Applications in Pharmaceutical Formulation or Technology
Sodium cyclamate is used as an intense sweetening agent in pharmaceutical formulations, foods, beverages and table-top sweeteners. In dilute solution, up to about 0.17% w/v, the sweetening power is approximately 30 times that of sucrose. However, at higher concentrations this is reduced and at a concentration of 0.5% w/v a bitter taste becomes noticeable. Sodium cyclamate enhances flavor systems and can be used to mask some unpleasant taste characteristics. In most applications, sodium cyclamate is used in combination with saccharin.

8. Description
Sodium cyclamate occurs as white, odorless or almost odorless crystals or as a crystalline powder with an intensely sweet taste.

9. Pharmacopeial Specifications

Test	PhEur 1992
Identification	+
Appearance of solution	+
pH (10% w/v aqueous solution)	5.5-7.5
Absorbance	+
Sulfamic acid	+
Aniline	$\leqslant$ 1 ppm
Cyclohexylamine	$\leqslant$ 10 ppm
Dicyclohexylamine	$\leqslant$ 1 ppm
Sulfates	+
Heavy metals	+
Loss on drying	$\leqslant$ 1.0%
Assay (dried basis)	98.5-101.0%

See also Section 19.

10. Typical Properties
Acidity/alkalinity: pH = 5.5-7.5 for a 10% w/v aqueous solution.
Solubility:

Solvent	Solubility at 20°C Unless otherwise stated
Benzene	practically insoluble
Chloroform	practically insoluble
Ethanol (95%)	1 in 250
Ether	practically insoluble
Propylene glycol	1 in 25
Water	1 in 5
	1 in 2 at 45°C

11. Stability and Storage Conditions
Sodium cyclamate is hydrolyzed by sulfuric acid and cyclohexylamine at a very slow rate which is proportional to the hydrogen ion concentration, such that for all practical considerations it can be regarded as stable. Solutions are stable to heat, light and air over a wide pH range.

Samples of tablets containing sodium cyclamate and saccharin have shown no loss in sweetening power following storage for approximately 20 years.

The bulk material should be stored in a well-closed container in a cool, dry, place.

12. Incompatibilities
—

13. Method of Manufacture
Cyclamates are prepared by the sulfonation of cyclohexylamine in the presence of a base. Commercially, the sulfonation can involve sulfamic acid, a sulfate salt or sulfur trioxide. Tertiary bases such as triethylamine or trimethylamine may be used as the condensing agent. The amine salts of cyclamate that are produced are converted to the sodium, calcium, potassium or magnesium salt by treatment with the appropriate metal oxide.

14. Safety
There has been considerable controversy concerning the safety of cyclamate following the FDA decision in 1970 to ban its use in the US.[1-3] This decision resulted from a feeding study in rats which suggested that cyclamate could cause an unusual form of bladder cancer. The study has however been criticized since it involved very high doses of cyclamate administered with saccharin, which has itself been the subject of controversy concerning its safety, *see* Saccharin. Although excreted almost entirely unchanged in the urine a potentially harmful metabolite of sodium cyclamate, cyclohexylamine, has been detected in humans.[4]

Extensive long-term animal feeding studies and epidemiological studies in humans have failed to show any evidence to support the belief that cyclamate is carcinogenic or mutagenic.[5,6] As a result, sodium cyclamate is now accepted in many countries for use in foods and pharmaceutical formulations. *See also* Section 16.

Few adverse reactions to cyclamate have been reported although its use has been associated with instances of photosensitive dermatitis.[7]

The WHO has set an estimated acceptable daily intake for sodium and calcium cyclamate, expressed as cyclamic acid, at up to 11 mg/kg body-weight.[8] In Europe, a temporary acceptable daily intake for sodium and calcium cyclamate, expressed as cyclamic acid, has been set at up to 1.5 mg/kg body-weight.

LD_{50} (mouse, IP): 1.15 g/kg[9]
LD_{50} (mouse, IV): 4.8 g/kg
LD_{50} (mouse, oral): 17 g/kg
LD_{50} (rat, IP): 1.35 g/kg
LD_{50} (rat, IV): 3.5 g/kg
LD_{50} (rat, oral): 15.25 g/kg

15. Handling Precautions

Observe normal precautions appropriate to the circumstances and quantity of material handled. Eye protection is recommended.

16. Regulatory Status

Sodium cyclamate is accepted for use in certain food applications in Europe and a number of other countries. The use of cyclamates in the US is currently not permitted although this position is under review. Included in nonparenteral medicines licensed in the UK.

17. Pharmacopeias

Eur, Fr, Neth, Rom and Swiss.

18. Related Substances

Calcium cyclamate; cyclamic acid.

Calcium cyclamate: $C_{12}H_{24}CaN_2O_6S_2.2H_2O$
Molecular weight: 432.57
CAS number:
[5897-16-5] for the dihydrate;
[139-06-0] for the anhydrous form.
Synonyms: calcium *N*-cyclohexylsulfamate dihydrate; *Cyclan*; cyclohexanesulfamic acid calcium salt; cyclohexylsulfamic acid calcium salt; *Sucaryl calcium*.
Pharmacopeias: Nord.
Appearance: white, odorless or almost odorless crystals or a crystalline powder with an intensely sweet taste.
Acidity/alkalinity: pH = 5.5-7.5 for a 10% w/v aqueous solution.
Solubility: freely soluble in water; practically insoluble in benzene, chloroform, ethanol and ether.

Cyclamic acid: $C_6H_{13}NO_3S$
Molecular weight: 179.23
CAS number: [100-88-9]
Synonyms: cyclamate; cyclohexanesulfamic acid; *N*-cyclohexylsulfamic acid; hexamic acid; *Sucaryl*.

Appearance: white, odorless or almost odorless crystals or a crystalline powder with an intensely sweet taste.
Melting point: 169-170°C
Solubility: slightly soluble in water.

19. Comments

The perceived intensity of sweeteners relative to sucrose depends upon their concentration, temperature of tasting, pH and on the flavor and texture of the product concerned.

Intense sweetening agents will not replace the bulk, textural or preservative characteristics of sucrose if the latter ingredient is removed from a formulation.

Synergistic effects for combinations of sweeteners have been reported, e.g. sodium cyclamate with saccharin sodium or acesulfame potassium.

Although sodium cyclamate is not included in the current BP or USPNF, monographs were included in the BP 1968 and USPNF XIII.

20. Specific References

1. Nabors LO, Miller WT. Cyclamate: a toxicological review. Commen Toxicol 1989; 3(4): 307-315.
2. Lecos C. The sweet and sour history of saccharin, cyclamate and aspartame. FDA Consumer 1981; 15(7): 8-11.
3. Cyclamate alone not a carcinogen. Am Pharm 1985; NS25(9): 11.
4. Kojima S, Ichibagase H. Studies on synthetic sweetening agents VIII. Cyclohexylamine, a metabolite of sodium cyclamate. Chem Pharm Bull 1966; 14: 971-974.
5. D'Arcy PF. Adverse reactions to excipients in pharmaceutical formulations. In: Florence AT, Salole EG, editors. Formulation factors in adverse reactions. London: Wright, 1990: 1-22.
6. Schmähl D, Habs M. Investigations on the carcinogenicity of the artificial sweeteners sodium cyclamate and sodium saccharin in rats in a two-generation experiment. Arzneimittelforschung 1984; 34: 604-606.
7. Yong JM, Sanderson KV. Photosensitive dermatitis and renal tubular acidosis after ingestion of calcium cyclamate. Lancet 1969; ii: 1273-1274.
8. FAO/WHO. Evaluation of certain food additives and contaminants. Twenty-sixth report of the joint FAO/WHO expert committee on food additives. Tech Rep Ser Wld Hlth Org 1982; No. 683.
9. Sweet DV, editor. Registry of toxic effects of chemical substances. Cincinnati: US Department of Health, 1987.

21. General References

—

22. Authors

UK: FR Higton, DM Thurgood.

Sodium Lauryl Sulfate

1. Nonproprietary Names

BP: Sodium lauryl sulphate
PhEur: Natrii laurilsulfas
USPNF: Sodium lauryl sulfate

2. Synonyms

Dodecyl sodium sulfate; *Elfan 240*; *Empicol LZ*; *Maprofix 563*; *Marlinat DFK30*; *Nutrapon W*; sodium dodecyl sulfate; sodium monododecyl sulfate; sodium monolauryl sulfate; *Stepanol WA 100*.

3. Chemical Name and CAS Registry Number

Sulfuric acid monododecyl ester sodium salt
[151-21-3]

4. Empirical Formula   Molecular Weight

$C_{12}H_{25}NaO_4S$ 288.38

The USPNF XVII describes sodium lauryl sulfate as a mixture of sodium alkyl sulfates consisting chiefly of sodium lauryl sulfate ($C_{12}H_{25}NaO_4S$). The BP 1993 and PhEur 1993 additionally state that sodium lauryl sulfate should contain not less than 85% of sodium alkyl sulfate calculated as $C_{12}H_{25}NaO_4S$.

5. Structural Formula

$CH_3(CH_2)_{10}CH_2OSO_3Na$
See also Section 4.

6. Functional Category

Anionic surfactant; detergent; emulsifying agent; skin penetrant; tablet and capsule lubricant; wetting agent.

7. Applications in Pharmaceutical Formulation or Technology

Sodium lauryl sulfate is an anionic surfactant employed in a wide range of nonparenteral pharmaceutical formulations and cosmetics. It is a detergent and wetting agent effective in both alkaline and acidic conditions.

Use	Concentration (%)
Anionic emulsifier, forms self-emulsifying bases with fatty alcohols	0.5-2.5
Detergent in medicated shampoos	≈ 10
Skin cleanser in topical applications	1
Solubilizer in concentrations greater than critical micelle concentration	> 0.0025
Tablet lubricant	1-2
Wetting agent in dentrifices	1-2

8. Description

Sodium lauryl sulfate consists of white or cream to pale yellow-colored crystals, flakes or powder having a smooth feel, a soapy, bitter taste and a faint odor of fatty substances.

SEM: 1
Excipient: Sodium lauryl sulfate
Manufacturer: Canadian Alcolac Ltd
Magnification: 120x

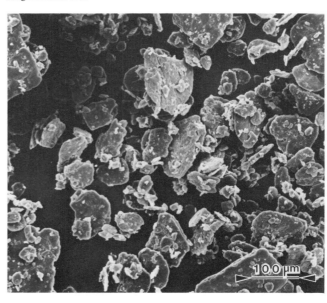

SEM: 2
Excipient: Sodium lauryl sulfate
Manufacturer: Canadian Alcolac Ltd
Magnification: 600x

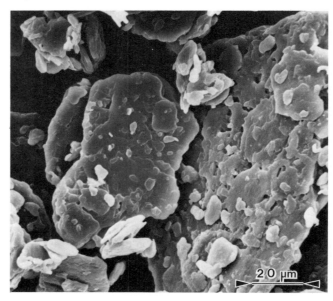

9. Pharmacopeial Specifications

Test	PhEur 1993	USPNF XVII
Identification	+	+
Alkalinity	+	+
Heavy metals	—	≤ 0.002%
Arsenic	—	≤ 3 ppm
Combined sodium chloride and sodium sulfate	≤ 8.0%	≤ 8.0%
Unsulfated alcohols	—	≤ 4.0%
Non-esterified alcohols	≤ 4.0%	—
Total alcohols	—	≥ 59.0%
Assay (as $C_{12}H_{25}NaO_4S$)	≥ 85.0%	—

10. Typical Properties

Acidity/alkalinity:
pH = 7.0-9.5 (1% w/v aqueous solution).
Acid value: 0
Antimicrobial activity: sodium lauryl sulfate has some bacteriostatic action against Gram-positive bacteria, but is ineffective against many Gram-negative microorganisms. It potentiates the fungicidal activity of certain substances such as sulfanilamide and sulfathiazole.
Critical micelle concentration:
8.2 mmol/L (0.23 g/L) at 20°C.
Density: 1.07 g/cm³ at 20°C
HLB value: ≈ 40
Interfacial tension: 11.8 mN/m (11.8 dynes/cm) for a 0.05% w/v solution (unspecified nonaqueous liquid) at 30°C.
Melting point: 204-207°C (for pure substance).
Moisture content: ≤ 5%; sodium lauryl sulfate is not hygroscopic.
Solubility: freely soluble in water, giving an opalescent solution; practically insoluble in chloroform and ether.
Spreading coefficient:
–7.0 (0.05% w/v aqueous solution) at 30°C.
Surface tension: 25.2 mN/m (25.2 dynes/cm) for a 0.05% w/v aqueous solution at 30°C.
Wetting time (Draize Test):
118 s (0.05% w/v aqueous solution) at 30°C.

11. Stability and Storage Conditions

Sodium lauryl sulfate is stable under normal storage conditions. However, in solution, under extreme conditions, i.e. pH 2.5 or below, it undergoes hydrolysis to lauryl alcohol and sodium bisulfate.
The bulk material should be stored in a well-closed container away from strong oxidizing agents in a cool, dry, place.

12. Incompatibilities

Sodium lauryl sulfate reacts with cationic surfactants causing loss of activity even in concentrations too low to cause precipitation. Unlike soaps, it is compatible with dilute acids and calcium and magnesium ions.
Solutions of sodium lauryl sulfate (pH 9.5-10.0) are mildly corrosive to mild steel, copper, brass, bronze and aluminum. Sodium lauryl sulfate is also incompatible with some alkaloidal salts and precipitates with lead and potassium salts.

13. Method of Manufacture

Sodium lauryl sulfate is prepared by sulfation of lauryl alcohol, followed by neutralization with sodium carbonate.

14. Safety

Sodium lauryl sulfate is widely used in cosmetics and oral and topical pharmaceutical formulations. It is a moderately toxic material with acute toxic effects including irritation to the skin, eyes, mucous membranes, upper respiratory tract and stomach. Repeated, prolonged exposure to dilute solutions may cause drying and cracking of the skin; contact dermatitis may develop. Prolonged inhalation of sodium lauryl sulfate will damage the lungs. Pulmonary sensitization is possible resulting in hyperactive airway dysfunction and pulmonary allergy. Animal studies have shown intravenous administration to cause marked toxic effects to the lung, kidney and liver. Mutagenic testing in bacterial systems has however proven negative.[1]
Adverse reactions to sodium lauryl sulfate in cosmetics and pharmaceutical formulations mainly concern reports of irritation to the skin[2-4] or eyes[5] following topical application.
Sodium lauryl sulfate should not be used in intravenous preparations for humans. The probable human lethal oral dose is 0.5-5 g/kg.
LD$_{50}$ (mouse, IP): 0.25 g/kg[6]
LD$_{50}$ (mouse, IV): 0.12 g/kg
LD$_{50}$ (rat, oral): 1.29 g/kg
LD$_{50}$ (rat, IP): 0.21 g/kg
LD$_{50}$ (rat, IV): 0.12 g/kg

15. Handling Precautions

Observe normal precautions appropriate to the circumstances and quantity of material handled. Inhalation and contact with the skin and eyes should be avoided; eye protection, gloves and other protective clothing, depending on the circumstances, are recommended. Adequate ventilation should be provided or a dust respirator worn. Prolonged or repeated exposure should be avoided. Sodium lauryl sulfate emits toxic fumes on combustion.

16. Regulatory Status

GRAS listed. Included in the FDA Inactive Ingredients Guide (oral capsules and tablets, and topical preparations). Included in nonparenteral medicines licensed in the UK.

17. Pharmacopeias

Aust, Belg, Br, Braz, Cz, Egypt, Eur, Fr, Gr, Hung, Ind, Jpn, Neth, Rom, Swiss, USPNF and Yug.

18. Related Substances

Magnesium lauryl sulfate.

Magnesium lauryl sulfate: $C_{12}H_{26}O_4S.\frac{1}{2}Mg$
CAS number: [3097-08-3]
Comments: a soluble tablet lubricant.[7]

19. Comments

—

20. Specific References

1. Mortelmans K, Haworth S, Lawlor T, Speck W, Tainer B, Zeiger E. Salmonella mutagenicity tests II: results from the testing of 270 chemicals. Environ Mutagen 1986; 8(Suppl 7): 1-119.
2. Blondeel A, Oleffe J, Achten G. Contact allergy in 330 dermatological patients. Contact Dermatitis 1978; 4(5): 270-276.
3. Bruynzeel DP, van Ketel WG, Scheper RJ, von Blomberg-van der Flier BME. Delayed time course of irritation by sodium lauryl

sulfate: observations on threshold reactions. Contact Dermatitis 1982; 8(4): 236-239.

4. Eubanks SW, Patterson JW. Dermatitis from sodium lauryl sulfate in hydrocortisone cream. Contact Dermatitis 1984; 11(4): 250-251.

5. Grant WM. Toxicology of the eye, 2nd edition. Springfield: Charles C Thomas, 1974: 964.

6. Sweet DV, editor. Registry of toxic effects of chemical substances. Cincinnati: US Department of Health, 1987.

7. Caldwell HC, Westlake WJ. Magnesium lauryl sulfate - soluble lubricant [letter]. J Pharm Sci 1972; 61: 984-985.

21. General References

Hadgraft J, Ashton P. The effect of sodium lauryl sulfate on topical drug bioavailability. J Pharm Pharmacol 1985; 37(Suppl): 85P.

Nakagaki M, Yokoyama S. Acid-catalyzed hydrolysis of sodium lauryl sulfate. J Pharm Sci 1985; 74: 1047-1052.

Vold RD, Mittal KL. Determination of sodium dodecyl sulfate in the presence of lauryl alcohol. Anal Chem 1972; 44(4): 849-850.

Wan LSC, Poon PKC. The interfacial activity of sodium lauryl sulfate in the presence of alcohols. Can J Pharm Sci 1970; 5: 104-107.

Wang L-H, Chowhan ZT. Drug-excipient interactions resulting from powder mixing V: role of sodium lauryl sulfate. Int J Pharmaceutics 1990; 60: 61-78.

22. Authors

UK: S Behn.

Sodium Metabisulfite

1. Nonproprietary Names

BP: Sodium metabisulphite
PhEur: Natrii metabisulfis
USPNF: Sodium metabisulfite

2. Synonyms

Disodium disulfite; disodium pyrosulfite; disulfurous acid disodium salt; E223; sodium acid sulfite.

3. Chemical Name and CAS Registry Number

Sodium pyrosulfite [7681-57-4]

4. Empirical Formula   Molecular Weight

$Na_2S_2O_5$ 190.1

5. Structural Formula

$$Na^+O^- \!-\! \underset{\displaystyle \|}{\overset{\displaystyle O}{S}} \!-\! O \!-\! \underset{\displaystyle \|}{\overset{\displaystyle O}{S}} \!-\! O^-\, Na^+$$

6. Functional Category

Antioxidant.

7. Applications in Pharmaceutical Formulation or Technology

Sodium metabisulfite is used as an antioxidant in oral, parenteral and topical pharmaceutical formulations. Primarily, sodium metabisulfite is used in acidic preparations; for alkaline preparations, sodium sulfite is usually preferred, *see* Sections 18 and 19. Sodium metabisulfite also has some antimicrobial activity, which is greatest at acid pH, and may be used as a preservative in oral preparations such as syrups.

In the food industry, and in wine production, sodium metabisulfite is similarly used as an antioxidant, antimicrobial preservative and anti-browning agent. However, at concentrations above about 500 ppm it imparts a noticeable flavor to preparations.

Sodium metabisulfite usually contains small amounts of sodium sulfite and sodium sulfate, *see* Section 18.

Use	Concentration (%)
Antioxidant	0.01-1.0

8. Description

Sodium metabisulfite occurs as colorless, prismatic crystals or as a white to creamy-white crystalline powder which has the odor of sulfur dioxide and an acidic, saline taste. Sodium metabisulfite crystallizes from water as a hydrate containing $7H_2O$.

9. Pharmacopeial Specifications

Test	PhEur 1993	USPNF XVII
Identification	+	+
Appearance of solution	+	—

Continued

Test	PhEur 1993	USPNF XVII
pH (5% w/v solution)	3.5-5.0	—
Chloride	—	⩽ 0.05%
Thiosulfate	+	⩽ 0.05%
Arsenic	⩽ 5 ppm	⩽ 3 ppm
Heavy metals	⩽ 20 ppm	⩽ 0.002%
Iron	⩽ 20 ppm	⩽ 0.002%
Assay (as $Na_2S_2O_5$)	95-100.5%	—
Assay (as SO_2)	—	65-67.4%

10. Typical Properties

Acidity/alkalinity: pH = 3.5-5.0 for a 5% w/v aqueous solution at 20°C.
Melting point: sodium metabisulfite melts with decomposition at less than 150°C.
Osmolarity: a 1.38% w/v aqueous solution is iso-osmotic with serum.
Solubility:

Solvent	Solubility at 20°C Unless otherwise stated
Ethanol (95%)	slightly soluble
Glycerin	freely soluble
Water	1 in 1.9
	1 in 1.2 at 100°C

11. Stability and Storage Conditions

On exposure to air and moisture, sodium metabisulfite is slowly oxidized to sodium sulfate with disintegration of the crystals.[1] Addition of strong acids, to the solid, liberates sulfur dioxide.

In water, sodium metabisulfite is immediately converted to sodium (Na^+) and bisulfite (HSO_3^-) ions. Aqueous sodium metabisulfite solutions also decompose in air, especially on heating, and solutions which are to be sterilized by autoclaving should therefore be filled into containers in which the air has been replaced with an inert gas, such as nitrogen. The addition of dextrose to aqueous sodium metabisulfite solutions results in a decrease in the stability of the metabisulfite.[2]

The bulk material should be stored in a well-closed container, protected from light, in a cool, dry, place.

12. Incompatibilities

Sodium metabisulfite reacts with sympathomimetics and other drugs which are *ortho-* or *para*-hydroxybenzyl alcohol derivatives to form sulfonic acid derivatives possessing little or no pharmacological activity. The most important drugs subject to this inactivation are adrenaline and its derivatives.[3] In addition, sodium metabisulfite is incompatible with chloramphenicol, due to a more complex reaction,[3] and inactivates cisplatin in solution;[4,5] it is also incompatible with phenylmercuric acetate when autoclaved in eye-drop preparations.[6]

Sodium metabisulfite may react with the rubber caps of multidose vials which should therefore be pre-treated with sodium metabisulfite solution.[7]

13. Method of Manufacture

Sodium metabisulfite is prepared by saturating a solution of sodium hydroxide with sulfur dioxide and allowing crystallization to occur; hydrogen is passed through the solution to exclude air. Sodium metabisulfite may also be prepared by saturating a solution of sodium carbonate with sulfur dioxide and allowing crystallization to occur, or by thermally dehydrating sodium bisulfite.

14. Safety

Sodium metabisulfite is widely used as an antioxidant in oral, topical and parenteral pharmaceutical formulations; it is also widely used in food products.

Although it is extensively used in a variety of preparations, sodium metabisulfite, and other sulfites, have been associated with a number of severe, or fatal, adverse reactions.[8-13] These are usually hypersensitivity type reactions and include bronchospasm and anaphylaxis. Allergy to sulfite antioxidants is estimated to occur in 5-10% of asthmatics although adverse reactions may also occur in non-asthmatics with no history of allergy.

Following oral ingestion, sodium metabisulfite is oxidized to sulfate and is excreted in the urine. Ingestion may result in gastric irritation due to the liberation of sulfurous acid, while ingestion of large amounts of sodium metabisulfite can cause colic, diarrhea, circulatory disturbances, CNS depression and death. In Europe, the acceptable daily intake of sodium metabisulfite, and other sulfites, used in foodstuffs has been set at up to 3.5 mg/kg body-weight, calculated as sulfur dioxide (SO_2). The WHO has similarly also set an acceptable daily intake of sodium metabisulfite, and other sulfites, at up to 7.0 mg/kg body-weight, calculated as sulfur dioxide (SO_2).[14]

LD_{50} (rat, IV): 0.12 g/kg[15]

15. Handling Precautions

Observe normal precautions appropriate to the circumstances and quantity of material handled. Sodium metabisulfite may be irritant to the skin and eyes; eye protection and gloves are recommended. In the UK, the long-term (8-hour TWA) occupational exposure limit for sodium metabisulfite is 5 mg/m³.[16]

16. Regulatory Status

GRAS listed. Accepted as a food additive in Europe. Included in the FDA Inactive Ingredients Guide (epidural, IM and IV injections, ophthalmic solutions and oral preparations). Included in nonparenteral and parenteral medicines licensed in the UK.

17. Pharmacopeias

Aust, Belg, Br, Cz, Egypt, Eur, Fr, Hung, Ind, Jpn, Mex, Neth, Nord, Turk, USPNF and Yug. Also in BP Vet.

18. Related Substances

Potassium bisulfite; potassium metabisulfite; sodium bisulfite; sodium sulfite.

Potassium bisulfite: KHSO$_3$
Molecular weight: 120.20
CAS number: [7773-03-7]
Synonyms: E228; potassium hydrogen sulfite.

Potassium metabisulfite: K$_2$S$_2$O$_5$
Molecular weight: 222.32
CAS number: [16731-55-8]
Synonyms: dipotassium pyrosulfite; E224; potassium pyrosulfite.
Appearance: white crystalline powder.

Pharmacopeias: Fr and USPNF.
Solubility: freely soluble in water; practically insoluble in ethanol (95%).

Sodium bisulfite: NaHSO$_3$
Molecular weight: 104.07
CAS number: [7631-90-5]
Synonyms: E222; sodium hydrogen sulfite.
Appearance: white crystalline powder.
Pharmacopeias: Jpn.
Density: 1.48 g/cm³
Solubility: soluble 1 in 3.5 parts of water at 20°C, 1 in 2 parts of water at 100°C, and 1 in 70 parts of ethanol (95%).
Comments: most substances sold as sodium bisulfite contain significant, variable, amounts of sodium metabisulfite, since the latter is less hygroscopic and more stable during storage and shipment. *See* Section 19.

Sodium sulfite: Na$_2$SO$_3$
Molecular weight: 126.06
CAS number: [7757-83-7]
Synonyms: anhydrous sodium sulfite; E221; exsiccated sodium sulfite.
Appearance: a white, odorless or almost odorless crystalline powder.
Pharmacopeias: Br, Eur, Fr, Jpn and Mex.
Acidity/alkalinity: pH = 9 for a saturated aqueous solution at 20°C.
Solubility: soluble 1 in 3.2 parts of water; soluble in glycerin; practically insoluble in ethanol (95%).
Comments: see Section 19.

19. Comments

Sodium metabisulfite is used as an antioxidant at low pH, sodium bisulfite at intermediate pH, and sodium sulfite at higher pH values.

20. Specific References

1. Schroeter LC. Oxidation of sulfurous acid salts in pharmaceutical systems. J Pharm Sci 1963; 52: 888-892.
2. Schumacher GE, Hull RL. Some factors influencing the degradation of sodium bisulfite in dextrose solutions. Am J Hosp Pharm 1966; 23: 245-249.
3. Higuchi T, Schroeter LC. Reactivity of bisulfite with a number of pharmaceuticals. J Am Pharm Assoc (Sci) 1959; 48: 535-540.
4. Hussain AA, Haddadin M, Iga K. Reaction of cis-platinum with sodium sulfite. J Pharm Sci 1980; 69: 364-365.
5. Garren KW, Repton AJ. Incompatibility of cisplatin and Reglan injectable. Int J Pharmaceutics 1985; 24: 91-99.
6. Collins AJ, Lingham P, Burbridge TA, Bain R. Incompatibility of phenylmercuric acetate with sodium metabisulfite in eye drop formulations. J Pharm Pharmacol 1985; 37(Suppl): 123P.
7. Schroeter LC. Sulfurous acid salts as pharmaceutical antioxidants. J Pharm Sci 1961; 50: 891-901.
8. Jamieson DM, Guill MF, Wray BB, May JR. Metabisulfite sensitivity: case report and literature review. Ann Allergy 1985; 54: 115-121.
9. Possible allergic-type reactions. FDA Drug Bull 1987; 17: 2.
10. Tsevat J, Gross GN, Dowling GP. Fatal asthma after ingestion of sulfite-containing wine [letter]. Ann Intern Med 1987; 107: 263.
11. Weiner M, Bernstein IL. Adverse reactions to drug formulation agents: a handbook of excipients. New York: Marcel Dekker Inc, 1989: 314-320.
12. Fitzharris P. What advances if any, have been made in treating sulphite allergy? Br Med J 1992; 305: 1478.

13. Smolinske SC. Handbook of food, drug, and cosmetic excipients. Boca Raton, FL: CRC Press Inc, 1992: 393-406.
14. FAO/WHO. Evaluation of certain food additives and contaminants. Thirtieth report of the joint FAO/WHO expert committee on food additives. Tech Rep Ser Wld Hlth Org 1987; No. 751.
15. Sweet DV, editor. Registry of toxic effects of chemical substances. Cincinnati: US Department of Health, 1987.
16. Health and Safety Executive. EH40/93 occupational exposure limits 1993. London: HMSO, 1993.

21. General References

Halaby SF, Mattocks AM. Absorption of sodium bisulfite from peritoneal dialysis solutions. J Pharm Sci 1965; 54: 52-55.
Wilkins JW, Greene JA, Weller JM. Toxicity of intraperitoneal bisulfite. Clin Pharmacol Ther 1968; 9: 328-332.

22. Authors

USA: JT Stewart.

Dibasic Sodium Phosphate

1. Nonproprietary Names

BP: Sodium phosphate
PhEur: Dinatrii phosphas dihydricus
         Dinatrii phosphas dodecahydricus
USP: Dibasic sodium phosphate
Note that the BP 1993 contains one monograph, for the dodecahydrate ($12H_2O$), whilst the PhEur 1987 and PhEur 1989 contain two separate monographs for the dihydrate ($2H_2O$) and the dodecahydrate. The USP XXII contains one monograph applicable to both the heptahydrate ($7H_2O$) and the anhydrous material.
See also Section 17.

2. Synonyms

Disodium hydrogen phosphate; disodium phosphate; E339; secondary sodium phosphate; sodium orthophosphate; phosphoric acid, disodium salt.

3. Chemical Name and CAS Registry Number

Anhydrous dibasic sodium phosphate [7558-79-4]
Dibasic sodium phosphate dihydrate [10028-24-7]
Dibasic sodium phosphate heptahydrate [7782-85-6]
Dibasic sodium phosphate dodecahydrate [10039-32-4]

4. Empirical Formula   Molecular Weight

Na_2HPO_4	141.96
$Na_2HPO_4.2H_2O$	177.98
$Na_2HPO_4.7H_2O$	268.03
$Na_2HPO_4.12H_2O$	358.08

5. Structural Formula

$Na_2HPO_4.xH_2O$
Where x = 0, 2, 7 or 12.

6. Functional Category

Buffering agent; sequestering agent.

7. Applications in Pharmaceutical Formulation or Technology

Dibasic sodium phosphate is used in a wide variety of pharmaceutical formulations as a buffering agent and as a sequestering agent. Therapeutically, dibasic sodium phosphate is used as a mild saline laxative and in the treatment of hypophosphatemia.[1,2]
Dibasic sodium phosphate is also used in food products, e.g. as an emulsifier in processed cheese.

8. Description

Anhydrous dibasic sodium phosphate occurs as a white powder. The dihydrate is a white or almost white, odorless, crystalline material. The heptahydrate occurs as colorless crystals or as a white, granular or caked salt that effloresces in warm, dry air. The dodecahydrate occurs as strongly efflorescent, colorless or transparent crystals.

9. Pharmacopeial Specifications

Test	PhEur*	USP XXII
Identification	+	+
Appearance of solution	+	—
Loss on drying		
(anhydrous form)	—	$\leqslant$ 5.0%
(dihydrate)	19.5-21.0%	—
(heptahydrate)	—	43.0-50.0%
(dodecahydrate)	57.0-61.0%	—
Insoluble substances	—	$\leqslant$ 0.4%
Reducing substances	+	—
Monosodium phosphate	+	—
Chloride		
(anhydrous form)	—	$\leqslant$ 0.06%
(dihydrate)	$\leqslant$ 400 ppm	—
(heptahydrate)	—	$\leqslant$ 0.06%
(dodecahydrate)	$\leqslant$ 200 ppm	—
Sulfate		
(anhydrous form)	—	$\leqslant$ 0.2%
(dihydrate)	$\leqslant$ 0.1%	—
(heptahydrate)	—	$\leqslant$ 0.2%
(dodecahydrate)	$\leqslant$ 500 ppm	—
Arsenic		
(anhydrous form)	—	$\leqslant$ 16 ppm
(dihydrate)	$\leqslant$ 4 ppm	—
(heptahydrate)	—	$\leqslant$ 16 ppm
(dodecahydrate)	$\leqslant$ 2 ppm	—
Heavy metals	$\leqslant$ 20 ppm	$\leqslant$ 0.002%
Iron		
(dihydrate)	$\leqslant$ 40 ppm	—
(dodecahydrate)	$\leqslant$ 20 ppm	—
Assay (dried basis)	98.0-101.0%	98.0-100.5%

* PhEur 1987 for the dodecahydrate and PhEur 1989 for the dihydrate.

10. Typical Properties

Acidity/alkalinity: pH = 9.1 for a 1% w/v aqueous solution of the anhydrous material at 25°C. A saturated aqueous solution of the dodecahydrate has a pH of about 9.5.
Dissociation constant:
pK_{a1} = 2.15 at 25°C;
pK_{a2} = 7.20 at 25°C.
Hygroscopicity: the anhydrous form is hygroscopic and will absorb 2-7 moles of water on exposure to air, whereas the heptahydrate is stable in air.
Osmolarity: a 2.23% w/v aqueous solution of the dihydrate is iso-osmotic with serum; a 4.45% w/v aqueous solution of the dodecahydrate is iso-osmotic with serum.
Solubility: very soluble in water, more so in hot or boiling water; practically insoluble in ethanol (95%). The anhydrous material is soluble 1 in 8 parts of water, the heptahydrate 1 in 4 parts of water and the dodecahydrate 1 in 3 parts of water.

11. Stability and Storage Conditions

The anhydrous form of dibasic sodium phosphate is hygroscopic. When heated to 40°C, the dodecahydrate fuses; at 100°C it loses its water of crystallization and at a dull-red heat, about 240°C, it is converted into the pyrophosphate, $Na_4P_2O_7$. Aqueous solutions of dibasic sodium phosphate are stable and may be sterilized by autoclaving.
The bulk material should be stored in an airtight container, in a cool, dry, place.

12. Incompatibilities

Dibasic sodium phosphate is incompatible with alkaloids, antipyrine, chloral hydrate, lead acetate, pyrogallol, resorcinol and calcium gluconate. Interaction between calcium and phosphate, leading to the formation of insoluble calcium-phosphate precipitates, is possible in parenteral admixtures.

13. Method of Manufacture

Either bone phosphate (bone ash), obtained by heating bones to whiteness, or the mineral phosphorite is used as a source of tribasic calcium phosphate, which is the starting material in the industrial production of dibasic sodium phosphate.

Tribasic calcium phosphate is finely ground and digested with sulfuric acid. This mixture is then leached with hot water, neutralized with sodium carbonate and dibasic sodium phosphate crystallized from the filtrate.

14. Safety

Dibasic sodium phosphate is widely used as an excipient in parenteral, oral and topical pharmaceutical formulations.

Phosphate occurs extensively in the body and is involved in many physiological processes since it is the principal anion of intracellular fluid. Most foods contain adequate amounts of phosphate and hence deficiency, hypophosphatemia,[1] is virtually unknown except for certain disease states[2] or in patients receiving total parenteral nutrition. Treatment is usually by the oral administration of up to 100 mmol of phosphate daily.

Approximately two-thirds of ingested phosphate is absorbed from the gastrointestinal tract, virtually all of it being excreted in the urine, the remainder being excreted in the feces.

Excessive administration of phosphate, particularly intravenously, rectally, or in patients with renal failure, can cause hyperphosphatemia which may lead to hypocalcemia or other severe electrolyte imbalances.[3,4] Adverse effects occur less frequently following oral consumption although phosphates act as mild saline laxatives when administered by this route or rectally. Consequently, gastrointestinal disturbances including diarrhea, nausea and vomiting may occur following the use of dibasic sodium phosphate as an excipient in oral formulations. Generally however, the level of dibasic sodium phosphate used as an excipient in a pharmaceutical formulation is not usually associated with adverse effects.

LD$_{50}$ (rat, oral): 17 g/kg[5]

15. Handling Precautions

Observe normal precautions appropriate to the circumstances and quantity of material handled. Dibasic sodium phosphate may be irritant to the skin, eyes and mucous membranes. Eye protection and gloves are recommended.

16. Regulatory Status

GRAS listed. Accepted in Europe as a food additive. Included in the FDA Inactive Ingredients Guide (injections, infusions, nasal, ophthalmic, oral, otic, topical and vaginal preparations). Included in nonparenteral and parenteral medicines licensed in the UK.

17. Pharmacopeias

Aust, Belg, Br, Cz, Egypt, Eur, Fr, Ger, Gr, Hung, Ind, It, Jpn, Mex, Neth, Nord, Port, Rom, Swiss, US and Yug.

These pharmacopeias may specify one or more states of hydration for dibasic sodium phosphate. Monographs or specifications can be found for the anhydrous form, the dihydrate, the dodecahydrate and the heptahydrate, although not all forms may necessarily be found in any one pharmacopeia.

18. Related Substances

Dibasic potassium phosphate; Monobasic Sodium Phosphate; tribasic sodium phosphate.

Dibasic potassium phosphate: K$_2$HPO$_4$
Molecular weight: 174.15
CAS number: [7758-11-4]
Synonyms: dipotassium hydrogen orthophosphate; dipotassium hydrogen phosphate; dipotassium phosphate; E340; potassium phosphate.
Appearance: colorless or white, granular, hygroscopic powder.
Pharmacopeias: Gr, Mex and US.
Acidity/alkalinity: pH = 8.5-9.6 for a 5% w/v aqueous solution at 25°C.
Osmolarity: a 2.08% w/v aqueous solution of dibasic potassium phosphate is iso-osmotic with serum.
Solubility: freely soluble in water; very slightly soluble in ethanol (95%).
Comments: each gram of dibasic potassium phosphate contains approximately 11.5 mmol of potassium and 5.7 mmol of phosphate.

Tribasic sodium phosphate: Na$_3$PO$_4$.xH$_2$O
Molecular weight: 163.94 for the anhydrous material; 380.06 for the dodecahydrate (12H$_2$O).
CAS number: [7601-54-9] for the anhydrous material.
Synonyms: E339; trisodium orthophosphate; trisodium phosphate; TSP.
Acidity/alkalinity: pH = 12.1 for a 1% w/v aqueous solution of the anhydrous material at 25°C. A 1% w/v aqueous solution of the dodecahydrate, at 25°C, has a pH of 12-12.2.
Density:
1.3 g/cm^3 for the anhydrous material;
0.9 g/cm^3 for the dodecahydrate.
Solubility: the anhydrous material is soluble 1 in 8 parts of water, whilst the dodecahydrate is soluble 1 in 5 parts of water at 20°C.

19. Comments

Each gram of anhydrous dibasic sodium phosphate represents approximately 14.1 mmol of sodium and 7.0 mmol of phosphate. Each gram of dibasic sodium phosphate dihydrate represents approximately 11.2 mmol of sodium and 5.6 mmol of phosphate. Each gram of dibasic sodium phosphate heptahydrate represents approximately 7.5 mmol of sodium and 3.7 mmol of phosphate. Each gram of dibasic sodium phosphate dodecahydrate represents approximately 5.6 mmol of sodium and 2.8 mmol of phosphate.

20. Specific References

1. Lloyd CW, Johnson CE. Management of hypophosphatemia. Clin Pharm 1988; 7: 123-128.
2. Holland PC, Wilkinson AR, Diez J, Lindsell DRM. Prenatal deficiency of phosphate, phosphate supplementation, and rickets in very-low-birthweight infants. Lancet 1990; 335: 697-701.
3. Haskell LP. Hypocalcaemic tetany induced by hypertonic-phosphate enema [letter]. Lancet 1985; ii: 1433.
4. Martin RR, Lisehora GR, Braxton M, Barcia PJ. Fatal poisoning from sodium phosphate enema: case report and experimental study. JAMA 1987; 257: 2190-2192.
5. Sweet DV, editor. Registry of toxic effects of chemical substances. Cincinnati: US Department of Health, 1987.

21. General References

—

22. Authors

USA: AS Kearney.

Monobasic Sodium Phosphate

1. Nonproprietary Names

BP: Sodium acid phosphate
PhEur: Natrii dihydrogenophosphas dihydricus
USP: Monobasic sodium phosphate
Note that the BP 1993 and the PhEur 1983 contain one monograph for the dihydrate ($2H_2O$), whilst the USP XXII has a single monograph applicable to either the dihydrate, monohydrate or the anhydrous material.
See also Section 17.

2. Synonyms

E339; monosodium orthophosphate; monosodium phosphate; phosphoric acid, monosodium salt; primary sodium phosphate; sodium biphosphate; sodium dihydrogen orthophosphate; sodium dihydrogen phosphate.

3. Chemical Name and CAS Registry Number

Anhydrous monobasic sodium phosphate [7558-80-7]
Monobasic sodium phosphate monohydrate [10049-21-5]
Monobasic sodium phosphate dihydrate [10028-24-7] or [13472-35-0]

4. Empirical Formula   Molecular Weight

NaH_2PO_4 119.98
$NaH_2PO_4.H_2O$ 137.99
$NaH_2PO_4.2H_2O$ 156.01

5. Structural Formula

$NaH_2PO_4.xH_2O$
Where x = 0, 1 or 2.

6. Functional Category

Buffering agent; emulsifying agent; sequestering agent.

7. Applications in Pharmaceutical Formulation or Technology

Monobasic sodium phosphate is used in a wide variety of pharmaceutical formulations as a buffering agent and as a sequestering agent. Therapeutically, monobasic sodium phosphate is used as a mild saline laxative and in the treatment of hypophosphatemia.[1,2]
Monobasic sodium phosphate is also used in food products, e.g. in baking powders, and as a dry acidulant and sequestrant.

8. Description

The hydrated forms of monobasic sodium phosphate occur as odorless, colorless or white-colored, slightly deliquescent, crystals. The anhydrous form occurs as a white crystalline powder or granules.

9. Pharmacopeial Specifications

Test	PhEur 1983	USP XXII (Suppl 6)
Identification	+	+
pH	4.2-4.5	4.1-4.5
Appearance of solution	+	—
Water		
(anhydrous form)	—	$\leqslant 2.0\%$
(monohydrate)	—	10.0-15.0%
(dihydrate)	21.5-24.0%	18.0-26.5%
Insoluble substances	—	$\leqslant 0.2\%$
Reducing substances	+	—
Chloride	$\leqslant 200$ ppm	$\leqslant 0.014\%$
Sulfate	$\leqslant 300$ ppm	$\leqslant 0.15\%$
Aluminum, cadmium and related elements	—	+
Arsenic	$\leqslant 2$ ppm	$\leqslant 8$ ppm
Heavy metals	$\leqslant 10$ ppm	$\leqslant 0.002\%$
Iron	$\leqslant 10$ ppm	—
Organic volatile impurities	—	+
Assay (dried basis)	98.0-100.5%	98.0-103.0%

10. Typical Properties

Acidity/alkalinity: pH = 4.1-4.5 for a 5% w/v aqueous solution of the monohydrate at 25°C.
Density: 1.915 g/cm³ for the dihydrate.
Dissociation constant: $pK_a = 2.15$ at 25°C.
Solubility: soluble 1 in 1 of water; very slightly soluble in ethanol (95%).

11. Stability and Storage Conditions

Monobasic sodium phosphate is chemically stable although it is slightly deliquescent. On heating at 100°C, the dihydrate loses all of its water of crystallization. On further heating, it melts with decomposition at 205°C forming sodium hydrogen pyrophosphate, $Na_2H_2P_2O_7$, and at 250°C it leaves a final residue of sodium metaphosphate, $NaPO_3$.
Aqueous solutions are stable and may be sterilized by autoclaving.
Monobasic sodium phosphate should be stored in an airtight container in a cool, dry, place.

12. Incompatibilities

Monobasic sodium phosphate is an acid salt and is therefore generally incompatible with alkaline materials and carbonates; aqueous solutions of monobasic sodium phosphate are acidic and will cause carbonates to effervesce.
Monobasic sodium phosphate should not be administered concomitantly with aluminum, calcium, or magnesium salts since they bind phosphate and could impair its absorption from the gastrointestinal tract. Interaction between calcium and phosphate, leading to the formation of insoluble calcium-phosphate precipitates, is possible in parenteral admixtures.[3,4]

13. Method of Manufacture

Monobasic sodium phosphate is prepared by adding phosphoric acid to a hot, concentrated solution of disodium phosphate until the liquid ceases to form a precipitate with barium chloride. This solution is then concentrated and the monobasic sodium phosphate crystallized.

14. Safety

Monobasic sodium phosphate is widely used as an excipient in parenteral, oral and topical pharmaceutical formulations.

Phosphate occurs extensively in the body and is involved in many physiological processes since it is the principal anion of intracellular fluid. Most foods contain adequate amounts of phosphate and hence deficiency, hypophosphatemia,[1] is virtually unknown except for certain disease states[2] or in patients receiving total parenteral nutrition. Treatment is usually by the oral administration of up to 100 mmol of phosphate daily.

Approximately two-thirds of ingested phosphate is absorbed from the gastrointestinal tract, virtually all of it being excreted in the urine, the remainder being excreted in the feces.

Excessive administration of phosphate, particularly intravenously, rectally, or in patients with renal failure, can cause hyperphosphatemia which may lead to hypocalcemia or other severe electrolyte imbalances.[5-7] Adverse effects occur less frequently following oral consumption although phosphates act as mild saline laxatives when administered by this route or rectally (2-4 g of monobasic sodium phosphate in an aqueous solution is used as a laxative). Consequently, gastrointestinal disturbances including diarrhea, nausea and vomiting may occur following the use of monobasic sodium phosphate as an excipient in oral formulations. Generally however, the level of monobasic sodium phosphate used as an excipient in a pharmaceutical formulation is not usually associated with adverse effects.

LD$_{50}$ (rat, IM): 0.25 g/kg[8]
LD$_{50}$ (rat, oral): 8.29 g/kg

15. Handling Precautions

Observe normal precautions appropriate to the circumstances and quantity of material handled. Monobasic sodium phosphate may be irritant to the skin, eyes and mucous membranes. Eye protection and gloves are recommended.

16. Regulatory Status

GRAS listed. Accepted as a food additive in Europe. Included in the FDA Inactive Ingredients Guide (injections, infusions, ophthalmic, oral, topical and vaginal preparations). Included in nonparenteral and parenteral medicines licensed in the UK.

17. Pharmacopeias

Aust, Belg, Br, Eur, Fr, Ger, Gr, Hung, Ind, It, Mex, Neth, Nord, Port, Swiss, and Yug; also BP Vet, specify the dihydrate.
Braz, Chin and Mex specify the monohydrate.
US specifies either the dihydrate, monohydrate or anhydrous form.

18. Related Substances

Dibasic Sodium Phosphate; monobasic potassium phosphate.

Monobasic potassium phosphate: KH$_2$PO$_4$
Molecular weight: 136.09
CAS number: [7778-77-0]
Synonyms: E340; monopotassium phosphate; potassium acid phosphate; potassium biphosphate; potassium dihydrogen orthophosphate.
Appearance: colorless crystals or a white, odorless granular or crystalline powder.
Pharmacopeias: Mex and USPNF.
Acidity/alkalinity: pH $\approx$ 4.5 for a 1% w/v aqueous solution at 25°C.
Solubility: freely soluble in water; practically insoluble in ethanol (95%).
Comments: each gram of monobasic potassium phosphate represents approximately 7.3 mmol of potassium and of phosphate.

19. Comments

Each gram of anhydrous monobasic sodium phosphate represents approximately 8.3 mmol of sodium and of phosphate. Each gram of monobasic sodium phosphate monohydrate represents approximately 7.2 mmol of sodium and of phosphate. Each gram of monobasic sodium phosphate dihydrate represents approximately 6.4 mmol of sodium and of phosphate.

20. Specific References

1. Lloyd CW, Johnson CE. Management of hypophosphatemia. Clin Pharm 1988; 7: 123-128.
2. Holland PC, Wilkinson AR, Diez J, Lindsell DRM. Prenatal deficiency of phosphate, phosphate supplementation, and rickets in very-low-birthweight infants. Lancet 1990; 335: 697-701.
3. Eggert LD, Rusho WJ, Mackay MW, Chan GM. Calcium and phosphorus compatibility in parenteral nutrition solutions for neonates. Am J Hosp Pharm 1982; 39: 49-53.
4. Niemiec PW, Vanderveen TW. Compatibility considerations in parenteral nutrient solutions. Am J Hosp Pharm 1984; 41: 893-911.
5. Haskell LP. Hypocalcaemic tetany induced by hypertonic-phosphate enema [letter]. Lancet 1985; ii: 1433.
6. Larson JE, Swigart SA, Angle CR. Laxative phosphate poisoning: pharmacokinetics of serum phosphorus. Hum Toxicol 1986; 5: 45-49.
7. Martin RR, Lisehora GR, Braxton M, Barcia PJ. Fatal poisoning from sodium phosphate enema: case report and experimental study. JAMA 1987; 257: 2190-2192.
8. Sweet DV, editor. Registry of toxic effects of chemical substances. Cincinnati: US Department of Health, 1987.

21. General References

—

22. Authors

USA: GW Radebaugh.

Sodium Propionate

1. Nonproprietary Names

USPNF: Sodium propionate

2. Synonyms

E281; ethylformic acid, sodium salt, hydrate; methylacetic acid, sodium salt, hydrate; sodium propanoate hydrate; sodium propionate hydrate.

3. Chemical Name and CAS Registry Number

Propanoic acid, sodium salt, hydrate [6700-17-0]

4. Empirical Formula   Molecular Weight

$C_3H_5NaO_2.xH_2O$ 114.06
                        (for monohydrate)

5. Structural Formula

$CH_3CH_2COONa.xH_2O$

6. Functional Category

Antimicrobial preservative.

7. Applications in Pharmaceutical Formulation or Technology

As an excipient, sodium propionate is used in oral pharmaceutical formulations as an antimicrobial preservative. Like propionic acid, sodium propionate and other propionic acid salts are fungistatic and bacteriostatic against a number of Gram-positive cocci. Propionates are more active against molds than sodium benzoate, but have essentially no activity against yeasts, *see* Section 10.

Therapeutically, sodium propionate has been used topically in concentrations up to 10% w/w alone or in combination with other propionates, caprylates, or other antifungal agents, in the form of ointments or solutions for the treatment of dermatophyte infections. Eye-drops containing 5% w/v sodium propionate have also been used. *See* Section 19.

In food processes, particularly baking, sodium propionate is used as an antifungal agent; it may also be used as a flavoring agent in food products. In veterinary medicine, sodium propionate is used therapeutically as a glucogenic substance in ruminants.[1]

8. Description

Sodium propionate occurs as colorless transparent crystals or as a granular, free-flowing, crystalline powder. It is odorless, or with a slight characteristic odor, and is deliquescent in moist air. Sodium propionate has a characteristic, slight cheese-like taste, although by itself it is unpalatable.

9. Pharmacopeial Specifications

Test	USPNF XVII (Suppl 6)
Identification	+
Alkalinity	+
Water	$\leqslant$ 1.0%
Arsenic	$\leqslant$ 3 ppm
Heavy metals	$\leqslant$ 0.001%
Organic volatile impurities	+
Assay (dried basis)	99.0-100.5%

10. Typical Properties

Antimicrobial activity: sodium propionate, propionic acid and other propionates possess mainly antifungal activity and are used as preservatives primarily against molds; they exhibit essentially no activity against yeasts. Although in general propionates exhibit little activity against bacteria, sodium propionate is effective against *Bacillus mesenterium*, the organism which causes 'rope' in bread. Antimicrobial activity is largely dependent upon the presence of the free acid and hence propionates exhibit optimum activity at acid pH, notably at less than pH 5. Synergistic effects occur between propionates and carbon dioxide or sorbic acid. *See* Section 18 for typical minimum inhibitory concentrations (MICs) for propionic acid.

Solubility: soluble 1 in 24 of ethanol (95%), 1 in 1 of water and 1 in 0.65 of boiling water; practically insoluble in chloroform and ether.

11. Stability and Storage Conditions

Sodium propionate is deliquescent and should therefore be stored in an airtight container in a cool, dry, place.

12. Incompatibilities

Incompatibilities for sodium propionate are similar to those of other weak organic acids.

13. Method of Manufacture

Sodium propionate is prepared by the reaction of propionic acid with sodium carbonate or sodium hydroxide. *See also* Section 18.

14. Safety

Sodium propionate and other propionates are used in oral pharmaceutical formulations, food products and cosmetics. The free acid, propionic acid, occurs naturally at levels up to 1% w/w in certain cheeses.

Following oral consumption, propionate is metabolized in mammals in a manner similar to fatty acids. Toxicity studies in animals have shown sodium propionate and other propionates to be relatively nontoxic materials.[2,3] In veterinary medicine, sodium propionate is used as a therapeutic agent in twice daily oral doses of 250 g for cows and 60 g for sheep, over four or five days.[1]

In humans, 6 g of sodium propionate has been administered daily without harm.[2] However, allergic reactions to propionates can occur.

LD_{50} (mouse, oral): 6.33 g/kg[4]
LD_{50} (mouse, SC): 2.1 g/kg
LD_{50} (rabbit, skin): 1.64 g/kg

15. Handling Precautions

Observe normal precautions appropriate to the circumstances and quantity of material handled. Sodium propionate may be irritant to the eyes and skin. Gloves, eye protection and a dust-mask are recommended. When heated to decomposition sodium propionate emits toxic fumes of sodium monoxide, Na_2O.

In the UK, the occupational exposure limits for propionic acid are 30 mg/m^3 (10 ppm) long-term (8-hour TWA) and 45 mg/m^3 (15 ppm) short-term.[5]

16. Regulatory Status

GRAS listed. Accepted for use as a food additive in Europe. In cheese products, propionates are limited to 0.3% w/w concentration; a limit of 0.32% w/w is applied in flour and white bread rolls, whilst a limit of 0.38% w/w is applied in whole wheat products.

Included in the FDA Inactive Ingredients Guide (oral capsules, powder, suspensions and syrups). Included in nonparenteral medicines licensed in the UK.

17. Pharmacopeias

Fr, Nord and USPNF. Also in BP Vet.

18. Related Substances

Anhydrous sodium propionate; calcium propionate; potassium propionate; propionic acid; zinc propionate.

Anhydrous sodium propionate: $C_3H_5O_2Na$
Molecular weight: 96.06
CAS number: [137-40-6]
Synonyms: E281; propanoic acid, sodium salt, anhydrous.
Safety:
LD_{50} (mouse, oral): 2.35 g/kg[4]
LD_{50} (rat, oral): 3.92 g/kg

Calcium propionate: $C_6H_{10}O_4Ca$
Molecular weight: 186.22
CAS number: [4075-81-4]
Synonyms: calcium dipropionate; E282; propanoic acid, calcium salt; propionic acid, calcium salt.
Appearance: white-colored crystalline powder.
Solubility: soluble in water; slightly soluble in ethanol and methanol; practically insoluble in acetone and benzene.
Method of manufacture: prepared by the reaction of propionic acid and calcium hydroxide.
Comments: occurs as the mono- or trihydrate.

Potassium propionate: $C_3H_5O_2K$
Molecular weight: 112.17
CAS number: [327-62-8]
Synonyms: E283; propanoic acid, potassium salt; propionic acid, potassium salt.
Appearance: white-colored crystalline powder.
Comments: occurs as the anhydrous form and the monohydrate. Decomposes in moist air to give off propionic acid.

Propionic acid: $C_3H_6O_2$
Molecular weight: 74.08
CAS number: [79-09-4]
Synonyms: carboxyethane; E280; ethylformic acid; methylacetic acid; propanoic acid.
Appearance: a corrosive, oily liquid having a slightly pungent, disagreeable, rancid odor.
Pharmacopeias: Fr and USPNF.
Antimicrobial activity: typical MICs for propionic acid at pH 3.9 are shown below.[6]

Microorganism	MIC (μg/mL)
Aspergillus niger	2000
Candida albicans	2000
Escherichia coli	2000
Klebsiella pneumoniae	1250
Penicillium notatum	2000
Pseudomonas aeruginosa	3000
Pseudomonas cepacia	3000
Pseudomonas fluorescens	1250
Staphylococcus aureus	2000

Autoignition temperature: 955°C
Boiling point: 141.1°C
Dissociation constant: $pK_a = 4.87$
Flash point: 58°C (open cup)
Melting point: -21.5°C
Partition coefficients: Octanol: water = 0.33.
Refractive index: $n_D^{25} = 1.3848$
Solubility: miscible with chloroform, ethanol (95%), ether and water.
Specific gravity: 0.9934
Surface tension: 27.21 mN/m (27.21 dynes/cm) at 15°C
Vapor density (relative): 2.56 (air = 1)
Viscosity (dynamic): 1.175 mPa s (1.175 cP) at 15°C; 1.020 mPa s (1.020 cP) at 25°C; 0.956 mPa s (0.956 cP) at 30°C; 0.668 mPa s (0.668 cP) at 60°C; 0.495 mPa s (0.495 cP) at 90°C.
Method of manufacture: propionic acid may be manufactured by the bacterial fermentation of wood pulp waste or other botanic materials. It may also be prepared by various synthetic routes such as: the reaction of ethanol and carbon monoxide in the presence of a boron trifluoride catalyst; the oxidation of propionaldehyde; or the oxidation of propan-1-ol with chromic acid.
Safety:
LD_{50} (mouse, IV): 0.63 g/kg[4]
LD_{50} (rabbit, skin): 0.5 g/kg
LD_{50} (rat, oral): 2.6 g/kg

Zinc propionate: $C_6H_{10}O_4Zn$
Molecular weight: 211.52
CAS number: [557-28-8]
Synonyms: propanoic acid, zinc salt; propionic acid, zinc salt.
Appearance: white-colored platelets or needle-like crystals (for the monohydrate).
Solubility: the anhydrous form is soluble 1 in 36 of ethanol (95%) at 15°C, 1 in 6 of boiling ethanol (95%) and 1 in 3 of water at 15°C.
Method of manufacture: prepared by dissolving zinc oxide in dilute propionic acid solution.
Comments: occurs as the anhydrous form and the monohydrate. Decomposes in moist air to give off propionic acid.

19. Comments

Propionates are used as antimicrobial preservatives in preference to propionic acid since they are less corrosive.

The therapeutic use of sodium propionate in topical antifungal preparations has been largely superseded by a new generation of antifungal drugs.

20. Specific References

1. Debuf Y, editor. The veterinary formulary, 2nd edition. London: The Pharmaceutical Press, 1994; 329-330.
2. Heseltine WW. A note on sodium propionate. J Pharm Pharmacol 1952; 4: 120-122.
3. Graham WD, Teed H, Grice HC. Chronic toxicity of bread additives to rats. J Pharm Pharmacol 1954; 6: 534-545.
4. Sweet DV, editor. Registry of toxic effects of chemical substances. Cincinnati: US Department of Health, 1987.
5. Health and Safety Executive. EH40/93: occupational exposure limits 1993. London: HMSO, 1993.
6. Wallhäusser KH. Propionic acid. In: Kabara JJ, editor. Cosmetic and drug preservation: principles and practice. New York: Marcel Dekker Inc, 1984: 665-666.

21. General References

Doores S. Organic acids. In: Branen AL, Davidson PM, editors. Antimicrobials in foods. New York: Marcel Dekker Inc, 1983: 85-87.

Furia TE, editor. CRC handbook of food additives. Cleveland, OH: CRC Press Inc, 1972: 137-141.

22. Authors

USA: GW Radebaugh.

Sodium Starch Glycolate

1. Nonproprietary Names

BP: Sodium starch glycollate
USPNF: Sodium starch glycolate

2. Synonyms

Carboxymethyl starch, sodium salt; *Explotab*; *Primojel*.

3. Chemical Name and CAS Registry Number

Sodium carboxymethyl starch [9063-38-1]

4. Empirical Formula   Molecular Weight

The BP 1993 states that sodium starch glycolate is the sodium salt of a poly-α-glucopyranose in which some of the hydroxyl groups are in the form of the carboxymethyl ether. The USPNF XVII states that it is the sodium salt of a carboxymethyl ether of starch. The molecular weight is typically 500 000-1 000 000. Sodium starch glycolate may be characterized by the degree of substitution and cross-linking.

5. Structural Formula

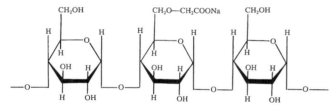

6. Functional Category

Tablet and capsule disintegrant.

7. Applications in Pharmaceutical Formulation or Technology

Sodium starch glycolate is widely used in oral pharmaceuticals as a disintegrant in capsule[1-6] and tablet formulations.[7-9] It is commonly used in tablets prepared by either direct compression[10,11] or wet granulation processes.[12] The usual concentration employed in a formulation is between 2-8%, with the optimum concentration about 4% although in many cases 2% is sufficient. Disintegration occurs by rapid uptake of water followed by rapid and enormous swelling.[13-15]

Although the effectiveness of many disintegrants is affected by the presence of hydrophobic excipients, such as lubricants, the disintegrant efficiency of sodium starch glycolate is unimpaired. Increasing the tablet compression pressure also appears to have no effect on disintegration time.

Sodium starch glycolate has also been investigated for use as a suspending vehicle.[16,17]

8. Description

Sodium starch glycolate is a white to off-white, odorless, tasteless, free-flowing powder. It consists of oval or spherical granules, 30-100 μm in diameter with some less-spherical granules ranging from 10-35 μm in diameter.

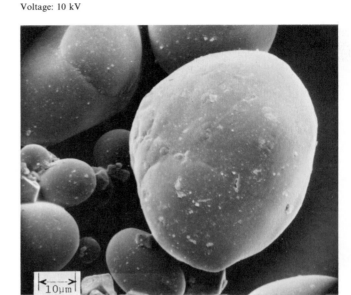

SEM: 1
Excipient: Sodium starch glycolate (*Primojel*)
Manufacturer: Avebe
Lot No.: 89A-1 (FXR-23)
Magnification: 1200x
Voltage: 10 kV

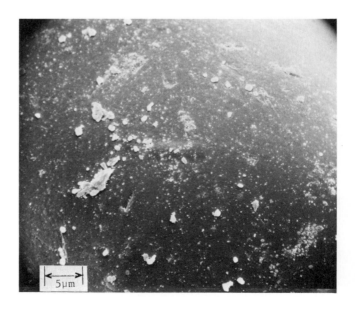

SEM: 2
Excipient: Sodium starch glycolate (*Primojel*)
Manufacturer: Avebe
Lot No.: 89A-1 (FXR-23)
Magnification: 2400x
Voltage: 10 kV

SEM: 3

Excipient: Sodium starch glycolate (*Explotab*)
Manufacturer: Edward Mendell Co Inc
Lot No.: 89A-2 (C-178)
Magnification: 1200x
Voltage: 10 kV

SEM: 4

Excipient: Sodium starch glycolate (*Explotab*)
Manufacturer: Edward Mendell Co Inc
Lot No.: 89A-2 (C-178)
Magnification: 2400x
Voltage: 10 kV

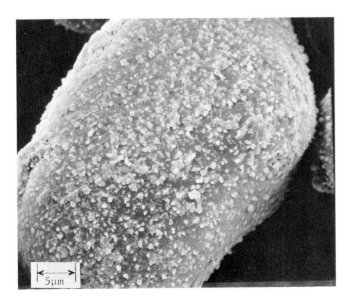

9. Pharmacopeial Specifications

Test	BP 1993	USPNF XVII (Suppl 7)
Identification	+	+
Microbial limits	—	+
Acidity or alkalinity	5.5-7.5	3.0-5.0 or 5.5-7.5
Heavy metals	$\leqslant$ 20 ppm	$\leqslant$ 0.002%
Iron	$\leqslant$ 20 ppm	$\leqslant$ 0.002%
Sodium chloride	$\leqslant$ 10.0%	$\leqslant$ 7.0%
Sodium glycolate	$\leqslant$ 2.0%	—
Loss on drying	$\leqslant$ 10.0%	$\leqslant$ 10.0%
Assay (of Na)	2.8-4.5%	2.8-4.2%

10. Typical Properties

Acidity/alkalinity: pH = 3.0-5.0% or, pH = 5.5-7.5% for a 3.3% aqueous dispersion. *See* Section 19.

Ash: $\leqslant$ 15%

Compressibility: *see* HPE Data.

Density (bulk): 0.85 g/cm^3 for *Primojel*, *see also* HPE Data.

Melting point: does not melt, but chars at approximately 200°C.

Moisture content: *see* HPE Data.

Particle size distribution: 100% of particles less than 104 μm in size. Average particle size is 42 μm for *Explotab*. *See also* HPE Data.

Solubility: sparingly soluble in ethanol (95%); practically insoluble in water. At a concentration of 2% w/v it disperses in cold water and settles in the form of a highly hydrated layer. *See also* HPE Data.

Swelling capacity: in water, sodium starch glycolate swells up to 300 times its volume.

Viscosity (dynamic): $\leqslant$ 200 mPa s (200 cP) for a 4% w/v aqueous dispersion.

	HPE Laboratory Project Data		
	Method	Lab #	Results
Average flow rate	FLO-1	14	13 g/s [a]
Bulk/tap density	BTD-1	1	B: 0.794 g/cm^3 [a]
			T: 1.000 g/cm^3 [a]
Bulk/tap density	BTD-7	14	B: 0.850 g/cm^3 [a]
			T: 1.000 g/cm^3 [a]
Compressibility	COM-5,6	29	*See* Fig. 1. [a]
Moisture content	MC-23	21	3.12% [b]
Moisture content	MC-22	2	1.20% [c]
Moisture content	EMC-1	2	*See* Fig. 2. [c]
Moisture content	SI-1	13	*See* Fig. 3. [a]
Particle friability	PF-1	36	0.037% [a]
Particle size	PSD-5A	21	*See* Fig. 4. [b]
Solubility			
Ethanol (95%)	SOL-1	1	20.8 mg/mL [a]
n-Hexane	SOL-1	1	0.1 mg/mL [a]
Water	SOL-1	1	Gels [a]

Supplier:

a. Avebe (*Primojel*, Lot No.: KYR 8);

b. Kingsley & Keith (Lot No.: 070);

c. Edward Mendell Co Inc (*Explotab*, Lot No.: 959).

11. Stability and Storage Conditions

Tablets prepared with sodium starch glycolate have good storage properties.[18-20] Sodium starch glycolate is stable and should be stored in a well-closed container to protect it from

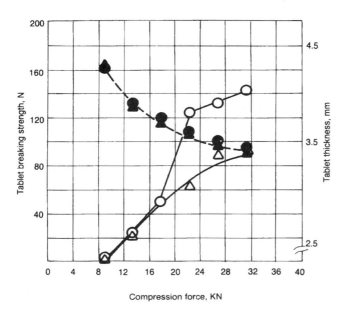

Fig. 1: Compression characteristics of sodium starch glycolate (*Primojel*).
○● Unlubricated Carver Laboratory Press (COM-5)
△▲ Lubricated Carver Laboratory Press (COM-6)

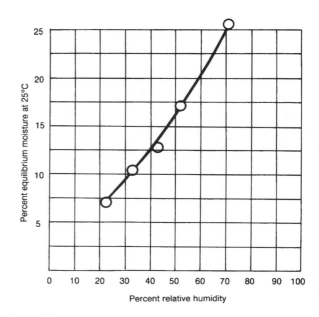

Fig. 3: Moisture sorption isotherm of sodium starch glycolate (*Primojel*).

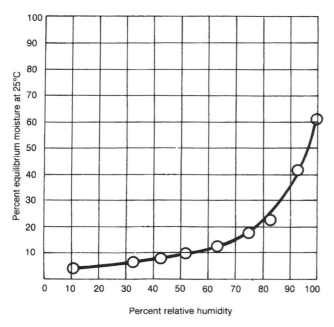

Fig. 2: Equilibrium moisture content of sodium starch glycolate (*Explotab*).

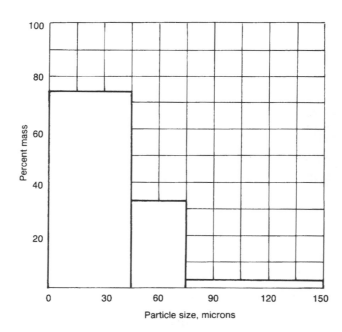

Fig. 4: Particle size distribution of sodium starch glycolate.

wide variations in humidity and temperature that may cause caking. The physical properties of sodium starch glycolate remain unchanged for up to four years if stored at moderate temperatures and humidity.

12. Incompatibilities

Sodium starch glycolate is incompatible with ascorbic acid.[21]

13. Method of Manufacture

Sodium starch glycolate is a substituted and cross-linked derivative of potato starch.

Starch is carboxymethylated by reacting it with sodium chloroacetate in an alkaline medium followed by neutralization with citric, or some other acid. Cross-linking may be achieved by either physical methods or chemically by using reagents such as phosphorus oxytrichloride or sodium trimetaphosphate.[22]

14. Safety

Sodium starch glycolate is widely used in oral pharmaceutical formulations and is generally regarded as a nontoxic and nonirritant material. However, oral ingestion of large quantities may be harmful.

15. Handling Precautions

Observe normal precautions appropriate to the circumstances and quantity of material handled. Sodium starch glycolate may be irritant to the eyes; eye protection and gloves are recommended. A dust mask or respirator is recommended for processes that generate a large quantity of dust.

16. Regulatory Status

Included in the FDA Inactive Ingredients Guide (oral capsules and tablets). Included in nonparenteral medicines licensed in the UK.

17. Pharmacopeias

Br, It, Mex and USPNF.

18. Related Substances

Pregelatinized Starch; Starch.

19. Comments

The physical properties of sodium starch glycolate, and hence its effectiveness as a disintegrant, are affected by the degree of cross-linkage and extent of carboxymethylation. Low substituted sodium starch glycolate, e.g. *Explotab Low pH* (Edward Mendell Co Inc) has a lower pH and, it is claimed, enhanced stability when used with acidic active ingredients which are sensitive to high pH values, such as acetylsalicylic acid.

20. Specific References

1. Newton JM, Razzo FN. The interaction of formulation factors and dissolution fluid and the *in vitro* release of drug from hard gelatin capsules. J Pharm Pharmacol 1975; 27: 78P.
2. Stewart AG, Grant DJW, Newton JM. The release of a model low-dose drug (riboflavine) from hard gelatin capsule formulations. J Pharm Pharmacol 1979; 31: 1-6.
3. Chowhan ZT, Chi L-H. Drug-excipient interactions resulting from powder mixing III: solid state properties and their effect on drug dissolution. J Pharm Sci 1986; 75: 534-541.
4. Botzolakis JE, Augsburger LL. Disintegrating agents in hard gelatin capsules part 1: mechanism of action. Drug Dev Ind Pharm 1988; 14: 29-41.
5. Hannula A-M, Marvola M, Jöns M. Release of ibuprofen from hard gelatin capsule formulations: effect of modern disintegrants. Acta Pharm Fenn 1989; 98: 189-196.
6. Marvola M, Hannula A-M, Ojantakanen S, Westermarck E, Rajamäki M. Effect of sodium bicarbonate and sodium starch glycolate on the *in vivo* disintegration of hard gelatin capsules - a radiological study in the dog. Acta Pharm Nord 1989; 1: 355-362.
7. Khan KA, Rooke DJ. Effect of disintegrant type upon the relationship between compressional pressure and dissolution efficiency. J Pharm Pharmacol 1976; 28: 633-636.
8. Rubinstein MH, Price EJ. *In vivo* evaluation of the effect of five disintegrants on the bioavailability of frusemide from 40 mg tablets. J Pharm Pharmacol 1977; 29: 5P.
9. Caramella C, Colombo P, Coute U, La Manna A. The influence of disintegrants on the characteristics of coated acetylsalicylic acid tablets. Farmaco (Prat) 1978; 33: 498-507.
10. Cid E, Jaminet F. Influence of adjuvants on the dissolution rate and stability of acetylsalicylic acid in compressed tablets [in French]. J Pharm Belg 1971; 26: 38-48.
11. Gordon MS, Chowhan ZT. Effect of tablet solubility and hygroscopicity on disintegrant efficiency in direct compression tablets in terms of dissolution. J Pharm Sci 1987; 76: 907-909.
12. Sekulović D, Tufegdžić N, Birmančević M. The investigation of the influence of Explotab on the disintegration of tablets. Pharmazie 1986; 41: 153-154.
13. Khan KA, Rhodes CT. Disintegration properties of calcium phosphate dibasic dihydrate tablets. J Pharm Sci 1975; 64: 166-168.
14. Khan KA, Rhodes CT. Water-sorption properties of tablet disintegrants. J Pharm Sci 1975; 64: 447-451.
15. Wan LSC, Prasad KPP. Uptake of water by excipients in tablets. Int J Pharmaceutics 1989; 50: 147-153.
16. Farley CA, Lund W. Suspending agents for extemporaneous dispensing: evaluation of alternatives to tragacanth. Pharm J 1976; 216: 562-566.
17. Smith G, McIntosh IEE. Suspending agents for extemporaneous dispensing [letter]. Pharm J 1976; 217: 42.
18. Horhota ST, Burgio J, Lonski L, Rhodes CT. Effect of storage at specified temperature and humidity on properties of three directly compressible tablet formulations. J Pharm Sci 1976; 65: 1746-1749.
19. Sheen P-C, Kim S-I. Comparative study of disintegrating agents in tiaramide hydrochloride tablets. Drug Dev Ind Pharm 1989; 15: 401-414.
20. Gordon MS, Chowhan ZT. The effect of aging on disintegrant efficiency in direct compression tablets with varied solubility and hygroscopicity, in terms of dissolution. Drug Dev Ind Pharm 1990; 16: 437-447.
21. Botha SA, Lötter AP, Du Preez JL. DSC screening for drug-excipient and excipient-excipient interactions in polypharmaceuticals intended for the alleviation of the symptoms of colds and flu III. Drug Dev Ind Pharm 1987; 13: 1197-1215.
22. Bolhuis GK, van Kamp HV, Lerk CF. On the similarity of sodium starch glycolate from different sources. Drug Dev Ind Pharm 1986; 12: 621-630.

21. General References

Avebe. Technical literature: *Primojel*, 1992.
Bhatia RP, Desai KJ, Sheth BB. Disintegration/compressibility of tablets using CLD and other excipients. Drug Cosmet Ind 1978; 122(4): 38, 39, 42, 44, 46, 52, 171-175.

Edward Mendell Co Inc. Technical literature: *Explotab*, 1990.

Gordon MS, Rudraraju VS, Dani K, Chowhan ZT. Effect of the mode of super disintegrant incorporation on dissolution in wet granulated tablets. J Pharm Sci 1993; 82: 220-226.

Khan KA, Rhodes CT. Further studies of the effect of compaction pressure on the dissolution efficiency of direct compression systems. Pharm Acta Helv 1974; 49: 258-261.

Kolarski K, Krówczyński L, Nowak-Goss M. Evaluation of starch sodium glycolate (Primojel) as a disintegrating substance for tablets [in Polish]. Farm Pol 1974; 30: 989-992.

Mendell E. An evaluation of carboxymethyl starch as a tablet disintegrant. Pharm Acta Helv 1974; 49: 248-50.

Rudnic EM, Kanig JL, Rhodes CT. Effect of molecular structure variation on the disintegrant action of sodium starch glycolate. J Pharm Sci 1985; 74: 647-650.

22. Authors

USA: UV Banakar.

Sodium Stearyl Fumarate

1. Nonproprietary Names

USPNF: Sodium stearyl fumarate

2. Synonyms

Fumaric acid, octadecyl ester, sodium salt; *Pruv*; sodium monostearyl fumarate.

3. Chemical Name and CAS Registry Number

2-Butenedioic, monooctadecyl ester, sodium salt [4070-80-8]

4. Empirical Formula   Molecular Weight

$C_{22}H_{39}NaO_4$ 390.5

5. Structural Formula

$$CH_3(CH_2)_{17}OOC \diagdown \qquad \diagup H$$
$$C = C$$
$$H \diagup \qquad \diagdown COONa$$

6. Functional Category

Tablet and capsule lubricant.

7. Applications in Pharmaceutical Formulation or Technology

Sodium stearyl fumarate is used as a lubricant in capsule and tablet formulations at 0.5-2.0% w/w concentration.[1-5] It is also used in certain food applications, *see* Section 16.

8. Description

Sodium stearyl fumarate is a fine, white powder with agglomerates of flat, circular shaped particles.

9. Pharmacopeial Specifications

Test	USPNF XVII
Identification	+
Water	≤ 5.0%
Arsenic	≤ 3 ppm
Lead	≤ 0.001%
Heavy metals	≤ 0.002%
Sodium stearyl maleate	≤ 0.25%
Stearyl alcohol	≤ 0.5%
Saponification value (anhydrous basis)	142.2-146.0
Assay (anhydrous basis)	99.0-101.5%

10. Typical Properties

Acidity/alkalinity: pH = 8.3 for a 5% w/v aqueous solution at 90°C.

SEM: 1

Excipient: Sodium stearyl fumarate (*Pruv*)
Manufacturer: Astra Pharmaceutical Production AB
Lot No.: 66
Magnification: 750x
Voltage: 10 kV

SEM: 2

Excipient: Sodium stearyl fumarate (*Pruv*)
Manufacturer: Astra Pharmaceutical Production AB
Lot No.: 66
Magnification: 1500x
Voltage: 10 kV

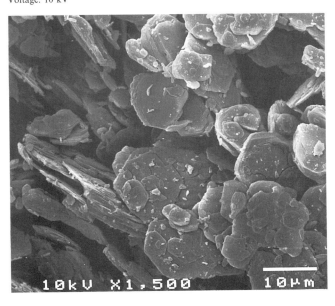

Density: 1.12-1.14 g/cm^3. *See* also HPE Data.
Density (bulk): 0.2-0.35 g/cm^3
Density (tapped): 0.3-0.5 g/cm^3
Melting point: 224-245°C (with decomposition)
Solubility:

Solvent	Solubility at 20°C Unless otherwise stated
Acetone	practically insoluble
Chloroform	practically insoluble
Ethanol	practically insoluble
Methanol	slightly soluble
Water	1 in 20 000 at 25°C
	1 in 10 at 80°C
	1 in 5 at 90°C

Specific surface area: 1.2-2.0 m^2/g. *See* also HPE Data.

	HPE Laboratory Project Data			
	Method	Lab #	Lot #	Results
Density	DE-1	37	90	1.14 g/cm^3 [a]
	DE-1	37	022	1.14 g/cm^3 [b]
Surface area	SSA-1	37	436-39	1.50 m^2/g [a]
	SSA-1	37	60	1.28 m^2/g [a]
	SSA-1	37	64	1.12 m^2/g [a]
	SSA-1	37	90	1.15 m^2/g [a]
	SSA-1	37	107	1.16 m^2/g [a]
	SSA-1	37	022	0.52 m^2/g [b]

Supplier: a. Astra Pharmaceutical Production AB; b. Syntex.

11. Stability and Storage Conditions

At ambient temperature, sodium stearyl fumarate is stable for up to three years when stored in amber glass bottles, with polyethylene screw caps.
The bulk material should be stored in a well-closed container in a cool, dry, place.

12. Incompatibilities

—

13. Method of Manufacture

Stearyl alcohol is reacted with maleic anhydride. The product of this reaction then undergoes an isomerization step followed by salt formation to produce sodium stearyl fumarate.

14. Safety

Sodium stearyl fumarate is used in oral pharmaceutical formulations and is generally regarded as a nontoxic and nonirritant material.
Metabolic studies of sodium stearyl fumarate in the rat and dog indicated that approximately 80% was absorbed and 35% rapidly metabolized. The fraction absorbed was hydrolyzed to stearyl alcohol and fumaric acid, with the stearyl alcohol further oxidized to stearic acid. Sodium stearyl fumarate that was not absorbed, in the dog, was excreted unchanged in the feces within 24 hours.[6]
Stearyl alcohol and stearic acid are naturally occurring constituents in various food products, whilst fumaric acid is a normal constituent of body tissue. Stearates and stearyl citrate have been reviewed by the WHO and an acceptable daily intake for stearyl citrate set at up to 50 mg/kg body-weight.[7] The establishment of an acceptable daily intake for stearates[7] and fumaric acid[8] was thought unnecessary. Disodium fumarate has been reported to have a toxicity not greatly exceeding that of sodium chloride.[9,10]
See Fumaric Acid, Stearic Acid and Stearyl Alcohol for further information.

15. Handling Precautions

Observe normal precautions appropriate to the circumstances and quantity of material handled. Sodium stearyl fumarate should be handled in a well-ventilated environment; eye protection is recommended.

16. Regulatory Status

GRAS listed. Permitted by the FDA for direct addition to food for human consumption as a conditioning or stabilizing agent in various bakery products, flour thickened foods, dehydrated potatoes and processed cereals up to 0.2-1.0% by weight of the food. Included in nonparenteral medicines licensed in the UK.

17. Pharmacopoeias

USPNF.

18. Related Substances

—

19. Comments

Sodium stearyl fumarate is supplied in a pure form and is often of value when the less pure stearate-type lubricants are unsuitable due to chemical incompatibility. Sodium stearyl fumarate is less hydrophobic than magnesium stearate or stearic acid and has a less retardant effect on tablet dissolution than magnesium stearate.

20. Specific References

1. Surén G. Evaluation of lubricants in the development of tablet formula. Dansk Tidsskr Farm 1971; 45: 331-338.
2. Hölzer AW, Sjögren J. Evaluation of sodium stearyl fumarate as a tablet lubricant. Int J Pharmaceutics 1979; 2: 145-153.
3. Hölzer AW, Sjögren J. Evaluation of some lubricants by the comparison of friction coefficients and tablet properties. Acta Pharm Suec 1981; 18: 139-148.
4. Saleh SI, Aboutaleb A, Kassem AA, Stamm A. Evaluation of some water soluble lubricants for direct compression. Lab Pharm Prob Tech 1984; 32: 588-591.
5. Shah NH, Stiel D, Weiss M, Infeld MH, Malick AW. Evaluation of two new tablet lubricants sodium stearyl fumarate and glyceryl behenate. Measurement of physical parameters (compaction, ejection and residual forces) in the tableting process and the effect on the dissolution rate. Drug Dev Ind Pharm 1986; 12: 1329-1346.
6. Figdor SK, Pinson R. The absorption and metabolism of orally administered tritium labelled sodium stearyl fumarate in the rat and dog. J Agr Food Chem 1970; 18(5): 872-877.
7. FAO/WHO. Toxicological evaluation of certain food additives with a review of general principles and of specifications. Seventeenth report of the joint FAO/WHO expert committee on food additives. Tech Rep Ser Wld Hth Org 1974; No. 539.
8. FAO/WHO. Evaluation of certain food additives and contaminants. Thirty-fifth report of the FAO/WHO expert committee on food additives. Tech Rep Ser Wld Hlth Org 1990; No. 789.
9. Bodansky O, Gold H, Zahm W. The toxicity and laxative action of sodium fumarate. J Am Pharm Assoc (Sci) 1942; 31: 1-8.

10. Locke A, Locke RB, Schlesinger H, Carr H. The comparative toxicity and cathartic efficiency of disodium tartrate and fumarate, and magnesium fumarate, for the mouse and rabbit. J Am Pharm Assoc (Sci) 1942; 31: 12-14.

21. General References

Chowhan ZT, Chi L-H. Drug-excipient interactions resulting from powder mixing IV: role of lubricants and their effect on in vitro dissolution. J Pharm Sci 1986; 75: 542-545.

Davies PN, Storey DE, Worthington HEC. Some pitfalls in accelerated stability testing with tablet and capsule lubricants. J Pharm Pharmacol 1987; 39: 86P.

Nicklasson M, Brodin A. The coating of disk surfaces by tablet lubricants, determined by an intrinsic rate of dissolution method. Acta Pharm Suec 1982; 19: 99-108.

22. Authors

UK: PN Davies.

Sorbic Acid

1. Nonproprietary Names

BP: Sorbic acid
PhEur: Acidum sorbicum
USPNF: Sorbic acid

2. Synonyms

E200; 2,4-hexadienoic acid; 2-propenylacrylic acid; (*E,E*)-sorbic acid; *Sorbistat*.

3. Chemical Name and CAS Registry Number

(*E,E*)-Hexa-2,4-dienoic acid [22500-92-1]

4. Empirical Formula   Molecular Weight

$C_6H_8O_2$ 112.13

5. Structural Formula

6. Functional Category

Antimicrobial preservative.

7. Applications in Pharmaceutical Formulation or Technology

Sorbic acid is an antimicrobial preservative, with antibacterial and antifungal properties used in pharmaceuticals, foods, enteral preparations and cosmetics. Generally, it is used at concentrations of 0.05-0.2% in oral and topical pharmaceutical formulations, especially those containing nonionic surfactants. Sorbic acid is also used with proteins, enzymes, gelatin and vegetable gums.[1]

Sorbic acid has limited stability and activity against bacteria and is thus frequently used in combination with other antimicrobial preservatives or glycols, where synergistic effects appear to occur, *see* Section 10.

8. Description

Sorbic acid is a tasteless, white to yellow-white crystalline powder with a faint characteristic odor.

9. Pharmacopeial Specifications

Test	PhEur 1989	USPNF XVII (Suppl 6)
Identification	+	+
Appearance of solution	+	—
Melting range	132-136°C	132-135°C
Water	⩽ 1.0%	⩽ 0.5%
Residue on ignition	—	⩽ 0.2%
Sulfated ash	⩽ 0.2%	—
Heavy metals	⩽ 10 ppm	⩽ 0.001%
Aldehyde (as C_2H_4O)	⩽ 0.15%	—
Assay (anhydrous basis)	99.0-101.0%	99.0-101.0%

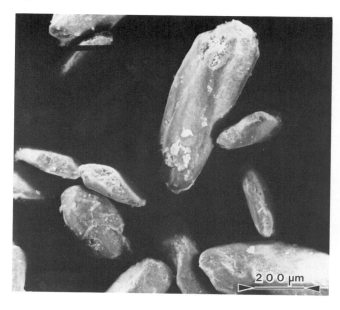

SEM: 1
Excipient: Sorbic acid
Manufacturer: Pfizer Ltd Chemical Division
Magnification: 60x

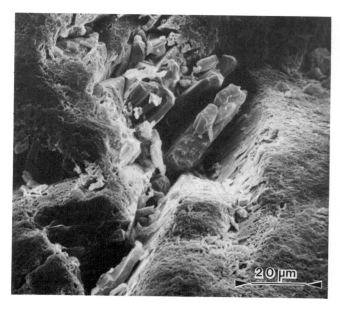

SEM: 2
Excipient: Sorbic acid
Manufacturer: Pfizer Ltd Chemical Division
Magnification: 600x

10. Typical Properties

Antimicrobial activity: sorbic acid is primarily used as an antifungal agent although it also possesses antibacterial properties. The optimum antibacterial activity is obtained at pH 4.5; practically no activity is observed above pH 6.[2,3] The efficacy of sorbic acid is enhanced when it is used in combination with other antimicrobial preservatives or glycols since synergistic effects occur.[4] Reported minimum inhibitory concentrations (MICs) at pH 6 are shown below:[5]

Microorganism	MIC (μg/mL)
Aspergillus niger	200-500
Candida albicans	25-50
Clostridium sporogenes	100-500
Escherichia coli	50-100
Klebsiella pneumoniae	50-100
Penicillium notatum	200-300
Pseudomonas aeruginosa	100-300
Pseudomonas cepacia	50-100
Pseudomonas fluorescens	100-300
Saccharomyces cerevisiae	200-500
Staphylococcus aureus	50-100

Boiling point: 228°C with decomposition.
Density: 1.20 g/cm^3
Dissociation constant: pK_a = 4.76
Flash point: 127°C
Melting point: 134.5°C
Solubility:

Solvent	Solubility at 25°C Unless otherwise stated
Acetone	1 in 11
Chloroform	1 in 15
Ethanol	1 in 8
Ethanol (95%)	1 in 10
Ether	1 in 30
Glycerin	1 in 320
Methanol	1 in 8
Propylene glycol	1 in 19
Water	1 in 400 at 30°C
	1 in 26 at 100°C

Vapor pressure: < 1.3 Pa (< 0.01 mmHg) at 20°C

11. Stability and Storage Conditions

Sorbic acid is sensitive to oxidation, particularly in the presence of light; oxidation occurs more readily in aqueous solution than in the solid form. Sorbic acid may be stabilized by phenolic antioxidants such as propyl gallate (0.02%).[4]
The bulk material should be stored in a well-closed container, protected from light, at a temperature not exceeding 40°C.

12. Incompatibilities

Sorbic acid is incompatible with bases, oxidizing agents and reducing agents. Some loss of antimicrobial activity occurs in the presence of nonionic surfactants and plastics. Oxidation is catalyzed by heavy metal salts.

13. Method of Manufacture

Naturally occurring sorbic acid may be extracted as the lactone (parasorbic acid) from the berries of the mountain ash *Sorbus aucuparia* L. Rosaceae. Synthetically, it may be prepared by the condensation of crotonaldehyde and ketene in the presence of boron trifluoride; the condensation of crotonaldehyde and malonic acid in pyridine solution; or from 1,1,3,5-tetraalkoxyhexane. Fermentation of sorbaldehyde or sorbitol, with bacteria in a culture media, has also been used.

14. Safety

Sorbic acid is used as an antimicrobial preservative in oral and topical pharmaceutical formulations and is generally regarded as a nontoxic material. However, adverse reactions to sorbic acid and potassium sorbate including irritant skin reactions[6-9] and, less frequently, allergic hypersensitivity skin reactions have been reported.[10-12]
Other adverse reactions which have been reported include exfoliative dermatitis due to ointments which contain sorbic acid[13] and allergic conjunctivitis caused by contact lens solutions preserved with sorbic acid.[14]
No adverse reactions have been described after systemic administration of sorbic acid and it is reported that patients who are allergic to sorbic acid topically can ingest it safely.[15] Peroral contact urticaria has however been reported.[9]
The WHO has set an estimated total acceptable daily intake for sorbic acid, calcium sorbate, potassium sorbate and sodium sorbate expressed as sorbic acid at up to 25 mg/kg body-weight.[16,17]
Animal toxicological studies have shown no mammalian carcinogenicity or teratogenicity for sorbic acid consumed at up to 10% of the diet.[18]
LD$_{50}$ (mouse, IP): 2.82 g/kg[19]
LD$_{50}$ (mouse, SC): 2.82 g/kg
LD$_{50}$ (rat, oral): 7.36 g/kg

15. Handling Precautions

Observe normal precautions appropriate to the circumstances and quantity of material handled. Sorbic acid can be irritant to the skin, eyes and respiratory system. Eye protection, gloves and a dust mask or respirator are recommended.

16. Regulatory Status

GRAS listed. Accepted as a food additive in Europe. Included in the FDA Inactive Ingredients Guide (oral capsules, solutions, syrups, tablets and topical preparations). Included in nonparenteral medicines licensed in the UK.

17. Pharmacopeias

Belg, Br, Eur, Fr, Ger, Hung, It, Neth, Swiss and USPNF. Aust, Cz, Mex and Yug include sorbic acid without specifying the (*E,E*)-form.

18. Related Substances

Calcium sorbate; Potassium Sorbate; sodium sorbate.

Calcium sorbate: $C_{12}H_{14}O_4Ca$
Synonyms: E203.
Molecular weight: 262.33
CAS number: [7492-55-9]
Appearance: white, odorless, tasteless, crystalline powder.
Solubility: soluble 1 in 83 parts of water; practically insoluble in fats.

Sodium sorbate: $C_6H_7O_2Na$
Synonyms: E201; sodium (*E,E*)-hexa-2,4-dienoate.
Molecular weight: 134.12
CAS number: [42788-83-0]
Appearance: light, white crystalline powder.

Solubility: soluble 1 in 3 parts of water.

19. Comments

—

20. Specific References

1. Weiner M, Bernstein IL. Adverse reactions to drug formulation agents: a handbook of excipients. New York: Marcel Dekker, 1989: 179.
2. Golightly LK, Smolinske SS, Bennett ML, Sutherland EW, Rumack BH. Adverse effects associated with inactive ingredients in drug products (part I). Med Toxicol 1988; 3: 128-165.
3. Eklund T. The antimicrobial effect of dissociated and undissociated sorbic acid at different pH levels. J Appl Bacteriol 1983; 54: 383-389.
4. Woodford R, Adams E. Sorbic acid. Am Perfum Cosmet 1970; 85(3): 25-30.
5. Wallhäusser KH. Sorbic acid. In: Kabara JJ, editor. Cosmetic and drug preservation principles and practice. New York: Marcel Dekker, 1984: 668-670.
6. Soschin D, Leyden JJ. Sorbic acid-induced erythema and edema. J Am Acad Dermatol 1986; 14: 234-241.
7. Fisher AA. Erythema limited to the face due to sorbic acid. Cutis 1987; 40: 395-397.
8. Clemmensen OJ, Schiodt M. Patch test reaction of the buccal mucosa to sorbic acid. Contact Dermatitis 1982; 8: 341-342.
9. Clemmensen O, Hjorth N. Perioral contact urticaria from sorbic acid and benzoic acid in a salad dressing. Contact Dermatitis 1982; 3: 1-6.
10. Saihan EM, Harman RRM. Contact sensitivity to sorbic acid in 'Unguentum Merck'. Br J Dermatol 1978; 99: 583-584.
11. Fisher AA. Cutaneous reactions to sorbic acid and potassium sorbate. Cutis 1980; 25: 350, 352, 423.
12. Fisher AA. Allergic reactions to the preservatives in over-the-counter hydrocortisone topical creams and lotions. Cutis 1983; 32: 222, 224, 230.
13. Coyle HE, Miller E, Chapman RS. Sorbic acid sensitivity from Unguentum Merck. Contact Dermatitis 1981; 7: 56-57.
14. Fisher AA. Allergic reactions to contact lens solutions. Cutis 1985; 36: 209-211.
15. Klaschka F, Beiersdorff HU. Allergic eczematous reaction from sorbic acid used as a preservative in external medicaments. Munch Med Wschr 1965; 107: 185-187.
16. FAO/WHO. Toxicological evaluation of certain food additives with a review of general principles and of specifications: seventeenth report of the joint FAO/WHO expert committee on food additives. Tech Rep Ser Wld Hlth Org 1974; No. 539.
17. FAO/WHO. Evaluation of certain food additives and contaminants: twenty-ninth report of the joint FAO/WHO expert committee on food additives. Tech Rep Ser Wld Hlth Org 1986; No. 733.
18. Walker R. Toxicology of sorbic acid and sorbates. Food Add Contam 1990; 7(5): 671-676.
19. Sweet DV, editor. Registry of toxic effects of chemical substances. Cincinnati: US Department of Health, 1987.

21. General References

Radus TP, Gyr G. Determination of antimicrobial preservatives in pharmaceutical formulations using reverse-phase liquid chromatography. J Pharm Sci 1983; 72: 221-224.

Sofos JN, Busta FF. Sorbates. In: Branen AL, Davidson PM, editors. Antimicrobials in foods. New York: Marcel Dekker, 1983: 141-175.

Warth A. Mechanism of resistance of *Saccharomyces bailii* to benzoic, sorbic and other weak acids used as food preservatives. J Appl Bacteriol 1977; 43: 215-230.

22. Authors

USA: DJ Harper.

Sorbitan Esters (Sorbitan Fatty Acid Esters)

1. Nonproprietary Names

BP: Sorbitan monolaurate
    Sorbitan mono-oleate
    Sorbitan monostearate

USPNF: Sorbitan monolaurate
       Sorbitan monooleate
       Sorbitan monopalmitate
       Sorbitan monostearate
       Sorbitan sesquioleate
       Sorbitan trioleate

2. Synonyms

See Table I.

3. Chemical Names and CAS Registry Numbers

See Table II.

Table I: Synonyms of selected sorbitan esters.

Name	Synonym
Sorbitan monoisostearate	1,4-Anhydro-D-glucitol, 6-isooctadecanoate; anhydrosorbitol monoisostearate; *Arlacel 987*; *Crill 6*; sorbitan isostearate.
Sorbitan monolaurate	*Arlacel 20*; *Armotan ML*; *Crill 1*; E493; *Glycomul L*; *Hodag SML*; *Liposorb L*; *Montane 20*; *Protachem SML*; *Sorbester P12*; *Sorbirol L*; sorbitan laurate; *Span 20*.
Sorbitan monooleate	*Arlacel 80*; *Armotan MO*; *Capmul O*; *Crill 4*; *Crill 50*; E494; *Glycomul O*; *Hodag SMO*; *Liposorb O*; *Montane 80*; *Protachem SMO*; *Sorbester P17*; *Sorbirol O*; sorbitan oleate; *Span 80*.
Sorbitan monopalmitate	1,4-Anhydro-D-glucitol, 6-hexadecanoate; *Arlacel 40*; *Armotan MP*; *Crill 2*; E495; *Glycomul P*; *Hodag SMP*; *Liposorb P*; *Montane 40*; *Protachem SMP*; *Sorbester P16*; *Sorbirol P*; sorbitan palmitate; *Span 40*.
Sorbitan monostearate	1,4-Anhydro-D-glucitol, 6-octadecanoate; anhydrosorbitol monostearate; *Arlacel 60*; *Armotan MS*; *Capmul S*; *Crill 3*; E491; *Glycomul S*; *Hodag SMS*; *Liposorb S*; *Liposorb SC*; *Liposorb S-K*; *Montane 60*; *Protachem SMS*; *Sorbester P18*; *Sorbirol S*; sorbitan stearate; *Span 60*.
Sorbitan sesqui-isostearate	*Protachem SQI*.
Sorbitan sesquioleate	*Arlacel C*; *Arlacel 83*; *Crill 43*; *Glycomul SOC*; *Hodag SSO*; *Liposorb SQO*; *Montane 83*; *Protachem SOC*.
Sorbitan trilaurate	*Span 25*.
Sorbitan trioleate	*Arlacel 85*; *Crill 45*; *Glycomul TO*; *Hodag STO*; *Liposorb TO*; *Montane 85*; *Protachem STO*; *Sorbester P37*; *Span 85*.
Sorbitan tristearate	*Crill 35*; *Crill 41*; E492; *Glycomul TS*; *Hodag STS*; *Liposorb TS*; *Liposorb TS-K*; *Montane 65*; *Protachem STS*; *Sorbester P38*; *Span 65*.

Table II: Chemical name and CAS registry number of selected sorbitan esters.

Name	Chemical name	CAS number
Sorbitan di-isostearate	Sorbitan di-isooctadecanoate	[68238-87-9]
Sorbitan dioleate	(Z,Z)-Sorbitan di-9-octadecanoate	[29116-98-1]
Sorbitan monolaurate	Sorbitan monododecanoate	[1338-39-2]
Sorbitan monoisostearate	Sorbitan monoisooctadecanoate	[71902-01-7]
Sorbitan monooleate	(Z)-Sorbitan mono-9-octadecenoate	[1338-43-8]
Sorbitan monopalmitate	Sorbitan monohexadecanoate	[26266-57-9]
Sorbitan monostearate	Sorbitan mono-octadecanoate	[1338-41-6]
Sorbitan sesqui-isostearate	Sorbitan sesqui-isooctadecanoate	[71812-38-9]
Sorbitan sesquioleate	(Z)-Sorbitan sesqui-9-octadecenoate	[8007-43-0]
Sorbitan sesquistearate	Sorbitan sesqui-octadecanoate	[51938-44-4]
Sorbitan tri-isostearate	Sorbitan tri-isooctadecanoate	[54392-27-7]
Sorbitan trioleate	(Z,Z,Z)-Sorbitan tri-9-octadecenoate	[26266-58-0]
Sorbitan tristearate	Sorbitan tri-octadecanoate	[26658-19-5]

4. Empirical Formula   Molecular Weight

Name	Formula	Molecular weight
Sorbitan di-isostearate	$C_{42}H_{80}O_7$	697
Sorbitan dioleate	$C_{42}H_{76}O_7$	693
Sorbitan monoisostearate	$C_{24}H_{46}O_6$	431
Sorbitan monolaurate	$C_{18}H_{34}O_6$	346
Sorbitan monooleate	$C_{24}H_{44}O_6$	429
Sorbitan monopalmitate	$C_{22}H_{42}O_6$	403
Sorbitan monostearate	$C_{24}H_{46}O_6$	431
Sorbitan sesqui-isostearate	$C_{33}H_{63}O_{6.5}$	564
Sorbitan sesquioleate	$C_{33}H_{60}O_{6.5}$	561
Sorbitan sesquistearate	$C_{33}H_{63}O_{6.5}$	564
Sorbitan tri-isostearate	$C_{60}H_{114}O_8$	964
Sorbitan trioleate	$C_{60}H_{108}O_8$	958
Sorbitan tristearate	$C_{60}H_{114}O_8$	964

5. Structural Formula

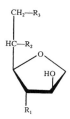

$R_1 = R_2 = OH$, $R_3 = R$ for sorbitan monoesters,
$R_1 = OH$, $R_2 = R_3 = R$ for sorbitan diesters,
$R_1 = R_2 = R_3 = R$ for sorbitan triesters,
Where R = $(C_{17}H_{35})COO$ for isostearate,
$\quad\quad\quad (C_{11}H_{23})COO$ for laurate,
$\quad\quad\quad (C_{17}H_{33})COO$ for oleate,
$\quad\quad\quad (C_{15}H_{31})COO$ for palmitate,
$\quad\quad\quad (C_{17}H_{35})COO$ for stearate.
The sesqui-esters are equimolar mixtures of monoesters and diesters.

6. Functional Category

Emulsifying agent; nonionic surfactant; solubilizing agent; wetting agent.

7. Applications in Pharmaceutical Formulation or Technology

Sorbitan esters are a series of mixtures of partial esters of sorbitol and its mono- and di-anhydrides with fatty acids. Sorbitan esters are widely used in cosmetics, food products and pharmaceutical formulations as lipophilic nonionic surfactants. They are mainly used in pharmaceutical formulations as emulsifying agents in the preparation of creams, emulsions and ointments for topical application. When used alone, sorbitan esters produce stable water-in-oil emulsions but are frequently used in combination with varying proportions of a polysorbate to produce water-in-oil or oil-in-water emulsions or creams of varying consistencies.

Sorbitan monolaurate, sorbitan monopalmitate and sorbitan trioleate have also been used at a concentration of 0.01-0.05% w/v in the preparation of an emulsion for intramuscular administration.

Use	Concentration (%)
Emulsifying agent	
Used alone in water-in-oil emulsions	1-15
Used in combination with hydrophilic emulsifiers in oil-in-water emulsions	1-10
Used to increase the water-holding properties of ointments	1-10
Solubilizing agent	
For poorly soluble, active constituents in lipophilic bases	1-10
Wetting agent	
For insoluble, active constituents in lipophilic bases	0.1-3

8. Description

Sorbitan esters occur as cream to amber-colored liquids or solids with a distinctive odor and taste, *see* below.

Name	Appearance
Sorbitan monoisostearate	Yellow viscous liquid
Sorbitan monolaurate	Yellow viscous liquid
Sorbitan monooleate	Yellow viscous liquid
Sorbitan monopalmitate	Cream solid
Sorbitan monostearate	Cream solid
Sorbitan sesquioleate	Amber viscous liquid
Sorbitan trioleate	Amber viscous liquid
Sorbitan tristearate	Cream/yellow solid

9. Pharmacopeial Specifications

Test	BP 1993 (Ad 1994)	USPNF XVII (Suppl 9)
Identification	+	+
Acid value		
Sorbitan monolaurate	⩽ 7.0	⩽ 8
Sorbitan monooleate	⩽ 8.0	⩽ 8
Sorbitan monopalmitate	—	⩽ 8
Sorbitan monostearate	⩽ 10.0	⩽ 10
Sorbitan sesquioleate	—	⩽ 14
Sorbitan trioleate	—	⩽ 17
Hydroxyl value		
Sorbitan monolaurate	330-358	330-358
Sorbitan monooleate	193-209	190-215
Sorbitan monopalmitate	—	275-305
Sorbitan monostearate	235-260	235-260
Sorbitan sesquioleate	—	182-220
Sorbitan trioleate	—	50-75
Iodine value		
Sorbitan monooleate	—	62-76
Sorbitan sesquioleate	—	65-75
Sorbitan trioleate	—	77-85
Saponification value		
Sorbitan monolaurate	158-170	158-170
Sorbitan monooleate	149-160	145-160
Sorbitan monopalmitate	—	140-150
Sorbitan monostearate	147-157	147-157
Sorbitan sesquioleate	—	143-165
Sorbitan trioleate	—	169-183
Water		
Sorbitan monolaurate	⩽ 1.5%	⩽ 1.5%
Sorbitan monooleate	⩽ 1.0%	⩽ 1.0%
Sorbitan monopalmitate	—	⩽ 1.5%
Sorbitan monostearate	⩽ 1.5%	⩽ 1.5%

Continued

Test	BP 1993 (Ad 1994)	USPNF XVII (Suppl 9)
Sorbitan sesquioleate	—	⩽ 1.0%
Sorbitan trioleate	—	⩽ 0.7%
Residue on ignition		
Sorbitan monolaurate	—	⩽ 0.5%
Sorbitan monooleate	—	⩽ 0.5%
Sorbitan monopalmitate	—	⩽ 0.5%
Sorbitan monostearate	—	⩽ 0.5%
Sorbitan sesquioleate	—	⩽ 1.4%
Sorbitan trioleate	—	⩽ 0.25%
Sulfated ash	⩽ 0.5%	—
Heavy metals	⩽ 10 ppm	⩽ 0.001%
Arsenic	⩽ 3 ppm	—
Specific gravity		
Sorbitan monolaurate	0.9-1.03	—
Sorbitan monooleate	0.985-1.005	—
Viscosity		
Sorbitan monolaurate	3.0-5.0 Pa s	—
Sorbitan monooleate	0.9-1.5 Pa s	—
Assay for fatty acids		
Sorbitan monolaurate	—	55.0-63.0%
Sorbitan monooleate	—	72.0-78.0%
Sorbitan monopalmitate	—	63.0-71.0%
Sorbitan monostearate	—	68.0-76.0%
Sorbitan sesquioleate	—	74.0-80.0%
Sorbitan trioleate	—	85.5-90.0%
Assay for polyols		
Sorbitan monolaurate	—	39.0-45.0%
Sorbitan monooleate	—	25.0-31.0%
Sorbitan monopalmitate	—	32.0-38.0%
Sorbitan monostearate	—	27.0-34.0%
Sorbitan sesquioleate	—	22.0-28.0%
Sorbitan trioleate	—	13.0-19.0%

Note: unless otherwise indicated, the above specifications apply to all of the sorbitan esters listed in the BP 1993 or USPNF XVII. The USPNF XVII contains 6 sorbitan ester monographs while the BP 1993 contains 3 monographs, *see* Sections 1 and 17.

10. Typical Properties

Acid value: see Table III
Density: see Table III
Flash point: > 149°C
HLB value: see Table III
Hydroxyl value: see Table III
Iodine number: see Table III
Melting point: see Table III
Moisture content: see Table IV
Pour point: see Table III
Saponification value: see Table IV
Solubility: sorbitan esters are generally soluble or dispersible in oils; they are also soluble in most organic solvents. In water, although insoluble they are generally dispersible.
Surface tension: see Table IV
Viscosity (dynamic): see Table IV

11. Stability and Storage Conditions

Gradual soap formation occurs with strong acids or bases; sorbitan esters are stable in weak acids or bases.
Sorbitan esters should be stored in a well-closed container in a cool, dry, place.

12. Incompatibilities

—

13. Method of Manufacture

Sorbitol is dehydrated to form a hexitan (1,4-sorbitan) which is then esterified with the desired fatty acid.

Table III: Typical properties of selected sorbitan esters.

Name	Acid value	Density (g/cm^3)	HLB value	Hydroxyl value	Iodine number	Melting point (°C)	Pour point (°C)
Sorbitan monoisostearate	⩽ 8	—	4.7	220-250	—	—	—
Sorbitan monolaurate	⩽ 7	1.01	8.6	159-169	⩽ 7	—	16-20
Sorbitan monooleate	⩽ 8	1.01	4.3	193-209	—	—	-12
Sorbitan monopalmitate	3-7	1.0	6.7	270-303	⩽ 1	43-48	—
Sorbitan monostearate	5-10	—	4.7	235-260	⩽ 1	53-57	—
Sorbitan sesquioleate	8.5-13	1.0	3.7	188-210	—	—	—
Sorbitan trioleate	10-14	0.95	1.8	55-70	—	—	—
Sorbitan tristearate	⩽ 7	—	2.1	60-80	—	—	—

Table IV: Typical properties of selected sorbitan esters (continued).

Name	Saponification value	Surface tension of 1% aqueous solution (mN/m)	Viscosity at 25°C (mPa s)	Water content (%)
Sorbitan monoisostearate	143-153	—	—	⩽ 1.0
Sorbitan monolaurate	159-169	28	3900-4900	⩽ 0.5
Sorbitan monooleate	149-160	30	970-1080	⩽ 0.5
Sorbitan monopalmitate	142-152	36	Solid	⩽ 1.0
Sorbitan monostearate	147-157	46	Solid	⩽ 1.0
Sorbitan sesquioleate	149-160	—	1500	⩽ 1.0
Sorbitan trioleate	170-190	32	200-250	⩽ 1.0
Sorbitan tristearate	172-185	48	Solid	⩽ 1.0

14. Safety

Sorbitan esters are widely used in cosmetics, food products, and oral and topical pharmaceutical formulations and are generally regarded as nontoxic and nonirritant materials. However, there have been occasional reports of hypersensitive skin reactions following the topical application of products containing sorbitan esters.[1-4]

The WHO has set an estimated acceptable daily intake of sorbitan monopalmitate, monostearate and tristearate,[5] and sorbitan monolaurate and monooleate[6] at up to 25 mg/kg body-weight calculated as total sorbitan esters.

Sorbitan monolaurate LD_{50} (rat, oral): 33.6 g/kg[7]

Sorbitan monostearate LD_{50} (rat, oral): 31 g/kg[7]

15. Handling Precautions

Observe normal precautions appropriate to the circumstances and quantity of material handled. Eye protection and gloves are recommended.

16. Regulatory Status

Certain sorbitan esters are accepted as food additives in Europe. Sorbitan esters are included in the FDA Inactive Ingredients guide (inhalations, IM injections, ophthalmic, oral, topical and vaginal preparations). Sorbitan esters are used in nonparenteral medicines licensed in the UK.

17. Pharmacopeias

Name	Pharmacopeia
Sorbitan monolaurate	Br, Hung, Mex and USPNF.
Sorbitan monooleate	Br, Mex and USPNF.
Sorbitan monopalmitate	Mex and USPNF.
Sorbitan monostearate	Br and USPNF.
Sorbitan sesquioleate	Jpn, Swiss and USPNF.
Sorbitan trioleate	USPNF.

18. Related Substances

Polyoxyethylene Sorbitan Fatty Acid Esters.

19. Comments

—

20. Specific References

1. Finn OA, Forsyth A. Contact dermatitis due to sorbitan monolaurate. Contact Dermatitis 1975; 1: 318.
2. Hannuksela M, et al. Allergy to ingredients of vehicles. Contact Dermatitis 1976; 2: 105-110.
3. Austad J. Allergic contact dermatitis to sorbitan monooleate (Span 80). Contact Dermatitis 1982; 8: 426-427.
4. Boyle J, Kennedy CTC. Contact urticaria and dermatitis to Alphaderm. Contact Dermatitis 1984; 10: 178.
5. FAO/WHO. Toxicological evaluations of certain food additives with a review of general principles and of specifications: seventeenth report of the joint FAO/WHO expert committee on food additives. Tech Rep Ser Wld Hlth Org 1974; No. 539.
6. FAO/WHO. Evaluation of certain food additives and contaminants: twenty-sixth report of the joint FAO/WHO expert committee on food additives. Tech Rep Ser Wld Hlth Org 1982; No. 683.
7. Sweet DV, editor. Registry of toxic effects of chemical substances. Cincinnati: US Department of Health, 1987.

21. General References

Konno K, Jinno T, Kitahara A. Solubility, critical aggregating or micellar concentration and aggregate formation of non-ionic surfactants in non-aqueous solutions. J Colloid Interface Sci 1974; 49: 383.
Mittal KL, editor. Micellization, solubilization and microemulsions, Volume 1. New York: Plenum Press, 1977.
Smolinske SC. Handbook of food, drug, and cosmetic excipients. Boca Raton, FL: CRC Press Inc, 1992: 369-370.
Suzuki E, Shirotani KI, Tsuda Y, Sekiguchi K. Studies on methods of particle size reduction of medicinal compounds VIII: size reduction by freeze-drying and the influence of pharmaceutical adjuvants on the micromeritic properties of freeze-dried powders. Chem Pharm Bull 1979; 27: 1214-1222.
Whitworth CW, Pongpaibul Y. The influence of some additives on the stability of aspirin in an oleaginous suppository base. Can J Pharm Sci 1979; 14: 36-38.

22. Authors

UK: RL Leyland.

Sorbitol

1. Nonproprietary Names

BP: Sorbitol
PhEur: Sorbitolum
USPNF: Sorbitol

2. Synonyms

E420; 1,2,3,4,5,6-hexanehexol; *Hydex*; *Neosorb*; sorbite; D-sorbitol; *Sorbitol instant*.

3. Chemical Names and CAS Registry Number

D-Glucitol [50-70-4]

4. Empirical Formula   Molecular Weight

$C_6H_{14}O_6$ 182.17

5. Structural Formula

```
            CH₂OH
             |
      H—C—OH
             |
   HO—C—H
             |
      H—C—OH
             |
      H—C—OH
             |
            CH₂OH
```

6. Functional Category

Humectant; plasticizer; sweetening agent; tablet and capsule diluent.

7. Applications in Pharmaceutical Formulation or Technology

Sorbitol is widely used as an excipient in pharmaceutical formulations. It is also used extensively in cosmetics and food products.

Sorbitol is used as a diluent in tablet formulations prepared by either wet granulation or direct compression.[1-5] It is particularly useful in chewable tablets due to its pleasant, sweet taste and cooling sensation. In capsule formulations it is used as a plasticizer for gelatin.

In liquid preparations[6] sorbitol is used as a vehicle in sugar-free formulations and as a stabilizer for drug,[7] vitamin[8,9] and antacid suspensions. In syrups it is effective in preventing crystallization around the cap of bottles. Sorbitol is additionally used in injectable[10] and topical preparations and therapeutically as an osmotic laxative.

Use	Concentration (%)
Humectant	3-15
IM injections	10-25
Moisture control agent in tablets	3-10
Oral solutions	20-35
Oral suspensions	70
Plasticizer for gelatin & cellulose	5-20
Prevention of 'cap locking' in syrups & elixirs	15-30

Continued

Use	Concentration (%)
Substitute for glycerin & propylene glycol	25-90
Tablet binder & filler	25-90
Toothpastes	20-60
Topical emulsions	2-18

8. Description

Sorbitol is D-glucitol. It is a hexahydric alcohol related to mannose and is isomeric with mannitol.

Sorbitol occurs as an odorless, white or almost colorless, crystalline, hygroscopic powder. Four crystalline polymorphs and one amorphous form of sorbitol have been identified which have slightly different physical properties, e.g. melting point.[3] Sorbitol is available in a wide range of grades and polymorphic forms such as granules, flakes or pellets which tend to cake less than the powdered form and have more desirable compression characteristics. Sorbitol has a pleasant, cooling, sweet taste and has approximately 50-60% the sweetness of sucrose.

9. Pharmacopeial Specifications

Test	PhEur 1985	USPNF XVII
Identification	+	+
Water	≤ 1.5%	≤ 1.0%
Acidity or alkalinity	+	—
Clarity and color of solution	+	—
Specific optical rotation	+4.0° to +7.0°	—
Residue on ignition	—	≤ 0.1%
Sulfated ash	≤ 0.1%	—
Chloride	≤ 50 ppm	≤ 0.0050%
Sulfate	≤ 100 ppm	≤ 0.010%
Arsenic	—	≤ 3 ppm
Lead	≤ 0.5 ppm	—
Nickel	≤ 1.0 ppm	—
Heavy metals	—	≤ 0.001%
Reducing sugars	+	+
Total sugars	—	+
Assay (anhydrous basis)	98.0-101.0%	91.0-100.5%

10. Typical Properties

Acidity/alkalinity:
pH = 4.5-7.0 for a 10% w/v aqueous solution.
Compressibility: compression characteristics and the degree of lubrication required vary, depending upon the particle size and grade of sorbitol used. *See* HPE Data.
Density: 1.49 g/cm³
Density (bulk & tapped): *see* HPE Data.
Flowability: flow characteristics vary depending upon the particle size and grade of sorbitol used. Fine powder grades tend to be poorly flowing while granular grades have good flow properties.
Heat of solution: -110.9 J/g (-26.5 cal/g)
Hygroscopicity: sorbitol is a very hygroscopic powder and relative humidities greater than 50% at 25°C should be avoided when sorbitol is added to direct compression tablet formulas.[1] *See also* HPE Data.
Melting point:
110-112°C for anhydrous form;
97.7°C for monohydrate;
93°C for metastable monohydrate form.

Osmolarity: a 5.48% w/v aqueous solution of sorbitol hemihydrate is iso-osmotic with serum.

Particle size distribution: particle size distribution varies depending upon the grade of sorbitol. For fine powder grades typically 87% < 125 μm in size while for granular grades 22% < 125 μm, 45% between 125-250 μm and 33% between 250-590 μm. Individual suppliers' literature should be consulted for further information.

Solubility:

Solvent	Solubility at 25°C
Chloroform	practically insoluble
Ethanol (95%)	1 in 25
Ethanol (82%)	1 in 8.3
Ethanol (62%)	1 in 2.1
Ethanol (41%)	1 in 1.4
Ethanol (20%)	1 in 1.2
Ethanol (11%)	1 in 1.14
Ether	practically insoluble
Methanol	slightly soluble
Water	1 in 0.5

	HPE Laboratory Project Data		
	Method	Lab #	Results
Bulk/tap density			
Coarse type	BTD-1	1	B: 0.667 g/cm³ [a]
			T: 0.833 g/cm³
Coarse type	BTD-7	14	B: 0.700 g/cm³ [a]
			T: 0.780 g/cm³
Tablet type	BTD-1	1	B: 0.505 g/cm³ [a]
			T: 0.641 g/cm³
Tablet type	BTD-7	14	B: 0.570 g/cm³ [a]
			T: 0.680 g/cm³
Compressibility			
Coarse type	COM-3	20	*See* Fig. 1.
Crystalline type	COM-3	20	*See* Fig. 2.
Moisture content			
Coarse type	MC-3	33	0.23% [a]
Crystalline type	MC-3	10	0.70% [b]
	MC-3	25	0.83% [a]
	EMC-1	10	*See* Fig. 3. [b]
Tablet type	MC-3	33	0.45% [a]

Supplier: a. Pfizer; b. ICI America (Lot No.: 2404JI).

11. Stability and Storage Conditions

Sorbitol is relatively chemically inert and compatible with most excipients. It is stable in air in the absence of catalysts and in cold, dilute acids and alkalis. Sorbitol does not darken or decompose at elevated temperatures or in the presence of amines. It is nonflammable, noncorrosive and nonvolatile.

Although resistant to fermentation by many microorganisms a preservative should be added to sorbitol solutions. Solutions may be stored in glass, plastic, aluminum and stainless steel containers. Solutions for injection may be sterilized by autoclaving.

The bulk material is hygroscopic and should be stored in an airtight container in a cool, dry, place.

12. Incompatibilities

Sorbitol will form water soluble chelates with many di- and trivalent metal ions in strongly acidic and alkaline conditions.

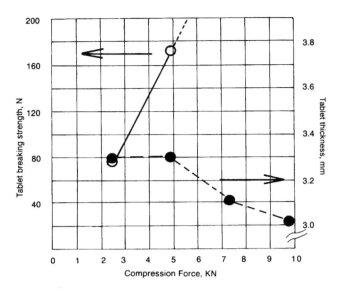

Fig. 1: Compression characteristics of sorbitol USPNF, crystalline tablet type (Lot No.: 95-1).
Mean tablet weight = 500 mg.
Minimum compressional force for compaction = 2.45 kN.
Compressional force resulting in capping = 14.7 kN.

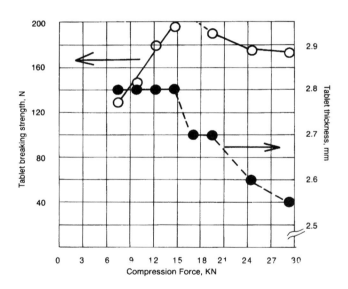

Fig. 2: Compression characteristics of sorbitol USPNF, coarse crystalline type (Lot No.: G92051-S6926).
Mean tablet weight = 500 mg.
Minimum compressional force for compaction = 7.35 kN.
Compressional force resulting in capping = 19.6 kN.
Lubricant required 1% w/w magnesium stearate.

Addition of liquid polyethylene glycols to sorbitol solution USP, with vigorous agitation, produces a waxy, water soluble gel with a melting point of 35-40°C. Sorbitol solutions also react with iron oxide to become discolored.

Sorbitol increases the degradation rate of penicillins in neutral and aqueous solutions. [11]

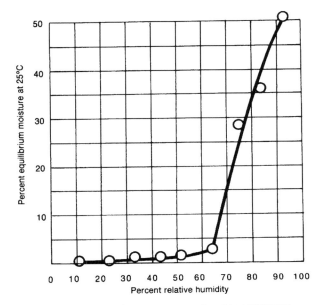

Fig. 3: Equilibrium moisture content of sorbitol USPNF.

13. Method of Manufacture

Sorbitol occurs naturally in the ripe berries of many trees and plants and was first isolated, in 1872, from the berries of the Mountain Ash (*Sorbus americana*).

Industrially, sorbitol is prepared by high-pressure hydrogenation with a copper-chromium or nickel catalyst, or by electrolytic reduction of glucose and corn syrup. If cane or beet sugars are used as a source, the disaccharide is first hydrolyzed to dextrose and fructose prior to hydrogenation.

14. Safety

Sorbitol is widely used in a number of pharmaceutical products and occurs naturally in many edible fruits and berries. It is absorbed more slowly from the gastrointestinal tract than sucrose and is metabolized in the liver to fructose and glucose. Its calorific value is approximately 16.7 J/g (4 cal/g). Sorbitol is better tolerated by diabetics than sucrose and is widely used in many sugar-free liquid vehicles. However, it is not considered to be unconditionally safe for diabetics.

Reports of adverse reactions to sorbitol are largely due to its action as an osmotic laxative when ingested orally,[12,13] which may be exploited therapeutically. Ingestion of large quantities of sorbitol (> 20 g/day in adults) should therefore be avoided. Sorbitol is not readily fermented by oral microorganisms and has little effect on dental plaque pH hence, it is generally considered to be noncariogenic.[14]

Sorbitol is generally considered to be more irritating than mannitol.

LD$_{50}$ (mouse, IP): 15 g/kg[15]
LD$_{50}$ (mouse, IV): 9.48 g/kg
LD$_{50}$ (mouse, oral): 17.8 g/kg
LD$_{50}$ (rat, IV): 7.1 g/kg
LD$_{50}$ (rat, oral): 15.9 g/kg

15. Handling Precautions

May be harmful if ingested in great quantities. May be irritant to the eyes. Observe normal precautions appropriate to the circumstances and quantity of material handled. Eye protection, gloves and a dust mask or respirator are recommended.

16. Regulatory Status

GRAS listed. Accepted for use as a food additive in Europe. Included in the FDA Inactive Ingredients Guide (intra-articular and IM injections, oral capsules, solutions, suspensions, syrups and tablets, rectal, topical and vaginal preparations). Included in parenteral and nonparenteral medicines licensed in the UK.

17. Pharmacopeias

Aust, Br, Cz, Egypt, Eur, Fr, Ger, Gr, Hung, Ind, It, Jpn, Mex, Neth, Port, Rom, Swiss, USPNF and Yug.

18. Related Substances

Mannitol; sorbitol solution 70%; Xylitol.

Sorbitol solution 70%
Synonyms: sorbitol liquid; *Sorbo*.
Appearance: a clear, colorless and odorless viscous liquid.
Pharmacopeias: Aust, Br, Cz, Egypt, Eur, Fr, Ger, Hung, Ind, It, Jpn, Neth, Port, Rom, Swiss, US and Yug.
Comments: sorbitol solution is an aqueous solution of hydrogenated, partly hydrolyzed starch. The PhEur 1985 specifies that it contains 68.0-72.0% w/w of solid matter and not less than 62.0% w/w of polyols expressed as D-glucitol. For physical properties *see* table I.

Table I: Physical properties of sorbitol in water solutions.

Concentration (% w/w) at 25°C	Density (g/cm³) at 25°C	Viscosity (mPa s) at 25°C	Refractive index	Freezing point (°C)
10	1.034	1.2	1.348	-1.1
20	1.073	1.7	1.365	-3.8
30	1.114	2.5	1.383	-8.0
40	1.155	4.4	1.400	-13.0
50	1.197	9.1	1.418	-26.0
60	1.240	26.0	1.437	—
70*	1.293	110.0	1.458	—
80	1.330	900.0	1.478	—

* Sorbitol solution PhEur 1985.

19. Comments

Sorbitol may be substituted, gram for gram, for sucrose to prepare 70-90% w/v syrups.

Several different grades of sorbitol, with different polymorphic form, particle size and other physical characteristics are commercially available, e.g. *Neosorb* (Roquette Frères). Pyrogen free grades are also available from some suppliers.

20. Specific References

1. Molokhia AM, Moustafa MA, Gouda MW. Effect of storage conditions on the hardness, disintegration and drug release from some tablet bases. Drug Dev Ind Pharm 1982; 8: 283-292.
2. Bolton S, Atluri R. Crystalline sorbitol tablets: effect of mixing time and lubricants on manufacturing. Drug Cosmet Ind 1984; 135(5): 44, 46, 47, 48, 50.
3. DuRoss JW. Modification of the crystalline structure of sorbitol and its effects on tableting characteristics. Pharmaceut Technol 1984; 8(9): 42-53.
4. Basedow AM, Möschl GA. Sorbitol instant - an excipient with unique tableting properties. Drug Dev Ind Pharm 1986; 12: 2061-2089.
5. Schmidt PC, Vortisch W. Influence of manufacturing method of fillers and binders on their tableting properties: comparison of 8

commercially available sorbitols [in German]. Pharm Ind 1987; 49: 495-503.

6. Daoust RG, Lynch MJ. Sorbitol in pharmaceutical liquids. Drug Cosmet Ind 1962; 90(6): 689-691, 773, 776, 777, 779, 781-785.

7. Sabatini GR, Gulesich JJ. Formulation of a stable and palatable oral suspension of procaine penicillin G. J Am Pharm Assoc (Pract Pharm) 1956; 17: 806-808.

8. Bandelin FJ, Tuschhoff JV. The stability of ascorbic acid in various liquid media. J Am Pharm Assoc (Sci) 1955; 44: 241-244.

9. Parikh BD, Lofgren FV. A further stability study of an oral multivitamin liquid preparation. Drug Standards 1958; 26: 56-61.

10. Lindvall S, Andersson NSE. Studies on a new intramuscular haematinic, iron-sorbitol. Br J Pharmacol 1961; 17: 358-371.

11. Bundgaard H. Drug allergy: chemical and pharmaceutical aspects. In: Florence AT, Salole EG, editors. Formulation factors in adverse reactions. London: Wright, 1990: 23-55.

12. Jain NK, et al. Sorbitol intolerance in adults. Am J Gastroenterol 1985; 80: 678-681.

13. Brown AM, Masson E. 'Hidden' sorbitol in proprietary medicines - a cause for concern? Pharm J 1990; 245: 211.

14. Ayers CS, Abrams RA. Noncariogenic sweeteners: sugar substitutes for caries control. Dental Hygiene 1987; 61: 162-167.

15. Sweet DV, editor. Registry of toxic effects of chemical substances. Cincinnati: US Department of Health, 1987.

21. General References

Barr M, Kohn SR, Tice LF. The solubility of sorbitol in hydroalcoholic solutions. Am J Pharm 1957; 129: 102-106.

Blanchard J, Fink WT, Duffy JP. Effect of sorbitol on interaction of phenolic preservatives with polysorbate 80. J Pharm Sci 1977; 66: 1470-1473.

Burgess S. Sorbitol instant: a unique excipient. Mfg Chem 1987; 58(6): 55, 57, 59.

Collins J. Metabolic disease: time for fructose solutions to go. Lancet 1993; 341: 600.

Rabinowitz MP, Reisberg P, Bodin JI. GLC assay of sorbitol as cyclic *n*-butylboronate. J Pharm Sci 1974; 63: 1601-1604.

Roquette Frères. Technical literature: Neosorb-sorbitol, 1992.

Shah DN, White JL, Hem SL. Mechanism of interaction between polyols and aluminum hydroxide gel. J Pharm Sci 1981; 70: 1101-1104.

Zatz JL, Lue R-Y. Flocculation of suspensions containing nonionic surfactants by sorbitol. J Pharm Sci 1987; 76: 157-160.

22. Authors

USA: RA Nash.

Soybean Oil

1. Nonproprietary Names

BP: Soya oil
USP: Soybean oil

2. Synonyms

Calchem IVO-114; *Lipex 107*; *Lipex 200*; soja bean oil; soya bean oil.

3. Chemical Name and CAS Registry Number

Soybean oil [8001-22-7]

4. Empirical Formula　　Molecular Weight

A typical analysis of refined soybean oil indicates the composition of the acids, present as glycerides, to be: linoleic acid 50-57%; linolenic acid 5-10%; oleic acid 17-26%; palmitic acid 9-13% and stearic acid 3-6%. Other acids are present in trace quantities.[1]

5. Structural Formula

See Sections 4 and 8.

6. Functional Category

Oleaginous vehicle; solvent.

7. Applications in Pharmaceutical Formulation or Technology

In pharmaceutical preparations, soybean oil emulsions are primarily used as a fat source in total parenteral nutrition (TPN) regimens.[2] Although other oils, such as peanut oil, have been used for this purpose, soybean oil is now preferred since it is associated with fewer adverse reactions. Emulsions containing soybean oil have also been used as vehicles for the oral and intravenous administration of drugs;[3] drug substances that have been incorporated into such emulsions include diazepam, oil soluble vitamins (A, D_2, E and K), poorly water soluble steroids[4] and fluorocarbons.[5,6] In addition, soybean oil has been included in formulations of liposomes.[7]

Soybean oil may also be used in cosmetics and is consumed as an edible oil. As soybean oil has emollient properties, it is used as a bath additive in the treatment of dry skin conditions.

8. Description

The USP XXII describes soybean oil as the refined fixed oil obtained from the seeds of the soya plant *Glycine soja* (Leguminosae). The BP 1993 describes soybean oil as the refined fixed oil obtained from the seeds of *Glycine max* (Leguminosae); it may contain a suitable antioxidant.

Soybean oil is a pale yellow colored, odorless or almost odorless liquid, with a bland taste.

9. Pharmacopeial Specifications

Test	BP 1993	USP XXII
Specific gravity	0.916-0.922	0.916-0.922
Refractive index	1.465-1.475	1.465-1.475
Heavy metals	—	$\leqslant$ 0.001%
Free fatty acids	—	+
Fatty acid composition	+	+
Acid value	$\leqslant$ 0.6	—
Iodine value	—	120-141
Saponification value	—	180-200
Unsaponifiable matter	$\leqslant$ 1.5%	$\leqslant$ 1.0%
Cottonseed oil	—	+
Peroxide	—	+
Stearin	+	—
Foreign fixed oils	+	—

10. Typical Properties

Autoignition temperature: 445°C
Density: 0.916-0.922 g/cm^3 at 25°C
Flash point: 282°C
Freezing point: -10 to -16°C
Hydroxyl value: 4-8
Interfacial tension: 50 mN/m (dynes/cm) at 20°C.
Refractive index: $n_D^{25} = 1.471$-1.475
Solubility: practically insoluble in ethanol (95%) and water; miscible with carbon disulfide, chloroform, ether and petroleum spirit (boiling range 40-60°C).
Surface tension: 25 mN/m (25 dynes/cm) at 20°C.
Viscosity (dynamic):
172.9 mPa s (172.9 cP) at 0°C;
99.7 mPa s (99.7 cP) at 10°C;
50.09 mPa s (50.09) cP at 25°C;
28.86 mPa s (28.86 cP) at 40°C.

11. Stability and Storage Conditions

Soybean oil is a stable material if protected from atmospheric oxygen.

The formation of undesirable flavors in soybean oil is accelerated by the presence of 0.01 ppm copper and 0.1 ppm iron which act as catalysts for oxidation; this can be minimized by the addition of chelating agents.

Prolonged storage of soybean oil emulsions, particularly at elevated temperatures, can result in the formation of free fatty acids with a consequent reduction in the pH of the emulsion; degradation is minimized at pH 6-7. However, soybean oil emulsions are stable at room temperature if stored under nitrogen, in a light-resistant, glass container. Plastic containers are permeable to oxygen and should not be used for long-term storage since oxidative degradation can occur.

The stability of soybean oil emulsions is considerably influenced by other additives in a formulation.[8-11]

Soybean oil should be stored in a well-filled, airtight, light-resistant container at a temperature not exceeding 25°C.

12. Incompatibilities

Soybean oil emulsions have been reported to be incompatible at 25°C with a number of materials including: calcium chloride; calcium gluconate; magnesium chloride; phenytoin sodium and tetracycline hydrochloride.[12] Lower concentrations of these materials, or lower storage temperatures, may result in improved compatibility. The source of the material may also affect compatibility, i.e. while one injection from a particular manufacturer may be incompatible with a fat emulsion, an injection with the same amount of active drug substance from another manufacturer may be compatible. Soybean oil emulsions are also incompatible with many other drug substances, IV infusion solutions and ions (above certain concentrations).

13. Method of Manufacture

Obtained by solvent extraction using petroleum hydrocarbons, or to a lesser extent by expression using continuous screw press operations, of the seeds of either *Glycine max* (Leguminosae) or *Glycine soja* (Leguminosae). The oil is refined, deodorized and clarified by filtration at about 0°C.

14. Safety

Soybean oil is widely used intramuscularly as a drug vehicle, or as a component of emulsions used in parenteral nutrition regimens; it is also consumed as an edible oil. Generally, soybean oil is regarded as an essentially nontoxic and nonirritant material. However, serious adverse reactions to soybean oil emulsions administered parenterally have been reported. These include cases of hypersensitivity,[13] CNS reactions[14] and fat embolism.[15]
Anaphylactic reactions have also been reported following the consumption of foods derived from, or containing, soya beans.
LD_{50} (mouse, IV): 22.1 g/kg[16]
LD_{50} (rat, IV): 16.5 g/kg

15. Handling Precautions

Observe normal precautions appropriate to the circumstances and quantity of material handled. Spillages of soybean oil are slippery and should be covered with an inert absorbent material prior to disposal.

16. Regulatory Status

Included in the FDA Inactive Ingredients Guide (IV injections, oral capsules, topical preparations). Included in nonparenteral and parenteral medicines licensed in the UK.

17. Pharmacopeias

Br, Chin, Jpn, Mex and US.

18. Related Substances

Canola Oil; Corn Oil; Cottonseed Oil; Peanut Oil; Sesame Oil.

19. Comments

The stability of soybean oil emulsions may be readily disturbed by the addition of other materials and formulations containing soybean oil should therefore be carefully evaluated for their compatibility and stability.

20. Specific References

1. British Standards Institute. Specification for crude vegetable fats, BS 7207. London: HMSO, 1990.
2. McNiff BL. Clinical use of 10% soybean oil emulsion. Am J Hosp Pharm 1977; 34: 1080-1086.
3. Jeppsson R. Effects of barbituric acids using an emulsion form intravenously. Acta Pharm Suec 1972; 9: 81-90.
4. Malcolmson C, Lawrence MJ. A comparison of the incorporation of model steroids into non-ionic micellar and microemulsion systems. J Pharm Pharmacol 1993; 45: 141-143.
5. Johnson OL, Washington C, Davis SS. Thermal stability of fluorocarbon emulsions that transport oxygen. Int J Pharmaceutics 1990; 59: 131-135.
6. Johnson OL, Washington C, Davis SS. Long-term stability studies of fluorocarbon oxygen transport emulsions. Int J Pharmaceutics 1990; 63: 65-72.
7. Stricker H, Müller H. The storage stability of dispersions of soybean-lecithin liposomes [in German]. Pharm Ind 1984; 46: 1175-1183.
8. Takamura A, Ishii F, Noro S, Tanifuji M, Nakajima S. Study of intravenous hyperalimentation: effect of selected amino acids on the stability of intravenous fat emulsions. J Pharm Sci 1984; 73: 91-94.
9. Driscoll DF, Baptista RJ, Bistrian BR, Blackburn GL. Practical considerations regarding the use of total nutrient admixtures. Am J Hosp Pharm 1986; 43: 416-419.
10. Washington C. The stability of intravenous fat emulsions in total parenteral nutrition mixtures. Int J Pharmaceutics 1990; 66: 1-21.
11. Manning RJ, Washington C. Chemical stability of total parenteral nutrition mixtures. Int J Pharmaceutics 1992; 81: 1-20.
12. Trissel LA. Handbook on injectable drugs, 7th edition. Bethesda, MD: American Society of Hospital Pharmacists, 1992: 372-383.
13. Hiyama DT, et al. Hypersensitivity following lipid emulsion infusion in an adult patient. J Parenter Enteral Nutr 1989; 13: 318-320.
14. Jellinek EH. Dangers of intravenous fat infusions [letter]. Lancet 1976; ii: 967.
15. Estebe JP, Malledant Y. Fat embolism after lipid emulsion infusion [letter]. Lancet 1991; 337: 673.
16. Sweet DV, editor. Registry of toxic effects of chemical substances. Cincinnati: US Department of Health, 1987.

21. General References

Benita S, Levy MY. Submicron emulsions as colloidal drug carriers for intravenous administration: comprehensive physicochemical characterization. J Pharm Sci 1993; 82: 1069-1079.
Delaveau P, Hotellier F. Oils of pharmaceutical, dietetic, and cosmetic interest, part I: maize, soybean, sunflower [in French]. Ann Pharm Fr 1971; 29: 399-412.
Mirtallo JM, Oh T. A key to the literature of total parenteral nutrition: update 1987. Drug Intell Clin Pharm 1987; 21: 594-606.
Smolinske SC. Handbook of food, drug, and cosmetic excipients. Boca Raton, FL: CRC Press Inc, 1992: 383-385.
Wolf WJ. In: Kirk-Othmer encyclopedia of chemical technology, volume 21; 3rd edition. New York: Wiley-Interscience, 1981: 417-442.

22. Authors

UK: CG Cable, PJ Weller.

Starch

1. Nonproprietary Names

BP: Maize starch
    Potato starch
    Rice starch
    Tapioca starch
    Wheat starch
PhEur: Maydis amylum (corn starch)
       Oryzae amylum (rice starch)
       Solani amylum (potato starch)
       Tritici amylum (wheat starch)
USPNF: Starch
Note that the USPNF XVII describes starch, in a single monograph, as being obtained from either the mature grain of corn, *Zea mays* or of wheat, *Triticum aestivum*, or from tubers of the potato *Solanum tuberosum*. The PhEur 1984 has individual monographs for each of these starches along with an additional monograph for rice starch, *Oryza sativa*. The BP 1993 similarly describes corn, potato, rice, tapioca and wheat starch in individual monographs, tapioca starch being obtained from the rhizomes of *Manihot utilissima* Pohl. *See also* Section 19.

2. Synonyms

Amido; amidon; amilo; amylum; *Aytex P*; cassava starch; *Fluftex W*; *Melojel*; *Paygel 55*; *Pure-Dent*; *Purity 21*; *Tablet White*.
See also Sections 1 and Section 19.

3. Chemical Name and CAS Registry Number

Starch [9005-25-8]

4. Empirical Formula   Molecular Weight

$(C_6H_{10}O_5)_n$
Where n = 300-1000.
Starch consists of amylose and amylopectin, two polysaccharides based on α-glucose. *See also* Sections 5 and 18.

5. Structural Formula

n = 300 to 1000

Amylose

glucose
unit

Segment of Amylopectin Molecule

6. Functional Category

Glidant; tablet and capsule diluent; tablet and capsule disintegrant; tablet binder.

7. Applications in Pharmaceutical Formulation or Technology

Starch is widely used as an excipient primarily in oral solid dosage formulations where it is utilized as a binder, diluent and disintegrant.
As a diluent, starch is used for the preparation of standardized triturates of colorants or potent drugs to facilitate subsequent mixing or blending processes in manufacturing operations. Starch is also used in dry-filled capsule formulations for volume adjustment of the fill matrix.[1]
In tablet formulations, freshly prepared starch paste is used at a concentration of 5-25% w/w in tablet granulations as a binder. Selection of the quantity required in a given system is determined by optimization studies, using parameters such as granule friability, tablet friability, hardness, disintegration rate and drug dissolution rate.
Starch is one of the most commonly used tablet disintegrants at concentrations of 3-15% w/w.[2-9] However, unmodified starch does not compress well and tends to increase tablet friability and capping if used in high concentrations. In granulated formulations, about half the total starch content is included in the granulation mixture and the balance as part of the final blend with the dried granulation.
Starch is also used in topical preparations, for example, it is widely used in dusting-powders for its absorbency, and is used as a protective covering in ointment formulations applied to the skin. Starch mucilage has also been applied to the skin as an emollient, has formed the base of some enemas and has been used in the treatment of iodine poisoning.
Therapeutically, rice starch based solutions have been used in the prevention and treatment of dehydration due to acute diarrheal diseases.

8. Description

Starch occurs as an odorless and tasteless, fine, white-colored powder comprised of very small spherical or ovoid granules whose size and shape are characteristic for each botanical variety.

SEM: 1
Excipient: Corn starch
Manufacturer: Anheuser Busch
Lot No.: 96A-3 (67)
Magnification: 2400x
Voltage: 20 kV

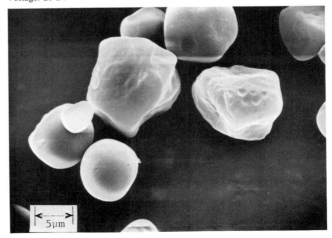

5μm

SEM: 2

Excipient: Corn starch
Manufacturer: AE Staley Mfg Co
Lot No.: 96A-4 (G77912)
Magnification: 2400x
Voltage: 20 kV

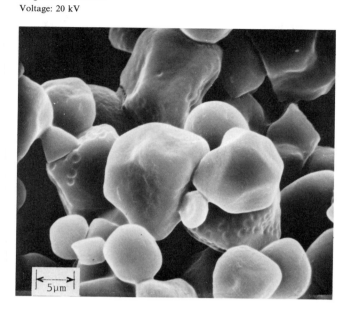

SEM: 4

Excipient: Rice starch
Supplier: Matheson, Coleman & Bell
Magnification: 600x

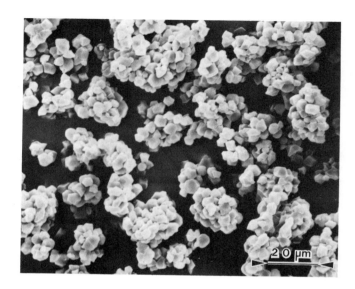

SEM: 3

Excipient: Potato starch
Manufacturer: Starchem
Lot No.: 96A-5 (1179)
Magnification: 2400x
Voltage: 20 kV

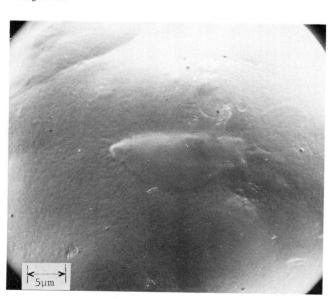

SEM: 5

Excipient: Rice starch
Supplier: Matheson, Coleman & Bell
Magnification: 3000x

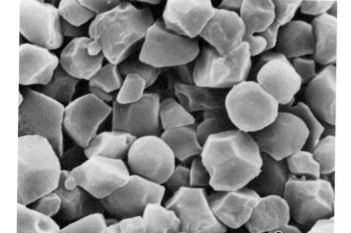

SEM: 6

Excipient: Wheat starch (*Paygel 55*)
Manufacturer: Henkel Corp
Lot No.: 96A-1 (2917D)
Magnification: 2400x
Voltage: 20 kV

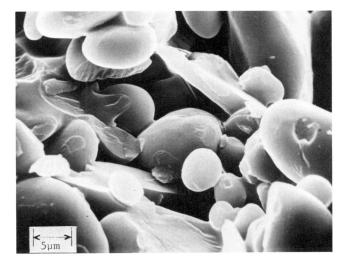

SEM: 7

Excipient: Wheat starch (*Aytex P*)
Manufacturer: Henkel Corp
Lot No.: 96A-2 (2919D)
Magnification: 2400x
Voltage: 20 kV

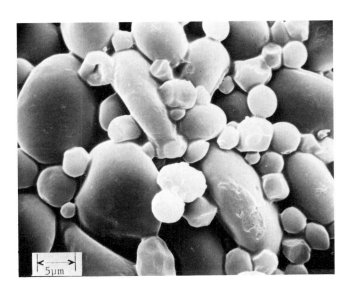

9. Pharmacopeial Specifications

Test	PhEur 1984	USPNF XVII
Identification	+	+
Botanic characteristics	+	+
Microbial limits	+	+
pH		
Corn starch	—	4.5-7.0
Potato starch	—	5.0-8.0
Wheat starch	—	4.5-7.0
Acidity	+	—
Loss on drying		
Corn starch	⩽ 15.0%	⩽ 14.0%
Rice starch	⩽ 15.0%	—
Potato starch	⩽ 20.0%	⩽ 14.0%
Wheat starch	⩽ 15.0%	⩽ 14.0%
Residue on ignition	—	⩽ 0.5%
Sulfated ash		
Corn starch	⩽ 0.6%	—
Rice starch	⩽ 1.0%	—
Potato starch	⩽ 0.6%	—
Wheat starch	⩽ 0.6%	—
Iron		
Corn starch	—	⩽ 0.002%
Rice starch	—	⩽ 0.002%
Potato starch	⩽ 10 ppm	⩽ 0.002%
Wheat starch	—	⩽ 0.002%
Oxidizing substances	—	⩽ 0.002%
Sulfur dioxide	—	⩽ 0.008%
Foreign matter	+	—

10. Typical Properties

Acidity/alkalinity: pH = 5.5-6.5 for a 2% w/v aqueous dispersion of corn starch, at 25°C.

Compressibility: *see* Fig. 1.

Density: 1.478 g/cm^3 for corn starch.

Density (bulk): 0.462 g/cm^3 for corn starch.

Density (tapped): 0.658 g/cm^3 for corn starch.

Flowability: 10.8-11.7 g/s for corn starch;[9] 30% for corn starch (Carr compressibility index).[10] Corn starch is cohesive and has poor flow characteristics.

Gelatinization temperature: 73°C for corn starch; 72°C for potato starch; 63°C for wheat starch.

Moisture content: all starches are hygroscopic and rapidly absorb atmospheric moisture.[11,12] Approximate equilibrium moisture content values at 50% relative humidity are: 11% for corn starch; 18% for potato starch; 14% for rice starch and 13% for wheat starch. Between 30-80% relative humidity, corn starch is the least hygroscopic starch and potato starch is the most hygroscopic starch. Commercially available grades of corn starch usually contain 10-14% water. *See also* HPE Data.

Particle size distribution: 2-32 μm for corn starch; 10-100 μm for potato starch; 2-20 μm for rice starch; 5-35 μm for tapioca starch; 2-45 μm for wheat starch. Median diameter for corn starch is 17 μm and for wheat starch is 23 μm.

Solubility: practically insoluble in cold ethanol (95%) and cold water. Starch swells instantaneously in water by about 5-10% at 37°C.[2,12] Polyvalent cations produce more swelling than monovalent ions, but pH has little effect.

Specific surface area: 0.60-0.75 m^2/g for corn starch.

Swelling temperature: 65°C for corn starch; 64°C for potato starch; 55°C for wheat starch.

Viscosity (dynamic): 13.0 mPa s (13.0 cP) for a 2% w/v aqueous dispersion of corn starch at 25°C

HPE Laboratory Project Data			
	Method	**Lab #**	**Results**
Corn Starch			
Bulk/tap density	BTD-1	1	B: 0.521 g/cm^3 [a]
			T: 0.806 g/cm^3
	BTD-1	1	B: 0.485 g/cm^3 [a]
			T: 0.694 g/cm^3
	BTD-1	1	B: 0.535 g/cm^3 [a]
			T: 0.820 g/cm^3
	BTD-1	1	B: 0.490 g/cm^3 [b]
			T: 0.769 g/cm^3
	BTD-1	14	B: 0.570 g/cm^3 [b]
			T: 0.670 g/cm^3
	BTD-1	1	B: 0.515 g/cm^3 [c]
			T: 0.758 g/cm^3
Moisture content	MC-20	2	7.10% [a]
	MC-15	14	9.80% [b]
	MC-15	34	9.90% [b]
	MC-15	34	9.86% [c]
	EMC-1	2	*See* Fig. 2. [a]
	SDI-1	14	*See* Fig. 3. [b]
Particle size	PSD-6	23	100% ⩽ 74 μm [a]
Solubility (at 25°C)			
Ethanol (95%)	SOL-1	1	0.030 mg/mL [b]
	SOL-1	1	0.020 mg/mL [c]
n-Hexane	SOL-1	1	0.005 mg/mL [b]
	SOL-1	1	0.011 mg/mL [c]
Water	SOL-1	1	0.063 mg/mL [b]
	SOL-1	1	0.084 mg/mL [c]
Potato Starch			
Moisture content	MC-29	23	15.30% [d]
	MC-15	34	15.85% [d]
Particle size	PSD-6	23	100% ⩽ 74 μm [d]
Wheat Starch			
Moisture content			
Aytex P	MC-15	14	7.94% [e]
Aytex P	MC-15	34	8.32% [e]
Paygel 55	MC-15	14	7.50% [e]
Paygel 55	MC-15	34	7.67% [e]
	SDI-1	14	*See* Fig. 4. [e]
Particle size	PSD-2	5	100% ⩽ 58 μm

Suppliers: a. National Starch & Chemicals Ltd; b. Anheuser Busch; c. AE Staley Mfg Co; d. Starchem; e. Henkel Corp.

11. Stability and Storage Conditions

Dry, unheated starch is stable if protected from high humidity. When used as a diluent or disintegrant in solid dosage forms, starch is considered to be inert under normal storage conditions. However, heated starch solutions or pastes are physically unstable and are readily attacked by microorganisms to form a wide variety of starch derivatives and modified starches which have unique physical properties.

Starch should be stored in an airtight container in a cool, dry, place.

12. Incompatibilities

—

13. Method of Manufacture

Starch is extracted from plant sources through a sequence of processing steps involving coarse milling, repeated water washing, wet sieving and centrifugal separation. The wet

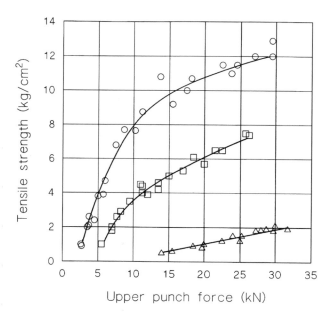

Fig. 1: Compression characteristics of corn, potato and wheat starches.
□ Corn starch.
○ Potato starch.
△ Wheat starch.
Tablet machine: Manesty F; speed: 50 per min; weight: 490-510 mg. Strength test: Diametral compression between flat-faced rams. Upper ram stationary, lower moving at 66 μm/s.

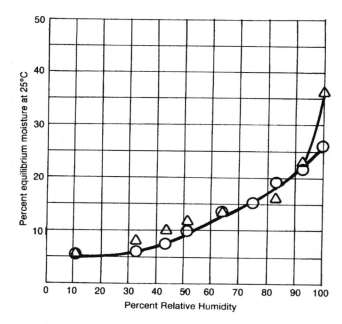

Fig. 2: Equilibrium moisture content of corn starch and pregelatinized starch.
○ Corn starch (National Starch & Chemicals Ltd; Lot #421).
△ Pregelatinized starch (National Starch & Chemicals Ltd; Lot #HJW 103).

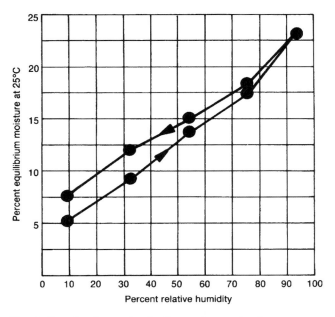

Fig. 3: Sorption-desorption isotherm of corn starch.
(Anheuser Busch; Lot #67).

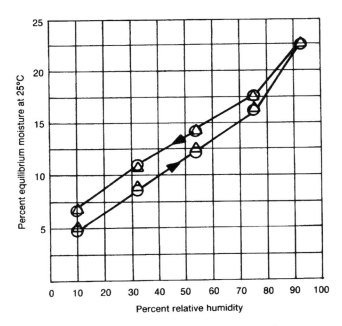

Fig. 4: Sorption-desorption isotherm of wheat starch.
○ *Paygel 55* (Henkel Corp; Lot #2917D).
△ *Aytex P* (Henkel Corp; Lot #2919D)

starch obtained from these processes is dried and milled before use in pharmaceutical formulations.

14. Safety

Starch is widely used as an excipient in pharmaceutical formulations, particularly oral tablets.

Starch is an edible food substance and is generally regarded as an essentially nontoxic and nonirritant material.[13] However, oral consumption of massive doses can be harmful due the formation of starch calculi which cause bowel obstruction.[14] Starch may also cause granulomatous reactions when applied to the peritoneum or the meninges. Contamination of surgical wounds with the starch glove powder used by surgeons has also resulted in the development of granulomatous lesions.[15] Allergic reactions to starch are extremely rare and individuals apparently allergic to one particular starch may not experience adverse effects with a starch from a different botanic source.

LD_{50} (mouse, IP): 6.6 g/kg[16]

15. Handling Precautions

Observe normal precautions appropriate to the circumstances and quantity of material handled. Eye protection and a dust-mask are recommended. Excessive dust generation should be avoided to minimize the risks of explosions.

In the UK, the long-term (8-hour TWA) occupational exposure limits for starch are: 10 mg/m^3 for total inhalable dust and 5 mg/m^3 for respirable dust.[17]

16. Regulatory Status

GRAS listed. Included in the FDA Inactive Ingredients Guide (buccal tablets, oral capsules, powders, suspensions and tablets, topical preparations and vaginal tablets). Included in nonparenteral medicines licensed in the UK.

17. Pharmacopeias

Aust, Br, Braz, Chin, Cz, Egypt, Eur, Fr, Ger, Gr, Hung, Ind, It, Jpn, Mex, Neth, Nord, Port, Rom, Swiss, Turk, Yug and USPNF. Also in BP Vet.

18. Related Substances

Amylopectin; α-amylose; Pregelatinized Starch; Sterilizable Maize Starch.

Amylopectin
CAS number: [9037-22-3]
Comments: amylopectin is a branched D-glucan with mostly α-D-(1→4) and approximately 4% α-D-(1→6) linkages.

α-Amylose
CAS number: [9005-82-7]
Comments: amylose is a linear (1→4)-α-D-glucan.

19. Comments

Note that corn starch is also known as maize starch and that tapioca starch is also known as cassava starch.

Whereas the USPNF XVII specifies that starch should be produced from corn, potato or wheat, the BP 1993 also permits starch to be produced from rice. In tropical and subtropical countries where these starches may not be readily available, the BP 1993 additionally permits the use of tapioca starch, subject to additional requirements.

Starches from different plant sources differ in their amylose/amylopectin ratio. For example, corn starch contains about 27% amylose, potato starch about 22%, and tapioca starch about 17%. In contrast, waxy corn starch contains almost entirely amylopectin, with no amylose. These differences modify the physical properties of the starches such that the various types may not be interchangeable in a given pharmaceutical application.

20. Specific References

1. York P. Studies of the effect of powder moisture content on drug release from hard gelatin capsules. Drug Dev Ind Pharm 1980; 6: 605-627.

2. Ingram JT, Lowenthal W. Mechanism of action of starch as a tablet disintegrant I: factors that affect the swelling of starch grains at 37°. J Pharm Sci 1966; 55: 614-617.

3. Patel NR, Hopponen RE. Mechanism of action of starch as a disintegrating agent in aspirin tablets. J Pharm Sci 1966; 55: 1065-1068.

4. Lowenthal W. Mechanism of action of tablet disintegrants. Pharm Acta Helv 1973; 48: 589-609.

5. Sakr AM, Kassem AA, Farrag NA. The effect of certain disintegrants on water soluble tablets. Mfg Chem Aerosol News 1973; 44(1): 37-41.

6. Shangraw RF, Wallace JW, Bowers FM. Morphology and functionality in tablet excipients for direct compression: part II. Pharmaceut Technol 1981; 5(10): 44-60.

7. Kitamori N, Makino T. Improvement in pressure-dependent dissolution of trepibutone tablets by using intragranular disintegrants. Drug Dev Ind Pharm 1982; 8: 125-139.

8. Rudnic EM, Rhodes CT, Welch S, Bernardo P. Evaluation of the mechanism of disintegrant action. Drug Dev Ind Pharm 1982; 8: 87-109.

9. Kottke MK, Chueh H-R, Rhodes CT. Comparison of disintegrant and binder activity of three corn starch products. Drug Dev Ind Pharm 1992; 18: 2207-2223.

10. Carr RL. Particle behaviour storage and flow. Br Chem Eng 1970; 15: 1541-1549.

11. Callahan JC, Cleary GW, Elefant M, Kaplan G, Kensler T, Nash RA. Equilibrium moisture content of pharmaceutical excipients. Drug Dev Ind Pharm 1982; 8: 355-369.

12. Wurster DE, Peck GE, Kildsig DO. A comparison of the moisture adsorption-desorption properties of corn starch, U.S.P., and directly compressible starch. Drug Dev Ind Pharm 1982; 8: 343-354.

13. Weiner M, Bernstein IL. Adverse reactions to drug formulation agents: a handbook of excipients. New York: Marcel Dekker Inc, 1989: 91-92.

14. Warshaw AL. Diagnosis of starch peritonitis by paracentesis. Lancet 1972; ii: 1054-1056.

15. Michaels L, Shah NS. Dangers of corn starch powder [letter]. Br Med J 1973; 2: 714.

16. Sweet DV, editor. Registry of toxic effects of chemical substances. Cincinnati: US Department of Health, 1987.

17. Health and Safety Executive. EH40/93: occupational exposure limits 1993. London: HMSO, 1993.

21. General References

—

22. Authors

USA: B Farhadieh.

Sterilizable Maize Starch

1. Nonproprietary Names
BP: Sterilisable maize starch
USP: Absorbable dusting powder

2. Synonyms
Bio-sorb; double-dressed, white maize starch; *Fluidamid R444P*; modified starch dusting powder; *Pure-Dent B851*; starch-derivative dusting powder; sterilizable corn starch.

3. Chemical Name and CAS Registry Number
Sterilizable maize starch

4. Empirical Formula   Molecular Weight
$(C_6H_{10}O_5)_n$
Where n = 300-1000.
Sterilizable maize starch is a modified corn (maize) starch that may also contain up to 2.2% of magnesium oxide.
See also Starch.

5. Structural Formula
See Starch.

6. Functional Category
Lubricant for surgeons' gloves; vehicle for medicated dusting powders.

7. Applications in Pharmaceutical Formulation or Technology
Sterilizable maize starch is a chemically or physically modified corn (maize) starch that does not gelatinize on exposure to moisture or steam sterilization. Sterilizable maize starch is primarily used as a lubricant for surgeons' gloves. It is also used as a vehicle for medicated dusting powders.

8. Description
Sterilizable maize starch occurs as an odorless, white-colored, free-flowing powder. Particles may be rounded or polyhedral in shape.

9. Pharmacopeial Specifications

Test	BP 1993	USP XXII
Identification	+	+
Stability to autoclaving	—	+
Sedimentation	+	+
pH (1 in 10 suspension)	9.5-10.8	10.0-10.8
Loss on drying	⩽ 15%	⩽ 12%
Residue on ignition	—	⩽ 3%
Acid-insoluble ash	⩽ 0.3%	—
Ash	⩽ 3.5%	—
Chloride	⩽ 0.15%	—
Formaldehyde	⩽ 0.01%	—
Heavy metals	—	⩽ 0.001%
Sulfate	⩽ 0.2%	—
Magnesium oxide	⩽ 2.2%	⩽ 2.0%

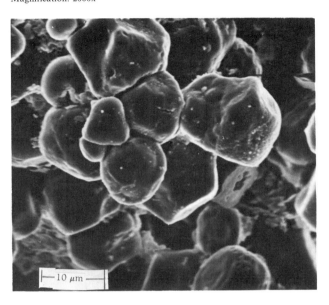

SEM: 1
Excipient: Sterilizable maize starch
Manufacturer: Corn Products
Magnification: 2000x

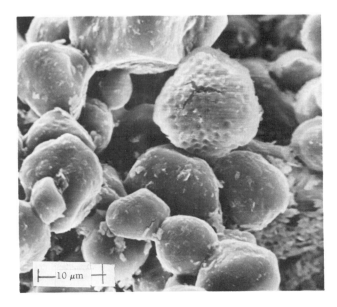

SEM: 2
Excipient: Sterilizable maize starch
Manufacturer: Biosorb
Magnification: 2000x

SEM: 3

Excipient: Sterilizable maize starch
Manufacturer: J & W Starches Ltd
Magnification: 2000x

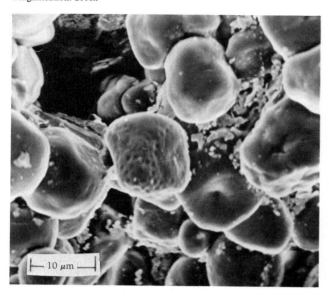

— 10 μm —

10. Typical Properties

Acidity/alkalinity: pH = 9.5-10.8 for a 10% w/v suspension at 25°C.
Density: 1.48 g/cm³
Density (bulk): 0.47-0.59 g/cm³
Density (tapped): 0.64-0.83 g/cm³
Flowability: 24-30% (Carr compressibility index)[1]
Moisture content: 10-15%
Particle size distribution: 6-25 μm; median diameter is 16 μm.
Solubility: very slightly soluble in chloroform and ethanol (95%); practically insoluble in water.
Specific surface area: 0.50-1.15 m²/g

11. Stability and Storage Conditions

Sterilizable maize starch may be sterilized by autoclaving at 121°C for 20 minutes, by ethylene oxide or by irradiation.[2] Sterilizable maize starch should be stored in a well-closed container in a cool, dry, place.

12. Incompatibilities

—

13. Method of Manufacture

Corn starch (maize starch) is physically or chemically modified by treatment with either phosphorus oxychloride or epichlorhydrin so that the branched and straight chain starch polymers cross-link. Up to 2.2% of magnesium oxide may also be added to the starch.
See also Starch.

14. Safety

Sterilizable maize starch is primarily used as a lubricant for surgeons' gloves and as a vehicle for topically applied dusting powders.

Granulomatous reactions and peritonitis at operation sites have been attributed to contamination with surgical glove powders containing sterilizable maize starch.[3,4] The use of excessive quantities of sterilizable maize starch on surgeons' gloves should therefore be avoided.
See also Starch.

15. Handling Precautions

Observe normal precautions appropriate to the circumstances and quantity of material handled. Eye protection and a dust-mask are recommended. Excessive dust generation should be avoided to minimize the risks of explosions.

In the UK, the long-term (8-hour TWA) occupational exposure limits for starch are: 10 mg/m³ for total inhalable dust and 5 mg/m³ for respirable dust.[5]

16. Regulatory Status

Included in the FDA Inactive Ingredients Guide (oral tablets and topical preparations). Included in nonparenteral medicines licensed in the UK.

17. Pharmacopeias

Br and US.

18. Related Substances

Pregelatinized Starch; Starch.

19. Comments

—

20. Specific References

1. Carr RL. Particle behaviour storage and flow. Br Chem Eng 1970; 15: 1541-1549.
2. Kelsey JC. Sterilization of glove powder by autoclaving. Mon Bull Minist Health 1962; 21: 17-21.
3. Neely J, Davis JD. Starch granulomatosis of the peritoneum. Br Med J 1971; 3: 625-629.
4. Michaels L, Shah NS. Dangers of corn starch powder [letter]. Br Med J 1973; 2: 714.
5. Health and Safety Executive. EH40/93: occupational exposure limits 1993. London: HMSO, 1993.

21. General References

El Saadany RMA, El Saadany FM, Foda YH. Degradation of corn starch under the influence of gamma irradiation. Staerke 1976; 28: 208-211.
Greenwood CT. The thermal degradation of starch. Adv Carbohydrate Chem Biochem 1967; 22: 483-515.
Greenwood CT. Starch. Adv Cereal Sci Technol 1976; 1: 119-157.

22. Authors

UK: G Rowley.
USA: B Farhadieh.

Pregelatinized Starch

1. Nonproprietary Names

BP: Pregelatinised maize starch
USPNF: Pregelatinized starch

2. Synonyms

Compressible starch; *Instastarch*; *Lycatab PGS*; *National 78-1551*; *Pharma-Gel*; *Prejel*; *Sepistab ST 200*; *Starch 1500*; *Sta-Rx 1500*.

3. Chemical Name and CAS Registry Number

Pregelatinized starch [9005-25-8]

4. Empirical Formula   Molecular Weight

$(C_6H_{10}O_5)_n$
Where n = 300-1000.
Pregelatinized starch is a starch that has been chemically and mechanically processed to rupture all or part of the starch granules and so render the starch flowable and directly compressible. Partially pregelatinized grades are also commercially available. Typically, pregelatinized starch contains 5% of free amylose, 15% of free amylopectin and 80% unmodified starch. The USPNF XVII does not specify the botanical origin of the original starch but the BP 1993 specifies that corn (maize) starch should be used. *See also* Starch and Section 13.

5. Structural Formula

See Starch.

6. Functional Category

Tablet and capsule diluent; tablet and capsule disintegrant; tablet binder.

7. Applications in Pharmaceutical Formulation or Technology

Pregelatinized starch is a modified starch used in oral capsule and tablet formulations as a binder, diluent[1] and disintegrant.[2]
In comparison to starch, grades of pregelatinized starch may be produced with enhanced flow and compression characteristics such that the pregelatinized material may be used as a tablet binder in dry compression processes.[3-11] In such processes, pregelatinized starch is self-lubricating. However, when used with other excipients it may be necessary to add a lubricant to a formulation. Although magnesium stearate 0.25% w/w is commonly used for this purpose, concentrations greater than this may have adverse effects on tablet strength and dissolution. Therefore, stearic acid is generally the preferred lubricant with pregelatinized starch.[12]
Pregelatinized starch may also be used in wet granulation processes.[13]

Use	Concentration (%)
Diluent (hard gelatin capsules)	5-75
Tablet binder (direct compression)	5-20
Tablet binder (wet granulation)	5-10
Tablet disintegrant	5-10

8. Description

Pregelatinized starch occurs as a moderately coarse to fine, white to off-white colored powder. It is odorless and has a slight characteristic taste.
Examination of fully pregelatinized starch as a slurry in cold water, under a polarizing microscope, reveals no significant ungelatinized granules. Examination of samples suspended in glycerin show characteristic forms depending upon the method of drying used during manufacture, e.g. either irregular chunks from drum drying or thin plates.

9. Pharmacopeial Specifications

Test	BP 1993	USPNF XVII (Suppl 5)
Identification	+	+
pH (10% w/v slurry)	4.5-7.0	4.5-7.0
Iron	—	$\leqslant 0.002\%$
Oxidizing substances	—	+
Sulfur dioxide	—	$\leqslant 0.008\%$
Microbial limits	+	+
Loss on drying	$\leqslant 15.0\%$	$\leqslant 14.0\%$
Residue on ignition	—	$\leqslant 0.5\%$
Sulfated ash	$\leqslant 0.5\%$	—
Protein	$\leqslant 0.5\%$	—

10. Typical Properties

Acidity/alkalinity: pH = 4.5-7.0 for a 10% w/v aqueous dispersion.
Angle of repose: 40.7°[6]
Flowability: 18-23% (Carr compressibility index)[14]
Moisture content: pregelatinized maize starch is hygroscopic.[11,15,16] *see* HPE Data.
Particle size distribution: 30-150 μm, median diameter 52 μm. For partially pregelatinized starch, greater than 90% through a US #100 mesh (149 μm), and less than 0.5% retained on a US #40 mesh (420 μm).
Solubility: practically insoluble in organic solvents. Slightly soluble to soluble in cold water, depending upon the degree of pregelatinization. Fully pregelatinized starch conforms to the completeness of solution test in the USP XXII. Pastes can be prepared by sifting the pregelatinized starch into stirred, cold water. Cold water soluble matter for partially pregelatinized starch is 10-20%.
Specific surface area: 0.21-0.22 m^2/g
Viscosity (dynamic): 8-10 mPa s (8-10 cP) for a 2% w/v aqueous dispersion at 25°C.

	HPE Laboratory Project Data		
	Method	**Lab #**	**Results***
Bulk/tap density			
Starch 1500	BTD-7	14	B: 0.650 g/cm³ (a)
			T: 0.820 g/cm³
Moisture content	MC-22	2	7.0% (b)
	MC-15	34	8.94% (b)
	EMC-1	2	*See* Fig. 1. (b)
Starch 1500	MC-15	34	11.12% (a)
Starch 1500	MC-15	14	11.30% (a)
Starch 1500	SDI-1	14	*See* Fig. 2. (a)
Wheat (*Paygel 90*)	MC-15	14	6.60% (c)
Wheat (*Paygel 90*)	SDI-1	14	*See* Fig. 2. (c)
Particle size	PSD-2	5	68 μm (b)
Starch 1500	PSD-2	5	80 μm (a)

Supplier: a. Colorcon Ltd; b. National Starch & Chemicals Ltd; c. Henkel Corp.

* Note that results are for pregelatinized corn starch unless otherwise indicated.

11. Stability and Storage Conditions

Pregelatinized starch is a stable, though hygroscopic material, which should be stored in a well-closed container in a cool, dry, place.

12. Incompatibilities

—

13. Method of Manufacture

Fully pregelatinized starch is prepared by heating an aqueous slurry containing up to 42% w/w of starch at 62-72°C. Chemical additives which may be included in the slurry are

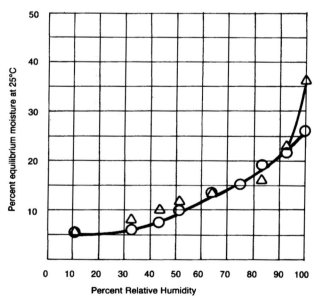

Fig. 1: Equilibrium moisture content of corn starch and pregelatinized starch.
○ Corn starch (National Starch & Chemicals Ltd; Lot #421).
△ Pregelatinized corn starch (National Starch & Chemicals Ltd; Lot #HJW 103).

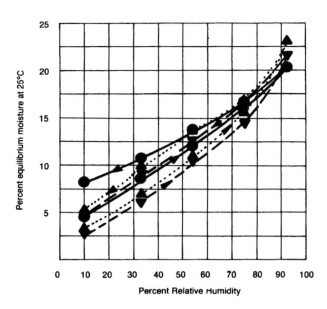

Fig. 2: Sorption-desorption isotherms of pregelatinized corn starch and pregelatinized wheat starch.
● Pregelatinized corn starch, *Sta-Rx 1500* (AE Staley Mfg Co; Lot #977912).
▲ Pregelatinized wheat starch, *Paygel 90* (Henkel Corp; Lot #289D).
▼ Pregelatinized corn starch, *Starch 1500* (Colorcon Ltd; Lot #904014)

gelatinization aids (salts or bases) and surfactants, added to control rehydration or minimize stickiness during drying. After heating, the slurry may be spray-dried, roll-dried, extruded or drum-dried. In the latter case, the dried material may be processed to produce a desired particle size range.

Partially pregelatinized starch is prepared by spreading an aqueous suspension of ungelatinized starch on hot drums where partial gelatinization and subsequent drying takes place.

14. Safety

Pregelatinized starch, and starch, are widely used in oral solid dosage formulations. Pregelatinized starch is generally regarded as a nontoxic and nonirritant excipient. However, oral consumption of massive amounts of pregelatinized starch may be harmful.
See Starch for further information.

15. Handling Precautions

Observe normal precautions appropriate to the circumstances and quantity of material handled. Eye protection and a dust-mask are recommended. Excessive dust generation should be avoided to minimize the risks of explosions.
In the UK, the long-term (8-hour TWA) occupational exposure limits for starch are, 10 mg/m³ for total inhalable dust and 5 mg/m³ for respirable dust.[17]

16. Regulatory Status

Included in the FDA Inactive Ingredients Guide (oral capsules, suspensions and tablets). Included in nonparenteral medicines licensed in the UK.

17. Pharmacopeias

Br and USPNF.

18. Related Substances

Starch; Sterilizable Maize Starch.

19. Comments

A low moisture grade of pregelatinized starch, *Starch 1500 L.M.* (Colorcon Ltd), containing less than 7% of water, is commercially available specifically intended for use as a diluent in capsule formulations.

20. Specific References

1. Small LE, Augsburger LL. Aspects of the lubrication requirements for an automatic capsule filling machine. Drug Dev Ind Pharm 1978; 4: 345-372.
2. Rudnic EM, Rhodes CT, Welch S, Bernardo P. Evaluations of the mechanism of disintegrant action. Drug Dev Ind Pharm 1982; 8: 87-109.
3. Manudhane KS, Contractor AM, Kim HY, Shangraw RF. Tableting properties of a directly compressible starch. J Pharm Sci 1969; 58: 616-620.
4. Underwood TW, Cadwallader DE. Influence of various starches on dissolution rate of salicylic acid from tablets. J Pharm Sci 1972; 61: 239-243.
5. Bolhuis GK, Lerk CF. Comparative evaluation of excipients for direct compression. Pharm Weekbl 1973; 108: 469-481.
6. Sakr AM, Elsabbagh HM, Emara KM. Sta-Rx 1500 starch: a new vehicle for the direct compression of tablets. Arch Pharm Chemi (Sci) 1974; 2: 14-24.
7. Schwartz JB, Martin ET, Dehner EJ. Intragranular starch: comparison of starch USP and modified cornstarch. J Pharm Sci 1975; 64: 328-332.
8. Rees JE, Rue PJ. Work required to cause failure of tablets in diametral compression. Drug Dev Ind Pharm 1978; 4: 131-156.
9. Shangraw RF, Wallace JW, Bowers FM. Morphology and functionality in tablet excipients for direct compression: part II. Pharmaceut Technol 1981; 5(10): 44-60.
10. Chilamkurti RW, Rhodes CT, Schwartz JB. Some studies on compression properties of tablet matrices using a computerized instrumental press. Drug Dev Ind Pharm 1982; 8: 63-86.
11. Malamataris S, Goidas P, Dimitriou A. Moisture sorption and tensile strength of some tableted direct compression excipients. Int J Pharmaceutics 1991; 68: 51-60.
12. Colorcon Ltd. Technical literature: *Starch 1500*, 1993.
13. Jaiyeoba KT, Spring MS. The granulation of ternary mixtures: the effect of the stability of the excipients. J Pharm Pharmacol 1980; 32: 1-5.
14. Carr RL. Particle behaviour storage and flow. Br Chem Eng 1970; 15: 1541-1549.
15. Callahan JC, Cleary GW, Elefant M, Kaplan G, Kensler T, Nash RA. Equilibrium moisture content of pharmaceutical excipients. Drug Dev Ind Pharm 1982; 8: 355-369.
16. Wurster DE, Peck GE, Kildsig DO. A comparison of the moisture adsorption-desorption properties of corn starch, U.S.P., and directly compressible starch. Drug Dev Ind Pharm 1982; 8: 343-354.
17. Health and Safety Executive. EH40/93: occupational exposure limits 1993. London: HMSO, 1993.

21. General References

Roquette Frères. Technical literature: *Lycatab PGS* excipient for wet granulation, 1992.
Sanghvi PP, Collins CC, Shukla AJ. Evaluation of Preflo modified starches as new direct compression excipients I: tabletting characteristics. Pharm Res 1993; 10: 1597-1603.

22. Authors

USA: NG Lordi.

Stearic Acid

1. Nonproprietary Names

BP: Stearic acid
USPNF: Stearic acid

2. Synonyms

570; *Crodacid*; *Crosterene*; *Glycon S-90*; *Hystrene*; *Industrene*; *Kortacid 1895*; *Pristerene*.

3. Chemical Name and CAS Registry Number

Octadecanoic acid [57-11-4]

4. Empirical Formula   Molecular Weight

$C_{18}H_{36}O_2$ 284.47 (for pure material)

The BP 1993 and the USPNF XVII describe stearic acid as a mixture of stearic acid ($C_{18}H_{36}O_2$) and palmitic acid ($C_{16}H_{32}O_2$). The content of stearic acid is not less than 40.0% and the sum of the two acids is not less than 90.0%. The USPNF XVII also contains a monograph for purified stearic acid, *see* Section 18.

5. Structural Formula

$CH_3(CH_2)_{16}COOH$

6. Functional Category

Emulsifying agent; solubilizing agent; tablet and capsule lubricant.

7. Applications in Pharmaceutical Formulation or Technology

Stearic acid is widely used in oral and topical pharmaceutical formulations. It is mainly used in oral formulations as a tablet and capsule lubricant[1-3] although it may also be used as a binder,[4] or in combination with shellac as a tablet coating.
In topical formulations, stearic acid is used as an emulsifying and solubilizing agent. When partially neutralized with alkalis or triethanolamine, stearic acid is used in the preparation of creams.[5,6] The partially neutralized stearic acid forms a creamy base when mixed with 5-15 times its own weight of aqueous liquid, the appearance and plasticity of the cream being determined by the proportion of alkali used.
Stearic acid is also widely used in cosmetics and food products.

Use	Concentration (%)
Ointments and creams	1-20
Tablet lubricant	1-3

8. Description

Stearic acid is a hard, white or faintly yellow colored, somewhat glossy, crystalline solid or a white, or yellowish white, powder. It has a slight odor and taste suggesting tallow. *See also* Section 13.

SEM: 1
Excipient: Stearic acid, 95% (*Emersol 153*)
Manufacturer: Emery Industries
Lot No.: 18895
Magnification: 120x
Voltage: 10 kV

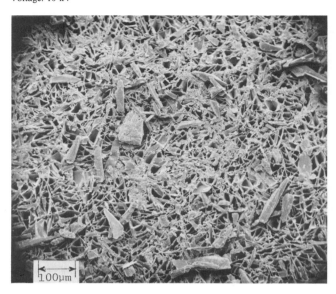

SEM: 2
Excipient: Stearic acid, food grade (*Emersol 6332*)
Manufacturer: Emery Industries
Lot No.: 18895
Magnification: 120x
Voltage: 10kV

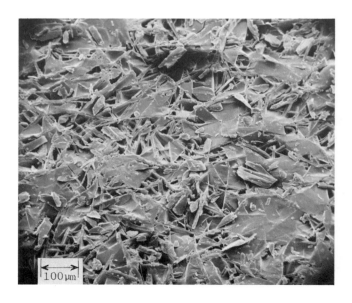

SEM: 3

Excipient: Stearic acid USP (*Hydrofol Acid 1655*)
Manufacturer: Sherex Chemical Company Inc
Lot No.: 9303-M639-521
Magnification: 120x
Voltage: 10kV

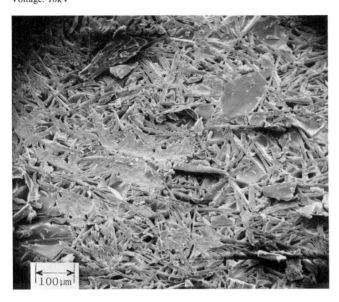

SEM: 4

Excipient: Stearic acid (*Hydrofol Acid 1870*)
Manufacturer: Sherex Chemical Company Inc
Lot No.: 9227-M635-421
Magnification: 120x
Voltage: 10kV

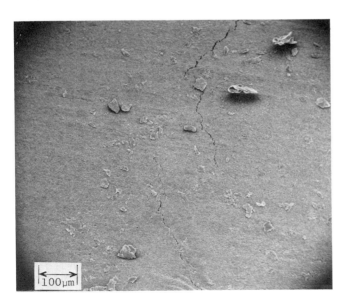

9. Pharmacopeial Specifications

Test	BP 1993	USPNF XVII (Suppl 6)
Identification	+	+
Congealing temperature	⩾ 54°C	⩾ 54°C
Residue on ignition	—	⩽ 0.1%
Sulfated ash	⩽ 0.1%	—
Heavy metals	⩽ 20 ppm	⩽ 0.001%
Mineral acid	+	+
Neutral fat or paraffin	—	+
Acid value	200-212	—
Iodine value	⩽ 4.0	⩽ 4.0
Organic volatile impurities	—	+
Assay of stearic acid	⩾ 40.0%	⩾ 40.0%
Assay of both acids	⩾ 90.0%	⩾ 90.0%

10. Typical Properties

Acid value: 200-212
Density (bulk): ≈ 0.8 g/cm^3
Melting point: ⩾ 54°C
Moisture content: contains practically no water.
Saponification value: 200-220
Solubility: freely soluble in benzene, carbon tetrachloride, chloroform and ether; soluble in ethanol, hexane and propylene glycol; practically insoluble in water.
See also Section 18.

11. Stability and Storage Conditions

Stearic acid is a stable material; an antioxidant may also be added to it, *see* Section 13. The bulk material should be stored in a well-closed container in a cool, dry, place.

12. Incompatibilities

Stearic acid is incompatible with most metal hydroxides and may be incompatible with oxidizing agents.

Insoluble stearates are formed with many metals; ointment bases made with stearic acid may show evidence of drying out or lumpiness due to such a reaction when compounded with zinc or calcium salts.

A number of differential scanning calorimetry studies have investigated the compatibility of stearic acid with drugs although such laboratory studies that have suggested incompatibilities, e.g. naproxen,[7] may not necessarily be applicable to formulated products.

Stearic acid has been reported to cause pitting in the film-coating of tablets coated using an aqueous film-coating technique; the pitting was found to be a function of the melting point of the stearic acid.[8]

13. Method of Manufacture

Stearic acid is manufactured by hydrolysis of fat by continuous exposure to a counter-current stream of high-temperature water and fat in a high-pressure chamber. The resultant mixture is purified by vacuum steam distillation and the distillates then separated using selective solvents.

Stearic acid may also be manufactured by hydrogenation of cottonseed and other vegetable oils; by the hydrogenation and subsequent saponification of olein followed by recrystallization from alcohol; and from edible fats and oils by boiling with sodium hydroxide, separating any glycerin and decomposing the resulting soap with sulfuric or hydrochloric acid. The

Table I: Specifications of different stearic acid grades (Witco Corporation).

Product	Stearic acid content (%)	Titer (°C)	Acid value	Iodine value	Saponification value	Unsaponifiable matter (%)
Hystrene 5016	44	54.5-56.5	206-210	$\leqslant 0.5$	206-211	$\leqslant 0.2$
Hystrene 7018	68.5	61.0-62.5	200-205	$\leqslant 0.5$	200-206	$\leqslant 0.2$
Hystrene 9718	90	66.5-68.0	196-201	$\leqslant 0.8$	196-202	$\leqslant 0.3$
Industrene 7018	65	58-62	200-207	$\leqslant 1.5$	200-208	$\leqslant 0.5$
Industrene 8718	87	64.5-67.5	196-201	$\leqslant 2.0$	196-202	$\leqslant 1.5$

stearic acid is then subsequently separated from any oleic acid by cold expression.

Stearic acid is derived from edible fat sources unless it is intended for external use, in which case nonedible fat sources may be used. Stearic acid may contain a suitable antioxidant such as 0.005% w/w butylated hydroxytoluene.

14. Safety

Stearic acid is widely used in oral and topical pharmaceutical formulations; it is also used in cosmetics and food products. Stearic acid is generally regarded as a nontoxic and nonirritant material. However, consumption of excessive amounts may be harmful.

LD_{50} (mouse, IV): 23 mg/kg[9]
LD_{50} (rabbit, skin): > 5 g/kg
LD_{50} (rat, IV): 21.5 mg/kg

15. Handling Precautions

Observe normal precautions appropriate to the circumstances and quantity of material handled. Stearic acid dust may be irritant to the skin, eyes and mucous membranes. Eye protection, gloves and a dust respirator are recommended. Stearic acid is combustible.

16. Regulatory Status

GRAS listed. Accepted as a food additive in the UK. Included in the FDA Inactive Ingredients Guide (buccal tablets, oral capsules, solutions, suspensions and tablets, topical and vaginal preparations). Included in nonparenteral medicines licensed in the UK.

17. Pharmacopeias

Aust, Belg, Br, Braz, Chin, Cz, Egypt, Fr, Hung, Ind, It, Jpn, Mex, Nord, Rom, Swiss, USPNF and Yug.

18. Related Substances

Calcium Stearate; Magnesium Stearate; palmitic acid; purified stearic acid; Zinc Stearate.

Palmitic acid: $C_{16}H_{32}O_2$
Molecular weight: 256.42
CAS number: [57-10-3]
Synonyms: cetylic acid; hexadecanoic acid; hexadecylic acid.
Appearance: the pure material is a white, crystalline powder.
Boiling point: 215°C
Density: 0.853 g/cm³ at 62°C
Melting point: 63-64°C
Refractive index: $n_D^{80} = 1.4273$
Solubility: freely soluble in chloroform; ether, propan-2-ol and hot ethanol (95%); sparingly soluble in ethanol (95%); practically insoluble in water.

Purified stearic acid: $C_{18}H_{36}O_2$
Molecular weight: 284.47
CAS number: [57-11-4]
Synonyms: octadecanoic acid.
Pharmacopeias: USPNF.
Acid value: 195-200
Boiling point: 361°C
Density: 0.847 g/cm³ at 70°C
Flash point: 196°C
Iodine number: $\leqslant 1.5$
Melting point: 66-69°C
Refractive index: $n_D^{80} = 1.4299$
Solubility: soluble 1 in 5 parts benzene, 1 in 6 parts carbon tetrachloride, 1 in 2 parts chloroform, 1 in 15 parts ethanol, 1 in 3 parts ether; practically insoluble in water.
Vapor density (relative): 9.80 (air = 1)
Comments: purified stearic acid contains not less than 96.0% of stearic and palmitic acid, of which, stearic acid constitutes not less than 90.0% of the total.

19. Comments

A wide range of different grades of stearic acid are commercially available which have varying chemical compositions and hence different physical and chemical properties, *see* Table I.[10]

20. Specific References

1. Iranloye TA, Parrott EL. Effects of compression force, particle size, and lubricants on dissolution rate. J Pharm Sci 1978; 67: 535-539.
2. Jarosz PJ, Parrott EL. Effect of tablet lubricants on axial and radial work of failure. Drug Dev Ind Pharm 1982; 8: 445-453.
3. Mitrevej KT, Augsburger LL. Adhesion of tablets in a rotary tablet press II: effects of blending time, running time, and lubricant concentration. Drug Dev Ind Pharm 1982; 8: 237-282.
4. Musikabhumma P, Rubinstein MH, Khan KA. Evaluation of stearic acid and polyethylene glycol as binders for tabletting potassium phenethicillin. Drug Dev Ind Pharm 1982; 8: 169-188.
5. Suzuki K. Rheological study of vanishing cream. Cosmet Toilet 1976; 91(6): 23-31.
6. Mores LR. Application of stearates in cosmetic creams and lotions. Cosmet Toilet 1980; 95(3): 79, 81-84.
7. Botha SA, Lötter AP. Compatibility study between naproxen and tablet excipients using differential scanning calorimetry. Drug Dev Ind Pharm 1990; 16: 673-683.
8. Rowe RC, Forse SF. Pitting: a defect on film-coated tablets. Int J Pharmaceutics 1983; 17: 347-349.
9. Sweet DV, editor. Registry of toxic effects of chemical substances. Cincinnati: US Department of Health, 1987.
10. Phadke DS, Keeney MP, Norris DA. Evaluation of batch-to-batch and manufacturer-to-manufacturer variability in the physical properties of talc and stearic acid. Drug Dev Ind Pharm 1994; 20: 859-871.

21. General References

Pilpel N. Metal stearates in pharmaceuticals and cosmetics. Mfg Chem Aerosol News 1971; 42(10): 37-40.

22. Authors

USA: LV Allen.

Stearyl Alcohol

1. Nonproprietary Names

BP: Stearyl alcohol
PhEur: Alcohol stearylicus
USPNF: Stearyl alcohol

2. Synonyms

Crodacol S95; *n*-octadecanol; octadecyl alcohol; stenol.

3. Chemical Name and CAS Registry Number

1-Octadecanol [112-92-5]

4. Empirical Formula

$C_{18}H_{38}O$

Molecular Weight

270.48
(for pure material)

The BP 1993 and PhEur 1992 describe stearyl alcohol as a mixture of solid alcohols containing not less than 95% of 1-octadecanol, $C_{18}H_{38}O$; the USPNF XVII states that it contains not less than 90% of 1-octadecanol.

5. Structural Formula

$CH_3(CH_2)_{16}CH_2OH$

6. Functional Category

Stiffening agent.

7. Applications in Pharmaceutical Formulation or Technology

Stearyl alcohol is used in cosmetics[1,2] and topical pharmaceutical creams and ointments as a stiffening agent. By increasing the viscosity of an emulsion stearyl alcohol increases its stability. Stearyl alcohol also has some emollient and weak emulsifying properties and is used to increase the water-holding capacity of ointments, e.g. petrolatum. In addition, stearyl alcohol has been used in controlled release tablets,[3,4] suppositories[5,6] and has been investigated for use as a transdermal penetration enhancer.[7]

8. Description

Stearyl alcohol occurs as hard, white, waxy pieces, flakes or granules with a slight characteristic odor and bland taste.

9. Pharmacopeial Specifications

Test	PhEur 1992	USPNF XVII
Identification	+	+
Appearance of solution	+	—
Melting range	57-60°C	55-60°C
Acid value	⩽ 1.0	⩽ 2.0
Iodine value	⩽ 2.0	⩽ 2.0
Hydroxyl value	197-217	195-220
Saponification value	⩽ 2.0	—
Assay (of $C_{18}H_{38}O$)	⩾ 95%	⩾ 90.0%

10. Typical Properties

Autoignition temperature: 450°C
Boiling point: 210.5°C at 2 kPa (15 mmHg)

100 μm

Density: 0.812 g/cm^3 at 50°C
Flash point: 191°C (open cup)
Freezing point: 55-57°C
Melting point: 59.4-59.8°C for the pure material.
Refractive index: $n_D^{60} = 1.4388$ at 60°C
Solubility: soluble in chloroform, ethanol (95%), ether and vegetable oils; practically insoluble in water. *See also* HPE Data.
Vapor pressure: 133.3 Pa (1 mmHg) at 150.3°C
Viscosity (dynamic): 1 Pa s (10 P) at 60°C

	HPE Laboratory Project Data		
	Method	Lab #	Results
Solubility			
Ethanol (95%) at 25°C	SOL-4	10	5.5 mg/mL
Ethanol (95%) at 37°C	SOL-4	10	17.6 mg/mL
Hexane at 25°C	SOL-4	10	9.5 mg/mL
Hexane at 37°C	SOL-4	10	148.1 mg/mL
Propylene glycol at 25°C	SOL-4	10	10 mg/mL
Water at 37°C	SOL-4	10	0.01 mg/mL

Supplier: A & S Company.

11. Stability and Storage Conditions

Stearyl alcohol is stable to acids and alkalis and does not usually become rancid. It should be stored in a well-closed container in a cool, dry, place.

12. Incompatibilities

Incompatible with strong oxidizing agents.

13. Method of Manufacture

Historically, stearyl alcohol was prepared from sperm whale oil but is now largely prepared synthetically by reduction of ethyl stearate with lithium aluminum hydride.

14. Safety

Stearyl alcohol is generally considered to be an innocuous, nontoxic material. However, adverse reactions to stearyl alcohol present in topical preparations have been reported. These include contact urticaria and hypersensitivity reactions which are possibly due to impurities contained in stearyl alcohol rather than stearyl alcohol itself.[8-10]

The probable lethal oral human dose is greater than 15 g/kg.

LD_{50} (rat, oral): 20 g/kg[11]

15. Handling Precautions

Observe normal precautions appropriate to the circumstances and quantity of material handled. Eye protection and gloves are recommended. Stearyl alcohol is not a fire hazard although it will burn and may give off noxious fumes containing carbon monoxide.

16. Regulatory Status

Included in the FDA Inactive Ingredients Guide (tablets and topical preparations). Included in nonparenteral medicines licensed in the UK.

17. Pharmacopeias

Br, Eur, Fr, It, Jpn, Mex and USPNF.

18. Related Substances

Cetostearyl Alcohol; Cetyl Alcohol.

19. Comments

—

20. Specific References

1. Egan RR, Portwood O. Higher alcohols in skin lotions. Cosmet Perfum 1974; 89(3): 39-42.
2. Alexander P. Organic rheological additives. Mfg Chem 1986; 57(9): 49,52.
3. Prasad CM, Srivastava GP. Study of some sustained release granulations of aspirin. Indian J Hosp Pharm 1971; 8: 21-28.
4. Kumar K, Chakrabarti T, Srivastava GP. Studies on the sustained release tablet formulation of diethylcarbamazine citrate (Hetrazan). Indian J Pharm 1975; 37: 57-59.
5. Kaiho F, Aoki T, Nakagane F, Nagano K, Kato Y. Application of fatty alcohols to pharmaceutical dosage forms. Yakuzaigaku 1984; 44: 99-102.
6. Tanabe K, Yoshida S, Yamamoto K, Itoh S, Yamazaki M. Effect of additives on release of ibuprofen from suppositories [in Japanese]. Yakuzaigaku 1988; 48: 262-269.
7. Chiang CH, Lai JS, Yang KH. The effects of pH and chemical enhancers on the percutaneous absorption of indomethacin. Drug Dev Ind Pharm 1991; 17: 91-111.
8. Fisher AA. Contact dermatitis from stearyl alcohol and propylene glycol. Arch Dermatol 1974; 110: 636.
9. Black H. Contact dermatitis from stearyl alcohol in Metosyn (flucinonide) cream. Contact Dermatitis 1975; 1: 125.
10. Cronin E. Contact Dermatitis. Edinburgh: Churchill Livingstone, 1980: 808.
11. Sweet DV, editor. Registry of toxic effects of chemical substances. Cincinnati: US Department of Health, 1987.

21. General References

Barry BW. Continuous shear, viscoelastic and spreading properties of a new topical vehicle, FAPG base. J Pharm Pharmacol 1973; 25: 131-137.
Madan PL, Luzzi LA, Price JC. Microencapsulation of a waxy solid: wall thickness and surface appearance studies. J Pharm Sci 1974; 63: 280-284.
Rowe RC. A quantitative assessment of the reactivity of the fatty alcohols with cetrimide using immersion calorimetry. J Pharm Pharmacol 1987; 39: 50-52.
Schott H, Han SK. Effect of inorganic additives on solutions of nonionic surfactants II. J Pharm Sci 1975; 64: 658-664.
Wan LSC, Poon PKC. The interfacial activity of sodium lauryl sulfate in the presence of alcohols. Can J Pharm Sci 1970; 5: 104-107.

22. Authors

UK: PJ Weller.

Sucrose

1. Nonproprietary Names

BP: Sucrose
PhEur: Saccharum
USPNF: Sucrose

2. Synonyms

Beet sugar; cane sugar; α-D-glucopyranosyl-β-D-fructofurano-side; refined sugar; saccharose; sugar.

3. Chemical Name and CAS Registry Number

β-D-fructofuranosyl-α-D-glucopyranoside
[57-50-1]

4. Empirical Formula   Molecular Weight

$C_{12}H_{22}O_{11}$ 342.30

5. Structural Formula

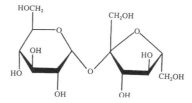

6. Functional Category

Base for medicated confectionery; granulating agent; sugar coating adjunct; suspending agent; sweetening agent; tablet and capsule diluent; viscosity-increasing agent.

7. Applications in Pharmaceutical Formulation or Technology

Sucrose is widely used in oral pharmaceutical formulations. Sucrose syrup, containing 50-67% w/w sucrose, is used in tableting as a binding agent for wet granulation. In the powdered form, sucrose serves as a dry binder (2-20% w/w) or as a bulking agent and sweetener in chewable tablets and lozenges. Tablets which contain large amounts of sucrose may harden to give poor disintegration.

Sucrose syrups are used as tablet coating agents at concentrations between 50-67% w/w. With higher concentrations, partial inversion of sucrose occurs which makes sugar coating difficult. Sucrose syrups are also widely used as vehicles in oral liquid dosage forms to enhance palatability or to increase viscosity. Sucrose is also widely used in foods, confectionery and therapeutically in sugar pastes which are used to promote wound healing.[1,2]

Use	Concentration (% w/w)
Syrup for oral liquid formulations	67
Sweetening agent	67
Tablet binder (dry granulation)	2-20
Tablet binder (wet granulation)	50-67
Tablet coating (syrup)	50-67

8. Description

Sucrose is a sugar obtained from sugar cane [*Saccharum officinarum* Linné (Fam. Gramineae)], sugar beet [*Beta vulgaris* Linné (Fam. Chenopodiaceae)], and other sources. It contains no added substances. Sucrose occurs as colorless crystals, crystalline masses or blocks, or as a white, crystalline powder; it is odorless and has a sweet taste.

SEM: 1

Excipient: Sucrose
Manufacturer: Great Western Sugar Co
Lot No.: 1-2-80
Magnification: 60x
Voltage: 10 kV

SEM: 2

Excipient: Sucrose
Manufacturer: Great Western Sugar Co
Lot No.: 1-2-80
Magnification: 600x
Voltage: 10 kV

SEM: 3

Excipient: Sucrose (Holly extra fine sugar)
Manufacturer: Holly Sugar Corp
Lot No.: TNG-2-2
Magnification: 60x
Voltage: 10 kV

SEM: 4

Excipient: Sucrose (Holly extra fine sugar)
Manufacturer: Holly Sugar Corp
Lot No.: TNG-2-2
Magnification: 600x
Voltage: 10 kV

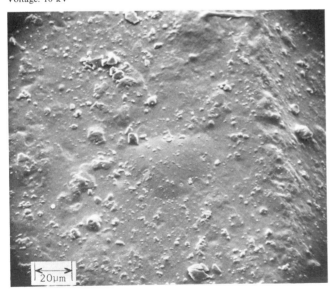

9. Pharmacopeial Specifications

Test	PhEur 1983	USPNF XVII
Identification	+	—
Appearance of solution	+	—
Acidity or alkalinity	+	—
Specific optical rotation	+66.2° to +66.8°	⩾ +65.9°
Coloring matter	+	—
Dextrins	+	—
Dextrose and invert sugar	+	—
Invert sugar	—	+
Chloride	—	⩽ 0.0035%
Sulfate	—	⩽ 0.006%
Sulfites	⩽ 15 ppm	—
Barium	+	—
Calcium	—	+
Heavy metals	—	⩽ 5 ppm
Lead	⩽ 0.5 ppm	—
Residue on ignition	—	⩽ 0.05%
Sulfated ash	⩽ 0.02%	—

10. Typical Properties

Compressibility: see Fig. 1. *See also* Compressible Sugar.
Density:
1.56 g/cm^3 (crystalline sucrose);
1.56 g/cm^3 (powdered sucrose).
Density (bulk):
0.93 g/cm^3 (crystalline sucrose);
0.60 g/cm^3 (powdered sucrose).
Density (tapped):
1.03 g/cm^3 (crystalline sucrose);
0.82 g/cm^3 (powdered sucrose).
Dissociation constant: $pK_a = 12.62$
Flowability: crystalline sucrose is free flowing whilst powdered sucrose is a cohesive solid.
Melting point: 160-186°C (with decomposition)
Moisture content: finely divided sucrose is hygroscopic and absorbs up to 1% water. See Fig. 2, 3 and 4.
Osmolarity: a 9.25% w/v aqueous solution is iso-osmotic with serum.
Particle size distribution: powdered sucrose is a white, irregular sized granular powder. The crystalline material consists of colorless crystalline, roughly cubic granules. See Fig. 5, 6 and 7.
Refractive index:

Concentration of aqueous sucrose solution (% w/w)	Refractive index at 20°C
2	1.0060
6	1.0219
10	1.0381
20	1.0810
30	1.1270
40	1.1764
50	1.2296
60	1.2865
70	1.3471
76	1.3854

Solubility:

Solvent	Solubility at 20°C Unless otherwise stated
Chloroform	practically insoluble
Ethanol	1 in 400
Ethanol (95%)	1 in 170
Propan-2-ol	1 in 400
Water	1 in 0.5
	1 in 0.2 at 100°C

Specific gravity:

Concentration of aqueous sucrose solution (% w/w)	Specific gravity at 20°C
2	1.0060
6	1.0219
10	1.0381
20	1.0810
30	1.1270
40	1.1764
50	1.2296
60	1.2865
70	1.3471
76	1.3854

HPE Laboratory Project Data			
	Method	Lab #	Results
Average flow rate	FLO-2	3	46.9 g/s [a]
Density	DE-1	7	1.62 ± 0.02 g/cm³ [b]
Moisture content	MC-8	5	0.15% [a]
	MC-10	10	< 0.10% [c]
	EMC-1	10	*See* Fig. 4. [c]
Particle friability	PF-1	36	0.01% [a]
Particle size	PSD-9	3	*See* Fig. 7. [c]

Supplier: a. Great Western Sugar Co; b. C & H Sugar; c. Amstar (Lot No.: 51995).

11. Stability and Storage Conditions

Sucrose has good stability at room temperature and at moderate relative humidity. It absorbs up to 1% moisture, which is released upon heating at 90°C. Sucrose caramelizes when heated to temperatures above 160°C. Dilute sucrose solutions are liable to fermentation by microorganisms but resist decomposition at higher concentrations, e.g. above 60% w/w concentration. Aqueous solutions may be sterilized by autoclaving or filtration.

When used as a base for medicated confectionery, the cooking process, at temperatures rising from 110°C to 145°C, causes some inversion to form dextrose and fructose (invert sugar). The fructose imparts stickiness to confectionery, but prevents cloudiness due to graining. Inversion is accelerated particularly at temperatures above 130°C and by the presence of acids.

The bulk material should be stored in a well-closed container in a cool, dry, place.

12. Incompatibilities

Powdered sucrose may be contaminated with traces of heavy metals which can lead to incompatibility with active ingredients, e.g. ascorbic acid. Sucrose may also be contami-

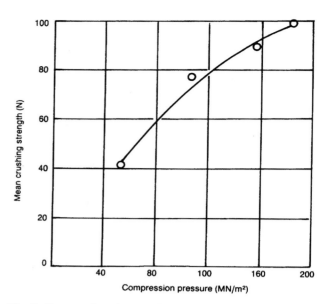

Fig. 1: Compression characteristics of crystalline sucrose.
Compression machine used: Manesty E2
Speed of compression: 50 strokes per minute (machine lubricated after each compression).
Diameter of compacts: 12.5 mm
Weight range of compacts: 675 $\pm$ 10 mg
Tablet strength instrument: Schleuniger
No lamination was encountered.

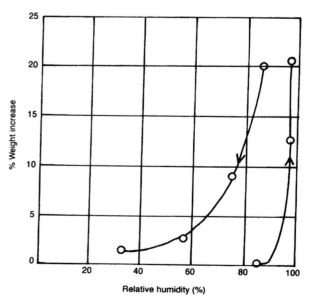

Fig. 2: Moisture sorption-desorption isotherm of crystalline sucrose.
Samples dried initially at 60°C over silica gel for 24 hours.
NOTE: at 97% relative humidity, sufficient water was absorbed to cause dissolution of the solid.

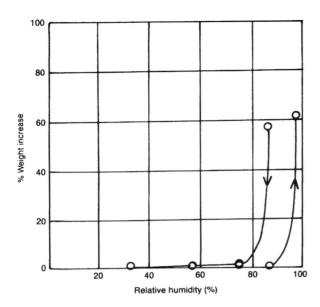

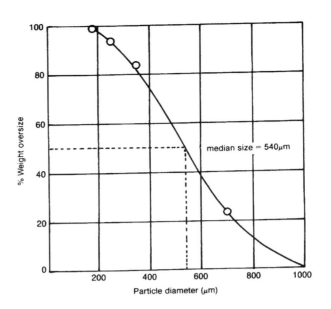

Fig. 3: Moisture sorption-desorption isotherm of powdered sucrose.
Samples dried initially at 60°C over silica gel for 24 hours. NOTE: at 90% relative humidity, sufficient water was absorbed to cause dissolution of the solid.

Fig. 5: Particle size distribution of crystalline sucrose.

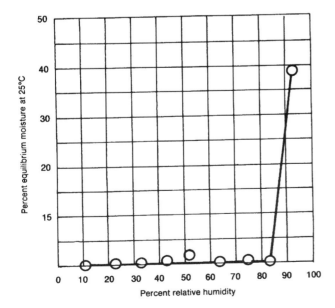

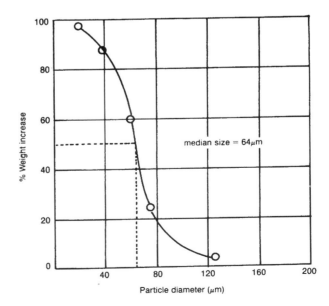

Fig. 4: Equilibrium moisture content of sucrose at 25°C.
Supplier: Amstar (Lot No.: 51995).

Fig. 6: Particle size distribution of powdered sucrose.

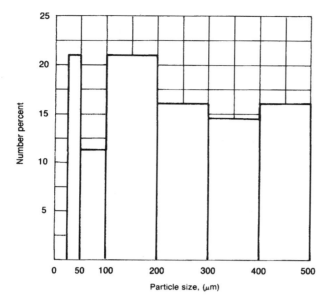

Fig. 7: Particle size distribution of sucrose.
Supplier: Amstar (Lot No.: 51995).

nated with sulfite from the refining process. With high sulfite content, color changes can occur in sugar coated tablets; for certain colors used in sugar coating the maximum limit for sulfite content, calculated as sulfur, is 1 ppm. In the presence of dilute or concentrated acids, sucrose is hydrolyzed or inverted to dextrose and fructose (invert sugar). Sucrose is also incompatible with aluminum.[3]

13. Method of Manufacture

Sucrose is obtained from the plants sugar cane, which contains 15-20% sucrose, and sugar beet, which contains 10-17% sucrose. Juice from these sources is heated to coagulate water soluble proteins which are removed by skimming. The resultant solution is then decolorized with an ion-exchange resin or charcoal and concentrated. Upon cooling, sucrose crystallizes out. The remaining solution is concentrated again and yields more sucrose, brown sugar, and molasses.

14. Safety

Sucrose is hydrolyzed in the small intestine by the enzyme sucrase to yield dextrose and fructose, which are then absorbed. When administered intravenously sucrose is excreted unchanged in the urine.
Although very widely used in foods and pharmaceutical formulations, sucrose consumption is a cause of concern and should be monitored in patients with diabetes mellitus or other metabolic sugar intolerance.[4]
Sucrose is also considered to be more cariogenic than other carbohydrates since it is more easily converted to dental plaque. For this reason, its use in oral pharmaceutical formulations is declining.
Although sucrose has been associated with obesity, renal damage and a number of other diseases, conclusive evidence linking sucrose intake with some diseases could not be established.[5,6] It was however recommended that sucrose intake in the diet should be reduced.[6]
LD_{50} (mouse, IP): 14 g/kg[7]
LD_{50} (rat, oral): 29.7 g/kg

15. Handling Precautions

Observe normal precautions appropriate to the circumstances and quantity of material handled. Eye protection and gloves are recommended. In the UK, the occupational exposure limit for sucrose is 10 mg/m^3 long-term (8-hour TWA) and 20 mg/m^3 short-term.[8]

16. Regulatory Status

GRAS listed. Included in the FDA Inactive Ingredients Guide (oral capsules, solutions, syrups and tablets). Included in nonparenteral and parenteral medicines licensed in the UK.

17. Pharmacopeias

Aust, Belg, Br, Chin, Cz, Egypt, Eur, Fr, Ger, Gr, Hung, Ind, It, Jpn, Mex, Neth, Nord, Port, Rom, Swiss, Turk, USPNF and Yug.

18. Related Substances

Compressible Sugar; Confectioner's Sugar; Dextrose; Fructose; invert sugar; Sugar Spheres.

Invert sugar: $C_6H_{12}O_6$
Molecular weight: 180.16
CAS number: [8013-17-0]
Comments: an equimolecular mixture of dextrose and fructose prepared by the hydrolysis of sucrose with a suitable mineral acid such as hydrochloric acid. Invert sugar may be used as a stabilizing agent to help prevent crystallization of sucrose syrups and graining in confectionery. A 10% aqueous solution is also used in parenteral nutrition.

19. Comments

Typical boiling points of sucrose syrups, without inversion of the sugar, are shown below:

Sucrose concentration (% w/v)	Boiling point (°C)
50	101.5
60	103
64	104
72	105.5
75	107
77.5	108.5
80	110.5

20. Specific References

1. Middleton KR, Seal D. Sugar as an aid to wound healing. Pharm J 1985; 235: 757-758.
2. Thomas S. Wound management and dressings. London: The Pharmaceutical Press, 1990: 62-63.
3. Tressler LJ. Medicine bottle caps [letter]. Pharm J 1985; 235: 99.
4. Golightly LK, Smolinske SS, Bennett ML, Sutherland EW, Rumack BH. Pharmaceutical excipients: adverse effects associated with 'inactive' ingredients in drug products (part II). Med Toxicol 1988; 3: 209-240.
5. Yudkin J. Sugar and disease. Nature 1972; 239: 197-199.
6. Report on health and social subjects 37. London: HMSO, 1989.
7. Sweet DV, editor. Registry of toxic effects of chemical substances. Cincinnati: US Department of Health, 1987.
8. Health and Safety Executive. EH40/93: occupational exposure limits 1993. London: HMSO, 1993.

21. General References

Barry RH, Weiss M, Johnson JB, DeRitter E. Stability of phenylpropanolamine hydrochloride in liquid formulations containing sugars. J Pharm Sci 1982; 71: 116-118.

Czeisler JL, Perlman KP. Diluents. In: Swarbrick J, Boylan JC, editors. Encyclopedia of pharmaceutical technology, volume 4. New York: Marcel Dekker, 1988: 37-84.

Jackson EB, editor. Sugar confectionery manufacture. Glasgow: Blackie, 1990.

Onyekweli AO, Pilpel N. Effect of temperature changes on the densification and compression of griseofulvin and sucrose powders. J Pharm Pharmacol 1981; 33: 377-381.

Wolraich ML, et al. Effects of diets high in sucrose or aspartame on the behavior and cognitive performance of children. N Engl J Med 1994; 330: 301-307.

22. Authors

UK: NA Armstrong, A Pickard.
USA: EE Hamlow.

Compressible Sugar

1. Nonproprietary Names
USPNF: Compressible sugar

2. Synonyms
Di-Pac; direct compacting sucrose; *Nu-Tab*.

3. Chemical name and CAS Registry Number
See Section 4.

4. Empirical Formula   Molecular Weight
The USPNF XVII states that compressible sugar contains not less than 95.0% and not more than 98.0% of sucrose ($C_{12}H_{22}O_{11}$). It may contain starch, maltodextrin, or invert sugar, and may contain a suitable lubricant.

Di-Pac (Domino Sugar Corporation) is a crystallized product consisting of about 97% sucrose and 3% maltodextrin. *Nu-Tab* (Crompton & Knowles Corp) consists of processed sucrose, about 4% invert sugar, and 0.1-0.2% each of corn starch and magnesium stearate.

5. Structural Formula
See Section 4.

6. Functional Category
Sweetening agent; tablet and capsule diluent.

7. Applications in Pharmaceutical Formulation or Technology
Compressible sugar is used primarily in the preparation of direct compression chewable tablets. Its tableting properties can be influenced by small changes in moisture level.[1,2]

Use	Concentration (%)
Dry binder in tablet formulations	5-20
Filler in chewable tablets	20-60
Filler in tablets	20-60
Sweetener in chewable tablets	10-50

8. Description
Compressible sugar is a sweet-tasting, white crystalline powder.

9. Pharmacopeial Specifications

Test	USPNF XVII
Identification	+
Microbial limits	+
Loss on drying	0.25-1.0%
Residue on ignition	$\leq$ 0.1%
Chloride	$\leq$ 0.014%
Sulfate	$\leq$ 0.010%
Calcium	+
Heavy metals	$\leq$ 5 ppm
Assay	95.0-98.0%

SEM: 1.
Excipient: Compressible Sugar (*Nu-tab*)
Manufacturer: Crompton & Knowles Corp
Lot No.: 101A-3 (10-105)
Magnification: 60x
Voltage: 20 kV

SEM: 2.
Excipient: Compressible Sugar (*Nu-tab*)
Manufacturer: Crompton & Knowles Corp
Lot No.: 101A-3 (10-105)
Magnification: 600x
Voltage: 20 kV

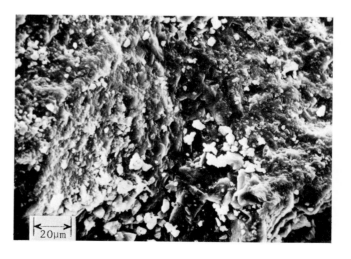

10. Typical Properties

Density (bulk): 0.6 g/cm³.
Density (tapped): 0.9 g/cm³.
Particle size distribution: for *Di-Pac*, 3% maximum retained on a #40 (425 μm) mesh; 75% minimum through a #100 (150 μm) mesh; 5% maximum through #200 (75 μm) mesh. For *Nu-Tab*, 50% maximum through a #60 (250 μm) mesh; 20% maximum through a #120 (125 μm) mesh.
Solubility: the sucrose portion is water soluble.

11. Stability and Storage Conditions

Compressible sugar is stable in air under normal storage conditions of room temperature and low relative humidity. The bulk material should be stored in a well-closed container in a cool, dry, place.

12. Incompatibilities

Incompatible with dilute acids which cause hydrolysis of sucrose to invert sugar, and alkaline earth hydroxides which react with sucrose to form sucrates.

13. Method of Manufacture

Compressible sugar is prepared by co-crystallization of sucrose with other excipients such as maltodextrin.[1]

14. Safety

See Sucrose.

15. Handling Precautions

See Sucrose.

16. Regulatory Status

Included in the FDA Inactive Ingredients Guide (capsules and tablets). Included in nonparenteral medicines licensed in the UK.

17. Pharmacopeias

USPNF.

18. Related Substances

Confectioner's Sugar; Sucrose; Sugar Spheres; *Sugartab*.

Sugartab:
Appearance: *Sugartab* (Edward Mendell Co Inc) is a compressible sugar which does not conform to the USPNF XVII specification. It is an agglomerated sugar product containing approximately 90-93% sucrose, the balance being invert sugar.
Density (bulk & tapped): see HPE Data.
Flowability: see HPE Data.
Moisture content: see HPE Data.
Particle size distribution: 30% through a #20 (850 μm) mesh; 3% through a #30 (600 μm) mesh.

HPE Laboratory Project Data			
	Method	**Lab #**	**Results**
Average flow rate	FLO-2	3	42.7 g/s
Bulk/tap density	BTD-1	1	B: 0.602 g/cm³
			T: 0.685 g/cm³
	BTD-7	14	B: 0.740 g/cm³
			T: 0.770 g/cm³
Moisture content	MC-3	33	0.57%
	MC-4	33	0.20%
Particle friability	PF-1	36	0.141%

Supplier: Edward Mendell Co Inc (*Sugartab*).

19. Comments

See Sucrose for further information.

20. Specific References

1. Rizzuto AB, Chen AC, Veiga MF. Modification of the sucrose crystal structure to enhance pharmaceutical properties of excipient and drug substances. Pharmaceut Technol 1984; 8(9): 32,34,36, 38-39.
2. Tabibi SE, Hollenbeck RG. Interaction of water vapor and compressible sugar. Int J Pharmaceutics 1984; 18: 169-183.

21. General References

Mendes RW, Gupta MR, Katz IA, O'Neil JA. Nu-tab as a chewable direct compression carrier. Drug Cosmet Ind 1974; 115(6): 42-46,130-133.

22. Authors

USA: W Wood.

Confectioner's Sugar

1. Nonproprietary Names
USPNF: Confectioner's sugar

2. Synonyms
Icing sugar; powdered sugar.

3. Chemical Name and CAS Registry Number
See Section 4.

4. Empirical Formula   Molecular Weight
The USPNF XVII describes confectioner's sugar as a mixture of sucrose ($C_{12}H_{22}O_{11}$) and corn starch that has been ground to a fine powder; it contains not less than 95.0% sucrose.

5. Structural Formula
See Section 4 and Sucrose.

6. Functional Category
Sugar coating adjunct; sweetening agent; tablet and capsule diluent.

7. Applications in Pharmaceutical Formulation or Technology
Confectioner's sugar is used in pharmaceutical formulations when a rapidly dissolving form of sugar is required for flavoring or sweetening. It is used as a diluent in solid dosage formulations when a small particle size is necessary to achieve content uniformity in blends with finely divided active ingredients. In solutions, at high concentrations (70% w/v), confectioner's sugar provides increased viscosity along with some preservative effects. Confectioner's sugar is also used in the preparation of sugar coating solutions and in wet granulations as a binder/diluent.
See also Section 19.

Use	Concentration (%)
Sugar coating	as desired
Sweetening agent in tablets	10-20
Tablet diluent	10-50

8. Description
Confectioner's sugar occurs as a sweet-tasting, fine, white, odorless powder.

9. Pharmacopeial Specifications

Test	USPNF XVII
Identification	+
Specific rotation	$\geqslant +62.6°$
Chloride	$\leqslant 0.014\%$
Calcium	+
Sulfate	$\leqslant 0.006\%$
Heavy metals	$\leqslant 5$ ppm
Microbial limits	+
Loss on drying	$\leqslant 1.0\%$
Residue on ignition	$\leqslant 0.08\%$

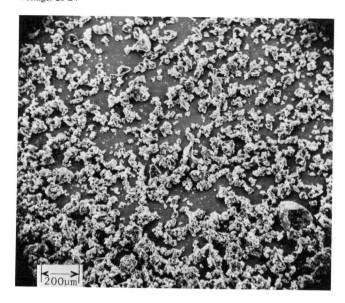

SEM: 1.
Excipient: Confectioner's sugar
Manufacturer: Frost
Lot No: 101A-1
Magnification: 60x
Voltage: 20 kV

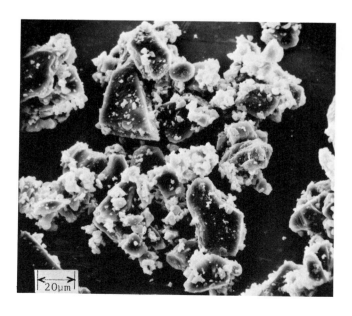

SEM: 2.
Excipient: Confectioner's sugar
Manufacturer: Frost
Lot No: 101A-1
Magnification: 600x
Voltage: 20 kV

10. Typical Properties

Density (bulk & tapped): *see* HPE Data.
Moisture content: *see* HPE Data.
Particle size distribution: various grades with different particle sizes are commercially available, e.g. 6X, 10X and 12X grades of confectioner's sugar from Domino Sugar Corporation. *See also* HPE Data.
For 6X, 94% through a #200 (75 μm) mesh; for 10X, 99.9% through a #100 (150 μm) mesh and 97.5% through a #200 (75 μm) mesh; for 12X, 99% through a #200 (75 μm) mesh and 96% through a #325 (45 μm) mesh.
Solubility: the sucrose portion is water soluble while the starch portion is insoluble in water although it forms a cloudy solution.

HPE Laboratory Project Data

	Method	Lab #	Results
Average flow rate	FLO-2	3	No flow
Bulk/tap density	BTD-1	1	B: 0.431 g/cm^3
			T: 0.694 g/cm^3
	BTD-7	14	B: 0.560 g/cm^3
			T: 0.710 g/cm^3
Moisture content	MC-3	33	0.31%
	MC-4	33	0.10%
Particle size	PSD-7	24	Mean = 14.3 μm
	PSD-9	3	*See* Fig. 1.

Supplier: Frost.

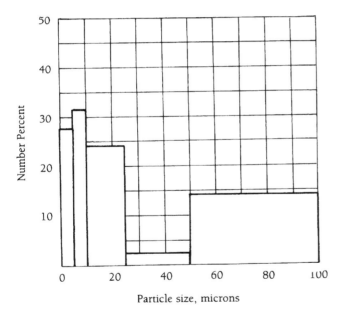

Fig. 1.: Particle size distribution of confectioner's sugar.

11. Stability and Storage Conditions

Confectioner's sugar is stable in air at moderate temperatures but may caramelize and decompose above 160°C. It is more hygroscopic than granular sucrose. Microbial growth may occur on dry storage if adsorbed moisture is present or in dilute aqueous solutions.
Confectioner's sugar should be stored in a well-closed container in a cool, dry, place.

12. Incompatibilities

Confectioner's sugar is incompatible with dilute acids which cause the hydrolysis of sucrose to invert sugar. It is also incompatible with alkaline earth hydroxides which react with sucrose to form sucrates.

13. Method of Manufacture

Confectioner's sugar is usually manufactured by grinding refined granulated sucrose with corn starch to produce a fine powder. Other anticaking agents, such as tricalcium phosphate and various silicates, have also been used but are less common.

14. Safety

See Sucrose.

15. Handling Precautions

See Sucrose.

16. Regulatory Status

Included in the FDA Inactive Ingredients Guide (capsules and tablets).

17. Pharmacopeias

USPNF.

18. Related Substances

Compressible Sugar; Sucrose; Sugar Spheres.

19. Comments

Confectioner's sugar is not widely used in pharmaceutical formulations because poor flow characteristics prevent its use in direct compression blends. However, confectioner's sugar is used when a smooth mouth feel or a rapidly dissolving sweetener is required, and when a milled/micronized active ingredient must be blended with a diluent of similar particle size for powders or wet granulations.
Low starch grades of confectioner's sugar containing 0.01% starch are also commercially available.

20. Specific References

See Sucrose.

21. General References

See Sucrose.

22. Authors

UK: A Pickard.
USA: MJ Jozwiakowski.

Sugar Spheres

1. Nonproprietary Names

USPNF: Sugar spheres

2. Synonyms

Non-pareil; *Non-pareil 103*; non-pareil seeds; *Nu-Core*; *Nu-Pareil*; sugar seeds.

3. Chemical Name and CAS Registry Number

—

4. Empirical Formula   Molecular Weight

See Section 8.

5. Structural Formula

See Section 8.

6. Functional Category

Tablet and capsule diluent.

7. Applications in Pharmaceutical Formulation or Technology

Sugar spheres are used as inert cores in capsule and tablet formulations particularly multiparticulate sustained release formulations.[1,2] They form the base upon which a drug is coated, usually followed by a release modifying polymer coating. Alternatively, a drug and matrix polymer may be coated onto the cores simultaneously. The active drug is released over an extended period either via diffusion through the polymer, or due to the controlled erosion of the polymer coating. Complex drug mixtures contained within a single dosage form may be prepared by coating the drugs onto different batches of sugar spheres with different protective polymer coatings.
Sugar spheres are also used in confectionery products.

8. Description

The USPNF XVII describes sugar spheres as approximately spherical granules of a labelled nominal size range with a uniform diameter and containing not less than 62.5% and not more than 91.5% of sucrose, calculated on the dried basis. The remainder is chiefly starch. Usually white in color, sugar spheres may also contain approved coloring agents.

9. Pharmacopeial Specifications

Test	USPNF XVII
Identification (starch)	+
Specific rotation	+41° to +61°
Microbial limits	+
Loss on drying	≤ 4.0%
Residue on ignition	≤ 0.25%
Heavy metals	≤ 5 ppm
Particle size distribution	≤ 10% oversize, ≤ 10% undersize

10. Typical properties

Particle size distribution: sugar spheres are of a uniform diameter. The following sizes are commercially available (US standard sieves):
35-40 mesh (425-500 μm)
30-35 mesh (500-600 μm)
25-30 mesh (600-710 μm)
20-25 mesh (710-850 μm)
18-20 mesh (850-1000 μm)
16-20 mesh (850-1180 μm)
14-18 mesh (1000-1400 μm)
Solubility: solubility in water varies according to the sucrose to starch ratio. The sucrose component is freely soluble in water whereas the starch component is insoluble in cold water.

11. Stability and Storage Conditions

Sugar spheres are stable when stored in a well-closed container in a cool, dry, place.

12. Incompatibilities

See Starch and Sucrose for information concerning the incompatibilities of the component materials of sugar spheres.

13. Method of Manufacture

Sugar spheres are prepared from crystalline sucrose which is coated using sugar syrup and a starch dusting powder.

14. Safety

Sugar spheres are used in oral pharmaceutical formulations. The sucrose and starch components of sugar spheres are widely used in edible food products and oral pharmaceutical formulations.
The adverse reactions and precautions necessary with the starch and sucrose components should be considered in any product containing sugar spheres. For example, sucrose is generally regarded as more cariogenic than other carbohydrates and in higher doses is also contraindicated in diabetic patients.
See Starch and Sucrose for further information.

15. Handling Precautions

Observe normal precautions appropriate to the circumstances and quantity of material handled.

16. Regulatory Status

Included in the FDA Inactive Ingredients Guide (oral capsules and tablets). Included in nonparenteral medicines licensed in the UK and Europe. The sucrose and starch components of sugar spheres are individually approved for use as food additives in Europe and the US.

17. Pharmacopeias

USPNF.

18. Related Substances

Compressible Sugar; Confectioner's Sugar; Starch; Sucrose.

19. Comments

—

20. Specific References

1. Narsimhan R, Labhasetwar VD, Lakhotia CL, Dorle A. Timed-release noscapine microcapsules. Indian J Pharm Sci 1988; 50: 120-122.
2. Bansal AK, Kakkar AP. Solvent deposition of diazepam over sucrose pellets. Indian J Pharm Sci 1990; 52: 186-187.

21. General References

Birch GG, Parker KJ, editors. Sugar: science and technology. London: Applied Science publications Ltd, 1979.

22. Authors

UK: RC Moreton.

Suppository Bases

1. Nonproprietary Names
BP: Hard fat
PhEur: Adeps solidus
USPNF: Hard fat

2. Synonyms
Adeps neutralis; hydrogenated vegetable glycerides; *Massa estarinum*; *Massupol*; *Novata*; semisynthetic glycerides; *Suppocire*; *Wecobee*; *Witepsol*.

3. Chemical Name and CAS Registry Number
Hard fat

4. Empirical Formula   Molecular Weight
Hard fat suppository bases consist mainly of mixtures of the triglyceride esters of the higher saturated fatty acids ($C_9H_{19}COOH$ to $C_{17}H_{35}COOH$) along with varying proportions of mono- and diglycerides. Special grades may contain additives such as beeswax, lecithin, polysorbates, ethoxylated fatty alcohols and ethoxylated partial fatty glycerides.

5. Structural Formula

```
          H
          |
    H—C—O—R
          |
    H—C—O—R
          |
    H—C—O—R
          |
          H
```

Where $R = -H$ or $-OC(CH_2)_n-CH_3$
$n = 8$ to 16
Not all Rs can be OH at the same time.

6. Functional Category
Suppository base.

7. Applications in Pharmaceutical Formulation or Technology
The primary application of hard fat suppository bases, or semisynthetic glycerides, is as a vehicle for the rectal administration of a variety of drugs, either to exert local effects or to achieve systemic absorption.

Selection of a suppository base cannot usually be made in the absence of knowledge of the physicochemical properties and intrinsic thermodynamic activity of the drug substance. Other drug-related factors that can affect release and absorption and which must therefore be considered are the particle size distribution of insoluble solids, the oil-water partition coefficient and the dissociation constant. The displacement value should also be known, as well as the ratio of drug to base. Properties of the suppository base which may or may not be modified by the drug, or which can influence drug release, are the melting characteristics, chemical reactivity and rheology. The presence of additives in the base can also affect performance.

Melting characteristics: fatty-based suppositories intended for systemic use should liquefy at just below body temperature.

Softening or dispersion may be adequate for suppositories intended for local action or modified release. High melting point bases may be indicated for fat-soluble drugs which tend to depress the melting point of bases or for suppositories used in warm climates. Drugs which dissolve in bases when hot may create problems if they deposit as crystals of different form or increased size on cooling or on storage. Low melting point bases, particularly those which melt to liquids of low viscosity, can be of value when large volumes of insoluble substances are to be incorporated; there is a risk of sedimentation in such instances. An important factor during processing is the time required for setting. This is affected by the temperature difference between the melting point and the solidification point.

Chemical reactivity: although the use of bases with low hydroxyl values (low partial ester content) is indicated to minimize the risk of interaction with chemically reactive compounds, formulators should be aware that hydroxyl values are also related to hydrophilic properties which, in turn, can modify both release and absorption rates. Bases with low hydroxyl values tend to be less plastic than those with higher values and, if cooled rapidly, may become excessively brittle. Peroxide values give a measure of the resistance of the base to oxidation and are a guide to the onset of rancidity.

Rheology: the viscosity of the melted base can affect the uniformity of distribution of suspended solids during manufacture. It can also influence the release and absorption of the drug in the rectum. Further reduction in the particle size of insoluble solids is the method of choice to minimize the risk of sedimentation. However, the presence of a high content of fine, suspended particles is likely to increase viscosity. It may also make pouring difficult, delay melting, and induce brittleness on solidification. Additives are sometimes included to modify rheological properties and to maintain homogeneity, but the extent of their effect on drug release should first be assessed. Release from a base in which viscosity has been enhanced by an added thickener may vary and be related to the aqueous solubility of the drug itself.

Additives: some grades of commercial bases already contain additives, and these are usually identified by the manufacturers by means of suitable letters and numbers. Additives may also be incorporated by formulators. Properties of suppositories which have been modified and additives or types of additives that have been used are listed below.

Property	Additive
Dispersants (release and/or absorber enhancers)	Surfactants
Hygroscopicity (reduction)	Colloidal silicon dioxide
Melting point	Ethoxylated partial fatty glycerides
	Saturated glyceride mixtures
Plasticity (plasticizers and hardeners)	Cetyl alcohol
	Glyceryl monostearate
	Myristyl alcohol
	Polysorbate 80 and 85
	Propylene glycol
	Stearic acid
	Stearyl alcohol
Viscosity	Aluminum monostearate, also di- and tri-stearates
	Bentonite
	Glyceryl monostearate
	Magnesium stearate
	Colloidal silicon dioxide

Water is undesirable as an additive because it enhances oxidation and the potential for a chemical reaction between suppository constituents. In low concentration, water plays little part in drug release and can serve as a medium for microbial growth. General guidance on the characteristics and potential applications of various grades of hard fat suppository bases appears in the following summaries.

Massa Estarinum (Hüls AG)

B: general purpose base suitable for use with both automatic and non-automatic equipment.

BC: similar to type B, but designed to reduce the sedimentation of crystalline medications.

C: material with a high melting range.

299: base with a very low hydroxyl value, for use with particularly reactive substances.

Massupol

Massupol: very hard base which sets rapidly on cooling.

Massupol 15: base designed for cold molding.

Novata (Henkel Chemicals Ltd)

A: general purpose suppository base suitable for use in both automatic and hand molding processes; rapid cooling can be used. The base has emulsifying properties.

AB: low melting range base used for formulations containing large quantities of powdery active ingredients; forced cooling can be used.

B: general purpose base for small or large-scale production equipment with or without forced cooling.

BBC: similar to type B, but with a lower solidification point and a higher melting point. Large quantities of powdery ingredients can be incorporated.

BC: particularly suitable for large-scale production and for the incorporation of crystalline substances with minimal sedimentation.

BCF: similar to type B, but with a higher melting range. Useful with active ingredients that produce a reduction in melting point or with dense crystalline substances. The base has emulsifying properties.

BD: material with a low hydroxyl value, can be used in large-scale equipment, although forced cooling should be avoided.

C: higher melting point base, suitable for large-scale equipment but forced cooling should be avoided.

D: high melting range base which can be used to adjust the melting point of suppository formulations.

E: base with good emulsifying properties, suitable for formulations containing up to 30% water, 20% alcohol or 40-50% glycerin; can be processed with forced cooling.

299: base with a particularly low hydroxyl value for use with reactive ingredients; can be used in automatic equipment, but forced cooling should be avoided.

PK, PKS37, and PKS39: bases with especially low hydroxyl values for use with reactive ingredients. These grades have different melting points to accommodate different quantities of the active ingredient.

Suppocire (Gattefossé Corp)

A: general purpose base suitable for both automatic and semiautomatic equipment.

AM: material with a low hydroxyl value; can be used on large-scale automatic equipment, but forced cooling should be avoided.

AML: similar to type AM, but contains phospholipid. Particularly suitable for formulations containing large quantities of powdery ingredients; can be used on automatic equipment.

AIML: similar to type AML, but with a lower melting range.

AS_2: similar to type A, but more suitable for use with automatic equipment with (or without) forced cooling.

AS_2X: similar to type AS_2, but contains a nonionic surfactant; can be used for formulations containing up to 10% water.

AT: material with intermediate hydroxyl value, suitable for large-scale production with forced cooling.

AP: lower melting range base with increased hydrophilic properties (intended to improve bioavailability).

AIP: similar to AP but with lower melting range.

AI, NAI: general purpose base used with large quantities of powdery actives. (The N indicates compatibility with solvents or essential oils).

AIX, NAIX: suitable for large quantities of actives and compatible with hydrophilic excipients, e.g. glycols.

AIM, NAI 5: standard bases for high speed manufacture, can be formulated with large amounts of actives.

NAI 10: similar to NAI 5 but more suited to medium or low speed manufacture.

NA 10: suitable for various machine speeds and small amounts of actives.

NAI 0: base with a low hydroxyl number for use with sensitive actives in large quantities.

NA 0: similar to NAI 0 but with a higher melting range suitable for use with small quantities of actives.

NA 5: similar to NA 0 but suitable for high speed manufacture.

NAIL: formulated to minimize thickening when used with large amounts of actives.

NAL: similar to NAIL but has a higher melting range that is more suited to small quantities of actives.

NAX: similar to NAIX but has a higher melting range that is more suited to small quantities of actives.

NBL: similar to NAIL but has a higher melting range suitable for use with small amounts of actives that are partially soluble in the base.

NBX: similar to NAIX but has a higher melting range suitable for use with small amounts of actives that are partially soluble in the base.

ND: base for medium speed manufacture and where the active is readily soluble in the base with consequent reduction in the melting point.

B: general purpose suppository base similar to type A, but with a higher melting range.

BM: similar to type AM, but with a higher melting range.

BML: similar to type AML, but with a higher melting range.

BS_2: similar to type AS_2, but with a higher melting range.

BS_2X: similar to type AS_2X, but with a higher melting range.

BT: similar to type AT, but with a higher melting range.

BP: similar to type AP, but with a higher melting range.

C: general purpose suppository base similar to type B, but with a higher melting range.

CM: similar to type BM, but with a higher melting range.

CS_2: similar to type BS_2, but with a higher melting range.

CS_2X: similar to type BS_2X, but with a higher melting range.

CT: similar to type BT, but with a higher melting range.

D: general purpose base similar to type C, but with a higher melting range.

DM: similar to type CM, but with a higher melting range.

NA: material with increased plasticity intended to improve the handling properties of formulations that are brittle or tend to fracture easily.

NB: similar to type NA, but with a higher melting range.

NC: similar to type NB, but with a higher melting range.

OSI: base with a low melting range and medium hydroxyl value. Particularly suited for ingredients which react with hydroxyl groups and/or produce an increase in the melting range. Can be processed on automatic equipment with forced cooling.

Witepsol (Hüls AG)

H5: base with a low hydroxyl value; rapid cooling should be avoided.

H12: material suitable for formulation with large amounts of crystalline or powdery ingredients; rapid cooling should be avoided.

H15: standard base designed to minimize the sedimentation of active material during processing; rapid cooling should be avoided.

H32: material with a very low hydroxyl value.

H35: similar to type H15, but with a very low hydroxyl value.

H37: similar to type H35, but with a higher melting range.

H39: similar to type H37, but with a higher melting range.

H42: similar to type H39, but with a higher melting range.

H175: base with a low hydroxyl value.

H185: base with a low hydroxyl value and a high melting range.

W25: general purpose base suitable for use on both automatic and nonautomatic production equipment; rapid cooling can be used.

W31: similar to type W25, but with a higher melting range.

W32: general purpose base for use with large quantities of powdery ingredients.

W35: general purpose base with a high hydroxyl value suitable for manufacture on large-scale automatic equipment; rapid cooling can be used.

W45: similar to type W35, but with a shorter setting time.

S51: material with added surfactant which improves dispersibility of active constituents. The base has a low melting range to allow for the incorporation of large amounts of medication; rapid cooling can be used.

S55: similar to S51, but with a higher melting range.

S58: similar to S55, but containing an additive intended to protect the rectal mucosa.

E75: high melting range base; rapid forced cooling should be avoided.

E76: similar to type E75, but more suitable for use with automatic equipment; forced cooling is recommended.

E85: very high melting range base used to adjust the melting range of suppository formulations; rapid cooling should be avoided.

8. Description

A white or almost white-colored, practically odorless, waxy, brittle mass. When heated to 50°C it melts to give a colorless or slightly yellowish liquid.

9. Pharmacopeial Specifications

Test	PhEur 1991	USPNF XVII
Identification	+	—
Melting range	30–45°C	27–44°C
Residue on ignition	—	≤ 0.05%
Total ash	≤ 0.05%	—
Acid value	≤ 0.5	≤ 1.0
Iodine value	≤ 3	≤ 7.0
Saponification value	210–260	215–255
Hydroxyl value	≤ 50	≤ 70
Peroxide value	≤ 3	—
Unsaponifiable matter	≤ 0.6%	≤ 3.0%
Alkaline impurities	+	+
1-Monoglycerides	≤ 5%	—
Heavy metals	≤ 10 ppm	—

10. Typical Properties

Acid value: *see* Table I.

Color number:

≤ 3 for *Massa estarinum* (iodine color index);

≤ 3 for *Novata* (iodine color index);

≤ 3 for *Suppocire* excluding L grades (Gardener scale);

≤ 5 for *Suppocire* L grades (Gardener scale);

≤ 3 for *Witepsol* (iodine color index).

Density:

0.955–0.975 g/cm^3 for *Massa estarinum* at 20°C;

0.955–0.975 g/cm^3 for *Novata* at 20°C;

0.950–0.960 g/cm^3 for *Suppocire* at 20°C;

0.950–0.980 g/cm^3 for *Witepsol* at 20°C.

Heat for melting (22–40°C):

≈ 145 J/g/°C for *Massa estarinum*;

≈ 125 J/g/°C for *Novata*;

100–130 J/g/°C for *Suppocire*;

≈ 145 J/g/°C for *Witepsol*.

Hydroxyl value: *see* Table I.

Iodine value: *see* Table I.

Melting point: *see* Table I.

Moisture content:

≤ 0.2% w/w for *Massa estarinum*;

≤ 0.1% w/w for *Novata*;

< 0.5% w/w for *Suppocire*;

≤ 0.2% w/w for *Witepsol*.

Peroxide value:

≤ 3 for *Massa estarinum*;

≤ 3 for *Novata*;

≤ 1.2 for *Suppocire*;

≤ 3 for *Witepsol*.

Saponification value: *see* Table I.

Solidification point: *see* Table I.

Solubility: freely soluble in carbon tetrachloride, chloroform, ether, toluene and xylene; slightly soluble in ethanol; practically insoluble in ethanol (95%) and water.

Specific heat:

≈ 2.6 J/g/°C for *Massa estarinum*;

1.9–2.1 J/g/°C for *Novata*;

1.7–2.5 J/g/°C for *Suppocire*;

≈ 2.6 J/g/°C for *Witepsol*.

Unsaponifiable matter: *see* Table I.

11. Stability and Storage Conditions

Hard fat suppository bases are fairly stable towards oxidation and hydrolysis with the peroxide value being a measure of their resistance to oxidation and rancidity. Water content is usually low and deterioration due to hygroscopicity rarely occurs. Melting characteristics, hardness and drug release profiles alter with time, and the melting point may rise by 0.5°C after storage for several months. Due to the complexity of bases, elucidation of the mechanisms which induce these changes on aging is difficult. Evidence has been presented[3] which supports a finite transition from amorphous to crystalline forms in which polymorphism, may or may not contribute, whereas other workers have found melting point changes to be closely associated with the conversion of triglycerides to more stable polymorphic forms.[4] Before melting point determinations are made, bases are 'conditioned' to a stable crystalline form.

Suppository bases should be stored protected from light in an airtight container at a temperature at least 5°C less than their stated melting point. Refrigeration is usually recommended for molded suppositories.

Table I: Typical properties of suppository bases.

Product		Acid value	Hydroxyl value	Iodine value	Melting point (°C)	Saponification value	Solidification point (°C)	Unsaponifiable matter (%)
Novata	A	≤ 0.3	35-45	≤ 3	33.5-35.5	225-240	29-31	≤ 0.5
	AB	≤ 0.3	25-40	≤ 3	29-31	230-245	26.5-28.5	≤ 0.5
	B	≤ 0.3	20-30	≤ 3	33-35.5	225-240	31-33	≤ 0.5
	BBC	≤ 0.3	20-30	≤ 3	34-36	225-240	30.5-32.5	≤ 0.5
	BC	≤ 0.3	30-40	≤ 3	33-35.5	225-240	30.5-35.5	≤ 0.5
	BCF	≤ 1.0	20-30	≤ 3	35-37	225-240	30-32	≤ 0.5
	BD	≤ 0.3	≤ 15	≤ 3	33.5-35.5	230-245	32-34	≤ 0.5
	C	≤ 0.3	20-30	≤ 3	36-38	220-235	33-35	≤ 0.5
	D	≤ 0.3	30-40	≤ 3	40-42	220-235	38-40	≤ 0.5
	E	≤ 1.0	45-60	≤ 3	34-36	215-230	29-31	≤ 2.0
	299	≤ 0.3	≤ 5	≤ 3	33.5-35.5	235-250	31.5-33.5	≤ 0.5
	PK	≤ 0.3	≤ 8	≤ 3	32-35	240-260	—	≤ 0.6
	PKS37	≤ 1.0	≤ 8	≤ 3	36-37.5	225-240	—	≤ 0.6
	PKS39	≤ 1.0	≤ 8	≤ 3	38-40	225-240	—	≤ 0.6
Massa Estarinum	B	≤ 0.3	20-30	≤ 3	33-35.5	225-240	31-33	≤ 0.3
	BC	≤ 0.3	30-40	≤ 3	33.5-35.5	225-240	30.5-32.5	≤ 0.3
	C	≤ 0.3	20-30	≤ 3	36-38	225-235	33-35	≤ 0.3
	299	≤ 0.3	≤ 2	≤ 3	33.5-35.5	240-255	32-34.5	≤ 0.3
Massupol		—	—	≤ 2	34-36	240-250	31-32.5	—
Massupol 15		—	—	≤ 3	35-37	220-230	31-33	—
Suppocire	A	< 0.5	20-30	< 2	35-36.5	225-245	—	≤ 0.5
	AM	< 0.2	≤ 6	< 2	35-36.5	225-245	—	≤ 0.5
	AML	< 0.5	≤ 6	< 2	35-36.5	225-245	—	≤ 0.6
	AIML	< 0.5	≤ 6	< 3	33-35	225-245	—	≤ 0.6
	AS$_2$	< 0.5	15-25	< 2	35-36.5	225-245	—	≤ 0.5
	AS$_2$X	< 0.5	15-25	< 2	35-36.5	225-245	—	≤ 0.6
	AT	< 0.5	25-35	< 2	35-36.5	225-245	—	≤ 0.5
	AP	< 1.0	30-50	< 1	33-35	200-220	—	≤ 0.5
	AI	< 0.5	20-30	< 2	33-35	225-245	—	≤ 0.5
	AIX	< 0.5	20-30	< 2	33-35	220-240	—	< 0.6
	AIM	< 0.3	< 6	< 2	33-35	225-245	—	≤ 0.5
	AIP	< 1.0	30-50	< 1	30-33	205-225	—	< 0.5
	B	< 0.5	20-30	< 2	36-37.5	225-245	—	≤ 0.5
	BM	< 0.2	< 6	< 2	36-37.5	225-245	—	≤ 0.5
	BML	< 0.5	< 6	< 3	36-37.5	225-245	—	≤ 0.6
	BS$_2$	< 0.5	15-25	< 2	36-37.5	225-245	—	≤ 0.5
	BS$_2$X	< 0.5	15-25	≤ 3	36-37.5	220-240	—	≤ 0.6
	BT	< 0.5	25-35	< 2	36-37.5	225-245	—	≤ 0.5
	BP	< 1.0	30-50	< 1	36-37	200-220	—	< 0.5
	C	< 0.5	20-30	< 2	38-40	220-240	—	≤ 0.5
	CM	< 0.2	< 6	< 2	38-40	225-245	—	≤ 0.5
	CS$_2$	< 0.5	15-25	< 2	38-40	220-240	—	≤ 0.5
	CS$_2$X	< 0.5	15-25	< 2	38-40	220-240	—	< 0.6
	CP	< 1.0	≤ 50	< 1	37-39	200-220	—	< 0.5
	D	< 0.5	20-30	< 2	42-45	215-235	—	≤ 0.5
	DM	< 0.2	< 6	< 2	42-45	215-235	—	≤ 0.5
	NA	< 0.5	< 40	< 2	35.5-37.5	225-245	—	< 0.5
	NB	< 0.5	< 40	< 2	36.5-38.5	215-235	—	< 0.5
	NC	< 0.5	< 40	< 2	38.5-40.5	220-240	—	< 0.5
	NAI 0	< 0.5	≤ 3	< 2	33.5-35.5	220-245	—	< 0.5
	NAI 5	< 0.5	≤ 5	< 2	33.5-35.5	220-245	—	< 0.5
	NAI 10	< 0.5	< 15	< 2	33.5-35.5	220-245	—	< 0.5
	NAI	< 0.5	< 40	< 2	33.5-35.5	225-245	—	< 0.5
	NAIL	< 1.0	< 40	< 3	33.5-35.5	225-245	—	< 0.6
	NAIX	< 0.5	< 40	< 2	33.5-35.5	220-240	—	< 0.6
	NA 0	< 0.5	≤ 3	< 2	35.5-37.5	225-245	—	< 0.5
	NA 5	< 0.5	≤ 5	< 2	35.5-37.5	225-245	—	< 0.5
	NA 10	< 0.5	≤ 15	< 2	35.5-37.5	225-245	—	< 0.5
	NAL	< 0.5	< 40	< 2	33.5-35.5	225-245	—	< 0.6
	NAX	< 0.5	< 40	< 2	35.5-37.5	220-240	—	< 0.6
	NBL	< 0.5	< 40	< 3	36.5-38.5	220-240	—	< 0.6
	NBX	< 0.5	< 40	< 2	36.5-38.5	215-235	—	< 0.6
	ND	< 0.5	< 40	< 2	42-45	210-230	—	< 0.5
Witepsol	H5	≤ 0.2	≤ 5	≤ 2	34-36	235-245	33-35	≤ 0.3
	H12	≤ 0.2	5-15	≤ 3	32-33.5	240-255	29-33	≤ 0.3
	H15	≤ 0.2	5-15	≤ 3	33.5-35.5	230-245	32.5-34.5	≤ 0.3
	H32	≤ 0.2	≤ 3	≤ 3	31-33	240-250	30-32.5	≤ 0.3
	H35	≤ 0.2	≤ 3	≤ 3	33.5-35.5	240-250	32-35	≤ 0.3
	H37	≤ 0.2	≤ 3	≤ 3	36-38	225-245	35-37	≤ 0.3
	H42	≤ 0.2	≤ 3	≤ 3	41-43	220-240	40-42.5	≤ 0.3
	H175	≤ 0.7	5-15	≤ 3	34.5-36.5	225-245	32-34.5	≤ 1.0
	H185	≤ 0.2	5-15	≤ 3	38-39	220-235	34-37	≤ 0.3
	W25	≤ 0.3	20-30	≤ 3	33.5-35.5	225-240	29-33	≤ 0.3
	W31	≤ 0.3	25-35	≤ 3	35-37	225-240	30-33	≤ 0.5
	W32	≤ 0.3	40-50	≤ 3	32-33.5	225-245	25-30	≤ 0.3
	W35	≤ 0.3	40-50	≤ 3	33.5-35.5	225-235	27-32	≤ 0.3
	W45	≤ 0.3	40-50	≤ 3	33.5-35.5	225-235	29-34	≤ 0.3
	S51	≤ 1.0	55-70	≤ 8	30-32	215-230	25-27	≤ 2.0
	S52	≤ 1.0	50-65	≤ 3	32-33.5	220-230	27-30	≤ 2.0
	S55	≤ 1.0	50-65	≤ 3	33.5-35.5	215-230	28-33	≤ 2.0
	S58	≤ 1.0	60-70	≤ 7	31.5-33	215-225	27-29	≤ 2.0
	E75	≤ 1.3	5-15	≤ 3	37-39	220-230	32-36	≤ 3
	E76	≤ 0.3	30-40	≤ 3	37-39	220-230	31-35	≤ 0.5
	E85	≤ 0.3	5-15	≤ 3	42-44	220-230	37-42	≤ 0.5

Table II: Typical properties of molded suppository bases.[*]

Product		Fracture index (kg)	Handling properties		Liquefaction time (min)
			ST (°C)	LT (°C)	
Novata	A	5.4+	33.7	35.3	15.3
	AB	5.4+	31.6	32.6	10.5
	B	5.4+	33.1	35.0	14.6
	BBC	5.4+	33.1	34.6	12.1
	BC	5.4+	33.2	35.0	14.0
	BCF	5.4+	34.4	35.8	20.4
	BD	5.4+	33.7	34.9	14.8
	C	5.4+	35.7	37.4	60.0+
	D	5.4+	40+	—	60.0+
	E	5.4+	32.9	35.5	14.0
	299	5.4+	33.9	35.9	11.7
Massa Estarinum	B	5.4+	32.8	34.8	12.6
	BC	5.4+	33.0	34.7	13.8
	C	5.4+	35.5	36.9	60.0+
	299	4.9	32.1	35.4	8.1
Suppocire	A	—	32.4	34.7	7.8
	AM	5.4+	32.7	35.0	8.7
	AML	5.4+	32.2	34.5	8.6
	AIML	4.3	31.4	33.9	5.3
	AS_2	4.4	32.2	34.6	9.9
	AS_2X	2.4	31.9	34.0	9.9
	AT	5.4	32.3	34.8	11.3
	AP	4.2	32.7	35.0	9.5
	B	5.4+	32.5	35.5	13.1
	BM	5.4+	33.0	35.7	13.1
	BML	5.4+	33.1	35.7	16.4
	BS_2	4.3	32.6	35.4	17.0
	BS_2X	1.4	32.4	35.0	14.0
	BT	3.2	33.4	36.3	29.3
	BP	3.9	32.8	35.4	16.0
	C	4.6	34.4	37.8	60.0+
	CM	5.4+	35.2	37.7	60.0+
	CS_2	5.4+	35.5	37.5	44.4
	CS_2X	5.4+	35.0	37.2	60.0
	CT	5.4+	34.7	37.4	60.0
	CP	5.4+	34.6	37.5	60.0
	D	5.4+	38.0	40.0+	60.0
	DM	5.4+	37.9	40.0+	60.0
	NA	5.4+	33.6	35.3	13.4
	NB	5.4+	34.7	36.7	22.9
	NC	5.4+	37.4	40.0+	60.0+
Witepsol	H5	5.4+	34.2	35.2	13.8
	H12	5.4+	30.0	32.7	3.7
	H15	5.4+	33.2	35.2	11.2
	H32	4.1	31.0	33.0	7.2
	H35	5.4+	33.7	34.7	17.4
	H37	5.4+	34.8	38.5	40.1
	H42	5.4+	34.7	38.3	50.2
	H175	5.4+	33.7	35.5	12.9
	H185	5.4+	35.5	37.0	48.8
	W25	5.4+	32.4	34.4	14.6
	W31	5.4+	34.9	36.5	31.0
	W32	4.3	31.5	34.3	8.7
	W35	5.4+	32.8	34.5	14.0
	W45	5.4+	32.6	34.3	12.9
	S51	3.2	30.3	32.8	6.8
	S55	5.4+	33.1	35.7	13.0
	S58	5.4+	31.5	33.7	7.7
	E75	5.4+	34.6	36.9	32.5
	E76	5.4+	34.9	38.0	60.0+
	E85	5.4+	39.0	40.0+	60.0+

[*] Samples for the above tests were prepared by melting the bases at 40-50°C and pouring into 2 g molds. When set, the suppositories were removed and stored at 20°C for 3 days prior to testing. **Fracture indexes** were determined using the Erweka apparatus at room temperature (22°C). **Handling properties** were determined by using an apparatus similar to that described by Setnikar and Fantelli.[1] The method used differed from that in the literature in that the test was started at 28°C (not 30°C), used a 500 g weight (not 460 g), and a 50 g rod (not 40 g). **ST** is the softening temperature, i.e. 5 mm displacement, and **LT** is the liquefaction temperature, i.e. 9 mm displacement. **Liquefaction times** were determined by the method described by Krówczyński.[2] The times quoted are for a 15 mm displacement of the glass rod. Note that the data presented in Table II should only be used as a guide. The tests are highly empirical, and the results can be influenced by factors such as the manufacturing conditions and storage history of the test sample, the physicochemical properties of the base, their location in either the middle or the ends of the defined ranges, and the presence of any drugs or adjuvants.

Suppositories which are not effectively packaged may develop a 'bloom' of powdery crystals at the surface. This is usually due to the presence of high melting point components in the base and can often be overcome by using a different base. Alternatively, the base can be pre-crystallized prior to pouring, since the crystals will cause a quick and complete crystallization into its end crystal form. This process is called 'tempering'.

12. Incompatibilities

Incompatibilities with suppository bases are now not extensively reported in the literature. The occurrence of a chemical reaction between a hard fat suppository base and a drug is relatively rare but any potential for such a reaction may be indicated by the magnitude of the hydroxyl value of the base. The risk of hydrolysis of aspirin, for example, may be reduced by the use of a base with a low hydroxyl value (< 5) and, additionally, by minimization of the water content of both the base and the aspirin.

There is evidence that aminophylline reacts with the glycerides in some hard fat bases to form diamides. On aging or exposure to elevated temperatures, degradation is accompanied by hardening and suppositories tend to exhibit a marked increase in melting point. The ethylene diamine content is also reduced.[5,6]

Certain fat-soluble medications, such as chloral hydrate, may depress the melting point when incorporated into a base. Similarly, when large amounts of an active substance, either solid or liquid, have to be dispersed into a base, the rheological characteristics of the resultant suppository may be changed with concomitant effects on release and absorption. Careful selection of bases or the inclusion of additives may therefore be necessary.

13. Method of Manufacture

The most common method of manufacture involves the hydrolysis of natural vegetable oils such as coconut or palm kernel oil, followed by fractional distillation of the free fatty acids produced. The C_{10} to C_{18} fractions are then hydrogenated and re-esterified under controlled conditions with glycerin to form a mixture of tri-, di- and monoglycerides of the required characteristics and hydroxyl value. This process is used for *Novata* and *Witepsol*.

In an alternative procedure, coconut or palm kernel oil is directly hydrogenated and then subjected to an interesterification with either itself or glycerin to form a mixture of tri-, di-, and monoglycerides of the required characteristics and hydroxyl value, e.g. *Suppocire*.

14. Safety

Suppository bases are generally regarded as nontoxic and nonirritant materials when used in rectal formulations. However, animal studies have suggested that some bases, particularly those types with a high hydroxyl value, may be irritant to the rectal mucosa.[7]

15. Handling Precautions

Observe normal precautions appropriate to the circumstances and quantity of material handled. There is a slight fire hazard when exposed to heat or flame.

16. Regulatory Status

Included in the FDA Inactive Ingredients Guide (rectal and vaginal preparations). Included in nonparenteral medicines licensed in the UK.

17. Pharmacopeias

Aust, Br, Eur, Fr, Ger, Gr, Hung, It, Neth, Nord, Port, Swiss and USPNF. Also in BP Vet.

18. Related Substances

Glycerin; Medium Chain Triglycerides; Polyethylene Glycol; theobroma oil.

Theobroma oil
CAS number: [8002-31-1]
Synonyms: cocoa butter; oleum cacao; oleum theobromatis.
Appearance: a yellowish or white-colored brittle solid with a slight odor of cocoa.
Pharmacopeias: Aust, Br, Cz, Egypt, Fr, Ger, Hung, It, Jpn, Mex, Neth, Nord, Rom, Rus, Turk, USPNF amd Yug. Also in BP Vet.
Melting point: 31-34°C
Solubility: freely soluble in chloroform, ether and petroleum spirit; soluble in boiling ethanol; slightly soluble in ethanol (95%).
Stability and storage conditions: heating theobroma oil to more than 36°C during the preparation of suppositories can result in an appreciable lowering of the solidification point due to the formation of metastable states; this may lead to difficulties in the setting of the suppository. Theobroma oil should be stored at a temperature not exceeding 25°C.
Comments: theobroma oil is a fat of natural origin used as a suppository base. It is comprised of a mixture of the triglycerides of saturated and unsaturated fatty acids, in which the unsaturated acid is preferentially situated on the 2-position of the glyceride. Theobroma oil is also a major ingredient of chocolate.

19. Comments

—

20. Specific References

1. Setnikar I, Fantelli S. Softening and liquefaction temperature of suppositories. J Pharm Sci 1963; 52: 38-43.
2. Krówczyński L. A simple device for testing suppositories [in Polish]. Diss Pharm 1959; 11: 269-273.
3. Coben LJ, Lordi NG. Physical stability of semisynthetic suppository bases. J Pharm Sci 1980; 69: 955-960.
4. Liversidge GG, Grant DJW, Padfield JM. Influence of physicochemical interactions on the properties of suppositories I: interactions between the constituents of fatty suppository bases. Int J Pharmaceutics 1981; 7: 211-223.
5. Brower JF, Juenge EC, Page DP, Dow ML. Decomposition of aminophylline in suppository formulations. J Pharm Sci 1980; 69: 942-945.
6. Taylor JB, Simpkins DE. Aminophylline suppositories: in vitro dissolution and bioavailability in man. Pharm J 1981; 227: 601-603.
7. De Muynck C, Cuvelier C, Van Steenkiste D, Bonnarens L, Remon JP. Rectal mucosa damage in rabbits after subchronical application of suppository bases. Pharm Res 1991; 8: 945-950.

21. General References

Anschel J, Lieberman HA. Suppositories. In: Lachman L, Lieberman HA, Kanig JL, editors. The theory and practice of industrial pharmacy, 2nd edition. Philadelphia: Lea and Febiger, 1976: 245-269.

Schoonen AJM, Moolenarr F, Huizinga T. Release of drugs from fatty suppository bases I: the release mechanism. Int J Pharmaceutics 1979; 4: 141-152.

Senior N. Review of rectal suppositories 1: formulation and manufacture. Pharm J 1969; 203: 703-706.

Senior N. Review of rectal suppositories 2: resorption studies and medical applications. Pharm J 1969; 203: 732-736.

Senior N. Rectal administration of drugs. In: Bean HS, Beckett AH, Carless JE, editors. Advances in pharmaceutical sciences, volume 4. London: Academic Press, 1974: 363-435.

22. Authors

UK: MC Meyer.
USA: B Pagliocca.

Talc

1. Nonproprietary Names
BP: Purified talc
PhEur: Talcum
USP: Talc

2. Synonyms
E553b; *Magsil Osmanthus*; *Magsil Star*; powdered talc; purified French chalk; *Purtalc*; soapstone; steatite.

3. Chemical Name and CAS Registry Number
Talc [14807-96-6]

4. Empirical Formula   Molecular Weight
Talc is a purified, hydrated, magnesium silicate, approximating to the formula $Mg_6(Si_2O_5)_4(OH)_4$. It may contain small, variable, amounts of aluminum silicate and iron.

5. Structural Formula
See Section 4.

6. Functional Category
Anticaking agent; glidant; tablet and capsule diluent; tablet and capsule lubricant.

7. Applications in Pharmaceutical Formulation or Technology
Talc is widely used in oral solid dosage formulations as a lubricant and diluent.[1,2] It is also used in topical preparations as a dusting powder, although it should not be used to dust surgical gloves, *see* Section 14. Since talc is a natural material it may frequently contain microorganisms and should therefore be sterilized when used as a dusting powder, *see* Section 11.
Talc is additionally used to clarify liquids and is also used, mainly for its lubricant properties, in cosmetics and food products.

Use	Concentration (%)
Dusting powder	90-99
Glidant and tablet lubricant	1-10
Tablet and capsule diluent	5-30

8. Description
Talc is a very fine, white to grayish-white colored, odorless, impalpable, unctuous, crystalline powder. It adheres readily to the skin, is soft to the touch, and free from grittiness.

9. Pharmacopeial Specifications

Test	PhEur 1985	USP XXII
Identification	+	+
Microbial limit	$\leqslant$ 100/g	$\leqslant$ 500/g
Loss on ignition	—	$\leqslant$ 6.5%
Loss on drying	$\leqslant$ 1.0%	—
Readily carbonizable substances	+	—

Continued

Test	PhEur 1985	USP XXII
Acid-soluble substances	+	$\leqslant$ 2.0%
Reaction and soluble substances	—	$\leqslant$ 0.1%
Water-soluble iron	—	+
Arsenic	—	$\leqslant$ 3 ppm
Calcium	$\leqslant$ 0.6%	—
Carbonate	+	—
Chloride	$\leqslant$ 140 ppm	—
Heavy metals	—	$\leqslant$ 0.004%
Lead	—	$\leqslant$ 0.001%

10. Typical Properties
Acidity/alkalinity:
pH = 6.5-10 for a 20% w/v aqueous dispersion.
Density (bulk & tapped): *see* HPE Data.
Hardness (Mohs): 1-1.5
Hygroscopicity: talc absorbs insignificant amounts of water at 25°C and relative humidities up to about 90%.
Particle size distribution: varies with the source and grade of material. Two typical grades are, $\geqslant$ 99% through a 74 μm (#200 mesh) or $\geqslant$ 99% through a 44 μm (#325 mesh). *See also* HPE Data.
Refractive index: n_D^{20} = 1.54-1.59
Solubility: practically insoluble in dilute acids and alkalis, organic solvents, and water.
Specific gravity: 2.7-2.8
Specific surface area: 12 m^2/g

	HPE Laboratory Project Data		
	Method	Lab #	Results
Bulk/tap density	BTD-1	1	B: 0.538 g/cm^3 [a]
			T: 0.862 g/cm^3
	BTD-1	1	B: 0.510 g/cm^3 [a]
			T: 0.833 g/cm^3
	BTD-1	1	B: 0.439 g/cm^3 [b]
			T: 0.694 g/cm^3
	BTD-1	1	B: 0.417 g/cm^3 [c]
			T: 0.667 g/cm^3
	BTD-7	14	B: 0.570 g/cm^3 [a]
			T: 0.710 g/cm^3
	BTD-7	14	B: 0.530 g/cm^3 [a]
			T: 0.610 g/cm^3
Compressibility	COM-1	21	No compacts [e]
	COM-7	12	No compacts [d]
Moisture content	MC-13	18	0.163% [a]
	MC-13	18	0.239% [a]
Particle size	PSD-5A	21	*See* Fig. 1.[e]

Supplier: a. Charles B Chrystal Co; b. Morelan; c. Whittaker, Clark & Daniels Inc; d. Pfizer Inc; e. Bate Chemical Co (Lot No.: A2349).

11. Stability and Storage Conditions
Talc is a stable material and may be sterilized by heating at 160°C for not less than 1 hour. It may also be sterilized by exposure to ethylene oxide or gamma irradiation.[3]
Talc should be stored in a well-closed container in a cool, dry, place.

12. Incompatibilities
Incompatible with quaternary ammonium compounds.

SEM: 1

Excipient: Talc
Manufacturer: Whittaker, Clark & Daniels Inc
Lot No.: 102A-4 (1745)
Magnification: 1200x
Voltage: 10 kV

SEM: 2

Excipient: Talc
Manufacturer: Cyprus Industrial Minerals Co
Lot No.: 102A-5 (375G)
Magnification: 1200x
Voltage: 10 kV

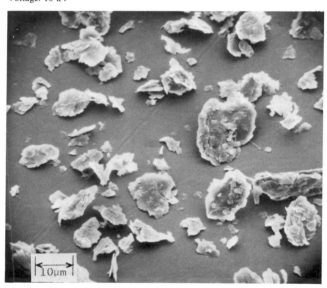

SEM: 3

Excipient: Talc (*Purtalc MC*)
Manufacturer: Charles B Chrystal Co Inc
Lot No.: 102A-1
Magnification: 1200x
Voltage: 10 kV

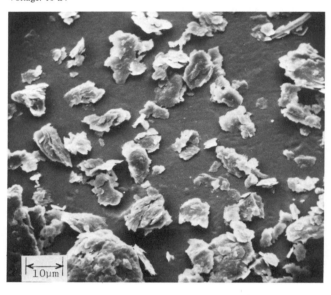

SEM: 4

Excipient: Talc (*Purtalc #325*)
Manufacturer: Charles B Chrystal Co Inc
Lot No.: 102A-2
Magnification: 1200x
Voltage: 10 kV

13. Method of Manufacture

Talc is a naturally occurring hydropolysilicate mineral found in many parts of the world including: Australia; China; Italy and the US.[4]

Naturally occurring talc is mined and pulverized before being subjected to flotation processes to remove various impurities such as: asbestos (tremolite); carbon; dolomite; iron oxide and various other magnesium and carbonate minerals. Following this process the talc is finely powdered, treated with dilute hydrochloric acid, washed with water and then dried.

14. Safety

Talc is mainly used in tablet and capsule formulations. Following oral ingestion talc is not absorbed systemically

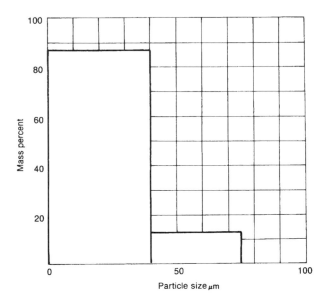

Fig. 1: Particle size distribution of talc.

and may thus be regarded as an essentially nontoxic material. However, intranasal or intravenous abuse of products containing talc can cause granulomas in body tissues, particularly the lungs.[5-7] Contamination of wounds or body cavities with talc may also cause granulomas, hence it should not be used to dust surgical gloves. Inhalation of talc causes irritation and may cause severe respiratory distress in infants,[8] *see also* Section 15.

Although talc has been extensively investigated for its carcinogenic potential, with some suggestion that there is an increased risk of ovarian cancer in women using talc, the evidence is inconclusive.[9,10] However, talc contaminated with asbestos has been concluded to be carcinogenic in humans and asbestos free grades should therefore be used in pharmaceutical products.[11]

15. Handling Precautions

Observe normal precautions appropriate to the circumstances and quantity of material handled. Talc is irritant if inhaled and prolonged excessive exposure may cause pneumoconiosis. In the UK, the occupational exposure limits for talc are 10 mg/m^3 of total inhalable dust long-term (8-hour TWA) and 1 mg/m^3 of respirable dust long-term (8-hour TWA).[12] Eye protection, gloves and a respirator are recommended.

16. Regulatory Status

Accepted in Europe as a food additive only when used in colors. Included in the FDA Inactive Ingredients Guide (buccal tablets, oral capsules and tablets, rectal and topical preparations). Included in nonparenteral medicines licensed in the UK.

17. Pharmacopeias

Aust, Br, Chin, Cz, Egypt, Eur, Fr, Ger, Gr, Hung, Ind, It, Jpn, Neth, Nord, Port, Rom, Swiss, Turk, US and Yug. Also in BP Vet.

18. Related Substances

—

19. Comments

Various different grades of talc are commercially available which vary in their chemical composition depending upon their source and method of preparation.[4,13]

20. Specific References

1. Dawoodbhai S, Rhodes CT. Pharmaceutical and cosmetic uses of talc. Drug Dev Ind Pharm 1990; 16: 2409-2429.
2. Dawoodbhai S, Suryanarayan ER, Woodruff CW. Optimization of tablet formulations containing talc. Drug Dev Ind Pharm 1991; 17: 1343-1371.
3. Bubik JS. Preparation of sterile talc for treatment of pleural effusion [letter]. Am J Hosp Pharm 1992; 49: 562-563.
4. Grexa RW, Parmentier CJ. Cosmetic talc properties and specifications. Cosmet Toilet 1979; 94(2): 29-33.
5. Schwartz IS, Bosken C. Pulmonary vascular talc granulomatosis. JAMA 1986; 256: 2584.
6. Johnson DC, et al. Foreign body pulmonary granulomas in an abuser of nasally inhaled drugs. Pediatrics 1991; 88: 159-161.
7. Sparrow SA, Hallam LA. Talc granulomas [letter]. Br Med J 1991; 303: 58.
8. Pairaudeau PW, Wilson RG, Hall MA, Milne M. Inhalation of baby powder: an unappreciated hazard. Br Med J 1991; 302: 1200-1201.
9. Longo DL, Young RC. Cosmetic talc and ovarian cancer. Lancet 1979; ii: 349-351.
10. Phillipson IM. Talc quality [letter]. Lancet 1980; i: 48.
11. International Agency for Research on Cancer/World Health Organisation. Silica and some silicates. IARC monographs on the evaluation of the carcinogenic risk of chemicals to humans 1987; 42.
12. Health and Safety Executive. EH40/93: occupational exposure limits 1993. London: HMSO, 1993.
13. Phadke DS, Keeney MP, Norris DA. Evaluation of batch-to-batch and manufacturer-to-manufacturer variability in the physical properties of talc and stearic acid. Drug Dev Ind Pharm 1994; 20: 859-871.

21. General References

Gold G, Campbell JA. Effects of selected USP talcs on acetylsalicylic acid stability in tablets. J Pharm Sci 1964; 53: 52-54.

22. Authors

USA: J Schirmer.

Tartaric Acid

1. Nonproprietary Names

BP: Tartaric acid
PhEur: Acidum tartaricum
USPNF: Tartaric acid

2. Synonyms

L-(+)-2,3-Dihydroxybutanedioic acid; (2R,3R)-2,3-dihydroxy-butane-1,4-dioic acid; 2,3-dihydroxysuccinic acid; E334; *d*-tartaric acid; L-(+)-tartaric acid.

3. Chemical Name and CAS Registry Number

$[R-(R^*,R^*)]$-2,3-dihydroxybutanedioic acid
[87-69-4]

4. Empirical Formula   Molecular Weight

$C_4H_6O_6$ 150.09

5. Structural Formula

```
        COOH
         |
   H — C — OH
         |
  HO — C — H
         |
        COOH
```

6. Functional Category

Acidifying agent; acidulant; flavor enhancer; sequestering agent.

7. Applications in Pharmaceutical Formulation or Technology

Tartaric acid is used in beverages, confectionery, food products and pharmaceutical formulations as an acidulant. It may also be used as an acidifying agent, a sequestering agent and as an antioxidant synergist. In pharmaceutical formulations, it is widely used in combination with bicarbonates, as the acid component of effervescent granules, powders and tablets.

8. Description

Tartaric acid occurs as colorless monoclinic crystals, or a white or almost white crystalline powder. It is odorless, with an extremely tart taste.

9. Pharmacopeial Specifications

Test	PhEur 1986	USPNF XVII (Suppl 6)
Identification	+	+
Appearance of solution	+	—
Specific rotation	+12.0° to +12.8°	+12.0° to +13.0°
Loss on drying	≤ 0.2%	≤ 0.5%
Sulfated ash	≤ 0.1%	—
Residue on ignition	—	≤ 0.1%
Organic volatile impurities	—	+

Continued

Test	PhEur 1986	USPNF XVII (Suppl 6)
Chloride	≤ 100 ppm	—
Oxalic acid	≤ 350 ppm	+
Sulfate	≤ 150 ppm	+
Calcium	≤ 200 ppm	—
Heavy metals	≤ 10 ppm	≤ 0.001%
Assay (dried basis)	99.5-101.0%	99.7-100.5%

10. Typical Properties

Acidity/alkalinity:
pH = 2.2 (1.5% w/v aqueous solution)
Density: 1.76 g/cm^3
Dissociation constant:
pK_{a1} = 2.93 at 25°C;
pK_{a2} = 4.23 at 25°C.
Heat of combustion: 1151 kJ/mol (275.1 kcal/mol)
Melting point: 168-170°C
Osmolarity: a 3.9% w/v aqueous solution is iso-osmotic with serum.
Solubility:

Solvent	Solubility at 20°C Unless otherwise stated
Chloroform	practically insoluble
Ethanol (95%)	1 in 2.5
Ether	1 in 250
Glycerin	soluble
Methanol	1 in 1.7
Propan-1-ol	1 in 10.5
Water	1 in 0.75
	1 in 0.5 at 100°C

Specific heat: 1.20 J/g (0.288 cal/g) at 20°C
Specific rotation: $[\alpha]_D^{20}$: +12.0° (20% w/v aqueous solution)

11. Stability and Storage Conditions

The bulk material is stable and should be stored in a well-closed container in a cool, dry, place.

12. Incompatibilities

Tartaric acid reacts with metal carbonates and bicarbonates (a property exploited in effervescent preparations).

13. Method of Manufacture

Tartaric acid occurs naturally in many fruits as the free acid or in combination with calcium, magnesium and potassium. Commercially, nearly all tartaric acid is manufactured from potassium tartrate (cream of tartar) a by-product of wine making. Potassium tartrate is treated with hydrochloric acid, followed by the addition of a calcium salt to produce insoluble calcium tartrate. This precipitate is then removed by filtration and reacted with 70% sulfuric acid to yield tartaric acid and calcium sulfate.

14. Safety

Tartaric acid is widely used in food products, oral, topical and parenteral pharmaceutical formulations and is generally regarded as a nontoxic and nonirritant material. However, strong tartaric acid solutions are mildly irritant and if ingested undiluted may cause gastroenteritis. Cardiovascular collapse and renal failure may follow.

An acceptable daily intake for L-(+)-tartaric acid has not been set by the WHO although an acceptable daily intake of up to 30 mg/kg body-weight for monosodium L-(+)-tartrate has been established.[1]

LD$_{50}$ (mouse, IV): 0.49 g/kg[2]
LD$_{50}$ (rat, oral): 1.29 g/kg

15. Handling Precautions

Observe normal precautions appropriate to the circumstances and quantity of material handled. Tartaric acid may be irritant to the eyes. Eye protection and rubber or plastic gloves are recommended. When heated to decomposition tartaric acid emits acrid smoke and fumes.

16. Regulatory Status

GRAS listed. Accepted as a food additive in Europe. Included in the FDA Inactive Ingredients Guide (IM and IV injections, oral solutions, syrups and tablets, rectal and vaginal preparations). Included in nonparenteral medicines licensed in the UK.

17. Pharmacopeias

Aust, Br, Braz, Cz, Egypt, Eur, Fr, Ger, Gr, Hung, Ind, It, Jpn, Mex, Neth, Nord, Port, Rom, Swiss, Turk, USPNF and Yug.

18. Related Substances

Citric Acid Monohydrate; Fumaric Acid; Malic Acid; D-(-)-tartaric acid; DL-(±)-tartaric acid.

D-(-)-Tartaric acid: C$_4$H$_6$O$_6$

Molecular weight: 150.09
CAS number: [147-71-7]
Synonyms: [S-(R^*,R^*)]-2,3-dihydroxybutanedioic acid; *l*-tartaric acid.
Appearance: colorless monoclinic crystals, or white or almost white crystalline powder.
Density: 1.76 g/cm^3
Dissociation constant: pK$_{a1}$ = 2.93; pK$_{a2}$ = 4.23.
Melting point: 168-170°C
Solubility:

Solvent	Solubility at 20°C Unless otherwise stated
Chloroform	practically insoluble
Ethanol (95%)	1 in 2.5
Ether	1 in 250
Glycerin	soluble
Methanol	1 in 1.7
Propan-1-ol	1 in 0.5
Water	1 in 0.75
	1 in 0.5 at 100°C

Specific rotation [α]$_D^{20}$: -12.0° (20% w/v aqueous solution)
Comments: prepared from DL-(±)-tartaric acid by reacting with a variety of microorganisms, and from salt formation with *d*-methylamphetamine. Has also been found to occur naturally.

DL-(±)-Tartaric acid: C$_4$H$_6$O$_6$

Molecular weight: 150.09
CAS number: [133-37-9]
Synonyms: 2,3-dihydroxybutanedioic acid; racemic tartaric acid; *dl*-tartaric acid.
Appearance: colorless triclinic crystals, or white or almost white crystalline powder.
Acidity/alkalinity: pH = 2.0 (1.5% w/v aqueous solution)
Density: 1.70 g/cm^3
Dissociation constant: pK$_{a1}$ = 2.96; pK$_{a2}$ = 4.24.
Melting point: 206°C
Solubility: 1 in 32 of ethanol (95%); 1 in 100 of ether; 1 in 4.85 of water.
Comments: not found in nature. Prepared by boiling L-(+)-tartaric acid in sodium hydroxide solution.

19. Comments

L-(+)-tartaric acid, the optical isomer usually encountered, is the naturally occurring form and is specified as tartaric acid in the BP 1993 and USPNF XVII.

20. Specific References

1. FAO/WHO. Evaluation of certain food additives. Twenty-first report of the joint FAO/WHO expert committee on food additives. Tech Rep Ser Wld Hlth Org 1978; No. 617.
2. Sweet DV, editor. Registry of toxic effects of chemical substances. Cincinnati: US Department of Health, 1987.

21. General References

Sendall FEJ, Staniforth JN. A study of powder adhesion to metal surfaces during compression of effervescent pharmaceutical tablets. J Pharm Pharmacol 1986; 38: 489-493.
Usui F, Carstensen JT. Interactions in the solid state I: interactions of sodium bicarbonate and tartaric acid under compressed conditions. J Pharm Sci 1985; 74: 1293-1297.

22. Authors

UK: KA Khan, KD Vaughan.

Tetrafluoroethane

1. Nonproprietary Names
None adopted.

2. Synonyms
Dymel 134a/P; fluorocarbon 134a; *Frigen 134a*; HFA 134a; HFC 134a; *Isceon 134a*; *Klea 134a*; propellant 134a; refrigerant 134a; *Suva 134a*.

3. Chemical Name and CAS Registry Number
1,1,1,2-Tetrafluoroethane [811-97-2]

4. Empirical Formula   Molecular Weight
$C_2H_2F_4$ 102.03

5. Structural Formula

$$F-\overset{\overset{\displaystyle F}{|}}{\underset{\underset{\displaystyle F}{|}}{C}}-\overset{\overset{\displaystyle H}{|}}{\underset{\underset{\displaystyle H}{|}}{C}}-F$$

6. Functional Category
Aerosol propellant.

7. Applications in Pharmaceutical Formulation or Technology
Tetrafluoroethane (propellant 134a) is currently under investigation for use in metered dose inhalers (MDIs)[1,2] as a non-ozone depleting replacement for dichlorodifluoromethane (propellant 12) which is subject to restrictions upon its use, under the terms of the Montreal Protocol.[3-8] *See* dichlorodifluoromethane for further information.
Tetrafluoroethane is presently in use as a refrigerant.

8. Description
Tetrafluoroethane is a liquefied gas and exists as a liquid at room temperature when contained under its own vapor pressure, or as a gas when exposed to room temperature and atmospheric pressure. The liquid is practically odorless and colorless. In high concentrations, the gas may have a slight ether-like odor. Tetrafluoroethane is noncorrosive, nonirritating and nonflammable.

9. Pharmacopeial Specifications
—

10. Typical Properties
Boiling point: -26.2°C
Critical pressure: 4.11 MPa (40.55 atm)
Critical temperature: 101.0°C
Density:
1.226 g/cm³ for liquid at 20°C;
1.207 g/cm³ for liquid at 25°C.
Flammability: nonflammable.
Freezing point: -108°C
Solubility: soluble in ethanol (95%), ether, and 1 in 1294 parts of water at 20°C.

Surface tension: 8.6 kN/m
Vapor density (absolute):
4.555 g/m³ at standard temperature and pressure.
Vapor density (relative): 3.53 (air = 1)
Vapor pressure:
569 kPa at 20°C;
662 kPa at 25°C.
Viscosity (dynamic):
0.222 mPa s (0.222 cP) for liquid at 20°C;
0.210 mPa s (0.210 cP) for liquid at 25°C.

11. Stability and Storage Conditions
Tetrafluoroethane is generally nonreactive at normal temperatures although it is less stable chemically than dichlorodifluoromethane and will decompose in the atmosphere.[1] The liquefied gas is however stable when used as a propellant or refrigerant. Tetrafluoroethane should be stored in metal cylinders in a cool location away from fire risks, direct sunlight or other sources of heat. Storage temperature should not exceed 45°C.

12. Incompatibilities
Tetrafluoroethane is thought to be compatible with the excipients frequently used in pharmaceutical aerosols. It has good miscibility with most organic solvents, less so with water. *See also* Section 19.

13. Method of Manufacture
Prepared by several possible routes. Any impurities are removed to produce a product greater than 99.9% pure.

14. Safety
Tetrafluoroethane is proposed as a replacement for dichlorodifluoromethane (propellant 12) for use in topical, oral and nasal aerosol formulations, including metered-dose inhalers (MDIs).
Propellants used for oral and nasal aerosol products generally vaporize quickly and most of the vapors escape and are not inhaled. However, a small amount of the propellant may be inhaled with the active ingredient and be carried to the respiratory system. These amounts of propellant do not present a toxicological problem and are quickly cleared from the lungs. Deliberate inhalation of excessive quantities of fluorocarbon propellant may result in death, and the following 'warning' statements must appear on the label of all aerosols:
WARNING: Avoid inhalation. Keep away from eyes or other mucous membranes. (Aerosols designed specifically for oral and nasal inhalation need not contain this statement).
WARNING: Do not inhale directly; deliberate inhalation of contents can cause death.
OR
WARNING: Use only as directed; intentional misuse by deliberately concentrating and inhaling the contents can be harmful or fatal.
Additionally, the label should contain the following information:
WARNING: Contents under pressure. Do not puncture or incinerate container. Do not expose to heat or store at room temperature above 120°F (49°C). Keep out of the reach of children.
When fluorocarbon propellants are used for topical aerosols they may cause a chilling effect on the skin although this effect has been somewhat overcome by the use of vapor tap valves. The propellants quickly vaporize from the skin, and are nonirritating when used as directed.

Extensive animal toxicity studies for tetrafluoroethane are currently in progress and include a lifetime inhalation study.

15. Handling Precautions

Tetrafluoroethane is usually encountered as a liquefied gas and appropriate precautions for handling such materials should be taken. Eye protection, gloves and protective clothing are recommended. Tetrafluoroethane should be handled in a well-ventilated environment. Fluorocarbon vapors are heavier than air and do not support life and therefore, when cleaning large tanks which have contained fluorocarbons, adequate provisions for oxygen in the tanks must be made in order to protect workers cleaning the tanks.

Although nonflammable, thermal degradation or hydrolysis will lead to the production of acidic, toxic fumes.

In the UK, a long-term (8-hour TWA) occupational exposure limit has not been specified as yet although an appropriate industrial standard for tetrafluoroethane exposure is 1000 ppm.

16. Regulatory Status

—

17. Pharmacopeias

—

18. Related Substances

Chlorodifluoroethane; Chlorodifluoromethane; Dichlorodifluoromethane; Dichlorotetrafluoroethane; Difluoroethane; Trichloromonofluoromethane.

19. Comments

Tetrafluoroethane has somewhat different solvent properties to earlier chlorofluorocarbon propellants so that the use of alternative lubricants and suspending agents may be necessary. Alternative rubber gasket compositions may also be necessary in aerosol containers.

For a discussion of the numerical nomenclature applied to fluorocarbon aerosol propellants *see* Dichlorodifluoromethane.

20. Specific References

1. Dalby RN, Byron PR, Shepherd HR, Papadopoulos E. CFC propellant substitution: P-134a as a potential replacement for P-12 in MDIs. Pharmaceut Technol 1990; 14(3): 26, 28, 30, 32, 33.
2. Reformulated MDIs plan from Glaxo. Pharm J 1994; 252: 217.
3. Fischer FX, Hess H, Sucker H, Byron PR. CFC propellant substitution: international perspectives. Pharmaceut Technol 1989; 13(9): 44, 48, 50, 52.
4. Kempner N. Metered dose inhaler CFCs under pressure. Pharm J 1990; 245: 428-429.
5. Dalby RN. Possible replacements for CFC-propelled metered-dose inhalers. Med Device Tech 1991; 2(4): 21-25.
6. Moren F. Chlorofluorocarbons and their replacement. Regulatory Affairs J 1991; 2(6): 385-389.
7. CFC-free aerosols: the final hurdle. Mfg Chem 1992; 63(7): 22-23.
8. Mackenzie D. Large hole in the ozone agreement. New Scientist 1992; Nov 28: 5.

See also Dichlorodifluoromethane for further information.

21. General References

Ravishankara AR, et al. Do hydrofluorocarbons destroy stratospheric ozone? Science 1994; 263: 71-75.

See also Dichlorodifluoromethane for further information.

22. Authors

UK: PJ Davies.

Thimerosal

1. Nonproprietary Names

BP: Thiomersal
USP: Thimerosal

2. Synonyms

[(*o*-Carboxyphenyl)thio]ethylmercury sodium salt; ethyl(2-mercaptobenzoato-*S*)-mercury, sodium salt; ethyl (sodium *o*-mercaptobenzoato)mercury; mercurothiolate; *Merfamin*; *Merthiolate*; *Mertorgan*; *Merzonin*; sodium ethylmercurithiosalicylate; thiomersalate.

3. Chemical Name and CAS Registry Number

Ethyl[2-mercaptobenzoato(2-)-*O*,*S*]-mercurate(1-) sodium
[54-64-8]

4. Empirical Formula   Molecular Weight

$C_9H_9HgNaO_2S$ 404.81

5. Structural Formula

COONa

SHgCH$_2$CH$_3$

6. Functional Category

Antimicrobial preservative; antiseptic.

7. Applications in Pharmaceutical Formulation or Technology

Thimerosal has been used as an antimicrobial preservative in biological and pharmaceutical preparations since the 1930s.[1] It is used as an alternative to benzalkonium chloride and other phenylmercuric preservatives and has both bacteriostatic and fungistatic activity. Increasing concerns over its safety have however led some to question its continued use in formulations, *see* Section 14. Thimerosal is also used in cosmetics (*see* Section 16) and to preserve soft contact lens solutions.

Use	Concentration (%)
IM, IV, SC injections	0.01
Ophthalmic solutions	0.001-0.15
Ophthalmic suspensions	0.001-0.004
Otic preparations	0.001-0.01
Topical preparations	0.01

8. Description

Thimerosal is a light, cream-colored crystalline powder with a slight, characteristic odor.

9. Pharmacopeial Specifications

Test	BP 1993	USP XXII
Identification	+	+
Acidity or alkalinity	6.0-8.0	—
Loss on drying	≤ 0.5%	≤ 0.5%
Ether-soluble substances	≤ 0.6%	≤ 0.8%
Mercury ions/mercuric salts	+	≤ 0.7%
Readily carbonizable substances	—	+
Assay (dried basis)	97.0-101.0%	97.0-101.0%

10. Typical Properties

Acidity/alkalinity: pH = 6.7 for a 1% w/v aqueous solution at 20°C.

Antimicrobial activity: thimerosal is bactericidal at acidic pH, bacteriostatic and fungistatic at alkaline or neutral pH. Thimerosal is not effective against spore-forming organisms. *See also* Section 12. Reported minimum inhibitory concentrations (MICs) are shown below:[2]

Microorganism	MIC (μg/mL)
Aspergillus niger	128
Candida albicans	32
Escherichia coli	4
Klebsiella pneumoniae	4
Penicillium notatum	128
Pseudomonas aeruginosa	8
Pseudomonas cepacia	8
Pseudomonas fluorescens	4
Staphylococcus aureus	0.2

Density (bulk): < 0.33 g/cm^3
Dissociation constant: pK_a = 3.05 at 25°C
Melting point: 232-233°C with decomposition.
Solubility: soluble 1 in 8 of ethanol (95%), 1 in 1 of water; practically insoluble in benzene and ether. *See also* HPE Data.

	HPE Laboratory Project Data		
	Method	Lab #	Results
Solubility			
Ethanol (95%) at 25°C	SOL-6	23	0.098-0.104 g/mL
Ethanol (95%) at 37°C	SOL-6	23	0.104-0.115 g/mL
Hexane at 25°C	SOL-6	23	0.005 g/mL
Hexane at 37°C	SOL-6	23	0.006 g/mL
Propylene glycol at 25°C	SOL-6	23	0.425-0.675 g/mL
Propylene glycol at 37°C	SOL-6	23	0.425-0.675 g/mL
Water at 25°C	SOL-6	23	1.007 g/mL
Water at 37°C	SOL-6	23	1.758 g/mL

11. Stability and Storage Conditions

Thimerosal is stable at normal temperatures and pressures; exposure to light may cause discoloration.

Aqueous solutions may be sterilized by autoclaving but are sensitive to light. The rate of oxidation in solutions is increased by the presence of trace amounts of copper and other metals. Edetic acid or edetates may be used to stabilize solutions but have been reported to reduce the antimicrobial efficacy of thimerosal solutions, *see* Section 12.

The solid material should be stored in a well-closed container, protected from light, in a cool, dry, place.

12. Incompatibilities

Incompatible with aluminum and other metals, strong oxidizing agents, strong acids and bases, sodium chloride solutions,[3] lecithin, phenylmercuric compounds, quaternary ammonium compounds, thioglycolate and proteins. The presence of sodium metabisulfite, edetic acid and edetates in solutions can reduce the preservative efficacy of thimerosal.[4] In solution, thimerosal may be adsorbed by plastic packaging materials, particularly polyethylene. It is strongly adsorbed by treated or untreated rubber caps that are in contact with solutions.[5,6]

13. Method of Manufacture

Thimerosal is prepared by the interaction of ethylmercuric chloride, or hydroxide, with thiosalicylic acid and sodium hydroxide, in ethanol (95%).

14. Safety

Thimerosal is widely used as an antimicrobial preservative in parenteral and topical pharmaceutical formulations. However, concern over the use of thimerosal in pharmaceuticals has increased as a result of a greater awareness of the toxicity of mercury and other associated mercury compounds. The increasing number of reports of adverse reactions, particularly hypersensitivity, to thimerosal and doubts as to its effectiveness as a preservative has led to suggestions that it should not be used as a preservative in eye-drops[7] or vaccines.[8-10]

The most frequently reported adverse reaction to thimerosal, particularly in vaccines,[8-12] is hypersensitivity, usually with erythema and papular or vesicular eruptions. Although not all thimerosal sensitive patients develop adverse reactions to vaccines containing thimerosal there is potential risk. Patch testing in humans, and animal experiments, have suggested that 0.1% w/v thimerosal can sensitize children.[13] The incidence of sensitivity to thimerosal appears to be increasing; a recent study of 256 healthy subjects showed approximately 6% with positive sensitivity.[14]

Adverse reactions to thimerosal used to preserve contact lens solutions have also been reported. Reactions include ocular redness, irritation, reduced lens tolerance and conjunctivitis.[15-17] One estimate suggests that approximately 10% of contact lens wearers may be sensitive to thimerosal.[18]

Thimerosal has also been associated with false positive reactions to old tuberculin,[19] ototoxicity[20] and an unusual reaction to aluminum[21] in which a patient suffered a burn 5 cm in diameter at the site of an aluminum foil diathermy electrode after preoperative preparation of the skin with a 0.1% w/v thimerosal solution in ethanol (50%). Investigation showed that considerable heat was generated when such a solution came into contact with aluminum.

An interaction between orally administered tetracyclines and thimerosal, which resulted in varying extents of ocular irritation, has been reported in patients using a contact lens solution preserved with thimerosal.[22]

LD$_{50}$ (rat, oral): 75 mg/kg[23]
LD$_{50}$ (rat, SC): 98 mg/kg

15. Handling Precautions

Observe normal precautions appropriate to the circumstances and quantity of material handled. Thimerosal is irritant to the skin and mucous membranes and may be systemically absorbed through the skin and upper respiratory tract.

Thimerosal should be handled in a well-ventilated environment. Eye protection, gloves and a respirator are recommended.

Chemical decomposition may cause the release of toxic fumes containing oxides of carbon, sulfur and mercury in addition to mercury vapor. In the UK, the occupational exposure limit for mercury containing compounds, calculated as mercury, is 0.05 mg/m^3 long-term (8-hour TWA) and 0.15 mg/m^3 short-term.[24]

16. Regulatory Status

Included in the FDA Inactive Ingredients Guide (IM, IV and SC injections, ophthalmic, otic and topical preparations). Included in nonparenteral and parenteral medicines licensed in the UK. In the UK, the use of thimerosal in cosmetics is limited to 0.003% w/w (calculated as mercury) as a preservative in shampoos and hair-creams, which contain nonionic emulsifiers that would render other preservatives ineffective. The total permitted concentration (calculated as mercury) when mixed with other mercury compounds is 0.007% w/w.[25]

17. Pharmacopeias

Br, Braz, Fr, Hung, Ind, It, Mex, Swiss and US.

18. Related Substances

Phenylmercuric Acetate; Phenylmercuric Borate; Phenylmercuric Nitrate.

19. Comments

Some variation between the results obtained when comparing different thimerosal assay methods has been reported.[26]

20. Specific References

1. Jamieson WA, Powell HM. Merthiolate as a preservative for biological products. Am J Hyg 1931; 14: 218-224.
2. Wallhäusser KH. Thimerosal. In: Kabara JJ, editor. Cosmetic and drug preservation principles and practice. New York: Marcel Dekker, 1984: 735-737.
3. Reader MJ. Influence of isotonic agents on the stability of thimerosal in ophthalmic formulations. J Pharm Sci 1984; 73: 840-841.
4. Richards RME, Reary JME. Changes in antibacterial activity of thiomersal and PMN on autoclaving with certain adjuvants. J Pharm Pharmacol 1972; 24(Suppl): 84P-89P.
5. Wiener S. The interference of rubber with the bacteriostatic action of thiomersalate. J Pharm Pharmacol 1955; 7: 118-125.
6. Birner J, Garnet JR. Thimerosal as a preservative in biological preparations III: factors affecting the concentration of thimerosal in aqueous solutions and in vaccines stored in rubber-capped bottles. J Pharm Sci 1964; 53: 1424-1426.
7. Ford JL, Brown MW, Hunt PB. A note on the contamination of eye-drops following use by hospital out-patients. J Clin Hosp Pharm 1985; 10: 203-209.
8. Cox NH, Forsyth A. Thiomersal allergy and vaccination reactions. Contact Dermatitis 1988; 18: 229-233.
9. Seal D, Ficker L, Wright P, Andrews V. The case against thiomersal [letter]. Lancet 1991; 338: 315-316.
10. Noel I, Galloway A, Ive FA. Hypersensitivity to thiomersal in hepatitis B vaccine [letter]. Lancet 1991; 338: 705.
11. Rietschel RL, Adams RM. Reactions to thimerosal in hepatitis B vaccines. Dermatol Clin 1990; 8(1): 161-164.
12. Golightly LK, Smolinske SS, Bennett ML, Sutherland III EW, Rumack BH. Pharmaceutical excipients: adverse effects

associated with inactive ingredients in drug products (part I). Med Toxicol 1988; 3: 128-165.

13. Osawa J, Kitamura K, Ikezawa Z, Nakajima H. A probable role for vaccines containing thimerosal in thimerosal hypersensitivity. Contact Dermatitis 1991; 24(3): 178-182.

14. Seidenari S, Manzini BM, Modenese M, Danese P. Sensitization after contact with thimerosal in a healthy population [in Italian]. G Ital Dermatol Venereol 1989; 124(7-8): 335-339.

15. Mondino BJ, Groden LR. Conjunctival hyperemia and corneal infiltrates with chemically disinfected soft contact lenses. Arch Ophthalmol 1980; 98: 1767-1770.

16. Sendele DD, Kenyon KR, Mobilia EF, Rosenthal P, Steinert R, et al. Superior limbic keratoconjunctivitis in contact lens wearers. Ophthalmology 1983; 90: 616-622.

17. Fisher AA. Allergic reactions to contact lens solutions. Cutis 1985; 21: 209-211.

18. Miller JR. Sensitivity to contact lens solutions. West J Med 1984; 140: 791.

19. Hansson H, Möller H. Intracutaneous test reactions to tuberculin containing merthiolate as a preservative. Scand J Infect Dis 1971; 3: 169-172.

20. Honigman JL. Disinfectant ototoxicity. Pharm J 1975; 215: 523.

21. Jones HT. Danger of skin burns from thiomersal. Br Med J 1972; 2: 504-505.

22. Crook TG, Freeman JJ. Reactions induced by the concurrent use of thimerosal and tetracyclines. Am J Optom Physiol Opt 1983; 60: 759-761.

23. Sweet DV, editor. Registry of toxic effects of chemical substances. Cincinnati: US Department of Health, 1987.

24. Health and Safety Executive. EH40/93: occupational exposure limits 1993. London: HMSO, 1993.

25. Statutory Instrument 2233. Consumer protection: the consumer products (safety) regulations 1989. London: HMSO, 1989.

26. Fleitman JS, Partridge IW, Neu DA. Thimerosal analysis in ketorolac tromethamine ophthalmic solution. Drug Dev Ind Pharm 1991; 17: 519-530.

21. General References

Axton JHM. Six cases of poisoning after a parenteral organic mercurial compound (Merthiolate). Postgrad Med J 1972; 48: 417-421.

Caraballo I, Rabasco AM, Fernández-Arévalo M. Study of thimerosal degradation mechanism. Int J Pharmaceutics 1993; 89: 213-221.

Rabasco AM, Caraballo I, Fernández-Arévalo M. Formulation factors affecting thimerosal stability. Drug Dev Ind Pharm 1993; 19: 1673-1691.

22. Authors

USA: DJ Harper.

Titanium Dioxide

1. Nonproprietary Names

BP: Titanium dioxide
PhEur: Titanii dioxidum
USP: Titanium dioxide

2. Synonyms

Anatase titanium dioxide; brookite titanium dioxide; color index number 77891, E171; *Kowett*; *Kronos 1171*; rutile titanium dioxide; titanic anhydride; *Tioxide*; *TiPure*.

3. Chemical Name and CAS Registry Number

Titanium oxide [13463-67-7]

4. Empirical Formula   Molecular Weight

TiO_2 79.88

5. Structural Formula

TiO_2

6. Functional Category

Coating agent; pigment.

7. Applications in Pharmaceutical Formulation or Technology

Titanium dioxide is widely used in confectionery, cosmetics, foods and topical and oral pharmaceutical formulations as a white pigment.

Due to its high refractive index titanium dioxide has unique light scattering properties which may be exploited in its use as a white pigment and opacifier. The range of light that is scattered can be altered by varying the particle size of the titanium dioxide powder. For example, titanium dioxide with an average particle size of 230 nm scatters visible light while titanium dioxide with an average particle size of 60 nm scatters ultraviolet light and reflects visible light.[1]

In pharmaceutical formulations titanium dioxide is used as a white pigment in film coating suspensions,[2,3] sugar coated tablets and gelatin capsules. In addition to titanium dioxide being used as a white pigment it may also be admixed with other pigments.

Titanium dioxide is also used in dermatological preparations and cosmetics, such as sunscreens.[1,4]

8. Description

White, amorphous, odorless and tasteless nonhygroscopic powder. Although the average particle size of titanium dioxide powder is less than 1 μm, commercial titanium dioxide generally occurs as aggregated particles of approximately 100 μm diameter. Titanium dioxide may occur in several different crystalline forms: rutile; anatase and brookite. Of these, rutile and anatase are the only forms of commercial importance. Rutile is the more thermodynamically stable and predominates.

SEM: 1
Excipient: Titanium dioxide (*Atlas white*)
Manufacturer: H Kohnstamm & Co
Magnification: 1200x
Voltage: 10 kV

SEM: 2
Excipient: Titanium dioxide (*Kowett*)
Magnification: 1200x
Voltage: 10 kV

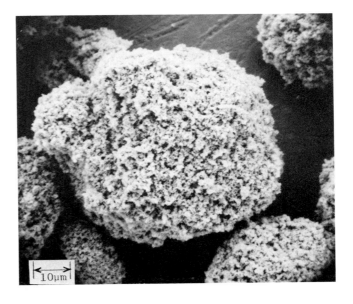

9. Pharmacopeial Specifications

Test	PhEur 1993	USP XXII
Identification	+	+
Loss on drying	—	≤ 0.5%
Loss on ignition	—	≤ 0.5%
Clarity and color of solution	+	—
Acidity or alkalinity	+	—
Water-soluble substances	≤ 0.5%	≤ 0.25%
Acid-soluble substances	—	≤ 0.5%
Antimony	≤ 100 ppm	≤ 2 ppm
Arsenic	≤ 5 ppm	≤ 1 ppm
Barium	+	—
Heavy metals	≤ 20 ppm	—
Iron	≤ 200 ppm	—
Lead	—	≤ 0.001%
Mercury	—	≤ 1 ppm
Assay (dried basis)	98.0-100.5%	99.0-100.5%

10. Typical Properties

Density:
3.8-4.1 g/cm³ for anatase;
3.9-4.2 g/cm³ for rutile.
See also HPE Data.
Density (bulk): 0.4 g/cm³ for *Kowett*.[5] *See also* HPE Data.
Density (tapped): 0.7 g/cm³ for *Kowett*.[5] *See also* HPE Data.
Dielectric constant: 48 for anatase; 114 for rutile.
Hardness (Mohs): 5-6 for anatase; 6-7 for rutile. *See also* Section 19.
Melting point: 1855°C
Moisture content: see HPE Data.
Particle size distribution: average particle size is 1.05 μm for *Kowett*.[5] *See also* HPE Data.
Refractive index: 2.55 for anatase; 2.76 for rutile.
Specific heat:
0.71 J/g (0.17 cal/g) for anatase;
0.71 J/g (0.17 cal/g) for rutile.
Specific surface area:
10.5 m²/g for *Kowett* (BET method).[5]
Solubility: practically insoluble in dilute sulfuric acid, hydrochloric acid, nitric acid, organic solvents and water. Soluble in hydrofluoric acid and hot concentrated sulfuric acid. Solubility depends on previous heat treatment; prolonged heating produces a less soluble material.
Tinting strength (Reynolds):
1200-1300 for anatase;
1650-1900 for rutile.

	HPE Laboratory Project Data		
	Method	Lab #	Results
Bulk/tap density	BTD-1	1	B: 0.431 g/cm³ [a]
			T: 0.625 g/cm³
	BTD-7	14	B: 0.620 g/cm³ [a]
		14	T: 0.830 g/cm³
(Food grade)	BTD-6	8	Volume: 20.5% [a]
			Weight: 21.0%
(Food grade)	BTD-6	8	Volume: 21.5% [a]
			Weight: 22.0%
	BTD-6	8	Volume: 22.0% [b]
			Weight: 23.0%

Continued

	HPE Laboratory Project Data		
	Method	Lab #	Results
Density	DE-2	36	3.461 g/cm³ [a]
Moisture content	MC-3	33	0.44% [a]
Particle size			
(Fine powder)	PSD-8	17	*See* Fig. 1. [b]
(Agglomerate)	PSD-4	17	*See* Fig. 2. [a]

Supplier:
a. Kerr-McGee;
b. Whittaker, Clark, Daniels, Inc (Lot #402302).

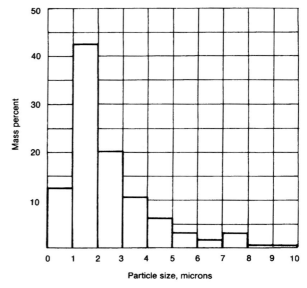

Fig. 1: Particle size distribution of titanium dioxide (fine powder).

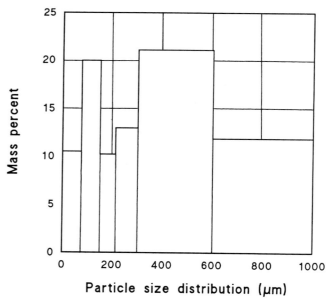

Fig. 2: Particle size distribution of titanium dioxide (agglomerated particles).

11. Stability and Storage Conditions

Titanium dioxide is extremely stable at high temperatures. The exceptional stability is due to the strong bond between the tetravalent titanium ion and the bivalent oxygen ions. Titanium dioxide can however lose small, unweighable amounts of oxygen by interaction with radiant energy. This oxygen can easily recombine again as a part of a reversible photochemical reaction, particularly if there is no oxidizable material available. These small oxygen losses are important because they can cause significant changes in the optical and electrical properties of the pigment. Titanium dioxide should be stored in a well-closed container, protected from light, in a cool, dry, place.

12. Incompatibilities

Due to a catalytic effect, titanium dioxide may interact with certain active substances.

13. Method of Manufacture

Titanium dioxide occurs naturally as the minerals rutile (tetragonal structure), anatase (tetragonal structure) and brookite (orthorhombic structure).

Commercially, titanium dioxide may be prepared by direct combination of titanium and oxygen; by treatment of titanium salts in aqueous solution; by the reaction of volatile inorganic titanium compounds with oxygen and by the oxidation or hydrolysis of organic compounds of titanium.

14. Safety

Titanium dioxide is widely used in foods and oral and topical pharmaceutical formulations. It is generally regarded as an essentially nonirritant and nontoxic excipient.

15. Handling Precautions

Observe normal precautions appropriate to the circumstances and quantity of material handled. Eye protection, gloves and a dust mask are recommended. Titanium dioxide is regarded as a relatively innocuous nuisance dust;[6] it may be irritant to the respiratory tract. In the UK, the long-term (8-hour TWA) exposure limit is 10 mg/m^3 for total inhalable dust and 5 mg/m^3 for respirable dust.[7]

16. Regulatory Status

Accepted as a food additive in Europe. Included in the FDA Inactive Ingredients Guide (oral capsules, suspensions, tablets, and topical preparations). Included in nonparenteral medicines licensed in the UK.

17. Pharmacopeias

Aust, Belg, Br, Braz, Eur, Fr, Gr, Hung, Ind, It, Jpn, Mex, Neth, Port, Swiss, US and Yug.

18. Related Substances

Coloring Agents.

19. Comments

Titanium dioxide is a hard, abrasive material. Coating suspensions containing titanium dioxide have been reported to cause abrasion and wear of a steel coating pan surface, which led to white colored tablets being contaminated with black specks.[8]

20. Specific References

1. Hewitt JP. Titanium dioxide: a different kind of sunshield. Drug Cosmet Ind 1992; 151(3): 26, 28, 30, 32.
2. Rowe RC. Quantitative opacity measurements on tablet film coatings containing titanium dioxide. Int J Pharmaceutics 1984; 22: 17-23.
3. Béchard SR, Quraishi O, Kwong E. Film coating: effect of titanium dioxide concentration and film thickness on the photostability of nifedipine. Int J Pharmaceutics 1992; 87: 133-139.
4. Alexander P. Ultrafine titanium dioxide makes the grade. Mfg Chem 1991; 62(7): 21,23.
5. Brittain HG, Barbera G, DeVincentis J, Newman AW. Titanium dioxide. In: Brittain HG, editor. Analytical profiles of drug substances and excipients, volume 21. San Diego: Academic Press, 1992: 659-691.
6. Driscoll KE, et al. Respiratory tract responses to dust: relationships between dust burden, lung injury, alveolar macrophage fibronectin release, and the development of pulmonary fibrosis. Toxicol Appl Pharmacol 1990; 106: 88-101.
7. Health and Safety Executive. EH40/93: occupational exposure limits 1993. London: HMSO, 1993.
8. Rosoff M, Sheen P-C. Pan abrasion and polymorphism of titanium dioxide in coating suspensions. J Pharm Sci 1983; 72: 1485.

21. General References

Judin VPS. The lighter side of TiO$_2$. Chem Br 1993; 29(6): 503-505.
Ortyl TT, Peck GE. Surface charge of titanium dioxide and its effect on dye adsorption and aqueous suspension stability. Drug Dev Ind Pharm 1991; 17: 2245-2268.
Rowe RC. Materials used in the film coating of oral dosage forms. In: Florence AT, editor. Critical reports on applied chemistry, volume 6: materials used in pharmaceutical formulation. Oxford: Blackwell Scientific Publications, 1984: 1-36.

22. Authors

USA: RD Gibson.

Tragacanth

1. Nonproprietary Names

BP: Tragacanth
PhEur: Tragacantha
USPNF: Tragacanth
Note that the BP 1993 also contains a monograph for powdered tragacanth.

2. Synonyms

E413; goat's thorn; gum dragon; gum tragacanth; persian tragacanth; trag; tragant.

3. Chemical Name and CAS Registry Number

Tragacanth gum [9000-65-1]

4. Empirical Formula   Molecular Weight

Tragacanth is a naturally occurring dried gum obtained from *Astragalus gummifer* Labillardière and other species of *Astragalus* grown in Western Asia, *see* Section 13.
The gum consists of a mixture of water-insoluble and water-soluble polysaccharides. Bassorin, which constitutes 60-70% of the gum, is the main water-insoluble portion whilst the remainder of the gum consists of the water-soluble material, tragacanthin. On hydrolysis, tragacanthin yields L-arabinose, L-fucose, D-xylose, D-galactose and D-galacturonic acid. Tragacanth gum also contains small amounts of cellulose, starch, protein and ash.
Tragacanth gum has an approximate molecular weight of 840 000.

5. Structural Formula

See Section 4.

6. Functional Category

Suspending agent; viscosity-increasing agent.

7. Applications in Pharmaceutical Formulation or Technology

Tragacanth gum is used as an emulsifying and suspending agent in a variety of pharmaceutical formulations. It is used in creams, gels and emulsions at various concentrations according to the application of the formulation and the grade of gum used.
Tragacanth gum is also similarly used in cosmetics and food products, and has been used as a diluent in tablet formulations.

8. Description

Tragacanth gum occurs as flattened, lamellated, frequently curved fragments or straight or spirally twisted linear pieces from 0.5-2.5 mm in thickness; it may also be obtained in a powdered form. White to yellowish in color, tragacanth is a translucent, odorless substance, with an insipid mucilaginous taste.

9. Pharmacopeial Specifications

Test	PhEur 1993	USPNF XVII
Identification	+	+
Botanic characteristics	+	+
Microbial limits	+	+
Flow time	+	—
Arsenic	—	≤ 3 ppm
Lead	—	≤ 0.001%
Heavy metals	—	≤ 0.004%
Acacia and other soluble gums	+	—
Foreign matter	≤ 1.0%	—
Karaya gum	—	+
Sterculia	+	—
Ash	≤ 4.0%	—

10. Typical Properties

Acidity/alkalinity:
pH = 5-6 for a 1% w/v aqueous dispersion.
Acid value: 2-5
Moisture content: ≤ 15% w/w
Particle size distribution: for powdered grades 50% w/w passes through a #200 (73.7 μm) mesh.
Solubility: practically insoluble in water, ethanol (95%) and other organic solvents. Although insoluble in water, tragacanth gum swells rapidly in 10 times its own weight of either hot or cold water to produce viscous colloidal sols or semi-gels. *See also* Section 19.
Specific gravity: 1.250-1.385
Viscosity (dynamic): the viscosity of tragacanth dispersions varies according to the grade and source of the material. Typically, 1% w/v aqueous dispersions may range in viscosity from 100-4000 mPa s (100-4000 cP) at 20°C. Viscosity increases with increasing temperature and concentration, and decreases with increasing pH. Maximum initial viscosity occurs at pH 8, although the greatest stability of tragacanth dispersions occurs at about pH 5. *See also* Sections 11 and 12.

11. Stability and Storage Conditions

Both the flaked and powdered forms of tragacanth are stable. Tragacanth gels are liable to microbial contamination with enterobacterial species, and stock solutions should therefore contain suitable antimicrobial preservatives. In emulsions, glycerin or propylene glycol are used as preservatives, whilst in gel formulations, tragacanth is usually preserved with either 0.1% w/v benzoic acid or sodium benzoate. A combination of 0.17% w/v methylparaben and 0.03% w/v propylparaben is also an effective preservative for tragacanth gels,[1] *see also* Section 12. Gels may be sterilized by autoclaving; sterilization by gamma irradiation causes a marked reduction in the viscosity of tragacanth dispersions.[2]
Tragacanth dispersions are most stable at pH 4-8 although stability is satisfactory at higher pH or as low as pH 2.
The bulk material should be stored in an airtight container in a cool, dry, place.

12. Incompatibilities

At pH 7, tragacanth has been reported to considerably reduce the efficacy of the antimicrobial preservatives benzalkonium chloride, chlorobutanol and methylparaben, and to a lesser extent phenol and phenylmercuric acetate.[3] However, at pH < 5 tragacanth was reported to have no adverse effects on the preservative efficacy of benzoic acid, chlorobutanol or methylparaben.[1]

The addition of strong mineral and organic acids can reduce the viscosity of tragacanth dispersions. Viscosity may also be reduced by the addition of alkali or sodium chloride particularly if the dispersion is heated. Tragacanth is compatible with relatively high salt concentrations and most other natural and synthetic suspending agents such as acacia, carboxymethylcellulose, starch and sucrose. A yellow colored, stringy, precipitate is formed with 10% w/v ferric chloride solution.

13. Method of Manufacture

Tragacanth gum is the air-dried gum obtained from *Astragalus gummifer* Labillardière and other species of *Astragalus* grown principally in Iran, Syria and Turkey. A low quality gum is obtained by collecting the natural air-dried exudate from *Astragalus* bushes. A higher grade material is obtained by making incisions in the trunk and branches of the bush which are held open with variously sized wooden pegs. The exudate is left to drain from the incision and dry naturally in the air before being collected. The size and position of the wooden wedges determines the physical form of the exudate whilst the drying conditions determine the color of the gum. After collection, the tragacanth gum is sorted by hand into various grades, such as ribbons or flakes.

14. Safety

Tragacanth has been used for many years in oral pharmaceutical formulations and food products, and is generally regarded as an essentially nontoxic material. However, hypersensitivity reactions, sometimes severe, have been reported following ingestion of products containing tragacanth.[4,5] Contact dermatitis has also been reported following the topical use of tragacanth formulations.[6]

The WHO has not specified an acceptable daily intake for tragacanth gum since the daily intake arising from the levels necessary to achieve a desired effect, and from its background levels in food, was not considered to be a hazard to health.[7]

LD_{50} (hamster, oral): 8.8 g/kg[8]
LD_{50} (mouse, oral): 10 g/kg
LD_{50} (rabbit, oral): 7.2 g/kg
LD_{50} (rat, oral): 10.2 g/kg

15. Handling Precautions

Observe normal precautions appropriate to the circumstances and quantity of material handled. Tragacanth gum may be irritant to the skin and eyes. Eye protection, gloves and a dust mask are recommended.

16. Regulatory Status

GRAS listed. Accepted for use as a food additive in Europe. Included in the FDA Inactive Ingredients Guide (buccal tablets, nasal solutions, oral powders, suspensions, syrups and tablets). Included in nonparenteral medicines licensed in the UK.

17. Pharmacopeias

Aust, Br, Cz, Egypt, Eur, Fr, Ger, Gr, Ind, It, Jpn, Mex, Neth, Nord, Port, Rom, Swiss, Turk, USPNF and Yug.

18. Related Substances

Hog gum (caramania gum), obtained from species of *Prunus*, and sterculia gum have been used in industrial applications as substitutes for tragacanth.

19. Comments

Tragacanth gum is a naturally occurring material whose physical properties vary greatly according to the grade and source of the material.

Powdered tragacanth gum tends to form lumps when added to water and aqueous dispersions should therefore be vigorously agitated by a high speed mixer. However, aqueous dispersions are more readily prepared by first pre-wetting the tragacanth with a small quantity of a wetting agent such as ethanol (95%), glycerin or propylene glycol. If lumps form, they usually disperse on standing. Dispersion is generally complete after one hour. If other powders, such as sucrose, are to be incorporated into a tragacanth formulation the powders are best mixed together in the dry state.

20. Specific References

1. Taub A, Meer WA, Clausen LW. Conditions for the preservation of gum tragacanth jellies. J Am Pharm Assoc (Sci) 1958; 47: 235-239.
2. Jacobs GP, Simes R. The gamma irradiation of tragacanth: effect on microbial contamination and rheology. J Pharm Pharmacol 1979; 31: 333-334.
3. Eisman PC, Cooper J, Jaconia D. Influence of gum tragacanth on the bactericidal activity of preservatives. J Am Pharm Assoc (Sci) 1957; 46: 144-147.
4. Danoff D, Lincoln L, Thomson DMP, Gold P. Big Mac attack [letter]. N Engl J Med 1978; 298: 1095-1096.
5. Rubinger D, Friedlander M, Superstine E. Hypersensitivity to tablet additives in transplant recipients on prednisone [letter]. Lancet 1978; ii: 689.
6. Coskey RJ. Contact dermatitis caused by ECG electrode jelly. Arch Dermatol 1977; 113: 839-840.
7. FAO/WHO. Evaluation of certain food additives and contaminants. Twenty-ninth report of the joint FAO/WHO expert committee on food additives. Tech Rep Ser Wld Hlth Org 1986; No. 733.
8. Sweet DV, editor. Registry of toxic effects of chemical substances. Cincinnati: US Department of Health, 1987.

21. General References

Fairbairn JW. The presence of peroxidases in tragacanth [letter]. J Pharm Pharmacol 1967; 19: 191.
Westwood N. Microbial contamination of some pharmaceutical raw materials. Pharm J 1971; 207: 99-102.

22. Authors

UK: PJ Weller.

Triacetin

1. Nonproprietary Names

USP: Triacetin

2. Synonyms

E1518; glycerol triacetate; glyceryl triacetate; *Priacetin 1579*; triacetyl glycerine.

3. Chemical Name and CAS Registry Number

1,2,3-Propanetriol triacetate [102-76-1]

4. Empirical Formula   Molecular Weight

$C_9H_{14}O_6$ 218.21

5. Structural Formula

$$
\begin{array}{c}
H_2C-O-\overset{\overset{O}{\|}}{C}-CH_3 \\
| \\
HC-O-\overset{\overset{O}{\|}}{C}-CH_3 \\
| \\
H_2C-O-\overset{\overset{O}{\|}}{C}-CH_3
\end{array}
$$

6. Functional Category

Antifungal agent; humectant; plasticizer; solvent.

7. Applications in Pharmaceutical Formulation or Technology

Triacetin is used as a hydrophilic plasticizer in both aqueous and solvent-based polymeric coating of capsules, tablets, beads and granules; typical concentrations used are 10-35% w/w. Triacetin is also reported to possess fungistatic properties due to the liberation of acetic acid and has been used as a 25% w/w cream or ointment in the treatment of superficial fungal conditions.

In addition, triacetin is used in cosmetics, perfumery and foods as a solvent and as a fixative in the formulation of perfumes and flavors.

8. Description

Triacetin is a colorless, viscous liquid with a slightly fatty odor.

9. Pharmacopeial Specifications

Test	USP XXII
Identification	+
Specific gravity	1.152-1.158
Refractive index	1.429-1.430
Acidity	+
Water	$\leqslant 0.2\%$
Assay (anhydrous basis)	97.0-100.5%

10. Typical Properties

Autoignition temperature: 432°C

Boiling point: 258°C
Density: 1.16 g/cm³ at 25°C
Explosive limits:
1.05% at 189°C lower limit;
7.73% at 215°C upper limit.
Flash point: 153°C (open cup)
Freezing point: 3.2°C (supercools to about -70°C)
Melting point: -78°C
Refractive index: $n_D^{25} = 1.4296$
Solubility:

Solvent	Solubility at 20°C
Chloroform	miscible
Ethanol (95%)	miscible
Ether	miscible
Water	1 in 14

Vapor density (relative): 7.52 (air = 1)
Vapor pressure: 133 Pa (1 mmHg) at 100°C
Viscosity (dynamic):
1111 mPa s (1111 cP) at -17.8°C;
107 mPa s (107 cP) at 0°C;
17.4 mPa s (17.4 cP) at 25°C;
1.8 mPa s (1.8 cP) at 100°C.

11. Stability and Storage Conditions

Triacetin is stable and should be stored in a well-closed, nonmetallic container, in a cool, dry, place.

12. Incompatibilities

Triacetin is incompatible with metals and may react with oxidizing agents.

13. Method of Manufacture

Triacetin is prepared by esterification of glycerin with acetic anhydride.

14. Safety

Triacetin is used in oral pharmaceutical formulations and is generally regarded as a nontoxic and nonirritant material at the levels employed as an excipient.
LD_{50} (dog, IV): 1.5 g/kg[1]
LD_{50} (mouse, IP): 1.4 g/kg
LD_{50} (mouse, IV): 1.6 g/kg
LD_{50} (mouse, oral): 1.1 g/kg
LD_{50} (mouse, SC): 2.3 g/kg
LD_{50} (rabbit, IV): 0.75 g/kg
LD_{50} (rat, IP): 2.1 g/kg
LD_{50} (rat, oral): 3 g/kg
LD_{50} (rat, SC): 2.8 g/kg

15. Handling Precautions

Observe normal precautions appropriate to the circumstances and quantity of material handled. Triacetin may be irritant to the eyes; eye protection and gloves are recommended.

16. Regulatory Status

GRAS listed. Accepted in Europe as a food additive in certain applications. Included in the FDA Inactive Ingredients Guide (oral capsules and tablets). Included in nonparenteral medicines licensed in the UK.

17. Pharmacopeias

US.

18. Related Substances

—

19. Comments

—

20. Specific References

1. Sax NI. Dangerous properties of industrial materials. New York: Van Nostrand Reinhold Company, 1984.

21. General References

Gutierrez-Rocca JC, McGinity JW. Influence of aging on the physical-mechanical properties of acrylic resin films cast from aqueous dispersions and organic solutions. Drug Dev Ind Pharm 1993; 19: 315-332.

Johnson K, Hathaway R, Leung P, Franz R. Effect of triacetin and polyethylene glycol 400 on some physical properties of hydroxypropyl methylcellulose free films. Int J Pharmaceutics 1991; 73: 197-208.

Lehmann KOR. Chemistry and application properties of polymethacrylate coating systems. In: McGinity JW, editor. Aqueous polymeric coatings for pharmaceutical dosage forms. New York: Marcel Dekker, Inc, 1989: 224.

Lin S-Y, Lee C-J, Lin Y-Y. The effect of plasticizers on compatibility, mechanical properties, and adhesion strength of drug-free Eudragit E films. Pharm Res 1991; 8: 1137-1143.

Rowe RC. Materials used in the film coating of oral dosage forms. In: Florence AT, editor. Critical reports on applied chemistry, volume 6: materials used in pharmaceutical formulation. Oxford: Blackwell Scientific Publications, 1984: 1-36.

Shah PS, Zatz JL. Plasticization of cellulose esters used in the coating of sustained release solid dosage forms. Drug Dev Ind Pharm 1992; 18: 1759-1772.

22. Authors

USA: NR Poola.

Trichloromonofluoro-methane

1. Nonproprietary Names

USPNF: Trichloromonofluoromethane

2. Synonyms

Arcton 11; *Dymel 11*; fluorotrichloromethane; *Freon 11*; *Frigen 11*; *Genetron 11*; *Isceon 11*; propellant 11; refrigerant 11.

3. Chemical Name and CAS Registry Number

Trichlorofluoromethane [75-69-4]

4. Empirical Formula   Molecular Weight

CCl_3F 137.37

5. Structural Formula

CCl_3F

6. Functional Category

Aerosol propellant.

7. Applications in Pharmaceutical Formulation or Technology

Trichloromonofluoromethane is used in combination with dichlorodifluoromethane as the propellant in metered-dose oral and nasal aerosols. It is also used in combination with mixtures of other chlorofluorocarbons.

Trichloromonofluoromethane has additionally been used as a refrigerant.

Under the terms of the Montreal Protocol the use of chlorofluorocarbons will be prohibited from January 1996. However, this prohibition does not apply to essential uses in pharmaceutical formulations. For further information *see* Dichlorodifluoromethane.

8. Description

Trichloromonofluoromethane is a clear, volatile liquid at room temperature. It has a characteristic carbon tetrachloride-like odor and is nonirritating and nonflammable.

9. Pharmacopeial Specifications

Test	USPNF XVII
Identification	+
Boiling temperature	24°C
Water	≤ 0.001%
High boiling residues	≤ 0.01%
Inorganic chlorides	+

10. Typical Properties

Boiling point: 23.7°C
Critical pressure: 4.38 MPa (43.2 atm)
Critical temperature: 198°C
Density:
1.485 g/cm^3 for liquid at 21°C;
1.403 g/cm^3 for liquid at 54.5°C.

Flammability: nonflammable
Freezing point: -111°C
Kauri-butanol value: 60
Refractive index: $n_D^{18.5} = 1.3865$
Solubility:

Solvent	Solubility at 20°C Unless otherwise stated
Ethanol (95%)	soluble
Ether	soluble
Water	1 in 909 at 25°C

Surface tension: 19 mN/m (19 dynes/cm) at 25°C
Vapor density (absolute): 6.133 g/m^3
Vapor density (relative): 4.76 (air = 1)
Vapor pressure:
92.4 kPa (13.4 psia) at 21°C;
268.9 kPa (39.0 psia) at 54.5°C.
Viscosity (dynamic):
0.439 mPa s (0.439 cP) for liquid at 21°C;
0.336 mPa s (0.336 cP) for liquid at 54.5°C.

11. Stability and Storage Conditions

Trichloromonofluoromethane is stable and should be stored in a metal cylinder in a cool, dry, place. Cylinders may be liable to corrosion, *see* Section 12.

12. Incompatibilities

The presence of greater than 5% water in solutions which contain trichloromonofluoromethane may lead to hydrolysis of the propellant and the formation of traces of hydrochloric acid which may be irritant to the skin or cause corrosion of metallic storage cylinders. Trichloromonofluoromethane may also react with aluminum, in the presence of ethanol, to cause corrosion within a cylinder with the formation of hydrogen gas. Similarly, alcohols in the presence of trace amounts of oxygen, peroxides, or other free radical catalysts may react with trichloromonofluoromethane to form trace quantities of hydrochloric acid.

Corrosion of metallic storage cylinders may be prevented by the inclusion of a free radical inhibitor.

13. Method of Manufacture

Trichloromonofluoromethane is prepared by the reaction of hydrogen fluoride with carbon tetrachloride in the presence of a suitable catalyst, such as polyvalent antimony; *see* Dichlorodifluoromethane.

14. Safety

Trichloromonofluoromethane and other chlorofluorocarbons have been used for a number of years as propellants in topical, oral and nasal aerosol formulations and are generally regarded as nontoxic and nonirritant materials. For further information *see* Dichlorodifluoromethane.

LC_{50} (guinea pig, inhalation): 25 pph/30 min[1]
LC_{50} (mouse, inhalation): 10 pph/30 min
LD_{50} (mouse, IP): 1.74 g/kg
LC_{50} (rabbit, inhalation): 25 pph/30 min

15. Handling Precautions

Observe normal precautions appropriate to the circumstances and quantity of material handled. Trichloromonofluoromethane may be harmful by inhalation or ingestion and may be irritant to the eyes. Eye protection, gloves and protective clothing are recommended. Trichloromonofluoromethane should be handled in a well-ventilated environment, *see* Dichlorodifluoromethane.

Although nonflammable, when heated to decomposition trichloromonofluoromethane emits toxic fumes containing chlorides and fluorides.

In the UK, the long-term (8-hour TWA) occupational exposure limit for trichloromonofluoromethane is 5600 mg/m^3 (1000 ppm) and the short-term (10-minutes) exposure limit is 7000 mg/m^3 (1250 ppm).[2]

16. Regulatory Status

Included in the FDA Inactive Ingredients Guide (aerosol formulations for inhalation, nasal, oral and topical applications). Included in nonparenteral medicines licensed in the UK.

17. Pharmacopeias

Mex and USPNF.
See also Section 19.

18. Related Substances

Chlorodifluoroethane; Chlorodifluoromethane; Dichlorodifluoromethane; Dichlorotetrafluoroethane; Difluoroethane; Tetrafluoroethane.

19. Comments

Blends of trichloromonofluoromethane and dichlorodifluoromethane (propellant 11/12) or propellant 11/114/12 produce vapor pressures of 103-484 kPa (15-70 psig) at 21°C which adequately cover the range of pressures required to produce the proper particle size distribution for satisfactory aerosol products. Trichloromonofluoromethane is unique amongst the chlorofluorocarbon propellants in that it is a liquid at cool room temperatures and can be used to prepare a slurry with insoluble medicinal agents.

Trichloromonofluoromethane has been omitted from the BP 1993, although it was present in the BP 1988.

For a discussion of the numerical nomenclature applied to fluorocarbon aerosol propellants *see* Dichlorodifluoromethane.

20. Specific References

1. Sweet DV, editor. Registry of toxic effects of chemical substances. Cincinnati: US Department of Health, 1987.
2. Health and Safety Executive. EH40/93: occupational exposure limits 1993. London: HMSO, 1993.

See also Dichlorodifluoromethane.

21. General References

Amin YM, Thompson EB, Chiou WL. Fluorocarbon aerosol propellants XII: correlation of blood levels of trichloromonofluoromethane to cardiovascular and respiratory responses in anesthetized dogs. J Pharm Sci 1979; 68: 160-163.

See also Dichlorodifluoromethane.

22. Authors

UK: PJ Davies.
USA: JJ Sciarra.

Triethanolamine

1. Nonproprietary Names

BP: Triethanolamine
USPNF: Trolamine

2. Synonyms

TEA; triethylolamine; trihydroxytriethylamine; tris(hydroxyethyl)amine.

3. Chemical Name and CAS Registry Number

2,2′,2″-Nitrilotriethanol [102-71-6]

4. Empirical Formula   Molecular Weight

$C_6H_{15}NO_3$ 149.19

5. Structural Formula

$N(CH_2CH_2OH)_3$

6. Functional Category

Alkalizing agent; emulsifying agent.

7. Applications in Pharmaceutical Formulation or Technology

Triethanolamine is widely used in topical pharmaceutical formulations primarily in the formation of emulsions.

When mixed in equimolecular proportions with a fatty acid, such as stearic or oleic acid, triethanolamine forms an anionic soap which may be used as an emulsifying agent to produce fine grained, stable, oil-in-water emulsions with a pH of about 8.

Triethanolamine soaps form emulsions that are more stable than those produced with an alkali soap although both the triethanolamine and alkali soaps break down in the presence of acids and high concentrations of ionisable salts.

Concentrations that are typically used for the emulsification of fixed oils are 2-4% of triethanolamine and 2-5 times as much fatty acid. For mineral oils the amount of the triethanolamine is increased to 5% with an appropriate increase in the amount of fatty acid used.

Preparations which contain triethanolamine soaps tend to darken on storage. However, discoloration may be reduced by avoiding exposure to light and contact with metals and metal ions.

Triethanolamine is also used in the formation of salts for injection, and in topical analgesic preparations. Other general uses are as a buffer, solvent, polymer plasticizer and humectant.

8. Description

The USPNF XVII describes triethanolamine as a variable mixture of alkanolamines consisting largely of triethanolamine with some diethanolamine and monoethanolamine.

Triethanolamine is a clear, colorless to pale yellow-colored viscous liquid having a slight ammoniacal odor.

9. Pharmacopeial Specifications

Test	BP 1993	USPNF XVII
Identification	+	+
Specific gravity	1.120-1.130	1.120-1.128
Refractive index	1.482-1.485	1.481-1.486
Water	—	$\leqslant 0.5\%$
Related substances	+	—
Total bases	+	—
Residue on ignition	—	$\leqslant 0.05\%$
Sulfated ash	$\leqslant 0.1\%$	—
Assay (anhydrous basis)	$> 80.0\%$	99.0-107.4%

10. Typical Properties

Acidity/alkalinity:
pH = 10.5 for a 0.1N aqueous solution
Autoignition temperature: 620°C
Boiling point: 335°C
Density:
1.1242 g/cm^3 at 20°C;
1.0985 g/cm^3 at 60°C.
Dissociation constant: pK_a = 7.8 at 25°C
Flash point (open cup): 180°C
Hygroscopicity: very hygroscopic.
Melting point: 20-21°C
Moisture content: *see* HPE Data.
Refractive index: n_D^{20} = 1.4852
Solubility:

Solvent	Solubility at 20°C
Acetone	miscible
Benzene	1 in 24
Chloroform	soluble
Ethanol (95%)	miscible
Ether	1 in 63
Methanol	miscible
Water	miscible

Surface tension:
47.5 mN/m (47.5 dynes/cm) at 20°C
Vapor density (relative): 5.1 (air = 1)
Vapor pressure: < 1 Pa at 20°C
Viscosity (dynamic):
590.5 mPa s (590.5 cP) at 25°C;
65.7 mPa s (65.7 cP) at 60°C.

HPE Laboratory Project Data			
	Method	Lab #	Results
Moisture content	MC-3	25	0.09%

Supplier: Olin Chemicals.

11. Stability and Storage Conditions

Triethanolamine may turn brown on exposure to air and light. The 85% grade of triethanolamine tends to stratify below 15°C; homogeneity can be restored by warming and mixing before use.

Triethanolamine should be stored in an airtight container, protected from light, in a cool, dry, place.

See Monoethanolamine for further information.

12. Incompatibilities

Triethanolamine is a tertiary amine which contains a hydroxy group. It is thus capable of undergoing reactions typical of tertiary amines and alcohols. The amine group usually exhibits the greater activity whenever it is possible for a reaction to take place at either the amine or the hydroxy group.

Triethanolamine will react with mineral acids to form crystalline salts and esters. With the higher fatty acids triethanolamine forms salts which are soluble in water and have the general characteristics of soaps. Triethanolamine will also react with copper to form complex salts. Discoloration and precipitation can take place in the presence of heavy metal salts.

Triethanolamine can react with reagents such as thionyl chloride to replace the hydroxy groups with halogens. The products of these reactions are very toxic, resembling other nitrogen mustards.

13. Method of Manufacture

Triethanolamine is prepared commercially by the ammonolysis of ethylene oxide. The reaction yields a mixture of mono-ethanolamine, diethanolamine and triethanolamine which is separated to obtain the pure products.

14. Safety

Triethanolamine is used primarily as an emulsifying agent in a variety of topical pharmaceutical formulations. Although generally regarded as a nontoxic material[1] triethanolamine may cause hypersensitivity or be irritant to the skin when present in formulated products. However, it is less irritant than monoethanolamine and diethanolamine.

The lethal human oral dose of triethanolamine is estimated to be 5-15 g/kg body-weight.

LD_{50} (guinea pig, oral): 2.2 g/kg[2]
LD_{50} (mouse, IP): 1.45 g/kg
LD_{50} (mouse, oral): 7.4 g/kg
LD_{50} (mouse, SC): 5.2 g/kg
LD_{50} (rabbit, oral): 2.2 g/kg
LD_{50} (rabbit, skin): > 20 g/kg
LD_{50} (rat, oral): 8.0 g/kg

15. Handling Precautions

Triethanolamine may be irritant to the skin, eyes and mucous membranes. Inhalation of vapor may be harmful. Protective clothing, gloves, eye protection and a respirator are recommended. Ideally, triethanolamine should be handled in a fume cupboard.

On heating, triethanolamine forms highly toxic nitrous fumes. Triethanolamine is combustible.

16. Regulatory Status

Included in the FDA Inactive Ingredients Guide (rectal, topical and vaginal preparations). Included in nonparenteral medicines licensed in the UK.

17. Pharmacopeias

Aust, Br, Braz, Cz, Egypt, Fr, Hung, It, Jpn, Mex, Neth, Pol, Swiss, USPNF and Yug.

18. Related Substances

Diethanolamine; Monoethanolamine.

19. Comments

Various grades of triethanolamine are commercially available, e.g. a standard grade of triethanolamine may contain 15% of diethanolamine and 0.5% of monoethanolamine.

20. Specific References

1. Maekawa A, et al. Lack of carcinogenicity of triethanolamine in F344 rats. J Toxicol Environ Health 1986; 19: 345-357.
2. Sweet DV, editor. Registry of toxic effects of chemical substances. Cincinnati: US Department of Health, 1987.

21. General References

Friberg SE, Wohn CS, Lockwood FE. The influence of solvent on nonaqueous lyotropic liquid crystalline phase formed by triethanolamine oleate. J Pharm Sci 1985; 74: 771-773.

Ramsay B, Lawrence CM, Bruce JM, Shuster S. The effect of triethanolamine application on anthralin-induced inflammation and therapeutic effect in psoriasis. J Am Acad Dermatol 1990; 23: 73-76.

22. Authors

USA: J Fleitman, JS Fujiki, JC Lee.

Triethyl Citrate

1. Nonproprietary Names

USPNF: Triethyl citrate

2. Synonyms

Citric acid, ethyl ester; *Citroflex 2*; E1505; ethyl citrate; TEC.

3. Chemical Name and CAS Registry Number

2-Hydroxy-1,2,3-propanetricarboxylic acid, triethyl ester [77-93-0]

4. Empirical Formula   Molecular Weight

$C_{12}H_{20}O_7$ 276.29

5. Structural Formula

$$
\begin{array}{c}
CH_2COOC_2H_5 \\
| \\
HO-C-COOC_2H_5 \\
| \\
CH_2COOC_2H_5
\end{array}
$$

6. Functional Category

Plasticizer.

7. Applications in Pharmaceutical Formulation or Technology

Triethyl citrate and other citrate esters are used as plasticizers for aqueous based coatings in oral sustained release or enteric coated capsule and tablet formulations.[1,2]
Triethyl citrate is also used in food products as a sequestrant and in cosmetics as a deodorizing agent.[3]

8. Description

Triethyl citrate occurs as a bitter tasting, odorless, practically colorless, oily liquid.

9. Pharmacopeial Specifications

Test	USPNF XVII (Suppl 7)
Specific gravity	1.135-1.139
Refractive index	1.439-1.441
Acidity	+
Water	$\leqslant 0.25\%$
Assay (anhydrous basis)	99.0-100.5%

10. Typical Properties

Boiling point: 288°C
Flash point: 155°C
Pour point: -45°C
Solubility: soluble 1 in 125 of peanut oil, 1 in 15 of water. Miscible with ethanol (95%) and ether.
Viscosity (dynamic): 35.2 mPa s (35.2 cP) at 25°C.

11. Stability and Storage Conditions

Triethyl citrate and other citrate esters are stable if stored in a well-closed container in a cool, dry, place.

12. Incompatibilities

Triethyl citrate and other citrate esters can react with oxidizing materials and strong alkalis.

13. Method of Manufacture

Triethyl citrate is prepared by the esterification of citric acid and ethanol.

14. Safety

Triethyl citrate and other citrate esters are used in oral pharmaceutical formulations and are generally regarded as nontoxic and nonirritant materials. However, ingestion of large quantities may be harmful.
LD_{50} (cat, oral): 3.5 g/kg[4]
LD_{50} (mouse, IP): 1.75 g/kg
LD_{50} (rabbit, skin): > 5 g/kg
LD_{50} (rat, IP): 4 g/kg
LD_{50} (rat, oral): 5.9 g/kg
LD_{50} (rat, SC): 6.6 g/kg

15. Handling Precautions

Observe normal precautions appropriate to the circumstances and quantity of material handled. Triethyl citrate is irritating to the eyes and may irritate the skin. Irritating to the respiratory system as a mist or at elevated temperatures. Gloves, eye protection and a respirator are recommended.

16. Regulatory Status

Accepted as a food additive in Europe. Included in the FDA Inactive Ingredients Guide (oral capsules and tablets).

17. Pharmacopeias

USPNF.

18. Related Substances

Acetyltributyl citrate; acetyltriethyl citrate; tributyl citrate.

Acetyltributyl citrate: $C_{20}H_{34}O_8$
Molecular weight: 402.54
CAS number: [77-90-7]
Synonyms: 2-acetyloxy-1,2,3-propanetricarboxylic acid, tri-*n*-butyl ester; ATBC; citric acid, tributyl ester, acetate; *Citroflex A-4*.
Appearance: practically colorless, oily liquid with a faint, sweet, herbaceous odor. At high concentrations (1000 ppm) it has a bitter taste.
Boiling point: 326°C
Flash point: 204°C
Pour point: -59°C
Solubility: practically insoluble in water. Miscible with most organic liquids.
Specific gravity: 1.048 at 25°C.
Viscosity (dynamic): 33 mPa s (33 cP) at 25°C.
Method of manufacture: prepared by the esterification of citric acid and butanol, followed by acetylation with acetic anhydride.
Comments: used as a plasticizer in pharmaceutical formulations and as a flavoring agent in food products.

Acetyltriethyl citrate: $C_{14}H_{22}O_8$
Molecular weight: 318.36
CAS number: [77-89-4]
Synonyms: 2-acetyloxy-1,2,3-propanetricarboxylic acid, triethyl ester; ATEC; *Citroflex A-2*; triethyl acetylcitrate.

Appearance: an odorless, practically colorless, oily liquid.
Boiling point: 294°C
Flash point: 188°C
Solubility: soluble 1 in 140 of water. Miscible with most organic liquids.
Viscosity (dynamic): 54 mPa s (54 cP) at 25°C.
Method of manufacture: prepared by the esterification of citric acid and ethanol, followed by acetylation with acetic anhydride.
Safety:
LD_{50} (mouse, IP): 1.15 g/kg[4]
LD_{50} (rat, oral): 7 g/kg
Comments: used as a plasticizer in pharmaceutical formulations.

Tributyl citrate: $C_{18}H_{32}O_7$
Molecular weight: 360.44
CAS number: [77-94-1]
Synonyms: butyl citrate; citric acid tributyl ester; *Citroflex 4*; 2-hydroxy-1,2,3-propanetricarboxylic acid, tri-*n*-butyl ester; TBC.
Appearance: an odorless, colorless or pale yellow colored, oily liquid.
Boiling point: 322°C
Flash point: 185°C
Pour point: -62°C
Refractive index: $n_D^{25} = 1.4440$
Solubility: practically insoluble in water. Miscible with most organic liquids.
Specific gravity: 1.045 at 25°C
Viscosity (dynamic): 32 mPa s (32 cP) at 25°C.

Method of manufacture: prepared by the esterification of citric acid and *n*-butanol.
Comments: used as a plasticizer in pharmaceutical formulations.

19. Comments

Triethyl citrate is listed in the Food Chemicals Codex (FCC).[5]

20. Specific References

1. Plaizier-Vercammen J, Suenens G. Evaluation of Aquateric, a pseudolatex of cellulose acetate phthalate, for its enteric coating properties on tablets. STP Pharma (Sci) 1991; 1: 307-312.
2. Gutierrez-Rocca JC, McGinity JW. Influence of aging on the physical-mechanical properties of acrylic resin films cast from aqueous dispersions and organic solutions. Drug Dev Ind Pharm 1993; 19: 315-332.
3. Osberghaus R. Nonmicrobicidal deodorizing agents. Cosmet Toilet 1980; 95(7): 48-50.
4. Sweet DV, editor. Registry of toxic effects of chemical substances. Cincinnati: US Department of Health, 1987.
5. National Academy of Sciences. Food chemicals codex, 3rd edition. Washington: National Academy Press, 1981.

21. General References

—

22. Authors

USA: SJ Kennedy.

Vanillin

1. Nonproprietary Names
BP: Vanillin
PhEur: Vanillinum
USPNF: Vanillin

2. Synonyms
4-Hydroxy-*m*-anisaldehyde; *p*-hydroxy-*m*-methoxybenzaldehyde; 3-methoxy-4-hydroxybenzaldehyde; methyl protocatechuic aldehyde; vanillic aldehyde.

3. Chemical Name and CAS Registry Number
4-Hydroxy-3-methoxybenzaldehyde [121-33-5]

4. Empirical Formula   Molecular Weight
$C_8H_8O_3$ 152.15

5. Structural Formula

6. Functional Category
Flavoring agent.

7. Applications in Pharmaceutical Formulation or Technology
Vanillin is widely used as a flavor in pharmaceuticals, foods, beverages and confectionery products to which it imparts a characteristic taste and odor of natural vanilla. It is also used in perfumes, as an analytical reagent and as an intermediate in the synthesis of a number of pharmaceuticals, particularly methyldopa. Additionally, it has been investigated as a potential therapeutic agent in sickle cell anemia[1] and is claimed to have some antifungal properties.[2]

As a pharmaceutical excipient, vanillin is used in tablets, solutions (0.01-0.02% w/v), syrups and powders to mask the unpleasant taste and odor characteristics of certain formulations, e.g. caffeine tablets and polythiazide tablets. It is similarly used in film coatings to mask the taste and odor of vitamin tablets.

Vanillin has also been investigated as a photostabilizer in frusemide 1% w/v injection, haloperidol 0.5% w/v injection and thiothixene 0.2% w/v injection.[3]

8. Description
White or cream, crystalline needles or powder with characteristic vanilla odor and sweet taste.

9. Pharmacopeial Specifications

Test	PhEur 1991	USPNF XVII
Identification	+	+
Clarity and color of solution	+	—
Melting range	81-84°C	81-83°C
Loss on drying	⩽ 1.0%	⩽ 1.0%
Sulfated ash	⩽ 0.05%	—
Residue on ignition	—	⩽ 0.05%
Related substances	+	—
Reaction with sulfuric acid	+	—
Assay	99.0-101.0%	97.0-103.0%

10. Typical Properties
Acidity/alkalinity: aqueous solutions are acid to litmus.
Boiling point: 284-285°C (with decomposition)
Density (bulk): 0.6 g/cm^3
Flash point: 153°C (closed cup)
Melting point: 81-83°C
Solubility:

Solvent	Solubility at 20°C Unless stated otherwise
Acetone	soluble
Alkali hydroxide solutions	soluble
Chloroform	soluble
Ethanol (95%)	1 in 2
Ethanol (70%)	1 in 3
Ether	soluble
Glycerin	1 in 20
Methanol	soluble
Oils	soluble
Water	1 in 100
	1 in 16 at 80°C

Specific gravity: 1.056 (liquid)

11. Stability and Storage Conditions
Vanillin slowly oxidizes in moist air and is affected by light. Solutions of vanillin in ethanol rapidly decompose in light to give a yellow-colored, slightly bitter tasting solution of 6,6'-dihydroxy-5,5'-dimethoxy-1,1'-biphenyl-3,3'-dicarbaldehyde. Alkaline solutions also decompose rapidly to give a brown-colored solution. However, by adding sodium metabisulfite 0.2% w/v, as an antioxidant, solutions stable for several months may be produced.[4]

The bulk material should be stored in a well-closed container, protected from light, in a cool, dry, place.

12. Incompatibilities
Incompatible with acetone, forming a brightly colored compound.[5] With glycerin a compound practically insoluble in ethanol is formed.

13. Method of Manufacture
Vanillin occurs naturally in many essential oils and particularly in the pods of *Vanilla planifolia* and *Vanilla tahitensis*. Industrially, vanillin is prepared from lignin, which is obtained from the sulfite wastes produced during paper manufacture. Lignin is treated with alkali at elevated temperature and

pressure, in the presence of a catalyst, to form a complex mixture of products from which vanillin is isolated. Vanillin is then purified by successive recrystallizations.

Vanillin may also be prepared synthetically by condensation, in weak alkali, of a slight excess of guaiacol with glyoxylic acid at room temperature. The resultant alkaline solution, containing 4-hydroxy-3-methoxymandelic acid is oxidized in air, in the presence of a catalyst and vanillin obtained by acidification and simultaneous decarboxylation. Vanillin is then purified by successive recrystallizations.

14. Safety

There have been few reports of adverse reactions to vanillin although it has been speculated that cross-sensitization with other structurally similar molecules, such as benzoic acid, may occur.[6] Adverse reactions that have been reported include contact dermatitis[7] and bronchospasm caused by hypersensitivity.[8]

The WHO has set an estimated acceptable daily intake for vanillin of up to 10 mg/kg body-weight.[9]

LD_{50} (mouse, IP): 0.48 g/kg[10]
LD_{50} (rat, IP): 1.16 g/kg
LD_{50} (rat, oral): 1.58 g/kg
LD_{50} (rat, SC): 1.5 g/kg

15. Handling Precautions

Observe normal precautions appropriate to the quantity of material handled. Eye protection is recommended. Heavy airborne concentrations of dust may present an explosion hazard.

16. Regulatory Status

GRAS listed. Included in the FDA Inactive Ingredients Guide (oral solutions, syrups, capsules and tablets). Included in nonparenteral medicines licensed in the UK.

17. Pharmacopeias

Aust, Belg, Br, Egypt, Eur, Fr, Ger, Hung, Ind, Mex, Nord, Swiss, USPNF and Yug.

18. Related Substances

Ethyl Vanillin.

19. Comments

One part of synthetic vanillin is equivalent to 400 parts of vanilla pods.

20. Specific References

1. Abraham DJ, Mehanna AS, Wireko FC, Whitney J, et al. Vanillin, a potential agent for the treatment of sickle cell anemia. Blood 1991; 77: 1334-1341.
2. Lisá M, Leifertová I, Baloun J. A contribution to the antifungal effect of propolis [in German]. Folia Pharm 1989; 13(1): 29-44.
3. Thoma K, Klimek R. Photostabilization of drugs in dosage forms without protection from packaging materials. Int J Pharmaceutics 1991; 67: 169-175.
4. Jethwa SA, Stanford JB, Sugden JK. Light stability of vanillin solutions in ethanol. Drug Dev Ind Pharm 1979; 5: 79-85.
5. Thakur AB, Dayal S. Schiff base formation with nitrogen of a sulfonamido group. J Pharm Sci 1982; 71: 1422.
6. Weiner M, Bernstein IL. Adverse reactions to drug formulation agents: a handbook of excipients. New York: Marcel Dekker, 1989: 238-239.
7. Wang X-S, Xue Y-S, Jiang Y, Ni H-L, et al. Occupational contact dermatitis in manufacture of vanillin. Chin Med J 1987; 100: 250-254.
8. Van Assendelft AHW. Bronchospasm induced by vanillin and lactose. Eur J Respir Dis 1984; 65: 468-472.
9. FAO/WHO. Specifications for the identity and purity of food additives and their toxicological evaluation: some flavouring substances and non-nutritive sweetening agents. Eleventh report of the joint FAO/WHO expert committee on food additives. Tech Rep Ser Wld Hlth Org 1968; No. 383.
10. Sweet DV, editor. Registry of toxic effects of chemical substances. Cincinnati: US Department of Health, 1987.

21. General References

Clark GS. Vanillin. Perfum Flav 1990; 15(Mar/Apr): 45-54.

22. Authors

UK: PJ Weller.

Hydrogenated Vegetable Oil, Type I

1. Nonproprietary Names

USPNF: Hydrogenated vegetable oil, type I
See also Sections 8, 9 and 18.

2. Synonyms

Sterotex
Trade names for materials derived from stated vegetable oils are shown below:
Hydrogenated cottonseed oil: *Lubritab*.
Hydrogenated palm oil: *Dynasan P60*; *Softisan 154*.
Hydrogenated soybean oil: *Sterotex HM*.

3. Chemical Name and CAS Registry Number

Hydrogenated vegetable oil [68334-00-9]
Hydrogenated soybean oil [8016-70-4]

4. Empirical Formula Molecular Weight

—

5. Structural Formula

$R_1COOCH_2 - CH(OOCR_2) - CH_2OOCR_3$
Where R_1, R_2 and R_3 are mainly C_{15} and C_{17}.

6. Functional Category

Tablet and capsule diluent; tablet and capsule lubricant; tablet binder.

7. Applications in Pharmaceutical Formulation or Technology

Hydrogenated vegetable oil, type I is used as a lubricant in tablet and capsule formulations.[1,2] It is used at concentrations of 1-6% w/w, usually in combination with talc. It may also be used as an auxiliary binder in tablet formulations.
Hydrogenated vegetable oil, type I is additionally used as the matrix forming material in lipophilic based controlled release formulations;[3-6] it may also be used as a coating aid in controlled release formulations.
Other uses of hydrogenated vegetable oil, type I include: as a viscosity modifier in the preparation of oil-based liquid and semi-solid formulations; in the preparation of suppositories, to reduce the sedimentation of suspended components and to improve the solidification process; and in the formulation of liquid and semi-solid fills for hard gelatin capsules.[7]
Fully hydrogenated vegetable oil products may also be used as alternatives to hard waxes in cosmetics and topical pharmaceutical formulations.

8. Description

Hydrogenated vegetable oil is a mixture of triglycerides of fatty acids. The two types which are defined in the USPNF XVII (Suppl 5) are characterised by their physical properties, *see* Section 9.
Hydrogenated vegetable oil, type I occurs in various forms, e.g. fine powder, flakes or pellets. The color of the material depends on the manufacturing process and the form. In general, the material is white to yellowish-white with the powder grades appearing more white-colored than the coarser grades.

SEM: 1
Excipient: Hydrogenated vegetable oil, type I (*Lubritab*)
Manufacturer: Edward Mendell Co Inc
Magnification: 100x
Voltage: 6 kV

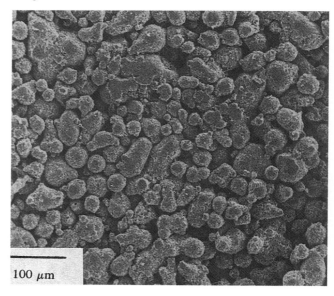

100 μm

SEM: 2
Excipient: Hydrogenated vegetable oil, type I (*Lubritab*)
Manufacturer: Edward Mendell Co Inc
Magnification: 1000x
Voltage: 6 kV

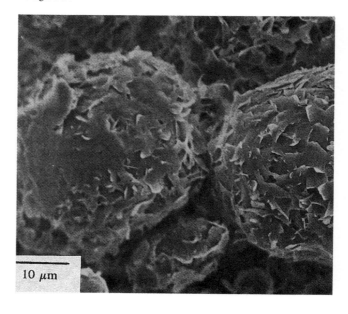

10 μm

9. Pharmacopeial Specifications

Test	USPNF XVII (Suppl 5) Type I	Type II
Melting range	57-70°C	20-50°C
Heavy metals	⩽ 10 ppm	⩽ 0.001%
Iodine value	0-5	55-80
Saponification value	175-205	185-200
Loss on drying	⩽ 0.1%	⩽ 0.1%
Acid value	⩽ 4.0	⩽ 4.0
Unsaponifiable matter	⩽ 0.8%	⩽ 0.8%

10. Typical Properties

Density (tapped): 0.57 g/cm^3 for *Lubritab*
Melting point: 61-66°C for *Lubritab*
Particle size distribution: mean size in range 50–70μm for *Lubritab*, by laser diffraction method.
Solubility: soluble in chloroform, petroleum spirit and hot propan-2-ol; practically insoluble in water.

11. Stability and Storage Conditions

Hydrogenated vegetable oil, type I is a stable material; typically it is assigned a three year shelf-life.
The bulk material should be stored in a well-closed container in a cool, dry, place.

12. Incompatibilities

Incompatible with strong oxidizing agents.

13. Method of Manufacture

Hydrogenated vegetable oil, type I is prepared from refined vegetable oils which are hydrogenated using a catalyst.

14. Safety

Hydrogenated vegetable oil, type I is used in food products and oral pharmaceutical formulations and is generally regarded as a nontoxic and nonirritant excipient.

15. Handling Precautions

Observe normal precautions appropriate to the circumstances and quantity of material handled. Gloves, eye protection and a dust mask are recommended when handling fine powder grades.

16. Regulatory Status

GRAS listed. Included in the FDA Inactive Ingredients Guide (oral capsules and tablets, and suppositories). Included in nonparenteral medicines licensed in the UK.

17. Pharmacopeias

Jpn and USPNF.

18. Related Substances

Hydrogenated Castor Oil; hydrogenated vegetable oil, type II; Medium Chain Triglycerides; Suppository Bases.

Hydrogenated vegetable oil, type II
Comments: hydrogenated vegetable oil, type II includes partially hydrogenated vegetable oils from different sources which have a wide range of applications. In general, type II materials have lower melting ranges and higher iodine values than type I materials. Many type II materials are prepared to meet specific customer requirements for use in cosmetics. Type II materials may also be used in the manufacture of suppositories. *See also* Section 9.

19. Comments

Products from different manufacturers may vary due to differences in the source of the vegetable oil used for hydrogenation.

20. Specific References

1. Hölzer AW, Sjögren J. Evaluation of some lubricants by the comparison of friction coefficients and tablet properties. Acta Pharm Suec 1981; 18: 139-148.
2. Staniforth JN. Use of hydrogenated vegetable oil as a tablet lubricant. Drug Dev Ind Pharm 1987; 13: 1141-1158.
3. Lockwood PJ, Baichwal AR, Staniforth JN. Influence of drug type and formulation variables on mechanisms of release from wax matrices. Proc Int Symp Control Rel Bioact Mater 1987; 14: 198-199.
4. Wang PY. Lipids as excipients in sustained release insulin implants. Int J Pharmaceutics 1989; 54: 223-230.
5. Çiftçi K, Çapan Y, Öztürk O, Hincal AA. Formulation and *in vitro-in vivo* evaluation of sustained release lithium carbonate tablets. Pharm Res 1990; 7: 359-363.
6. Watanbe Y, Kogoshi T, Amagai Y, Matsumoto M. Preparation and evaluation of enteric granules of aspirin prepared by acylglycerols. Int J Pharmaceutics 1990; 64: 147-154.
7. Dürr M, Fribolin HU, Gneuss KD. Dosing of liquids into liquid gelatin capsules at the production scale: development of compositions and procedures [in German]. Acta Pharm Technol 1983; 29(3): 245-251.

21. General References

Banker GS, Peck GE, Baley G. Tablet formulation and design. In: Lieberman HA, Lachman L, editors. Pharmaceutical dosage forms: tablets I. New York: Marcel Dekker Inc, 1989.
Bardon J, Sébert P, Chaumat C, Robelin N, Rollet M. Temperature elevation undergone by mixtures of powders or granules during their transformation into tablets II: influence of nature and rate of lubricant [in French]. STP Pharma 1985; 1: 948-955.
Miller TA, York P. Pharmaceutical tablet lubrication. Int J Pharmaceutics 1988; 41: 1-19.
Staniforth JN, Cryer S, Ahmed HA, Davies SP. Aspects of pharmaceutical tribology. Drug Dev Ind Pharm 1989; 15: 2265-2294.

22. Authors

UK: RC Moreton.

Water

1. Nonproprietary Names
BP: Purified water
PhEur: Aqua purificata
USP: Purified water
See also Sections 8 and 18.

2. Synonyms
Aqua; hydrogen oxide.

3. Chemical Name and CAS Registry Number
Water [7732-18-5]

4. Empirical Formula   Molecular Weight
H_2O 18.02

5. Structural Formula
H_2O

6. Functional Category
Solvent.

7. Applications in Pharmaceutical Formulation or Technology
Water is a very widely used solvent and vehicle for many types of pharmaceutical formulation. Specific grades of water are used for particular applications in concentrations up to 100%, *see* Table I.

Table I: Typical applications of specific grades of water.

Type	Use
Bacteriostatic water for injection	Diluent for ophthalmic and multiple-dose injections.
Potable water	Public supply suitable for drinking, the purity of which is unlikely to be suitable for use in the manufacture of pharmaceuticals.
Purified water	Vehicle and solvent for the manufacture of drug products and pharmaceutical preparations; not suitable for use in the manufacture of parenteral products.
Sterile water for inhalation	Diluent for inhalation therapy products.
Sterile water for injection	Diluent for injections.
Sterile water for irrigation	Diluent for internal irrigation therapy products.
Water for injections in bulk	Water for the bulk preparation of medicines for parenteral administration.

8. Description
The term 'water' is used to describe potable water freshly drawn direct from the public supply and suitable for drinking. The chemical composition of potable water is variable and the

Table II: Pharmacopeial specifications of water for different pharmaceutical applications.

Test	Purified water PhEur	USP	Water for injection PhEur	USP	Sterile water for injection PhEur	USP	Bacteriostatic water for injection USP	Sterile water for inhalation USP	Sterile water for irrigation BP	USP
Identification	+	+	+	+	+	+	+	+	+	+
pH	+	5.0-7.0	+	5.0-7.0	+	+	4.5-7.0	4.5-7.5	+	5.0-7.0
Chloride	+	+	+	+	≤ 0.5 ppm	≤ 0.5 ppm	—	≤ 0.5 ppm	≤ 0.5 ppm	≤ 0.5 ppm
Sulfate	+	+	+	+	+	+	+	+	+	+
Ammonia	+	≤ 0.3 ppm	+	≤ 0.3 ppm	+	≤ 0.6 ppm[c] ≤ 0.3 ppm[d]	—	≤ 0.6 ppm[c] ≤ 0.3 ppm[d]	≤ 0.2 ppm	≤ 0.6 ppm[c] ≤ 0.3 ppm[d]
Calcium	+	+	+	+	+	+	+	+	+	+
Magnesium	+	—	+	—	+	—	—	—	+	—
Nitrate	≤ 0.2 ppm	—	≤ 0.2 ppm	—	+	—	—	—	≤ 0.2 ppm	—
Carbon dioxide	—	+	—	+	—	+	+	+	—	+
Heavy metals	≤ 0.1 ppm	+	≤ 0.1 ppm	+	≤ 0.1 ppm	+	+	+	≤ 0.1 ppm	+
Oxidizable substances	+	+	+	+	+	+	—	+	+	+
Total solids	≤ 0.001%	≤ 0.001%	≤ 0.001%	≤ 0.001%	≤ 0.004%[a] ≤ 0.003%[b]	≤ 0.004%[e] ≤ 0.003%[f] ≤ 0.002%[g]	—	≤ 0.004%[e] ≤ 0.003%[f] ≤ 0.002%[g]	≤ 0.003%	≤ 0.004%[e] ≤ 0.003%[f] ≤ 0.002%[g]
Bacterial endotoxins	—	—	—	+	+	+	+	+	+	+
Antimicrobial agents	—	—	—	+	—	—	+	—	—	—
Sterility	—	—	—	+	+	+	+	+	+	+
Particulate matter	—	—	—	+	—	+	+	—	—	—

Note: + = tested for; — = not tested for.
[a] For containers of nominal volume 10 mL or less.
[b] For containers of nominal volume more than 10 mL.
[c] For containers of nominal volume 50 mL or less.
[d] For containers of nominal volume more than 50 mL.
[e] For containers of nominal volume 30 mL or less.
[f] For containers of nominal volume between 30-100 mL.
[g] For containers of nominal volume more than 100 mL.
Pharmacopeial standards are from BP 1993, PhEur 1989, PhEur 1990 and USP XXII.

nature and concentration of the impurities in it depend upon the source from which it is drawn. Although potable water must be both palatable and safe to drink, for most pharmaceutical applications potable water is purified by distillation, ion exchange treatment, reverse osmosis or some other suitable process to produce 'purified water'. For certain applications, water with pharmacopeial specifications differing from purified water should be used, e.g. water for injection, *see* Sections 9 and 18.

Water is a clear, colorless, odorless and tasteless liquid.

9. Pharmacopeial Specifications

See Table II.

10. Typical Properties

Boiling point: 100°C
Critical pressure: 22.1 MPa (218.3 atm)
Critical temperature: 374.2°C
Dielectric constant: $D^{25} = 78.54$
Dipole moment:
1.76 in benzene at 25°C;
1.86 in dioxane at 25°C.
Ionization constant: 1.008×10^{-14} at 25°C
Latent heat of fusion: 6 kJ/mole (1.436 kcal/mole)
Latent heat of vaporization:
40.7 kJ/mole (9.717 kcal/mole)
Melting point: 0°C
Refractive index: $n_D^{20} = 1.3330$
Solubility: miscible with most polar solvents.
Specific gravity: 0.9971 at 25°C.
Specific heat (liquid):
4.184 J/g/°C (1.00 cal/g/°C) at 14°C
Surface tension:
71.97 mN/m (71.97 dynes/cm) at 25°C.
Vapor pressure: 3.17 kPa (23.76 mmHg) at 25°C
Viscosity (dynamic): 0.89 mPa s (0.89 cP) at 25°C.

11. Stability and Storage Conditions

Water is chemically stable in all physical states (ice, liquid and steam). Water for specific purposes should be stored in an appropriate container, *see* Table III.

Table III: Storage requirements for different grades of water.

Type	Storage requirements*
Bacteriostatic water for injection	Preserve in single-dose and multiple-dose containers, preferably of Type I or Type II glass, not larger than 30 mL in size.
Potable water	Preserve in tightly sealed containers.
Purified water	Preserve in tightly sealed containers. If stored in bulk, the conditions of storage should be designed to limit the growth of microorganisms and avoid any other contamination.
Sterile water for inhalation	Preserve in single-dose containers, preferably of Type I or Type II glass.
Sterile water for injection	Preserve in single-dose containers, preferably of Type I or Type II glass, not more than 1000 mL in size.

Table III: *Continued*

Type	Storage requirements*
Water for injection	Preserve in tightly sealed containers.
Water for injections in bulk	Collected and stored in conditions designed to prevent growth of microorganisms and avoid any other contamination.

* To prevent evaporation and to maintain quality.

12. Incompatibilities

In pharmaceutical formulations, water can react with drugs and other excipients that are susceptible to hydrolysis (decomposition in the presence of water or moisture) at ambient and elevated temperatures.

Water can react violently with alkali metals and rapidly with alkaline metals and their oxides, such as calcium oxide and magnesium oxide. Water also reacts with anhydrous salts to form hydrates of various compositions, and with certain organic materials and calcium carbide.

13. Method of Manufacture

To produce potable or drinking water, insoluble matter is first removed from a water supply by coagulation, settling and filtering processes. Pathogenic microorganisms present are then destroyed by aeration, chlorination or some other means. Water may also be rendered free of viable pathogenic microorganisms by active boiling for 15-20 minutes. Finally, the palatability of the water is then improved by aeration and charcoal filtration.

Purified water suitable for use in pharmaceutical formulations is usually prepared by purifying potable water by one of several processes, such as: distillation; de-ionization; or reverse osmosis.[1-7]

Distillation: a wide variety of stills are available to produce purified or distilled water. A typical design consists of an evaporator, vapor separator and compressor. The distilland (raw feed water) is heated in the evaporator to boiling and the vapor produced separated from entrained distilland in the separator. The vapor then enters a compressor where the temperature of the vapors is raised to 107°C. Superheated vapors are then condensed on the outer surface of the tubes of the evaporator containing cool distilland circulating within.

Vapor compression stills of various sizes are commercially available and can be used to produce water of high purity when properly constructed. A high-quality distillate, such as water for injection, can be obtained if the water is first de-ionized. The best stills are constructed of types 304 or 316 stainless steel and coated with pure tin, or are made from chemical-resistant glass.

De-ionization: cationic and anionic ion-exchange resins are used to purify potable water by removing any dissolved ions. Dissolved gases are also removed, whilst chlorine, in the concentrations generally found in potable water, is destroyed by the resin itself. Some organics, and colloidal particles, are removed by adsorption and filtration. Resin beds may however foster microbial life and produce pyrogenic effluent unless adequate precautions are taken to prevent contamination. Mixed bed units produce purer water (decreased conductivity) than stills. However, the organic matter content is usually higher. Ion-exchange units are normally used today to treat raw feed water prior to distillation or reverse osmosis processing.

Reverse osmosis: water is forced through a semi-permeable membrane in the opposite direction to normal osmotic diffusion. A very small proportion of inorganic salts passes through, but undissolved materials (bacteria and large molecules, such as viruses, pyrogens and high molecular weight organics) are removed.

14. Safety

Water is the base for many biological life forms, and its safety in pharmaceutical formulations is unquestioned provided it meets standards of quality for potability[8] and microbial content, *see* Sections 9 and 19. Plain water is considered slightly more toxic upon injection to laboratory animals than physiological salt solutions such as normal saline or Ringer's solution.

Ingestion of excessive quantities of water can lead to water intoxication with disturbances of the electrolyte balance.

Water for injection should be free from pyrogens.

15. Handling Precautions

Observe normal precautions appropriate to the circumstances and quantity of material handled.

16. Regulatory Status

Included in nonparenteral and parenteral medicines licensed in the UK and US.

17. Pharmacopeias

Aust, Belg, Br, Chin, Cz, Egypt, Eur, Fr, Ger, Gr, Hung, Ind, It, Jpn, Mex, Neth, Nord, Port, Rom, Rus, Swiss, Turk, US and Yug. Also in BP Vet.

18. Related Substances

Bacteriostatic water for injection; carbon dioxide-free water; de-aerated water; hard water; soft water; sterile water for inhalation; sterile water for injection; sterile water for irrigation; water for injection; water for injections in bulk.

Bacteriostatic water for injection
Pharmacopeias: US.
Comments: the USP XXII describes bacteriostatic water for injection as sterile water for injection which contains one or more suitable antimicrobial agents.

Carbon dioxide-free water
Comments: purified water that has been boiled vigorously for 5 minutes and allowed to cool while protecting it from absorption of atmospheric carbon dioxide.

De-aerated water
Comments: purified water that has been boiled vigorously for 5 minutes and cooled to reduce the air (oxygen) content.

Hard water
Comments: water containing the equivalent to not less than 120 mg/L and not more than 180 mg/L of calcium carbonate.

Soft water
Comments: water containing the equivalent to not more than 60 mg/L of calcium carbonate.

Sterile water for inhalation
Pharmacopeias: US.
Comments: the USP XXII describes sterile water for inhalation as water purified by distillation or by reverse osmosis and rendered sterile. It contains no antimicrobial agents or other added substances, except where used in humidifiers or other similar devices, and where liable to contamination over a period of time.

Sterile water for injection
Pharmacopeias: Br, Eur and US.
Comments: the USP XXII describes sterile water for injection as water for injection sterilized and suitably packaged. It contains no antimicrobial agents or other substances. The BP 1993 and PhEur 1990 describes such water, used for dissolving or diluting substances or preparations for parenteral administration, as 'sterilised water for injections'.

Sterile water for irrigation
Pharmacopeias: Br and US.
Comments: the USP XXII describes sterile water for irrigation as water for injection sterilized and suitably packaged. It contains no antimicrobial agents or other substances.

Water for injection
Pharmacopeias: Aust, Belg, Br, Chin, Cz, Egypt, Eur, Fr, Ger, Gr, Hung, Ind, It, Jpn, Mex, Neth, Nord, Port, Rus, Swiss, Turk, US and Yug. Also in BP Vet.
Comments: the USP XXII describes water for injection as water purified by distillation or reverse osmosis. It contains no added substances. The BP 1993 and PhEur 1990 title is 'water for injections' and is comprised two parts, 'water for injections in bulk' and 'sterilised water for injections'. The BP 1993 and PhEur 1990 describes water for injections as apyrogenic distilled water.

Water for injections in bulk
Pharmacopeias: Br and Eur.
Comments: the BP 1993 and PhEur 1990 describe water for injections in bulk as water produced from potable or purified water by distillation which is free from pyrogens. The distillate is collected and stored in conditions designed to prevent the growth of microorganisms and to avoid any other contamination.

19. Comments

In most pharmacopeias, the term 'water' now refers to purified or distilled water.

Without further purification, 'water' may be unsuitable for certain pharmaceutical applications, e.g. the presence of calcium in water affects the viscosity and gel strength of algins and pectin dispersions, while the use of potable water affects the clarity and quality of cough mixtures, and the stability of antibiotic liquid preparations.

Water commonly contains salts of aluminum, calcium, iron, magnesium, potassium, sodium and zinc. Toxic substances such as arsenic, barium, cadmium, chromium, cyanide, lead, mercury and selenium may constitute a danger to health if present in excessive amounts. Ingestion of water containing high amounts of calcium and nitrate is also contra-indicated. National standards generally specify the maximum limits for these inorganic substances in potable water. Limits have also been placed on microorganisms, detergents, phenolics, chlorinated phenolics and other organic substances. The WHO,[9] and other national bodies, have issued guidelines for water quality although many countries have their own standards for water quality embodied in specific legislation.[10] *See* Table IV.

Table IV: Limits for inorganic substances in potable water (mg/L).

Contaminant	UK (mg/L)	WHO (mg/L)
Aluminum	0.2	0.2
Ammonium	0.5	—
Antimony	0.01	—
Arsenic	0.05	0.05
Barium	1.0	No limit
Beryllium	—	No limit
Boron	2.0	—
Cadmium	0.005	0.005
Calcium	250	—
Chloride	400	250
Chromium	0.05	0.05
Copper	3.0	1.0
Cyanide	0.05	0.1
Fluoride	1.5	1.5
Iron	0.2	0.3
Lead	0.05	0.05
Magnesium	50	—
Manganese	0.05	0.1
Mercury	0.001	0.001
Nickel	0.05	No limit
Nitrate (as N)	—	10
Nitrate (as NO_3)	50	—
Nitrite (as NO_2)	0.1	—
Phosphorus	2.2	—
Potassium	12	—
Selenium	0.01	0.01
Silver	0.01	No limit
Sodium	150	200
Sulfate	250	400
Zinc	5.0	5.0

20. Specific References

1. Thomas WH, Harvey H. Achieving purity in pharmaceutical water. Mfg Chem Aerosol News 1976; 47(10): 32, 36, 39, 40.
2. Honeyman T. Purified water for pharmaceuticals. Mfg Chem 1987; 58(3): 53, 54, 57, 59.
3. Cross J. Treating waters for the pharmaceutical industry. Mfg Chem 1988; 59(3): 34-35.
4. Cross J. Steam sterilisable ultrafiltration membranes. Mfg Chem 1989; 60(3): 25-27.
5. Horry JM, Cross JR. Purifying water for ophthalmic and injectable preparations. Pharm J 1989; 242: 169-171.
6. Smith VC. Pure water. Mfg Chem 1990; 61(3): 22-24.
7. Burrows WD, Nelson JH. IV fluidmakers: preparation of sterile water for injection in a field setting. J Parenter Sci Technol 1993; 47(3): 124-129.
8. Walker A. Drinking water - doubts about quality. Br Med J 1992; 304: 175-178.
9. World Health Organization. Guidelines for drinking-water quality, volume 1: recommendations. Geneva: World Health Organization, 1984.
10. Statutory Instrument 1147. The water supply (water quality) regulations 1989. London: HMSO, 1989.

21. General References

Rössler R. Water and air, two important media in the manufacture of sterile pharmaceuticals, with regard to the GMP. Drugs Made Ger 1976; 19: 130-136.

22. Authors

UK: JM Horry.
USA: RA Nash.

Anionic Emulsifying Wax

1. Nonproprietary Names
BP: Emulsifying wax

2. Synonyms
Collone HV; *Crodex A*; *Cyclonette Wax*; *Lanette wax SX BP*; *Polawax*.

3. Chemical Name and CAS Registry Number
Anionic emulsifying wax [8014-38-8]

4. Empirical Formula   Molecular Weight
Anionic emulsifying wax contains cetostearyl alcohol, purified water, and either sodium lauryl sulfate or a sodium salt of a similar higher primary aliphatic alcohol. *See also* Sections 13 and 19.

5. Structural Formula
See Section 4.

6. Functional Categories
Emulsifying agent; stiffening agent.

7. Applications in Pharmaceutical Formulation or Technology
Anionic emulsifying wax is used in cosmetics and topical pharmaceutical formulations primarily as an emulsifying agent. The wax is added to fatty or paraffin bases to facilitate the production of oil-in-water emulsions which are nongreasy. In concentrations of about 2%, emulsions are pourable; stiffer emulsions, e.g. aqueous cream BP may contain up to 10% of anionic emulsifying wax.

Creams should be adequately preserved and can usually be sterilized by autoclaving. A better quality emulsion is produced by incorporating some alkali into the aqueous phase although care should be taken not to use an excess.

Anionic emulsifying wax (3-30%) may also be mixed with soft and liquid paraffins to prepare anhydrous ointment bases such as emulsifying ointment BP. A preparation of 80% anionic emulsifying wax in white soft paraffin has been used as a soap substitute in the treatment of eczema.

In addition, anionic emulsifying wax (10%) has been added to theobroma oil to produce a suppository base with a melting point of 34°C.

8. Description
An almost white, or pale yellow colored, waxy solid or flakes which when warmed become plastic before melting. Anionic emulsifying wax has a faint characteristic odor and a bland taste.

9. Pharmacopeial Specifications

Test	BP 1993
Identification	+
Acidity	+
Alkalinity	+
Alcohols	+
Iodine value	⩽ 3.0
Saponification value	⩽ 2.0
Sodium alkyl sulfates	⩾ 8.7%
Unsaponifiable matter	⩾ 86.0%
Water	⩽ 4.0%

10. Typical Properties
Density: 0.97 g/cm^3
Flash point: > 100°C
Melting point: 52°C
Solubility: soluble in chloroform, ethanol (95%), ether and on warming in fixed oils and mineral oil; practically insoluble in water, forming an emulsion.

11. Stability and Storage Conditions
Solid anionic emulsifying wax is chemically stable and should be stored in a well-closed container in a cool, dry, place.

12. Incompatibilities
Incompatibilities of anionic emulsifying wax are essentially those of sodium alkyl sulfates and include: cationic compounds (quaternary ammonium compounds, acriflavine, ephedrine hydrochloride, antihistamines and other nitrogenous compounds); salts of polyvalent metals (aluminum, zinc, tin and lead); and thioglycollates. Anionic emulsifying wax is compatible with most acids above pH 2.5. It is also compatible with alkalis and hard water.

Iron vessels should not be used when heating anionic emulsifying wax; stainless steel containers are satisfactory.

13. Method of Manufacture
Anionic emulsifying wax is prepared by melting cetostearyl alcohol and heating to about 95°C. Sodium lauryl sulfate, or some other suitable anionic surfactant, and purified water is then added. The mixture is heated to 115°C and while this temperature is maintained the mixture is vigorously stirred until any frothing ceases. The wax is then rapidly cooled.

The BP 1993 specifies that the formula of anionic emulsifying wax is:

Cetostearyl alcohol 90 g
Sodium lauryl sulfate 10 g
Purified water 4 mL

14. Safety
Anionic emulsifying wax is used primarily in topical pharmaceutical formulations and is generally regarded as a nontoxic and nonirritant material. However, sodium lauryl sulfate, a constituent of anionic emulsifying wax, is known to be irritant to the skin at high concentrations; sodium cetyl sulfate is claimed to be less irritating.

Emulsifying ointment BP, which contains anionic emulsifying wax, has been found to have major sunscreen activity in clinically normal skin and should therefore not be used before phototherapy procedures.[1]

15. Handling Precautions

Observe normal precautions appropriate to the circumstances and quantity of material handled. Eye protection is recommended.

16. Regulatory Status

Included in nonparenteral medicines licensed in the UK.

17. Pharmacopeias

Belg, Br, Ger, Ind, Nord, Swiss and Yug.

Note that the Belgian Pharmacopeia includes anionic emulsifying wax prepared from 9 parts cetostearyl alcohol and 1 part sodium cetostearyl sulfate. The German Pharmacopeia includes anionic emulsifying wax prepared from 12.5 parts cetostearyl alcohol and 1 part sodium cetostearyl sulfate.

18. Related Substances

Cetostearyl alcohol; Nonionic Emulsifying Wax; Sodium Lauryl Sulfate.

A number of emulsifying waxes are commercially available which contain different sodium alkyl sulfates and may not meet official compendial specifications. *See also* Section 19.

19. Comments

The nomenclature for emulsifying wax is confused since there are three groups of emulsifying waxes with different titles in the UK and US:

	UK	US
Nonionic	Cetomacrogol emulsifying wax	Emulsifying wax
Anionic	Emulsifying wax	—
Cationic	Cetrimide emulsifying wax	—

Each wax has similar physical properties, but varies in the type of surfactant used which, in turn, affects the range of compatibilities. Emulsifying wax BP and emulsifying wax USPNF contain anionic and nonionic surfactants respectively and are therefore not interchangeable in formulations.

20. Specific References

1. Cox NH, Sharpe G. Emollients, salicylic acid, and ultraviolet erythema [letter]. Lancet 1990; 335: 53-54.

21. General References

Eccleston GM. Properties of fatty alcohol mixed emulsifiers and emulsifying waxes. In: Florence AT, editor. Materials used in pharmaceutical formulation: critical reports on applied chemistry, volume 6. Oxford: Blackwell Scientific Publications, 1984: 124-156.

22. Authors

UK: AJ Winfield.

Carnauba Wax

1. Nonproprietary Names
BP: Carnauba wax
PhEur: Cera carnauba
USPNF: Carnauba wax

2. Synonyms
903; brazil wax; caranda wax.

3. Chemical Name and CAS Registry Number
Carnauba wax [8015-86-9]

4. Empirical Formula   Molecular Weight
Carnauba wax consists primarily of a complex mixture of esters of acids and hydroxyacids. Also present are acids, oxypolyhydric alcohols, hydrocarbons, resinous matter and water.

5. Structural Formula
See Section 4.

6. Functional Category
Coating agent.

7. Applications in Pharmaceutical Formulation or Technology
Carnauba wax is widely used in cosmetics, certain foods and pharmaceutical formulations.
Carnauba wax is the hardest and highest melting of the waxes commonly used in pharmaceutical formulations and is used primarily as a 10% w/v aqueous emulsion to polish sugar-coated tablets. Aqueous emulsions may be prepared by mixing carnauba wax with an ethanolamine compound and oleic acid. The carnauba wax coating produces tablets of good luster without rubbing. Carnauba wax may also be used in powder form to polish sugar-coated tablets.
Carnauba wax (10-50% w/w) has also been used alone or with stearyl alcohol to produce sustained release solid dosage formulations.[1-4]

8. Description
Carnauba wax occurs as a light brown to pale yellow colored powder, flakes, or irregular lumps of a hard, brittle wax. It possesses a characteristic bland odor and practically no taste. It is free from rancidity. Commercially, various types and grades are available.

9. Pharmacopeial Specifications

Test	PhEur 1989	USPNF XVII
Identification	+	—
Appearance of solution	+	—
Melting range	80-88°C	81-86°C
Residue on ignition	—	$\leqslant$ 0.25%
Total ash	$\leqslant$ 0.25%	—
Heavy metals	–	$\leqslant$ 0.004%
Acid value	2-7	2-7
Saponification value	78-95	78-95

10. Typical Properties
Flash point: 270-330°C
Refractive index: $n_D^{90} = 1.450$
Solubility: soluble in warm chloroform, and warm toluene; slightly soluble in boiling ethanol (95%); practically insoluble in water.
Specific gravity: 0.990-0.999 at 25°C
Unsaponified matter: 50-55%

11. Stability and Storage Conditions
Carnauba wax is stable and should be stored in a well-closed container, in a cool, dry, place.

12. Incompatibilities
—

13. Method of Manufacture
Carnauba wax is obtained from the leaf buds and leaves of *Copernicia cerifera* Mart. (Fam. Palmae). The leaves are dried and shredded and the wax then removed by the addition of hot water.

14. Safety
Carnauba wax is widely used in oral pharmaceutical formulations, cosmetics, and certain food products and is generally regarded as an essentially nontoxic and nonirritant material.

15. Handling Precautions
Observe normal precautions appropriate to the circumstances and quantity of material handled.

16. Regulatory Status
GRAS listed. Accepted for use in certain foods in the UK. Included in the FDA Inactive Ingredients Guide (oral capsules and tablets, also topical preparations). Included in nonparenteral medicines licensed in the UK.

17. Pharmacopeias
Br, Eur, Fr, Ger, Jpn, Neth, Swiss and USPNF.

18. Related Substances
—

19. Comments
In cosmetics, carnauba wax is mainly used to increase the stiffness of formulations, e.g. lipsticks and mascaras.

20. Specific References
1. Wiseman EH, Federici NJ. Development of a sustained-release aspirin tablet. J Pharm Sci 1968; 51: 1535-1539.
2. Prasad CM, Srivastava GP. Study of some sustained release granulations of aspirin. Indian J Hosp Pharm 1971; 8: 21-28.
3. Dave SC, Chakrabarti T, Srivastava GP. Sustained release tablet formulation of diphenhydramine hydrochloride (Benadryl) - part II. Indian J Pharm 1974; 36: 94-96.
4. Kumar K, Chakrabarti T, Srivastava GP. Sustained release tablet formulation of diethylcarbamazine citrate (Hetrazan). Indian J Pharm 1975; 37: 57-59.

21. General References
Briquet F, Brossard C, Ser J, Duchêne D. Optimization of a sustained release formulation containing spherical microgranules produced

by extrusion-spheronization [in French]. STP Pharma 1986; 2: 986-994.

22. Authors

USA: NH Kobayashi.

Microcrystalline Wax

1. Nonproprietary Names

USPNF: Microcrystalline wax

2. Synonyms

Amorphous wax; petroleum ceresin; petroleum wax (microcrystalline).

3. Chemical Name and CAS Registry Number

Microcrystalline wax [63231-60-7]

4. Empirical Formula   Molecular Weight

Microcrystalline wax is composed of a mixture of straight-chain and randomly branched saturated alkanes obtained from petroleum. The carbon chain lengths range from C_{41}-C_{57}; cyclic hydrocarbons are also present.

5. Structural Formula

See Section 4.

6. Functional Category

Coating agent; stiffening agent.

7. Applications in Pharmaceutical Formulation or Technology

Microcrystalline wax is used mainly as a stiffening agent in topical creams and ointments. The wax is used to modify the crystal structure of other waxes (particularly paraffin wax) present in a mixture so that changes in crystal structure, usually exhibited over a period of time, do not occur. Microcrystalline wax also minimizes the sweating or bleeding of oils from blends of oils and waxes. Microcrystalline wax generally has a higher melting point and higher viscosity when molten, thereby increasing the consistency of creams and ointments when incorporated.

Microcrystalline wax is also used as a tablet and capsule coating agent, and in confectionery, cosmetics and food products.

8. Description

Microcrystalline wax occurs as odorless and tasteless waxy lumps or flakes containing small irregularly shaped crystals. It may vary in color from white to yellow, amber, brown or black depending on the grade of material; pharmaceutical grades are usually white or yellow-colored.

9. Pharmacopeial Specifications

Test	USPNF XVII
Color	+
Melting range	54-102°C
Consistency	3-100
Acidity	+
Alkalinity	+
Residue on ignition	⩽ 0.1%
Organic acids	+
Fixed oils, fats, and rosin	+

10. Typical Properties

Acid value: 1.0
Density: 0.928-0.941 g/cm³
Freezing point: 60-75°C
Refractive index: n_D^{100} = 1.435-1.445
Saponification value: 0.05-0.10
Solubility: soluble in benzene, chloroform and ether; slightly soluble in ethanol; practically insoluble in water. When melted, microcrystalline wax is miscible with volatile oils and most warm fixed oils. *See also* HPE Data.
Viscosity (dynamic):
10-30 mPa s (10-30 cP) at 100°C.

	HPE Laboratory Project Data		
	Method	Lab #	Results
Solubility			
Ethanol (95%) at 25°C	SOL-4	10	0.003 mg/mL
Ethanol (95%) at 37°C	SOL-4	10	0.003 mg/mL
Hexane at 25°C	SOL-4	10	0.053 mg/mL
Hexane at 37°C	SOL-4	10	0.088 mg/mL
Propylene glycol at 25°C	SOL-4	10	0.001 mg/mL

Supplier: International Wax Refining Co.

11. Stability and Storage Conditions

Microcrystalline wax is stable in the presence of acids, alkalis, light and air. The bulk material should be stored in a well-closed container in a cool, dry, place.

12. Incompatibilities

—

13. Method of Manufacture

Microcrystalline wax is obtained by solvent fractionation of the still bottom fraction of petroleum by suitable dewaxing or de-oiling.

14. Safety

Microcrystalline wax is mainly used in topical pharmaceutical formulations but is also used in some oral products. It is generally regarded as a nontoxic and nonirritating material.

15. Handling Precautions

Observe normal precautions appropriate to the circumstances and quantity of material handled. Eye protection is recommended.

16. Regulatory Status

GRAS listed. Included in the FDA Inactive Ingredients Guide (oral capsules and topical preparations). Included in nonparenteral medicines licensed in the UK.

17. Pharmacopeias

Swiss and USPNF.

18. Related Substances

Ceresin; Paraffin.

Ceresin

Pharmacopeias: Swiss and Yug.
Comments: ceresin is a mixture of solid hydrocarbons obtained by the purification of ozokerite, a naturally occuring solid paraffin.

19. Comments
—

20. Specific References
—

21. General References
—

22. Authors
USA: LD Bighley.

Nonionic Emulsifying Wax

1. Nonproprietary Name

BP: Cetomacrogol emulsifying wax
USPNF: Emulsifying wax

2. Synonyms

Collone NI; Crodex N; Ritachol; T-Wax.

3. Chemical Name and CAS Registry Number

Nonionic emulsifying wax [977069-99-0]

4. Empirical Formula   Molecular Weight

The USPNF XVII describes nonionic emulsifying wax as emulsifying wax, prepared from cetostearyl alcohol and containing a polyoxyethylene derivative of a fatty acid ester of sorbitan. However, the BP 1993 describes nonionic emulsifying wax as cetomacrogol emulsifying wax prepared from cetostearyl alcohol and cetomacrogol 1000. The UK and US materials may therefore be constitutionally different. *See also* Section 19.

5. Structural Formula

See Section 4.

6. Functional Category

Emulsifying agent; stiffening agent.

7. Applications in Pharmaceutical Formulation or Technology

Nonionic emulsifying wax is used as an emulsifying agent in the production of oil-in-water emulsions which are unaffected by moderate concentrations of electrolytes and are stable over a wide pH range. The concentration of wax used alters the consistency of a product due to its 'self-bodying action'; at concentrations up to about 5% a product is pourable.
Concentrations of about 15% of nonionic emulsifying wax are commonly used in creams, but concentrations as high as 25% may be employed, e.g. in chlorhexidine cream BP. Nonionic emulsifying wax is particularly recommended for use with salts of polyvalent metals and medicaments based on nitrogenous compounds. Creams are susceptible to microbial spoilage and should be adequately preserved.
Nonionic emulsifying wax is also used in nonaqueous ointment bases, such as cetomacrogol emulsifying ointment BP and in barrier creams.

8. Description

Nonionic emulsifying wax is a white or off-white colored waxy solid or flakes which melt when heated to give a clear, almost colorless liquid. Nonionic emulsifying wax has a faint odor characteristic of cetostearyl alcohol.

9. Pharmacopeial Specifications

Test	BP 1993	USPNF XVII (Suppl 7)
Identification	+	—
Melting range	—	50-54°C
Solidifying point	45-53°C	—
pH (3% dispersion)	—	5.5-7.0
Alkalinity	+	—
Acid value	≤ 0.5	—
Hydroxyl value	175-192	178-192
Iodine value	—	≤ 3.5
Refractive index (at 60°C)	1.435-1.439	—
Saponification value	≤ 2.0	≤ 14.0

10. Typical Properties

Density: 0.94 g/cm^3
Flash point: > 55°C
Solubility: freely soluble in aerosol propellants, chloroform, ether, and hydrocarbons; soluble in ethanol (95%); insoluble in water (forms emulsions).

11. Stability and Storage Conditions

Nonionic emulsifying wax is stable and should be stored in a well-closed container in a cool, dry, place.

12. Incompatibilities

Nonionic emulsifying wax is incompatible with tannin, phenol and phenolic materials, resorcinol and benzocaine. It may reduce the antibacterial efficacy of quaternary ammonium compounds.

13. Method of Manufacture

The BP 1993 specifies that cetomacrogol emulsifying wax (nonionic emulsifying wax) may be prepared by melting and mixing together 80 g of cetostearyl alcohol and 20 g of cetomacrogol 1000. The mixture is then stirred until cold.
The USPNF XVII formula for nonionic emulsifying wax is a mixture of unstated proportions of cetostearyl alcohol and a polyoxyethylene derivative of a fatty acid ester of sorbitan.

14. Safety

Nonionic emulsifying wax is used in cosmetics and topical pharmaceutical formulations and is generally regarded as a nontoxic and nonirritant material.

15. Handling Precautions

Observe normal precautions appropriate to the circumstances and quantity of material handled. Eye protection is recommended.

16. Regulatory Status

Included in the FDA Inactive Ingredients Guide (topical aerosols, emulsions, lotions and ointments). Included in nonparenteral medicines licensed in the UK.

17. Pharmacopeias

Br and USPNF. Also in BP Vet.

18. Related Substances

Anionic Emulsifying Wax; cationic emulsifying wax; Cetostearyl Alcohol; Polyoxyethylene Alkyl Ethers.

It should be noted that there are many similar nonionic emulsifying waxes composed of different nonionic surfactants and fatty alcohols.

Cationic emulsifying wax

Synonyms: cetrimide emulsifying wax; *Crodex C.*

Method of manufacture: cetrimide emulsifying wax is prepared similarly to nonionic emulsifying wax and contains 90 g of cetostearyl alcohol and 10 g of cetrimide.

Comments: cationic emulsifying wax is claimed to be of particular value in cosmetic and pharmaceutical formulations when cationic characteristics are important. Thus it can be used in medicated creams, germicidal creams, ointments and lotions, hair conditioners, baby creams and skin care products in which cationic compounds are included. Cationic emulsifying wax is compatible with cationic and nonionic materials, but is incompatible with anionic surfactants and drugs. Additional antimicrobial preservatives should be included in creams. Cetrimide may cause irritation to the eye, *see* Cetrimide.

19. Comments

The nomenclature for emulsifying wax is confused since there are three groups of emulsifying waxes with different titles in the UK and US:

	UK	US
Nonionic	Cetomacrogol emulsifying wax	Emulsifying wax
Anionic	Emulsifying wax	—
Cationic	Cetrimide emulsifying wax	—

Each wax has similar physical properties, but varies in the type of surfactant used which, in turn, affects the range of compatibilities. Emulsifying wax BP and emulsifying wax USPNF contain anionic and nonionic surfactants respectively and are therefore not interchangeable in formulations.

20. Specific References

—

21. General References

Eccleston GM. Properties of fatty alcohol mixed emulsifiers and emulsifying waxes. In: Florence AT, editor. Materials used in pharmaceutical formulation: critical reports on applied chemistry, volume 6. Oxford: Blackwell Scientific Publications, 1984: 124-156.

Hadgraft JW. The emulsifying properties of polyethyleneglycol ethers of cetostearyl alcohol. J Pharm Pharmacol 1954; 6: 816-829.

22. Authors

UK: AJ Winfield.

White Wax

1. Nonproprietary Names

BP: White beeswax
PhEur: Cera alba
USPNF: White wax

2. Synonyms

Bleached wax; E901.

3. Chemical Name and CAS Registry Number

White beeswax [8012-89-3]

4. Empirical Formula   Molecular Weight

White wax is the chemically bleached form of natural beeswax, *see* Section 13.

Beeswax consists of 70-75% of a mixture of various esters of straight chain monohydric alcohols with even number carbon chains from C_{24}-C_{36} esterified with straight chain acids which also have even numbers of carbon atoms up to C_{36} together with some C_{18} hydroxy acids. The chief ester is myricyl palmitate. Also present are free acids (about 14%) and carbohydrates (about 12%) as well as approximately 1% free wax alcohols and stearic esters of fatty acids.

5. Structural Formula

See Section 4.

6. Functional Category

Emulsion stabilizer; stiffening agent.

7. Applications in Pharmaceutical Formulation or Technology

White wax is a chemically bleached form of yellow wax and is used in similar applications, such as to increase the consistency of creams and ointments, and to stabilize water-in-oil emulsions. White wax is also used to polish sugar-coated tablets and to adjust the melting point of suppositories.
See also Yellow Wax.

8. Description

White wax consists of tasteless, white or slightly yellow-colored sheets or fine granules with some translucence. Odor is similar to yellow wax although it is less intense.

9. Pharmacopeial Specifications

Test	PhEur 1981	USPNF XVII
Melting range	61-65°C	62-65°C
Saponification cloud test	—	+
Saponification value	87-104	—
Fats, or fatty acids, Japan wax, rosin and soap	—	+
Acid value	17-24	17-24
Ester value	70-80	72-79
Ratio number	3.3-4.3	—
Ceresin, paraffin and certain other waxes	+	—
Glycerin and other polyhydric alcohols	$\leqslant$ 0.5%	—

10. Typical Properties

Arsenic: $\leqslant$ 3 ppm
Density: 0.95-0.96 g/cm^3
Flash point: 245-258°C
Heavy metals: $\leqslant$ 0.004%
Iodine number: 8-11
Lead: $\leqslant$ 10 ppm
Melting point: 61-65°C
Peroxide value: $\leqslant$ 8
Solubility: soluble in chloroform, ether, fixed oils, volatile oils and warm carbon disulfide; sparingly soluble in ethanol (95%); practically insoluble in water.
Unsaponified matter: 52-55%

HPE Laboratory Project Data			
	Method	Lab #	Results
Density	DE-1	7	0.958 ± 0.006 g/cm^3

11. Stability and Storage Conditions

When heated above 150°C esterification occurs with a consequent lowering of acid value and elevation of melting point. White wax is stable when stored in a well-closed container, protected from light.

12. Incompatibilities

Incompatible with oxidizing agents.

13. Method of Manufacture

Beeswax (yellow wax) is obtained from the honeycomb of the bee [*Apis mellifera* Linné (Fam. Apidae)], *see* Yellow Wax. Subsequent treatment with oxidizing agents bleaches the wax to yield white wax.

14. Safety

Used in both topical and oral formulations, white wax is generally regarded as being an essentially nontoxic and nonirritant material. However, although rare, hypersensitivity reactions to beeswax, attributed to contaminants in the wax, have been reported.[1,2]

15. Handling Precautions

Observe normal precautions appropriate to the circumstances and quantity of material handled.

16. Regulatory Status

GRAS listed. Accepted as a food additive in Europe. Included in the FDA Inactive Ingredients Guide (oral capsules and tablets, rectal, topical and vaginal preparations). Included in nonparenteral medicines licensed in the UK.

17. Pharmacopeias

Aust, Belg, Br, Cz, Egypt, Eur, Fr, Ger, Gr, Hung, Ind, It, Jpn, Mex, Neth, Nord, Port, Rom, Swiss, USPNF and Yug. Also in BP Vet.

18. Related Substances

Yellow Wax.

19. Comments

—

20. Specific References

1. Cronin E. Contact dermatitis from cosmetics. J Soc Cosmet Chem 1967; 18: 681-691.
2. Rothenborg HW. Occupational dermatitis in beekeeper due to poplar resins in beeswax. Arch Dermatol 1967; 95: 381-384.

21. General References

Puleo SL. Beeswax. Cosmet Toilet 1987; 102(6): 57-58.

22. Authors

USA: LD Bighley.

Yellow Wax

1. Nonproprietary Names

BP: Yellow beeswax
PhEur: Cera flava
USPNF: Yellow wax

2. Synonyms

E901; refined wax.

3. Chemical Name and CAS Registry Number

Yellow beeswax [8012-89-3]

4. Empirical Formula   Molecular Weight

Yellow wax is naturally obtained beeswax, *see* Section 13. Beeswax consists of 70-75% of a mixture of various esters of straight chain monohydric alcohols with even number carbon chains from C_{24}-C_{36} esterified with straight chain acids which also have even numbers of carbon atoms up to C_{36} together with some C_{18} hydroxy acids. The chief ester is myricyl palmitate. Also present are free acids (about 14%) and carbohydrates (about 12%) as well as approximately 1% free wax alcohols and stearic esters of fatty acids.

5. Structural Formula

See Section 4.

6. Functional Category

Emulsion stabilizer; stiffening agent.

7. Applications in Pharmaceutical Formulation or Technology

Yellow wax is used in food, cosmetics and confectionery products. However, its main use is in topical pharmaceutical formulations, where it is used at a concentration of 5-20%, as a stiffening agent in ointments and creams. Yellow wax is also employed in emulsions since it enables water to be incorporated into water-in-oil emulsions.
In some oral formulations, yellow wax is used as a polishing agent for sugar-coated tablets; it is also used in sustained release formulations.
Yellow wax forms a soap with borax.

8. Description

Yellow or light brown pieces or plates with a fine-grained matt, noncrystalline fracture and a faint characteristic odor. The wax becomes soft and pliable when warmed.

9. Pharmacopeial Specifications

Test	PhEur 1981	USPNF XVII
Melting range	61-65°C	62-65°C
Saponification cloud test	—	+
Saponification value	87-102	—
Fats, or fatty acids, Japan wax, rosin and soap	—	+
Acid value	17-22	17-24
Ester value	70-80	72-79

Continued

Test	PhEur 1981	USPNF XVII
Ratio number	3.3-4.3	—
Ceresin, paraffin and certain other waxes	+	—
Glycerin and other polyhydric alcohols	⩽ 0.5%	—

10. Typical Properties

Acid value: 20
Arsenic: ⩽ 3 ppm
Density: 0.950-0.960 g/cm^3
Flash point: 245-258°C
Heavy metals: ⩽ 0.004%
Iodine number: 8-11
Lead: ⩽ 10 ppm
Melting point: 61-65°C
Peroxide value: ⩽ 8
Refractive index: 1.440-1.445
Solubility: soluble in chloroform, ether, fixed oils, volatile oils, and warm carbon disulfide; sparingly soluble in ethanol (95%); practically insoluble in water.
Unsaponified matter: 52-55%
Viscosity (kinematic):
1470 mm^2/s (1470 cSt) at 99°C

11. Stability and Storage Conditions

When heated above 150°C esterification occurs with a consequent lowering of acid value and elevation of melting point. Yellow wax is stable when stored in a well-closed container, protected from light.

12. Incompatibilities

Incompatible with oxidizing agents.

13. Method of Manufacture

Yellow wax is a natural secretion of bees [*Apis mellifera* Linné (Fam. Apidae)] and is obtained commercially from honeycombs. Honey is abstracted from combs either by draining or centrifugation and water added to the remaining wax to remove soluble impurities. Hot water is then added to form a floating melt which is strained to remove foreign matter. The wax is then poured into flat dishes or molds to cool and harden.

14. Safety

Used in both topical and oral formulations, yellow wax is generally regarded as being an essentially nontoxic and nonirritant material. However, hypersensitivity reactions attributed to contaminants in the wax, although rare, have been reported.[1,2]

15. Handling Precautions

Observe normal precautions appropriate to the circumstances and quantity of material handled.

16. Regulatory Status

GRAS listed. Accepted as a food additive in Europe. Included in the FDA Inactive Ingredients Guide (oral capsules and tablets, and topical preparations). Included in nonparenteral medicines licensed in the UK.

17. Pharmacopeias

Aust, Belg, Br, Chin, Egypt, Eur, Fr, Ger, Ind, It, Jpn, Neth, Nord, Port, Rom, Swiss, USPNF and Yug.

18. Related Substances

White Wax.

19. Comments

—

20. Specific References

1. Cronin E. Contact dermatitis from cosmetics. J Soc Cosmet Chem 1967; 18: 681-691.
2. Rothenborg HW. Occupational dermatitis in beekeeper due to poplar resins in beeswax. Arch Dermatol 1967; 95: 381-384.

21. General References

Puleo SL. Beeswax. Cosmet Toilet 1987; 102(6): 57-58.

22. Authors

USA: LD Bighley.

Xanthan Gum

1. Nonproprietary Names

USPNF: Xanthan gum

2. Synonyms

Corn sugar gum; E415; *Keltrol*; *Merezan*; polysaccharide B-1459; *Rhodigel*; xantham gum.

3. Chemical Name and CAS Registry Number

Xanthan gum [11138-66-2]

4. Empirical Formula   Molecular Weight

The USPNF XVII describes xanthan gum as a high molecular weight polysaccharide gum. It contains D-glucose and D-mannose as the dominant hexose units, along with D-glucuronic acid, and is prepared as the sodium, potassium, or calcium salt. The molecular weight is approximately 2×10^6.

5. Structural Formula

Each xanthan gum repeat unit contains five sugar residues: two glucose; two mannose and one glucuronic acid. The polymer backbone consists of four β-D-glucose units linked at the 1 and 4 positions, and is therefore identical in structure to cellulose. Trisaccharide side chains on alternating anhydroglucose units distinguish xanthan gum from cellulose. Each side chain comprises a glucuronic acid residue between two mannose units. At most of the terminal mannose units is a pyruvate moiety; the mannose nearest the main chain carries a single group at C-6. The resulting stiff polymer chain may exist in solution, as a single, double or triple helix which interacts with other xanthan gum molecules to form complex, loosely bound networks.[1,2]

6. Functional Category

Stabilizing agent; suspending agent; viscosity-increasing agent.

7. Applications in Pharmaceutical Formulation or Technology

Xanthan gum is widely used in oral and topical pharmaceutical formulations, cosmetics, and foods as a suspending and stabilizing agent.[3,4]

It is nontoxic, compatible with most other pharmaceutical ingredients and has good stability and viscosity properties over a wide pH and temperature range, *see* Section 11.

When mixed with certain inorganic suspending agents, such as magnesium aluminum silicate, or organic gums, synergistic rheological effects occur.[5] In general, mixtures of xanthan gum and magnesium aluminum silicate in ratios between 1:2 and 1:9 produce the optimum properties. Similarly, optimum synergistic effects are obtained with xanthan gum:guar gum ratios of between 3:7 and 1:9.

Although primarily used as a suspending agent xanthan gum has also been used to prepare sustained release matrix tablets.[6-8]

8. Description

Xanthan gum occurs as a cream or white-colored, odorless, free-flowing, fine powder.

9. Pharmacopeial Specifications

Test	USPNF XVII (Suppl 6)
Identification	+
Viscosity	+
Microbial limits	+
Loss on drying	$\leqslant$ 15.0%
Ash	6.5-16.0%
Arsenic	$\leqslant$ 3 ppm
Heavy metals	$\leqslant$ 0.003%
Lead	$\leqslant$ 5 ppm
Isopropyl alcohol	$\leqslant$ 0.075%
Pyruvic acid	$\geqslant$ 1.5%
Assay	91.0-108.0%

10. Typical Properties

Acidity/alkalinity: pH = 6-8 for a 1% w/v aqueous solution.
Freezing point: 0°C for a 1% w/v aqueous solution.
Heat of combustion: 14.6 J/g (3.5 cal/g)
Melting point: chars at 270°C
Particle size distribution: 100% less than 250 μm, 95% less than 177 μm in size for *Rhodigel*; 100% less than 177 μm, 92% less than 74 μm in size for *Rhodigel 200*.
Refractive index:
n_D^{20} = 1.333 for a 1% w/v aqueous solution.
Solubility: practically insoluble in ethanol and ether; soluble in cold or warm water.
Specific gravity: 1.600 at 25°C
Viscosity (dynamic): 1200-1600 mPa s (1200-1600 cP) for a 1% w/v aqueous solution at 25°C.

11. Stability and Storage Conditions

Xanthan gum is a stable material. Aqueous solutions are stable over a wide pH range (pH 3-12) and temperatures between 10-60°C. Xanthan gum solutions less than 1% w/v concentration may be adversely affected by higher than ambient temperatures, e.g. viscosity is reduced. Solutions are also stable in the presence of enzymes, salts, acids and bases.

The bulk material should be stored in a well-closed container in a cool, dry, place.

12. Incompatibilities

Xanthan gum is an anionic material and is not usually compatible with cationic surfactants, polymers and preservatives since precipitation occurs. Anionic and amphoteric surfactants at concentrations above 15% cause precipitation of xanthan gum from a solution.

Under highly alkaline conditions polyvalent metal ions, such as calcium, cause gelation or precipitation; this may be inhibited by the addition of a glucoheptonate sequestrant. The presence of low levels of borates (< 300 ppm) can also cause gelation. This may be avoided by increasing the boron ion concentration or by lowering the pH of a formulation to less than pH 5. The addition of ethylene glycol, sorbitol, or mannitol may also prevent this gelation.

Xanthan gum is compatible with most synthetic and natural viscosity-increasing agents. If it is to be combined with cellulose derivatives then xanthan gum free of cellulase should be used to prevent depolymerization of the cellulose derivative.

The viscosity of xanthan gum solutions is considerably increased, or gelation occurs, in the presence of some materials such as guar gum, locust bean gum and magnesium aluminum silicate.[5] This effect is most pronounced in deionized water and reduced by the presence of salt. This interaction may be desirable in some instances and can be exploited to reduce the amount of xanthan gum used in a formulation, *see* Section 7.

Xanthan gum solutions are stable in the presence of up to 60% water-miscible organic solvents such as acetone, methanol, ethanol or propan-2-ol. However, above this concentration precipitation or gelation occurs.

Xanthan gum is also incompatible with oxidizing agents, some tablet film-coatings,[4] carboxymethylcellulose sodium,[9] dried aluminum hydroxide gel[10] and some active ingredients such as amitriptyline, tamoxifen and verapamil.[3]

13. Method of Manufacture

Xanthan gum is a polysaccharide produced by a pure-culture aerobic fermentation of a carbohydrate with *Xanthomonas campestris*. The polysaccharide is then purified by recovery with propan-2-ol, dried, and milled.[11,12]

14. Safety

Xanthan gum is widely used in oral and topical pharmaceutical formulations, cosmetics and food products and is generally regarded as nontoxic and nonirritant at the levels employed as a pharmaceutical excipient.

The estimated acceptable daily intake for xanthan gum has been set by the WHO at up to 10 mg/kg body-weight.[12]

LD_{50} (dog, oral): > 20 g/kg [13]
LD_{50} (rat, oral): > 45 g/kg

15. Handling Precautions

Observe normal precautions appropriate to the circumstances and quantity of material handled. Eye protection and gloves are recommended.

16. Regulatory Status

GRAS listed. Accepted for use as a food additive in Europe. Included in the FDA Inactive Ingredients Guide (oral solutions, suspensions and tablets; rectal and topical preparations). Included in nonparenteral medicines licensed in the UK.

17. Pharmacopeias

Mex and USPNF.

18. Related Substances

-

19. Comments

Xanthan gum is available in several different grades which have varying particle sizes, e.g. *Rhodigel EZ*, *Rhodigel* and *Rhodigel 200* (Rhône-Poulenc Chemicals) where *Rhodigel EZ* is the coarsest and *Rhodigel 200* the finest material. Fine mesh grades of xanthan gum are used in applications where high solubility is desirable since they dissolve rapidly in water. However, fine mesh grades disperse more slowly than coarse grades and are best used dry blended with the other ingredients of a formulation. In general, it is preferable to dissolve xanthan gum in water first and then add the other ingredients of a formulation.

20. Specific References

1. Jansson PE, Kenne L, Lindberg B. Structure of extracellular polysaccharide from *Xanthamonas campestris*. Carbohydrate Res 1975; 45: 275-282.
2. Melton LD, Mindt L, Rees DA, Sanderson GR. Covalent structure of the polysaccharide from *Xanthamonas campestris*: evidence from partial hydrolysis studies. Carbohydrate Res 1976; 46: 245-257.
3. Bumphrey G. 'Extremely useful' new suspending agent. Pharm J 1986; 237: 665.
4. Evans BK, Fenton-May V. Keltrol [letter]. Pharm J 1986; 237: 736-737.
5. Kovacs P. Useful incompatibility of xanthan gum with galactomannans. Food Technol 1973; 27(3): 26-30.
6. Lu MF, Woodward L, Borodkin S. Xanthan gum and alginate based controlled release theophylline formulations. Drug Dev Ind Pharm 1991; 17: 1987-2004.
7. Dhopeshwarkar V, Zatz JL. Evaluation of xanthan gum in the preparation of sustained release matrix tablets. Drug Dev Ind Pharm 1993; 19: 999-1017.
8. Talukdar M, Plaizier-Vercammen J. Evaluation of xanthan gum as a hydrophilic matrix for controlled-release dosage form preparations. Drug Dev Ind Pharm 1993; 19: 1037-1046.
9. Walker CV, Wells JI. Rheological synergism between ionic and non-ionic cellulose gums. Int J Pharmaceutics 1982; 11: 309-322.
10. Zatz JL, Figler D, Livero K. Fluidization of aluminum hydroxide gels containing xanthan gum. Drug Dev Ind Pharm 1986; 12: 561-568.
11. Jeanes AR, Pittsley JE, Senti FR. Polysaccharide B-1459: a new hydrocolloid polyelectrolyte produced from glucose by bacterial fermentation. J Appl Polym Sci 1961; 5(17): 519-526.
12. Godet P. Fermentation of polysaccharide gums. Process Biochem 1973; 8(1): 33.
13. FAO/WHO. Evaluation of certain food additives and contaminants. Twenty-ninth report of the joint FAO/WHO expert committee on food additives. Tech Rep Ser Wld Hlth Org 1986; No. 733.
14. The Boots Company Ltd. Technical literature: xanthan gum, 1981.

21. General References

Gamini A, De Bleijer J, Leute JC. Physicochemical properties of aqueous solutions of xanthan: an NMR study. Carbohydrate Res 1991; 220: 33-47.
Kelco Division of Merck & Co Inc. Technical literature: xanthan gum - natural biogum for scientific water control, 3rd edition, 1991.
Rhône-Poulenc Chemicals. Technical literature: *Rhodigel* - food grade xanthan gum, 1991.
Shatwell KP, Sutherland IW, Ross-Murphy SB. Influence of acetyl and pyruvate substituents on the solution properties of xanthan polysaccharide. Int J Biol Macromol 1990; 12(2): 71-78.
Whitcomb PJ. Rheology of xanthan gum. J Rheology 1978; 22(5): 493-505.
Zatz JL. Applications of gums in pharmaceutical and cosmetic suspensions. Ind Eng Chem Prod Res Dev 1984; 23: 12-16.

22. Authors

USA: SA Daskalakis.

Xylitol

1. Nonproprietary Names
USPNF: Xylitol

2. Synonyms
E967; *Klinit*; *Xilitol*; *Xylifin*; *Xylit*; *Xylitab*; *meso*-xylitol; *Xylitolo*.

3. Chemical Name and CAS Registry Number
xylo-Pentane-1,2,3,4,5-pentol [87-99-0]

4. Empirical Formula   Molecular Weight
$C_5H_{12}O_5$ 152.15

5. Structural Formula

$$\begin{array}{c} CH_2OH \\ | \\ H-C-OH \\ | \\ HO-C-H \\ | \\ H-C-OH \\ | \\ CH_2OH \end{array}$$

6. Functional Category
Sweetening agent.

7. Applications in Pharmaceutical Formulation or Technology
Xylitol is used as a non-cariogenic sweetening agent in tablets, syrups and coatings. It is also used as an alternative to sucrose in foods, confectionery and toiletries. Xylitol has additionally been proposed as an energy source for intravenous infusion after trauma.[1]

8. Description
Xylitol occurs as a white, granular solid comprising crystalline, equi-dimensional particles having a mean diameter of about 0.4-0.7 mm. It is odorless, with a sweet taste that imparts a cooling sensation. Xylitol is also commercially available in powdered form and several granular, directly compressible forms.[2] *See also* Section 18.

9. Pharmacopeial Specifications

Test	USPNF XVII
Identification	+
Water	≤ 0.5%
Residue on ignition	≤ 0.5%
Arsenic	≤ 3 ppm
Heavy metals	≤ 0.001%
Reducing sugars (as dextrose)	≤ 0.2%
Other polyols	≤ 2.0%
Assay (anhydrous basis)	98.5-101.0%

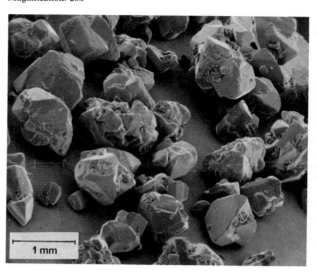

SEM: 1
Excipient: xylitol
Magnification: 20x

1 mm

10. Typical Properties
Acidity/alkalinity:
pH = 5.0-7.0 (5% w/v aqueous solution).
Boiling point: 215-217°C for metastable form.
Compressibility: *see* Fig. 1. Xylitol, under the same test conditions, produces 11.2 mm tablets of 40 N hardness at 20 kN compression force.
Density: 1.52 g/cm^3
Density (bulk): 0.5-0.7 g/cm^3
Melting point:
61.0-61.5°C for metastable form;
92.0-95.0°C for stable form.
Moisture content: at 20°C and 52% relative humidity the equilibrium moisture content of xylitol is 0.1% w/w. After drying in vacuum, over P_2O_5 at 80°C for 4 hours, xylitol loses less than 0.5% w/w water. *See also* Fig. 2.
Osmolarity: a 4.56% w/v aqueous solution is iso-osmotic with serum.
Particle size distribution: *see* Fig. 3, 4 and 5.
Solubility:

Solvent	Solubility at 20°C
Ethanol	1 in 80
Glycerin	very slightly soluble
Methanol	1 in 16.7
Peanut oil	very slightly soluble
Propan-2-ol	1 in 500
Propylene glycol	1 in 15
Pyridine	soluble
Water	1 in 1.6

Specific rotation: not optically active.
Viscosity (dynamic): *see* Fig. 6.

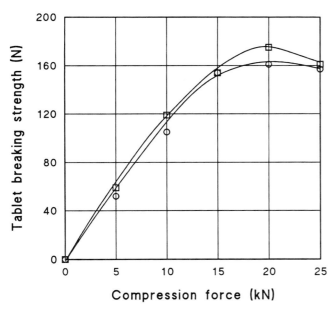

Fig. 1: Compression characteristics of *Xylitab 100* and *Xylitab 200* [Xyrofin (UK) Ltd].
○ Xylitol with 3% polydextrose (*Xylitab 100*).
□ Xylitol with 1.5% carboxymethylcellulose (*Xylitab 200*).
Tablet weight: 550 mg
Tablet size: 11.2 mm, flat bevelled
Lubricant: 1% w/w magnesium stearate
Tablets produced using Manesty Betapress.

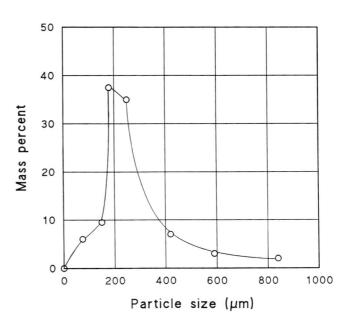

Fig. 3: Particle size distribution of Xylitol with 3% polydextrose [*Xylitab 100*, Xyrofin (UK) Ltd].

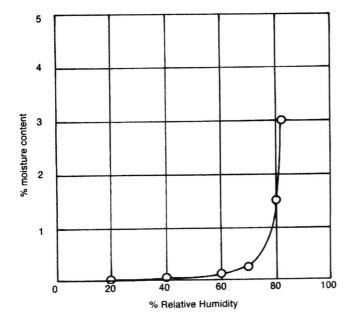

Fig. 2: Moisture sorption isotherm of xylitol at 20°C.

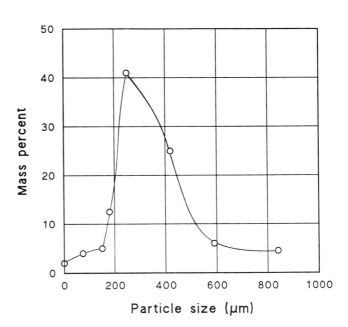

Fig. 4: Particle size distribution of Xylitol with 1.5% carboxymethylcellulose [*Xylitab 200*, Xyrofin (UK) Ltd].

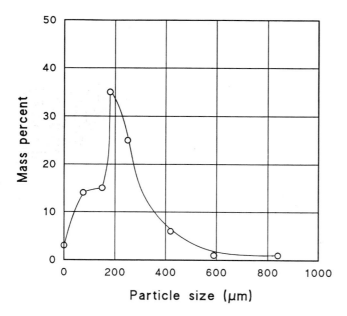

Fig. 5: Particle size distribution of Xylitol [*Xylitab 300*, Xyrofin (UK) Ltd].

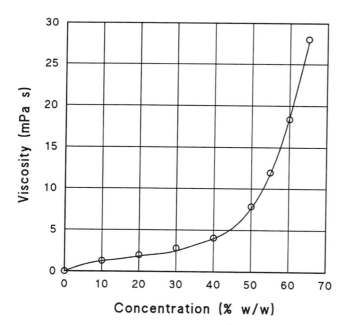

Fig. 6: Viscosity of aqueous xylitol solutions at 20°C.

11. Stability and Storage Conditions

Xylitol is stable to heat but is slightly hygroscopic. Caramelization can occur only if it is heated for several minutes near its boiling point. It is stable for at least one year if stored at less than 65% relative humidity and 25°C. Aqueous xylitol solutions have been reported to be stable, even on prolonged heating and storage. Since it is not utilized by most microorganisms, products made with xylitol are usually safe from fermentation and microbial spoilage.[3,4]

Xylitol should be stored in a well-closed container in a cool, dry, place.

12. Incompatibilities

Incompatible with oxidizing agents.

13. Method of Manufacture

Xylitol is derived from various types of cellulose obtained from such sources as wood, straw, cane pulp, seed hulls and shells. These materials usually contain 20-35% xylan, which is readily converted to xylose by hydrolysis; xylose is then converted to xylitol by hydrogenation. Possible impurities are mannitol, sorbitol, galactitol or arabitol.

Xylitol can also be made biologically through yeast fermentation or by oxalic acid treatment of cellulose products.

14. Safety

Xylitol is used in oral pharmaceutical formulations and food products and is generally regarded as an essentially nontoxic and nonirritant material.

Up to 200 g of xylitol in divided oral doses may be tolerated daily although like other polyols large doses have a laxative effect. The laxative threshold depends on a number of factors including individual sensitivity, mode of ingestion, daily diet and previous adaption to xylitol. Single doses of 20-30 g are usually tolerated. Approximately 20% of ingested xylitol is absorbed.

An acceptable daily intake for xylitol has not been specified by the WHO, since the level of use in foods does not represent a hazard to health.[5]

LD_{50} (mouse, IV): 3.77 g/kg[6]
LD_{50} (mouse, oral): 12.5 g/kg
LD_{50} (rabbit, IV): 4 g/kg
LD_{50} (rabbit, oral): 25 g/kg
LD_{50} (rat, oral): 17.3 g/kg

15. Handling Precautions

Observe normal precautions appropriate to the circumstances and quantity of material handled. Xylitol may be harmful if ingested in large quantities; may also be irritant to the eyes. Eye protection is recommended. Xylitol is flammable.

16. Regulatory Status

GRAS listed. Accepted as a food additive in Europe. Included in nonparenteral medicines licensed in the UK.

17. Pharmacopeias

Cz, Jpn and USPNF.

18. Related Substances

Various directly compressible forms of xylitol which contain other excipients are commercially available, e.g. *Xylitab* (Edward Mendell Co Inc) which contains 3% sorbitol; *Xylitab 100* which contains 3% polydextrose, and *Xylitab*

200 which contains 1.5% carboxymethylcellulose [both Xyrofin (UK) Ltd].

Pyrogen free grades of xylitol suitable for parenteral use are also commercially available.

19. Comments

The sweetening power of xylitol is approximately equal to that of sucrose, although it has been shown to be pH, concentration, and temperature dependent; it is 2.5 times as sweet as mannitol.

Xylitol does not promote dental caries[7-9] and has a negative heat of solution which is larger than alternative common sweetening agents, *see* below:

Sweetening agent	Heat of solution (J/g)
Mannitol	- 120.9
Sorbitol	- 111.3
Sucrose	- 18.0
Xylitol	- 153.1

20. Specific References

1. Georgieff M, Moldawer LL, Bistrian BR, Blackburn GL. Xylitol, an energy source for intravenous nutrition after trauma. J Parenter Enteral Nutr 1985; 9: 199-209.
2. Garr JSM, Rubinstein MH. Direct compression characteristics of xylitol. Int J Pharmaceutics 1990; 64: 223-226.
3. Emodi A. Xylitol: its properties and food applications. Food Technol 1978; (Jan): 28-32.
4. Makinen KK, Soderling E. Effect of xylitol on some food spoilage microorganisms. J Food Sci 1981; 46(3): 950-951.
5. FAO/WHO. Evaluation of certain food additives and contaminants: twenty-seventh report of the joint FAO/WHO expert committee on food additives. Tech Rep Ser Wld Hlth Org 1983; No. 696.
6. Sweet DV, editor. Registry of toxic effects of chemical substances. Cincinnati: US Department of Health, 1987.
7. Scheinin A. Xylitol in relation to oral and general health. Int Dent J 1979; 29: 237-243.
8. Bär A. Caries prevention with xylitol: a review of the scientific evidence. Wld Rev Nutr Diet 1988; 55: 183-209.
9. Makinen KK. Latest dental studies on xylitol and mechanism of action of xylitol in caries limitation. In: Grenby TH, editor. Progress in sweeteners. London: Elsevier, 1989: 331-362.

21. General References

Counsell JN. Xylitol. London: Applied Science Publishers Ltd, 1978.
Thomas SE, Ali MA, Craig DQM, Taylor J, Chatham SM. The use of xylitol as a carrier for liquid-filled hard-gelatin capsules. Pharm Technol Int 1991; 3(9): 36-40.
Ylikahri R. Metabolic and nutritional aspects of xylitol. Adv Food Res 1979; 25: 159-180.

22. Authors

UK: HEC Worthington.
USA: PM Olinger.

Zein

1. Nonproprietary Names
USPNF: Zein

2. Synonyms
—

3. Chemical Name and CAS Registry Number
Zein [9010-66-6]

4. Empirical Formula   Molecular Weight
— $\approx 38\,000$

5. Structural Formula
See Section 8.

6. Functional Category
Coating agent; extended release agent; tablet binder.

7. Applications in Pharmaceutical Formulation or Technology
Zein is used as a tablet binder in wet granulation processes or as a tablet coating agent. It is primarily used as an enteric coating agent or in extended release oral tablet formulations.[1] Zein is also used in food applications as a coating agent.

Use	Concentration (%)
Tablet coating agent	15
Tablet sealer	20
Wet granulation binder	30

8. Description
Zein is a prolamine obtained from corn [*Zea mays* Linné (Fam. Gramineae)]. It occurs as a granular, straw to pale yellow-colored amorphous powder or fine flakes and has a characteristic odor and bland taste.
For amino acid composition, *see* Section 19.

9. Pharmacopeial Specifications

Test	USPNF XVII
Identification	+
Microbial limits	+
Loss on drying	$\leqslant 8.0\%$
Residue on ignition	$\leqslant 2.0\%$
Arsenic	$\leqslant 3$ ppm
Heavy metals	$\leqslant 0.002\%$
Nitrogen content	13.1-17.0%

10. Typical Properties
Density: 1.23 g/cm³
Melting point: when completely dry it may be heated to 200°C without visible signs of decomposition.
Particle size distribution: 100% < 840 μm in size.
Solubility: practically insoluble in acetone, ethanol and water; soluble in aqueous alcohol solutions, aqueous acetone solutions (60-80% v/v) and glycols. Also soluble in aqueous alkaline solutions of pH 11.5 and above.

11. Stability and Storage Conditions
Zein should be stored in an airtight container, in a cool, dry, place.

12. Incompatibilities
Incompatible with oxidizing agents.

13. Method of Manufacture
Zein is extracted from corn gluten meal with dilute propan-2-ol.

14. Safety
Zein is used in oral pharmaceutical formulations and food products and is generally regarded as an essentially nontoxic and nonirritant material at the levels employed as an excipient. However, it may be harmful if ingested in large quantities. *See also* Section 19.

15. Handling Precautions
Observe normal precautions appropriate to the circumstances and quantity of material handled. Zein may be irritant to the eyes and may evolve toxic fumes on combustion. Eye protection and gloves are recommended.

16. Regulatory Status
GRAS listed. Included in the FDA Inactive Ingredients Guide (oral tablets).

17. Pharmacopeias
USPNF.

18. Related Substances
—

19. Comments
Zein is a protein derivative that does not contain lysine or tryptophan. The approximate amino acid content is shown below:

Alanine	8.3%	Lysine	0.0%
Arginine	1.8%	Methionine	2.0%
Asparagine	4.5%	Phenylalanine	6.8%
Cystine	0.8%	Proline	9.0%
Glutamic acid	1.5%	Serine	5.7%
Glutamine	21.4%	Threonine	2.7%
Glycine	0.7%	Tryptophan	0.0%
Histidine	1.1%	Tyrosine	5.1%
Isoleucine	6.2%	Valine	3.1%
Leucine	19.3%		

Zein may be safely consumed by persons sensitive to gluten.

20. Specific References
1. Katayama H, Kanke M. Drug release from directly compressed tablets containing zein. Drug Dev Ind Pharm 1992; 18: 2173-2184.

21. General References
—

22. Authors
USA: EL Brunson.

Zinc Stearate

1. Nonproprietary Names

BP: Zinc stearate
PhEur: Zinci stearas
USP: Zinc stearate

2. Synonyms

HyQual; stearic acid zinc salt; zinc distearate.

3. Chemical Name and CAS Registry Number

Octadecanoic acid zinc salt [557-05-1]

4. Empirical Formula   Molecular Weight

$C_{36}H_{70}O_4Zn$ 632.33
(for pure material)

The USP XXII describes zinc stearate as a compound of zinc with a mixture of solid organic acids obtained from fats, and consists chiefly of variable proportions of zinc stearate and zinc palmitate. It contains the equivalent of 12.5-14.0% of zinc oxide (ZnO).

The BP 1993 and PhEur 1984 similarly describe zinc stearate as consisting mainly of zinc stearate $[(C_{17}H_{35}COO)_2Zn]$ with variable proportions of zinc palmitate $[(C_{15}H_{31}COO)_2Zn]$ and zinc oleate $[(C_{17}H_{33}COO)_2Zn]$. It contains the equivalent of 10.0-12.0% of zinc.

5. Structural Formula

$(C_{17}H_{35}COO)_2Zn$

6. Functional Category

Tablet and capsule lubricant.

7. Applications in Pharmaceutical Formulation or Technology

Zinc stearate is primarily used in pharmaceutical formulations as a lubricant in tablet and capsule manufacture at concentrations up to 1.5% w/w. It has also been used as a thickening and opacifying agent in cosmetic and pharmaceutical creams and as a dusting powder.

Use	Concentration (%)
Tablet lubricant	0.5-1.5
Water repellent ointments	2.5

8. Description

Zinc stearate occurs as a fine, white, bulky, hydrophobic powder, free from grittiness and with a faint characteristic odor.

9. Pharmacopeial Specifications

Test	PhEur 1984	USP XXII
Identification	+	+
Acidity or alkalinity	+	—
Alkalis and alkaline earths	—	+
Appearance of solution	+	—

Continued

Test	PhEur 1984	USP XXII
Acid value of the fatty acids	195-210	—
Appearance of solution of fatty acids	+	—
Arsenic	—	≤ 1.5 ppm
Cadmium	≤ 5 ppm	—
Lead	≤ 25 ppm	≤ 0.001%
Chlorides	≤ 250 ppm	—
Sulfates	≤ 0.6%	—
Assay (as Zn)	10.0-12.0%	—
Assay (as ZnO)	—	12.5-14.0%

SEM: 1
Excipient: Zinc stearate
Magnification: 600x

SEM: 2
Excipient: Zinc stearate
Magnification: 2400x

10. Typical Properties

Autoignition temperature: 421°C
Density: 1.09 g/cm^3
Density (tapped): 0.26 g/cm^3 for Standard grade (Durham Chemicals).
Flash point: 277°C
Melting point: 120-122°C
Particle size distribution: 100% through a 44.5 μm sieve (#325 mesh).
Solubility: practically insoluble in ethanol (95%), ether and water; soluble in benzene.

11. Stability and Storage Conditions

Zinc stearate is stable and should be stored in a well-closed container in a cool, dry, place.

12. Incompatibilities

Zinc stearate is decomposed by dilute acids.

13. Method of Manufacture

An aqueous solution of zinc sulfate is added to sodium stearate solution to precipitate zinc stearate. The zinc stearate is then washed with water and dried. Zinc stearate may also be prepared from stearic acid and zinc chloride.

14. Safety

Zinc stearate is used in oral and topical pharmaceutical formulations and is generally regarded as a nontoxic and nonirritant excipient. However, following inhalation, it has been associated with fatal pneumonitis particularly in infants. As a result, zinc stearate has now been removed from baby dusting powders.

15. Handling Precautions

Observe normal precautions appropriate to the circumstances and quantity of material handled. Eye protection and gloves are recommended. Zinc stearate may be harmful on inhalation and should be used in a well ventilated environment; a respirator is recommended. In the UK, the long-term (8-hour TWA) occupational exposure limit for zinc stearate is 10 mg/m^3 for total inhalable dust and 5 mg/m^3 for respirable dust.[1]
When heated to decomposition zinc stearate emits acrid smoke and fumes of zinc oxide.

16. Regulatory Status

GRAS listed. Included in the FDA Inactive Ingredients Guide (oral capsules and tablets). Included in nonparenteral medicines licensed in the UK.

17. Pharmacopeias

Aust, Br, Eur, Fr, Gr, Ind, It, Mex, Neth, Port, Swiss, Turk and US.

18. Related Substances

Calcium Stearate; Magnesium Stearate; Stearic Acid.

19. Comments

See Magnesium Stearate for further information and references.

20. Specific References

1. Health and Safety Executive. EH40/93: occupational exposure limits 1993. London: HMSO, 1993.

21. General References

—

22. Authors

USA: LV Allen.

Appendix I: Suppliers' Directory

Excipients List

Acacia
UK
AF Suter & Co Ltd
Arthur Branwell & Co Ltd
Berk Chemicals Ltd
Courtin & Warner Ltd
Eggar & Co (Chemicals) Ltd
Gale & Mount Ltd
Guinness Chemical (Ireland) Ltd
Interpharm Ltd
John Kellys (Merchants) Ltd
LS Raw Materials Ltd
Medex Medical Export Co Ltd
Merck Ltd
Pacegrove Ltd
Raught Ltd
Rhône-Poulenc Chemicals
SA Shepherd & Co Ltd
SBP Ltd
Thew, Arnott & Co Ltd

Other European
Alland & Robert
Colloides Naturels International
E. Merck
Polysciences Ltd

USA
Chart Corp Inc
EM Industries Inc
Functional Foods
Gumix International Inc
Meer Corp
Mutchler Chemical Co Inc
Penta Manufacturing Co
Spectrum Chemical Mfg Corp
The Lebermuth Co Inc
Van Waters & Rogers Inc
Zumbro Inc

Acesulfame Potassium
UK
Hoechst UK Ltd
MDA Chemicals Ltd

Albumin
UK
Chesham Chemicals Ltd
Ubichem Ltd

Other European
Bayer Diagnosticos SA
Kraeber GmbH & Co

Organon Teknika NV

USA
Amresco Inc
Organon Teknika Corp
Penta Manufacturing Co
Viobin Corp

Alcohol
UK
Alcohols Ltd
BP Chemicals Ltd
Hayman Ltd
Joseph Mills (Denaturants) Ltd
Merck Ltd
Pacegrove Ltd
Tunnel Refineries Ltd

Other European
E. Merck
Polysciences Ltd

USA
Ashland Chemical Company
Biospur Inc
EM Industries Inc
Grain Processing Corporation
Penta Manufacturing Co
Spectrum Chemical Mfg Corp
Van Waters & Rogers Inc
Vista Chemical Company

Alginic Acid
UK
Arthur Branwell & Co Ltd
Chesham Chemicals Ltd
Grinsted Products Ltd
Kelco International Ltd
LS Raw Materials Ltd
MDA Chemicals Ltd
Protan Ltd
Sanofi Bio-Industries Ltd

Other European
Grinsted Products
Laserson SA
Polysciences Ltd
Protan A/S
Sobalg

USA
Edward Mendell Co Inc
Functional Foods
Grinsted Products Inc
Kelco Division of Merck & Co Inc
Meer Corp
Penta Manufacturing Co
Protan Inc
Spectrum Chemical Mfg Corp

Others
Sansho Co

Alpha Tocopherol
UK

A & E Connock (Perfumery & Cosmetics) Ltd
BASF Plc
Blagden Chemicals Ltd
Cornelius Chemical Co Ltd
Eastman Fine Chemicals
Eisai Pharma-Chem Europe Ltd
Henkel Organics
LS Raw Materials Ltd
MDA Chemicals Ltd
Merck Ltd
Rhône-Poulenc Chemicals
Roche Products Ltd
Ubichem Ltd

Other European
E. Merck
Henkel KGaA
Hoffmann-La Roche AG
Jan Dekker BV
Laserson SA

USA
BASF Corporation
Eastman Fine Chemicals
Eisai USA Inc
EM Industries Inc
Helm New York Chemical Corp
Hoffmann-La Roche Inc
Penta Manufacturing Co
Protameen Chemicals Inc
Rhône-Poulenc Inc
Schweizerhall Inc
Spectrum Chemical Mfg Corp
Vitamins Inc
Vivion Inc

Others
Eisai Co Ltd

Ascorbic Acid
UK
Allchem International Ltd
AMC Chemicals
BASF Plc
Berk Chemicals Ltd
Cornelius Chemical Co Ltd
Courtin & Warner Ltd
Farleyway Chemicals Ltd
Forum Chemicals Ltd
Harbottle (Pharmaceuticals) Ltd
Interpharm Ltd
John Kellys (Merchants) Ltd
LS Raw Materials Ltd
Magnesia UK
Medex Medical Export Co Ltd
Merck Ltd
MDA Chemicals Ltd
Pacegrove Ltd
Paldena Ltd
Peter Whiting (Chemicals) Ltd
Pfizer Food Science Group
Pointing Group
Raught Ltd
Roche Products Ltd
SBP Ltd

Scan Chem UK Ltd
TA Chemicals

Other European
E. Merck
Hoffmann-La Roche AG
Laserson SA
Polysciences Ltd
Takeda Europe GmbH

USA
American Ingredients Inc
Amresco Inc
Ashland Chemical Company
BASF Corporation
Chemco Industries Inc
EM Industries Inc
Functional Foods
Harrisons Trading Co Inc
Helm New York Chemical Corp
Hoffmann-La Roche Inc
International Sourcing Inc
Jungbunzlauer Inc
Kraft Chemical Company
Merona Chemicals Ltd
Penta Manufacturing Co
Pfizer Food Science Group
Schweizerhall Inc
Spectrum Chemical Mfg Corp
The Lebermuth Co Inc
Van Waters & Roger Inc
Vitamins Inc
Vivion Inc
Weinstein Nutritional Products

Others
Chorney Chemical Co

Ascorbyl Palmitate
UK
Merck Ltd
Roche Products Ltd

Other European
E. Merck
Grinsted Products
Hoffmann-La Roche AG
Jan Dekker BV
Laserson SA

USA
EM Industries Inc
Hoffmann-La Roche Inc

Aspartame
UK
Cerestar UK Ltd
Cornelius Chemical Co Ltd
DSM United Kingdom
Forum Chemicals Ltd
Interpharm Ltd
John Kellys (Merchants) Ltd
LS Raw Materials Ltd
Magnesia UK
MDA Chemicals Ltd
NutraSweet AG

Sanofi Bio-Industries Ltd
SBP Ltd
Scan Chem UK Ltd
TA Chemicals
Thew, Arnott & Co Ltd

Other European
Cerestar International Sales
Chemag AG
DSM Special Products BV
Holland Sweetener Company
NutraSweet AG

USA
DSM Fine Chemicals USA Inc

Others
Chorney Chemical Co

Bentonite
UK
A & E Connock (Perfumery & Cosmetics) Ltd
Bromhead & Denison Ltd
Bush Beach Ltd
Cornelius Chemical Co Ltd
Courtin & Warner Ltd
Farleyway Chemicals Ltd
Laporte Absorbents
Magnesia UK
Medex Medical Export Co Ltd
Pacegrove Ltd
Raught Ltd
Redland Minerals Ltd
SBP Ltd
Ubichem Ltd
Volclay Ltd
Wilfrid Smith Ltd

USA
American Colliod Co
Charles B Chrystal Co Inc
Laporte Inc
Penta Manufacturing Co
RT Vanderbilt Co Inc
Spectrum Chemical Mfg Corp
Van Waters & Rogers Inc
Whittaker, Clark & Daniels Inc

Benzalkonium Chloride
UK
Albright & Wilson Ltd
Alfa Chemicals Ltd
Berk Chemicals Ltd
Cochrane & Keane (Chemicals) Ltd
Eastman Fine Chemicals
Lonza (UK) Ltd
LS Raw Materials Ltd
MDA Chemicals Ltd
Medex Medical Export Co Ltd
Millchem UK Ltd
Pacegrove Ltd
Pentagon Chemicals Ltd
Pointing Group
Raught Ltd
Rewo Chemicals Ltd
SBP Ltd

Stan Chem International Ltd
Ubichem Ltd

Other European
FEF Chemicals A/S
Laserson SA
Polysciences Ltd
Stepan Europe

USA
Amresco Inc
Eastman Fine Chemicals
EM Industries Inc
Functional Foods
Millmaster Onyx International
Penta Manufacturing Co
Sherex Chemical Company Inc
Spectrum Chemical Mfg Corp
Triple Crown America Inc

Others
Boehme Filatex Canada Inc

Benzethonium Chloride
UK
Lonza (UK) Ltd
LS Raw Materials Ltd
Millchem UK Ltd

USA
Amresco Inc
Millmaster Onyx International
Penta Manufacturing Co
Spectrum Chemical Mfg Corp

Benzoic Acid
UK
Berk Chemicals Ltd
Bush Beach Ltd
Cornelius Chemical Co Ltd
Courtin & Warner Ltd
DSM United Kingdom
Interpharm Ltd
LS Raw Materials Ltd
Magnesia UK
MDA Chemicals Ltd
Medex Medical Export Co Ltd
Merck Ltd
Pacegrove Ltd
Paldena Ltd
Pentagon Chemicals Ltd
Pointing Group
Raught Ltd
Resource Chemical Ltd
SBP Ltd
Sparkford Chemicals Ltd
TA Chemicals
Tennants (Lancashire) Ltd

Other European
DSM Special Products BV
E. Merck
Jan Dekker BV
Mallinckrodt Speciality Chemicals Europe
  GmbH
Polysciences Ltd

USA
Amresco Inc
Ashland Chemical Company
DSM Fine Chemicals USA Inc
EM Industries Inc
Fisher Scientific
Mallinckrodt Speciality Chemicals Co
Merona Chemicals Ltd
Mutchler Chemical Co Inc
Penta Manufacturing Co
Schweizerhall Inc
Spectrum Chemical Mfg Corp
Triple Crown America Inc
Van Waters & Rogers Inc

Others
San Fu Chemical Co Ltd

Benzyl Alcohol
UK
Alcohols Ltd
Berk Chemicals Ltd
Bush Beach Ltd
DSM United Kingdom
Gale & Mount Ltd
Haarmann & Reimer Ltd
K & K Greeff Ltd
LS Raw Materials Ltd
MDA Chemicals Ltd
Merck Ltd
Raught Ltd
RC Treatt & Co Ltd
SBP Ltd
Tennants (Lancashire) Ltd
Ubichem Ltd

Other European
Akzo Chemicals BV
DSM Special Products BV
E. Merck
Haarmann & Reimer GmbH
Laserson SA
Polysciences Ltd
Tessenderlo Chemie SA

USA
Aceto Corporation
Akzo Chemicals Inc
Ashland Chemical Company
Charkit Chemical Corp
DSM Fine Chemicals USA Inc
EM Industries Inc
Haarmann & Reimer Corp
Penta Manufacturing Co
Schweizerhall Inc
Spectrum Chemical Mfg Corp
Van Waters & Rogers Inc

Benzyl Benzoate
UK
Berk Chemicals Ltd
Bush Beach Ltd
DSM United Kingdom
Haarmann & Reimer Ltd
Interpharm Ltd
LS Raw Materials Ltd

Magnesia UK
MDA Chemicals Ltd
Medex Medical Export Co Ltd
Merck Ltd
Pacegrove Ltd
Pentagon Chemicals Ltd
Pointing Group
Raught Ltd
Rhône-Poulenc Chemicals

Other European
DSM Special Products BV
E. Merck
Haarmann & Reimer GmbH
Laserson SA
Polysciences Ltd

USA
Aceto Corporation
DSM Fine Chemicals USA Inc
EM Industries Inc
Haarmann & Reimer Corp
Penta Manufacturing Co
Rhône-Poulenc Inc
Schweizerhall Inc
Spectrum Chemical Mfg Corp
The Lebermuth Co Inc

Bronopol
UK
Allchem International Ltd
Blagden Chemicals Ltd
Boots Chemicals
Honeywill & Stein Ltd
LS Raw Materials Ltd
MDA Chemicals Ltd
Millchem UK Ltd
Raught Ltd

Other European
Dynamit Nobel AG

USA
Angus Chemical Company
Inolex Chemical Co
Millmaster Onyx International
Tri-K Industries Inc
Vivion Inc

Butane
UK
Air Products Plc
BOC Ltd
BP Chemicals Ltd
Calor Gas Ltd
Distillers MG Ltd
Phillips Petroleum Chemicals UK

Other European
E. Merck

USA
Aeropres Corp
Phillips 66 Company
Van Waters & Rogers Inc

Butylated Hydroxyanisole
UK
Blagden Chemicals Ltd
Eastman Fine Chemicals
Gale & Mount Ltd
MDA Chemicals Ltd
Rhône-Poulenc Chemicals
Sparkford Chemicals Ltd

Other European
Jan Dekker BV
Laserson SA

USA
Aceto Corporation
Amresco Inc
Eastman Fine Chemicals
Kraft Chemical Company
Mutchler Chemical Co Inc
Nipa Laboratories Inc
Penta Manufacturing Co
Rhône-Poulenc Inc
Spectrum Chemical Mfg Corp

Butylated Hydroxytoluene
UK
Blagden Chemicals Ltd
Chance & Hunt
Eastman Fine Chemicals
Ferro Metal and Chemical Corporation Ltd
Gale & Mount Ltd
K & K Greeff Ltd
MDA Chemicals Ltd
Peter Whiting (Chemicals) Ltd
Rhône-Poulenc Chemicals

Other European
Derivados Fenolicos SA
Jan Dekker BV
Laserson SA
Polysciences Ltd

USA
Aceto Corporation
Ashland Chemical Company
Eastman Fine Chemicals
Gallard-Schlesinger Industries Inc
Kraft Chemical Company
Mutchler Chemical Co Inc
Nipa Laboratories Inc
Penta Manufacturing Co
PMC Specialities Group Inc
Rhône-Poulenc Inc
Spectrum Chemical Mfg Corp
Triple Crown America Inc
Van Waters & Rogers Inc

Butylparaben
UK
LS Raw Materials Ltd
MDA Chemicals Ltd
Nipa Laboratories Ltd

Other European
Chemag AG
Laserson SA

Mallinckrodt Speciality Chemicals Europe GmbH

USA
Amresco Inc
Ashland Chemical Company
Avatar Corp
Functional Foods
Inolex Chemical Co
International Sourcing Inc
Kalama Chemical Inc
Mallinckrodt Speciality Chemicals Co
Mutchler Chemical Co Inc
Napp Technologies Inc
Nipa Laboratories Inc
Penta Manufacturing Co
Protameen Chemicals Inc
Spectrum Chemical Mfg Corp
Sutton Laboratories Inc
Tri-K Industries Inc
Vivion Inc

Others
Chorney Chemical Co
San Fu Chemical Company Ltd

Calcium Carbonate
UK
Berk Chemicals Ltd
Cornelius Chemical Co Ltd
Croxton & Garry Ltd
LS Raw Materials Ltd
Magnesia UK
MDA Chemicals Ltd
Medex Medical Export Co Ltd
Merck Ltd
Pacegrove Ltd
Pennine Darlington Magnesia Ltd
Resource Chemical Ltd
Rhône-Poulenc Chemicals
TA Chemicals
Thew, Arnott & Co Ltd

Other European
Dr Paul Lohmann GmbH
E. Merck
Janssen Chimica
Schaefer Kalk

USA
American Ingredients Inc
Amresco Inc
Ashland Chemical Company
Charles B Chrystal Co Inc
Crompton & Knowles Corp
EM Industries Inc
Fisher Scientific
International Sourcing Inc
JWS Delavau Co Inc
Mutchler Chemical Co Inc
Noah Chemical
Particle Dynamics Inc
Penta Manufacturing Co
Pharmaceutical Ingredients Ltd
Rhône-Poulenc Inc
Spectrum Chemical Mfg Corp

Van Waters & Rogers Inc
Vivion Inc
Whittaker, Clark & Daniels Inc

Dibasic Calcium Phosphate Dihydrate
UK
Albright & Wilson Ltd
Cornelius Chemical Co Ltd
Edward Mendell Co Inc
Forum Chemicals Ltd
Honeywill & Stein Ltd
Interpharm Ltd
K & K Greeff Ltd
LS Raw Materials Ltd
Magnesia UK
MDA Chemicals Ltd
Pacegrove Ltd
Peter Whiting (Chemicals) Ltd
Prayon (UK) Plc
Rhône-Poulenc Chemicals

Other European
Chemische Fabrik Budenheim Rudolf A. Oetker
Dr Paul Lohmann GmbH
E. Merck
FMC Europe NV
Gelatine Delft BV
Lehmann & Voss & Co
Mallinckrodt Speciality Chemicals Europe GmbH

USA
Amresco Inc
Ashland Chemical Company
Edward Mendell Co Inc
FMC Corporation
Gallard-Schlesinger Industries Inc
Mallinckrodt Speciality Chemicals Co
Mutchler Chemical Co Inc
Penta Manufacturing Co
Rhône-Poulenc Basic Chemicals Co
Spectrum Chemical Mfg Corp
Van Waters & Rogers Inc
Vivion Inc

Tribasic Calcium Phosphate
UK
Albright & Wilson Ltd
Interpharm Ltd
K & K Greeff Ltd
LS Raw Materials Ltd
Magnesia UK
MDA Chemicals Ltd
Merck Ltd
Pacegrove Ltd
Peter Whiting (Chemicals) Ltd
Prayon (UK) Plc
Rhône-Poulenc Chemicals

Other European
Chemische Fabrik Budenheim Rudolf A. Oetker
Dr Paul Lohmann GmbH
E. Merck

Mallinckrodt Speciality Chemicals Europe GmbH

USA
Amresco Inc
Ashland Chemical Company
EM Industries Inc
Gallard-Schlesinger Industries Inc
JWS Delavau Co Inc
Mallinckrodt Speciality Chemicals Co
Mutchler Chemical Co Inc
Penta Manufacturing Co
Rhône-Poulenc Basic Chemicals Co
Spectrum Chemical Mfg Corp
Van Waters & Rogers Inc
Vivion Inc

Others
Gadot Petrochemical Industries Ltd

Calcium Stearate
UK
Akcros Chemicals
Berk Chemicals Ltd
Bush Beach Ltd
Croda Chemicals Ltd
Croxton & Garry Ltd
Durham Chemicals
Fina Chemicals
James M Brown Ltd
K & K Greeff Ltd
LS Raw Materials Ltd
Magnesia UK
Megret Ltd
Merck Ltd
SBP Ltd
Sparkford Chemicals Ltd
TA Chemicals
Woburn Chemicals Ltd

Other European
Akcros Chemicals v.o.f.
Dr Paul Lohmann GmbH
E. Merck
Fina Chemicals
Mallinckrodt Speciality Chemicals Europe GmbH

USA
Aceto Corporation
Akcros Chemicals America
Croda Inc
Edward Mendell Co Inc
EM Industries Inc
Harrisons Trading Co Inc
Mallinckrodt Speciality Chemicals Co
Merona Chemicals Ltd
Mutchler Chemical Co Inc
Penta Manufacturing Co
Spectrum Chemical Mfg Corp
Triple Crown America Inc
Van Waters & Rogers Inc
Vivion Inc

Calcium Sulfate
UK

British Gypsum Ltd
Edward Mendell Co Inc
Forum Chemicals Ltd
Honeywill & Stein Ltd
LS Raw Materials Ltd
Merck Ltd
Magnesia UK
Pacegrove Ltd

Other European
Dr Paul Lohmann GmbH
E. Merck

USA
American Ingredients Inc
Amresco Inc
Charles B Chrystal Co Inc
Crompton & Knowles Corp
Edward Mendell Co Inc
EM Industries Inc
Mutchler Chemical Co Inc
Particle Dynamics Inc
Penta Manufacturing Co
Pharmaceutical Ingredients Ltd
Spectrum Chemical Mfg Corp
United States Gypsum Co
Van Waters & Rogers Inc
Whittaker, Clark & Daniels Inc

Canola Oil
UK
Brightstern Ltd
Bush Beach Ltd
Chesham Chemicals Ltd
Karlshamns UK Ltd

Other European
Aarhus Oliefabrik A/S
Karlshamns Lipids for Care

USA
Arista Industries
Avatar Corp
Biospur Inc
Calgene Chemical Inc
International Sourcing Inc
Karlshamns USA Inc
Lipo Chemicals Inc
Penta Manufacturing Co
Tri-K Industries Inc
Van Waters & Rogers Inc

Carbomer
UK
BFGoodrich Chemical (UK) Ltd
Cornelius Chemical Co Ltd
Croxton & Garry Ltd

USA
BFGoodrich Company
Protameen Chemicals Inc
RITA Corp

Carbon Dioxide
UK
Air Products Plc

BOC Ltd
CryoService Ltd
Distillers MG Ltd

Other European
Air Liquide

USA
Van Waters & Rogers Inc

Carboxymethylcellulose Calcium
UK
LS Raw Materials Ltd
Metsä-Serla Chemicals Ltd
SBP Ltd

Other European
Lehmann & Voss & Co
Metsä-Serla Chemicals BV
Wolff Walsrode AG

USA
Aceto Corporation
Kraft Chemical Company
Metsä-Serla Chemicals Inc

Carboxymethylcellulose Sodium
UK
Arthur Branwell & Co Ltd
Chesham Chemicals Ltd
Cornelius Chemical Co Ltd
Courtaulds Chemicals
Hercules Ltd
Honeywill & Stein Ltd
Interpharm Ltd
LS Raw Materials Ltd
Magnesia UK
Metsä-Serla Chemicals Ltd
Stan Chem International Ltd

Other European
Aqualon France
Laserson SA
Metsä-Serla Chemicals BV
Polysciences Ltd
Wolff Walsrode AG

USA
Aceto Corporation
Amresco Inc
Aqualon
Ashland Chemical Company
Harrisons Trading Co Inc
Metsä-Serla Chemicals Inc
Penta Manufacturing Co
Spectrum Chemical Mfg Corp
Van Waters & Rogers Inc

Others
Sansho Co

Hydrogenated Castor Oil
UK
Berk Chemicals Ltd
Henkel Organics
LS Raw Materials Ltd

Pacegrove Ltd
SBP Ltd
The White Sea & Baltic Company Ltd

Other European
Alberdingk Boley GmbH
Henkel KGaA
Jan Dekker BV
Laserson SA
Seppic

USA
Arista Industries
Avatar Corp
Caschem Inc
Lipo Chemicals Inc
Mutchler Chemical Co Inc
Seppic Inc
Van Waters & Rogers Inc

Others
Freund Industrial Co Ltd
Kawaken Fine Chemicals Co Ltd

Microcrystalline Cellulose
UK
Allchem International Ltd
Becpharm Ltd
Cornelius Chemical Co Ltd
Edward Mendell Co Inc
Forum Chemicals Ltd
Honeywill & Stein Ltd
Interpharm Ltd
K & K Greeff Ltd
LS Raw Materials Ltd
Magnesia UK
Medex Medical Export Co Ltd
Pacegrove Ltd

Other European
FMC Europe NV
J. Rettenmaier & Söhne GmbH
Lehmann & Voss & Co

USA
Ashland Chemical Company
Barrington Chemical Corporation
Edward Mendell Co Inc
FMC Corporation
Functional Foods
Gallard-Schlesinger Industries Inc
Harrisons Trading Co Inc
Mutchler Chemical Co Inc
Pharmaceutical Ingredients Ltd
Resources Industry Inc
RW Greeff & Co Inc
Spectrum Chemical Mfg Corp
Van Waters & Rogers Inc

Others
Chorney Chemical Co

Powdered Cellulose
UK
Chemical Exchange (1987) Ltd
Courtaulds Chemicals

Croxton & Garry Ltd
Degussa Ltd
Edward Mendell Co Inc
Interpharm Ltd
LS Raw Materials Ltd

Other European
Degussa AG
E. Merck

USA
American Ingredients Inc
Barrington Chemical Corporation
Edward Mendell Co Inc
Functional Foods
Harrisons Trading Co Inc
Presperse Inc
United Mineral & Chemical Corp

Cellulose Acetate Phthalate
UK
Chemical Exchange (1987) Ltd
Eastman Fine Chemicals
Forum Chemicals Ltd
Honeywill & Stein Ltd
LS Raw Materials Ltd

Other European
FMC Europe NV
Lehmann & Voss & Co
Polysciences Ltd
Takeda Europe GmbH

USA
Eastman Fine Chemicals
FMC Corporation

Others
Chorney Chemical Co

Cetostearyl Alcohol
UK
A & E Connock (Perfumery & Cosmetics) Ltd
Albright & Wilson Ltd
Berk Chemicals Ltd
Chesham Chemicals Ltd
Courtin & Warner Ltd
Croda Chemicals Ltd
Croxton & Garry Ltd
Efkay Chemicals Ltd
Eggar & Co (Chemicals) Ltd
Fina Chemicals
Henkel Organics
H. Foster & Co (Stearines) Ltd
Interpharm Ltd
LS Raw Materials Ltd
Millchem UK Ltd
Pacegrove Ltd
Rewo Chemicals Ltd
The White Sea & Baltic Company Ltd

Other European
Aarhus Oliefabrik A/S
Fina Chemicals

Henkel KGaA
Laserson SA

USA
Ashland Chemical Company
Croda Inc
Lipo Chemicals Inc
Millmaster Onyx International
M Michel & Co Inc
Sherex Chemical Company Inc

Cetrimide
UK
Allchem International Ltd
Berk Chemicals Ltd
Cochrane & Keane (Chemicals) Ltd
Courtin & Warner Ltd
Efkay Chemicals Ltd
Harbottle (Pharmaceuticals) Ltd
Interpharm Ltd
LS Raw Materials Ltd
Magnesia UK
MDA Chemicals Ltd
Millchem UK Ltd
Pacegrove Ltd
Pentagon Chemicals Ltd
Raught Ltd
Rewo Chemicals Ltd
Rhône-Poulenc Chemicals
SBP Ltd

Other European
Chemische Fabrik Berg GmbH
FEF Chemicals A/S

USA
Accurate Chemical & Scientific Corp
Aceto Corporation
Millmaster Onyx International
Rhône-Poulenc Inc
Sherex Chemical Company Inc
Triple Crown America Inc

Cetyl Alcohol
UK
A & E Connock (Perfumery & Cosmetics) Ltd
Berk Chemicals Ltd
Chesham Chemicals Ltd
Cornelius Chemical Co Ltd
Croda Chemicals Ltd
Croxton & Garry Ltd
Efkay Chemicals Ltd
Eggar & Co (Chemicals) Ltd
Henkel Organics
Interpharm Ltd
Kimpton Brothers Ltd
LS Raw Materials Ltd
MDA Chemicals Ltd
Merck Ltd
Millchem UK Ltd
Rewo Chemicals Ltd
SBP Ltd
The White Sea & Baltic Company Ltd

Other European
Aarhus Oliefabrik A/S
E. Merck
Henkel KGaA
Jan Dekker BV
Laserson SA

USA
Amresco Inc
Ashland Chemical Company
Avatar Corp
Croda Inc
EM Industries Inc
Lipo Chemicals Inc
Millmaster Onyx International
M Michel & Co Inc
Mutchler Chemical Co Inc
Penta Manufacturing Co
RITA Corp
Sherex Chemical Company Inc
Spectrum Chemical Mfg Corp
Van Waters & Rogers Inc
Vivion Inc

Cetyl Esters Wax
UK
A & E Connock (Perfumery & Cosmetics) Ltd
AF Suter & Co Ltd
Chesham Chemicals Ltd
Croda Chemicals Ltd
Eggar & Co (Chemicals) Ltd
Henkel Organics
K & K Greeff Ltd
Rewo Chemicals Ltd

Other European
Henkel KGaA

USA
Avatar Corp
Calgene Chemical Inc
Caschem Inc
Croda Inc
Koster Keunen Inc
Lipo Chemicals Inc
Protameen Chemicals Inc
RITA Corp
Robeco Chemicals Inc
Sherex Chemical Company Inc
Spectrum Chemical Mfg Corp
Strahl & Pitsch Inc
Werner G Smith Inc

Chlorhexidine
UK
Allchem International Ltd
Becpharm Ltd
Berk Chemicals Ltd
Cochrane & Keane (Chemicals) Ltd
Harbottle (Pharmaceuticals) Ltd
Interpharm Ltd
K & K Greeff Ltd
LS Raw Materials Ltd
Magnesia UK
MDA Chemicals Ltd

Medex Medical Export Co Ltd
Pacegrove Ltd
Raught Ltd
Rhône-Poulenc Chemicals

Other European
Laserson SA

USA
Accurate Chemical & Scientific Corp
Amresco Inc
George Uhe Co Inc
Napp Technologies Inc
Rhône-Poulenc Inc

Chlorobutanol
UK
Blagden Chemicals Ltd
Courtin & Warner Ltd
IDIS Ltd
LS Raw Materials Ltd
Pacegrove Ltd

Other European
Akzo Chemicals BV
E. Merck
Riedel-de Haën AG

USA
Akzo Chemicals Inc
Amresco Inc
Penta Manufacturing Co
Spectrum Chemical Mfg Corp
Van Waters & Rogers Inc

Chlorocresol
UK
IDIS Ltd
LS Raw Materials Ltd
Merck Ltd
Nipa Laboratories Ltd
Pacegrove Ltd

Other European
E. Merck

USA
EM Industries Inc

Chlorodifluoroethane
UK
Du Pont (UK) Ltd
Fluorochem Ltd
Rhône-Poulenc Chemicals (Fluorinated
   Products)

USA
EI Du Pont de Nemours & Co Inc

Chlorodifluoromethane
UK
BOC Ltd
Du Pont (UK) Ltd
Fluorochem Ltd
Hoechst UK Ltd
ICI Chemicals and Polymers Ltd

Rhône-Poulenc Chemicals (Fluorinated
   Products)

USA
EI Du Pont de Nemours & Co Inc
ICI Chemicals and Polymers America

Cholesterol
UK
A & E Connock (Perfumery & Cosmetics)
   Ltd
Cornelius Chemical Co Ltd
Croda Chemicals Ltd
Honeywill & Stein Ltd
LS Raw Materials Ltd
MDA Chemicals Ltd
Merck Ltd
Ubichem Ltd

Other European
Bayer Diagnosticos SA
E. Merck
Laserson SA
Polysciences Ltd

USA
Amresco Inc
Ashland Chemical Company
Charkit Chemical Corp
Croda Inc
EM Industries Inc
Freeman Industries Inc
Presperse Inc
RITA Corp
Spectrum Chemical Mfg Corp
Vitamins Inc

Citric Acid Monohydrate
UK
AMC Chemicals
British Traders & Shippers Ltd
Bush Beach Ltd
Cargill Plc
Cerestar UK Ltd
Corcoran Chemicals Ltd
Cornelius Chemical Co Ltd
Courtin & Warner Ltd
Farleyway Chemicals Ltd
Forum Chemicals Ltd
Haarmann & Reimer Ltd
Harbottle (Pharmaceuticals) Ltd
IDIS Ltd
Interpharm Ltd
John Kellys (Merchants) Ltd
LS Raw Materials Ltd
Magnesia UK
MDA Chemicals Ltd
Medex Medical Export Ltd
Merck Ltd
Pacegrove Ltd
Paldena Ltd
Peter Whiting (Chemicals) Ltd
Pointing Group
Raught Ltd
Resource Chemical Ltd
Roche Products Ltd

SBP Ltd
Scan Chem UK Ltd
TA Chemicals
Takasago (UK) Ltd
Tennants (Lancashire) Ltd
Ubichem Ltd
Woburn Chemicals Ltd

Other European
Cerestar International Sales
Dr Paul Lohmann GmbH
E. Merck
Jungbunzlauer International AG
Laserson SA
Polysciences Ltd
SA Citrique Belge NV

USA
Amresco Inc
Ashland Chemical Company
Chemco Industries Inc
EM Industries Inc
Fisher Scientific
Harrisons Trading Co Inc
Helm New York Chemical Corp
Jungbunzlauer Inc
Kraft Chemical Company
Merona Chemicals Ltd
Mutchler Chemical Co Inc
Penta Manufacturing Co
Schweizerhall Inc
Spectrum Chemical Mfg Corp
Takasago International Corp (USA)
The Lebermuth Co Inc
Van Waters & Rogers Inc
Vivion Inc

Others
Gadot Petrochemical Industries Ltd
Takasago International Corp

Coloring Agents
UK
Chesham Chemicals Ltd
Cornelius Chemical Co Ltd
Guinness Chemical (Ireland) Ltd
Interpharm Ltd
K & K Greeff Ltd
MDA Chemicals Ltd
Pacegrove Ltd
Paldena Ltd
Pointing Group
Rhône-Poulenc Chemicals
Roche Products Ltd
Sanofi Bio-Industries Ltd
SBP Ltd
Stan Chem International Ltd
Warner Jenkinson Europe
William Ransom & Son Plc
WS Simpson & Co Ltd

USA
BASF Corporation
Crompton & Knowles Corp
Freeman Industries Inc
Penta Manufacturing Co

Presperse Inc
Tricon Colors Inc
Van Dyk Inc
Virginia Dare
Whittaker, Clark & Daniels Inc

Corn Oil
UK
A & E Connock (Perfumery & Cosmetics) Ltd
Alembic Products Ltd
Brightstern Ltd
Cargill Plc
Cerestar UK Ltd
Croda Chemicals Ltd
Karlshamns UK Ltd
MDA Chemicals Ltd
Paldena Ltd
SBP Ltd
The White Sea & Baltic Company Ltd
Tunnel Refineries Ltd

Other European
Aarhus Oliefabrik A/S
Cerestar International Sales
Karlshamns Lipids for Care
Laserson SA

USA
Arista Industries
Avatar Corp
Calgene Chemical Inc
Corn Products
Croda Inc
Karlshamns USA Inc
Mutchler Chemical Co Inc
Penta Manufacturing Co
Spectrum Chemical Mfg Corp
Tri-K Industries Inc
Van Waters & Rogers Inc

Cottonseed Oil
UK
A & E Connock (Perfumery & Cosmetics) Ltd
Alembic Products Ltd
Brightstern Ltd
Croda Chemicals Ltd
Forum Chemicals Ltd
Karlshamns UK Ltd
MDA Chemicals Ltd
Pacegrove Ltd
Paldena Ltd
SBP Ltd
The White Sea & Baltic Company Ltd

Other European
Karlshamns Lipids for Care
Laserson SA

USA
Amresco Inc
Arista Industries
Avatar Corp
Calgene Chemical Inc
Croda Inc

Fisher Scientific
Karlshamns USA Inc
Mutchler Chemical Co Inc
Penta Manufacturing Co
Spectrum Chemical Mfg Corp
Tri-K Industries Inc
Van Waters & Rogers Inc

Cresol
UK
IDIS Ltd
LS Raw Materials Ltd
Pointing Group
PPK Products (UK) Ltd

USA
Amresco Inc
Penta Manufacturing Co
Van Waters & Rogers Inc

Croscarmellose Sodium
UK
Avebe UK Ltd
Honeywill & Stein Ltd
Metsä-Serla Chemicals Ltd

Other European
Avebe BA
FMC Europe NV
Lehmann & Voss & Co
Metsä-Serla Chemicals BV

USA
Avebe America Inc
FMC Corporation
Generichem Corp
George Uhe Co Inc
Harrisons Trading Co Inc
JWS Delavau Co Inc
Metsä-Serla Chemicals Inc
Pharmaceutical Ingredients Ltd

Others
Chorney Chemical Co

Crospovidone
UK
BASF Plc
ISP Europe

USA
BASF Corporation
ISP

Cyclodextrins
UK
Forum Chemicals Ltd
MDA Chemicals Ltd
Rhône-Poulenc Chemicals
Roquette (UK) Ltd
RW Unwin & Co Ltd
Wacker Chemicals Ltd

Other European
Jan Dekker BV
Janssen Biotech NV

Roquette Frères
Wacker-Chemie GmbH

USA
American Maize Products Co
Cyclodextrin Technologies Development Inc
Pfanstiehl Laboratories Inc
Pharmatec Inc
Rhône-Poulenc Inc
Roquette America Inc
Wacker Silicones Corp

Dextrates
UK
Edward Mendell Co Inc
Forum Chemicals Ltd

USA
Amresco Inc
Barrington Chemical Corporation
Edward Mendell Co Inc

Dextrin
UK
Avebe UK Ltd
Cerestar UK Ltd
MDA Chemicals Ltd
Roquette (UK) Ltd
SBP Ltd
Tunnel Refineries Ltd

Other European
Avebe BA
Campo Ebro Industrrial SA
Cerestar International Sales
E. Merck
Polysciences Ltd
Roquette Frères

USA
American Maize Products Co
Avebe America Inc
Pfanstiehl Laboratories Inc
Roquette America Inc
Van Waters & Rogers Inc
Zumbro Inc

Dextrose
UK
Cargill Plc
Cerestar UK Ltd
Corcoran Chemicals Ltd
Edward Mendell Co Inc
IDIS Ltd
Interpharm Ltd
Magnesia UK
MDA Chemicals Ltd
Medex Medical Export Co Ltd
Merck Ltd
Pacegrove Ltd
Paldena Ltd
Peter Whiting (Chemicals) Ltd
Raught Ltd
Roquette (UK) Ltd
RW Unwin & Co Ltd
Tunnel Refineries Ltd

Ubichem Ltd
Xyrofin (UK) Ltd

Other European
Amylum NV
Campo Ebro Industrial SA
Cerestar International Sales
E. Merck
Mallinckrodt Speciality Chemicals Europe
   GmbH
Polysciences Ltd
Roquette Frères
Xyrofin AG

USA
American Xyrofin Inc
Amresco Inc
Ashland Chemical Company
Barrington Chemical Corporation
Chemco Industries Inc
Corn Products
Edward Mendell Co Inc
EM Industries Inc
Functional Foods
Jungbunzlauer Inc
Mallinckrodt Speciality Chemicals Co
Merona Chemicals Ltd
Mutchler Chemical Co Inc
Penta Manufacturing Co
Pfanstiehl Laboratories Inc
Roquette America Inc
Spectrum Chemical Mfg Corp
Van Waters & Rogers Inc
Vivion Ltd

Dibutyl Sebacate
USA
Aceto Corporation

Dichlorodifluoromethane
UK
BOC Ltd
Du Pont (UK) Ltd
Fluorochem Ltd
Hoechst UK Ltd
ICI Chemicals and Polymers Ltd
Rhône-Poulenc Chemicals (Fluorinated
   Products)

USA
EI Du Pont de Nemours & Co Inc
ICI Chemicals and Polymers America

Dichlorotetrafluoroethane
UK
BOC Ltd
Du Pont (UK) Ltd
Fluorochem Ltd
Hoechst UK Ltd
ICI Chemicals and Polymers Ltd
Rhône-Poulenc Chemicals (Fluorinated
   Products)

USA
EI Du Pont de Nemours & Co Inc
ICI Chemicals and Polymers America

Diethanolamine
UK
BASF Plc
Berk Chemicals Ltd
BP Chemicals Ltd
Brenntag (UK) Ltd
Dow Chemical Company Ltd
Honeywill & Stein Ltd
Interpharm Ltd
MDA Chemicals Ltd
SBP Ltd
TA Chemicals
Texaco Chemical Europe Ltd
Union Carbide Ltd

Other European
Texaco Services (Europe) Ltd

USA
Amresco Inc
Ashland Chemical Company
Dow Chemical Company
Mutchler Chemical Co Inc
Penta Manufacturing Co
Texaco Chemical International Trader Inc
Van Waters & Rogers Inc

Diethyl Phthalate
UK
BASF Plc
BP Chemicals Ltd
Chesham Chemicals Ltd
Eastman Fine Chemicals
Haarmann & Reimer Ltd
MDA Chemicals Ltd
Pacegrove Ltd
Tennants (Lancashire) Ltd
Ubichem Ltd

Other European
Chemial Spa
Haarmann & Reimer GmbH
Laserson SA
Polysciences Ltd

USA
Ashland Chemical Company
Eastman Fine Chemicals
Haarmann & Reimer Corp
Penta Manufacturing Co
Van Waters & Rogers Inc

Difluoroethane
UK
BOC Ltd
Du Pont (UK) Ltd

USA
EI Du Pont de Nemours & Co Inc

Dimethyl Ether
UK
Akzo Chemicals Ltd
BOC Ltd
BP Chemicals Ltd
Condea Chemicals UK Ltd

Distillers MG Ltd
Du Pont (UK) Ltd
LS Raw Materials Ltd
MDA Chemicals Ltd

USA
EI Du Pont de Nemours & Co Inc
Van Waters & Rogers Inc

Docusate Sodium
UK
Croda Chemicals Ltd
LS Raw Materials Ltd

Other European
Mallinckrodt Speciality Chemicals Europe
   GmbH

USA
Croda Inc
Gallard-Schlesinger Industries Inc
Mallinckrodt Speciality Chemicals Co
Spectrum Chemical Mfg Corp

Edetic Acid
UK
Hampshire Chemical Ltd
Pacegrove Ltd
Rhone-Poulenc Chemicals
Ubichem Ltd

Other European
E. Merck
Hampshire Chemical GmbH
Laserson SA

USA
Amresco Inc
Ashland Chemical Company
Hampshire Chemical Corp
International Sourcing Inc
Spectrum Chemical Mfg Corp
Van Waters & Rogers Inc
Vivion Inc

Others
Boehme Filatex Canada Inc

Ethyl Maltol
UK
Forum Chemicals Ltd
Gale & Mount Ltd
John Kellys (Merchants) Ltd
MDA Chemicals Ltd
Pfizer Food Science Group
Scan Chem UK Ltd

Other European
Laserson SA

USA
Aceto Corporation
Ashland Chemical Company
Penta Manufacturing Co
Pfizer Food Science Group

Ethyl Oleate
UK
A & E Connock (Perfumery & Cosmetics)
  Ltd
Akzo Chemicals Ltd
Bush Beach Ltd
Chesham Chemicals Ltd
Croda Chemicals Ltd
K & K Greeff Ltd
LS Raw Materials Ltd

USA
Croda Inc
Penta Manufacturing Co

Ethyl Vanillin
UK
AMC Chemicals
Courtin & Warner Ltd
Gale & Mount Ltd
Haarmann & Reimer Ltd
John Kellys (Merchants) Ltd
Kimpton Brothers Ltd
LS Raw Materials Ltd
MDA Chemicals Ltd
Pointing Group
RC Treatt & Co Ltd
Rhône-Poulenc Chemicals
Scan Chem UK Ltd
Takasago (UK) Ltd

Other European
Haarmann & Reimer GmbH
Laserson SA

USA
Ashland Chemical Company
Avatar Corp
Chart Corp Inc
Haarmann & Reimer Corp
Mutchler Chemical Co Inc
Penta Manufacturing Co
Rhône-Poulenc Inc
Spectrum Chemical Mfg Corp
Takasago International Corp (USA)
The Lebermuth Co Inc
Van Waters & Rogers Inc
Virginia Dare

Others
Chorney Chemical Co
Takasago International Corp

Ethylcellulose
UK
Colorcon Ltd
Dow Chemical Company Ltd
Hercules Ltd
Honeywill & Stein Ltd
K & K Greeff Ltd
LS Raw Materials Ltd

Other European
Aqualon France
FMC Europe NV
Laserson SA

USA
Aqualon
Ashland Chemical Company
Colorcon
Dow Chemical Company
FMC Corporation
Spectrum Chemical Mfg Corp

Others
Sansho Co

Ethylparaben
UK
Interpharm Ltd
LS Raw Materials Ltd
Magnesia UK
MDA Chemicals Ltd
Merck Ltd
Nipa Laboratories Ltd

Other European
Chemag AG
E. Merck
Jan Dekker BV
Laserson SA
Mallinckrodt Speciality Chemicals Europe
  GmbH

USA
Amresco Inc
Ashland Chemical Company
Avatar Corp
EM Industries Inc
Helm New York Chemical Corp
International Sourcing Inc
Kalama Chemical Inc
Mallinckrodt Speciality Chemicals Co
Mutchler Chemical Co Inc
Napp Technologies Inc
Nipa Laboratories Inc
Penta Manufacturing Co
Protameen Chemicals Inc
Spectrum Chemical Mfg Corp
Tri-K Industries Inc

Others
Chorney Chemical Co

Fructose
UK
Brenntag (UK) Ltd
Cambridge Research Biochemicals
Cerestar UK Ltd
Corcoran Chemicals Ltd
Forum Chemicals Ltd
IDIS Ltd
Interpharm Ltd
MDA Chemicals Ltd
Merck Ltd
Peter Whiting (Chemicals) Ltd
Tunnel Refineries Ltd
Xyrofin (UK) Ltd

Other European
Amylum NV
Campo Ebro Industrial SA

Cerestar International Sales
E. Merck
Polysciences Ltd
Xyrofin AG

USA
AE Staley Mfg Co
American Maize Products Co
American Xyrofin Inc
Amresco Inc
Ashland Chemical Company
Barrington Chemical Corporation
Chemco Industries Inc
EM Industries Inc
Mutchler Chemical Co Inc
Penta Manufacturing Co
Pfanstiehl Laboratories Inc
Schweizerhall Inc
Spectrum Chemical Mfg Corp
Van Waters & Rogers Inc
Vivion Inc

Fumaric Acid
UK
Berk Chemicals Ltd
Bush Beach Ltd
Chemie Linz UK Ltd
Forum Chemicals Ltd
LS Raw Materials Ltd
Magnesia UK
MDA Chemicals Ltd
Medex Medical Export Co Ltd
Merck Ltd
Monsanto Plc
Peter Whiting (Chemicals) Ltd
Sparkford Chemicals Ltd
Stan Chem International Ltd
TA Chemicals

Other European
E. Merck
Hüls AG

USA
Amresco Inc
Ashland Chemical Company
Chemco Industries Inc
Chemie Linz US Inc
EM Industries Inc
Gallard-Schlesinger Industries Inc
Hüls America Inc
Jungbunzlauer Inc
Merona Chemicals Ltd
Penta Manufacturing Co
Schweizerhall Inc
Spectrum Chemical Mfg Corp
Van Waters & Rogers Inc
Vivion Inc

Others
Gadot Petrochemical Industries Ltd

Gelatin
UK
Arthur Branwell & Co Ltd
Berk Chemicals Ltd

Chemical Exchange (1987) Ltd
Croda Chemicals Ltd
Davis Gelatine
Eggar & Co (Chemicals) Ltd
Gale & Mount Ltd
Harbottle (Pharmaceuticals) Ltd
LS Raw Materials Ltd
Magnesia UK
Medex Medical Export Co Ltd
Merck Ltd
PB Gelatins UK
Sanofi Bio-Industries Ltd
Thew, Arnott & Co Ltd

Other European
E. Merck
Extraco
Gelatine Delft BV
PB Gelatins
Willi Kruger KG

USA
Aceto Corporation
Amresco Inc
Ashland Chemical Company
Chemco Industries Inc
Croda Inc
EM Industries Inc
Functional Foods
Grayslake Gelatin
Hormel Foods Corporation
Pectagel Inc
Penta Manufacturing Co
Pfanstiehl Laboratories Inc
Spectrum Chemical Mfg Corp
Van Waters & Rogers Inc
Vyse Gelatin Co

Liquid Glucose
UK
Cargill Plc
Cerestar UK Ltd
Corcoran Chemicals Ltd
IDIS Ltd
Interpharm Ltd
LS Raw Materials Ltd
Paldena Ltd
Roquette (UK) Ltd
Tunnel Refineries Ltd

Other European
Amylum NV
Campo Ebro Industrial SA
Cerestar UK Ltd
Roquette Frères

USA
Corn Products
EI Dupont de Nemours & Co Inc
Jungbunzlauer Inc
Merona Chemicals Ltd
Penta Manufacturing Co
Roquette America Inc

Glycerin
UK

A & E Connock (Perfumery & Cosmetics)
  Ltd
Akzo Chemicals Ltd
Alembic Products Ltd
Berk Chemicals Ltd
Blagden Chemicals Ltd
Brightstern Ltd
Bush Beach Ltd
Caldic (UK) Ltd
Chemical Exchange (1987) Ltd
Chesham Chemicals Ltd
Corcoran Chemicals Ltd
Courtin & Warner Ltd
Croda Chemicals Ltd
Dow Chemical Company Ltd
Farleyway Chemicals Ltd
Fina Chemicals
Harbottle (Pharmaceuticals) Ltd
H. Foster & Co (Stearines) Ltd
Interpharm Ltd
K & K Greeff Ltd
Kimpton Brothers Ltd
Lonza (UK) Ltd
LS Raw Materials Ltd
Magnesia UK
Medex Medical Export Co Ltd
Merck Ltd
Millchem UK Ltd
Pacegrove Ltd
Paldena Ltd
Raught Ltd
Resource Chemical Ltd
Stan Chem International Ltd
Tennants (Lancashire) Ltd
Thew, Arnott & Co Ltd
The White Sea & Baltic Company Ltd
Ubichem Ltd
Unichema Chemicals Ltd
Woburn Chemicals Ltd

Other European
E. Merck
Fina Chemicals
Karlshamns Lipids for Care
Laserson SA
Polysciences Ltd
Simel Spa

USA
Amresco Inc
Ashland Chemical Company
Avatar Corp
Chemco Industries Inc
Croda Inc
Dow Chemical Company
EM Industries Inc
Fisher Scientific
Kraft Chemical Company
Lonza Inc
Millmaster Onyx International
Mutchler Chemical Co Inc
Penta Manufacturing Co
Spectrum Chemical Mfg Corp
Unichema North America
Van Waters & Rogers Inc
Vivion Inc

Witco Corporation

Others
Chorney Chemical Co

Glyceryl Monooleate
UK
A & E Connock (Perfumery & Cosmetics)
  Ltd
AP Chemicals Ltd
Bush Beach Ltd
Chesham Chemicals Ltd
Cornelius Chemical Co Ltd
Croda Chemicals Ltd
Eastman Fine Chemicals
Fina Chemicals
Honeywill & Stein Ltd
K & K Greeff Ltd
Lonza (UK) Ltd
LS Raw Materials Ltd
MDA Chemicals Ltd
TH Goldschmidt Ltd
Unichema Chemicals Ltd

Other European
Dr W. Kolb AG
Fina Chemicals
Gattefossé SA
Grinsted Products
ICI Surfactants
Laserson SA

USA
Ashland Chemical Company
Avatar Corp
Calgene Chemical Inc
Croda Inc
Eastman Fine Chemicals
Gallard-Schlesinger Industries Inc
Gattefosse Corp
Inolex Chemical Co
Karlshamns USA Inc
Lonza Inc
Penta Manufacturing Co
PPG Industries Inc
Unichema North America
Witco Corporation

Glyceryl Monostearate
UK
A & E Connock (Perfumery & Cosmetics)
  Ltd
Akzo Chemicals Ltd
Alfa Chemicals Ltd
AP Chemicals Ltd
Berk Chemicals Ltd
Blagden Chemicals Ltd
Bush Beach Ltd
Chesham Chemicals Ltd
Cornelius Chemical Co Ltd
Croda Chemicals Ltd
Croxton & Garry Ltd
Eastman Fine Chemicals
Fina Chemicals
Henkel Organics
H. Foster & Co (Stearines) Ltd

Honeywill & Stein Ltd
Hüls (UK) Ltd
K & K Greeff Ltd
Lonza (UK) Ltd
LS Raw Materials Ltd
MDA Chemicals Ltd
TA Chemicals
TH Goldschmidt Ltd
Unichema Chemicals Ltd

Other European
Dr W. Kolb AG
Fina Chemicals
Gattefossé SA
Grinsted Products
Henkel KGaA
Hüls AG
ICI Surfactants
Laserson SA
Seppic
Stepan Europe

USA
Ashland Chemical Company
Avatar Corp
Calgene Chemical Inc
Croda Inc
Eastman Fine Chemicals
Gallard-Schlesinger Industries Inc
Gattefosse Corp
Hüls America Inc
Inolex Chemical Co
Karlshamns USA Inc
Lipo Chemicals Inc
Lonza Inc
Mutchler Chemical Co Inc
Penta Manufacturing Co
PPG Industries Inc
Protameen Chemicals Inc
RITA Corp
Unichema North America
Van Dyk Inc
Van Waters & Rogers Inc
Vivion Inc
Witco Corporation

Glyceryl Palmitostearate
UK
Alfa Chemicals Ltd
Chesham Chemicals Ltd
Croda Chemicals Ltd
Hüls (UK) Ltd

Other European
Gattefossé SA
Hüls AG
ICI Surfactants

USA
Avatar Corp
Gattefosse Corp
Hüls America Inc

Glycofurol
Other European
Co Farmaceutica Milanese Spa

Hoffmann-La Roche AG

Guar Gum
UK
AF Suter & Co Ltd
Arthur Branwell & Co Ltd
Berk Chemicals Ltd
Chemical Exchange (1987) Ltd
Chesham Chemicals Ltd
Cornelius Chemical Co Ltd
Eggar & Co (Chemicals) Ltd
Gale & Mount Ltd
Guinness Chemical (Ireland) Ltd
Interpharm Ltd
LS Raw Materials Ltd
Magnesia UK
MDA Chemicals Ltd
Rhône-Poulenc Chemicals
Sanofi Bio-Industries Ltd
SBP Ltd
Stan Chem International Ltd
Thew, Arnott & Co Ltd

Other European
Alland & Robert
Colloides Naturels International

USA
American Ingredients Inc
Ashland Chemical Company
Barrington Chemical Corporation
Chart Corp Inc
Gallard-Schlesinger Industries Inc
Gumix International Inc
Meer Corp
Rhône-Poulenc Inc
Spectrum Chemical Mfg Corp
Van Waters & Rogers Inc
Vivion Inc
Weinstein Nutritional Products

Others
Sansho Co

Hydrochloric Acid
UK
Farleyway Chemicals Ltd
Hays Chemical Distribution Ltd
MDA Chemicals Ltd
Merck Ltd
Pacegrove Ltd
Resource Chemical Ltd
Rhône-Poulenc Chemicals
Tennants (Lancashire) Ltd
Woburn Chemicals Ltd

Other European
E. Merck
Polysciences Ltd

USA
Amresco Inc
Ashland Chemical Company
EM Industries Inc
Fisher Scientific
Rhône-Poulenc Inc

Spectrum Chemical Mfg Corp
Van Waters & Rogers Inc

Hydroxyethyl Cellulose
UK
Chesham Chemicals Ltd
Cornelius Chemical Co Ltd
Croxton & Garry Ltd
Hercules Ltd
LS Raw Materials Ltd
Paroxite Ltd
Union Carbide Ltd

Other European
Amerchol Europe
Aqualon France
Polysciences Ltd
Vevy Europe Spa

USA
Amerchol Corp
Aqualon
Spectrum Chemical Mfg Corp
Van Waters & Rogers Inc

Others
Sansho Co

Hydroxypropyl Cellulose
UK
Dow Chemical Company Ltd
Hercules Ltd
Honeywill & Stein Ltd
LS Raw Materials Ltd
Stancourt Sons & Muir Ltd

Other European
Aqualon France
Polysciences Ltd

USA
Aqualon
Barrington Chemical Corporation
Biddle Sawyer Corporation
Dow Chemical Company
Van Waters & Rogers Inc

Others
Nippon Soda Co Ltd
Sansho Co
Shin-Etsu Chemical Co Ltd

Hydroxypropyl Methylcellulose
UK
Colorcon Ltd
Courtaulds Chemicals
Dow Chemical Company Ltd
Hercules Ltd
LS Raw Materials Ltd
Stancourt Sons & Muir Ltd

Other European
Aqualon France
Polysciences Ltd
Seppic
Wolff Walsrode AG

USA
Aceto Corporation
Aqualon
Ashland Chemical Company
Biddle Sawyer Corporation
Colorcon
Dow Chemical Company
Seppic Inc
Van Waters & Rogers Inc

Others
Nippon Soda Co Ltd
Shin-Etsu Chemical Co Ltd

Hydroxypropyl Methylcellulose Phthalate
UK
Eastman Fine Chemicals
Honeywill & Stein Ltd
LS Raw Materials Ltd
Stancourt Sons & Muir Ltd

USA
Biddle Sawyer Corporation
Eastman Fine Chemicals
Van Waters & Rogers Inc

Others
Shin-Etsu Chemical Co Ltd

Imidurea
UK
Blagden Chemicals Ltd
Chesham Chemicals Ltd
Nipa Laboratories Ltd

Other European
Chemag AG
Laserson SA

USA
International Sourcing Inc
Lipo Chemicals Inc
Nipa Laboratories Inc
Sutton Laboratories Inc
Tri-K Industries Inc

Isobutane
UK
Air Products Plc
BOC Ltd
Calor Gas Ltd
Distillers MG Ltd
Phillips Petroleum Chemicals UK

USA
Aeropres Corp
Phillips 66 Company

Isopropyl Alcohol
UK
Alcohols Ltd
Berk Chemicals Ltd
Blagden Chemicals Ltd
BP Chemicals Ltd
Brenntag (UK) Ltd
Caldic (UK) Ltd

Chemoxy International Plc
Condea Chemicals UK Ltd
Corcoran Chemicals Ltd
Farleyway Chemicals Ltd
Hayman Ltd
Honeywill & Stein Ltd
ICI Chemicals and Polymers Ltd
Interpharm Ltd
LS Raw Materials Ltd
MDA Chemicals Ltd
Merck Ltd
Millchem UK Ltd
Pacegrove Ltd
Tennants (Lancashire) Ltd
Ubichem Ltd
Woburn Chemicals Ltd

Other European
E. Merck
Polysciences Ltd

USA
Amresco Inc
Ashland Chemical Company
Avatar Corp
EM Industries Inc
Millmaster Onyx International
Mutchler Chemical Co Inc
Penta Manufacturing Co
Spectrum Chemical Mfg Corp
Van Waters & Rogers Inc

Isopropyl Myristate
UK
A & E Connock (Perfumery & Cosmetics)
  Ltd
Akzo Chemicals Ltd
Berk Chemicals Ltd
Blagden Chemicals Ltd
Bush Beach Ltd
Chemoxy International Plc
Chesham Chemicals Ltd
Cornelius Chemicals Co Ltd
Croda Chemicals Ltd
Fina Chemicals
Henkel Organics
K & K Greeff Ltd
LS Raw Materials Ltd
Pentagon Chemicals Ltd
TA Chemicals
Ubichem Ltd
Unichema Chemicals Ltd

Other European
Amerchol Europe
Fina Chemicals
Henkel KGaA
ICI Surfactants
Laserson SA
Stepan Europe

USA
Amerchol Corp
Ashland Chemical Company
Caschem Inc
Croda Inc

Inolex Chemical Co
Lipo Chemicals Inc
Penta Manufacturing Co
Protameen Chemicals Inc
Spectrum Chemical Mfg Corp
Unichema North America

Isopropyl Palmitate
UK
A & E Connock (Perfumery & Cosmetics)
  Ltd
Akzo Chemicals Ltd
Berk Chemicals Ltd
Chesham Chemicals Ltd
Croda Chemicals Ltd
Fina Chemicals
Henkel Organics
K & K Greeff Ltd
LS Raw Materials Ltd
Pentagon Chemicals Ltd
TA Chemicals
Unichema Chemicals Ltd

Other European
Fina Chemicals
Henkel KGaA
ICI Surfactants
Laserson SA
Stepan Europe

USA
Ashland Chemical Company
Caschem Inc
Croda Inc
Inolex Chemical Co
Lipo Chemicals Inc
Penta Manufacturing Co
Protameen Chemicals Inc
Spectrum Chemical Mfg Corp
Unichema North America
Van Waters & Rogers Inc

Kaolin
UK
Chemical Exchange (1987) Ltd
Cornelius Chemicals Co Ltd
Courtin & Warner Ltd
ECC International (Sales) Ltd
Harbottle (Pharmaceuticals) Ltd
Interpharm Ltd
LS Raw Materials Ltd
Magnesia UK
MDA Chemicals Ltd
Medex Medical Export Co Ltd
Pacegrove Ltd
Raught Ltd
Richard Baker Harrison Ltd
SBP Ltd
TA Chemicals
Ubichem Ltd

Other European
E. Merck
Mallinckrodt Speciality Chemicals Europe
  GmbH
Riedel-de Haën AG

USA
Charles B Chrystal Co Inc
Engelhard Corporation
Kaopolite Inc
Mallinckrodt Speciality Chemicals Co
Mutchler Chemical Co Inc
RT Vanderbilt Co Inc
Spectrum Chemical Mfg Corp
Van Waters & Rogers Inc
Whittaker, Clark & Daniels Inc

Lactic Acid
UK
A & E Connock (Perfumery & Cosmetics) Ltd
AMC Chemicals
Berk Chemicals Ltd
Borculo Whey Products UK Ltd
Bush Beach Ltd
Cambridge Research Biochemicals
Cornelius Chemical Co Ltd
Farleyway Chemicals Ltd
Honeywill & Stein Ltd
John Kellys (Merchants) Ltd
LS Raw Materials Ltd
MDA Chemicals Ltd
Medex Medical Export Co Ltd
Merck Ltd
Pacegrove Ltd
Peter Whiting (Chemicals) Ltd
Pointing Group
SBP Ltd
TA Chemicals
Ubichem Ltd

Other European
Dr Paul Lohmann GmbH
E. Merck
Janssen Chimica
Laserson SA
Purac Biochem BV

USA
Amresco Inc
Ashland Chemical Company
Chemco Industries Inc
Ecochem
EM Industries Inc
Fisher Scientific
Gallard-Schlesinger Industries Inc
International Sourcing Inc
Jungbunzlauer Inc
Merona Chemicals Ltd
Mutchler Chemical Co Inc
Penta Manufacturing Co
Pfanstiehl Laboratories Inc
Purac America Inc
RITA Corp
Spectrum Chemical Mfg Corp
Tri-K Industries Inc
Van Waters & Rogers Inc
Vivion Inc

Lactose
UK
Allchem International Ltd

Borculo Whey Products UK Ltd
Cambridge Research Biochemicals
Cerestar UK Ltd
Chesham Chemicals Ltd
Forum Chemicals Ltd
Gale & Mount Ltd
Harbottle (Pharmaceuticals) Ltd
Honeywill & Stein Ltd
IDIS Ltd
Interpharm Ltd
K & K Greeff Ltd
LS Raw Materials Ltd
Magnesia UK
MDA Chemicals Ltd
Medex Medical Export Co Ltd
Merck Ltd
Pacegrove Ltd
Peter Whiting (Chemicals) Ltd
Quest International UK Ltd
Ubichem Ltd

Other European
Borculo Whey Products
Cerestar International Sales
DMV International
E. Merck
HMS Hollandse Melksuikerfabriek
Janssen Chimica
Meggle GmbH

USA
Amresco Inc
Crompton & Knowles Corp
DMV Campina Inc
EM Industries Inc
Foremost Ingredients Group
Forum Products Inc
Helm New York Chemical Corp
Mutchler Chemical Co Inc
Penta Manufacturing Co
Pfanstiehl Laboratories Inc
Quest International Inc
Spectrum Chemical Mfg Corp
Van Waters & Rogers Inc
Vivion Inc

Others
Freund Industrial Co Ltd

Lanolin
UK
Cornelius Chemical Co Ltd
Croda Chemicals Ltd
Harbottle (Pharmaceuticals) Ltd
Henkel Organics
LS Raw Materials Ltd
MDA Chemicals Ltd
Pacegrove Ltd
SBP Ltd
Takasago (UK) Ltd
Westbrook Lanolin Company

Other European
Amerchol Europe
Henkel KGaA
ICI Surfactants

Laserson SA

USA
Amerchol Corp
Brooks Industries Inc
Charkit Chemical Corp
Croda Inc
Gallard-Schlesinger Industries Inc
Mutchler Chemical Co Inc
Protameen Chemicals Inc
Spectrum Chemical Mfg Corp
Takasago International Corp (USA)

Others
Chorney Chemical Co
Takasago International Corp

Lanolin Alcohols
UK
Cornelius Chemical Co Ltd
Croda Chemicals Ltd
Henkel Organics
LS Raw Materials Ltd
Pacegrove Ltd
SBP Ltd
Westbrook Lanolin Company

Other European
Amerchol Europe
Henkel KGaA

USA
Amerchol Corp
Ashland Chemical Company
Brooks Industries Inc
Charkit Chemical Corp
Croda Inc
Gallard-Schlesinger Industries Inc
RITA Corp
Van Waters & Rogers Inc

Others
Chorney Chemical Co

Hydrous Lanolin
UK
Cornelius Chemical Co Ltd
Harbottle (Pharmaceuticals) Ltd
Henkel Organics
Interpharm Ltd
LS Raw Materials Ltd
Magnesia UK
MDA Chemicals Ltd
Medex Medical Export Co Ltd
Pacegrove Ltd
SBP Ltd
Westbrook Lanolin Company

Other European
Henkel KGaA
Laserson SA

USA
Charkit Chemical Corp
Fisher Scientific
Gallard-Schlesinger Industries Inc

Mutchler Chemical Co Inc
RITA Corp
Spectrum Chemical Mfg Corp
Van Waters & Rogers Inc

Others
Chorney Chemical Co

Lecithin
UK
A & E Connock (Perfumery & Cosmetics) Ltd
Alembic Products Ltd
Berk Chemicals Ltd
Brightstern Ltd
Chesham Chemicals Ltd
Cornelius Chemical Co Ltd
Croda Chemicals Ltd
Genzyme Pharmaceuticals and Fine Chemicals
Harbottle (Pharmaceuticals) Ltd
Interpharm Ltd
K & K Greeff Ltd
LS Raw Materials Ltd
Lucas Meyer (UK) Ltd
Merck Ltd
Paldena Ltd
Rhône-Poulenc Chemicals
SBP Ltd
The White Sea & Baltic Company Ltd

Other European
Aarhus Oliefabrik A/S
E. Merck
Laserson SA
Lucas Meyer GmbH & Co

USA
Aceto Corporation
Amresco Inc
Ashland Chemical Company
Avatar Corp
Biospur Inc
Croda Inc
EM Industries Inc
Genzyme Corporation
Lucas Meyer Inc
Penta Manufacturing Co
Pfanstiehl Laboratories Inc
Rhône-Poulenc Inc
Spectrum Chemical Mfg Corp
Van Waters & Rogers Inc
Vivion Inc

Magnesium Aluminum Silicate
UK
Bromhead & Denison Ltd
Bush Beach Ltd
Cornelius Chemical Co Ltd
Interpharm Ltd
K & K Greeff Ltd
LS Raw Materials Ltd
Magnesia UK
Medex Medical Export Co Ltd
SBP Ltd

Other European
E. Merck

USA
American Colloid Co
Engelhard Corporation
RT Vanderbilt Co Inc
Van Waters & Rogers Inc
Whittaker, Clark & Daniels Inc

Magnesium Carbonate
UK
Berk Chemicals Ltd
Cornelius Chemical Co Ltd
Courtin & Warner Ltd
Farleyway Chemicals Ltd
Honeywill & Stein Ltd
Intermag Co Ltd
Interpharm Ltd
LS Raw Materials Ltd
Magnesia UK
MDA Chemicals Ltd
Medex Medical Export Co Ltd
Merck Ltd
Pacegrove Ltd
Pennine Darlington Magnesia Ltd
Peter Whiting (Chemicals) Ltd
Raught Ltd
Richard Baker Harrison Ltd

Other European
Dr Paul Lohmann GmbH
E. Merck
Lehmann & Voss & Co
Magnesia GmbH
Mallinckrodt Speciality Chemicals Europe GmbH

USA
Amresco Inc
Barrington Chemical Corporation
EM Industries Inc
Gallard-Schlesinger Industries Inc
Generichem Corp
Mallinckrodt Speciality Chemicals Co
Marine Magnesium Co
Mutchler Chemical Co Inc
Particle Dynamics Inc
Penta Manufacturing Co
Spectrum Chemical Mfg Corp
Van Waters & Rogers Inc
Vivion Inc
Whittaker, Clark & Daniels Inc

Magnesium Oxide
UK
Berk Chemicals Ltd
Cornelius Chemical Co Ltd
Hoechst UK Ltd
Honeywill & Stein Ltd
IDIS Ltd
Intermag Co Ltd
LS Raw Materials Ltd
Magnesia UK
MDA Chemicals Ltd
Medex Medical Export Co Ltd

Merck Ltd
Pacegrove Ltd
Pennine Darlington Magnesia Ltd
Peter Whiting (Chemicals) Ltd
Ubichem Ltd

Other European
Dr Paul Lohmann GmbH
E. Merck
Lehmann & Voss & Co
Magnesia GmbH
Mallinckrodt Speciality Chemicals Europe GmbH

USA
Amresco Inc
Ashland Chemical Company
Barrington Chemical Corporation
Chemco Industries Inc
Edward Mendell Co Inc
EM Industries Inc
Fisher Scientific
Gallard-Schlesinger Industries Inc
Generichem Corp
JWS Delavau Co Inc
Mallinckrodt Specialty Chemicals Co
Marine Magnesium Co
Mutchler Chemical Co Inc
Noah Chemical
Particle Dynamics Inc
Penta Manufacturing Co
Spectrum Chemical Mfg Corp
United Mineral & Chemical Corp
Van Waters & Rogers Inc
Vivion Inc
Whittaker, Clark & Daniels Inc

Others
Chorney Chemical Co

Magnesium Stearate
UK
Akcros Chemicals
Berk Chemicals Ltd
Bush Beach Ltd
Croxton & Garry Ltd
Durham Chemicals
Fina Chemicals
Hoechst UK Ltd
Intermag Co Ltd
Interpharm Ltd
James M Brown Ltd
K & K Greeff Ltd
LS Raw Materials Ltd
Magnesia UK
Medex Medical Export Co Ltd
Megret Ltd
Merck Ltd
Pacegrove Ltd
Richard Baker Harrison Ltd
SBP Ltd

Other European
Akcros Chemicals v.o.f.
Dr Paul Lohmann GmbH
E. Merck

Fina Chemicals
Janssen Chimica
Laserson SA
Magnesia GmbH
Mallinckrodt Speciality Chemicals Europe
  GmbH

USA
Aceto Corporation
Akcros Chemicals America
Barrington Chemical Corporation
Chemco Industries Inc
EM Industries Inc
Gallard-Schlesinger Industries Inc
Generichem Corp
Harrisons Trading Co Inc
Mallinckrodt Speciality Chemicals Co
Merona Chemicals Ltd
Mutchler Chemical Co Inc
Penta Manufacturing Co
Spectrum Chemical Mfg Corp
Triple Crown America Inc
Van Waters & Rogers Inc
Vivion Inc
Weinstein Nutritional Products

Magnesium Trisilicate
UK
Courtin & Warner Ltd
Intermag Co Ltd
Interpharm Ltd
Joseph Crosfield & Sons Ltd
LS Raw Materials Ltd
Magnesia UK
Medex Medical Export Co Ltd
Merck Ltd
Pacegrove Ltd
Raught Ltd

Other European
Crosfield BV
Dr Paul Lohmann GmbH
E. Merck
Magnesia GmbH

USA
Amresco Inc
Barrington Chemical Corporation
Crosfield Co
EM Industries Inc
Gallard-Schlesinger Industries Inc
Generichem Corp
Mutchler Chemical Co Inc
Penta Manufacturing Co
Spectrum Chemical Mfg Corp

Malic Acid
UK
Berk Chemicals Ltd
Bush Beach Ltd
Cornelius Chemical Co Ltd
Croda Chemicals Ltd
Farleyway Chemicals Ltd
Haarmann & Reimer Ltd
Lonza (UK) Ltd
LS Raw Materials Ltd

MDA Chemicals Ltd
Merck Ltd
Paldena Ltd
Peter Whiting (Chemicals) Ltd
Pointing Group
TA Chemicals

Other European
E. Merck

USA
Amresco Inc
Ashland Chemical Company
Chemco Industries Inc
EM Industries Inc
Gallard-Schlesinger Industries Inc
Haarmann & Reimer Corp
International Sourcing Inc
Penta Manufacturing Co
Schweizerhall Inc
Spectrum Chemical Mfg Corp
Van Waters & Rogers Inc
Vivion Inc

Maltitol Solution
UK
Forum Chemicals Ltd
Roquette (UK) Ltd
Tunnel Refineries Ltd

Other European
Roquette Frères
Xyrofin AG

USA
Roquette America Inc

Maltodextrin
UK
Avebe UK Ltd
Cerestar UK Ltd
Corcoran Chemicals Ltd
Rhône-Poulenc Chemicals
Roquette (UK) Ltd
Tunnel Refineries Ltd

Other European
Avebe BA
Campo Ebro Industrial SA
Cerestar International Sales
Roquette Frères

USA
Avebe America Inc
Chemco Industries Inc
Corn Products
Functional Foods
Genetichem Corp
Grain Processing Corporation
Rhône-Poulenc Inc
Roquette America Inc
Van Waters & Rogers Inc
Vivion Inc
Zumbro Inc

Maltol
UK
Forum Chemicals Ltd
Gale & Mount Ltd
John Kellys (Merchants) Ltd
MDA Chemicals Ltd
Pfizer Food Science Group
RC Treatt & Co Ltd
Scan Chem UK Ltd
Takasago (UK) Ltd

Other European
Laserson SA

USA
Aceto Corporation
Ashland Chemical Company
Penta Manufacturing Co
Pfizer Food Science Group
Takasago International Corp (USA)
Van Waters & Rogers Inc

Others
Takasago International Corp

Mannitol
UK
Allchem International Ltd
Berk Chemicals Ltd
Cerestar UK Ltd
Chemical Exchange (1987) Ltd
Corcoran Chemicals Ltd
IDIS Ltd
Interpharm Ltd
LS Raw Materials Ltd
Magnesia UK
MDA Chemicals Ltd
Medex Medical Export Co Ltd
Merck Ltd
Pacegrove Ltd
Raught Ltd
Roquette (UK) Ltd

Other European
Cerestar International Sales
E. Merck
Polysciences Ltd
Roquette Frères

USA
American Xyrofin Inc
Amresco Inc
Avatar Corp
Chemco Industries Inc
EM Industries Inc
Functional Foods
Harrisons Trading Co Inc
Helm New York Chemical Corp
International Sourcing Inc
Mutchler Chemical Co Inc
Penta Manufacturing Co
Pfanstiehl Laboratories Inc
Roquette America Inc
Schweizerhall Inc
Spectrum Chemical Mfg Corp
Tri-K Industries Inc

Van Waters & Rogers Inc

Medium Chain Triglycerides
UK
Alfa Chemicals Ltd
Allchem International Ltd
Brightstern Ltd
Castrol (UK) Ltd
Chesham Chemicals Ltd
Croda Chemicals Ltd
Henkel Organics
Hüls (UK) Ltd
Karlshamns UK Ltd
MDA Chemicals Ltd
Paroxite Ltd
Quest International UK Ltd
The White Sea & Baltic Company Ltd

Other European
Gattefossé SA
Henkel KGaA
Hüls AG
ICI Surfactants
Karlshamns Lipids for Care
Stepan Europe
Vevy Europe Spa

USA
Avatar Corp
Calgene Chemical Inc
Gattefosse Corp
Hüls America Inc
Karlshamns USA Inc
Lipo Chemicals Inc

Meglumine
UK
Merck Ltd
Rhône-Poulenc Chemicals

Other European
E. Merck

USA
EM Industries Inc
Rhône-Poulenc Inc

Menthol
UK
A & E Connock (Perfumery & Cosmetics)
   Ltd
AMC Chemicals
Berk Chemicals Ltd
Bush Boake Allen Ltd
Courtin & Warner Ltd
Gale & Mount Ltd
Haarmann & Reimer Ltd
Interpharm Ltd
John Kellys (Merchants) Ltd
LS Raw Materials Ltd
Magnesia UK
MDA Chemicals Ltd
Medex Medical Export Co Ltd
Merck Ltd
Pacegrove Ltd
Paldena Ltd

Raught Ltd
RC Treatt & Co Ltd
SA Shepherd & Co Ltd
Scan Chem UK Ltd
Takasago (UK) Ltd

Other European
E. Merck
Haarmann & Reimer GmbH
Jan Dekker BV
Laserson SA
Polysciences Ltd

USA
Chart Corp Inc
EM Industries Inc
Gallard-Schlesinger Industries Inc
Haarmann & Reimer Corp
Mutchler Chemical Co Inc
Penta Manufacturing Co
Spectrum Chemical Mfg Corp
Takasago International Corp (USA)
The Leburmuth Co Inc

Others
Takasago International Corp +

Methylcellulose
UK
Arthur Branwell & Co Ltd
Colorcon Ltd
Courtaulds Chemicals
Dow Chemical Company Ltd
Hercules Ltd
Honeywill & Stein Ltd
IDIS Ltd
Interpharm Ltd
LS Raw Materials Ltd
Stancourt Sons & Muir Ltd

Other European
Aqualon France
Laserson SA

USA
Aceto Corporation
Aqualon
Ashland Chemical Company
Biddle Sawyer Corporation
Colorcon
Dow Chemical Company
Fisher Scientific
Penta Manufacturing Co
Spectrum Chemical Mfg Corp
Van Waters & Rogers Inc

Others
Shin-Etsu Chemical Co Ltd

Methylparaben
UK
Interpharm Ltd
LS Raw Materials Ltd
Magnesia UK
MDA Chemicals Ltd
Medex Medical Export Co Ltd

Merck Ltd
Nipa Laboratories Ltd
Pacegrove Ltd
Pointing Group
SBP Ltd

Other European
Chemag AG
E. Merck
Jan Dekker BV
Laserson SA
Mallinckrodt Speciality Chemicals Europe
   GmbH

USA
Aceto Corporation
Amresco Inc
Ashland Chemical Company
Avatar Corp
EM Industries Inc
Functional Foods
Helm New York Chemical Corp
Inolex Chemical Co
International Sourcing Inc
Kalama Chemical Inc
Kraft Chemical Company
Mallinckrodt Speciality Chemicals Co
Mutchler Chemical Co Inc
Napp Technologies Inc
Nipa Laboratories Inc
Penta Manufacturing Co
Protameen Chemicals Inc
Spectrum Chemical Mfg Corp
Sutton Laboratories Inc
Tri-K Industries Inc
Vivion Inc

Others
Chorney Chemical Co
San Fu Chemical Company Ltd

Mineral Oil
UK
Castrol (UK) Ltd
Condea Chemicals UK Ltd
Eggar & Co (Chemicals) Ltd
K & K Greeff Ltd
Merck Ltd
Mobil Oil Company Ltd
Pacegrove Ltd
Poth, Hille & Co Ltd
SBP Ltd
Silkolene Lubricants Plc

Other European
E. Merck
Laserson SA
Parafluid Mineraloelgesellschaft MbH
USOCO BV

USA
Amresco Inc
Ashland Chemical Company
Avatar Corp
EM Industries Inc
Fisher Scientific

Mobil Oil Corporation
Mutchler Chemical Co Inc
Penta Manufacturing Co
Spectrum Chemical Mfg Corp
Van Waters & Rogers Inc
Vivion Inc

Mineral Oil and Lanolin Alcohols
UK
Croda Chemicals Ltd
Henkel Organics
Westbrook Lanolin Company

Other European
Amerchol Europe
Henkel KGaA

USA
Amerchol Corp
Amresco Inc
Brooks Industries Inc
Croda Inc
Protameen Chemicals Inc
Van Waters & Rogers Inc

Light Mineral Oil
UK
Condea Chemicals UK Ltd
Eggar & Co (Chemicals) Ltd
K & K Greeff Ltd
Medex Medical Export Co Ltd
Merck Ltd
Mobil Oil Company Ltd
Pacegrove Ltd
Poth, Hille & Co Ltd
SBP Ltd
Silkolene Lubricants Plc
Woburn Chemicals Ltd

Other European
E. Merck
Laserson SA

USA
Amresco Inc
Ashland Chemical Company
Avatar Corp
EM Industries Inc
Mobil Oil Corporation
Mutchler Chemical Co Inc
Penta Manufacturing Co
Spectrum Chemical Mfg Corp
Van Waters & Rogers Inc
Vivion Inc

Monoethanolamine
UK
BASF Plc
Berk Chemicals Ltd
Brenntag (UK) Ltd
Bush Beach Ltd
Corcoran Chemicals Ltd
Dow Chemical Company Ltd
Honeywill & Stein Ltd
Interpharm Ltd
K & K Greeff Ltd

MDA Chemicals Ltd
Merck Ltd
SBP Ltd
TA Chemicals
Tennants (Lancashire) Ltd
Texaco Chemical Europe
Union Carbide Ltd
Woburn Chemicals

Other European
E. Merck
Texaco Services (Europe) Ltd

USA
Ashland Chemical Company
Dow Chemical Company
EM Industries Inc
Mutchler Chemical Co Inc
Penta Manufacturing Co
Texaco Chemical International Trader Inc
Van Waters & Rogers Inc

Nitrogen
UK
Air Products Plc
BOC Ltd
CryoService Ltd
Distillers MG Ltd

Other European
Air Liquide

USA
Van Waters & Rogers Inc

Nitrous Oxide
UK
Air Products Plc
BOC Ltd
Distillers MG Ltd

Oleic Acid
UK
Bush Beach Ltd
Chesham Chemicals Ltd
Croda Chemicals Ltd
Fina Chemicals
H. Foster & Co (Stearines) Ltd
K & K Greeff Ltd
LS Raw Materials Ltd
Merck Ltd
Pacegrove Ltd
SBP Ltd
Tennants (Lancashire) Ltd
The White Sea & Baltic Company
Unichema Chemicals Ltd

Other European
E. Merck
Fina Chemicals
Laserson SA

USA
Amresco Inc
Arista Industries
Croda Inc

EM Industries Inc
Fisher Scientific
Mutchler Chemical Co Inc
Penta Manufacturing Co
Schweizerhall Inc
Spectrum Chemical Mfg Corp
Unichema North America
Van Waters & Rogers Inc

Paraffin
UK
AF Suter & Co Ltd
Chemical Exchange (1987) Ltd
Condea Chemicals UK Ltd
Courtin & Warner Ltd
LS Raw Materials Ltd
Magnesia UK
Medex Medical Export Co Ltd
Merck Ltd
Mobil Oil Company Ltd
Pacegrove Ltd
Poth, Hille & Co Ltd
Silkolene Lubricants Plc

Other European
E. Merck
Janssen Chimica
Laserson SA
Parafluid Mineraloelgesellschaft MbH
Polysciences Ltd

USA
Avatar Corp
EM Industries Inc
Koster Keunen Inc
Mobil Oil Corporation
Mutchler Chemical Co Inc
Penta Manufacturing Co
Presperse Inc
Strahl & Pitsch Inc
Van Waters & Rogers Inc
Vivion Inc

Peanut Oil
UK
A & E Connock (Perfumery & Cosmetics) Ltd
Alembic Products Ltd
Allchem International Ltd
Anglia Oils Ltd
Brightstern Ltd
Chemical Exchange (1987) Ltd
Chesham Chemicals Ltd
Croda Chemicals Ltd
John L Seaton & Co Ltd
K & K Greeff Ltd
Karlshamns UK Ltd
Pacegrove Ltd
Paldena Ltd
SBP Ltd
The White Sea & Baltic Company Ltd

Other European
Aarhus Oliefabrik A/S
Karlshamns Lipids for Care

USA
Arista Industries
Avatar Corp
Calgene Chemical Inc
Croda Inc
Karlshamns USA Inc
Mutchler Chemical Co Inc
Penta Manufacturing Co
Spectrum Chemical Mfg Corp

Petrolatum
UK
Condea Chemicals UK Ltd
Eggar & Co (Chemicals) Ltd
LS Raw Materials Ltd
Magnesia UK
Merck Ltd
Mobil Oil Company Ltd
Silkolene Lubricants Plc

Other European
E. Merck
Laserson SA
Parafluid Mineraloelgesellschaft MbH
USOCO BV

USA
Avatar Corp
EM Industries Inc
Mobil Oil Corporation
Mutchler Chemical Co Inc
Penta Manufacturing Co
Spectrum Chemical Mfg Corp
Van Waters & Rogers Inc
Vivion Inc

Petrolatum and Lanolin Alcohols
UK
Henkel Organics
LS Raw Materials Ltd
Westbrook Lanolin Company

Other European
Amerchol Europe
Henkel KGaA

USA
Amerchol Corp
Brooks Industries Inc
RITA Corp
Van Waters & Rogers Inc

Phenol
UK
BP Chemicals Ltd
Brenntag (UK) Ltd
Chance & Hunt
Croda Chemicals Ltd
IDIS Ltd
Interpharm Ltd
LS Raw Materials Ltd
Merck Ltd
Pacegrove Ltd
Paldena Ltd
Pointing Group
PPK Products (UK) Ltd

Raught Ltd
SBP Ltd
Tennants (Lancashire) Ltd
Ubichem Ltd

Other European
E. Merck

USA
Amresco Inc
Dow Chemical Company
EM Industries Inc
Fisher Scientific
Functional Foods
Penta Manufacturing Co
Spectrum Chemical Mfg Corp
Van Waters & Rogers Inc

Phenoxyethanol
UK
BASF Plc
Chesham Chemicals Ltd
Haarmann & Reimer Ltd
Hüls (UK) Ltd
K & K Greeff Ltd
LS Raw Materials Ltd
MDA Chemicals Ltd
Nipa Laboratories Ltd

Other European
Haarmann & Reimer GmbH
Huls AG
Laserson SA

USA
Functional Foods
Haarmann & Reimer Corp
Hüls America Inc
Nipa Laboratories Inc
Penta Manufacturing Co
Tri-K Industries Inc

Phenylethyl Alcohol
UK
BASF Plc
Berk Chemicals Ltd
Courtaulds Chemicals
Gale & Mount Ltd
Haarmann & Reimer Ltd
IFF (Great Britain) Ltd
LS Raw Materials Ltd
MDA Chemicals Ltd
RC Treatt & Co Ltd
Takasago (UK) Ltd

Other European
Haarmann & Reimer GmbH
Laserson SA

USA
Aceto Corporation
Haarmann & Reimer Corp
Penta Manufacturing Co
Takasago International Corp (USA)

Others
Takasago International Corp

Phenylmercuric Acetate
UK
LS Raw Materials Ltd
Magnesia UK
MDA Chemicals Ltd

USA
Amresco Inc
Noah Chemical
Spectrum Chemical Mfg Corp

Phenylmercuric Borate
UK
LS Raw Materials Ltd
Magnesia UK
MDA Chemicals Ltd

USA
Noah Chemical

Phenylmercuric Nitrate
UK
LS Raw Materials Ltd
Magnesia UK
MDA Chemicals Ltd

Other European
Janssen Chimica

USA
Amresco Inc
Noah Chemical
Spectrum Chemical Mfg Corp

Polacrilin Potassium
UK
Rohm and Haas (UK) Ltd

Other European
Röhm Pharma

USA
Rohm and Haas Company

Poloxamer
UK
BASF Plc
ICI Surfactants

Other European
ICI Surfactants
Laserson SA

USA
BASF Corporation
Calgene Chemical Inc
PPG Industries Inc

Polyethylene Glycol
UK
BASF Plc
Berk Chemicals Ltd
Brenntag (UK) Ltd

Corcoran Chemicals Ltd
Dow Chemical Company Ltd
Hoechst UK Ltd
Honeywill & Stein Ltd
Interpharm Ltd
K & K Greeff Ltd
LS Raw Materials Ltd
Medex Medical Export Co Ltd
Pacegrove Ltd
Raught Ltd

Other European
ICI Surfactants
Laserson SA
Polysciences Ltd

USA
Amresco Inc
Ashland Chemical Company
Calgene Chemical Inc
Dow Chemical Company
Lipo Chemicals Inc
Mutchler Chemical Co Inc
PPG Industries Inc
Spectrum Chemical Mfg Corp
Union Carbide Corporation
Van Waters & Rogers Inc

Polymethacrylates
UK
Albright & Wilson Ltd
Chesham Chemicals Ltd
SBP Ltd

Other European
Polysciences Ltd
Röhm Pharma

USA
Presperse Inc

Polyoxyethylene Alkyl Ethers
UK
Albright & Wilson Ltd
Blagden Chemicals Ltd
Chesham Chemicals Ltd
Croda Chemicals Ltd
Hüls (UK) Ltd

Other European
Dr W. Kolb AG
Hüls AG
ICI Surfactants

USA
Calgene Chemical Inc
Croda Inc
Hüls America Inc
Karlshamns USA Inc
Protameen Chemicals Inc
Spectrum Chemical Mfg Corp
Van Waters & Rogers Inc

Polyoxyethylene Castor Oil Derivatives
UK
BASF Plc

Blagden Chemicals Ltd
Chesham Chemicals Ltd
Croda Chemicals Ltd
Honeywill & Stein Ltd
Hüls (UK) Ltd
Karlshamns UK Ltd

Other European
Dr W. Kolb AG
Hüls AG
ICI Surfactants
Karlshamns Lipids for Care
Laserson SA
Seppic

USA
BASF Corporation
Calgene Chemical Inc
Croda Inc
Hüls America Inc
Karlshamns USA Inc
Lipo Chemicals Inc
Protameen Chemicals Inc

Polyoxyethylene Sorbitan Fatty Acid Esters
UK
A & E Connock (Perfumery & Cosmetics)
    Ltd
Akzo Chemicals Ltd
Albright & Wilson Ltd
AP Chemicals Ltd
Blagden Chemicals Ltd
Chesham Chemicals Ltd
Croda Chemicals Ltd
Croxton & Garry Ltd
Henkel Organics
Honeywill & Stein Ltd
ICI Surfactants
K & K Greeff Ltd
Karlshamns UK Ltd
Lonza (UK) Ltd

Other European
Dr W. Kolb AG
Henkel KGaA
ICI Surfactants
Karlshamns Lipids for Care
Laserson SA
Seppic

USA
Calgene Chemical Inc
Croda Inc
Karlshamns USA Inc
Lipo Chemicals Inc
Lonza Inc
Protameen Chemicals Inc
Seppic Inc
Spectrum Chemical Mfg Corp
Witco Corporation

Polyoxyethylene Stearates
UK
Akzo Chemicals Ltd
Albright & Wilson Ltd
AP Chemicals Ltd

Blagden Chemicals Ltd
Chesham Chemicals Ltd
Croda Chemicals Ltd
Hüls (UK) Ltd
K & K Greeff Ltd
Karlshamns UK Ltd
Lonza (UK) Ltd

Other European
Dr W. Kolb AG
Hüls AG
ICI Surfactants
Karlshamns Lipids for Care
Laserson SA

USA
Calgene Chemical Inc
Croda Inc
Hüls America Inc
Karlshamns USA Inc
Lipo Chemicals Inc
Lonza Inc
Protameen Chemicals Inc
RITA Corp
Spectrum Chemical Mfg Corp

Polyvinyl Alcohol
UK
Berk Chemicals Ltd
Blagden Chemicals Ltd
Brenntag (UK) Ltd
British Traders & Shippers Ltd
Du Pont (UK) Ltd
Harlow Chemical Company Ltd
Honeywill & Stein Ltd
SBP Ltd
Tennants (Lancashire) Ltd
Wacker Chemicals Ltd

Other European
Denka
Polysciences Ltd
Wacker-Chemie GmbH

USA
Air Products and Chemicals Inc
Amresco Inc
Chemco Industries Inc
Denka
EI Du Pont de Nemours & Co Inc
Functional Foods
Van Waters & Rogers Inc
Wacker Silicones Corp

Others
Denka

Potassium Chloride
UK
Berk Chemicals Ltd
Farleyway Chemicals Ltd
Forum Chemicals Ltd
Gale & Mount Ltd
Hoechst UK Ltd
Interpharm Ltd
K & K Greeff Ltd

Klinge Chemicals Ltd
LS Raw Materials Ltd
Magnesia UK
MDA Chemicals Ltd
Merck Ltd
Pacegrove Ltd
Raught Ltd
Resource Chemical Ltd
Stan Chem International Ltd
TA Chemicals
Tennants (Lancashire) Ltd
Ubichem Ltd

Other European
Dr Paul Lohmann GmbH
E. Merck
Mallinckrodt Speciality Chemicals Europe
   GmbH

USA
American Ingrdients Inc
Amresco Inc
Ashland Chemical Company
EM Industries Inc
Functional Foods
International Sourcing Inc
Kraft Chemical Company
Mallinckrodt Speciality Chemicals Co
Mutchler Chemical Co Inc
Penta Manufacturing Co
Reheis Inc
Spectrum Chemical Mfg Corp
Van Waters & Rogers Inc
Vivion Inc

Potassium Citrate
UK
AMC Chemicals
Bush Beach Ltd
Courtin & Warner Ltd
Forum Chemicals Ltd
Hoechst UK Ltd
Interpharm Ltd
John Kellys (Merchants) Ltd
LS Raw Materials Ltd
Magnesia UK
MDA Chemicals Ltd
Medex Medical Export Co Ltd
Merck Ltd
Pacegrove Ltd
Paldena Ltd
Rhône-Poulenc Chemicals
Roche Products Ltd
TA Chemicals
Ubichem Ltd

Other European
Dr Paul Lohmann GmbH
E. Merck
Jungbunzlauer International AG
Mallinckrodt Speciality Chemicals Europe
   GmbH

USA
American Ingredients Inc
Amresco Inc

Ashland Chemical Company
Chemco Industries Inc
EM Industries Inc
Helm New York Chemical Corp
International Sourcing Inc
Jungbunzlauer Inc
Kraft Chemical Company
Mallinckrodt Speciality Chemicals Co
Mutchler Chemical Co Inc
Penta Manufacturing Co
Rhône-Poulenc Inc
Schweizerhall Inc
Spectrum Chemical Mfg Corp
Van Waters & Rogers Inc
Weinstein Nutritional Products

Others
Chorney Chemical Co
Gadot Petrochemical Industries Ltd

Potassium Sorbate
UK
Blagden Chemicals Ltd
Cornelius Chemical Co Ltd
Eastman Fine Chemicals
Farleyway Chemicals Ltd
Hoechst UK Ltd
Interpharm Ltd
LS Raw Materials Ltd
Magnesia UK
MDA Chemicals Ltd
Medex Medical Export Co Ltd
Pacegrove Ltd
Peter Whiting (Chemicals) Ltd
Pointing Group

Other European
E. Merck
Laserson SA

USA
Ashland Chemical Company
Chemco Industries Inc
Eastman Fine Chemicals
Helm New York Chemical Corp
International Sourcing Inc
Jungbunzlauer Inc
Kraft Chemical Company
Merona Chemicals Ltd
Mutchler Chemical Co Inc
Penta Manufacturing Co
Protameen Chemicals Inc
Schweizerhall Inc
Spectrum Chemical Mfg Corp
Van Waters & Rogers Inc
Vivion Inc

Povidone
UK
BASF Plc
Interpharm Ltd
ISP Europe
LS Raw Materials Ltd
MDA Chemicals
Medex Medical Export Co Ltd
Pacegrove Ltd

Raught Ltd

Other European
Laserson SA

USA
Amresco Inc
BASF Corporation
ISP

Propane
UK
Air Products Plc
BOC Ltd
BP Chemicals Ltd
Calor Gas Ltd
Distillers MG Ltd
Phillips Petroleum Chemicals UK

USA
Aeropres Corp
Phillips 66 Company
Van Waters & Rogers Inc

Propyl Gallate
UK
Berk Chemicals Ltd
Eastman Fine Chemicals
LS Raw Materials Ltd
Magnesia UK
MDA Chemicals Ltd
Medex Medical Export Co Ltd
Nipa Laboratories Ltd
Rhône-Poulenc Chemicals

Other European
Jan Dekker BV
Laserson SA

USA
Eastman Fine Chemicals
Penta Manufacturing Co
Rhône-Poulenc Inc
Triple Crown America Inc

Propylene Carbonate
UK
Berk Chemicals Ltd
Honeywill & Stein Ltd
Hüls (UK) Ltd
MDA Chemicals Ltd
Merck Ltd
Texaco Chemical Europe

Other European
E. Merck
Hüls AG
Texaco Services (Europe) Ltd

USA
Aceto Corporation
EM Industries Inc
Hüls America Inc
Texaco Chemical International Trader Inc
Van Waters & Rogers Inc

Propylene Glycol
UK
Alcohols Ltd
Arco Chemical Europe Inc
BASF Plc
Berk Chemicals Ltd
Blagden Chemicals Ltd
BP Chemicals Ltd
Chemoxy International Plc
Corcoran Chemicals Ltd
Dow Chemical Company Ltd
Eastman Fine Chemicals
Farleyway Chemicals Ltd
Haarmann & Reimer Ltd
Hayman Ltd
Honeywill and Stein Ltd
Hüls (UK) Ltd
Interpharm Ltd
K & K Greeff Ltd
LS Raw Materials Ltd
Magnesia UK
Medex Medical Export Co Ltd
Merck Ltd
Pacegrove Ltd
Raught Ltd
SBP Ltd
TA Chemicals
Woburn Chemicals Ltd

Other European
E. Merck
Haarmann & Reimer GmbH
Hüls AG
Laserson SA
Polysciences Ltd

USA
Amresco Inc
Arco Chemical Co
Ashland Chemical Company
Avatar Corp
Chemco Industries Inc
Dow Chemical Company
Eastman Fine Chemicals
EM Industries Inc
Fisher Scientific
Haarmann & Reimer Corp
Hüls America Inc
Meer Corp
Mutchler Chemical Co Inc
Penta Manufacturing Co
PPG Industries Inc
Spectrum Chemical Mfg Corp
The Lebermuth Co Inc
Van Waters & Rogers Inc
Vivion Inc

Propylene Glycol Alginate
UK
Chesham Chemicals Ltd
Kelco International Ltd
Protan Ltd

Other European
Laserson SA
Protan A/S

USA
Ashland Chemical Company
Functional Foods
Kelco Division of Merck & Co Inc
Meer Corp
Protan Inc
Van Waters & Rogers Inc

Others
Sansho Co

Propylparaben
UK
Interpharm Ltd
LS Raw Materials Ltd
Magnesia UK
MDA Chemicals Ltd
Medex Medical Export Co Ltd
Merck Ltd
Nipa Laboratories Ltd
Pacegrove Ltd
Pointing Group
SBP Ltd

Other European
Chemag AG
E. Merck
Jan Dekker BV
Laserson SA
Mallinckrodt Speciality Chemicals Europe
  GmbH

USA
Amresco Inc
Ashland Chemical Company
Avatar Corp
EM Industries Inc
Inolex Chemical Co
International Sourcing Inc
Kalama Chemical Inc
Kraft Chemical Company
Mallinckrodt Speciality Chemicals Co
Mutchler Chemical Co Inc
Napp Technologies Inc
Nipa Laboratories Inc
Penta Manufacturing Co
Protameen Chemicals Inc
Spectrum Chemical Mfg Corp
Sutton Laboratories Inc
Tri-K Industries Inc
Triple Crown America Inc
Vivion Inc

Others
San Fu Chemical Co Ltd

Saccharin
UK
Berk Chemicals Ltd
Boots Chemicals
British Traders & Shippers Ltd
Bush Beach Ltd
Cornelius Chemical Co Ltd
Farleyway Chemicals Ltd
Harbottle (Pharmaceuticals) Ltd
IDIS Ltd

Interpharm Ltd
K & K Greeff Ltd
LS Raw Materials Ltd
Magnesia UK
MDA Chemicals Ltd
Medex Medical Export Co Ltd
Pacegrove Ltd
Paldena Ltd
Pointing Group
TA Chemicals
Ubichem Ltd

Other European
Chemag AG
Co Farmaceutica Milanese Spa
Jan Dekker BV
Productos Aditivos SA

USA
Chemco Industries Inc
Helm New York Chemical Corp
International Sourcing Inc
Jungbunzlauer Inc
Merona Chemicals Ltd
Mutchler Chemical Co Inc
Penta Manufacturing Co
RW Greeff & Co Inc
Spectrum Chemical Mfg Corp
Tri-K Industries Inc
Triple Crown America Inc

Others
Chorney Chemical Co

Saccharin Sodium
UK
AMC Chemicals
Berk Chemicals Ltd
Boots Chemicals
British Traders & Shippers Ltd
Bush Beach Ltd
Corcoran Chemicals Ltd
Cornelius Chemical Co Ltd
Gale & Mount Ltd
Harbottle (Pharmaceuticals) Ltd
IDIS Ltd
Interpharm Ltd
John Kellys (Merchants) Ltd
K & K Greeff Ltd
LS Raw Materials Ltd
Magnesia UK
MDA Chemicals Ltd
Medex Medical Export Co Ltd
Pacegrove Ltd
Paldena Ltd
Peter Whiting (Chemicals) Ltd
PMC Specialties International Ltd
Pointing Group
Scan Chem UK Ltd
TA Chemicals
Ubichem Ltd

Other European
Chemag AG
Co Farmaceutica Milanese Spa
Jan Dekker BV

Productos Aditivos SA

USA
Chemco Industries Inc
Harrisons Trading Co Inc
Helm New York Chemical Corp
International Sourcing Inc
Jungbunzlauer Inc
Merona Chemicals Ltd
Mutchler Chemical Co Inc
Penta Manufacturing Co
PMC Specialities Group Inc
RW Greeff & Co Inc
Schweizerhall Inc
Spectrum Chemical Mfg Corp
Tri-K Industries Inc

Others
Chorney Chemical Co

Sesame Oil
UK
A & E Connock (Perfumery & Cosmetics) Ltd
Alembic Products Ltd
Anglia Oils Ltd
Blagden Chemicals Ltd
Brightstern Ltd
Bush Beach Ltd
Chesham Chemicals Ltd
Cornelius Chemical Co Ltd
Croda Chemicals Ltd
Efkay Chemicals Ltd
Eggar & Co (Chemicals) Ltd
IDIS Ltd
John Kellys (Merchants) Ltd
K & K Greeff Ltd
Paldena Ltd
SBP Ltd
Takasago (UK) Ltd
The White Sea & Baltic Company Ltd

Other European
Aarhus Oliefabrik A/S
Jan Dekker BV

USA
Arista Industries
Avatar Corp
Barrington Chemical Corporation
Croda Inc
Desert Balm
Helm New York Chemical Corp
International Sourcing Inc
Lipo Chemicals Inc
Mutchler Chemical Co Inc
Penta Manufacturing Co
Spectrum Chemical Mfg Corp
Takasago International Corp (USA)
Tri-K Industries Inc
Van Waters & Rogers Inc
Vitamins Inc
Vivion Inc

Others
Takasago International Corp

Shellac
UK
AF Suter & Co Ltd
Angelo Rhodes Ltd
Batewell Ltd
British Traders & Shippers Ltd
Eggar & Co (Chemicals) Ltd
Hax Co Ltd
K & K Greeff Ltd
LS Raw Materials Ltd
Pointing Group
SA Shepherd & Co Ltd
SBP Ltd
Thew, Arnott & Co Ltd
Warner Jenkinson Europe Ltd

Other European
Alland & Robert

USA
Functional Foods
Mantrose-Haeuser Co
Van Waters & Rogers Inc

Colloidal Silicon Dioxide
UK
Blagden Chemicals Ltd
Cabot Carbon Ltd
Cornelius Chemical Co Ltd
Degussa Ltd
K & K Greeff Ltd
Merck Ltd
Wacker Chemicals Ltd
WR Grace Ltd

Other European
Cabot GmbH
Degussa AG
E. Merck
Grace GmbH
Wacker-Chemie GmbH

USA
Cabot Corporation
Charles B Chrystal Co Inc
EM Industries Inc
Noah Chemical
Presperse Inc
Van Waters & Rogers Inc
Wacker Silicones Corp
WR Grace & Co

Others
Freund Industrial Co Ltd

Sodium Alginate
UK
Berk Chemicals Ltd
Chesham Chemicals Ltd
Grindsted Products Ltd
Guinness Chemical (Ireland) Ltd
Kelco International Ltd
LS Raw Materials Ltd
MDA Chemicals Ltd
Protan Ltd
Sanofi Bio-Industries Ltd

Other European
Grinsted Products
Laserson SA
Protan A/S
Sobalg

USA
Ashland Chemical Company
Edward Mendell Co Inc
Functional Foods
Grindsted Products Inc
Kelco Division of Merck & Co Inc
Meer Corp
Penta Manufacturing Co
Protan Inc
Spectrum Chemical Mfg Corp

Others
Sansho Co

Sodium Ascorbate
UK
AMC Chemicals
BASF Plc
Forum Chemicals Ltd
Harbottle (Pharmaceuticals) Ltd
LS Raw Materials Ltd
Magnesia UK
MDA Chemicals Ltd
Merck Ltd
Pfizer Food Science Group
Roche Products Ltd
Scan Chem UK Ltd
Ubichem Ltd

Other European
E. Merck
Laserson SA
Takeda Europe GmbH

USA
Ashland Chemical Company
BASF Corporation
EM Industries Inc
Functional Foods
Hoffman-La Roche Inc
Pfizer Food Science Group
Schweizerhall Inc
Spectrum Chemical Mfg Corp
Van Waters & Rogers Inc

Others
Chorney Chemical Co

Sodium Benzoate
UK
AMC Chemicals
Bush Beach Ltd
Corcoran Chemicals Ltd
Cornelius Chemical Co Ltd
Courtin & Warner Ltd
DSM United Kingdom
Farleyway Chemicals Ltd
Forum Chemicals Ltd
Hoechst UK Ltd
Interpharm Ltd

LS Raw Materials Ltd
Magnesia UK
MDA Chemicals Ltd
Medex Medical Export Co Ltd
Merck Ltd
Millchem UK Ltd
Pacegrove Ltd
Pentagon Chemicals Ltd
Peter Whiting (Chemicals) Ltd
Pointing Group
Raught Ltd
Resource Chemicals Ltd
Scan Chem UK Ltd
TA Chemicals
Tennants (Lancashire) Ltd
Ubichem Ltd
Woburn Chemicals Ltd

Other European
Dr Paul Lohmann GmbH
DSM Special Products
E. Merck
Mallinckrodt Speciality Chemicals Europe
 GmbH
Verdugt BV

USA
Amresco Inc
Ashland Chemical Company
DSM Fine Chemicals USA Inc
DuCoa LP
EM Industries Inc
Fisher Scientific
Functional Foods
Helm New York Chemical Corp
International Sourcing Inc
Jungbunzlauer Inc
Kalama Chemical Inc
Kraft Chemical Company
Mallinckrodt Speciality Chemicals Co
Merona Chemicals Ltd
Millmaster Onyx International
Mutchler Chemical Co Inc
Penta Manufacturing Co
Schweizerhall Inc
Spectrum Chemical Mfg Corp
Van Waters & Rogers Inc
Vivion Inc

Others
San Fu Chemical Co Ltd

Sodium Bicarbonate
UK
Brunner Mond & Company Ltd
Courtin & Warner Ltd
Farleyway Chemicals Ltd
LS Raw Materials Ltd
Magnesia UK
MDA Chemicals Ltd
Medex Medical Export Co Ltd
Merck Ltd
Pacegrove Ltd
Peter Whiting (Chemicals) Ltd
Resource Chemicals Ltd
TA Chemicals

Tennants (Lancashire) Ltd
Woburn Chemicals Ltd

Other European
Dr Paul Lohmann GmbH
E. Merck
Mallinckrodt Speciality Chemicals Europe
 GmbH
Polysciences Ltd

USA
Amresco Inc
Ashland Chemical Company
Church & Dwight Co Inc
EM Industries Inc
Fisher Scientific
Gallard-Schlesinger Industries Inc
Mallinckrodt Speciality Chemicals Co
Mutchler Chemical Co Inc
Penta Manufacturing Co
Spectrum Chemical Mfg Corp
Van Waters & Rogers Inc

Sodium Chloride
UK
Berk Chemicals Ltd
British Salt Ltd
Courtin & Warner Ltd
Farleyway Chemicals Ltd
Hoechst UK Ltd
K & K Greeff Ltd
LS Raw Materials Ltd
Magnesia UK
Maldon Crystal Salt Ltd
MDA Chemicals Ltd
Medex Medical Export Co Ltd
Merck Ltd
Pacegrove Ltd
Raught Ltd
Stan Chem International Ltd
TA Chemicals
Tennants (Lancashire) Ltd
Woburn Chemicals Ltd

Other European
E. Merck
Mallinckrodt Speciality Chemicals Europe
 GmbH
Polysciences Ltd

USA
Amresco Inc
Ashland Chemical Company
EM Industries Inc
Fisher Scientific
Heico Chemicals Inc
Mallinckrodt Speciality Chemicals Co
Mutchler Chemical Co Inc
Penta Manufacturing Co
Spectrum Chemical Mfg Corp
Van Waters & Rogers Inc
Vivion Inc

Sodium Citrate Dihydrate
UK
AMC Chemicals

Bush Beach Ltd
Courtin & Warner Ltd
Forum Chemicals Ltd
Haarmann & Reimer Ltd
LS Raw Materials Ltd
Magnesia UK
MDA Chemicals Ltd
Merck Ltd
Pacegrove Ltd
Peter Whiting (Chemicals) Ltd
Pointing Group
Rhône-Poulenc Chemicals
Ubichem Ltd

Other European
Dr Paul Lohmann GmbH
E. Merck
Jungbunzlauer International AG
Mallinckrodt Speciality Chemicals Europe
 GmbH
Polysciences Ltd
SA Citrique Belge NV

USA
Amresco Inc
Ashland Chemical Company
Chemco Industries Inc
EM Industries Inc
Fisher Scientific
Gallard-Schlesinger Industries Inc
Haarmann & Reimer Corp
Helm New York Chemical Corp
International sourcing Inc
Jungbunzlauer Inc
Kraft Chemical Company
Mallinckrodt Speciality Chemicals Co
Merona Chemicals Ltd
Mutchler Chemical Co Inc
Penta Manufacturing Co
Rhône-Poulenc Inc
Spectrum Chemical Mfg Corp
Van Waters & Rogers Inc
Vivion Inc

Others
Gadot Petrochemical Industries Ltd

Sodium Cyclamate
UK
LS Raw Materials Ltd
MDA Chemicals Ltd
RW Unwin & Co Ltd
Stan Chem International Ltd

Other European
Chemag AG
Co Farmaceutica Milanese Spa
Jan Dekker BV
Productos Aditivos SA

USA
Abbott Laboratories
George Uhe Co Inc
Helm New York Chemical Corp

Others
Chorney Chemical Co
San Fu Chemical Co Ltd

Sodium Lauryl Sulfate
UK
Akzo Chemicals Ltd
Albright & Wilson Ltd
Alfa Chemicals Ltd
Blagden Chemicals Ltd
Henkel Organics
Hüls (UK) Ltd
LS Raw Materials Ltd
Magnesia UK
Merck Ltd
Millchem UK Ltd
Pacegrove Ltd
Rewo Chemicals Ltd
SBP Ltd
Ubichem Ltd

Other European
E. Merck
Henkel KGaA
Hüls AG
Laserson SA
Stepan Europe

USA
Accurate Chemical & Scientific Corp
Aceto Corporation
Amresco Inc
Ashland Chemical Company
EM Industries Inc
Fisher Scientific
Hüls America Inc
Millmaster Onyx International
Mutchler Chemical Co Inc
Pilot Laboratories Inc
Sherex Chemical Company Inc
Spectrum Chemical Mfg Corp
Van Waters & Rogers Inc

Others
Boehme Filatex Canada Inc

Sodium Metabisulfite
UK
LS Raw Materials Ltd
MDA Chemicals Ltd
Merck Ltd
Pacegrove Ltd
Peter Whiting (Chemicals) Ltd
Raught Ltd
Resource Chemicals Ltd
TA Chemicals
Tennants (Lancashire) Ltd
William Blythe Ltd
Woburn Chemicals Ltd

Other European
E. Merck
Mallinckrodt Speciality Chemicals Europe
GmbH

USA
Amresco Inc
Ashland Chemical Company
EM Industries Inc
Kraft Chemical Company
Mallinckrodt Speciality Chemicals Co
Penta Manufacturing Co
Spectrum Chemical Mfg Corp
Van Waters & Rogers Inc
Vivion Inc

Dibasic Sodium Phosphate
UK
Albright & Wilson Ltd
Berk Chemicals Ltd
Forum Chemicals Ltd
Honeywill & Stein Ltd
K & K Greeff Ltd
LS Raw Materials Ltd
Magnesia UK
MDA Chemicals Ltd
Merck Ltd
Monsanto Plc
Pacegrove Ltd
Paldena Ltd
Peter Whiting (Chemicals) Ltd
Prayon (UK) Plc
TA Chemicals
Tennants (Lancashire) Ltd

Other European
Chemische Fabrik Budenheim Rudolf A.
Oetker
Dr Paul Lohmann GmbH
E. Merck
Mallinckrodt Speciality Chemicals Europe
GmbH
Monsanto Europe SA
Polysciences Ltd

USA
Amresco Inc
Ashland Chemical Company
EM Industries Inc
Fisher Scientific
Gallard-Schlesinger Industries Inc
Heico Chemicals Inc
Mallinckrodt Speciality Chemicals Co
Merona Chemicals Ltd
Monsanto Chemical Co
Penta Manufacturing Co
Spectrum Chemical Mfg Corp
Van Waters & Rogers Inc
Vivion Inc

Others
Gadot Petrochemical Industries Ltd

Monobasic Sodium Phosphate
UK
Albright & Wilson Ltd
Berk Chemicals Ltd
Forum Chemicals Ltd
Honeywill & Stein Ltd
K & K Greeff Ltd
LS Raw Materials Ltd

Magnesia UK
MDA Chemical Ltd
Monsanto Plc
Pacegrove Ltd
Peter Whiting (Chemicals) Ltd
TA Chemicals
Tennants (Lancashire) Ltd

Other European
Chemische Fabrik Budenheim Rudolf A.
Oetker
Mallinckrodt Speciality Chemicals Europe
GmbH
Monsanto Europe SA
Polysciences Ltd

USA
Amresco Inc
Ashland Chemical Company
Fisher Scientific
Gallard-Schlesinger Industries Inc
Heico Chemicals Inc
Mallincrodt Speciality Chemicals Co
Merona Chemicals Ltd
Monsanto Chemical Co
Penta Manufacturing Co
Spectrum Chemical Mfg Corp
Van Waters & Rogers Inc
Vivion Inc

Others
Gadot Petrochemical Industries Ltd

Sodium Propionate
UK
Forum Chemicals Ltd
Honeywill & Stein Ltd
LS Raw Materials Ltd
Stan Chem International Ltd
Ubichem Ltd

Other European
Dr Paul Lohmann GmbH
Verdugt BV

USA
Ashland Chemical Company
DuCoa LP
Penta Manufacturing Co
Spectrum Chemical Mfg Corp
Van Waters & Rogers Inc

Sodium Starch Glycolate
UK
Avebe UK Ltd
Edward Mendell Co Inc
Forum Chemicals Ltd
Interpharm Ltd
Magnesia UK

Other European
Avebe BA

USA
Aceto Corporation
American Ingredients Inc

Avebe America Inc
Barrington Chemical Corporation
ChorChem Inc
Edward Mendell Co Inc
Functional Foods
Generichem Corp
Pharmaceutical Ingredients Ltd

Others
Chorney Chemical Co

Sodium Stearyl Fumarate
UK
Edward Mendell Co Inc
Forum Chemicals Ltd

Other European
Astra Pharmaceutical Production AB

USA
Edward Mendell Co Inc
Functional Foods

Sorbic Acid
UK
Blagden Chemicals Ltd
Cornelius Chemical Co Ltd
Hoechst UK Ltd
LS Raw Materials Ltd
Magnesia UK
MDA Chemicals Ltd
Merck Ltd
Pacegrove Ltd
Pointing Group
Takasago (UK) Ltd

Other European
E. Merck
Jan Dekker BV
Laserson SA

USA
Amresco Inc
Ashland Chemical Company
Avatar Corp
Chemco Industries Inc
EM Industries Inc
Helm New York Chemical Corp
International Sourcing Inc
Merona Chemicals Ltd
Penta Manufacturing Co
Protameen Chemicals Inc
Schweizerhall Inc
Spectrum Chemical Mfg Corp
Takasago International Corp (USA)
Van Waters & Rogers Inc
Vivion Inc

Others
Takasago International Corp

Sorbitan Esters (Sorbitan Fatty Acid Esters)
UK
A & E Connock (Perfumery & Cosmetics)
   Ltd
Akzo Chemicals Ltd

AP Chemicals Ltd
Blagden Chemicals Ltd
British Traders & Shippers Ltd
Chesham Chemicals Ltd
Cornelius Chemical Co Ltd
Croda Chemicals Ltd
Croxton & Garry Ltd
Henkel Organics
Honeywill & Stein Ltd
K & K Greeff Ltd
Karlshamns UK Ltd
Lonza (UK) Ltd
Magnesia UK
MDA Chemicals Ltd
Medex Medical Export Co Ltd

Other European
Dr W. Kolb AG
Grinsted Products
Henkel KGaA
ICI Surfactants
Karlshamns Lipids for Care
Laserson SA
Seppic

USA
Ashland Chemical Company
Calgene Chemical Inc
Croda Inc
Karlshamns USA Inc
Kraft Chemical Company
Lipo Chemicals Inc
Lonza Inc
PPG Industries Inc
Protameen Chemicals Inc
Spectrum Chemical Mfg Corp

Sorbitol
UK
Berk Chemicals Ltd
Cerestar UK Ltd
Chemical Exchange (1987) Ltd
Corcoran Chemicals Ltd
Cornelius Chemical Co Ltd
Forum Chemicals Ltd
Interpharm Ltd
Lonza (UK) Ltd
LS Raw Materials Ltd
Magnesia UK
MDA Chemicals Ltd
Medex Medical Export Co Ltd
Merck Ltd
Pacegrove Ltd
Paldena Ltd
Resource Chemicals Ltd
Roquette (UK) Ltd
Sparkford Chemicals Ltd
Tunnel Refineries Ltd
Ubichem Ltd
Xyrofin (UK) Ltd

Other European
Amylum NV
Campo Ebro Industrial SA
Cerestar International Sales
E. Merck

Laserson SA
Polysciences Ltd
Roquette Frères

USA
American Xyrofin Inc
Ashland Chemical Company
Avatar Corp
Chemco Industries Inc
EM Industries Inc
Kraft Chemical Company
Lipo Chemicals Inc
Lonza Inc
Merona Chemicals Ltd
Mutchler Chemical Co Inc
Penta Manufacturing Co
Pfanstiehl Laboratories Inc
Roquette America Inc
Schweizerhall Inc
Spectrum Chemical Mfg Corp
Van Waters & Rogers Inc
Vivion Inc

Others
Chorney Chemical Co

Soybean Oil
UK
A & E Connock (Perfumery & Cosmetics)
   Ltd
Alembic Products Ltd
Anglia Oils Ltd
Blagden Chemicals Ltd
Brightstern Ltd
Chesham Chemicals Ltd
Cornelius Chemical Co Ltd
Croda Chemicals Ltd
John L Seaton & Co Ltd
K & K Greeff Ltd
Karlshamns UK Ltd
MDA Chemicals Ltd
Paldena Ltd
SBP Ltd
The White Sea & Baltic Company Ltd

Other European
Aarhus Oliefabrik A/S
Karlshamns Lipids for Care

USA
Arista Industries
Ashland Chemical Company
Avatar Corp
Calgene Chemical Inc
Croda Inc
Karlshamns USA Inc
Lipo Chemicals Inc
Mutchler Chemical Co Inc
Penta Manufacturing Co
Spectrum Chemical Mfg Corp
Van Waters & Rogers Inc

Starch
UK
Avebe UK Ltd
Blagden Chemicals Ltd

Cargill Plc
Cerestar UK Ltd
Colorcon Ltd
Corcoran Chemicals Ltd
Interpharm Ltd
Magnesia UK
National Starch & Chemical Ltd
Pacegrove Ltd
Paldena Ltd
Richard Baker Harrison Ltd
Roquette (UK) Ltd
SBP Ltd
Stan Chem International Ltd
Tunnel Refineries Ltd

Other European
Amylum NV
Avebe BA
Campo Ebro Industrial SA
Cerestar International Sales
Polysciences Ltd
Roquette Frères

USA
AE Staley Mfg Co
American Maize Products Co
Amresco Inc
Avebe America Inc
Colorcon
Corn Products
Generichem Corp
Grain Processing Corporation
Mutchler Chemical Co Inc
Penta Manufacturing Co
Roquette America Inc
Spectrum Chemical Mfg Corp
Van Waters & Rogers Inc
Zumbro Inc

Others
Sansho Co

Sterilizable Maize Starch
UK
Blagden Chemicals Ltd
Cerestar UK Ltd
Corcoran Chemicals Ltd
Interpharm Ltd
National Starch & Chemical Ltd
Paldena Ltd
Roquette (UK) Ltd
Tunnel Refineries Ltd

Other European
Amylum NV
Campo Ebro Industrial SA
Roquette Frères

USA
American Maize Products Co
Roquette America Inc
Van Waters & Rogers Inc

Pregelatinized Starch
UK
Avebe UK Ltd

Cerestar UK Ltd
Colorcon Ltd
Corcoran Chemicals Ltd
Honeywill & Stein Ltd
Interpharm Ltd
National Starch & Chemical Ltd
Paldena Ltd
Peter Whiting (Chemicals) Ltd
Roquette (UK) Ltd
Tunnel Refineries Ltd

Other European
Amylum NV
Avebe BA
Campo Ebro Industrial SA
Cerestar International Sales
Roquette Frères
Seppic

USA
AE Staley Mfg Co
American Maize Products Co
Avebe America Inc
Colorcon
Crompton & Knowles Corp
Functional Foods
Generichem Corp
Mutchler Chemical Co Inc
Roquette America Inc
Seppic Inc
Zumbro Inc

Stearic Acid
UK
A & E Connock (Perfumery & Cosmetics)
   Ltd
Berk Chemicals Ltd
Bush Beach Ltd
Caldic (UK) Ltd
Chesham Chemicals Ltd
Corcoran Chemicals Ltd
Croda Chemicals Ltd
Croxton & Garry Ltd
Eggar & Co (Chemicals) Ltd
Farleyway Chemicals Ltd
Fina Chemicals
H. Foster & Co (Stearines) Ltd
Interpharm Ltd
K & K Greeff Ltd
Lonza (UK) Ltd
LS Raw Materials Ltd
Magnesia UK
Merck Ltd
Pacegrove Ltd
Poth, Hille & Co Ltd
Rewo Chemicals Ltd
SBP Ltd
TA Chemicals
Tennants (Lancashire) Ltd
Thew, Arnott & Co Ltd
The White Sea & Baltic Company Ltd
Unichema Chemicals Ltd

Other European
E. Merck
Fina Chemicals

Karlshamns Lipids for Care
Laserson SA
Mallinckrodt Speciality Chemicals Europe
   GmbH
Polysciences Ltd
Simel Spa

USA
Aceto Corporation
Amresco Inc
Ashland Chemical Company
Croda Inc
EM Industries Inc
Generichem Corp
Koster Keunen Inc
Lonza Inc
Mallinckrodt Speciality Chemicals Co
Mutchler Chemical Co Inc
Penta Manufacturing Co
Sherex Chemical Company Inc
Spectrum Chemical Mfg Corp
Unichema North America
Van Waters & Rogers Inc
Vivion Inc
Witco Corporation

Others
Kawaken Fine Chemicals Co Ltd

Stearyl Alcohol
UK
A & E Connock (Perfumery & Cosmetics)
   Ltd
Chesham Chemicals Ltd
Croda Chemicals Ltd
Croxton & Garry Ltd
Efkay Chemicals Ltd
Eggar & Co (Chemicals) Ltd
Henkel Organics
Kimpton Brothers Ltd
LS Raw Materials Ltd
Millchem UK Ltd
Rewo Chemicals Ltd
SBP Ltd
The White Sea & Baltic Company Ltd

Other European
Aarhus Oliefabrik A/S
Henkel KGaA
Jan Dekker BV
Laserson SA

USA
Ashland Chemical Company
Croda Inc
Lipo Chemicals Inc
Millmaster Onyx International
M Michel & Co Inc
Mutchler Chemical Co Inc
Penta Manufacturing Co
RITA Corp
Sherex Chemical Company Inc
Spectrum Chemical Mfg Corp
Van Waters & Rogers Inc
Vivion Inc

Sucrose
UK
British Sugar Plc
Interpharm Ltd
MDA Chemicals Ltd
Pacegrove Ltd
Tate & Lyle Sugars
Ubichem Ltd

Other European
E. Merck
Polysciences Ltd

USA
Amresco Inc
Austin Chemical Company Inc
Domino Sugar Corporation
EM Industries Inc
Mutchler Chemical Co Inc
Penta Manufacturing Co
Pfanstiehl Laboratories Inc
Schweizerhall Inc
Spectrum Chemical Mfg Corp
Van Waters & Rogers Inc

Others
Chorney Chemical Co

Compressible Sugar
UK
Roquette (UK) Ltd
Tate & Lyle Sugars
Wilfrid Smith Ltd

USA
Austin Chemical Company Inc
Barrington Chemical Corporation
Crompton & Knowles Corp
Domino Sugar Corporation
JWS Delavau Co Inc

Others
Chorney Chemical Co

Confectioner's Sugar
UK
Paldena Ltd
Roquette (UK) Ltd
Wilfrid Smith Ltd

USA
Domino Sugar Corporation
Mutchler Chemical Co Inc

Sugar Spheres
UK
Edward Mendell Co Inc
Forum Chemicals Ltd
Honeywill & Stein Ltd

Other European
NP Pharm SA
Seppic

USA
Barrington Chemical Corporation

Crompton & Knowles Corp
Edward Mendell Co Inc
Mutchler Chemical Co Inc
Ozone Confectioners & Bakers Supply Co
  Inc
Seppic Inc

Others
Freund Industrial Co Ltd

Suppository Bases
UK
Chesham Chemicals Ltd
Efkay Chemicals Ltd
Henkel Organics
Hüls (UK) Ltd

Other European
Aarhus Oliefabrik A/S
Gattefossé SA
Henkel KGaA
Hüls AG

USA
Functional Foods
Gattefosse Corp
Hüls America Inc
Karlshamns USA Inc

Talc
UK
Chemical Exchange (1987) Ltd
Chesham Chemicals Ltd
Cornelius Chemical Co Ltd
Hays Chemical Distribution Ltd
Interpharm Ltd
Luzenac UK Ltd
Magnesia UK
Medex Medical Export Co Inc
Merck Ltd
Pacegrove Ltd
Raught Ltd
Richard Baker Harrison Ltd
Tennants (Lancashire) Ltd
Thew, Arnott & Co Ltd

Other European
E. Merck
Janssen Chimica
Luzenac Europe
Mallinckrodt Speciality Chemicals Europe
  GmbH

USA
Amresco Inc
Charles B Chrystal Co Inc
EM Industries Inc
Kraft Chemical Company
Luzenac America Technical Center
Mallinckrodt Speciality Chemicals Co
Mutchler Chemical Co Inc
Penta Manufacturing Co
Presperse Inc
Spectrum Chemical Mfg Corp
Van Waters & Rogers Inc
Whittaker, Clark & Daniels Inc

Tartaric Acid
UK
Berk Chemicals Ltd
Brenntag (UK) Ltd
Bromhead & Denison Ltd
Bush Beach Ltd
Cornelius Chemical Co Ltd
Farleyway Chemicals Ltd
Ferro Metal and Chemical Corporation Ltd
Forum Chemicals Ltd
Harbottle (Pharmaceuticals) Ltd
LS Raw Materials Ltd
Magnesia Ltd
MDA Chemicals Ltd
Medex Medical Export Co Ltd
Merck Ltd
Pacegrove Ltd
Paldena Ltd
Pointing Group
Prayon (UK) Plc
Raught Ltd
TA Chemicals
Tennants (Lancashire) Ltd

Other European
Dr Paul Lohmann GmbH
E. Merck
Pahi SA

USA
Ashland Chemical Company
Chemco Industries Inc
EM Industries Inc
Helm New York Chemical Corp
International Sourcing Inc
Jungbunzlauer Inc
Merona Chemicals Ltd
Mutchler Chemical Co Inc
Penta Manufacturing Co
Schweizerhall Inc
Spectrum Chemical Mfg Corp
Van Waters & Rogers Inc
Vivion Inc

Tetrafluoroethane
UK
BOC Ltd
Du Pont (UK) Ltd
Hoechst UK Ltd
ICI Chemicals and Polymers Ltd
Rhône-Poulenc Chemicals (Fluorinated
  Products)

USA
EI Du Pont de Nemours & Co Inc
ICI Chemicals and Polymers America

Thimerosal
UK
Berk Chemicals Ltd
LS Raw Materials Ltd
Magnesia UK
MDA Chemicals Ltd
Medex Medical Export Co Ltd
Raught Ltd
Ubichem Ltd

Other European
Biosynth AG

USA
Accurate Chemical & Scientific Corp
Amresco Inc
Atomergic Chemetals Corp
Barrington Chemical Corporation
Gallard-Schlesinger Industries Inc
Generichem Corp
Noah Chemical
Spectrum Chemical Mfg Corp

Titanium Dioxide
UK
Brenntag (UK) Ltd
Chesham Chemicals Ltd
Cornelius Chemical Co Ltd
Degussa Ltd
Du Pont (UK) Ltd
K & K Greeff Ltd
Kronos Ltd
Merck Ltd
Pointing Group
SBP Ltd
TA Chemicals
Tennants (Lancashire) Ltd
Tioxide Europe Ltd
Warner Jenkinson Europe Ltd

Other European
Degussa AG
E. Merck
Janssen Chimica
Laserson SA

USA
Amresco Inc
Brooks Industries Inc
Calgene Chemical Inc
EI Du Pont de Nemours & Co Inc
EM Industries Inc
Kraft Chemical Company
Merona Chemicals Ltd
Penta Manufacturing Co
Presperse Inc
Spectrum Chemical Mfg Corp
Van Waters & Rogers Inc

Others
Freund Industrial Co Ltd

Tragacanth
UK
AF Suter & Co Ltd
Arthur Branwell & Co Ltd
Berk Chemicals Ltd
Cornelius Chemical Co Ltd
Eggar & Co (Chemicals) Ltd
Gale & Mount Ltd
Guinness Chemical (Ireland) Ltd
Interpharm Ltd
LS Raw Materials Ltd
Merck Ltd
Pacegrove Ltd
Rhône-Poulenc Chemicals

SA Shepherd & Co Ltd
Thew, Arnott & Co Ltd

Other European
Alland & Robert
Colloides Naturels International
E. Merck

USA
Ashland Chemical Company
Chart Corp Inc
EM Industries Inc
Fisher Scientific
Gumix International Inc
Meer Corp
Mutchler Chemical Co Inc
Spectrum Chemical Mfg Corp
Van Waters & Rogers Inc

Triacetin
UK
Blagden Chemicals Ltd
Croda Chemicals Ltd
Eastman Fine Chemicals
Haarmann & Reimer Ltd
Honeywill & Stein Ltd
LS Raw Materials Ltd
Stan Chem International Ltd
Unichema Chemicals Ltd

Other European
Haarmann & Reimer GmbH

USA
Aceto Corporation
Avatar Corp
Eastman Fine Chemicals
Haarmann & Reimer Corp
Penta Manufacturing Co
Spectrum Chemical Mfg Corp
Unichema North America

Trichloromonofluoromethane
UK
BOC Ltd
Du Pont (UK) Ltd
Fluorochem Ltd
Hoechst UK Ltd
ICI Chemicals and Polymers Ltd
Rhône-Poulenc Chemicals (Fluorinated
  Products)

USA
EI Du Pont de Nemours & Co Inc
Functional Foods
ICI Chemicals and Polymers America

Triethanolamine
UK
Berk Chemicals Ltd
Brenntag (UK) Ltd
Bush Beach Ltd
Corcoran Chemicals Ltd
Cornelius Chemical Co Ltd
Dow Chemical Company Ltd
Farleyway Chemicals Ltd

H. Foster & Co (Stearines) Ltd
Honeywill & Stein Ltd
Interpharm Ltd
K & K Greeff Ltd
MDA Chemicals Ltd
Merck Ltd
Pacegrove Ltd
SBP Ltd
Tennants (Lancashire) Ltd
Texaco Chemical Europe
Ubichem Ltd
Union Carbide Ltd

Other European
E. Merck
Laserson SA
Polysciences Ltd
Texaco Services (Europe) Ltd

USA
Amresco Inc
Ashland Chemical Company
Dow Chemical Company
EM Industries Inc
Fisher Scientific
Penta Manufacturing Co
Spectrum Chemical Mfg Corp
Texaco Chemical International Trader Inc
Van Waters & Rogers Inc

Triethyl Citrate
UK
Henkel Organics
MDA Chemicals Ltd
Ubichem Ltd

Other European
Henkel KGaA

USA
Morflex Inc
Penta Manufacturing Co
Van Waters & Rogers Inc

Vanillin
UK
AMC Chemicals
Bush Boake Allen Ltd
Chemical Exchange (1987) Ltd
Cornelius Chemical Co Ltd
Courtin & Warner Ltd
Gale & Mount Ltd
Haarmann & Reimer Ltd
Interpharm Ltd
John Kellys (Merchants) Ltd
Kimpton Brothers Ltd
LS Raw Materials Ltd
MDA Chemicals Ltd
Merck Ltd
Paldena Ltd
Pointing Group
Raught Ltd
RC Treatt & Co Ltd
Rhône-Poulenc Chemicals
SBP Ltd

Scan Chem UK Ltd
Takasago (UK) Ltd

Other European
E. Merck
Haarmann & Reimer GmbH
Laserson SA
Polysciences Ltd

USA
Amresco Inc
Ashland Chemical Company
Avatar Corp
Chart Corp Inc
EM Industries Inc
Fisher Scientific
Freeman Industries Inc
Haarmann & Reimer Corp
Helm New York Chemical Corp
Kraft Chemical Company
Mutchler Chemical Co Inc
Penta Manufacturing Co
Rhône-Poulenc Inc
Schweizerhall Inc
Spectrum Chemical Mfg Corp
Takasago International Corp (USA)
The Lebermuth Co Inc
Van Waters & Rogers Inc
Virginia Dare

Others
Chorney Chemical Co
Takasago International Corp

Hydrogenated Vegetable Oil, Type I
UK
Anglia Oils Ltd
Croda Chemicals Ltd
Edward Mendell Co Inc
Efkay Chemicals Ltd
Eggar & Co (Chemicals) Ltd
Forum Chemicals Ltd
Hüls (UK) Ltd
K & K Greeff Ltd
Karlshamns UK Ltd
Paldena Ltd

Other European
Aarhus Oliefabrik A/S
Hüls AG
Karlshamns Lipids for Care
Laserson SA

USA
Avatar Corp
Croda Inc
Edward Mendell Co Inc
Hüls America Inc
Karlshamns USA Inc
Lipo Chemicals Inc
Van Waters & Rogers Inc
Vivion Inc

Others
Freund Industrial Co Ltd

Anionic Emulsifying Wax
UK
Blagden Chemicals Ltd
British Wax Refining Co
Chesham Chemicals Ltd
Courtin & Warner Ltd
Croda Chemicals Ltd
Eggar & Co (Chemicals) Ltd
Henkel Organics
Hoechst UK Ltd
Interpharm Ltd
Kimpton Brothers Ltd
LS Raw Materials Ltd
Medex Medical Export Co Ltd
Pacegrove Ltd
SBP Ltd
Thew, Arnott & Co Ltd

Other European
Henkel KGaA

USA
Brooks Industries Inc
Caschem Inc
Croda Inc
Lipo Chemicals Inc
PPG Industries Inc

Carnauba Wax
UK
AF Suter & Co Ltd
BASF Plc
British Wax Refining Co
Bush Beach Ltd
Eggar & Co (Chemicals) Ltd
Interpharm Ltd
K & K Greeff Ltd
Kimpton Brothers Ltd
LS Raw Materials Ltd
Pacegrove Ltd
Pointing Group
Poth, Hille & Co Ltd
SBP Ltd
Thew, Arnott & Co Ltd

Other European
Alland & Robert
Laserson SA

USA
Frank B Ross Co Inc
Koster Keunen Inc
Mutchler Chemical Co Inc
Penta Manufacturing Co
Strahl & Pitsch Inc
Van Waters & Rogers Inc
Vivion Inc

Others
Freund Industrial Co Ltd

Microcrystalline Wax
UK
AF Suter & Co Ltd
Blagden Chemicals Ltd
British Wax Refining Co

Bush Beach Ltd
Condea Chemicals UK Ltd
Eggar & Co (Chemicals) Ltd
Kimpton Brothers Ltd
LS Raw Materials Ltd
Mobil Oil Company Ltd
Poth, Hille & Co Ltd
SBP Ltd
Thew, Arnott & Co Ltd

USA
Avatar Corp
Frank B Ross Co Inc
Functional Foods
Koster Keunen Inc
Mobil Oil Corporation
Strahl & Pitsch Inc
Van Waters & Rogers Inc
Vivion Inc

Nonionic Emulsifying Wax
UK
British Wax Refining Co
Chesham Chemicals Ltd
Croda Chemicals Ltd
Efkay Chemicals Ltd
Eggar & Co (Chemicals) Ltd
Henkel Organics
Kimpton Brothers Ltd
LS Raw Materials Ltd
Magnesia UK
Medex Medical Export Co Ltd
Pacegrove Ltd
SBP Ltd
Stan Chem International Ltd

Other European
Henkel KGaA

USA
Caschem Inc
Croda Inc
Koster Keunen Inc
Lipo Chemicals Inc
PPG Industries Inc
RITA Corp
Tri-K Industries Inc

White Wax
UK
A & E Connock (Perfumery & Cosmetics)
    Ltd
AF Suter & Co Ltd
British Wax Refining Co
Bush Beach Ltd
Condea Chemicals UK Ltd
Courtin & Warner Ltd
Croda Chemicals Ltd
Eggar & Co (Chemicals) Ltd
Hax Co Ltd
Hoechst UK Ltd
Kimpton Brothers Ltd
Merck Ltd
Pacegrove Ltd
Poth, Hill & Co Ltd

SBP Ltd
Thew, Arnott & Co Ltd

Other European
E. Merck
Laserson SA

USA
Avatar Corp
Croda Inc
EM Industries Inc
Frank B Ross Co Inc
Koster Keunen Inc
Mantrose-Haeuser Co
Mutchler Chemical Co Inc
Penta Manufacturing Co
Spectrum Chemical Mfg Corp
Strahl & Pitsch Inc
Van Waters & Rogers Inc
Vivion Inc

Yellow Wax
UK
AF Suter & Co Ltd
British Wax Refining Co
Bush Beach Ltd
Condea Chemicals UK Ltd
Courtin & Warner Ltd
Eggar & Co (Chemicals) Ltd
Hoechst UK Ltd
Impag (Great Britain) Ltd
Kimpton Brothers Ltd
Pacegrove Ltd
Poth, Hille & Co Ltd
SBP Ltd
Thew, Arnott & Co Ltd

Other European
Laserson SA

USA
Avatar Corp
Frank B Ross Co Inc
Koster Keunen Inc
Mutchler Chemical Co Inc
Penta Manufacturing Co
Spectrum Chemical Mfg Corp
Strahl & Pitsch Inc
Van Waters & Rogers Inc
Vivion Inc

Xanthan Gum
UK
A & E Connock (Perfumery & Cosmetics)
  Ltd
AF Suter & Co Ltd
Arthur Branwell & Co Ltd
Berk Chemicals Ltd
Cerestar UK Ltd
Cornelius Chemical Co Ltd

Courtaulds Chemicals
Eggar & Co (Chemicals) Ltd
Gale & Mount Ltd
Guinness Chemical (Ireland) Ltd
Interpharm Ltd
Kelco International Ltd
LS Raw Materials Ltd
MDA Chemicals Ltd
Raught Ltd
Rhône-Poulenc Chemicals
Sanofi Bio-Industries Ltd
Thew, Arnott & Co Ltd

Other European
Cerestar International Sales
Jungbunzlauer International AG
Laserson SA

USA
Ashland Chemical Company
Chart Corp Inc
Functional Foods
Gumix International Inc
Jungbunzlauer Inc
Kelco Division of Merck & Co Inc
Meer Corp
Rhône-Poulenc Inc
RT Vanderbilt Co Inc
Spectrum Chemical Mfg Corp
Van Waters & Rogers Inc
Zumbro Inc

Others
Sansho Co

Xylitol
UK
Cerestar UK Ltd
Edward Mendell Co Inc
Forum Chemicals Ltd
Interpharm Ltd
MDA Chemicals Ltd
Raught Ltd
Roquette (UK) Ltd
Scan Chem UK Ltd
Xyrofin (UK) Ltd

Other European
Cerestar International Sales
Roquette Frères
Xyrofin AG

USA
American Xyrofin Inc
Amresco Inc
Edward Mendell Co Inc
Functional Foods
Penta Manufacturing Co
Pfanstiehl Laboratories Inc
Roquette America Inc

Others
Eisai Co Ltd

Zein
UK
Hax Co Ltd
Interpharm Ltd
MDA Chemicals Ltd
Pointing Group

USA
Freeman Industries Inc
Mantrose-Haeuser Co
Vivion Inc
Zumbro Inc

Zinc Stearate
UK
Akcros Chemicals
Berk Chemicals Ltd
Bush Beach Ltd
Chesham Chemicals Ltd
Cornelius Chemical Co Ltd
Croxton & Garry Ltd
Durham Chemicals
Fina Chemicals
James M Brown Ltd
K & K Greeff Ltd
LS Raw Materials Ltd
MDA Chemicals Ltd
Megret Ltd
Pacegrove Ltd
Peter Whiting (Chemicals) Ltd
Richard Baker Harrison Ltd
SBP Ltd
Sparkford Chemicals Ltd
Woburn Chemicals Ltd

Other European
Akcros Chemicals v.o.f.
Dr Paul Lohmann GmbH
Fina Chemicals
Laserson SA
Mallinckrodt Speciality Chemicals Europe
  GmbH

USA
Aceto Corporation
Akcros Chemicals America
Fisher Scientific
Mallinckrodt Speciality Chemicals Co
Merona Chemicals Ltd
Mutchler Chemical Co Inc
Penta Manufacturing Co
Spectrum Chemical Mfg Corp
Van Waters & Rogers Inc
Vivion

Suppliers' List: UK

A & E Connock (Perfumery & Cosmetics) Ltd
Alderholt Mill House
Fordingbridge
Hampshire
SP6 1PU
Tel: 0425 653367
Fax: 0425 656041
Trade names: *Armotan MS; Armotan MO; Armotan ML; Armotan MP; Armotan PML 20; Armotan PMS 20; Armotan PMO 20; Kortacid 1895.*

AF Suter & Co Ltd
Swan Wharf
60 Dace Road
London
E3 2NQ
Tel: 081 986 8218
Fax: 081 985 0747
Trade names: *Swanlac.*

Air Products Plc
Speciality Gases Department
Weston Road
Crewe
Cheshire
CW1 1DF
Tel: 0270 583131
Fax: 0270 500024

Akcros Chemicals
Lankro House
PO Box 1
Eccles
Manchester
M30 0BH
Tel: 061 789 7300
Fax: 061 788 7886

Akzo Chemicals Ltd
1-5 Queens Road
Hersham
Walton-on-Thames
Surrey
KT12 5NL
Tel: 0932 247891
Fax: 0932 231204
Trade names: *Armotan ML; Armotan MO; Armotan MP; Armotan MS; Armotan PML 20; Armotan PMO 20; Armotan PMS 20; Elfan 240; Kessco EO; Kessco GMS; Kessco IPM 95; Kessco IPP; Kessco PEG 400 DS; Kessco PEG 6000 DS.*

Albright & Wilson Ltd
PO Box 3
210-222 Hagley Road West
Oldbury
Warley
West Midlands
B68 0NN

Tel: 021 429 4942
Fax: 021 420 5151

Alcohols Ltd
Charringtons House North
The Causeway
Bishop's Stortford
Hertfordshire
CM23 2EW
Tel: 0279 658464
Fax: 0279 757613

Alembic Products Ltd
River Lane
Saltney
Chester
CH4 8RQ
Tel: 0244 680147
Fax: 0244 680155

Alfa Chemicals Ltd
Arc House
Terrace Road South
Binfield
Bracknell
Berkshire
RG12 5PZ
Tel: 0344 861800
Fax: 0344 862010
Trade names: *Compritol 888; Precirol ATO 5.*

Allchem International Ltd
Broadway House
21 Broadway
Maidenhead
Berkshire
SL6 1JE
Tel: 0628 776666
Fax: 0628 776591
Trade names: *Bergabest; Vivacel.*

AMC Chemicals
10 Charterhouse Square
London
EC1M 6EH
Tel: 071 626 4521
Fax: 071 490 2726

Angelo Rhodes Ltd
Corolin Road
Lower Tuffley
Gloucester
GL2 6DQ
Tel: 0452 305021
Fax: 0452 306545

Anglia Oils Ltd
King George Dock
Hull
North Humberside
HU9 5PX
Tel: 0482 701271
Fax: 0482 709447

AP Chemicals Ltd
Station Road
Cheddleton
Nr Leek
Staffordshire
ST13 7EF
Tel: 0538 361302
Fax: 0538 361330

Arco Chemical Europe Inc
Arco Chemical House
Bridge Avenue
Maidenhead
Berkshire
SL6 1YP
Tel: 0628 775000
Fax: 0628 775180

Arthur Branwell & Co Ltd
Bronte House
58-62 High Street
Epping
Essex
CM16 4AE
Tel: 0992 577333
Fax: 0992 575043

Avebe UK Ltd
Thornton Hall
Thornton Curtis
Ulceby
South Humberside
DN39 6XD
Tel: 0469 32222
Fax: 0469 31488
Trade names: *Avebe; Avedex; Prejel; Primellose; Primojel.*

BASF Plc
PO Box 4
Earl Road
Cheadle Hulme
Cheadle
Cheshire
SK8 6QG
Tel: 061 485 6222
Fax: 061 486 0891
Trade names: *Cremophor EL; Cremophor RH40; Kollidon; Kollidon CL; Lutrol E; Palatinol A; Pluronic.*

Batewell Ltd
Meadow Cottage
Ferbies
Speldhurst
Kent
TN3 0NS
Tel: 0892 863015
Fax: 0892 862443

Becpharm Ltd
7 Spire Green Centre
Flex Meadow
Harlow
Essex
CM19 5TR

Tel: 0279 434567
Fax: 0279 429664

Berk Chemicals Ltd
PO Box 56
Priestley Road
Basingstoke
Hampshire
RG24 9QB
Tel: 0256 29292
Fax: 0256 64711

BFGoodrich Chemical (UK) Ltd
The Lawn
100 Lampton Road
Hounslow
Middlesex
TW3 4EB
Tel: 081 570 4700
Fax: 081 570 0850
Trade names: *Carbopol.*

Blagden Chemicals Ltd
A.M.P. House
Dingwall Road
Croydon
Surrey
CR9 3QU
Tel: 081 681 2341
Fax: 081 688 5851

Blythe Ltd *see* **William Blythe Ltd**

BOC Ltd
Special Gases
The Priestley Centre
10 Priestley Road
The Surrey Research Park
Guildford
Surrey
GU2 5XY
Tel: 0483 579857
Fax: 0483 32115
Trade names: *Suva 134a.*

Boots Chemicals
Thane Road
Nottingham
NG2 3AA
Tel: 0602 591643
Fax: 0602 591680
Trade names: *Britsol; Bronopol-Boots; Myacide.*

Borculo Whey Products UK Ltd
Unit 2
Brymau Four Estate
River Lane
Saltney
Nr Chester
CH4 8RQ
Tel: 0244 680127
Fax: 0244 671703
Trade names: *L18; Lactochem; Microfine; Zeparox.*

BP Chemicals Ltd
6th Floor
Brittania House
1 Finsbury Circus
London
EC2M 7BA
Tel: 071 496 5005
Fax: 071 496 4516
Trade names: *Breox PEG.*

Branwell Ltd *see* **Arthur Branwell & Co Ltd**

Brenntag (UK) Ltd
Brenntag House
High Street
Hampton Wick
Kingston-upon-Thames
Surrey
Tel: 081 977 3200

Brightstern Ltd
24 Haigh Park
Haigh Avenue
Stockport
Cheshire
SK4 1QR
Tel: 061 429 9552
Fax: 061 429 7662

British Gypsum Ltd
Industrial Products Division
Jericho Works
Bowbridge Road
Newark
Nottinghamshire
NG24 3BZ
Tel: 0636 703351
Fax: 0636 73542
Trade names: *Ground Gypsum Superfine White; Ground Gypsum FG200.*

British Salt Ltd
Cledford Lane
Middlewich
Cheshire
CW10 0JP
Tel: 0606 832881
Fax: 0606 835999
Trade names: *Aquasol; Granulite.*

British Sugar Plc
PO Box 26
Oundle Road
Peterborough
PE2 9QU
Tel: 0733 63171
Fax: 0733 63068

British Traders & Shippers Ltd
6-7 Merrielands Crescent
Dagenham
Essex
RM9 6SL
Tel: 081 595 4211
Fax: 081 593 0933

British Wax Refining Co
29 St John's Road
Redhill
Surrey
RH1 6DT
Tel: 0737 761242
Fax: 0737 761472

Bromhead & Denison Ltd
7 Stonebank
Welwyn Garden City
Herts
AL8 6NQ
Tel: 0707 331031
Fax: 0707 325012
Trade names: *BentoPharm; Carrisorb; Gelsorb.*

Brown Ltd *see* **James M Brown Ltd**

Brunner Mond & Company Ltd
PO Box 4
Mond House
Northwich
Cheshire
CW8 4DT
Tel: 0606 724183
Fax: 0606 781353

Bush Beach Ltd
Paul Ungerer House
Earl Road
Stanley Green
Handforth
Wilmslow
Cheshire
SK9 3RL
Tel: 061 485 8231
Fax: 061 486 6212

Bush Boake Allen Ltd
Natural Products Division
Blackhorse Lane
London
E17 5QP
Tel: 081 531 4211
Fax: 081 531 7413

Cabot Carbon Ltd
Cab-O-Sil Division
Barry Site
Sully Moors Road
Sully
South Glamorgan
CF6 2XP
Tel: 0446 736999
Trade names: *Cab-O-Sil.*

Caldic (UK) Ltd
Unit 10
Kidlington Buisness Park
Lakesmere Close
Kidlington
Oxfordshire
OX5 1LG

Tel: 0865 841311
Fax: 0865 841288

Calor Gas Ltd
Southern Region
Third Avenue
Milbrook Trading Estate
Southampton
SO9 1WE
Tel: 0703 777244
Fax: 0703 789228

Cambridge Research Biochemicals
Gadbrook Park
Northwich
Cheshire
CW9 7RA
Tel: 0606 41100
Fax: 0606 49366

Cargill Plc
Milling Division
Tilbury Docks
Essex
RM18 7PU
Tel: 0375 851122
Fax: 0375 850665

Castrol (UK) Ltd
Burmah Castrol House
Pipers Way
Swindon
Wiltshire
SN3 1RE
Tel: 0793 512712
Fax: 0793 513506
Trade names: *Puremor WOM; Vitalube RA; Whitemor WOT.*

Cerestar UK Ltd
Trafford Park
Manchester
M17 1PA
Tel: 061 872 5959
Fax: 061 848 8760

Chance & Hunt
Alexander House
Crown Gate
Runcorn
Cheshire
WA7 2UP
Tel: 0928 793000
Fax: 0928 714351

Chemical Exchange (1987) Ltd
Chemexel House
11 Sunderland Road
London
SE23 2PS
Tel: 081 699 0466
Fax: 081 291 6290

Chemie Linz UK Ltd
12 The Green
Richmond

Surrey
TW9 1PX
Tel: 081 948 6966
Fax: 081 948 8923

Chemoxy International Plc
All Saints Refinery
Cargo Fleet Road
Middlesborough
Cleveland
TS3 6AF
Tel: 0642 248555
Fax: 0642 244340

Chesham Chemicals Ltd
Cunningham House
Westfield Lane
Kenton
Middlesex
HA3 9ED
Tel: 081 907 7779
Fax: 081 909 1053

Cochrane & Keane (Chemicals) Ltd
Chichester Street
Rochdale
Lancashire
OL16 2AU
Tel: 0706 54341
Fax: 0706 46811

Colorcon Ltd
Murray Road
St. Pauls Cray
Orpington
Kent
BR5 3QY
Tel: 0689 838301
Fax: 0689 878342
Trade names: *Methocel; Starch 1500; Starch 1500 L.M.; Surelease.*

Condea Chemicals UK Ltd
Millennium House
21 Eden Street
Kingston-upon-Thames
Surrey
KT1 1BL
Tel: 081 547 3006
Fax: 081 547 3608
Trade names: *Merkur.*

Connock Ltd *see* **A & E Connock (Perfumery & Cosmetics) Ltd**

Corcoran Chemicals Ltd
Oak House
Oak Close
Wilmslow
Cheshire
SK9 6DF
Tel: 0625 532731
Fax: 0625 539096

Cornelius Chemical Co Ltd
St. James's House

27-43 Eastern Road
Romford
Essex
RM1 3NN
Tel: 0708 722300
Fax: 0708 768204

Courtaulds Chemicals
PO Box 5
Spondon
Derbyshire
DE21 7BP
Tel: 0332 661422
Fax: 0332 280610
Trade names: *Celacol; Courlose; Courcel.*

Courtin & Warner Ltd
19 Phoenix Place
Lewes
Sussex
BN7 1JX
Tel: 0273 480611
Fax: 0273 472249

Croda Chemicals Ltd
Cowick Hall
Snaith
Goole
North Humberside
DN14 9AA
Tel: 0405 860551
Fax: 0405 860205
Trade names: *Cithrol 4MS; Cithrol GMO N/E; Cithrol GMS N/E; Cithrol GMS S/E; Corona; Crill; Crillet; Crodacid; Crodacol CS; Crodacol C70; Crodacol C90; Crodacol C95; Crodacol S95; Crodamol IPM; Crodamol IPP; Crodamol SS; Croderol; Crodet S8; Crodet S40; Crodet S50; Crodex A; Crodex N; Crodolene; Croduret 40; Crodyne BY19; Cropol 35; Cropol 60; Cropol 70; Crosterene; Etocas 35; Hartolan; Volpo CS20; Volpo N10; Volpo O10.*

Crosfield & Sons Ltd *see* **Joseph Crosfield & Sons Ltd**

Croxton & Garry Ltd
Curtis Road
Dorking
Surrey
RH4 1XA
Tel: 0306 886688
Fax: 0306 887780
Trade names: *Cellosize; Cepo; Millicarb; Sorbirol.*

CryoService Ltd
Blackpole Trading Estate East
Blackpole Road
Worcester
WR3 8SG
Tel: 0905 754500
Fax: 0905 754060

Davis Gelatine
Upper Grove Street
Leamington Spa
Warwickshire
CV32 5AN
Tel: 0926 422795
Fax: 0926 335126

Degussa Ltd
Paul Ungerer House
Earl Road
Stanley Green
Handforth
Wilmslow
Cheshire
SK9 3RL
Tel: 061 486 6211
Fax: 061 485 6445
Trade names: *Aerosil; Elcema.*

Dinoval Ltd *see* **Pointing Group**

Distillers MG Ltd
Cedar House
39 London House
Reigate
Surrey
RH2 9QE
Tel: 0737 241133
Fax: 0737 241842

Dow Chemical Company Ltd
Lakeside House
Stockley Park
Uxbridge
Middlesex
UB11 1BE
Tel: 081 848 8688
Fax: 081 848 5400
Trade names: *Ethocel; Methocel.*

DSM United Kingdom
Kingfisher House
Redditch
Worcestershire
B97 4EZ
Tel: 0527 68254
Fax: 0527 68949

Du Pont (UK) Ltd
Wedgewood Way
Stevenage
Hertfordshire
SG1 4QN
Tel: 0438 734487
Fax: 0438 734621
Trade names: *Dymel 11; Dymel 12; Dymel 22; Dymel 114; Dymel 134a/P; Dymel 142b; Dymel 152a; Dymel A; Elvanol; TiPure.*

Durham Chemicals
Birtley
Chester-le-Street
County Durham
DH3 1QX

Tel: 091 410 2361
Fax: 091 410 6005

Eastman Fine Chemicals
Hadrian House
Edgefield Avenue
Fawdon
Newcastle Upon Tyne
NE3 3TT
Tel: 091 285 3311
Fax: 091 284 5975
Trade names: *Kodaflex DBP; Kodaflex DEP; Kodaflex DMP; Myvaplex 600P.*

ECC International (Sales) Ltd
John Keay House
St. Austell
Cornwall
PL25 4DJ
Tel: 0726 74482
Fax: 0726 6230191

Edward Mendell Co Inc
Church House
48 Church Street
Reigate
Surrey RH2 0SN
Tel: 0737 222323
Fax: 0737 222545
Trade names: *Caridex; Compactrol; Emcocel; Emcompress; Emcompress Anhydrous; Emdex; Emvelop; Explotab; Lubritab; Nonpareil seeds; Pruv; Solka-Floc; Sugartab.*

Efkay Chemicals Ltd
204 Banderway House
156-162 Kilburn High Road
London
NW6 4JD
Tel: 071 625 4445
Fax: 071 328 9101

Eggar & Co (Chemicals) Ltd
High Street
Theale
Reading
Berkshire
RG7 5AR
Tel: 0734 302379
Fax: 0734 323224

Eisai Pharma-Chem Europe Ltd
Commonwealth House
Hammersmith International Centre
London
W6 8DW
Tel: 081 741 1330
Fax: 081 913 0019

Farleyway Chemicals Ltd
Ham Lane
Kingswinford
West Midlands
DY6 7JU
Tel: 0384 400222
Fax: 0384 400020

Ferro Metal and Chemical Corporation Ltd
179 Kings Road
Reading
Berkshire
RG1 4EX
Tel: 0784 591961
Fax: 0734 509216

Fina Chemicals
Fina House
Ashley Avenue
Epsom
Surrey
KT18 5AD
Tel: 03727 26226
Fax: 03727 45821

Fluorochem Ltd
Wesley Street
Old Glossop
Derbyshire
SK13 9RY
Tel: 0457 868921
Fax: 0457 869360

Forum Chemicals Ltd
Forum House
41-51 Brighton Road
Redhill
Surrey
RH1 6YS
Tel: 0737 773711
Fax: 0737 773116
Trade names: *C-97; CCal-97; Finmalt L; NutraSweet; SA-99.*

Foster & Co *see* **H. Foster & Co (Stearines) Ltd**

Gale & Mount Ltd
Liverpool Road
Eccles
Manchester
M30 7RT
Tel: 061 787 7136
Fax: 061 787 3341

Genzyme Pharmaceuticals and Fine Chemicals
37 Hollands Road
Haverhill
Suffolk
CB9 8PU
Tel: 0440 703522
Fax: 0440 707783

Grace Ltd *see* **WR Grace Ltd**

Grindsted Products Ltd
Northern Way
Bury St Edmonds
Suffolk
IP32 6NP
Trade names: *Sobalg.*

Guinness Chemical (Ireland) Ltd
33 London Street
Reading
Berkshire
RG1 4PS
Tel: 0734 391222
Fax: 0734 393871
Trade names: *Merezan.*

Haarmann & Reimer Ltd
Fieldhouse Lane
Marlow
SL7 1NA
Tel: 0628 472051
Fax: 0628 472238

Hampshire Chemical Ltd
Northdale House
North Circular Road
London
NW10 7UH
Tel: 081 961 9366
Fax: 081 963 0928
Trade names: *Detarex.*

Harbottle (Pharmaceuticals) Ltd
Seabright House
72-76 River Road
Barking
Essex
IG11 0DY
Tel: 081 594 9617
Fax: 081 591 8563

Harcross Chemical Group *see* **Durham Chemicals**

Harlow Chemical Company Ltd
Templefields
Harlow
Essex
CM20 2BH
Tel: 0279 436211
Fax: 0279 444025

Hax Co Ltd
306 Archway Road
Highgate
London
N6 5AU
Tel: 081 341 1010
Fax: 081 348 0504
Trade names: *Mantrolac R-49.*

Hayman Ltd
70 Eastways Industrial Park
Witham
Essex
CM8 3YE
Tel: 0376 517517
Fax: 0376 510709

Hays Chemical Distribution Ltd
Rawdon House
Green Lane
Yeadon
Leeds
LS19 7XX
Tel: 0532 505811

Henkel Organics
Henkel House
292-308 Southbury Road
Enfield
Middlesex
EN1 1TS
Tel: 081 804 3343
Fax: 081 443 4392
Trade names: *Controx; Cutina; Dehymuls; Emery; Eumulgin; Hydagen; Lanette; Myritol; Texapon.*

Hercules Ltd
Langley Road
Pendlebury
Salford
M6 6JU
Tel: 061 736 4461
Fax: 061 745 7009
Trade names: *Benecel; Blanose; Culminal MC; Culminal MHPC; Klucel; Natrosol.*

H. Foster & Co (Stearines) Ltd
103 Kirkstall Road
Leeds
Yorkshire
LS3 1JL
Tel: 0532 439016
Fax: 0532 422418

Hoechst UK Ltd
Chemicals Division
Hoechst House
Salisbury Road
Hounslow
TW4 6JH
Tel: 081 570 7712
Fax: 081 577 1854
Trade names: *Frigen.*

Honeywill & Stein Ltd
Times House
Throwley Way
Sutton
Surrey
SM1 4AF
Tel: 081 770 7090
Fax: 081 770 7295
Trade names: *Ac-Di-Sol; Aquacoat; Aquateric; Avicel; Benecel; Blanose; Breox PEG; Calstar; Destab; Eco-Lac; Montane; Montanox; Myverol 18-99; Nu-Pareil; Poval; Sepistab ST 200; Simulsol; Simulsol 165; Zeparox.*

Hüls (UK) Ltd
Featherstone Road
Wolverton Mill South
Milton Keynes
MK12 5TB
Tel: 0908 226444
Fax: 0908 224950

Trade names: *Dynasan P60; Imwitor; Lipoxol; Marlinat DFK30; Marlosol; Marlowet; Massa Estrarinum; Miglyol Softisan 154; Witepsol.*

ICI Chemicals and Polymers Ltd
PO Box 14
The Heath
Runcorn
Cheshire
WA7 4QG
Tel: 0928 514444
Fax: 0928 513890
Trade names: *Arcton 11; Arcton 12; Arcton 22; Arcton 114; Klea 134a.*

ICI Surfactants
PO Box 90
Wilton
Middlesborough
Cleveland
TS6 8JE
Tel: 0642 454144

IDIS Ltd
Unit 9
Canbury 2000 Business Centre
Elm Crescent
Kingston-upon-Thames
Surrey
KT2 6HJ
Tel: 081 549 1355
Fax: 081 547 1372

IFF (Great Britain) Ltd
Duddery Hill
Haverhill
Suffolk
CB9 8LG
Tel: 0440 704488
Fax: 0440 62199

Impag (Great Britain) Ltd
Draycott Business Park
Cam
Dursley
GL11 5DQ
Tel: 0453 890077
Fax: 0453 890040

Intermag Co Ltd
Bath Road
Felling Industrial Estate
Gateshead
NE10 0LG
Tel: 091 495 2220
Fax: 091 438 4717

Interpharm Ltd
Unit 1
99b Cobbold Road
Willesden
London
NW10 9SL
Tel: 081 830 0803
Fax: 081 830 0804

ISP Europe
40 Alan Turing Road
Surrey Research Park
Guildford
Surrey
GU2 5YF
Tel: 0483 301757
Fax: 0483 302175
Trade names: *Plasdone; Polyplasdone XL; Polyplasdone XL-10.*

James M Brown Ltd
Napier Street
Fenton
Stoke-on-Trent
Staffordshire
ST4 4NX
Tel: 0782 744171
Fax: 0782 744473

John Kellys (Merchants) Ltd
Prescot House
Prescot Street
London
E1 8BB
Tel: 071 481 2110
Fax: 071 480 5030

John L Seaton & Co Ltd
Bankside
Hull
HU5 1RR
Tel: 0482 41345
Fax: 0482 447 157

Joseph Crosfield & Sons Limited
Crosfield Group
Bank Quay
Warrington
Cheshire
WA5 1AB
Tel: 0925 416100
Fax: 0925 59828

Joseph Mills (Denaturants) Ltd
3 Tower Way
Liverpool
L25 6ED
Tel: 051 421 0014
Fax: 051 428 1315

K & K Greeff Ltd
Suffolk House
George Street
Croydon
CR9 3QL
Tel: 081 686 0544
Fax: 081 686 4792
Trade names: *Fast Flo Lactose 316; Veegum; Wacker HDK.*

Karlshamns UK Ltd
189-197 Wincolmlee
Hull
North Humberside
HU1 0QA

Tel: 0482 586747
Fax: 0482 587004
Trade names: *Acconon; Capmul; Captex; Lipex; Sterotex.*

Kelco International Ltd
Westminster Tower
3 Albert Embankment
London
SE1 7RZ
Tel: 071 735 0333
Fax: 071 735 1363
Trade names: *Kelacid; Kelcoloid; Kelcosol; Keltone; Keltrol; Manucol; Manucol ester; Manugel.*

Kellys Ltd *see* **John Kellys (Merchants) Ltd**

Kimpton Brothers Ltd
10-14 Hewett Street
London
EC2A 3HA
Tel: 071 247 2072
Fax: 071 247 2784
Trade names: *Palmera; Picol.*

Klinge Chemicals Ltd
7 Albion Way
Kelvin Industrial Estate
East Kilbride
G75 0YN
Tel: 03552 38464
Fax: 03552 64328
Trade names: *LoSalt.*

Kronos Ltd
Barons Court
Manchester Road
Wilmslow
Cheshire
SK9 1BG
Tel: 0625 529511
Fax: 0625 533123
Trade names: *Kronos 1171.*

Lactochem *see* **Borculo Whey Products UK Ltd**

Laporte Absorbents
PO Box 2
Moorfield Road
Widnes
Cheshire
WA8 0JU
Tel: 051 495 2222
Fax: 051 420 4088

Lonza (UK) Ltd
Imperial House
Lypiatt Road
Cheltenham
GL50 2QJ
Tel: 0242 513211
Fax: 0242 222294
Trade names: *Aldo MO; Aldo MS; Glyco-mul; Glycon G-100; Glycon S-90; Glycos-*

perse; Hyamine 1622; Hyamine 3500; Hydex; Pegosperse 400 MS.

LS Raw Materials Ltd
Rodary House
Alderton Crescent
London
NW4 3XX
Tel: 081 202 4166
Fax: 081 202 8903

Lucas Meyer (UK) Ltd
42 City Road
Chester
CH1 3AE
Tel: 0244 348447
Fax: 0244 346988
Trade names: *Epikuron; Espholip; Ovothin.*

Luzenac UK Ltd
Dunphy House
Queensway
Rochdale
OL11 2 RF
Tel: 0706 355048
Fax: 0706 860605

Magnesia UK
10 Main Street
Great Oxendon
Market Harborough
Liecestershire
LE16 8NE
Tel: 0858 431425
Fax: 0858 433132

Maldon Crystal Salt Ltd
The Downs
Maldon
Essex
CM9 7HR
Tel: 0621 853315
Fax: 0621 858191

MDA Chemicals Ltd
Willow Mill
Caton
Lancaster
LA2 9RA
Tel: 0524 771881
Fax: 0524 771882

Medex Medical Export Co Ltd
10 Main Street
Great Oxendon
Market Harborough
LE16 8NE
Tel: 0858 431425
Fax: 0858 433132

Megret Ltd
Coburg Dock
Queens Gate
Liverpool
L3 4AP
Tel: 051 708 7034

Fax: 051 708 6929

Merck Ltd
Freshwater Road
PO Box 11
Dagenham
Essex
RM8 1QJ
Tel: 081 599 5141
Fax: 081 599 0876
Trade names: *Sorbitol instant.*

Metsä-Serla Chemicals Ltd
St. George House
Station Approach
Cheam
Surrey
SM2 7AT
Tel: 081 642 9560
Fax: 081 642 9478
Trade names: *Cekol; Nymcel; Nymcel ZSC; Nymcel ZSX.*

MG Gas Products *see* **Distillers MG Ltd**

Millchem UK Ltd
Broseley House
81 Union Street
Oldham
OL1 1PF
Tel: 061 624 6415
Fax: 061 627 0329
Trade names: *Maprofix 563.*

Mobil Oil Company Ltd
Process Products
Mobil House
54/60 Victoria Street
London
SW1E 6QB
Tel: 071 830 3000
Fax: 071 830 3549

Monsanto Plc
Monsanto House
Chineham Court
Chineham
Basingstoke
Hampshire
RG24 0UL
Tel: 0256 57288

National Starch & Chemical Ltd
Prestbury Court
Greencourts Business Park
333 Styal Road
Manchester
M22 5LW
Tel: 061 435 3200
Fax: 061 435 3300
Trade names: *National 78-1551; Purity 21.*

Nipa Laboratories Ltd
Llantwit Fardre
Pontypridd
Mid Glamorgan

CF38 2SN
Tel: 0443 205311
Fax: 0443 207746
Trade names: *Biopure 100; Nipabutyl; Nipacide PC; Nipagin A; Nipagin M; Nipasol M; Phenoxetol; Progallin P.*

Nutrasweet AG
St. Georges Court
131 Putney Bridge Road
London
SW15 2PA

Pacegrove Ltd
Unit 13
Courtyard Workshops
Bath Street
Market Harborough
Leicestershire
LE16 7ET

Paldena Ltd
49 Ridge Hill
London
NW11 8PR
Tel: 081 455 3020
Fax: 081 458 0264

Paroxite Ltd
Office Unit 2
7 Dryden Court
Renfrew Road
London
SE11 4NH
Tel: 071 735 2425
Fax: 071 735 4408

PB Gelatins UK
Treforest
Mid Glamorgan
South Wales
CF37 5SU
Tel: 0443 842464
Fax: 0443 844209
Trade names: *Cryogel; Instagel; Slimgel; Solugel.*

Pennine Darlington Magnesia Ltd
Radnor Park Trading Estate
Back Lane
Congleton
Cheshire
CW12 4XJ
Tel: 0260 279631
Fax: 0260 278263

Pentagon Chemicals Ltd
Northside
Workington
Cumbria
CA14 1JJ
Tel: 0900 604371
Fax: 0900 66943
Trade names: *Pentonium.*

Peter Whiting (Chemicals) Ltd
5 Lord Napier Place
Upper Mall
London
W6 9UB
Tel: 081 741 4025
Fax: 081 741 1737

Pfizer Food Science Group
10 Dover Road
Sandwich
Kent
CT13 0BN
Tel: 0304 615518
Fax: 0304 615529
Trade names: *Veltol; Veltol Plus.*

Phillips Petroleum Chemicals UK
Phillips Quadrant
35 Guildford Road
Woking
Surrey
GU22 7QT
Tel: 0837 52314
Fax: 0837 52371

PMC Specialties International Ltd
65b Wigmore Street
London
W1H 9LG
Tel: 071 935 4058
Fax: 071 935 9895
Trade names: *Syncal CAS; Syncal S.*

Pointing Group
Prudhoe
Northumberland
NE42 6NJ
Tel: 0661 830215
Fax: 0661 830118

Poth, Hille & Co Ltd
37 High Street
Stratford
London
E15 2QD
Tel: 081 534 7091
Fax: 081 534 2291

PPK Products (UK) Ltd
Unit 3
Tinsley Industrial Estate
Shepcote Lane
Sheffield
S9 1TL
Tel: 0742 540414
Fax: 0742 540703

Prayon (UK) Plc
Rivers Lodge
West Common
Harpenden
Hertfordshire
AL5 2JD
Tel: 0582 769999
Fax: 0582 769989

Trade names: *A-TAB; DI-TAB; TRI-TAB.*

Protan Ltd
PO Box 8
Alton
Hampshire
GU34 1YL
Tel: 0420 82503
Fax: 0420 83360
Trade names: *Pronova; Protacid; Protanal.*

Quest International UK Ltd
Bromborough Port
Wirral
Merseyside
L62 4SU
Tel: 051 645 2060
Fax: 051 645 6975

Raught Ltd
38 Cambridge Road
Barking
Essex
IG11 8NW
Tel: 081 591 6933
Fax: 081 507 8066

RC Treatt & Co Ltd
Northern Way
Bury St. Edmunds
Suffolk
IP32 6NL
Tel: 0284 702500
Fax: 0284 703809

Redland Minerals Ltd
PO Box 2
Retford Road
Worksop
Nottinghamshire
S81 7QQ
Tel: 0909 475511
Fax: 0909 486532

Resource Chemical Ltd
Dunstable Road
Redbourne
St Albans
Hertfordshire
AL3 7PR
Tel: 0582 794433
Fax: 0582 794957

Rewo Chemicals Ltd
Gorsey Lane
Widnes
Cheshire
WA8 0HE
Tel: 051 495 1989
Fax: 051 495 2003

Rhône-Poulenc Chemicals
Oak House
Reeds Crescent
Watford
Hertfordshire

WD1 1QH
Tel: 0923 211700
Fax: 0923 211580
Trade names: *A-TAB; DI-TAB; TRI-TAB*
Embanox; Rhodiarôme; Rhodigel; Sturcal;
TRI-CAL WG; TRI-TAB.

Rhône-Poulenc Chemicals (Fluorinated Products)
PO Box 46
Avonmouth
Bristol
BS11 9YF
Tel: 0272 823631
Fax: 0272 820759
Trade names: *Isceon.*

Richard Baker Harrison Ltd
253 Cranbrook Road
Ilford
Essex
IG1 4TQ
Tel: 081 554 0102
Fax: 081 554 9282
Trade names: *Magsil Osmanthus; Magsil*
Star.

Roche Products Ltd
Vitamin & Fine Chemical Division
PO Box 8
Welwyn Garden City
Hertfordshire
AL7 3AY
Tel: 0707 366000
Fax: 0707 329587

Rohm and Haas (UK) Ltd
Lennig House
2 Mason's Avenue
Croydon
CR9 3NB
Tel: 081 686 8844
Fax: 081 686 8329
Trade names: *Amberlite.*

Roquette (UK) Ltd
The Pantiles House
2 Nevill Street
Tunbridge Wells
Kent
TN2 5TT
Tel: 0892 540188
Fax: 0892 510872
Trade names: *Fluidamid R444P; Glucidex;*
Kleptose; Lycasin 80/55; Lycatab DSH;
Lycatab PGS; Neosorb.

RW Unwin & Co Ltd
Prospect Place
Welwyn
Hertfordshire
AL6 9EW
Tel: 0438 716441
Fax: 0438 716067

Sanofi Bio-Industries Ltd
Sanofi House
Kelvin Road
Newbury
Berkshire
RG13 2DB
Tel: 0635 38343
Fax: 0635 37896

SA Shepherd & Co Ltd
PO Box 528
Polegate
East Sussex
BN26 5TQ
Tel: 0323 870972

SBP Ltd
The Old Coachhouse
103a Devonport Road
London
WI2 8PB
Tel: 081 749 5752

Scan Chem UK Ltd
16 Jordangate
Macclesfield
Cheshire
SK10 1EW
Tel: 0625 511222
Fax: 0625 511391

Seaton & Co Ltd *see* **John L Seaton & Co Ltd**

Shepherd Ltd *see* **SA Shepherd & Co Ltd**

Silkolene Lubricants Plc
Silkolene Oil Refinery
Belper
Derbyshire
DE56 1WF
Tel: 0773 824151
Fax: 0773 823659

Simpson Ltd *see* **WS Simpson & Co Ltd**

Smith Ltd *see* **Wilfred Smith Ltd**

Sparkford Chemicals Ltd
72 Portswood Road
Southampton
SO2 1FW
Tel: 0703 228747
Fax: 0703 586682

Stan Chem International Ltd
4 Kings Road
Reading
Berkshire
RG1 3AA
Tel: 0734 580247
Fax: 0734 589580

Stancourt Sons & Muir Ltd
County House
76 St John's Road
Tunbridge Wells

Kent
TN4 9PH
Tel: 0892 539277
Fax: 0892 511840
Trade names: *L-HPC; Metolose; Nisso HPC; Pharmacoat.*

Suter Ltd *see* **AF Suter & Co Ltd**

TA Chemicals
10 Allied Business Centre
Coldharbour Lane
Harpenden
Hertfordshire
AL5 4UT
Tel: 0582 469990
Fax: 0582 468830

Takasago (UK) Ltd
Standbrook House
2-5 Old Bond Street
London
W1X 3TB
Tel: 071 491 1473
Fax: 071 629 9490

Tate & Lyle Sugars
Thames Refinery
Silvertown
London
E16 2EW
Tel: 071 476 4455
Fax: 071 511 0938

Tennants (Lancashire) Ltd
Hazelbottom Road
Cheetham
Manchester
M8 7GR
Tel: 061 205 4454
Fax: 061 203 4298

Texaco Chemical Europe
195 Knightsbridge
London
SW7 1RU
Tel: 071 581 5500
Fax: 071 581 9163

Thames Chemicals (UK) *see* **Pointing Group**

Thew, Arnott & Co Ltd
Newman Works
270 London Road
Wallington
Surrey
SM6 7DJ
Tel: 081 669 3131
Fax: 081 669 7747

The White Sea & Baltic Company Ltd
Arndale House
Otley Road
Headingley
Leeds
LS6 2UU

Tel: 0532 304774
Fax: 0532 304770

TH Goldschmidt Ltd
Tego House
Victoria Road
Ruislip
Middx
HA4 0YL
Tel: 081 422 7788
Fax: 081 864 8159
Trade names: *Tegin.*

Tioxide Europe Ltd
Haverton Hill Road
Billingham
Cleveland
TS23 1PS
Tel: 0642 370300
Fax: 0642 370290
Trade names: *Tioxide.*

Treatt Ltd *see* **RC Treatt & Co Ltd**

Tunnel Refineries Ltd
Thames Bank House
Tunnel Avenue
Greenwich
London
SE10 0PA
Tel: 081 858 3033
Fax: 081 305 0981

Ubichem Ltd
Mayflower Close
Chandlers Ford Industrial Estate
Eastleigh
Hampshire
SO5 3AR
Tel: 0703 263030
Fax: 0703 263012

Unichema Chemicals Ltd
Pool Lane
Bebington
Wirral
Merseyside
L62 4UF
Tel: 051 645 2020
Fax: 051 645 9197
Trade names: *Estol 1473; Estol 1514; Estol 1517; Priacetin 1579; Pricerine; Priolene; Priolube 1408; Pristerene.*

Union Carbide Ltd
Union Carbide House
93-95 High Street
Rickmansworth
Hertfordshire
WD3 1RB
Tel: 0923 720366
Fax: 0923 775462
Trade names: *Cellosize HEC.*

Unwin Ltd *see* **RW Unwin & Co Ltd**

Volclay Ltd
Leonard House
Scotts Quays
Birkenhead
Merseyside
L41 1FB
Tel: 051 638 0967
Fax: 051 638 7000
Trade names: *Volclay.*

Wacker Chemicals Ltd
The Clock Tower
Mount Felix
Bridge Street
Walton-on-Thames
Surrey
KT12 1AS
Tel: 0932 246111
Fax: 0932 240141
Trade names: *Gamma W8; Polyviol; Vinnol; Wacker HDK.*

Warner Jenkinson Europe Ltd
Oldmedow Road
Kings Lynn
Norfolk
PE30 4JJ
Tel: 0553 763236
Fax: 0533 766891

Westbrook Lanolin Company
Argonaut Works
Laisterdyke
Bradford
BD4 8AU
Tel: 0274 663331
Fax: 0274 667665
Trade names: *Argowax; Argobase EU.*

Whiting Ltd *see* **Peter Whiting (Chemicals) Ltd**

Wilfred Smith Ltd
Gemini House
High Street
Edgware
Middlesex
HA8 7ET
Tel: 081 952 6655
Fax: 081 952 6694

William Blythe Ltd
Holland Banks Works
Church
Accrington
Lancashire
BB5 4PD
Tel: 0254 872872
Fax: 0254 872000

William Ransom & Son Plc
104 Bancroft
Hitchin
Hertfordshire

SG5 1LY
Tel: 0462 437615
Fax: 0462 420528

Woburn Chemicals Ltd
Chesney Wold
Bleak Hall
Milton Keynes
MK6 1LQ
Tel: 0908 670081
Fax: 0908 670084

WR Grace Ltd
Davison Product Line
Northdale House
North Circular Road
London
NW10 7UH
Tel: 081 965 0611
Fax: 081 961 8620

WS Simpson & Co Ltd
1-23 Linden Way
Old Southgate
London
N14 4LT
Tel: 081 886 0196
Fax: 081 886 1958

Xyrofin (UK) Ltd
41-51 Brighton Road
Redhill
Surrey
RH1 6YS
Tel: 0737 773732
Fax: 0737 773117
Trade names: *Xylitab*.

Suppliers' List: Other European

Aarhus Oliefabrik A/S
M P Bruusgade 27
DK-8100 Aarhus C
Denmark
Tel: 45 86 12 60 00
Fax: 45 86 18 38 39

Air Liquide
Asklipiou 26
10679 Athens
Greece
Tel: 1 3608411
Fax: 1 3625431

Akcros Chemicals v.o.f.
Haagen Site
Molenweg 10
PO Box 44
6040 AA Roermond
Netherlands
Tel: 4750 91777
Fax: 4750 17489

Akzo Chemicals BV
4 Stationsplein/38
PO Box 247
3800 AB Amersfoort
Netherlands
Fax: 33 676150

Alberdingk Boley GmbH
PO Box 446/448
47815 Krefeld
Germany
Tel: 2151 5280
Fax: 2151 573643
Trade Names: *DAB; DRO.*

Alland & Robert
9 Rue de Saintonge
75003 Paris
France
Tel: 42 72 90 55
Fax: 42 72 54 38

Amerchol Europe
Havenstraat 86
B-1800
Vilvoorde
Belgium
Tel: 02 2524012
Fax: 02 2524909
Trade names: *Amerchol CAB; Amerchol L-101; Cellosize; Promyr.*

Amylum NV
Burchtstraat 10
9300 Aalst
Belgium
Tel: 53 733333
Fax: 53 783183

Aqualon France
3 Rue Eugene et Armand Peuguot
92508 Rueil-Malmaison
France
Tel: 47 51 29 19
Fax: 47 77 06 14

Astra Pharmaceutical Production AB
S-151 85 Södertälje
Sweden
Tel: 31 7761000
Fax: 31 7763727
Trade names: *Pruv.*

Avebe BA
Sales, Marketing and Logistics
Avebe-weg 1
9607 PT Foxhol
Netherlands
Tel: 5980 42234
Fax: 5980 97892
Trade names: *Avebe; Avedex; Prejel; Primellose; Primojel.*

Bayer Diagnosticos SA
Pentex
Plaza de Espana 10
28008 Madrid
Spain
Tel: 1 5425729
Fax: 1 5420522

Biosynth AG
Rietlistrasse 4
PO Box 125
9422 Staad
Switzerland
Tel: 71 430190
Fax: 71 425859

Borculo Whey Products
Postbus 46
7270AA
Borculo
Netherlands
Tel: 5457 56789
Fax: 5457 56787
Trade names: *L18; Lactochem; Microfine; Zeparox.*

Cabot GmbH
Cab-O-Sil Division
Postfach 1766
Cesar-Stünzi-Strasse 15
D-7888 Rheinfelden
Germany
Tel: 7623 9090
Fax: 7623 90932
Trade names: *Cab-O-Sil.*

Campo Ebro Industrial SA
76-78 Avenda Salvadore Allende
50015 Zaragoza
Spain
Tel: 76 738100
Fax: 76 738128

Cerestar International Sales
Avenue Louis 149
BTE 13
B-1050 Brussels
Belgium
Tel: 02 5351711
Fax: 02 5376837

Chemag AG
Postfach 150103
D-6000 Frankfurt am Main 1
Germany
Tel: 69 74340
Fax: 69 7434377

Chemial Spa
Via Arsenale 27/E
10121 Turin
Italy
Tel: 11 5620331
Fax: 11 5620910
Trade names: *Chemial DEP; Chemial GTA.*

Chemische Fabrik Berg GmbH
Postfach 1347
D-5880 Lüdenscheid
Germany
Tel: 2351 36130

Chemische Fabrik Budenheim Rudolf A. Oetker
D-55257 Budenheim
Germany
Tel: 6139 890
Fax: 6139 89264
Trade names: *Cafos; Di-Cafos; Di-Cafos A; Tri-Cafos.*

Colloides Naturels International
4 Rue Frederic-Passy
BP 3-92205 Neuilly-sur-Seine
France
Tel: 47 47 18 50
Fax: 47 47 18 91

Co Farmaceutica Milanese Spa
Via Gallarate 37
20151 Milan
Italy
Tel: 2 3085441
Fax: 2 38001028

Crosfield BV
Postbus 1
6245 ZG Eijsden
Netherlands
Tel: 4409 9333
Fax: 4409 4478

Degussa AG
Postfach 110533
D-6000 Frankfurt 11
Germany
Tel: 69 21801
Trade names: *Aerosil; Elcema.*

Denka
4000 Düsseldorf 1
Koenigs Allee 92a
Germany
Tel: 211 133379
Trade names: *Poval.*

Derivados Fenolicos SA
08470 Sant Celoni
Barcelona
Spain
Tel: 3 8674997
Fax: 3 8674168
Trade names: *Ionol CP.*

DMV International
PO Box 13
5460 BA Veghel
Netherlands
Tel: 4130 72222
Fax: 4130 43695
Trade names: *Pharmatose.*

Dr Paul Lohmann GmbH
PO Box 1220
D-3254 Emmerthal 1
Germany
Tel: 5155 630
Fax: 5155 63118

Dr W. Kolb AG
Chemische Fabrik
CH-8908 Hedingen
Switzerland
Tel: 1 7614646
Fax: 1 7611757
Trade names: *Kosteran; Kotilen; Sympatens-A; Sympatens-BS; Sympatens-GMO; Sympatens-GMS; Sympatens-TR.*

DSM Special Products
PO Box 81
5900 AB Venlo
Netherlands
Tel: 77 899555
Fax: 77 899300

Dynamit Nobel AG
PO Box 1261
53839 Troisdorf
Germany
Tel: 2241 891084
Fax: 2241 891706

E. Merck
PO Box 4119
Frankfurter Strasse 250
D-6100 Darmstadt 1
Germany
Tel: 6151 720
Fax: 6151 723368
Trade names: *Sorbitol instant.*

Extraco
Box 502
S-264 23 Klippan

Sweden
Tel: 435 26500
Fax: 435 26590

FEF Chemicals A/S
PO Box 230
Københavnsvej 216
4600 Køge
Denmark
Tel: 45 53 65 40 55
Fax: 45 53 65 72 25

Fina Chemicals
A Division of Petrofina SA
Nijverheidsstraat 52
Rue de L'Industrie 52
B-1040 Brussels
Belgium
Tel: 02 2889111
Fax: 02 2883388

FMC Europe NV
Avenue Louise 480 B9
1050 Brussels
Belgium
Tel: 02 6459211
Fax: 02 6406350
Trade names: *Ac-Di-Sol; Aquacoat; Aquateric; Avicel; Calstar.*

Gattefossé SA
36 Chemin de Genas
BP 603
69804 Saint-Priest
France
Tel: 72 22 98 00
Fax: 78 90 45 67
Trade names: *Geloel; Labrafac Lipo; Maisine; Olicine; Precirol ATO5; Suppocire AM.*

Gelatine Delft
Rotterdamseweg 268-270
Postbus 3
2600 AA Delft
Netherlands
Tel: 15 569301
Fax: 15 560101

Grace GmbH
Postfach 1445
In der Hollerhecke 1
6520 Worms
Germany
Tel: 6241 4030
Fax: 6241 403211
Trade names: *Syloid AL1-FP; Syloid 244FP.*

Grinsted Products
Edwin Rahrs Vej 38
DK-8220 Brabrand
Denmark
Tel: 45 86 25 33 66
Fax: 45 86 25 10 77

Haarmann & Reimer GmbH
Rumohrtalstrasse 1

Postfach 1253
3450 Holzminden
Germany
Tel: 5531 7011
Fax: 5531 120911

Hampshire Chemical GmbH
Postfach 103007
D-69020 Heidelberg
Germany
Tel: 6221 700111
Fax: 6221 700115
Trade names: *Detarex.*

Henkel KGaA
Marketing Cospha
PO Box 101100
D-40191 Dusseldorf
Germany
Tel: 211 7971
Fax: 211 7987696
Trade names: *Controx; Cutina; Dehymuls; Emery; Eumulgin; Hyaden; Lanette; Myritol; Texapon.*

HMS Hollandse Melksuikerfabriek
PO Box 4
1910 AA Uitgeest
Netherlands
Tel: 2513 10373
Fax: 2513 15591

Hoffmann-La Roche AG
4002 Basel
Switzerland

Holland Sweetener Company
PO Box 1201
6201 BE Maastricht
Netherlands
Tel: 43 212228
Fax: 43 216633
Trade names: *Sanecta.*

Hüls AG
Postfach 1320
D-45764 Marl
Germany
Tel: 2365 491
Fax: 2365 492000
Trade names: *Dynasan P60; Imwitor; Lipoxol; Marlinat DFK30; Marlosol; Marlowet; Massa Estrarinum; Miglyol; Softisan 154; Witepsol.*

ICI Surfactants
Everslaan 45
B-3078 Everberg
Belgium
Tel: 02 7589211
Fax: 02 7589652
Trade names: *Arlacel 129; Arlacel 186; Arlamol IPM; Arlamol IPP; Arlamol M812; Arlatone 285; Arlatone 289; Arlatone 650; Arlatone 983; Atlas G-695; Atlas G-3713; Atlas G-4829; Atlas G-4909; Atmos 150;*

Atmul 84K; Brij; Myrj; Renex; Sorbo; Span; Synperonic; Tween.

Jan Dekker BV
PO Box 10
1520 AA Wormerveer
Netherlands
Tel: 75 278278
Fax: 75 213883

Janssen Biotech NV
Lammerdries 55
B-2430 Olen
Belgium
Tel: 14 224015
Fax: 14 231533
Trade names: *Encapsin.*

Janssen Chimica
Janssen Pharmaceutica NV
B-2440 Geel
Belgium
Tel: 14 604200
Fax: 14 604220

J. Rettenmaier & Söhne GmbH
D-7092 Ellwangen-Holzmühle
Germany
Tel: 7967 1520
Fax: 7967 6111
Trade names: *Vivacel.*

Jungbunzlauer International AG
St Alban-Vorstadt 90
Postfach
4002 Basel
Switzerland
Tel: 61 2955100
Fax: 61 2955108

Karlshamns Lipids for Care
S-374 82 Karlshamn
Sweden
Tel: 454 82300
Fax: 454 12911
Trade names: *Acconon; Capmul; Captex; Lipex; Sterotex.*

Kraeber GmbH & Co
Hochallee 80
2000 Hamburg 13
Germany
Tel: 40 445061
Fax: 40 455163

Laserson SA
BP 57
Zone Industrielle
91151 Etampes
France
Tel: 64 94 31 24
Fax: 64 94 98 97

Lehmann & Voss & Co
Postfach 303424
20311 Hamburg

Germany
Tel: 40 441970
Fax: 40 44197219

Lucas Meyer GmbH & Co
Ausschläger Elbdeich 62
D-2000 Hamburg 26
Germany
Tel: 40 789550
Fax: 40 7898329
Trade names: *Epikuron; Espholip; Ovothin.*

Luzenac Europe
BP 1162
31036 Toulouse
France
Tel: 61 40 63 33
Fax: 61 40 06 23

Magnesia GmbH
Kurt-Hobold StraBe 6
Industriegebiet Hafan
D-21337 Luneburg
Germany
Tel: 41 3152011
Fax: 41 3153050

Mallinckrodt Speciality Chemicals Europe GmbH
Josef-Dietzgen-Strasse 3
D-5202 Hennef/Sieg 1
Postfach 1445
Germany
Tel: 2242 8850
Fax: 2242 885109
Trade names: *HyQual.*

Meggle GmbH
Megglestrasse 6-12
83512 Wasserburg
Germany
Tel: 8071 730
Fax: 8071 73444
Trade names: *Cellactose; CapsuLac; CrystaLac; GranuLac; SorboLac; SpheroLac; Tablettose.*

Metsä-Serla Chemicals BV
PO Box 31
Winselingseweg 12
NL-6500 AA Nijmegen
Netherlands
Tel: 80 772182
Fax: 80 788160
Trade names: *Cekol; Nymcel; Nymcel ZSC; Nymcel ZSX.*

Monsanto Europe SA
270 Avenue de Tervuren
B-1150 Brussels
Belgium
Tel: 02 7614111

NP Pharm SA
54 Bis Route de Paris
BP 5

F-78550 Bazainville
France
Tel: 34 87 78 97
Fax: 34 87 78 96

NutraSweet AG
Innere Güterstrasse 2-4
6304 Zug
Switzerland
Tel: 42 226622
Fax: 42 214246
Trade names: *NutraSweet.*

Organon Teknika NV
Veedijk 58
B-2300 Turnhout
Belgium
Tel: 14 404040
Fax: 14 421700
Trade names: *Boseral.*

Pahi SA
Avenida De Madrid 66
Barcelona
Spain
Tel: 3 6562409

Parafluid Mineraloelgesellschaft MbH
Uberseering 9
D-22297 Hamburg
Germany
Tel: 40 6370400
Fax: 40 63704100
Trade names: *Parafluid.*

PB Gelatins
Division of Tessenderlo Chemie
Marius Duchestraat 260
1800 Vilvoorde
Belgium
Tel: 02 2513061
Fax: 02 2516428
Trade names: *Cryogel; Instagel; Slimgel; Solugel.*

Polysciences Ltd
Nielderlassung Eppelheim
D-6904 Eppelheim
Germany
Tel: 6221 765767
Fax: 6221 764620

Productos Aditivos SA
Paseo de Gracia 89
5a Planta
08008 Barcelona
Spain
Tel: 3 2160645
Fax: 3 2160571

Protan A/S
PO Box 420
N-3002 Drammen
Norway
Tel: 3 83 76 60
Fax: 3 83 32 42

Trade names: *Pronova; Protacid; Protanal.*

Purac Biochem BV
Arkelsedijk 46
PO Box 21
4200 AA Gorinchem
Netherlands
Tel: 1830 41799
Fax: 1830 29202
Trade names: *Purac 88 PH.*

Riedel-de Haën AG
Wunstorfer Strasse 40
D-3016 Seelze 1
Germany
Tel: 5137 707630

Röhm Pharma
Postfach 4347
D-6100 Darmstadt 1
Germany
Tel: 6151 8770
Fax: 6151 877602
Trade names: *Eudragit.*

Roquette Frères
F-62136 Lestrem
France
Tel: 21 57 99 11
Fax: 21 02 55 06
Trade names: *Fluidamid R444P; Glucidex;
Kleptose; Lycasin 80/55; Lycatab DSH;
Lycatab PGS; Neosorb.*

SA Citrique Belge NV
Pastorijstraat 249
B-3300 Tienen
Belgium
Tel: 16 821100
Fax: 16 822214

Schaefer Kalk
Postfach 1361
D-6252 Diez/Lahn
Germany
Tel: 6432 5030
Fax: 6432 503269

Seppic
Division Cosmétique-Pharmacie
75 Quai d'Orsay
75321 Paris
France
Tel: 40 62 55 55

Fax: 40 62 52 53
Trade names: *Montane; Montanox; Non-
pareil 103; Sepistab ST 200; Simulsol.*

Simel Spa
Division of Unichema International Italia
Via Bergamo 66
26100 Cremona
Italy
Tel: 372 4871
Fax: 372 412123

Sobalg
Societe Bretonne des Algues et Colloides
BP 6
F-29207 Landerneau
France
Tel: 98 85 45 45
Fax: 98 85 45 40
Trade names: *Sobalg.*

Stepan Europe
Chemin Jonking
BP 127
38340 Voreppe
France
Tel: 76 50 51 00
Fax: 76 53 71 65
Trade names: *Catigene; Neobee M5; Seloster
SDG; Steol; Stepan IP01; Stepan IPP.*

Takeda Europe GmbH
Domstrasse 17
D-20095 Hamburg
Germany
Tel: 40 329050
Fax: 40 327506
Trade names: *C-97; CCal-97; SA-99.*

Tessenderlo Chemie SA
1 Square de Meeûs
B-1040 Brussels
Belgium
Tel: 02 5191811
Fax: 02 5135580

Texaco Services (Europe) Ltd
Technologiepark
Zwijnaarde 2
B-9052 Ghent
Zwijnaarde
Belgium
Tel: 09 1407342

Fax: 09 1407340

USOCO BV
Mandenmakerstraat 21
NL 2984 AS
Ridderkerk
Netherlands
Tel: 1804 16155
Fax: 1804 12836

Verdugt BV
PO Box 60
4000 AB Tiel
Netherlands
Tel: 3440 15221
Fax: 3440 11475

Vevy Europe Spa
Via Semeria 18
16131 Genoa
Italy
Tel: 10 5221515
Fax: 10 5221530

Wacker-Chemie GmbH
Hanns-Seidel-Platz 4
D-81737 Munich
Germany
Tel: 89 627901
Fax: 89 62791771
Trade names: *Gamma W8; Polyviol; Vinnol;
Wacker HDK.*

Willi Kruger KG
Preussenstrasse 56
D-4030 Ratingen 6
Germany
Tel: 21 0268640
Fax: 21 0266682

Wolff Walsrode AG
Postfach 1515
29355 Walsrode
Germany

Xyrofin AG
PO Box 157
Seestrasse 5
CH 6301 Zug
Switzerland
Tel: 41 42 21 02 30
Fax: 41 42 21 14 33
Trade names: *Finmalt L; Xylitab.*

Suppliers' List: USA

Abbott Laboratories
Chemical and Agricultural Products Division
1401 Sheridan Road
North Chicago
IL 60064
Tel: (708) 937 8800
Fax: (708) 937 6676

Aceto Corporation
One Hollow Lane
Lake Success
NY 11042-1215
Tel: (516) 627 6000
Fax: (516) 627 6093

Accurate Chemical & Scientific Corp
300 Shames Drive
Westbury
NY 11590
Tel: (516) 333 2221
Fax: (516) 997 4948

Aeropres Corp
PO Box 78588
Shreveport
LA 71137-8588
Tel: (318) 221 6282
Fax: (318) 429 6739
Trade names: *Aeropres 17; Aeropres 31; Aeropres 108.*

AE Staley Mfg Co
PO Box 151
Decatur
IL 62525
Tel: (217) 421 2301
Trade names: *Krystar; Sta-Rx 1500.*

Air Products and Chemicals Inc
Polymer Chemicals Division
7201 Hamilton Boulevard
Allentown
PA 18195-1501
Tel: (215) 481 6799
Fax: (215) 481 4184
Trade names: *Airvol.*

Akcros Chemicals America
500 Jersey Avenue
PO Box 638
New Brunswick
NJ 08903
Tel: (908) 247 2202
Fax: (908) 247 2287

Akzo Chemicals Inc
Meadow Road
Edison
NJ 08817
Tel: (908) 985 6262
Fax: (908) 777 2203

Amerchol Corp
136 Talmadge Road
PO Box 4051
Edison
NJ 08818-4051
Tel: (908) 248 6056
Fax: (908) 287 3109
Trade names: *Amerchol CAB; Amerchol L-101; Cellosize; Promyr.*

American Colloid Co
One North Arlington
1500 West Shure Drive
Arlington Heights
IL 60004-1434
Tel: (708) 392 4600
Fax: (708) 506 6199
Trade names: *Magnabrite; Polargel; Volclay NF.*

American Ingredients Inc
956 North Elm Street
Orange
CA 92667
Tel: (714) 633 1301
Fax: (714) 771 5627

American Maize Products Co
Corn Processing Division
1100 Indianapolis Boulevard
Hammond
IN 46320-1094
Tel: (800) 348 9896
Fax: (219) 659 1045
Trade names: *Cavitron; Fluftex W; Tablet White.*

American Xyrofin Inc
1400 North Meacham Road
Shaumburg
IL 60173
Tel: (708) 843 3200
Fax: (708) 843 3368
Trade names: *Dextrofin; Sorbifin; Xylitab.*

Amresco Inc
30175 Solon Industrial Parkway
Solon
OH 44139-4300
Tel: (216) 349 2805
Fax: (216) 349 1182

Angus Chemical Company
1500 East Lake Cook Road
Buffalo Grove
IL 60089
Tel: (708) 215 8600
Fax: (708) 215 8626

Aqualon
Little Falls Center One
2711 Centerville Road
Wilmington
DE 19850-5417
Tel: (302) 996 2000
Fax: (302) 996 2049

Trade names: *Benecel; Blanose; Culminal MC; Culminal MHPC; Klucel; Natrosol.*

Arco Chemical Co
3801 West Chester Pike
Newtown Square
PA 19073
Tel: (215) 359 2000
Fax: (215) 359 5759

Arista Industries
1082 Post Road
Darien
CT 06820
Tel: (203) 655 0881
Fax: (203) 656 0328

Ashland Chemical Company
Fine Ingredients
PO Box 2219
Columbus
OH 43216
Tel: (614) 889 4343
Fax: (614) 889 3465

Atomergic Chemetals Corp
222 Sherwood Avenue
Farmingdale
NY 11735
Tel: (516) 694 9000
Fax: (516) 694 9177

Austin Chemical Company Inc
9655 West Bryn Mawr Avenue
Rosemont
IL 60018
Tel: (708) 671 6565
Fax: (708) 671 6569
Trade names: *Di-Pac.*

Avatar Corp
Special Chemicals Division
7728 West 99 Street
Hickory Hills
IL 60457
Tel: (312) 430 4200
Trade names: *Avatech; Citation; LSC; Snow white; Soft white.*

Avebe America Inc
Princeton Corporate Center
4 Independence Way
Princeton
NJ 08540
Tel: (609) 520 1400
Fax: (609) 520 1473
Trade names: *Avebe; Avedex; Prejel; Primellose; Primojel.*

Barrington Chemical Corporation
540 West Boston Post Road
Mamaroneck
NY 10543
Tel: (914) 833 1283
Fax: (914) 833 1765

BASF Corporation
100 Cherry Hill Road
Parsippany
NJ 07054
Tel: (201) 316 3000
Trade names: *Cremophor EL; Cremophor RH40; Kollidon; Kollidon CL; Pluronic.*

BFGoodrich Company
9911 Brecksville Road
Cleveland
OH 44141-3247
Tel: (216) 447 5000
Fax: (216) 447 5740
Trade names: *Carbopol.*

Biddle Sawyer Corporation
2 Penn Plaza
New York
NY 10121-0034
Tel: (212) 736 1580
Fax: (212) 239 1089
Trade names: *Metolose; Pharmacoat.*

Biospur Inc
PO Box 17379
Milwaukee
WI 53217
Tel: (414) 352 4229
Fax: (414) 352 6075

Brooks Industries Inc
70 Tyler Place
S Plainfield
NJ 07080

Cabot Corporation
Cab-O-Sil Division
PO Box 188
Tuscola
IL 61953
Tel: (217) 253 3370
Fax: (217) 253 4334
Trade names: Cab-O-Sil.

Calgene Chemical Inc
7247 North Central Park Avenue
Skokie
IL 60076-4093
Tel: (708) 675 3950
Fax: (708) 675 3013
Trade names: *Calchem C-102; Calchem H-102; Calchem IVO-108; Calchem IVO-109; Calchem IVO-112; Calchem IVO-114; Hodag; Hodag PEG; Nonionic.*

Caschem Inc
40 Avenue A
Bayonne
NJ 07002
Tel: (201) 858 7900
Fax: (201) 858 0308

Charkit Chemical Corp
330 Post Road
PO Box 1725

Darien
CT 06820
Tel: (203) 655 3400
Fax: (203) 655 8643

Charles B Chrystal Co Inc
30 Vesey Street
New York
NY 10007
Tel: (212) 227 2151
Fax: (212) 233 7916
Trade names: *Purtalc.*

Chart Corp Inc
787 East 27th Street
Paterson
NJ 07504
Tel: (201) 345 5554
Fax: (201) 345 2139

Chemco Industries Inc
500 Citadel Drive
Suite 120
Los Angeles
CA 90040

Chemie Linz US Inc
65 Challenger Road
Ridgefield Park
NJ 07660
Tel: (201) 641 6410
Fax: (201) 641 2323

ChorChem Inc
158 Mount Olivet Avenue
Newark
NJ 07114
Tel: (201) 824 6461
Fax: (201) 824 6763

Church & Dwight Co Inc
Speciality Products Division
Performance Products Group
469 N Harrison Street
Princeton
NJ 08543-5297
Tel: (609) 683 5900
Fax: (609) 497 7176

Colorcon
415 Moyer Boulevard
PO Box 24
West Point
PA 19486-0024
Tel: (215) 699 7733
Fax: (215) 661 2605
Trade names: *Methocel; Starch 1500; Starch 1500 L.M.; Surelease.*

Corn Products
Unit of CPC International Inc
6500 Archer Road
PO Box 345
Summit-Argo
IL 60501-0345
Tel: (708) 563 2400

Fax: (708) 563 6852

Croda Inc
183 Madison Avenue
New York
NY 10016
Tel: (212) 683 3089
Fax: (212) 532 8718
Trade names: *Cithrol 4MS; Cithrol GMO N/E; Cithrol GMS N/E; Cithrol GMS S/E; Corona; Crill; Crillet; Crodacid; Crodacol CS; Crodacol C70; Crodacol C90; Crodacol C95; Crodacol S95; Crodamol IPM; Crodamol IPP; Crodamol SS; Croderol; Crodet S8; Crodet S40; Crodet S50; Crodex A; Crodex N; Crodolene; Croduret 40; Crodyne BY19; Cropol 35; Cropol 60; Cropol 70; Crosterene; Etocas 35; Hartolan; Volpo CS20; Volpo N10; Volpo O10.*

Crompton & Knowles Corp
Ingredient Technology Division
1533 Union Avenue
Pennsauken
NJ 08110
Tel: (609) 662 2746
Fax: (609) 486 9853
Trade names: *Cal-Carb; Cal-Tab; Nu-Core; Nu-Pareil; Nu-Tab; Pharma-Carb; Pharma-Gel.*

Crosfield Co
101 Ingalls Avenue
Joliet
IL 60435
Tel: (815) 727 3651
Fax: (815) 727 5312

Cyclodextrin Technologies Development Inc
Suite A 108
2632 NW 43rd Street
Gainesville
FL 32606
Tel: (904) 375 6822
Fax: (904) 375 8287

Delavau Co Inc *see* **JWS Delavau Co Inc**
Denka
Pan American Building
200 Park Avenue
New York
NY 10166
Tel: (212) 867 1381
Trade names: *Poval.*

Desert Balm
PO Box 4310
San Luis Obispo
CA 93403
Tel: (805) 781 3208
Fax: (805) 781 3209

DMV Campina Inc
PO Box 1628
La Crosse
WI 54602-1628

Tel: (608) 781 2345
Fax: (608) 781 3299
Trade names: *Pharmatose.*

Domino Sugar Corporation
1114 Avenue of the Americas
New York
NY 10036-7783
Tel: (212) 789 9700
Fax: (212) 789 9754
Trade names: *Di-Pac.*

Dow Chemical Company
2020 Willard H Dow Center
Midland
MI 48674
Tel: (800) 441 4369
Trade names: *Ethocel; Methocel.*

DSM Fine Chemicals USA Inc
5 Paul Kohner Place
Elmwood Park
NJ 07407-2614
Tel: (201) 796 9025
Fax: (201) 796 6996

DuCoa LP
115 Executive Drive
Suite 103
PO Box 219
Highland
IL 62249
Tel: (618) 654 2070
Fax: (618) 654 1818
Trade names: *ProBenz.*

Du Pont *see* **EI Du Pont de Nemours & Co Inc**

Eastman Fine Chemicals
1999 East Stone Drive
One Executive Park
PO Box 431
Kingsport
TN 37662
Tel: (615) 229 8124
Fax: (615) 229 8133
Trade names: *Kodaflex DBP; Kodaflex DEP; Kodaflex DMP; Myvaplex 600P.*

Ecochem
PO Box 299
W5280S County Trunk A
Adell
WI 53001
Tel: (414) 994 4969
Fax: (414) 994 9103
Trade names: *Eco-Lac.*

Edward Mendell Co Inc
2981 Route 22
Patterson
NY 12563-9970
Tel: (914) 878 3414
Fax: (914) 878 3484

Trade names: *Caridex; Compactrol; Emcocel 50 M; Emcocel 90 M; Emcompress; Emcompress Anhydrous; Emdex; Emvelop; Explotab; Lubritab; Magnyox; Non-pareils; Pruv; Satialgine; Satialgine-H8; Solka-Floc; Sugartab.*

EI Du Pont de Nemours & Co Inc
Brandywine Building
Wilmington
DE 19898
Tel: (302) 774 4784
Fax: (302) 774 8416
Trade names: *Dymel 11; Dymel 12; Dymel 22; Dymel 114; Dymel 134a/P; Dymel 142b; Dymel 152a; Dymel A; Elvanol; TiPure.*

Eisai USA Inc
Glenpoint Center East
300 Frank W. Burr Boulevard
Teaneck
NJ 07666-6741
Tel: (201) 692 0999
Fax: (201) 692 1972

EM Industries Inc
Fine Chemicals Division
5 Skyline Drive
Hawthorne
NY 10532
Tel: (914) 785 5860
Fax: (914) 592 9469
Trade names: *Sorbitol instant.*

Engelhard Corporation
101 Wood Avenue
Iselin
NJ 08830-0770
Tel: (908) 205 7140
Fax: (908) 321 0250

Fisher Scientific
711 Forbes Avenue
Pittsburgh
PA 15219-4785
Tel: (201) 467 6400
Fax: (201) 379 7415

FMC Corporation
1735 Market Street
Philadelphia
PA 19103
Tel: (215) 299 6534
Fax: (215) 299 6821
Trade names: *Ac-Di-Sol; Aquacoat; Aquateric; Avicel; Calstar.*

Foremost Ingredients Group
Division of Wisconsin Dairies Cooperative
PO Box 111
Baraboo
WI 53913
Tel: (608) 356 8316
Fax: (608) 356 9005
Trade names: *Fast-Flo.*

Forum Products Inc
321 Clock Tower Commons
Brewster
NY 10509
Tel: (914) 278 4978
Fax: (914) 278 4980

Frank B Ross Co Inc
22 Halladay Street
PO Box 4085
Jersey City
NJ 07304-0085
Tel: (201) 433 4512
Fax: (201) 332 3555

Freeman Industries Inc
100 Marbledale Road
Tuckahoe
NY 10707
Tel: (914) 961 2100
Fax: (914) 961 5793

Functional Foods
470 Route 9
Englishtown
NJ 07726
Tel: (908) 972 2232
Fax: (908) 536 9179

Gallard-Schlesinger Industries Inc
584 Mineola Avenue
Carle Place
NY 11514
Tel: (516) 333 5600
Fax: (516) 333 5628

Gattefosse Corp
189 Kinderkamack Road
Westwood
NJ 07675
Tel: (201) 573 1700
Fax: (201) 573 9671
Trade names: *Geloel; Labrafac Lipo; Maisine; Olicine; Precirol ATO5; Suppocire.*

Generichem Corp
85 Main Street
PO Box 369
Little Falls
NJ 07424
Tel: (201) 256 9266
Fax: (201) 256 0069
Trade names: *Primellose; Primojel.*

Genzyme Corporation
One Kendall Square
Cambridge
MA 02139
Tel: (617) 252 7500
Fax: (617) 252 7772

George Uhe Co Inc
12 Route 17 North
PO Box 970
Paramus
NJ 07653-0970

Tel: (201) 843 4000
Fax: (201) 843 7517

Grace & Co *see* **WR Grace & Co**

Grain Processing Corporation
1600 Oregon Street
Muscatine
IA 52761
Tel: (319) 264 4265
Fax: (319) 264 4289
Trade names: *Maltrin; Pure-Dent; Pure-Dent B851.*

Grayslake Gelatin
PO Box 248
40 Railroad Avenue
Grayslake
IL 60030
Tel: (708) 223 8141
Fax: (708) 223 8144

Grindsted Products Inc
201 Industrial Parkway
Industrial Airport
KS 66031
Trade names: *Sobalg.*

Greeff & Co *see* **RW Greeff & Co Inc**

Gumix International Inc
2160 North Central Road
Fort Lee
NJ 07024-7552
Tel: (201) 947 6300
Fax: (201) 947 9265

Haarmann & Reimer Corp
70 Diamond Road
Springfield
NJ 07081
Tel: (908) 686 3132
Fax: (908) 467 3514

Hampshire Chemical Corp
55 Hayden Avenue
Lexington
MA 02173
Tel: (617) 861 9700
Fax: (617) 862 3869

Harrisons Trading Co Inc
303 South Broadway
Tarrytown
NY 10591
Tel: (914) 332 4600
Fax: (914) 332 8575
Trade names: *Solutab.*

Heico Chemicals Inc
Route 611
PO Box 160
Delaware Water Gap
PA 18327-0160
Tel: (717) 420 3900
Fax: (717) 421 9012

Helm New York Chemical Corp
1110 Centennial Avenue
Piscataway
NJ 08855-1333
Tel: (909) 981 1160
Fax: (908) 981 0528

Hoffmann-La Roche Inc
340 Kingsland Street
Nutley
NJ 07110
Tel: (201) 235 8091
Fax: (201) 235 8023

Hormel Foods Corporation
1 Hormel Place
Austin
MN 55912-3680
Tel: (507) 437 5609
Fax: (507) 437 5120

Hüls America Inc
PO Box 456
Piscataway
NJ 08855
Tel: (908) 980 6940
Fax: (908) 980 6970
Trade names: *Dynasan P60; Imwitor; Lipoxol; Marlinat DFK30; Marlosol; Marlowet; Massa Estrarinum; Miglyol; Softisan 154; Witepsol.*

Humko see **Witco Corporation**
ICI Chemicals and Polymers America
Concord Plaza
3411 Silverside Road
PO Box 15391
Wilmington
DE 19850
Tel: (302) 887 3000
Fax: (302) 887 1818
Trade names: *Arcton 11; Arcton 12; Arcton 22; Arcton 114; Klea 134a.*

Inolex Chemical Co
Jackson & Swanson Streets
Philadelphia
PA 19148-3497
Tel: (215) 271 0800
Fax: (215) 289 9065

International Sourcing Inc
121 Pleasant Avenue
Upper Saddle River
NJ 07458
Tel: (201) 934 8900
Fax: (201) 934 8291

ISP
1361 Alps Road
Wayne
NJ 07470-3688
Tel: (201) 628 3000
Fax: (201) 628 4117
Trade names: *Plasdone; Polyplasdone XL; Polyplasdone XL-10.*

Jungbunzlauer Inc
75 Wells Avenue
Newton Center
MA 02159-3214
Tel: (617) 969 0900
Fax: (617) 964 2921

JWS Delavau Co Inc
2140 Germantown Avenue
Philadelphia
PA 19122
Tel: (215) 235 1100
Fax: (215) 235 2206

Kalama Chemical Inc
Bank of California Center
Suite 1110
Seattle
WA 98164

Kaopolite Inc
2444 Morris Avenue
Union
NJ 07083
Tel: (908) 789 0609
Fax: (908) 851 2974

Karlshamns USA Inc
PO Box 569
Columbus
OH 43216-0569
Tel: (614) 299 3131
Fax: (614) 299 8279
Trade names: *Acconon; Capmul; Captex; Lipex; Sterotex.*

Kelco Division of Merck & Co Inc
PO Box 23576
8355 Aero Drive
San Diego
CA 92123
Tel: (619) 292 4900
Fax: (619) 292 8763
Trade names: *Kelacid; Kelcoloid; Kelcosol; Keltone; Keltrol; Manucol; Manucol ester; Manugel.*

Koster Keunen Inc
90 Bourne Boulevard
PO Box 447
Sayville
NY 11782
Tel: (516) 589 0456
Fax: (516) 589 0120

Kraft Chemical Company
Pharm & Cosmetic Division
1975 North Hawthorne Avenue
Melrose Park
IL 60160-1103
Tel: (708) 345 5200
Fax: (708) 345 4005

Laporte Inc
3701 Algonquin Road
Suite 390

Rolling Meadows
IL 60008
Tel: (708) 670 8870
Fax: (708) 670 8874

Lebermuth Co *see* **The Lebermuth Co Inc**

Lipo Chemicals Inc
207 19th Avenue
Paterson
NJ 07504
Tel: (201) 345 8600
Fax: (201) 345 8365

Lonza Inc
2210 Route 208
Fair Lawn
NJ 07410
Tel: (201) 794 2400
Trade names: *Aldo MO; Aldo MS; Glyco-mul; Glycon G-100; Glycon S-90; Glycos-perse; Hydex; Pegosperse 400 MS.*

Lucas Meyer Inc
765 East Pythian Avenue
Decataur
IL 62526
Tel: (217) 875 3660
Fax: (217) 877 5046
Trade names: *Epikuron; Espholip; Ovothin.*

Luzenac America Technical Center
8985 East Nichols Avenue
Englewood
CO 80112
Tel: (303) 643 0451
Fax: (303) 799 8926

Mallinckrodt Speciality Chemicals Co
Drug and Cosmetic Chemicals Division
PO Box 5439
St. Louis
MO 63147
Tel: (800) 325 8888
Fax: (314) 539 1641
Trade names: *HyQual.*

Mantrose-Haeuser Co
500 Post Road East
Westport
CT 06880
Tel: (203) 454 1800
Fax: (203) 227 0558
Trade names: *Mantrolac R-49.*

Marine Magnesium Co
995 Beaver Grade Road
Coraopolis
PA 15108
Tel: (412) 264 0200
Fax: (412) 264 9020

Meer Corp
9500 Railroad Avenue
North Bergen
NJ 07047

Tel: (201) 861 9500
Fax: (201) 861 9267

Merona Chemicals Ltd
10 South Broadway
The Equity Building
Nyack
NY 10960
Tel: (914) 353 0066
Fax: (914) 353 0206

Metsä-Serla Chemicals Inc
Suite 260
3000 Corporate Center Drive
Morrow
GA 30260
Tel: (404) 960 9967
Fax: (404) 960 1267
Trade names: *Cekol; Nymcel; Nymcel ZSC; Nymcel ZSX.*

Millmaster Onyx International
134 Clinton Road
PO Box 1045
Fairfield
NJ 07007
Tel: (201) 227 3995
Fax: (201) 227 9213
Trade names: *Maprofix 563.*

M Michel & Co Inc
90 Broad Street
NY 10004
Tel: (212) 344 3878
Fax: (212) 344 3880
Trade names: *Cachalot.*

Mobil Oil Corporation
Marketing Refining Division
3225 Gallows Road
Fairfax
VA 22037-0001
Tel: (703) 846 2642
Fax: (703) 846 2647

Monsanto Chemical Co
800 North Lindbergh Boulevard
St. Louis
MO 63167
Tel: (314) 694 1000

Morflex Inc
2110 High Point Road
Greensboro
NC 27403
Tel: (919) 292 1781
Fax: (919) 854 4058
Trade names: *Citroflex 2; Citroflex 4; Citroflex A-2; Citroflex A-4.*

Mutchler Chemical Co Inc
99 Kinderkamack Road
Westwood
NJ 07675
Tel: (201) 666 7002
Fax: (201) 666 3652

Napp Technologies Inc
199 Main Street
PO Box 900
Lodi
NJ 07644
Tel: (201) 773 3900
Fax: (201) 773 2010

Nipa Laboratories Inc
104 Hagley Building
3411 Silverside Road
Wilmington
DE 19810
Tel: (302) 478 1522
Fax: (302) 478 4097
Trade names: *Biopure 100; Nipabutyl; Nipagin A; Nipagin M; Nipasol M; Nipanox BHA; Nipanox BHT; Phenoxetol.*

Noah Chemical
Division of Noah Technologies Corporation
7001 Fairgrounds Parkway
San Antonio
TX 78238-4541
Tel: (210) 680 9000
Fax: (210) 521 3323

Organon Teknika Corp
100 Akzo Avenue
Durham
NC 27712
Tel: (800) 523 7620
Fax: (919) 620 2107

Ozone Confectioners & Bakers Supply Co Inc
55 Bank Street
PO Box 234
Elmwood Park
NJ 07407
Tel: (201) 791 4444
Fax: (201) 791 2893

Particle Dynamics Inc
2503 South Hanley Road
St. Louis
MO 63144
Tel: (314) 968 2376
Fax: (314) 968 5208
Trade names: *Destab.*

Pectagel Inc
98 Cutter Mill Road
Suite 258 South
PO Box 465
Great Neck
NY 11021
Tel: (516) 829 0350
Fax: (516) 829 0354

Penta Manufacturing Co
PO Box 1448
Fairfield
NJ 07007
Tel: (201) 575 7475
Fax: (201) 575 8907

Pfanstiehl Laboratories Inc
1219 Glen Rock Avenue
Waukegan
IL 60085-0439
Tel: (708) 623 0370
Fax: (708) 623 9173

Pfizer Food Science Group
230 Brighton Road
Clifton
NJ 07012
Tel: (800) 245 4495
Trade names: *Veltol; Veltol Plus.*

Pharmaceutical Ingredients Ltd
5-10 Homestead Road
Belle Mead
NJ 08502
Tel: (908) 281 9419
Fax: (908) 281 9594
Trade names: *Solutab.*

Pharmatec Inc
PO Box 730
2054 County Road
Alachua
FL 32615
Tel: (904) 462 1210
Fax: (904) 462 5401

Phillips 66 Company
A division of Phillips Petroleum Company
874-B Adams Building
Bartlesville
OK 74004
Tel: (918) 661 9092
Fax: (918) 661 8379

Pilot Laboratories Inc
Parkway 109 Office Center
328 Newman Springs Road
Redbank
NJ 07701
Tel: (908) 576 1900
Fax: (908) 530 0844

PMC Specialities Group Inc
501 Murray Road
Cincinatti
OH 45217
Tel: (513) 482 7374
Fax: (513) 482 7315
Trade names: *Syncal CAS; Syncal S.*

PPG Industries Inc
Speciality Chemicals, Chemicals Group
3938 Porett Drive
Gurnee
IL 60031
Tel: (800) 552 1912
Fax: (708) 249 6790

Presperse Inc
PO Box 735
South Plainfield
NJ 07080

Tel: (908) 756 2023
Fax: (908) 756 8754

Protameen Chemicals Inc
PO Box 166
Totowa
NJ 07511
Tel: (201) 256 4374
Fax: (201) 256 6764
Trade names: *Procol; Protachem; Protalan M-16; Protalan M-26; Protamate; Protasorb.*

Protan Inc
135 Commerce Way
Suite 201
Portsmouth
NH 03801
Tel: (603) 433 1231
Fax: (603) 433 1348
Trade names: *Pronova; Protacid; Protanal.*

Purac America Inc
111 Barclay Boulevard
Lincolnshire Coroporate Center
Lincolnshire
IL 60069
Tel: (708) 634 6330
Fax: (708) 634 1992
Trade names: *Purac 88 PH.*

Quest International Inc
Sheffield Products Division
PO Box 630
Norwich
NY 13815
Tel: (607) 334 9951
Fax: (607) 334 5022

Reheis Inc
PO Box 609
Berkeley Heights
NJ 07922
Tel: (908) 464 1500
Fax: (908) 464 8094

Resources Industry Inc
172 North 36th Street
Lafayette
IN 47905
Tel: (317) 447 5725
Fax: (317) 447 1325
Trade names: *Fibrocel.*

Rhône-Poulenc Basic Chemicals Co
One Corporate Drive
PO Box 881
Shelton
CT 06484
Tel: (203) 925 3300
Fax: (203) 925 3627
Trade names: *A-TAB; DI-TAB; TRI-CAL WG; TRI-TAB.*

Rhône-Poulenc Inc
Speciality Chemicals Division

Cranbury
NJ 08512-7500
Trade names: *Embanox; Rhodiarôme; Rhodigel; Sturcal.*

RITA Corp
PO Box 585
Woodstock
IL 60098
Tel: (815) 337 2500
Fax: (815) 337 2522
Trade names: *Acritamer; Forlan 200; Ritachol; Ritachol SS; RITA-GMS; Ritapeg 400 MS; Ritawax.*

Robeco Chemicals Inc
99 Park Avenue
New York
NY 10016
Tel: (212) 986 6410
Fax: (212) 986 6419
Trade names: *Spermwax.*

Rohm and Haas Company
Independent Mile West
Philadelphia
PA 19105
Tel: (215) 592 3424
Trade names: *Amberlite.*

Roquette America Inc
1550 Northwestern Avenue
Gurnee
IL 60031-2392
Tel: (708) 249 5950
Fax: (708) 578 1027
Trade names: *Fluidamid R444P; Glucidex; Kleptose; Lycasin 80/55; Lycatab DSH; Lycatab PGS; Neosorb.*

Ross Co *see* **Frank B Ross Co Inc**

RT Vanderbilt Co Inc
30 Winfield Street
PO Box 5150
Norwalk
CT 06856-5150
Tel: (203) 853 1400
Fax: (203) 853 1452
Trade names: *Rhodigel; Vanclay; Veegum; Veegum HS.*

RW Greeff & Co Inc
777 West Putnam Avenue
Greenwich
CT 06830
Tel: (203) 532 2900
Fax: (203) 532 2980

Schweizerhall Inc
10 Corporate Place South
Piscataway
NJ 08854
Tel: (908) 981 8200
Fax: (908) 981 8282

Seppic Inc
30 Two Bridges Road
Suite 225
Fairfield
NJ 07006
Tel: (201) 882 5597
Fax: (201) 882 5178
Trade names: *Montanox; Non-pareil 103;
Sepifilm; Sepistab ST 200; Simulsol.*

Sheffield Products *see* **Quest International Inc**

Sherex Chemical Company Inc
PO Box 646
Dublin
OH 43017
Tel: (614) 764 6500
Fax: (614) 764 6650

Spectrum Chemical Mfg Corp
755 Jersey Avenue
New Brunswick
NJ 08901
Tel: (908) 214 1300
Fax: (908) 220 6553

Staley Mfg Co *see* **AE Staley Mfg Co**

Strahl & Pitsch Inc
PO Box 1098
West Babylon
NY 11704
Tel: (516) 587 9000
Fax: (516) 587 9120

Sutton Laboratories Inc
PO Box 837
116 Summit Avenue
Chatham
NJ 07928-0837
Tel: (201) 635 1551
Fax: (201) 635 4964
Trade names: *Germall 115; Germall II.*

Takasago International Corp (USA)
11 Volvo Drive
Rockleigh
NJ 07647
Tel: (201) 767 9001
Fax: (201) 767 8062

Texaco Chemical International Trader Inc
3040 Post Oak Boulevard
Houston
TX 77056
Tel: (713) 235 6520
Fax: (713) 235 6436

The Lebermuth Co Inc
PO Box 4103
South Bend
IN 46634
Tel: (219) 259 7000
Fax: (219) 258 7450

Tricon Colors Inc
16 Leliarts Lane
Elmwood Park
NJ 07407-3291
Tel: (201) 794 3800
Fax: (201) 797 4660

Tri-K Industries Inc
27 Bland Street
PO Box 312
Emerson
NJ 07630
Tel: (201) 261 2800
Fax: (201) 261 1432
Trade names: *Tristat BNP; Tri-stat IU; T-Wax.*

Triple Crown America Inc
13 North Seventh Street
Perkasie
PA 18944
Tel: (215) 453 2500
Fax: (215) 453 2508

Unichema North America
4650 South Racine Avenue
Chicago
IL 60609
Tel: (312) 376 9000
Fax: (312) 376 0095
Trade names: *Estol 1473; Estol 1514; Estol
1517; Priacetin 1579; Pricerine; Priolene;
Priolube 1408; Pristerene.*

Union Carbide Corporation
Industrial Chemicals Division
39 Old Ridgebury Road
Danbury
CT 06817-0001
Tel: (203) 794 5300
Trade names: *Carbowax; Cellosize HEC.*

United Mineral & Chemical Corp
1100 Valley Brook Avenue
Lyndhurst
NJ 07071-3608
Tel: (201) 507 3300
Fax: (201) 507 1506

United States Gypsum Co
PO Box 803832
Chicago
IL 60680-3832
Tel: (312) 606 5840
Fax: (312) 606 5443
Trade names: *Snow White; USG Terra Alba.*

Vanderbilt Co *see* **RT Vanderbilt Co Inc**

Van Dyk Inc
Main and William Streets
Belleville
NJ 07109
Tel: (201) 759 3225

Van Waters & Rogers Inc
PO Box 34325
Seattle
WA 98124-1325
Tel: (206) 889 3400
Fax: (206) 889 4133

Viobin Corp
PO Box 158
Waunakee
WI 53597
Tel: (608) 849 5944
Fax: (608) 849 4053

Virginia Dare
882 Third Avenue
Brooklyn
NY 11232
Tel: (718) 788 1776
Fax: (718) 788 3978

Vista Chemical Company
900 Threadneedle
Houston
TX 77079-2990
Tel: (713) 588 3214
Fax: (713) 588 3119

Vitamins Inc
200 East Randolph Drive
Chicago
IL 60601-7799
Tel: (312) 861 0700
Fax: (312) 861 0708

Vivion Inc
929 Bransten Road
San Carlos
CA 94070
Tel: (415) 595 3600
Fax: (415) 595 2094

Vyse Gelatin Co
5010 North Rose Street
Schiller Park
IL 60176
Tel: (708) 678 4780
Fax: (708) 678 0329
Trade names: *Vee Gee.*

Wacker Silicones Corp
3301 Sutton Road
Adrian
MI 49221-9397
Tel: (517) 264 8500
Fax: (517) 264 8246
Trade names: *Gamma W8; Polyviol; Vinnol;
Wacker HDK.*

Weinstein Nutritional Products
666 Baker Street
Suite 253
Costa Mesa
CA 92626
Tel: (714) 754 0901
Fax: (714) 754 0936

Werner G Smith Inc
1730 Train Avenue
Cleveland
OH 44113
Tel: (216) 861 3676
Fax: (216) 861 3680

Whittaker, Clark & Daniels Inc
1000 Coolidge Street
South Plainfield
NJ 07080
Tel: (800) 732 0562
Fax: (800) 833 8139

Wisconsin Dairies *see* **Foremost Ingredients Group**

Witco Corporation
Humko Chemical Division
PO Box 125
Memphis
TN 38101-0125
Tel: (901) 684 7000
Fax: (901) 682 6531
Trade names: *Hystrene; Industrene; Kemstrene; Polycon T 60 K.*

WR Grace & Co
Davison Chemical Division

PO Box 2117
Baltimore
MD 21203
Tel: (410) 659 9000
Fax: (410) 659 9190

Zumbro Inc
Route 1
PO Box 83
Hayfield
MN 55940
Tel: (507) 365 8400
Fax: (507) 365 8288
Trade names: *Instastarch; Maltagran.*

624   Appendix I: Suppliers' Directory

Suppliers' List: Others

Boehme Filatex Canada Inc
PO Box 1017
St-Jean-sur-Richelieu
Quebec J3B 7B5
Canada
Tel: 514 346 6848
Fax: 514 346 7263
Trade names: *Exameen 3580; Nutrapon W;*
Questal Di; Questric acid 5286.

Chorney Chemical Co
138 Sunrise Avenue
Toronto
Ontario M4A 1B3
Canada
Tel: 416 752 9562
Fax: 416 752 2021

Denka
Sanshin Building
4-1 Yuraku-cho, 1-chome
Chiyoda-ku
Tokyo 100
Japan
Tel: 507 5405
Trade names: *Poval.*

Eisai Co Ltd
6-10 Koishikawa 4 chome
Bunkyo-ku
Tokyo 112-88
Japan
Tel: 03 3817 5149
Fax: 03 3811 1459

Freund Industrial Co Ltd
14-2 Takadanobaba 2-Chome
Shinjuku-ku
Tokyo 169
Japan
Tel: 03 3200 9611
Fax: 03 3232 0359

Gadot Petrochemical Industries Ltd
155 Bialik St Ramat-Gan
PO Box 3366
Ramat-Gan 52133
Israel
Tel: 03 75 10811
Fax: 03 75 18042

Kawaken Fine Chemicals Co Ltd
2-3-3 Nihombashi Horidome-cho
Chuo-ku
Tokyo 103
Japan
Tel: 03 3663 9521
Fax: 03 3661 5630

Nippon Soda Co Ltd
2-1 Ohtemachi 2-chome
Chiyoda-ku
Tokyo 100
Japan
Tel: 03 3245 6152
Fax: 03 3245 6059
Trade names: *Nisso HPC.*

San Fu Chemical Company Ltd
5th Floor
21 Changshan N. Road Sec. 2
Taipei 104
Taiwan
Tel: 02 521 4161
Fax: 02 581 8359

Sansho Co
The 2nd Kitahama Building
1-29 Kitahama-Higashi
Chuoh-Ku
Osaka City 540
Japan
Tel: 06 941 7271
Fax: 06 941 7278

Shin-Etsu Chemical Co Ltd
6-1, Ohtemachi 2-chome
Chiyoda-ku
Tokyo 100
Japan
Tel: 03 3246 5261
Fax: 03 3246 5372
Trade names: *L-HPC; Metolose; Pharma-coat.*

Takasago International Corp
19-22 Takanawa 3-Chome
Minato-Ku
Tokyo 108
Japan
Tel: 03 3442 1211
Fax: 03 3442 1285

Appendix II: HPE Laboratory Methods

Compression Characteristics

COM-1: Lab #21

Instrumentation and Calibration of a Manesty B3B Rotary Tablet Press.

Compressional force was monitored from a remote site using pairs of metal foil strain gauges[1] (in Wheatstone bridge configuration) bonded to turned down sections on opposite sides of the pressure rod. The unbalance in the bridge circuit caused by elongation of the pressure rod during tablet compression was monitored using a carrier amplifier,[2] that also served to activate the bridge. Compression events were recorded on a storage-type oscilloscope.[3] Responses were read directly as units of scope deflections that were later converted into units of force.

The instrumented site was previously calibrated against an upper punch that had been instrumented by bonding strain gauges[1] (in Wheatstone bridge configuration) to turned down sections on opposite sides of the punch. Bridge excitation voltage was provided by a DC power supply.[4] Bridge unbalance voltage was amplified by one of the differential amplifiers of the oscilloscope. The punch was calibrated in a Carver press[5] by observing scope deflection versus applied compressional force. The punch was then inserted into the tablet press and scope deflection from the punch and pressure rod were recorded simultaneously and compared while manually turning the press under varying compressional loads. The signal deflection produced by the pressure rod was found to be directly proportional to the punch compressional force.

COM-2: Lab #21

Use of the Carver Press in the Preparation of Compacts.

Apparatus:
Carver Press
Stainless steel baseplate
Flat faced bolt for bolt hole in press head
½-inch round die (from tests using rotary press)
½-inch round lower punch (from tests using rotary press)

Method:
The die, baseplate and punch face were lubricated with a 10% solution of stearic acid in chloroform, applied using a cotton-tipped applicator. The die and baseplate were then centered on the platen and a measured amount of powder introduced into the die cavity. The plug was inserted into the bolt hole and the punch inserted into the die cavity.

The desired pressure was then applied and released immediately. While holding the die with the punch inverted, the head of the punch was tapped on the base of the press to force the tablet from the die. The die, baseplate, and punch face were then re-lubricated prior to formation of the next compact.

A diagram of the assembly is shown in Fig. 1.

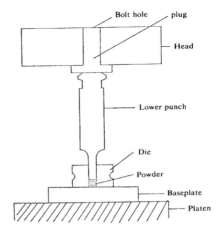

Fig. 1: Set up of the Carver Press for compact formation.

COM-3: Lab #20

Procedure for Compression-Hardness Testing.

Approximately 1 kg of each material was blended with 0.25% magnesium stearate for 5 minutes in an Erweka cube blender. Compression was accomplished on a 16 station Stokes B-2 rotary press using 4 stations set up with 7/16-inch standard concave tooling; compression and ejection forces were monitored through strain gauges on a Tektronix dual-beam storage oscilloscope.

Edge thicknesses were measured with a vernier calliper and hardnesses were measured with a Schleuniger model 2E hardness tester; each reported data point is the mean of 20 determinations.

Profiles were drawn as a 2nd degree regression curve with a Tektronix programmable calculator and X-Y plotter, except in the cases of microcrystalline cellulose (*Avicel PH101* and *Avicel PH102*), which were drawn by 3rd degree regression.

COM-4: Lab #29

Procedure for Stokes, Model F, Single Punch Press.

Apparatus:
Stokes model F, single punch press equipped with ½-inch, round, flat-faced tooling and instrumented with piezo electric transducers leading to an instrument panel with an oscilloscope and to a computer.

Method:
The fill volume (lower punch) was first adjusted to obtain compacts of 600 mg then a preliminary test performed under machine power to determine that tablet weight was reasonably uniform (tablets were collected in groups of 10).

Ten tablets compressed under machine power were then collected and the applied compressional force reading from the computer output recorded. The procedure was then repeated at other pressure settings with the press operating at 60 tablets per minute.

COM-5: Lab #29

Unlubricated Granulation, Carver Press, Manual Operation.

Equipment and procedure were the same as for COM-6.

COM-6: Lab # 29

Lubricated Granulation, Carver Press, Manual Operation.

Apparatus:

Hydraulic press equipped with ½-inch, round, flat-faced upper and lower punches and the appropriate die supports for the die with lower punch at a constant height to allow for the die fill. A pressure gauge, graduated to 10 000 pounds with 100 pound increments.

Method:

A 5% solution of stearic acid in denatured alcohol was applied to the punch face and sides and to the die bore. The die was placed on the supports with the lower punch in place and a pre-weighed 600 mg portion of material transferred to the die cavity.

The top punch was positioned in the die cavity and pressure manually applied to a specified setting; the pressure was maintained at the maximum pressure for 5 seconds then released.

The upper punch was then removed and the assembly inverted on the supports. By pushing against the lower punch the press was used to eject the compact downward without causing undue stress on the structural strength of the compact.

The process was repeated four times at each level of applied force.

Physical Property Measurements.

Tablet weight:

Tablets were weighed individually on a Mettler semi-micro analytical balance and the tablet weight recorded in mg.

Tablet thickness:

Tablets were measured individually with an Ames Dial Comparator calibrated in 0.01 mm and tablet thickness recorded in mm.

Tablet breaking strength:

Tablets with a breaking strength less than 16 kg were measured individually in an Heberlein electric hardness tester and the breaking strength recorded in kg.

Tablets with a breaking strength greater than 16 kg were measured individually using a Stokes Gun equipped with a heavy duty spring. The initial and final readings were recorded and breaking strength calculated in kg using the following formula:

$$(Reading_{final} - Reading_{initial}) \times 3 = Breaking\ strength$$

COM-7: Lab #12

Compression Characteristics

Evaluations of compression characteristics were carried out with a Model B Carver Laboratory Press[5]. A set of 16/32-inch F.F.B.E. punches and appropriate die was fitted into the standard Carver Press retention chuck and 500 mg of test material weighed into the die. Alternatively, depending on the material evaluated, sufficient powder to fill the die to 70-80% of capacity was weighed into the die. Pressure at the required compression force was applied and immediately released when the desired value was obtained.

At least five tablets were prepared at a minimum of four different compression forces if acceptable tablets could be compressed. Dies were lubricated with a 10% stearic acid in chloroform solution. Tablet hardness values were obtained using the Schleuniger Model 2E hardness tester.

Note:
1. FAET 25-B-35-56-E half bridge T-rosettes, Type SR-4, BLH Electronics, Waltham, MA.
2. Sanborn Model 311A, Hewlett Packard Co, Palo Alto, CA.
3. Model 5113 with 4B12N time base and two 5A26 dual differential amplifiers, Tektronix Inc Mfg Co, Beaverton, OR.
4. Model 21-200 Calex Mfg Co, Pleasant Hill, CA.
5. Fred S. Carver Inc, Summit, NJ.

Density

DE-1: Lab #7 & Lab #31

Helium air pycnometer (Micromeritic Instrument Corp).

DE-2: Lab #36

Pycnometer method for solids insoluble in and heavier than water (Osol A et al, editors. Remington's Pharmaceutical Sciences, 15th edition. Easton, PA. Mack Publishing Company, 1975: 94): titanium dioxide.

DE-3: Lab #36

Sinker method for solids insoluble in and lighter than water (Osol A et al, editors. Remington's Pharmaceutical Sciences, 15th edition. Easton, PA. Mack Publishing Company, 1975: 95). Each sample was first melted and resolidified prior to determination, and stearic acid saturated water used as the displaced liquid: stearic acid.

DE-4: Lab #36

Pycnometer method for solids soluble in water using heptane as the displaced liquid (Osol A et al, editors. Remington's Pharmaceutical Sciences, 15th edition. Easton, PA. Mack Publishing Company, 1975: 95): lactose (anhydrous).

DE-5: Lab #30

Using a 30 mL, capillary bore stopper pycnometer; exact volume determined by weighing water at 24°C in accordance with standard data tables that correlate density with temperature.

Bulk and Tap Density or Volume

BTD-1: Lab #1 & Lab #14

Samples were passed through a US #20 mesh screen prior to density measurement. Bulk density was determined by pouring 25 g of material into a 100 mL graduated cylinder and measuring the volume to the nearest mL. Tapped density was determined by placing the graduated cylinder in the Tap-Pak Volunteer[6] and operating the unit through a series of taps until the powder contained in the graduated cylinder attained a constant tapped volume. Results presented represent an average of two determinations per sample.

BTD-2: Lab #1

Determined using 25 g of material placed in a 250 mL graduated cylinder.

BTD-3: Lab #1

As for BTD-1 except samples were not passed through a US #20 mesh screen prior to density determination.

BTD-4: Lab #1

Determined using 6 g of material placed in a 250 mL graduated cylinder.

BTD-5: Lab #6

Weighed samples of not more than 130 g and not less than 40 g were placed in a 250 mL graduated cylinder using a glassine type weighing paper to facilitate ease of flow. Transfer of the weighed powder to the cylinder was done as rapidly as flow would permit with the cylinder being held at approximately a 45° angle. The cylinder containing the sample was brought to the vertical and given a sharp shake to level the volume for reading.

After reading the loose bulk volume, each sample was placed on the Tap-Pak device[6] and run in 100 tap increments from 100, through 500, and then 1000 taps. At 1000 taps, the sample was run in 1000 tap increments up to a total of 4000 taps. The volume of each tap increment was recorded in mL.

The data indicated that a relative constant volume was achieved between 3000 to 4000 taps using this apparatus.

After each 100 taps the volume was recorded until three consecutive readings were the same; this was defined as the tap volume of the sample.

BTD-8: Lab #36

A weighed portion of each sample was gently poured through a glass funnel into a 250 mL graduated cylinder supported at an angle of 45° on a ring stand. The graduated cylinder was then rotated to an upright position, the powder surface gently levelled and the bulk volume of the sample recorded. The graduated cylinder loaded with the powder sample was then subjected to the action of an apparatus (Tap-Pak Volumeter, model 2, Shandon Scientific Co Inc, Sewickley, PA) which was adjusted to operate for 100 taps.

Note:

6. Model #JEL ST2 manufactured by J Engelsmann, Germany. Available through Shandon Scientific Co Inc, Sewickley, PA.

Flowability

FLOW-3: Lab #24

The powder flowmeter used consisted of an aluminum pan attached to a beam equipped with four strain gauges capable of measuring weight differences in microseconds, and a strain gauge activation and measuring unit which converted the strain gauge signal to an electrical impulse measurable by a 10-inch, variable speed, strip chart recorder. The sample to be evaluated was placed in a funnel (70°) held above the pan and equipped with an electrically triggered trap door. The strip chart recorder was adjusted so that 250 g would be represented by 100% of scale. The sample was allowed to flow onto the pan and the time required for the sample to empty from the funnel recorded. The rate of flow was determined from the strip chart recorder and expressed as a flow rate in g/s.

All samples were passed through a US #30 mesh screen to remove any lumps. All measurements were repeated three times.

Moisture Content

MC-1

USP XXII (page 1621), water determination, gravimetric, method III, 5 hours at 60°C.

MC-2

USP XXII (page 1621), water determination, gravimetric, method III, 16 hours at 60°C.

MC-3

USP XXII (page 1619), water determination, titrimetric, method I.

MC-4

USP XXII (page 1586), loss on drying, thermogravimetric.

MC-5

USP XXII (page 1586), loss on drying, 2 hours at 60°C.

MC-6

USP XXII (page 1586), loss on drying, 3 hours at 60°C.

MC-7

USP XXII (page 1586), loss on drying, 3 hours at 105°C.

MC-8

USP XXII (page 1586), loss on drying, 4 hours at 105°C.

MC-9

USP XXII (page 1586), loss on drying, 5 hours at 105°C.

MC-10

USP XXII (page 1586), loss on drying, 16 hours at 105°C.

MC-11

USP XXII (page 1586), loss on drying, 17 hours at 105°C.

MC-12

USP XXII (page 1586), loss on drying, heat to constant weight at 105°C.

MC-13

USP XXII (page 1586), loss on drying, heat to constant weight at 110°C.

MC-14

USP XXII (page 1586), loss on drying, 2 hours at 105°C.

MC-15

USP XXII (page 1586), loss on drying, 4 hours at 120°C.

MC-16

USP XXII (page 1586), loss on drying, 1 hour at 105°C, then 3 hours at 120°C.

MC-17

USP XXII (page 1586), loss on drying, 2 hours at 105°C then 16 hours at 120°C.

MC-18

USP XXII (page 1586), loss on drying under vacuum.

MC-19

USP XXII (page 1586), loss on drying under vacuum, 8 hours at 45°C.

MC-20

USP XXII (page 1586), loss on drying under vacuum, 16 hours at 60°C.

MC-21

USP XXII (page 1586), loss on drying under vacuum, 17 hours at 60°C.

MC-22

USP XXII (page 1586), loss on drying under vacuum, 20 hours at 60°C.

MC-23

USP XXII (page 1586), loss on drying under vacuum, 3 hours at 105°C and 10 mmHg.

MC-24

USP XXII (page 1586), loss on drying under vacuum, 3 hours at 200°C and 76 mmHg.

MC-25

USP XXII (page 1586), loss on ignition.

MC-26

Horwitz W, editor. Official methods of analysis of the Association of Official Analytical Chemists, 12th edition. Washington, DC: American Association of Official Analytical Chemists, 1975: 221.

MC-27

Loss on drying. Food Chemicals Codex, 3rd edition. Washington, DC: National Academy Press, 1981: 518.

MC-28

USP XXII (page 1527), residue on ignition.

MC-29

Approximately 1 g of a sample was accurately weighed on a watch glass then dried for 24 hours at 110°C and weighed. The sample was then dried for an additional 24 hours and weighed again. Loss on drying was then converted to percent moisture content.

MC-30

No direct method for determining the water content of dibasic calcium phosphate dihydrate was available; in compendial tests, the loss on ignition is used. This loss includes loss of free water, water of hydration and the elimination of one mole of water for every two moles of $CaHPO_4$ as it converts to the pyrophosphate ($Ca_2P_2O_7$). The following calculation was used to arrive at the stated values:

$$\% \ H_2O = \frac{Gram \ sample - (Residue \ on \ ignition \times \frac{272.12}{254.12} \times 100}{Gram \ sample}$$

Where $(CaHPO_4) = 272.12$
$Ca_2P_2O_7 = 254.12$
H_2O = Water of crystallization and absorbed water

Theory for $CaHPO_4 \cdot 2H_2O$ is 20.9% H_2O.

MC-31

USP XXII (page 1621), water determination, gravimetric, method III, 16 hours at 105°C.

Equilibrium Moisture Content

EMC-1: Lab #2, 10, 15, 18 and 22

Materials:

Nine plastic desiccators (Nalge/Sybron Corporation) approximately 9-inches in diameter, were obtained from a local laboratory supply house. Glass desiccators of equivalent size may be substituted for the plastic containers.

A supply of glass analytical weighing bottles with standard taper covers (25 mm outside diameter x 40 mm height, with 12 mL capacity) were used to contain samples for testing. Samples were weighed on an analytical balance to the nearest 0.1 mg. A series of saturated salt solutions were prepared as described in Table I.

Table I: Saturated salt solutions for maintaining constant relative humidity conditions in desiccators.

Saturated salt solution[*]	Percent relative humidity at indicated temperatures			
	20°C	25°C	30°C	37°C
Lithium chloride	12	11	11	11
Potassium acetate	24	23	23	23
Magnesium chloride	33	33	32	31
Potassium carbonate	44	43	42	41
Magnesium nitrate	53	52	52	51
Sodium nitrite	66	64	63	62
Sodium chloride	76	75	75	75
Potassium bromide	84	83	82	81
Potassium nitrate	94	93	92	91

[*] Prepared from reagent grade salts dissolved in purified water.

Method:

Equilibrium moisture content (EMC) determinations were made by placing accurately weighed samples of each material (100-200 mg) in 2 or 3 open, tared, and numbered weighing bottles and then into a labelled desiccator containing one of the saturated salt solutions described in Table I. A liberal amount of the saturated salt solution (with excess crystals) was placed in the well of the desiccator.

Samples were stored in each of the nine securely closed individual desiccators, each containing a different moisture atmosphere. At equilibrium (7 days storage at controlled room temperature 25 ± 2°C) the samples were removed from the desiccators and the moisture increase or decrease determined for each sample by obtaining the final equilibrium weight with the aid of an analytical balance. These data were recorded on moisture analysis data sheets.

EMC values were calculated from P (% moisture dry basis). Initial moisture content (A) of each excipient was accurately determined by a suitable method, such as loss on drying to constant weight, and used to calculate P. EMC values, at each relative humidity tested, were tabulated and plotted, using coordinate graph paper, to obtain EMC versus relative humidity curves.

Particle Friability

PF-1: Lab #36

A 50 g portion of each sample was sieved through a series of selected standard sieves with the aid of a Ro-Tap Testing Sieve Shaker (WS Tyler Company, Cleveland, OH) for 5 minutes. The powder retained on each sieve was weighed to obtain a weight-size distribution of the sample. The arithmetic mean particle size was then calculated.[7]

A second 50 g portion of each sample was attrited by placing 100 g of 5 mm glass beads and the sample in the sieve collector and subjecting both to the action of the Ro-Tap Testing Sieve Shaker for 5 minutes.

The weight size distribution of the attrited sample was determined by the method outlined above, and the arithmetic mean particle size calculated.

The difference between the arithmetic mean particle sizes obtained before and after attrition was divided by the size before attrition to obtain a number which was defined as the Friability Index.

Note:

7. Parrott E, Saski W. Experimental pharmaceutical technology, 3rd edition. Minneapolis, MN: Burgess Publishing Company, 1971: 286.

Particle Size Distribution Methods

PSD-1: Lab #1

Sieve analysis using a Syntrol Sieve Shaker, model TSS-31-C. Amplitude was set at 0.08-inch and sieving time was 15 minutes. All sieves were US Standard Sieve Series. Samples identified as PSD-15 were passed through a US #20 mesh screen to break up lumps before analysis.

PSD-2: Lab #5

Sieve analysis using USP XXII (page 1602), method for powder fineness, with US Standard Sieves (Fisher Scientific Co) made of stainless steel. Sample size was approximately 10 g and each sample was screened for 35 minutes on a mechanical sieve shaker (Fritsch Co). The arithmetic mean diameter, d_{av}, was determined using the following equation:[8]

$$d_{av} = \frac{\sum (nd)}{\sum n}$$

Weight size is the product of the arithmetic mean size of the openings and the percentage retained on the smaller sieve.

PSD-3: Lab #12

A 100 g sample was placed in the top screen of a series on a Cenco Meinzer Sieve Shaker (Central Scientific Co) and shaken at intensity #7 for 5 minutes. The results were then reported as percentage retained on each screen size.

PSD-4: Lab #17

The tare weight of each sieve and the pan used in the ATM Sonic Sifter (ATM Corporation) was determined, then 4 g of the excipient was weighed and transferred to the top sieve of the sieve assembly. The sifter was run for 2 minutes using the sift/pulse mode, with the amplitude of sift set to '8' (on a scale of 1-10). After the sifting, each sieve and the pan were weighed. The weight and the weight percent of excipient retained on each sieve was then calculated. The analysis was performed in triplicate and the weight percent and standard deviation retained on sieves of different opening sizes reported.

PSD-5A: Lab #21

The Alpine Jet Sieve, model 200, was operated at '8' reading on the manometer using water. A 10 g sample was run for 10 minutes per screen size and the results reported as percentage retained on each sieve.

PSD-5B: Lab #21

A 10 g sample was placed on a nest of sieves which had been previously wetted. A stream of cold distilled water was passed over the sample until no more passed through the sieve. The material retained on each sieve was then dried and weighed.

PSD-6: Lab #23

A 100 g sample was accurately weighed and placed on the top sieve of a sieve series (Tyler Sieves) with meshes 35, 48, 60, 80, 100, 150, 200 and the Pan. The tare weight of each sieve and the pan was obtained. The nest of sieves were then placed on the Tyler Portable Sieve Shaker, model RX21, which was operated for 5 hours. Each sieve and the pan were then accurately weighed and the nest of sieves operated for an additional 2 hours. If there was no change in the weights, the weight of the excipient retained on each sieve was then converted to the percent of total weight.

PSD-7: Lab #24

Analysis using the Fisher Sub-Sieve Particle Size Analyzer.

The Fisher Sub-Sieve Particle Size Analyzer operates on the air-permeability principle for measuring the average particle size of powders, i.e. particles in the path of a regulated air flow will affect that air flow according to the particle size. This principle is based on the property that a current of air flows more readily through a bed of coarse powder than through an otherwise equal bed of fine powder that is equal to the shape of bed, apparent volume and percentage of voids. By reason of differences in the general coarseness of materials and differing average pore diameter and total interstitial surface, measurements of average particle sizes are obtained. The particle size data reported represent an average of 3 determinations and lie within ± 0.3 μm.

PSD-8: Lab #33

The Micromerograph (Sharples Type XC) was used to determine the particle size distribution of the samples with the data represented in terms of equivalent spherical diameters in microns (μm). The principle involved is sedimentation in an air column. Samples of hydrogenated castor oil and *Witepsol* were unsuitable for particle size distribution measurement because of their physical properties.

PSD-9: Lab #3

The method used, microscopy, is considered to be adequate for narrowly distributed samples, whereas highly dispersed samples will be prone to errors due to sampling. The parameter obtained in this case is simply a supporting parameter. A small sample of the excipient, 20 mg at the most, was dispersed in 3-4 drops of mineral oil, and a sample of this dispersion further diluted with mineral oil and transferred to a hemocytometer slide, so that the concentration was sufficiently large to allow counting but not too large to prevent counting. A cover slip was placed on the sample and care taken not to entrap air. The slide was then mounted on the microscope and photographed using a Polaroid camera. Particle size distributions were then determined from the photograph.

Note:

8. Lachman L, Lieberman HA, Kanig JL, editors. The theory and practice of industrial pharmacy, 2nd edition. Philadelphia: Lea and Febiger, 1976: 466.

Scanning Electron Microscopy

The purpose of this study was to obtain a topographical characterization of pharmaceutical excipients through the use of scanning electron microscopy (SEM).

The aluminum stubs used for SEM were first polished with a metal polish, *Wenol* (Tedd Pella Inc) and ultrasonified for 5 minutes in a bath of acetone. The stubs were then rinsed with ethanol and coated with a thin layer of adhesive, *Mikrostik* (Tedd Pella Inc). Prior to the evaporation of the adhesive, the excipient sample was placed uniformly on the stub. By this procedure, the excipient sample was fastened to the surface of the stub. A thin layer of gold was then coated on the surface in a vacuum evaporator and the SEM micrographs were taken with a Cambridge Scanning Electron Microscope (model IIA) at the required magnifications.

Solubility

SOL-1: Lab #1

An excess of each excipient was added to approximately 30 mL of purified water, ethanol (95%) or *n*-hexane. The excipient-solvent mixtures were agitated on a wrist-action shaker for 1 hour. The mixtures were then filtered through 0.45 μm Millipore-MF filters in the case of ethanol and *n*-hexane. Samples (10 mL) of the filtrates were pipetted into tared culture dishes and the solvents permitted to evaporate at ambient conditions. The dishes were reweighed and examined for residue until all of the solvent evaporated.

SOL-2: Lab #1

Weighed increments of each excipient were added to 1.0 mL of purified water, ethanol and *n*-hexane. The mixtures were agitated on a Vortex Genie until the material dissolved. Since the mixtures were warmed by the Vortex Genie, each mixture was allowed to cool to room temperature. The mixtures were examined to determine if the excipient dissolved and remained in solution. If a precipitate was present or if the solution became cloudy, the previous increment was considered to be the limit of solubility. In the case of povidone, reported solubilities in purified water and ethanol (95%) are not

maximum solubilities, but are values limited by high viscosities which made mixing impossible.

SOL-3: Lab #10

A saturated solution of the excipient was either filtered or decanted; 10 mL of the clear solution was evaporated to dryness and the residue weighed. Most determinations were performed in quadruplicate and weighings made on a single-pan analytical balance (accuracy 0.1 mg). In the absence of any measurable residue, the material was considered as insoluble.

SOL-4: Lab #10

For solubility in propylene glycol, an excess of weighed material was dissolved and suspended in a measured volume of solvent. When no more of the excipient would dissolve, the suspension was filtered through a medium pore, tared, sintered glass funnel. The filtrate was then used to rinse all suspended material into the funnel. When all of the material was in the funnel, the funnel had its contents briefly rinsed with cold water (none of the materials tested were appreciably soluble in water), the funnel was dried and the recovered material dried to determine the solubility. The above procedure was not feasible at 37°C.

The measurement of the solubility of stearyl alcohol in *n*-hexane presented problems due to its high solubility, its tendency to supersaturate, and its considerable tendency to crystallize upon a very slight temperature change such as inevitably would occur during an attempt to filter a saturated solution. Therefore, this solubility was estimated by preparing a series of concentrated solutions and noting the highest concentration attainable after making sure that the solution was not supersaturated.

SOL-5: Lab #11

The general method involved the equilibration of a large excess of solid solute in the solvent. Samples were drawn with warmed glass pipettes possessing glass-wool wrapped tips. Solutions were maintained at specified temperatures by placing the containers in jacketed beakers and circulating water at the indicated temperatures within the jacket. Control of temperature was within 0.1°C. Vigorous magnetic stirring of the slurries continued until sampling time. With this method, equilibrium was obtained in less than one hour.

Experimental data on the aqueous solubility of benzoic acid was determined in water acidified with HCl to a pH of 2.14. The analytical method employed in all cases was spectrophotometry with appropriate standards, i.e. Beer's Law plots in each solvent.

Experimental data on the aqueous solubility of sodium benzoate was determined at the natural pH taken by the excipient. Determination of the solubility of sodium benzoate in propylene glycol proved to be difficult as a cloudy, colloidal (in appearance) supernatant was obtained. Filtering through glass-wool was tested and found to be satisfactory. The data reported represent the combined values of two trials.

SOL-6: Lab #23

For purified water, ethanol (95%) and *n*-hexane, a known volume of saturated solvent was placed in a weighing pan and the solvent evaporated. For propylene glycol, a solute was added to the solvent in accurately weighed increments until dissolution failed to take place within 48 hours. All determinations were performed in duplicate and reported as the combined values of the two trials.